ENCYCLOPEDIA
OF THE
U.S. MILITARY

William M. Arkin
Joshua M. Handler
Julia A. Morrissey
Jacquelyn M. Walsh

AN INSTITUTE FOR POLICY STUDIES BOOK

1817

Harper & Row, Publishers, New York

BALLINGER DIVISION

Grand Rapids, Philadelphia, St. Louis, San Francisco
London, Singapore, Sydney, Tokyo, Toronto

90 - 5114

International Standard Book Number: 0-88730-215-7

Library of Congress Catalog Card Number: 89-45783

Printed in the United States of America

Library of Congress Cataloging-in-Publication Data

Encyclopedia of the U. S. military / by William M. Arkin. . .[et al.]
    p. cm.
  "An Institute for Policy Studies book."
  Includes bibliographical references
  ISBN 0-88730-215-7
  1. United States–Armed Forces–Dictionaries. 2. United States–Defenses–Dictionaries.
  I. Arkin, William M.
UA23.E57   1990
355.00973–dc20–dc20   89-45783
                                                                      CIP

90 91 92 92 93 HC 9 8 7 6 5 4 3 2 1

Contents

Acknowledgments

The *Encyclopedia of the U. S. Military* is a product of many years of inquiry conducted on dozens of aspects of U. S. military affairs. As such, the book represents the collective experience and knowledge of numerous individuals who have provided insight into the workings of the massive military and national security establishment. The authors wish to acknowledge the persons, both inside and outside the government, who have contributed to the final product.

First, we offer our gratitude to our colleague and friend Robert S. Norris, who enthusiastically reviewed and commented on virtually every entry in the *Encyclopedia* from A to Z. We also wish to thank those persons who helped conceive of and provide direction to the book, including Robert Borosage, former Director of the Institute for Policy Studies; Marcus Raskin, Senior Fellow of the Institute for Policy Studies; and Carol Franco, former president of Ballinger Publishing Company.

We would like to acknowledge our former colleagues David Chappell, Richard Fieldhouse, Andrew Burrows, and Kathleen Clark for their countless hours of research and collection of information and documents central to this work, and to Julia Sweig, who researched and wrote the entries associated with foreign military sales and military assistance programs. We also offer our appreciation to our assistants Matthew Carlson, Damian Durrant, Kristen Richards, Sean Riley, Jennifer Southard, and Amy Wickenheiser for the administrative and substantive help they provided. We would also like to recognize Greenpeace USA's Disarmament Campaign for the support it offered during the editing stage of the book's production. To those whose work advanced our knowledge of particular subjects covered in the book, we acknowledge the expertise and assistance provided by Thomas Cochran, Colin Danby, Pauline Kerr, Andrew Mack, Jeffrey Richelson, John Pike, and Paul Stares. We are also grateful to those agencies and individuals who provided much of the detailed and specialized information contained within the Military Occupational Specialties appendix, including J. L. Brumbaugh, FOIA [Freedom of Information Act] Officer, U. S. Total Army Personnel Agency; and LT R. G. Thompson, USNR, Naval Military Personnel Command.

We are grateful to many government departments—especially the Department of Defense and its commands and agencies—for their responsiveness to our numerous requests for official source information used throughout the text. Therefore, we would like to acknowledge the assistance provided the project by the staffs of the DOD and government public affairs and history offices, including the Air University (Public Affairs and Library staff), Arms Control and Disarmament Agency, Army War College, Chief of Naval Education and Training,

Central Intelligence Agency, Defense Security Assistance Agency, Department of Energy, Department of Justice (Public Affairs and Office of Intelligence Policy and Review), Department of State, Federal Aviation Administration, Federal Bureau of Investigation, Federal Emergency Management Agency, Forces Command, Information Security Oversight Office, Marine Corps Combat Development Command, Military Airlift Command, National Aeronautics and Space Administration, National Defense University (Library staffs), National Guard Bureau, National Security Agency/Central Security Service, National Security Council, Naval Air Systems Command, Naval War College (Library staff), Pentagon Library (Reference and Law Reference staff), Office of the Air Force Reserve, Office of the Army Reserve, Office of the Assistant Secretary of Defense (Public Affairs) (American Forces Information Service, Directorate for Defense Information, Armed Forces News Branch, Defense News Branch, and Research and Distribution Branch), Office of the Chief of Naval Operations, Office of the Chief of Staff of the Air Force, Office of the Chief of Staff of the Army, Office of the Joint Chiefs of Staff, Office of the Secretary of Defense, Office of the Secretary of the Air Force (Public Affairs and Resource Library), Office of the Secretary of the Army (Public Affairs and Readiness and Support), Office of the Secretary of the Navy (CHINFO), Strategic Air Command, Supreme Allied Command Atlantic (Washington liaison office), Supreme Headquarters Allied Powers Europe (Washington liaison office), U. S. Army Western Command, U. S. Central Command (History office), U. S. Coast Guard, U. S. European Command, U. S. Marine Corps, U. S. Pacific Command, U. S. Southern Command, and U. S. Special Operations Command (Washington office).

Further, we would like to extend our special gratitude to the staff members of the offices that, over many years, administered our requests for documents and data under the Freedom of Information Act (FOIA). These FOIA heads of staff and individuals include G. R. Aitken, Head, PA/FOIA Branch, Chief of Naval Operations; Carlton W. Brown, Jr. and Samuel McKinney, Freedom of Information Officers, and staff at the Defense Nuclear Agency; Barbara A. Carmichael, Freedom of Information Manager, Department of the Air Force; John H. Carter, Chief of Freedom of Information and Privacy Acts, Office of Administrative Services, Department of Energy; Bernard F. Cavalcante, Head, Operational Archives Branch, Naval Historical Center, Department of the Navy; Jean S. Conover, Information and Privacy Coordinator, Naval Security and Investigative Command; Defense Communications Agency FOIA staff; Department of the Army FOIA staff; Gladys T. Gentry, Freedom of Information Officer, U. S. Readiness Command and U. S. Special Operations Command; Robert C. Hardzog, Freedom of Information Act Officer, Defense Intelligence Agency; Sharon B. Kotok, Chief, Information Access Branch, Department of State; Doris M. Lama, FOIA Manager, Chief of Naval Operations; Frank M. Machak, Information and Privacy Coordinator, Department of State; W. M. McDonald, Director, Freedom of Information and Security Review, Office of the Assistant Secretary of Defense (Public Affairs); Nancy V. Menan, FOI/Mandatory

Review Office, National Security Coucil; Military Airlift Command FOIA staff; Brenda S. Reger, Senior Director, Office of Information Policy and Security Review, National Security Council; Strategic Air Command FOIA staff; Lee S. Strickland, Information and Privacy Coordinator, Central Intelligence Agency; Sharon P. Thiele, Command FOIA Manager, Directorate of Administration, United States Air Forces in Europe; Training and Doctrine Command FOIA staff; Anne W. Turner, USAF Freedom of Information Manager, Department of the Air Force; U. S. Atlantic Command FOIA staff; U. S. Central Command FOIA staff; U. S. Marine Corps FOIA staff; U. S. Pacific Command FOIA staff; U. S. Southern Command FOIA staff; Robert J. Walsh, Jr., Chief, Freedom of Information/Privacy Office, Army Intelligence and Security Command; Julie B. Wetzel, Director of Policy, National Security Agency/Central Security Service; and Judy P. Wise, Head, Freedom of Information and Privacy, Naval Sea Systems Command.

The Institute for Policy Studies and the authors also wish to acknowledge the financial support and encouragement provided the *Encyclopedia* by Ruth Adams, Robert Allen, Harriet Barlow, James Compton, the Patrick and Anna M. Cudahy Fund, Larry Janss, the W. Alton Jones Foundation, Inc., Stewart R. Mott and Associates, and the Winston Foundation for World Peace.

And, finally, we would like to express our gratitude to Virginia Smith and Lee Watson of Harper & Row, who helped shepherd this book through a long editorial process, and special thanks to Tom Novack and James Osborne of Publication Services for their tireless production work on the *Encyclopedia*.

Introduction

The *Encyclopedia of the U. S. Military* is published at the onset of a new decade; one that will be characterized by continuing changes in U. S.–Soviet and international relations, a new focus on the environment, decreases in U. S. military spending, and the emergence of new priorities for national economic growth, and new opportunities for disarmament. In the course of this decade, the U. S. military will undergo its most significant reform since the end of the Second World War. Many of the rules and assumptions regarding the political and military structures established during this era will be reexamined.

As we stand poised at the edge of this new world, the nation faces enormous questions: How might the United States decrease its burden of defense while maintaining security and an international perspective? How will national institutions determine and implement cutbacks in military forces and personnel? What criteria should be applied in determining the size and composition of the future military? What is the process by which threats to U. S. security are reevaluated? How might U. S. war plans and national guidance reflect these threat assessments in order for the military to fulfill its constitutional responsibilities? In short, how might the nation make a positive transition from the nuclear arms race and preparations for protracted conventional war to the needs of the post–Cold War world?

Clearly, the exploration of such vital questions is determined by the availability and dissemination of information, which in turn provides a basis for public and private debates on these issues of national importance. To defense specialists and nonspecialists alike, an access to and understanding of the military establishment provides the key to reevaluation and change.

In the course of any reevaluation of the national system of defense, the specialists—policymakers, defense analysts, economists, and the like—will surely be cognizant of the roles and status afforded the U. S. military establishment in American society. High levels of defense spending, perhaps the most visible sign of this status, give the defense structure an influence on all sectors of the U. S. economy. Cutbacks in defense will have reverberating effects on peacetime civilian life as well as on local communities, making the coming fight over the remaining defense dollar very likely to be dominated by domestic and local politics, intramural battling, and greed, rather than by dispassionate and forward-looking analyses of national needs.

But defense politics aside, we should be mindful that there has never existed a scientific formula for determining the "proper defense." Indeed, in the darkest days of the Cold War, subjective judgments were made to quantify the unquantifiable. Competing systems analysts and operations researchers marshaled their information to make their respective cases for specific weapons, strategies, and courses of action. Sometimes they were right, sometimes wrong. But military decisions were all too often made on the basis of spotty, partial, or inaccurate information about national adversaries. Unfortunately, even in this age of *glasnost*, where both the East and the West are, in theory, less constrained by a lack of information, we can reasonably expect national military specialists and special interest groups to cling to institutional positions and established notions of defense. The strides made in areas such as arms control verification and U. S.–Soviet exchanges, in addition, may yield information that is as spotty, complex, and inaccessible as ever.

Nonspecialists, those who reside outside of the capital beltway and away from information institutions, will find few sources at their disposal to help them understand the new world of threats and defense needs. The very nature of defense organization and military decision making makes these activities largely inaccessible to the layperson, and the modes of thinking, logical connections, and values shaped by an immersion in the defense language are mostly impenetrable to the outsider. Additionally, the possibility of providing more, perhaps even better, information to specialists neither facilitates the access to such information nor ensures its clarity to the general citizenry.

Therefore, it is with both groups in mind—the defense specialists and the general public—that the *Encyclopedia of the U. S. Military* was written. Whether our readers be journalists, students, activists, researchers, defense contractors, government bureaucrats, soldiers, civilians, defense experts, or novices to defense affairs, it is our intent that the *Encyclopedia* serve as a practical and comprehensive reference tool on the major and current subjects related to U. S. military and defense activities. It exists not as an apolitical tome, but rather its publication is predicated on the democratic principle that values the rights and obligations of citizens to participate in the public debates of the time. It is understood that such participation requires not only the opportunity for involvement, but also the accessibility of information and the public's understanding of the issues.

As a detailed reference work, the *Encyclopedia* represents another in a series of such materials produced through the efforts of the Arms Race and Nuclear Weapons Research Project of the Institute for Policy Studies. Since 1981, when it published the *Research Guide to Current Military and Strategic Affairs*, the Project has sought to provide the public with analyses on all aspects of nuclear weapons, policy, and the arms race. But most importantly, it has sought to assemble and disseminate authoritative information in order to provide an access point for members of the public to participate in defense decision making.

Having surveyed the existing reference literature on defense, we believe that no other single-volume work can better aid those concerned with the generalities and particulars of the defense world—its history, terminology, trends, and organization. The major categories of information contained in the *Encyclopedia* are

- Major weapons/weapon systems (nuclear and conventional)
- Command, control, and communications programs/procedures
- Combat units and hierarchy
- Operations and exercises
- Intelligence collection and analysis
- Planning, budgeting, programming, and management systems
- U. S. military commands and organizations
- NATO military commands and organizations
- Major U. S. laws affecting national security
- International treaties and arms control agreements
- Codewords

The *Encyclopedia* comprises over 2,000 entries ranging from single-sentence definitions of specific terms to extended discussions of military concepts and systems. Definitions were compiled from hundreds of authoritative sources, including U. S. government documents, military manuals, books, fact sheets, internal studies, glossaries, and specialized dictionaries. Entries were composed using official source materials whenever possible and are presented without extraneous commentary. An attempt was made to present language in political and military contexts to aid the reader. Throughout the *Encyclopedia*, direct quotes and officially approved definitions and information have been used when most appropriate, and sources are provided within the text only for the attribution of such quotes, official material, and specialized information.

Insofar as the military and defense community is a massive, multifaceted, and ever-evolving institution, it should be noted that a great effort has been made to include the most timely, pertinent, and up-to-date information available. For example, only current weapon systems and technologies have been included, together with details of such programs from the last available fiscal year, in most cases FY 1989. A large portion of the entries, however, such as those defining operational military terms and concepts, are relatively ageless.

It is our hope that as events move forward in the world—when crises erupt, when accidents occur, when budget decisions are made, when new weapons are developed—the *Encyclopedia* will be readily able to clarify ambiguous information, to provide precision where generalities will not suffice, and to put into a political and organizational context events and systems that often seem unconnected to larger values and decisions. It is our profound belief that to make accessible to the layperson the mysterious processes that often surround the Pentagon and its actions is to make a worthwhile contribution to democracy, and, ultimately, American security.

Acronyms and Abbreviations

AB	Air Base	EMP	electromagnetic pulse
AFB	Air Force Base	EO	Executive Order
AFM	Air Force Manual	FM	Field Manual
AFR	Air Force Regulation	FOIA	Freedom of Information
AFS	Air Force Station		Act
ANGB	Air National Guard Base	FPO	Fleet Post Office
APO	Air Post Office	ft	foot/feet
AR	Army Regulation	FY	fiscal year
AS	Air Station	GLCM	ground-launched cruise
ASAT	anti-satellite		missile
ASROC	anti-submarine rocket	HF	high frequency
ASW	anti-submarine warfare	Hz	hertz
AWACS	Airborne Warning and Control	ICBM	intercontinental
	System		ballistic missile
AY	Academic Year	IOC	initial operational
blk	block		capability
C2	command and control	IR	infrared
C3	command, control,	JCS	Joint Chiefs of Staff
	and communication	km	kilometer(s)
C3I	command, control,	kph	kilometer(s) per hour
	communication, and	Kt	Kiloton(s)
	intelligence	kt	knot(s)
CEP	circular error probable	lb	pound(s)
CINC	Commander-in-Chief	MAC	Military Airlift
CONUS	continental United States		Command
CY	calendar year	MaRV	maneuvering re-entry
DARPA	Defense Advanced		vehicle
	Research Projects	MCAS	Marine Corps
	Agency		Air Station
Dir	Directive	MIRV	multiple independently tar-
DOD	Department of Defense		geted re-entry vehicle
DOE	Department of Energy	Mk	mark
EAM	emergency action	MHz	Megahertz
	message	MOU	Memorandum of
ELF	extremely low frequency		Understanding

mph	mile(s) per hour	Reg	Regulation
nm	nautical mile(s)	SAC	Strategic Air Command
NAS	Naval Air Station	SDI	Strategic Defense Initiative
NATO	North Atlantic Treaty Organization	SDIO	Strategic Defense Initiative Organization
NORAD	North American Aerospace Defense Command	SLBM	submarine-launched ballistic missile
NSDD	National Security Decision Directive	SLCM	sea-launched cruise missile
OCONUS	outside the continental United States	SIOP	Single Integrated Operational Plan
OJCS	Office of the Joint Chiefs of Staff	SM	Staff Memorandum
OMB	Office of Management and Budget	TAC	Tactical Air Command
		USAF	United States Air Force
OSD	Office of the Secretary of Defense	USC	United States Code
		VLF	very low frequency
PD	Presidential Directive	V/STOL	vertical/short take-off and landing
RAF	Royal Air Force		
R&D	research and development	VTOL/	vertical take-off and
RDT&E	research, development, testing, and evaluation	STOL	landing/short take-off and landing

A

A: Prefix designating **1.** Attack aircraft with the primary functions of interdiction and close air support (e.g., A-6, A-10). **2.** Auxiliary Navy ships (e.g., AE: ammunition ship). **3.** Air-launched missiles (e.g., AGM-86: air-launched cruise missile).

A-3 Skywarrior (see **EA-3 Skywarrior**)

A-4 Skyhawk: A currently deployed Marine Corps, all-weather, day or night, single-seat, single-engine, subsonic, turbojet, dual-capable, light attack aircraft. The first version was deployed in 1956; the current version is the A-4M. The A-4 is armed with two internal 20 mm cannons and externally can carry up to 10,000 lb of weapons, including rockets, bombs, torpedoes, and cannons, and a single B43 or B57 nuclear bomb. Its maximum speed at sea level is 670 mph, or 646 mph with 4,000 lb of weapons. Its combat radius is 335 nm with 4,000 lb of weapons and it has a range of 2,000 nm with external fuel tanks. The A-4 can act as a tanker and can itself be refueled. There are approximately 100 A-4M operational aircraft left in the Marine

Corps inventory as of 1989, deployed in two active and five reserve attack squadrons (designated VMA), each with 19 and 12 aircraft, respectively. The last two Marine Corps active squadrons are to transition to **AV-8B Harriers** by 1990, and the reserve squadrons are scheduled to transition to AV-8Bs and **F/A-18 Hornets** in the 1990s. McDonnell Douglas, St. Louis, MO, was the prime contractor.

The A-4 was developed in the early 1950s (the first serial production airplane was designated the A-4D). The plane was designed to be a lightweight, day only nuclear strike aircraft for use in large numbers from aircraft carriers. It entered both Navy and Marine Corps service in 1956 with first fleet delivery to Navy attack squadron 72 (VA-72) in November 1956. Over 2,900 A-4s in attack, trainer, support, and export configurations (A-4A, A-4B, A-4C, A-4E, A-4F, A-4J, and A-4M) were produced, with the last A-4 delivered to the Marine Corps in February 1979. The last year an active Navy squadron flew the A-4 was 1974. The only remaining version in the U.S. inventory is the nuclear capable A-4M. Foreign nations operating A-4 variants include Australia, Israel,

New Zealand, Kuwait, Argentina, and Singapore.

A-6E Intruder: A currently deployed Navy and Marine Corps carrier-based, all-weather, two-seat, twin-engine, subsonic, turbojet, dual-capable, medium attack aircraft. The A-6A entered the fleet in 1964; the current updated version is the A-6E. The A-6E has five external store stations, allowing it to carry up to 18,000 lb of weapons, including bombs, mines, 20 mm guns, missiles, rockets (including **Harpoon**, **HARM**, and **Sidewinder**), and B43, B57, and B61 nuclear bombs. It has an integrated attack/navigation computer system to locate targets while at a low altitude. It has a maximum speed of 650 mph at sea level and cruises at 475 mph at optimum altitude. It has a combat radius of 1,000 mi with combat load and a maximum range of 3,100 mi with external fuel tanks. It can act as a tanker and can itself be refueled. There are approximately 280 Navy and Marine Corps A-6Es in the operational inventory as of 1989. These are distributed among 19 Navy attack squadrons (designated VA) — 16 active, 2 fleet readiness and training, and 1 reserve — and 5 Marine Corps all-weather attack squadrons (VMAAW) of ten aircraft each. Atlantic and Pacific Fleet squadrons are located at NAS Oceana, VA, and NAS Whidbey Island, WA, respectively, and two squadrons are forward-based at NAF Atsugi, Japan, as part of the aircraft carrier USS Midway's (CV-41) airwing. The Marine Corps squadrons are divided between MCAS El Toro, CA, and MCAS Cherry Point, NC, but may occasionally deploy on carriers or to overseas Marine bases. Prime contractors are Grumman Aerospace Corporation of Bethpage, Long Island, NY, and Pratt and Whitney, East Hartford, CT, for the engine.

The A-6 was developed in the late 1950s, and the first test flight took place in 1963. Seven variants of the basic design have been built, of which the A-6A, A-6B, and A-6C are no longer operational. The current attack version is the A-6E equipped with a TRAM (Target Recognition Attack Multisensor) system, a turreted electro-optical/infrared system matched with laser-guided weapons. The Navy was planning to produce a new variant, the A-6F, in the late 1980s, which would have incorporated digital avionics, high-resolution radar, a night attack system, state-of-the-art electronic counter-measure equipment, and new engines. Budgetary constraints led to the cancellation of the A-6F program in the FY 1989 defense budget in favor of an A-6E upgrade and continued work on the A-6's future replacement, the **A-12 Advanced Tactical Aircraft**. The upgrade, designated the A-6G, would have included some of the improvements developed in the A-6F program. However, budgetary problems led to the termination of the A-6G program in the FY 1990 defense budget. Instead, the A-6E is scheduled to receive modest avionics updates and wing replacements. Two non-attack derivatives of the A-6 currently active are the **KA-6D** aerial refueling aircraft and the **EA-6B Prowler** electronic warfare plane.

A-7 Corsair II: A currently deployed Air Force, Air National Guard, and Navy all-weather, single-seat, single-engine, subsonic, turbofan, dual-capable, light attack aircraft. It is used for close air support, interdiction, and search and rescue missions. The A-7A first entered Navy service in 1966 and deliveries to the Air Force began in 1968. It is armed with an internal 20 mm multi-barrel gatling gun and a Vulcan cannon, and it can carry up to 15,000 lb of bombs and missiles. The A-7E variant can carry B43, B57, and B61 nuclear bombs. The A-7 has a maximum speed of 680 mph, or 640 mph at 5,000 feet with 12 Mk 82 conventional bombs. It has a combat radius of 490 mi with external fuel tanks, or 630 mi without tanks, and a maximum range of 2,900 miles with external fuel tanks. As of 1989, there are approximately 540 A-7s in the U.S. operational inventory, 170 A-7Es with the Navy, and 340 A-7Ds and 30 A-7Ks with the Air Force and Air National Guard. The deployments are

- Navy (A-7E): As of 1989, 10 active squadrons are based at NAS Cecil Field, FL, and NAS Lemoore, CA, and three reserve squadrons are at NAS Cecil Field, FL; NAS New Orleans, LA; and NAS Atlanta, GA, each with 12 aircraft. One fleet readiness training squadron with TA-7Cs is also at NAS Lemoore, CA.
- Air Force (A-7D/K): As of 1988, 14 Air National Guard units have about 340 combat and trainer aircraft. No major active Air Force units exist, but some 30 aircraft are at two

active Air Force locations, Nellis AFB, NV, and Edwards AFB, CA, and are used for training.

The prime contractors are Vought Corporation (LTV Inc.), Dallas, TX (prime/airframe), and Detroit Diesel, Allison Division, Indianapolis, IN (engine).

The A-7 was developed in the early 1960s for the Navy as a light attack, close air support aircraft. Its design was based on the F-8 Crusader airframe to reduce costs. Between 1966 and 1983, 1,567 A-7s were produced in several versions: 199 A-7As, 196 A-7Bs, 67 A-7Cs, 459 A-7Ds, 596 A-7Es, and 30 A-7Ks. The A-7E became operational in 1969 and is the current Navy version. It is based on the A-7D design, but it has a Navy specified air-refueling system. It is the only current nuclear-capable version. The A-7D/K are the current Air Force and Air National Guard versions. The A-7D had a new engine, 20 mm cannon, air-refueling system, and navigation/weapons system installed. A-7Ds were delivered to the Air National Guard between 1973 and 1981. The A-7K is a two-seat version of the A-7D for service with the Air National Guard. The prototype, converted from an A-7D, was first flown in 1980, and the last delivery of an A-7K was in 1984. There are also export versions for the Greek and Portuguese air forces. Some 367 A-7Ds were modified with Pave Penny laser spot tracker target pods from 1978 to 1982. LTV is modifying another 72 A-7Ds and 8 A-7Ks for low-altitude night attack (LANA) capability, with forward-looking infrared sensors (FLIR) and automatic ter-

rain following (ATF) systems to provide round-the-clock effectiveness.
The first LANA-equipped aircraft was
delivered June 1987. Under a contract
awarded May 1987, LTV is upgrading
A-7Ds to the A-7 "Plus" configuration, designated A-7F. Modifications
include a lengthened fuselage to
accommodate a new engine and additional fuel and provisions for **Maverick** and **Sidewinder** missiles. Plans as
of 1988 call for up to 335 aircraft to
be so modified.

The number of Navy A-7 squadrons
has been and will continue to decline
as they are replaced by **F/A-18 Hornet** squadrons. Moreover, plans call
to replace another A-7 Navy reserve
squadron with A-6Es in 1990 (one
squadron was replaced in 1988–89).
All Navy A-7 squadrons are scheduled to be replaced by F/A-18s by the
early 1990s.

A-10 Thunderbolt II: A currently
deployed Air Force, single-seat, twin-
engine, subsonic, turbofan, conventionally armed, close air support
aircraft. The A-10 was the first modern Air Force aircraft built especially
for the close air support role. It is
designed to operate from short-field,
unimproved surfaces and is capable
of long endurance in the target area
while being refueled in flight. Pilot
and flight control systems are surrounded by titanium armor plates to
protect them from armor-piercing and
high-explosive 23 mm projectiles. It
can carry non-nuclear ordnance such
as bombs, cluster bombs, **Maverick**, **Sidewinder**, and laser-guided
missiles. A GAU-8/A Avenger 30 mm
cannon is installed to give the A10

an antitank killing capability. The A-
10 can also be equipped with electronic jammer pods. Chaff and flares
are carried internally to counter radar
and infrared-guided missiles. The A-
10's combat speed without loads is
439 mph. Combat radius with 9,500
lb of ordnance and almost two hours
on station is 290 mi. As of 1988,
some 650 aircraft were distributed
among Air Force, Air National Guard,
and Air Force Reserve squadrons in
the United States and overseas. The
prime contractor is Fairchild-Republic
Company, a division of Fairchild
Industries.

The A-10 was developed in the
early 1970s as a specialized close air
support aircraft. It was first flown
in 1972 and the first operational
unit, the 354th Tactical Fighter Wing,
was activated at Myrtle Beach AFB,
SC, in June 1977, achieving operational status in October. Delivery of
over 700 aircraft to the Air Force
was completed in March 1984. The
first A-10s assigned to U.S. Air
Forces in Europe (USAFE) were stationed at RAF Bentwaters, UK, in
1979. In 1982, squadrons of A-10s
were assigned to Pacific Air Forces
at Suwon AB, South Korea, and
Alaskan Air Command's 18th Tactical Fighter Squadron at Eielson AFB,
AK. The FY 1990 defense budget
calls for phasing out of the A-10
force beginning in FY 1992. Possible
replacements include an attack version of the F-16 fighter (designated
the A-16), as well as a new aircraft.
Some 26 A-10s are being designated
OA-10s and will be used for forward
air control, search and rescue, and
visual reconnaissance.

A-12 Advanced Tactical Aircraft (ATA): A Navy two-seat, all-weather, long-range, carrier-based attack aircraft under development, to be deployed in the 1990s as a replacement for the **A-6 Intruder**. It will incorporate advanced low-observable (stealth) technologies. The pilot and the bombardier/navigator will sit in tandem. The Air Force is also a major participant in the program in order to produce a joint service attack aircraft (**Advanced Tactical Fighter**) at reduced costs. On 23 December 1987, the Navy chose a McDonnell Douglas/General Dynamics team over a Grumman/Northrop team to develop and produce the A-12. The plane will be powered with the F-404 engine. Reportedly, the Navy wishes to build some 450-500 aircraft at an estimated cost of $35-45 billion, with an initial operating capability scheduled for the middle to late 1990s. The first planes will be based at NAS Whidbey Island, WA. The aircraft designation A-12A was established on 3 October 1988.

AAC (see **Alaskan Air Command**)

AACE (see **Aircraft Alerting Communications Electromagnetic Pulse**)

AAFCE (see **Allied Air Forces, Central Europe**)

AAM (see **air-to-air missile**)

ABM (anti-ballistic missile): A missile designed to intercept and destroy a strategic or theater **ballistic missile** or its **reentry vehicle(s)**. A complete ABM system consists of long- or short-range interceptor missiles, launchers in silos or on the ground, acquisition and tracking radars, and command and control and fire support equipment. The only U.S. ABM system ever deployed was located at Grand Forks, ND, and consisted of nuclear-armed Sprint and Spartan missiles, radars, and support equipment. The missiles were deployed in 1974 and removed in 1976 because of high costs and technical ineffectiveness. Further deployment of ABM systems is limited by the **ABM Treaty** of 1972 and **ABM Protocol** of 1974.

ABM Protocol: A protocol to the 1972 **ABM Treaty** that reduced the number of allowed ABM deployment areas in the United States and the Soviet Union from two to one. It was signed in Moscow on 3 July 1974, and it entered into force on 24 May 1976. It also allowed the Soviet Union and the United States to move their ABM systems from the national capital to a missile site or vice versa, with advance notice. The Soviet ABM system, originally called Galosh, surrounds Moscow. The American system, **Safeguard**, was deployed to protect a missile site in Grand Forks, ND.

ABM Treaty: (**"Treaty between the United States and the USSR on the Limitation of Anti-Ballistic Missile Systems"**) The ABM Treaty is part of the **SALT I** agreements signed by President Richard Nixon and General Secretary Leonid Brezhnev on 26 May 1972 and ratified by the U.S. Senate on 30 September 1972. The treaty entered into force on 3 October 1972. The treaty limited the use of U.S. and Soviet anti-ballistic missile systems, and it committed the Soviet Union and the United States not to develop, test, or deploy ABM systems or components that are sea-based, air-based, space-based, or mobile land-based.

The ABM Treaty figures prominently in current debates surrounding the RDT&E phases of the **Strategic Defense Initiative (SDI)**. Critics of SDI claim that a strict interpretation of the ABM Treaty limits SDI development to the laboratory. The Reagan Administration argued for a looser interpretation that would allow the development and even the deployment of certain technologies. In 1985, the Soviet Union proposed a fifteen-year moratorium on the deployment of new missile defenses. In 1986, the Reagan Administration proposed a seven-and-a-half-year delay in deploying space- and ground-based weapons but proposed permitting development and testing. At the 1986 Iceland summit, the United States was willing to compromise on this proposal to a 10-year delay, but the Soviet Union demanded that SDI be confined to the laboratory with no testing and development of the system during that 10 years. The United States found this unacceptable, and the issue has simmered since, awaiting progress in the **START** talks, pending final resolution.

Provisions of the ABM Treaty are as follows

- *Article I:* Agree to limit ABM systems and not deploy these systems for defense of its own country.
- *Article II:* An ABM system includes ABM interceptor missiles, launch-

ers, and radars that are operational; under construction; undergoing testing, overhaul, repair, or conversion; or mothballed.
- *Article III:* Exceptions to deploying an ABM system: each party may deploy one system around its capital and not exceeding a radius of 150 km; no more than 100 ABM launchers and no more than 100 ABM interceptor missiles at launch sites; ABM radars within no more than six ABM radar complexes. Within one ABM system deployment area containing ICBM missile silos the following may be deployed: no more than 100 ABM launchers or missiles; two large phased-array ABM radars comparable to those radars operational or under construction as of May 1972; no more than 18 ABM radars each with a lesser potential of the larger phased-array radars. These provisions for two ABM systems within each country were changed by the 1974 Protocol to allow only one system per country.
- *Article IV:* "The limitations provided for in Article III shall not apply to ABM systems or their components used for development or testing, and located within current or additionally agreed test ranges. Each Party may have no more than a total of 15 ABM launchers at test ranges." Test ranges include White Sands, NM, and Kwajalein Atoll (U.S.) and Sary Shagan, Kazakhstan (Soviet Union).
- *Article V:* "Each Party undertakes not to develop, test, or deploy ABM systems or components which are sea-based, air-based, space-based or mobile land-based." Also pro-

hibited is the development of a capability to launch more than one ABM interceptor missile at once from each launcher and a capability for rapid reload of ABM launchers. Development of MIRVed ABM missiles is therefore banned.

- *Article VI:* Each party undertakes "not to give missiles, launchers, or radars, other than ABM interceptor missiles, ABM launchers, or ABM radars, capabilities to counter strategic ballistic missiles or their elements in flight trajectory, and not to test them in an ABM mode." Also agreed upon is that neither party will "deploy in the future radars for early warning of strategic ballistic missile attack except at locations along the periphery of its national territory and oriented outward."
- *Article VII:* Modernization and replacement of ABM systems or their components may be carried out.
- *Article VIII:* ABM systems or components outside the numbers or areas specified in the treaty "shall be destroyed or dismantled under agreed procedures within the shortest possible agreed period of time."
- *Article IX:* The United States and the Soviet Union agree "not to transfer to other States, and not to deploy outside its national territory, ABM systems or their components limited by this treaty." The Reagan plan to share SDI technology with allies would therefore violate the treaty. Cooperative laboratory research efforts are allowed, but joint development, testing, production, and deployment of ABM systems or components are prohibited. Despite these restric-

tions, the United States began in 1984 to brief its allies on the scope and progress of SDI research.
- *Article X:* "Each Party undertakes not to assume any international obligations which would conflict with this Treaty."
- *Article XI:* "The Parties undertake to continue active negotiations for limitations on strategic offensive arms."
- *Article XII:* To comply with the treaty, both signatories will use "**national technical means of verification**" under the guidelines of international law. These means of verification are not to be impeded by the other country or by concealment measures.
- *Article XIII:* Establishes a Standing Consultative Commission to deal with compliance questions and verification, changing strategic forces technologies, destruction of ABM systems as proscribed by the treaty, amendments to the treaty, and future arms control proposals.
- *Article XIV:* Both parties may submit amendments to the treaty. Also, "five years after entry into force of this Treaty, and at five-year intervals thereafter, the Parties shall together conduct a review of this Treaty." The third treaty review was held from 24–31 August 1988.
- *Article XV:* "This Treaty shall be of unlimited duration . . . . Each Party shall, in exercising its national sovereignty, have the right to withdraw from this Treaty if it decides that extraordinary events related to the subject matter of this Treaty have jeopardized its supreme interests." Notice of withdrawal must be given six months in advance and

must outline the events justifying withdrawal. On 9 May 1972, U.S. negotiator Gerard Smith stated, "If an agreement providing for more complete strategic offensive arms limitations were not achieved within five years, U.S. supreme interests could be jeopardized. Should that occur, it would constitute a basis for withdrawal from the ABM Treaty."

- *Article XVI:* Registers the treaty with the United Nations and provides for its ratification by both countries.

Accusations made by the United States of Soviet violations to the Treaty include

- construction of restricted large lasers for ABM purposes;
- nonpermanently-fixed ABM radar on the Kamchatka peninsula; and
- construction of a restricted large phased-array radar station at Krasnoyarsk, Siberia.

Soviet accusations of U.S. violations include

- use of the phased-array radar station at Shemya Island, AK;
- shelters used at anti-missile launcher sites;
- work on mobile ABM systems and space-based missile systems;
- testing Minuteman ICBMs to give them ABM capabilities;
- development of multiple warheads for anti-missile weapons;
- development of PAVE PAW radars for ABM defense; and
- development of SDI.

(see also **SALT I**)

ABNCP (see **airborne command post**)

Abrams (see **M-1 Abrams**)

ABRES (Advanced Ballistic Reentry System): Missile reentry system research program that is the Air Force predecessor to the **Advanced Strategic Missile System (ASMS)**.

AC-130 A/H Spectre: A currently deployed, Air Force, limited/all-weather, four-engine, turboprop, close air support and **special operations** gunship version of the **C-130 Hercules** transport aircraft. Its mission is to provide fire support for regular and unconventional warfare forces, as well as conduct interdiction and armed reconnaissance missions. It is able to loiter for hours over a target area while providing heavy fire support. It was first used extensively in 1968 in the Vietnam War. It has a maximum speed of 390 mph and a range of 2,500 mi when fully loaded. Two versions of the AC-130 are in service: the AC-130A equipped with two 40 mm cannons, two 20 mm Vulcan cannons, and two 7.62 mm miniguns; and the AC-130H with similar armament except that one 40 mm cannon is replaced with a 105 mm howitzer. Both models are equipped with sensors and target acquisition systems, including **forward-looking infrared (FLIR)** and low-light-level TV (LLLTV). AC-130Hs are equipped for in-flight refueling as well. As part of an improvement program to be finished in the early 1990s, AC-130Hs are being fitted with new fire control computers, navigation equipment, and sensors. Twenty aircraft are deployed in two squadrons: 10 AC-130As with the

711th Special Operations Squadron (SOS); and 10 AC-130Hs with the 16th SOS, both at Eglin AFB, FL.

A new AC-130 version, the AC-130U, is in production with a planned 12 aircraft to be delivered by FY 1992. The AC-130Us will replace aging AC-130As and will be modified from new C-130H airframes. AC-130Us will have enhanced capability, improved reliability and maintainability, and more survivability than the older AC-130A gunships, and they will include new precision navigation, infrared countermeasures, covert lighting, and secure communications. AC-130Us will have a highly accurate suite of 105 mm, 40 mm, and 25 mm guns that can be remotely controlled by FLIR, LLLTV, or strike radar, permitting night and adverse weather operations. They will also have electronic countermeasure systems to improve survivability. The airframe contractor is Lockheed and the avionics integrations contractor is Rockwell International. In July 1987, Rockwell was awarded a research and development contract for the AC-130U. Total RDT&E and production costs in FY 1990 are $307.6 million, for the procurement of five aircraft. FY 1991 will be the final year of procurement funding ($60.3 million requested) for initial spares and completion of evaluation.

ACCHAN (see **Allied Command Channel**)

Accident Measures Agreement (see **Agreement on Measures to Reduce the Risk of Outbreak of Nuclear War**)

accidental war: According to the JCS, the term "accidental war" is "not to be used" [*JCS Pub 1*, 1 April 1984, p. 2]. (see **Agreement on the Prevention of Nuclear War, Agreement on Measures to Reduce the Risk of Outbreak of Nuclear War**)

ACDA (see **Arms Control and Disarmament Agency**)

ACE (see **Allied Command Europe**)

Ace High: NATO tropospheric forward-scatter communications network extending from northern Norway to eastern Turkey as part of the **NATO Integrated Communications System (NICS)**. Ace High is the primary fixed ground transmission system for **Allied Command Europe (ACE)**. About 80 troposcatter links exist, each with 60 voice channels. Branch routes span to Belgium (via **Supreme Headquarters Allied Powers Europe (SHAPE)**) from southern Norway, and to the United Kingdom. Ace High has been operational since 1960, and in 1980 the move was made to convert the troposcatter systems to digital operations. The NICS plan for replacement was to be completed by 1988. Its links in Norway are being phased out.

ACE Mobile Force (AMF): Major subordinate command of NATO's **Allied Command Europe (ACE)** and its rapid deployment force. Established in 1960, AMF provides rapid air and land deployment reinforcements to the northern and southern flanks. AMF is a multilateral brigade strength force consisting of combat battalions from seven nations—Belgium, West Germany, Luxembourg, the United States, Canada, Italy, and the United Kingdom—plus other air, land, and support elements. There are no air units permanently assigned to AMF, but when deployed, the air component is composed of squadrons from Belgium, Canada, West Germany, Italy, the Netherlands, the United Kingdom, and the United States. It has no central headquarters, but when operational, AMF comes under the command of the regional NATO command or Allied Tactical Air Force to which it is deployed. Its exercises are most often held in Norway or Turkey, where it practices rapid reinforcement of the flanks of NATO.

Headquarters AMF
(L), Heidelberg, West Germany

ACINT (see **acoustical intelligence**)

acoustical intelligence (ACOUSTINT/ACINT): Type of **intelligence** information collected from acoustic waves emitted either intentionally or unintentionally. In naval usage, ACINT usually refers to intelligence derived specifically from the analysis of underwater acoustic waves radiated from ships and submarines. ACINT can provide identifying or "signature" information on a vessel. Navy ACINT systems include the **Sound Surveillance System (SOSUS)**, the Fixed Distributed Surveillance (FDS) system, the Rapidly Deployable Surveillance System (RDSS), and the **Surface Towed Array Surveillance System (SURTASS)**.

acoustics: The science of sound dealing with its propagation, transmission, and effects. Acoustic detection techniques are used to locate ships and submarines and, in conjunction with seismic detection, to identify nuclear explosions.

acquisition: **1.** Process of searching for and detecting a potentially threatening object, in air or in space. A sensor searches large areas, distinguishing between potential targets and decoys. **2.** The process of acquiring military items, such as materiel. (see also **acquisition cycle**)

acquisition cycle: The process by which military materiel and systems are acquired. The cycle normally consists of five phases: Conception, Validation, Full-Scale Development, Production, and Deployment, with key decision points between each of the first three phases: Program, Ratification, and Production Decisions.

action officer (AO): Designated at the JCS, a unified or specified command, a service headquarters, or a major command to work on a particular action or series of related actions requiring decisions. The AO is responsible for developing, coordinating, and completing the required analysis; formulating recommendations; presenting the action for decision; and preparing a message or other correspondence implementing the recommendations. AO responsibility continues during the internal routing of the implementing document and ends only when that document has been dispatched or further action is not required [*Joint Staff Officer's*

Guide 1988, Armed Forces Staff College Publication 1, p. 72].

activate: To bring into existence a unit or facility that has been previously constituted or is in reserve status. In the Navy, a new unit is commissioned.

active component: The largest portion of the **Total Force**, composed of "men and women who serve in units that engage enemy forces, units that provide support in the combat theater, other support units, and those people who are in special accounts (transients, students, etc.). These men and women are on call 24 hours a day and receive full-time military pay." The active component numbers approximately 2.1 million military personnel [DOD, *Manpower Requirements Report: FY 1989*, March 1988, p. I-1]. (see also **reserves**)

activity: **1.** An organizational unit of the Navy with a separate **table of distribution and allowance (TDA)** (e.g., Naval Security Group Activity). **2.** A function or mission (e.g., recruiting or training activity).

actual ground zero (AGZ):   "The point on the surface of the earth at, or vertical below or above, the center of an actual nuclear detonation" [*JCS Pub 1*, 1 April 1984, p. 4]. (see also **desired ground zero**)

AD: Designation for **destroyer tender** ship.

Ada: DOD's standard computer software language. It is named for Augusta Ada Byron (1815–1852),

daughter of Lord Byron and Annabella Milbanke Byron, the first computer programmer. Before the development of Ada, DOD and contractors were using more than 450 different programming languages and dialects on their computer systems. DARPA was charged with managing the development of a new language and, in 1977, opened bids to develop a new language based on either PL/I, Algol 68, or Pascal. In 1979, the new language based on Pascal was chosen and named Ada. The Ada Joint Program Office was opened in 1980, and it then created the Ada Information Clearinghouse and Ada Compiler Validation Capability. Responsibility for Ada then switched to DOD. The Canadian Ministry of Defence and the Federal Aviation Administration also use Ada, as does NATO.

adaption kit: Components required to adapt a DOE nuclear warhead to a DOD weapon. The adaption kit normally includes the arming, safing, and fuzing systems, the necessary power supplies, hardware, support structure and in some cases, the warhead compartment.

adaptive HF: Communications system designed to adapt to the most hostile ionospheric environments and to provide long-range connectivity and command and control information to military forces. HF frequency systems are used for long-haul mobile communications since they are small, affordable, and enduring, but they are considered vulnerable and largely obsolete. As a part of the **Minimum Essential Emergency Communications Network (MEECN)**, the purpose of adaptive HF is to provide a modular family of radios that will improve reliability of two-way HF communications in a nuclear or jamming environment. The system was developed to reduce vulnerability to jamming and to provide a back-up to satellite intraforce communications. Adaptive HF radios will be able to automatically select the optimum transmit and receive frequencies to rapidly adapt to both natural and induced ionospheric changes. It includes netted, broadcast, and point-to-point capabilities for voice, teletype, and 2.4 KBPs data transmission. The system is software controlled and programmed.

ADATS (Air Defense Antitank System) (see **Forward Area Defense System**)

Adjutant General (AG):   1. Adjutant General Corps, **combat service support** branch of the Army.   **2. Staff officer** with administrative duties, such as personnel, publications, postal service, and bands.

ADM   (see **atomic demolition munition**)

administration/administrative support: Management of all military matters not included in strategy and tactics (e.g., personnel management of units).

administration and associated activities: Program 9 of the 11 **major force programs** that represent all of the major missions of the services and are the most basic structural elements of the **Five Year Defense**

Program. It consists of resources for the administrative support of departmental and major administrative headquarters, field commands, administration, and associated activities not accounted for elsewhere. It also includes construction support and other miscellaneous activities.

administrative chain of command: Command hierarchy established for normal, non-operational functions prior to assignment of forces and units for combat missions. The Navy's typical administrative chain of command is illustrated below. Note that fleet commanders-in-chief (CINCs) fall in both the administrative and operational chains of command, as do group, ship squadron, and air wing commanders. (see also **administrative command, operational chain of command, task organization, type command**)

President
:
Secretary of Defense
:
Secretary of the Navy
:
Chief of Naval Operations
:
Area Fleet CINCs
:
Type Commander
:
Group Commander
:
Ship Squadron/Air Wing Commander
:
Commanding officers of individual units

administrative control: Authority of a commander to manage the non-operational matters of subordinate units or organizations, such as supply, personnel, and administration. (see also **operational control**)

Admiral: 1. The highest officer rank in the Navy, equivalent to a General in the Air Force, Army, or Marine Corps. Also referred to as a **flag officer**, since Admirals are authorized to fly flags with stars to denote their rank. **2.** A four-star Navy Admiral.

Advanced air-to-air missile (AAAM): A Navy anti-air missile under development to replace the AIM-54C **Phoenix**. It will be much lighter than the Phoenix, allowing it greater range and speed. It also will be compatible with a greater variety of aircraft than the Phoenix (which can only be used by the F-14 Tomcat), including the **F/A-18 Hornet**, **F-15 Eagle**, **F-14 Tomcat**, the **A-12 Advanced Tactical Aircraft (ATA)**, and **Advanced Tactical Fighter (ATF)**. It will have an improved electronic counter-countermeasures capability and will be effective against stealth targets. Proposed FY 1990 and FY 1991 RDT&E costs are respectively $74.7 million and $84.9 million.

Advanced Attack Helicopter (AAH): Developmental name for the **AH-64 Apache**.

Advanced Antitank Weapon System: Army program to develop and acquire advanced medium and heavy antitank weapons for the replacement of existing Dragon and **TOW** missiles. The systems will be capable of operating at day or night, in smoke and other battlefield obscurants, and

in a countermeasures environment. These systems include

- Advanced Antitank Weapon System-Heavy (AAWS-H): Joint program with the Marine Corps to replace the TOW. AAWS-H is a family of weapons consisting of an Advanced Missile System-Heavy (AMS-H) and a Kinetic Energy Missile (KEM) System. The KEM will be developed as a line-of-sight antitank replacement for the M-901 Improved TOW Vehicle dedicated antitank vehicle; the AMS-H will be for use on the **M-2 Bradley Fighting Vehicle**, High Mobility Multipurpose Wheeled Vehicle (HMMWV), and potentially attack helicopters. Both missiles are to have a range greater than TOW (3,750 meters). In 1989, AAWS-H was in the pre-Full Engineering Development phase. The **fiber optic-guided missile (FOG-M)**, which is being developed for both an air defense and antitank applications, is also under consideration to be the AAWS-H.

- Advanced Antitank Weapon System-Medium (AAWS-M): Army one-man portable antitank weapon employed at the infantry platoon level. The AAWS-M will be developed to replace the Dragon, and address many of its operational deficiencies. These deficiencies include poor lethality, short range, gunner vulnerability, high launch signature and long time of flight. The system will consist of a round (missile and throw-away launch tube) and reusable command and launch unit (CLU). The CLU will include a day or night sight and be capable of operating several hours before replenishing batteries. One of three candidate technologies—Laser Beamrider, Fiber Optic, and fire-and-forget Imaging Infrared—currently under development will be used for guidance of the missile. AAWS-M is to weigh less than 45 lb and have a range of greater than 1,500 meters. Contracts for the Proof of Principle phase were awarded in August 1986 and the Full Scale Development contract was to be awarded in April 1989. Contractor teams for the Proof of Principle phase included Ford Aerospace (Laser Beamrider concept), Hughes Aircraft (Fiber Optic guidance), and Texas Instruments (infrared seeker).

The FY 1990 and FY 1991 RDT&E request for advanced antitank weapon systems is $228.3 and $148.8 million, respectively.

Advanced Cruise Missile (ACM) (AGM 129): An Air Force air-launched nuclear-armed **cruise missile** under development and scheduled to augment and replace the currently deployed AGM-86B **air-launched cruise missile (ALCM)** on **B-52H** and **B-1B** bombers in the 1990s. The ACM will be more accurate and will be able to operate at longer ranges than the existing ALCM. This extra range will allow bombers to deliver their weapons at greater distance from Soviet territory, thereby avoiding airborne warning systems and long-range interceptors that are expected to extend Soviet air defense coverage in the 1990s. The ACM also will be able to circumvent some

defenses due to its added range. Low-observable (stealth) technologies will enhance the missile's ability to penetrate and attack highly defended areas.

In July 1982, the Air Force concluded an assessment of the requirements for a next-generation cruise missile. In August 1982, President Reagan approved the ACM program, and development efforts began in 1983, with General Dynamics being the prime contractor, making use of DARPA work on advanced cruise missile technology. After the initial flight test program failed and quality assurance manufacturing problems were identified in General Dynamics' development effort, McDonnell Douglas received an Air Force contract involving technology transfer and became a second source producer in November 1987. Approximately 1,500 ACMs will be built, with the first operational missile scheduled to be deployed in 1992–1993 on B-52Hs at K. I. Sawyer AFB, MI.

advanced development: Line item **research and development** projects that have advanced to a point where the development of experimental hardware for technical or operational testing is required prior to the determination of whether these items should be designed or engineered for eventual service use.

Advanced Field Artillery System (AFAS): The next generation of Army and Marine Corps self-propelled **howitzers**. They will be more mobile and have longer ranges and higher rates of fire. Advanced technology, such as robotics and artificial intelligence, and new propellants, including modular charge, unicharge, liquid propellent, and electromagnetic propulsion, will be incorporated. These howitzers are scheduled for deployment in the late 1990s, and they will replace 155 mm howitzers currently deployed.

Advanced Field Artillery Tactical Data System (AFTADS): Army field artillery and short-range missile fire support command, control and communications system under development. It will replace and modernize the Army's **Tactical Fire Direction (TACFIRE)** command, control and communications system. It will meet automated fire support requirements of the Army Tactical Command and Control System (ATACCS) during the 1990–2010 timeframe. The fully automated AFTADS will support close, rear, and deep operations and nuclear, nonnuclear, and chemical fire planning. It will coordinate the employment of all Army and joint fire support assets (mortars, close air support aircraft, naval gunfire, attack helicopters, offensive electronic warfare, field artillery cannons, rockets and guided missiles) on the battlefield. Compatibility will be provided with all existing and planned U.S. and allied field artillery sensors and systems. A Milestone III full-scale development and procurement decision was scheduled for FY 1989. The contractor is Magnavox, Fort Wayne, IN.

advanced inertial reference sphere (AIRS): **MX** and **Small ICBM** missile guidance system (in miniature version for the Small ICBM) that,

unlike conventional inertial guidance systems, can continually adjust the flight and accuracy of the missile through external navigation corrections provided by systems such as **NAVSTAR/GPS** satellites.

Advanced Lightweight Torpedo (ALWT) (see **MK-50 Barracuda Torpedo**)

Advanced Medium-Range Air-to-Air Missile (see **AMRAAM**)

Advanced Range Instrumentation Aircraft (ARIA): An Air Force instrumentation aircraft modified from former American Airlines Boeing 707-320 transports and used to support DOD and NASA space launch and missile testing programs. The ARIA aircraft have a primary mission of tracking U.S. missiles during flight tests and monitoring unmanned satellites, covering gaps in land- and sea-based tracking capabilities. They are also used to gather intelligence on the terminal phase of Soviet missile tests, particularly those terminating in the Pacific. There have been two generations of ARIA aircraft: the EC-135N, and the new **EC-18B**, which replaced the **EC-135**. The new EC-18B has a completely new cockpit configuration and houses the world's largest airborne steerable antenna in its bulbous nose, with a probe antenna on each wingtip. It has a larger volume and payload than the EC-135s previously used, allowing it to hold the new ARIA Scoring System, a surveillance and processing suite that will allow broad ocean area coverage for reentry vehicle splashdown. The ARIA Scoring System includes the Sonobuoy Missile Impact Location System (SMILS), which acquires and processes missile impact data of multiple reentry vehicles, using either deep ocean transponders or **NAVSTAR/GPS**. The EC-18B will also collect optical data on reentry vehicles during the terminal phase of flight. The SMILS functions previously required both the EC-135 ARIA and Navy **P-3** aircraft but will now be combined. Following the modification of aircraft, the first EC-18B flew on 27 February 1985, and entered operational service in January 1986. By the end of 1988, four EC-18B ARIA aircraft replaced the four EC-135N ARIAs operated by the 4950th Test Wing of the Aeronautical Systems Division, Air Force Systems Command, at Kirtland AFB, NM.

Advanced Research Projects Agency (see **Defense Advanced Research Projects Agency**)

Advanced Short Range Air-to-Air Missile (see **ASRAAM**)

Advanced Space Technology Program (see **LIGHTSAT**)

Advanced Strategic Missile System (ASMS): An Air Force research project formerly known as ABRES (Advanced Ballistic Reentry Systems). It is a continuing research program that develops, applies, and proves ballistic missile technologies by conducting advanced development for operational intercontinental ballistic missile (**ICBM**) applications. Early development work is pursued to gain confidence in engineering feasi-

bility of new technologies and concepts to ensure their readiness for full scale development, and to provide timely solutions for identified ICBM force deficiencies, mission changes, and evolving threats. The ASMS mission also includes intercontinental range flight testing of exploratory **reentry vehicles** and **penetration aid** systems for all three services.

The majority of the current work focuses on penetration systems for ICBMs to counter ongoing Soviet improvements in ballistic missile defenses. These systems include maneuvering reentry vehicles, decoys, chaff, optical, and other countermeasures. Future programs will study technologies that will allow ICBMs to attack relocatable and underground targets. About $150 million annually is spent on the research program.

Advanced Tactical Fighter (ATF): An Air Force conventionally armed, single-seat, supersonic **stealth** fighter aircraft under development. The ATF, designated the F-23, is scheduled to replace the **F-15 Eagle**, with initial deployment starting in the mid- to late-1990s. The Air Force anticipates arming the ATF with the advanced medium-range air-to-air missile (**AMRAAM**), advanced short-range air-to-air missiles (**ASRAAM**), and **Sidewinders**, as well as with an internal gun. As an air superiority fighter, the ATF will protect allied interdiction forces through offensive counterair operations in hostile territory with first-look, first-kill capability facilitated by integrated avionics and weapon control systems that permit simultaneous engagement of multiple targets. Use of **VHSIC** common signal processors will result in integrated communications, sensors, and weapons control. The ATF will be designed to survive enemy air-defense systems through a combination of sustained supersonic speed without the use of afterburners, improved maneuverability, and reduced radar and infrared detection signature. The ATF will have a short takeoff and landing (STOL) capability resulting from a high thrust-to-weight-ratio engine. Advances in fly-by-wire flight controls will optimize stability and handling characteristics. Substantial reductions in the number of ground support personnel and equipment are planned. The aircraft is expected to include advanced propulsion, flight control, fire control, and a greatly increased combat radius. The ATF will incorporate the joint Air Force/Navy integrated electronic warfare system (INEWS). The two competing prime contractor teams for the ATF are Northrop/McDonnell Douglas and Lockheed/Boeing/General Dynamics. The winner of the competition will get a contract to build as many as 750 Air Force fighters with a possibility of building several hundred more for the Navy (which is also developing the **A-12 Advanced Tactical Aircraft**). The RDT&E request for FY 1988 was $498.1 million, for FY 1989 was $702.3 million ($684.6 appropriated), for FY 1990 is $1,111.5 million, and for FY 1991 is $1,618.1 million.

The original need for an advanced fighter was released in 1973, but the need for a new aircraft was withdrawn from consideration due to development of the **A-10 Thunderbolt**, the **F-15 Eagle**, and the **F-16 Fighting Falcon**. The deployment of these aircraft led to the resurrection of the program in 1981. In November 1981, the Defense Resources Board approved the program as a new start in the FY 1983 budget request. The ATF program was restructured in FY 1986 to reduce technical and cost risk, emphasize fly-before-buy prototyping and competition, and implement recommendations of the Packard Commission. In October 1986, the Air Force awarded 50-month contracts to two development teams, one led by Northrop Corporation and one by Lockheed, to begin a four-year demonstration and validation phase. Affordability was stressed by the Air Force, which set a unit fly-away cost of $35 million in FY 1985 dollars as a goal. Each contractor team is to build two flying prototypes, one with a Pratt and Whitney engine and one with a General Electric engine, and one avionics demonstrator. The flying prototypes are to be known as YF-22As (Lockheed's) and YF-23As (Northrop's). First flight of the prototypes is scheduled for FY 1990, and full-scale development is planned for FY 1991.

The Navy also is participating in the ATF program, with a possibility that the aircraft could be used to replace the **F-14D Tomcat** carrier-based fighter aircraft in the late 1990s. The Navy estimates that it will need 400–600 ATFs, excluding Marine Corps fighter demands. Also, a Memorandum of Understanding (MOU) was signed between the

Navy and Air Force to facilitate cross-service utilization of ATF and A-12 Advanced Tactical Aircraft technologies.

Advanced Technology Bomber (ATB)   (see **B-2**)

Advanced Warning System (AWS): An **early-warning** satellite scheduled to be deployed in the 1990s as a follow-on to the **Defense Support Program (DSP)** but currently incorporated in the **Boost Surveillance and Tracking System (BSTS)**. The research program will incorporate improved survivability of the satellite, as well as earlier detection of targets and more accurate target identification, particularly for submarine-launched missiles. AWS is composed of the following: the **High Altitude Large Optics (HALO)**/Mini-HALO DARPA system to detect dual-capable aircraft and missiles, the Air Force Mosaic sensor, and the DARPA **HI-CAMP** mosaic millimeter-wave receiver.

AE: Designation for **ammunition ship.**

AEDS   (see **Atomic Energy Detection System**)

AEGIS Combat System: A fast-reaction, integrated shipboard air and ship defense system that combines fire control computers, the AN/SPY-1 phased-array radar, sonar navigational systems, and Standard surface-to-air missiles. It is capable of automatically detecting, tracking, and destroying airborne, seaborne, and land-launched weapons. It is installed in the Ticonderoga class (CG-47) cruisers and will be installed on the Arleigh Burke (DDG-51) class destroyers. RCA, Mooristown, NJ, is the AEGIS combat system agent responsible for designing, engineering, producing, and integrating shore and ship systems.

AEGIS Extended Range Missile: Standard Missile 2 (SM-2) Block IV version for use in AEGIS ships (Ticonderoga class cruisers and Burke class destroyers) equipped with the **vertical launching system (VLS)**. Part of Standard Missile "family," the anti-air missiles will be employed in **Terrier** and **TARTAR** weapon control systems. The new missile will incorporate major guidance, airframe, and missile-booster improvements. The FY 1989 cost for RDT&E is $100.7 million.

aerial refueling: The transfer of fuel from a tanker aircraft to another aircraft while in flight. Aerial tanker aircraft include **KC-135 Stratotankers, KC-10A Extenders, KA-6D Intruders, KC-130s,** and **KA-3B Skywarriors**. All strategic bombers and some tactical fighter aircraft and long-range helicopters have the capability for in-flight refueling. Aerial tankers usually position themselves above and ahead of the receiving aircraft. They either trail a probe that inserts into a refueling port atop the aircraft to be refueled, or trail a receptacle into which the refueling aircraft inserts a probe. The long-range aerial refueling aircraft (KC-135, KC-10) are operated and controlled by the Air Force's Strategic Air Command. The KA-6D version of the

A-6 Intruder attack aircraft is operated by the Navy. The KC-130 is operated by the Marine Corps. The KA-3Bs are operated by the Naval Air Reserve.

aeromedical airlift: Units operated by the 23rd Air Force of the Military Airlift Command and the Air Force Reserve that provide medical evacuation and transport of patients using specially configured C-9A Nightingale, C-12F, and C-21 aircraft.

Aerospace Corporation (see **Federally-Funded Research and Development Center**)

Aerospace Defense Center (ADC): Facility subordinate to **Air Force Space Command**, established 18 October 1979, responsible for unilateral U.S. continental air defense warning, commands, and operations. ADC is collocated with the NORAD command center and is composed of the Air Defense Operations Center, an **E-3A AWACs** squadron committed to NORAD at Tinker AFB, OK, and a support squadron at the NORAD alternate command center at North Bay, Canada. The Commander of ADC is also the Commander of the **U.S. Space Command**.

Headquarters
Cheyenne Mountain Complex, CO
80914

Aerospace Defense Command (ADCOM):   Former Air Force **specified command**, established in 1975 and disestablished 19 December 1986. The responsibilities were transferred to to **Air Force Space Command** and **U.S. Space Command**.

Aerospace Defense, Tactical Air Command (ADTAC): Component of the Air Force's **Tactical Air Command**. ADTAC provides fighter interceptor and air defense forces to **Aerospace Defense Center** and **NORAD**.

Headquarters
Langley AFB, VA 23665

AF: Designation for stores ship.

AFB   (see **Air Force Base**)

AFB 888   (see **Teal Ruby**)

afloat prepositioning force (APF): Navy program comprised of commercially-chartered ships that provide increased sealift capability to areas where host nation support of prepositioned supplies on land is not allowed (e.g., Southwest Asia). In 1989, there were 12 ships in the APF. The program is managed by the **Military Sealift Command**. (see also **maritime prepositioning force**)

AFS: Designation for combat stores ship.

AFSATCOM (Air Force Satellite Communications System): Model designation: AN/GSC-40. Worldwide, low-data rate teletype communications system to provide the Joint Chiefs of Staff (JCS), the National Command Authorities (NCAs), and Commanders in Chief (CINCs) with reliable communications for command and control of nuclear-capable forces and communications for other selected priority tasks. AFSATCOM, code-named Giant Star, provides designated high-priority users with a means for dissemination of **emergency action messages (EAMs)**, JCS/CINC internetting, and **Single Integrated Operational Plan (SIOP)** and non-strategic nuclear force direction and report-back. The force elements are primarily strategic bombers, reconnaissance forces, and both ground- and sea-launched ballistic missiles. The AFSATCOM program was established in March 1974, became initially operational in May 1979, and was fully operational in December 1983. AFSATCOM provides two-way, 100-words-per-minute communications as part of the **Minimum Essential Emergency Communications Network (MEECN)**. The AFSATCOM program does not use dedicated satellites; rather, it uses communications packages that ride as "guest" payloads on the following satellites:

- **Fleet Satellite Communications (FLTSATCOM)** 12 AFSATCOM channels on four FLTSATCOM satellites;
- **Satellite Data Systems (SDS)** AFSATCOM coverage of the polar region;
- **Defense Satellite Communications System (DSCS) III** Worldwide, single-channel (one-way) transponder AFSATCOM coverage; and
- **NAVSTAR/GPS** Worldwide, single-channel (one-way) transponder AFSATCOM coverage.

Single channel transponders (SCT) provide backup for transmitting EAMs to the forces, receiving the EAM in either SHF or UHF and then rebroadcasting to AFSATCOM terminals. The first SCT was put into space in March 1975.

There are AFSATCOM terminals in all **airborne command posts**, **FB-111**, **B-52** and **B-1B** bombers, **RC-135** reconnaissance aircraft, and Navy **TACAMO** aircraft. Over 150 ground terminals are located at command centers, **SAC command posts**, ICBM **launch control centers**, and nuclear weapons storage sites. The AFSATCOM consolidated ground terminal and master control center is located at Offutt AFB, NB. The information system for AFSATCOM is the Advanced AFSATCOM Monitoring Subsystem (AAMS), a computer-controlled satellite communications payload monitoring system for managing and scheduling AFSATCOM space segment access [Air Force Communications Command, *Information Handbook*. Prepared by the Directorate of Cost, DCS Comptroller, HQ AFCC, July 1987, released under the FOIA].

afterwinds: Wind currents sent up in the vicinity of a nuclear explosion directed toward the burst center, resulting from the updraft accompanying the rise of the fireball.

AFT Spacecraft   (see **Zenith Star**)

AG: Designation for miscellaneous support ship.

AGDS: Designation for deep submergence support ship.

AGF: Designation for miscellaneous command ship.

AGM: **1.** Model designation abbreviation for an **air-to-ground missile**. Types of AGMs include

AGM-12	Bullpup
AGM-28	Hound Dog
AGM-45	**Shrike**
AGM-53	Condor
AGM-62	Walleye
AGM-65	**Maverick**
AGM-69	**SRAM**
AGM-78	**Standard Arm**
AGM-84	**Harpoon**
AGM-86	**Air-launched Cruise Missile**
AGM-88	**HARM**
AGM-114	**Hellfire**
AGM-119	Penguin
AGM-123	Skipper
AGM-129	**Advanced Cruise Missile**
AGM-130	Improved version of GBU-15 bomb
AGM-131	**SRAM II**
AGM 136	**Tacit Rainbow**

2. Designation for missile range instrumentation ship.

AGOR: Designation for **oceanographic research ship**.

AGOS: Designation for ocean surveillance ship.

Agreement Governing the Activities of States on the Moon and Other Celestial Bodies (see **Moon Agreement**)

Agreement on Measures to Reduce the Risk of Outbreak of Nuclear War: U.S.–Soviet agreement signed in Washington on 30 September 1971 in which both sides pledged to maintain and improve their safeguards against the accidental or unauthorized use of nuclear weapons. The agreement entered into force on the same day. Each party agrees to notify the other immediately should the risk of nuclear war arise due to accidents, unauthorized use, or the detection of unidentified objects that could lead to the potential detonation of a nuclear weapon. Both countries also agree to supply notification of missile warning alerts and advance information on any missile launches that could be interpreted by the other party as threatening. On the same day, an agreement improving the **Direct Communications Link (DCL)** (Washington-Moscow "hot line") was also signed. The DCL was established in 1963 for use "in situations requiring prompt clarification." Both agreements are designed to work together in reducing the risk of accidental war and are both of unlimited duration. The Soviet Union has similar bilateral Agreements to Avoid Nuclear Accidents concluded with France (1976) and with the United Kingdom (1977).

Agreement on Notifications of Launches of Intercontinental Ballistic Missiles and Submarine-launched Ballistic Missiles: Agreement between the United States and the Soviet Union concluded in 1988 that stipulates 24 hours advance notification of missile test launches. "Believing that nuclear war cannot be won and must never be fought," the parties agree to notify each other of all missile launches at least 24 hours in advance, via the Nuclear Risk Reduction Centers (NRRCs) in Washington and Moscow. The time of the launch, area of launch, and impact of launch is to be made known. The agreement entered into force on 31 May 1988.

Agreement on the Establishment of Nuclear Risk Reduction Centers: Agreement signed on 15 September 1987 to establish Nuclear Risk Reduction Centers (**NRRCs**) in Washington and Moscow. The agreement entered into force on the same date. The NRRCs are designed to build confidence and reduce the risk of nuclear war originating from miscalculation, accident, or misunderstanding, and to reaffirm previous treaty obligations. The NRRCs will also be used to receive information, exchange data, and provide notifications as dictated by the **INF Treaty**. The NRRCs, which began operation in April 1988, are connected by satellite and capable of receiving and sending both textual and graphic information.

Protocols I and II, both also signed on 15 September 1987, made the following provisions for transmitting information through the NRRCs:

- Notifications of ballistic missile launches are to be made in accordance with the **Agreement on Measures to Reduce the Risk of Outbreak of Nuclear War** (September 1971) and the **Agreement on the Prevention of Incidents On and Over the High Seas** (May 1972). Other information may be transmitted based on U.S. and Soviet discretion.
- All communications transmitted will be confidential unless otherwise agreed. Soviet transmissions will be made in Russian; U.S. transmissions in English.
- Direct facsimile communications between the Centers will be provided by an INTELSAT and STATSIONAIR satellite circuit.

Each satellite circuit also has secure orderwire communications capability.

- The orderwire will use the same modem and communications link as used for the facsimile message transmission, and its printer will provide a record copy of all information exchanged.
- Facsimile equipment and procedures are to conform to those used with the **Direct Communications Link**.
- Meetings of NRRC representatives are to be held at least once a year to discuss operations of the centers.

Agreement on the Prevention of Dangerous Military Activities: Agreement signed on 12 June 1989 by the United States and Soviet Union to help prevent accidental war between the two nations. The agreement was signed in Moscow by Chairman of the JCS Admiral Crowe and Chief of the General Staff of the Soviet Armed Forces General Mikhail Moiseyev. The accord states that both sides "shall take measures to ensure expeditious termination and resolution by peaceful means without resort to the threat or use of force, of any incident which may arise as a result of dangerous military activities." The accord refers only to unintentional acts by armed forces and was precipitated by events such as the KAL-007 shoot down by the Soviet Union. The agreement is part of the ongoing **Confidence and Security Building Measures (CSBM)** process between the two countries.

Agreement on the Prevention of Incidents On and Over the High Seas: Agreement between the

United States and the Soviet Union signed in Moscow by Secretary of the Navy John Warner and Soviet Defense Minister Andrey A. Grechko on 25 May 1972 to reduce peacetime naval tensions. The agreement establishes rules of conduct for surveillance and aircraft carrier ships. Both countries agree to notify the other of actions on the high seas that may pose a danger to shipping or aircraft and/or collisions or incidents at sea between ships and aircraft. A Protocol signed in Washington on 22 May 1973 further provides that ships and aircraft will not aim their weapons at the other country's civilian vessels in attack simulations and that launches and drops will be conducted so as not to endanger civilian shipping.

Agreement on the Prevention of Nuclear War: The U.S.–Soviet agreement signed in Washington on 22 June 1973 by President Richard Nixon and General Secretary Leonid Brezhnev that calls for both signatories to make the prevention of nuclear war their national policy. The agreement entered into force on its signature date. Both parties commit themselves to removing the danger of nuclear war and averting situations capable of causing military confrontation. To this end, the United States and the Soviet Union agree to "enter into urgent consultations with each other" in the event of a crisis and to "refrain from the threat or use of force not only against each other, but also against the allies of the other Party and against other countries, in circumstances which may endanger international peace and security." The agreement is of unlimited duration.

AGS: Designation for surveying ship.

AGSS: Designation for auxiliary research submarine.

AH: Designation for hospital ship.

AH-1G/S Cobra: An Army limited-weather, two-crew, single-engine, conventionally armed, light antitank, armed escort, and reconnaissance helicopter gunship. First flown in 1965, the current **TOW**-armed version entered service in 1977. The AH-1S carries an internal turret-mounted 20 mm cannon and can be armed with either 8 TOW antitank missiles or 76 2.75 inch rockets on external wing stores. It has a normal cruise speed of about 120 kts and a combat radius of 250 nm with 2.5 hours endurance. The original AH-1G Huey Cobra was a gunship version with miniguns, grenade launchers, and rockets deployed in the Army and Marine Corps. It could attack personnel and light armored vehicles but not tanks. The AH-1 helicopters are being partially replaced by **AH-64 Apache** helicopters. Older AH-1 models will be displaced by AH-64s, whereas newer, fully modernized AH-1 models will be consolidated, and AH-1s will fill Army National Guard and Army Reserve units. Prime contractor is Bell Helicopter Textron, Fort Worth, TX.

AH-1J/T/W Sea Cobra: A Marine Corps two-seat, dual-engine, conventionally armed version of the **AH-1S Cobra** helicopter gunship. Its missions are to escort and protect troop assault helicopters during amphibious assaults, and to conduct fire suppression and fire support during subsequent operations ashore. The AH-1J first flew in 1971, the AH-1T in 1977, and the AH-1W, known as the "Super Cobra," in 1986. The AH-1J had an armament similar to the AH-1G except with a 20 mm XM197 cannon. The AH-1T added a **TOW** capability and **Sidewinder** anti-air missiles. The AH-1W version also has **Hellfire** and **Sidearm** missile capability. The Sea Cobras have a maximum speed of just over 200 mph and a range of 360 nm. The first production model AH-1W Super Cobra was tested in April 1987 at the Naval Air Test Center's Rotary Wing Aircraft Test Directorate. It has a head-up display, increased firepower, and bigger engines. Approximately 100 helicopters of all variants are in service. As of 1989, 44 new production AH-1Ws are deployed and another 34 will be delivered by FY 1991. They replace older AH-1J/Ts on a one-for-one basis. Additionally, 37 AH-1Ts will be converted to AH-1Ws. The Marine Corps has six 24-helicopter composite squadrons (with 12 UH-1s and 12 AH-1s), as well as two 12-aircraft reserve squadrons (AH-1Js). Bell Helicopter Textron, Fort Worth, TX, is the prime contractor, and General Electric, Lynn, MA, produces the engines. Total funding in FY 1988 for procuring the last 34 AH-1W helicopters was $241.4 million.

AH-64 Apache: An Army day-and-night, all-weather, two-crew, twin-engine, conventionally armed, anti-tank attack helicopter gunship. The Apache began deployment in FY 1986. It can be armed with up to 16 **Hellfire** laser-guided antitank missiles, 1,200 rounds of 30 mm cannon, and 76 Hydra 70 2.75 inch rockets. The helicopter has a maximum speed of approximately 150 kts and a range of 370 nm with a mission endurance of 1.8 hours. The helicopter is equipped with a Target Acquisition Designation Sight and Pilot Night Vision Sensor (TADS/PNVS), which includes TV and infrared sensors. The Airborne Adverse-Weather Weapon System (AAWWS) provides the AH-64 with a fire-and-forget Hellfire capability. Over 400 helicopters have been delivered as of 1989 and the Army wants to acquire a total of 975. As of 1989, the Army has equipped 11 of a total 48 planned battalions. The helicopter partially replaces and complements the AH-1S Cobra gunship. Fifteen AH-64 battalions will eventually be assigned to the Army National Guard. Prime contractor is McDonnell Douglas, Mesa, AZ; General Electric, Lynn, MA, builds the engines; and Martin Marietta, Orlando, FL, is the contractor for the target acquisition and night vision systems. The Army requested to buy 72 helicopters a year in FY 1990 and FY 1991, requesting $899.7 million and $847.1 million, respectively. The AH-64 was called Advanced Attack Helicopter (AAH) while under development.

A-hour (Alert Hour):   1. The time designated by the Joint Chiefs of Staff at which generation of non-alert forces will commence.   **2.** The hour nuclear forces begin force generation. (see also **military time**)

aim point: The target of an attack, particularly of a nuclear attack.

AIM: Model designation abbreviation for an air-intercept missile. Types of AIMs include

AIM-4 Falcon
AIM-7 **Sparrow**
AIM-9 **Sidewinder**
AIM-26 Super Falcon
AIM-54 **Phoenix**
AIM-120 advanced medium-range air-to-air missile (**AMRAAM**)
AIM-xxx* advanced short-range air-to-air missile (**ASRAAM**)
AIM-xxx* **advanced air-to-air missile (AAAM)**
* model number to be assigned

AIR: Model designation abbreviation for an air-intercept rocket. The last AIR in the U.S. inventory was the AIR-2 Genie.

air assault division: One of six types of Army **divisions**, it conducts air assault operations alone or as part of a larger force, including rear-area, covering force, active defense, riverine, mobile counterattack, surveillance, reconnaissance, and target acquisition operations. It can "exploit success, including the effects of nuclear, biological, chemical, and conventional fires." An air assault division can conduct operations in the enemy's rear, employing helicopter-borne vertical envelopment techniques. The division has limited ground vehicle mobility; has no armor battalions; requires a large amount of continuing logistical support, particularly aircraft maintenance and fuel; has limited heavy artillery support; and has less antitank defense than other divisions. Air assault divisions have nine **air assault infantry battal-**

ions as well as divisional units. There are three 155 mm towed artillery battalions with 54 howitzers assigned, with the primary means of deploying the howitzers being the **CH-47** helicopter. There is an aviation maintenance battalion to support more than 400 helicopters in the division. The Army has one air assault division, the 101st Airborne Division (Air Assault), located at Ft. Campbell, KY.

Air assault operations are those operations involving the movement of combat forces about the battlefield in helicopters. Air assault operations may involve the use of assault and medium-lift helicopters and combinations of internal and external sling loading of combat equipment. In the late 1950s, the Howze board, chaired by General Hamilton H. Howze, conducted an examination of the mobility requirements of the Army, recommending that the helicopter be integrated into the ground combat structure. During Vietnam, the air assault concept was tested by the 1st Cavalry Division (Airmobile), and later by the 101st Airborne Division (Air Assault), which was organized in 1967.

air assault infantry battalion: The smallest of the **infantry battalions,** with a total strength of about 761 officers and enlisted personnel. It differs from the infantry battalion only in its headquarters and the addition of an anti-armor company. Since it is designed, equipped, and trained to be transported about the battle area in the aircraft organic to the air assault division, all equipment in the combat and combat support elements are transportable by helicopter. There are no 4.2 inch mortars in the battalion. It has little ground vehicle mobility but is capable of maintaining operations at a very rapid tempo because of its air mobility.

Air Base (AB): 1. Air Force facility, composed of an airfield and its installations, personnel, and activities for the flight operation, maintenance, and supply of aircraft. **2. Air Force Base** located outside of the United States. **3.** Wing, group, or squadron that operates the facilities of an Air Base or Air Force Base.

airborne: 1. Operation involving movement and delivery of combat forces and their logistic support by air. **2.** State of an aircraft when entirely sustained by air.

airborne alert: A state of **readiness** where bombers and airborne command posts are maintained aloft on a continuing basis to reduce the enemy's reaction time and to increase survivability of the planes against land attack. A portion of the U.S. bomber force, normally 12 to 15 planes, was kept on airborne alert from 1957 until 1968. This alert condition ended after two nuclear weapons accidents involving B-52 bombers, one over Greenland on 23 January 1968 and one near Palomares, Spain, on 17 January 1966. Currently, a single **EC-135 "Looking Glass"** airborne command post is on airborne alert at all times, as well as a single **TACAMO** radio relay aircraft in the Atlantic. Continuous airborne alert by Looking Glass has been maintained since 3 February 1961.

Airborne Battlefield Command and Control Center (ABCCC): Air Force **EC-130E** aircraft equipped with communications, data links, and display equipment and capable of operating as either an airborne command post or a communications and intelligence relay facility for tactical forces. The ABCCC serves as an airborne extension of the **Tactical Air Control Center** in areas beyond radio range of the **Tactical Air Command System (TACS)**. It provides an on-scene battle staff and communications capability to any area of operations but has no radar surveillance or control capability. Along with **Airborne Warning and Control System (AWACS)**, the ABCCC may often be the first TACS element present in a crisis area.

airborne command post: Specially equipped large aircraft, normally converted from commercial airliner designs, that contain communications and computer equipment enabling it to operate as a mobile command center. Airborne command centers back up land-based command centers and can take over the functions of command and control in the pre-, trans-, and post-attack phases of nuclear war. There are three major airborne command center programs:

- **National Emergency Airborne Command Posts (NEACP) (E-4A/B):** Program to support the National Command Authorities and the Jointl Chiefs of Staff, codenamed **Nightwatch**;
- **Post Attack Command and Control System (PACCS)(EC-135):** Program to support the Strategic Air Command and Joint Chiefs

of Staff, codenamed **Cover All** (CINCSAC) and **Looking Glass** (airborne launch control center); and
• **Worldwide Airborne Command Post System (WWABNCP)** (EC-135): Program to support the unified commands, including **Silk Purse** for the U.S. European Command, **Blue Eagle** for the U.S. Pacific Command, **Scope Light** for the U.S. Atlantic Command, and codename unknown for the U.S. Central Command.

Aircraft are equipped with a wide variety of communications means, including satellite links, but there are only 14 ground entry points that allow the National Emergency Airborne Command Posts and Strategic Air Command airborne command posts to access ground-based communications networks. Two other airborne programs, the **TACAMO** Navy communications planes and the **Crown Helo** specially configured helicopters to support the President, do not have battle staffs.

airborne division: One of six types of Army **divisions**, it conducts airborne operations alone or as part of a larger force, conducts operations deep in the enemy's rear area, deploys rapidly by air, conducts air assaults, and conducts riverine operations. The division has limited ground vehicle mobility, requires a large amount of initial and continuing Air Force support, has limited organic medium-artillery fire support, and has less anti-tank defense than other divisions. The division is composed of nine **airborne infantry battalions,** one armor battalion, and divisional support. Artillery

support consists of three 155 mm towed howitzer battalions. The Army has one airborne division, the 82nd Airborne Division, located at Ft. Bragg, NC. The division maintains a portion of its units in an advanced state of deployability at all times, in order that the first battalion task force can be alerted and "wheels up" in no more than 18 hours.

Airborne operations involve Army and Air Force elements, whether the operation is a major forced entry into a hostile country or a simple proficiency training jump. The first U.S. airborne parachute unit was formed in 1940. Today, active Army airborne forces number 27,500 personnel and include elements of the XVIII Airborne Corps; the 82nd Airborne Division; the 509th Airborne Battalion Combat Team at Vicenza, Italy; the Special Forces Groups; and the three Ranger battalions.

airborne early warning (AEW): The airborne detection of air or surface units by radar or other electronic equipment. AEW is provided by radar-equipped aircraft, either Navy **E-2 Hawkeyes**, which operate from aircraft carriers, or Air Force **E-3 Airborne Warning and Control System (AWACS)** aircraft.

airborne infantry battalion: Specially trained and designed **infantry battalion** with 768 officers and enlisted persons. It is capable of all roles of the infantry battalion but has the additional capability to carry out airborne assaults by parachute or assault aircraft. All personnel are parachute-qualified and all equipment is air-transportable in medium-cargo

Air Force aircraft. The battalion is organized into three rifle companies and a headquarters company. Combat service support is very limited and must be augmented when committed to sustained combat operations. It has limited ground mobility and is relatively vulnerable to enemy armor.

Airborne Launch Control System (ALCS): The system installed in specially equipped **EC-135** airborne command posts of the **Post Attack Command and Control System** to monitor the status and command the launch of certain ICBMs while airborne.

Airborne Optical Adjunct (AOA): Experimental program begun in 1984 to determine how airborne optical sensors can best provide early warning and tracking of enemy ballistic missile warheads. AOA is applicable to boost, midcourse, and terminal phases of ballistic missile flight and would discriminate decoys, chaff, and debris from enemy warheads. The air-based AOA sensor emerged from other range instrumentation and intelligence collection aircraft, such as the RC-135 Optical Aircraft Measurement Program (OAMP) aboard **Cobra Eye**. AOA consists of a long-wave infrared (LWIR) sensor and data processor on a modified Boeing 767 commercial aircraft. The LWIR sensor detects the heat of objects against the cold space background. The U.S. Army Strategic Defense Command is also considering the airborne laser experiment (ALE) for active tracking to follow AOA's passive sensing system. Test flights of AOA will be conducted in CONUS, and flights against objects in

space will be held at Kwajalein Atoll. The first AOA flight was scheduled for 1987, but calls for performance upgrades delayed this test. Boeing of Kent, WA, is the prime contractor; Hughes, Clearwater, FL, is producing the sensors; and Honeywell, El Segundo, CA, is responsible for data processing.

Airborne Self-protection Jammer (ASPJ): Model designation: AN/ALQ-165. Joint Air Force/Navy development program for an internally mounted electronic countermeasures (ECM) system for **F-16Cs, F-14Ds, F/A-18s**, and **AV-8Bs**. It is designed to detect and analyze enemy radar signals and select the correct **electronic countermeasures** to jam them. Flight tests began in FY 1988 and it will be deployed in the early 1990s on both new and existing aircraft. The proposed funding for FY 1990 and FY 1991 is $15.9 and $18.8 million, respectively.

Airborne Warning and Control System (AWACS): Model designation: 411L. An Air Force airborne, long-range radar air surveillance platform to support strategic defense and tactical air operations. AWACS provides radar coverage beyond and below that of ground-based elements. The system has four missions: surveillance of enemy areas, early warning of attack, control of airborne resources against enemy aircraft or in support of friendly ground forces, and providing of information on friendly ground and air forces. The AWACS is mounted in a Boeing 707 modified aircraft (designated **E-3A sentry**) with a radome mounted above the aft fuselage. The radar provides 360 degree coverage for 200 miles for low-altitude targets and farther for higher altitudes. An on-board data processor provides uncluttered coverage of airborne targets over all types of terrain for directing interceptors. AWACS communications use UHF, VHF, and HF radios to communicate with ground and air units, as well as the Tactical Data Link (TADIL). AWACSs are assigned to the 552d Airborne Warning and Control Wing, Tinker AFB, OK. Eight AWACSs are assigned to NORAD. Canadian personnel serve in crews of AWACS in Canadian airspace.

AWACS aircraft routinely stay on station for 18 hours, using augmented crews and air refueling. The E-3As can stay airborne for 12 hours without refueling. AWACS random patrols were used to supplement land-based radars while the **DEW Line** was upgraded and before the **OTH-B** radars were partially operational. The Peace Shield program has been to assist Saudi Arabia in obtaining command, control, and communications systems and ground-based long-range radars in support of their AWACS operations.

air breathing: A term that describes aircraft or missiles (normally cruise missiles) with engines that intake external air to provide oxygen for combustion of their fuel. Air breathing systems are typically contrasted to other weapons that carry their oxidizers internally, such as ballistic missiles.

airburst: An explosion of a nuclear warhead above the surface at such a height that the radius of the expanding fireball does not touch the Earth's surface, as distinguished from an explosion on contact with the surface or after penetration into the Earth. High airburst refers to the "fallout-safe" **height of burst** for a nuclear weapon that maximizes damage to soft targets and reduces induced radiation contamination at **actual ground zero**. Low airburst is the fallout-safe height of burst for a nuclear weapon that maximizes damages to surface targets.

Aircraft Alerting Communications Electromagnetic Pulse (AACE): Strategic Air Command program to harden all 24 bomber and aerial refueling wing command posts against **electromagnetic pulse (EMP)**. Its purpose is to provide assured, EMP-hardened, end-to-end communications from CINCSAC to alert aircraft and to provide CINCSAC and SAC main operating base commanders with indications of an EMP event that could signal a nuclear attack. AACE provides shielded enclosures for equipment for SAC bases in CONUS and protects communications equipment used to relay **emergency action messages (EAMs)** from the command post to bomber crews in the alert facility or in the cockpit.

aircraft carrier (CV/CVN): Largest warship of the U.S. Navy, ranging from 64,000 to 91,400 tons at full load. Aircraft carriers are mobile floating airfields whose aircraft are able to attack targets up to 1,000 nm (1,900 km) away. Aircraft carriers themselves have no offensive weaponry, only some short-range missiles and guns for limited self-defense. For attacks and more extensive defensive measures, they rely on their complement of aircraft, which can conduct anti-surface, anti-air, and anti-submarine attacks, electronic warfare, reconnaissance, and land strikes. Aircraft carriers store a wide variety of conventional weapons for these aircraft, as well as B43, B57, and B61 nuclear bombs for surface attacks by their attack aircraft, and B57 nuclear depth bombs for their anti-submarine warfare aircraft. Aircraft carriers routinely carry about 100 nuclear weapons.

Aircraft carriers operate worldwide and typically spend months in forward deployment before being relieved by another carrier. Four or five aircraft carriers generally are forward-deployed at any given time, divided among the Mediterranean Sea, Indian Ocean, and Western Pacific. The other carriers are either in overhaul or participating in exercises and training off the east and west coasts of the United States or in the northern Atlantic. When underway, carriers are accompanied by several escort ships, forming **carrier battlegroups (CVBGs)**. The escort ships provide additional protection to the carrier from air, surface, and submarine attacks; in turn, the carriers' planes give similar protection to the escort ships. In peacetime, a carrier battlegroup usually consists of 1 carrier, 1–2 cruisers, 2–3 destroyers or frigates, 1–3 attack submarines, and support ships, particularly fuel and ammunition supply. In wartime, 2–4 carrier battle groups would operate together along with additional escort ships.

The United States currently has 15 deployable aircraft carriers distributed among Midway (CV-41) class, Forrestal (CV-59) class, Kitty Hawk (CV-63) class, John F. Kennedy (CV-67) class, Enterprise (CVN-65) class, and **Nimitz** (CVN-68) **class**. Five of these cariers are nuclear-powered. The original nuclear-powered carrier, the USS Enterprise (CVN-65), was commissioned in 1961 and has eight nuclear reactors. The four later Nimitz class carriers, USS Nimitz (CVN-68), USS Eisenhower (CVN-69), USS Carl Vinson (CVN-70), USS Theodore Roosevelt (CVN-71) and USS Abraham Lincoln (CVN-72), each have two reactors. The nuclear-powered carriers have an estimated steaming life of 13 years and one million miles before refueling.

Eight older carriers are undergoing a **Service Life Extension Program (SLEP)** to increase their service life from 30 to 45 years. The USS Saratoga (CV-60), USS Forrestal (CV-59), and USS Independence (CV-62) have completed their SLEPs. The USS Kitty Hawk (CV-63) began its SLEP in January 1988, and four other carriers are programmed for SLEP in future years: USS Constellation (CV-64), USS Ranger (CV-61), USS America (CV-66), and USS John F. Kennedy (CV-67).

The latest Nimitz class carriers, the USS Theodore Roosevelt (CVN-71) and the USS Abraham Lincoln (CVN-72), were commissioned on 25 October 1986, and 11 November 1989, respectively. An additional nuclear-powered aircraft carrier of the Nimitz class, USS George Washington (CVN-73), is under construction and is scheduled to be delivered in 1991. Two Nimitz class carriers (CVN-74/75) were authorized in the

FY 1988 budget to replace the USS Midway (CV-41) and USS Forrestal (CV-59) in the mid- to late 1990s. The Navy's goal, with new construction and SLEP, and taking retirements into account, is to have 15 deployable aircraft carriers. As the centerpiece of the 600 ship fleet planned under the Reagan Administration, this goal was to have been achieved by 1990 with the commissioning of the USS Abraham Lincoln; it now appears, however, that that objective will be short-lived. (The Navy does not consider carriers undergoing SLEP to be deployable; therefore, 16 carriers are required to support 15 deployable carriers.)

The Navy hopes to maintain a 15 carrier force by starting the construction of one nuclear-powered carrier every three years, commencing in FY 1990 with CVN-74. These carriers would be built by Newport News Shipbuilding in Newport News, VA, the only shipyard in the United States currently capable of building nuclear-powered large-deck aircraft carriers.

Aircraft carriers deploy with a 65–95 **carrier air wing**, depending on the size of the carrier and the mission. Aircraft include **F/A-18 Hornets** for surface attack and air-to-air combat; **F-14 Tomcats** for air-to-air combat; **A-6E Intruders** and **A-7E Corsairs** for attack missions; **S-3A/B Viking** jets and **SH-3D/H Sea King** helicopters for anti-submarine warfare; **EA-6B Prowlers** for electronic warfare; **KA-6D** aerial refueling tankers; and **E-2C Hawkeyes** for airborne early warning and command and control. Several electronic reconnaissance and logistic planes are also usually on board. The F/A-18s, A-6Es,

A-7Es, S-3A/Bs, and SH-3D/Hs are all nuclear-capable.

These aircraft are organized into squadrons, and the squadrons in turn collectively constitute the carrier air wing. A typical carrier air wing includes two squadrons of A-7s or F/A-18s (24 aircraft), one squadron of A-6s (14 aircraft consisting of 10 A-6Es and 4 KA-6Ds), one squadron of S-3s (10 aircraft); one squadron of SH-3s (6 helicopters); two squadrons of F-14s (24 aircraft); one squadron of EA-6s (4 aircraft); one squadron of E-2Cs (4 aircraft); and detachments of electronic reconnaissance and transport aircraft.

This carrier air wing mixture is changing as F/A-18s enter the fleet to replace A-7s. The Navy is introducing a nominal new air wing of 86 aircraft: 20 F-14s, 18 F/A-18s, 20 A-6s, 10 S-3s, 8 SH-60Fs (a replacement for the SH-3, due to become operational in 1989), 5 E-2Cs, and 5 EA-6Bs. The two oldest aircraft carriers, the Midway and the Coral Sea, cannot support F-14s and will have four squadrons of F/A-18s instead. They also do not support S-3 aircraft.

As of 1989, eight aircraft carriers were assigned to the **Pacific Fleet** and seven to the **Atlantic Fleet**. Pacific-based aircraft carriers currently are home-ported in Yokosuka, Japan (the USS Midway), and Alameda (San Francisco) and North Island (San Diego), CA. Moreover, the USS Nimitz's homeport recently was changed to Bremerton, WA, in preparation for a move to a homeport currently under construction at Everett, WA, as part of the Navy's strategic homeporting plan. In the Atlantic, carriers are stationed at Norfolk, VA, and Mayport,

Aircraft Carriers (1989)

	Nimitz (CVN-68)	Enterprise (CVN-65)	Kennedy (CV-67)	Kitty Hawk (CV-63)	Forrestal (CV-59)	Midway (CV-41)
Number Deployed	5	1	1	3*	4	2
Nuclear Weapons	B43, B57, B61	B43, B57, B61	B43, B57, B61	B43, B57, B61	B43, B57, B61	B43, B57, B61
Displacement (full load) (tons)	91,487	89,600	82,000	80,800	75,900–79,300	62,000
Length (ft)	1,040	1,040	1,052	1,046	1,063–1,086	979
(m)	(317)	(317)	(320.6)	(318.8)	(324–331)	(298)
Draft (ft)	36	39	37	37	37	36
(m)	(11)	(12)	(11.3)	(11.3)	(11.3)	(11)
Beam (ft)	134	133	130	130	129	121
(m)	(40.8)	(40.5)	(39.6)	(39.6)	(39.3)	(36.9)
Nuclear Reactors	2 A4W	8 A2W	—	—	—	—
Speed (knots)	30+	30+	30+	30+	30+	30+
(kph)	(56)	(56)	(56)	(56)	(56)	(56)
(mph)	(35)	(35)	(35)	(35)	(35)	(35)
Ship's Complement	3,200	3,350	3,117	3,150	3,019	2,533
Air Wing Complement	2,480	2,480	2,480	2,480	2,480	2,239
Aircraft (approx.)	85	85	85	85	75	65
IOC	1975	1961	1968	1961	1955	1945

* The USS Kitty Hawk (CV-63) entered SLEP in January 1988.

FL. A training carrier, the Lexington (AVT-16), is homeported at Pensacola, FL.

Though not generally considered part of the Navy's aircraft carrier force, the five Tarawa (LHA-1) class general-purpose amphibious assault ships and seven Iwo Jima (LPH-2) class helicopter amphibious assault ships are, in effect, small aircraft carriers (respectively, 39,300 and 18,000 tons at full load). (see also **amphibious warfare ships**)

aircraft carrier, training (AVT): Training aircraft carrier specifically used for aviator training purposes. The U.S. Navy operates one carrier of this type, the USS Lexington (AVT-16), at Pensacola, FL, the last of the World War II Essex class carriers still in use. At full load, it displaces about 42,500 tons. It is scheduled to be replaced by the Coral Sea (CV-43) sometime in the 1990s.

Aircraft Monitoring and Control (AMAC): That equipment installed in aircraft to permit monitoring and control of the safing, arming, and fuzing functions of a nuclear bomb or nuclear missile delivered by the aircraft. The AMAC is normally integral to the cockpit controls in modern aircraft, and is used to transmit signals from the pilot (or weapons officer) to the nuclear weapon(s) on board. It is the avenue for transmission of the **permissive action link (PAL)** codes.

air cushion landing craft (LCAC): Operational Navy amphibious assault hovercraft deployed with the Atlantic and Pacific Fleets. The LCAC is a gas turbine-powered craft that carries amphibious assault troops from ships to the beach. The craft is transported by **dock landing ships** and Wasp class amphibious assault ships (depending on the ship class, up to four LCACs can be carried at once). Its troop capacity is 24. The LCAC is equipped with the LN-66 navigation radar with processed video, UHF/VHF/HF communications, and gyrocompass. The speed of 30 + kts and range of 200 nm provides great flexibility; for instance, the craft can be launched from over the horizon and reach the beach in roughly the same time a conventional landing craft can traverse the standard 5,000–10,000-yard boat lane. It is able to glide over 80 percent of the world's beaches without **SEAL** or other preparatory forces being used to survey a boat lane. The first deployed LCAC detachment is on board the USS Germantown (LSD-42) as part of Amphibious Squadron Five. The Germantown is the second ship of the Whidbey Island (LSD-41) class, specially designed to support LCAC. Plans are to procure eight ships of the LSD-41 class for LCAC duties. LCACs are assigned to assault units based at Little Creek, VA, and Camp Pendleton, CA. About 40 personnel are assigned to a three- or four-unit detachment for an operation or deployment. The LCAC can also carry tanks, artillery, light armored vehicles, and tracked personnel landing vehicles. The LSD does not need to ballast or deballast to embark LCACs. Capabilities for the LCAC include conventional assault, general unloading, advance force support, and amphibious rapid capabilities. Survivability depends on its ability to hit a wide range of beaches at high speed with little warning.

air cushion vehicle: Used to designate military versions of hovercraft, which have the ability to float over either land or sea, depending on design.

air defense: Defensive measures or systems designed to destroy or nullify the effectiveness of attacking aircraft or cruise missiles. Air defense systems consist of groundbased radars, surveillance aircraft, interceptor aircraft, anti-aircraft artillery, **surface-to-air missiles (SAMs)**, and the ancillary identification equipment and decision-making systems. Deception, chaff, decoys, and **electronic countermeasures** such as jamming are also part of air defense measures. (see also **NORAD**)

air defense artillery: 1. Air defense assets in the Army deployed at all echelons. Theater air defense assets consist of the **Patriot surface-to-air missile (SAM)**. Corps assets consist of the **Hawk** SAM, or the Chaparral short-range missile and Vulcan gun. Division assets consist of **Chaparral**/Vulcan, and handheld systems (e.g., **Stinger**, Redeye) at lower echelons. The Air Force component commander is normally designated the area air defense commander and is responsible for specifying air defense rules of engagement and procedures to all air defense units. **2.** Weapons for combating air targets from the ground (e.g., Vulcan, Chaparral). Vulcan batteries provide forward air defense for fixed and mobile installations against low-

flying aircraft when the aircraft can be engaged visually. Chaparral batteries provide forward-area coverage along low-altitude avenues of approach, or, in the absence of definable avenues, they may be dispersed throughout the division area. The towed Vulcan Battalion is organic to the airborne and air assault divisions. A self-propelled Chaparral/Vulcan (C/V) Battalion is organic to the infantry, armored, and mechanized infantry divisions. **3.** A **combat arms** branch of the Army.

air defense emergency: One of two types of emergency conditions within the **alert conditions (LERTCONs)** system. An air defense emergency "exists when attack upon the continental United States, Alaska, Canada, or U.S. installations in Greenland by hostile aircraft or missiles is considered probable, is imminent, or is taking place." An air defense emergency is declared by the CINCNORAD. The exercise term for an air defense emergency is "Big Noise" [JCS, *Alert System of the Joint Chiefs of Staff, Part II, LERTCON ACTIONS,* SM-522-69, 13 August 1969, p. 254, released under the FOIA]. An air defense emergency declaration will be accompanied by an **air defense warning condition**. (see also **defense emergency**)

air defense ground environment (ADGE): Network of ground radar sites and regional command and control centers used to provide early warning and weapons control for tactical air control of air defense and interceptor operations. NADGE (NATO air defense ground environment) is operational throughout

Europe; BADGE (Base ADGE), in Japan; GEADGE, (German ADGE) in West Germany; and "Combat Grande," in Spain.

Air Defense Identification Zone (ADIZ): "Airspace of defined dimensions within which the ready identification, location, and control of airborne vehicles are required" [*JCS Pub 1*, p. 15].

Air Defense Initiative (ADI): Research program to develop defenses capable of locating, tracking, and engaging manned bomber aircraft and unmanned cruise missiles attacking North America. The ADI program was created by National Security Decision Directive 178 (July 1985), which called for a near-term air defense capability for CONUS. The Office of the Secretary of Defense manages the ADI program with the assistance of an interagency steering committee, and the Air Force, Navy, and DARPA are tasked to execute it. The program is under the operational purview of the U.S. Space Command and **NORAD**, and it includes the participation of the Canadian government. President Reagan directed that ADI deployment decisions should occur within the same time frame as **Strategic Defense Initiative (SDI)** deployment decisions. Although SDI received DOD authorization to begin its demonstration phase in September 1987, ADI is running behind schedule and will not reach this stage until FY 1990. Funding for ADI is in both the Air Force and Navy budgets. Total funding for FY 1987 was $32.9 million and for FY 1988 was $49.2 million,

with $6.4 million going to classified activities. The FY 1989 appropriation is for $156.1 million (less than the requested $213.5 million). The Air Force has requested $257.2 million for FY 1990 and $296.1 million for FY 1991.

The current ADI program is divided into three main research groups: surveillance technology, engagement, and system architecture. Initial emphasis has been on surveillance technology. The Navy is to develop undersea surveillance and air engagement technology options. The plan is to integrate into ADI the Navy tracking of submarines capable of carrying cruise missiles within the range of North America.

Surveillance

- Ground, airborne, and space-based radars and infrared optical sensors, including **Teal Ruby**;
- Undersea surveillance, including acoustic testing and measurement;
- The **North Warning System** to replace the DEW Line;
- **Seek Igloo** radars in Alaska;
- Long-range, over-the-horizon **(OTH) radars** of the Navy and Air Force; and
- The **Airborne Warning and Control System (AWACS)**.

Engagement

- **Surface-to-air missiles, air-to-air missiles**, fire control systems, and guns;
- Long-endurance attack systems;
- Sensors to detect and track air targets;
- Air defense interceptor aircraft and forward-operating locations in northern Canada; and

- The DARPA Long-Range Interceptor Experiment (**Loraine**) and the joint Air Force/DARPA **hypersonic glide vehicle (HGV)** technology prototype program.

Battle Management and C3

- Command and control simulation facility at Rome Air Development Center, Griffiss AFB, NY;
- ADI communications system; and
- Upgrades to NORAD headquarters at Cheyenne Mountain, CO.

Since SDI and ADI respond to different threats, they are classified as different initiatives; however, some of the surveillance technology is similar. In early 1986, the Air Force Space Division elevated the Director of its Teal Ruby program (infrared satellite sensor technology) to the post of Deputy for Strategic Experiments. Two SDI pointing and tracking experiments were added to the new Deputy's area of responsibility, as well as the retainment of Teal Ruby, consolidating both programs.

Air Defense Operations Center (ADOC): Highest-level air defense **command post** in North America, under the operational control of NORAD. It is tasked to monitor air activity, inform others on the air situation, and coordinate with regional commanders through **Regional Operational Control Centers (ROCCs)** to assess resource utilization and direct air interception [JCS, *Emergency Conferences for Tactical Warning and Attack Assessment,* EAPJCS Volume VI, 1 December 1986, released under the FOIA].

air defense warning condition: 1. "A degree of air raid probability . . . applicable to forces and units afloat and/or deployed to forward areas" [*JCS Pub 1,* p. 16]. **2.** An imminence-of-attack condition specified concurrently with the declaration of an **air defense emergency**, one of two military emergency conditions (EMERGCONs) [REDCOM, *Emergency Action Procedures,* pp. 3–4, released under the FOIA]. There are three conditions:

- *Air Defense Warning White:* Attack by hostile aircraft and/or missiles is not considered immediately probable or imminent. Air Defense Warning White will only be declared subsequent to a previous Red or Yellow condition. The exercise term is "Snow Man."
- *Air Defense Warning Yellow:* Attack by hostile aircraft and/or missiles is probable. The exercise term is "Lemon Juice."
- *Air Defense Warning Red:* Attack by hostile aircraft and/or missiles is imminent or in progress. The exercise term is "Apple Jack."

air defense weapons control status: The degree of fire control imposed upon Army air defense units, measured at one of three levels: Weapons Free, Weapons Tight, and Weapons Hold.

air division: Major Air Force aviation combat organization, usually consisting of two or more **wings** and service units. The air division is under an **Air Force** in the chain of command.

airdrop: Aerial delivery of personnel or materiel from an aircraft in flight. Delivery of cargo may be by parachute, by free drop, or by cargo extraction techniques such as **High-Altitude Low Opening (HALO)** and Low-Altitude Parachute Extraction System (LAPES). Airdrops are categorized in the following height bands:

- Ultra low level: ground level to 50 ft above ground level;
- Low level: 51 ft to 500 ft above ground level;
- Medium level: 501 ft to 2,500 ft (this height divides conventional parachuting, or "airdrop," from stabilized fall, or "free drop"); and
- High level: 2,501 ft to 12,000 ft.

Air Force: 1. Common name for the **Department of the Air Force**. **2.** Largest combat echelon of the Air Force, consisting of divisions, wings, or groups (e.g., 9th Air Force (Tactical Air Command)). The Air Forces currently deployed include

- 1st AF (TAC), Langley AFB, VA 23665
- 3rd AF (USAFE), RAF Mildenhall UK, APO NY 09127
- 4th AF (MAC)*, McClellan AFB, CA 95652
- 5th AF (PACAF), Yokota AB, Japan, APO SF 96328
- 7th AF (PACAF), Osan AB, South Korea, APO SF 96570
- 8th AF (SAC), Barksdale AFB, LA 71110
- 9th AF (TAC), Shaw AFB, SC 29152
- 10th AF (TAC/SAC)*, Bergstrom AFB, TX 78743

- 12th AF (TAC), Bergstrom AFB, TX 78743
- 13th AF (PACAF), Clark AB, Phil, APO SF 96274
- 14th AF (MAC)*, Dobbins AFB, GA 30069
- 15th AF (SAC), March AFB, CA 92518
- 16th AF (USAFE), Torrejon AB, Spain, APO NY 09283
- 17th AF (USAFE), Sembach AB, West Germany, APO NY 09130
- 21st AF (MAC), McGuire AFB, NJ 08641
- 22nd AF (MAC), Travis AFB, CA 94535
- 23rd AF (MAC), Hurlburt Field, FL 32544

(* designates reserve unit)

Air Force Accounting and Finance Center (AFAFC):   Air Force **separate operating agency**. AFAFC is the pay center for all Air Force members (more than 769,000 personnel, involving more than $21 billion annually). In addition, it makes accounting reports to the Department, Congress, and other federal agencies; provides accounting assistance to the Air Force worldwide; and manages the accounting, billing, and collecting of DOD foreign military sales contracts. Its personnel strength is approximately 2,340.

Headquarters
Lowry AFB, CO 80230

Air Force Audit Agency (AFAA):   Air Force **separate operating agency**, established in 1950 by the Budgeting and Accounting Procedures Act. It conducts independent evaluations of Air Force operational, financial, and support activities. Its personnel strength is approximately 950 civilian and military personnel.

Headquarters
Norton AFB, CA 92409

Directorates

- Acquisition and Logistics Audit, Wright-Patterson AFB, OH 45433
- Financial and Support Audit, Norton AFB, CA 92409
- Field Activities, Norton AFB, CA 92409

Air Force Base (AFB): Facility located within the United States for support of Air Force units and components. It is under the operating responsibility of the service, and its area usually is not more than 20 square miles. Smaller facilities are called Air Force Stations. Overseas, AFBs are called **Air Bases**.

Air Force Civilian Personnel Management Center (AFCPMC): Air Force **direct reporting unit** responsible for civilian personnel management.

Headquarters
Randolph AFB, TX 78150

Air Force Combat Operations Staff (AFCOS): Air Force **direct reporting unit** supporting the Chief of Staff of the Air Force and operating the Air Force Emergency Operations Center in the Pentagon. It is responsible for monitoring the daily readiness status of Air Force combat and support forces for the JCS. AFCOS provides staff support as well as facilities

to unified and specified commands in crisis operations and exercises. Its personnel strength is approximately 260 military and civilian personnel.

Air Force Commissary Service (AFCOMS): Air Force **separate operating agency** responsible for operating base commissaries, exchanges, and snack bars.

Headquarters
Kelly AFB, TX 78245

Air Force Communications Command (AFCC): Air Force **major command**, established in 1984 from the Air Force Communications Service. Its predecessor agencies include the Army Airways Communications System (established in 1938). Today, AFCC engineers, manages, and maintains communications systems for the department and other federal agencies. Its services include telephone systems, base communications centers, computer integration and facilities, radio and satellite stations, and air traffic control. Systems include the Automatic Voice Network (**AUTOVON**) telephone service and the Automatic Digital Network (**AUTODIN**) teletype and computer-to-computer communications service. AFCC operates and maintains a major part of the **Defense Communications System**; the **National Emergency Airborne Command Post** ground entry points; the **PAVE PAWS** early warning radars; the SAC's communications systems, including **Giant Talk**; and one half of the **Defense Satellite Communications System's** ground terminals. AFCC operates 700 units at 400 locations around the world. Its total personnel strength is approximately 55,000 military and civilian personnel.

Headquarters
Scott AFB, IL 62225

Communications Divisions

- Airlift Communications Division: Scott AFB, IL 62225
- Air Training Communications Division: Randolph AFB, TX 78150
- Engineering Installation Division: Tinker AFB, OK 73145
- European Communications Division: Kapaun AS, West Germany
- Logistics Communication Division: Wright-Patterson AFB, OH 45433
- Pacific Communications Division: Hickam AFB, HI 96853
- Research and Acquisition Communications Division: Andrews AFB, MD 20331
- Space Communications Division: Colorado Springs, CO 80914
- Strategic Communications Division: Offutt AFB, NB 68113
- Tactical Communications Division: Langley AFB, VA 23665

Air Force-Controlled (AFCON): "A unit for which the legal authority is controlled by HQ [headquarters] USAF. AFCON units are constituted by HQ USAF and assigned to MAJCOMs [**major commands**] for activation. All HQ above wing level, combat and operational flying units, combat support units, and named units are AFCON units. All units with a combat or operational role are normally designated AFCON units" [*NORAD Dictionary*].

Air Force District of Washington (AFDW): Air Force **direct reporting unit** that administers Air Force military and civilian personnel and facilities in the Washington, DC, area, including Bolling AFB and Andrews AFB, MD. It consists of the 1100th Air Base Group, 1100th Resource Management Group, and ceremonial units including the U.S. Air Force Honor Guard and the Air Force Band. Its personnel strength is approximately 2,500 military and civilian personnel.

Headquarters
Bolling AFB,
Washington, DC 20332

(see also **Military District of Washington**, **Naval District of Washington**)

Air Force Electronics Security Command (ESC) (see **Electronics Security Command**)

Air Force Engineering and Services Center (AFESC): Air Force **separate operating agency**, and an extension of the Directorate of Engineering and Services of headquarters, Department of the Air Force. AFESC provides guidance and assistance to Air Force installations and commands in the following areas: engineering services, environmental and energy planning, housing services, fire protection, mortuary services, and operations and maintenance of installations. It conducts readiness exercises in which **Prime BEEF**, **Prime RIBS**, and RED HORSE forces participate. Its personnel strength is approximately 945 military and civilian personnel.

Headquarters
Tyndall AFB, FL 32403

Air Force Inspection and Safety Center (AFISC): Air Force **separate operating agency**. Its mission is to assess the capabilities and effectiveness of various Air Force programs, including nuclear weapons systems safety and **nuclear surety** programs. Its personnel strength is approximately 500 military and civilian personnel.

Headquarters
Norton AFB, CA 92409

Directorates

- Directorate of Medical Inspection: Norton AFB, CA 92409
- Directorate of Nuclear Surety: Kirtland AFB, NM 87117
- Directorate of Aerospace Safety: Norton AFB, CA 92409
- Directorate of Inspection: Norton AFB, CA 92409

Air Force Intelligence Agency (AFIA): Air Force **separate operating agency**, activated 27 June 1972 as the Air Force Intelligence Service, redesignated in 1988. AFIA is responsible for intelligence collection and analysis within the Air Force, (excluding signals intelligence, which is under the Electronics Security Command; strategic intelligence collection, which is under the Strategic Air Command; and tactical intelligence organic to Air Force combat units). AFIA reports directly to the Assistant Chief of Staff for Intelligence (ACS/I) and provides intelligence support to the Air Staff and combatant commands. Analytic support includes preparation of the Air Force portion of **National Intelligence Estimates**, Air Force and defense intelligence projections, and other finished intelligence assessments. AFIA is composed of 11 directorates, responsible to either the Deputy Commander for Assessments or the Deputy Commander for Resources. Additional activities include the Air Force Special Activities Center, at Ft. Belvoir, VA, which manages all Air Force **human intelligence (HUMINT)** operations; the Pacific Special Activities Area, located at Hickam AFB, HI, with detachments in Japan and South Korea; and the European Special Activities Area, located at Lindsey AS, West Germany, with detachments throughout Europe. AFIA also manages the Air Force Special Security Office, which operates back-channel communications and controls special compartmented information programs within the Air Force. Personnel strength worldwide is approximately 2,300 civilian and military personnel.

Headquarters
Pentagon, Washington, DC
20330-5110

Directorates

- Regional Estimates
- Research and Soviet Studies
- Threat and Technology
- Warning and Current Intelligence
- Targets
- Security and Communications Management
- Intelligence Data Management
- Personnel/Force Management
- Intelligence Reserve Forces
- Attaché Affairs
- Joint Services Support

Air Force Legal Services Center (AFLSC): Air Force **separate operating agency** operating within the office of the Air Force Judge Advocate General.

Headquarters
Pentagon, Washington, DC
20330-5120

Air Force Logistics Command (AFLC): Air Force **major command**, redesignated in 1962 from the Air Materiel Command. AFLC provides logistics support, including procurement, supply, transport, and maintenance of equipment and weapons systems for the Air Force as well as for other services and allies. It operates five logistics centers and over a dozen specialized centers. AFLC manages over 600,000 procurement contracts annually, and it manages approximately 850,000 different Air Force supply items. Its personnel strength worldwide is approximately 92,000 military and civilian personnel, including some 4,300 scientists and engineers.

Headquarters
Wright-Patterson AFB, OH
45433-5001

Air Logistics Centers

• Ogden Air Logistics Center: Hill AFB, UT 84056
• Oklahoma City Air Logistics Center: Tinker AFB, OK 73145
• San Antonio Air Logistics Center: Kelly AFB, TX 78241
• Sacramento Air Logistics Center: McClellan AFB, CA, 91652
• Warner Robins Air Logistics Center: Robins AFB, GA, 31098

Air Force Management Engineering Agency (AFMEA): Air Force **separate operating agency** responsible for the development of **manpower** organization and standards via the Functional Review Program.

Headquarters
Randolph AFB, TX 78150

Air Force Military Personnel Center (AFMPC): Air Force **separate operating agency** responsible for personnel management of enlisted personnel and officers.

Headquarters
Randolph AFB, TX 78150

Air Force Office of Medical Support (AFOMS): Air Force **separate operating agency** that acts as an agent of the Air Force Surgeon General for the development and delivery of health care services for Air Force personnel.

Headquarters
Brooks AFB, TX 78235

Air Force Office of Security Police (AFOSP): Air Force **separate operating agency** established 1 September 1979, reporting to the Air Force Inspector General. AFOSP coordinates the security and law enforcement functions of the Air Force. The basic missions of security police units are the physical protection of Air Force resources and personnel, including base security; base law enforcement and crime prevention; narcotics and explosives detection; the administration of **information security**; confrontation management with the public; emergency services; criminal investigations; and corrections. AFOSP also provides support to the Secret Service, Department of State, and other federal agencies in the area of explosives detection. In wartime, security police units function as rear-area ground defense forces, protecting air bases and facilities, and they administer the **Wartime Information Security Program**. The commander of AFOSP is also the Assistant Inspector General for Security and the Air Force Chief of Security Police. Personnel strength worldwide is approximately 50,000 civilian and military personnel, including contracted security guards.

Headquarters
Kirtland AFB, NM 87117

Other Activities

- Air Force Security Clearance Office: Pentagon, Washington, DC 20330-6440
- Air Force Corrections Program: Lowry AFB, CO 80230
- Air Force Security Police Academy: Lackland AFB, TX 78236

Air Force Office of Special Investigations (AFOSI): Air Force **separate operating agency** activated 31 December 1971 to consolidate Air Force investigative activities throughout the world. AFOSI's primary mission is to provide investigative and **counterintelligence** services, including internal criminal and personnel security investigations; counter-espionage and counter-terrorism investigations; and protective services for DOD and U.S. government officials and foreign dignitaries. AFOSI

operates in 19 districts, with detachments on all major Air Force bases. Personnel strength is approximately 2,500 military and civilian personnel, of whom two thirds are special agents.

Headquarters
Bolling AFB, DC 20332

Air Force One: A radio call signal used to denote the Air Force aircraft the President is aboard, whether it is either of two specially configured Boeing 707s (AF-designated VC-137Cs or VC-25As) or any other Air Force aircraft. The VC-137C aircraft are part of MAC's 89th Military Airlift Wing fleet at Andrews AFB, MD. The VC-137C cruises at 540 mph at a maximum altitude of 42,000 ft and has a range of 7,140 mi. Maximum passenger load is 50. Differences between the standard Boeing 707 and the VC-137C include electronic and communications equipment, the interior configuration, and the furnishings. The passenger cabin is divided into a communications center, presidential quarters, staff/office compartment, and seating for the press.

One of the VC-137Cs, No. 26000, currently serves as the backup presidential plane. This plane joined the fleet in October 1962, flying President Kennedy to Dallas and serving as the site of Lyndon Johnson's inauguration at Love Field, TX. President Nixon used No. 26000 for his around-the-world trip in 1969 and his trip to the PRC in 1972. No. 27000 joined the fleet in 1972 and has been used extensively by Presidents Ford, Carter, and Reagan. Two new aircraft, modified Boeing 747s designated as **VC-25As**, will replace the VC-137Cs in late 1989. (See also **Mystic Star**)

Air Force Operational Test and Evaluation Center (AFOTEC): Air Force **separate operating agency** that conducts independent operational testing of new or modified weapons systems and components developed for Air Force or multiservice use. AFOTEC is currently planning or conducting tests on the **Consolidated Space Operations Center**, the Next-Generation Weather Radar, the **B-1B**, the **F-15E**, the **MX** missile, the **AMRAAM**, and the **Advanced Tactical Fighter**. AFOTEC consists of 5 detachments and 24 test teams. Its personnel strength is approximately 700 military and civilian personnel, with approximately 2,400 personnel under its operational control.

Headquarters
Kirtland AFB, NM 87117

Detachments

- Eglin AFB, FL 32542
- Nellis AFB, NV 89191
- Edwards AFB, CA 93523
- Colorado Springs, CO 80914
- Kapaun Barracks, West Germany

Air Force Reserve (AFRES, AFR, or USAFR): The federal **reserve** component and a **separate operating agency** of the Air Force. It consists of 58 flying **squadrons** tasked to the **Military Airlift Command**, **Strategic Air Command**, or **Tactical Air Command**, and 450 mission support (nonflying) units responsible for aeromedical evacuation, natural disaster support, civil engineering, electronics security, communications, and logistics support. The AFRES provides a significant portion of the capabilities of the total force in many mission areas, including 100 percent of aerial spraying capability, 25 percent of theater airlift, 25 percent of air rescue and recovery capability, 47 percent of weather reconnaissance, 72 percent of aeromedical evacuation, 50 percent of the crews for strategic airlift and aerial refueling aircraft, 60 percent of aerial port units, 60 percent of combat logistics support, and 20 percent of civil engineering.

Units report to the Air Force Chief of Staff through the Commander Air Force Reserve, who also serves as the Chief of the Air Force Reserve. Personnel matters are administrated by the Air Reserve Personnel Center, Denver, CO. During FY 1988, the AFRES received 11 percent of the total reserve appropriations. In 1987, reservists participated in 46 training events in approximately 40 countries, including training exercises Valiant Oak, Airlift Rodeo, Gunsmoke, Team Spirit, Valiant Partner, and the European Tanker Task Force. The personnel strength of the Ready Reserve is about 129,000, plus 24,000 in the Standby Reserve and 100,000 in the Retired Reserves.

Administrative Headquarters
Robins AFB, GA 31098

Office of the AFRES
Pentagon, Washington, DC
20330-5440

Air Force Reserve (Associate) unit: Reserve unit of the Air Force collocated with and using the equipment and facilities of an active force unit but providing augmentation crews and support personnel, particularly in strategic airlift and aerial refueling.

Air Force Satellite Communications System   (see **AFSATCOM**)

Air Force Satellite Control Facility (AFSCF)/Air Force Satellite Control Network: Command and communications network for onboard real time communications of DOD satellites.   AFSCF includes seven remote tracking stations (RTS); a communications satellite calibration site at Camp Parks, CA; and a satellite recovery group at Hickam AFB, HI. AFSCF provides primary tracking, telemetry and command (TT&C) for the **Defense Satellite Communications System**, **Satellite Data System**, **NATO Integrated Communications System (NATO II/III)**, **Fleet Satellite Communications System** and **NAVSTAR/GPS** satellites, and backup TT&C for the **Defense Support Program** and the **Defense Meteorological Satellite Program**. The RSTs receive and record telemetry data about the health and status of the satellite. Each RTS transmits a variety of commands to satellites, particularly reconnaissance satellites.

Headquarters
Patrick AFB, FL 32925

Remote Tracking Stations

- Thule AB Tracking Station, Greenland (northernmost, can provide on-orbit support for all polar orbiting satellites on each revolution);
- Guam Tracking Station, Andersen AFB (orbital support for synchronous and near-synchronous spacecraft);
- Indian Ocean Tracking Station, Mahe, Seychelles Islands (monitors orbit injection during high altitude satellite launches);
- United Kingdom Oakhanger Tracking Station, Borden Haunts;
- Vandenberg AFB Tracking Station, CA (dual station that can support two satellites simultaneously);
- Tracking Station, New Boston, NH (dual station); and
- Hawaii Tracking Station, Kaena Point AFS, HI (dual station assists with ballistic missile tests).   (see also **Spacetrack**)

Air Forces Atlantic (AFLANT)   (see **U.S. Air Forces Atlantic**)

Air Force Security Service (AFSS): Former name of Air Force **Electronics Security Command**.

Air Force Service Information and News Center (AFSINC):   Air Force **separate operating agency** activated 1 June 1978. It acts as a clearinghouse for DOD and Air Force news and public affairs products. It operates the Internal Information Directorate, the Army and Air Force Hometown News Service, the Air Force Broadcasting Service, and the Air Force Office of Youth Relations. Its personnel strength is approximately 850 military and civilian personnel.

Headquarters
Kelly AFB, TX 78245

Air Forces Iceland (AFI): Highest-level Air Force command in Iceland and, in wartime, a component command of the **Iceland Defense Force**. AFI provides for the air defense of the island on behalf of NATO. It consists of the 57th Fighter Interceptor Squadron (NAS Keflavik), equipped with **F-15s**; forward-based **E-3A** AWACS (on rotation from Tinker AFB, OK); the 932d Aircraft Control and Warning squadron at Rockville, operating an air defense radar; and the 667th Aircraft Control and Warning squadron at Hofn, operating an air defense radar.

Headquarters
NAS Keflavik, Iceland
(FPO New York 09571)

Air Force Space Command (AF-SPACECOM): Air Force **major command** and component of the unified **U.S. Space Command**, established 1 September 1982 to consolidate Air Force space activities and unilateral U.S. aerospace warning functions. Its missions include satellite surveillance (tracking, early orbit determination, space object identification, impact prediction), protection (collision avoidance, Space Shuttle support), and negation (deterrence of threats, space defense). AFSPACECOM is responsible for organizing, training, equipping, and administering forces in support of NORAD and U.S. Space Command; managing the **Defense Support Program (DSP)**; and managing the **Defense Meteorological Satellite Program (DMSP)**. It will also manage the **NAVSTAR** and **MILSTAR** systems when they are fully operational. Its 1st Space Wing manages 20 operational satellite, ground-based missile warning, and space sensor sites. The wing's space and optical sensor systems track more than

7,000 man-made objects in space and make over 48,000 observations daily. AFSPACECOM's 2d Space Wing manages the **Air Force Satellite Control Network**; the **Consolidated Space Operations Center**; and ground stations for the **DMSP, NAVSTAR**, and **DSP**. It also provides support for the **Defense Satellite Communications System**, the **Fleet Satellite Communications System**, and MILSTAR (when activated). The command operates at 35 installations worldwide. Its personnel strength is approximately 7,900 Air Force military and civilian personnel and 5,400 contractor personnel.

Headquarters
Peterson AFB, CO 80914

Major subordinate units

• 1st Space Wing, Peterson AFB, CO 80914
• 2d Space Wing, Falcon AFB, CO 80912
• 3d Space Support Wing, Peterson AFB, CO 80914

Air Force Systems Command (AFSC): Air Force **major command**, redesignated from the Air Research and Development Command on 1 April 1961. AFSC is responsible for research, development, and testing of all Air Force weapons and aeronautical and space technologies. It also manages RDT&E of satellites, boosters, space probes, and related systems in support of DOD and **National Aeronautics and Space Administration (NASA)**. It administers over 48,000 active contracts totaling approximately $305 billion, plus approximately $35 billion in foreign military sales cases. It operates 5 product divisions, 3 supporting divisions, 14 laboratories, and 5 test centers. Its personnel strength is approximately 51,000 military and civilian personnel.

Headquarters
Andrews AFB, MD 20334

Products Divisions

- Aeronautical Systems Division: Wright-Patterson AFB, OH 85433
- Ballistic Systems Division: Norton AFB, CA 92409
- Contract Management Division: Kirtland AFB, NM 87117
- Electronics Systems Division: Hanscom AFB, MA 01731
- Foreign Technology Division: Wright-Patterson AFB, OH 85433
- Human Systems Division: Brooks AFB, TX 78235
- Munition Systems Division: Eglin AFB, FL 32542
- Space Systems Division: Los Angeles AFB, CA 90009

Air Force Technical Applications Center (AFTAC): Air Force **direct reporting unit**. Its mission is to detect, assess, and report technical information related to nuclear explosions by foreign powers, and to monitor foreign compliance with nuclear testing treaties. AFTAC operates and maintains the **Atomic Energy Detection System**, which monitors nuclear activities worldwide—on land, at sea, in space, and in the atmosphere. Treaties monitored include the **Limited Test Ban Treaty**, the **Non-Proliferation Treaty**, the **Threshold Test Ban Treaty**, the **Peaceful Nuclear Explosion Treaty**, and the

INF Treaty (through support to the **On-Site Inspection Agency**). AFTAC operates or receives information from satellite sensors, seismic stations, high frequency receivers, airborne samplers, and hydroacoustic detectors. It consists of 3 headquarters units, 11 detachments, 6 operating sites, and 70 equipment locations in over 35 countries (some of them clandestine). Its personnel strength is approximately 1,300 military and civilian personnel.

Headquarters
Patrick AFB, FL 32925

Major elements

- Technical Operations Division: McClellan AFB, CA 95652
- Pacific Technical Operations Area: Wheeler AFB, HI 96854
- European Technical Operations Area: Lindsey AB, West Germany, APO New York 09634

Air Intercept Missile (see **AIM**)

Air Intercept Rocket (see **AIR**)

airland battle: Army operational concept, used particularly for European-based forces but applicable worldwide, that describes how it expects to fight. Two ideas—extending the battlefield well forward of friendly forces in both depth and time, and integrating conventional, nuclear, chemical, and electronic means—are blended to describe a battlefield where the enemy is attacked to the full depth of its formations. It therefore concentrates not only on defeating first-echelon Warsaw Pact forces but also on disrupting and destroying second-echelon follow-on forces. Air-land battle focuses mainly on combat operations at the corps level and below.

The airland battle concept was adopted in 1980. It stresses the tenets of Army **doctrine**: initiative, agility, and synchronized actions. Doctrine-established common techniques that are used at all levels of command are

- Ensure unity of effort;
- Direct friendly strengths against enemy weaknesses;
- Sustain the fight;
- Move fast, strike hard, and finish rapidly;
- Use terrain and weather; and
- Protect the force.

Offensive operations are undertaken to carry the fight to the enemy and seek decision on our terms. The purpose of these operations is to accomplish one or more of the following

- Destroy enemy forces;
- Secure key terrain;
- Deprive the enemy of resources and demoralize enemy forces;
- Deceive and divert the enemy;
- Develop intelligence information; and
- Hold the enemy in position.

Types of offensive operations include movement to contact, hasty attack, deliberate attack, exploitation, and pursuit. Forms of offensive maneuvers include frontal attack, envelopment, and penetration.

Defensive operations are intended to

- Cause an enemy attack to fail;
- Gain time;
- Concentrate forces elsewhere;
- Control essential terrain;

- Wear down enemy forces as a prelude to offensive operations; and
- Retain tactical, strategic, and political objectives.

Types of defensive operations include defense, delay, defense of an encircled force, and rear-area protection. Corps and division commanders assigned a defensive mission usually organize their forces for operations in four areas: the area of influence, covering force area, main battle area, and the rear area. In the airland battle concept, air-delivered weapons, field artillery fires, nuclear forces, air maneuver units, and unconventional warfare forces are the principal weapons of the deep battle. Deep battle operations are designed to affect the closure tomes of follow-on forces and thereby create windows of opportunity for decisive action against the leading enemy echelons. They aim to prevent the enemy from concentrating overwhelming combat power.

The Army's airland battle concept is compatible with NATO's **follow-on forces attack (FOFA)** concept, although there are some differences. The airland battle focuses on corps and below, whereas FOFA concentrates on the theater. FOFA is therefore more of an operational- and strategic-level concept whose primary emphasis is on deterrence, whereas the airland battle is a tactical and operational concept with primary emphasis on war-fighting. Further, while airland battle is concerned with near-term battle and has worldwide applications, FOFA is concerned with the overall war and is limited in applicability to NATO operations.

Air-launched Cruise Missile (AL-CM): Model designation AGM-86B. An Air Force subsonic, guided, air-to-ground, long-range, nuclear-armed **cruise missile**. It is a small (12 ft wingspan; 20 ft, 9 in. length; 24 in. diameter) winged missile powered by a turbofan jet engine with low-altitude flight capability. Armed with a 200 kiloton W80 nuclear warhead, the ALCM is extremely accurate (30 meter CEP). It uses a Litton inertial navigation element with a **terrain contour-matching (TERCOM)** guidance system.

The ALCM is currently launched from **B-52G/H** bombers (each bomber can carry six missiles on each of two external pylons). The **Strategic Air Command** plans to equip 98 B-52Gs and 96 B-52Hs for ALCMs. As of 1989, all 98 B-52Gs and about 70 B-52Hs were equipped for cruise missiles. All B-52H aircraft will be equipped for external carriage of ALCMs by the end of FY 1989. Internal bomb bay rotary launchers for eight additional missiles are scheduled to be on all B-52Hs by the end of FY 1993. With the deployment of the B-1B and B-2 bombers, the B-52G force is scheduled to be eventually retired from its nuclear mission, and the B-52H force will serve as the primary cruise missile carriers. B-1B bombers could be equipped to launch ALCMs in the future.

ALCMs were first deployed in 1982 with the 416th Bombardment Wing (BW) at Griffiss AFB, NY. Other wings equipped with the ALCM are 379th BW, Wurtsmith AFB, MI; 2nd BW, Barksdale AFB, LA; 92nd BW, Fairchild AFB, WA; 97th BW, Blytheville AFB, AR; and 7th BW,

Carswell AFB, TX. The 410th BW, K.I. Sawyer AFB, MI, and 5th BW, Minot AFB, ND, are scheduled to receive ALCMs.

The missile has a top speed of about 550 mph and a range of 2,500 km. The Air Force began full-scale development in January 1977. Production of an initial 225 missiles began in FY 1980. The first-alert capability (one B-52G bomber capable of alert status) was reached in September 1981. Originally, 4,348 ALCMs were planned, but developments in **stealth** technology led to a cutback in the program to 1,715, of which production was completed in October 1986. The follow-on **Advanced Cruise Missile** is under development. The prime contractor is Boeing.

airlift: The operation of aircraft for the purpose of transporting passengers, cargo, and mail. (see also **Military Airlift Command**)

airlift and sealift forces: Program 4 of the 11 **major force programs** that represent all of the major missions of the services and are the most basic structural elements of the **Five Year Defense Program (FYDP)**. The category consists of airlift, sealift, traffic management, and water terminal activities, both industrially funded and non-industrially funded (including command, logistics, and support) units.

air-mobile: 1. The process of using assigned or attached fixed-wing and rotary aircraft to maneuver rapidly within given areas of operations.   **2.** Units that have or are given air-mobile capability. (see also **air assault**)

Air National Guard (ANG): Federal **reserve** component of the Air Force whose members are **National Guard** personnel. Its missions are to augment active forces during wartime or national emergencies and provide assistance in natural disasters and **civil disturbances**. It consists of over 1,000 separate units, including 24 **wings**, 67 groups, and 91 squadrons; these are assigned to the **Strategic Air Command**, **Tactical Air Command**, **Military Airlift Command**, **Pacific Air Forces**, or **U.S. Air Forces Europe** upon activation. ANG provides a significant portion of the capabilities of the total force in many mission areas, including about 78 percent of CONUS interceptor forces, 35 percent of theater airlift, 54 percent of tactical reconnaissance, 40 percent of tactical air support, 25 percent of tactical fighters, 67 percent of airborne warning and control units, 67 percent of combat communications and engineering installations, 55 percent of tactical control, and 24 percent of civil engineering. Units are under the control of the state governors until mobilized for federal service, and they are supervised by the National Guard Bureau, as well as the Air National Guard Support Center. The Air National Guard constitutes approximately three percent of the AF's total budget and 20 percent of the total reserve appropriations for FY 1988. It makes up 11 percent of the Air Force's total personnel strength. The personnel strength of the ANG Ready Reserve is about 115,000.

Headquarters
Pentagon, Washington, DC
20310-2500

air operation: Strategic or tactical military operation conducted in conjunction with land or sea forces. Strategic operations seek the progressive destruction of enemy war-making capacity. Tactical air operations, in conjunction with land or sea forces, are of the following types:

• Counter-air (CA): Attain and maintain air superiority by attacking air and air defense assets;
• Air interdiction (AI): Prevent movement of enemy forces into combat zones and destroy forces and supporting installations; and
• Offensive air support (OAS): Assist in accomplishment of ground/naval objectives.

There are three functional missions in the conduct of offensive air support:

• Close air support (CAS): Air actions against enemy targets in close proximity to friendly forces, particularly in support of ground forces;
• Battlefield air interdiction (BAI): Air actions nominated and approved by the ground commander; and
• Tactical air reconnaissance (REC-CE): Reconnaissance by forces organic to combat units.

Counter-air and offensive air support operations require close cooperation with ground forces, whereas air interdiction requires no cooperation. Interdiction is generally beyond the range of ground forces and has little direct effect on ground maneuver.

Air Staff: The executive part of the **Department of the Air Force**. It serves to assist the Secretary of the Air Force in carrying out his or her responsibilities and is organized to include the Chief of Staff; Vice Chief; Deputy Chiefs for personnel, logistics and engineering, plans and operations, and programs and resources; Assistant Chiefs for information systems, intelligence, and studies and analyses; and the Special Staff, consisting of the Surgeon General, Judge Advocate General, the Chief of Chaplains, and the Chief of the National Guard Bureau. (see also **Chief of Staff of the Air Force**)

air superiority: One of the functions of air forces—dominance in the air to a degree that permits ground and naval forces to operate without prohibitive interference by enemy air forces.

Air Support Operations Center (ASOC): Air Force facility designated to operate with a corps-level tactical operations center (TOC). The ASOC, normally located at the Corps Tactical Operations Center, manages the planning and execution of CAS operations. Its primary tasks are to provide a fast-reaction capability to satisfy immediate requests from Army forces for close air support, and to process preplanned air support requests. ASOCs in Europe, which exist one per corps, are subordinate to **Allied Tactical Operations Centers (ATOCs),** two of which exist in each Allied Tactical Air Force. An ASOC can request additional offensive air support through the ATOCs, which task the Air Force fighter wings. Subordinate to ASOCs are tactical air control points (TACPs) and forward-air controllers (FACs), which exist at the battalion level.

air target materials program: "A DOD program established for the production of medium- and large-scale target materials and related items in support of long-range, worldwide requirements of the unified and specified commands, the military departments, and allied participants. It is under the management control of the **Defense Intelligence Agency** and encompasses the determination of production and coverage requirements, standardization of products, establishment of production priorities and schedules, and the production, distribution, storage, and release/exchange of the air target materials items and related products" [*JCS Pub 1*, p. 22].

air-to-air missile (AAM): A missile launched from an aircraft at a target above the surface. The designation is **AIM.** (see also **AMRAAM, ASRAAM, Phoenix, Sidewinder, Sparrow**)

air-to-ground missile (see **AGM**)

air-to-surface missile (ASM): A missile launched from an aircraft to impact on a surface target, also called an air-to-ground missile. Its designation is **AGM.** (see also **Air-launched Cruise Missile, Harpoon, HARM, Maverick, Shrike, SRAM, Standard Arm**)

Air Training Command (ATC): Air Force **major command** established in 1943 that recruits and trains officers and enlisted personnel. ATC conducts a number of training schools:

• *Basic training* Lackland AFB, TX 78236;

- *Technical training* Lowry AFB, CO 80230; Chanute AFB, IL 61868; Keesler AFB, MS 39534; Sheppard AFB, TX 76311; Lackland AFB, TX 78236; and Goodfellow AFB, TX 76908;
- *Pilot training* Columbus AFB, MS 39701; Laughlin AFB, TX 78843; Reese AFB, TX 79489; Vance AFB, OK 73705; and Williams AFB, AZ 85240;
- *NATO pilot training* Sheppard AFB, TX 76311;
- *Navigator training* Mather AFB, CA 95655; and
- *Space training* Lowry AFB, CO 80230.

ATC also manages the Officer Training School (Lackland AFB, TX); the Air Force Reserve Officer Training Corps (Maxwell AFB, AL); the **Air University** (Maxwell AFB, AL); the School of Health Care Sciences (Sheppard AFB, TX); and the Defense Language Institute English Language Center (Lackland AFB, TX). In total, ATC conducts more than 6,300 training courses in more than 350 specialties. It is composed of 13 major installations within CONUS, 97 field training detachments worldwide, and 150 Reserve Officer Training Corps (ROTC) detachments on CONUS college and university campuses. Its Recruiting Service (Randolph AFB, TX) is composed of 5 recruiting groups, 35 squadrons, and approximately 1,350 recruiting offices. It gains approximately 60,000 recruits a year. Personnel strength of the command is approximately 71,000 military and civilian personnel.

Headquarters
Randolph AFB, TX 78150

Air University (AU): Air Force **major command** managed by the **Air Training Command** and consisting of the Air War College; Air Command and Staff College; Squadron Officer School; Center for Aerospace Doctrine, Research, and Education (CADRE); Educational Development Center; and the Leadership Management Development Center.

Headquarters
Maxwell AFB, AL 36112

Air Weather Service (AWS): Air Force technical command subordinate to **Military Airlift Command**. Redesignated from the Army Air Forces Weather Service on 13 March 1946, AWS is responsible for tactical and base-level weather forecasting support for the Air Force and Army worldwide and for providing operational weather support to DOD. It operates at more than 290 locations worldwide and employs approximately 4,800 military and civilian personnel.

Headquarters
Scott AFB, IL 62225

AK: Designation for cargo ship.

AKR: Designation for vehicle cargo ship.

ALASAT (Air-launched anti-satellite weapon) (see **anti-satellite (ASAT)**)

Alaskan Air Command (AAC): Air Force **major command** and component command of the joint **Alaskan Command**, redesignated from the Eleventh Air Force, 18 December

1945. It is responsible for the tactical air defense of Alaska and North America, and would provide forces to the Alaskan Command when directed. It consists of three main bases and two forward operating locations; one tactical control wing; one air base group; two tactical fighter wings; and two combat support groups. The 11th Tactical Control Wing operates 13 long-range radar sites (LRRS) throughout Alaska, currently being integrated into the **Joint Surveillance System** (**JSS**) through AAC's modernization program, "Seek Igloo." The wing also operates the Alaskan Tactical Air Control System, serves as the operating agency for AAC's Alternate Command Post (ALCOP), and is responsible for the Alaskan NORAD **Regional Operational Control Center**. AAC also operates the Elmendorf Rescue Coordination Center (RCC) for military and civilian emergency search and rescue efforts. The AAC Commander, an Air Force Lieutenant General, also serves as the Commander of the Alaskan **NORAD** Region and the Alaskan Command. A Canadian Forces brigadier general is assigned as the AAC deputy commander for NORAD operations. AAC personnel strength is about 9,000 military and civilian employees.

Headquarters
Elmendorf AFB, AK 99506

Alaskan Command (ALASCOM): Subunified command of **U.S. Pacific Command** responsible for the strategic air, ground and sea defense of Alaska, including Aleutian Island bases, and the coordination of statewide civil disasters. The command was reactivated on 7 July 1989 to take on the responsibilities of predecessor agencies including: the Alaskan Command (comprised of the naval Alaskan Sea Frontier and the U.S. Army Alaska) which was established 1 January 1947 and disestablished in 1975; and Joint Task Force Alaska, which was disestablished with the activation of Alaskan Command. The new joint Alaskan Command is comprised of units from the Air Force's **Alaskan Air Command**, the Army's 6th Infantry Division (Light), and Navy units assigned to the 17th U.S. Coast Guard District. Its commander, an Air Force Lieutenant General, also serves as the Commander of the Alaskan Air Command and the Alaskan **NORAD** Region. Its combined personnel strength is approximately 30,000 military members.

Headquarters
Elmendorf AFB, AK 99506

ALCOP (Alternate Command Post): Any location, fixed or mobile, designated to assume **command post** functions in the event that the primary command post becomes inoperative. It is primarily a term used by the Air Force. An ALCOP may be partially or fully equipped and manned and may be the command post of a subordinate unit. The ALCOPs of some commands are specially configured train cars.

ALCOR (ARPA Lincoln Coherent Observables Radar): MIT Lincoln Laboratory field research facility, including L-band radar, "Firepond" infrared tracking radar for precise tracking, "Haystack" X-band radar for geosynchronous orbit observations, and a very long-baseline interferometry observatory. It is located in Westford, MA, at the Millstone Hill facility [*Nuclear Battlefields*, p. 194].

alert: 1. "Readiness for action, defense, or protection" [*JCS Pub 1*, p. 23]. **2.** The level of preparedness directed by competent authority to be attained by deploying units. This refers to the state of an organization (alerted) when it has been notified of its selection for employment in support of a specific operation plan or operation order. There are three general states of alert for strategic forces:

- Day-to-day alert
- Generated alert
- Airborne alert

A ballistic missile submarine, on station and prepared to fire its missiles at assigned targets when so notified, is considered on day-to-day alert. Submarines in transit to and from stations or involved in training are referred to as "mod alert" (modified alert) submarines and could be generated to full alert levels. **3.** "A warning signal of a real or threatened danger, such as an air attack" [*JCS Pub 1*, p. 23]. Alert systems used include

- Alert system of the Joint Chiefs of Staff and the unified and specified commands, which specifies different **alert conditions**;
- Civil readiness levels and warning conditions of the Federal Emergency Management Agency; and
- NATO alert system. The alert status of NATO forces is expressed in four levels: military vigilance, simple alert, reinforced alert, and general alert. (see also **air defense emergency**, **ALFA**, **conflict**, **crisis**, **Crisis Action System**)

alert condition (LERTCON): System used to achieve a uniform state of command readiness for U.S. military forces. "The Alert System of the Joint Chiefs of Staff is designed for use in crisis management. It is adaptable to a full spectrum of crises, from general war and execution of the **Single Integrated Operational Plan (SIOP)** to operations and regional tensions in a limited area, with or without the use of nuclear weapons. It is intended to be used as a directive as well as an authorization for the commanders of the unified and specified commands to implement preplanned actions to increase force readiness, which may include the execution of portions of some plans or entire plans during a particular alert condition. The attainment of a specific LERTCON does not indicate, in itself, the attainment of a specific level of combat readiness by a command, but rather that all actions considered appropriate have been completed that will bring a command up to a desired readiness in a time consistent with the existing situation and the LERTCON declared" [JCS, *Alert System of the Joint Chiefs of Staff,* Part 1, Concept, 29 January 1981, p. 2-1, released under the FOIA].

The alert system of the Joint Chiefs of Staff consists of seven LERTCONs, which are divided into two subsystems, **Defense Readiness Conditions (DEFCONs)** and Emer-

Alert Condition	Exercise Term
DEFCON 5	Fade Out
DEFCON 4	Double Take
DEFCON 3	Round House
DEFCON 2	Fast Pace
DEFCON 1	Cocked Pistol
Defense Emergency	Hot Box
Air Defense Emergency	Big Noise
Air Defense Warning Red	Big Noise Apple Jack
Air Defense Warning Yellow	Big Noise Lemon Juice
Air Defense Warning White	Big Noise Snow Man

gency Conditions (EMERGCONs). There are five DEFCONs, with DEFCON 5 being the lowest and DEFCON 1 being the highest. There are two EMERGCONs, **Defense Emergency** and **Air Defense Emergency**, with three attack warning conditions.

Each LERTCON level is restricted in terms of the authority that different officers or commands have to declare changes. The Joint Chiefs of Staff or higher authorities are authorized to declare all DEFCONs and defense emergencies. Commander in Chief **NORAD** is authorized to declare an Air Defense Emergency. There are actions common to all LERTCONs, as well as actions specific to commands for each separate LERTCON. The **Strategic Air Command (SAC)** and forces in South Korea are always on DEFCON 4. During the Cuban Missile Crisis, SAC was moved to DEFCON 2 and the rest of the U.S. forces were moved to DEFCON 3.

alert order: Formal directive issued by the **Chairman of the Joint Chiefs of Staff** to initiate execution planning. It is part of Phase IV of the **Crisis Action System (CAS)**, which follows a decision by the NCA that U.S. military forces may be required. It pro- vides the essential guidance for planning the ongoing situation and marks the outset of CAS, Phase V, execution planning. An alert order requires approval by the Secretary of Defense, as it reflects the NCA decision and identifies the military course(s) of action selected for execution planning. (see also **planning order**)

ALFA: Name of the day-to-day alert force of the Strategic Air Command.

Allied Air Forces Central Europe (AAFCE): Principle subordinate command of NATO's **Allied Forces Central Europe (AFCENT)**, established in 1974. It is responsible for all air operations in Central Europe and has operational command of all NATO air forces in the central region. It is commanded by a U.S. Air Force general (who is also the U.S. Air Forces Europe commander) and is composed of two **Allied Tactical Air Forces**, each consisting of approximately 1,500 tactical aircraft. AAFCE, in coordination with Northern Army Group (NORTHAG) and Central Army Group (CENTAG), recommends to AFCENT the apportionment of the air effect, either by priority or percentages in terms of missions. AFCENT and AAFCE have a joint command center, the AAFCE portion of which is called the Central Region Air Operations Center (CRAOC).

Headquarters
Ramstein AB, W. Germany
APO New York 09094

Subordinate Forces

- 4th Allied Tactical Air Force: Heidelberg, West Germany
- 2d Allied Tactical Air Force: Mönchen-Gladbach, West Germany

Allied Air Forces Southern Europe (AIRSOUTH): Principle subordinate command of NATO's **Allied Forces Southern Europe (AFSOUTH)**, established in August 1951. It is responsible for air operations in southern Europe. It is commanded by a U.S. Air Force general (who is also the commander of the 16th Air Force, headquartered in Spain) and is composed of two **Allied Tactical Air Forces**. Long range plans call for the resubordination of the Hellenic Tactical Air Force to NATO as the 7th ATAF.

Headquarters
Naples, Italy FPO New York 09524

Subordinate Forces

- 5th Allied Tactical Air Force: Vicenza, Italy
- 6th Allied Tactical Air Force: Izmir, Turkey

Allied Command Atlantic (ACLANT): One of three **major NATO commands (MNCs)**. ACLANT, which became operational 10 April 1952, is responsible for the defense of the ocean area from the north pole to the Tropic of Cancer, and from the coastal waters of North America to the coasts of Europe and Africa, including the land areas of Greenland, Iceland, Bermuda, the Faroes, the Azores, and Madeira. The ACLANT area includes Portugal but does not encompass the English Channel or the British Isles. The area covers approximately 12 million square miles of the Atlantic Ocean. Its three missions are **1**. to "maintain intact the Atlantic Ocean communication lines"; **2**. to "conduct conventional and nuclear operations against enemy naval bases and air fields"; and **3**. to "support operations carried out by **SACEUR (Supreme Allied Commander Europe)**" [JCS, *Systems Description, Exercise Poll Station 81,* 9 January 1981, p. G-1-B-EX-11, released under the FOIA]. It is commanded by **Supreme Allied Commander Atlantic (SACLANT)**, an American admiral who also serves as the Commander-in-Chief of the **U.S. Atlantic Command (CINCLANT)**. SACLANT has the right of direct access to Chiefs of Staff of NATO forces and, under certain defined circumstances, to Defense Ministers and heads of government. The only operating force assigned to ACLANT in peacetime is the **Standing Naval Force Atlantic (STANAVFORLANT)**, which normally consists of four destroyer-type ship. Forces earmarked for ACLANT, primarily naval forces, are provided by the United Kingdom, Canada, Denmark, West Germany, the Netherlands, Portugal, and the United States. Only the United States has committed naval forces to ACLANT. There are also arrangements for cooperation with French naval forces. (see also **Island Command**)

Headquarters
Norfolk, VA 23511

Major Subordinate Commands

- **Western Atlantic Command (WESTLANT):** Norfolk, VA 23511-5102
- **Eastern Atlantic Command (EASTLANT):** Northwood, UK (APO New York 09083)
- **Striking Fleet Atlantic:** afloat (APO New York 09501)
- **Submarines Allied Command Atlantic:** Norfolk, VA 23511
- **Iberian Atlantic Command (IBERLANT):** Lisbon, Portugal (APO New York 09678)

Principle Subordinate Commands

EASTLANT:
- Carrier Striking Force, afloat
- Bay of Biscay Sub Area, Northwood, UK
- Central Sub Area, Plymouth, UK
- Maritime Air Central Sub Area, Plymouth, UK
- Maritime Air Eastern Atlantic Area, Northwood, UK
- Maritime Air Northern Sub Area, Pitreavie, UK
- Northern Sub Area, Rosyth, UK

WESTLANT:
- Canadian Atlantic Sub Area, Halifax, Canada B3K 2XO
- Ocean Sub Area, Norfolk, VA
- Striking Fleet and Special Task Forces (when assigned)
- Submarine Forces Eastern Atlantic Area, Northwood, UK
- Submarine Forces Western Atlantic Area, Norfolk, VA

Island Commands

- Island Commander Azores, San Miguel, Azores, Portugal
- Island Commander Bermuda, Hamilton, Bermuda
- Island Commander Faroes, Thorshavn, Faroes, Denmark
- Island Commander Greenland, Gronnedal, Greenland
- Island Commander Iceland, Keflavik, Iceland
- Island Commander Madeira, Funchal, Madeira, Portugal

Allied Command Channel (ACCHAN): One of three **major NATO commands (MNCs)**, established 21 February 1952. ACCHAN's area of responsibility is the English Channel and the southern North Sea. Its mission is the defense of this area and, in cooperation with Allied Command Europe, the air defense of the Channel. ACCHAN is commanded by **Allied Commander-in-Chief Channel (CINCHAN)**, a British Admiral who also serves as the Commander-in-Chief Eastern Atlantic Command of **Allied Command Atlantic**. The only force assigned to ACCHAN in peace-time is the **Standing Naval Force Channel (STANAVFORCHAN)**, formed in 1973 and consisting of mine countermeasures ships from Belgium, West Germany, the Netherlands, and the United Kingdom. Other forces earmarked for ACCHAN are predominantly naval but include maritime air forces as well. CINCHAN has a Maritime Air Advisor on staff who is also

Allied Commanders-in-Chief Channel

Adm of the Fleet Sir Arthur John Power	Feb 1952
Adm Sir John H. Edelsten	Jun 1952
Adm of the Fleet Sir George E. Creasey	Sep 1954
Adm Sir Guy Grantham	May 1957
Adm Sir Manley L. Power	Feb 1959
Adm Sir Alexander N.C. Bingley	Oct 1961
Adm Sir Varyl C. Begg	Aug 1965
Adm Sir John B. Frewen	Jan 1966
Adm Sir John Bush	Oct 1967
Adm Sir William O'Brien	Feb 1970
Adm Sir Edward Ashmore	Sep 1971
Adm Sir Terence Lewin	Dec 1973
Adm Sir John Treacher	Oct 1975
Adm Sir Henry Leach	Mar 1977
Adm Sir James Eberle	May 1979
Adm Sir John Fieldhouse	Apr 1981
Adm Sir Benjamin Bathurst	May 1989

the Commander Allied Maritime Air Forces Channel. The United States has no forces assigned to ACCHAN. There are arrangements also for cooperation with French naval forces. The Channel Committee, located in London and consisting of Naval Chiefs of Staff from Belgium, the Netherlands, and the United Kingdom, serves as CINCHAN's advisory and consultative body.

Headquarters
Northwood, UK
(APO New York 09083)

Major Subordinate Commands

- **Nore Sub Area,** Pitreavie, UK
- **Plymouth Sub Area,** Plymouth, UK
- **Benelux Sub Area,** Den Helder, Netherlands
- **Allied Maritime Air Force Channel,** Northwood, UK

Principle Subordinate Commands

- Maritime Air Nore Sub Area, Pitreavie, UK
- Maritime Air Plymouth Sub Area, Plymouth, UK

Allied Commander-in-Chief Channel (CINCHAN): Commander of NATO's **Allied Command Channel,** always a British Admiral and equal in rank to the **Supreme Allied Commander Europe** and **Supreme Allied Commander Atlantic**.

Allied Command Europe (ACE): One of three **major NATO commands (MNCs)**. ACE, which became operational 2 April 1951, is responsible for the defense of the land area from the north cape of Norway to North Africa, and from the Atlantic, including the Mediterranean Sea, to the eastern border of Turkey, excluding the United Kingdom, France, Iceland, Spain, and Portugal. Its mission also includes the air defense of the United Kingdom. ACE's headquarters is the **Supreme Headquarters Allied Powers Europe (SHAPE)** and its commander is the **Supreme Allied Commander Europe (SACEUR)**. SACEUR is an American general who also serves as Commander-in-Chief of **U.S. European Command (USEUCOM)**. USEUCOM operational forces committed to NATO come under the operational control of ACE. In addition to their usual military advisors, SACEUR and the Deputy Supreme Allied Commander also have political and scientific advisors. Fourteen NATO-member countries have National Military Representatives at SHAPE who serve as liaisons with their respective chiefs of staff. France has a military liaison mission at SHAPE. SACEUR shares command of airborne early warning and control with SACLANT and CINCHAN.

Headquarters
Casteau Mons, Belgium
(APO New York 09055)

Major Subordinate Commands

- **Allied Forces Northern Europe (AFNORTH):** Kolsaas, Norway (APO New York 09085)
- **Allied Forces Central Europe (AFCENT):** Brunssum, Netherlands (APO New York 09011)
- **Allied Forces Southern Europe (AFSOUTH):** Naples, Italy (FPO New York 09524)
- **ACE Mobile Force (Land):** Heidelberg, West Germany
- **United Kingdom Air Command Region (UKAIR):** High Wycombe, UK

- **NATO Airborne Early Warning Force (NAEWF) Command:** Geilenkirchen, West Germany

Principle Subordinate Commands

AFNORTH
- **Allied Forces Baltic Approaches:** Karup, Denmark
- **Allied Forces North Norway:** Reitan, Norway
- **Allied Forces South Norway:** Oslo, Norway

AFCENT
- **Allied Air Forces Central Europe:** Ramstein, West Germany
- **Central Army Group:** Seckenheim, West Germany
- **Northern Army Group:** Mönchen-Gladbach, West Germany

AFSOUTH
- **Allied Naval Forces Southern Europe:** Naples, Italy
- **Allied Air Forces Southern Europe:** Naples, Italy
- **Allied Land Forces Southern Europe:** Verona, Italy
- **Allied Land Forces Southeastern Europe:** Izmir, Turkey
- Hellenic 1st Army
- **Striking and Support Forces Southern Europe:** Naples, Italy

Allied Command Europe Mobile Force (AMF) (see **ACE Mobile Force**)

Allied Forces Baltic Approaches (BALTAP): Principle subordinate command of NATO's **Allied Forces Northern Europe (AFNORTH)**, established in 1962. Its area of responsibility includes Denmark; Schleswig-Holstein and Hamburg, West Germany north of the Elbe river; and the

Baltic Sea approaches. Its operational forces include land, air, and naval forces provided by Denmark and West Germany. It is also supplemented by the Danish Home Guard of 77,000 volunteers.

Headquarters
Karup, Denmark
(APO New York 09870)

Subordinate Commands

- Allied Land Forces SchelswigHolstein and Jutland (LANDJUT): Rendsburg, West Germany
- Land Forces Zealand and Bornholm (LANDZEALAND): Ringsted, Denmark
- Allied Naval Forces Baltic Approaches (NAVBALTAP): Karup, Denmark
- Allied Air Forces Baltic Approaches (AIRBALTAP): Karup, Denmark

Allied Forces Central Europe (AFCENT): Major subordinate command of NATO's **Allied Command Europe (ACE)**, established in 1951. It has operational command of land and air forces in the central European region, minus Belgium and the Netherlands. It is commanded by a West German general and consists of two army groups, the **2d Allied Tactical Air Force** and the **4th Allied Tactical Air Force**, provided by seven nations. The bulk of the U.S. commitment to NATO is to AFCENT.

Headquarters
Brunssum, Netherlands
(APO New York 09011)

Principle Subordinate Commands

- **Central Army Group**: Seckenheim, West Germany
- **Allied Air Forces Central Europe**: Ramstein, West Germany
- **Northern Army Group**: Moenchen-Gladbach, West Germany

Allied Forces Northern Europe (AFNORTH): Major subordinate command of NATO's **Allied Command Europe**, established in April 1951. It is responsible for the defense of Norway; Denmark; Schleswig-Holstein and Hamburg, West Germany north of the Elbe river; and the Baltic approaches. It is commanded by a British general and consists of one West German division, two West German naval air wings, the Baltic Fleet, and most of the armed forces of Norway and Denmark. Some U.S. forces are earmarked for the command.

Headquarters
Kolsaas, Norway
(APO New York 09085)

Principle Subordinate Commands

- **Allied Forces Baltic Approaches**: Karup, Denmark
- **Allied Forces North Norway**: Reitan, Norway
- **Allied Forces South Norway**: Oslo, Norway

Allied Forces North Norway: Principle subordinate command of NATO's **Allied Forces Northern Europe**, established 1 September 1971. It is commanded by a Norwegian general and consists of land, air, and naval units.

Headquarters
Reitan, Norway
(APO New York 09085)

Subordinate Commands

- Allied Land Forces North Norway (LANDNONOR)
- Allied Naval Forces North Norway (NAVNONOR)
- Allied Air Forces North Norway (AIRNONOR)

Allied Forces Southern Europe (AFSOUTH): Major subordinate command of NATO's **Allied Command Europe (ACE)**, established June 1951. AFSOUTH is the largest of the ACE regions and is responsible for the defense of Turkey, Italy, Greece, the Black Sea, and the entire Mediterranean Sea. It is commanded by an American admiral and consists of naval and land forces from the United States, Italy, Turkey, and the United Kingdom, as well as two **Allied Tactical Air Forces**. Long-range plans call for the creation of LANDSOUTHEAST Northern Greece, and the subordination of the Hellenic Tactical Air Force as 7th Allied Tactical Air Force.

Headquarters
Naples, Italy
(FPO New York 09524)

Principle Subordinate Commands

- **Allied Naval Forces Southern Europe (NAVSOUTH):** Naples, Italy
- **Allied Air Forces Southern Europe (AIRSOUTH):** Naples, Italy
- **Striking and Support Forces Southern Europe (STRIKFOR-SOUTH):** Naples, Italy
- **Allied Land Forces Southern Europe (LANDSOUTH):** Verona, Italy

- **Allied Land Forces Southeastern Europe (LANDSOUTHEAST):** Izmir, Turkey
- Hellenic First Army

Allied Forces South Norway: Principle subordinate command of NATO's **Allied Forces Northern Europe**. It is commanded by a Norwegian general or admiral and consists of land, air, and naval forces plus Norway's Home Guard of 60,000 personnel.

Headquarters
Oslo, Norway
(APO New York 09085)

Subordinate Commands

- Allied Air Forces South Norway (AIRSONOR)
- Allied Naval Forces South Norway (NAVSONOR)
- Allied Land Forces South Norway (LANDSONOR)

Allied Land Forces Southeastern Europe (LANDSOUTHEAST): Principle subordinate command of NATO's **Allied Forces Southern Europe**, established 8 September 1952. It is responsible for land operations in defense of Greece and Turkey. It is commanded by a Turkish general and includes forces from Turkey. Command of Greek forces within NATO is currently under negotiation.

Headquarters
Izmir, Turkey
(APO New York 09118)

Allied Land Forces Southern Europe (LANDSOUTH): Principle subordinate command of NATO's

Allied Forces Southern Europe. It is responsible for land operations in defense of northeast Italy. It is commanded by an Italian general and includes forces from six nations—Italy, West Germany, Greece, Turkey, Portugal, and the United States. The U.S. **Southern European Task Force (SETAF)**, headquartered in Vicenza, Italy, was established in 1955 from the major and support units in the region.

Headquarters:
Verona, Italy
(APO New York 09453)

Allied Maritime Air Force Channel Command: Major subordinate command of NATO's **Allied Command Channel**.

Headquarters
Northwood, UK
(APO New York 09083)

Allied Naval Forces Southern Europe (NAVSOUTH): Principle subordinate command of NATO's **Allied Forces Southern Europe**. It is responsible for naval operations in southern Europe, including the Mediterranean Sea from the Straits of Gibraltar to the coast of Syria; the Adriatic, Ionian, and Aegean Seas; and the Sea of Marmara and the Black Sea outside Soviet waters. It is commanded by a U.S. admiral.

Headquarters
Naples, Italy
(FPO New York 09524)

Subordinate Commands

- Maritime Air Forces, Med (MARAIRMED): Naples, Italy

- Central Med (MEDCENT): Santa Rosa (Rome), Italy
- Eastern Med (MEDEAST): Athens, Greece
- North East Med (MEDNOREAST): Ankara, Turkey
- Gibraltar Med (GIBMED): Gibraltar

Allied Tactical Air Force (ATAF): Multinational air force supporting NATO's allied forces. ATAFs maintain operational control of assigned forces and receive apportionment decisions from Allied Air Forces commanders in the region. In conjunction with army groups, ATAFs determine the priority for offensive air support, match priorities with sorties available, and agree with the army group on the mix of preplanned and immediate sorties. ATAFs send a daily operations order to subordinate Allied Tactical Operations Centers (ATOCs) at the army group, and an air allocation message to the corps. Each ATAF has two subordinate ATOCs. Two ATAFs support **Allied Forces Central (AFCENT)** and **Southern Europe (AFSOUTH)**. The Hellenic Tactical Air Force is slated for resubordination to NATO as the 7th ATAF.

AFCENT
- **2nd ATAF (TWOATAF):** Moenchen-Gladbach, West Germany
- **4th ATAF (FOURATAF):** Heidelberg, West Germany

AFSOUTH
- **5th ATAF (FIVEATAF):** Vicenza, Italy
- **6th ATAF (SIXATAF):** Izmir, Turkey

Allied Tactical Operations Center (ATOC): Air Force command center located at the army group level in Europe and responsible for tactical control of allocated air sorties in support of ground forces. It receives orders from **Allied Tactical Air Forces (ATAFs),** which have operational control of assigned forces. There are two active ATOCs in each ATAF in Central Europe: 2nd ATAF has ATOCs at Kalkar, West Germany, and Maastricht, Netherlands; and 4th ATAF has ATOCs at Mestetten and Sembach, West Germany. The ATOCs build mission packages, select types of aircraft and units to fly ordered missions, are responsible for air route coordination with Army air defense units, and task Air Force wings to carry out missions. Army liaison personnel are located in the ATOCs.

all-source: Intelligence information that is not segregated on the basis of the source, such as **signals intelligence** collection, **human intelligence**, or **satellite reconnaissance** sources. Separation is imposed so as to restrict dissemination of information where the source is considered to be as sensitive as the derived information. Compartmented intelligence information collection, both generic and specific, particularly that in **special access** categories or **special compartmented information (SCI)**, prevents the creation and dissemination of all-source intelligence products.

all-weather: An aircraft or other weapon system with radar and other special equipment that allow it to intercept, find its target, navigate, or otherwise perform its mission in dark or daylight weather conditions that do not permit visual identification.

Alpha: Strategic Defense Initiative (SDI) research program to develop a continuous-wave hydrogen-fluoride laser to be launched as a space-based weapon. The Alpha laser is an element of **Zenith Star**, a space-based laser experiment. TRW is the prime contractor and DARPA is the government organization with responsibility for overseeing the project. The prototype Alpha laser is located at TRW's San Juan Capistrano test site in California. On 10 April 1989, the first test fire of the Alpha took place. The test lasted only one fifth of a second and the laser did not reach full power (approximately two megawatts), which takes several seconds to achieve [*Air Force Magazine*, June 1989, p. 34].

The Alpha wavelength is 2.7 microns and it produces a brighter beam than other chemical lasers such as the deuterium-fluoride Mid-Infrared Chemical Laser (**MIRACL**), which operates at 3.8 microns. Alpha's cavity pressure is much lower than MIRACL's, which allows Alpha to operate in the vacuum of space. To form the laser beam, hydrogen and fluoride are mixed, and optical mirrors are used to extract an infrared beam from the excited hydrogen fluoride molecules. The design of the Alpha is cylindrical, which allows the chemical fuel to flow in an even radial pattern to increase stability. The mirrors produce a ring-shaped beam that is directed to a beam compactor, which then narrows the beam.

With **LODE** and **LAMP**, Alpha is part of a three-part SDI-directed energy weapons development program. The LODE/LAMP mirror is to be merged with Alpha by 1990 to be used for ground-based testing against ground targets.

Alternate Command Post
(see **ALCOP**)

Alternate Joint Communications Center (AJCC): Air Force-operated communications facility for the JCS at Raven Rock, PA. It is collocated with the **Alternate National Military Command Center**.

Alternate National Military Command Center (ANMCC): One of the four National Command Authority (NCA) command centers. The ANMCC is the JCS backup underground command post to the **National Military Command Center** in the Pentagon. It is in the chain of command for communications to military forces, including the release of nuclear weapons, and serves as the hub for the JCS and a representative of the NCA during crises and wartime. Built in 1955 inside Raven Rock Mountain, on the Pennsylvania/Maryland border, 70 miles north of Washington, the facility is also referred to as "Site R" or Raven Rock. It is located near, and supported by, Ft. Ritchie, MD. The ANMCC is connected to the Pentagon through a wide variety of communications channels, including the **AUTODIN**, **AUTOVON**, **Improved Emergency Message Automated Transmission System (IEMATS)**, **WASHFAX**, and **AUTOSEVOCOM** systems. Messages from U.S. military forces worldwide are normally routed

to the ANMCC before they are routed to the Pentagon. Destruction of the Pentagon and not the ANMCC will leave the communications network open into Washington. The ANMCC is permanently manned with a core staff, and exercises are constantly run to test evacuation and activation procedures. (see also **Joint Emergency Evacuation Plan**)

altimeter: An instrument that measures an aircraft's or cruise missile's elevation above a given reference point, such as sea level. Barometric, radar, radio, and electronic altimeters are common.

ammunition: "A device charged with explosives, propellants, pyrotechnics, initiating composition, or nuclear, biological, or chemical material for use in connection with defense or offense, including demolitions. Certain ammunition can be used for training, ceremonial, or non-operational purposes" [*JSC Pub 1*, p. 26]. Types of ammunition include

• Fixed ammunition: The cartridge case is permanently attached to the projectile;
• Semifixed ammunition: The cartridge case is not permanently attached to the ammunition; and
• Separate-loading ammunition: The projectile and charge are loaded separately into the gun.

Tank projectile types include

• Armor-piercing (AP): Designed to penetrate armor;
• Armor-piercing incendiary (API): Designed to set fires after piercing armor;

- Armor-piercing fin-stabilized discarding sabot-tracer (APFSDS-T): M829 120 mm kinetic energy projectile with depleted uranium penetrator;
- Armor-piercing sabot (APS): Incorporates a sabot;
- Armor-piercing tracer (APT): Fitted with a tracer for spotting; and
- High-explosive antitank multipurpose with tracer (HEAT-MP-T): M830 120 mm shaped-charge warhead.

Artillery projectile types include

- Aerial denial artillery munitions (ADAM): 155 mm artillery projectile;
- Copperhead: Guided 155 mm artillery projectile;
- Dual-purpose improved conventional munitions (DPICM): 105 mm, 155 mm, and 8 inch artillery projectile;
- Extended-range dual-purpose improved conventional munitions (ERDPICM): 155 mm artillery projectile;
- High explosive (HE): 155 mm artillery;
- High explosive rocket-assisted (HERA): 105 mm artillery;
- Improved conventional munitions (ICM): 8 inch artillery;
- Remote anti-armor mine system (RAAMS): 155 mm artillery;
- **Sense and destroy armor (SADARM)**: 155 mm artillery or MLRS-launched anti-armor projectile with a sensing submunition; and
- Smoke: 155 mm artillery.

In addition, there are chemical ammunition where the filler is primarily a **chemical agent** or, in the case of binary chemical ammunition, two types of chemicals that are only mixed as the projectile flies towards the target; and nuclear ammunition for either 155 mm or 8 inch artillery.

ammunition ship (AE): Ship that delivers ammunition either independently or with other combat logistic ships to combatants and/or battle groups at sea or on land. At sea, movement of ammunition and weapons uses both connected and vertical replenishment. The Navy has 13 ammunition ships in three classes: Kilauea (AE-26) class, Suribachi (AE-21) class, and Nitro (AE-23) class. One of the Kilauea class ships, the Kilauea (AE-26) itself, is operated by the Military Sealift Command.

All ammunition ships are regularly certified to carry and stow nuclear weapons, except ballistic missile warheads. Builders of ammunition ships include GD Shipbuilding, Quincy Shipbuilding Division (AE-26, 27); Bethlehem Steel, Sparrows Point, MD (AE-21 to 25, 28, 29); and Ingalls Shipbuilding (AE-32 to 35).

The USS Suribachi (AE-21), USS Nitro (AE-23), and USS Butte (AE-27) are homeported at Earle, NJ. The USS Mauna Kea (AE-22), USS Pyro (AE-24), USS Mount Hood (AE-29), USS Flint (AE-32), USS Shasta (AE-33), and USS Kiska (AE-35) are homeported at Concord, CA. The USS Haleakala (AE-25) is homeported in Guam. The USS Santa Barbara (AE-28) and USS Mount Baker (AE-34) are homeported at Charleston, SC.

Ammunition Ships

	Suribachi (AE-21)	Nitro (AE-23)	Kilauea (AE-26)
Number Deployed	2	3	7 (+1 MSC T-AE)
Displacement (tons) (full load)	15,500	15,500	18,088
Length (ft) (m)	512 (156)	512 (156)	564 (172)
Draft (ft) (m)	29 (8.8)	29 (8.8)	26 (7.9)
Beam (ft) (m)	72 (22)	72 (22)	81 (25)
Speed (kts)	20	20	20
Crew	390	390	410
Helicopters	Landing area only	Landing area only	2 CH-46s
IOC	1956	1959	1968

AMOS: Strategic Defense Initiative laser test facility at Maui, HI, used for testing the **ground-based laser**. In early 1987, laser beams from AMOS successfully tracked U.S. Navy sounding rockets fired from nearby Barking Sands Missile Range.

amphibious assault: "An attack launched from the sea by naval and landing forces embarked in ships or craft involving a landing and establishing of forces on a hostile shore" [*NWP 3*].

amphibious assault ship (LHA) (see **amphibious warfare ship**)

amphibious cargo ship (LKA) (see **amphibious warfare ship**)

amphibious command ship (LCC) (see **amphibious warfare ship**)

amphibious construction battalion: Naval beach group unit that provides ship-to-shore fuel systems, pontoon causeways and lighterage, and beach salvage and limited construction capabilities.

amphibious group (PHIBGRU): A permanent administrative unit of a **Navy Surface Force** similar to an Army corps headquarters. It is composed of a staff, headquarters staff, and a command ship, and is assigned organic operating forces. When established for operational duty, it is assigned amphibious and landing ship squadrons in support of a reinforced ground division. PHIBGRUs are assigned to the Atlantic Fleet and the Pacific Fleet. Amphibious groups include

Amphibious Group 1   White Beach, Okinawa

Amphibious Warfare Landing Craft

	LCAC	LCU 1610	LCM-8 Mk3/4	LCM-8 Mk2	LCM-6	LCVP	LCPL
Displacement (tons)							
light	88	190	34	37	27	—	—
loaded	200	390	120	107	62	14	13
Length (ft)	88	135	74	74	56	36	36
Draft (ft)	n.a.	6	5	5	3	4	4
Beam (ft)	47	30	21	21	14	11	13
Speed (kts) (max)	50	11	12	12	10	9	19
Cargo	60 t	190 t	58 t	65 t	34 t	4 t	17 people
Manning	5	14	5	5	5	2–3	3

Amphibious Group 2   Norfolk, VA 23511

Amphibious Group 3   San Diego, CA 92135

amphibious ship: Naval vessel specifically designed to transport, land, and support forces in amphibious operations, loading and unloading without external assistance. The Navy operates 63 major active and reserve amphibious warfare ships, as well as numerous smaller associated landing craft. The Marine Corps operates the tracked assault amphibian vehicles used for landings. (see also **amphibious warfare ship**, **amphibious warfare landing craft**, **assault amphibian vehicle**)

amphibious task force (ATF): A major naval **task organization** formed for the purpose of conducting amphibious operations. An ATF always includes Navy forces and a landing force, with their organic aviation, and may include Air Force forces when appropriate. An ATF consists of

- 1–2 carrier battle groups;
- 16–18 destroyers or frigates; and
- amphibious ships, including 2 amphibious command and control ships (LCCs), 5 general-purpose amphibious assault ships (LHAs), 5 amphibious cargo ships (LKAs), 10 amphibious transport docks (LPDs), 6 helicopter amphibious assault ships (LPHs), 10 dock landing ships (LSDs), 15 tank landing ships (LSTs), and 8 support ships.

amphibious transport dock (LPD) (see **amphibious warfare ship**)

amphibious warfare landing craft: The Navy operates several hundred landing craft for transporting troops and materiel ashore during amphibious assaults. The larger craft, **landing craft air cushion (LCAC)** and utility landing craft (LCU), are usually identified by their hull numbers. The smaller craft are usually identified by the ships, units, or stations to which they are assigned. All are operated by Navy personnel. These craft are carried by **amphibious warfare**

ships of the LHA, LPD, and LSD classes for ferrying troops, vehicles, and materiel to shore. They also can receive equipment from LKA class ships. Some craft are also stored on **maritime prepositioning force ships (MPs)**.

The six most common types include the Utility Landing Craft (LCU 1610 class); Mechanized Landing Craft (LCM-8 Mk 3/4, LCM-8 Mk 2, and LCM-6); Landing Craft Vehicle and Personnel (LCVP); and Landing Craft Personnel Light (LCPL).

The LCAC is the latest design landing craft. In a departure from traditional designs, the LCAC is a hovercraft. It is capable of operating from existing and planned ships.

amphibious warfare ship: There are seven types of major amphibious warfare ships: general-purpose amphibious assault ships (LHAs), helicopter amphibious assault ships (LPHs), amphibious transport docks (LPDs), amphibious cargo ships (LKAs), dock landing ships (LSDs), tank landing ships (LSTs), and amphibious command and control ships (LCCs). An eighth type, the amphibious assault ship (LHDs), is under construction.

The largest ships carry helicopters, **AV-8B Harrier II** short-takeoff and landing fighters, troops, weapons, materiel, and the transport craft that ferry troops and materiel to shore for amphibious landings. The five TARAWA (LHA-1) class general-purpose amphibious assault ships and seven IWO JIMA (LPH-2) class helicopter amphibious assault ships are, in effect, small aircraft carriers

(39,300 and 18,000 tons at full load, respectively) that serve as the lead ships of amphibious task forces. They are equipped with a complement of transport and attack helicopters and AV-8Bs. The ships can carry nuclear bombs for the AV-8B, and transport nuclear projectiles for use ashore by Marine Corps 155 mm and 8 inch (203 mm) artillery.

Other amphibious assault ships—amphibious transport docks, amphibious cargo ships, dock landing ships, and tank landing ships—carry troops, materiel, or smaller landing craft for conveying troops and material ashore. Similarly, they can transport nuclear weapons for use by Marine artillery units. Amphibious command and control ships can provide amphibious command and control in major amphibious operations and also can be used to transport nuclear weapons if necessary. The nuclear weapons can be transported ashore by smaller tracked landing vehicles or helicopters, with helicopters being the preferred mode of transportation.

In 1984, Congress appropriated money for a new class of amphibious assault ships designated LHDs. The first ship in this class, the USS Wasp (LHD-1), entered the fleet in 1989. The Navy has requested authorization for the fourth and fifth ships in the FY 1989 and FY 1991 budgets, respectively. Additional ships are planned to replace the LPHs, which are scheduled to be retired in the mid-1990s. The Wasp class ships will displace 40,600 tons at full load and have capabilities similar to the LHAs in operating AV-8Bs and transporting nuclear weapons.

AMRAAM (Advanced Medium Range Air-to-Air Missile): Model designation AIM-120A. An Air Force and Navy supersonic, guided, air-to-air, beyond-visual range, conventionally armed missile under development. It is scheduled to replace the **Sparrow** missile as the all-environment, all-aspect air-to-air missile in the 1990s. It is smaller, faster, and lighter than the Sparrow and better able to attack targets at low level. AMRAAM will have an active radar seeker that gives it a "launch-and-leave" capability. The Sparrow, on the other hand, has semi-active radar and must be fired and guided to its target; since the firing plane can only guide one missile at a time, this leaves the firing plane vulnerable if it is being attacked by more than one aircraft. AMRAAM will be employed by Navy **F-14 Tomcats** and **F/A-18 Hornets** and Air Force **F-16 Falcons** and **F-15 Eagle** fighters, as well as by NATO aircraft. The Air Force is the executive service for its development. The first production missiles are scheduled to be delivered in mid-1989 and are scheduled to become operational on the F-15 in the first quarter of FY 1990. The Air Force is expected to buy 17,000 missiles and the Navy 7,320 in an 11-year production run. AMRAAM has a speed of more than 760 mph and a range of greater than 35 nm. The prime contractors are Hughes Aircraft Company, Tuscon, AZ, and Raytheon Corporation, Lowell, MA (second source). The proposed funding for FY 1990 for 1,600 missiles and for FY 1991 for 3,000 missiles is $1,048.6 million and $1,305.8 million, respectively.

The AMRAAM development program began in 1975. Development and production problems almost resulted in the cancellation of the program in FY 1986. The missile received intense Congressional scrutiny, with the General Accounting Office and Congress expressing doubts about testing, production, cost, and effectiveness. Congress set a ceiling in FY 1987 of $7 billion in total production cost for the 24,335 AMRAAMs for both Air Force and Navy aircraft.

AN: Prefix designating standard nomenclature for electronic equipment.

ANGLICO (Air Naval Gunfire Liaison Company): An organization of Navy and Marine Corps personnel specially qualified for shore control of naval gunfire and close air support.

Antarctic Treaty: Multilateral agreement establishing Antarctica as the first **nuclear free zone**, which is now contiguous with the Latin American and South Pacific Nuclear Free Zones. The treaty opened for signature in Washington on 1 December 1959 and was signed by 12 countries that routinely conduct research in Antarctica (the United States, the Soviet Union, France, the United Kingdom, Argentina, Australia, Belgium, Chile, Japan, New Zealand, Norway, and South Africa). Since then, 25 other nations have signed the treaty. The United States ratified the treaty on 18 August 1960, and the treaty entered into force on 23 June 1961. As of 1988, 38 parties had signed the treaty.

The Antarctic Treaty originates in 1957–58, during International Geophysical Year (IGY), when 12 countries were in Antarctica carrying out unprecedented international scientific collaborations. Concerns were raised, especially by the United States, that when the IGY ended, issues of territorial claims in the region would make such scientific collaboration impossible to continue. To waylay such an event, the United States in May 1958 invited the 11 other IGY participants to a conference to negotiate the peaceful uses of Antarctica. The three goals of the conference, in order of importance, were 1. to freeze the legal status quo to prevent politics from interfering with scientific study; 2. to provide a basis for future scientific cooperation; and 3. to ensure that Antarctica be used for peaceful purposes only. The conference was held in Washington from October–December 1959, and, on 1 December 1959, all 12 nations signed the treaty. It was the first multilateral treaty to apply intrusive verification measures to NATO and Warsaw Pact members.

The treaty forbids deploying and testing nuclear weapons, establishing military bases or fortifications, conducting military maneuvers, and disposing of radioactive waste in the region south of 60 degrees south latitude, including all ice shelves but excluding the high seas. Key provisions include

- The use of military equipment or personnel in Antarctica only for peaceful scientific purposes.
- Freedom of scientific investigation and cooperation between signatories, including exchanges of plans, personnel, and observations. The Scientific Committee on Antarctic Research of the International Council of Scientific Unions (ICSU), as well as other groups such as UNESCO, advise the Treaty parties on scientific research issues.
- Preservation of the status quo with regard to sovereignty. "No acts may constitute a basis for asserting, supporting, or denying a claim to territorial sovereignty in Antarctica, or create any rights of sovereignty, and no new claims or enlargement of existing ones can be asserted."
- On-site inspection of stations, installations, equipment, ships, and aircraft, as well as aerial observation, for verification. The first inspection took place in November 1963 when New Zealand visited three U.S. stations. The United States has several times inspected the Soviet Antarctic sites.
- Periodic meetings to be held in Canberra, Australia, to discuss amendments, modifications, and withdrawals. The first review session is scheduled for 1991.

anti-ballistic missile   (see **ABM**)

Anti-ballistic Missile Protocol   (see **ABM Protocol**)

Anti-ballistic Missile Treaty   (see **ABM Treaty**)

anti-satellite (ASAT) negotiations: In March 1977, agreement was reached to establish several U.S.-Soviet working groups to consider a variety of arms control topics including ASAT. In June 1978, the United States and Soviet Union met in Helsinki, Finland, for an initial discussion. Two subsequent rounds were held in Bern, Switzerland, from 23 January–16 February 1979, and in Vienna, Austria, from 23 April–17 June 1979.

The talks were abandoned after the Soviet invasion of Afghanistan. In June 1984, President Reagan expressed U.S. willingness to resume the talks and the Soviets expressed interest.

ASAT technology overlaps with that of **Strategic Defense Initiative** and anti-ballistic missile (**ABM**) systems, since weapons to destroy satellites can also be used to destroy missiles in flight. In his space policy directive of July 1982 (NSDD-42), President Reagan made a commitment to the operational deployment of an ASAT system. This will have to be reconciled with the provisions of the ABM Treaty. In August 1983, the Soviet Union stopped ASAT testing and called for a bilateral moratorium on ASAT testing. Congress then passed legislation calling for the Administration to negotiate on ASAT control, and, in the FY 1985, a DOD appropriations bill prohibited the testing of ASAT against objects (but not points) in space until 1 March 1985 or until 15 days after the President certifies that he is making a good-faith attempt to negotiate with the Soviets on ASAT.

anti-satellite (ASAT) weapon: System for the destruction of enemy satellites. ASAT weapons can be ground-launched, air-launched, or space-based. The first ASAT was the Air Force Bold Orion program, which began in the fall of 1959. Bold Orion was a two-stage air-launched missile and served as a prototype for the modern ASAT system launched from F-15s. The next ASAT program was the SAINT (Satellite Inspector), a coorbital system, which was designed with television cameras and a radar in the nose of an Agena B rocket. SAINT was canceled in December 1962. With the demise of SAINT, the United States embarked on new concepts of direct-ascent ASATs and air-launched missiles. The Navy was also working on ASAT programs, and, from 1960–1964, under Early Spring, it evaluated the use of Polaris SLBMs for direct ascent attacks. The Navy's project Hi-Ho, similar to Bold Orion, used an F-4B Phantom to carry a missile to high altitudes and then launch it upwards to its target. Hi-Ho was tested in the spring of 1962 but abandoned when the Navy lost interest in ASATs. Hi-Ho was revived in 1970 with the appearance of Soviet ocean reconnaissance satellites. The Army ASAT program, code-named Mudflap, used the Nike Zeus rocket. Mudflap was tested at White Sands Missile Range, NM, and Kwajalein Atoll during 1962–63 and pronounced operational on 1 August 1963, with one nuclear-tipped Nike Zeus ready to be fired at one satellite passing over the Pacific. Following the Army's lead, the Air Force began, in February 1962, Program 437 for a direct-ascent ASAT using the Thor booster. The supply of Thors was plentiful, since IRBMs were being removed from Europe at that time, and Thor had a sufficient range. On 10 June 1964, a pair of these missiles were put on alert in the Pacific on Johnston Island. Testing continued through 1970, but when interest again flagged in ASATs, Program 437 ended. Although the testing of systems continued into the early 1970s, U.S. interest in ASAT systems and technologies effectively died during 1963. The increasing number of satellites in space made it impossible to track and kill all of them.

In 1988, the Air Force disbanded its ASAT program consisting of F-15 aircraft launchers based at Langley AFB, VA, and McChord AFB, WA, after Congress imposed bans on testing the F-15-launched MHV system. The F-15s fired missiles consisting of a lower stage of an SRAM missile, a Thiokol-manufactured Altair III solid-propellent second stage (the fourth stage of the Scout rocket), a Vought MHV kill mechanism, a Hughes IR terminal seeker, and Singer-Kearfott guidance. The types of ASAT devices often discussed are

- **Directed energy weapons (DEWs)** ground-based: high-power radio waves, lasers, and electro-optical counter-measures;space-based:high-power radio waves, lasers, and neutral particle beams
- **Isotropic nuclear warheads (INWs)** ground-based: coorbital interceptors and direct-ascent interceptors; space-based: space mines and
- **Kinetic energy weapons (KEWs)** ground-based: coorbital interceptors and direct-ascent interceptors; space-based: noncoorbital interceptors.

In early March 1989, Acting Secretary of Defense William Taft IV approved program initiation (Milestone 0) for kinetic energy and directed energy ASAT systems. The Defense Acquisition Board deter-

mined that a Milestone I review for a kinetic energy system was to occur by December 1989 and for a directed energy system during FY 1991. The new ASAT program includes space surveillance and battle management/ C3 elements. The less risky kinetic energy weapons will be emphasized over directed energy technologies, which could take years to become operational. Each DOD service is responsible for a particular aspect of the ASAT program.

The new ASAT will, according to the DOD, "address imbalances in space control capabilities" and, by destroying Soviet low-orbit ocean surveillance satellites, maintain **sea lines of communication (SLOCs)** in times of conflict [DOD, *Annual Report to the Congress, FY 1990,* p. 212]. The Soviet ASAT system, which became operational in the late 1970s, has not been tested in several years. A CIA assessment of the Soviet system determined that it was rather rudimentary; this conclusion is, however, not universally accepted within Congress and DOD. According to former Secretary of Defense Frank Carlucci, "As the President, the Chairman of the JCS, and I have stated repeatedly, the development and deployment of a comprehensive ASAT capability is an absolute necessity to prevent the Soviets from using hostile space systems to the detriment of our forces." The FY 1990–91 budget request by the Reagan Administration for the total ASAT program was $431.4 million.

The Air Force is responsible for a single comprehensive space surveillance and battle management system to control all ASAT activities. It is also responsible for coordinating the integration of those elements into the kinetic energy and directed energy programs. A joint program office was established to develop, test, and produce a hit-to-kill ground-based kinetic energy interceptor missile system derived from SDI technology. The initial design is likely to be a surface-launched rocket carrying an optical homing device. The Army was designated to manage the program, under the direction of the U.S. Army Strategic Defense Command in Huntsville, AL. The Navy provides a Deputy Program Manager. At Milestone I, lead-service responsibility and options for sea- and land-based KE systems will be evaluated in the future.

The Navy began a budget line item for ASAT research in FY 1990. The Navy will conduct research using the Mid-Infrared Chemical Laser (MIRACL). Funds for this part of the project had been eliminated by DOD in 1988 but were reinstated after congressional protests, particularly from the New Mexico delegation. Another funding review of the MIRACL facility is scheduled for the spring of 1989.

A joint program office has not yet been established for the directed energy ASAT system. The Army will continue to include ASAT technology in the design of the SDI free electron laser (FEL) through FY 1991. The Air Force will conduct a parallel program of alternative concepts for an FY 1991 selection decision.

anti-ship missile   (see **Harpoon, Tomahawk anti-ship missile**)

anti-submarine rocket
(see **ASROC**)

anti-submarine warfare (ASW): Operations to detect, classify, locate, track, and destroy enemy submarines. The Navy describes its ASW operations as a defense-in-depth, which consists of a series of protective screens of sensors, aircraft, ships, and submarines the enemy must penetrate to get into position to attack sea- or land-based targets. The first defensive layer is "forward offensive operations" by **attack submarines**, utilizing **torpedoes**, **mines**, and nuclear-armed **SUBROC** ASW missiles in waters near the Soviet Union (SUB-ROCS, however, will be withdrawn from the fleet by 1991). The next layer consists of attack submarines and **P-3 Orion** land-based maritime patrol aircraft conducting open ocean "area" ASW between waters close to the Soviet Union and narrower choke points such as the Greenland–Iceland–United Kingdom gap (**GIUK gap**). At these chokepoints, attack submarines, surface ships, aircraft, and mines perform "barrier" ASW operations. A submarine that makes it through these first three screens faces "local" ASW forces attached to a carrier battle group or other surface group. More P-3s or attack submarines operating in direct support of battle groups, or carrier-launched **S-3A/B Viking** aircraft, constitute local forces for long-range protection at 250–300 miles from the ship concentration. Mid-zone local protection is provided by surface ships with towed-sonar arrays and their **SH-2F** or **SH-60B** helicopters. Finally, **SH-3** Sea King helicopters launched from aircraft carriers and employing active-dipping sonar furnish inner-zone protection (approximately within 50 miles). At each layer of attack, there are strategic, regional, and local sources of surveillance information on ocean activity, which seek to identify submarine activity and transmit that information to the anti-submarine weapons platforms.

Forward operations to destroy Soviet attack submarines, according to the **Maritime Strategy**, would also include attacks on ballistic missile submarines. Former Chief of Naval Operations Admiral James Watkins wrote that the Navy's Maritime Strategy has three phases that constitute a timeline of action for Navy and Marine Corps forces. In the second phase, the Maritime Strategy calls for anti-submarine warfare forces to wage "an aggressive campaign against all Soviet submarines, including ballistic missile submarines." And, as a follow-up, in the third phase antisubmarine warfare forces "would continue to destroy Soviet submarines, including ballistic missile submarines, thus reducing the attractiveness of nuclear escalation by changing the nuclear balance in our favor."

Attacks on ballistic missile submarines usually are referred to as part of "strategic" ASW. This is contrasted to tactical ASW, which involves operations against cruise missile and attack submarines to defend battlegroups and convoys. However, since many of the same sensors, platforms, and weapons are used for both purposes, and tactical operations may take place near ballistic missile submarines, the two are not necessarily distinct in practice.

An extensive sensor and command and control system supports U.S. ASW efforts. Early warning of enemy submarine deployments is provided by signals intelligence and satellite observations. Acoustic information is important to identify the approximate open ocean positions of submarines and is obtained primarily through fixed-placed underwater hydrophones known as the **Sound Surveillance System (SOSUS)**. Hydrophones in the SOSUS arrays are found off the east and west coasts of the United States, as well as near chokepoints and off allied shores. SOSUS is supplemented by special sonars known as **SURTASSs** towed by TAGOS **ocean surveillance ships** deployed in the Atlantic and Pacific oceans. Other intelligence information pertinent to ASW is gathered and coordinated at a tactical level in a battle-group and at regional centers in the Pacific and Atlantic, as well as centrally in the United States as part of the **Ocean Surveillance Information System**. Similarly, there are tactical and regional coordinators of ASW assets and operations.

anti-submarine warfare operations center (ASWOC): An **antisubmarine warfare (ASW)** control facility, located at a shore **P-3 Orion** patrol squadron base or aboard an aircraft carrier (called an ASW operations module). ASWOCs are responsible for planning, briefing, conducting, debriefing, and analyzing air anti-submarine warfare operations. ASWOCs were previously called tactical support centers (TSCs) and carrier-based tactical support centers (CVTSCs).

anti-submarine warfare standoff weapon (ASWSOW) (see **Sea Lance**)

anti-tactical missile (ATM)/anti-tactical ballistic missile (ATBM): Short-range, high-speed, anti-air missiles designed to provide battlefield defense against ballistic missiles, cruise missiles, and air-to-surface missiles. The United States has had programs to develop ATMs/ATBMs since the early 1980s. A comprehensive battlefield defense system has not been fielded, but modifications to **Patriot** missiles allowed Patriots to attain an initial self-defense capability against tactical missiles in July 1988. (see also **Joint Tactical Missile Defense**)

anti-terrorism: Defensive or preventative measures taken to minimize or eliminate the vulnerability of individuals or property to terrorist acts (e.g., airport security measures, **physical security** enhancements). (see also **counterterrorism, terrorism**)

Anti-Terrorist Assistance Program: State Department program that provides anti-terrorism assistance to civilian/law enforcement agencies of foreign governments. In 1984, exchange and training programs were established with 15 foreign governments. A total of 500 foreign officials are involved, from countries including Italy, Egypt, Turkey, the United Kingdom, Costa Rica, Honduras, and Columbia.

ANZUS (Australia-New Zealand-U.S.): Pacific Security Treaty signed in September 1951 by Australia, New Zealand, and the United States. The treaty entered into force in April 1952. ANZUS was the first collective security agreement for the Pacific region. Each party undertakes to help the others in the event of an armed attack on their territories or military forces in the Pacific. The treaty originated in response to the fall of China in 1949, the outbreak of the Korean War, the 1951 U.S.-Japanese Security Treaty, and threats of Communist expansion in southeast Asia, all of which raised apprehensions about security in Australia and New Zealand.

In 1985, the New Zealand government implemented a policy denying nuclear-armed and powered ships New Zealand port calls. In retaliation, in June 1986, Secretary of State George Schultz announced that the United States could no longer extend its security guarantee to New Zealand, thus excluding New Zealand from the protection resulting from the ANZUS Treaty and suspending almost all joint military exchanges. The pact today remains between Australia and the United States and could again be expanded to include New Zealand.

AO: Designation for fleet **oiler**.

AOE: Designation for **fast combat support ship.**

AOG: Designation for gasoline tanker ship.

AOR: Designation for replenishment oiler ship.

AOT: Designation for transport oiler ship.

AP: Designation for **transport ship**.

Apple Jack: Exercise name for Air Defense Warning Red, one of three **air defense warning conditions**.

appropriation: Congressional legislation used to permit the DOD to obligate the U.S. Treasury to pay for goods and services. The Congress passes two pieces of legislation dealing with the DOD budget, the Defense Appropriations Bill and the Military Construction (MilCon) Appropriations Bill. Appropriations are only made for purposes authorized by law. Most defense legislation requires both authorization and appropriation. The Congressional committees that appropriate funds are the House and Senate Appropriations Committees. There are 13 appropriations bills and 13 subcommittees, two with DOD (DOD and MilCon) responsibilities and one with responsibilities for the DOE (Energy and Water Development Appropriations). The other subcommittees and appropriation bills deal with civil agencies.

When it was decided to centralize budget preparation in the Executive Branch, Congress decided it was equally desirable to centralize responsibility for appropriations in the appropriations committees of the two Houses (previously, the jurisdiction of the appropriations committees was limited to activities at the seat of government). However, to retain some power within the substantive committees, a rule was made in the House of Representatives that appropriations could not be recommended by the appropriations committee for purposes not authorized by law. Similarly, there has been a rule that appropriations could not

be included in bills reported by the substantive committees. The areas and accounts subject to authorization and/or appropriation are

Authorization	*Appropriation*
RDT&E	RDT&E
Aircraft Procurement	Aircraft Procurement
Missile Procurement	Missile Procurement
Other Procurement	Other Procurement
National Guard and Reserve Equipment	National Guard and Reserve Equipment
Military Construction	Military Construction
Military Family Housing	Military Family Housing
Operations and Maintenance	Operations and Maintenance
Stock Fund	Stock Fund
Military End Strength	Military Personnel
Civilian End Strength	Reserve Personnel
Training Loads	National Guard Personnel
Selected Reserve Average Strength	

The DOD Appropriations Bill is divided into a number of titles, which are then further broken down by service:

Title I	Military Personnel
Title II	Operations and Management
Title III	Procurement
Title IV	Research, Development, Testing, & Evaluation
Title V	Other
Title VI	Revolving and Management Funds

Before FY 1971, procurement appropriations were "no-year accounts"; that is, available for obligation until expended. Since FY 1971, these appropriations have been designated "multi-year" appropriations, and they are available for obligation for only three years. The RDT&E appropriation, also a no-year account before FY 1971, is now a multi-year appropriation, but it is available for obligation purposes for only two years. The military construction and military family housing accounts were no-year before FY 1979; after FY 1979, they were designated a multi-year, five-year appropriation. Single-year appropriations, such as operations and maintenance and military personnel accounts, expire for obligation purposes on 30 September, the end of the fiscal year. (see also **authorization**)

AQM-34   (see **Firebee**)

Aquacade: **Byeman** code name for a former class of **signals intelligence (SIGINT)** satellites, previously called **Rhyolite**. The system was renamed following its "compromise" to the Soviet Union in 1975 by spies Christopher Boyce and Andrew Daulton Lee, who were later dramatized in the book and movie, *The Falcon and the Snowman*. Five Rhyolite/Aquacade satellites were launched into geosynchronous orbit between 19 June 1970 and 7 April 1978. The satellites' primary function was the collection of Soviet and Chinese telemetry intelligence and other signals intelligence collection. The system was controlled from the Central Intelligence Agency facility located in Alice Springs, Australia (often called **Pine Gap**).

Intelligence obtained by Aquacade and other SIGINT satellites is marked by the codeword **Zarf** [Jeffrey Richelson, *American Espionage and the Soviet Target*, 1987, pp. 226, 277].

Aquila: Army target-acquisition **remotely piloted vehicle (RPV)**, powered by a two-cylinder, 26-horsepower engine, that can detect and identify stationary and moving targets beyond the range of ground-based observers and sensors, adjust artillery fire, and designate targets for destruction by laser-seeking munitions. It can also perform general surveillance, reconnaissance, and damage assessment. Aquila is six feet long, has a wingspan of almost 13 feet, and weighs about 260 lbs. It can cruise for three hours, achieving a service ceiling of 12,000 ft. Aquila has a daylight television camera or **forward-looking infrared (FLIR)** sensor, and it carries a laser range finder and designater. Rail-launched from a specially configured wheeled truck and recovered in a net after its mission, it is controlled by an operator on the ground. The total Aquila system involves an air vehicle, a ground station, a remote ground terminal antenna, launch and recovery equipment, and support and maintenance equipment. All of this equipment is either mounted on or stored within a fleet of mobile trucks. As a corps asset, an RPV battery will have 13 air vehicles. Initial operating capability of the Aquila is scheduled for FY 1992.

The launch system catapults the air vehicle into the air. The vehicle is then controlled from the ground station through a jam-resistant data communication link. Aquila detects and identifies targets, transmitting information back to the field artillery unit as it is collected. An automated recovery system guides the air vehicle into a net near the ground station at the completion of its mission.

Development of the Aquila began in 1974, and the program is beset with technical and financial problems. As costs have risen for individual components of Aquila, the Army has scaled down the number of systems it wishes to procure. A special task force established by the Army in May 1985, the Red Team, reported serious performance limitations and a shortage of test air vehicles. Program management was changed from Aviation Systems Command to the Missile Command (of the Army Material Command). Operational testing began in November 1986 at Fort Hood, TX. Problems still remain with adequate test evaluations: criteria to evaluate survivability, reliability, availability, and maintainability were never specified. The main rationale behind the Aquila is the FLIR sensor, which allows use of the system at night. However, development of the sensor has been plagued by technical problems, resulting in major funding cuts. Design changes implemented in 1985 increased costs for the sensor and resulted in Congressional action that cut the Aquila FY 1987 development budget by $30 million.

AR: Designation for **repair ship**.

ARC: Designation for cable-repairing ship.

Arctic   Reconnaissance   Group (ARG):   Unique   Alaskan   **Army**   National Guard** unit of regimental size specially trained for movement over snow and ice and survival in arctic conditions. The mission of the Group is to conduct border patrol and reconnaissance at long distances from military facilities. Manning of the ARG is mostly by Alaskans who use traditional skills of survival.

area commander: The commander of a military organization within a general or specific geographical area. An area commander directs forces assigned within the area of responsibility and integrates service component commands and forces assigned to the area. The commander is not restricted to operations only within his area but may operate forces wherever to carry out an assigned mission. When forces not assigned to the commander are assigned missions within the area, the commander provides assistance to the forces, but the forces do not necessarily fall in the area commander's chain of command. (see also **commander/commanding officer, unified command, specified command**)

area defense: **1.** Measures to protect large areas (e.g., cities) by engaging enemy forces at a considerable distance, as opposed to protecting a point target (e.g., an underground missile silo).   **2. Anti-submarine warfare (ASW)** and anti-air warfare (AAW) over a broad area, as opposed to around a battle group or individual ship.

area of influence: "A geographical area wherein a commander is directly capable of influencing operations by maneuver or fire support systems normally under his command or control" [*JCS Pub 1,* p. 34].

area of responsibility (AOR): 1. "A defined area of land in which responsibility is specifically assigned to the commander of the area for the development and maintenance of installations, control of movement, and the conduct of tactical operations involving troops under his control, along with parallel authority to exercise these functions.   **2.** In naval usage, a pre-defined area of enemy terrain for which supporting ships are responsible for covering by fire on known targets or targets of opportunity and by observation" [*JCS Pub 1,* p. 34].

Argus: Codename for **signals intelligence** collection satellite.

ARIA (Advanced Range Instrumentation Aircraft)   (see **Advanced Range Instrumentation Aircraft**)

ARL: Designation for small **repair ship**.

Arleigh Burke (DDG-51) class guided-missile destroyer: The newest class of Navy destroyers. The lead ship's keel was laid down at Bath Iron Works, ME, on 31 July 1986, and it is scheduled to be delivered in FY 1990. Twenty-nine Burke class ships will be constructed and deployed in the 1990s, replacing the Adams (DDG-2) and Farragut (DDG-37) classes. The ship will have a full **AEGIS Combat System**, equipped with one AN/SPY-1D multi-function phased array radar. It will be outfitted with one 61-cell and one 29-cell **vertical launch**

system. Armaments will include **Tomahawk** sea-launched cruise missiles (nuclear and conventional variants), vertical launch **ASROCs, Harpoons, Standard missile** 2s (SM-2), one five inch gun, two **Phalanx** close-in-weapons systems (CIWS), anti-submarine torpedoes, and **Light Airborne Multi-purpose System (LAMPS)** Mk III SH-60B Sea hawk ASW helicopters. It will also have a towed-array sonar. The Burke destroyers are all steel, which is better able to limit the effects of electromagnetic pulse. The ship is also designed to withstand a nuclear blast overpressure of seven psi, compared to three psi in most other Navy surface combatants. (see also **destroyer**)

arm   (see **branch**)

armed: "The configuration of a nuclear weapon in which a single signal will initiate the action required for obtaining a nuclear detonation" [DNA, *Nuclear Weapon Accident Response Procedures (NARP) Manual,* Janaury 1984, p. 154, released under the FOIA].

armed forces censorship: The control and review of personal communications to or from those persons involved with the U.S. armed forces. In peacetime, such censorship is directed by the President, Secretary of Defense, or Commander of a unified or specified command. Upon declaration of war by the United States, censorship outside of the United States is imposed immediately and within the United States by order of the Secretary of Defense or other military authorities as justified.

Armed Forces Courier Service: Joint organization operated by the Department of the Army that provides couriers for the secure transmission of material that is not authorized to be mailed or cannot be electronically transmitted (e.g., codes, highly sensitive intelligence, and targeting tapes).

arming system: The system of components in a nuclear weapon that serves to ready (prearm), safe, or resafe (dearm) the fusing system and firing system, and prevents premature detonation.

armor: 1. Combat arms branch of the Army.   **2.** Combat units or forces such as tanks, antitank weapons, and mechanized artillery. (see also **armored cavalry**, **armored division**)

armored cavalry: Army combat units characterized by a high degree of mobility and shock action. The units are designed to accomplish a variety of missions, including reconnaissance and counter-reconnaissance operations, utilizing organic surface or air modes of transport. To maintain some of the cavalry tradition, armored cavalry units have different labels than standard units:

Standard Unit	*Armored Cavalry Unit*
Platoon	Platoon
Company	Troop
Battalion	Squadron
Brigade	Regiment

armored cavalry regiment (ACR): Army unit normally assigned to the **corps**. For special operations or for support of other combat maneuver elements, the regiment itself, or squadrons of the regiment, may be attached to a division. The ACR is organized into a headquarters and headquarters troop, one air cavalry troop, and three regimental armored cavalry squadrons. In Europe, two ACRs, one assigned to each U.S. corps, provide border surveillance duties. Armored cavalry regiments currently formed include

2d ACR	Nürnberg, West Germany (APO New York 09093)
3d ACR	Ft. Bliss, TX 79916
11th ACR	Fulda, West Germany (APO New York 09146)
107th ACR*	Cleveland, OH 44101
116th ACR*	Twin Falls, ID 83301
163d ACR	Bozeman, MT 59715
278th ACR*	Knoxville, TN 37901

(* designates reserve unit)

armored division: One of six types of Army **divisions**, it is the heaviest of all divisions. The armored division can conduct sustained combat operations, including active defense, rapid movement, deep penetration and pursuit, covering force, and mobile counterattack. It can disperse over great distances and concentrate rapidly from widely separated areas. The division can also conduct limited air assault operations. Limitations of the armored division include a minimum of rapid movement over long distances due to limited air transportability. Rail or highway transport of tracked vehicles is required for long administrative moves. The division has restricted mobility in jungles, dense forest, or untrafficable, steep, rugged terrain. The division requires large quantities of supplies and other heavy logistical support, particularly maintenance, fuel, lubricants, and ammunition. An armored division typically consists of 6 **tank battalions**, 4 **mechanized infantry battalions,** and 16,800 personnel. Some armored divisions, particularly in Europe, have four, rather than three, **brigades**.

arms control: "A concept that connotes **1.** any plan, arrangement, or process, resting upon explicit or implicit international agreement, governing any aspect of the following: the numbers, types, and performance characteristics of weapon systems (including the command and control, logistics support arrangements, and any related intelligence-gathering mechanisms); and the numerical strength, organization, equipment, deployment, or employment of the armed forces retained by the parties (It encompasses 'disarmament') and **2.** on some occasions, those measures taken for the purpose of reducing instability in the military environment" [*JCS Pub 1,* p. 36].

Arms Control and Disarmament Agency (ACDA): Executive branch agency established on 26 September 1961 by President Kennedy. It succeeded the smaller White House and Department of State Offices of Disarmament and the U.S. Disarmament Administration established by the Eisenhower Administration. ACDA was created largely in response to the ad hoc nature in which prior arms control agreements were negotiated

and was made specifically responsible for the development, implementation, and support of arms control and disarmament policies. In the 1960s and early 1970s, ACDA enjoyed an influential reign, but it then declined until the Carter Administration restored some of its prestige. Under President Reagan, ACDA's budget was cut severely, raising questions about the Agency's future role.

The Director of the Agency is required to serve as the "principal advisor" to the Secretary of State, National Security Council, and the President on matters concerning arms control and disarmament. ACDA has led U.S. delegations to the **Conference on Disarmament** (formerly the Eighteen-Nation Disarmament Committee (ENDC)) at which the following treaties were negotiated in full or in part: the **Limited Test Ban Treaty** (1963), the **Non-Proliferation Treaty** (1968), the **Seabed Treaty** (1971), the **Biological Weapons Convention** (1972), and the **ENMOD [Environmental Modification] Convention** (1977). In addition, ACDA has participated in the negotiation of the major arms control agreements between the United States and the Soviet Union, including the "hotline" (**direct communications link**) agreements (1963, 1971, and 1984), the **Agreement on Measures to Reduce the Risk of Outbreak of Nuclear War** (1971), the **Threshold Test Ban Treaty** (1974), the **Peaceful Nuclear Explosion Treaty** (1976), **SALT I** and **SALT II**, the **ABM Treaty**, **START**, and the **INF Treaty**, as well as the current **Nuclear and Space Talks (NST)**. In addition to its Director and Deputy Director, ACDA's Assistant Directors run the Agency's functional bureaus, including those dealing with strategic programs, multilateral negotiations, bilateral negotiations, non-proliferation of nuclear weapons, assessment of arms control impact, and verification. Also, the Agency has offices of law, administration, public information, and Congressional affairs. Its personnel strength is approximately 250.

FY 1990 budget is approximately $30 million.

Headquarters
Washington, DC 20451

ACDA Directors

William C. Foster	1961–1969
Gerard C. Smith	1969–1973
Fred C. Iklé	1973–1977
Paul C. Warnke	1977–1978
Gen. George C. Seignious, USAF (Ret)	1978–1980
Ralph W. Earle II	1980–1981
Eugene V. Rostow	1981–1983
Kenneth L. Adelman	1983–1987
Gen. William F. Burns, USA (Ret)	1988–1989
Ronald F. Lehman II	1989–present

Arms Export Control Act of 1976 (AECA): Congressional act signed into law that authorizes the sale of U.S. material and services to eligible foreign and international organizations as carried out through **security assistance programs**. Under the law, the locus of arms sales regulation is the Department of State. As stated by Section 2 of the AECA, "the Secretary of State . . . shall be responsible for the continuous supervision and general direction of sales and exports . . . to the end that . . . the foreign policy of the United States is best served thereby." In practice, this function is shared among many departments and agencies, including DOD, the Treasury Department, the Central Intelligence Agency, and the National Security Council. The AECA declares that "the President is authorized to control the import and export of defense articles and defense services and to provide guidance to persons of the United States involved in the export or import of such articles and services." The act emphasizes cooperative projects with fellow member countries of NATO. It authorizes sales to NATO, Japan, Australia, and New Zealand made on a grant or credit basis, as well as the lease of U.S. defense items to other nations. It established the **Special Defense Acquisition Fund (SDAF)**, which finances the acquisition of material specifically for security assistance purposes. (see also **Foreign Assistance Act of 1961**)

Army: 1. An echelon above **corps** that provides command, control, and support to the basic unit of ground combat power, the division. There are three types of armies: army group, **field army**, and **theater army**. In an established theater of operations, the army component under a unified command is termed "the theater army." If the war or the number of corps is so large that the span of control of the theater army is too great, field armies and/or army groups may be organized in echelons between corps and theater army. **2.** A CONUS-based formation responsible for commanding

Army Reserve units in a geographic area.   **3.** The colloquial name for the **Department of the Army**. Armies currently formed include

1st U.S. Army	Ft. Meade, MD 20755
2nd U.S. Army	Ft. Gillem, GA 30050
3rd U.S. Army	Ft. McPherson, GA 30330
4th U.S. Army	Ft. Sheridan, IL 60037
5th U.S. Army	Ft. Sam Houston, TX 78234
6th U.S. Army	Presidio of San Francisco, CA 94129
Seventh U.S. Army	Heidelberg, West Germany (APO New York 09102)
Eighth U.S. Army	Seoul, South Korea (APO San Francisco 96301)
Combined Field Army	(ROK/US), Uijong-bu, S. Korea (APO San Francisco 96358)

Army Communications Command (USACC): Former name of the **Army Information Systems Command**.

Army Corps of Engineers (USACE): 1. Army **major command** founded in 1775 and designated as a major command on 16 June 1979. It is normally referred to as the Corps of Engineers. The Corps has dual engineering tasks, which include both military functions and civil works. The USACE fulfills the responsibilities for the Department of the Army as the principal construction agency of the federal government. Besides being heavily engaged in civil works construction programs, the Corps builds military facilities for the Air Force and Navy (as required), as well as for the Army. The Corps also performs construction for non-defense agencies such as NASA and the U.S. Postal Service, and for foreign governments. The Corps is responsible for the care of rivers, harbors, and waterways to facilitate navigation throughout the United States. In this capacity, the Corps is the principal developer of the nation's water resources. It reports through the Assistant Secretary of the Army (Civil Works) to the Secretary on Civil Works Matters.

Military functions include operation and maintenance of certain Army and Air Force installations; real estate management; mobilization planning; and military engineering research, development, testing, and evaluation. USACE operates 13 divisions in different geographical regions and numerous districts, several laboratory centers, and specialized engineering activities.

Headquarters
Washington, DC 20314

2. The colloquial name often used to describe the **branch** of assignment of engineers, even though they are assigned to engineer combat units that train to participate in combat operations including construction, demolition, cover and deception, topographic activities, and use of explosives.

Army Criminal Investigations Command (CIDC): Army **major com-**

mand that conducts and manages criminal investigations of service personnel in support of the Army Staff and field commanders. CIDC operates the U.S. Army Crime Records Repository and is involved in protective service operations for Army high-level commanders and other ranking government officials. Its worldwide personnel strength is approximately 2,000 military and civilian personnel.

Headquarters
Falls Church, VA 22041

Army Data Distribution System (ADDS): Army data distribution system under development which will support battlefield tactical operations (division and corps) with reliable real-time, secure, jam resistant data communications, position/location assistance, and unit identification capabilities. It will link the high priority elements of each battlefield functional area (fire support, air defense, intelligence/electronic warfare, maneuver control, and combat service support) and automatically identify the location of units. The hardware will include a control station which performs net management and command functions. The FY 1989/90 program will be for low rate initial production of equipment. The FY 1991/92 program will fund the start of full-scale production.

ADDS was formerly known as the PLRS (Position Location Reporting System)/JTDS (Joint Tactical Information Distribution System) Hybrid (PJH). ADDS will modify, combine, and integrate components of PLRS and JTDS in an evolutionary five-phase program to take advantage of the advanced state of development of these two projects.

The ADDS contains three primary equipment elements: Enhanced PLRS User Units (EPUU), JTIDS terminals, and Net Control Stations (NCS). The EPUUs are assigned to almost all units in the division area that participate in near real-time data communications, identification and position location/navigation. JTIDS terminals are assigned to those users whose data requirements exceed the capability of the EPUU and who participate heavily in interservice communications. For example, air defense users pass high volume tracking data internally and exchange friendly identification information with the Air Force. The NCS will provide overall system network management. The FAAD C^2I (**Forward Area Air Defense** Command, Control, and Intelligence) System is totally dependent on ADDS for data distribution.

ADDS entered its final phase of development in 1985 with a low rate production award scheduled for March 1989. The FY 1989/90 program will be for the preplanned program improvement (P3I) low rate initial production equipment. The FY 1991/92 program will fund the start of full-scale production. The total procurement RDT&E request for FY 1990 and FY 1991 is $69.5 and $242 million, respectively. The contractors are Hughes Aircraft Company, Ground Systems Group, Fullerton, CA; and the Singer Company, Kearfott Division, Little Falls, NJ.

Army Forces Atlantic (see **U.S. Army Forces, Atlantic Command**)

Army Forces Command   (see **Forces Command**)

Army group   (see **Army**)

Army Health Services Command (HSC): Army **major command** responsible as the single manager for the Army's combat-oriented and peacetime health services. It commands and supervises three major installations, medical centers, medical and dental laboratories, medical area commands, and the Academy of Health Sciences. Besides providing health services, it also provides professional education and training for Army medical personnel and develops concepts, doctrine, and material requirements for Army medical units in the field.

Headquarters
Ft. Sam Houston, TX 78234

Army Helicopter Improvement Program (AHIP)   (see **OH-58 Kiowa**)

Army Information Systems Command (AISC): Army **major command**, redesignated from the Army Communications Command on 15 May 1984. It is responsible for the Army's communications-electronics facilities and equipment, and for engineering, installing, operating, and maintaining the Army portion of the **Defense Communications System (DCS)**. AISC operates and maintains the **AUTODIN, AUTOVON,** and **AUTOSEVOCOM** systems. It also conducts Army air traffic control and is the Army's telecommunications leasing agency. Furthermore, AISC provides communications sup-

port to other federal agencies involved in domestic disturbances, continuity of government, natural disasters, and other special operations. AISC's personnel strength is approximately 40,000 military and civilian personnel.

Headquarters
Ft. Huachuca, AZ 85613

Subcommands and Units

- 1st Signal Brigade: Seoul, South Korea (APO San Francisco 96301)
- 5th Signal Command (Europe): Worms, West Germany (APO New York 09056)
- 7th Signal Command (CONUS): Ft. Ritchie, MD 17268
- 11th Signal Brigade: Ft. Huachuca, AZ 85613
- Information Systems Engineering Command: Ft. Belvoir, VA 22060
- Information Systems Command, Japan: Camp Zama, Japan (APO San Francisco 96503)
- Information Systems Command, Western: Ft. Shafter, HI 96858

Army Intelligence Agency (AIA): A **field operating agency** reporting to the Office of the Assistant Chief of Staff for Intelligence, Department of the Army. AIA is the primary analytic intelligence organization of the Army that is not involved in the production of tactical intelligence but produces and disseminates scientific and technical intelligence, general **intelligence**, **counterintelligence**, and **counterterrorism** analysis. The AIA also does threat projections and analyses for the Department and manages the Foreign Materiel Exploitation Program, which evaluates military equipment for intelligence information. It consists of 3 intelligence production centers—the Intelligence and Threat Analysis Center (ITAC), the Foreign Science and Technology Center (FSTC), and the Missile and Space Intelligence Center (MSIC)—and 23 Army reserve strategic military intelligence detachments. Its authorized personnel strength is 1,500.

Headquarters
Washington Navy Yard,
Washington, DC 20374

Army Intelligence and Security Command (INSCOM): Army **major command** and service component of the Central Security Service of the **National Security Agency**. INSCOM was created in October 1977 by the merger of the Army Intelligence Command and the Army Security Agency. It conducts **intelligence** functions at the echelons-above-corps level in support of the Department of the Army as well as other major commands and field commanders. INSCOM operational intelligence activities include **human intelligence (HUMINT)**, **signals intelligence (SIGINT)**, **counterintelligence**, **communications security**, **electronic warfare**, **technical surveillance countermeasures**, surveys, and polygraphs.

INSCOM operates major nontactical SIGINT collection stations (called field stations) in West Berlin and Augsburg, West Germany; Okinawa and Misawa, Japan; Pyongtaek, South Korea; San Antonio, TX; Homestead AFB, FL; and Kunia, HI.

Headquarters
Arlington Hall Station, VA 22212

Army Materiel Command (AMC): Army **major command** activated on 1 August 1962. It was called the U.S. Army Materiel Development and Readiness Command (DARCOM) from 1974–1984. AMC performs logistical functions for all Army materiel systems including research, development, and acquisition; test and evaluation; production; distribution; maintenance; and storage. In addition, it is the Army's executive director for security assistance and foreign military sales, and DOD's lead agency for chemical, biological, and radiological defense materiels development. AMC is also responsible for the readiness of war reserve equipment, pre-positioning of material configured to unit sets (**POMCUS**) stocks, and management of operational stocks. It operates at approximately 65 installations, 18 subinstallations, and 100 additional locations worldwide, and consists of ten subordinate commands, two separate-reporting activities, and two command and control elements. Its personnel strength is approximately 114,000 military and civilian personnel.

Headquarters
Alexandria, VA 22333-0001

Subordinate Activities

- Armament, Munition, and Chemical Command (AMCCOM): Rock Island, IL 61299
- AMC-Europe: Seckenheim, West Germany (APO NY 09333)
- Aviation Systems Command (AVSCOM): St. Louis, MO 63120
- Communications-Electronics Command (CECOM): Ft. Monmouth, NJ 07703

- Depot System Command (DESCOM): Chambersburg, PA 17201
- Laboratory Command: Chambersburg, PA 20783
- Missile Command (MICOM): Redstone Arsenal, AL 35898
- Security Affairs Command (USA-SAC): Alexandria, VA 22333
- Tank-Automotive Command (TACOM): Warren, MI 48090
- Test and Evaluation Command (TECOM): Aberdeen Proving Ground, MD 21005
- Troop Support Command (TROSCOM): St. Louis, MO 63120

Army Medical Department: Combat service support arm and special **branch** of the Army composed of the Medical Corps, the Army Nurse Corps, the Dental Corps, the Veterinary Corps, the Medical Service Corps, and the Army Medical Specialist Corps.

Army Military District of Washington   (see **Military District of Washington**)

Army Military Traffic Management Command (see **Military Traffic Management Command**)

Army National Guard (ARNG): The federal **reserve** component of the Army whose members are **National Guard** personnel. The ARNG is the successor to the Colonial Militia of pre-Revolution days and still is under the control of the state governments unless called to federal service by the President. The state mission is to supply organized units that are equipped and trained to function in the pro-

tection of life and property and the preservation of peace, order, and public safety under competent orders of federal or state authorities. The primary federal mission is to supply properly trained and equipped units capable of immediate participation in combat through timely mobilization in accordance with operations plans. The wartime missions include deploying early to overseas commands, rounding out active component forces with units as required, and constituting a strategic reserve in CONUS. ARNG units can perform, under federal control, the same emergency functions they perform for their state governments.

ARNG major combat units consist of 10 **divisions** (two armored, two mechanized, five infantry, one light infantry); 8 round-out **brigades** or **battalions** of active divisions; 14 **separate brigades** (with 16 planned by FY 1989); 4 **armored cavalry regiments**; and 188 separate **maneuver battalions** (with 189 planned by FY 1989). The ARNG provides a significant portion of the total force and capabilities in certain mission areas, including 36 percent of combat divisions, 46 percent of Pathfinder units, 30 percent of supply and service units, 74 percent of infantry battalions, 47 percent of mechanized infantry battalions, 36 percent of armored battalions, 48 percent of non-divisional engineer bridge companies, 57 percent of armored cavalry regiments, and 25 percent of special forces groups.

Personnel matters are administered by the Army National Guard Personnel Center. During FY 1988, the ARNG received 34 percent of the total reserve appropriations. ARNG units are located in 4,600 facilities and 2,858 locations throughout CONUS. Together with the Army Reserve, the ARNG makes up almost 50 percent of the Army's personnel strength. The personnel strength of the ARNG Ready Reserve is 460,000. Inactive ARNG personnel are assigned to the Inactive National Guard. (see also **Army Reserve**)

Headquarters
Pentagon, Washington, DC
20310-2500

Army Nuclear and Chemical Agency (see **U.S. Army Nuclear and Chemical Agency**)

Army Operations Center (AOC): The primary command and control facility for Headquarters, Department of the Army, located in the Pentagon. It routinely operates as a 24-hour emergency action facility and operations information center. During periods of national or international crisis, the AOC is the Army point of contract for the exchange of operational information with the **National Military Command System** and other **Worldwide Military Command and Control System (WWMCCS)** operations centers.

Army Reserve (USAR): Federal **reserve** component of the Army. Like the **Army National Guard**, the USAR is based on the principle that citizen-soldiers, trained in peacetime, should contribute to the nation's defense in emergencies, but it differs from the National Guard in that its origins are more recent and its responsibilities are to fill out the force

structure of the active Army during mobilization, rather than augment its ranks. There are some combat units in the USAR, and currently one brigade and two battalions are designated to round-out active Army divisions, but the majority of USAR units are **combat support** and **combat service support** units, as well as area commands and units prepared to assume training mission from the active forces in case of emergency. Unlike the Army National Guard, the USAR supplies trained individuals for filling critical positions in case of mobilization, as well as supplies replacements for losses in active Army, Army National Guard, and USAR units.

The USAR consists of 13 **separate brigades** (one round-out), 13 **maneuver battalions** (two round-out battalions), 12 training divisions, and 3 training battalions. The USAR provides a significant portion of the total Army force in various mission areas, including 100 percent of training divisions and brigades, 100 percent of railroad units, 97 percent of civil affairs, 46 percent of Pathfinder units, 59 percent of supplies and services units, 89 percent of psychological operations units, 78 percent of chemical smoke generation units, 29 percent of bridging, 51 percent of conventional ammunition companies, and 25 percent of special forces groups. During FY 1988, the USAR received 18 percent of the total reserve appropriations. Units report to the Army Chief of Staff through the Commander-in-Chief, Forces Command, who exercises his or her authority through the numbered CONUS Armies, Army Reserve Commands (ARCOMs), and General Officer Commands (GOCOMs). ARCOMs command Army Reserve units within certain geographic areas. GOCOMs are functional organizations such as training divisions, maneuver area commands, and other units authorized to have general officers as commands. The Chief, Army Reserve, is a special staff officer on the Army Staff and advises the Chief of Staff and Secretary of the Army on matters concerning the component. Personnel matters are administered by the Army Reserve Personnel Center. Together with the Army National Guard, the USAR makes up almost 50 percent of the Army's personnel strength. The personnel strength of the USAR Ready Reserve for FY 1988 was about 600,000, with an additional 400 in the Standby Reserve and 179,000 in the Retired Reserve.

Administrative Headquarters
Ft. Derussy, HI 96815

Office of the USAR
Pentagon, Washington, DC
20310-0300

Army South   (see **U.S. Army South**)

Army Space Command   (see **U.S. Army Space Command**)

Army Special Forces   (see **Special Forces, First Special Operations Command, psychological operations, civil affairs, Task Force 160**)

Army Staff: An executive component of the **Department of the Army**. It exists to assist the **Secretary of the Army** in his or her responsibilities and includes the Chief of Staff; Vice Chief; Deputy Chiefs for Personnel, Intelligence, Operations and Plans, and Logistics; and the Special Staff, including the Chief of Engineers, Surgeon General, Judge Advocate General, Chief of Chaplains, Chief of the National Guard Bureau, and Chief of the Army Reserve.

Army Strategic Defense Command (see **U.S. Army Strategic Defense Command**)

Army Tactical Missile System (ATACMS):   Army improved, all-weather, semiguided, conventional **ballistic missile** system assigned to the corps with the mission to attack targets beyond the range of cannons and rockets, to replace the conventional **Lance** missile. The ATACMS will be used to attack tactical surface-to-surface missile sites, air defense systems, logistic elements, C3 complexes, and second-echelon maneuver units arrayed in depth throughout the corps' area of influence. It is transported and launched from a modified M270 **Multiple-Launch Rocket System (MLRS)** launcher. Each launcher will be able to fire either MLRS rockets or ATACMS munitions. The missile will have an anti-personnel/anti-materiel (APAM) warhead. The system will use targeting systems, engagement systems, and command control systems that are the same as in the MLRS. The ATACMS has a higher rate of fire and longer range and uses less manpower than the Lance missile system. Plans to use the ATACMS as a nuclear follow-on to the Lance missile have been canceled. The prime contractor is Vought Corporation, Dallas, TX.

Medium and Heavy Artillery Gun Types

Model	Type	Caliber (mm)	Weight (t)	Range (km)	Crew	Nuclear
M101A1	HT	105	2.5	11.3/14.5*		no
M102	HT	105	1.5	11.5/15		no
M119	HT	105	2	14/19.5	7	no
M114A1/A2	HT	155	6.5	14.6/19.7	11	yes
M198	HT	155	8	22/30.1	11	yes
M109A2/A3	HSP	155	30	23.7/24.5	6	yes
M109HIP	HSP	155	27.5	22/30	6	yes
M110A2	HSP	203	31	23/29	13	yes

*unassisted range/rocket-assisted projectile range
M = mortar; HT = towed howitzer; HSP = self-propelled howitzer; G = gun

The system is scheduled for fielding in FY 1991. The Army purchased 66 missiles and spent $146.7 million on ATACMS in FY 1989. The FY 1990 and 1991 requests for ATACMS are $187.7 million for 276 missiles in 1990 and $188.9 million for 452 missiles in 1991.

Army Test and Evaluation Management Agency: Army **field operating agency** responsible for the coordination and programming of Army developmental, operational, and production testing and evaluation in support of Army activities and commands and Office of the Secretary of Defense. The Agency reports to the Office of the Chief of Staff of the Army through the Deputy Under Secretary of the Army for Operations Research.

Army Training and Doctrine Command (TRADOC) (see **Training and Doctrine Command**)

Army Western Command (see **U.S. Army Western Command**)

array: 1. Two or more connected sensors (such as hydrophones or seismometers) feeding into a common receiver.   **2.** A set of connected communications antennae. (see also **Atomic Energy Detection System**, **Sound Surveillance System (SOSUS)**, **Surface Towed Array Sensor (SURTASS)**)

ARS: Designation for salvage ship.

artillery: 1. The branch of Army equipped with artillery weapons. (see also **Multiple-Launch Rocket System**, **Lance**, **Pershing**)   **2.** Weaponry exceeding small-arms caliber (0.6 inch/15 mm or more). Also refers to rockets and rocket launchers assigned to the artillery branch of the Army. Guns, howitzers, and mortars are all classic artillery. In artillery, which is also frequently referred to as cannon (as opposed to rockets or missiles), the projectile is projected through a barrel by the expansion of gases produced by the explosion of the propelling charge. The cannon fires projectiles of various types and consists of a breach, firing mechanism, and tube or barrel. The range and accuracy depend on the power of the explosive cartridge and the length of the barrel. Projectiles are stabilized by the spinning effect created by the rifling of the barrel, or through fin-stabilized ammunition fired through smooth barrels. Mortars are generally short-barrelled, low-muzzle velocity, high-angle fire weapons. Howitzers have a barrel length between that of a mortar and a gun, have medium muzzle velocity, and are capable of both low and high angle of fire. Guns have a relatively long barrel in relation to caliber, high muzzle velocity, and low angles of fire. Artillery cannon can fire a wide variety of ammunition: high explosive, illumination, white phosphorous, laser-guided, rocket-assisted (to increase range), anti-personnel, remote-mine laying, chemical, and nuclear.

Artillery Fired Atomic Projectile (AFAP): Artillery projectile that contains a nuclear warhead. The United States has four types of AFAPs: the M422 203 mm projectile with the W33 warhead, the M454 155 mm projectile with the W48 warhead, the M753 203 mm projectile with the W79 warhead, and the M785 155 mm projectile with the W82 warhead. The W79 and W82 are replacing the W33 and W48. The Army and Marine Corps both use these four weapons. These artillery can be fired from numerous U.S. and Allied 155 mm and 203 mm howitzers and have yields in the sub-kiloton to 12 kiloton range.

AS: Designation for submarine tender.

ASAT (see **anti-satellite weapon**)

ASM (see **air-to-surface missile**)

ASPJ (see **Airborne Self-Protection Jammer**)

ASR: Designation for submarine rescue ship.

ASRAAM (Advanced Short-Range Air-to-Air Missile): A missile under development to replace the **Sidewinder**. The ASRAAM requirements call for the missile to have 2.5 times greater seeker acquisition range and effective launch range than the Sidewinder. Also, it will be faster, be more maneuverable, provide a significant increase in fighter-to-target separation at missile intercept, and provide a significant improvement in flare rejection over the Sidewinder.

In 1980, the Secretaries and Ministers of Defense of the United States, France, West Germany, and the United Kingdom signed a Memorandum of Understanding for a cooperative program to develop a new family of advanced air-to-air missile systems. To avoid duplication of effort and increase NATO standardization, the European nations are responsible for the development of ASRAAM whereas the United States is in charge of developing the **AMRAAM** (advanced medium range air-to-air missile). The ASRAAM Allied Joint Project Office (AJPO) is located in Koblenz, West Germany, and is in the course of conducting engineering development activities in 1988–1989. In the United States, ASRAAM is a joint Navy and Air Force program, with the Air Force designated as the executive service. For FY 1990 and FY 1991, the DOD requested $5 million and $6.5 million, respectively, for ASRAAM development.

ASROC (Anti-Submarine Rocket):
Model designation RUR-5. Navy unguided, surface ship-launched, short-
range, dual-capable, anti-submarine
rocket. It is armed with either a Mk-
46 lightweight acoustic homing torpedo or a W44 1 kt nuclear depth
charge. The conventional version is
known as a Rocket Thrown Torpedo (RTT) and the nuclear version
as a Rocket Thrown Depth Charge
(RTDC). ASROC is used for self-
defense against submarines and can be
launched from an eight-cell directable
launcher or from launching rails that
also fire **Terrier** and **Standard** surface-to-air missiles. It also has a
surface-to-surface capability against
ships. The missile has a range of 0.9–
5 nm (1.8–9 km). It has been operational since 1961. Approximately 500
W44 ASROC nuclear warheads were
in the stockpile in 1988, but the
U.S. Navy decided in August 1988
to accelerate retirement of the nuclear
versions. They are in the process of,
or already have been removed from,
surface ships in the fleet. The ASROC
is deployed on 151 surface ships,
including 32 cruisers (all but the vertical launch system (VLS)–equipped
Ticonderoga cruisers), 62 destroyers
(all but the Kidd and VLS-equipped
Spruance destroyers), and 57 frigates
(all except the Oliver Hazard Perry
frigates). Honeywell, Inc., is the
prime contractor, and Naval Weapons Center, White Oak, MD, is
responsible for the nuclear depth
charge section.

A **Vertical Launched ASROC
(VLA)** program to extend ASROC
capability to VLS-equipped ships began in March 1982. The VLA is a new
rocket, with quicker reaction time,

greater range (10 nm), and increased
kill probability (due to an acoustical
terminal guidance system) than the
current ASROC. It was originally intended to be armed with either a new
nuclear warhead or a lightweight
torpedo. A joint DOD/DOE Phase 2
feasibility study to investigate the
nuclear requirements and characteristics for the VLA took place between
October 1983 and October 1984 but
did not advance. Congress denied
funds for the new nuclear warhead
and now the VLA will be conventionally armed. It is scheduled to
enter the fleet in the 1990s and eventually will be on Ticonderoga class
cruisers, Arleigh Burke class destroyers, and Spruance class destroyers
equipped with VLS.

assault amphibian vehicles (AAV):
Light armored, box-shaped, tracked
vehicle used for ship-to-shore movement of Marines from **landing ship,
tank (LST)** amphibious warfare ships.
AAVs are able to land troops and
material on beaches through heavy
surf. The Marines operate over 1,200
AAVs. Most of these are troop
carriers (AAVP7A1) but about 100
are configured as command vehicles (AAVC7A1) and another 60 as
recovery repair vehicles (AAVR7A1).
Several hundred are pre-positioned
on maritime pre-positioning force
ships and some are pre-positioned in
Norway. The AAV was formerly designated landing vehicle, tracked, personnel (LVTP-7), but this was formally changed to AAV in 1985; likewise,
the term "amtrac" for amphibious
tractor was officially abandoned for
the AAV terminology. The vehicle
weighs 40,000–50,000 lb and, on

land, has a top speed of 40 mph and a cruise speed of 20–30 mph. In water, it can get get up to 8.4 mph, with a cruise speed of 8 mph. It has a range of 300 mi at 25 mph on land and 300 mi at 8 mph in water. The crew of the personnel carrier numbers 3, with the AAV able to carry an additional 21 troops. A stern ramp drops to allow the troops to exit. The command vehicle has a crew of 12: three crewmen, five radiomen, and four unit commanders and staff. The recovery/repair vehicles have a 6,000 lb capacity telescoping boom-type crane, a 30,000 lb pull winch, and maintenance equipment. All AAVs are armed with a single machine gun, and the personnel carrier also has a grenade launcher.

Assault Breaker: Army program during the Reagan Administration to develop high-technology conventional weapons with advanced submunitions capable of engaging and destroying armored forces at long ranges. Examples of submunitions being considered for Assault Breaker are

- T16 and T22 missiles: Capable of carrying terminally guided submunitions that analyze the shape of the target while in flight, then, while slowed by parachutes, drop vertically onto the target. These submunitions have the capability to discriminate between massed, dispersed, and strung-out targets and to adjust by infrared sensor their descent spins to meet each situation. They are also capable of carrying Avco-manufactured Skeet munitions, which are fin-stabilized, parachute-slowed

submunitions. Skeets are ejected horizontally in pairs from the missile and infrared sensors home them to tank engine com partments. If no tanks are hit, the skeets will home in on personnel and light armored vehicles.

- Extended-range antitank mine (ERAM): Dropped from the air ahead of enemy tank formations, it buries itself in the ground. ERAM explodes when a tank passes over it.
- WASP mini-missile: Air-launched and capable of independently sighting and tracking after launch and attacking armored targets in a "swarm" of up to a dozen rounds at once.

assault craft unit (ACU): Permanent naval operating organization, subordinate to the **naval beach group**. Consists of landing craft and crews for support of amphibious operations. (see also **amphibious warfare landing craft**)

assign: 1. To place under the primary or relatively permanent **operational command** or **operational control** of a commander. Assigned forces are combat forces placed under the operational command or operational control of a commander. **2.** To detail individuals to specific duties or functions. (see also **chop**)

assured destruction: "The capability to destroy an aggressor as a viable society, even after a well planned and executed surprise attack on our forces" [*U.S. Air Force Glossary*]. (see also **Mutual Assured Destruction**)

ASW (see **anti-submarine warfare**)

ASW Standoff Weapon (ASWSOW): Navy program to develop a follow-on anti-submarine standoff weapon to the **SUBROC** and **ASROC**. The ASWSOW program became the **Sea Lance** program.

ATA (see **A-12 Advanced Tactical Aircraft**)

ATARS: Umbrella concept for the full-scale development of electro-optical (EO) sensors to upgrade Air Force and Navy manned and unmanned reconnaissance systems. ATARS is designed to assist tactical commanders with detection, location, and classification of tactical targets by providing sufficient location accuracy to permit delivery of air- and ground-launched weapons. ATARS is composed of two elements: Tactical Air Reconnaissance System (TARS) and Unmanned Air Reconnaissance System (UARS). TARS, an Air Force/Navy medium-range unmanned system, focuses on sensor development for fighter and reconnaissance aircraft and on tactical ground control of manned and unmanned Air Force systems. UARS is a Navy/Air Force medium-range unmanned system. Although an unmanned system can be developed at a lower cost and does not endanger crew lives, it lacks the mission flexibility of a manned system: it cannot detect, avoid, or react to air or mobile ground-based threats nor adjust to inclement weather in the target area. UARS is therefore designed to complement, not replace, Air Force manned tactical reconnaissance systems. (see also **electro-optics**)

ATC: Designation for coastal **patrol combatant**.

ATF: **1.** Designation for fleet ocean tug. **2. Advanced Tactical Fighter (ATF).**

Athens Guidelines on Nuclear Defense: Concepts for the development of current NATO nuclear strategy and tactics adopted in May 1962 at the Athens meeting of NATO Ministers. The Guidelines outline the circumstances in which nuclear weapons may be used in response to aggression against NATO countries and discuss the feasibility of political consultation at such a time. The Guidelines were established in the midst of the growing NATO nuclear stockpile. The ambiguous nuclear strategy and tactics became, as it is today, a major political issue within the allied countries. The Athens meeting attempted to alleviate political and strategic unrest by introducing procedures for the exchange of information among NATO countries concerning the role of nuclear weapons in defense. Many of these arrangements were institutionalized by the formation of the **Nuclear Planning Group** in 1967. (see also **General Political Guidelines for the Use of Nuclear Weapons**)

Atlantic Command (LANTCOM) (see **U.S. Atlantic Command**)

Atlantic Fleet (LANTFLT): Navy **operating force** and the largest service component command of

U.S. Atlantic Command. Its mision area includes portions of the Atlantic, Pacific, and Arctic Oceans, and the Caribbean Sea. CINCLANTFLT (Commander-in-Chief LANTFLT) falls in both the administrative and operational chains of command. In the administrative role, CINCLANTFLT readies and provides naval forces for the **2d Fleet**, the **6th Fleet**, the **Middle East Force** in the Indian Ocean, and other Navy commands as directed. In his or her operational role, CINCLANTFLT exercises command of subordinate **Commander Task Forces (CTFs)**, when activated, and directs operations of the Commander, 2d Fleet. In addition to his or her subordinate, type, and special commands, CINCLANTFLT serves as Commander of NATO's Western Atlantic Command and Oceans Atlantic, of the **Allied Command Atlantic**. At full activation, LANTFLT is composed of approximately 312 active and reserve ships, ballistic missile submarines in the Atlantic, 1,100 aircraft, and 250,000 personnel.

Headquarters
Norfolk, VA 23511

Subordinate Operating Forces

- **Second Fleet (2d FLT)**
- **Submarine Force Atlantic (COMSUBLANT)**

Type Commands

- **Naval Surface Force** (CTF 40)
- **Naval Air Force** (CTF 41)
- **Submarine Force** (CTF 42)
- **Fleet Marine Force** (CTF 45)

Special Commands (selected)

- Training Command (CTF 43)

- **Mine Warfare Command** (CTF 46)
- Patrol Air Task Force (CTF 86)
- **U.S. Naval Forces Caribbean** (CTF 134)
- Eastern Atlantic (CTF 137)
- South Atlantic Force (CTF 138)

Atlas II: Medium-launch vehicle rocket operated by the Air Force and NASA and based on retired and modified Atlas **ICBMs**. In May 1988, the Air Force selected General Dynamics to build an upgraded Atlas/ Centaur vehicle, known as Atlas II, to meet its continuing space launch needs. Eleven vehicles were procured as of 1989. The supply of already manufactured Atlas rockets has been exhausted. Changes to the older Atlas rockets will include lower-cost avionics, improved flight computers, greater thrust, and larger propellant tanks.

Two versions, Atlas E and Atlas G/Centaur rockets, were used to launch Air Force, Navy, and National Oceanic and Atmospheric Administration satellites. The Air Force's Atlas E was a refurbished version of the retired Air Force Atlas ICBM with radio guidance and liquid fuel rocket engines. NASA's Atlas G utilized a Centaur D-1A version high-energy upper stage. The Atlas E was capable of delivering a payload of 3,800 lb into a low-earth polar orbit. The Atlas G/Centaur could put a 13,500 lb payload into low-earth polar orbit or a 5,200 lb payload into geosynchronous transfer orbit. The Atlas II will be capable of putting 11,200 lb into a low-earth orbit and 6,100 lb into a geosynchronous transfer orbit. Atlas II will have its first flight in 1991 and will launch a **Defense Satellite Communications System (DSCS)** satellite. The prime contractor for Atlas and Centaur is General Dynamics Corporation, Convair Division.

ATMX: The designation assigned to a special railcar used to transport nuclear weapons in the United States. Only series 500 and 600 ATMX cars are nuclear weapons transporting railcars.

ATOMAL: NATO codeword for nuclear weapons-related information that circulates among the NATO governments. U.S. nuclear weapons-related information is either designated **restricted data** or **formerly restricted data** and is not circulated within NATO. **Programs of cooperation** with individual governments allow the exchange of nuclear information on a bilateral basis, but information that is to circulate among many governments and the international staffs of NATO headquarters is designated ATOMAL. (see also **security classification**)

atomic demolition munition (ADM): Nuclear land mine designed to be detonated on or below the surface to block, deny, and/or canalize enemy forces. The only version of the ADM remaining in the U.S. arsenal is the **Special ADM (SADM)**, which is used by special operations units of the Army, Navy, and Marine Corps. The Medium ADM, assigned to specially trained engineer units, was retired in 1984.

Atomic Energy Act of 1946: Congressional act, also known as the McMahon Act, signed into law on 1 August 1946, a year after the first atomic bomb blast (42 USC §§ 1801). It was amended 30 August 1954 by the Atomic Energy Act of 1954 (42 USC §§ 2011-), as well as by subsequent amendments. The act abolished the Army's Manhattan Project; placed control of nuclear weapons, energy, and materiel under civilian authority; established the Atomic Energy Commission (abolished 19 January 1975 and replaced by the Energy Research and Development Administration and subsequently by the Department of Energy); and placed stringent controls on the export and exchange of U.S. nuclear technology and information. The first section states

> Atomic energy is capable of application for peaceful as well as military purposes. It is therefore declared to be the policy of the United States that:
>
> (a) the development, use, and control of atomic energy shall be directed so as to make the maximum contribution to the general welfare, subject at all times to the paramount objective of making the maximum contribution to the common defense and security; and
>
> (b) the development, use, and control of atomic energy shall be directed so as to promote world peace, improve the general welfare, increase the standard of living, and strengthen free competition in private enterprise.

(see also **restricted data**)

Atomic Energy Commission (AEC): Former civilian nuclear management organization established by the **Atomic Energy Act of 1946**, originally responsible for control and supervision of U.S. nuclear weapons development. From 1946–1954, the AEC also held physical custody of nuclear weapons and materials in the U.S. stockpile. The AEC was abolished in 1974, and its nuclear weapons functions were assumed by the Energy Research and Development Administration. (see also **Department of Energy**)

Atomic Energy Detection System (AEDS): Worldwide network of under-water, land-based, air-based, and space-based instruments to detect and identify nuclear explosions, whether conducted underground, above ground, in the high atmosphere, or in space. The monitoring system is operated by the **Air Force Technical Applications Center (AFTAC)**.

Atomic Music Principle: Codeword for information dealing with nuclear weapons that is exchanged between the United States and the United Kingdom.

ATS: Designation for salvage and rescue ship.

attach: To temporarily assign combat and support units or personnel not organic to a command to an organization. The commander, according to the attachment order, exercises the same degree of command and control over the attached unit or person as with those organizations organic to the command. The responsibility for transfer and promo-

tion of personnel is retained by the parent unit. (see also **assign**)

attaché: Defense Attaché System of the **Defense Intelligence Agency**. (see also **defense attaché**)

attack aircraft carrier (see **aircraft carrier**)

attack assessment: "An evaluation of information to determine the potential or actual nature and objectives of an attack for the purpose of providing information for timely decisions" [*JCS Pub 1*, p. 40]. "The performance of attack assessment includes the process of deriving projected attack patterns and impact points from sensed attack events to determine the character and expected effectiveness of an attack. The process includes evaluation of the effects of the projected attack on U.S. force Capability" [JCS, *Policy and Procedures for Management of Joint Command and Control Systems*, 11 January 1982, p. 5, released under the FOIA]. After warning information is received, NORAD would initiate conferences with the other National Command Authority (NCA) centers to determine warning validity and attack severity.

Approximately halfway into the flight of an incoming ballistic missile, the following inferred data would be available to decision makers from a wide variety of attack assessment systems (e.g., **BMEWS, Perimeter Acquisition Radar Attack Characterization System PARCS, PAVE PAWS**):

- The cumulative number of individual warheads detected, including the identification of type or re-entry vehicle;

• Cumulative or individual warhead impact points given in longitude and latitude;

• Identification of the target as coded in the Selected Target for Attack Characterization (STAC) database (city, military facility, missile field, early-warning facility);

• Time of first event and impact time of each warhead, including Washington impact time and "next impact";

• "Class" of attack as a way to interpret intentions: Class I: urban/industrial; Class II: missile fields; Class III: bomber/tanker bases; Class IV: command and control centers; and Class V: Washington, DC;

• Cumulative number impacted and number not yet impacted; and

• Launch points of each missile in the Soviet Union by latitude and longitude, and number and location of submarines launching missiles.

In less than 30 minutes, all of this information would be used to develop the options to respond to a nuclear attack. (see also **CINCNOR-AD assessment**, **USCINCSPACE assessment**, **emergency conference**)

attack condition: The description of the nature of a nuclear attack on the United States. Attack condition alpha is the military term for a surprise attack when "there is inadequate warning of attack, and the command post or headquarters of a decision authority becomes ineffective prior to the performance of essential functions

[responding to the attack]" [*JCS Pub 1*, p. 40]. Attack condition bravo "considers there is sufficient effective warning of impending attack to relocate personnel required to perform essential functions to alternate command facilities" [*JCS Pub 1*, p. 40].

attack helicopter battalion: Army **maneuver battalion** assigned to the **combat aviation brigade** and composed of one headquarters and headquarters company and three attack helicopter companies. Each attack company has an attack platoon with either seven **AH-1S Cobras** or six **AH-64 Apaches** and a scout platoon with four **OH-58** helicopters.

attack option: Options for the use of nuclear forces derived from Annex C (Nuclear) of the **Joint Strategic Capabilities Plan**. The options are incorporated into the **Single Integrated Operational Plan** and the non-strategic nuclear plans of the regional unified commands.

attack submarine (SS/SSN): Diesel-electric (SS) or nuclear-powered (SSN) submarines optimized for attacking other submarines or surface ships. Of the approximately 100 attack submarines in the U.S. fleet, all but three are nuclear-powered. The diesel-electric submarines are armed with torpedoes. The nuclear-powered submarines can be armed with torpedoes, mines, nuclear **SUBROCs**, **Harpoon** missiles, or **Tomahawk** sea-launched cruise missiles, depending on the class and submarine. The older attack submarines are being retired and replaced by newly con-

Attack Submarines

SUB:	Nuclear Weapons	Torpedo Tube (inches)	Displacement (tons)	Length (ft)	Draft (ft)	Beam (ft)	Speed (kts)	Submerged Complement	IOC
Seawolf (SSN-21)	Tomahawk	8 30	9,150	353	34	40	35	108	1994
Los Angeles (SSN-688)	Tomahawk SUBROC*	4 21	6,900	360	32	33	30+	142	1976
Lipscomb (SSN-684)	SUBROC	4 21	6,480	365	29	32	20+	141	1974
Narwhal (SSN-671)	SUBROC	4 21	5,350	314	26	38	20+	141	1969
Sturgeon (SSN-637)	Tomahawk SUBROC	4 21	4,640	292	29	32	20+	121-134	1967
Permit (SSN-594)	SUBROC	4 21	4,200	278-297	29	32	20+	143	1962
Ethan Allen (SSN-609)	none	4 21	7,880	410	30	33	20+	143	1962/1980
Skate (SSN-578)	none	8	2,860	268	20	25	20	139	1957
Skipjack (SSN-585)	none	6	3,513	252	28	31	20+	143	1959
Barbel (SS-580)	none	6 21	2,640	219	28	29	25	85	1959
Darter (SS-576)	none	8 21	2,250	268	19	27	14	93	1956

*The number of submarines able to fire the SUBROC will decline as SUBROC is retired.

structed Los Angeles class (SSN-688) submarines. The Navy plans to buy a total of 63 SSN-688s. As of 1989, 40 submarines of this type have been delivered to the service. The Navy is requesting $1.6 billion in FY 1990 to build two Los Angeles class submarines. The Seawolf class (SSN-21) submarine is under development and scheduled to enter the fleet in the mid-1990s at a cost of $1–1.5 billion apiece.

In the 1950s and 1960s, nuclear-powered attack submarines were constructed at several commercial and Navy shipyards; now, only General Dynamics, Electric Boat Division, in Groton, CT, and Newport News Shipbuilding, in Newport News, VA, build submarines.

attack transport (LPA) (see **amphibious ship**)

augmentation forces: Combat forces transferred to the operational command of a supported commander during the execution of an operation.

Aurora: Laser system at the Los Alamos National Laboratory, NM, that uses an array of computer-controlled relay mirrors to direct laser beams to their targets.

authentication: 1. Communication security measure designed to provide protection against fraudulent transmission and hostile imitative communications deception by establishing the validity of a transmission, message, station, or designator. Challenge-and-reply authentication is a prearranged procedure whereby an individual requests authentication (challenge) of another individual, who establishes authenticity with a proper reply (reply). **2.** "A cryptosystem or a **cryptographic** process used for authentication" [CENTCOM, *Emergency Action Procedures*, Volume I, p. 4-1, released under the FOIA]. (see also **Sealed Authentication System**)

authorization: 1. Congressional permission to carry out a program (generally procurement of ships, aircraft, or weapons) involving the expenditure of funds. Actual appropriation of the funds is necessary before they can be spent (or obligated). **2.** An act of Congress giving authority to buy certain things when the appropriations are also made by Congress. The Congress passes four pieces of authorizing legislation dealing with the DOD budget—the Defense Authorizations Bill and Military Construction Authorizations Bill of both the House and the Senate. **Appropriations** are only made for purposes authorized by law. The Congressional committees that authorize DOD programs are the House and Senate Armed Services Committees. The House and Senate Intelligence Committees also provide oversight of the intelligence and intelligence-related activities (IRA) portion of the budget.

Authorized Level of Organization (ALO): An Army term for the ratio of authorized **manpower** spaces to the full **tables of organization** and equipment structure spaces, against which a unit is authorized to requisition personnel and equipment. ALO allows the Army to manage manpower shortages by having the core of a desired number of units even though some

Air Force AUTODIN Terminals

Command Supported	CONUS	Overseas	Total	Percent of Total
PACAF	1	40	41	9.0
USAFE	0	102	102	22.3
TAC	54	0	54	11.8
AFLC	16	0	16	3.5
MAC	34	3	37	8.1
SAC	40	17	57	12.5
AFSC	26	0	26	5.7
AAC	0	6	6	1.3
ATC	16	0	16	3.5
AFCC	16	0	16	3.5
AFSPACECOM	20	0	20	4.4
Other*	35	31	66	14.4
Total	258	199	457	100.00

*Headquarters Air Force and separate operating agencies and staff offices, Electronics Security Command, Air Force Reserve, and Air National Guard.

of those units may be manned at reduced strength. ALO is expressed in a numeric code from 1 (100 percent) to 0 (10 percent), or in an alphabetic code of Z (0 percent), B (designed to conserve personnel by substitution of non-U.S. personnel), C (cadre-organized), and E (exception, none of the above). The 82nd Airborne Division and the 24th Infantry Division are the only active divisions at ALO-1. Both are part of the U.S. Central Command rapid deployment force.

AUTODIN (Automatic Digital Network): General-purpose worldwide DOD communications network that provides high-speed data communications. It was established in 1963 from the Air Force Data Communications System (AFDATACOM). It is the primary DOD system for secure record transmission and is capable of providing paper tape, punched card, magnetic tape, computer interface, and teletype copy. AUTODIN serves DOD, other federal agencies including the Federal Aviation Administration, the Federal Emergency Management Agency, the General Services Administration, quasi-government agencies, and defense contractors. The network consists of computer-controlled high-speed Automatic Switching Centers (ASCs), interswitch trunks, and about 1,300 subscribers. A packet-switched AUTODIN II network took over in 1985–1986. The planned replacement is the Integrated Automatic Digital Network System (IAS).

AUTODIN is the usual and preferred medium for transmission of **joint reporting system** reports and general service message traffic, and it is the primary system for transferring and receiving **emergency action messages (EAMs)** among **Worldwide Military Command and Control System (WWMCCS)** subscribers. AUTODIN interfaces with

IEMATS terminals and is the transmission system for IEMATS-originated EAMs. Commands without IEMATS terminals receive IEMATS-originated EAMs at their normal AUTODIN terminals. The USCENT-COM Command Center AUTODIN input/output is an Air Force Automatic Message Processing Exchange (AFAMPE) terminal. The AFAMPE terminal interfaces with the terminals of component forces, components, supporting CINCs, and the JCS/National Military Command Center (NMCC) via the AUTODIN system [CENTCOM, *Emergency Action Procedures, Volume 1: System Description,* 20 February 1986, p. 5-1, released under the FOIA].

Automatic Digital Network (see · **AUTODIN**)

Automatic Voice Network (see **AUTOVON**)

AUTOSEVOCOM (Automatic Secure Voice Communications): System designation 493L. A worldwide DOD network of switching centers providing secure telephone communications. It provides DOD's primary encrypted voice communications capability, though it also serves certain non-DOD subscribers. Phase I was approved on 11 July 1967. AUTOSEVOCOM consists of 11 automatic government-owned switches; one leased automatic switch in the Pentagon; and 101 manual government-owned switches. It has about 1,500 DOD users, plus additional switches at the White House, Department of State, and the Central Intelligence Agency. Its two types of services are (1) encrypted call of superior voice quality within and between local areas at key locations, such as Washington and HQ SAC; and (2) lower quality encrypted calls. In 1976, work began on AUTO-SEVOCOM II to serve over 10,000 users. AUTOSEVOCOM is to be replaced by the **Secure Voice System (SVS)**.

AUTOVON (Automatic Voice Network): "The principal long-haul, unsecure voice communications network within the **Defense Communications System**" [*JCS Pub 1,* p. 43]. AUTOVON operates worldwide and provides the primary means of direct-dial, non-secure telephone connections between military forces, and between the National Command Authority (NCA) and the unified and specified commands. It was conceived to "meet the growing demands for command and control, operation, intelligence, logistic, diplomatic, and administrative voice communications" [DCA, *Overseas AUTOVON Network Control Procedures,* p. 1-1, released under the FOIA]. AUTOVON provides multi-level voice precedence calling capability and ensures 100 percent completion of Flash/Flash Override traffic under given JCS scenarios. AUTOVON incorporates many features to ensure a high degree of survivability, reliability, and routing flexibility not found in normal telephone networks. As of 30 June 1987, AUTOVON switch locations were as follows: 47 CONUS and 16 overseas, for a total of 63 (48 switching centers are leased from commercial carriers and 15 are government-owned).

AUTOVON Switching Centers

Air Force: Dau (Clark AB), Philippines; Feldberg, West Germany; Yokota, Japan; Hillingdon, UK; Torrejon, Spain; Langerkopf, West Germany; Martlesham-Heath, UK; Mt. Pateras, Greece; Mt. Vergine, Italy; and Schoenfeld, West Germany.

Army: Coltano, Italy; Corozal, Panama; Donnersberg, West Germany; and Ft. Buckner, Okinawa, Japan.

Navy: Finnegayan, Guam; and Wahiawa, HI.

Autumn Forge: The name given an annual series of NATO **exercises** held each fall under a common scenario. The exercises began in 1975 to link a number of training exercises together. Major Autumn Forge exercises that the United States sponsors and/or participates in include **REFORGER**, Crested Cap, Cold Fire, and Display Determination.

AUW   (Advanced   Underwater Weapon):   Euphemism used to describe naval anti-submarine weapons delivered by aircraft, specifically torpedoes and B57 nuclear depth bombs. The weapons are stored mainly at **P-3 Orion** operating bases and Naval Air Stations in AUW shops or modified AUW shops (MAUW shops). (see also **anti-submarine warfare**)

auxiliary oiler   (see **oiler**)

AV-8B (V/STOL) Harrier II: Marine Corps single-seat, single-engine, turbojet, subsonic, dual-capable, **vertical/short takeoff and landing** **(V/STOL)** light attack aircraft and follow on to the AV-8A/C Harrier. It was purchased to provide close air support of Marine forces in amphibious operations and direct support of ground forces from forward bases. It entered service in 1985. It can carry a 25 mm gatling gun, conventional bombs, **Sidewinder** air-to-air missiles, **Maverick** air-to-surface missiles, and a B61 nuclear bomb. Its combat radius varies from 100 nm to 650 nm depending on weapons load and takeoff/landing mode. It has a 2,500 nm ferry range. Its distinct vertical takeoff and landing ability allows it to operate from small unimproved fields or from large amphibious assault ships. There were approximately 100 aircraft in the operating inventory in 1988, and the Marine Corps' requirement is 13 squadrons of 20 aircraft each. AV-8Bs are deployed at MCAS Cherry Point, NC, and MCAS Yuma, AZ. The current aviation plans call for an increase to eight squadrons of 20 aircraft and a training squadron of 33 aircraft by 1990. The acquisition objective to support this plan is 328 aircraft. By 1988, however, a projected lower-than-expected attrition rate based on operational experience led the Navy to reduce its total acquisition objective. The Navy expects that fewer aircraft will still permit the operation of the same total number of squadrons. The prime contractor is McDonnell-Douglas, St. Louis, MO. Rolls Royce Ltd., Bristol, UK, is the engine contractor. To purchase 24 aircraft in both FY 1990 and FY 1991, the Navy is requesting $562.7 and $520.4 million, respectively.

The original Harrier was developed and built for the Royal Air Force and the Marine Corps in the early 1970s by Hawker Siddeley (now British Aerospace). The Marine Corps' 110 AV-8A/TAV-8As began service in 1971. The U.S. prime contractor was McDonnell Douglas Corp., St. Louis, MO, for the airframe, and Rolls Royce Ltd., of Bristol, UK, for the engine. Approximately one half of the AV-8A aircraft were subsequently modified to the AV-8C configuration, but all were phased out of active squadrons by 1987. The AV8A/Cs were not nuclear-certified. The AV-8B has a modified engine and airframe, a new graphite wing, and twice the range and payload of the AV-8A/C. Plans are underway to phase in a "night attack" AV-8B, beginning with aircraft number 160, which will add a new **forward-looking infrared (FLIR) system**, moving map display, digital control unit, modified cockpit lighting, night vision goggles, and avionics modifications.

The AV-8B replaced the AV-A/Cs in four squadrons (VMA-231, VMA-331, VMA-513, and VMA-542) and one training squadron (VMAT-203). It is also replacing the Marine Corps' four active **A-4M Skyhawk** squadrons. One A-4M squadron had shifted to AV-8Bs by spring 1988, and the transition will be finished by the early 1990s.

availability   (see **overhaul**)

AVB: Designation for aviation logistic support ship.

aviation: Combat arms branch of the Army.

AVM: Designation for guided missile ship.

AVT: Designation for **aircraft carrier, training**.

AWACS (see **Airborne Warning and Control System**, **E-3 Sentry AWACS**)

B

B: Prefix designating **1.** Vehicle capable of being launched from multiple environments. **2.** Bomber aircraft (e.g., B-1, B-52).

B-1/B-1B: Air Force supersonic, swing-wing, four-person, four-engine, long-range strategic bomber designed to replace the B-52. It is smaller than the B-52 but carries more weapons, with three weapons bays that provide the flexibility to launch B28, B61, and B83 nuclear bombs, as well as the **short-range attack missile (SRAM)** and a wide variety of conventional bombs, mines, and other weapons. A movable bulkhead was incorporated in the forward weapons bay of the last 91 aircraft produced to allow the plane to carry the **air-launched cruise missile**. The airplane is equipped with sophisticated offensive and defensive avionics and can penetrate defended territory at very low levels at supersonic speeds. The use of radar absorption materials and designs, and the AN/ALQ-161 electronic countermeasures suite, further decreases the detectability of the airplane.

The B-1B is assigned to the Strategic Air Command (SAC). The original B-1 program was canceled in June 1977 by President Carter, then rein-

troduced as the B-1B in October 1981 by the Reagan Administration. The first production B-1B entered testing at Edwards AFB, CA, in October 1984, and the first delivery to SAC at Dyess AFB, TX, occurred on 2 July 1985. The first B-1B became operational on 30 September 1986. The last of 100 B-1B bombers was delivered to the Air Force on 30 April 1988. Aircraft are deployed at Dyess AFB, TX; Ellsworth AFB, SD; Grand Forks AFB, ND; and McConnell AFB, KS. Since the bomber was deployed, there have been three B-1B crashes: 28 September 1987; 8 November 1988; and 17 November 1988. The 97 remaining bombers are assigned strategic and theater roles. Rockwell International, North American Aircraft Operations was the prime contractor. Eaton Corporation, AIL Division; Boeing Military Airplanes; and General Electric are other major contractors. The total cost for the program was approximately $35 billion.

B-2: Air Force long-range, all-weather, two-or-three-person, "stealth" strategic bomber under development for assignment to the Strategic Air Command (SAC) to replace the B-52. The B-2 has a length of 69 ft, but it is essentially a "flying wing" with a wingspan of 172 ft. On 22 November 1988, the first B-2 was rolled out at Air Force Plant 42 at Palmdale, CA. The B-2 will first be based at Whiteman AFB, MO. The B-2 uses new designs and technologies to reduce radar and infrared detectability. DOD announced its intention to develop such a bomber in August 1980. Current plans are to build 132 aircraft at a cost of $70–80 billion. Northrop Corporation and General Electric are the main contractors, with Boeing and LTV other major contractors. IOC is planned for 1993–94. The B-2 was called the Advanced Technology Bomber (ATB) while being developed.

B-52 Stratofortress: Air Force long-range, all-weather, air refuelable, six-person, strategic heavy bomber powered by eight turbojet engines. It can carry the entire range of nuclear bombs as well as **air-launched cruise missiles (ALCMs)** and **short-range attack missiles (SRAMs)**. Conventional weapon capabilities include **Harpoons**, bombs, and mines, among others. Missions in recent years have included sea surveillance flights, aerial minelaying and anti-surface warfare operations in cooperation with the Navy, and support for NATO exercises. B-52s have a top speed of 595 mph during high-altitude level flight and an unrefueled range of more than 7,500 miles.

There were eight versions of the B-52 (designated A–H), and a total of 742 (plus 2 experimental) aircraft were built. However, only two of the eight versions, the B-52G and B-52H, are currently deployed, with 261 operational aircraft. The B-52G

introduced some important changes, including a redesigned wing containing integral fuel tanks, fixed underwing external tanks, a new tail fin of reduced height, and a remotely controlled tail gun turret that allows the gunner to be positioned with the rest of the crew. B-52G deliveries began in February 1959, and 193 were built. The B-52H, the final version of the B-52, has improved turbofan engines that give it a greater unrefueled range, and improved defensive armament, including a 20 mm **Vulcan** multibarrel tail gun. B-52H deliveries began in May 1961, and 102 were built.

During the early 1970s, all B-52G/Hs were modified to carry SRAMs. In addition, all G/H models were equipped with an AN/ASQ-151 electro-optical viewing system (EVS) using **forward-looking infrared (FLIR)** and low-light level TV sensors to improve low-level flight capabilities. Under an Air Force improvement program begun in 1974, these models have been progressively updated with Phase IV avionics. These improvements include ALQ-122 SNOE (smart noise operation equipment) and ALQ-155(V) advanced **electronic countermeasures (ECM)**; an **AFSATCOM** kit permitting worldwide communications via satellite; a Dalmo Victor ALR-46 digital radar warning receiver; Westinghouse ALQ-135 pulse Doppler tail warning radar; and an improved ITT Avionics ALQ-117 Pave Mint or ALQ-172 ECM jamming system. The G/H models also have been fitted with digital-based solid-state offensive avionics systems (OASs) that include inertial guidance, **terrain contour matching**

(TERCOM) guidance, and micropro-cessors to upgrade the aircraft's navigation and weapons delivery systems. This improvement program was completed in 1986.

Two B-52G wings have been assigned to support conventional operations by employing airpower over great distances at short notice. With the deployment of the B-2 bomber, the B-52s will be primarily ALCM carriers. A typical profile would see multiple ALCM launches at high altitude, often followed by B-52 low-level descent to attack additional targets using SRAMs and bombs. In December 1984, the Air Force completed deployment of the ALCM on 98 on-line B-52Gs, each with 12 external cruise missiles. As B-1Bs entered service, the Air Force also began deployment of ALCMs on 95 B-52Hs. Completion of this program is scheduled for FY 1990. Full-scale production of the **Common Strategic Rotary Launcher (CSRL)**, which will permit internal carriage of eight additional ALCMs in the B-52H, is under way. Full operational capability for this system at all SAC bases is scheduled for late summer 1993.

All 69 non-ALCM-modified B-52Gs, equipping four SAC units, had assumed a primary conventional role by 1 October 1988. They achieved full operational capability in June 1985, supporting naval anti-surface warfare operations through Harpoon employment (each B-52G can carry 8–12 Harpoons in underwing clusters). Two full squadrons are equipped for this role; one is based at Loring AFB, ME, for Atlantic operations, and the other at Andersen AFB, Guam, for Pacific operations.

Additionally, flight testing began in 1986 of an integrated conventional stores management system (ICSMS) for installation on the 69 non-ALCM B-52Gs. The ICSMS enables aircraft normally configured for the carriage of nuclear weapons to carry conventional weapons by rearranging data stored in the weapon systems computer, using a preprogrammed removable software cassette. Plans call for an increase in the number of B-52G/Hs assigned to the dual-role mission and capable of both nuclear and theater warfare, although the FY 1990 budget calls for the deactivation of one squadron beginning in FY 1990.

The prime contractor for the original B-52 was Boeing. Two hundred seventy-seven aircraft were built in Seattle, WA; another 467 were built at Wichita, KS. The unit flyaway cost was approximately $50 million, and it costs over $7 million a year to operate and maintain each B-52.

back channel: 1. General officers' personal and sensitive message traffic, not handled by ordinary communications centers. Back channels give officers the opportunity to express themselves frankly and off the record. **2.** Informal communications between two countries, particularly during negotiations, that rely on personal and private discussions outside of the formal framework.

backscattering   (see **Over-the-horizon (OTH) radar**)

backup aircraft authorization: Aircraft over and above the primary authorized aircraft to permit scheduled and unscheduled maintenance, modifications, inspections, and repair without a reduction of aircraft available for the operational mission. No operating resources are allocated for these aircraft in the defense budget.

Baker-Charlie: VHF communications system operated by the Secret Service and connected to the **National Emergency Airborne Command Post**.

Baker-Nunn camera: Satellite-tracking camera used for long-range observations. Most radar systems can track satellites up to 3,000 miles above the earth; above this altitude, optical sensors must be used. NORAD operates six Baker-Nunn deep space cameras, which are capable of photographing a basketball-sized object from 20,000 miles. The cameras are located at Pulmosan, South Korea; Mt. John, New Zealand; San Vito dei Normanni, Italy; and Edwards AFB, CA. A Canadian camera is located at St. Margarets, New Brunswick. The Baker-Nunn camera is being replaced by the **Ground-based Electro-optical Detection System (GEODSS)**.

ballistic missile: A pilotless missile propelled into space by one or more rocket boosters and designed to follow a trajectory determined predominantly by gravity and aerodynamic drag after thrust is terminated. Ballistic missiles typically fly outside the atmosphere for a substantial portion of their flight paths and are unpowered during most of the flight. The missile is most vulnerable during the boost phase, when it moves relatively slowly, laden as it is with warheads, decoys, and fuel.

Guidance and control of a ballistic missile are as follows

- Pre-launch: desired missile position and velocity are entered into the flight computer;
- Boost: booster rocket propels the missile into the atmosphere; an inertial sensing system measures and records changes in velocity, position, and altitude;
- Post-boost: releases missile at correct velocity and altitude; changes altitude with thrusters and torques; and
- Terminal: reentry vehicle(s) coasts in an ellipse until entering the atmosphere.

Currently deployed major U.S. ballistic missiles include **Minuteman** II and III, **MX**, **Lance**, **Pershing** II, **Poseidon**, and **Trident** I. Most of the costs of ballistic missiles are for the boosters and launchers. (see also **ICBM (intercontinental ballistic missile), intermediate-range ballistic missile, modern large ballistic missile, older heavy ballistic missile launcher, medium-range ballistic missile, short-range ballistic missile, submarine-launched ballistic missile)**

Ballistic Missile Defense (BMD): A system of measures for defending against an attack by ballistic missiles. These defense systems used to be called anti-ballistic missile (ABM) systems, but this usage declined after the demise of the **Sentinel** and **Safeguard** ABM systems in the early 1970s. The first types of BMD systems used by both the United States and the Soviet Union were ground-based interceptors and radars designed to intercept ballistic **reentry vehicles (RVs)** as they descended to earth. Past U.S. systems in this design include the Nike surface-to-air missile; BAMBI (ballistic missile boost intercept); Dynosoar, a shuttle-like vehicle; the Saint sensor; Sentinel, an ABM system relying on nuclear interceptors to protect population centers; and Safeguard, the Sentinel system reconfigured to protect Minuteman missile silos. These systems were mostly point defense systems, meaning they were designed to defend localized positions such as missile silos or cities, rather than area defense systems which attempt to defend whole territories. The U.S. ABM system at Grand Forks, ND, was dismantled after the signing of the **ABM Treaty** and after expenditures of $5.7 billion.

Present-day BMD systems are designed to intercept RVs at all stages of flight, not just the reentry stage. BMD can operate in the following forms: completely preferential, semipreferential, and random subtractive. In a completely preferential system, only selected RVs are marked to be destroyed. A semipreferential system would shoot at selected RVs previously determined to be hostile. A random subtractive system would shoot at as many RVs as possible without attempting to distinguish among them.

A theoretically effective BMD system would be composed of the following:

- boost-phase defensive layer,
- sensors/computers to discriminate between decoys and RVs,
- sensors to function during attack,
- battle-management computers and software,
- target-tracking system,
- space-based power supply stations,
- protection for space-based BMD, and
- ground-based, exo-atmospheric interceptors for the mid-course, and endo-atmospheric interceptors for the terminal layer.

Current U.S. systems that could contribute to BMD missions are

- **BMEWS** radars in Alaska, Greenland, and the United Kingdom;
- the **PAVE PAWS** phased array radars in the United States; and
- **Defense Support Program (DSP)** early warning satellites.

(see also **Strategic Defense Initiative**)

Ballistic Missile Early Warning System   (see **BMEWS**)

ballistic missile submarine (see fleet ballistic missile)

bargaining chip: An arms control term meaning a weapons system or other military asset that one party expresses a willingness to downgrade or discard in return for concessions by the other party; used pejoratively in reference to a weapons system being developed or deployed specifically to achieve leverage in arms control negotiations, but whose stated military need is questionable.

Barnacle: Code name for a Navy attack submarine reconnaissance program, formerly called Holystone. The operations involved include the covert collection of electronic, acoustic, telemetric, and photographic intelligence against Soviet and other enemy submarines, as well as operations close to the ports and shores of foreign countries to collect intelligence information on land. Operations involve deep penetration of enemy territorial waters and tapping of underwater communications cables. Thirty-eight nuclear-powered Sturgeon class attack submarines were specially equipped with the AN/WLR-6 "Waterboy" Signals Intelligence collection system and the newer AN/WLQ-4 **Sea Nymph** system for the conduct of Barnacle missions [Jeffrey Richelson, *The U.S. Intelligence Community*, 2d ed., pp. 190–191].

Base Air Defense Ground Environment (BADGE): Operational early warning and weapons control system that provides tactical air control of Japanese air interceptor forces. BADGE is tied into U.S. networks.

Hughes/Fullerton and Nippon Aviotronics were prime contractors. (see also **air defense ground environment**)

Base and Installation Security System (see **BISS**)

base surge: The cloud that rolls out from the bottom of the column produced by a subsurface burst of a nuclear weapon. For underwater bursts, the surge is in effect a cloud of liquid droplets that has the property of a homogeneous fluid. For subsurface land bursts, the surge is made up of small, solid particles but still behaves like a fluid.

basic load: The quantity of ammunition a unit is required to have available and able to transport for its weapon systems. As a unit's basic load is consumed in combat, it must be replenished from an ammunition transfer point or ammunition storage point at the division level.

battalion (bn): Army and Marine Corps formation, subordinate to a **brigade**, grouped in different combinations to form the types of Army **divisions**. There are nine types of battalions in the current Army structure, each with individual characteristics and composition. Each battalion is composed of a headquarters and two or more **companies** or **batteries**, depending on its mission. Armored cavalry or air cavalry units of equivalent size are called **squadrons**. Battalions are composed of 500–880 personnel.

A battalion may operate as part of a **regiment** or brigade, or as a separate unit with both administrative and tactical functions. Normally, a battalion is commanded by a Lieutenant Colonel. Battalions are also called maneuver or combat maneuver battalions. Although the divisional cavalry squadron and the attack helicopter battalion have always had a combat mission, it is only with their recent pairing in the divisional combat aviation brigade—a maneuver brigade—that they have been labeled as maneuver battalions.

Battalion Types

• Air Assault Infantry Battalion.
• Airborne Infantry Battalion.
• Armored Cavalry Squadron.

- Attack Helicopter Battalion.
- Infantry Battalion.
- Light Infantry Battalion.
- Mechanized Infantry Battalion.
- Motorized Infantry Battalion.
- Tank Battalion.

Battalion Landing Team (BLT): Marine infantry battalion and combat and service reinforcements, specially organized for an amphibious landing.

battery: 1. An Army or Marine Corps artillery unit, equivalent in size to a **company**. **2.** A naval ship's guns of the same caliber or used for the same purpose (e.g., main, secondary, and anti-aircraft batteries).

battle force: A general term referring to a type of naval **task organization** composed of aircraft carriers, surface ships, and submarines, and assigned to numbered fleets. A battle force is subdivided into battle groups (e.g., carrier battle group).

battle group: A general term referring to a naval **task organization** of Navy ships centered around at least one aircraft carrier. (see also **carrier battle group**)

battle management: 1. A network or system of command and control, personnel, equipment, and procedures for coordination of all aspects of a defense system. **2.** Battle Management and Command, Control, and Communications (BM/C3) Program of the **Strategic Defense Initiative**.

battleship (BB): Navy conventionally powered, major surface warship.

The Navy operates four Iowa (BB-61) class battleships. Battleships have several missions. As the capital ships in battleship battle groups (BBBGs), they can substitute for aircraft carriers to ease the peacetime deployment schedules of carriers. They can also operate with **carrier battle groups** in battles at sea or amphibious operations, providing support with their 16 inch guns, **Harpoon** missiles, and **Tomahawk** cruise missiles. In wartime, plans call for one battleship to operate with the Sixth Fleet in the Mediterranean, one to deploy with the Second Fleet in the Atlantic, and two to be assigned to the Seventh Fleet for use in the western Pacific and Indian Oceans, including one operating in the South China Sea. (see also **Iowa class**)

battle staff exercise (BSX): An Air Force or Strategic Air Command exercise designed to provide ground and airborne battle staff personnel with experience and training in **emergency action procedures** and the **Crisis Action System**. The exercise objectives are to evaluate the transition to battle staff operations during an escalating crisis; to train personnel in procedures required for managing forces in SIOP execution; to evaluate procedures for responding to emergency action messages; and to evaluate continuity of operations and command, control, and communications during all phases of a nuclear war, including recovery, reconstitution, retargeting, and restrike [SAC, *SAC Exercise Program*, SACR 55–38, Vol. I, p. 2–1, released under the FOIA].

BB: Designation for **battleship**.

beachmaster: In amphibious operations, the unit or officer designated to take charge of logistic activities on the beach once the assault phase of the landing has been conducted.

Beartrap: Code name for **P-3C Orion** planes specially modified for the collection, recording, and analysis of **acoustic intelligence (ACINT)**. The plane's primary targets are Soviet submarines, sonar systems, and underwater communications. The P-3Cs have a range of 4,000 nm, an operational altitude of 200–10,000 ft, and an endurance of 12 hours. There are presently five of these modified P-3Cs. They operate from Patrol Squadron Special Project Unit One (NAS Brunswick, ME) and Patrol Squadron Special Project Unit Two (NAS Barbers Point, HI) [Jeffrey Richelson, *The U.S. Intelligence Community*, 2d ed., p. 203].

Benelux Sub Area: Major subordinate command of NATO's **Allied Command Channel**.

Headquarters
The Hague, Netherlands
(APO New York 09159)

Bent Spear: Code name for a **nuclear weapon incident**.

BIDDS (Base Information Digital Distribution System): Air Force program to integrate several communications elements at Air Force bases worldwide under a single manager. BIDDS combines telephone switches and associated automated test equipment, on-base distribution systems, certain end instruments, and a telecommunications management and control subsystem (TMCS). BIDDS also addresses follow-on maintenance, life cycle support, and configuration management to ensure cost-effective logistic support. BIDDS will support on-base common user requirements, including those of the on-base medical center. Air Force responsibilities for the European Telephone System (ETS) and the Defense Switched Network (DSN) will be accomplished under BIDDS. In FY 1988, BIDDS replaced the Scope Exchange Initiative to replace/upgrade leased telephone systems at selected CONUS bases [Air Force Communications Command, *Information Handbook*, prepared by the Directorate of Cost, DCS Comptroller, July 1987].

Biennial Planning, Programming, and Budgeting System (see **Planning, Programming, and Budgeting System**)

Big Bird (see **Hexagon**)

Bigeye: Binary chemical glide bomb that can be dropped from aircraft up to four miles away from the target. On impact, the bomb releases a cloud of lethal chemical droplets that last for some time, killing troops in the area well after the initial attack. Bigeye does not contain a bursting charge. Initial delivery of unfilled bombs began in December 1988, with full production beginning in April 1989. Bigeye replaces aircraft-mounted spray tanks, with which aircraft fly low and slow over enemy territory spraying chemicals. The other two systems to deploy new chemical weapons to U.S. forces are the 155 mm artillery projectile for short-range use, and the **Multiple Launch Rocket System (MLRS)**, both of which are also **binary chemical munitions**.

Big Noise: Exercise term to designate an **air defense emergency**.

Big Safari: Code name for RC-135 signals intelligence missions of the Strategic Air Command.

billet: "A programmed manpower structure space that defines by **grade** and **occupation** a job to be performed which is associated with a specific unit or organization" [DOD, *Manpower Requirements Report FY 1989*, March 1988, p. B-1]. (see also **manpower**)

binary chemical munition: Chemical weapon in which a lethal chemical agent is formed from two nonlethal components by means of a chemical reaction caused by forces created during flight of a weapon to a target. The binary design is advantageous over conventional unitary chemical weapons in safety, transportation, production, storage, and handling. It is lethal only if the two components are mixed.

The Army is pursuing the development of two binary chemical munitions — a binary chemical warhead for the **Multiple Launch Rocket System (MLRS)**, and a 155 mm binary chemical artillery projectile. Both the Air Force and the Navy are developing the **Bigeye** binary chemical bomb and are scheduled to field the new weapon in the early 1990s.

The 155 mm binary chemical artillery projectile entered initial production in 1988. In 1989, the MLRS binary warhead was in the engineering development phase. The MLRS binary warhead is to complement the 155 mm projectile by providing greater range and area coverage than front line artillery and to engage rear area military targets.

Contractors for the Army systems include the Marquardt Company, Van Nuys, CA; the Morton Thiokol Corp., Shreveport, LA; the Combustion Engineering Operations and Maintenance Corp., Pine Bluff, AK; the LTV Corp., Dallas, TX; KDI Corp., Cincinnati, OH; and the Parsons Co., San Diego, CA. (see also **chemical and biological agents**)

biographical intelligence: Foreign intelligence information on the views, traits, habits, skills, importance, relationships, health, and curriculum vitae of foreign personalities such as government officials, corporate officials, or terrorists. The information is used as part of preparations for negotiations and government meetings and for the formulation of offensive **counterintelligence** and **covert operations**.

biological weapon: Living microorganisms (such as bacteria and viruses), toxic agents derived from dead microorganisms, or plant growth regulators used to produce casualties in humans, animals, and/or plants. (see also **chemical and biological agents**)

Biological Weapons Convention: Convention formally known as the "Convention on the Prohibition of the

Development, Production, and Stockpiling of Bacteriological (Biological) and Toxin Weapons and on Their Destruction." Signed in Washington, London, and Moscow on 10 April 1972 and ratified by the United States on 22 January 1975, the convention entered into force on 26 March 1975. Over 100 countries have signed the convention. The convention prohibits the development, production, stockpiling, and means of delivery of biological and toxic agents and weapons "with no justification for prophylactic, protective, or other peaceful purposes" (Article I), and it mandates their destruction or conversion to peaceful uses. The convention gained fame for being the first multilateral total disarmament agreement since 1945, but it was criticized for its lack of verification methods. The lack of military uses for the weapons themselves has been cited as the prime reason for treaty compliance. Key provisions are

- Existing weapons of this type are to be destroyed within nine months of the treaty's coming to force;
- The indirect or direct transfer of these weapons to another state is forbidden;
- Compliance complaints are to be lodged with the U.N. Security Council;
- The convention does not limit or detract from but enhances the obligations of the **Geneva Protocol** of 1925, which prohibited the use of chemical and/or bacteriological warfare;
- Scientific access to the use of biological weapons for peaceful purposes is to be encouraged;

- The convention is open to all states for signature and amendment; and
- The convention is of unlimited duration.

Review conferences were held in 1980 and 1986 in Geneva. In the spring of 1987, a meeting of scientific and technical experts submitted a report on modes to exchange information and data.

U.S. accusations of Soviet noncompliance include the use of biological/toxic weapons in Afghanistan; transfer to Vietnam of toxic agents and their use in Laos and Kampuchea; and an outbreak of anthrax in the Soviet city of Sverdlovsk in 1979, which killed several hundred people (and led to the suspicion that the Soviet Union was producing biological weapons). Soviet accusations of U.S. violations include the U.S. refusal to enter into talks with the Soviet Union on a ban of chemical weapons; negative U.S. reaction to a draft treaty banning chemical weapons; and new production of chemical weapons.

BISS (Base and Installation Security System): Nickname for the Air Force Physical Security System. BISS provides for the development of perimeter area intrusion detection systems for the protection of Air Force resources. A related program known as SAFE provides for the acquisition and deployment of Air Force intrusion detection sensor programs worldwide. (see also **physical security**)

Black Berets: Nickname for the Army's 75th Infantry Regiment (**Rangers**).

Blackbird: Nickname for **SR-71** strategic reconnaissance aircraft.

black box: **1.** "A term which generally refers to electronic equipment, usually relatively small, that can be readily inserted into, or removed from, a specified place in a large system without benefit of extensive knowledge of its internal structure. The input and output requirements, and the transfer function, are usually all that are known" *[NWP 3].* **2.** Onboard electronic equipment, so called because of the usual shape and color of the container. The term has come to mean electronic equipment in general.

Black Hawk (see **UH-60 Black Hawk**)

blackout: The disturbance of radio and radar signals caused by nuclear detonation; also the severe absorption of radio frequency signals near a nuclear fireball.

black phone: Emergency communications link to the **National Military Command Center (NMCC)** from the **NORAD Cheyenne Mountain Complex (NCMC)**, activated solely by the NMCC.

black program: Unofficial nickname for a highly classified item "hidden" within the defense budget. An item may be associated with a stated dollar amount but only be identified by a code name or nondescript title to conceal its specific nature. Other black programs may be named but costs associated with the programs are considered classified. A program may be designated black in order for it to proceed without formal Congressional or public support or with secret presidential and Congressional consent. The current list of large black programs includes the stealth technology programs such as the B-2 bomber, F-117A stealth fighter, and the Advanced Cruise Missile, and portions of the Strategic Defense Initiative. Collectively, such programs are referred to as the "black budget." The number of black programs is unknown, as is the size of the black budget, but *The National Journal* estimates the budget totaled $5.5 billion in FY 1981 and $22 billion in FY 1988. It is estimated that up to 20 percent of the FY 1990 defense budget is hidden in black [David C. Morrison, "Pentagon's Top Secret 'Black' Budget Has Skyrocketed During Reagan Years," *National Journal*, 1 March 1986, p. 492; "Dancing in the Dark," *National Journal*, 11 April 1987, p. 867]. (see also **special access program**)

blast: The brief and rapid movement of air vapor or fluid away from a center of outward pressure, and, in an explosion or in the combustion of rocket fuel, the pressure accompanying this movement. This term is commonly used as a synonym for explosion, but the two terms are distinguishable.

blast yield: That portion of the total energy of a nuclear detonation that manifests as a **blast** or shock wave. Blast is often expressed in terms of overpressure.

Blind Bat: Program for the relay of selected **emergency action mes-**

sages by the Federal Aviation Administration (FAA) to bombers and aerial refueling aircraft during the positive control launch phase of their operations. The messages are transmitted from the JCS to the Federal Aviation Administration (FAA) via **AUTODIN**, then formatted and transmitted to FAA flight service stations for further ground-to-air transmission.

blockade: A military operation that attempts to isolate a place or region, whether the nation of registry is participating in the conflict or not. Of the different degrees of blockade, one type is absolute; its objective is to cut off enemy communications and commerce. The target nation may consider such a total blockade an "act of war." A lesser degree of blockade has been called a "pacific blockade." This type may or may not be perceived as an act of war. It is often limited to carriers flying the flag of the state against which retaliatory measures are taken. International law has generally held that to be meaningful, a blockade must be physically enforced at the spot (i.e., a neutral nation blockade runner is not subject to capture merely because she had, sometime previously, run a blockade).

BLU: Designation for a bomb or mine unit (e.g., BLU-35).

Blue Eagle: Code name for the U.S. Pacific Command **airborne command post**, a part of the **Worldwide Airborne Command Post (WWABNCP)**. Blue Eagle was activated in 1965 and logged 40,000 hours of continuous airborne alert from 1965–69. It consists of four EC-135J aircraft and a van with ground access to the **Defense Communications System**. The aircraft are based at Hickam AFB, HI.

blue out: The inability of sonar systems to operate effectively due to the interference caused by an underwater nuclear explosion. An underwater nuclear explosion releases large amounts of thermal and nuclear radiation, most of which is absorbed by the water surrounding the explosion area. During the early stages of the explosion, the bomb attains a very high temperature (millions of degrees) and very high pressure. Energy generated by the bomb is transfered to the layer of water closest to the bomb, which is heated and compressed and which then heats and compresses the next outward layer. A wave of compression is formed that moves outward from the bomb. Soon after the burst, a bubble of vaporized water with radioactive debris at its center is formed. A second shock wave begins after this bubble reaches its minimum volume. This wave has a lower peak overpressure but a longer duration than the initial shock wave. The second cycle of bubble expansion and contraction then begins. These shock waves make the use of sonar impossible [DNA, *Capabilities of Nuclear Weapons*, DNA-EM 1, Part II, 1 July 1972, released under the FOIA].

BMEWS (Ballistic Missile Early Warning System): Model designation 474L. Air Force radar system, and the major sensor for confirming **Defense Support Program** early warning satellite detection of ballistic missile launches and for providing attack assessment and identification of time-urgent targets under attack. The detection fans that emanate from the giant football field-sized radar antennae consist of narrow beams of energy at two different angles of elevation. A hostile missile passing successively through the two fans gives enough information for computers to establish position, direction, and velocity. BMEWS is composed of three early warning radar sites to detect and warn of ICBM attacks from the north and the east against CONUS and southern Canada. BMEWS also covers the Arctic Ocean to warn of ballistic missile attacks against northern Europe. The BMEWS radars would be the first ground-based radars to detect a Soviet ICBM attack, giving 15 minutes pre-attack warning. First deployed in 1960, BMEWS consists of 12 primary radars operated by NORAD at three sites: Thule, Greenland; Clear, AK; and Fylingdales, United Kingdom. All high-speed data circuits from BMEWS travel to NORAD via redundant transmission facilities. RAF Fylingdales transmits data to both NORAD and RAF operations centers. BMEWS also includes two troposcatter communications systems and a rearward communications system. Raytheon phased array radars are replacing standard radars at Thule and Fylingdales. BMEWS was operated by SAC until the creation of **Air Force Space Command**, which took over responsibility. BMEWS is augmented by the **Cobra Dane** radar at Shemya, AK.

Bollard: Former code name of the Navy's Holystone submarine reconnaissance system, now called **Barnacle**.

bomber: Aircraft specifically designed to carry and drop bombs. Long-range or heavy bombers are capable of a tactical operating radius of over 2,500 miles; medium bombers have an operating radius of between 1,000 and 2,500 miles; and light bombers have an operating radius of under 1,000 miles. U.S. long-range bombers are **B-52** and **B-1B** (and the **B-2** when deployed). The only U.S. medium-range bomber is the **FB-111**.

boomer: Nickname used to describe a ballistic missile submarine.

booster: The section of a rocket that provides thrust after launch. The booster lifts the payload from surface to ballistic trajectory in the atmosphere. (see also **Titan**, **expendable launch vehicle**)

boost phase: The phase of a **ballistic missile** trajectory from launch to burnout of the final stage. Both the booster and sustainer engines operate until the missile reaches an altitude of about 1200 km (which normally takes about 3–5 minutes in current ICBMs). At that point, rocket-powered flight ends, and the missile continues on its flight. Other phases of a missile flight (mid-course and reentry) can take up to 30 minutes. During the boost phase, the rocket emits an easily detected trail of hot exhaust gases. Defensive systems using infrared sensors are able to identify missiles by this trail. Solid-fuel rockets burn fuel faster than do liquid-fuel rockets and so leave a less discernable signature for detection.

Boost Surveillance and Tracking System (BSTS): Major **SDI** research program to develop new early warning satellites capable of detecting and identifying ballistic missiles and other objects entering space while at the same time being survivable to attack. Formerly known as the Advanced Warning System, BSTS is a program that seeks to replace the current **Defense Support Program (DSP)**. Like DSP, the BSTS infrared sensors will detect and track missiles in their boost phases; they will not track MIRVed warheads released in the post-boost phase. However, BSTS could provide tracking information to be relayed for use by post-boost-phase interceptors.

The main BSTS equipment is a large telescope and a wide field of view infrared sensor. The system will be designed to identify targets within seconds after the boosters clear atmospheric effects, by using plume intensity and launch profile information to categorize targets. BSTS will have satellite-to-satellite communications crosslink capability, as well as downlink with ground terminals, other SDI platforms, and perhaps other DOD satellites. The BSTS satellites will most likely be launched on Titan IV boosters.

The transition from the DSP to BSTS could take place as early as the mid- to late-1990s. BSTS development and deployment costs are estimated at $8 billion. Full-scale devel-

opment funds for the program are expected to appear in the Air Force budget for FY 1992. The Air Force and the SDIO are working on the program jointly. The Air Force plans to begin its purchase with four satellites and two ground terminals (one fixed and one mobile), and to eventually purchase six satellites. Lockheed and Grumman are competing for this development and production contract.

BQM-34   (see **Firebee**)

Bradley Fighting Vehicle   (see **M-2 Bradley Fighting Vehicle**)

branch: 1. A subdivision of any military organization.   **2.** A geographically separate element of an organization that performs all or part of the organization's primary functions, only on a smaller scale.   **3.** A functional arm or service of the Army for assignment of personnel. The branch system of the Army provides a framework for some compartmentation of missions and broad functions, thereby facilitating the development and adaptation of weapons, tactics, and techniques, especially in the areas of education, training, assignment, and overall career development. The branch system also facilitates the provision of personnel and units having the specialized technical and administrative skills necessary for planning and support of combat operations. The system promotes morale and esprit de corps; branch identity and traditions are a source of pride and psychological support to the branches' units and members. The career field branches, in the order of official anniversary dates, are **Infantry, Adjutant General Corps, (Army) Corps of Engineers, Finance Corps, Quartermaster Corps, Air Defense Artillery, Artillery, Armor, Ordnance Corps,** Signal Corps, **Chemical Corps, Military Police** Corps, Transportation Corps, **Military Intelligence, Aviation,** and **Civil Affairs.** The special branches are every corps of the Army Medical Department (Medical Corps, Army Nurse Corps, Dental Corps, Veterinary Corps, Medical Service Corps, and Army Medical Specialist Corps), the **Chaplain Corps,** and the **Judge Advocate General Corps.** (see also **combat arms, combat support, combat service support**)

Bravo Net: Medium-power HF single-sideband radio system operated by the Strategic Air Command.

breakout: A change in the military balance caused when one party violates provisions of an arms control treaty quantitatively or qualitatively and improves its forces, either before being detected or after abrogating the terms of an agreement. In general, the term is used to express the concern that a party to a treaty could be surprised by a sudden improvement in capabilities deployed by the other side even though an agreement wasn't officially broken.

breeder: A **nuclear reactor** that produces more atomic fuel than it consumes while generating power. A nonfissionable isotope, bombarded by neutrons, is transformed into a fissionable material, such as plutonium, that can be used as fuel.

brevity code: A code used to shorten frequently used unclassified phrases, sentences, or groups of sentences. It is not employed for information or communication security purposes, however: "[T]his type of code must be used in conjunction with a means of encipherment to provide security" [Army, *EW [Electronic Warfare] —A Weapons Qualification Course,* Training Circular 100-32-1, September 1977, p. B1].

Brick Bat: Urgency designator established by the JCS to show the relative priority between programs. Brick Bat gives defense contractors precedence over other commercial companies in obtaining critical materials. Brick Bat has higher priority than **CUE-CAP**.

briefing: A type of military oral or written report designed to impart information, obtain a decision, exchange information, or review details. The objective common to every briefing is to facilitate a rapid, coordinated response. There are four types of military briefings:

• *Information briefing*:   To present facts to keep listeners abreast of the current situation or to supply requested information. It does not require a decision.
• *Decision briefing*: The same as an information briefing except with a more comprehensive scope. It is presented in order to make a decision on a course of action.
• *Staff briefing*: Used at every military echelon to keep a commander and staff mutually informed of the

current situation. The anticipated response is a coordinated effort.

- *Mission briefing*: Designed especially for combat operations to impart combat last-minute information, to give specific instructions, or to instill an appreciation of the overall mission.

brigade (bde): Major combat unit of the Army, subordinate to a division and larger than a **battalion**. It consists of a tactical headquarters, 2–5 attached maneuver battalions, and combat support and combat service support units, depending on its mission. It is capable of independent and semi-independent operations. Brigades are usually organized as battalion task forces, with each grouping under one commander, to conduct a specific operation or mission. A brigade is commanded by a Colonel or Brigadier General and is composed of 4,000–5,000 personnel. (see also **regiment, maneuver brigade, separate brigade**)

Bright Star: JCS-sponsored, biannual, large-scale field training exercise **(FTX)** conducted by U.S. Central Command (CENTCOM) in Southwest Asia. The exercise "demonstrates the U.S. capability to project military forces into that region should the need arise" [JCS, *FY 1989 Military Posture*, p. 74]. Bright Star 83 was the first of the Bright Star exercises. Bright Star 89 emphasized rapid deployment, mobility, host nation agreements, and the combat readiness of CONUS-based forces allocated to CENTCOM.

Brilliant Pebbles: Nickname for **SDI** research program to develop space-based miniaturized interceptors, with possible offensive uses as well against satellites and strategic mobile missiles. The program has an estimated cost of $10 billion. R&D is being conducted at Lawrence Livermore National Laboratory, Livermore, CA. The program is presently undergoing two years of sounding rocket tests. Competing with Brilliant Pebbles is the space-based interceptor, a more sophisticated and costlier program also being developed under SDI auspices.

Brim Frost: JCS-sponsored, biannual, large-scale, joint field training exercise **(FTX)** conducted by Alaskan Air Command/Joint Task Force Alaska and held in Alaska. It is the largest-scale military maneuver to practice Alaskan defense, and the largest regular defense exercise for North America.

Broken Arrow: Code word for a **nuclear weapon accident**.

Bronco   (see **OV-10 Bronco**)

budget authority: Authority conferred by law to enter into obligations (i.e., appropriations) that will result in immediate or future outlays involving government funds. Budget authority is usually associated with the year the authority takes effect. Budget authority is composed of New Obligational Authority (NOA) (the amount Congress appropriates for agency use over and above earlier appropriations, and other funds the agency may have or expects to have from other sources), plus loan authority (the authority to incur obligations for loans; for example, debt payment on mortgages for military family housing)

budget estimate submission (BES): The service budget proposal (also called the budget submission), part of the **Planning, Programming, and Budgeting System**. The BES is derived from the **Program Objective Memorandum**, as approved and adjusted by the **Program Decision Memorandum** of the **Defense Resources Board**. The OSD provides updated guidance on projected budget levels and anticipated economic assumptions. After further review by OSD and OMB to reprice the items and resolve any outstanding differences, the BES becomes part of the President's annual budget submission to Congress. Military service and DOD agency estimates are based on approved programs in the Program Decision Memoranda and most recent fiscal guidelines.

buff: The former nickname of a report prepared by a Directorate in the Joint Staff and circulated to other Directorates in the Joint Staff and to the Service points of contact for coordination and approval. The name is taken from the color of the paper. An "instant buff" referred to a buff report without a **flimsy**, when substantive agreement existed or time limitations precluded full processing. A July 1985 change in JCS procedures eliminated use of the "buff" name.

build-down: A nuclear arms control proposal introduced in early 1983 by Senators William Cohen and Sam Nunn that called on the United States and the Soviet Union each to eliminate "two older nuclear warheads for each newly deployed nuclear warhead." The proposal provided for reductions in the number of weapons while modernization was occurring. On 4 October 1983, President Reagan announced that the United States would incorporate a more detailed form of the proposal into the U.S. **START** negotiating position, but the Soviets broke off negotiations with the U.S. deployment of the **Pershing II** and **Ground-launched cruise missile** in Europe, and the position was never fully developed.

Bullseye: Code name for the Navy's network of land-based high-frequency direction-finding (HFDF) ocean surveillance stations operated by the **Naval Security Group Command**. Formally known as Bulldog and Classic Bullseye, its mission is monitoring naval activity. It operates in the Caribbean Sea; the Atlantic, Indian, and Pacific Oceans; and the Mediterranean Sea. There are 22 stations within the Atlantic and Pacific Fleets assigned to support U.S. Naval Forces Europe. Most stations employ the AN/FRD-10 antenna array. Stations include Card Sound, FL; Sugar Grove, WV; Northwest, VA; and Winter Harbor, ME, in the Atlantic; Edzell, UK; Keflavik, Iceland; and Terceira, Azores, Portugal, in Europe; and Diego Garcia; Clark AB, Philippines; Torri Station, Okinawa, Japan; Guam; Adak, AK; Wahiawa, HI; Imperial Beach, CA; and Skaggs Island, CA, in the Pacific.

BUNO (Bureau Number): An un-hyphenated serial number, not ex-ceed ing six digits, used to identify individual airframes within the naval aircraft inventory. Each number is unique to a particular airframe.

Burke class guided missile destroyer (DDG 51): Next-generation Navy guided missile destroyer under devel-opment for deployment in the 1990s, officially called the Arleigh Burke class. The Burke class is a gas turbine ship armed with a **vertical launch system (VLS)** able to carry 90 missiles, in-cluding **Tomahawk** sea-launched cruise missiles, **Standard missile 2 (SM-2)** surface-to-air missiles, and **ASROC**. Special features include an AN/SPY-1D phased array radar, AN/SQS-53C sonar, and AN/SQR-19 TACTAS. The ship is also armed with a 5 inch/54 rapid fire gun with the Seafire fire control system, the Pha-lanx close-in-weapon system, and the AN/SLQ-32 electronic warfare system. Builders are Bath Iron Works, Bath, ME, and Ingalls Shipbuilding Division. Bath was awarded the initial contract for construction in 1985 after competition with two other shipyards. The Burke class will be tasked to function with carrier battle groups and surface action groups, and to support Marine Corps amphibious forces against air, surface, and subsurface threats. The first ship is scheduled to complete construction in February 1991. The FY 1990 and FY 1991 requests for five ships per year are $3,672.1 million and $3,697.5 million, respectively. Total cost of the program as of December 1988 for procurement of 33 ships is $27.057 billion.

Burning Star   (see **Cobra Ball**)

burst communications: Communi-cations systems that compress and then transmit data at extremely high speeds in order to reduce the possi-bility of detection. They are used by unconventional warfare forces and by covert intelligence agents. The Army Special Forces Burst Communications System consists of the HF/VHF Man Pack Radio (AN/PRC-70) and the UHF backpack tactical satellite ter-minal (Single Channel Manpack Sys-tem AN/PSC-1). This system is used by Special Forces and Army Rangers on long patrols and special missions. A vehicle-mounted version (AN/VSC-7) controls the nets. (see also **meteor burst communications**)

bus: 1. The front end of a missile, containing reentry vehicles (RVs), a guidance system, propellant, and thrust devices for altering the bal-listic flight path so that the RVs can be ejected sequentially toward their respective targets. The bus is also known as a post-boost vehicle (PBV). Once the bus releases the RVs, it may deploy shields, decoys, or other countermeasures.   **2.** The main body of the satellite except for the mission payload itself. This includes the structural frame as well as the subsystems responsible for tracking, telemetry, command, system status monitoring, position keeping, altitude control, thermal control, and electric power.

Busy Brewer: Code name of pro-gram whereby SAC bombers provide conventional support to NATO exer-cises [SAC, *SAC Exercise Program*, SACR 55–38, Vol. I, p. 2–2, released under the FOIA].

Byeman: One of the four major types of **sensitive compartmented information**. Byeman information is used by the National Security Agency to mark certain products and details of satellite intelligence collection systems. Access to Byeman information requires a special security clearance that is a subset of the **Talent Keyhole** compartment, usually called a TK-"B" clearance. Byeman codewords are given to **signals intelligence** satellites, including **Rhyolite**, **Aquacade**, **Chalet**, **Vortex**, **Jumpseat**, and **Magnum**. Byeman codewords also used for present, future, and past imaging satellites, including **Kennan**, **Lacrosse**, **Gambit**, **Hexagon**, and **Corona** [Jeffrey Richelson, *The U.S. Intelligence Community*, 2d ed., p. 418].

C

C: Prefix designating **1.** Captive test vehicle carried on a launch platform but incapable of being fired. **2.** Transport aircraft (e.g., C-5, C-130).

C-1A Trader: Navy reciprocating-engine transport aircraft used for carrier on-board delivery of supplies, repair parts, and personnel. The Navy's last operational C-1A (Bureau Number 146048) was retired from active service on 30 September 1988 at NAS Pensacola, FL.

C-2A Greyhound: Navy twin-turboprop transport aircraft based on the airframe of the **E-2 Hawkeye** and used for carrier on-board delivery of supplies, repair parts, and personnel. The C-2 replaced the **C-1A Trader**. Prime contractor is Grumman Aerospace, Bethpage, NY. General Motors, Allison Division, Indianapolis, IN, is the contractor for the engine. Cost in FY 1987 for purchase of the final nine aircraft was $103.4 million; ongoing costs are for spares.

C3 (see **command, control, and communications**)

C3CM (see **command, control, and communications countermeasures**)

C-5A/B Galaxy: Air Force long-range, five-person, air refuelable, heavy-lift cargo transport powered by four turbofan engines. This is the largest U.S. cargo aircraft used for **strategic airlift**; it is capable of carrying outsize cargo weighing up to 291,000 lb, such as two M60 tanks or three CH-47 Chinook helicopters, over transoceanic ranges. Its maximum speed at 25,000 ft is 571 mph. Its range is 3,434 miles with its maximum payload, and 6,469 with its maximum fuel. It can carry 75 troops and 36 standard pallets or assorted vehicles, or an additional 270 troops. There is a rest area for 15 persons, which can be used by a relief crew and loaders. The aircraft are assigned to the **Military Airlift Command**.

Delivery of 81 basic C-5As began in December 1969 and was completed in May 1973. Under a major modification program, initiated in 1978, Lockheed produced component kits to extend the service lives of the C-5A wings by 30,000 flight hours each without load restrictions. Installation of the kits began in 1982, and modification of all 77 C-5A aircraft in the inventory was complete by July 1987.

The Air Force is acquiring 50 new C-5Bs, generally similar to the C-5A but embodying all the improvements that have been introduced since the completion of C-5A production, including strengthened wings, better engines, and updated avionics. The first C-5B flew on 10 September 1985 and was delivered to Altus AFB, OK, on 8 January 1986. Deliveries are scheduled for completion in 1989. The two operational C-5B units (each with 23 aircraft) are the 60th Military Airlift Wing (MAW) at Travis AFB, CA, and the 436th MAW at Dover AFB, DE. As C-5Bs are delivered, C-5As are transferred to the **Air National Guard (ANG)** and **Air Force Reserve (AFRES)**. In December 1984, the 433rd MAW at Kelly AFB, TX, became the first AFRES unit to be equipped with C-5As. The ANG's 105th Military Airlift Group at Newburgh, NY, received its first C-5As in July 1985. In October 1987, the 439th MAW at Westover AFB, MA, began replacing its C-130s with C-5As.

The 50 C-5Bs plus the remaining 77 C-5As means the Air Force will have a total C-5 inventory of 127 aircraft. Prime contractors are Lockheed Georgia and General Electric. The cost in FY 1987 for purchase of the final 21 C-5B aircraft was $1,627.2 million.

C-9A/C Nightingale: Air Force twin-engine, two-person aeromedical evacuation and passenger transport.

C-9B Skytrain II: Navy reserve, twin-engine, two-person passenger transport, used to ferry naval personnel and reservists to and from training sites. The C-9 is based on the commercial DC-9 and is built by McDonnell Douglas. The last C-9s were pur-

chased in FY 1985, and the fleet of 27 is being upgraded to fly into the year 2000.

C-12 Huron: Air Force small, twin-engine, two-person passenger/cargo utility airplane powered by two turboprop engines. C-12s are military versions of civilian Beechcraft Super King Air 200/1900C aircraft and are used for priority transportation of high-level officials, supply of spare parts for **National Emergency Airborne Command Post** aircraft, medical evacuation, and intelligence collection. The C-12A and C-12E are used to support attaché and military assistance advisory missions throughout the world. **Military Airlift Command (MAC)** also uses two C-12As to train aircrews and to supplement support airlift. C-12As refitted with PT6A-42 engines are redesignated C-12Es. The C-12F, a cargo and passenger Super King Air B200C, is used by MAC for the time-sensitive movement of people and cargo. The C-12Fs, along with the C-21As, replaced the CT-39 fleet. The C-12J, a military version of the 19-passenger Beechcraft 1900C, is assigned to the **Air National Guard**. The first C-12J was ordered in FY 1985 and delivered in September 1987. Prime contractor was Beech Aircraft Corporation, Wichita, KS. The C-12A has a top speed of 301 mph at 14,000 ft and a maximum range at cruising speed of 1,824 miles. (see also **RC-12**)

C-17: Air Force long-range, two-person, air refuelable, heavy-lift cargo transport aircraft powered by four turbofan engines. Developed to meet U.S. force projection requirements, the C-17 will provide both inter- and intratheater airlift of all classes of military cargo including outsize materials. Its estimated normal cruising speed is 518 mph. The maximum range with a 167,000-lb payload is 2,765 miles. It will be able to operate routinely from small, austere airfields (3,000 ft by 90 ft) previously restricted to the **C-130**, and it will provide the first capability to airland or airdrop/extract outsize cargo on battlefields. The C-17 will be capable of intertheater delivery of troops and all types of cargo to both main operating bases and forward bases.

McDonnell Douglas was selected as the prime contractor in August 1981. Full-scale development was approved in February 1985. Initial procurement was approved in the FY 1987 budget, together with continued RDT&E. The first two production aircraft were funded in FY 1988. The FY 1989 budget approved $941.1 million for continued RDT&E as well as procurement of four more production aircraft. The FY 1990 budget requests $1,979.3 million for six aircraft as well as $915.2 million for RDT&E. Current plans call for the first flight in FY 1990 and an initial capability of 12 aircraft in FY 1992. Delivery of the planned buy of 210 C-17s would be completed by the year 2000. The C-17 will replace the C-130A and **C-141** as they begin to leave the airlift force in the 1990s. The 437th Military Airlift Wing at Charleston AFB, SC, has been designated as the first C-17 unit. Aircraft will be assigned to the Military Airlift Command, **Air Force Reserve**, and Air National Guard.

Major contractors are McDonnell Douglas Aircraft Co., Long Beach, CA (airframe), and Pratt-Whitney, East Hartford, CT (engine).

C-20 Gulfstream: Air Force five-person, midsize, medium-to long-range passenger aircraft powered by twin turbofan engines. C-20s are off-the-shelf Gulfstream III transports, each with accommodations for 14–18 passengers. They have a maximum cruising range of 561 mph and an intercontinental range of 4,050 miles. They can operate from short runways. They are for VIP transport duties and replace the C-140 in the **Military Airlift Command**. Three C-20As and one C-20B were delivered to the 89th Military Airlift Wing, Andrews AFB, MD, in FY 1983 and FY 1984 under a lease purchase agreement; the aircraft were subsequently purchased. Another seven C-20Bs with advanced mission communications equipment and revised in interiors were ordered in January 1986 and delivered to Andrews as well. The original three C-20As were then transferred to Ramstein AB, West Germany, in support of the 58th Military Airlift Squadron. Prime contractor was Gulfstream Aerospace Corporation. Two planes were procured in FY 1987 for a total of $40 million. In FY 1988, the final plane was procured for $20 million.

C-21: Air Force twin-turbofan, small passenger and light cargo transport aircraft that, along with the C-12, replaced the CT-39. The C-21 is a military version of the Learjet 35A. It is operated by the **Military Air-**

lift **Command** and the **Air National Guard**.

C-23 Sherpa: Air Force twin-turboprop, light cargo transport aircraft. The C-23 is an all-weather, day- and night-capable plane used to ferry spare parts and engines to Air Force bases throughout Europe. They are operated by the **Military Airlift Command**. The first aircraft flew on 23 December 1982, and a fleet of 20 are based at Zweibruecken AB, West Germany.

C-130 Hercules: Air Force, Navy, Marine Corps, and Air National Guard medium-size, mid-range, four-turbojet troop and cargo transport aircraft specially designed with integral ramp for use in airdrop delivery of airborne troops and equipment. The Hercules is the standard and venerable mid-range airlift aircraft flown by the **Military Airlift Command**, particularly for intertheater support, but it is also considered the most versatile tactical transport ever built. It is used for transport, electronic surveillance, search and rescue, space and film capsule recovery, helicopter refueling, Arctic operations, special operations, and communications.

The initial production model, the C-130A, which was first flown in April 1955, began delivery in December 1956. The D model is ski-equipped for use in the Arctic. The E model has additional fuel capacity for extended range. The H model has upgraded turboprops and avionics. The in-flight tanker configuration is designated HC-130 and is also used for aerial rescue and re-covery missions. The gunship and special operations version is designated **AC-130**. The drone control version is designated DC-130. Ski-equipped C-130Hs will be designated LC-130H. The **MC-130 Combat Talon** is a modified special operations aircraft. Weather-modified aircraft are designated WC-130. The Navy uses the C-130 as the basis for its **TACAMO** VLF communication relay plane. The Marine Corps uses the plane for both assault transport and aerial refueling, with the Marine Corps Reserve taking delivery of the latest **KC-130T** versions. Prime contractor is LASC Georgia Division of Lockheed Corporation. Cost in FY 1988 for 14 aircraft for the Air Force Reserve and Air National Guard was $3,284.9 million.

C-141 Starlifter: Air Force air refuelable, long-range transport aircraft powered by four turbofan engines, and capable of intercontinental range with heavy payloads and airdrop potential. It has a maximum cruising speed of 566 mph and a range with maximum payload of 2,293 miles. The C-141 began operation with the **Military Airlift Command** in April 1965. Two hundred and eighty-five were built. In the 1970s, the Air Force began modifying the entire C-141 fleet to the C-141B model, except for four aircraft used by the Air Force Systems Command for test purposes. The C141-B has a lengthened fuselage and an added in-flight refueling capability. The first production C-141B was delivered in December 1979 and the last in June 1982. Plans currently call for a center-wing modification program to extend the planes' flying lives by 15,000 hours each. Two hundred sixty-six aircraft are in the Air Force inventory as of 1989.

Prime contractor was Lockheed-Georgia Co.

CA: Designation for gun cruiser.

CADIN (Continental Air Defense Integration North)/Pinetree Line: A line of radars across southern Canada for air defense warning, airspace control, and command of interceptor forces against Soviet bomber attack. In 1951, the United States and Canada extended the CADIN/-Pinetree Line, which had started as a U.S. project, along latitude 50 degrees north. The United States was responsible for two thirds of the Canadian station costs. The line was completed in 1954 and consisted of 39 radars. During 1954, the Mid-Canada Line was positioned 500 km further north along the 55th parallel. This was not a radar line but an electronic screen that could detect but not track aircraft penetration. In 1957, the completion of the **DEW Line** began the process of phasing out the CADIN/Pinetree system. Twenty-four CADIN/Pinetree radars were situated in southern Canada close to the Canadian–U.S. border, and 21 DEW Line radars stretched across the northern part of Canada. Both radars reported to a NORAD Regional Operations Control Center at North Bay, Ontario. From this hardened command center, U.S. and Canadian operators could run the entire NORAD aircraft early warning system, directing U.S. and Canadian aircraft to intercept attack-

ing bombers. The line has since been replaced.

cadre status: A unit that possesses a nucleus of administrative personnel and/or equipment but does not have sufficient personnel to conduct combat operations.

Caeser: Code name for the first ocean-bottom array in the **Sound Surveillance System (SOSUS)**, placed off the east coast of the United States. It became operational in 1954 [Jeffrey Richelson, *American Espionage and the Soviet Target*, 1987, pp. 168–69].

caliber: Diameter of a gun's bore or projectile measured in inches.

Canada–United States Regional Planning Group (CUSRPG): A joint organization that develops and recommends plans for the defense of North America. It reports such plans to the NATO **Military Committee**. The group meets alternately in Washington and Ottawa.

U.S. Headquarters:
Arlington, VA 22209.

CAOSOP: Acronym for Standing Operating Procedures for the Coordination of Atomic Operations, one of the reports in the **Joint Reporting Structure**.

CAP (see **Civil Air Patrol, combat air patrol**)

Capsule: General ground-to-air call sign meaning "all MAC [Military Airlift Command] aircraft." The signal is sent by **Global Command and Control System** HF communications stations.

Captor: Deep-water mine involving an encapsulated Mk-46 torpedo (the name is derived from a contraction of "encapsulated torpedo") inserted in a mine casing. The mine is inserted in deep water under routes traveled by submarines, and it detects and classifies submarine targets before releasing the torpedo. The triggered torpedo homes in on the source that activated the release mechanism. Captor can be launched by surface ships, submarines, and aircraft, including the B-52. The last Captors were purchased in FY 1985, although improvement kits are being procured.

carrier air wing (CVW): Naval administrative unit assigned to a **Naval Air Force** that serves as the headquarters for aircraft squadron operations and activities. CVWs vary in their aircraft squadron composition depending on mission and on the capabilities of the carriers from which they operate. The fleet is composed of a mixture of types of CVWs. The most common type of CVW is the Conventional CVW, which was created from the merger of attack carrier airwings (CVAs) and anti-submarine warfare airwings (CVSs) in the early 1970s. The Conventional CVW is composed of 86 aircraft and features 24 each of the F-14 and F/A-18 or A-7. The Coral Sea CVW is the smallest air wing type in the fleet, with only 66 aircraft, mostly F/A-18s and A-6s. The Theodore Roosevelt CVW was designed as a follow-on to other CVWs in the 1990s and is intended to strengthen the medium attack capabilities of the Conventional CVW. It is composed of 86 aircraft (20 each of the F-14, F/A-18, and the A-6). The Kennedy CVW was an experimental type of air wing that featured 24 medium attack aircraft (A-6s) but no F/A-18s; this type was formerly employed aboard the USS Kennedy and will soon be abandoned from aboard the USS Ranger. The Transitional CVW will first appear in FY 1990. It is composed of fewer medium attack and fixed-wing anti-submarine aircraft than the Roosevelt CVW. The Reserve CVW type is the same as a Conventional CVW less S-3s.

There are currently 13 organized CVWs in the active force, each assigned to an aircraft carrier. Shifts in squadron and CVW assignments to carriers occur as a result of the commissioning of new carriers, the permanent decommissioning of carriers, changes in homeport assignments, and the removal of individual carriers from active duty for extensive, multi-year refueling and overhaul operations (see also **Service Life Extension Program (SLEP)**). The assignments of CVWs as of fall 1989 were as shown above. (see also **aircraft carrier**)

carrier battle group (CVBG): An aircraft carrier and its accompanying escort ships configured for combat operations. This is the backbone of the offensive forces. It can remain independent of shore bases almost indefinitely due to techniques for the **underway replenishment** of fuel and provisioning at sea. As task organizations, CVBGs vary in size and composition

Carrier Air Wing	Name	Hull No.	Fleet	Type	Homeport
CVW-1	America	CV-66	LANTFLT	Conv.	Norfolk, VA, 23511
CVW-2	Ranger	CV-61	PACFLT	Kennedy	San Diego, CA, 92136
CVW-3	John F. Kennedy	CV-67	LANTFLT	Conv.	Norfolk, VA, 23511
CVW-5	Midway	CV-41	PACFLT	Coral Sea	Yokosuka, Japan
CVW-6	Forrestal	CV-59	LANTFLT	Conv.	Mayport, FL, 32228
CVW-7	Dwight D. Eisenhower	CVN-69	LANTFLT	Conv.	Norfolk, VA, 23511
CVW-8	Theodore Roosevelt	CVN-71	LANTFLT	Roosevelt	Norfolk, VA, 23511
CVW-9	Nimitz	CVN-68	PACFLT	Conv.	Bremerton, WA, 98315
CVW-[a]	Independence	CV-62	PACFLT		San Diego, CA, 92136
CVW-11[b]	Enterprise	CVN-65	PACFLT	Conv.	NAS Alameda, CA, 94501
CVW-13	Coral Sea	CV-43	LANTFLT	Coral Sea	Norfolk, VA, 23511
CVW-14[c]	Constellation	CV-64	PACFLT	Conv.	San Diego, CA, 92136
CVW-15	Carl Vinson	CVN-70	PACFLT	Conv.	NAS Alameda, CA, 94501
CVW-17	Saratoga	CV-60	LANTFLT	Conv.	Mayport, FL, 32228
CVW-[d]	Kitty Hawk	CV-63	LANTFLT		Philadelphia, PA
CVW-[e]	Abraham Lincoln	CVN-72	PACFLT		NAS Alameda, CA, 94501

[a] No unit or type assigned. The carrier has completed its SLEP and is scheduled to receive CVW-14.
[b] The Enterprise is scheduled to be transferred to Norfolk, VA for a major refueling and overhaul.
[c] Carrier is scheduled to enter SLEP. Its air wing will be transferred to CV-62.
[d] No unit number or type assigned. The carrier is currently in the SLEP.
[e] No unit number or type assigned. The new carrier was commissioned on 11 November 1989.

depending on their assigned missions. The attack range of a CVBG is dependent on its aircraft assignment and specific ship capabilities.

Nominal Peacetime Composition

- 1 aircraft carrier (CV/CVN);
- 1–2 guided missile cruisers (CG/CGNs);
- 2–3 guided missile destroyers (DDGs);
- 2–3 destroyers (DDs); and
- 1–3 nuclear-powered attack submarines (SSNs).

Nominal Wartime Composition

- 2–4 aircraft carriers (CV/CVNs);
- 4–8 guided missile cruisers (CG/CGNs);
- 4–8 guided missile destroyers (DDGs);
- 4–8 destroyers (DDs); and
- 3–4 nuclear-powered attack submarines (SSNs).

carrier group (CARGRU): Principle subordinate administrative unit of a **Naval Air Force**, consisting of one or more aircraft carriers and employed operationally as a **task force**, **task group**, or **task unit** under the operational control of a numbered fleet. Its commander may occasionally exercise operational control of a carrier task force/**carrier battle group** as assigned by a fleet commander. A CARGRU is commanded by a Rear Admiral. There are eight active carrier groups:

- Carrier Group 1, NAS North Island, CA 92135
- Carrier Group 2, NAS Norfolk, VA 23511

- Carrier Group 3, NAS Alameda, CA 94501
- Carrier Group 4, NAS Norfolk, VA 23511
- Carrier Group 5, NAS Cubi Point, Philippines
- Carrier Group 6, Mayport, FL 32228
- Carrier Group 7, NAS North Island, CA 92135
- Carrier Group 8, NAS Norfolk, VA 23511

carrier on-board delivery (COD): "The delivery of passengers and/or light freight on board an aircraft carrier at sea by carrier aircraft. COD aircraft are a carrier-type aircraft especially adapted for this purpose" [*NWP 3*]. The primary Navy COD aircraft is the **C-2A Greyhound**.

CAS (see **close air support, Crisis Action System**)

cavalry: 1. The "eyes and ears" of the division through the conduct of reconnaissance, security, surveillance, and command and control roles. 2. One of eight types of **maneuver battalions** of the Army assigned to the **division**, it is called a squadron in the tradition of the cavalry. The cavalry squadron has a strength of approximately 630 personnel and is composed of a headquarters and headquarters troop (company), two air cavalry troops, two ground cavalry troops, and one long-range surveillance detachment. The squadron may operate under the control of the division, the combat aviation brigade, or another maneuver command. When assigned to a **light infantry division**, it is no longer a cavalry squadron but a reconnaissance squadron and has only one ground troop, although its mission remains the same. (see also **armored cavalry**)

Cayuse   (see **OH-6**)

C-day: 1. The unnamed day on which movement from origin in a deployment operation in support of a crisis commences or is to commence. The deployment may be the movement of troops, cargo, weapon systems, or a combination of these elements utilizing any or all types of transport. All movement required for C-day preparatory actions or pre-positioning of deployment support are expressed relative to this day as negative days (e.g., N-5). For execution, the actual day is established under the authority and direction of the Secretary of Defense [JCS, *Joint Operation Planning System, Volume I Deliberate Planning Procedures*, p. xxii]. **2.** The day on which U.S. Central Command (USCENTCOM) deployment/redeployment commences or is scheduled to commence. This applies to movement of USCENTCOM-deploying elements from on-load air bases, surface ports or embarkations, and tactical unit departure bases. The movement of select deployment support elements to pre-positioned locations may precede C-day. USCENTCOM operations plans (OPLANS) designate C-day [HQ, USCENTCOM, *Emergency Action Procedures. Volume I: System Description*, 20 Feb 1986, p. 4–2]. (see also **military time**)

Cemetery Network: Code name for the U.S. European Command HF/SSB radio communications network operated by the Army and used for command and control of nuclear forces in Europe, and for the release of nuclear weapons, particularly those intended for use by NATO allies. Cemetery Net main stations in Europe are located at Boeblingen, Bann, and Edingen, West Germany; Mildenhall, UK; and Sigonella, Italy. A subnet of the Cemetery Network is code-named "Gangbusters." The Cemetery Network is being replaced by the **Regency Network**.

censorship   (see **armed forces censorship, civil censorship, national censorship, public media censorship**)

Central Army Group (CENTAG): Principle subordinate command of **Allied Forces Central Europe**, established in 1953 and restructured in 1970. It is responsible for land operations in central Europe. It consists of two West German corps, two U.S. corps (V and VII Corps), and a mechanized brigade group from Canada. It is commanded by a U.S. General, who also serves as the Commander-in-Chief **U.S. Army Europe**. The **4th Allied Tactical Air Force (ATAF)** assigned to CENTAG is collocated with CENTAG.

Headquarters
Seckenheim, West Germany
(APO New York 09099)

Central Command   (see **U.S. Central Command**)

Central European Pipeline System (CEPS): Underground NATO-operated and controlled pipeline extending 6300 km and running through Belgium, France, West Germany, and the Netherlands. It directly serves 54 major NATO airbases. It is operated multilaterally by eight nations through the Central Europe Operating Agency, formed in 1958. It stores 1.8 million cubic meters of fuel. The first leg of the pipeline from LeHavre to Paris was built in 1952. The second leg, from the North Sea to West Germany, was built in 1958. The five other NATO pipelines include the North European Pipeline System (600 km from Jutland to northern Germany), and lines running through Italy (600 km), Greece (600 km), Turkey (1000 km east-west), and the United Kingdom (providing jet fuel only to U.S. bases).

Central Intelligence Agency (CIA): Executive branch agency created by the **National Security Act of 1947** (50 USC § 403) and further defined by the **Central Intelligence Agency Act of 1949**. It is responsible for the collection and coordination of foreign intelligence information. The Agency was modeled after previous intelligence services, namely the Coordinator of Information (COI), which operated from 11 July 1941–13 June 1942; the Office of Strategic Services (OSS), which existed from 13 June 1942–20 September 1945; and the Central Intelligence Group (CIG), which operated from 20 January 1946–25 July 1947. The Director of the CIA is also the Director of Central Intelligence (DCI), the senior intelligence official of the U.S.

government. CIA's powers and duties are stated as the following:

- To provide advice and recommendations to the National Security Council in matters concerning intelligence activities relating to national security.
- To provide for the coordination of intelligence activities relating to national security with other government departments and agencies. Other government intelligence agencies are responsible for continued departmental intelligence activities.
- To "correlate," "evaluate," and provide for the "dissemination" of intelligence information.
- To protect intelligence sources and methods from unauthorized disclosure. The CIA is not afforded any police, subpoena, or law enforcement powers, or internal security functions. The only exception to this as foreseen by the enacting Congress was the open collection of foreign intelligence information from American citizens.
- To provide "services of common concern," as determined by the National Security Council, for the benefit of other intelligence agencies.
- To conduct other intelligence-related functions and duties relating to national security as directed by the National Security Council. This clause serves as the basis for the Agency's covert action operations and activities, although there is disagreement regarding whether this action was intended by the enactment of the 1947 act.

Headquarters
Mclean, VA.
(Washington, DC 20305)

CIA Directors/Directors of Central Intelligence

RADM Sidney W. Souers, USNR	3 Jan 1946–10 Jun 1946
LTG Hoyt S. Vandenberg, USA	10 Jun 1946–1 May 1947
RADM Roscoe H. Hillenkoetter, USN	1 May 1947–7 Oct 1950
GEN Walter B. Smith, USA	7 Oct 1950–9 Feb 1953
Allen W. Dulles	26 Feb 1953–29 Nov 1961
John A. McCone	29 Nov 1961–28 Apr 1965
VADM William F. Raborn, Jr., USN (Ret.)	28 Apr 1965–30 Jun 1966
Richard M. Helms	30 Jun 1966–2 Feb 1973
James R. Schlesinger	2 Feb 1973–2 Jul 1973
William E. Colby	4 Sep 1973–30 Jan 1976
George H. W. Bush	30 Jan 1976–20 Jan 1977
ADM Stansfield Turner, USN (Ret.)	9 Mar 1977–20 Jan 1981
William J. Casey	28 Jan 1981–29 Jan 1987
William H. Webster	26 May 1987–present

Central Intelligence Agency Act of 1949: Congressional act signed into law on 20 June 1949 (50 Title § 403a-403n, as amended) that further defined the operating procedures of the CIA as first outlined in the **National Security Act of 1947**. Its sections detail the special administrative regulations for CIA operations as distinguished from other federal agencies and departments. Its provisions include

- Appropriations or other monies made available to the CIA "may be expended without regard to provisions of law and regulations relating to the expenditure of government funds." This allows that "objects of a confidential, extraordinary or emergency nature may be accounted for (solely) on the certificate of the Director."
- The CIA may transfer and receive funds from other agencies and departments as approved by the Office of Management and Budget and without public notice.
- The CIA may hire and fire employees without regard to Civil Service regulations.
- The CIA may admit up to 100 aliens per year into permanent residence in the United States if deemed essential to the national security or intelligence missions, bypassing normal immigration procedures.

Central Security Service (CSS) (see **National Security Agency/Central Security Service**)

central supply and maintenance: Program 7 of the 11 **major force programs** that represent all of the major missions of the services and are the most basic structural elements of the **Five-Year Defense Program**. It consists of resources related to supply, maintenance, and service activities. both industrially and nonindustrially funded, and other supporting activities such as first- and second-destination transportation, overseas port units, industrial preparedness, commissaries, and logistics and maintenance support.

central system: Common name for offensive nuclear weapons that are considered basic to the issue of the strategic nuclear relationship between the United States and the Soviet Union.

CEP (see **circular error probable**)

CG/CGN: Designation for guided missile **cruiser**/nuclear-powered guided missile cruiser.

CH-3: Air Force transport and special operations helicopter developed as a variant of the Sikorsky S-61 helicopter and based on the Navy's **SH-3**. Many were modified for a combat search and rescue role and renamed HH-3E Jolly Green Giants. Prime contractor was Sikorsky Aircraft, a division of United Technologies Corporation.

CH-46 Sea Knight: Navy and Marine Corps tandem-rotor, medium-lift helicopter used for personnel and cargo transport and designed for both land and ship operations. The CH-46D/E is used by the Marine Corps for troop assault and by the Navy for vertical replenishment of ships at sea. The HH-46 is configured for search and rescue. It has a speed of 165 mph and a range of 206 nm. The Navy and Marine Corps took delivery of 624 Sea Knights from 1961–77. Prime contractor was Boeing Vertol.

CH-47 Chinook: Army turbine-powered, all-weather heavy transport for artillery, engineering equipment, bulk cargo, and personnel (it can carry up to 40 troops). The heli-copter provides a capability for the recovery of downed aircraft and medical evacuation. The CH-47 is currently undergoing a modernization program to extend operations beyond the year 2000. The latest version, the CH-47D, is equipped with advanced avionics, and it has a maximum speed of 300 kph and a mission range of 185 km. Boeing Vertol of Philadelphia, PA, is the prime contractor. Estimated cost for FY 1989 was $248.1 million. The requests for FY 1990 and FY 1991 are $326.6 million and $259.9 million, respectively.

CH-53 Sea Stallion/Super Stallion: Navy, Marine Corps, and Air Force single-rotor, three-engine, heavy-lift helicopter utilized for personnel and cargo transport. The helicopter can accommodate 55 troops. It is replacing the **CH-3**/HH-3. The Air Force also uses some CH-53Cs to provide transport for the tactical air control system. The HH-53 version is specially modified for combat search and rescue and is assigned to the Air Force. The RH-53 is a mine countermeasures version. The **MH-53** is significantly modified for Air Force special operations, and it is called Pave Low. The CH-53 has a maximum range of 492 km and a maximum speed of 315 kph. The RH-53D was used in the attempt to free American hostages in Tehran in 1979.

The CH-53E Super Stallion is a Marine Corps and Navy shipboard-capable heavy-lift helicopter used for fleet vertical on-board delivery (VOD) of ships at sea, airborne mine countermeasures (AMCM) operations, and recovery of downed or damaged aircraft and equipment. It is the largest and most powerful U.S. helicopter. The first were delivered in 1981. The MH-53E minesweeping version, heavier and with a greater fuel capacity than the CH-53E, first flew in 1983. Prime contractors are United Technologies, Sikorsky Aircraft of Stratford, CT; and General Electronics of West Lynn, MA, for the engine. Cost in FY 1989 for the CH/MH-53E Super Stallion was $244.3 million. The final three Super Stallions are being procured in FY 1990 for $73.2 million.

chaff: The general name for reflectors of enemy radar signals meant to create a false target or screen an actual target. Chaff is usually dropped by aircraft and missiles or streamed from surface ships. It consists of magnetic foil or wire, metalized glass fiber, and confetti-like metal foil ribbons of various lengths and frequency responses. One type of chaff is known as "kite." Chaff is nicknamed "Window." (see also **electronic countermeasures**)

chain of command: Hierarchy of command of a military organization or set of organizations. (see also **administrative chain of command, command, Department of Defense Reorganization Act of 1986, operational chain of command**)

Chairman of the Joint Chiefs of Staff (CJCS): Highest-ranking member and presiding officer of the **Joint Chiefs of Staff**; principal military advisor to the President, the National Security Council, and the Secretary of Defense; and executive of the Organization of the Joint Chiefs of Staff. The position was established by the **National Security Act of 1949**. The principle role of the CJCS was strengthened by the Goldwater-Nichols **Department of Defense Reorganization Act of 1986** out of the recommendations of the President's Blue Ribbon Commission on Defense Management (Packard Commission). As provided by the act, the CJCS acquired many of the functions previously performed by the corporate JCS, including preparation of "fiscally contrained" strategic plans; conduct of military net assessments; establishment of unified and specified command readiness evaluation systems; development of joint service doctrine and joint tactics, techniques, and procedures; and providing of advice on the budget priorities of the unified and specified commands and services. The act also clarified the relationship of the CJCS to the unified and specified combatant commands. The CJCS, as directed by the Secretary of Defense, oversees the activities of the unified and specified combatant commands. The roles of the CJCS in the chain of command to the combatant commands are

• Relayer of communications between the National Command Authority (NCA) and the combatant commands. Passage of the Goldwater-Nichols Act placed the CJCS in the communications chain of command, and communications between the NCA and the combatant commanders now pass through the Chairman. Furthermore, the Secretary of Defense is permitted

Chairmen of the Joint Chiefs of Staff

GEN Omar N. Bradley, USA	16 Aug 1949–14 Aug 1953
ADM Arthur W. Radford, USN	15 Aug 1953–14 Aug 1957
GEN Nathan W. Twining, USAF	15 Aug 1957–30 Sep 1960
GEN Lyman L. Lemnitzer, USA	1 Oct 1960–30 Sep 1962
GEN Maxwell D. Taylor, USA	1 Oct 1962–3 Jul 1964
GEN Earle W. Wheeler, USA	3 Jul 1964–2 Jul 1970
ADM Thomas H. Moorer, USN	3 Jul 1970–30 Jun 1974
GEN George S. Brown, USAF	1 Jul 1974–20 Jun 1978
GEN David C. Jones, USAF	21 Jun 1978–18 Jun 1982
GEN John W. Vessey Jr., USA	18 Jun 1982–30 Sep 1985
ADM William J. Crowe, Jr., USN	1 Oct 1985–1 Oct 1989
GEN Colin L. Powell, USA	1 Oct 1989–present

wide latitude to assign oversight responsibilities to the Chairman in the Secretary's control and coordination of the combatant commanders.

- Overseer of the activities of combatant commands in matters dealing with the statutory responsibility of the Secretary of Defense. This includes recommending changes in assignment of functions, roles, and missions to achieve maximum effectiveness of the armed forces.
- Spokesman for the combatant commanders, including the summary and analysis of requirements, programs, and budgets.

As a result of the DOD Reorganization Act, there is now a Vice Chairman, who performs such duties as the Chairman may prescribe. By law, the Vice Chairman is the second highest-ranking member of the armed forces and replaces the Chairman in the event of absence or disability. The Vice Chairman is not, by definition, a member of the Joint Chiefs of Staff, but he may participate in all meetings. He votes on matters before the Joint Chiefs of Staff only when acting in the capacity of Chairman.

Chalet: Initial code name for a class of **signals intelligence** satellites, renamed **Vortex**.

change of operational control (see **chop**)

Channel Command (see **Allied Command Channel**)

Chaparral: Model designation MIM-72. Army short-range, low-altitude, division-level, **air defense surface-to-air missile** system adapted from the **Sidewinder** infrared homing missile. Four missiles are mounted on a tracked launcher, with another four stowed. Chaparral features the Rosette Scan Seeker (RSS) developed by Ford Aerospace. First fielded in 1969, Chaparral will remain in Army and National Guard stocks until the 1990s and will provide short-range air defense for mechanized infantry and armored divisions. Prime contractor is Philco-Ford. FY 1989 total cost was $61.2 million.

Chaplain Corps: Combat service support branch of the Army.

Checkered Flag: Air Force training program practicing the deployment of U.S.-based tactical air units to Europe, Alaska, and the Pacific so that the units may become familiar with operating areas and procedures. The European deployment program is given the nickname "Coronet," with each individual deployment separately identified (e.g., Coronet Gauntlet, Coronet Castle). When the deployment is sponsored by the Tactical Air Command, the nickname "Creek" is applied to deployments to West Germany, and "Salty" (e.g., Salty Bee) to deployments to Italy.

chemical and biological agents: Chemical agents are "intended for use in military operations to kill, seriously injure, or incapacitate through its physiological effects. " This category excludes riot control agents, herbicides, smoke, and flame. Biological agents are microorganisms that cause "disease in man, plants, or animals, or cause the deterioration of material" [*JCS Pub 1*, pp. 52, 65]. Types of chemical and biological agents are

- *Anticrop*: "An agent that reduces the harvest yield of food or economic crops. These agents may or may not kill plants. As used in the field, they are nontoxic and noninfectious to human beings and animals and do not cause permanent soil sterility."
- *Antimaterial*: "A living organism or chemical that causes deterioration of, or damage to, selected material."
- *Antiplant*:   "A microorganism or chemical that causes disease or damage to plants."
- *Casualty*: "An agent that is capable of producing serious injury or death when used in field concentrations."
- *Defoliant*: "A chemical used for the premature removal of leaves from plants."
- *Herbicide*: "Any preparation used to kill or inhibit the growth of plants."
- *Incapacitating*: "An agent that produces temporary physiological or mental effects, or both, which will render individuals incapable of concerted effort in the performance of their assigned duties."
- *Riot control*: "A chemical that produces temporary irritating or disabling effects when in contact with the eyes or when inhaled." [*NWP 3*]

In January 1989, 151 national representatives gathered in Paris for the Conference on the Prohibition of Chemical Weapons. This complemented the 40-nation Geneva Conference on Disarmament, which was negotiating a verifiable, comprehensive, and global ban on chemical weapons. (see also **Biological Weapons Convention, Geneva Protocol**)

Chemical Corps: Combat support and **combat service support** branch of the Army.

chemical defense: The military methods, plans, and procedures involved in establishing and executing defensive measures against attacks utilizing chemical agents. (see also **chemical and biological agents**)

Chess: Control marking and security clearance applied to **Talent-Keyhole**

information relating to **SR-71** and **U-2** photography. (see also **security classification**)

Cheyenne Mountain (see **NORAD Cheyenne Mountain Complex**)

Chief of Naval Education and Training (CNET):   Naval **shore establishment** reporting to the Chief of Naval Operations, renamed from the Chief of Naval Training on 21 August 1973. It provides shore-based education and training to Navy personnel and dependents and some Marine Corps personnel, as well as interservice training for Security Assistance Program personnel.

Headquarters
NAS Pensacola, FL 32508

Major Operations

- Chief of Naval Air Training, Corpus Christi, TX 78419
- Chief of Naval Technical Training, Millington, TN 38054
- Naval Education and Training Program Management Support Activity, Fausley Field, Pensacola, FL 32509
- Naval Education and Training Center, Great Lakes, IL 60088

Type Commands

- Training Command, **Atlantic Fleet**
- Training Command, **Pacific Fleet**

Chief of Naval Operations (CNO): Senior active military officer of the **Department of the Navy**, equivalent to the **Chief of Staff of the Air Force** and the **Chief of Staff of the Army**. The office of the CNO was established in 1915, with the CNO having responsibility for both

fleet operations and war plan preparation and readiness. Operational duties were transferred to the Commander-in-Chief of the U.S. Fleet in the 1920s, but they were restored in March 1942 to the CNO. In the 1960s, the CNO gained complete responsibility for naval operations, logistics, and administration. Today, the CNO serves as an advisor to the President, the **National Security Council**, the **Secretary of Defense**, and the **Secretary of the Navy** and is a member of the **Joint Chiefs of Staff (JCS)**. The CNO "shall command the operating forces of the Navy (consistent with the operational command vested in the commanders of unified or specified combatant commands)" as well as the **Naval Material Command**, the Bureau of Naval Personnel, the **Naval Medical Command**, and other shore activities as directed. Under present law, as reiterated in the **Department of Defense Reorganization Act of 1986**, the CNO's operational command authority has been de-emphasized. Naval forces assigned to the unified commands are not subject to the personal operational command of the CNO in any JCS or DOD capacity, but only as the Secretary of the Navy may determine. Major commands directly under the administrative command of the Chief of Naval Operations include the **Atlantic Fleet** and **Pacific Fleet**, **U.S. Naval Forces Europe**, and the **Military Sealift Command**. The CNO is responsible for Navy efficiency and readiness and therefore manages logistical, maintenance, personnel management, procurement, and R&D in support of the operational commanders. The CNO is appointed for a term of four years by the president

Chiefs of Naval Operations

FADM Chester W. Nimitz	15 Dec 1945–15 Dec 1947
ADM Louis E. Denfield	15 Dec 1947–2 Nov 1949
ADM Forrest P. Sherman	2 Nov 1949–22 Jul 1951
ADM William M. Fechteler	16 Aug 1951–17 Aug 1953
ADM Robert B. Carney	17 Aug 1953–16 Aug 1955
ADM Arleigh A. Burke	17 Aug 1955–1 Aug 1961
ADM George W. Anderson	1 Aug 1961–31 Jul 1963
ADM David L. McDonald	1 Aug 1963–31 Jul 1967
ADM Thomas H. Moorer	1 Aug 1967–1 Jul 1970
ADM Elmo R. Zumwalt, Jr.	1 Jul 1970–29 Jun 1974
ADM James L. Holloway III	29 Jun 1974–1 Jul 1978
ADM Thomas B. Hayward	1 Jul 1978–30 Jun 1982
ADM James D. Watkins	1 Jul 1982–30 Jun 1986
ADM C.A.H. Trost	1 Jul 1986–present

through the Secretary of Defense and is approved by the Senate.

The Office of the Chief of Naval Operations (OCNO) consists of

- Chief of Naval Operations;
- Vice Chief of Naval Operations;
- Deputy CNOs for Manpower, Personnel, and Training; Program Planning; Logistics; and Plans, Policy, and Operations;
- Assistant CNOs for Air Warfare; Surface Warfare; and Submarine Warfare;
- Offices of Naval Intelligence; Surgeon General; Space, Command, and Control; Naval Reserve; Oceanographer; Chief of Chaplains; Research and Development Requirements; and Test and Evaluation.

(see also **chiefs of military services**)

chief of staff: 1. Senior active military officer of a military department. (see also **Chief of Staff of the Air Force, Chief of Staff of the Army, Chief of Naval Operations, chiefs of**

military services) 2. Senior assistant to a commanding officer or staff officer who supervises the staff of a command. At lower echelons, the chief of staff is usually called the executive officer.

Chief of Staff of the Air Force (CSAF or AF/CC): Senior active military officer of the **Department of the Air Force**, equivalent to the **Chief of Staff of the Army** and the **Chief of Naval Operations**. The office was first recognized in June 1941 within the Army Air Forces as the Office of the Chief of the Air Force. It has undergone many staff reorganizations and arrangements. Today, the CSAF serves as an advisor to the President, the **National Security Council**, the **Secretary of Defense**, and the **Secretary of the Air Force** and is a member of the **Joint Chiefs of Staff**. The CSAF "presides over the Air Staff and supervises members and organizations of the Air Force as the Secretary of the Air Force deter-

Chiefs of Staff of the Air Force

GEN Carl Spaatz	26 Sep 1947–29 Apr 1948
GEN Hoyt S. Vandenberg	30 Apr 1948–29 Jun 1953
GEN Nathan F. Twining	30 Jun 1953–30 Jun 1957
GEN Thomas D. White	1 Jul 1957–30 Jun 1961
GEN Curtis E. LeMay	30 Jun 1961–31 Jan 1965
GEN John P. McConnell	1 Feb 1965–31 Jul 1969
GEN John D. Ryan	1 Aug 1969–31 Jul 1973
GEN George S. Brown	1 Aug 1973–30 Jun 1974
GEN David C. Jones	1 Jul 1974–21 Jun 1978
GEN Lew Allen, Jr.	1 Jul 1978–30 Jun 1982
GEN Charles A. Gabriel	1 Jul 1982–30 Jun 1986
GEN Larry D. Welch	1 Jul 1986–present

mines, consistent with full operational command assigned to commanders of specified and unified combatant commands." CSAF is responsible for Air Force efficiency and readiness, which includes the management of logistics, maintenance, personnel, procurement, and R&D. The CSAF is appointed for a term of four years by the President through the Secretary of Defense and is approved by the Senate.

The Office of the CSAF, also known as the Air Staff, consists of

- Chief of Staff;
- Vice Chief of Staff;
- Assistant Vice Chief of Staff;
- Deputy Chiefs of Staff for Personnel; Programs and Resources; Plans and Operations; and Logistics and Engineering;
- Assistant Chiefs of Staff for Intelligence; Studies and Analysis; and Information Systems;
- Offices of Air Force History; Surgeon General; Chief of Chaplains; the Judge Advocate General; Chief of Air Force Reserve; and Chief of

National Guard Bureau/Director of the Air National Guard.

(see also **chiefs of military services**)

Chief of Staff of the Army (CSA): Senior active military officer of the **Department of the Army**, equivalent to the **Chief of Staff of the Air Force** and the **Chief of Naval Operations**. The Office of the CSA was first established by Congress in 1903 as the Chief of the U.S. Army General Staff. It was composed of 44 officers and was subordinate to the Chief of Staff of the War Department. Today, the CSA serves as an advisor to the President, the **National Security Council**, the **Secretary of Defense**, and the **Secretary of the Army** and is a member of the **Joint Chiefs of Staff**. The CSA presides over the activities of the **Army Staff** and is responsible for the efficiency and readiness of the Army. The CSA is appointed for a four year term by the President through the Secretary of Defense and is approved by the Senate.

The Office of the CSA, also known as the Army Staff, consists of

Chiefs of Staff of the Army

GEN Dwight D. Eisenhower	19 Nov 1945–7 Feb 1948
GEN Omar N. Bradley	7 Feb 1948–15 Aug 1949
GEN J. Lawton Collins	16 Aug 1949–14 Aug 1953
GEN Matthew B. Ridgway	15 Aug 1953–30 Jun 1955
GEN Maxwell D. Taylor	30 Jun 1955–30 Jun 1959
GEN Lyman L. Lemnitzer	1 Jul 1959–30 Sep 1960
GEN George H. Decker	30 Sep 1960–30 Sep 1962
GEN Earle G. Wheeler	1 Oct 1962–3 Jul 1964
GEN Harold K. Johnson	3 Jul 1964–2 Jul 1968
GEN William C. Westmoreland	3 Jul 1968–30 Jun 1972
GEN Creighton W. Abrams	12 Oct 1972–4 Sep 1974
GEN Fred C. Weyand	7 Oct 1974–30 Sep 1976
GEN Bernard W. Rogers	1 Oct 1976–21 Jun 1979
GEN Edward C. Meyer	22 Jun 1979–21 Jun 1983
GEN John A. Wickham	23 Jul 1983–23 Jun 1987
GEN Carl E. Vuono	23 Jun 1987–present

- Chief of Staff;
- Vice Chief of Staff;
- Director of the Army Staff;
- Deputy Chiefs of Staff for Intelligence; Personnel; Operations and Plans; and Logistics;
- Offices of the Chief of Chaplains; Judge Advocate General; Chief of Engineers; Surgeon General; Chief of Army Reserve; Chief of National Guard Bureau.

(see also **chiefs of military services**)

chiefs of military services: The **Chief of Naval Operations**, the **Chief of Staff of the Air Force**, and the **Chief of Staff of the Army**. These military service chiefs are dual-hatted: as members of the **Joint Chiefs of Staff (JCS)**, they offer advice to the President, the **Secretary of Defense**, and the **National Security Council (NSC)**; as chiefs of military services, they are responsible to the secretary of the military department for management of the services. The chiefs serve for four years. By custom, the vice chiefs are delegated the authority to act for their chiefs in most matters having to do with day-to-day operation of the services. The duties of the chiefs as members of the JCS take precedence over all their other duties. (see also **chief of staff**)

Chinook   (see **CH-47 Chinook**)

chop (change of operational control):   In the Navy, the date and time (GMT) at which the responsibility for naval operational control of a force or unit passes from the operational control of one authority to another as it moves through the ocean. Usually used as "chopped-to," "in-chopped," "out-chopped," or a similar variation.

CIMEX: Civil-military exercise conducted by NATO, usually referred to as

WINTEX/CIMEX (Winter exercise/ civil-military exercise).

CINC (see **Commander-in-Chief**)

CINCHAN (see **Allied Commander in-Chief Channel**)

CINCNORAD Assessment: An e-valuation by the Commander-in-Chief North American Aerospace Defense Command (**NORAD**) that a missile attack is in progress against North America. If CINCNORAD is unable to perform the assessment, USCINC-SPACE will make the assessment for the continental United States.

The evaluations include

- Domestic: Indications correspond to known domestic or cooperative launch activity and do not constitute a missile attack against North America;
- No: In the judgement of CINC-NORAD, a missile attack against North America is not in progress;
- Concern: In the judgement of CINCNORAD, events are occurring that have raised the level of concern. Further assessment is necessary in order to determine the nature of the activity involved. Pending completion of the ongoing assessment, precautionary measures to enhance responsiveness or survivability are suggested; and
- High: In the judgement of CINC-NORAD, a missile attack against North America is in progress.

[JCS, *EAP-Emergency Conferences for Tactical Warning and Attack Assessment*, 1 December 1986, p. II-B-2, released under the FOIA]

cipher: A **cryptographic** system in which the cryptographic treatment (i.e., the method of transforming plain text by predetermined rules to obscure or conceal its meaning) is applied to plain text elements such as letters, digits, polygraphs, or bits that either have no intrinsic meaning or are treated without regard to their meaning in cases where the element is a natural-language word.

circular error probable (CEP): "An indicator of the delivery accuracy of a weapon system, used as a factor in determining probable damage to a target. It is the radius of a circle within which half of a missile's projectiles are expected to fall" [*JCS Pub 1*, p. 67].

CIRVIS: Acronym standing for "communications instructions for reporting vital intelligence sightings," used by U.S.–Canadian intelligence agencies.

civil affairs (CA): 1. Type of **special operation** that seeks to enhance civil-military cooperation in an occupied country or area where U.S. forces are present. It includes "minimizing local population interference with U.S. military operations"; supporting **unconventional warfare** forces; assisting indigenous governments; identifying and procuring useful local resources for military missions; and establishing civil administration in enemy territory occupied by U.S. forces. CA organizations function within the Army's **Special Forces** ("Green Berets") and are subordinate to the Army's **First Special Operations Command**. There are 36 CA units, stationed in 22 states, with a total personnel strength of 4,800. The only active CA unit is at Ft. Bragg, NC; the Army Reserve CA units are headquartered at Mountain View, CA; Riverdale, MD; and Bronx, NY. **2. Combat arms** branch of the Army.

Civil Air Patrol (CAP): Auxiliary organization of the Air Force, composed of civilian volunteers. CAP is a federally chartered, nonprofit corporation designated by Congress in 1948. Its mission is to provide air support services during local and national emergencies, recruit youth for careers in the Air Force, and further Air Force interests through education and training. It is composed of 64,000 members from more than 2,000 communities throughout the United States.

Headquarters
Maxwell AFB, AL 36112

civil censorship: Control and review of civilian communications (messages, printed matter, and films) entering, leaving, or circulating within areas or territories occupied or controlled by U.S. forces. Censorship may be initiated by the Secretary of Defense or the commander of a unified or specified command. The degree of censorship required is made according to an assessment of the "status of hostilities" and the "attitude of the people" — "if the populace remains hostile, uncooperative, and belligerent, the percentages of censorship control will remain high in order to counter subversive activity." Persons or groups believed to be especially threatening are entered on a watch list or white list [Department

of the Army, *Civil Censorship*, FM 45-20, December 1965]. (see also **armed forces censorship**)

civil defense (CD):   A type of **domestic emergency** that encompasses those activities and measures designed or undertaken to

- Minimize the effects upon the civilian population caused or that would be caused by an enemy attack upon the United States;
- Deal with the immediate emergency conditions that would be created by any such attack; and
- Effect emergency repairs to, or the emergency restoration of, vital utilities and facilities destroyed or damaged by any such attack.

The U.S. civil defense program is managed by the **Federal Emergency Management Agency (FEMA)**. **Forces Command** (formerly under the responsibility of U.S. Readiness Command) is responsible for coordinating the DOD's **Military Support to Civil Defense (MSCD)** program.

The Army was given responsibility for the CD program after WWII, but it argued that the key to CD was citizen "self help," that local government should take the lead role, and that the military should not be too involved. Civil defense planning languished until the spring of 1950, after the Soviets detonated their A-bomb, and the Joint Committee on Atomic Energy held the first hearings on civil defense in case of atomic attack. On 20 February 1950, Congressman Chet Holifield introduced a bill in the House "proposing that a commission be created to investigate the measures which can be taken to insure the continuous operations of the U.S. government in the event of a nuclear attack by a foreign power." The bill was never reported out of the Judiciary Committee. On 12 January 1951, President Truman established the Federal Civil Defense Administration (FCDA) and Congress passed the Federal Civil Defense Act of 1950 (in January 1951). Among other plans, the Truman Administration drew up plans for government evacuation and **continuity of government (COG)**.

The civil defense program after the Eisenhower Administration has largely reflected public perceptions of imminent nuclear danger. President Kennedy instituted a five-year $3.5 billion nationwide fallout shelter program in January 1962, but the government began to retreat almost immediately from the program when it became controversial. A new Office of Civil Defense was established in the Office of the Secretary of Defense. In March 1964, the Office was moved to the Office of the Secretary of the Army. Between 1964 and the late 1970s, civil defense faded. Attention was shifted to civil preparedness rather than national security-related defense measures. Executive Order 11490, 28 October 1969, as amended, issued by President Nixon, charged the departments and agencies of the federal government with the duty of assuring the continuity of the federal government in any national emergency that might confront the nation.

President Carter signed Presidential Directive 41, "U.S. Civil Defense Policy," on 29 September 1978, providing new interagency guidance. The Carter directive delineated a role for civil defense in terms of the strategic balance. In the directive, President Carter stated

I have reviewed the recommendations of the Policy Review Committee meeting on PRM-32. Based on them, I direct that the U.S. Civil Defense program seek to "provide some increase in the number of surviving population and for greater continuity of government, should deterrence and escalation control fail, in order to provide an improved basis for dealing with the crisis and carrying out eventual national recovery."

In the Summer of 1979, **FEMA** was created by Executive Order 12148, 20 July 1979, and was charged with establishing federal policies and coordinating all civil defense and emergency planning functions, including continuity of government. A 1980 amendment to the Federal Civil Defense Act, taking into account the creation of FEMA, also stated that "an improved civil defense program should be implemented which . . . enhances the survivability of the American people *and its leadership* [author's italics] in the event of nuclear war and thereby improves the basis for eventual recovery."

On 26 February 1982, President Reagan signed National Security Decision Directive (NSDD) 26, "U.S. Civil Defense Policy," which called for a large-scale program of urban population crisis relocation planning and an expansion of civil defense efforts. An unclassified version of the NSDD-26 released by the government states "Civil Defense, along with an effective Continuity of Government program, emergency mobilization, and secure and reconstitutable telecommunications systems, is an essential ingredient of our nuclear deterrent forces." On 22 July 1982, Reagan also signed NSDD-47, "Emergency Mobilization Preparedness" (which rescinded PD-57 of the Carter Administration), which stated that:

> It is the policy of the United States to have an emergency mobilization preparedness capability that will ensure the government at all levels, in partnership with the private sector and the American people, can respond decisively and effectively to any major national emergency with the defense of the U.S. as first priority.

To carry out the policy, the NSDD stated the following about government operations in an emergency:

> It is the policy of the United States to develop systems and plans that will ensure the maintenance of necessary government functions at the Federal, State, and local levels and provide for a timely and effective transition into emergency modes of operation.

The program will

- Ensure continuous performance of essential government functions;
- Provide timely and effective transition to emergency government operations;
- Provide a mechanism for the reconstitution of the operations of government following a nuclear attack, as required; and
- Ensure that government officials at all levels are capable of responding predictably and effectively to emergency conditions.

In NSDD-47, President Reagan appointed the **Emergency Mobiliza-** **tion Preparedness Board** to support the overall civil defense and COG effort, and to prepare a national "Plan of Action."

The President's FY 1986 budget request, released 4 February 1985, marked a significant turning point in the CD program. In FY 1985 hearings before the House Appropriations Committee, FEMA provided out-year budget figures showing that they planned to request $345.5 million in FY 1986 and $410.5 million in FY 1987, with requests of over $500 million in each fiscal year through FY 1990. Instead of requesting $345 million, however, the Administration request, citing "severe fiscal pressures," was for $119 million. Although the Administration stated that this level of funding was adequate to maintain existing programs at current levels, it essentially abandoned the crisis relocation program. The FY 1986 appropriation for civil defense ended up being the all-time low in real dollars in the funding history of the civil defense program. A new policy document, NSDD-259, "U.S. Civil Defense," was signed on 4 February 1987, replacing NSDD-26. The new directive stated that the civil defense program will continue to support all-hazard integrated emergency management at state and local levels, "to the extent that this is consistent with and contributes to preparedness of the Nation in the event of an attack, whether by nuclear or non-nuclear means." It further states that federal funds and assistance for all elements of the civil defense program will be applied to develop capabilities required for attack preparedness and other disasters having national security implications (such as terrorism). The components of the program, as stated in the NSDD, are

1. Population protection.
2. State and local government crisis management in support of the population.
3. Promoting public information regarding "threats, including nuclear attacks, which may affect their localities and on actions they should take to increase their chances of survival."
4. Assisting U.S. business and industry with information regarding "measures to protect their work forces and physical assets."
5. "Voluntary participation by citizens and institutions in community civil defense activities and emphasis on citizen protective actions."
6. "Plans for sustaining survivors and for post-attack recovery."
7. Plans regarding the "gradual mobilization of civil defense capabilities in a period of gradually increasing world tensions, and for a civil defense surge in an international crisis."

[NSDD-259 reprinted in U.S. Congress, House Armed Services Committee, *Civil Defense*, hearing, National Defense Authorization Act for FY 1988/1989, 27 March 1987, p. 14]

civil disturbance (CD): A type of **domestic emergency** defined as "group acts of violence and disorders prejudicial to public law and order" that include "all domestic conditions requiring or likely to require the use of Federal Armed Forces" [Department of the Army, *Civil Disturbances*, AR 500-50, 21 April 1972, p. 1-1]. The Secretary of the Army, as the DOD executive

agent for coordination of military assistance to civil law enforcement agencies in peacetime domestic emergencies, is charged with the lead in all matters regarding the use of federal military force and military involvement in domestic terrorist incidents and civil disturbances. The Army's **operation plan (OPLAN)** for civil disturbances is called **GARDEN PLOT**. Army policy states that in a CD situation, federal military resources are employed

- After "state and local civil authorities have utilized all of their own forces . . . available for use, and are unable to control the situation."
- When the situation exceeds the "capabilities" of state or local law enforcement.
- When civil authorities "will not take appropriate action." [*Civil Disturbances*, p. 1-1].

The employment of the armed forces in a CD is made only upon a request to the U.S. Attorney General and, normally, upon the authorization of the President through a presidential directive or executive order. A request for employment must include a formal request made by a state legislature or Governor, a proclamation issued by the President ordering that "insurgents cease and desist from acts of violence and disperse and retire peacefully," and approval by the Department of the Army. When employed, the mission of armed forces in CD situations is "to assist civil authorities in the restoration of law and order," not supplant civil authority [Department of the Army, Director of Military Support, *DA Civil Disturbance Plan GARDEN PLOT*, 1 March 1984, p. 3].

National Guard Civil Disturbance Call-ups
(by Fiscal Year)

Year	Total Number[a]	Number of CDs/Possible CDs[b]	Number of Demonstrations
1976	5	4	
1977	9	6	
1978	22	9	
1979	27	3	1 demonstration 1 nuclear demonstration
1980	20	9	2 demonstrations 2 nuclear demonstrations
1981	14	4	2 nuclear demonstrations 1 anti-nuclear demonstration
1982	6	4	
1983	10	2	1 anti-nuclear demonstration
1984	8	8	
1985	4	4	
1986	2	2	
1988	1	1	

[a] all CD call-ups of any kind (e.g., labor strikes, prison disorders, and group demonstrations)
[b] disorders specifically labeled "civil disturbances" or "possible civil disturbances."
Source: National Guard Bureau, *Annual Review*, various years.

In addition to the much-publicized use of military forces in CDs during the 1960s, the armed forces maintain readiness for CD operations, and occasionally are employed (primarily the National Guard). Military response forces include GARDEN PLOT task forces, normally composed of one brigade and headquarters, two battalions, and a support element. A task force is composed of a minimum of 1,210 and a maximum of 2,150 personnel and is commanded by a Major General. Forces Command trains, equips, and maintains 10 brigades for CD deployment in CONUS, six battalions for deployment with Task Force Military District of Washington (TF MDW), and other units, including Strategic Army Forces (STRAF) Military Police companies, CONUS-based infantry units, and a Quick Reaction Force (QRT), whose brigade and task force

headquarters is on 24-hour alert status. In addition, the Commander of the Marine Corps trains, equips, and maintains two CD battalions in the eastern United States and units for employment with TF MDW [*DA Civil Disturbance Plan GARDEN PLOT*, p. A-4].

Civil Disturbance Conditions (CIDCONs), levels of preparedness to be attained by military forces in preparation for CD deployment, range from CIDCON-5 (the normal readiness status for military response to CDs) to CIDCON-1 (the level at which U.S. forces become involved). Marine Corps CD exercises are designated by the term "Grown Tall." Laws that govern the use of federal forces in civil law enforcement include the **Posse Comitatus Act**. (see also **civil disturbance readiness conditions**)

civil disturbance readiness conditions: "Required conditions of preparedness to be attained by military forces in preparation for deployment to an objective area in response to an actual or threatened **civil disturbance**" [*JCS Pub 1*, p. 68]. The civil readiness alert status ranges from communications watch, to initial alert, to advanced alert, to attack warning, to termination of attack warning.

Civil Reserve Air Fleet (CRAF): Program of the **Military Airlift Command (MAC)** that provides emergency civilian airlift in support of DOD requirements. It was established in 1952 and is composed of American commercial aircraft and crews—approximately 380 planes from 26 civilian airlines—that, if mobilized, would represent about half of the airlift available to DOD. Since the entire CRAF is not needed for all contingencies, it is separated into three states:

- Stage I of mobilization ("Committed Expansion") is initiated by the CINC-TRANSCOM and consists of about 50 aircraft.
- State II ("Airlift Emergency") is initiated by the Secretary of Defense and adds about 25 long-range and 30 domestic planes.
- Stage III ("National Emergency") is ordered by the Secretary of Defense upon declaration of an emergency by Congress or by the President.

During Stage III, the CRAF would provide close to half of MAC's strategic airlift needs (25 percent of DOD cargo airlift, 95 percent of its passenger transport). In peacetime, CRAF contractors earn revenue by providing daily transportation for the DOD. Additional contracts with civilian airliners for the modification of commercial transports are being sought by the U.S. Transportation Command and MAC in order to meet the DOD's goal of 66 million ton-miles per day in cargo capacity by the year 2000.

Civil Situation Report (CIVSIT-REP): Principal federal-level reporting system as part of the civil government mobilization planning and management system. During wartime, the CIVSITREP would be prepared daily by the **Federal Emergency Management Agency** to summarize the major civilian activities during the previous 24-hour period.

CIWS (Close-in Weapon System) (see **Phalanx**)

cladding: A thin layer of metal, totally enclosing nuclear fuel in a reactor, that protects the fuel from chemical corrosion by the coolant, prevents the escape of fission products, and provides structural support.

clandestine: "Activity to accomplish intelligence, counter intelligence, and other activities sponsored or conducted by governmental departments, or agencies in such a way as to assure secrecy or concealment of the operation. In common usage: hide the act" [*USAF SOF Master Plan*].

Clarinet Merlin: Emergency **satellite communications** system using submarine-launched one-way transmissions to communicate from submarines to the National Command Authority.

Clarinet Merlin is used to report the loss or "in extremis" situation of a strategic submarine. The system is composed of an AN/BST-1 buoy and an AN/FRR-93 receiver system. The buoy broadcasts a continuous signal at 12–15 words per minute in the HF band upon its release. The HF direction finding net can then find the approximate position of the submarine.

Clarinet Pilgrim: Shore-to-submarine communications by superimposing Navy fleet broadcasts on the LF carrier wave transmitted by **LORAN-C** navigation stations worldwide. The 30 LORAN-C LF stations serve as backups to the Navy VLF stations, and in turn are backed up by HF stations that broadcast the same information. The Clarinet Pilgrim system is equipped to broadcast command and control messages to ballistic missile submarines during all weather conditions but only within a limited part of the world, principally in the northern hemisphere. Transmitted information is in the form of a radio teletype stream of binary data. The system is in use all of the time and is installed in the Northwest Pacific LORAN-C chain, which includes Iwo Jima, Volcano Island, Marcus Island, Hokkaido, Okinawa, and Yap Island. All stations in the chain transmit the same data. A receiver usually receives information from the three strongest stations and then combines the information into a single best estimate of the data.

Classic: General Navy code word designation for intelligence, signals security, and sensitive command, control, and communications programs. Examples of Classic programs include Classic Alpine, Classic Ascot/Nomad, Classic Baritone, Classic Coyote, Classic Flaghoist, Classic Fox, Classic Julep, Classic Music (Multiuse Special Intelligence Communications), Classic Oracle, and Classic Seacoast. Classic Outboard is the code name for the Navy over-the-horizon ocean surveillance equipment employed aboard U.S. surface ships. It operates on 30 ships to detect, classify, and locate hostile vessels through the collection of electronic data. Targets include ships, aircraft, and submarines. (see also **Classic Wizard, Bullseye, Hydrus**)

Classic Wizard: Code name for the Navy's first ocean surveillance satellite system, initially launched 30 April 1976. It consists of a space-based component (called **White Cloud**) and a ground-based network of receiving and transmitting stations for satellite information. Classic Wizard ground stations are located at **Naval Security Group** activities at Adak, AK; Winter Harbor, ME; Edzell, Scotland, UK; Diego Garcia; and Guam. (see also **Classic, satellite reconnaissance**)

classification: The determination that official government information or material requires a specific degree of protection against unauthorized disclosure, coupled with a designation signifying that such a determination has been made by a classification authority, because revelation of the information would damage national security. (see also **security classification**)

classified (see **security classification**)

clean weapon: A nuclear weapon with an absence of **fission** or the production of fission products. The cleanliness of a nuclear weapon is a matter of degree; if the total yield is due only to thermonuclear or **fusion** reactions, the weapon is said to be completely "clean."

Clipper Bow: Code name of a planned Navy ocean surveillance satellite system to be equipped with active radar for the detection of surface vessels. It would have complemented the **White Cloud** ocean surveillance satellite system in the identification of ships, by allowing the comparison of **radar intelligence** and **signals intelligence** information.

close air support: Air strikes against targets near enough to ground combat units that detailed coordination between air and ground elements is required. It is one of three functional missions of offensive air support, and a part of tactical **air operations**.

close-hold: **1.** Control on information designating a special sensitivity, particularly to protect intelligence sources or operational options. **2.** Security control placed on **operation plan (OPLAN)** information during its development stage, restricting access to only certain personnel and **Worldwide Military Command and Control (WWMCCS)** System terminals. (see also **limited access, normal access security classification**)

CNO (see **Chief of Naval Operations**)

coastal minehunter (see **mine warfare ship**)

coastal patrol combatant (see **patrol combatant**)

coastal river squadron: An operational Navy unit with expertise in all facets of riverine and inshore coastal warfare, including riverine patrol, assault coastal patrol and interdiction, and support of naval special warfare units.

Coast Guard (USCG): Separate military service operating within the Department of Transportation. It was established 4 August 1790 as the Revenue Marine of the Department of Treasury, with responsibilities for duty collection, enforcement of embargos and quarantines, pirate hunting, and other law enforcement tasks. In 1915, the Revenue Cutter service merged with the U.S. Lifesaving Service to form the U.S. Coast Guard. Its duties expanded to include port safety and security, vessel safety, icebreaking, and marine environmental protection. In 1939, it was joined by the Lighthouse Service and gained navigation aids functions. The USCG was transferred to the Department of Transportation upon its formation in 1967.

Today, the USCG is assigned both peacetime and wartime missions. The statutory basis for its functions and missions, as amended, are found within 14 U.S. Code. Its primary peacetime mission is the enforcement of U.S. laws and treaties in coastal waters and on the high seas subject to U.S. jurisdiction. This includes enforcement of U.S. customs and immigration laws, illegal drug and immigration interdiction, enforcement of fisheries laws, and enforcement of the 200-mile economic zone. Other missions include recreational boating safety, merchant marine safety, port and environmental safety, search and rescue, and operation of approximately 400 lighthouses and 13,000 minor navigational lights. In addition, a March 1984 memorandum of understanding between the Secretaries of the Navy and Transportation designated the commanders of the Atlantic and Pacific USCG Regions as **Maritime Defense Zone** area commanders, with peacetime and wartime coastal defense responsibilities. Also in peacetime, in preparation for its wartime role, the Secretary of Transportation provides for the readiness of the USCG as a reserve force of the U.S. military. Its wartime role commences upon declaration of war or when directed by the President. At such time, the USCG becomes a functioning military service within and reporting to the Navy, providing units to the operational commanders of the area fleets (Commander **Task Force** 44 of the **Atlantic Fleet**, or a similar task force of the **Pacific Fleet**). Its specific wartime missions largely parallel its peacetime activities, with greater emphasis placed on its civil maritime traffic control responsibilities.

The USCG organization consists of an administrative headquarters, 2 area commands, 10 districts, 7 training schools, and numerous support and supply centers. Large floating units, those longer than 180 ft, operate within a district under the command of an area commander, a Vice Admiral. Smaller floating units, air units, and marine safety units report to a district comman-

der, a Rear Admiral. The total personnel strength of the USCG is approximately 87,000 active, reserve, civilian, and auxiliary (volunteer) personnel, including just under 37,000 on active duty. Its FY 1989 budget was close to $3 billion.

Headquarters

- Administrative: Washington, DC 20593
- Atlantic Area: Governors Island, NY 10004
- Pacific Area: Coast Guard Island, Alameda, CA 94501

Coast Guard Districts

- 1st CG District, Boston, MA 02210-2209
- 2d CG District, St. Louis, MO 63103
- 5th CG District, Portsmouth, VA 23705
- 7th CG District, Miami, FL 33130
- 8th CG District, New Orleans, LA 70130
- 9th CG District, Cleveland, OH 44199
- 11th CG District, Long Beach, CA 90882
- 13th CG District, Seattle, WA 98174
- 14th CG District, Honolulu, HI 96813
- 17th CG District, Juneau, AK 99801

(see also **Coast Guard Reserve**)

Coast Guard Reserve: Federal **reserve** component of the U.S. **Coast Guard**. It contributes approximately 56 percent of the Coast Guard's total port safety and security forces. Reservists augmenting active units report to the Commandant of the Coast Guard through the

Chief, Office of Readiness and Reserves, and area and district offices. During FY 1988, the Coast Guard Reserve received less than one percent of the total reserve appropriations. It makes up approximately 26 percent of the Coast Guard's personnel strength, or about 19,000 reservists, including 13,000 in the Selected Reserve, 5,000 in the Individual Ready Reserve, 373 in the Standby Reserve, and 776 in the Retired Reserve.

Cobra   (see **AH-1 G/S Cobra**)

Cobra Ball: Nickname for the **RC-135S** intelligence collection aircraft operated by the **Strategic Air Command**. The RC-135S is modified from the C-135B. There are two Cobra Ball planes, stationed at Eielson AFB, AK, and operating from Shemya AFB, AK. Their mission, named Burning Star, is the collection of **signals intelligence** on ballistic missile tests, specifically the reentry phases of Soviet and Chinese ICBM, SLBM, and IRBM research and development tests. Cobra Ball aircraft remain on alert to receive notification from the Defense Special Missile and Astronautics Center (DEFSMAC) of an impending test. The planes are equipped with three sensor systems: the Advanced Telemetry System (ATS); Ballistic Framing Camera System; and Medium Resolution Camera (MRC) System. [Jeffrey Richelson, *The U.S. Intelligence Community*, 2d Ed., pp. 176–78].

Cobra Dane: Air Force-operated phased array radar located on Shemya Island, AK, at the tip of the Aleutian Island chain. It was fully activated 13 July 1977. Its primary mission is the collection and verification of **signals intelligence** regarding Soviet ballistic missile tests that terminate in the Pacific or Asian region. Its secondary missions are to provide augmentation to the **BMEWS** (Ballistic Missile Early Warning System), to compute predicted impact points, and to track satellites. Cobra Dane consists of an AN/FPS-108 radar facility and a Precision Measurement Equipment Laboratory (PMEL). It has a 28,000-mile range and the capability to track "a basketball-sized object at a range of 2,000 miles with a 120-degree field of view extending from the northern half of Sakhalin Island to just short of the easternmost tip of the Soviet Union nearing the Bering Strait" [Jeffrey Richelson, *The U.S. Intelligence Community*, 2d Ed., pp. 181–83].

Cobra Dane can be transferred to a full-time early warning function. When employed for space surveillance or early warning purposes, it can track up to 200 satellites and 300 incoming warheads. The radar is limited, however, in that Soviet reentry vehicles in their final, near-earth trajectories are not visible due to line-of-sight constraint from the curvature of the earth.

Cobra Eye: Air Force-operated, specially equipped **RC-135** reconnaissance aircraft equipped with the Army's Optical Airborne Measurements Program (OAMP) sensor. The aircraft operate from Shemya AFB, AK. They are used for SDI data collection and research, particularly to take measurements of and photograph Soviet missile reentry vehicles during tests.

Cobra Judy: Navy-operated phased array radar mounted aboard the USNS

Observation Island and used to collect **signals intelligence** on Soviet missile tests into the Pacific Ocean. It consists of an AN/SPQ-11 phased array radar, a complex of passive receiving antennae, and an X-band radar with parabolic dish antennae. Cobra Judy enables the United States to monitor Soviet reentry vehicles in their final, near-earth trajectories, which are untrackable by **Cobra Dane** due to line-of-sight constraint from the curvature of the earth [Jeffrey Richelson, *American Espionage and the Soviet Target*, 1987, p. 167].

Cocked Pistol: Exercise term for **Defense Readiness Conditon (DEF-CON)** 1.

code: A **cryptographic** system in which the cryptographic equivalents (usually called code groups), typically consisting of letters or digits (or both) in otherwise meaningless combinations, are substituted for plain text elements such as words, phrases, or sentences.

coded switch system (CSS): "A system installed in an aircraft or missile which, with associated ground equipment, precludes prearming of a nuclear weapon until the insertion of a prescribed discrete code." The code that will cause or permit the operation of a CSS device is called a "coded switch system command" [AF, *Communications Security for Nuclear Command and Control Communications*, AFR 205-28, 10 August 1973, released under the FOIA].

code word: 1. A word that conveys a special, prearranged meaning other than the conventional one; it is normally assigned a classification and a

classified meaning to safeguard information regarding a classified plan or operation. **2.** Codeword: "Any of the series of designated words or terms used with a **security classification** to indicate that the material so classified was derived through a sensitive source or method, constitutes a particular type of **sensitive compartmented information (SCI)**, and is therefore accorded limited distribution" [*DIC Glossary*]. **3.** "A word selected from those listed in JANAP [Joint Army Navy Air Force Publication] 299 and subsequent volumes assigned a classified meaning by appropriate authority to ensure proper security intentions, and to safeguard information pertaining to actual, 'real world' military plans or operations classified as confidential or higher. A code word shall not be assigned to text, drill or exercise activities" [SAC, *Strategic Air Command Regulations: Operations. SAC Exercise Program*, SACR 55-38 Vol. 1, 16 November 1984. p. 2-2, released under the FOIA]. (see also **nickname**)

Cohesion Operational Readiness and Training (COHORT) program: One of two subsystems of the new **Unit Manning System** of the Army, adopted in 1981 to move from a system of exclusive reliance on individual replacements toward one based on movement of entire units, beginning with combat units. The theory of the program is that "by keeping soldiers together with their leaders in units longer, soldiers possess more horizontal cohesion, demonstrate more self-confidence, and are more psychologically ready for combat. COHORT soldiers also exhibit better teamwork and are generally more dedicated to unit service vice individual service." The two types of COHORT units and their characteristics are

- *Traditional COHORT unit*: Fixed life cycle (usually 36 months); initial-term soldiers normally enlisted under three- or four-year Variable Enlistment Legislation (VEL) contracts; soldiers (both career and first-term) are stabilized in the unit for the duration of the unit's life cycle.
- *Sustained COHORT unit*: Initially established as traditional COHORT unit but not given a fixed life cycle; initial-term soldiers may be assigned regardless of enlistment term, providing they can otherwise meet OCONUS tour length requirements, and package replacement cycles are not necessarily required to be VEL; soldiers are stabilized based on tour length or other non-COHORT specific policies; soldiers are assigned to and from units as members of a package during a scheduled assignment window (usually every four months).

Since 1981, 197 companies were built and sustained in the COHORT program. A 1987 plan between the U.S. Army in Europe, Forces Command, U.S. Army Western Command, and the Army called for the formation of up to 33 traditional COHORT companies to be deployed to South Korea each year for manning combat units of the 2d Infantry Division. All four Light Infantry Divisions formed units using the traditional COHORT methodology and have received approval to convert to sustained units [DOD, *Manpower Requirements Report FY 1989*, March 1988, pp. III-28, 29]. (see also **Regimental System**)

cold launch: A "pop up" technique that ejects **ballistic missiles** from silos or submarines by emitting compressed gas or steam into the air before the main engine is ignited. Ignition is delayed until the missile is safely clear of the launcher.

cold war: "A state of international tension wherein political, economic, technological, sociological, psychological, paramilitary, and military measures short of overt armed conflict involving regular military forces are employed to achieve national objectives" [*JCS Pub 1*, p. 72]. (see also **conflict, crisis**)

collateral damage: Physical harm inflicted by intent or otherwise on persons and property as a result of an attack on a primarily military target.

collocated operating base (COB): A civil or military airfield in a NATO country earmarked for wartime use by U.S. forces. This alleviates, to some extent, the congestion of U.S. forces on U.S. airfields in the host country. Under the COB **Host Nation Support** program, the U.S. concludes agreements for the use of alirfields and for operations of the facilities at the airfield, including communications facilities and the minimum supply of fuel.

Colossus: Code name for an ocean-bottom array of the **Sound Surveillance System (SOSUS)**. It was employed in the late 1960s and is an upgraded version of **Caesar**, the first sonar in the network. It was placed off the Pacific coast of the United States [Jeffrey Richelson, *American Espio-*

nage and the Soviet Target, 1987, p. 169].

COM: Prefix used in the Navy with the short title of a **command** indicating reference to the commander rather than the command (e.g., COMSUBLANT indicates Commander, Submarine Forces, Atlantic Fleet, not the force SUBLANT). (see also **commander/ commanding officer**)

combat air patrol (CAP):   Aerial operations conducted over a naval task force or air defense area for the purpose of intercepting hostile aircraft before they reach their target. A "dawn and dusk combat air patrol" is referred to as a DADCAP [*JCS Pub 1*, p. 73].

combat alert status (CAS)   (see **quick reaction alert**)

combatant command: A unified command or **specified command**. The commander of a combatant command is designated Commander-in-Chief (CINC). The **Department of Defense Reorganization Act of 1986** requires that all forces under the jurisdiction of the military department be assigned to unified and specified combatant commands with the exception of forces assigned to perform the mission of the military department (i.e., recruit, supply, equip, maintain, etc.). In addition, all forces in a CINC's area of responsibility will be under the command of the combatant command.

combat area: That part of the Army theater of operations required by combat forces to conduct operations. It includes the geographical area extending from the enemy-controlled area to the rear boundary of the highest land combat operational echelon. Lateral and rear boundaries are designated by the theater commander and include all areas necessary for maneuver, combat support, and combat service support of organic forces. The area from the rear of the combat area to the rear of the theater of operations is known as the **communications zone (COMMZ)**.

combat arm: Branch of the Army whose primary mission is combat: **Infantry, Armor, Field Artillery, Air Defense Artillery,** and **Aviation**. (see also **combat service support, combat support**)

combat aviation brigade: A new Army maneuver brigade formed with the grouping of two of the **division**-base combat assets, the **cavalry** squadron and the **attack helicopter** battalion. It provides the division commanders with a fourth maneuver headquarters and provides unity of command for divisional aviation assets. In addition to attack helicopter and cavalry forces, the aviation brigade provides maneuver capabilities to dismounted infantry in **air assault** operations; combat support by repositioning of artillery, air defense, and engineer assets; and immediate personnel or logistical transport of personnel and equipment.

combat control team (CCT):   1. Air Force **special operations** personnel dropped into enemy or unsecured territory to give navigational and communications aid to follow-on airborne assault elements.   **2.** "Air

Force personnel organized, trained, and equipped to establish and operate navigational or terminal guidance aids, communications, and aircraft control facilities within the objective area of an airborne operation" [USCENTCOM, *Operations Standing Operating Procedures*, CENTCOM Reg. 525-1, 30 March 1984, p. C-10-B-3, released under the FOIA].

combat electronic warfare intelligence (CEWI):   Army tactical intelligence activities assigned to the field command that integrate **signals intelligence** collection, **signals security, reconnaissance, human intelligence, counterintelligence**, and analysis in support of a combat commander, particularly at the division level or above. The CEWI battalion at the division consists of four organic companies: headquarters and operations company, ground surveillance company, collection and jamming company, and service support company.

combat information center (CIC): The section of a ship manned and equipped to collect, collate, and display tactical information. It is not the bridge of a ship but its command center, and it is usually located to the rear of or directly beneath the bridge.

combat maneuver battalion (see **battalion**)

combat radius: The maximum distance an operational aircraft at design gross weight characteristically armed for a combat mission can fly unrefueled from base to target and return safely, allowing for fuel expenditure involved in combat action (at differing angles, speeds, and altitudes) typical of the mission profile. Also called operating radius.

combat ready: Synonymous with **operational readiness.** (see also **readiness**)

Combat Sent: Nickname for Air Force **RC-135U** airborne reconnaissance aircraft, a modified RC-135C. There are two Combat Sent planes assigned to the **Strategic Air Command**. Their mission is the collection of **electronics intelligence** and other noncommunications intelligence along the periphery of the Soviet Union and Warsaw Pact countries. Targets include Soviet radar systems. The planes are equipped with the Precision Power MeasurementSystem, a high-resolution camera, and TV and radar sensors. One of the planes contains Compass Era, an infrared thermal imaging, interferometer-spectrometer, and radiometer sensor system [Jeffrey Richelson, *The U.S. Intelligence Community*, 2d Ed. pp. 177–78].

combat service support: **1.** Indirect combat assistance provided by one military organization to another.   **2.** **Branch** of the Army whose primary mission is combat service support and administrative support: **Adjutant General Corps, (Army) Corps of Engineers, Chemical Corps, Finance Corps, Ordnance Corps, Quartermaster Corps, Military Police Corps, Signal Corps, Judge Advocate General Corps, Transportation Corps, Army Medical Depart-**

ment, and the **Chaplain Corps**. Their functions range from participation as organic elements in forward combat units, through support commands, through services at the national level. Three of the combat service support arms (Corps of Engineers, Signal Corps, and Military Police Corps) are also categorized as **combat support** branches.

combat support: 1. Operational combat assistance provided by a military organization to combat elements. In the Air Force, combat support groups operate and maintain an installation and provide base-level support to other units and organizations located on-base. A combat support group normally consists of a commander; several squadrons: security police, civil engineering, and services; an administrative staff; and a training and headquarters squadron section. **2. Branch** of the Army whose primary mission is combat support: **Corps of Engineers, Signal Corps, Military Police Corps, Chemical Corps, and Military Intelligence**. Three of the combat support arms (Corps of Engineers Signal Corps, and Military Police Corps) are also categorized as services because units of these arms also provide **combat service support**.

Combat Talon (see **MC-130H Combat Talon**)

combat unit: A unit that is expected to be offensively or defensively employed to fire weapons, release bombs, drop or land assault forces, conduct reconnaissance or surveillance, or engage in other operational activity directly related to combat.

combined: Military planning, organization, or activity in which forces or agencies of more than one nation participate under a single command. The concepts of **unified commanders** are generally applicable to combined commanders; however, since combined commands are binational or multinational, their missions and responsibilities (including command responsibilities) are established by agreements. The North American Aerospace Defense Command **(NORAD), Combined Forces Command (CFC)**, and **NATO** are examples of combined commands.

Combined Arms Initiative (CAI) (see **Forward Area Air Defense System (FAADS)**)

Combined Field Army (ROK/U.S.) (see **Combined Forces Command**)

Combined Forces Command (CFC): Joint **combined** command of the Republic of Korea and the United States, established 7 November 1978, with operational control of designated ROK and U.S. military forces for bilateral defense of South Korea. Commander-in-Chief, CFC is also the commander of the **United Nations Command** in Korea and **U.S. Forces Korea (USFK)** and is the Commanding General of the **Eighth U.S. Army** (the U.S. component of the ROK/U.S. Combined Field Army). The CFC's command staff structure is binational, and it receives guidance from an ROK/U.S. military committee, co-chaired by the respective chairpersons of the JCS. In wartime, the CFC would activate additional forces, including the Combined Unconventional Warfare Task Force and U.S. Marine Forces Korea. Its peacetime personnel strength is about 615,000.

U.S. component forces

- U.S. Forces Korea;
- Eighth U.S. Army;
- U.S. Air Forces Korea; and
- U.S. Naval Forces Korea.

COMINT (see **communications intelligence**)

command: 1. Authority vested in an individual for the direction, coordination, and control of military forces. There are two types of command: **operational command** and **operational control**. Operational command is authority to assign missions, deploy units, reassign forces, and delegate those functions as necessary. Operational control is limited in time and does not include authority to task components of the units assigned. Full command is authority over every aspect of military operations and administration. No NATO commander exercises full command as administration and logistics are national functions. The non-operational command of military organizations is called **administrative command. 2.** Order directing a particular action in a specific way. **3.** Unit, activity, or area under the command of one individual. (see also **commander/commanding officer, commander-in-chief, major command, major NATO command, major subordi-**

nate command, principle subordinate command, specified command, unified command).

command and control (C2): "The exercise of authority and direction by properly designated commanders over assigned forces to complete their mission. Command and control functions are performed through an arrangement of personnel, equipment, communications, facilities, and procedures that are used by commanders to plan and control forces and operations to complete their mission." [AFR 55-23]. "The NCA [National Command Authority] exercises operational direction and administrative support of U.S. forces worldwide, under all force postures. The capability to exercise these functions is provided by interoperating command and control (C2) systems, which also provide appropriate capabilities at the various command echelons for which they were designed. The total capability created by these interoperating systems is not a single system, nor is it planned to become one. Some C2 systems are dedicated to the support of the NCA and the JCS; however, for the most part, C2 systems are designed, developed, procured, and employed to satisfy mission requirements of the Service or command that normally uses them. Hence, individual systems must exhibit certain attributes to insure that C2 is not the limiting factor in U.S. warfighting capability but rather provides options for execution of plans and aids exploitations of battlefield opportunities." [JCS, *Policy and Procedures for Management of Joint Command and Control*

Commandants of the Marine Corps

GEN Lemuel C. Shepard	1 Jan 1952–31 Dec 1955
GEN Randolph McC. Pate	1 Jan 1956–31 Dec 1959
GEN David M. Shoup	1 Jan 1960–31 Dec 1963
GEN Wallace M. Greene, Jr.	1 Jan 1964–31 Dec 1967
GEN Leonard F. Chapman, Jr.	1 Jan 1968–31 Dec 1971
GEN Robert E. Cushman, Jr.	1 Jan 1972–30 Jun 1975
GEN Louis H. Wilson	1 Jul 1975–1 Jul 1979
GEN Robert H. Barrow	1 Jul 1979–30 Jun 1983
GEN Paul X. Kelley	1 Jul 1983–1 Jul 1987
GEN Alfred M. Gray, Jr.	1 Jul 1987–present

Systems, SM-7-82, 11 January 1982, pp. 1–10, released under the FOIA].

Tasks supported by command and control systems:

- Monitor the current situation, including the status of U.S. and non-U.S. forces.
- Formulate responses to warning and threat assessment.
- Select options, employ forces, and execute operation plans.
- Perform attack, strike, damage, and residual capability assessment.
- Reconstitute and redirect forces.
- Terminate hostilities and active operations to insure that the conflict terminates under conditions favorable to the United States.

The general components of the command and control system are

- Command facilities;
- Communications;
- Warning systems;
- Command and control procedures; and
- Command and control data collection and processing.

Commandant of the Marine Corps (CMC): Senior military officer in the **Marine Corps** and a member of the **Joint Chiefs of Staff**. He is responsible for keeping the **Secretary of the Navy** fully informed on the status of the Marine Corps and is responsible to the President and the Secretary of Defense for duties external to the Department of the Navy, as prescribed by law. Internal to the administration of the Department of the Navy, the Commandant is responsible for the administration, discipline, internal organization, training, requirements, efficiency, and readiness of the Corps; for the operations of the material support system; and for the performance of the Marine Corps. The Commandant is directly responsible to the **Chief of Naval Operations** for the organization, training, and readiness of those elements of the operating forces of the Marine Corps assigned to the operating forces of the Navy. The Commandant however, does not exercise operational control of combat forces, except when so directed by the Secretary of Defense or the Joint Chiefs of Staff. Operational control of the Marine Corps is exercised through the **Fleet Marine Forces** by the CINCs of the **U.S. Atlantic Command** and **U.S. Pacific Command** or other unified commands.

command center: A facility from which forces and operations are directed. Command centers are capable of gathering, processing, analyzing, displaying, and disseminating planning and operational data to commanded forces. Command centers "achieve survivability through mobility, redundancy, hardness, deception, dispersal, or combinations thereof for continuity of operations under the worst probable conditions of conflict, including nuclear, biological, and chemical attacks.

(a) Within any definable command structure, at least one command center must survive the threat projected by latest JCS-approved documents.

(b) The surviving command center(s) must be capable of supporting all mission-required C2 functional tasks of the supported command throughout all phases of any conflict.

(c) Alternate operating facilities are required to assure the survival of a military command and control capability" [JCS, *Policy and Procedures for Management of Joint Command and Control Systems*, SM-7-82, 11 January 1982, pp. 7–8, released under the FOIA].

The national-level major U.S. military command centers are

- **National Military Command Center (NMCC)**, Pentagon, Washington, DC
- **Alternate National Military Command Center (ANMCC)** (Site R), Raven Rock, PA;
- **SAC (Strategic Air Command) Command Post**, Offutt AFB, NE;
- Alternate SAC headquarters, Beale AFB, CA, and Barksdale AFB, LA;
- **NORAD Cheyenne Mountain Complex (NCMC)**, Colorado Springs, CO; and

- Alternate NORAD headquarters, North Bay, Canada.

(see also **combat information center, command post**)

Command Center Processing and Display System (CCPDS): A system of dedicated computers, software, display control elements, consoles, and associated system support hardware at the **National Military Command Center (NMCC), Alternate National Military Command Center (ANMCC), SAC** command center, and **NORAD Cheyenne Mountain Complex (NCMC)**. CCPDS is dedicated to the receipt, processing, and common display of missile, space, and atmospheric tactical warning and attack assessment information. The information derived from CCPDS is used by the National Command Authority (NCA), CINCSAC, and CINC NORAD, in decisions relating to the retaliatory execution of the **Single Integrated Operational Plan**, force survival, and the use of strategic reserves during the trans- and post-attack periods of a protracted nuclear war. The goal of the CCPDS-R replacement program is to upgrade the current CCPDS system at NCMC, ANMCC, SAC, and NMCC, and provide for a duplicate of the NCMC CCPDS to be placed in the Offutt Processing and Correlation Center at Offutt AFB, NE.

command, control, and communications (C3): Facilities, personnel, equipment, and procedures used to exercise authority and direction over military forces, particularly strategic nuclear forces. With respect to nuclear weapons, a "strategic" C3 system has been developed with "those capabilities required to provide survivable, reconstitutable, and secure means for management of the strategic nuclear forces and for technical support of operations of these forces prior to, during, and following global nuclear conflict" [DOD, *C3I Program Management Structure and Major Programs*, 10 December 1980, p. 12, released under the FOIA]. The FY 1990 budget for C3 programs is $21.3 billion.

There are three components of C3 systems:

- Command authorities: Control systems and command centers to analyze data, make decisions, carry out directions, and control forces. The basis of the command structure is to give civilian control over military forces and nuclear weapons.
- Sensors: Intelligence systems to provide warning of enemy attacks, assessments of enemy actions, results of own-force strikes, and targeting data for the use of U.S. forces. Strategic early-warning systems operate 24 hours a day to analyze potential enemy actions while tactical warning systems provide immediate data on pre-launch and actual launch actions. Tactical warning is done with ground- and satellite-based sensors of three types: satellites for infrared detection of land- and submarine-based missile launchers; land-based radars for detection of missiles in flight; and land-based radars for detection of bombers and airborne objects in flight.
- Communications links: Networks to distribute warning data from sensors to interconnected command cen-

ters and to transmit orders from command centers to forces and between forces. Redundant communications links (ELF, VLF, LF, MF, HF, VHF, UHF, SHF, EHF) connect the National Command Authority (NCA) and nuclear forces. According to DOD, strategic communications must "provide for rapid and certain delivery of Emergency Action Messages to the strategic forces, report-back from the forces, and support reconstitution of forces and command entities following an initial attack" [*C3I Program Management Structure and Major Programs*, p. 7]. The various systems "achieve flexibility, survivability, and security (including physical) of communications in support of operations throughout the spectrum of force postures." [JCS, *Policy and Procedures for Management of Joint Command and Control Systems*, SM-7-82, 11 January 1982].

Communication links include rearward communications systems to transmit early-warning information from satellites and radars to command centers; inter-military communications to evaluate warning information and plan response options; command communications for crisis management and direction of military forces; special networks for the control of nuclear weapons; special networks for discussions with the United States and the Soviet Union; and war-termination communications.

Programs related to strategic command and control systems under the Reagan Administration focused on enduring survivability. Priorities were the control of nuclear weapons, connectivity to forces to provide long-term endurance, and greater invulnerability to "cheap shots," such as electromagnetic pulse, sabotage, and jamming.

command, control, and communications countermeasures (C3CM): Techniques designed to deny access to command, control, and communications (**C3**) systems and information by unfriendly forces and a-gents. C3CM strategy is implemented through the use of disruption, deception, and physical destruction to degrade and destroy the enemy's command and control while protecting U.S. systems. C3CM include operations security, military deception, jamming, and physical destruction. There are two divisions of C3CM:

- Counter-C3: Measures taken to lessen the ability of enemy leaders to command and control their forces effectively; and
- C3 protection: Measures taken to maintain the effectiveness of U.S. and friendly C3 systems and activities. [*JCS Pub 1*, change 2, 1 December 1984, p. B-5]

command, control, communications, and intelligence (C3I): "Command and control systems are made up of people, equipment, and information systems designed to assist in planning, directing and controlling military forces. Command, control, communications and intelligence systems must enhance the inherent deterrent capabilities of both offensive and defensive forces. They must provide our commanders at all echelons with accurate, timely and credible information, provide a means to process, dis-

play and evaluate data and also provide the commander with the capabilities to transmit orders and decisions to our forces and weapons systems. We must also deny our adversaries the benefits they gain by disrupting our C3I systems and by using their own capabilities with impunity. Thus, the C3I mission area goals also include the development and operation of effective electronic warfare and command, control and communications countermeasures systems" [*C3I Handbook: Command Control Communications Intelligence*, 1986, p. 21].

C3I mission areas

- Nuclear force management:
  surveillance and warning;
  communications connectivity; and
  command and control elements.
- Conventional force management:
  information collection;
  information distribution; and
  command and control elements.
- Defense-wide information and communications:
  navigation and location systems;
  common-user communications;
  information systems; and
  communications and computer security.
- Electronic warfare:
  electronic countermeasures;
  electronic counter-counter-measures; and
  electronic warfare support systems.
- Defense intelligence:
  National Foreign Intelligence Program;
  tactical intelligence and related activities; and
  intelligence oversight.

- C3 countermeasures:
  C3 protection; and
  counter-C3.

command disable system (CDS): A device integrated into a storage container to disable a nuclear warhead by destroying critical components of the warhead. The CDS cannot be activated until a code is inserted. (see also **permissive action link**)

commander/commanding officer: Officer in command of a unit or activity. May be a staff officer in special cases. (see also **command, commander-in-chief, administrative command, operational command**)

Commander-in-Chief (CINC): 1. Title of the officer in supreme command of a military or naval force. The President is the Commander-in-Chief of all U.S. armed forces. **2.** The highest-ranking officer of a **combatant command**: a **unified command**, a **specified command**, and certain commands of **NATO** who have operational authority over military forces. The Goldwater-Nichols **Department of Defense Reorganization Act of 1986** makes commanders responsible to the National Command Authority (NCA) for the performance of their assigned missions. With this responsibility comes the assignment of all authority, direction, and control that Congress considers necessary to execute that responsibility. The act defines the command authority ("operational command") of the CINC to

- Give authoritative direction to subordinate commands, including all aspects of military operations, joint training, and logistics;
- Prescribe the chain of command within the command;
- Organize commands and forces to carry out assigned missions;
- Employ forces necessary to carry out assigned missions;
- Coordinate and approve administration, support, and discipline; and
- Exercise authority to select subordinate commanders and combatant command staff.

The Commanders-in-Chief are

- Commander-in-Chief **Allied Command Channel** (NATO)
- Commander-in-Chief **Forces Command**
- Commander-in-Chief **NORAD** (North American Aerospace Defense Command)
- Commander-in-Chief **Strategic Air Command**
- Commander-in-Chief **United Nations Command** (Korea)
- Commander-in-Chief **U.S. Atlantic Command**
- Commander-in-Chief **U.S. Central Command**
- Commander-in-Chief **U.S. European Command**
- Commander-in-Chief **U.S. Pacific Command**
- Commander-in-Chief **U.S. Southern Command**
- Commander-in-Chief **U.S. Space Command**
- Commander-in-Chief **U.S. Special Operations Command**
- Commander-in-Chief **U.S. Transportation Command**

The commanders of the **Allied Command Atlantic** and **Allied Command**

Europe (NATO) are called **Supreme Allied Commanders**.

Commander's Availability Checks: Calls initiated by the **National Military Command Center** periodically and received at the headquarters of unified and specified commanders to test the degree of their accessibility to the JCS and National Command Authorities via voice communications. These tests are termed "FLASH Availability Checks," "Command Conference Tests," and "Presidential Conference Tests."

Commander Task Force (CTF): Operational naval force under one commander. (see also **task force**)

Commando Escort: U.S. Pacific Command HF/SSB air-to-ground communications network providing point-to-point communications for USCINC-PAC command and control elements and the primary HF ground entry system for the Pacific airborne command post. Locations of transmitting and receiving stations in Japan: Kadena AB, Okinawa; Iruma, Owada (receiver); and Tokorozawa (transmitter). Yokota AB serves as the Global Command and Control System station for both Commando Escort and **Giant Talk**/Scope Signal III. An HF receiver is located at Hickam AFB, Honolulu, HI with a transmitter at Bellows AFS, Oahu, HI.

Commando Fox: Project name for the installation of the Air Combat Maneuvering Instrumentation (ACMI) range in the Pacific to provide enhanced capabilities for Air Force F-15s based at Kadena AB, Japan. Commando Fox includes five semi-submersible buoys in the Pacific Ocean for remote station monitoring of air combat maneuvers, an underwater fiber optics cable, and a microwave system that relays data back to the air base. The ACMI became operational in mid-1985.

command post (CP): Headquarters, usually located in the field, where the commander and staff direct actions in support of the unit's assigned mission. It is the focal point of the unit's operation and receives and disseminates orders, information, and requests pertinent to the assigned task. A higher level command post is normally referred to as a **command center**. (see also **airborne command post, command post exercise**)

command post exercise (CPX): A military exercise that involves the commander, staff, and communications within and between headquarters, where the participation by actual combat and support units is usually simulated. CPXs provide commanders and staffs with opportunities to develop and test procedures under adverse or stressful conditions and to recover from emergency-producing events. A CPX tests crisis or contingency plans, policies, procedures, supporting systems, staff functions, and organizational interfaces. CPXs provide the necessary environments to activate the alert system and to exercise and evaluate the capability of the National Military Command Center (NMCC) and unified and specified commands to react to regional contingency situations. CPXs vary in duration from a few hours to days or weeks. They may be compact procedural exercises or expanded, full-staff exercises following a pre-planned scenario. CPXs have great utility since they are relatively inexpensive in both time and funds compared to **field training exercises** [Air Force, *Air Force Participation in the Military Exercise Program*, AFR 55-37, 7 June 1985, p. 5, released under the FOIA].

Commercial sales: Security assistance-related program in which private U.S. firms sell small arms and combat support equipment such as firearms, chemical munitions, helicopters, radios, jeeps, and transport planes to foreign police and military agencies. Commercial sales are approved under the **Arms Control Export Act of 1976 (ACEA)**. Private weapons firms must apply for an export license to the **Office of Munitions Control (OMC)** in the State Department's Bureau of Politico-Military Affairs. The distinction between commercial sales and **foreign military sales (FMS)** is that large defense contractors undertake FMS projects in the course of their ongoing work for the DOD, whereas thousands of smaller firms receive some FMS orders but rely on commercial sales channels for their export sales. Commercial sales are reported in the State Department's Congressional Presentation for Security Assistance Programs because they are regulated and licensed by the OMC.

Commissioned officer   (see **officer**)

Common Strategic Rotary Launcher (CSRL): Rotary launcher for the internal carriage of weapons on Strategic Air Command **B-52H** and **B-1B** bombers. The CSRL program will develop a multipurpose launcher that is capable of uniform or mixed weapons payloads and that can accommodate current and projected cruise missiles, short-range attack missiles, and nuclear bombs. The prime contractor is the Boeing Military Airplane Co.

communications intelligence (COMINT): Type of **signals intelligence** information collected by the interception of voice communications. COMINT targets include governmentcommunications, communications of foreign diplomats while overseas, military command centers, local military units, political parties and opposition movements, terrorist groups, and narcotics traffickers. COMINT does not include communications obtained during the course of a counterintelligence investigation held within the United States.

communications satellite: A satellite that relays signals between communications stations. Military satellite communications are known as MilSatCom. The United States currently operates, or has under development, a number of distinct communications satellites for military purposes:

- **Defense Satellite Communications System (DSCS);**
- **Fleet Satellite Communications (FLTSATCOM);**
- **MILSTAR;**
- **AFSATCOM (Air Force Satellite Communications);**

- **LEASAT**;
- **LES-8/9**; and
- **Satellite Data System (SDS)**.

(see also **satellite communication**)

communications security (COM-SEC): "Protective measures taken to deny unauthorized persons information derived from telecommunications of the United States government related to national security and to ensure the authenticity of these communications." Security measures include cryptosecurity, transmission security, emissions security, and physical security. COMSEC measures related to the command and control of nuclear weapons include

- Nuclear command and control COM-SEC material: All material, including documents, devices, and equipment, used to encrypt, decrypt, or authenticate telecommunications that support nuclear weapons control and decision making, such as **coded switch systems** and **permissive action links**.
- Secure Voice Program: Common-user secure telephone systems under the Automated Secure Voice Communications Network (**AUTO-SEVOCOM**). The tactical secure voice program utilizes a wide variety of communications security devices, including Vinson, Parkhill, Bancroft, and ANDVT in aircraft, groundmobile, and fixed radio applications.

There are a number of techniques and devices used to achieve COM-SEC:

- Codes: Systems of communications in which arbitrary groups of symbols represent units of plain text of varying length. Codes may be used for brevity or for security.
- Ciphers: Any cryptographic systems in which arbitrary symbols or groups of symbols represent units of plain text of regular length, usually single letters, or in which units of plain text are rearranged, or both, in accordance with predetermined rules.
- Authenticators: Any security measures designed to protect communication systems against fraudulent transmissions.
- Call signs: Any combinations of characters or pronounceable words that identify communications facilities, communications activities, units, or authorities. Call signs are used primarily for establishing communications. Daily changing of call signs is one means of denying adversaries information on order of battle.

The Secretary of Defense acts as executive agent for COMSEC. Overall responsibility for COMSEC matters related to federal telecommunications is delegated to the Director of the **National Security Agency**. COMSEC policy and guidance is provided by the Systems Security Steering Group and its interagency subcommittee, the National Telecommunications and Information Systems Security Committee (NTISSC) [AF, *War Planning: USAF Operation Planning Process*, AFR 28-3, 30 June 1986, p. 330; Air Force, *Communications Security for Nuclear Command and Control Communications*, AFR 205-28, 10 August 1973, released under the FOIA].

communications zone (COMMZ): That part of an established theater of operations that extends from the rear area of the combat area to the rear of the theater of operations. The COMMZ includes lines of communications (LOCs), establishments for supply and evacuation, and the area necessary for area support groups to set up operations to support the combat forces.

Community On-Line Intelligence System (COINS): A network of **defense intelligence community** computer systems and computer terminals that have been interconnected for interagency sharing of machine-formatted files in real time.

community relations: "The relationship between military and civilian communities." The military community relations program is "that command function that evaluates public attitudes, identifies the mission of a military organization with the public interest, and executes a program of action to earn public understanding and acceptance" [*JCS Pub 1*, p. 81].

company (co): Largest Army or Marine Corps fighting formation commanded by a commissioned officer, and the basic tactical and administrative element of the maneuver **battalion**. A company typically consists of three or four platoons and support elements. An artillery unit of equivalent size is called a battery; an armored or air cavalry unit of equivalent size is called a troop. A company is normally commanded by a Captain and varies in strength from about 90 personnel and 17 tanks in a tank company to about 150 personnel and 9 infantry carriers in a mechanized infantry company.

compartmentation: The special management of an intelligence or **special operations** organization or activity so that information about the personnel, organization, or activities is kept secret from other intelligence or special operations components. (see also **sensitive compartmented information**)

Compass Call: Air Force **EC-130H** airborne **command, control, and communications countermeasures (C3CM)** platform used to intercept, analyze, and jam enemy C3 systems. Compass Call operates together with the **EF-111 Raven** and the **F-4G Wild Weasel:** the Wild Weasels destroy enemy missile sites and the EF-111s and Compass Call planes work to confuse adversary signals. During wartime, the EC-130H Compass Call aircraft would serve to protect allied tactical fighter planes involved in close air support and air interdiction missions.

Ten modified Lockheed EC-130H aircraft are equipped with an electronic warfare system to receive and process signals and disrupt selected targets. Although designed to support tactical air operations, Compass Call can be adapted for use in ground operations. The EC-130H has a crew of 12: 1 electronic warfare officer; 6 signal analysts; 1 maintenance technician; and 4 flight crew. Each aircraft has several added blade and trailing wire antennas mounted in housing pods under each wing and behind the tail. The wire antennas can be extended several hundred feet behind the aircraft while in flight for receiving enemy communications signals. The first EC-130H was delivered in July 1980 and assigned to the 41st Electronic Combat Squadron at Davis-Monthan AFB, AZ. Compass Call aircraft are stationed with the 43rd Electronic Combat Squadron at Sembach AB, West Germany. The systems operators are assigned to the 6919th Electronic Security Squadron, Electronics Security Command. The unit can be deployed worldwide and includes its own command, operations, and maintenance functions.

component command: "Service component commands with each **unified command** or **subordinate unified command**, if established, will be designated as the U.S. Army forces, the U.S. Naval forces, or the U.S. Air Force forces of the appropriate command. Each will be commanded by the senior officer of that component eligible to exercise command. Service forces assigned to a unified or **specified command** will be organized by the Service to support accomplishment of the missions of the commander of the unified or specified command. Headquarters staff and facilities for component commanders will be provided by the respective Services" [JCS, *Unified Command Plan*, SM-729-83, 28 October 1983, p. 3, released under the FOIA].

Comprehensive Test Ban (CTB): Negotiations from 1977–1980 between the United States, the Soviet Union, and the United Kingdom to ban all nuclear explosions in all environments.

President Carter began the CTB negotiations although the **Threshold Test Ban Treaty (TTBT)** and **Peaceful Nuclear Explosions Treaty (PNET)** were still unratified. In September 1977, the Soviet Union dropped its previous precondition to agreement that all nuclear nations must be a party to any comprehensive test ban agreement (France and China would not agree to any test ban and this had been a major stumbling block to the negotiations). In November 1977, the Soviet Union announced that it would suspend active peaceful nuclear testing, an important point since the difficulty of distinguishing weapons tests from peaceful tests was great. In 1978, the United States proposed in-country seismic verification stations and proposed "challenge" on-site inspections, a verification system the Soviets agreed to in March 1978.

Opposition to a total test ban slowed progress during 1978–1980. Internal U.S. government opposition to the CTB centered on the conviction by some that the reliability and safety of nuclear weapons would deteriorate, and a lack of confidence in seismic verification measures. The United States stepped back from its earlier position of an unlimited duration agreement to one lasting only three years without any specifications for renewal. In retaliation, the Soviet Union stipulated that the United Kingdom would have to accept an equal number of seismic stations in the British Isles as well as in overseas territories, to which the United Kingdom objected. This problem of seismic stations in the United Kingdom, however, remained unresolved.

President Carter then decided to press for the ratification of **SALT II** rather than to conclude the details of the CTB negotiations. CTB talks continued after the withdrawal of SALT II from Senate consideration (after the Soviet invasion of Afghanistan), but President Carter left office without any further progress on the CTB.

Following the election of President Reagan, U.S. participation in CTB negotiations was limited to general discussions at the **Conference on Disarmament** in Geneva rather than the tripartite discussions held under the Carter Administration. Verification issues were the major topic of discussion. Although the United States maintained that it was interested in the CTB, administration officials stated private opposition. Richard Perle, then-Assistant Secretary of Defense for International Security Policy, expressed the private administration position that "it would be irresponsible and unwise to enter into [the CTB] at this time. I happen to believe that the distant future in which it might make sense is sufficiently distant so that it is unwise for us even to discuss with the Soviets at this point a comprehensive ban on nuclear testing" [U.S. Congress, Senate Foreign Relations Communications, Nuclear Testing Issues, Hearing, 8 May 1986]. In July 1982, the CTB was formally tabled.

On 6 August 1985, the Soviet Union unilaterally declared a moratorium on underground nuclear tests, which it extended on 14 May 1986 and again on 8 August to last until 1 January 1987. The United States declined to join the moratorium: in August 1986, President Reagan's spokesperson Larry Speakes said that "a nuclear test ban is not in the security interests of the United States, our friends or allies" [Michael Gordon, "U.S. Again Says It Won't Join Soviet Moratorium," *New York Times*, 19 August 1986].

On 26 February 1986, the U.S. House passed H. J. Res. 3, "To Prevent Nuclear Testing," calling for the immediate ratification of the TTBT and PNET and a resumption of negotiations towards a CTB. The resolution did not meet with agreement from the Reagan Administration. In a letter to Senate Majority Leader Robert Dole dated 7 March 1986, President Reagan stated that H. J. Res. 3 "would undercut the initiatives I have proposed to make progress on nuclear test limitations issues, and they would set back prospects on a broad range of arms control efforts, including the achievement of deep, stabilizing, and verifiable arms reductions." On 14 March 1986, President Reagan proposed to the Soviet Union that they begin bilateral discussions on verification issues for the TTBT and PNET, particularly with regard to an on-site verification system known as CORRTEX. In October 1986, a joint House/Senate conference committee dropped earlier testing legislation, including H. J. Res. 3, in order to give President Reagan negotiating leeway at the Reykjavik summit. The House bill would have placed a one-year ban on U.S. tests of more than one kiloton as long as the Soviet Union maintained the same ban. The Senate resolution urged Reagan to resume the CTB talks. In February 1987, the Senate

Foreign Relations Committee sent the TTBT and PNET to the full Senate for consideration. On 26 February 1987, the Soviet Union ended their moratorium with a test at Semipalatinsk. The United States conducted 26 tests during the 19-month Soviet moratorium. Subsequent to the flurry of activity in 1987, the United States and Soviet Union have held a number of meetings at the government "expert" level to discuss verification and have conducted joint experiments at each other's test sites, but little progress has been made on negotiations to conclude the CTB Treaty. (see also **Limited Test Ban Treaty**)

compression wave: A seismic wave that vibrates through the crust and mantle of the earth. This wave is known as a P wave (for primary) because it is the first wave to arrive at a seismometer. An underground explosion is a source of nearly pure P waves because it applies a uniform pressure to the walls of the cavity it creates.

concept of operations: Commander's outline of an intended operation or series of operations. The concept is often embodied in campaign plans and **operation plans** [*JCS Pub 1*, p. 83].

Conceptual Military Framework (CMF):   The basic long-term NATO planning document, produced by the **Military Committee** and adopted at MC 299 in May 1985. It elaborates on guidance of MC 48/3 and is the first NATO policy to deal strictly with conventional issues. The CMF is designed to give broad conceptual guidance and project long-term requirements into

the early 1990s. There are seven key mission areas, covering defense against the first echelon, **follow-on forces attack (FOFA)**, counter-air operations, **command, control, communications, and intelligence (C3I)**, and three maritime areas. Eleven specific issues in emerging technology needs have been identified (e.g., NATO **Identification, Friend or Foe (IFF)** system). From this CMF, two more detailed statements have been prepared: the SACEUR CMF and the Tri-MNC (major NATO commanders) Maritime CMF. The SACEUR CMF is the detailed supporting analysis for the FOFA key mission area. These documents are translated into planning guidelines, force development goals, and technological needs.

conceptual phase: The initial period in the development of a weapon system when the technical, military, and economic bases for acquisition programs are established through studies and experimental hardware development and evaluation. The outputs are alternative concepts and their characteristics (estimated operational, schedule, procurement, costs, and support parameters) that serve as inputs to the Development Concept Paper on major systems, to memoranda on smaller systems and equipment, and to service decision documents (Program Management Directives) for programs that do not require OSD decisions.

Conference on Disarmament (CD): United Nations international forum held in Geneva for negotiating multilateral disarmament issues, particularly the **Comprehensive Test Ban**.

The Conference is represented by over 40 countries, including the 5 nuclear nations, with membership of non-nuclear states reviewed periodically. Predecessors to the CD include the Ten-Nation Committee on Disarmament (1959–1960), the Eighteen-Nation Committee on Disarmament (1962–1969), and the Conference of the Committee on Disarmament (1969–1978). From 1979 to 1983, the CD was known as the Committee on Disarmament. The first session of the present CD structure was held in 1979. Although the CD is not a subsidiary body of the General Assembly, it takes Assembly recommendations into account in forming its agenda. The Secretary General of the CD is appointed by the U.N. Secretary General, the CD budget is included in the U.N. overall budget, and CD meetings are held on U.N. premises and staffed by U.N. personnel. The CD meets annually in Geneva for approximately 6 months, usually when the General Assembly is not in session. The CD held its 1988 session in two parts: 2 February to 29 April and 7 July to 20 September.

In 1979, the following 10 items were decided on as the permanent CD agenda:

- Nuclear weapons in all aspects
- Chemical weapons
- Other weapons of mass destruction
- Conventional weapons
- Reduction of military budgets
- Reduction of armed forces
- Disarmament and development
- Disarmament and international security
- Collateral measures; confidence-building measures; effective verifi-cation methods in relation to appropriate disarmament measures, acceptable to all parties concerned
- Comprehensive program of disarmament leading to general and complete disarmament under effective international control

Conference on Disarmament in Europe (CDE):   Multilateral outgrowth of the **Conference on Security and Cooperation in Europe (CSCE)** review conference held in Madrid in August 1983. Originally conceived in 1978 by French President Giscard d'Estaing, the conference aimed to bring about new political and military **confidence-building measures**. Held in Stockholm from 1984–1987, the conference heard proposals from both NATO and the Warsaw Pact. NATO proposals included information exchange, early notification of military exercises, and improved verification techniques. The Warsaw Pact proposals stressed general themes, such as the no-first use pledge. On 1 January 1987, the Stockholm **Confidence- and Security-Building Measures (CSBMs)** went into effect. Known as the Stockholm Document, these measures impose tolerable constraints on military systems not planning aggression.

Conference on Security and Cooperation in Europe (CSCE):   An ongoing conference of the United States, Soviet Union, Canada, and 32 European countries (excluding Albania). The CSCE was established to discuss the political status quo in Europe, as well as economic, scientific, and cultural cooperation and human rights. First held in November 1972 in Helsinki, the CSCE produced agreements on 31 July and 1 August 1975 referred to as the "Helsinki Accords." In the 1975 Final Act of the conference, the United States, Canada, and 33 European NATO, neutral, and Warsaw Pact countries agreed to multilateral **confidence-building measures**, the most important of which provided for prior notification of, and voluntary invitation of observers to, military maneuvers and exercises involving more than 25,000 troops in the CSCE area. The Accords included three major provisions (called "Baskets"):

- Basket I: "The participating states regard as inviolable each other's frontiers, as well as the frontiers of all states in Europe." The use of force was also discarded as a legitimate way to settle disputes between states.
- Basket II: Trade and scientific and cultural exchange across European borders were reaffirmed as desirable.
- Basket III: Regard for human rights in Europe.

Review conferences have been held in Belgrade (1977–1978), Madrid (1980–1983), and Vienna (1987–1989). The Madrid Conference led to the **Conference on Disarmament in Europe (CDE)** at Stockholm in 1984. The CSCE review conference in Vienna continued from 1987–January 1989 and produced agreement for new negotiations on Conventional Forces in Europe (CFE) to begin 9 March 1989. Participants in CFE are the 16 NATO nations and the 7 Warsaw Pact countries. The 15-year-old **Mutual and Balanced Force Reduction (MBFR) Talks**

are scheduled to end once the CFE talks begin, with the last MBFR session to be held on 2 February 1989. Another series of talks arising from the CSCE deals with **confidence- and security-building measures (CSBMs)**, and include NATO, Warsaw Pact, and 12 other European countries as participants. The CSBM talks are designed to increase the willingness to talk openly about respective force levels.

Confidence- and Security-Building Measures (CSBMs): Series of talks held in Vienna to reduce political confrontation and to establish stable and cooperative relationships in all fields of international relations. The talks emerged from a recommendation made during the Madrid review session (1980–83) of the **Conference on Security and Cooperation in Europe (CSCE)**. The first series of talks convened on 17 January 1984. The second stage of the negotiations began in 1989. Guidelines for **confidence-building measures (CBMs)** as outlined by the U.N. General Assembly are to "reduce the dangers of misunderstanding or miscalculation of military activities, to help prevent military confrontation as well as covert preparations for the commencement of a war, to reduce the risk of surprise attacks and of the outbreak of war by accident, and thereby, finally, to give effect and concrete expression to the solemn pledge of all nations to refrain from the threat or use of force in all its forms and to enhance security and stability." On 7 December 1988, the U.N. General Assembly adopted without a vote the draft resolution entitled "Confidence- and

Security-Building Measures and Conventional Disarmament in Europe." The resolution reaffirmed the goals of the CSCE: to build confidence, to lessen the risk of military confrontation, and to enhance mutual security.

confidence-building measures (CB-Ms): Agreements designed to increase mutual understanding, knowledge, and communications between hostile states and alliances by making the intentions and, more particular, the military activities of each more predictable and less threatening during peacetime or crisis. CBMs are to reduce the possibility of conflict — especially nuclear conflict — through accident, miscalculation, or failure of communications. CBMs complement negotiated arms reductions. The use of CBMs is conceivable under two different scenarios:

- "Routine" situations, where the problem is to provide the communications and protocols to help prevent or sort out unexpected developments, unintended actions, or accidents; and
- Crisis situations, where it is necessary to resolve the issues giving rise to serious confrontations between nations.

CBMs in existence currently include

- The Washington-Moscow **Direct Communications Link** (Hotline), 1963; with addition of a facsimile machine in July 1984;
- Agreement on Measures to Reduce the Risk of Outbreak of Nuclear War, 1971;
- Agreement on the Prevention of Incidents On and Over the High Seas, 1972;

- **Agreement on the Prevention of Nuclear War**, 1973;
- Helsinki Accords, **Conference on Security and Cooperation in Europe**, 1975;
- **START** negotiations, including notification of ICBM and SLBM launches; advance notice of major military exercises; and expanded exchange of data on strategic nuclear forces;
- On-site inspections established by the **INF Treaty**; and
- Agreement on the Establishment of Nuclear Risk Reduction Centers (NRRCs) (1988).

confidential (C):   Security classification category applied to national security-related information "that requires protection and the unauthorized disclosure of which could reasonably be expected to cause damage to the national security." Of the three major classification levels, confidential is a lower category than both **secret (S)** and **top secret (TS)**. The transmission of confidential information is controlled in accordance with **communications security (COMSEC)** guidelines. Transmission is generally done through the Protected Distribution System (PDS) (formerly named Approved Circuits), which includes "all equipment and cabling used for the clear text transmission of classified information." However, "during hostilities, Confidential and Secret information may be electrically transmitted in-the-clear by unsecured means (such as telephone, teletypewriter, and radio) as an emergency measure" under certain conditions. Prior to the transmission of confidential information, a PDS must be evaluated, approved, and authorized at the service staff and major command level. In a tactical environment, authority to approve circuits for transmission of confidential information lies with the battalion commander and higher echelons.

Authorized access to confidential information is granted to an individual by a government agency based upon a local records check and the commander's consent. In FY 1986, confidential clearances were held by approximately 427,000 DOD and industry personnel [*JCS Pub 1*, p. 328].

conflict: Term used to describe all types of military activities that require the specification of **rules of engagement** and **operations plans**. The Joint Chiefs of Staff define five levels of conflict:

1. Day-to-day operations;
2. Crisis actions;
3. Application of conventional and limited nuclear forces;
4. Transattack in a general nuclear war environment; and
5. Postnuclear attack, including reconstitution.

[JCS, *WWMCCS ADP Concept of Operations and General Requirements for Post 1985*, SM-101-81, 6 Feb 1981, p. A-6].

(see also **crisis**)

CONPLAN (Concept Plan): An **operations plan (OPLAN)** in concept format, which requires expansion into an OPLAN or **operations order (OPORD)** prior to implementation.

Consolidated Cryptologic Program: Budget program managed by the

National Security Agency/Central Security Service and including all **signals intelligence (SIGINT)** resources within the National Foreign Intelligence Program (NFIP).

Consolidated Space Operations Center (CSOC): Organization of the **Air Force Space Command**. It operates in conjunction with (and as a backup for) the Air Force Systems Command's Satellite Test Center to manage the worldwide **Air Force Satellite Control Facility** network, which supports DOD satellites and plans, manages, and controls all DOD Space Shuttle flights at the Shuttle Operations and Planning Complex. CSOC is the focal point for day-to-day space operations. In 1987, CSOC personnel strength was approximately 2,000 personnel.

Headquarters
Falcon AFS, CO 80912

Constant Shotgun: Nickname identifying certain Soviet and People's Republic of China aircraft flights authorized to enter the United States and its territorial possessions. These flights are usually accompanied by Air Force flight crews who serve as escorts. Communication requirements for Constant Shotgun flights are provided by the **Global Command and Control System**.

Constant Watch: Combined Air Force/South Korean Air Force (ROK-AF) program to construct and equip a hardened command and control facility at Osan AB, South Korea, and harden and automate the **Tactical Air**

Control System in Korea. Phase I will construct a 87,000 sq ft hardened tactical air control center; provide space for a master control reporting center; baseline automation of intelligence functions; and consolidate upgraded and expanded communications. Phase II will install automated subsystems and automate the Korean combat operations intelligence center. Phase III will install automated systems in air support operations centers and wing operations centers; provide for operations/intelligence integration; and provide enhanced information and tasking dissemination.

constant-year dollars: The purchasing power of a dollar of any specific year, past, present, or future.

construction battalion unit (CBU): Naval organization within a fleet or shore establishment. Fleet CBUs fulfill long-term facilities-improvement requirements at specific locations. Shore CBUs are used for construction, alteration, repair, and non-recurring maintenance.

containment vessel: A gas-tight shell or other enclosure around a nuclear reactor, designed to contain the releases from accidents with little or no significant escape to the environment.

Continental Air Defense Integration North/Pinetree Line (see **CADIN**)

continental U.S. (see **CONUS**)

Continental U.S. Airborne Reconnaissance for Damage Assessment

(CARDA): Joint plan overseen by the Air Force for **reconnaissance** in the United States following an attack, to assess damage and report on the state of U.S. forces that might have been cut off by the destruction of communications. CARDA is governed by USAF OPLAN 2-84, 14 March 1984. It calls for automatic preplanned T-43 missions by the Air Training Command, and missions by training aircraft of the Navy and Marine Corps. Under CARDA, reconnaissance aircraft would submit "Glass Eye" reports to **NORAD** and remaining **command centers** for evaluating the reconstitution of U.S. forces. Reconnaissance in the Soviet Union following a nuclear strike falls under the **Single Integrated Operational Plan (SIOP)** Reconnaissance Plan (SRP).

contingency plan: "A plan for major contingencies that can reasonably be anticipated in the principal geographic subareas of the command" [*JCS Pub 1*, p. 86]. (see also **operation plan**)

continuity of government (COG): Federal emergency preparedness programs to ensure the survival of the presidency and to ensure that the "essential uninterruptible functions" of civilian government agencies, in support of the President, continue without interruption. The goals of COG are to organize the resources of the United States after an attack for utilization by the military, and to guarantee that the federal government is able to keep control of the economy, including the control of banks, credits, labor, food, and transportation.

Each federal agency has been charged to prepare COG plans, and 33 agencies and departments are designated as "essential and uninterruptible." Essential functions are

a. Provide the coordinating mechanism and a central emergency management operations center within the Executive branch for the collection and evaluation of information concerning an actual or impending crisis, or national emergency.

b. Provide advice and assistance to the National Security Council concerning:

1. Determination and assessment of the impact on the Nation of an actual or impending crisis or emergency.
2. Actions to be taken to avoid or reduce the effect on the Nation of an actual or impending crisis or emergency.
3. Emergency economic stabilization matters.
4. Actions to be taken to accelerate the readiness posture of the Federal civilian departments and agencies, and State and local governments.
5. Emergency succession to the Office of the Presidency.
6. Continuity of the Executive Branch of the Federal Government.
7. The status and the management of national security.
8. **Civil defense**.
9. The issuance of specific emergency action guidance of the Federal Government . . . .

d. Provide, in conjunction with the Federal departments and agencies concerned, an initial analysis of the transattack and immediate postattack situation, and make recommendations regarding measures and actions needed to ensure attainment of initial postattack objectives for the health and welfare of the people and the continuity of government and the reconstitution of the economy [FEMA, *Central Office Emergency Readiness Instructions*, FEMA Manual 8500.1, 5 March 1980, Chapter 2, p. 1, released under the FOIA].

The major COG effort is related to nuclear war, not natural disaster or conventional war (conventional war is the domain of "mobilization" preparedness). Each agency plan establishes lines of succession and authority; provides guidelines for the use of alternate headquarters and for the evacuation of key personnel; provides for communications; and provides for the protection and availability of records and information.

The centerpiece of COG plans is the dispersal of personnel to relocation sites in an area within 300 miles of Washington, DC, an area designated the "Federal Arc." Within this area is Mt. Weather, the civil government's site, as well as the **Alternate National Military Command Center**. Movement would be through the activation of the **Joint Air Transportation Service**.

The Kennedy assassination led to the adoption of the 25th Amendment to the Constitution, which deals with succession in the case of disability or inability. The amendment dealt with the flaw that there was no way to select a Vice President under the existing laws, and no way to determine and declare presidential disability. The 25th Amendment was ratified in 1967 and, together with the Presidential Succession Act of 1947, forms the legal basis for succession. On 9 February 1977, the Federal Preparedness Agency issued the secret "Plan for Succession to the Presidency Under Certain Emergency Conditions," coordinated with DOD and the White House Military Office. In 1980, President Carter issued a new directive on COG, emphasizing multiple locations and greater dispersal to protect the line of succession. A key part of the program was joint FEMA/DOD efforts to create enduring communications. The Reagan Administration kept COG planning and presidential-succession preparedness at a high level, creating the National Security Emergency Planning Senior Interagency Group (NSEP SIG) to oversee the effort. (see also **continuity of operations, Federal Emerergency Plan D**)

continuity of operations (COOP): Military programs equivalent to the civilian government programs for **continuity of government** but applying to the DOD and its components. The DOD Directive, "Continuity of Operations Policies and Planning," contains internal Defense Department planning in the event of "strategic nuclear attack upon the United States." It specifically states that "because a decision to relocate, particularly at the national level, might appear provocative, potentially escalating the crisis, the NCA [national command authorities] can be expected to initiate relocation in

a covert manner" [DOD, *Continuity of Operations Policies and Planning*, DOD Dir 3020.26, 24 October 1985, p. 2]. Parts of the COOP program are the **Joint Air Transportation System (JATS)** and the **Joint Emergency Evacuation Plan (JEEP)**.

The JCS prepares on an annual basis "Annex H, Nuclear Weapons Damage Considerations, Civil Defense, Recovery, and Reconstitution" of the **Joint Strategic Capabilities Plan**, which serves as the guide for the creation of Continuity of Operations Plans. The office of the Under Secretary of Defense (Policy) is designated as the principal point of contact between the DOD and other government agencies on COG operations and planning.

The DOD identifies two attack conditions, Alpha and Bravo, which are the basis of planning for COOP. Under attack condition Bravo, the DOD "assumes that there will be sufficient warning of impending attack for emergency staff personnel to relocate." Under attack condition Alpha, the DOD

assumes that a surprise nuclear attack will destroy peacetime headquarters of DOD components. Only those few personnel from these headquarters prelocated in hardened, mobile, or dispersed facilities are expected to survive. Planning under condition ALPHA shall incorporate use of existing facilities, designation of alternate headquarters and successors . . . [DOD, *Continuity of Operations*, 24 October 1985, p. 3].

continuous wave   (see **CW**)

control rod: A solid element used to control the multiplication factor of a **nuclear reactor**. The reactor functions through the splitting of nuclear fuel by neutrons. The control rod absorbs neutrons that would normally split atoms of the fuel. Hence, inserting the rod into the reactor core reduces the multiplication factor, decreases reactivity, and thus produces a decrease or shut-down in power production. Pulling the rod out increases power. Another type of control rod operates with a rotary motion.

controlled area: A security area adjacent to or encompassing a **limited area** or **exclusion area**. The controlled area is designed for the principal purpose of providing administrative control and safety, and a buffer of security restrictions for limited or exclusion areas.

CONUS (Continental United States): United States territory within the North American continent between Canada and Mexico, including adjacent territorial waters. Alaska and Hawaii, and overseas territories and possessions, are not part of CONUS.

conventional: Organizations, hostilities, and hardware that exclude nuclear, chemical, and biological capabilities.

Conventional Weapons Ban: Formally known as the "Convention on the Prohibition or Restriction on the Use of Specific Conventional Weapons Which May Be Deemed to Be Excessively Injurious or to Have Indiscriminate Effects." Opened for signature at the United Nations on 10 April 1981, the convention entered into force on 2 December 1983. The United States signed the convention on 8 April 1982 but never ratified it because of objections to a lack of treaty-stipulated compliance measures. The substance of the convention is contained in three protocols. Protocol I on Non-Detectable Fragments prohibits the use of "any weapon the primary effect of which is to injure by fragments which in the human body escape detection by X-rays." Protocol II prohibits and/or restricts the use of land mines (antiship mines are excluded), booby traps, and other similar devices against civilian populations. Restrictions on the use of mines, which cover both remotely and non-remotely delivered mines, as determined by Protocol II include

- In populated areas, warning signs or the like must be posted or placed in close proximity to military locations (Article 4); and
- Remotely delivered mines are permitted only within a military objective area, unless there is a self-activating neutralizing mechanism for when the mine is no longer needed or notification is given of pre-planned mine fields (Article 5).

Booby traps associated with the following are prohibited: international protective emblems; sick, wounded, or dead people; burial sites; medical facilities and equipment; children's toys and goods; food and drink; kitchen utensils (except for those in military establishments); religious objects; historic monuments and works of art; or animals or their carcasses (Article 6).

Protocol III covers Prohibitions or Restrictions on the Use of Incendiary Weapons. It sets limits on weapons designed to "set fire to objects or to cause burn injury to persons through the action of flame, heat, or a combination thereof, produced by a chemical reaction of a substance delivered on the target" (Article 1).

Restrictions on the use of incendiary weapons include

- Civilian populations may not be the object of attack (Article 20);
- Military objectives located within civilian areas are prohibited from attack by air-delivered incendiary weapons;
- Attack on military objectives within civilian areas by incendiary weapons other than the air-delivered variety is permitted only when precautions have been taken to separate the military from the civilian objectives and to avoid or minimize incidental loss of civilian life (Article 2).

On 23 September 1979, the Resolution on Small-Calibre Weapon Systems was adopted. The resolution calls for the continued research and discussion of wound ballistics as generated by small-calibre weapons. Although the resolution recognizes the deleterious effects of bullets that expand or flatten within the body, it makes no recommendations for their discontinued use.

convoy escort group (CEG): A group of warships assigned to escort a convoy of transport ships. Typically, a CEG consists of 10 destroyers or frigates and a nuclear-powered attack submarine.

coolant: A substance circulated through a **nuclear reactor** to remove or transfer heat. Common coolants are water, air, carbon dioxide, liquid sodium, and sodium-potassium alloy (NaK). In a pressurized water reactor, the water passes through the core to remove the heat liberated in the **fission** process. A coolant may also be referred to as a primary coolant.

cooperative measures: Measures taken by a party to an arms control agreement in order to enhance the ability of the other to verify compliance. Cooperative measures can be voluntary or negotiated. Examples include data exchanges or unilateral dismantling or destruction of older weapons.

COPAN (Command Post Alerting Network): Air Force non-secure voice communications alerting network between operations centers of selected major commands.

Copperhead: Marine Corps precision guided 155 mm artillery projectile fired from howitzers, at ranges of 3 to 16 km. One thousand eighty-eight are planned for FY 1987 at a cost of $37.8 million. The Copperhead M712 model is a laser-homing and cannon-launched guided projectile (CLGP) designed for antitank operations. The M712 has a maximum range of 16,400 meters. Prime contractor for the Copperhead is Martin Marietta.

core: The heart of a **nuclear reactor**, where the nuclei of the fuel **fission** (split) and release energy. The core is usually surrounded by a reflecting material, which bounces stray neutrons back to the fuel. The reactor core contains the fuel elements, moderator and support structures, and the **coolant** that passes through it.

core melt   (see **meltdown**)

Corona: Byeman code name for the Central Intelligence Agency's first photographic **satellite reconnaissance** system. Project Corona was approved by President Eisenhower in February 1958 by NSC document 5814/1, "Preliminary U.S. Policy in Outer Space," in response to the 4 October 1957 launching of the Soviet's Sputnik satellite. The early effort consisted of three programs:

- Discoverer satellite program, which served as a cover for Corona by placing an emphasis on biomedical research missions. Its first mission, Discoverer 1, failed to be launched on its intended date, 21 January 1959. It was launched in February but malfunctioned, as did the following 12 Discoverers for a variety of reasons. In all, 38 satellites were launched during 28 February 1959–27 February 1962. Among other information, the Discoverer program yielded intelligence on Soviet ballistic missiles and facilities. Corona, a specifically military reconnaissance system, subsequently launched six satellites on 7 March 1962, 26 April 1962, 17 June 1962, 18 July 1962, 5 August 1962, and 11 November 1962.
- Sentry reconnaissance satellite program, developed by the Air Force. It was initially called the Advance Reconnaissance System, or Pied Piper, until its name appeared in an article in *Aviation Week* and the program was renamed SAMOS (the Satellite and Missile Observation System). SAMOS 1 was launched on 11 October 1960 (but did not reach orbit). Thirty spacecraft were launched in all, the last on 27 November 1963.
- Missile Alarm Defense System (MIDAS), developed by the Air Force. It was the first early-warning satellite equipped with infrared detection scanners for the monitoring of Soviet ballistic missile launches. It was to be followed by the **Defense Support Program**.

(see also **keyhole**)

corps: 1. The largest Army combat organization capable of sustained administrative, logistical, and tactical operations. Smaller than a **field army**, a corps directs the combat operations of assigned **divisions** and provides them with **combat support** and **combat service support**. Its traditional missions are command and control and support of assigned divisions, but, under the **airland battle** doctrine, a corps functions as a principal operational maneuver unit as well. A corps is normally assigned a specific area of responsibility (AOR) and is organized depending on its mission. It typically consists of a headquarters, a **corps support command (COSCOM)**, two or more divisions, and other support units. The types of corps are forward-deployed corps predeployed in the theater of operations; corps contingency forces deployed in an area where no U.S. bases have been established; heavy corps consisting of armor and/or mechanized divisions;

and lights corps consisting of infantry, air-mobile, or airborne divisions. A corps is commanded by a Lt. General. The active Army Corps organized in peacetime are

- I Corps, Ft. Lewis, WA 98373;
- III Corps, Ft. Hood, TX 76544;
- V Corps, Frankfurt, West Germany;
- VII Corps, Stuttgart, West Germany;
- IX Corps, Camp Zama, Japan;
- IX Corps (R), Ft. DeRussey, HI 96815; and
- XVIII Airborne Corps, Ft. Bragg, NC 28307.

2. Organization of career field on special **branch** of the Army.

Corps of Engineers (see **Army Corps of Engineers**)

corps support command (COS-COM): Organization responsible for providing **combat service support** (minus water, communications security equipment, and construction) within the corps area of operations. The COSCOM organization is flexible, and the theater army commander may add or remove units to support changes in corps missions or composition of forces. The COSCOM has two types of subordinate elements: corps-wide services organization, which provide health services, personnel and administration, ammunition, and civil affairs; and support groups, which are assigned to provide supply, maintenance, and field services on an area basis. The COSCOM commander is considered to be on the same level as the division commander.

corrigendum: A modification of a JCS paper that requires that the paper be reissued in whole or in part.

CORRTEX (Continuous Reflectometry for Radius versus Time Experiment): Hydrodynamic yield measurement technique that measures the propagation of the underground shock wave from a nuclear explosion. CORRTEX uses a coaxial cable that can be placed in a hole parallel to the device-emplacement hole. Precise measurements are made of the length of the cable by timing the return of low energy electrical pulses sent down to, and reflected from, the cable end. When the nuclear device is detonated, a shock wave emanates through the ground, crushing and shortening the cable. The rate by which the cable length changes is recorded via measurements of the changing pulse transit times. This rate is a measure of the propagation rate of the explosive shock wave through the ground, which is, in turn, a measure of the yield of the nuclear explosion. The electronic device providing the timing signals is a battery-powered, suitcase-sized unit that may be remotely controlled. All equipment for power, recording, and data reduction can be contained in a small trailer. (see also **Comprehensive Test Ban**)

Corsair II   (see **A-7 Corsair II**)

COSMIC: NATO code word designating **top secret** information that originated in NATO organizations or commands and that circulates freely within the alliance among properly cleared individuals. It is treated with the same security requirement as top secret information in the United States except that it requires a special NATO access agreement. (see also **ATOMAL, security classification**)

counterespionage: Counterintelligence activity "designed to detect, destroy, neutralize, exploit, or prevent espionage activities through identification, penetration, manipulation, deception, and repression of individuals, groups, or organizations conducting or suspected of conducting espionage activities" [*JCS Pub 1*, p. 93].

counterforce: "The employment of strategic air and missile forces in an effort to destroy, or render impotent, selected military capabilities of an enemy force under any of the circumstances by which hostilities may be initiated" [*JCS Pub 1*, p. 94]. (see also **countervalue**)

counterinsurgency: "Those military, paramilitary, political, economic, psychological, and civic actions taken by a government to defeat insurgency" [*JCS Pub 1*, p. 94]. (see also **special operations**)

counterintelligence: Intelligence activity intended to detect, counteract, and/or prevent espionage and other clandestine intelligence activities, sabotage, or terrorism. The Defense Intelligence Agency (DIA) Office of Security produces counterintelligence analysis and terrorist threat studies and coordinates all service counterintelligence. Air Force counterintelligence falls under the **Air Force Office of Special Investigations**. The Army's counterintelligence effort is headed by the **Army Intelligence Agency** and the **Army Intelligence and Security Command**, depending on whether the effort is strategic or in direct support of field commands and units. Naval counterintelligence is the responsibility of the **Naval Investigative Service**. The Marine Corps has 11 Counter Intelligence Teams within the Fleet Marine Force assigned to major installations. Their responsibilities include terrorist intelligence, threat assessments, antiterrorist plans, and methodology. (see also **counterespionage, counterterrorism**)

counterterrorism (CT): Offensive measures taken to respond, deter, or prevent terrorism, including counterintelligence, threat analyses, hostage rescue operations, and military raids. The Department of State's Office for Counter-Terrorism and Emergency Planning is the lead agency responsible for all CT activities of the U.S. government, including "terrorist incident management" and administration of the **Anti-terrorist Assistance Program**. Military counterterrorism units and terrorism-response teams have been specially trained to evacuate bystanders, negotiate for and rescue hostages, snipe, employ riot control agents, and conduct surreptitious entries. Counterterrorist supervision in the U.S. military is provided by the **Joint Special Operations Command (JSOC)** and the Counterterrorist Joint Task Force Group (CTJTFG), Ft. Bragg, NC. Counterterrorist military units are Air Force units of the 23d Air Force; Army **Delta Force**

(Special Forces Operational Detachment, Delta), Ft. Bragg, NC; Army **Task Force 160** (160th Aviation Battalion), Ft. Campbell, KY; and Navy **SEAL** Team 6, Dam Neck, VA. Emergency response forces include 16 Medical Emergency Response Teams, established in December 1985 and based in Europe; numerous U.S.and Pacific-based emergency teams; four-member Air Force Emergency Service Teams (ESTs), comprised of mobile, volunteer security police officers; five-member Army Special Reaction Teams (SRTs); and Marine Corps Crisis Management Teams (CMTs) and Threat Management Forces (TMFs), assigned to major commands and installations. Nuclear terrorism response is the responsibility of the DOE's **Nuclear Emergency Search Teams**. (see also **antiterrorism**)

countervailing: Nuclear weapons employment policy adopted in the Carter Administration and implemented by Presidential Directive 59 (**PD-59**), 25 June 1980.

countervalue: Strategies or attacks against an opponent's civilian population and general economic centers that constitute the social fabric of the nation. (see also **counterforce**)

coupling: **1.** The linking of a lower-level **conflict**, such as a NATO/Warsaw Pact European war, to the use of U.S. strategic nuclear forces. With the advent of nuclear parity, some argued that U.S. strategic nuclear forces no longer served to deter Warsaw Pact aggression in Western Europe. This argument rested on the assumption that the United States would not risk strategic nuclear warfare in the defense of Europe. The issue of coupling was thus one of the theoretical bases for deployment of long-range **Pershing II** and **ground-launched cruise missiles** in Europe in 1983, thereby linking more closely U.S. forces defending Western Europe with U.S. strategic forces. **2.** In seismology, the extent of the total energy released in an underground explosion that is transformed into seismic waves in the earth. The greater the coupling of a particular explosion, the larger will be the seismic waves and the easier will be the detection by seismographs.

Cover All: Code name for the **airborne command post** for the Commander-in-Chief Strategic Air Command (CINCSAC). Cover All is an **EC-135** aircraft specially designated for the use of the CINCSAC or his representative. Cover All is a component of the **Post Attack Command and Control System**, which also includes SAC's complementary airborne launch control center, named **Looking Glass**. Cover All is available to CINCSAC at all times and is usually based at Offutt AFB, NE.

cover and deception: Cover: "Concealment to prevent enemy recognition of friendly forces' capabilities, disposition, and intentions." Deception: "Those measures designed to mislead the enemy by manipulation, distortion, or falsification of evidence to induce him to react in a manner beneficial to friendly interest" [*NWP 3*].

covert operations: "Operations that are so planned and executed as to conceal the identity of or permit plausible denial by the sponsor. They differ from **clandestine** operations in that emphasis is placed on concealment of identity of sponsor rather than on concealment of the operation" [*JCS Pub 1*, p. 96].

CP   (see **command post**)

C-rating: The rating of a unit's **readiness**, based on a composite of the unit's C-rating in the four resource areas: equipment and supplies on hand, equipment condition, personnel, and training. There are five C-rating categories:

- *C-1, Fully Combat Ready:* A unit possesses its prescribed levels of wartime resources and is trained so that it is capable of performing the wartime mission for which it is organized, designed, and tasked.
- *C-2, Substantially Combat Ready:* A unit has only minor deficiencies in its wartime level of resources or training.
- *C-3, Marginally Combat Ready:* A unit has major deficiencies in wartime resources or training that limit performance capability.
- *C-4, Not Combat Ready:* A unit has major deficiencies in wartime resources or training and cannot effectively perform its wartime mission.
- *C-5, Service Programmed, Not Combat Ready:* Due to service programs, a unit does not possess the prescribed wartime resources or cannot perform the wartime mission for

which it is organized, designed, or tasked (for example, ships in overhaul and units undergoing major equipment conversion or transition).

Crested Cap: Annual Air Force exercise, held in conjunction with the **REFORGER** exercise and part of the NATO **Autumn Forge** exercises held each fall, which practice and test procedures for receiving, exercising, and returning dual-based air force units to Europe, and provide tactical training for and operational readiness testing of those units. Army dual-based units are tested under REFORGER. Redeployment of U.S. air units to Europe occurs under the 1967 Trilateral Agreement and under U.S. war plans. The drawdown of Air Force personnel and equipment under the 1967 agreement involved the return of four tactical squadrons, including 96 F-4 aircraft, to U.S. bases. During the Crested Cap exercises, squadrons from Seymour Johnson AFB, NC, and other U.S. bases deploy nonstop to European bases using aerial refueling, and take up intense operations.

Criminal Investigation Command (see **Army Criminal Investigation Command**)

crisis: 1. "A crisis is defined as an incident or situation involving a threat to the United States, its territories, and possessions that rapidly develops and creates a condition of such diplomatic, economic, political, or military importance to the U.S. Government that commitment of U.S. military forces and resources is contemplated to achieve U.S. national objectives" [JCS, *Joint Operations Planning System (JOPS)*, Vol. IV, p. I-2, released under the FOIA]. **2.** "A crisis is defined as an incident or situation involving a threat from a source external to the United States, its territories/possessions that rapidly develops and creates a condition of such diplomatic, political, or military importance to the U.S. Government that commitment of U.S. armed forces and/or resources is contemplated to achieve U.S. national objectives" [CINCPAC, *USPACOM Crisis Command and Control Procedures*, USCINCPACINST C3100.1F, 16 May 1985, p. 1, released under the FOIA]. (see also **conflict, cold war**)

crisis action procedures (CAP) (see **Crisis Action System**)

Crisis Action System (CAS): Joint Chiefs of Staff system that provides guidance and procedures for joint operation planning by military forces during emergency or time-sensitive **crisis** situations. Crisis action procedures give the JCS information to develop recommendations to the National Command Authority (NCA) for decisions involving the use of U.S. military forces. "The CAS provides a framework for the timely development and exchange of information for evaluating and recommending specific military COAs [courses of action] during time-sensitive situations" [JCS, *Joint Operations Planning System (JOPS)*, Vol. IV, p. II-1, released under the FOIA]. The CAS is intended to be conducted in six phases. Each phase begins with

a deliberate action (order, report, or event) and ends with a decision. Decisions must be made to continue planning, hold at a certain planning phase, or revert to a previous planning phase. "In certain fast-moving situations, phases may be compressed, conducted concurrently, or eliminated, depending on conditions. The decision to commit forces may be made shortly after an event occurs, thereby necessitating compression of Phase II through V" [JCS, *JOPS*, II-2].

Crisis Action Phases

- Phase I: Situation Development
- Phase II: Crisis Assessment
- Phase III: Course of Action Development
- Phase IV: Course of Action Selection
- Phase V: Execution Planning
- Phase VI: Execution

(see also **plans**)

crisis relocation: Civil defense measure that involves the evacuation of civilians from cities to comparative havens in the surrounding countryside as one means of constraining casualties in a **countervalue** nuclear war.

CRITIC (Critical Intelligence Communication): A National Security Agency/Central Security Service (NSA/CSS) message. A CRITIC is one of two formal reports (the other is an **OPREP**-3 PINNACLE) that could initiate actions under the **Crisis Action System**. It contains "intelligence that is crucial and requires the immediate attention of the commander. It is required to enable the commander to make decisions that will provide a timely and appropriate response to actions by the potential/actual enemy. It includes but is not limited to the following: **a.** strong indications of the imminent outbreak of hostilities of any type (warning of attack); **b.** aggression of any nature against a friendly country; **c.** indications or use of nuclear-biological-chemical weapons (targets); and **d.** significant events within potential enemy countries that may lead to modification of nuclear strike plans" [*JCS Pub 1*]. CRITIC is of such urgent importance that it is transmitted at the highest priority to the President and other national decision makers before passing through regular evaluative channels. CRITICs are transmitted over the NSA-operated Critical Intelligence Communications System (CRITICOM).

Critical Nuclear Weapon Design Information (CNWDI):   Type of classified weapons data, designated by DOE to apply to "Top Secret **Restricted Data** or Secret Restricted Data revealing the theory of operation or design of the components of a thermo-nuclear or implosion-type fission bomb, warhead, demolition munition or test device." Access to CNWDI requires a **top secret** or **secret** security clearance for DOD personnel, or a **Q clearance** for DOE personnel. Excluded from the CNWDI category is information regarding

- Arming, fuzing, and firing systems;
- Limited-life components (tritium);
- Total contained quantities of fissionable; fusionable, and high-explosive materials by type; and

- Components that DOD personnel set, maintain, operate, test, or replace.

[DOD, *Information Security Program Regulation*, DOD 5200.1-R, 28 April 1987, p. 19]. (see also **Sigma Security Classification**)

Crown Helo: Specially configured, Air Force-operated **VH-60** helicopters, modified from the Navy **SH-60 Seahawks**, operated to transport the National Command Authorities and other presidential successors in an emergency. Crown Helo helicopters operate as a type of **airborne command post**, and they are stationed at Andrews AFB, MD.

cruise missile: A pilotless, winged, jet-propelled, guided, air-breathing missile that, like an aircraft, uses aerodynamic lift to offset gravity and propulsion to counteract drag. A cruise missile's flight remains within the earth's atmosphere and maintains thrust throughout its flight. In 1977, the DOD initiated a major program to develop a new generation of long-range cruise missiles. These weapons are extremely accurate due to a combination of inertial guidance and terrain contour matching (TERCOM) sensors. The United States has three long-range cruise missiles deployed and one in development:

- **Air-launched cruise missile:** Can be launched from B-52 bombers and B-1B bombers in the future.
- **Ground-launched cruise missile:** Will be eliminated under the INF Treaty.

- **Tomahawk sea-launched cruise missile:** Launched from surface ships and attack submarines.
- **Advanced Cruise Missile:** To be deployed in the early 1990s to arm B-52H and B-2 bombers.

(see also **EC-18**)

cruiser (CG/CGN): Large, long-endurance, guided-missile, conventionally powered (CG) or nuclear-powered (CGN) warship capable of limited independent offensive operations against surface ships and land targets. Cruisers are almost exclusively employed as anti-air warfare escorts to protect aircraft carriers or other ships against air attack. The Navy has about 30 cruisers in eight classes: Long Beach (CGN-16) (1), Leahy (CG-16) (9), Bainbridge (CGN-25) (1), Belknap (CG-26) (9), Truxton (CGN-35) (1), California (CGN-36) (2), Virginia (CGN-38) (4), and Ticonderoga (CG-47). The Ticonderoga class is in production.

cruiser-destroyer group (CRUDES-GRU): A permanent administrative unit of a **naval surface force** assigned to the Atlantic and Pacific Fleets, which provides ships to the numbered fleets for operations, when directed. A CRUDESGRU typically consists of a battleship, missile cruisers, missile destroyers, destroyer tender, frigates, missile frigates, and ammunition ships. There are six organized cruiser-destroyer groups in peacetime:

- Cruiser Destroyer Group 1, San Diego, CA 92155;
- Cruiser Destroyer Group 2, Charleston, SC 29408;
- Cruiser Destroyer Group 3, San Diego, CA 92155;
- Cruiser Destroyer Group 5, San Diego, CA 92155;
- Cruiser Destroyer Group 8, Norfolk, VA 23511; and
- Cruiser Destroyer Group 12, Mayport, FL 32228.

cryptanalysis: The steps or processes involved in converting encrypted messages into plain text without initial knowledge of the system employed in the encryption.

CRYPTO: A designation or marking applied to classified, operational keying material. It indicates that the information requires special accounting and safeguarding. The CRYPTO marking identifies all **communications security (COMSEC)** keying material used to protect or authenticate telecommunications carrying national security-related information. The CRYPTO marking also identifies COMSEC equipment with installed, hardwired, operational keying variables. (See also **security classification**)

cryptography: The branch of **cryptology** used to provide a means of encryption and deception of plain text so that its meaning may be concealed. Cryptographic systems are all associated items of cryptomaterial (e.g., equipment and its removable components that perform cryptographic functions, operating instructions, and maintenance manuals) that are used as a unit to provide a single means of encryption and decryption of plain text so that its meaning may be concealed;

also any mechanical or electrical device or method used for the purpose of disguising, authenticating, or concealing the contents, significance, or meanings of communications. Current cryptographic systems in use include

- TSEC/ST-51: Automatic test equipment (ATE) for depot repair of the new generation of cryptographic equipment. This equipment employs micro-miniature technology in its construction, making conventional test equipment unsatisfactory for trouble-shooting and repair.
- TSEC/KG-30: Micro-miniaturized electronic key generators for tactical encryption of various intelligence from ASW centers and **Fleet Satellite Communications (FLTSAT-COM)** terminals. This equipment is contracted by the National Security Agency (NSA) on consolidated tri-service multi-year procurement.
- TSEC/KY-57/58 VINSON: Half-duplex wide-band tactical speech security equipment that includes KY-57, manpack model; and KY-58, airborne and shipboard model.
- TSEC/KYV-2: Secure Voice Modules (SVMs) for encryption in the TENLEY Crypto System of the handheld PRC-68 radio. This equipment is essential to be compatible with Marine Corps communications and to avoid plain text intra-Navy communications.
- TSEC/KY-65/75: Narrow-band, half-duplex, portable, tactical speech security equipment. KY-65/75 application to HF radios requires cryptographic protection.
- CSS Secure Voice/Record: Components of the Communication Security System (CSS) for secure voice installations aboard ships.
- CI-3 Walburn: A full-duplex, high-speed digital data encryption system used for bulk encryption of vital Defense Communication System (DCS) links.
- TSEC/KY-67 VHR Bancroft: Integrated radio-crypto.

(see also **cypher, code**)

Cryptologic Support Group (CSG): Liaison staff that provides **signals intelligence (SIGINT)** support between the National Security Agency/Central Security Service (NSA/CSS) and major combatant commands and unified and specified commands. The CSG provides point-to-point operator communications between the National SIGINT Operations Center at NSA headquarters and the command [CENTCOM, *Operations SOP*, 30 March 1984, p. B-2-2, released under the FOIA].

cryptology: The science of producing **signals intelligence** and maintaining **signals security**.

CSS (see **National Security Agency/Central Security Service**)

CUE-CAP: An urgency designator of the JCS to show relative priority for resources among nationally-designated programs. CUE-CAP is lower than **Brick Bat**.

current, or then-year, dollars: Price level at the time when expenditures are actually made; includes estimated inflation for out-years.

current force: The actual, day-to-day force structure and personnel strength available to meet present contingencies or a planning period. It is identified in the **Joint Strategic Capabilities Plan** and forms the basis for operation and contingency plans and orders.

custodial unit: Military organization responsible for guarding, safekeeping, and maintaining accountability for U.S. nuclear weapons, components, and nuclear materials, to be delivered by allied forces. Custodial units are normally collocated with allied units and are responsible for guarding and arming the weapons. Allied units have access to U.S. nuclear weapons under **Programs of Cooperation**.

custody: "Responsibility for the control of, transfer and movement of, and access to, weapons and components. Custody also includes the maintenance of accountability for weapons and components" [DNA, *Nuclear Weapon Accident Response Procedures (NARP) Manual*, January 1984,

p. 155, released under the FOIA].

CVA: Designation for attack **aircraft carrier**.

CV/CVN: Designation for **aircraft carrier**/nuclear-powered aircraft carrier.

CVS: Designation for anti-submarine warfare **aircraft carrier**.

CV-22 (see **V-22 Osprey**)

CVAN (see **USCINCPAC Voice Alert Network**)

CW (continuous wave): HF (high-frequency communications) operating mode, commonly known as "Morse code." With CW, the transmitter is keyed on and off by a hand-operated telegraph key. Maximum efficiency depends on the operator efficiency with the international Morse Code. Many HF stations use CW because of the relatively simple equipment and reliability of communications. It is one of the most common sources of **signals intelligence**.

D

D: Prefix designating **1.** Director aircraft that control drone aircraft or missiles (e.g., DC-130). **2.** Decoy. **3.** Dummy, nonflyable vehicle used for training.

Daily Intelligence Summary (DI-SUM): Intelligence report prepared by unified and specified commands to give the Joint Chiefs of Staff, the National Military Intelligence Center, the military services, and selected U.S. government agencies a daily analysis of an actual or simulated (training exercise) crisis and a summary of relevant intelligence information produced during the preceding 24-hour period.

damage expectancy: "The probability of achieving a desired level of damage, considering pre-launch survivability, weapon system reliability, weather/darkness factors, penetration probability and weapons effects" [*U.S. Air Force Glossary*].

damage limitation: "The capability to limit the effects of nuclear destruction on population and industry by using offensive and defensive measures to reduce the weight of enemy attacks" [*U.S. Air Force Glossary*].

DARCOM (Materiel Development and Readiness Command) (see Army Materiel Command)

Dark Eyes: Navy submarine electro-optics intelligence collection program.

DARPA: Acronym for **Defense Advanced Research Projects Agency**.

DARPA Triad: DOD research program to develop a space-based chemical laser weapon as part of the **Strategic Defense Initiative**. The Triad refers to three research projects: **Alpha** (the laser); **Talon Gold** (means of detecting and tracing targets); and **LODE** (Large Optics Demonstration Experiment). The ultimate goal of the Triad is to develop optical systems to focus and aim large lasers.

Date-Time-Group (DTG): The date and time at which a message is prepared for transmission. Expressed as six digits followed by the time zone suffix and month/year (e.g., 192040Z Nov 81). The first pair of digits represents the date, the second pair the hours, and the third pair the minutes. The DTG of all messages is based on the 24-hour clock time and expressed in **Zulu time**.

DCI   (see **Director of Central Intelligence, Central Intelligence Agency**)

DD/DDG: Designation for **destroyer/ guided missile destroyer.**

D-day: **1.** The unnamed day on which a particular operation, such as a land assault, air strike, naval bombardment, parachute assault, or amphibious assault, commences or is to commence. It may be the commencement of hostilities or the date an employment phase is implemented. The senior headquarters directing the operation will specify the D-day. C-, D-, and M-days end at 2400Z and are assumed to be 24 hours long for planning [USCENTCOM, *Emergency Action Procedures, Volume I: System Description*, 20 February 1976, p. 4-3, released under the FOIA]. **2.** The unnamed day on which a nuclear test takes place. D+7 means seven days after D-day. (see also **military time**)

deadly force: The physical force that a person uses, such as firing a weapon, with the purpose of causing, or which is likely to cause, death or serious body harm.

DEB (Digital European Backbone): Air Force program to extend the digital wideband communications system through central Europe, the United Kingdom, and in conjunction with the **Defense Communications System (DCS)** Mediterranean Improvement Program, Turkey, Greece, Spain, and Italy. DEB upgrade projects have the code name "Creek."

declared facility: A facility or area that has been designated by agreement as a place where treaty-related activities (e.g., missile production, testing) take place. The exchange of data about declared facilities in the form of a memorandum of understanding can help to facilitate verification.

declassified: Information that has been removed from a state of **security classification**.

decoy: A deception device intended to divert or mislead an opponent's early-warning and defense systems so as to increase the probability of penetration and weapon delivery. Decoys carried on ballistic missiles are released with the reentry vehicle(s) in order to penetrate ballistic missile defenses. Several types of decoys are currently in use or under development: **chaff**, aerosols, and dummy warheads.

deep submergence rescue vehicle (DSRV): Navy small (37 ton), conventionally powered, three-person submarine designed for rescuing submariners trapped in disabled submarines. It is able to connect with virtually all U.S. submarines. It is configured to be launched and recovered by a submerged attack submarine or by Pigeon (ASR-21) class submarine rescue ships. After launching, the DSRV descends to the disabled submarine, mates to one of the submarine's escape hatches, takes onboard up to 24 persons, and returns to the mother submarine or ship. The DSRV can be air-transported in C-141 or C-5A aircraft or ground-transported by a special trailer. It has specially constructed propulsion systems to allow precise maneuvering, as well as elaborate search navigation equipment. DSRVs can operate up to depths of 5,000 ft.

DSRVs were developed after the loss of the nuclear-powered attack submarine Thresher in 1963. Originally 12 were planned, each capable of carrying 12 survivors. This capability was subsequently doubled and the number required was cut in half. Only two were built, however, both becoming operational in 1977. The prime contractor was Lockheed Missiles and Space Co., Sunnyvale, CA. The total development, construction, test, and support cost of the two DSRVs was more than $220 million.

DEFCON (see **Defense Readiness Conditions**)

Defense Acquisitions Board (DAB): Board chaired by the Under Secretary of Defense (Acquisition) and composed of 10 committees responsible for milestone and program reviews, policy formulations, and acquisition recommendations dealing with the **major defense acquisition programs**. The committees are

- Science & Technology Committee
- Strategic Systems Committee
- C3I Systems Committee
- Production & Logistics Committee
- International Programs Committee
- Nuclear & Chemical Committee
- Conventional Systems Committee
- Test & Evaluation Committee
- Installation Support & Military Construction Committee
- Policy & Initiatives Committee.

Defense Advanced Research Projects Agency (DARPA): One of 13 agencies of the **Department of Defense**, established 7 February 1958, partly in reaction to the Soviet launching of Sputnik, as the Advanced Research Projects Agency (ARPA). It was redesignated from ARPA in March 1972. Its mission, in support of DOD components, the Joint Chiefs of Staff, military services, and other federal agencies, is to conduct basic and applied research and development of advanced technologies beyond the immediate and specific requirements of the military services. In addition, DARPA conducts prototype projects embodying technologies that may be used in joint programs and provides assistance to the services with prototype projects on request. DARPA reports to the Under Secretary of Defense (Acquisition) through the Director, Defense Research and Engineering. Its personnel strength is about 150 military and civilian personnel, and its annual budget is approximately $670 million. It has directorates and offices dealing with Aerospace Technology, Defense Science, Directed Energy, Information Sciences and Technology, Naval Technology, Nuclear Monitoring, Strategic Technology, and Tactical Technology.

Headquarters
Arlington, VA 22209

Defense Attaché System: Program of the **Defense Intelligence Agency** responsible for staffing, training, and administering the placement of attachés in the U.S. embassies overseas. The joint program places intelligence officers in countries overseas, primarily to report on the states and capabilities of foreign military forces.

defense budget: The culmination of the **Planning, Programming, and Budgeting System**, and part of the President's annual budget submitted to Congress. Section 1405, Public Law 99-145, the DOD Authorization Act, 1986, requires that the Department submit a two-year budget beginning with FY 1988. Thereafter, a two-year budget is to be submitted every other year. The DOD submitted the first biennial budget for FY 1988 and 1989 on 5 January 1987 (other agencies continued with their annual budgets for only FY 1988). During Congressional hearings, little emphasis was placed on the FY 1989 columns by either the authorization or appropriations committees.

Defense Civil Preparedness Agency (DCPA) (see **Federal Emergency Management Agency**)

Defense Commercial Telecommunications Network (DCTN): Bulk-leased switch and dedicated-voice channel and wideband communications service used by the DOD within the United States and Puerto Rico.

Defense Communications Agency (DCA): One of 13 agencies of the **Department of Defense (DOD)**, established 12 May 1960. Its function is to provide technical and operational communications support to the National Command Authorities, DOD agencies, the military services, the Joint Chiefs of Staff, and commanders of the unified and specified commands. Its original mission, operation of the **Defense Communications System**, has been expanded to include the conduct of joint war-gaming; development and planning of the Defense Special Security Communications System; the providing of technical support for the **Worldwide Military Command and Control System**'s Standard Automation Data Processing System and engineering activities; management of the **Minimum Essential Emergency Communications Network**, the **Military Satellite Communications System Office**, the Theater Mission Planning System, the Defense Data Network, and the Defense Switched Network; and the providing of software support for the **National Emergency Airborne Command Post**. The DCA supervises the **White House Communications System**. The DCA reports to the Under Secretary of Defense (Acquisition) through the Assistant Secretary of Defense (Command, Control, Communications, and Intelligence). Its personnel strength is approximately 2,000 civilian and 2,000 military personnel, and its annual budget is approximately $450 million. (see also **National Military Command System**)

Headquarters
Washington, DC 20305-2000

Directorates
- Engineering and Technology
- Communication System Organization

- Joint Data Support Center
- Resource Management
- Joint Tactical Command, Control, Communications Agency
- Information Management Organization
- Personnel and Administration
- Center for Command, Control, Communications Systems
- Acquisition Management/Defense Commercial Communications Office

Defense Communications System (DCS): The main communications links between U.S. armed forces, composed of land lines, submarine cables, high- and low-frequency stations, tropospheric scattering facilities, and orbiting satellites. The DCS is the largest communications system in the world, serving about 3,200 locations in 75 countries and islands. Nearly two thirds of the DCS sites are overseas. The DCS provides for global common-user military communications in support of peacetime and crisis communications and operations. The DCS systems generally support nuclear weapons, although they are not specifically designated for strategic communications. Every command center, headquarters, submarine, missile silo, and bomber constantly receives messages over the DCS. Management control and operational direction of the DCS comes from the **Defense Communications Agency**.

A number of DCS upgrade programs are underway:

- **DEB (Digital European Backbone).**
- DCS Mediterranean Improvement Plan (DMIP): Increases the capacity, connectivity, and survivability of the DCS in Turkey, Greece, Italy, and Spain through the use of the leased satellite capacity and submarine fiber optic cables. The DMIP will reduce the manning requirements at or shut down approximately 12 communications sites. The upgrade of the DCS in Greece and Turkey is called "Scope Axis."
- Hawaii Area Wideband System (HAWS): Provides a digital wideband interconnect system (DCS) in Hawaii.
- Philippine Digital Upgrade: Joint Air Force/Navy project for digital upgrade of DCS in the Philippines using microwave equipment and adding bulk encryption.

Defense Contract Audit Agency (DCAA): One of 13 agencies of the **Department of Defense (DOD)** and other government agencies and foreign allies, as directed, that provides accounting and financial advice and services to all DOD components. The DCAA provides services to approximately 30 non-DOD agencies, including the National Aeronautics and Space Administration (NASA), Environmental Protection Agency (EPA), and the Departments of Transportation, Health and Human Services, and the Interior. Its personnel strength is approximately 6,000 civilians, and its annual budget is approximately $200 million.

Headquarters
Cameron Station,
Alexandria, VA 22314

Defense Data Network (DDN): Common-user packet-switching transmission media for all long-haul data communications users to replace dedicated circuits. The DDN consists of MILNET, which serves the unclassified general services community, and networks serving secret, top secret, and compartmented applications. In FYs 1988-89, independent DDN classified segments were merged into one multilevel secure network. DDN connects over 600 host computers and more than 30,000 terminal users. DDN replaces **AUTODIN II**, which was cancelled on 2 April 1982.

defense emergency: One of two uniform **alert conditions (LERTCONs)** used to notify U.S. military forces. "An emergency condition which exists when: **a.** A major attack is made upon U.S. Forces overseas, or allied forces in any area, and is confirmed either by the commander of a unified or specified command or higher authority. **b.** An overt attack of any type is made upon the United States and is confirmed by the commander of a unified or specified command or higher authority" [JCS, *Alert System of the Joint Chiefs of Staff, Part II, LERTCON ACTIONS*, SM-522-69, 13 August 1969, p. 219, released under the FOIA]. The exercise term for a defense emergency is "hot box." (see also **Air Defense Emergency**)

Defense Guidance (DG): Annual statement of the **Secretary of Defense** containing threat assessment, policy, strategy, force planning, resource planning, and fiscal guidance for program development. It covers a five-year period beginning with the next fiscal year. The report provides firm guidance, including fis-

cal constraints, for the development of the **Program Objective Memoranda** by the military departments and the defense agencies. The **Joint Strategic Planning Document** provides the Secretary of Defense with JCS inputs to the DG on strategic and military objectives and on planning force levels. These are considered along with **Program Decision Memoranda** and the Congressional budget. The DG reflects the Secretary's policy, strategy, force planning, resource planning, and fiscal guidance. Fiscal guidance is provided at total obligational authority level for each of the next five years. The document is drafted by a number of teams, guided by a DG steering group, which resolves issues, and links the various sections into a coherent package. The Under Secretary of Defense for Policy takes the lead in drafting the DG. The final DG draft is reviewed by the Chairman of the JCS, the Commanders-in-Chief, and the **Defense Resources Board** before the Secretary signs it.

Defense Intelligence Agency (DIA): One of 13 agencies of the **Department of Defense (DOD)**, established 21 August 1961, in reaction to the missile gap "crisis" of the late 1950s, to consolidate the military services' non-cryptologic intelligence analysis activities. It is responsible for producing and disseminating foreign intelligence and **counterintelligence** in support of the Secretary of Defense, JCS, unified and specified commands, and major DOD components. It coordinates all service intelligence production; issues DOD-wide manuals and regulations governing intelligence procedures; supervises the DOD **indications-and-warning (I&W)** system; manages the General Defense Intelligence Program (GDIP); manages the **Defense Attaché System**; is responsible for Target Data Inventory, which becomes the basis for nuclear war plans; and contributes to **national intelligence estimates/special national intelligence estimates (NIEs/SNIEs)**. The DIA's director serves as intelligence advisor to the Secretary of Defense and as intelligence staff officer of the JCS and is a member of the **National Foreign Intelligence Board (NFIB)**. The DIA reports to the Secretary of Defense through the JCS. Staff supervision is provided by the Assistant Secretary of Defense (Command, Control, Communication, and Intelligence). DIA personnel strength is believed to be approximately 5,000 employees, with a budget in the $200–250 million range.

Headquarters
Bolling AFB,
Washington, DC 20332

defense intelligence community: The **Defense Intelligence Agency**, the **National Security Agency**, and the military services' intelligence offices and commands including Department of Defense collectors of specialized intelligence through reconnaissance programs. (see also **intelligence community**)

Defense Intelligence Notice (DIN): Intelligence report prepared by the **Defense Intelligence Agency** to provide the Joint Chiefs of Staff, unified and specified commands, military services, and selected government agencies timely, finished intelligence about developments that could have a significant effect on current and future planning and operations. (see also **Special Defense Intelligence Notice**)

Defense Investigative Service (DIS): One of 13 agencies of the **Department of Defense (DOD)**, established 1 October 1972. It conducts Personnel Security Investigations (PSIs) and background investigations for DOD components and other government activities, as directed. PSIs are conducted for all federal, military, civilian, and private industry personnel with access to classified defense documents. The DIS also manages the Industrial Security Program (ISP), which investigates and inspects private contractor organizations with access to classified information and materials, to ensure their proper handling and physical security. The DIS also has limited law enforcement responsibilities regarding the unauthorized release of government information. Its personnel strength is approximately 4,000 personnel, and its annual budget is approximately $150 million. (see also **Inspector General, Security Classification**)

Headquarters
Buzzards Point,
Washington, DC 20324

Defense Legal Services Agency (DLSA): One of 13 agencies of the **Department of Defense (DOD)**. Its director serves as the DOD General Counsel. The DLSA provides legal advice and services for the Office of the Secretary of Defense, DOD Field Agencies, and Defense Agencies. It also provides technical support and assistance for the DOD Legislative Program; coordinates DOD positions on legislation and Presidential Executive Orders; serves as DOD's central reference and distribution point for legislative and Congressional documents; and maintains DOD's historical legislative files.

Headquarters
Pentagon, Washington, DC 20301

Defense Logistics Agency (DLA): One of 13 agencies of the **Department of Defense (DOD)** established 1 October 1961 as the Defense Supply Agency (DSA), and redesignated as DLA in 1977. It provides material support, contract administration, and logistical and technical services to DOD components, the military services, unified and specified commands, federal agencies, foreign governments, and international organizations worldwide. It operates 6 procurement and supply centers, 6 service centers, 36 military depots, and numerous regional contract administration services. Approximately 30 million requisitions are processed annually by the DLA on over 4.8 million types of items, ranging from clothing and medical supplies to fuel and heavy construction equipment. Through its Weapon System Support Program, the DLA assists in the design and purchase of 900,600 items and components of over 1,000 major weapons systems. DLA works with approximately 30,000 U.S. manufacturers and suppliers on some 412,000 on-going contracts totaling $311 billion. It also manages the DOD's inventory program for heavy industrial equipment, the Federal Catalog System, a portion of the Defense Standardization and Value Engineering Programs, the Retail Interservice Support Program, and DOD reutilization programs. Additionally, as of February 1988, the DLA is responsible for the management of the National Defense Stockpile, a responsibility taken over from the General Services Administration. DLA reports to the Under Secretary of Defense (Acquisition) through the Assistant Secretary of Defense (Production and Logistics). Its personnel strength is approximately 54,000 military and civilian personnel.

Headquarters
Cameron Station,
Alexandria, VA 22314

defense manpower (see **manpower**)

Defense Mapping Agency (DMA): One of 13 agencies of the **Department of Defense (DOD)**, established 1 January 1972 by consolidating the separate mapping organizations of the three services. It conducts mapping, charting, and geodetic (MC&G) activities, including the production and distribution of maps, charts, precise positioning, and digital data for strategic and non-strategic military operations, in support of the DOD, the Joint Chiefs of Staff, military services, unified and specified commands, and foreign allies, as well as merchant marine and private vessels. It reports to the Under Secretary of Defense (Acquisition) through the Assistant Secretary of Defense (Command, Control, Communications, and Intelligence). Its personnel strength is approximately 450 military and 8,500 civilian personnel, and its annual budget is approximately $800 million.

Headquarters
Naval Observatory,
Washington, DC 20007

Directorates

- Aerospace Center
- Hydrographic/Topographic Center
- Defense Mapping School
- Inter-American Geodetic Survey
- Telecommunications Service Center
- Combat Support Center
- Reston Center
- System Center

Defense Meteorological Satellite Program (DMSP): Joint satellite system managed by the Air Force that provides the Air Force Global Weather Central, the Fleet Numerical Oceanographic Center, and other military users with weather and meteorological data for military use. Satellite-borne sensors scan an 1,800 mile-wide swath on each pass and provide real-time imagery and mission sensor data to tactical users. The data are recorded, stored on-board the satellites, and relayed via commercial satellites to the Global Weather Control at Offutt AFB, NE, and the Navy's Fleet Numerical Oceanographic Center at Monterey, CA. The prime sensor is the Operational Linescan System, capable of providing global cloud imagery in the visible and infrared spectral regions, day or night. Other sensors measure temperature, water vapor, auroral effects, ocean surface wind speed, ice coverage, areas and intensity of precipitation, cloud water content, and land surface moisture. The control segment includes a Satellite Operations Center at Offutt AFB, NE, and remote Command Read-out Stations at Loring AFB, ME, and Fairchild AFB, WA. The data are kept on file at the depository at the University of Wisconsin. RCA is the prime contractor. Cost in FY 1989 was $212.7 million.

The current DMSP satellites are designated the Block 5D Integrated Spacecraft System. The first Block 5D satellite was launched from Vandenberg AFB, CA, in September 1976 and became operational in March 1977. The second satellite was launched in June 1977; the third in May 1978; the fourth in June 1979; and the fifth in July 1980. All of the satellites were launched on Thor (LV-2F) boosters. The satellites are in sun-synchronous 500-mile near-polar orbits, typically overflying the noon/midnight line or the dawn/dusk line. The satellites are powered by a deployable, sun-tracking solar array. The follow-on to the Block 5D-1 satellites are the Block 5D-2 DMSP satellites, two of which will be delivered in 1989. The Block 5D-2 satellites will be launched by an Atlas E. Plans are to acquire five Block 5D-3 satellites with multi-year funding covering FYs 1989–92. The Block 5D-3 satellites, considerably heavier than their predecessors, will be launched by Titan 2 SLVs. RCA, Hightstown, NJ, is the prime contractor. The procurement and RDT&E cost for one satellite is $190 million in FY 1990 and $199.7 million in FY 1991.

Defense Nuclear Agency (DNA): One of 13 agencies of the **Department of Defense (DOD)**, established

in 1971 from the Defense Atomic
Support Agency (DASA), which was
preceded by the Armed Forces Special Weapons Project, the organization responsible for the Manhattan
Project. The DNA's mission, in support of the Secretary of Defense,
DOD components, the Joint Chiefs
of Staff, unified and specified commands, and other federal agencies, includes the management of
the Department of Defense nuclear
stockpile; nuclear weapons systems
acquisitions; nuclear weapons effects
research and explosive testing; and
nuclear test readiness (with the
Department of Energy). In addition,
the DNA coordinates nuclear weapons
and facilitates security enhancement
programs, theater nuclear weapons
survivability programs, and the JCS's
Accident Response Planning program.
Regarding its research, development, programming, and budgeting
activities, the DNA reports to the
Under Secretary of Defense (Acquisition) through the Director, Defense
Research and Engineering. On operational matters, DNA reports to the
Chairman of the Joint Chiefs of Staff.
DNA personnel strength is approximately 550 military and 850 civilian
personnel, and its annual budget is
approximately $370 million.

Headquarters
Alexandria, VA 22310

DNA Field Command
Kirtland AFB, NM 87117

**Defense Planning and Program-
ming Categories (DPPC):**   Elements
of the defense **manpower** program,
used by the DOD for **force structure**
planning and its annual manpower

requirement requests to Congress. The
categories are based on the same program elements as the 11 major defense
programs of the **Five-Year Defense
Plan**. The DPPCs aggregate activities
performing similar functions.

DPPC Categories

1. Strategic
     Offensive Strategic Forces
     Defensive Strategic Forces
     Strategic Control and Sur-
     veillance
2. Tactical/Mobility
     Land Forces
         Division Forces
         Theater Forces
     Tactical Air Forces
     Naval Forces
         Warships and Anti-sub-
         marine Warfare Forces
         Amphibious Forces
         Naval Support Forces
     Mobility Forces
3. Communications and Intelligence
     Centrally Managed Com-
     munications
     Intelligence
4. Combat Installations
5. Force Support Training
6. Medical Support
7. Joint Activities
     International Military Orga-
     nizations
     Unified Commands
     Federal Agency Support
     Joint Chiefs of Staff
     OSD/Defense Agencies/Ac-
     tivities
8. Central Logistics
     Supply Operations
     Maintenance Operations
     Logistics Support Opera-
     tions

9. Service Management Headquarters
   Combat Commands
   Support Commands
10. Research and Development
    Research and Develop-
    ment Activities
    Geophysical Activities
11. Training and Personnel
    Individual Training
    Personnel Support
12. Support Activities
    Support Installations
    Centralized Support Ac-
    tivities
13. Individuals
    Transients
    Patients, Prisoners, and
    Holdees
    Trainees, Students, and
    Cadets/Midshipmen

[DOD, *Manpower Requirements Report FY 1989*, March 1988, Appendix C]

Defense Planning Committee (DP-C): A component of NATO's civil structure. The DPC deals only with NATO defense matters. It is composed of the defense ministers of member countries taking part in NATO's integrated defense structure (this excludes France, Spain, and Iceland). The defense ministers meet twice a year with NATO ambassadors representing them in permanent session at other times. It is chaired by NATO's Secretary General. (see also **North Atlantic Council**)

Defense Planning Questionnaire (DPQ): Annual inquiry sent by the international staff and NATO headquarters to all NATO-member governments asking for information on

their defense plans for the coming year. The DPQ forms the basis for NATO-member government commitments of forces to NATO in peacetime and wartime.

defense readiness conditions (DEFCONS): One of two uniform **alert conditions (LERTCONs)** used to notify U.S. military forces. DEFCONs are the system of five progressive readiness conditions, with DEFCON 5 signifying normal readiness and DEFCON 1 signifying maximum readiness posture. DEFCONs prescribe the amount and type of military force that can be committed in a particular span of time. Each DEFCON is specified by a general indication of the type of action that is required to bring a command's readiness into consonance with the general description of circumstances specified in operational plans. The JCS describe DEFCONs as "a uniform system of progressive alert postures for use between the Joint Chiefs of Staff and the commanders of unified and specified commands and for use by the Services. DEFCONs are graduated to match situations of varying military severity (status of alert)" [*JCS Pub 1*, p. 107]. The Strategic Air Command and U.S. troops in South Korea are always at DEFCON 4. U.S. strategic forces are kept at DEFCON 5. During the Cuban Missile Crisis, the status of U.S. forces was raised to DEFCON 2.

- DEFCON 5 (exercise term: Fade Out): "Normal peacetime situation exists."
- DEFCON 4 (exercise term: Double Take): "Tensions exist which re-

quire greater military vigilance. No U.S. forces involved."

- DEFCON 3 (exercise term: Round House)
- DEFCON 2 (exercise term: Fast Pace)
- DEFCON 1 (exercise term: Cocked Pistol)

[LANTCOM, *Atlantic Command Alert System*, CINCLANTINST S3301.3B, 13 January 1982, released under the FOIA]

(see also **defense emergency**)

Defense Resources Board (DRB): Corporate review body that provides assistance to the Secretary of Defense in the review and management of the **Planning, Programming, and Budgeting System (PPBS)** and the systems acquisition process. The DRB is chaired by the Deputy Secretary of Defense. Members of the DRB include the service secretaries, the Chairman of the Joint Chiefs of Staff, appropriate Under Secretaries of Defense and Assistant Secretaries of Defense, the DOD's General Counsel, and participants from the government Office of Management and Budget (OMB). Final authority on program issues following service and agency Program Objectives Memorandum inputs rests with the Deputy Secretary. (see also **Defense Acquisition Board**)

Defense Satellite Communications System (DSCS II/III): Standard military **communications satellite** that provides long-haul SHF 7/8 GHz voice and high-data rate communications for fixed and transportable ter-

minals and extends mobile service to ships and aircraft. DSCS provides connectivity to the **Worldwide Military Command and Control System (WWMCCS)**, ground mobile forces, Navy vessels, the National Command Authorities (NCA), overseas bases, and the Department of State diplomatic telecommunications system for U.S. embassies. The NCA can conduct threat assessments through the DSCS, connecting through the **National Emergency Airborne Command Post (NEACP)** or a mobile command center. The user segment includes the Defense Communications Agency (DCA) Operations Center (DCAOC), which manages the program, and several DSCS operations centers. Operational control of DSCS ground control facilities is exercised by the **U.S. Army Space Command**. The ground control facilities include the Air Force Operations Facility at Onizuka AFS, CA, Army ground control centers, and a planned Navy operations center. Technical control of DSCS is exercised by the **DCA** and satellite command rests with the **Air Force Space Command**.

An important subset of the DSCS is the **Electronic Counter-Counter Measures (ECCM)** network to support secure voice conferencing for the major WWMCCS commanders.

Phase I: Twenty-six small communications satellites, designed to last three years, were launched between June 1966 and June 1968. DSCS I became operational in July 1967. Each satellite had only one channel and relayed voice, imagery, computerized digital data, and teletype transmissions. The satellites operated in a circular orbit 20,930 miles above the earth at a speed that kept each satellite positioned over the equator. Prime contractor was Ford Aerospace.

Phase II: Phase II replaced Phase I satellites with three active satellites and four spares in a synchronous equatorial orbit at 23,230 miles above the Earth. The DSCS Phase II satellites are located over the Atlantic, East and West Pacific, and Indian Oceans and provide world coverage except over the polar regions (this is provided by **Satellite Data Systems** satellites). The satellites provided voice, teletype, computerized digital data, and video transmissions, including those used by **AFSATCOM**. The Phase II satellites are electrically powered by solar arrays. With a design life of five years, Phase II satellites have four channels and propulsion systems for repositioning themselves in orbit. Five antennas are mounted on the satellite platforms: two dish-shaped antennas steerable by ground command to cover different portions of the earth; two horn-shaped antennas used for transmitting and receiving uniform coverage information on the earth; and an omnidirectional antenna for transmitting and receiving signals for satellite command and control (C2). The Air Force Satellite Test Center controls the satellites through a network of satellite control facility stations. TRW is the prime contractor.

Phase III: DSCS III-AI was launched on 30 October 1982 by a Titan III rocket. The Atlas II will be used in the future to launch the satellite. The switch to DSCS III began on 30 April 1983 with the first DSCS III satellite launch. DCS dispersed, EMP-hardened ground control facilities control the satellite communications and orbital positions. Phase III satellites have six active communications transmitter channels and are designed to last for 10 years. DSCS III is dual-compatible with the space shuttle and with rocket launches and will have a longer life, increased channelization, increased user flexibility, and improved anti-jam protection over DSCS II. DSCS III plans include four active satellites on-orbit (and two spares) and ground terminal components for secure, long-distance worldwide communications for C2, intelligence, and Presidential use. The prime contractor is General Electric of Valley Forge, PA. Procurement and RDT&E funding for FY 1990 is $77.2 million and for FY 1991 is $78.5 million.

Together, DSCS III and LEASAT provide near-global coverage from **airborne command posts**, and ground-based command posts to SAC bombers and tankers, ICBM launch control centers, and strategic reconnaissance aircraft. The DSCS carries a single channel transponder for AFSATCOM. It receives Emergency Action Messages (EAM) on either SHF or UHF, then rebroadcasts them to all AFSATCOM terminals.

Defense Science Board (DSB): Senior scientific and technical advisory body, composed of individuals from the private sector, providing support to the Secretary of Defense, Under Secretary of Defense (Acquisition), and the Chairman of the Joint Chiefs of Staff. The DSB Summer Study group normally evaluates a contemporary defense issue and reports its findings and recommendations to the Secretary of Defense. It can have a major influence on policy decisions.

Defense Security Assistance Agency (DSAA): One of 13 agencies of the **Department of Defense (DOD)** established in September 1971 to direct, supervise, and administer **security assistance programs** such as **Foreign Military Sales (FMS)** and the **Military Assistance Program**. The Assistant Secretary of Defense (International Security Affairs) is empowered to conduct international logistics and sales negotiations with foreign countries; to "serve as the DOD focal point for liaison with U.S. industry with respect to security assistance activities;" and to "direct and supervise the organization, functions and staffing of DOD elements in foreign countries responsible for managing the security assistance program" [DOD, *Defense Security Assistance Agency,* DOD Directive 5105.38, 1978, released under the FOIA]. The DSAA is staffed by approximately 100 military and civilian specialists and is headed by a director (usually a two- or three-star General) and a civilian chief of operations. Its annual budget is approximately $10 million. (see also **Military Assistance Advisory Group**)

Headquarters
Pentagon, Washington, DC 20301

Defense Special Missile Astronautics Center (DEFSMAC): **National Security Agency**-operated early-warning center responsible for alerting intelligence-collection activities worldwide of time-sensitive opportunities to collect information. DEFSMAC, for instance, upon receiving information from the most sensitive **signals intelligence** sources, will alert airborne collectors, such as the **Cobra Ball** and **Cobra Eye** aircraft, to get into position to collect information on a Soviet test.

Defense Special Security Communications System: Intelligence communications system supervised by the **National Security Agency** and used to transmit **back-channel** and **special compartmented information (SCI)**. It is separate from general-service (GENSER) message traffic systems, which can transmit classified information but not compartmented information.

Defense Support Program (DSP): Model designation 647. The satellite **early-warning** system of the DOD used to detect the launch of ICBMs or SLBMs "virtually instantaneously" and relay warning data to NORAD and SAC. The DSP consists of three satellites carrying infrared sensors in geosynchronous orbits, one above South America, another above the central Pacific, and the third over the Indian Ocean. The infrared detecting telescope, which always points toward the earth, scans a conical area below as the satellite spins at a rate of seven revolutions per minute. A countermotion wheel in the satellite spins in the opposite direction to maintain stability. Infrared energy is collected into the telescope and reflected off a mirror onto a series of 2,000 angled, two-dimensional lead sulphide detector cells. Each cell calculates the intensity of the signals and the earth locations where the signals originated.

In the event of a missile launch, the satellite senses the infrared heat within a minute of lift-off, making DSP the first warning system to detect launches. A computer library compares the data to characteristics of previous test flights and satellite launches to determine if the launch is threatening. These data are then computed and analyzed within the satellite and transmitted to ground stations: two large processing stations (Nurungar, Australia, and Buckley Air National Guard Base, CO), a Simplified Processing Station at Kapaun, West Germany, and six Mobile Ground Stations in New Mexico. The Mobile Ground Stations consist of a Mobile Ground Terminal (for data processing) and Mobile Communications Terminal and involve a number of 18-wheel tractor-trailers that continuously change locations in order to avoid being targeted. Jam Resistant Secure Communications mobile communications terminals (MCT) support the mobile ground terminals.

The data are simultaneously transmitted from the ground stations by satellite to the four National Command Authority (NCA) command centers. Every Soviet and Chinese launch is monitored by the United States. When the DSP detects a rocket plume from a launch, ground controllers first inform the Missile Warning center at the **NORAD Cheyenne Mountain Complex**. After taking no more than two minutes to verify an actual launch, the Warning Center passes the information to the NORAD command post in the Mountain. DSP sensors are sensitive enough to have reportedly detected 166 tactical missile attacks between Iran and Iraq. The sensors responsible for confirming DSP detection and providing attack assessments include **BMEWS**, **PAVE PAWS**, and **Perimeter Acquisition Radar Attack Characterization System (PARCS)**.

The first DSP satellite was launched on 5 May 1971. It weighed over 2,000 lb and carried an Aeroject telescope with 2,000 infrared detectors. Approximately eight second-generation DSP satellites were launched, the last on 29 November 1987. The new Block 14 satellite, under contract to TRW, includes a new focal plane with dual-wavelength capability on the telescope to protect it from Soviet laser attack. The Block 14 satellites, of which at least nine launches are planned, weigh about 5,200 lb and will be boosted into orbit on Titan IV/IUSs. Since 1971, the Air Force has launched 13 DSP satellites, although some of these launches may in fact have been cover launches for **Rhyolite** and **Chalet** satellites. The first Block 14 satellite was launched in the spring of 1989; the second, to be launched in 1990, will initiate a laser communications system enabling DSP satellites to transmit missile warning and intelligence information to other DSP satellites via laser beams. All three satellites would then transmit data directly to ground stations.

There are plans to replace the DSP with the **Boost Surveillance and Tracking System (BSTS)**, which would perform the same missile warning and intelligence functions but could also guide SDI weapons to intercept missiles heading towards CONUS. However, the projected cost of $8 billion for the new BSTS will be subject to cutbacks, and the Air Force officials are worried about phasing out DSP for an uncertain future with BSTS. As of mid-1989, BSTS exists only on paper with the sole purpose of supporting Phase I SDI deployment. Nonetheless, the **Advanced Warning System**, the previous follow-on to DSP, has been canceled.

TRW is the prime contractor for the DSP, having built the satellites since the late 1960s. Aerojet Electrosystems is constructing the infrared telescope and sensor subsystem; IBM provides the software. DSP satellites are operated by the **Air Force Space Command**. TRW is on a multi-year $743 million contract for DSP.

Defense Switched Network (DSN): Replacement telephone system for **AUTOVON**. The DSN is an interbase telecommunications system that will provide end-to-end, common-user, and dedicated telephone service for the DOD, with the capability of incorporating data, video, and other traffic. The DSN includes the architecture for all switched systems and networks and includes virtually all of the systems in the **Defense Communications System**, including secure voice networks, and the **Defense Data Network**.

Defense Telephone Service-Washington (DTS-W): An organizational entity under the Secretary of the Army assigned responsibility pursuant

to DOD Directive 5160.9 to provide administrative telephone communications, including **AUTOVON** and **Defense Switched Network**, to DOD elements located in the **National Capital Region**.

degaussing: 1. The erasure of magnetically recorded information through the application of an alternating magnetic field.   **2.** "The method of making ships safer against magnetic influence mines and other devices using magnetic exploders by temporarily neutralizing the ship's magnetic field with electric coils installed in the ship" [*NWP 3*]. (see also **deperming**)

degaussing range: "An array of underwater sensing devices, either permanently installed on the bottom of a harbor channel or on a mobile unit capable of being established in forward areas by ship or boat, used to measure the magnetic field of ships or boats in order to determine the effectiveness of their **degaussing** system" [*NWP 3*].

deliberate concealment: "SALT II provides that verification of compliance with the provisions of the agreement shall be by **national technical means (NTM)**. The sides have agreed not to use deliberate concealment measures which impede verification by NTM of compliance with the provisions of the agreement. Deliberate concealment measures are measures carried out deliberately to hinder or deliberately to impede verification by NTM of compliance with the provisions of the Treaty. Deliberate concealment measures could include, for example, camouflage, use of coverings, or deliberate denial of telemetric information, such as through the use of telemetry encryption, whenever such measures impede verification of compliance with the provisions of the agreement" [ACDA, *SALT II: Glossary of Terms*, 1979].

deliberate escalation: The second option in NATO's **flexible response** strategy, which includes **direct defense**, deliberate escalation, and **general nuclear response**.

deliberate planning: Operation planning and review in peacetime situations as a result of the **Joint Strategic Capabilities Plan (JSCP)** or other tasking directive using **Joint Operation Planning System (JOPS)** procedures. Time-sensitive planning procedures are used in emergency situations under the **Crisis Action System**. The deliberate planning process has five formal phases:

- Phase I: Initiation;
- Phase II: Concept development;
- Phase III: Plan development;
- Phase IV: Plan review; and
- Phase V: Supporting plans.

Deliberate planning is followed by plan maintenance, execution (under the Crisis Action System), and implementation.

delivery mode: The way in which a nuclear gravity bomb is delivered by the attacking aircraft, depending on defenses of the target and desired height of burst. A freefall weapon has no apparatus or device, such as a parachute, to retard its rate of fall after release of the weapon in air. Retarded weapons can be slowed from the normal freefall acceleration rate by a parachute or mechanical means to allow the delivery aircraft sufficient time to escape from the hazards created by the detonation of the weapon. There are two types of delivery modes:

- Laydown: a weapon designed to detonate at some finite time after it comes to rest on land or in water.
- Blind toss: a weapon-delivery maneuver executed under instrument conditions using radar to identify the target. The aircraft is pulled up and the weapon is released in such a manner that it is tossed onto the target.

delivery system: A generic term used to describe the aircraft, vehicle, ship, or missile that launches, releases, carries, or fires a particular piece of ordnance. It is usually applied to aircraft or missiles. It is also sometimes referred to as a "weapons platform," particularly for naval ships. Thus, an aircraft is the delivery system for bombs or air-to-air or air-to-surface rockets. An ICBM is a delivery system for reentry vehicles and warheads. A battleship is a delivery system or weapons platform for Tomahawk sea-launched cruise missiles.

Delphi: **SDI** concept that would use a high-energy pulse of electrons in the upper atmosphere to discriminate between decoys and warheads. At higher power levels, Delphi could be used to destroy incoming warheads.

The signal emitted by Delphi to discriminate targets would destroy all electronics aboard the vehicle, negating most fuzing mechanisms and reentry maneuvering capabilities. The Delphi ground-based system would be launched into the exoatmosphere just before use. Delphi would use long-pulse duration electron beams, which last for several millionths of a second. The beams are designed to hit a target with increased amounts of energy without increasing the weapon's electron energy level. The Delphi research is conducted at the Electron Propagation on Channels (Epoch) facility at Sandia Laboratories, Albuquerque, NM. The laboratory and research is paid for by the Strategic Defense Initiative Organization (SDIO). (see also **Space-Based Particle Beam**)

Delta II: An Air Force medium-payload space launch vehicle (also known as a Medium Launch Vehicle [MLV], along with the **Atlas II** rocket). It is a slightly larger, modified version of the Delta rocket, configured to launch **NAVSTAR/GPS** satellites. When fully operational, the rocket will consist of a three-stage booster surrounded by nine solid-propellant, graphite epoxy motors (GEMs). As of 1989, the GEMs were still under development and would not be available for the first nine GPS flights. These flights therefore employ a modified version of the current Delta rocket's Castor IV engine, designated the Castor IVA. Delta II differs from the earlier version in having a twelve-foot stretch in the first-state fuel tanks and, beginning with the tenth rocket, an increased expansion ratio on the first-state engine.

The prime contractor is McDonnell Douglas Astronautics Corp. On January 1987, McDonnell Douglas was selected by the Air Force to build 20 Delta II rockets. All 20 rockets are to be launched by 1991. The first launch took place on 14 February 1989 and was successful. Additional Delta IIs are planned for procurement for GPS replenishment after the required satellite constellation is achieved.

Delta Force: The nickname for the Army's counterterrorist Special Operations Detachment (Delta), subordinate to the **Joint Special Operations Command**. It was created in the 1970s as the U.S. Blue Light Team, and redesignated as the Delta detachment in October 1980 from recommendations of the Holloway Commission. It became operational in January 1981, although its existence is only obliquely acknowledged by the DOD. Its name has probably been changed to maintain its secret existence. The primary mission of the unit is the conduct of **counterterrorism** operations OCONUS. It also provides **special operations** assistance to conventional forces. It is aided by the Air Force's 8th Special Operations Squadron, Navy **SEAL** Team 6, and the Army's **Task Force 160**, which provides aviation support. Delta Force was involved in Operation Eagle Claw (Iranian hostage rescue attempt, 1979), the invasion of Grenada (1983), and the 1985 Achille Lauro intercept. Delta Force is thought to consist of 100–200 personnel from the three services.

Headquarters
Ft. Bragg, NC 23824

demilitarized zone (DMZ): A defined area in which the stationing or concentrating of military forces, or the retention or establishment of military installations of any description, is prohibited.

demonstration: A show of force. A demonstration employs forces, but it does so in a manner designed to warn or threaten the opposition rather than engage in combat. A demonstration can warn the potential aggressor that the United States has the capability and the will to escalate if necessary. A demonstration can also be staged to deceive the enemy as to our true actions. Feints and **cover and deception** movements are a form of demonstration. Normally, deception operations are used in conjunction with other military actions.

department: Separately organized entity under a civilian secretary who supervises the service chief (or chiefs) in matters of a service nature. The functions of departments are to recruit, supply, train, mobilize, administer, construct, outfit, repair, organize, equip, service, demobilize, and maintain. Common functions of the military departments are to

- Prepare forces and establish reserves of manpower, equipment, and supplies for the effective prosecution of war and military operations short of war; and plan for the expansion of peacetime components to meet the needs of war;
- Maintain in readiness mobile reserve forces, properly organized, trained, and equipped for employment in emergency;

- Recruit, organize, train, and equip interoperable forces for assignment to unified and specified commands;
- Prepare and submit budgets for their respective departments;
- Develop, garrison, supply, equip, and maintain bases and other installations, and furnish administrative and logistics support for forces and bases; and
- Assist each other in the accomplishment of their respective functions.

The **Department of Defense Reorganization Act of 1986** removed the military departments from the operational chain of command and clarified their support and administrative responsibilities.

Department of Defense (DOD): Executive branch agency of the U.S. government, formally established by the **National Security Act of 1949**. DOD was previously designated the Department of War in 1789, and redesignated as the National Military Establishment on 18 September 1947 by the **National Security Act of 1947**. The statutory basis for the Department's functions and composition is found at 10 USC §111 and within 10 USC Subtitle A. The DOD is headed by the civilian **Secretary of Defense**. As stated in its implementing directive, the DOD's responsibility is to

- Support and defend the Constitution of the United States against all enemies, foreign and domestic;
- Ensure, by timely and effective military action, the security of the United States, its possessions, and areas vital to its interest; and

- Uphold and advance the national policies and interests of the United States.

The organization of the DOD has undergone several major restructurings and is constantly changing its staff structure and agency structure. The DOD is currently composed of

- Office of the Secretary of Defense;
- DOD Inspector General;
- Defense Agencies;
- DOD Field Activities;
- Organization of the **Joint Chiefs of Staff;**
- The three military services—
  Department of the Air Force, Department of the Army, and **Department of the Navy**;
- **unified commands**;
- U.S. **Marine Corps**, reporting through the Department of the Navy; and
- U.S. **Coast Guard**, reporting to the Department of the Navy in wartime.

The DOD operates at over 1,265 major military installations worldwide, with approximately 870 installations within the United States, 375 overseas in 21 countries, and 20 in U.S. territories. Its force strength consists of more than five million personnel: 2,100,000 active-duty military personnel, 1,670,000 national guard and reserve personnel, and 1,000,000 civilian employees.

The Defense Agencies are

- **Defense Advanced Research Projects Agency (DARPA)**;
- **Defense Communications Agency (DCA)**;
- **Defense Contract Audit Agency (DCAA)**;
- **Defense Intelligence Agency (DIA)**;
- **Defense Investigative Service (DIS)**;
- **Defense Logistics Agency (DLA)**;
- **Defense Legal Services Agency (DLSA)**;
- **Defense Mapping Agency (DMA)**;
- **Defense Nuclear Agency (DNA)**;
- **Defense Security Assistance Agency (DSAA)**;
- **National Security Agency (NSA)**;
- **On-Site Inspection Agency (OSIA)**; and
- **Strategic Defense Initiative Organization (SDIO)**.

The DOD Field Activities are

- American Forces Information Service (ASD (Public Affairs)), Alexandria, VA 22314
- Defense Medical Support Activity (ASD (Health Affairs)), Falls Church, VA 22041
- Defense Technology Security Administration (USD (Policy)), Arlington, VA 20301
- Department of Defense Dependents Schools (ASD (Force Management and Personnel)), Alexandria, VA 22331-1100
- Office of Civilian Health and Medical Program of the Uniformed Services (OCHAMPUS) (ASD (Health Affairs)), Aurora, CO 80045-6900
- Office of Economic Adjustment (ASD (Force Management and Personnel)), Arlington, VA 20301
- Washington Headquarters Services (ASD (Comptroller)), Pentagon, Washington, DC 20301

(see also **Department of Defense Reorganization Act of 1958, Department of Defense Reorganization Act of 1986**)

Department of Defense Reorganization Act of 1958:   Congressional act signed into law on 6 August 1958 (PL 85-599, Title 50 U.S. Code §401) that instituted the first major reorganization of the Department of Defense since the **National Security Act of 1947**. It outlined the operational chain of command of the armed forces from the President (Commander-in-Chief), through the **Secretary of Defense**, to the commanders of the **unified and specified commands**. The act thereby strengthened the authority of the unified and specified commanders by placing them under the direct operational control of the **Joint Chiefs of Staff**, and by assigning forces to the commands on a full-time, operational basis (power to withdraw forces from this arrangement rests with the Secretary of Defense upon approval by the President). It also transferred operational command for air forces from the Air Force to the unified and specified commands to equal the authority of the Army and Navy. It created within the DOD the Office of the Secretary of Defense and asserted the control of the Secretary of Defense over the executive department. In addition, it established within the Office a Director of Defense for Research and Engineering and seven Assistant Secretaries. The law also granted a vote to the **Chairman of the Joint Chiefs of Staff** and increased the personnel strength of the Joint Staff from 210 to 400 officers. (see also **Department of Defense Reorganization Act of 1986**)

Department of Defense Reorganization Act of 1986:   Congressional act, also known as the Goldwater-Nichols Act, signed into law on 1 October 1986. It is the most significant restructuring of the Department since the **Department of Defense Reorganization Act of 1958**. It was enacted following the recommendations of the President's Blue Ribbon Commission on Defense Management (Packard Commission). The act designated the **Chairman of the Joint Chiefs of Staff (CJCS)** the principal military advisor to the President and Secretary of Defense, transferred duties of corporate JCS to the chairman, created the position of Vice Chairman, created the Operational Plans and Interoperability (J-7) and Force Structure, Resource, and Assessment (J-8) directorates, limited the Joint Staff to 1,627 military and civilian personnel, and specified the operational chain of command to run from the President to the combatant commanders.

Until the 1986 Act, there was confusion over the role of the JCS in the chain of command. The **National Security Act of 1947** stated that "combatant commands . . . are responsible to the President and to the Secretary [of Defense] for such military missions as may be assigned to them by the Secretary." This had been interpreted to cloud the statutory command authority of the Secretary and the subsequent role of the JCS. Further complication arose when, in the **Department of Defense Reorganization Act of 1958**, the Joint Chiefs of Staff, contrary to statute, were placed in the chain of command between the National Command Authority (NCA) and the combatant commanders. Congressional intent in the 1986 Act was to clarify the command line to the combatant commanders and preserve civilian control of the military. The act clearly resolved the issue of whether the JCS have executive authority to command combatant forces: "The Secretaries of the Military departments shall assign all forces under their jurisdiction to unified and specified combatant commands to perform missions assigned to those commands" and the chain of command "runs from the President to the Secretary of Defense and from the Secretary of Defense to the commander of the combatant commands." A provision of the act permits the President to authorize communications through CJCS.

Chief provisions of the act:

- Upgrades the authority and responsibility of the Chairman of the Joint Chiefs of Staff to that of the principal military advisor to the President, the **National Security Council**, and the Secretary of Defense;
- Clarifies the role of the Chairman of the Joint Chiefs of Staff in the operational chain of command to be communications-, not command-, oriented;
- Allows a third two-year term for the Chairman;
- Creates the position of Vice Chairman to serve as the nation's second-ranking military officer;
- Transfers several functions from the corporate Joint Chiefs of staff to the Chairman. Specified that the Joint Staff is to assist the Chairman, and is to be managed and supervised by the Chairman;
- Increases the authority of the **Commanders-in-Chief** to direct training, operations, and logistical functions of assigned forces;

- Requires that all operational communications from the President or the Secretary of Defense to the unified and specified commands flow through the Chairman of the Joint Chiefs of Staff;
- Clarifies the position of the Secretary of Defense in the operational chain of command;
- Formalizes the responsibilities of the Secretary of Defense to issue guidance on the services' programs and budgets;
- Requires the Secretary of Defense to provide written guidance to the Chairman of the Joint Chiefs of Staff regarding strategic planning and the preparation and review of contingency plans;
- Removes the statutory titles of the 11 Assistant Secretaries of Defense (ASDs) except for those for ASD (Reserve Affairs) and ASD (C3I);
- Revokes the authority of the Secretary of Defense to reorganize DOD activities established by law;
- Outlines specific supervisory and oversight responsibilties of the Secretary of Defense with regard to defense agencies and field activities;
- Requires a 10 percent reduction in the number of defense agency and field personnel by 30 September 1989;
- Requires services to consolidate similar functions performed both within their Staff and within civilian Secretariat offices, and places them within the Secretariat. These functions are acquisition, auditing, comptroller, information management, inspector general, legislative affairs, public affairs, and R&D (minus military requirements and operational testing); and

• Places limits on the numbers of service headquarters staffs, and mandates a 15 percent reduction in the number of general and flag officers and other personnel assigned to each headquarters staff by 30 September 1988.

The act also established new joint officer personnel policy towards the management and promotion of "joint-duty specialty" officers and other joint (interservice) officers.

Department of Energy (DOE): Executive branch agency created by the Department of Energy Organization Act on 4 August 1977, and activated 1 October 1977. Its predecessor organizations include the Federal Energy Administration, the Atomic Energy Commission, the Energy Research and Development Administration, and the Federal Power Commission. The Federal Energy Regulatory Commission was established as an independent agency within the DOE. The DOE, together with the DOD, is responsible for the production of nuclear warheads and components. The DOE's role in the production process includes the design, testing, manufacturing, assembly, and retirement of warheads (all according to DOD specifications and requirements). The DOE also processes the uranium, plutonium, and tritium used in nuclear warheads; monitors the quality of the stockpile; and, together with the DOD, is responsible for the safety and security of nuclear weapons and components. The independent Defense Nuclear Facilities Safety Board conducts safety oversight of certain DOE defense facilities. The DOE's

Assistant Secretary for Nuclear Energy is responsible for nuclear reactor and non-reactor facility safety [DOE, *Departmental Organization and Management Arrangements*, Secretary of Energy Notice 6-89].

The nuclear production complex consists of 36 laboratories and centers, including

• Nuclear warhead research and design laboratories:
    Lawrence Livermore National Laboratory
    Los Alamos National Laboratory
• Nonnuclear design laboratory
    Sandia National Laboratory
• Army, Air Force, and Navy supporting laboratories
• Nevada Testing Site
• Processing/manufacturing plants
    Rocky Flats Plant (Golden, CO)
    Y-12 Plant (Oak Ridge, TN)
    Savannah River Plant (Aiken, SC)
    Mound Facility (Miamisburg, OH)
    Pinellas Plant (St. Petersburg, FL)
    Kansas City Plant (Kansas City, MO)
    Pantex Plant (Amarillo, TX)

The DOE Assistant Secretary for Defense Programs (ASDP) acts as the manager of the nuclear weapon program and production complex including all aspects of nuclear weapons safety and is principal advisor to the Secretary of Energy on national security matters. Performing various defense tasks are four subordinate deputy assistant secretariats and nine program offices. The DOE Assistant Secretary for Nuclear Energy (ASNE) manages three weapons-related programs: the Naval Nuclear Propulsion Program (NNPP); space power research programs related to Strategic Defense Initiative platforms; and the uranium enrichment program.

The DOE production complex Employs approximately 45,000 people. The total DOE budget request for FY 1990 is $15 billion, of which approximately $9 billion is for Atomic Energy Defense Activities.

Headquarters
Germantown, MD
and Washington, DC 20545

Operations Offices

- Albuquerque Operations Office;
- San Francisco Operations Office;
- Nevada Operations Office;
- Richland Operations Office;
- Idaho Operations Office;
- Chicago Operations Office;
- Oak Ridge Operations Office; and
- Savannah River Operations Office.

Naval Reactors Offices

- Schenectady Naval Reactors Office;
- Knolls Atomic Power Lab;
- Pittsburgh Naval Reactors Office;
- Bettis Atomic Power Lab; and
- Naval Reactors Facility.

Secretaries of Energy

James R. Schlesinger	5 Aug 1977– 23 Aug 1979
Charles W. Duncan	24 Aug 1979– 20 Jan 1981
James Burrows Edwards	23 Jan 1981– 5 Nov 1982
Donald Paul Hodel	5 Nov 1982– 7 Feb 1985
John S. Herrington	7 Feb 1985– 19 Jan 1989
Adm James D. Watkins	20 Jan 1989– present

Department of the Air Force: The executive component and central headquarters of the U.S. Air Force, together with all the field headquarters, forces, reserve components, installations, activities, and functions operating under the **Secretary of the Air Force**. It was first organized in 1935 from the Army Air Corps as the General Headquarters Air Force, operating under the Army Chief of Staff and the War Department. The Air Force was separately established by the **National Security Act of 1947**. The first Secretary of the Air Force was sworn in on 18 September 1947. The statutory basis for the functions and composition of the Air Force is found at 10 U.S. Code §8062 and within 10 U.S. Code Subtitle D. The Department's role is to

> . . . organize, train, and equip the Air Forces to conduct prompt and sustained combat operations in the air— specifically, forces to defend the United States against air attack, gain and maintain general air supremacy, defeat enemy air forces, conduct space operations, control vital air areas, and establish local air superiority. . .

The Department is organized by functional, not regional, lines and is composed of three components: the Secretariat, known as the Office of the Secretary of the Air Force (SAF); the **Air Staff**, also known as the Office of the **Chief of Staff of the Air Force (CSAF)**; and the field activities, including **major commands, separate operating agencies**, and **direct reporting units**. Its combat forces include 18 strategic bomber wings, 15 interceptor squadrons, 46 tactical fighter wings,

343 strategic airlift aircraft, and 429 tactical airlift aircraft. The total force strength of the Air Force is about 595,000 active-duty military personnel; 268,000 **Air National Guard** and **Air Force Reserve** personnel; and 260,000 civilian employees.

Department of the Air Force Command and Control System (DAFCCS): Command and control system directly responsive to the **Secretary of the Air Force** and **Chief of Staff of the Air Force**. DAFCCS conducts resource and capability monitoring and supports contingency planning to ensure that Air Force components of unified and specified commands can meet the requirements of commanders. The command and control systems of the Air Force major commands are elements of DAFCCS and support the **National Military Command System (NMCS)** through the Air Force Operations Center (AFOC) and the Air Force Emergency Operations Center. AFOC correlates DAFCCS with the **Worldwide Military Command and Control System (WWMCCS)**. DAFCCS responsibilities are to

- Facilitate planning, directing, coordinating, and controlling operational activities of subordinate elements;
- Provide designated authorities with essential information to permit effective decision making;
- Provide the capability to transmit decisions in a timely manner to the authorities charged with execution responsiblity;

- Support the controlled commitment and timely application and withdrawal of forces in support of national objectives; and
- Ensure the continuity of essential military functions by providing for survival and secure command, control, and communications facilities.

[USAF, *USAF Command Posts*, AFR 55-23, 2 July 1982, released under the FOIA]

Department of the Army (DA or HQDA): The executive component and central headquarters of the U.S. Army, together with all the field headquarters, forces, reserve components, installations, activities, and functions operating under the **Secretary of the Army**. The Army was established as the American Continental Army by the Continental Congress on 14 June 1775. Its first Commander-in-Chief, George Washington, was named the same day. The Continental Army was redesignated as the United States Army on 29 September 1789 and subsequently became an arm of the War Department. Eventually, the Army was established as one of three military departments subordinate to the Department of Defense by the **National Security Act of 1947**, as amended. The statutory basis for the functions and composition of the Army are found at 10 U.S. Code §3062 and within 10 U.S. Code Subtitle B. Section 3062 states "It is the intent of Congress to provide an Army that is capable, in conjunction with the other armed forces, of

1. preserving the peace and security, and providing for the de-

fense, of the United States, the Territories, Commonwealths, and possessions, and any areas occupied by the United States;

2. supporting the national policies;
3. implementing the national objectives; and
4. overcoming any nations responsible for aggressive acts that imperil the peace and security of the United States.

. . . It shall be organized, trained, and equipped primarily for prompt and sustained combat incident to operations on land. . ."

The Department is composed of the Office of the Secretary of the Army and the **Army Staff**, also known as the Office of the **Chief of Staff of the Army**. Additionally, the Army consists of reserve components and numerous **major commands**. Its combat force consists of 28 combat divisions and 22 combat brigades. The total force strength of the Army is 770,000 active-duty military personnel; 1,000,000 **Army National Guard** and **Army Reserve** personnel; and 440,000 civilian employees. Headquarters, Department of the Army (HQDA) is the executive part of the Department of the Army at the seat of government. It exercises directive and supervisory functions.

Department of the Navy: The executive component and central headquarters of the U.S. Navy together with all the field headquarters, forces, reserve components, installations, activities, and functions under the **Secretary of the Navy**. The Navy was established 30 April 1798 (just prior to the undeclared war with France) by an act of Congress, which removed naval activities from the jurisdiction of the War Department. Congress established the U.S. **Marine Corps** as a separate service within the Navy Department on 11 July 1798. The statutory basis for the Navy's function and composition is found at 10 U.S. Code Subtitle C. Primary roles of the Navy are to

. . . organize, train, and equip Navy and Marine Corps forces to conduct prompt and sustained combat operations at sea, including operations of sea-based aircraft and land-based naval air components; specifically, forces to seek out and destroy enemy naval forces and to suppress enemy sea commerce; to gain and maintain general naval supremacy; to control vital sea areas; to protect vital sea lines of communication; to establish and maintain local superiority (including air) in an area of naval operations; to seize and defend advanced naval bases; and to conduct such land and air operations as may be essential to the prosecution of naval campaign.

The Department establishes policy and exercises direction and control over the other two components of the Navy establishment: the **operating forces** of the Navy; and the administrative organizations (known as the **shore establishment**). The Navy Department is composed of the Office of the Secretary of the Navy; the Office of the **Chief of Naval Operations (CNO)**; the Headquarters, U.S. **Marine Corps**; the Headquarters, **Naval Material Command; Bureau of Naval Personnel**; and Headquarters, U.S. **Coast Guard**. As a bilinear organization, the Navy consists of two separate but overlapping chains of command: an **administrative chain of command** and an **operational chain of command**. Its combat forces include 14 aircraft carriers and air wings, 35 fleet ballistic missile submarines, and 100 attack submarines. The total Navy force strength is 580,000 active-duty military personnel; 240,000 **Naval Reserve** personnel; and 360,000 civilian employees.

deperming: "The process to permanently decrease the magnetic condition of a ship by wrapping a large conductor around it a number of times and energizing the coil thus formed" [*NWP 3*]. (see also **degaussing**)

depleted uranium: Uranium depleted in the U-235 isotope; the composition is in the range of 99.28 percent to approximately 99.85 percent U-238 and less than 0.711 percent U-235, with a trace of U-234.

deployment: **1.** The act of relocating forces to desired areas of operation. **2.** The designated location of units. **3.** The act of spreading out offensive and defensive forces, according to a plan, such as to meet a military situation. **4.** The final stage of weapons development and acquisition process.

deployment order/deployment preparation order: An order issued by competent authority to move forces or prepare forces for movement. "Upon designation of actual units to participate in a planned operation, the Joint Chiefs of Staff may issue a deployment preparation order by the authority of the Secretary of Defense

that directs supporting commanders to place their units in an alert or deployability posture appropriate to the priority for deployment" [JCS, *Joint Operations Planning System,* Vol. IV, p. II–18, released under the FOIA]. A deployment/deployment preparation order can

- Increase the deployability posture of units;
- Decrease the deployability posture of units;
- Deploy forces;
- Redeploy forces;
- Establish **joint task forces (JTFs)**, activate JTF headquarters, and designate commanders of JTFs;
- Disestablish headquarters of JTFs; and
- Direct any other action that would signal planned U.S. military action or the termination thereof in response to a particular crisis event or incident.

deployment phase: The period in a weapon system's life beginning with the user's acceptance of the first operational unit and extending until the system is phased out of the inventory. It overlaps the production phase.

depressed trajectory: The trajectory of a **ballistic missile** fired at an angle to the ground significantly lower than the angle of a minimum energy trajectory (the usual ballistic missile trajectory). Such a missile rises above the line-of-sight radar horizon at a later state of flight and has a shorter time of flight, thus making detection and tracking more difficult and reducing warning time. The use of submarine-launched ballistic missiles close to enemy coasts in the depressed trajectory mode is of concern to nuclear strategists.

depth bomb/depth charge: A depth bomb is an **anti-submarine warfare (ASW)** explosive dropped from aircraft. A depth charge is an ASW explosive dropped or fired from ships. The primary conventional air-launched ASW depth bomb is actually the Mk46 lightweight torpedo. The nuclear depth bomb is the B57. The classic "ash can" depth charges rolled off the back of a ship are no longer in use on modern Navy ships. The primary conventional surface ship-launched ASW depth charge is the **ASROC**-launched Mk46 lightweight torpedo, or Mk46 torpedoes launched over the sides of the ships. The nuclear depth charges, which consist of ASROCs armed with W44 warheads and which are known as rocket-thrown depth charges (RTDCs), are being retired in FY 1990.

desired ground zero (DGZ):   That point on the surface of the earth at, or vertically below or above, the center of a planned nuclear detonation. (see also **actual ground zero, ground zero**)

destroyer   (DD-/DDG-):   Heavily armed small warship (smaller in size than a cruiser but larger than a frigate) designed to operate offensively with strike forces — **carrier battle groups** or **surface action groups** — and in support of amphibious operations, or defensively to protect support forces against submarine, air, and surface threats. As of 1989, there are about 68 active destroyers in four classes: Spruance class (DD-963), Charles F. Adams class (DDG-2), Farragut class (DDG-37), and Kidd class (DDG-993). The Navy plans to build a new series of destroyers, the Arleigh **Burke** class (DDG-51), in the 1990s.

destroyer tender: A mobile logistics type ship for material support, designated AD. Current classes of destroyer tenders include

- AD-14 Dixie class;
- AD-37 Samuel Gompers class; and
- AD-41 Yellowstone class.

detachment (det):   1. A portion of a unit separated from its main organization for a mission elsewhere. **2.** A temporary military or naval unit formed from other units or parts of units.

deterrence: "The prevention from action by fear of the consequences. Deterrence is a state of mind brought about by the existence of a credible threat of unacceptable counteraction" [*JCS Pub 1.*, p. 114].

DEW   (Distant   Early   Warning) Line: A line of 31 AN/FPS-19 and AN/FPS-30 air defense radars a-long the 70th parallel about 350 km north of the Arctic Circle, stretching from northern Alaska across northern Canada and into Greenland. Two radars are also in Iceland. Completed in July 1957, the DEW Line was a follow-on to the **CADIN/Pinetree** Line and the Mid-Canada Line, and it has itself been replaced by the **North Warning System (NWS)**. The DEW line warned against manned bomber attacks in Canada and CONUS, but fell into obsolescence with the advent of ballistic missiles. The DEW Line was jointly conceived and planned by the United States and Canada, but funded and staffed by the United States.

DIA (see **Defense Intelligence Agency**)

DIA Periodic Intelligence Summary (DIA INTSUM): Intelligence report for the JCS, unified and specified commands, military services, military commanders worldwide, and selected U.S. government agencies providing periodic intelligence summaries about an actual or simulated (training exercises) crisis that could have an immediate effect on U.S. military planning and preparations.

DIKTER (see **sensitive compartmented information**)

direct action mission: "A specified act of **special operations** involving operations of an overt, covert, clandestine, or low visibility nature conducted in hostile or denied areas by a sponsoring power's special operations forces" [MAC, *Contingency Planning Policies and Procedures*, MACR 28-2, 29 December 1986, p. 103 released under the FOIA].

Direct Air Support Center (DASC): Operational component of the Air Force **Tactical Air Control System**. DASC is designated to coordinate and direct tactical air support operations, providing fast reaction to requests from ground forces for close air support, tactical air reconnaissance, and tactical airlift. It consists of the following functional components:

- Close air support operations;
- Tactical air reconnaissance operations; and
- Tactical airlift operation, intelligence, and support.

It is collocated with the senior Tactical Operations Center (TOC) of the supported Army forces, usually at the corps level. In NATO, the DASC is called the **Air Support Operations Center**. The DASC processes requests from tactical air control parties at lower-level ground units. Previously allocated resources and resources diverted from lower-priority missions are used to fulfill the requests. The DASC also advises Army commanders on preplanned air operations through Air Liaison Officers (ALOs) at the corps, division, and brigade levels.

Direct Communications Link (DCL): The Washington-Moscow "hot line" for emergency communications between the leaders of the United States and the Soviet Union. During the 1962 Cuban Missile Crisis, both the Soviet Union and the United States decided that a better means of communication between the leaders of the two countries was needed to reduce the risk of nuclear war through accident, miscalculation, or failure of communications. The two countries therefore initiated the following agreements:

- *Memorandum of Understanding between the USA and the USSR Regarding the Establishment of a*

Direct Communications Link: The first DCL agreement, it entered into force on 20 June 1963. The DCL was one of several proposals put forth by the United States at the Eighteen-Nation Disarmament Committee meeting in Geneva. On 30 August 1963 a wire-telegraph circuit and printer between the Pentagon and the Kremlin (called "MOLINK") went into service. Teletype was chosen over telephone communications because it would not rely on rapid translation and printed messages would give more time before responding than would verbal messages.

- *Agreement on Measures to Improve the USA–USSR Direct Communications Link*: An update to the 1963 agreement, this went into effect on 30 September 1971. Two satellite communications circuits replaced the radio circuits (becoming fully operational in January 1978), but the wire telegraph circuit was retained as a backup. The U.S. terminal is located in the **National Military Command Center**, and the Soviet terminal is located in a similar unhardened facility. Both countries have identical facilities: two satellite earth stations, encryption devices, expert linguists, and secure teletype terminals. The DCL is tested daily.

- *Additional Hotline Modernization*: On 17 July 1984, the United States and Soviet Union signed an agreement upgrading the DCL line speed and flexibility. The new system can transmit graphs, maps, and other documents via facsimile. This new system was proposed by President Reagan in 1983, and Sen-

ators Jackson and Nunn also had recommendations for improvement. The Soviet Union turned down two proposals: one would have established a DCL between the Pentagon and the Soviet Ministry of Defense; the other would have linked each nation's capital with its embassy in the other country. The Soviet rejection of these proposals was based on its wish not to decentralize defense establishment and fears that the United States would use its link to its Moscow embassy for intelligence gathering.

The Soviet Union also has a DCL with France (established in 1966) and one with the United Kingdom (1967).

direct defense: The first option in NATO's **flexible response** strategy, which includes direct defense, **deliberate escalation**, and **general nuclear response**.

directed energy weapon (DEW): Weapon (chemical laser, particle beam, microwave generator, or excimer or free-electron beam) that destroys targets with highly concentrated beams of energy. The advantage of DEWs is the speed with which they can hit a target; they deliver energy to the target at or near the speed of light. DEWs involve three types of kill mechanisms:

- Functional kill: Damage rendered may not be detected immediately but it is enough to disable the target (incapacitates without obliterating);
- Impulse kill: Delivers a mechanical shock wave to the target (most effective against boosters); and

• Thermal kill: Intense heat (10 to 100 kilojoules) directed onto a small part of the target to disable it.

direction finding: A procedure for obtaining bearings on radio frequency emitters with the use of a directional antenna and display unit on an intercept receiver or ancillary equipment.

directive: Military communication in which policy is established or a specific action is ordered.

Director of Central Intelligence (DCI):   The central authority for the coordination and operation of intelligence activities by member agencies and offices of the U.S. **intelligence community**, and principal foreign intelligence adviser to the President. The DCI also serves as the Director of the **Central Intelligence Agency** and is a non-statutory member of the **National Security Council**. The DCI is appointed by the President with the consent of the Senate.

direct reporting unit (DRU):   Air Force organization, usually an office or center with a single, specialized, and continuing mission, operating from one location. DRUs report directly to the **Air Staff** or the **Chief of Staff of the Air Force**.

Air Force Direct Reporting Units

• Air Force Center for International Programs;
• Air Force Civilian Personnel Management Center (AFCPMC);
• Air Force District of Washington (AFDW);
• Air Force Technical Applications Center (AFTAC);
• Air National Guard Support Center;

• U.S. Air Force Academy (USAFA); and
• U.S. Air Force Historical Research Center (USAFHRC).

(see also **major command, separate operating agency**)

direct support (DS): 1. Support provided by one subordinate unit or force to another, such as direct support artillery. A direct support unit is under the operational command of the supported unit. **2.** Use of an attack submarine for the protection of a specific force, such as a carrier battle group. (see also **general support**)

dirty weapon: A nuclear weapon that produces a larger amount of radioactive residues than a "normal" weapon of the same yield.

Discoverer   (see **Corona**)

dispersed operating base: An airbase or civilian airport equipped, manned, and maintained in a reduced operational status, with the capability to receive aircraft before **H-hour** on either a temporary or permanent basis and from which the aircraft can conduct exercise, contingency, or general war operations.

displacement: The weight of water displaced by a vessel, expressed in long tons.

division: 1. An organizational part of a headquarters or naval ship that deals with a particular military function or area (e.g. plans division, weapons division). **2.** In the Air Force, a subordinate organization to an air force but higher in echelon than a wing, called an **air division**.

3. In the Navy, an operational and administrative group of naval ships of similar type, or a tactical unit of a naval aircraft squadron consisting of two or more sections. **4.** In the Army and Marine Corps, a major administrative and tactical unit for ground combat operations, subordinate to a **corps**. It is the smallest combat unit capable of conducting sustained combat operations for an extended time. A division consists of from 10,000–18,000 personnel, depending on type and mission. Its division base is composed of a relatively fixed headquarters company and staff; reconnaissance, combat support, and combat service support units; a combat aviation brigade; and three or four maneuver **brigades**, each with two to five **maneuver battalions** (infantry, mechanized infantry, airborne infantry, air assault infantry, tank, etc.) depending on its mission. Units subordinate to the division other than the brigade are

- Division Artillery;
- Division Support Command;
- Division Engineer Battalion;
- Division Signal Battalion;
- Air Defense Artillery (ADA) Battalion;
- Military Intelligence (CEWI) Battalion;
- Division Military Police Company;
- Division Chemical Company (NBC Defense); and
- Band.

A division is designated as a particular type based on the number and types of its maneuver combat battalions. There are presently seven types of Army divisions:

- **Airborne division;**
- **Air assault division;**
- **Armored division;**
- **Infantry division;**
- **Mechanized infantry division;**
- **Motorized infantry division; and**
- **Light infantry division.**

Although the organization, strength, and equipment of a division are based on its anticipated mission and area of operations, its actual capabilities and limitations also depend on its final type structure. All divisions are characteristically able to perform ground operations in a nuclear, biological, and chemical environment; control and administer additional combat battalions; conduct long-range patrolling; and perform all organizational and direct support maintenance on their organic equipment. The division headquarters provides command, control, and coordination of the tactical operations of the division, and administration of the division and its organic, attached, and supporting units. The division commander exercises command through the commanders of the brigades, division artillery, and other commands of the division. To assist a division Commander (normally a Major General) during combat operations, a Division Tactical Operations Center (DTOC) is established.

Current Army divisions are

- 1st Armored Div, Ansbach, West Germany (APO New York 09177);
- 1st Cavalry Div, Ft. Hood, TX 76544;
- 1st Infantry Div (Mech), Ft. Riley, KS 66442;
- 2d Armored Div, Ft. Hood, TX 76544;

- 2d Infantry Div, Tongduchon, South Korea (APO San Francisco 96224);
- 3d Infantry Div (Mech), Wuerzburg, West Germany;
- 3d Armored Div, Frankfurt, West Germany;
- 4th Infantry Div (Mech), Ft. Carson, CO 80913;
- 5th Infantry Div (Mech), Ft. Polk, LA 71459;
- 6th Infantry Div (Light), Ft. Richardson, AK 99505;
- 7th Infantry Div (Light), Ft. Ord, CA 93941;
- 8th Infantry Div (Mech), Bad Kreuznach, West Germany;
- 9th Infantry Div (Motorized), Ft. Lewis, WA 98373;
- 10th Mountain Div (Light Inf), Ft. Drum, NY 13601;
- 24th Infantry Div (Mech), Ft. Stewart, GA 31314;
- 25th Infantry Div (Light), Schonfield Barracks, HI 96786;
- 26th Infantry Div (ARNG), Boston, MA 02210;
- 28th Infantry Div (ARNG), Harrisburg, PA 17105;
- 29th Infantry Div (Light) (ARNG), Ft. Belvoir, VA 22060;
- 35th Inf Div (Mech) (ARNG), Ft. Leavenworth, KS 66027;
- 38th Infantry Div (ARNG), Indianapolis, IN 46216;
- 40th Infantry Div (Mech) (ARNG), Los Alamitos, CA 90720;
- 42d Infantry Div (ARNG), New York, NY 10305;
- 47th Infantry Div (ARNG), St. Paul, MN 55101;
- 49th Armored Div (ARNG), Austin, TX 78743;
- 50th Armored Div (ARNG), Somerset, NJ 08873;
- 82d Airborne Div, Ft. Bragg, NC 28307; and
- 101st Airborne Div (Air Assault), Ft. Campbell, KY 42223.

(see also **Marine division**)

division artillery (DIVARTY):   One of two major subordinate commands subordinate to the division for command and control of the combat support and combat service support units. It provides close and continuous fire support to the division. It is augmented by corps and army artillery units assigned tactical missions to support the division with all or part of their fires. The primary function of DIVARTY is to support the maneuver elements of the division by neutralizing with fire those targets most likely to hinder accomplishment of the missions. It also provides counterbattery, interdiction, and flank suppression fires. (see also **division support command**)

division support command (DISCOM):   One of two major subordinate commands subordinate to the division for command and control of the combat support and combat service support units. The division support command is at the same echelon as the brigades and **division artillery**. The DISCOM is the logistic operator for the division and is responsible to the division commander for accomplishing the division logistics plan. Functions include supply and operation of supply distribution points, except for communications security equipment; direct support maintenance, except for clothing, medical, and communications security

(COMSEC) equipment; medical services; maintenance management; personnel services and finance support; and transportation support.

dock landing ship (LSD): Navy conventionally powered amphibious ship, designed to support Navy and Marine Corps amphibious operations, including landings on hostile shores. LSDs can transport and launch amphibious vehicles and craft with their crews and embarked personnel in amphibious assault operations. The latest class, the Whidbey Island (LSD-41) class, will be able to provide limited docking and repair service for the **Landing Craft Air Cushion (LCAC)**. The Navy operates just over a dozen LSDs, with more being added to the fleet. Lockheed Shipbuilding and Avondale Shipyards are the contractors. The end costs for the first two LSD-41s were $411 million and $344 million respectively. (see also **amphibious warfare ship**)

doctrine: Experience, theory, capabilities, understanding, and guesswork that governs the use of military forces. The principles of war for the U.S. military are contained in service publications such as Army Field Manual 100-1, *The Army*; Air Force Manual 1-1, *Basic Doctrine of the U.S. Air Force*; and Fleet Marine Force Manual FMFM 6-4, *Marine Rifle Company/Platoon*. Doctrine is developed from parameters that include the agreed strategy, conceptual ideas, operational concepts, and available technologies. Doctrine is based on military expertise and experience derived from sources such as military history.

Basic aerospace doctrine describes and guides the proper use of air forces in combat. Since 1943, this basic doctrine has capitalized on the speed, range, and flexibility of air forces and **air operations**. Tactical air forces fly offensive and defensive counterair to control the skies; reconnaissance and surveillance to avoid surprise; and close air support and interdiction to support forces in the land battle.

Basic Army doctrine emphasizes initiative, depth, agility, and synchronization. Initiative implies an offensive spirit in the conduct of all operations. The underlying purpose of every encounter is to seize or retain independence of action. The goals of the battle in depth are to delay, disrupt, or destroy the enemy's noncommitted forces and to isolate his committed forces so that they may be destroyed. Agility means commanders must stay informed of critical events as they occur and must take necessary actions faster than the enemy. Synchronization of operations is necessary to achieve maximum combat power at the point of decision. Flexible Army doctrine requires readiness for combat in any terrain or climate, and under whatever conditions the enemy, the geography, or the nature of objectives may impose.

Field Manual 100-5, *Operations* (20 August 1982), is the authoritative statement of Army combat doctrine for worldwide applications, and the basic statement of the Army's **airland battle** concept. It provides general guidelines to units, primarily corps and below. On 21 April 1983, the Air Force confirmed that FM 100-5 would guide their forces as well in joint airland combat operations.

In NATO, Army operations in either direct defense or deliberate escalation using either conventional or nuclear weapons are governed by NATO doctrine, the strategy of **flexible response** (MC 14/3), and NATO's **General Political Guidelines for the Employment of Nuclear Weapons in Defense of NATO**.

Field Manual 100-5 states "The U.S. Army must meet a variety of situations and challenges. In the 1980's it can expect to be committed in either of two environments. It may fight on a sophisticated battlefield with an existing infrastructure of communications, air defense, logistic facilities, and ports. Or on a relatively unsophisticated battlefield where it may have to create an infrastructure or choose to fight without one. The Army recognizes nine principles of war: objective, offensive, mass, economy of force, maneuver, unity of command, security, surprise, and simplicity."

- *Objective*: The direction of every military operation toward a clearly defined and attainable objective. The Army's primary objective is to win the land battle. The intermediate objective of each operation must contribute to this ultimate objective through the destruction of the enemy's armed forces and his will to fight.
- *Offensive*: Offensive action necessary to achieve decisive results and maintain freedom of action. It permits the commander to exercise initiative and impose his will upon the enemy; to set the pace and determine the course of battle; to exploit enemy weaknesses and rapidly changing situations; and

to meet unexpected developments. The defensive may be forced on the commander, but doctrine states that he should deliberately adopt it only temporarily while awaiting an opportunity or offensive action. Even on the defensive, the commander is to seek every opportunity to seize the initiative and achieve decisive results by offensive action.
- *Mass*: Superior combat power concentrated at the critical time and place for a decisive purpose. Superiority results from the proper combination of the elements of combat power. Numerically inferior forces can achieve decisive combat superiority at the critical point on the battlefield by consideration of this principle.
- *Economy of Force*: The skillful and prudent use of combat power, which enables the commander to accomplish the mission with a minimum expenditure of resources. This principle is the corollary of the principle of mass. By economizing in less critical areas, the commander can achieve superiority at the point of decision.
- *Maneuver*: To dispose forces to place the enemy at a disadvantage and thus achieve results that would otherwise be more costly in men and materiel. Successful maneuver requires flexibility in organization, administrative support, and command and control.
- *Unity of Command*: Unity of command is vital to the coordinated action of all forces toward a common goal. This is best achieved by giving a single commander the requisite authority.
- *Security*: Preventing surprise, preserving freedom of action, and

denying the enemy information during military operations. Application of the principle does not imply undue caution or avoidance of risk. Bold seizure and retention of the initiative frequently deny the enemy the opportunity to interfere.

- *Surprise*: Taking decisive action where success is out of proportion to the effort expended. Surprise results from striking an enemy at a time and place and in a manner for which he is not prepared.
- *Simplicity*: Direct, simple plans and clear, concise orders, which minimize misunderstanding and confusion. If other factors are equal, the simplest plan is preferred.

NATO, guided by the Military Agency for Standardization (MAS), has developed a broad variety of agreed tactical principles and doctrine. These encompass a series of about 30 Allied Tactical Publication (ATPs). ATP-35(A), "Land Force Tactical Doctrine," states that

> it will be essential for the land forces of the Alliance to operate together in the event of an attack on the NATO area. Formations of different nations will deploy alongside or pass through one other's area of responsibility or even be grouped in multinational formations. This will demand a high degree of interoperability. Therefore it is essential that they possess a common understanding of the principles of land combat and apply the same doctrine in tactical operations. ATP-35(A) has been developed to ensure this common understanding and approach. It outlines the doctrine for combined arms operations at the brigade level and above.

ATP-35(A) defines the operational-level doctrine, but each nation has its own tactical doctrine. ATP-35(A) organizes the battlefield into three areas: the Covering Force Area, the Main Battle Area, and the Rear Area. Within this basic division each nation can decide how its forces will fight. The developed doctrine for the conduct of amphibious operations is set forth in FM 31-11, *Doctrine for Amphibious Operations*. In July 1962, the Army approved the doctrine for joint use.

DOD   (see **Department of Defense**)

dome: The mound of water spray thrown into the air when the shock wave from an underwater detonation of a nuclear weapon reaches the surface.

domestic emergency: General term encompassing those emergencies "that effect the public welfare and occur within the 50 states, District of Columbia, Commonwealth of Puerto Rico, U.S. possessions and territories, or any political subdivision thereof, as a result of enemy attack, insurrection, civil disturbance, earthquakes, fire, flood, and other public disasters of equivalent emergencies that endanger life and property or disrupt the usual processes of government" [*JCS Pub 1*, p. 119]. Domestic emergencies include

- **Civil defense** emergencies;
- **Civil disturbances**;
- Major disasters; and
- Natural disasters.

Military policy concerning domestic emergencies (excluding civil disturbances) includes the provision of certain military assistance to civil authorities; loan of military resources according to certain provisions; maintenance or support of "the reestablishment of law and order and protection of life and property in the event civil control or leadership is destroyed or overwhelmed"; and coordination with those civil authorities "to ensure maximum military-civil cooperation and understanding during emergencies."

The Department of the Army has primary responsibility for the coordination of military assistance to civil authorities in peacetime domestic emergencies. In enemy attack situations, such responsibility is transferred to commanders in the operational chain of command as determined by the Secretary of Defense or the Chairman of the JCS. "In the event of a nuclear attack upon the United States, military forces will have a priority commitment initially to mount offensive and defensive actions and to assist civil authorities in assessing damage and danger areas within the continental limits of the United States. It is possible that extensive damage will require evaluation of the priorities to be assigned to civil support as opposed to military requirements for planned combat and combat support operations" [JCS, *Unified Action Armed Forces (UNAAF)*, JCS Pub 2, December 1986, Chapter 4, pp. 38–42]. (see also **martial law, Military Support of Civil Defense**)

domestic intelligence: "Intelligence relating to activities or conditions within the United States that threaten internal security and that might require the employment of troops; and intelligence relating to activities of individuals or agencies potentially or actually dangerous to the security of the Department of Defense" [*JCS Pub 1*, p. 119].

Doomsday plane: Nickname often applied by the media to the President's **National Emergency Airborne Command Post**.

Double Take: Exercise term to describe **Defense Readiness Condition (DEFCON) 4**.

downgrade: To change a **security classification** from a higher to a lower level.

drone: Any aircraft or missile modified or produced as a target for weapon evaluation and crew training, or for reconnaissance and data gathering purposes, and which has incorporated into its prime design the capability to be flown by remote control.

DRUID (see **sensitive compartmented information**)

DSCS (see **Defense Satellite Communications System**)

DSP (see **Defense Support Program**)

DSRV: Designation for **deep submergence rescue vehicle**.

DSV: Designation for deep submergence vehicle.

dual-based: A tactical combat unit whose tenant location is separate from its area of responsibility and parent command. Prior to or during hostilities, the dual-based unit would deploy to a predesignated base. For example, a handful of combat-ready tactical fighter squadrons from the Tactical Air Command, which are stationed in the United States, are under day-to-day operational control of U.S. European Command. They practice the deployment to Europe annually as part of the Crested Cap exercises.

dual-capable: Delivery system that can be equipped with either a nuclear or nonnuclear (conventional high explosive, chemical, etc.) weapon.

dual-hatted: Describes a commander who commands two commands (e.g., the U.S. Commander-in-Chief U.S. European Command is also the NATO Supreme Allied Commander Europe (SACEUR)) and thus is "dual-hatted." Another usage is to describe the commander as "wearing two hats." Similarly, commanders who simultaneously command more than two commands may be described as "triple-hatted" or "wearing four hats," and so on.

dual-key: Euphemism for an allied nuclear-capable system that, under programs of cooperation, can fire U.S. nuclear warheads. The dual-key is intended to ensure that both nations share in the decision to use nuclear weapons. Artillery guns, aircraft, and missile systems of Belgium, Greece, Italy, the Netherlands, Turkey, the United Kingdom, and West Germany are currently certified for dual-key nuclear use. Also called "two-key" or "double-key" systems.

dual-purpose: A military force or weapon system that is adaptable for use in two or more functions, such as conventional and strategic operations. The term is generally used to refer to military forces; weapon systems are more frequently called **dual-capable**.

dual-warning phenomenology: The practice of deriving warning data from two different systems (e.g., radar and infrared, visible light and x-ray) in order to double-check the validity of the information. U.S. early warning and attack assessment is based upon the principle of dual-warning phenomenology.

Dull Sword: Code name for a naval **nuclear weapon incident**.

duress system: A method by which personnel who control entry into, vouch for, or escort visitors in a **limited area** and/or **exclusion area** containing nuclear weapons can covertly communicate a situation of duress to other operating or security personnel.

E

E: Prefix designating **1.** Special Electronic Installation: aircraft designed for electronic countermeasures, airborne early-warning radar, airborne command, control, and communications, and tactical data communications link for all nonautonomous modes of flight (e.g., E-6, EC-135). **2.** Vehicle with special electronic installation for communications, countermeasures, electronic radiation sounding, or other electronic recording or relay mission.

E-2C Hawkeye: Navy all-weather, carrier-based, five-person, twin-engine, turboprop **airborne early-warning (AEW)** aircraft. The Hawkeye is used for airborne early-warning and command and control under all weather conditions, detecting approaching enemy units and vectoring interceptors into attack positions. It also provides strike control, air traffic control, radar surveillance, search and rescue assistance, communications relay, and automatic tactical data exchange. The Hawkeye has three primary sensors—radar, **Identification, Friend or Foe (IFF)**, and a passive detection system for **electronic warfare support measures**—which are integrated with a general-purpose computer to accomplish its missions. Its most distinctive feature is the 24 ft rotodome mounted above the fuselage. The equipment is able to track simultaneously more than 250 targets and control up to 30 interceptors. Its range/endurance is 3.6 hours on station at 200 nm from the aircraft carrier.

The first E-2s flew in the early 1960s, with the first production-version test flight in April 1961. A total of 59 E-2As were built and delivered to the Navy beginning in 1964. The operational E-2As were upgraded to E-2Bs by 1971, the same year production of the E-2Cs began. IOC of the E-2Cs was reached in November 1973. The E-2Cs are organized into 13 deployable and two readiness training air early-warning squadrons (VAW), with a four-plane squadron usually assigned to a carrier air wing. When not deployed aboard an aircraft carrier, the planes are located at NAS Norfolk, VA, and NAS Miramar, CA, with one squadron at NAF Atsugi, Japan. About 90 E-2Cs are in the inventory, and the Navy plans to purchase 160 more, adding 6 per year to its inventory. Prime contractors are Grumman Aerospace Corp. of Bethpage, NY, and General Motors, Allison Division, of Indianapolis, IN (engine). The requested budget to purchase four planes in FY 1990 is $559.7 million.

E-3 Sentry AWACS (Airborne Warning and Control System): Air Force **airborne early warning** aircraft to provide survivable airborne surveillance capability and command, control, and communications functions. AWACS aircraft could also take over the command center function for continental air defense missions from **NORAD's Regional Operational Control Centers** if the centers were destroyed or disabled. The aircraft are assigned to the 552nd AWACS Wing of the Tactical Air Command, Tinker AFB, OK, which is also the main operating base for AWACS. Forward detachments are located at Kadena AB, Okinawa, Japan; Keflavik, Iceland; and Elmendorf AFB, AK.

Boeing delivered the first E-3A to the Air Force in 1977. The E-3As have a radius of 1,600 nm with an operating ceiling of 8,850 meters and six-hour endurance. The total number of aircraft procured by the Air Force is 34. In the mid-1980s, the Air Force ordered the modification of all E-3As; when this is complete, 24 aircraft will be redesignated E-3Bs and 10 as E-3Cs. The modifications include added crew stations and radios, color display screens, and an improved computer system. Boeing also delivered 18 aircraft to NATO during 1981–1985 for use in the European Airborne Early-Warning Force. The European main operating base is at Geilenkirchen, West Germany; forward operating bases are located at Preveza, Greece; Trapani, Italy; Konya, Turkey; and Oerland, Norway. The government of Saudi Arabia purchased five E-3As for delivery in the mid-1980s.

The AWACS planes are modified by Boeing from basic 707-320B commercial jet aircraft, with the Westinghouse rotating, saucer-shaped radar added topside. The standard Boeing 707 turbofan engines are replaced with Pratt & Whitney TF-33 turbofan engines. The radar is capable of detecting airborne targets as far away as 350 miles at all altitudes.

Plans to procure an additional 12 aircraft between FY 1985 and 1988 were scrapped in favor of land-based over-the-horizon radars. As of FY 1986, DOD had spent over $4.5 billion on AWACS, making it the largest DOD commitment to a single tactical command and control system. A major radar upgrade for AWACS E-3 aircraft was begun in 1989. The older AN/APY-1 radar has been replaced in the last 10 aircraft modified (The E-3Cs) by the AN/APY-2, which allows AWACS to detect ships at sea. The E-3B does not have this radar capability, but it is able to detect slow-moving ships through computer software upgrades. Another modification is the addition of the **Joint Tactical Information Distribution System (JTIDS)**, which increases data handling capability, protects against jamming, and adds nuclear hardening. Modified Westinghouse APY-1 and APY-2 radar systems will provide improved performance against low-radar cross section fighters and cruise missiles. The Air Force plans to upgrade 24 core E-3s with the APY-1 (with limited maritime surveillance capability) and 10 standard E-3s with APY-2 (with full maritime surveillance capability). The upgrade to the E-3 prime sensor will cost over $500 million, with an expected completion date in 1998. The improvement program is the most substantial update to the AWACS fleet since they were first fielded in 1977. The modernization program will extend to the 18 NATO E-3s with APY-2 radars. The modified radar will use a pulse compressed waveform; 19 old circuit boards will be replaced and an additional 17 boards will be installed in five AWACS radar system line replaceable units. The radar data correlator will also be replaced by a general-purpose processor, and the digital doppler processor will be replaced by a new signal processor: together, these will form a new surveillance radar computer. The radar control and maintenance console will be modified so that a fast Fourier transform radar signal analyzer display can be placed next to the maintenance display. This means that one operator will be able to keep track of the environment in which the AWACS radar is working with the signal analyzer while monitoring the maintenance status of the system.

E-4B National Emergency Airborne Command Post (NEACP): Air Force-operated **airborne command post** aircraft to support the National Commmand Authority and JCS in the command and control of forces during and after an attack on the United States. The E-4Bs supplement the ground **National Military Command Center (NMCC)** located in the Pentagon and the **Alternate National Military Command Center (ANMCC)** near Ft. Richie, MD. The aircraft are assigned to the 1st Airborne Command and Control Squadron at Offutt AFB, NE, with a forward detachment at Grissom AFB, IN. The alert force aboard the NEACP consists of a JCS joint service operations team, SAC flight crew, maintenance crew, security forces, and a communications team from the **Air Force Communications Command**.

The aircraft are derived from the Boeing 747-200B commercial airliner. Onboard communications systems, ranging from VLF to SHF frequencies, allow the E-4B to link with land, sea, air, and space systems, as well as with the commercial telephone and broadcast systems. These systems include **AUTODIN, AFSATCOM,** and an LF/VLF antenna-trailing system similar to **TACAMO** that links NEACP to TACAMO and the **EC-135** airborne command posts. The Rockwell AN/ASC-24 SHF terminal allows NEACP to link with **Defense Satellite Communications System (DSCS)** satellites. The air frame is EMP-hardened to protect its 150,000 lb of communications equipment. The interior of the plane is divided into six main functional areas; a command work area; conference room; battlestaff work area; communications control center; briefing room; and rest area.

Three aircraft were built in the earlier E-4A configuration with communications equipment taken from EC-135 airborne command posts. The fourth NEACP had more modern communications and was designated the E-4B. In 1980, Boeing was awarded a $163.4 million contract to upgrade the three E-4As to the E-4B configuration. RCA is the contractor for the SHF dish antenna and pointing system. The E-4B has an endurance of 12 hours or up to 72 hours if refueled in flight. There are no plans to add to the fleet. Modernization plans include adding **Ground-Wave Emergency Network** terminals and EHF terminals to operate with the **MILSTAR** satellites. (see also **National Emergency Airborne Command Post**)

E-6 Hermes (TACAMO II): Navy wide-body, radio relay communications platform scheduled to replace the current **EC-130Q TACAMO** aircraft. The primary mission of the E-6s is to provide a link between the National Command Authorities and ballistic missile submarines at sea. The E-6As will be capable of receiving **emergency action messages** from **MILSTAR** and then relaying these messages to the ballistic submarines using a high-power VLF transmitter. The E-6As also will feature increased endurance to allow longer station time and improved chances of recovery and reconstruction at a surviving airfield, and increased on-board spare parts for recovery at remote fields with little or no logistic support. The aircraft are survivable, EMP-hardened, and part of the **Minimum Essential Emergency Communications Network (MEECN)**. The prime contractor is Boeing Co., Seattle, WA. Procurement costs for FY 1989 were $399.4 million

for the purchase of seven aircraft. FY 1990 and 1991 requested budgets include $60 million for initial spares and construction. The first production model arrived at NATC Patuxent River, MD, for extensive electromagnetic testing on 16 May 1988. (see also **TACAMO**)

E-8A: Air Force-operated **Joint Surveillance Target Attack Radar System (JSTARS)** aircraft modified to operate a target attack radar system to detect and track both moving and fixed enemy ground targets in the second echelon to support the **Airland Battle** and **Follow-on Forces Attack** strategies in Europe. Research and development costs in the requested FY 1990 and 1991 budgets are $153.5 million and $114.4 million, respectively.

EA-3 Skywarrior: Navy carrier-based, twin-turbojet, six-person, subsonic signals and electronics intelligence collection aircraft. The A-3 first flew in 1952, and the EA-3B prototype in 1958. The EKA-3B is a tanker variant. TA-3B and VA-3B are the VIP transport configurations. The prime contractor was Douglas Aircraft. The last EA-3Bs were removed from active service aboard aircraft carriers in 1988. Sixteen converted electronic warfare and signals intelligence-equipped **S-3As** (designated ES-3s) are scheduled to replace the EA-3Bs.

EA-6B Prowler: Navy and Marine Corps four-seat, twin-engine derivation of the **A-6** attack aircraft equipped with a computer-controlled electronic surveillance and control system and high-power jamming transmitters. Its primary mission is to support strike aircraft and amphibious operations and provide a counter-targeting capability for carrier battle groups by suppressing and degrading an enemy's electronic systems through tactical jamming. Secondary missions include passive early-warning for fleet defense and the obtaining of tactical electronic intelligence within a combat area. The EA-6B is the only carrier-based aircraft that provides these capabilities. The aircraft is a fully integrated **electronic warfare** weapon system that combines long-range, all-weather capability with advanced electronic countermeasures and electronic support measures system. It features a computer-controlled electronic surveillance and control system, and 12 high-power jamming transmitters in various frequency bands. It can carry up to five jammer pods, which house the high-power jamming transmitters capable of operating against various threat emitters. It is designed for carrier and/or advanced base operations and has an in-flight refueling capability.

Older versions of the Prowler are being updated to match the capabilities of newly produced aircraft. EA-6Bs are organized into 10 deployable and 3 training fleet electronic warfare squadrons, with a four-plane squadron usually assigned to a carrier air wing. When not aboard aircraft carriers, they are located at NAS Whidbey Island, WA, except for one squadron supporting the Japan-based USS Midway (CV-41). The first flight was in May 1968, and the first squadron became operational in July 1971. A total of 146 aircraft are in the inventory. The recurring fly-away cost is about $24 million each. Contractors are Grumman Aerospace Corporation, Bethpage, Long Island, NY (airframe); and Pratt and Whitney, East Hartford, CT (engine). FY 1990 and 1991 budget requests for remanufacture and upgrade of the EA-6 fleet are $159.9 million and $396.2 million, respectively.

Eagle (see **F-15 Eagle**)

EAM (see **emergency action message**)

early-warning (EW): A variety of satellite, air-, and ground-based sensors designed to detect an attack soon after it has been launched. Early-warning systems:

(a) Provide warning regardless of enemy tactics or technology, natural disturbance, or U.S. situation through a system combination of availability, detection probability, and geographic coverage of all known and probable attack launch points.

(b) Insure that neither a strategic weapon impact on the United States nor an attack upon a U.S. satellite occurs without prior warning having been received by the NCA (National Command Authorities).

(c) Insure that warning/characterization information has sufficient validity so that immediate force preservation actions can be initiated for those elements where appropriate.

(d) Provide credible warning/characterization information as soon as possible after initiation of an attack and continually thereafter.

(e) Provide sufficiently accurate data to support meaningful sensor information correlations [JCS, *Policy and Procedures for Management of Joint Command and Control Systems,* SM-7-82, 11 January 1982, p. 10, released under the FOIA].

For ballistic missile attacks, EW consists of the **Defense Support Program** satellites that detect the launch of ICBMs and SLBMs, coupled with radar correlation provided by **BMEWS, Cobra Dane**, and **Perimeter Aquisition Radar Attack Characterization System** in case of ICBM attack, and by **PAVE PAWS** in case of SLBM attacks. For bomber and cruise missile attacks, EW consists of tactical warning radars along Canada's northern border and in Greenland (**DEW Line** and **North Warning System**), in Alaska (**Seek Igloo**), and in Iceland (Iceland Surveillance).

earmarked: Forces and/or equipment designated specifically for assignment or attachment to a commander in the event of mobilization or war.

Eastern Atlantic Command (EAST-LANT): Major subordinate command of NATO's **Allied Command Atlantic**.

Headquarters
Northwood, UK
(APO New York 09083)

Principle Subordinate Commands

- Submarine Forces Eastern Atlantic Area, Northwood, UK (APO New York 09083)
- Bay of Biscay Sub-Area, Northwood, UK (APO New York 09083)
- Island Command Iceland, Keflavik, Iceland (FPO New York 09571)
- Island Command Faroes, Thorshavn, Faroes, Denmark
- Striking Fleet and Special Task Forces (when assigned) (APO New York 09083)
- Maritime Air Eastern Atlantic Area, Northwood, UK (APO New York 09083)
- Northern Sub-Area, Rosyth, UK (APO New York 09083)
- Maritime Air Northern Sub-Area, Pitreavie, UK (APO New York 09083)
- Central Sub-Area, Plymouth, UK (APO New York 09083)
- Maritime Air Central Sub-Area, Plymouth, UK (APO New York 09083)

EC-18:   Two Boeing 707s are being modified by Electrospace Systems, Inc. for use as dedicated cruise missile mission control aircraft; they are designated EC-18Ds. They are scheduled to become operational in 1992 and will be operated by the 4750th Test Wing, Air Force Systems Command, Wright-Patterson AFB, OH, in support of Navy and Air Force flight testing. (see also **Advanced Range Instrumentation Aircraft**)

EC-130H Compass Call: Air Force aircraft system modified to intercept, analyze, and jam enemy command, control, and communications systems. **Compass Call** includes 10 Lockheed C-130 aircraft as replacements for the retired EC-121s. Modifications included adding blade antennas and trailing wire antennas mounted in pods under each wing and behind the tail. The antennas are extended several hundred feet while in flight to pick up enemy communications signals. The first EC-130H was delivered to Tactical Air Command at Davis-Monthan AFB, AZ, in July 1980. The EC-130H carries a crew of 12: one electronic warfare officer, six signal analysts, one maintenance technician, and four flight crew. The prime contractor is Lockheed.

EC-130Q TACAMO: Navy airborne communications relay version of the **C-130 Hercules**, which has been modified to provide long-range VLF communication links from the National Command Authority to submarines. They have the USC-13 airborne communications suite using 200-watt VLF communications gear, which utilizes a trailing wire antenna of over 30,000 ft in length. The Lockheed EC-130Q aircraft are being replaced with Boeing **E-6 Hermes**. The EC-130Qs are propeller-driven and lack the range, speed, and time-on-station needed for the **TACAMO** command, control, and communications mission, especially with the advent of new Navy missiles such as Trident.

EC-135: Air Force-operated, specially modified platforms for the Strategic Air Command's **Post Attack Command and Control System (PACCS)** and the **Worldwide Airborne Command Post (WWABNCP).** PACCS is a strategic system that would be used to control SAC bomber and ICBM forces in the event that the underground command centers, alternate command posts, or ground-based communications are destroyed. The EC-135s have the capability to order the launch of Minuteman

and Peacekeeper (mx) missiles and to transmit bomber attack orders. Although the **E-4B National Emergency Airborne Command Post (NEACP)** serves as a survivable backup for the **National Military Command Center (NMCC)** for the National Command Authority to direct all U.S. forces, the PACCS mission is more narrowly defined as commanding and controlling SAC's nuclear forces. PACCS components are the SAC Airborne Command Post (**Looking Glass**), the East and West Auxiliary Command Posts, three airborne launch control centers, and two radio relay aircraft. In the WWABNCP, the EC-135s provide the platforms for command and control by the Commanders-in-Chief of the Atlantic, Pacific, European, and Central commands.

The EC-135s, like the E-4Bs, have a variety of on-board communications systems, linking the aircraft with the NMCC, SAC command posts, and alert forces. An AN/ARC-96 transmitter allows VLF communications in the manner of **TACAMO** submarine communications; however, it uses a single long trailing wire rather than the dual long- and short-antenna system installed in TACAMO and the E-4Bs. Miniature receive terminals (MRT) were installed by Rockwell Collins in SAC's B-1B, B-52, and FB-111 bombers to receive VLF messages from NEACP and PACCS. The aircraft are equipped with **AFSATCOM**.

The EC-135s are modified versions of the **KC-135** stratotankers. Improvements on the 39 EC-135s are being made by Electrospace Systems of Richardson, TX, under the Pacer Link program. UHF line-of-sight

Army/Marine Corps	Navy/Marine Corps	Air Force
Army Group	Fleet	Division
Field Army	Force	Wing
Corps	Group/Brigade	Squadron
Division	Squadron	Flight
Brigade	Unit	
Regiment	Element	
Battalion/Squadron		
Company/Troop		
Platoon		
Squad		

equipment, Ground-Wave Emergency Network terminals, MILSTAR terminals, and nuclear detonation detection terminals will be installed through the early 1990s. The Air Force may replace the EC-135 fleet during the 1990s with the McDonnell Douglas **C-17** (designated EC-17), which is currently being developed as the Air Force's new airlifter.

echelon: 1. A subdivision of a headquarters (e.g., rear echelon or reserve echelon).   **2.** A level of command of an operational fighting force. Combat echelons are listed in descending order. Navy operational organization is described under **task organization**.

Economic Support Fund (ESF):   A part of the **security assistance program** officially designated under the Foreign Assistance Act of 1961 as amended in 1974 and implemented by the Agency for International Development (AID). ESF is best understood as the political component to military security assistance. Economic Support Funds are mainly cash transfers to governments with chronic bal-ance-of-payments deficits. ESF supports development projects and funds Commodity Import Programs (CIPs). ESF frees up local currency for the recipient governments' programs.

ESF was preceded by the Security Supporting Assistance Program, of which South Vietnam was the biggest single recipient from 1962–1974. Adjusting for inflation, South Vietnam remains the biggest all-time ESF grantee: in 1982 dollars, the total program exceeded $50 billion, far ahead of current front-runner Israel, which has received $5.5 billion dollars since FY 1986. ESF now makes up almost half of the total economic aid part of the foreign assistance budget, mainly because of large annual transfers to Israel and Egypt since the 1978 Camp David Accords. Currently, of roughly $5 billion annually in ESF, Israel receives almost $1.2 billion and Egypt nearly $1 billion, mostly without conditions of any sort. Pakistan has become the third highest-ranking ESF recipient, receiving over $200 million a year. ESF programs target Costa Rica, Honduras, and El Salvador in Central America.

Countries in which the United States maintains military bases are also recipients of ESF, such as Spain, Portugal, Turkey, and the Philippines.

ESF is disbursed in three categories: cash transfer; project aid; and import financing through the Commodity Import Program.

- Cash transfer: The greatest part of ESF is in the form of cash transfers, under which checks from the U.S. Treasury are written to foreign governments. When the recipient government receives the check, it places an equivalent amount of its local currency in a special account, then reimburses itself by exchanging dollars with its Central Bank for local currency. ESF cash transfers supply foreign exchange to the local economy and thereby avert the damaging effects of a foreign exchange shortfall. For this reason, cash transfers are often called "Balance of Payments Assistance," producing "counterpart funds" in local currency for the national government for its own expenditures.
- Project Aid: ESF program used for the development of infrastructure such as roads and dams and for development and agrarian reform programs, allocated to Development Assistance (DA) for the Agency for International Development's missions abroad.
- Commodity Import Program: ESF program that is a more restrictive version of cash transfers, in which dollars are made available for specific imports of U.S. products.

Economic Support Fund Narcotics Control Initiative: A part of the

Economic Support Fund (ESF) security assistance program budget that earmarks aid for countries engaged in attempts to eradicate narcotics production and trafficking. The FY 1990 budget earmarks $61 million to be distributed to Colombia, Bolivia, Ecuador, Jamaica, and Peru. The security-related nature of the ESF Narcotics Control Initiative stresses the military's preparedness to increase its involvement in eradication at the "supply end of the problem . . . Efforts to date have involved mostly work with local law enforcement people, eradication, and the very occasional and temporary use of U.S. military transportation to assist the law enforcement people. We believe the local military forces are ready to and must take a larger role in these efforts . . . In the struggle against the traffic in illicit drugs, military establishments need our assistance in funding of material, training, and support . . . We seek through our military assistance programs to enhance these countries military forces' ability both to combat insurgencies and effectively contribute to the antinarcotics effort" [Lt. Gen. Charles W. Brown, Director of the Defense Security Assistance Agency, *FY 1990 presentation to the International Security Subcommittee of the House Foreign Affairs Committee*, 8 March 1989].

E-day: The day on which an exercise commences. (see also **military time**)

EF-111A Raven: Air Force all-weather, two-person, two-engine, supersonic, unarmed, electronic warfare aircraft. The EF-111A is a conversion of the basic General Dynamics **F-111** airframe fitted with off-the-shelf components that enable it to accomplish defense suppression and electronic countermeasures missions worldwide. Its AN/ALQ-99E primary jammer is a modification of the Navy AN/ALQ-99 and is carried internally. The powerful and versatile system's frequency coverage and reliability enable the EF-111A to suppress extremely dense electronic defenses. Other equipment includes self-protection systems from the **FB-111**. An upgrade program is currently under way, with improvements to the ALQ-99E being done to counter advanced electronic defenses for the 1990s and beyond. The aircraft has a maximum combat speed of 1,377 mph and a combat radius with fuel reserves of 900 miles.

Forty-two EF-111As were produced for missions that include barrier surveillance jamming, degradation of acquisition radars during close air support operations, and escort jamming for deep-strike missions. Flight testing began in March 1977, and the first EF-111s were delivered in late 1981 to the 366th Tactical Fighter Wing at Mountain Home AFB, ID, where they became operational in December 1983 with the 389th Electronic Combat Squadron. The second operational location was RAF Upper Heyford, UK, where the first EF-111 arrived in February 1984 for the 42nd Electronic Combat Squadron. Aircraft from this unit took part in the attack on Libya in April 1986. Grumman Aerospace was the prime contractor.

EH-1/EH-60 Quick Fix: Army helicopters configured for carrying the Quick Fix airborne tactical jamming and direction-finding suite. Several interim EH-1H Quick Fix I and interim EH-1X Quick Fix II systems based upon the **UH-1** airframe are currently fielded. The EH-60A Quick Fix II is in production. The EH-1H has three crew, a mission payload of 1,050 lb, a cruise speed of 100 knots, an endurance of 1.7 hours, and a maximum range of 250 nm. The EH-1X has four crew, a mission payload of 1,557 lb, a cruise speed of 100 knots, an endurance of 1.5 hours, and a maximum range of 250 nm. The EH-60A has four crew, a mission payload of 2,130 lb, a cruise speed of 137 knots, an endurance of two hours, and a maximum range of 266 nm. The first Army unit was equipped with the Quick Fix II in May 1988. The Army plans to buy 66 Quick Fix II aircraft. Eventually, the EH-60A will replace Quick Fix I/II capabilities in the EH-1H and EH-1X. Prime EH-60 contractors are Sikorsky Aircraft, Stratford, CT, and Tracor, Inc., Austin, TX.

E-hour: Single Integrated Operational Plan execution hour. (see also **military time**)

EIFEL (Elektronisches Informations und Führungssystem für die Einsatzbereitschaft der Luftwaffe): Computer network developed by the West German Air Force to provide automated assistance for the command and control of tactical air forces in Central Europe. EIFEL is used by the **Allied Tactical Operations Center (ATOC)** to plan, task, and monitor offensive air operations. In operation since 1974, EIFEL provides automatic data processing (ADP) support to the squadrons, wings, air divisions, and major German air commands on logistics, personnel, and intelligence. Access to EIFEL is through the DIA-LOG language.

The U.S. Air Forces Europe EIFEL 1 system aids mission planning, control, tasking, monitoring, and evaluation functions performed at Sembach, West Germany. ADP is provided for wings, control and reporting posts, NATO command and control facilities, and other associated facilities. Five nations (United Kingdom, Belgium, Netherlands, United States, West Germany) agreed to a multinational management structure for EIFEL 1 in December 1983 [MITRE, *USAF EIFEL 1 Functional Description*, MITRE Technical Report MTR-8446, September 1981].

Eighth U.S. Army (EUSA):   Army **major command** and component command of **U.S. Forces Korea (USFK)**, the **United Nations Command (UNC)**, and the **Combined Forces Command (CFC)**. The Commanding General Eighth U.S. Army also serves as the Commander-in-Chief USFK, UNC, and CFC. U.S. Army personnel in South Korea number approximately 31,000.

Headquarters
Seoul, South Korea

Subordinate Units

- Combined Field Army (ROK/US), Uijongbu, South Korea
- 2d Infantry Division, Tongduchon, South Korea
- 8th Personnel Command, Seoul, South Korea
- 18th Medical Command, Seoul, South Korea

- 19th Support Command, Taegu, South Korea

electromagnetic gun: A kinetic energy gun using electromagnetic forces to accelerate the projectile, rather than chemical explosives as in a conventional gun. It is also known as a hypervelocity gun, electromagnetic rail gun, or electromagnetic launcher. This type of gun uses an electromagnetic accelerator with a magnetic field to impart great velocities to electrically conducting projectiles. For an SDI system, these particles would have to be acccelerated hundreds of thousands of times that of gravity. It is estimated that an electromagnetic gun's range could be 1600 km, but it would require a power source large enough to power a small town for each shot. It would also require the capability to deliver energy in short pulses; depend on guidance systems that could withstand rapid accelerations; and have proven accuracy, recoil momentum, and refiring capabilities. The SDI Innovative Science and Technology (IST) program developed operating specifications for an electromagnetic launcher that could accelerate 100 gram projectiles to five km/second. Land-based electromagnetic railguns are being researched by the Strategic Defense Initiative Organization (SDIO) to demonstrate launchings of guided and unguided projectiles. Space-based gun experiments are testing the potential uses of the gun against anti-satellite interceptors.

SDIO is working on several electromagnetic guns, including the Scientific Ultrahigh Velocity Accelerator (Suvac), a sub-project for a larger launcher called Thunderbolt. SDIO has also funded projects on small, lightweight projectiles to be used with the **Space-Based Interceptor** and the **Exoatmospheric Reentry Interceptor Subsystem (ERIS)**. In 1977, the Army Gremlin and Air Force Sagittar programs were combined into the Lightweight Exoatmospheric Advanced Projectiles (LEAP) program to develop and test hardware for miniature projectiles and fire control systems. The Theater Missile Defense program of kinetic-energy weapon research sponsors subsystem research into the electromagnetic railgun switches, barrels, projectiles, instrumentation, and EMP effects by the United Kingdom [*SDI Dictionary,* pp. 53–54].

electromagnetic pulse (EMP): Electromagnetic radiation from a nuclear explosion, caused by Compton-recoil electrons and photoelectrons from photons scattered in the materials of a nuclear device or in a surrounding medium. The resulting electric and magnetic fields may couple with electronic circuitry to produce damaging current and voltage sources. EMP may also be caused by nonnuclear means. High-altitude EMP (HEMP) is the electromagnetic pulse produced in a nuclear explosion outside of the earth's atmosphere. EMP was first detected during a nuclear test at Johnston Island in the Pacific in 1962.

electromagnetic radiation: A form of propagated energy, arising from electric charges in motion, that produces a simultaneous wave-like variation in electric and magnetic fields in space. The highest frequencies, with the shortest wavelengths, are gamma rays. At lower frequencies,

the electromagnetic spectrum includes x-rays, ultraviolet light, visible light, infrared light, microwaves, and radio waves [U.S. Congress, Office of Technology Assessment, *Anti-Satellite Weapons, Countermeasures, and Arms Control,* OTA-ISC-281, September 1985].

electronic counter-countermeasures (ECCM): Electronic warfare measures taken to ensure effective use of the electromagnetic spectrum despite enemy electronic warfare efforts. Preventive ECCM bar enemy attempts to conduct **electronic warfare support measures** and **electronic countermeasures**. Remedial ECCM are taken in response to enemy electronic warfare operations. Frequency agility is a common ECCM technique. The standard response to ECCM is to use a signal with complex frequency modulations.

electronic countermeasures (ECM): Electronic warfare involving actions taken to prevent or reduce the effectiveness of enemy radar and electronic systems. ECM includes both confusion measures (e.g., hiding real targets by cluttering enemy radars) and deception measures (e.g., producing false echoes to simulate real targets). Confusion **jamming** can be done by high-power continuous wave transmissions on the enemy's radar frequency; however, this requires a great deal of power to transmit, which is difficult when airborne, and the enemy frequencies are not always known, in which case the entire bandwidth must be covered. "Spot jamming" occurs when the enemy's frequencies are known and all energy is concentrated on them. A counter to this would be to switch rapidly from one frequency to another, leaving the spot-jammer behind (this is called frequency agility). Another confusion technique is "sweep-through jamming," which sweeps through a wide range of frequencies, jamming many different radars briefly at the same time until the next sweep comes along.

Deception measures require less power but more information and advanced technology. A "repeater jammer" picks up enemy signals and sends them out as their own. When given a false delay, they mislead enemy radars as to the range and position of the target. Transponders are used for the **Identification, Friend or Foe** system. The transponder automatically switches on when the beams of the enemy radar set sweep over the aircraft; it then transmits a stored replica for the signal and displaces the radar "image" of the target. Tracking radars keep a beam circling the expected course of the target so that deviations are registered and the course is adjusted. A "range-gate stealer" sends a signal to meet with and strengthen the real echo. The signal is then slowly shifted to create a false target position.

Passive ECM techniques rely on **chaff** (e.g., foil strips whose length "fits" the frequency of enemy radars), decoys, or radar cross-section reduction (e.g., Stealth). Spot chaff deceives by simulating targets; corridor chaff confuses by releasing bundles of chaff, which create a radar cloud through which other aircraft can pass. Problems with chaff are that high-speed aircraft can leave chaff

behind and enemy radars can distinguish between chaff and targets by comparing velocities. The use of decoys to simulate aircraft and missiles is more reliable, although the decoys must have a range and speed similar to real targets to be effective. Radar cross-section reduction is accomplished at the design stage by using materials with poor reflecting qualities.

electronic intelligence (ELINT): Type of **signals intelligence** information collected by the interception of noncommunications electromagnetic radiations (e.g., radar signals, navigation aids, and countermeasures equipment). ELINT targets include air defense radar systems; intelligence radars; space tracking radars; and ballistic missile early-warning radars. ELINT does not include information derived from nuclear detonations or radioactive sources. **Foreign instrumentation signals intelligence (FISINT)** is a subcategory of ELINT. (see also **radiation intelligence**)

electronic security (ELSEC): Measures designed to deny unauthorized persons information of value that might be derived from the interception and study of electromagnetic and non-communications-related radiations, such as radar. (see also **signals security, communications security**)

Electronic Security Command (ESC): Air Force **major command** and component of the **National Security Agency/Central Security Services (NSA/CSS)**. Redesignated from the Air Force Security Service on 1 August 1979, ESC supports the

Air Force and unified and specified commands in the areas of **electronic warfare**; **signals intelligence (SIG-INT)**; communications support; **command, control, and communication countermeasures**; operational security; **communications security**; and computer security. ESC is composed of three Electronic Security Divisions and major command staffs, six wings, seven groups, an Electronic Warfare Center, a Cryptologic Support Center, and numerous detachments worldwide. It employs approximately 13,700 military and civilian personnel. (see also **Army Intelligence and Security Command, Naval Security Group**)

Headquarters
Kelly AFB, TX 78245

electronic warfare (EW): "Military action involving the use of electromagnetic energy to determine, exploit, reduce, or prevent hostile use of the electromagnetic spectrum and action to retain its effective use by friendly forces" [*JCS Pub 1*, Change 2, pp. 8–9]. EW is composed of **electronic countermeasures** (jamming, deception), **electronic countercountermeasures** (protection), and **electronic warfare support measures** (listening, locating).

electronic warfare support measures (ESM): Actions used in **electronic warfare** to search for, intercept, locate, record, and analyze radiated electromagnetic energy for the purpose of exploiting such radiation in support of military operations. ESM provides a source of electronic warfare information that may be used for immediate action, as opposed to collection of information for later use. ESM information is primarily collected from electronic systems including communications systems such as voice and continuous wave networks, and noncommunication systems such as radar and missile guidance systems.

electro-optics   (EO): Technology based on the union of optics and electronics, which uses the electromagnetic spectrum ranging from ultraviolet (0.01 micrometers) through far (long-wavelength) infrared (1,000 micrometers). EOs include lasers, photometry, infrared, and other types of visible and infrared imaging systems. Electro-optical guidance for missiles and bombs makes use of the visible optical contrast patterns of the target or surrounding area to effect guidance (seeker) lock-on and terminal homing. Three types are

- Contrast edge tracker, such as the Mk-84 EO guided bomb and **Walleye** air-to-surface missile;
- Contrast centroid tracker, such as **Maverick** air-to-surface missile; and
- Optical area correlator, which scans contrast patterns in a large area surrounding the target.

ELF (extremely low frequency)(see **frequency, extremely low frequency (ELF) communications**)

ELINT (see **electronic intelligence**)

ELV (see **expendable launch vehicle**)

EMCON   (see **emission control**)

emergency: "Major disaster or another catastrophe in any part of the United States, which, in the determination of the President, requires federal emergency assistance to supplement state and local efforts to save lives and protect property, public health, and safety, or to avert or lessen the threat of a disaster" [Air Force, *Disaster Preparedness: Planning and Operations,* AFR 355-1, 17 November 1986, p. 84, released under the FOIA].

emergency action: The term used by command and control agencies identifying actions, procedures, and communications used during periods of tension or increased readiness, whether or not an increased **Defense Readiness Condition (DEFCON)** has been declared.

emergency action message (EAM): "Messages through which the Joint Chiefs of Staff and the National Command Authorities (National Command Authoritiess), through the Joint Chiefs of Staff, pass significant directives to the commanders of the unified and specified commands, their forces, and other military and Government agencies" [JCS, *Emergency Action Procedures,* Volume I, 1 April 1984, p. 1–14]. EAMs are specially formatted messages to authorize implementation of specific preplanned actions when authorized by proper authority. There are two basic types of EAMs: alerting, preparation, and warning messages; and nuclear control orders (including nuclear execution and nuclear termination messages). EAMs are used to pass significant, time-sensitive orders,

directives, authorization, and information. Specific functions include

• To direct the execution of the **Single Integrated Operational Plan**;
• To authorize the use and release of chemical and nuclear weapons;
• To direct the change in readiness conditions (**Defense Readiness Conditions (DEFCONs)** and **Alert Conditions (LERTCONs)**) for one or more of the unified and specified commands; and
• To designate a change in the location of the primary command center of the **National Military Command System**.

Alerting, preparing, and warning messages are used to "direct changes in alert readiness conditions, general warning, denial of selective release, rapid response, and relay of additional information not suitable for a specific formatted message" [USCINCLANT, *Emergency Action Procedures,* 17 July 1985, Ch. 10, p. 5-1, released under the FOIA].

Great care is used in ensuring the authenticity of the EAM. "Minimum staffing of center/facilities that compose/transpose/voice relay any EAM will provide for a cross-check of all actions. Two persons are considered minimum staffing" [CENTCOM, *Emergency Action Procedures,* Volume I, p. 2-1, released under the FOIA]. Each EAM has a unique message designator and action consistent with the message designator (e.g., 100 message format: nuclear execution; 222 message format: LERTCON and A-Hour alert and preparation; 228 message format: general-purpose alert and preparation; 326 message format: special NCA or JCS instructions regarding the transfer of authority for U.S. forces to NATO). The identical format and alphabetic sequence of each message requires authentication, attainment confirmation, and notification of attainment exceptions or deviations, as well as progress reports.

There are two types of EAMs, those that require approval by the NCA and those that do not. EAMs that do not require approval by the NCA are prepared and released by the JCS or the CINCs. EAMs are normally dispatched by secure-record communications over the Improved Emergency Message Automated Transmission System to national and high-level command posts, and over common user circuits (e.g., AUTODIN) to other commands. They can also be transmitted by secure voice [JCS, *Crisis Staffing Procedures of the Joint Chiefs of Staff*, SM-481-83, 12 July 1983, pp. 4–28ff, released under the FOIA; JCS, *Crisis Staffing Procedures of the Joint Chiefs of Staff*, SM-205-80, 27 March 1980, pp. 4–30ff, released under the FOIA; JCS, *Emergency Action Procedures*, Volume I, 24 April 1981, p. 3-4; JCS, *Continuity of Operations Plan*, 20 December 1973, p. 7, released under the FOIA; USSOUTHCOM, *Emergency Action Procedures, Volume I—General*, 1 October 1983, released under the FOIA]. (see also **Red Rocket**)

emergency action procedures (E-AP): The **emergency action messages** and procedures used by the Joint Chiefs of Staff, the unified and specified commands, and the services to maintain command and control of U.S. forces and nuclear weapons. EAPs are "procedures designed to be used under conditions of emergency wherein an increase in the readiness conditions may be required or when the emergency might result in general war" [JCS, *Alert System of the Joint Chiefs of Staff, Part II—LERTCON Actions*, SM-415-76, 8 June 1976, p. 1, released under the FOIA].

Emergency Broadcast System: Civil emergency communication system overseen by NORAD to allow the President "to address the nation under an emergency condition."

emergency combat capability: The condition exclusive of primary alert status whereby elements essential to launch a missile are present at the launch base and can effect a launch under conditions of strategic warning.

emergency condition (EMERG-CON): One of two uniform **alert conditions (LERTCONs)** used to notify U.S. military forces of countersurprise alerts. There are two EMERGCONs:

- Defense Emergency: An emergency condition that exists when a major attack is made upon U.S. or allied forces in any area or upon the United States. The exercise term is "Hot Box."
- Air Defense Emergency: An emergency condition that exists when attack upon the United States, Canada, or U.S. installations in Greenland is considered probable, is imminent, or is taking place. An air defense emergency declaration will be accompanied by an Air Defense Warning Red (imminent or taking place), Yellow (probable), or White (not probable or immi-

nent) [CINCLANT, *Atlantic Command Alert System,* 12 January 1982, released under the FOIA].

emergency conferences: The short-notice systems, procedures, and conferences used in reporting and assessing crises and attacks upon the United States. "In emergency situations, the NCA [National Command Authority] and the Joint Chiefs of Staff may convene emergency conferences in a conference room in the Pentagon, at the ANMCC **[Alternate National Military Command Center]**, aboard the NEACP **[National Emergency Airborne Command Post]**, or by means of telephone" [JCS, *Crisis Staffing Procedures of the Joint Chiefs of Staff,* SM-481-83, 12 July 1983, pp. 4–9, released under the FOIA]. Emergency conferences include

• Air Event Conference (formerly Air Activity Conference).
• Air Threat Conference.
• Emergency Telephone Conference (formerly LERTCON Conference): changes in **alert conditions**.
• Missile Event Conference (formerly Missile Attack Conference).
• Missile Threat Conference (formerly Routine Missile Display/Missile Display Conference).
• Missile Warning Systems Conference.
• NUCFLASH Conference.
• Significant Event Conference.
• Space Event Conference (formerly Space Activity Conference).
• Space Threat Conference.

[JCS, *EAP-Emergency Conferences for Tactical Warning and Attack Assessment,* 1 December 1986, released under the FOIA]

Emergency Mobilization Preparedness Board (EMPD): Interagency group established 18 December 1981, following **Nifty Nugget**/Rex 78 and **Proud** Saber/Rex-80 Bravo, by President Reagan to help guide and coordinate federal mobilization preparedness planning. It is chaired by the Assistant to the President for National Security Affairs. NSDD-47, "Emergency Mobilization Preparedness," 22 July 1982, reestablished mobilization and emergency planning as visible and indispensable functions of federal civil agencies and called on the EMPD to establish effective policy to ensure the maintenance of necessary government functions at the federal, state, and local levels and provide for a timely and effective transition into emergency modes of operation, and to prepare a national plan of action. The National Plan of Action on Emergency Mobilization preparedness was completed on 27 April 1983. (see also **REX-Bravo**)

Emergency Rocket Communications System (ERCS): Program designation 494L. A set of 10 **Minuteman II** missiles deployed at Whiteman AFB, MO, where the nose cones of the missiles carry UHF radio transmitters instead of nuclear warheads. The ERCS program began in 1961 as a part of the **Minimum Essential Emergency Communications Network (MEECN)** to provide a last-resort, back-up, rocket-launched emergency means of communications ensuring that communications from **airborne command posts** could be received by bombers and submarines. ERCS became operational in 1965 aboard Blue Scout boosters. In 1970, the ERCS transmitters were switched to Minuteman II missiles. If all other means of communications fail or are destroyed, ERCS missiles with a pre-recorded launch order injected into the radio package would be launched by airborne command posts. The missiles would be boosted into a suborbital trajector, where they could broadcast the EAM for about 30 minutes on two UHF frequencies for reception by bomber aircraft, **TACAMO**, and others within the line of sight. Coverage is augmented by **Giant Talk** and Green Pine broadcast systems. In FY 1987, SAC canceled procurement of replacement ERCS payloads but retained sufficient funds to procure batteries to keep the current system operational.

emergency war order (EWO): "The order issued by competent authority to launch combat-ready weapon systems maintained in readiness for or generated for first strike wartime operations" [*U.S. Air Force Glossary*].

emission control (EMCON): A Navy term for electronic silence by the controlled use of electronic, acoustic, or other emitters as a countermeasure against detection by the enemy.

EMP (see **electromagnetic pulse**)

employment: The use of a weapon or combat force in an operation.

enable: The unlocked state of a **permissive action link (PAL)** system that permits the normal launching or arming of a nuclear weapon or nuclear weapons system.

encrypted for transmission only (EFTO): A message whose information is placed into code form during transmission to avoid hostile interception but whose contents are unclassified. (see also **communications security**, **security classification**)

encryption: "Encoding communications for the purpose of concealing information. In **SALT II**, this term has been applied to a practice whereby a side alters the manner by which it transmits telemetry from a weapon being tested in order to render the information deliberately undecipherable" [ACDA, *SALT II: Glossary of Terms,* 1979]. (see also **deliberate concealment**)

end-strength: A manpower term meaning the sum of the **operating strength** plus the **individuals** category on the last day for the fiscal year. (see also **manpower**)

endurance: "The ability to continue operating under unfavorable circumstances and conditions. Such abilities include graceful degradation, restart and recovery, and manual backup in order to fulfill missions" [JCS, *WWMCCS ADP Concept of Operations and General Requirements for Post–1989,* SM-101-81, 6 February 1981].

Energy Research and Development Administration (ERDA) (see **Department of Energy**)

enhanced radiation: The effects of, and the technology employed in, the class of controlled-effects nuclear weapons designed to produce more and/or higher output(s) of neutrons, x-rays, and gamma rays, or a combination thereof, than a **fission** weapon of the same total yield. Enhanced radiation/reduced blast refers to the increase in nuclear radiation in the target area at the same time as attenuating blast and heat. Enhanced radiation weapons are commonly known as "neutron bombs."

enlisted: General term for the category of military personnel at various ranks but all below that of Warrant Officer.

ENMOD Convention: Formally known as the "Convention on the Prohibition of Military or Any Other Hostile Use of Environmental Modification Techniques." It opened for signature at the United Nations on 18 May 1977 and entered into force on 5 October 1978. The Convention has 31 signatories, including the United States and the Soviet Union. It bans "military or other hostile use of environmental modification techniques having widespread, long-lasting or severe effects as the means of destruction, damage or injury to any other State Party" (Article I). Environmental modification is defined as any technique for changing the dynamics, composition, or structure of the earth that could cause earthquakes, tidal waves, inundation, and so on. Provisions are

- Environmental modifications for peaceful purposes are permitted;
- Each party to the Convention is to use measures in accordance with its consitutional processes to pro-

hibit harmful environmental modifications from taking place;
- Compliance complaints are to be made to the U.N. Security Council;
- The Convention is of unlimited duration and open to signature by all nations; and
- Five years after the Convention comes into force, a review conference will be held in Geneva. This was held in 1984.

Enterprise (CVN-65) class aircraft carrier: Navy nuclear-powered, nuclear-armed aircraft carrier, only one of the class. The USS Enterprise (CVN-65) is the world's first nuclear-powered aircraft carrier and the second nuclear-powered surface vessel. The ship displaces 91,000 tons at full load, is powered by eight nuclear reactors, and has a top speed of 30-plus knots. Built by Newport News Shipbuilding, VA, at a cost of $440 million, it was commissioned in November 1961. (see also **aircraft carrier, naval nuclear propulsion**)

environmental sensing device (ESD): A safety device placed in the arming circuit of a nuclear weapon to prevent inadvertent function of the circuit until after the weapon, having been launched or released, experiences an environmental change peculiar to its delivery method. Differential pressure switches and integrating accelerometers are commonly employed for this use.

EP-3B/E: Navy signals intelligence and reconnaissance aircraft modified from the **P-3** airframe. Over a dozen of these are deployed in two fleet air reconnaissance squadrons, VQ-1 at Agana, Guam, and VQ-2 at Rota, Spain. Some operate as part of electronic warfare squadrons out of Key West, FL. The EP-3 aircraft are equipped with the ARIES/DEEP-WELL intelligence collection system.

equivalent megatonnage (EMT): A computed function of yield that compensates approximately for the fact that blast damage resulting from a nuclear detonation does not increase linearly with an increase in yield. EMT calculations are used by targeters in estimating the effects of small numbers of high-yield nuclear warheads in contrast to a larger number of smaller-yield warheads against the same targets. EMT is computed from the expression $EMT = N \times Y \times X$, where N is the number of actual warheads of yield Y; Y is the yield of the actual warheads in megatons; and X is a scaling factor. Scaling factors vary with the size and characteristics of the target base and the number of targets attacked.

ERA-3: Navy reconnaissance aircraft based on the **A-3 Skywarrior** airframe. About a dozen of these aircraft are part of electronic warfare squadrons at Key West, FL, and Point Mugu, CA.

ERCS (see **Emergency Rocket Communications System**)

ERIS (Exoatmospheric Reentry Vehicle Interceptor System): Army SDI-related research program to develop a ground-launched, mid-course interceptor to destroy incoming ICBM and SLBM warheads above the atmosphere within a deployed SDI system. ERIS is the advanced follow-on to the **Homing Overlay Experiment (HOE)** but uses a smaller interceptor kill vehicle, allowing the use of multiple warheads. ERIS does not contain nuclear warheads; it will destroy targets through kinetic energy by colliding with them at high speeds. ERIS will be a dormant system requiring no power or maintenance prior to launch. Mid-course sensors will acquire, track, and pass target information to the battle manager for target identification and the assignment of ERIS interceptors to targets, trajectory and launch data to the interceptor, and target upgrades to the in-flight interceptors.

ERIS is expected to weigh about 270 lb, above the expected 70 lb weight of the targets. When mounted on its booster, ERIS will actually fly backwards. Once clear of the earth's atmosphere, the assembly will rotate 180 degrees so that the seeker looks in the direction of motion to locate its target. The mercury-cadmium-telluride sensing element is mounted directly on the ERIS main body in a smaller package. A set of thrusters on the body adjacent to the seeker will orient the ERIS around three axes as it searches for targets. Avionics, including a mechanical inertial measurement unit, and the propulsion section are located aft of the seeker. The fourth section holds communications systems, batteries, encryption devices, and the seeker-cooling system. The fifth section is the kill-enhancement device (KED). KED is an expanding device using air bag technology similar to that in automobiles. Total system cost is estimated at more than $3.5 billion. Lockheed is the prime contractor, and the U.S. Army Strategic Defense Command is the program manager.

Three Functional Technology Validation (FTV) tests are scheduled for FY 1990–1991 at Kwajalein Atoll to test increasingly stressful threat levels. Advanced Technology Validation (ATV) tests are scheduled to look at improved three-color staring seekers; cooled optics; fiber optics gyro; improved avionics; and reduced system size. Some of these tests will be against targets resembling Soviet warheads. ERIS will be launched on Aries 2 rockets and will be test-targeted against converted Minuteman I ICBMs launched from Vandenberg AFB, CA.

Espionage Act of 1917: Congressional act signed into law on 15 June 1917. As amended, its sections are found at 18 U.S. Code §11, 791-4, 1288, 3241; 22 U.S. Code §213, 220-2, 401-8; and 50 U.S. Code §191-2, 194. The various espionage-related statutes, as amended, include Chapter 37 of Title 18: Espionage and Censorship:

- *Sec. 792:* Prohibits the harboring or concealing of persons known or reasonably suspected of being involved in illegal espionage activities. The penalty is a fine of $10,000, and/or imprisonment up to 10 years.
- *Sec. 793:* Makes illegal the unauthorized "gathering, transmitting or losing" of "information respecting the national defense with intent or reason to believe that the information is to be used to the injury of the United States, or to the advantage of any foreign nation." "In-

formation" as defined includes "any document, writing, code book, signal book, sketch, photograph, photographic negative, blueprint, plan, map, model, instrument, appliance, or note relating to the national defense."
- *Sec. 794:* Prohibits the gathering or delivering of defense information "used to the injury of the United States or to the advantage of a foreign nation." It specifically prohibits communications to the enemy in wartime regarding the "movement, numbers, description, condition, or disposition" as well as plans and conduct of any armed forces (a provision added 30 June 1953). The penalty is death or imprisonment of any term including life.
- *Sec. 795:* Prohibits the photographing and sketching of "vital military and naval installations or equipment" (as defined by the President, "in the interests of national defense") without prior permission of the installation commander or higher authority. Penalty is a fine of up to $1,000 and/or imprisonment of up to one year.
- *Sec. 796:* Makes illegal the use or permission for use of an aircraft for the purpose of obtaining illegal photographs per section 795. Penalty is a fine of up to $1,000 and/or imprisonment of up to one year.
- *Sec. 787:* Prohibits the publication and sale of photographs of vital installations, "on and after thirty days" from the date the installation is defined as such, without the permission of the installation commander or higher authority.
- *Sec. 798* (added 31 October 1951): Makes illegal the knowing and will-

ful disclosure of classified information to an unauthorized person, and the publishing and use of such information "in any manner prejudicial to the safety or interest of the United States or for the benefit of any foreign government to the detriment of the United States." Classified information protected by this section includes U.S. and foreign codes, ciphers, and cryptographic systems used for communications intelligence purposes; and information relating to the activities, procedures, and methods employed for communications intelligence purposes. Penalty is a fine of up to $10,000 and/or imprisonment of up to 10 years.

- *Sec. 799* (added 29 July 1958): Prohibits the violation of any NASA regulation or order regarding the protection and security of facilities and equipment. Penalty is a fine of up to $5,000 and/or imprisonment of up to one year.

[U.S. Congress, House Permanent Select Committee on Intelligence, *Compilation of Intelligence Laws and Related Laws and Executive Orders of Interest to the National Intelligence Community*, March 1987]. (see also **censorship, security classification**)

European Command (EUCOM) (see **U.S. European Command**)

European Command and Control Console System (ECCCS): Terrestrial teletype conferencing system connecting nuclear units with Europe, and used as the primary means for the Commander-in-Chief U.S. European Command to release nuclear weapons

to delivering units or for the passage of **emergency action messages** related to the command and control of nuclear weapons.

European Telephone System (ETS): The upgrade/replacement of all telephone switching systems in Europe to include systems in West Germany, Belgium, the Netherlands, Luxemburg, the United Kingdom, Spain, Italy, Greece, and Turkey. The Army is the lead military department for acquisition in West Germany, Belgium, the Netherlands, Luxemburg, and Italy. The Air Force is the lead for the United Kingdom, Greece, and Turkey.

European Troop Strength Ceiling (ETS): Congressionally mandated limit placed on the number of U.S. troops that may be deployed in the European theater. The ceiling is intended to encourage NATO allies to increase their share of the total NATO defense burden. A ceiling was set by Congress in FY 1983 and FY 1984 for NATO European countries. In FY 1987, a permanent ETS was set at 326,412. The ETS has received much criticism from the DOD and the services, as it is viewed as "arbitrary" and largely divorced from U.S. security needs in the theater. The DOD, in its FY 1989 manpower report to Congress, warns that "the ceiling has outlived its usefulness and will, in fact, be a detriment, if the U.S. is to implement the **INF Treaty**. While the Department has no intention of significantly increasing forces (if for no other reason than fiscal constraints), DOD needs the flexibility during the transition years to make appropriate force structure changes" [DOD, *Manpower Requirements Report FY 1989,* March 1988, p. II-12]. The Army section of the report states that the ETS "continues to limit CINCEUR's flexibility to structure his forces to meet the threat as he sees it. The Army strongly supports removal of the ceiling" [DOD, *Manpower Requirements,* p. III-11]. The Air Force section states "theater ceilings, and this one in particular, have severe flaws. [The ETS] continues to be the single most significant management obstacle to performance of the Air Force mission in Europe" [DOD, *Manpower Requirements,* p. VI-6]. (see also **manpower**, **force structure**)

evasion and escape (E & E): Procedures and operations by which military personnel (particularly pilots) are able to survive and be recovered from enemy-held or hostile territory.

event: "An event is an occurrence out of the ordinary that might have future implications for the U.S. Government or its allies. This event is detected through situation monitoring" [JCS, *Joint Operations Planning System,* Vol. IV, p. II-4, released under the FOIA].

Excalibur: Code name for an underground test of a proposed missile defense system using x-ray laser energy to destroy enemy missiles in the boost or mid-course stages. Kept secret by the U.S. government, Excalibur has now become the common name for the U.S. program in which x-rays are to be produced by the detonation of nuclear devices in space.

Excess Defense Articles (EDA):   A security assistance program in which "no longer needed" defense articles are sold either under the **Foreign Military Sales (FMS)** program or transferred under the provisions of Section 516 of the Foreign Assistance Act of 1961, as amended, also referred to as the **Southern Region Amendment (SRA)**. In determining which defense articles are excess, the following definition from the **Foreign Assistance Act** is applied

> Excess defense articles means the quantity of defense articles owned by the United States Government, and not procured in anticipation of military assistance or sales requirements, or pursuant to a military assistance or sales order, which is in excess of the Approved Force Acquisition Objective and Approved Force Retention stock of all Department of Defense components at the time such articles are dropped from inventory by the supplying agency for delivery to countries or international organizations. . .

As items actually become excess, they are screened for transfer to eligible countries under SRA or are made available for purchase by eligible countries under FMS procedures. Only EDA items sold through FMS are made public to Congress. Those items transferred under SRA are presented in a classified report to Congress under the provisions of Section 516 of the Foreign Assistance Act of 1961, as amended. The Department of State's FY 1990 Congressional presentation for security assistance programs lists Costa Rica, Japan, Korea, Philippines, Taiwan, Thailand, Austria, the United Kingdom, Israel, and Pakistan as recipients of EDA, with nearly one third of the $1.4 billion FY 1988 value in sales to international organizations. The Arms Export Control Act limits the annual acquisition value of EDA to $250 million per country. Items acquired under EDA are also referred to as "SRA items" but are not necessarily the same items sold to the same country [Department of State, *Congressional Presentation of Security Assistance Program, FY 1990*, pp. 56–57]. (see also **Special Defense Acquisition Fund**)

exclusion area: Any **restricted area**, designated by a nuclear storage site or alert site commander, that contains one or more nuclear weapons. An exclusion area can be an individual storage structure such as a maintenance/assembly building, a helipad or aircraft holding area, or vehicle parking area when a vehicle or aircraft is carrying a nuclear load.

execute order: An order issued by the Joint Chiefs of Staff to direct execution of an **operation order (OPORD)** or other military operation to implement a National Command Authority decision. "The execute order will be issued by authority and direction of the Secretary of Defense" [JCS, *Joint Operations Planning System*, Vol. IV, p. H-1, released under the FOIA]. Under Phase VI of the **Crisis Action System**, the execute order will establish the execution time and provide the latest guidance on execution of the operations order.

executing commander: "A commander to whom nuclear weapons are released for delivery against specific targets in accordance with approved plans" [USCINCLANT, *Emergency Action Procedures*, 17 July 1985, Ch. 10, p. 2-6, released under the FOIA]. (see also **commander/commanding officer**)

execution planning: The phase of planning in which an approved **operation plan (OPLAN)** or other National Command Authority-designated course of action is adjusted and refined, as required by the prevailing situation, and converted into an **operations order (OPORD)** that can be executed at a designated time. Execution planning can proceed on the basis of prior deliberate planning, or it can take place under a NOPLAN situation as part of Phase V of the **Crisis Action System**. The execution planning phase of a crisis begins upon receipt of a planning order or alert order, which defines the politico-military situation, the mission to be undertaken, the strategic guidance, and the anticipated date of execution (**D-day**).

executive agent: A person, command, or service given primary responsibility and authority for a particular mission. For example, the Department of the Army is the designated executive agent for the Department of Defense regarding military involvement in domestic civil disturbance control and regarding highways for national defense.

executive officer (XO):   The second-in-command of a ship, aircraft, or squadron.

exercise: A military maneuver or simulated wartime operation involving planning, preparation, and execution. Exercises give all individuals and units the opportunity to train under simulated stressful conditions. Performance during an exercise is measured, recorded, and analyzed to identify systemic problems requiring corrective action, but this is done from a no-fault perspective. Unlike **inspections**, which are conducted to grade performance of personnel, exercises are carried out for the purpose of training and evaluation.

A military exercise may be combined, unified, joint, or uniservice, depending on participating organizations. Exercises may be designed and conducted as **command post exercises (CPXs)**, field training exercises **(FTXs)**, or combined CPXs and FTXs. An exercise is considered a significant "Part I" military exercise, and requires presidential approval, if it falls into one or more of the following categories:

- An exercise that involves comparatively large-scale participation of U.S. or foreign forces or commands;
- An exercise that requires the granting of rights or approval by another nation, or representatives thereof, except where such approval is sought by NATO authorities;
- An exercise planned for geographical areas considered politically sensitive by the Department of State;
- An exercise that has particular political significance or implications;
- An exercise in which the situation, mission, intelligence, buildup,

concepts of operations, politico-military scenario and/or public affairs guidance deals with counterinsurgency activities by U.S. forces, unless the exercise is held in the United States or is a unilateral training event in normal U.S. training areas outside the continental United States; and

- Any exercise which is of such a nature as to receive prominent attention by public information media.

A significant "Part II" exercise does not meet the above criteria but is designated by the commanders of unified or specified commands to be of interest to the **Joint Chiefs of Staff (JCS)**. A significant "Part III" exercise does not meet the above criteria but is designated to be of interest to unified or specified commanders.

Joint and combined exercises can also be designated JCS-Directed Exercises or JCS-Coordinated Exercises. A JCS-Directed Exercise is a joint and combined exercise addressing the most urgent military requirements and priority resources that are specifically directed by the JCS. A JCS-Coordinated Exercise is a joint and combined exercise whose scheduling requires coordination by the JCS but is not directed. These exercises are scheduled by the Joint Chiefs of Staff, the Services, Defense agencies, or unified and specified commands for the purposes of

- Conforming to national policy and military strategy guidance;
- Conforming to guidance from the Joint Chiefs of Staff or higher U.S. government authority;

- Participating in mutual defense arrangements with allied nations;
- Testing operation plans or contingency plans; and
- Meeting command joint readiness and training objectives.

There are a number of different exercise types, particularly in the Navy:

- AAWEX: anti-air warfare exercise;
- AIRBAREX: air barrier exercise;
- AIRLEX: air landing exercise;
- AIRTRANSEX: air transport(ation) exercise;
- AMTREX: amphibious training exercise;
- ASWEX: anti-submarine warfare exercise;
- BLTLEX: battalion landing team landing exercise;
- BOMBEX: bombing exercise;
- CASEX: close air support exercise;
- CAX: combined arms exercise;
- CINTEX: combined in-port tactical exercise;
- COMBEX: combined exercise;
- COMBINEX: combined exercise;
- COMCONEX: command and control exercise;
- COMPUTEX: composite training unit exercise;
- CONVEX: convoy exercise;
- COREX: coordinated electronic countermeasures exercise;
- COWEALEX: cold weather exercise;
- COWLEX: cold weather landing exercise;
- CPX: command post exercise;
- EWEX: electronic warfare exercise;
- EWEXIPT: electronic warfare exercise in port;
- FAIRDEX: fleet air defense exercise;
- FLEETEX/FLTEX: fleet exercise;

- FLTSTRIKEX: full general-emergency striking force exercise;
- FTX: field training exercise;
- GUNEX: gunnery exercise;
- HARDEX: harbor defense exercise;
- HELILEX: helicopter landing exercise (amphibious);
- JAMEX: jamming exercise;
- LOADEX: loading exercise;
- LOGEX: logistics exercise;
- MARAAWEX: Marine anti-air warfare exercise;
- MARFIREX: Marine firing exercise;
- MEFFEX: Marine expeditionary force field exercise;
- MEFLEX: Marine expeditionary force landing exercise;
- MINEX: Mine warfare exercise;
- MISSILEX: missile exercise;
- NAVEX: navigation exercise;
- NOREX: nuclear operational readiness exercise;
- NUCEX/NUKEX: nuclear exercise;
- NUCLEX: nuclear load-out exercise;
- PACSTRIKEX: full general-emergency striking force exercise;
- PASSEX: passing exercise;
- PHIBLEX: amphibious landing exercise;
- PHIBTRAEX: amphibious training exercise;
- PLANEX: planning exercise;
- RADEX: radar exercise;
- READEX: readiness exercise;
- RECONEX: raid/reconnaissance exercise;
- RIMEX: ship-launched intercept guided missile exercise;
- SECEX: SSBN-security exercise;
- SINKEX: target/hull sinking/destruction exercise;
- SLAMEX: submarine-launched assault missile exercise;

- SMASHEX: search for simulated-submarine casualty exercise;
- SNORKEX: snorkel detection exercise;
- SNOWFLEX: field exercise under snow conditions;
- SPECWEPS LOADEX: nuclear weapons loading exercise;
- STRIKEX: striking force exercise;
- SUBASWEX: submarine-versus-submarine exercise; and
- TRANSITEX: transit exercise.

[JCS, *Significant Military Exercise Program*, MJCS 95-81, 29 May 1981, released under the FOIA; JCS, *Procedural Guidance for the JCS-Directed and JCS-Coordinated Exercise Program*, SM-48-84, 25 January 1984, released under the FOIA; AF, *Air Force Participation in the Military Exercise Program*, AFR 55-37, 7 June 1985, released under the FOIA; PACOM, *USPACOM Military Exercises*, USCINCPAC Instruction C3550.1K, 31 May 1984, released under the FOIA; EUCOM, *Exercise Scheduling and Reporting*, ED 55-29, 14 September 1984, released under the FOIA.]

exercise term: "A combination of two words, normally unclassified, used exclusively to designate a test, drill, or **exercise**. An exercise term is employed to preclude the possibility of confusing exercise directions with actual operations directives" [SAC, *Strategic Air Command Regulation: Operations. SAC Exercise Program*, SACR 55-38, Vol. 1, 16 November 1984, p. 2-2, released under the FOIA].

Exoatmospheric Reentry Vehicle Interceptor Subsystem   (see **ERIS**)

expendable launch vehicle (ELV): The transition to a new family of ELVs is planned for the 1990s to give the DOD its own launch capability. This family includes **Delta II** and **Titan II** rockets, which have already had their first flights, and Titan IV and Atlas II, which have not yet been introduced. Nearly all DOD launches in the 1990s will be made on ELVs.

- *Medium-class ELVs*:   The Air Force is procuring Titan II rockets for use as launch platforms for navigation satellites to half-geosynchronous altitudes. Payloads include the **Defense Meteorological Satellite Program** and **N-Ross**. Titan II space launch vehicles (SLVs) are being refurbished for smaller payloads with launch capability established in late 1988 from Vandenberg AFB, CA. Unmanned vehicles will be used for payloads not requiring a manned presence in space.
- *Complementary ELVs (CELVs)*: Launch vehicles complementing the space shuttle. CELVs ensure access to space when launching the manned shuttle is considered too risky or when the shuttle is unavailable to meet launch-on-demand requirements. In February 1985, the Air Force awarded Martin Marietta a contract for $5 million to design a successor to the Titan 34D, designated Titan IV. In June 1985, the Air Force ordered 10 Titan/Centaur CELVs from Martin Marietta at a cost of $2.09 billion and is exercising its option to buy 13 more. Titan

IV consists of a 119 ft tall, two-stage liquid propellant core, plus a pair of seven-segment solid rocket motors. Titan IV has three different configurations:

- Titan IV/Centaur: Will lift a 40 ft long, 10,000 lb payload to geostationary orbit;
- Titan IV/IUS: Will deliver a 38,784 lb IUS and satellite to a low earth orbit. The IUS will then lift about 5,000 lb to geosynchronous orbit;
- Titan IV/NUS: No specific payload requirements.

[SDIO, *Report to the Congress on the SDI,* April 1987, p. VI-C-14]

explosive ordnance: "All munitions containing explosives, nuclear fission, or fusion materials and biological and chemical agents. This includes bombs and warheads; guided and ballistic missiles; artillery, mortar, rocket and small arms ammunition; all mines, torpedoes, and depth charges; pyrotechnics; clusters and dispensers; cartridges and propellant actuated devices; electro-explosive devices; clandestine and improvised explosive devices; and all similar or related items or components explosive in nature" [DNA, *Nuclear Weapon Accident Response Procedures (NARP) Manual,* January 1984, p. 156, released under the FOIA].

explosive ordnance disposal (EOD): The detection, identification, field evaluation, rendering safe, recovery, evacuation, and disposal of explosive ordnance that constitutes a hazard to operations, installations, personnel, or material. It also includes the rendering safe and/or disposal or ordnance that has become hazardous or unserviceable by damage or deterioration when the disposal of such items is beyond the capabilities of personnel normally assigned the responsibility for routine disposition. EOD procedures are those particular courses or modes of action for access to, recovery, rendering safe, and final disposal of explosive ordnance or any hazardous material associated with an explosive ordnance disposal incident:

- Access procedures: Those actions taken to locate and gain access to unexploded ordnance.
- Diagnostic procedures: Those actions taken to identify and evaluate ordnance.
- Rendersafe procedures: Those actions involving the application of special explosive ordnance disposal methods and tools to provide for the interruption of functions or separation for essential components of unexploded ordnance to prevent an unacceptable detonation.
- Recovery procedures: Those actions taken to recover unexploded explosive ordnance.
- Final disposal procedures: Those actions taken to eliminate the ordnance by burning, removal, or other means.

extended-range interceptor (ER-INT): SDI research program to develop a kinetic-energy weapon that adds to the **Flexible Lightweight Agile-Guided Experiment (FLAGE)** technologies an advanced radar seeker performance, a reduced-weight warhead with a fuzing function, and a more powerful rocket motor.

extremely low-frequency (ELF) communications: Navy one-way, low-data rate communications system for communicating with submerged submarines. The radio signal from the ELF transmitter can penetrate sea water to hundreds of feet, much deeper than the VLF signal from **TACAMO**. This allows submarines to remain in constant contact while operating at optimum patrol speeds and depths, which is important for special missions and deep-depth operations such as arctic or surveillance operations. It is also important for fleet ballistic missile submarines in training or en route to station to relieve a submarine that is on alert. ELF significantly increases a submarine's ability to evade antisubmarine search operations. ELF is a bellringer: it cannot send **emergency action messages**. If the system goes off the air, the submarine knows something has happened and can surface to receive other communications. The transmitter consists of 28 miles of overhead antenna in Wisconsin and 56 miles of overhead antenna near K.I. Sawyer AFB, MI, which sends three-character, preformatted ELF messages. ELF is EMP-protected.

extremely sensitive information (ESI)   (see **SIOP ESI**)

F

F: Prefix designating **1.** Fighter aircraft used to intercept and destroy other aircraft and missiles as well as for ground support missions of interdiction and close air support (e.g., F-14, F-16). **2.** Individual missile: hand-carried and launched by combat personnel.

F-4 Phantom/Phantom II: Air Force, Navy, and Marine Corps all-weather, twin-seat, twin-engine, supersonic, dual-capable fighter-attack jet. The F-4 has a maximum speed of Mach 2.0 at 40,000 feet and a range with a typical tactical load of 700 miles. F-4s can carry AIM-7 **Sparrow**, AIM-9 **Sidewinder**, AGM-45A **Shrike**, and AGM-88A **HARM** missiles and other bombs and are armed with one 20 mm multibarrel gun.

Designed in the mid-1950s, the F-4 has moved to a predominately air-to-ground role, although it retains residual air-to-air capability. Continuous updating has maintained the effectiveness of the F-4, and, under a 1986 contract, the navigation and weapons delivery systems of some Air Force and Air National Guard F-4s will be modified. The first version supplied to the Air Force was the F-4C, a two-seat, twin-engine, all-weather tactical fighter with inertial navigation and boom flight refueling.

The F-4D introduced major system changes, including new weapon ranging and release computers to increase accuracy in air-to-air and air-to-surface weapon delivery. The F-4E was developed as a multi-role fighter capable of performing counterair, close support, and interdiction missions. A 20 mm **Vulcan** multibarrel gun is fitted, together with an improved fire control system and an additional fuselage fuel tank. Leading-edge slats, to improve maneuverability, were fitted on all Air Force F-4Es. In addition, from early 1973, some were fitted with an improved target-identification system. Overall aircraft improvements include the Pave Tack system, which provides day/night adverse-weather capability to acquire, track, and designate ground targets for laser, infrared, and electro-optically guided weapons; the Pave Spike day tracking/laser ordnance designator pod, for use with smart weapons; and a digital intercept computer that includes launch computations for AIM-9 and AIM-7 missiles. All Air National Guard F-4Ds and F-4Es are being modified to carry AIM-9L/M Sidewinder missiles. The F-4E version will also be equipped with improved AGM-65D Maverick TV-guided missiles and a new area-denial submunition.

The F-4G Advanced Wild Weasel is a modified F-4E with its gun replaced by AN/APR-38 electronic warfare equipment, which allows it to detect, identify, and locate enemy radars and attack them. A performance upgrade is underway. The Wild Weasel's primary armaments are the Shrike and HARM missiles.

In the Air Force, the last of the F-4s are being replaced by **F-15s** and **F-16s** in active units. F-4Cs still equip a few Air National Guard units. F-4Ds equip both Air Force Reserve and Air National Guard units.

F-4s are no longer operated by active Navy squadrons. The last two Marine Corps F-4S squadrons are currently transitioning to the **F/A-18 Hornet**. There are three Marine Reserve F-4S squadrons; these will transition to F/A-18s in the early 1990s. An RF-4B reconnaissance version is operated by the Marine Corps photo-reconnaissance squadron. Plans call for the replacement of the RF-4B with the new F/A-18D reconnaissance-capable aircraft in the 1990s. The prime contractor is McDonnell Douglas Corp.

F-5E/F Tiger II: Air Force single- or dual-seat, twin-engine, supersonic, day/night, limited all-weather, lightweight jet fighter used primarily in adversary aggressor training. Its maximum level speed is Mach 1.64 at 36,000 ft and its maximum range with external fuel is 1,543 miles. It can carry AIM-9 **Sidewinder** air-to-air missiles and a mix of bombs under its wings and fuselage, and it is armed with two 20 mm cannon in its nose.

The F-5E was developed as a successor to Northrop Corporation's F-5A export fighter. The Tiger II was primarily meant to provide U.S. allies with an uncomplicated air-superiority tactical fighter that could be operated and maintained relatively inexpensively. The single-seat F-5E, first flown in August 1972, is basically a VFR day/night fighter with limited all-weather capability. Design emphasis is on maneuverability rather than on high speed. Well over 1,000 F-5Es and two-seat F-5Fs were delivered to foreign countries through early 1987, when the last two aircraft were exported.

Tactical Air Command, assisted by Air Training Command, trains pilots and technicians of user air forces. For this purpose, 20 F-5Es were supplied to the Air Force beginning in April 1973, before deliveries to foreign governments began in 1974. TAC also operates two aggressor squadrons of camouflaged F-5Es simulating late-model Soviet MiG threat aircraft in "Red Flag" exercises at Nellis AFB, NV. Similar training is provided by F-5Es of the 527th Tactical Fighter Training Aggressor Squadron at RAF Alconbury, UK, and the 26th Tactical Fighter Training Squadron at Clark AB, Philippines. F-16s will replace F-5s for the aggressor mission. There are plans to upgrade the Air Forces's 74 F-5Es and F-5Fs to improve target-detection range and tracking. The prime contractor is Northrop Corp.

F-14 Tomcat: Navy twin-engine, two-person, supersonic, conventionally armed jet fighter that is the Navy's premier air-superiority and fleet defense interceptor. The airplane is carrier-based, with a sophisticated all-weather fire control system and compatibility with **Sidewinder, Sparrow,** and **Phoenix** air-to-air missiles. It is also capable of limited air-to-ground attack. The F-14 entered the active force in 1974, and 22 former F-4 squadrons have completed transition. The inventory of aircraft is about 400 operational and 50 training. They are assigned to NAS Oceana, VA, and NAS Miramar, CA. A version of the F-14 (designated F-14D) was projected for deployment in the early 1990s but was canceled in the FY 1990 budget by the Secretary of Defense. On 11 April 1988, the Navy's first operational F-14A Plus was accepted by VF-101 at NAS Oceana, VA. The F-14A Plus has two GE F-110 engines that each develop 7,000 lb more thrust than the original Tomcat power plants.

Prime contractors are Grumman Aerospace of Bethpage, NY; and General Electric of Lynn, MA, for the engines. The FY 1990 and FY 1991 budget requests for 18 and 24 F-14D new and remanufactured aircraft were $1,397.8 million and $1,467.3 million, respectively.

F-15 Eagle: Air Force one- or two-person, twin-engine, supersonic, dual-capable, day/night, all-weather jet fighter. It is the Air Force's primary air-superiority fighter and has been progressively replacing F-4s since the mid-1970s. The latest version, the F-15C, has a maximum speed of Mach 2.5 and a ferry range of more than 2,800 miles with external fuel tanks and of 3,570 miles with conformal fuel tanks (CFTs). It can carry AIM-9L/M **Sidewinder** and AIM-7F/M **Sparrow** missiles and is armed with one internally mounted 20 mm six-barrel cannon.

The original single-seat F-15A and two-seat F-15B were followed in June 1979 by the F-15C and F-15D, which had greater internal and external fuel capacities. Under ongoing contracts initiated in 1983, the F-15 is undergoing a multi-stage improvement program (MSIP) to improve offensive and defensive avionics and add an **AMRAAM** capability. Delivery of the MSIF-equipped planes began in June 1985. Also, a g-force overload indicator is being added to permit safe maneuver of up to 9g throughout most of the flight envelope.

The F-15E Strike Eagle is the Air Force's new two-seat, dual-role, totally integrated fighter for all-weather air-to-air and deep-interdiction missions. The F-15E has front- and rear-cockpit modifications, with improved CRT screens and displays for radar, weapons selection, and monitoring of enemy tracking systems, and a greater field of view. The F-15E can carry up to 24,500 lb of ordnance, including nuclear bombs and the nuclear-armed **tactical air-to-surface missile (TASM)** under development. Its flight control system provides for coupled automatic terrain-following and improved navigational accuracy. For low-altitude, high-speed penetration and precision attack on tactical targets at night and in adverse weather, the F-15E carries the high-resolution AN-APG-70 radar and **LANTIRN** (Low-Altitude Navigation and Targeting Infrared for Night) pods with wide-field **forward-looking infrared (FLIR).**

The F-15Es have reduced internal fuel space to accommodate the new avionics, but they are fitted with external conformal fuel tanks. In addition to its primary load of guided and unguided bombs and other air-to-ground weapons, the F-15E retains its air-superiority performance and weapons. The first three F-15E prototypes flew in December 1986, and the first production F-15E was delivered to the 505th Tactical Training Wing at Luke AFB, AZ, in April 1988. The first operational F-15E wing will be the 4th Tactical Fighter Wing at Seymour Johnson AFB, NC, which received its first aircraft on 29 December 1988. Total procurement of 350 F-15Es is planned, with 134 already procured through 1989. The plane will be deployed to Europe and South Korea.

A short-take-off-and-landing version, the F-15 S/MTC (STOL/Maneuvering Technology Demonstrator), is being developed and tested by McDonnell Douglas at the request of the Air Force.

Planned production of all F-15 models will total 1,266 aircraft for the Air Force plus the original 20 R&D models by the mid-1990s. The prime contractor is McDonnell Douglas. The FY 1990 and FY 1991 budget requests for 36 F-15E aircraft each year are $1,713.3 million and $1,643.3 million, respectively, including RDT&E and military construction.

F-16 Fighting Falcon: Air Force and Navy single- or twin-seat, single-engine, supersonic, dual-capable fighter and attack jet. The latest model, the F-16C, has a maximum speed of Mach 2 and a ferry range of over 2,000 miles. It can carry 9L/M **Side-**winder and AIM-7F/M **Sparrow** air-to-air missiles, air-to-surface munitions, and nuclear bombs and is armed with one 20 mm multibarrel cannon.

The F-16 was developed to replace the F-4s in the Air Force and modernize the air reserve forces. Advanced technologies incorporated from the start into the single-seat F-16A and twin-seat F-16B made them two of the most maneuverable fighters ever built. The advances include decreased structural weight through the use of composite materials, fly-by-wire flight controls with a stick controller, decreased drag, and a high g tolerance/high visibility cockpit. Equipment includes a multi-mode radar with clutter-free look-down capability, and an advanced warning receiver, a head-up display, internal chaff and flare dispensers, and a 20 mm internal gun. The aircraft also have provisions for electronic countermeasures.

The F-16 entered operational service with Tactical Air Command's 388th Tactical Fighter Wing at Hill AFB, UT, in January 1979. Production of the F-16A and F-16B for the Air Force ended in 1985. The Air Force and NATO are cooperating in an operational-capabilities upgrade (OCU) program to improve the planes' avionics, and giving the planes the ability to operate next-generation air-to-air and air-to-ground weapons systems.

A multinational staged improvement program (MSIP) was implemented by the Air Force in February 1980 to assure the aircraft's capability to accept systems under development and thereby minimize refit costs. As a first stage, all F-16s delivered since November 1981 have had built-in structural and wiring architecture that expand the F-16A's multi-role flexibility. Stage two was applied to improved single-seat F-16C and twin-seat F-16D versions, deliveries of which to the Air Force began in July 1984. Current aircraft have improved avionics, ECCM, and navigation/attack systems, and **Shrike** and **AMRAAM** capabilities were recently added to F-16C/Ds.

Up to 270 of the original F-16As are being modified to a F-16(ADF) standard under a contract awarded in October 1986, to meet the Air Force's requirement for an air-defense fighter to replace aging F-106s and **F-4s** in 11 Air National Guard air defense squadrons assigned to NORAD. These new aircraft will enter service starting in 1989, and the last modified aircraft is due in 1991.

A further version known as Agile Falcon or MSIP IV is being pursued, with the possibility of continuing a codevelopment and coproduction program with allies who fly the F-16. A parallel effort is under way for an F-16A/B mid-life upgrade (MLU).

Derivatives of the F-16 are being considered as close-air-support/battlefield air-interdiction (CAS/BAI) aircraft (the A-16) and as tactical air-reconnaissance platforms. Future development and applications of the F-16 will be monitored under a program known as Falcon Century. A sophisticated research variant of the F-16, the AFTI/F-16, is used at Edwards AFB, CA, to test and evaluate advanced fighter technologies.

The Air Force plans a total buy of 2,609 F-16s through FY 1994. By 1989, 1,859 had been funded, with 1,562 expected to be delivered by fall of 1989. F-16s are standard equipment with 27 Tactical Air Command, U.S. Air Forces Europe, and Pacific Air Forces units, and they are progressively replacing older aircraft in the Air Force Reserve and Air National Guard. F-16s also equip the Air Force's Thunderbirds air-demonstration squadron. The 50th Tactical Fighter Wing at Hahn Air Base, West Germany, became the first operational unit to field the F-16C/D fighters in 1986. The 944th Tactical Fighter Group, Luke AFB, Arizona, became the first Air Force Reserve unit to receive the F-16C/D on 24 October 1987. Over 1,100 more have been delivered to, or ordered for, the air forces of Bahrain, Belgium, Denmark, Egypt, Greece, Indonesia, Israel, the Netherlands, Norway, Pakistan, Singapore, South Korea, Thailand, Turkey, Venezuela, and the U.S. Navy.

The Navy has acquired F-16Ns to play the role of adversary training aircraft and to provide realistic air-combat maneuvering (ACM) training at the Naval Fighter Weapons School ("Top Gun") at NAS Miramar, CA. The performance characteristics of the F-16N match those of several Soviet aircraft.

The prime contractor is General Dynamics, Fort Worth, TX. The FY 1990 and FY 1991 budget requests for 150 aircraft each year are $3,317.6 million and $3,218.4 million, respectively, including RDT&E and military construction.

F/A-18 Hornet: Navy and Marine Corps single-seat or twin-seat, twin-engine, supersonic, dual-capable, multimission fighter and attack aircraft, replacing both the **F-4** and **A-7** aircraft. It was designed for traditional strike applications such as interdiction and close air support without compromising its fighter capabilities. It also supplements the **F-14 Tomcat** in fleet air defense. F/A-18s can operate from both carriers and ground bases. The plane has a top speed of over Mach 1.7, a combat radius of 400 nm for fighter missions and 575 nm for attack missions, and a ferry range of more than 2,000 nm. It can carry **Sparrow** and **Sidewinder** air-to-air missiles, air-to-ground ordnance, and nuclear bombs and is armed with an internal 20 mm **Vulcan** cannon.

Over 700 aircraft had been delivered by 1989. The first F/A-18C single-seat was delivered on 21 September 1987. The newest version is the first airplane to include the AN/ALQ-165 Airborne Self-Protection Jammer (ASPJ), and it is capable of firing the **AMRAAM** and the imaging infrared **Maverick**. The Navy plans to buy more than 700 F/A-18Cs and two-seat F/A-18Ds. By 1990, the Marines expect to have 12 F/A-18 squadrons, each equipped with eight single-seat and eight two-seat models. The overall projected buy is 1,168 aircraft. They are assigned to MCAS El Toro, CA; NAS Lemore, CA; and NAS Cecil Field, FL.

The prime contractors are McDonnell Douglas Corporation of St. Louis, MO, for the airframe, and General Electric, Lynn, MA, for the engines. The FY 1990 and FY 1991 budget requests for 72 aircraft each year are $2,683.3 million and $2,183.2 million, respectively.

F-23 (see **Advanced Tactical Fighter (ATF)**)

F-111 Aardvark: Air Force twin-seat, twin-engine, supersonic, day/night, all-weather, medium-range, dual-capable fighter-bomber. It is operated by Tactical Air Command and U.S. Air Forces Europe in five versions for tactical attacks. Its maximum speed is Mach 2.5, and the F-111F version has a range of 2,925 miles with external fuel. The plane uses a variable-geometry swing-wing. First flown in 1964, it was originally also developed for the Navy and Marine Corps.

Four versions of the F-111 are deployed with the Tactical Air Command to provide the Air Force with a 24 hour, long-range interdiction capability. Deliveries of production F-111As to the first operational wing began in October 1967, and 141 were built. This version was used in the Vietnam War and currently equips the 366th Tactical Fighter Wing. The F-111A was replaced in production by the F-111E, which has modified air intakes that improve engine performance above Mach 2.2. Ninety-four F-111Es were built, and most of these serve with the 20th Tactical Fighter Wing at RAF Upper Heyford, UK. The replacement of current analog bombing and navigation systems with digital equipment is scheduled to begin in 1989 and to be completed in 1993. This replacement will enable F-111A/E aircraft to handle modern guided munitions and advanced sensors, as well as future systems such as the **NAVSTAR/GPS**. The F-111D was designed with advanced avionics, offering improvements in navigation and air-to-air weapon delivery. Ninety-six were built, and they equip the 27th Tactical Fighter Wing, Cannon AFB, NM. The F-111F, of which 106 were built, has uprated turbofan engines. They equip the 48th Tactical Fighter Wing, RAF Lakenheath, UK, and can carry in the weapons bay the Pave Tack system, which provides a day/night capability to acquire, track, and designate ground targets for laser, infrared, and electro-optically guided weapons. Production of the F-111 was completed in 1976. Currently, its electronic warfare capabilities are being updated, and future improvements include adding an AIM-9L/M Sidewinder capability. In addition to its nuclear and conventional-bombing and missile-attack capabilities, the F-111 can carry up to 12 French-made Durandal parachute-retarded, rocket-boosted, runway attack bombs for low-altitude, high-speed delivery, as well as Gators. There is also an **EF-111 Raven** electronic warfare version of the F-111. Prime contractor was General Dynamics.

F-117A Stealth fighter: Air Force single-seat, twin-engine, probably subsonic, stealth jet fighter. A secret program since 1978, details of the fighter were finally revealed by the Air Force in November 1988. It was frequently referred to as the F-19 until its true designation was revealed. The plane first flew in June 1981 and became operational in October 1983. Fifty-nine aircraft have been ordered to date, of which 52 were delivered by November 1988. They are operated by the 4450th Tactical Group based at the Tonopah Test Range airfield, adjacent to Nellis AFB and the Nevada Test Site in Nevada. They have been restricted mainly to night-flying to maintain secrecy. At least three have been lost in much-publicized accidents.

The F-117A designers at Lockheed used several methods to give the aircraft its low-observable, or stealth, characteristics. The skin panels of the arrowhead-shaped airframe are divided into many small, perfectly flat surfaces, which reflect away at a variety of angles all signals from probing hostile ground or airborne radars. This is known as "faceting." Much of the aircraft's external surface is made of radar absorbent composite materials. The engine air intakes and exhaust nozzles are above the wings and the stubby rear fuselage, respectively, to shield them from infrared sensors.

The F-117A can be carried onboard a **C-5 Galaxy** with its wings folded or removed. Its engines are said to be non-afterburning turbofans, implying low noise emissions and subsonic performance. Fly-by-wire flight controls and a powerful stability augmentation system are said to be fitted and seem to be important features of an aircraft known to pilots as the "Wobbly Goblin." Its primary role would appear to be low-level precision attack on high-priority targets using internally stowed air-to-surface missiles. The prime contractor is Lockheed Corp., Burbank, CA.

FAADS (see **Forward Area Air Defense System**)

Faded Giant: Code name for a **nuclear reactor accident**.

Fade Out: Exercise term to describe **Defense Readiness Condition (DEFCON) 5**.

fail-safe: "A design feature of a nuclear weapon system or component which ensures that a *critical* function or personnel injury will not occur because of a failure in the system or component" (emphasis in original) [AFR 122-10, Attachment 1, 5 January 1982, released under the FOIA].

fast combat support ship (AOE): Navy conventionally powered multi-product support ship. AOEs are the largest combat logistic ships and have the speed and armament to remain with fast-moving **aircraft carrier battlegroups**. They receive petroleum products, ammunition, and stores from shuttle logistic ships and redistribute these items simultaneously to ships in the battlegroups using both connected and vertical replenishment. AOEs operate as an integral unit of the carrier battlegroup. They serve as a fuel/ammunition reservoir, delivering customer-configured loads. AOEs' simultaneous multi-product delivery reduces the vulnerability of individual ships by minimizing along-side time. They can carry more than 177,000 barrels of oil, 2,150 tons of ammunition including nuclear weapons, 500 tons of dry stores, and 250 tons of refrigerated stores. The Sacramento

(AOE-1) class of four ships is active. Each ship displaces 53,000 tons at full load, is 793 ft long, and has a beam of 107 ft, a speed of 26 kts, and a complement of 615 personnel. The lead ship of the four-ship Supply (AOE-6) class was authorized in FY 1987 and is currently under construction for delivery in 1991. These will displace 48,500 tons at full load, be 753 ft long, and have a beam of 107 ft, a speed of 26 kts, and a complement of 667 personnel. Ships of both classes have **Sea Sparrow** missiles and the **Phalanx** close-in-weapons-system for self-defense and two **CH-46 Sea Knight** helicopters for **underway replenishment**. The prime contractor for the AOE-6s is National Steel and Shipbuilding Company, San Diego, CA. The FY 1990 and FY 1991 budget requests for one AOE-6 in each year are $363.1 million and $365.9 million, respectively, including RDT&E. (see **logistic ships**)

Fast Pace: Exercise term to describe **Defense Readiness Condition (DEFCON) 2**.

FB-111: Air Force twin-seat, twin-engine, supersonic, day/night, all-weather, medium-range, dual-capable strategic bomber. Its maximum speed is Mach 2.5 and it has a range of 4,100 miles with external fuel. The FB-111As belong to the Strategic Air Command (SAC). They are a medium-range strategic version of the swing-wing **F-111** and are capable of providing high-precision, low-altitude weapons delivery in all weather conditions, day or night. FB-111As were developed to provide SAC with a replacement for early versions of the **B-52** and supersonic B-58 Hustlers. The first of 76 production aircraft flew in July 1968, and the initial delivery was made in October 1969 to the 340th Bomb Group. Sixty-one aircraft remain in the inventory as of 1989. Although the FB-111's primary mission is delivering nuclear bombs or **Short-Range Attack Missiles (SRAMs)**, it can also be used to deliver conventional weapons. It can carry up to four SRAMs on external pylons plus two in the weapons bay, or six nuclear bombs (of either the B28, B57, B61, or B83 types). FB-111s are currently scheduled to remain operational until after the year 2000, although they will be transferred from SAC to the tactical air forces after the **B-2** is deployed.

FEBA (see **forward edge of the battle area**)

Federal Aviation Administration (FAA): Executive branch agency operating within the Department of Transportation. Its predecessor organizations include the Civil Aeronautics Authority (1938), the Civil Aeronautics Board and the Civil Aeronautics Administration (1940), and the Federal Aviation Agency (1958). The Agency's functions were transferred to the FAA upon its establishment on 1 April 1967. Its missions include aviation safety and security, law enforcement, responsibility for civil-military airnavigation air-traffic-control systems, research, and development. It operates the National Airspace System (NAS), which serves civil and Depart-

ment of Defense air-traffic control and navigation needs.

Headquarters
Washington, DC 20951

*Administrators of
the Federal Aviation Administration*

Elwood R. Quesada	1 Nov 1958–
20 Jan 1961
Najeeb E. Halaby	3 Mar 1961–
1 Jul 1965
William F. McKee	1 Jul 1965–
31 Jul 1968
John H. Shaffer	24 Mar 1969–
14 Mar 1973
Alexander P. Butterfield	14 Mar 1973–
31 Mar 1975
John L. McLucas	24 Nov 1975–
1 Apr 1977
Langhorne M. Bond	4 May 1977–
20 Jan 1981
J. Lynn Helms	22 Apr 1981–
31 Jan 1984
Donald D. Engen	10 Apr 1984–
2 Jul 1987
T. Allan McArtor	22 Jul 1987–
17 Feb 1989
James B. Bufey	30 Jun 1989–
present

Federal Bureau of Investigation (FBI): Executive branch agency, established 1 July 1935 within the Department of Justice. It was originally referred to as the Special Agent Force (26 July 1908) and has been designated as the Bureau of Investigation (16 March 1909), the United States Bureau of Investigation (1 July 1932), and Division of Investigation (10 August 1933). The FBI is responsible for domestic **counterintelligence** and **counterterrorist** investigations, and it works closely with the military counterintelligence organizations in the conduct of investigations on DOD personnel. It is the lead agency for the operational response to a domestic terrorist incident [DOD–DOJ–FBI MOU, *Use of Federal Military Force in Domestic Incidents*, 5 August 1983].

Headquarters
Washington, DC 20535

Directors/Heads,
Federal Bureau of Investigation

Stanley W. Finch	
(Special Agent Force)	26 Jul 1908
(Bureau of Investigation)	16 Mar 1909
A. Bruce Bielaski	
(Bureau of Investigation)	30 Apr 1912
William E. Allen*	
(Bureau of Investigation)	10 Feb 1919
William J. Flynn	
(Bureau of Investigation)	1 Jul 1919
William J. Burns	
(Bureau of Investigation)	22 Aug 1921
John Edgar Hoover*	
(Bureau of Investigation)	10 May 1924
(BOI/USBOI/Div. of Invest.)	10 Dec 1924
L. Patrick Gray*	3 May 1972
William D. Ruckelshaus*	27 Apr 1973
Clarence M. Kelley	9 Jul 1973
William H. Webster	23 Feb 1978
John Otto*	26 May 1987
William Steele Sessions	2 Nov 1987
*acting	

Federal Contract Research Center (FCRC)(see Federally Funded Research and Development Center.)

Federal Emergency Management Agency (FEMA): Independent executive branch agency, established by President Carter (as proposed In Reorganization Plan No. 3 of 1978) by Executive Orders 12127 and 12148, 20 July 1979. Its predecessor organizations include the Council of National Defense (August 1916–December 1918), National Defense Advisory Commission (est. 28 May 1940), Office of Civil Defense (May 1941–June 1945), Office of Civil Defense Planning (est. 1948), National Security Resources Board (est. 1949), Federal Civil Defense Administration (est. 12 January 1951), the military's Office of Civil Defense (est. 1 August 1961), and the Defense Civil Preparedness Agency (est. 5 May 1972). The functions and responsibilities of the following agencies were assigned to FEMA: Federal Disaster Assistance Administration and the Federal Flood Insurance Program (transferred from HUD), the Defense Civil Preparedness Agency (transferred from DOD), the National Fire Prevention and Control Administration and the Emergency Broadcast System (transferred from Commerce), the Federal Preparedness Agency (transferred from GSA), and the Earthquake Hazards Reduction Office (transferred from the Office of Science and Technology Policy).

FEMA is responsible for federal emergency preparedness, policies, planning, and coordination for both peacetime disasters and wartime emergencies. Its areas of responsibility include **civil defense**, crisis relocation, mobilization of emergency resources, **continuity of government**, disaster relief and rescue, fire and flood preparedness and response, emergency food and shelter programs, and emergency communications and broadcasting. Its civil emergency programs specifically relate to nuclear weapons attacks and accidents and nuclear power plant accidents. FEMA's civil defense program for FY 1988 included

- State/local emergency management (providing support to numerous emergency staffs in 2,700 locations around the country; managing military reserve support to 850 state/local governments), $56 million.
- Radiological defense (support to 52 state radiological officers; maintenance support for state radiological instruments), $13 million.
- Population protection (assistance in the development of state and local emergency plans; surveys of potential emergency shelters (FEMA has identified approximately 394 million buildings for nuclear fallout protection and emergency lodging), $14 million.
- State/local direction control and warning (development of fallout-protected operations centers; protection of approximately 20 emergency broadcast system stations), $4 million.
- Research (plans for surge improvement of civil defense capabilities in time of escalating tension), $900,000.
- Training and education (training at National Emergency Training Center and in states; development of public information), $10 million.
- Telecommunications and warning networks and systems, $24 million.

FEMA provides assistance to state and local governments in response to emergency situations and is also responsible for the coordination of other federal agencies' emergency programs and efforts. FEMA and DOD have provided for participation in civil defense programs involving reservists (through the National Guard Bureau), installations, the Army Corps of Engineers, and DOD command, control, and communications programs and facilities. The Under Secretary of Defense (Policy) represents the DOD in FEMA matters, and the Secretary of the Army is designated the DOD's executive agent for FEMA except for matters related to civil defense.

FEMA's civilian director reports directly to the President. FEMA's FY 1989 budget was approximately $700 million. Its personnel strength is approximately 2,400.

Headquarters
Washington, DC 20472

Major Directorates

- Training and Education Directorate/ National Emergency Training Center
- Federal Insurance Administration
- National Preparedness Programs Directorate
- State and Local Programs and Support Directorate
- U.S. Fire Administration
- Resource Management and Administration Directorate

Regional Offices

- Region I, Boston, MA 02109
- Region II, New York, NY 10278
- Region III, Philadelphia, PA 19106
- Region IV, Atlanta, GA 30309
- Region V, Chicago, IL 60606

- Region VI, Denton, TX 76201
- Region VII, Kansas City, MO 64106
- Region VIII, Denver, CO 80225
- Region IX, San Francisco, CA 94129
- Region X, Bothell, WA 98021

*Directors, Federal
Emergency Management Agency*

John Williams Macy, Jr.
    1 Aug 1979   20 Jan 1981
Louis O. Giuffrida
    19 May 1981   Sep 1985
Julius W. Becton, Jr.
    28 Oct 1985   present

Federal Emergency Plan D: Basic federal emergency plan issued in 1969 and revised in March 1970, as the "basic Federal emergency plan for use in a crippling nuclear attack on the United States." Plan D establishes a system and structure for management of critical resources during a **general war:**

- "to ensure the **continuity of government** and order;
- to support military operations and military alliances;
- to ensure survival of the remaining population and recovery of the nation;
- to ensure the most effective use of resources; and
- to maintain free-world unity" [NCS, Briefing, *Federal Emergency Plan D,* AH 134–35, released under the FOIA].

Plan D contains a basic plan and three annexes:

- Annex A: Presidential Emergency Action Directives;
- Annex B: Office of Defense Resources Management Assignments; and
- Annex C: Resource Management Implementation Plans and Instructions.

Plan D can be implemented only by Presidential declaration. Annex A, prepared by the Department of Justice, is a set of 22 Presidential Emergency Action Directives (PEADS), which are "draft executive orders that might be utilized by a President" in the event of nuclear war. These standby orders deal with "the full range of powers that might be [used] during an emergency." Annex A was last revised in full in May 1980. (see also **Federal Emergency Management Agency**)

Federal Financing Bank (FFB): Branch of the Department of the Treasury that, under the U.S. **security assistance programs**, extends loans for **Foreign Military Sales (FMS)**. The **Defense Security Assistance Agency (DSAA)** guarantees the loans and is accountable to the FFB to make the interest payments on the loans when borrowing countries do not. (see also **Guaranteed Reserve Fund**)

Federally-Funded Research and Development Center (FFRDC): A government-sponsored nonprofit contract research center. A FFRDC does not compete with private firms for government contracts, nor does it manufacture products or contract for systems, subsystems, or hardware. It performs directed research in the fields of science and technology, program analysis, policy and management, or communications on behalf of its sponsor or other government agency. The six FFRDCs operating in support of a military service or DOD are the following

Air Force

- Aerospace Corporation, El Segundo, CA 90245
- RAND Corporation—Project Air Force, Washington, DC 20330

Department of Defense/Joint Chiefs of Staff

- Institute for Defense Analyses, Alexandria, VA 22311
- Logistics Management Institute, Bethesda, MD 20817-5886
- MITRE Corporation, McLean, VA 22102

Navy

- Center for Naval Analyses, Alexandria, VA 22302

Federal Regional Center (FRC): A series of eight underground bunkers operated by the **Federal Emergency Management Agency** and intended for the evacuation and wartime operation of the civil government, particularly the **civil defense**-related officials. The eight regions are

- Region I: Maynard, MA 01754
- Region III: Olney, MD 20832
- Region IV: Thomasville, GA 31792
- Region V: Battle Creek, MI 49016
- Region VI: Denton, TX 76201
- Region VIII: Denver, CO 80201
- Region IX: Santa Rosa, CA 92402
- Region X: Bothell, WA 98011.

FEMA (see **Federal Emergency Management Agency**)

FEMA Special Facility (SF): Emergency Operations Facility (EOF) of the **Federal Emergency Management Agency (FEMA)**, also known as Mt. Weather, located about 80 miles from Washington along Virginia Route 601 between the towns of Bluemont and Paris. The SF is the evacuation bunker of the civil government, particularly of **civil defense**-related officials and agencies. A skeletal staff keeps the facility operating, but the day-to-day command center of FEMA is actually in Washington, with a backup in Laytonsville, MD, close to Olney.

ferret: 1. Type of **signals intelligence (SIGINT)** satellite. Referred to as "balls" within the U.S. intelligence community, several classes of these electronic reconnaissance, low-earth orbiting satellites have been deployed since 1962 to intercept Soviet, Chinese, and other foreign signals. Since 1972, only ferret subsatellites have been launched as secondary pay-loads on imaging satellite deployments (the KH-9 **Hexagon** and possibly the KH-11 **Kennan**). The Air Force second-generation satellite is to be superceded by a new Hughes design Code 711. Ferret's main contractors are Lockheed and Sanders. (see also **satellite reconnaissance**) **2.** Flight whose purpose is to evoke enemy-radar and air-defense activity in order to monitor, analyze, and record electro magnetic emissions.

FF/FFG: Designation for **frigate/ guided missile frigate**.

F-hour: The effective time of an announcement by the Secretary of

Defense to the military departments of a decision to mobilize reserve units. (see also **military time**)

Fiber Optics-Guided Missile (FOG-M): An Army short-range, mobile, indirect fire (non–line of sight), fiber optic–guided air defense missile under development. It is the Non–Line of Sight (NLOS) missle component of the **Forward Area Air Defense System (FAADS)**, integrating with other parts of the FAAD system. As designed, its primary mission is to provide low altitude defense for ground forces against attacks by low-flying masked and stand-off helicopter targets. Its secondary mission is to provide defense against moving and stationary armored targets. The Army is currently evaluating contractor proposals for the development of the Block I system. The Army plans to buy 403 systems, with the first unit to be equipped in FY 1993.

The fiber-optic–guided missile (FOG-M) has been chosen to prove the technological feasibility of the NLOS missile. It was designed and built at the Army Missile Command's Research, Development and Engineering Center, Redstone Arsenal, AL. The program is now assembling hardware for the initial operational evaluation (IOE), in which the user will run multiple "hands-on" exercises with this notional system, which has a 10-kilometer range. Lessons learned from the IOE and early user employment will be channeled into full-scale development of the longer-range Block I system.

FOG-M utilizes a fiber optic data link for command guidance by one operator who guides the missile to impact via video display console. The launcher/gunner station can be mounted on either a high-mobility multipurpose wheeled vehicle (HMMWV) or **Multiple Launch Rocket System (MLRS)**-type tracked vehicle. The FOG-M IOE system consists of a HMMWV prime mover, launcher, six-missile launch pad, a gunner's station, and communications equipment. The FOG-M is launched vertically and then programmed to pitch over to level flight. The low-cost seeker mounted in the nose of the missile sends pictures of the battlefield to the gunner via a bi-directional fiber optic data link. A bobbin located at the rear of the missile allows the fiber optic cable to play out like fishing line from a spinning reel.

The capabilities of the gunner's station include premission missile route planning, digital terrain map displays, built-in training devices that give the operator a three-dimensional perspective, and multiple missile flight control. The gunner can survey the battlefield; select a target; and activate the automatic tracker, or, if preferred, manually fly the missile into the target. Built-in flight recording devices allow the gunner to replace stored video images transmitted by the seeker and to perform reconnaissance and damage assessment.

The contractors are Boeing Aerospace, Renton, WA, and Hughes Aircraft, El Segundo, CA. The total procurement and RDT&E requests for FY 1990 and FY 1991 are $171.9 and $229.5 million, respectively.

field army: An **Army** administrative and tactical organization at the combat echelon above corps. It consists of a headquarters, a variable number of corps, a variable number of divisions, certain organic Army troops, and service support troops.

field artillery: 1. Branch and arm of the Army whose personnel and units employ cannons, rockets, and missile systems, with target acquisition means. **2.** That portion of the Army and Marine Corps that employs field artillery weapon systems and traditionally has been the largest casualty producer on the battlefield. U.S. field artillery is almost 100 percent self-propelled on tracked vehicles, providing mobility required to ensure flexibility and responsiveness. In addition, field artillery can serve as an effective antitank arm by employing small, scatterable antitank mines and munitions in standard cannon tubes. The precision-guided projectile, also fired from standard artillery and capable of first-round hits, can also be employed an antitank role. Automated fire control procedures reduce the response time for the delivery of on-target fires and eliminate manual computation methods. Field artillery forward observers are equipped with laser rangefinders, which allow them to send accurate range data with requests for fire. (see also **ammunition, artillery, division artillery**)

Field Artillery Ammunition Support Vehicle (FAASV): Model designation M992. Army full-tracked, self-propelled armored ammunition vehicle, which gives protection to its crew and ammunition from hostile fires. FAASV replaced the can-vas-topped M548 ammunition carrier, which was in service in Europe and South Korea. There was an urgent need for an armored ammunition vehicle, since the canvas-topped M548 was extremely vulnerable to hostile fire. Acquisition began in FY 1983, and deployment began in the mid-1980s.

One FAASV accompanies one self-propelled **howitzer** and can carry 90 155 mm and 48 203 mm rounds. The vehicle has a hydraulic-powered conveyor for self-loading of projectiles and propellant charges and for moving fuzed projectiles and propellant charges up to the breach of the howitzer. Projectiles are stored in racks and are moved into the howitzer by a conveyor. An armored rear door of the FAASV swings up to provide overhead protection during ammunition transfer to the howitzer. It is a derivative of the M109A2 155 mm howitzer chassis, with the same cross-country mobility and armored protection.

The prime contractor is Browen-McLauglin-York, York, PA. The FY 1987 and FY 1988 budget requests for 141 and 48 FAASVs were $62.9 million and $28.7 million, respectively (FY 1988 was the last procurement year).

field operating agency (FOA): Army organization smaller than a **major command** but subordinate to the **Army Staff, Chief of Staff of the Army**, and the Department of the Army. FOAs usually perform a specialized service and operate from one location. They are equivalent to Air Force **separate operating agencies**.

Army Field Operating Agencies

- Army Claims Service
- Army Intelligence Agency
- Army National Guard Personnel Center
- Army Research Institute
- Army Reserve Personnel Center
- Army Physical Disability Agency
- Army Safety Center
- Army Space Program Office
- Army War College
- Center of Military History
- Civilian Appellate Review Agency
- Command and Control Support Agency
- Community and Family Support Center
- Concepts Analysis Agency
- Cost and Economic Analysis Center
- Development and Employment Agency
- Finance and Accounting Center
- Force Development Support Agency
- Judge Advocate General's School
- Legal Services Agency
- Logistics Evaluation Agency
- Manpower Requirements and Documentation Agency
- Medical Research and Development Command
- Military Academy
- Operational Test and Evaluation Agency
- Plans and Operations Information Support Agency
- Recruiting Command
- Total Army Personnel Agency
- Troop Support Agency
- U.S. Army Nuclear and Chemical Agency
- U.S. Army Strategic Defense Command

field storage location (FSL): Army nuclear weapons storage point located in the corps area that supplies nuclear weapons to the Special Ammunition Storage Point (SASP) for delivery to the using unit.

field training exercise (see **FTX**)

Fifth Air Force (5th AF): Major subordinate unit of the **Pacific Air Forces** and a service component command of **U.S. Forces Japan**. Its mission is to provide tactical fighter and reconnaissance support for Japanese and South Korean operations. Its personnel strength is approximately 23,000.

Headquarters
Yokota AB, Tokyo, Japan

Subordinate Units

- 313th Air Division, Kadena AB, Japan
- 18th Tactical Fighter Wing, Kadena AB, Japan
- 432d Tactical Fighter Wing, Misawa, AB, Japan
- 475th Air Base Wing, Yokota AB, Japan

Fifth Allied Tactical Air Force (FIVEATAF): NATO air organization assigned to **Allied Air Forces Southern Europe**, established 1 January 1956. Its area of responsibility includes the Italian peninsula, its islands, and adjacent waters. The bulk of its assigned forces are provided by Italy and the United States.

Headquarters
Vicenza, Italy

Fifth Fleet (5th FLT): Numbered operating fleet of the Navy in a reserve, nonoperational status. Upon activation, it is assigned to the **Pacific Fleet**. Commander, 5th FLT exercises operational control over assigned commander task forces, most of which do not exist in peacetime. Operating Task Forces, when activated, are

- CTF 50: Commander Battle Force
- CTF 51: Commander Command and Coordination Force
- CTF 52: Commander Patrol and Reconnaissance Force
- CTF 53: Commander Logistic Support Force
- CTF 54: Commander Submarine Force
- CTF 55: Commander Surface Combatant Force
- CTF 56: Commander Amphibious Force
- CTF 57: Commander Carrier Strike Force
- CTF 59: Commander Landing Force

Finance Corps: A **combat service support** branch of the Army.

fireball: The luminous sphere of hot gases that forms a few millionths of a second after a nuclear explosion as the result of the absorption by the surrounding medium of the thermal x-rays emitted by the extremely hot (several tens of million Degrees) weapon residues. The exterior of the fireball in air is initially sharply defined by the luminous shock front and later by the limits of the hot gases themselves (radiation front).

Firebee: An Air Force remotely piloted drone, currently deployed and designated AQM-34M. Firebees have a preprogrammed digital computer, with a doppler guidance system. They are 30 ft long, have a wingspan of 14 1/2 ft, and have a maximum launch weight of 3,100 lb. Eighteen AQM-34 Firebee drones were reactivated for tests of the **over-the-horizon (OTH)** backscatter and north warning radar systems. The first was successfully tested in September 1987. The drones, which were stored at the Warner Robins Air Logistics Center, GA for 10 years, are being used by the 6514th Test Squadron at Hill AFB, UT. The prime contractor is Teledyne Ryan Aeronautical.

fire control: Equipment required and used to directly aim guns or control missiles to fly at a particular target. Fire control equipment includes all instruments used in calculating and adjusting the proper elevation and deflection of guns and missiles in flight, including radars, telescopes, range finders, predictors, directors, other computers, power plants, and communication control systems connecting the elements.

Firefinder: An army radar system that enables friendly forces to locate and bring immediate fire upon enemy mortar, artillery, and rocket-launching positions to silence them before they can adjust their fire on friendly units and positions. The two types of Firefinders are the AN/TPQ-37 Artillery Locating Radar and the AN/TPQ-36 mortar Locating Radar.

Firefinder radars are the world's first automatic hostile-weapon-locating systems. They use advanced phased array antenna techniques complete with computer-controlled signal processing. Firefinder radars function by spotting enemy projectiles in flight and mathematically backplotting their trajectory. The position of the weapon is reported in grid coordinates that can be fed automatically into artillery fire direction centers, enabling them to target enemy weapons with guns, rockets, or other ordnance. Upon fielding of the **Army Data Distribution System (ADDS)**, the link from the radars to fire direction centers will pass this position data on a nearly real-time basis. In tests, both radars, in combination with fire control devices, enabled an artillery unit to have accurate counterfire on the way before the first enemy projectile struck the ground. In actual combat action in Lebanon (1984), the Mortar Locating Radar performed equal to or better than the test results. Each Army division is being equipped with two artillery-locating radars and three mortar-locating radars. Fielding of the two types of radars to the active Army was completed in 1987. Completion of fielding to the reserves is scheduled for July 1990. A Firefinder II is under development and will upgrade the current system to a more capable radar on a single vehicle. The prime contractor is Hughes Aircraft, Fullerton, CA.

fire storm: Stationary mass fire, generally in built-up urban areas, generating strong, inrushing winds from all sides, which keep the fires from spreading while adding fresh oxygen to increase its intensity.

fire support vehicle: Model designation M981. Army target acquisition vehicle, laser designator, and range finder mounted on a modified M113 armored personnel carrier. Over 700 are deployed in artillery units.

firing system: The system of components in a nuclear weapon that converts (if necessary), stores, and releases electrical energy to detonate the weapon when commanded by the fuzing system.

First Special Operations Command (1st SOCOM):   Army **Major Command** subordinate to **Forces Command** and the Army's service component command of **U.S. Special Operations Command**. It was established 6 October 1983 to oversee Army special operations revitalization, including training, doctrine and contingency planning, and assistance to unified and specified commands (except for those counterterror forces assigned to the **Joint Special Operations Command**). 1st SOCOM exercises responsibility for the Army **Special Forces**, the **Rangers, psychological operations** groups, **civil affairs** groups, **Task Force 160**, and the John F. Kennedy Special Warfare Center and School. [U.S. Army, *SOF Master Plan,* 4 April 1984, pp. V-4–5, released under the FOIA].

Headquarters
Ft. Bragg, NC 23824

first strike: "The first offensive move of a war. (Generally associated with nuclear operations)" [*JCS Pub 1,* p. 147].

first use: The initial employment of nuclear weapons in response to a conventional attack. U.S. Secretary of Defense James Schlesinger publicly declared the U.S. no-first-use policy on 30 May 1975, and it remains a part of current NATO **flexible response** strategy as articulated in the **General Political Guidelines for the Employment of Nuclear Weapons in Defense of NATO**. In July 1982, at the U.N. Second Special Session on Disarmament, the Soviet Union unilaterally pledged that it would not be the first to use nuclear weapons, and expected other nations to do the same.

fiscal year (FY): The period beginning 1 October and ending 30 September.

FISINT (see **foreign instrumentation signals intelligence**)

fission: The process whereby the nucleus of a particular heavy element (isotope of plutonium or uranium) splits into (generally) two nuclei of lighter elements, with the release of a substantial amount of energy. For this to happen, the atom must be inherently unstable — its nuclear binding forces must be inadequate to hold it together. Uranium-238 is stable in normal circumstances and can absorb low-energy neutrons without splitting, though under great heat it will undergo **fusion**. Uranium-235 is unstable even in its natural state, since it has three neutrons fewer than U-238 and neutrons are essential to the nuclear binding process. A few U-235 atoms disintegrate spontaneously at any one moment, emitting neu-

trons and pure energy in the form of gamma rays. Other fissile elements are plutonium and thorium-232, which decays into U-233. Fission is also used for nuclear power generation: a slow release of energy is obtained by using a mixture of uranium with about three percent U-235. The most common way to control the reaction is to insert and/or withdraw graphite rods to absorb the radioactivity. Fission provides the trigger for fusion weapons. A fission weapon is a nuclear warhead that applies fission. A chemical explosive detonation creates the critical mass needed to create an explosion. The complete fission of one pound of fissionable material would have a yield equivalent to 8,000 tons of TNT.

Five-Year Defense Program (FY-DP): The official document that summarizes the Secretary of Defense-approved programs for DOD. It is a detailed compilation of the total resources (forces, manpower, procurement, construction, research and development, and dollars) programmed for DOD, structured along two dimensions: 11 **Major Force Programs (MFPs)** and the **program element** appropriation categories. Annexes to the FYDP provide additional information on procurement, construction, and research, development, testing, and evaluation. The dual organization allows for both internal DOD and Congressional review. The FYDP projects five years for all data except forces, which extend an additional three years. The Assistant Secretary of Defense (Comptroller) maintains the FYDP.

It is updated three times each year, to reflect the president's budget, the service **Program Objective Memoranda**, and the Service budget estimate submissions.

fixed-price incentive contract: Type of procurement contract that provides for the adjustment of profit and price according to the difference between the estimated cost and the final, total cost.

fixed-price type contract: Type of procurement contract that generally provides for a firm price, although it may provide for an adjustable price in certain circumstances.

flag officer: Army, Marine, or Air Force officer above the rank of Colonel, or Navy or U.S. Coast Guard officer above the rank of Captain. A flag officer is equivalent to a **general officer** or **Admiral** and is authorized to fly a personal flag.

flag plot: "A tactical and navigation center located in a space adjacent to the flag bridge and used by the flag officer and his staff in evaluating current tactical and strategic information" [*NWP3*]. (see also **combat information center**)

flagship: The ship for which an Admiral or other **task organization** commander exercises command.

flaming arrow: U.S. Air Forces Europe (USAFE) UHF communications network used for nuclear weapons command, control, and communications. The Army is planning to upgrade flaming arrow and to provide SHF-receive capability.

FLASH: 1. Regarding communications, a **precedence** category assigned to a message to indicate the relative order and speed at which it is to be communicated. Usually reserved for initial enemy contact messages of extreme urgency, FLASH messages are marked "ZZ" and are to be handled "as fast as possible (less than 10 minutes)." (see also **Immediate, Priority, Routine**) **2.** In the Navy, the Force Level Alerting System, which receives correlated real-time radar track and uses the OPS-83 expert system language to identify potential threat situations. FLASH considers different factors and informs the battlegroup commander on whether the battlegroup is undetected, generally located, or targeted by enemy forces. FLASH also allows specific alert conditions to be set by the user. The complete FLASH system will have over 2,000 rules, supplemented by the capabilities of OPS-83. The goal is to have FLASH perform 20–30 rule firings per second, but it is likely that in some situations over 10,000 rules per second will be needed. In January 1986, FLASH was installed on the USS Carl Vinson. The system was developed by Carnegie-Mellon University and the Naval Ocean Systems Center. **3.** Regarding nuclear weapons, the intense pulse of heat and light emitted by a nuclear explosion.

flash burn: A burn caused by excessive exposure (of bare skin) to thermal radiation.

fleet: Naval organization composed of ships, aircraft, Marines, and shore-based fleet activities. Area fleets of the U.S. Navy are the **Atlantic Fleet** and the **Pacific Fleet**. Each fleet commander-in-chief exercises his authority through two separate chains of command: the type (administrative) chain of command and the task fleet (operational) command chain. The area fleet commanders thus have **operational command** and **administrative command** over assigned forces. Numbered fleets are operationally subordinate to area fleets; they are the **2d Fleet** in the western Atlantic; the **3d Fleet** in the eastern and northeastern Pacific; the **5th Fleet** in the Indian Ocean; the **6th Fleet** in the Mediterranean; and the **7th Fleet** in the western and northwestern Pacific.

fleet air wing: Composite Navy administrative unit that includes patrol squadrons and land- and carrier-based aircraft, with supporting units.

fleet ballistic missile (FBM):   Shipborne **ballistic missile**, either **Polaris, Poseidon**, or **Trident**, designed to be carried by strategic submarines often referred to as "FBM submarines."

fleet ballistic missile submarine (SSBN):   Nuclear-powered submarine designed to deliver **ballistic missiles** from either a submerged or surfaced condition.

Fleet Marine Force (FMF):   Marine Corps organization, assigned as an operating force of the Navy for the conduct of amphibious assault operations. An FMF is composed of a **Marine division**, a **Marine aircraft wing**, force troops, and a **force service support group**. FMFs are an integral part of the Atlantic and Pacific Fleets and function as naval "type" commands (i.e., they are responsible for particular types of ships or operations). FMFs are under the operational control of the Fleet commanders and under the administrative control of the Commandant of the Marine Corps (CMC), unless they are assigned to unified combatant commanders. A reserve Division/Wing team is also maintained by the Marine Corps to be an FMF but is not now assigned to an existing FMF. (see also **Fleet Marine Force Atlantic, Fleet Marine Force Pacific, Marine Air-Ground Task Force**)

Fleet Marine Force Atlantic (FMFLANT):   Service component command of **U.S. Atlantic Command**; one of five type commands of the Navy's **Atlantic Fleet**; and a Marine Corps **major command**. The Commanding General reports to the Commandant of the Marine Corps on all training, readiness, and administrative matters, and to the Commander-in-Chief Atlantic Fleet on all operational matters. In wartime, FMFLANT provides forces to the **II Marine Expeditionary Force (II MEF)**, and its Commander assumes the role of commander of the II MEF. FMFLANT also has limited type command responsibilities to **U.S. Naval Forces Europe**. Its personnel strength is approximately 40,000.

Headquarters
Norfolk, VA 23511

Fleet Oilers

	Cimarron (AO-177)	Ashtabula (AO-51)
Number active	5	2
Displacement (tons)	27,500 (full)	34,750 (full)
Length (ft)	592	644
Beam (ft)	88	75
Speed (kt)	20	18
Cargo Capacity (barrels)	120,000	143,000
Complement	215	372
Aircraft	None	None; but small area for vertical replenishment
Builder	Avondale Shipyards, LA	Bethlehem Steel, MD
Commissioned	1981–83	1945

Subordinate Commands

- 2d Marine Division, Camp Lejeune, NC 28542
- 2d Marine Aircraft Wing, Cherry Point, NC 28533
- 2d Force Service Support Group, Camp Lejeune, NC 28542

Fleet Marine Force Pacific (FMF-PAC): Service component command of **U.S. Pacific Command**; one of six type commands of the Navy's Pacific Fleet; and a Marine Corps **major command**. It was originally established in 1933 and was redesignated as FMFPAC in 1944. Today, it is the largest single Marine Corps command, with its force consisting of two of the three active Marine divisions and two of three active aircraft wings. The Commanding General reports to the Commandant of the Marine Corps on all training, readiness, and administrative matters, and to the Commander-in-Chief Pacific Fleet on all operational matters. In wartime, it provides forces to the **I Marine Expeditionary Force (I MEF)** and/or the

III Marine Expeditionary Force (MEF). Its commander is also the Commander, Marine Corps Bases, Pacific and is responsible for the management of all area camp, station, and base facilities reporting to the Pacific Command. Its personnel strength is approximately 72,000.

Headquarters
Camp H.M. Smith, HI 96602

Subordinate Commands

- 1st Marine Division, Camp Pendleton, CA 92055
- 1st Marine Air Wing, Iwakuni and Okinawa, Japan
- 1st Marine Brigade, Kaneohe Bay, HI 96868
- 3d Marine Division, Okinawa, Japan
- 3d Marine Aircraft Wing, MCAS El Toro, CA 92709

fleet oiler (AO): Navy conventionally powered ships that have the mission of operating as a unit of an **underway replenishment** group, furnishing replenishment of petroleum products to the fleet at sea. Oilers transport bulk petroleum and lubricants from depots to aircraft carrier battlegroup ships, effecting delivery and consolidation under way. In addition, they are support forces by alongside and/or vertical replenishment.

The Navy operates two classes of fleet oilers. It is also "jumboizing" all five ships of the Cimarron (AO-177) class. The AO Jumbo program is designed to increase the 120,000 barrel fuel capacity of these ships to 180,000 barrels. The FY 1990 funding request of $35.7 million will jumboize the last ship.

The number of Navy-manned fleet oilers has diminished, as more and more Military Sealift Command ships, all civilian-manned, have assumed responsibilities for supplying ships of the fleet. The Military Sealift Command oilers, designated T-AOs, have a similar mission of transporting petroleum products to forward-deployed, underway ships to make them as independent as possible of overseas fuel sources. The Military Sealift Command operates 11 oilers in three classes: Henry J. Kaiser (T-AO-187), Mispillion "jumboized" (T-AO-105), and Neosho (T-AO-143) classes. The Henry J. Kaiser class is under construction, with the lead ship delivered in September 1986. The Navy would like to procure 20 ships, and, as new oilers join the fleet, this will permit the retirement of some of the older Mispillion and Neosho class ships. The Kaiser class is a commercial version of the AO-177 class fleet oiler, with a 180,000 barrel capacity and a speed of up to 20 knots. The ships accommodate a

106 person Military Sealift Command crew; a Navy command, control, and communications team of 21 persons and 10 transient personnel. The ships are capable of replenishing from five stations simultaneously. Contractors are Avondale Shipyard, New Orleans, LA, and Pennsylvania Shipbuilding, Chester, PA. (see also **logistic ships**)

Fleet Satellite Communications System (FLTSATCOM): Navy **satellite communications** system that supplies data to Navy tactical mobile units for fleet operations. It also hosts the Air Force satellite communications systems (**AFSATCOM**). FLTSATCOM's basic mission is to provide the UHF and SHF anti-jam communications between all Navy ships and submarines, aircraft, and shore stations, as well as to connect the National Command Authority with field commanders. FLTSATCOM will be replaced by **MILSTAR**. FLTSATCOM consists of geosynchronous satellites that orbit over the equator to provide worldwide coverage except for the polar regions, where the **Satellite Data System** operates. Six UHF communication satellites of this generation were launched from Cape Canaveral, FL, by NASA Atlas-Centaur rockets, the first in February 1978 and the last on 25 September 1989.

FLTSATCOM has two communications support responsibilities. The first is the Submarine Satellite Information Exchange System (SSIXS), which is used for non-urgent shore-to-submarine broadcasting. FLTSATCOM in the SSIXS mode uses a teletype and cannot connect a submarine with another submarine or a surface vessel. FLTSATCOM's second communications option provides for direct ship-to-ship voice link when both ships are in line-of-sight of the same satellite. Conversations can only last less than one minute, since ships need to be prepared to receive higher-priority messages from ashore. FLTSATCOM overcomes HF transmission deficiencies by using the SHF/UHF band to conduct aircraft, ship, submarine, and ground communications. The ground portion of FLTSATCOM consists of communications links between fixed and mobile users, including most U.S. Navy ships, selected Air Force and Navy aircraft, and ground stations. Additionally, **acoustic intelligence** collected by systems including the **Sound Surveillance System (SOSUS)** is sent via FLTSATCOM to processing facilities. Twelve of the 23 UHF and SHF channels are used by the Air Force for communications between SAC and its bomber force and ICBM installations (AFSATCOM). Ten channels are for exclusive Navy use. One 500 KHz channel is reserved for the National Command Authorities.

The **Space and Naval Warfare Systems Command** has program management responsibility for FLTSATCOM, and the **Air Force Space Command** manages the acquisition of spacecraft for the program. The satellite consists of two major portions, each with a basic hexagonal body 7.5 ft in diameter and 4.17 ft high. The payload contains UHF and prototype EHF communications equipment and antennas. Weight at lift-off is 4,100 lb; 1,950 lb once in orbit. Each of

six side panels carry related communications components. A UHF transmit antenna, 16 ft in diameter, consists of an 80 inch solid center surrounded by a wire mesh screen that folds to fit inside the Atlas-Centaur. In orbit, the screen is opened by ground command and resembles an umbrella. Outside of the transmit antenna dish is a 13 ft spiral receive antenna, which is also folded inside the rocket until ground command unfolds it. Earth sensors, altitude and velocity controls, telemetry, tracking and command, electrical power and distribution, and the apogee kick motor equipment are carried in the spacecraft module. Primary electrical power is provided by two deployable solar array paddles that together provide 1200 watts. Three nickel-cadmium batteries provide power during an eclipse. The prime contractor is TRW.

A UHF follow-on series to FLTSATCOM known as UFO satellites, has been ordered from Hughes Aircraft. The Navy ordered one satellite, with an option for nine more. The first launch of the UFO satellites is planned for 1992. RDT&E and procurement costs for two FLTSATCOM satellites for FY 1990 is $328.7 million. The cost for three satellites in FY 1991 is $215.1 million.

Fleet Training Command: A Navy type organization operating within the two fleets and responsible for coordinating non-unit training:

- Training Command, Pacific Fleet, San Diego, CA 92147-5030
- Training Command, Atlantic Fleet, Norfolk, VA 23511-6597

flexible lightweight agile-guided experiment (FLAGE): Nine SDI experiments using **kinetic-energy weapons (KEW)** to intercept tactical ballistic missiles in the terminal stage. A small kinetic-energy weapon is fitted onto a Patriot surface-to-air missile or follow-on SAM. The original KEW, tested in 1986, was 12 ft long and guided by 216 solid rocket motors with its own radar and computer systems. The FLAGE prime contractor is LTV of Dallas. A modified version of the KEW is the **extended-range interceptor (ERINT)** with a nonnuclear fuzed warhead. FLAGE has possible applicability for the **Air Defense Initiative**. It has successfully used its radar and steering rockets to lock onto and destroy targets during tests.

flexible response: 1. "The capability of military forces for effective reaction to any enemy threat or attack with actions appropriate and adaptable to the circumstances existing" [*JCS Pub 1,* p. 149]. Also known as "flexible response counterforce," this is the basis of U.S. strategic nuclear employment policy.   **2.** NATO's official strategy, which, in 1967, replaced that of massive retaliation. The NATO communiqué describing flexible response, *Overall Strategic Concept for the Defense of the North Atlantic Treaty Organization Area* (MC 14/3), of NATO's Military Committee, calls for "a flexible and balanced range of appropriate responses, conventional and nuclear, to all levels of aggression or threats of aggression. These responses, subject to appropriate political control, are designed, first to deter aggression and thus preserve peace; but should

aggression unhappily occur, to maintain the security of the North Atlantic Treaty area within the concept of forward defense." Flexible response calls for three types and levels of response to enemy aggression: direct defense, deliberate escalation, and general nuclear response.

- *Direct Defense:* "Meet initially any aggression short of general nuclear attack with a direct defense at the level chosen by the aggressor. This may include the use of nuclear weapons, if the enemy were the first to use such weapons. The theory is that as a result, either the aggression fails or the burden of escalation is placed upon the aggressor."
- *Deliberate Escalation:* "Conduct a deliberate escalation if aggression cannot be contained and the situation restored by direct defense." Repulse an attack by persuading the aggressor to take the political decision to cease hostilities, since his prospects of success and the risk he is running are no longer in an acceptable ratio. As a potential means of convincing the aggressor of such a fact, the Alliance preserves the option of the selective use of nuclear weapons, including the "first use" of nuclear weapons.
- *General Nuclear Response:* "Initiate an appropriate general nuclear response to a major nuclear attack." Escalation against the aggressor's strategic potential and means using the Alliance's strategic nuclear weapons.

(see also **General Political Guidelines for the Employment of Nuclear Weapons in Defense of NATO, PD-59**)

flight: **1.** Basic tactical air unit in the Air Force, consisting of four or more aircraft in two or more elements and subordinate to a **squadron**. **2.** Specified group of Navy or Marine Corps aircraft, usually engaged in a common mission. **3.** Single aircraft airborne on a nonoperational mission. (see also **sortie**)

flimsy: **1.** Formerly, the preliminary draft report on a JCS paper, prepared by a Joint Staff Directorate and circulated to action officers for comment and recommendation. In July 1985, the flimsy stage was replaced by new JCS rules for handling draft reports. **2.** Formerly, an information memorandum to the JCS used primarily to propose changes to JCS paper when time does not permit submission of a slant.

FLIR (see **forward-looking infrared (FLIR) system**)

flotilla: Naval administrative or tactical organization composed of two or more squadrons of destroyers or smaller types, plus additional ships as assigned. Archaic term—more commonly referred to as a "group."

FLT (see **fleet**)

FLTSATCOM (see **Fleet Satellite Communications System**)

flyaway cost: The total recurring and nonrecurring procurement expenditures required to produce the primary and secondary mission equipment, excluding production base support and modifications. Within the individual weapon-system line item in the budget, the costs related to the production of usable end items of military hardware are commonly referred to as "flyaway cost." Also called "rollaway cost" and "sailaway cost" for vehicles and ships, respectively, and "mission equipment cost" for other classes of hardware.

focal point: Communications system, liaison, and joint operations between the Central Intelligence Agency and the DOD dealing with matters relating to special operations and intelligence.

FOG-M (see **Fiber Optics-Guided Missile**)

Follow-On Forces Attack (FOFA): NATO doctrine of theater-conducted operations designed to destroy, disrupt, or delay all enemy forces not directly engaged at **forward line of own troops (FLOT)**. The doctrine was developed in 1979 under the direction of Supreme Allied Commander Europe (SACEUR) General Rogers. Formally referred to as a sub-concept of operations, FOFA was approved by the Defense Planning Committee in November 1984 and has been accepted by the United States. FOFA locates and tracks Warsaw Pact troops from the initial deployment to commitment and attacks these forces when and where they are most vulnerable. FOFA also calls for the exploitation of Warsaw Pact vulnerabilities in the reinforcement process, inflexibility of plans, dense forces on limited attack routes, and dependence on rail transportation systems.

NATO Long Term Planning Guidelines define improvements for locating and engaging troops from 50–500 km. With its theater orientation, FOFA is heavily dependent on the use of air assets and is compatible with **airland battle** doctrine.

Airland Battle	Follow On Forces Attack
corps and below	
Focus	theater
tactical/operational	
Level	operational/strategic
war fighting	
Emphasis	deterrence
near-term battle	
Impact	affect on war
decentralized	
Air	centralized
worldwide	
Use	NATO only

Follow-On To Lance (FOTL): Army program to replace the **Lance** missile. Begun in FY 1989, it is a major new program to meet requirements predating the **INF Treaty**. The FOTL will replace the Lance with a modern, longer-range system (just under the minimum range permitted by the INF Treaty). Current plans call for the use of the **Multiple-Launch Rocket System (MLRS)** M270 type launcher for the FOTL. The Army was previously considering the **Army Tactical Missile System (ATACMS)** as a potential FOTL, but this option was rejected in 1988. It is now considering five different models as a potential new missile: a derivative of the **Pershing** missile; a derivative of the **Patriot** surface-to-air missile; the French Hades short-range nuclear missile; an upgraded Lance missile; and a completely new missile.

football: Nickname for the briefcase containing the nuclear weapons release codes and attack options. The football is carried at all times by a military aide to the President who is assigned to the White House Military Office.

Footlight: Secure communications system operated by the National Security Agency/Central Security Service (NSA/CSS) and the Army Communications Command. NSA/CSS is the Footlight project manager.

forces afloat: The several active and reserve fleets, the **Military Sealift Command**, the **Coast Guard** (when operating as a service in the Navy), special duty ships and craft and specialized units, and other fleets and forces as assigned by the Secretary of the Navy.

Forces Command (FORSCOM): U.S. **specified command** (as of 26 July 1987); Army **major command**; and, for planning purposes, the Army component command of **U.S. Atlantic Command**. Its primary mission is to organize, equip, train, and maintain the combat readiness of assigned units within CONUS, and, on order, mobilize and deploy these forces in support of the **combatant commands**. Additional missions, partly assumed from the deactivated U.S. Readiness Command (REDCOM), include primary responsibility for the defense of CONUS and Alaska; coordination with Canada for the defense of North America; military support to civil authorities in **civil defense** and **civil**

disturbance operations; and protection of key assets. The FORSCOM Commanding General is charged with the administrative and operational command of the six numbered armies within CONUS, together with the numerous CONUS-based commands, combat organizations, and facilities assigned to the Department of the Army within the United States, territories and possessions, and the Republic of Panama. The Commanding General also commands the U.S. **Army Reserve**, supervises training of the **Army National Guard**, and is designated Commander-in-Chief, **U.S. Army Forces, Atlantic**. FORSCOM is the largest DOD command, with an active personnel strength of 326,000 military and civilian personnel. Its reserve strength is 288,000 personnel, plus an additional 450,000 Army National Guard personnel, when mobilized.

Headquarters
Ft. McPherson, GA 30050

Continental
United States Armies (CONUSA)

- 1st Army, Ft. Meade, MD 22427
- 2d Army, Ft. Gillem, GA 30050
- 3d Army, Ft. McPherson, GA 30050
- 4th Army, Ft. Sheridan, IL 60037
- 5th Army, Ft. Houston, TX 78234
- 6th Army, Presidio of San Francisco, CA 94129

Commanders-in-Chief,
Forces Command

- GEN Joseph T. Palastra, Jr.
1 July 1987–4 Apr 1989

- GEN Colin L. Powell
4 Apr 1989–27 Sep 1989
- GEN Edwin H. Burba, Jr.
27 Sep 1989–present

force service support group (FSSG): Basic service and combat support organization of the Marine Corps. An FSSG operates as a component of a **Marine Expeditionary Force** and as an organic element of the two **Fleet Marine Forces**. There are three FSSGs, one organic to FMF Atlantic and two organic to FMF Pacific. An FSSG is typically composed of a headquarters and service battalion; a maintenance battalion; a supply battalion; an engineer support battalion; a motor transport battalion; a medical battalion; a dental company; and a landing support battalion. Personnel strength is approximately 10,000 Marine Corps and Navy personnel.

force structure: "Numbers, size, and composition of the units that comprise our Defense forces; e.g., divisions, ships, airwings" [*JCS Pub 1*, p. 229]. As used by the DOD, force structure is an element of **military capability** that also includes modernization, readiness, and sustainability. The force structure is based upon the DOD's **Total Force** policy and consists of active, reserve, civilian, retired, and host nation forces. The programmed force structure refers to the composite of units and organizations that exists for each year of the **Five-Year Defense Program (FYDP)**, including the major combat and tactical support forces expected to meet U.S. strategic and security objectives [DOD. *Manpower Requirements Report FY 1989*, Mar 1988, p. B-3]. (see also **manpower**)

forcible entry: The use of military forces, ranging from an administrative unopposed landing in order to conduct police-type operations to an outright invasion under a state of war.

Foreign Assistance Act of 1961 (FAA): Congressional act signed into law on 4 September 1961 (PL 87-195, Title 22, various sections) that serves as the legal guidance for U.S. foreign aid and security assistance programs. As amended, the act:

- *Part I:* Establishes policy on U.S. economic and humanitarian assistance to other nations and authorizes such aid.
- *Part II:* Authorizes military assistance, **international military education and training (IMET), Foreign Military Sales (FMS)**, economic support, air base construction, and peacekeeping support to eligible countries and international organizations.
- *Part III:* Provides for private participation in the foreign assistance program and outlines the responsibilities for the administration of the program.

The Hughes-Ryan Amendment (§2422) places limitations on intelligence activities by stating that "no funds appropriated under the authority of this or any other Act may be expended by or on behalf of the Central Intelligence Agency for operations in foreign countries" except when authorized by the President by the proper process. (see also **commercial sales, Office of Munitions Control**)

Foreign Broadcast Information Service (FBIS): Central Intelligence Agency-operated organization that monitors open commercial and governmental radio transmissions worldwide for the purpose of producing foreign intelligence information. Clandestine radio networks are also monitored. FBIS does not monitor internal governmental and military radio transmissions, which remain the responsibility of the National Security Agency and the service cryptologic authorities.

foreign instrumentation signals intelligence (FISINT): Category of **electronics intelligence** information collected by the interception of electromagnetic emissions (e.g., signals from telemetry, fuzing, arming, command systems, and video data links). FISINT includes emissions from the testing and operational deployment of aerospace, surface, and subsurface systems. **Telemetry intelligence (TELINT)** is a subcategory of FISINT [Jeffrey Richelson, *The U.S. Intelligence Community*, 2d Edition, p. 169].

Foreign Intelligence Surveillance Act (FISA) of 1978: Congressional act signed into law 25 October 1978 and into full effect 16 August 1979 (50 U.S. Code §§1801-11). FISA outlines the procedures by which government agencies are authorized to covertly collect foreign intelligence information from "foreign powers," "agents of a foreign power," and U.S. persons, who knowingly engage in hostile and clandestine intelligence activities, sabotage, or international terrorism on behalf of a foreign power. The law was proposed by the Department of Justice following the Church and Pike Committees hearings in order to ensure the ability of the U.S. government to conduct electronic surveillance against hostile foreign forces operating within the United States. "Foreign intelligence information" is defined as that information with respect to a foreign power relating to "the national defense or the security of the United States; or the conduct of the foreign affairs of the United States"; and that information relating to the "ability of the U.S. to protect against:

(A) actual or potential attack or other grave hostile acts of a foreign power or an agent of a foreign power;

(B) sabotage or international terrorism by a foreign power or an agent of a foreign power; or

(C) clandestine intelligence activities by an intelligence service or network of a foreign power or an agent of a foreign power."

Government intelligence agencies wishing to collect intelligence on an individual for purposes outlined above must apply for surveillance approval through the Office of Intelligence Policy and Review of the Department of Justice. In turn, all FISA applications are made to a specially designated court with national jurisdiction, the Foreign Intelligence Surveillance Court (FISC), which grants or denies the requests. The Court con-

sists of seven U.S. District Court judges assigned by the Chief Justice, on a rotational basis. Emergency applications may be made to an available court judge. In addition, three federal judges comprise the Foreign Intelligence Court of Review, to review FISA application appeals. FISA orders relating to foreign powers or agents are granted for a term of one year; all others are limited to a period of up to 90 days (subject to extension). According to the law, the Attorney General may approve certain types of electronic surveillance activities that only involve communications used exclusively between foreign governments or factions, or technical intelligence not involving spoken communications and not involving U.S. persons. Following a declaration of war, the President through the Attorney General may authorize electronic surveillance without a court order for a period of up to 15 days.

FISA Orders Granted

1979 (May–Dec):	199
1980:	319
1981:	431
1982:	473
1983:	549
1984:	635
1985:	587
1986:	573
1987:	512
1988:	534

The number of approved FISA applications does not necessarily reflect the number of surveillance targets, as more than one order may be issued for a single surveillance (due to surveillance of a target at more than one location, or extensions of an order) [Mary C. Lawton, Counsel for Intelligence Policy, Office of Intelligence Policy and Review, Department of Justice, House Subcommittee on Courts, Civil Liberties, and the Administration of Justice, 8 June 1983].

Foreign Internal Defense (FID): "Participation by civilian and military agencies of a government in any of the action programs taken by another government to free and protect its society from subversion, lawlessness, and insurgency." As one aspect of **special operations**, FID activities include: "nation building," military/paramilitary training, intelligence, **psychological operations**, and **civil affairs** operations [*JCS Pub 1*, p. 152]. FID operations are

- Performed in remote, urban, or rural environments during peacetime and wartime to promote national and regional stability;
- Involve the use of political, economic, psychological, and military powers of a government to defeat an insurgency;
- Operations where Special Forces engaged in FID are oriented toward the development and training of military organizations; and
- Operations where Special Forces mobile training teams organize, train, and advise host country military and paramilitary forces.

Foreign Military Construction Sales (FMCS):   A part of the **Foreign Military Sales (FMS) security assistance program** of loans and grants to

foreign countries for defense-related purchases from the U.S. government or private U.S. firms. For some countries, mostly in the Middle East and North and East Africa, portions of the FMS budget are earmarked for purchases related specifically to military-related construction, as opposed to purchases of weapons systems or combat support equipment. Since FY 1987, portions of the FMS grant or loan have been *post facto* described as FMSC in the case of Egypt, Saudi Arabia, El Salvador, Honduras, Central African Republic, Djibouti, Kenya, Madagascar, and Somalia.

Foreign Military Sales (FMS):   A **security assistance program** that provides for the sale of major military equipment by the U.S. government to foreign governments for cash or credit. FMS is a government-to-government weapons supply program under which the U.S. government resells weapons systems from private companies to foreign governments. It also includes sales of military construction services under the **Foreign Military Construction Sales (FMCS)** program. A significant proportion of FMS transactions involve mixed-use systems (i.e., equipment that is usable for both external and internal security operations), or weapons intended exclusively for paramilitary purposes. Such equipment is often sold to military forces that perform civil security functions under martial law decree, or to paramilitary organizations with an exclusive internal-security function. The use of FMS channels for sales of this sort is permitted under Section

4 of the **Arms Export Control Act**, which states that "defense articles and defense services shall be sold by the United States Government . . . for internal security [and] legitimate self-defense." The largest recipients of FMS are Israel, Egypt, Jordan, Pakistan, Turkey, Greece and, in the Third World, El Salvador, Honduras, Indonesia, Morocco, the Philippines, and Thailand.

Foreign Military Sales Credit: A **security assistance program** synonymous and commonly used interchangeably with **Foreign Military Sales (FMS)** to refer to concessional-interest rate loans or grants the U.S. government makes to cash-poor nations to facilitate arms purchases.

Foreign Military Sales Debt Reform/Restructuring: A type of financing for **security assistance programs** established in 1986 to redress the debt burden incurred by developing countries' **Foreign Military Sales (FMS)** loans for defense-related purchases. In 1987, Congress approved a debt-reform plan after an unsuccessful 1986 Administration initiative that offered FMS loan recipients a refinancing plan of either prepaying high-interest FMS loans or restructuring the repayment schedule so that a portion of the loans would be capitalized for repayment with interest when the loan matures. The debt refinancing plan permits countries to refinance outstanding FMS loans that fall due after September 1989 and that carry an interest rate of 10 percent or above. The legislation limits the guarantee to 90 percent of the total amount refinanced and establishes a new 90-day deadline on FMS arrears for countries that participate in the program. Countries whose arrears exceed the 90-day deadline face a cutoff of all U.S. assistance until they make up their arrears. The law permits countries to refinance through FY 1991. To date, the principal beneficiaries of this program tend to be the recipients of the largest security assistance packages: Israel, Jordan, and Turkey [Department of State, *Congressional Presentation of Security Assistance Program,* FY 1990, p. 40].

Foreign Military Sales Financing (FMSF): The financing system of the **Foreign Military Sales (FMS)** program, developed in response to the foreign debt accrued in the 1970s by Third World and Middle Eastern countries that participated in FMS but were unable to meet scheduled interest payments on loans. In order to pay cash for commercial and government sales of defense articles, these countries were forced to take out high-interest loans. FMSF was initiated in its previous form in the Mutual Defense Security Act of 1954 and continued in the **Foreign Assistance Act** of 1961. In 1971, credit financing exceeded grant assistance for the first time. In 1976, the **Arms Export Control Act (AECA)** consolidated existing government and commercial sales legislation. The AECA provided for authorization of FMSF direct loans and guaranteed loans. In 1985, FMSF was restructured into two forms of loans, forgiven loans and concessional- (low-) interest rate loans. FMS loans to Israel and Egypt are fully forgiven. Loans to Pakistan and Turkey are partially forgiven. The FY 1990 security assistance requests to Congress ask for the entire FMS budget request of $5.027 billion to be appropriated as grants to finance commercial purchases not possible under the **Military Assistance Program (MAP)** [Department of State, *Congressional Presentation of Security Assistance Program, FY 1990,* p. 11].

Forest Green: Code name for the program of sensors aboard **Nuclear Detonation Detection System** satellites that are capable of detecting high-energy, laser, and particle beam attacks.

formerly restricted data (FRD): Type of classified information designated by the DOD and DOE. It applies to weapons "information removed from the **restricted data** category upon a joint determination by the DOE (or antecedent agencies) and DOD that such information relates primarily to the military utilization of atomic weapons and that such information can be adequately safeguarded as classified defense information. (Section 142d, Atomic Energy Act of 1954, as amended.)" For example, specific locations of nuclear weapons storage sites and information on the presence of nuclear weapons are generally classified at the confidential formerly restricted data (CFRD) level [*JCS Pub 1; Joint DOE/DOD Nuclear Weapons Classification Guide,*] CG-W-5, January 1984, released under the FOIA]. (see also **security classification, Sigma**)

For Official Use Only (FOUO): Control marking applied by the DOD to unclassified or declassified information and material "which have been determined to require protection from disclosure to the general public, and which for a significant reason should not be given general circulation" [Department of the Army. *Safeguarding 'For Official Use Only' Information.* AR 340-16, 26 June 1973, p. 1, released under the FOIA]. (See also **security classification**)

Forward Area Air Defense System (FAADS): An Army air defense weapon system intended to protect Army maneuver elements on the battlefield from attack. It is specifically intended to fight in the division area, in and near the places where tanks and infantry fighting vehicles are in contact with enemy forces. The system is composed of five major elements: the Line of Sight–Forward component (the air defense antitank system—ADATS); the Line of Sight–Rear component (the pedestal-mounted Stinger—PMS); the Non–Line of Sight component (the **Fiber Optic-Guided Missile—(FOG-M)**; the FAAD Command, Control, and Intelligence component; and the Combined Arms Initiative (CAI).

The FAADS was created in reaction to the termination of the Sergeant York air defense gun system by the Secretary of Defense in August 1985. After the cancellation, the Army working group that studied the nature of the total air threat concluded that the Army needed an affordable and quickly available weapon system to counter the threat and that the system should be capable of expansion through preplanned product improvement to keep ahead of the air threat as it evolves. It is believed that by the mid-1990s, the Warsaw Pact will have electronic warfare aircraft that can stand off beyond 10 km and jam U.S. communications and air defense radars. These stand-off jammers will be capable of supporting air operations that will be carried out by helicopters, planes, and unmanned aircraft. The helicopters will be able to use terrain masking to find attack positions from which they will deliver an increasingly lethal arsenal of stand-off antitank weapons or begin strafing runs with guns and rockets. Planes will continue to be a significant threat to friendly forces on the battlefield and to facilities in the division, corps, and theater rear. Unmanned aerial vehicles will attempt to decoy air defense weapons and provide the enemy commander a significant reconnaissance ability.

The Army is acquiring the FAADS as quickly as it can, using nondevelopmental items (NDI) where possible to accelerate the process. Individual components of the system will be fielded as they become available. On 30 November 1987, the Army announced the selection of the air defense antitank system (ADATS) as the line-of-sight forward, heavy (LOS-F-H) component of FAADS. ADATS is a laser beam rider missile system designed specifically to counter the low-level flying helicopter and plane threats and is mounted on the M3A1 Bradley cavalry fighting vehicle chassis. The system has a crew of three: a driver, a commander, and a gunner. Targets are detected using the on-board search radar; the target track is established using either **forward-looking-infrared (FLIR)** or TV sensors; and the eight ready-to-fire missiles are guided to the target using a carbon dioxide laser. ADATS can be employed autonomously or as part of FAADS. The component is scheduled to undergo extensive technical and operational testing in the fall of 1989, when a decision to enter full-scale production will be made. The Army plans to buy 562 systems, with the first unit to be equipped in FY 1992. ADATS was developed by Martin Marietta Corporation in cooperation with Oerlikon-Buehrle of Switzerland for deployment with Canadian forces.

The pedestal-mounted Stinger (PMS) is the line of sight-rear component of FAADS needed to counter planes attacking targets in the division rear or passing through to attack deeper targets. An NDI acquisition, PMS will be the first element of FAADS fielded. The system mounts eight Stinger missiles and a .50 caliber machine gun on the high-mobility, multipurpose wheeled vehicle (HMMWV). A FLIR device, laser range finder, and missile seeker display are integrated into the fire control system. The first production units will be delivered in the first quarter of fiscal 1989, with initial fielding in the third quarter. This PMS system, also known as Avenger, is manufactured by the Boeing Aerospace Company. The Army plans to buy 1,207 units.

The non-line of sight (NLOS) component of FAADS will be capable of defeating terrain-masked helicopters and armored ground targets while firing from hidden, protected positions. The system developed to prove basic technological principles is the fiber optic-guided missile (FOG-M).

FAAD Command, Control, and Intelligence (C^2I) element integrates FAADS components into a synergistic system by providing rapid and reliable targeting, air situation information, and air battle management information. FAAD C^2I will assist in planning, directing, coordinating, and controlling the FAAD. FAAD C^2I consists of four separate but interrelated efforts: C^2 hardware and software, ground based sensor, mass target sensors, and positive hostile identification equipment. The C^2, Ground Based Sensor, and passive identification components are scheduled for initial fielding in FY 1993. The FAAD C^2I Software contractor is TRW, Redondo Beach, CA.

The Combined Armed Initiative (CAI) provides ground and aerial combat elements an enhanced capability for self-defense against enemy helicopters. Air-to-air Stinger is in production for the OH-58C/D helicopter. A **Bradley Fighting Vehicle** sight reticle was changed to allow improved viewing and was cut into the production line in May 1987. Engineering development to provide 120 mm tank ammunition for anti-helicopter capability continues. Total cost of the FAADS program is approximately $11.5 billion.

forward-based system (FBS): A term originally introduced by the Soviet Union during the **SALT** negotiations to refer to those U.S. nuclear systems based in Europe or on aircraft carriers with less than intercontinental range but capable of delivering a nuclear strike against Soviet territory. U.S. FBSs include **F-111** and other fighters land-based in Europe, and **A-6** and **A-7** attack aircraft on aircraft carriers in the northern Atlantic and in the Mediterranean Sea.

forward edge of the battle area (FEBA): The foremost limits of a series of areas in which ground combat units are deployed, excluding the areas in which the covering or screening forces are operating. Designated to coordinate fire support, the positioning of forces, or the maneuver of units.

forward line of own troops (FLOT): A line that indicates the most forward positions of friendly forces in any kind of military operation at a specific time.

forward-looking infrared (FLIR) system: An infrared imaging system that scans the scene viewed by internal means, both horizontally and vertically. FLIR systems can be mounted on satellites, air or ground vehicles, and ships. The field of view is determined by the optics used, the scanning mechanism, and the dimensions of the detector array.

forward operating base (FOB): An airfield used to support tactical operations without establishing full support facilities. The base may be used for an extended time period. Support by a main operating base will be required to provide backup support for a FOB [MAC, *Contingency Planning Policies and Procedures,* MACR 28-2, 29 December 1986, p. 103, released under the FOIA].

Forward Operating Location (FOL):   One of five sites for air-defense fighters under the North American Air Defense modernization program. Most of the work will be at Rankin Inlet; other sites include Inuvik, Yellowknife, Iqaluit, and Kuujjuaq in Canada.

Fourth Allied Tactical Air Force (FOURATAF):   NATO air organization assigned to **Allied Air Forces, Central Europe (AAFCE)**. It is responsible for the air defense of Central Europe, sharing its area with NATO's **Central Army Group**. Its assigned forces are provided by Canada, the United States, and West Germany. If French air units are provided to NATO in the region, they would be coordinated through FOURATAF. U.S. air assets placed in the United Kingdom primarily support FOURATAF. FOURATAF is commanded by a West German General, with an American Chief of Staff.

Headquarters
Heidelberg, W. Germany

fractionation: "The division of the payload of a missile into several warheads. The use of a MIRV [multiple independently targetable reentry vehicle] payload is an example of fractionation. The term 'fractionation limits' is used to describe the treaty limitations on the maximum number of reentry vehicles per missile" [ACDA, *SALT II: Glossary of Terms,* 1979].

fragmentary order (frag order):   A shorter type of **operations order (OPORD)**, usually issued on a day-to-day basis.

Freedom of Information Act (FOIA):   Congressional act signed into law on 6 September 1966 (5 U.S. Code §552). The act, significantly amended in 1974 and, most recently, by the Freedom of Information Reform Act of 1986, requires the release of certain government information to the public upon request. The FOIA applies to records held by agencies in the executive branch of the federal government. Elected officials of the federal government, including the President, Vice President, senators, congressmen, and the federal judiciary, are not subject to the law, nor does it apply to private companies, federal contractors, or state or local governments. Requests may be made for unclassified, nonclassified, declassified, or classified records. Submissions may also include a request for a full or partial waiver of fees incurred in the search, copying, or review of documents. Upon receipt of a request, the agency reviews the documents for their possible full or partial release. This review may involve the declassification or downgrading of a document (or portions) that are classified. Based upon this review, the agency either releases or denies the release of the documents and makes a determination regarding the costs to the requester or the waiver of fees, if applicable. A document that contains exempt portions is not necessarily exempt from disclosure in its entirety, as the agency is required to release any reasonably segregable portions of a record after the deletion of exempt portions. All determinations are subject to administrative appeal by the requester and court appeals may be sought. The "operational files" of the Central Intelligence Agency and other intelligence agencies are generally exempt from the FOIA, as provided in the **National Security Act**, as amended (50 U.S. Code §431). Agencies' records may be withheld from release based upon statutory protections of national security information. The Department of Energy generally invokes the atomic energy information protections contained within the **Atomic Energy Act of 1954**. The National Security Agency (NSA) frequently invokes provisions against disclosure of personnel and operations data from the National Security Agency Act of 1959 (50 U.S. Code §402 note, Section 6). Both the NSA and the Navy cite the statute that prohibits public disclosure of communications intelligence information (18 U.S. Code §798). The Air Force is the primary DOD organization that cites the statute that protects against the disclosure of "technical data with military or space application" potential or usefulness (10 U.S. Code §130). There are nine specific exemptions to the FOIA that can be applied to certain records in order to withhold their release, seven of which are used by the Department of Defense:

- (b)(1): Applies to material that is properly classified pursuant to an executive order in the interest of national defense or foreign policy (invoked in 11 percent of all initial determinations by DOD agencies during CY 1987);
- (b)(2): Applies to information that pertains solely to the internal rules and practices of the agency (invoked in 14 percent of all initial determinations by DOD agencies during CY 1987);
- (b)(3): Applies to the director's statutory obligations to protect from disclosure intelligence sources and methods, as well as the organization, functions, names, official titles, salaries, and numbers of personnel employed by the agency, in accord with the National Security Act of 1947 and the CIA Act of 1949, respectively (invoked in 4 percent of all initial determinations by DOD agencies during CY 1987);
- (b)(4): Applies to information such as trade secrets and commercial or financial information obtained from a person on a privileged or confidential basis (invoked in 15 percent of all initial determinations by DOD agencies during CY 1987);
- (b)(5): Applies to inter- and intra-agency memoranda that are advisory in nature (invoked in 20 percent of all initial determinations by DOD agencies during CY 1987);
- (b)(6): Applies to information the release of which would constitute an unwarranted invasion of the personal privacy of other individuals (invoked in 20 percent of all initial determinations by DOD agencies during CY 1987); and

• (b)(7): Applies to all records or information compiled for law enforcement purposes, but only to the extent that the production of such law enforcement records or information (a) could reasonably be expected to interfere with enforcement proceedings, (b) would deprive a person of a right to a fair trial or an impartial adjudication, (c) could reasonably be expected to constitute an unwarranted invasion of personal privacy, (d) could disclose the identity of a confidential source, (e) would disclose techniques and procedures for law enforcement investigation or prosecution, or (f) could reasonably be expected to endanger the life or physical safety of any individual (invoked in 15 percent of all initial determinations by DOD agencies during CY 1987).

In CY 1987, the Department of Defense and all its agencies processed 97,669 requests under the FOIA, 75 percent of requests were initially granted in some form, 7,483 were denied on the basis of one or more exemptions, and 16,210 were unfulfilled by the department for other reasons ("no record found," lack of specificity of the request, transferred to another agency, etc.). During the same period, 587 appeals were submitted, and, of those, 65 were granted in full, 202 were partially granted, and 315 were denied on appeal. Administrative cost for these requests was approximately $13,000,000, or approximately $140 per request [OAS-D(PA), *Department of Defense Freedom of Information Act Program CY87: Summary of the Report to Congress*].

frequency: "The number of cycles per second of an alternating current, a sound wave, or a vibrating object. The bands and channels are established to provide one standard system of frequency band designations for electromagnetic emissions and to facilitate the operational control of electronic emissions and interceptions. Frequencies of electromagnetic emissions are given in hertz. One hertz is equal to one cycle per second" [*NWP 3*].

Electronic countermeasures (ECM) and **radar** frequencies: "Standard bands are identified in alphabetical sequence. Each band is divided into ten numerical channels. The **phonetic alphabet** and numerical channel number will be used to identify the frequency of EW [**electronic warfare**] operations. To identify an exact frequency use the band/channel plus frequency in Mega-Hertz above the base frequency" [*NWP 3*].

Band	Frequency (MHz)	Channel Width (MHz)
A	0–250	25
B	250–500	25
C	500–1000	50
D	1000–2000	100
E	2000–3000	100
F	3000–4000	100
G	4000–6000	200
H	6000–8000	200
I	8000–10000	200
J	10000–20000	1000
K	20000–40000	2000
L	40000–60000	2000
M	60000–100000	4000

Radio Frequency

Band	*Frequency*
ELF	Below 3 kHz
VLF	3–30 kHz
LF	30–300 kHz
MF	300–3000 kHz
HF	3–30 MHz
VHF	30–300 MHz
UHF	300–3000 MHz
SHF	3–30 GHz
EHF	30–300 GHz

frigate (FF/FFG): Small Navy surface warship configured to escort and protect ships less important than aircraft carriers against surface, air, and submarine attack. There are about 100 active frigates in six classes: Bronstein, Garcia, Knox, Glover, Brooke, and Oliver Hazard Perry.

front burner: Flagword used on an **OPREP-3 PINNACLE** message to immediately report any occurrence having the potential of rapidly moving into a military crisis or general war, such as an armed attack, harassment, or hostile act against U.S. shipping or forces, or the following:

- Contact between U.S. or friendly forces and those of an antagonistic nation when the situation could lead to a confrontation.
- Violations of the claimed territory, air space, or territorial waters of U.S. or friendly nations by an antagonistic nation or nations.
- Unauthorized U.S. or friendly force ingress or alleged ingress into the claimed territory, air space, or territorial waters of an antagonistic nation or nations.

- Violation of international agreements on the high seas.

FTX (field training exercise): A military **exercise** conducted in the field under simulated war conditions and involving active play by combat and support units. An FTX is designed to exercise plans, procedures, and systems for deploying, employing, and redeploying forces [AF, *Air Force Participation in the Military Exercise Program,* AFR 55-37, 7 June 1985, p. 5, released under the FOIA]. (see also **command post exercise**)

fuel air explosive: Munition whose effects result from an explosive mixture of atmospheric oxygen and a selected fuel that, by itself, does not contain oxidizers in sufficient quantity to constitute an explosive mix.

fuel element: A rod, tube, plate, or other mechanical shape or form into which the nuclear fuel is fabricated for use in a reactor.

full-fuzing option (FUFO): The capability that a nuclear bomb has for airburst, contact burst, laydown operations, and depth bomb or subsurface detonation.

full operational capability (FOC): The state of a weapon system at full operation, that is, at the completion of deployment. (see also **Initial Operational Capability**)

full-scale development phase: The period when a weapon system and the principal items necessary for its support are designed, fabricated, tested, and evaluated. The intended output is, at a minimum, a pre-production system that closely approximates the final product, the documentation necessary to enter the production phase, and the test results that demonstrate that the production product will meet stated requirements.

functionally related observable differences (FRODs): A term introduced in **SALT II** designating the means whereby aircraft can be distinguished in terms of their SALT-limited or allowed functions. "FRODs are differences in the observable features of airplanes which specifically determine whether or not these airplanes can perform the mission of a heavy bomber, or whether or not they can perform the mission of a bomber equipped for cruise missiles capable of a range in excess of 600 km, or whether or not they can perform the mission of a bomber equipped for ASBMs [air-launched ballistic missiles]" [ACDA, *SALT II: Glossary of Terms,* 1979].

fusion: 1. The process accompanied by the release of tremendous amounts of energy in which the nuclei of light elements combine to form the nucleus of a heavier element. The most common substances used for this are deuterium (one neutron plus one proton in the nucleus) and tritium (two neutrons plus one proton). These can be made to fuse at temperatures over 1,000,000 degrees centigrade to form helium and, in the process, convert a small quantity of their matter into a vast amount of energy. A hydrogen fusion bomb, also known as a thermonuclear weapon, works by exploding a small fission bomb to generate the heat necessary for the fusion process. The fission reaction drives the hydrogen isotopes into a tiny lump of matter of very high density in which the thermonuclear burn wave takes place, attaining the required temperature and density of the material needed for a fusion reaction. The energy released is more than three times that of an equivalent amount of fissionable material. The enormous amount of heat generated by the fusion reaction can be used to drive a secondary **fission** reaction. **2.** The blending of intelligence information from multiple sources to produce a single intelligence product, usually done in a fusion center. (see also **Joint Tactical Fusion Program**)

fuze: 1. Mechanical, electrical, electronic, or magnetic device for detonating the explosive charge of a weapon. **2.** The union of one or more subassemblies or major components that, when combined with other major assemblies as required (bomb, power supply, etc.), is capable either in itself or in conjunction with a firing set, of controlling the electrical or mechanical arming and firing of a weapon.

fuzing system: The system of components in a nuclear weapon that determines the time and place to detonate the weapon.

FYDP   (see **Five-Year Defense Program**)

G

G: Prefix designating **1.** General Staff such as G-1 (formerly the personnel division of the U.S. War Department), G-2 (formerly the intelligence division), G-3 (formerly the operations and training division), and G-4 (formerly the supply division). The letter designations for staff offices are still used in Army and Marine Corps tactical organizations above the battalion level. **2.** Surface attack missile to destroy land or sea targets. **3.** Permanently grounded aircraft. **4.** Glider aircraft. **5.** Missile launched from a runway.

Galaxy   (see **C-5A/B Galaxy**)

Gallant: First word of a two-word nickname (e.g., Gallant Knight) for **U.S. Central Command**-sponsored exercises. Gallant Eagle 88, held in several western U.S. locations in August 1988, involved rapid deployment of forces for ground combat operations in a desert environment. Gallant Knight 88, conducted in California in late July 1988, provided a simulated desert combat environment for U.S. Central Command headquarters and multi-service units to practice tactical employment.

Gambit: **Byeman** code name for the former KH-8 class of photographic reconnaissance satellites. Some 30 Gambits were launched between 20 July 1966 and 15 June 1971, and they remained operational until 1984. It was a close-look, low-altitude, film-return, high-resolution system. Intelligence obtained by Gambit and other imaging satellites is marked by the codeword **Ruff**. (see also **keyhole**)

gamma ray: X-ray emitted by the nuclei of an atom. Gamma rays are high energy bursts of radiation released by nuclear explosions and are extremely dangerous to living organisms. A gamma ray laser, known as a graser, would generate a beam of gamma rays. Although it would employ nuclear reactions, it need not necessarily employ nuclear fission or fusion reactions or explosions.

GAPFILLER: Navy satellite system used prior to **Fleet Satellite Communications System** that relied on leased UHF **satellite communications** service from the commercial **MARISAT**. GAPFILLER consisted of three satellites covering the Atlantic, Pacific, and Indian Oceans and operated until 1984. The satellites were launched on 19 February 1976, 9 June 1976, and 14 October 1976.

Garden Plot: Code name for the Department of the Army's **operations plan (OPLAN)** for military involvement in **civil disturbances**.

GBU-15: Air Force conventionally armed air-launched glide bomb. It has a guidance system designed to give it pinpoint accuracy from low or medium altitudes over short standoff ranges. Development began in 1974 based on experience gained in Vietnam with the earlier Pave Strike GBU-8 HOBO modular weapons program. The GBU-15 is intended for tactical use to suppress enemy defenses and destroy heavily defended targets. The target-detecting device is carried on the front of the warhead; the control module, with autopilot and data link module, attaches to the rear.

The weapon offers two modes of attack. In direct attack, it is locked onto the target before launch and flies in a near line-of-sight profile to impact. In indirect mode, the seeker can be locked onto the target after launch, or the operator can fly the weapon manually to impact, using guidance updates provided through the data link. The profile uses a midcourse guide phase and extends standoff range. The GBU-15 is deployed with the **F-4E** and **F-111** aircraft and has been test launched from the **F-15E** and **F-16D**. The GBU-15(V)1/B TV-guided variant qualified for operational service in 1983. The GBU-15(V)2/B imaging infrared (IIR) version entered service in 1987. GBU-15 procurement was completed in FY 1987.

Development of the **AGM-130** rocket-powered version of the GBU-15 was terminated under the amended FY 1988-89 DOD budget requests. However, testing has continued through the completion of the originally contracted program. The prime contractor is Rockwell International Corporation.

G-day: The day on which the decision to deploy a specific force or forces is directed by competent authority. (see also **military time**)

general nuclear response: The third option in NATO's **flexible response** strategy, which also includes **direct defense** and **deliberate escalation**. A general nuclear response could consist of an all-out nuclear strike on the Soviet Union including the use of strategic nuclear weapons.

general officer: The rank of brigadier general or above. An **officer** of the Army, Air Force or Marine Corps whose rank insignia is one or more stars. Equivalent to a Navy or Coast Guard **flag officer** and often referred to as flag officers because they are authorized to fly personal flags.

general order: **1.** Permanent order which applies to all members of a command, usually concerning policy or administrative matters. (see also **special order**) **2.** A series of permanent orders governing the duties of a sentry guard on post.

General Political Guidelines for the Employment of Nuclear Weapons in Defense of NATO: During the NATO Minister's meeting in Gleneagles, Scotland, on 20–21 October

1986, NATO adopted new political guidelines for the use of its nuclear forces. Although a process of reevaluating NATO's nuclear capabilities had been ongoing for about eight years, the deployment of long-range nuclear forces and the withdrawal of major portions of NATO's European stockpile necessitated a restatement of nuclear strategy as it related to the initiation of the use of nuclear weapons, follow-on nuclear strikes, and strikes on Soviet territory.

These new General Political Guidelines are the NATO equivalent of the Carter Administration's Presidential Directive 59 (**PD-59**), the Nuclear Weapons Employment Policy for strategic forces that was approved in 1980. The new General Political Guidelines, like PD-59 (and the Reagan Administration affirmation of basic strategy in **National Security Decision Directive 13**), sought to better articulate a counterforce nuclear doctrine that had been evolving during the 1970s.

The new General Political Guidelines were prepared by a NATO working group under the **Defense Planning Committee**, which resulted in four drafts (the last was in 1982) that were discussed and debated at numerous Defense Planning Committee, **Nuclear Planning Group**, and Ministerial meetings. The new guidelines updated and replaced both the 1969 "Provisional" Political Guidelines (known as the PPGs) on the initial (aka "first") use of nuclear weapons and the 1970 "General Release" guidelines, which, together with two previous NATO statements on the use of nuclear weapons, constituted NATO's nuclear employment policy:

- *Provisional Political Guidelines for the Initial Defensive Tactical Use of Nuclear Weapons By NATO* [DPC/D(69)58 (Revised), November 1969].
- *Concept for the Role of Theater Nuclear Strike Forces in ACE* (Allied Command Europe) [DPC/D(70)59 (Revised), October 1970].
- Guidelines for consultation procedures on use of nuclear weapons (November 1969).
- Political guidelines for use of atomic demolition munitions (October 1970).

The General Political Guidelines (GPG) specify the following:

- Reaffirm NATO's **flexible response** strategy, which calls for NATO to defend itself against attack in three phases: "direct defense," "deliberate escalation," and "general nuclear response."
- Reaffirm the policy of initial ("first") use of NATO nuclear weapons in response to a Soviet conventional attack.
- Discuss in great detail the selective use of NATO nuclear weapons. The GPG put greater emphasis on "follow-on" nuclear strikes, assuming a Warsaw Pact nuclear response to "initial" use. Since the assumption is one of a series of selective strikes, the priority for the "deliberate escalation" phase of the flexible response strategy is evidence of strikes beyond the battlefield (i.e., not on NATO territory). Under the GPG, initial attacks will be made "mainly on the

territory of the aggressor, including the Soviet Union" [Lothar Ruehl (State Secretary of the Ministry of Defense, West Germany), "The Nuclear Balance in the Central Region and Strategic Stability in Europe," *NATO's Sixteen Nations*, August 1987, p. 19].   Strikes on Soviet homeland territory in previous NATO employment policy were highly restricted to specific circumstances, such as warfare on the Soviet-Turkish border.

- State that nuclear weapons will be developed and deployed to implement the new long-range employment doctrine. "TNF [Theater Nuclear Force] modernization in Europe has shifted the weight of regional nuclear armaments and target options away from the battlefield toward the adversary's side with a tendency of striking deep in WP [Warsaw Pact] territory" [Ruehl, p. 19].
- Contain guidance for nuclear targeting, stating that priority be given to militarily significant (counterforce) strikes as a means to convey political messages, rather than countervalue strikes. This is in contrast to the 1969 guidelines, which stated that the objective of the initial NATO use of nuclear weapons "would be essentially political and that initial use would therefore be very selective" [J. Michael Legge, *Theater Nuclear Weapons and the NATO Strategy of Flexible Response*, Rand Corporation R-2964-FF, April 1983, p. 20].
- Contain new guidance on NATO declaratory policy dealing with nuclear weapons.

- Contain new guidance on communicating NATO intentions to the Soviet Union in a crisis, as well as after selective use of nuclear weapons (such as in the case of demonstration nuclear strikes).
- Provide new guidelines for political consultation to ensure control over battlefield commanders. Reaffirms the traditional **Athens guidelines** that consultation would be subject to "time and circumstances permitting."
- Provide guidelines on the use of sea-based nuclear weapons for the first time. The 1969 guidelines only considered the initial use of land-based nuclear weapons in response to an attack.

general purpose forces: 1. All combat forces not designed primarily to accomplish strategic offensive/defensive or mobility missions. **2.** Program 2 of the 11 **major force programs** that represent all of the major missions of the services and are the most basic structural elements of the **Five Year Defense Program**. Consists of combatant force-oriented program elements other than those in Program 1, Strategic Forces, and includes the command organizations associated with these forces, the logistics organizations organic to these forces, and the related support units deployed or deployable as part of the military forces and field organizations.

general staff: Headquarters staff of a commander of a service component, division, or wing, comprising officers, to assist in the planning and conduct of operations. Directorates within a **joint staff** are designated as J-1, J-2, and so forth. The Army and Marine Corps may use the designations G-1, G-2, and so on to identify staff divisions. Navy staffs may be designated by N-1, N-2, and so forth. Staffs within Army and Marine Corps units smaller than a brigade or aircraft wing are designated by S-2, and the like. The Air Force uses letter designations.

Nominal General Staff Composition

- G, J, N, S-1, Personnel
- G, J, N, S-2, Intelligence
- G, J, N, S-3, Operations
- G, J, N, S-4, Logistics
- G, J, N, S-5, Plans
- G, J, N, S-6, Communications

Air Force
Nominal General Staff Composition

- DP, Personnel
- IN, Intelligence
- DO, Operations
- LG, Logistics
- XP, Plans
- SC, Communications Systems

The general staff model derives from the general staff organization adapted by General Pershing from the French in World War I and developed by the Army and Marine Corps. The term joint staff is generally used at high levels in lieu of general staff to avoid confusion with General Staff, a unique organizational concept of professional senior military staff with command authority, an arrangement forbidden in the U.S. military because it threatens civilian control of the military.

general support: Logistic and administrative assistance provided to several combat units by elements that operate independently. Supply, maintenance, and service forces at depot level are representative. (see also **direct support**)

general war: "Armed conflict between major powers in which the total resources of the belligerents are employed, and the national survival of a major belligerent is in jeopardy" [*JCS Pub 1*, p. 159]. In a general war, the military is directed to strike back at an aggressor, to defend the homeland, and to withstand enemy offensives towards strategic areas. The term *general war* is commonly reserved for a showdown between the United States and the Soviet Union. For planning purposes, general war is divided into three phases: preattack, transattack, and postattack [Air Force, *Disaster Preparedness: Planning and Operations*, AFR 355-1, 17 November 1986, p. 87, released under the FOIA]. (see also **limited war**)

generated alert: An increase in the readiness of strategic forces from day-to-day (peacetime) alert levels. Actions include an increase in the percentage of bombers that are armed and ready to take off instantly from main or dispersal bases, bringing ICBMs that are "down" for maintenance to full capability, and preparing submarines that are in homeports or in transit for military operations.

generation time: "The time required to progress from day-to-day status to a posture directed by the

Force Generation Order. SLBM forces may have generation times to both Advanced Readiness and Maximum Readiness" [CINCPAC, *CINCPAC Standing Operating Procedures [SOP] for Nuclear Operations*, 18 April 1983, released under the FOIA].

Geneva Conventions: Series of agreements regulating international law as it applies to warfare. They supplemented the earlier Red Cross Convention of 1864 and the Hague Conventions of 1899 and 1907. The 1947 Conventions deal with the treatment of military personnel, prisoners of war, and the protection of civilians during wartime. A protocol was concluded in 1977 relating to the rights of combatants and noncombatants in **unconventional warfare**.

Geneva Protocol: Formally known as the Protocol for the Prohibition of the Use in War of Asphyxiating, Poisonous or Other Gases, and of Bacteriological Methods of Warfare. Signed by 38 countries on 17 June 1925. As of December 1988, 114 countries had agreed to the terms of the protocol. The protocol condemns "the use in war of asphyxiating, poisonous or other gases, and of all analogous liquids, materials or devices" and calls for their prohibition by international law. (see also **chemical and biological agents**, **biological weapon**)

GEODSS (see **Ground-Based Electro-Optical Deep Space Surveillance System**)

geostationary orbit: A particular **geosynchronous** orbit, also called a Clarke orbit. The geostationary orbit is circular at an altitude of 35,786 km (orbital radius of 42,164 km) with zero inclination (in the plane of the Earth's equator) and direct (in the same direction as the rotation of the Earth). A satellite in geostationary orbit revolves around the Earth once per day, maintaining the same position relative to the surface of the Earth, making the satellite appear to be stationary. Given their "stationary" position satellites in geostationary orbit can be used as communications relays or as intelligence collection or early warning platforms.

geosynchronous orbit: A satellite orbit at approximately 35,800 km above the equator. Objects at this altitude travel at the same speed as the earth, thus their position remains stationary in reference to the planet. A satellite in geosynchronous orbit revolves around the Earth once per day. (see also **geostationary orbit**)

Giant: Strategic Air Command nickname and exercise term to designate systems and activities:

- Giant Drill: Battle staff exercise of the airborne command and control system.
- Giant Lance: Selective employment of tanker task forces and bomber orbits in air/ground alert including airborne carriage of nuclear weapons.
- Giant Link: Communications system located at March AFB, CA.
- Giant Look: Special exercise activities.
- Giant Star: **AFSATCOM** system.
- **Giant Talk**: HF/SSB communications network.

[SAC, *SAC Exercise Program*, SACR 55-38, Vol. I, p. 2-2, released under the FOIA; Strategic Communications Division (AFCC) *33rd Communications Group,* SCD Regulation 23-15, 15 July 1982, released under the FOIA].

Giant Talk: SAC HF/SSB long-distance HF communications network operated by the **Air Force Communications Command** that provides CINCSAC with a means of positive control over the SAC bomber and tanker force. It also provides the National Command Authority, through CINCSAC, the means to exercise command and control of tactical and strategic aircraft. The Giant Talk system is under the operational control of SAC and is composed of 14 worldwide stations that operate continuously. The CONUS Net consists of stations at Barksdale AFB, LA; Offutt AFB, NE; March AFB, CA; and Westover AFB, MA. The Pacific Net consists of stations at Kadena AB, Okinawa, Japan; Andersen AB, Guam; and Hickam AFB, HI. The European Net consists of stations at RAF Mildenhall, UK; Torrejon AB, Spain; and Incirlik AB, Turkey. Stations are also operated at Thule AB, Greenland; and Eielson AFB, AK. Giant Talk is being upgraded and replaced under the **Scope Signal** program.

GIN gap: The Greenland-Iceland-Norway gap. The "gap" in this term connotes a narrowing in NATO's defensive line across the north Atlantic ocean region where a "choke-point" could be established by naval and air forces to cut off the main Atlantic Ocean **sea lines of communi-**

nications (SLOCs) from the United States to Europe. This gap is roughly marked by a line drawn from Greenland to Iceland and then to northern Norway. Also this gap marks a rough transitional area above which U.S./NATO forces would be considered to be conducting offensive operations close to the Soviet Union (and the Soviets would be conducting defensive operations) and at and below which U.S./NATO forces would be conducting defensive operations against Soviet forces seeking to disrupt the SLOCs (and the Soviets would be conducting offensive operations against the SLOCs).

GIUK gap: Greenland-Iceland-U.K. gap. Like the **GIN gap**, connotes a "choke-point" where U.S./NATO forces can be concentrated to mount naval and aerial operations to defend the **sea lines of communications (SLOCs)**. This gap is roughly marked by a line drawn from Greenland to Iceland and then to the northern United Kingdom. In recent years, use of the GIUK gap has fallen into disuse, replaced by the GIN gap, which connotes operations further north, particularly to defend Norway, a member of NATO.

glide bomb: A bomb fitted with airfoils to provide lift; it may be remotely controlled (e.g., **GBU-15**).

Global Command and Control System (GCCS): Air Force HF communications system providing reliable, rapid, two-way voice connections between ground stations and DOD aircraft. GCCS was redesignated from the USAF Aeronautical

Station System on 1 October 1983. For effective dissemination of information, 14 command control zones (CCZs) dividing the globe are assigned a GCCS command and control station. That station is responsible for its zone's communications, but any GCCS station can provide information to authorized users anywhere in the world. The stations consist of control, receiver, and transmitter sites, with the control site located 10 to 20 miles from the transmitter and receiver. The sites are linked by microwave and landline. Control stations are also linked to **AUTOVON**, **AUTODIN**, and dedicated direct lines.

GCCS zones and stations

- Zone 1: Clark AB, Philippines (APO San Francisco 96274)
- Zone 2: Andersen AB, Guam (APO San Francisco 96334)
- Zone 3: Yokota AB, Japan (APO San Francisco 96328)
- Zone 4: Hickam AFB, HI 96853
- Zone 5: Elmendorf AFB, AK 99506
- Zone 6: McClellan AFB, CA 95652
- Zone 7: Scott AFB, IL 62225
- Zone 8: Albrook AFS, Panama
- Zone 9: MacDill AFB, FL 33608
- Zone 10: Thule AB, Greenland (APO New York 09023)
- Zone 11: RAF Croughton, UK
- Zone 12: Lajes AB, Azores (APO New York 09406)
- Zone 13: Ascension Island
- Zone 14: Incirlik AB, Turkey (APO New York 09289)

Command, control, and communications support provided by these stations includes

- **Mystic Star** (presidential communications support);
- Air-to-ground communications to support the **airborne command posts**;
- **Electronic Security Command**;
- Major command aircraft deployment/redeployment;
- Foxtrot broadcasts and **emergency action messages**;
- Weather reconnaissance;
- Disaster and rescue missions; and
- Mercy missions.

Airborne Warning and Control System (AWACS) air-ground-air communications support is provided by GCCS on request. In CONUS, this support consists of phone patch or message relay service to the **NORAD Cheyenne Mountain Complex**, NORAD Regional Operation Control Centers, and aircraft military control agencies [AF, *Standard Procedures for Operation of USAF Global Command Control System Stations*, AFCC R100-20, Vol. IV, 1 May 1984, released under the FOIA].

Global Decision Support System (GDSS): Command and control system for the **Military Airlift Command (MAC)** to track personnel, parts, status of bases, maintenance, cargo, and airplanes. GDSS began with a memorandum of agreement between the Chairman of the JCS, the Air Force Chief of Staff, CINC-MAC, and the Defense Communications Agency (DCA) to develop a flexible and reliable system for tracking MAC's 1100 aircraft. Before the advent of GDSS, MAC used telephones and **AUTODIN** messages to pass along command and control information. When an aircraft landed, a telephone call was placed from the base to the Airlift Division, then passed to the numbered Air Force level and finally to headquarters. With GDSS, this flow of information to the appropriate levels occurs automatically, as well as providing decision-level information. There are seven GDSS sites: Scott AFB, IL (headquarters); McGuire AFB, NJ; Travis AFB, CA; Hurlburt Field, FL; Air National Guard Support Center, Andrews AFB, MD; and Airlift Divisions at Hickam AFB, HI, and Ramstein AB, West Germany.

Global Positioning System (GPS) (see **NAVSTAR/GPS**)

Global Shield: Annual JCS-directed exercise sponsored by the Strategic Air Command (SAC). Global Shield is a large scale readiness exercise "designed to enhance force readiness and project the positive perception that SAC's strategic forces are capable of responding effectively throughout the spectrum of conflict" [SAC, *SAC Exercise Program*, SACR 55-38, Vol. I, p. 2–2, released under the FOIA].

Golden Thrust 88: Operation conducted from 6–22 November 1987, the largest peacetime reserve component mobilization exercise since World War II. The exercise involved more than 24,000 Army National Guard and Army Reserve soldiers from 115 units. Some 34,000 support personnel in the 12-state First

Army region of mid-Atlantic and New England states participated. The units underwent a five-phase process to assess mobilization plans, including pre-alert activities, alert procedures, assembly and actions at home stations, movement of personnel and equipment to mobilization stations, and preparation for movement overseas.

Gold Phone: 1. Nickname for the White House/Secretary of Defense Command Hot Line connected during crises. Use of this hot line is limited to the Secretary of Defense or his designated agent. Extensions are located in the **National Military Command Center (NMCC)** and the White House or other presidential locations [JCS, *Crisis Staffing Procedures,* J-3 Instruction 3180.11B, 29 September 1983, Annex G, released under the FOIA]. **2.** Nickname for the phone used to connect the Commanders of unified and specified commands to the NMCC for use during a **Commander's Availability Check**.

gold room: Nickname for the **tank**, where the Joint Chiefs of Staff meet.

Goldwater-Nichols Act (see **Department of Defense Reorganization Act of 1986**)

Government-owned, contractor-operated (GOCO): Term applied to a manufacturing plant that is owned by the government and operated by a contractual civilian organization.

Government-owned, government-operated (GOGO): Term applied to a manufacturing plant that is both owned and operated by the government.

grade: Refers to the "pay grade requirement of a **billet** or the pay grade possessed by a service member" [DOD, *Manpower Requirements Report FY 1989*, May 1988, p. B-2].

Granite Sentry: Five-phase upgrade plan in automatic data processing (ADP) equipment at NORAD's **Air Defense Operations Center** at Cheyenne Mountain, Colorado Springs, CO. The first phase, begun in late 1986, concentrated on computers and display terminals used for assessment and warning of bomber and cruise missile attacks. The new computers and 60 inch wall screen replace equipment originally procured in the 1960s. Phase II focuses on improved missile warning displays; Phase III involves improved space warning systems; Phase IVa will link the upgrades to an improved command center processing and display system; Phase V will upgrade the battle staff support center and weather support unit. Full Granite Sentry upgrade is scheduled for completion by the end of 1993. **Air Force Space Command** and the **Air Force Systems Command**'s Electronic Systems Division (ESD) have joint program responsibility. ESD manages the overall program while Air Force Space Command is responsible for software development.

grant aid: Military assistance rendered under the authority of the **Foreign Assistance Act** (as amended) for which the United States receives no dollar reimbursement. (see also **Military Assistance Program**)

gravity bomb: Used to describe bombs (or other ordnance) dropped from aircraft that do not have any other forces propelling them toward the ground beyond the pull of gravity. The term is not usually used to refer to guided glide bombs and is roughly synonymous with free-fall bombs. It does encompass bombs which have parachutes or other devices to slow their descent. It usually is used to differentiate a bomb from missiles or rockets that have other sources of propulsion. Nuclear gravity bombs currently deployed include the B28, B43, B53, B57, B61, and B83.

gray   (see **rad**)

gray phone: Secure **National Security Agency (NSA)** telephone network that provides direct links from unified and specified commands and field intelligence stations to the NSA secure switchboard in Washington, D.C.

green: 1. An obsolete term that refers to a paper circulated by the Secretary of the **Joint Chiefs of Staff (JCS)**. The name is from the color of the paper. An instant green refers to a formal report for JCS consideration, without **flimsy** or **buff** stage, when there are no substantive issues or when time limitations preclude formal coordination at a planner's conference. Also known as "short green" or "short-form green." To turn green is the process involved in reprinting a flimsy or a buff paper as a green paper, preparatory to consideration by the JCS. **2.** The restricted telephone system connecting the **National Military Command Center** with the **Central Intelligence Agency**.

Green Berets   (see **Special Forces**)

Green Pine: A remote early-warning UHF radio network providing line-of-sight communications between strategic aircraft in the Arctic regions, where HF/SSB is not always reliable, and the SAC command post. Green Pine is a SAC communication system that supplements **Giant Talk** and **Scope Signal** and that utilizes the infrastructure of the **DEW Line** system. Green Pine also supports emergency air and ground operational communications. The system consists of 13 UHF-equipped sites, reaches from the Aleutian Islands in Alaska to Iceland, and is connected by land and satellite circuits. Green Pine primary sites are located at Adak, Cold Bay, Point Barrow, Barter Island, AK; Cape Parry, Cambridge Bay, Hall Beach, Cape Dyer, Melville, Argentina, Canada; Thule, Greenland; and Keflavik, Iceland. Network control is from Elkhorn, NE [Strategic Communications Division (AFCC), *1st Aerospace Communications Group,* SCD Regulation 23-2, 31 July 1981, p. 4, released under the FOIA; Maj. Louis J. Casamayou, *A Guide to U.S. Air Force Command Control Communications*, Air Command and Staff College, Air University, Maxwell AFB, AL, Report #83-0380. April 1983, released under the FOIA].

ground alert: State of readiness in which aircraft on the ground are fully serviced and armed and combat crews are ready to take off within short notice (usually 15 minutes) after receipt of a mission order. Approximately 30 percent of strategic bombers are on ground alert at any one time. (see also **alert**)

Ground-Based Electro-Optical Deep Space Surveillance System (GEODSS):   Air Force television-telescope network of six sites used to identify and track objects in space out to geosynchronous orbits. GEODSS replaces the **Baker-Nunn camera**. Instead of using photographic film like the Baker-Nunn camera, GEODDS uses television cameras that permit rapid analysis of any satellite under observation. The telescopes move at a rate that is exactly counter to the rotation of the earth, an effect that "freezes" the stars in place so they appear not to move. But satellites in orbit do move against this background of stars. The GEODDS computers erase everything that has not moved from one picture to the next, while objects that have moved are recorded and relayed to the Space Surveillance Center computers for analysis.

GEODDS is supplemented with two telescopic cameras: Teal Amber located at Malabar, FL, and Teal Blue located at Mount Haleakala, Maui, HI. Both cameras provide NORAD with computer-enhanced close-up photographs of spacecraft in real time.

The system is tied via computer to NORAD at Cheyenne Mountain to provide near-real-time information. The first site at White Sands Missile Range, NM, was activated in 1981, and the system reached initial operational capability in 1983. Other sites are located at Maui, HI; Taegu, South Korea; Diego Garcia; and southern Portugal. GEODSS can spot an object the size of a soccer ball at geosynchronous orbit and has discovered about 40,000 1-cm-sized objects in low and medium Earth orbit. It also provides the interim primary satellite detection capability from 3,000 to 20,000 nm. TRW is the prime contractor.

Ground-Based Laser (GBL): Series of **Strategic Defense Initiative (SDI)** laser experiments conducted at White Sands Missile Range, NM, by the **U.S. Army Strategic Defense Command**. The GBL would be fired from the ground, reflected off a high-altitude relay mirror in orbit, then reflected off another mirror from which it could hit enemy missiles in the boost phase. The experimental program has several tasks to demonstrate: that multimegawatt lasers can be built, that a laser beam can be directed to and its energy deposited on a space-based target, and that these components can be integrated into an operational system. The GBL experiments will use either a linear accelerator or a radio frequency laser, whichever freeelectron laser (FEL) technology provides the better laboratory results. Contractors: Boeing, Seattle, WA, and TRW, Redondo Beach, CA (radio frequency FEL); Lockheed, Sunnyvale, CA (beam control); TRW, Redondo Beach, CA (system engineering); and Fluor, Irvine, CA (facililties). (see also **Alpha**, **LODE**)

Ground-Based Radar (GBR-X): Experimental prototype **Strategic Defense Initiative (SDI)**-related radar to discriminate targets in midcourse and high endoatmospheric phases. The program is being conducted by the **U.S. Army Strategic Defense Command**. GBR-X is an SDI Phase I experiment forming the basis for an operational GBR, a high-powered single-face, dual-use, phased-array radar. Its 100-meter-tall surface contains over 21,000 elements for steering the antenna beam. It is expected that the GBR-X will be operational in 1993 at its site at Kwajalein Atoll. Raytheon, Boston, MA, is the prime contractor. Software is provided by TRW, Redondo Beach, CA.

The GBR experiment is the **Terminal Imaging Radar (TIR)**, a large phased-array high-resolution microwave radar that senses incoming missile warheads in the mid-course and terminal phases. TIR will be installed at Kwajalein Atoll in the early 1990s. GBR/TIR will support both the **High Endoatmospheric Defense Interceptor (HEDI)** terminal-phase interceptor and the **Exoatmospheric Reentry Interceptor Subsystem (ERIS)** mid-course kinetic energy weapon.

Ground-Based Surveillance Tracking System (GSTS): **U.S. Army Strategic Defense Command**/Strategic Defense Initiative Organization research program to support tracking and discrimination in the mid-course phase using rocket-carried boosters in space. GSTS would incorporate pairs of long-wave infrared sensors, launched after warning of attack given by boost-phase sensors, to relay data on mid-course missiles to battle commanders. GSTS will be integrated with the **Boost Surveillance and Tracking System (BSTS)** and mid-course sensors of the **Space Surveillance and Tracking System (SSTS)** and the **Ground-Based Radar (GBR-X)**. Demonstration and validation of the GSTS is expected in the mid-1990s. The prime contractor is McDonnell Douglas, Huntington Beach, CA. Hughes and Rockwell subcontracted for sensors; TRW has contracted for the software.

ground entry point: A ground-based station connected to air-to-ground communications networks such as **Mystic Star** or **Giant Talk** and **Scope Signal** that are used by **airborne command posts** to access terrestrial network. There are 14 ground-entry points that allow the **National Emergency Airborne Command Post (NEACP)** and the **Strategic Air Command's Post Attack Command and Control System** to access ground-based communications networks.

Ground-Launched Cruise Missile (GLCM): Model designation BGM-109G. Nickname: Gryphon. Air Force, subsonic, guided, long-range surface-to-surface nuclear missile being phased out under the **INF Treaty**. The missile is 20 ft long and has a range of 1,500 mi. The first GLCM operational base, in 1983, was at RAF Greenham Common, UK, followed by Comiso AB, Sicily, Italy; and Florennes AB, Belgium, both in 1984, Wueschiem AB, West Germany, in 1986, and RAF Molesworth, UK, in 1987. A GLCM mobile flight consists of four transporter/erector/launchers (TELs), each carrying four missiles, and two launch-control and communications vehicles. The missile is armed with a W84 nuclear warhead with a yield of .3 to 80 kilotons. It is a modified version of the Navy's **Tomahawk sea-launched cruise missile**. A total of 464 missiles were planned for deployment by 1988, but deployment was halted at 19 flights with the signing of the INF Treaty. The first GLCMs were removed from Europe in September 1988, and all GLCMs and TELs will be eliminated by 31 May 1991 as required by the INF Treaty. Contractors were General Dynamics, Convair Division, San Diego, CA; and McDonnell Douglas.

Ground Mobile Command Center (GMCC): National-level **special access program**, codenamed Island Sun, to provide a series of truck-based command centers to accommodate the **National Command Authorities** and other presidential successors. The Army operates the national mobile command centers (MCCs) and the Defense Communications Agency is the proponent group. One of the components of preparing the MCC has been the preparation and maintenance of distributed data bases, available outside of Washington at all times, that would provide basic information to decisionmakers following a protracted nuclear war. One set of GMCCs is reportedly located at Ft. Ritchie, MD, and the other is located at Hill AFB, Utah. Brunswick Corporation is the major contractor. (see also **Rapier, HERT**)

ground wave: 1. Radio frequency energy that remains near the earth's surface when a transmitted signal leaves a radio antenna. Standard broadcast stations use ground waves for distances of 100 km or more. As the frequency is increased, the signals are attenuated; consequently, ground waves are of little use except for local communications up to about 160 km for frequencies below four MHz. The ground-wave signal can be received at much greater distances over sea water than over average soil or dry terrain. (see also **sky wave**) **2.** A wave formed in the ground by the blast from an explosion. These waves are of three types: longitudinal waves (compression), transverse waves (shear), and surface waves (similar to water rippling). Ground waves are sometimes referred to as seismic waves or stress waves; stress waves in soil are not classical shock waves since dissipative and dispersive effects tend to increase markedly the rise time to the order of milliseconds.

Ground-Wave Emergency Network (GWEN): Air Force LF ground-wave two-way communications system designed to relay messages during a nuclear war. A part of the **Minimum Essential Emergency Communications Network (MEECN)**, GWEN is designed to provide U.S. strategic forces with the ability to maintain CONUS long-range command and control connectivity despite disruptions by nuclear explosions and the resulting **electromagnetic pulse (EMP)**. As such, GWEN will carry the positive control launch (PCL) and initial **Single Integrated Operational Plan** execution messages directly to the forces. The GWEN nodes will interact directly with the **Improved Emergency Message Automatic Transmission System (IEMATS)**.

There are three types of GWEN stations. The first, an input/output terminal, is able to both transmit and receive messages. They use 50-watt transmitters 60 to 150 ft atop unmanned EMP-hardened relay radio towers to broadcast UHF signals. The second type of stations are receive-only, meaning that they cannot transmit messages. Generally located on the roofs of buildings, they use LF signals of 150–175 MHz. While both of these types of stations are located on military installations, the third type are scheduled for deployment at 150–200 mile intervals across CONUS on 11-acre plots of private or government-leased land. These 300 ft tall LF radio relay nodes distribute messages throughout the GWEN system via computerized traffic controllers. It is this third type of GWEN tower that has met with opposition in local communities.

A partial GWEN network begun by the Air Force in 1985, the Thin Line Connectivity Capability, contains eight input/output stations, 30 receive-only stations at bomber bases, and 56 relay nodes. The Final Operational Capability phase plans to add four more fixed input/output receive-only terminals, 70 unmanned relay nodes, 34 airborne input/output terminals and portable receive-only terminals. In 1988, however, funding for GWEN relay towers was cut off at 96, about 30 less than was planned. Thin Line sites as of November 1988 are

- Grady, Hackleburg, AL
- Flagstaff (Navajo Army Depot), AZ
- Fayetteville, AR
- Bakersfield, Biggs, Fenner, Roseville, CA
- Aurora (Lowry AFB), Pueblo, Pueblo Army Depot, Rocky Flats, CO
- Macon, Savannah Beach, GA
- Glenwood/Pacific Junction, Mechanicsville, IA
- Goodland, Topeka, KS
- Herseytown, Penobscot, ME
- Hagerstown, Crownsville, Waldorf, MD
- Barre Falls, Acushnet, MA
- Onondaga, MI
- Alligator Township, MS
- Billings, Great Falls, Ronan, MT
- Ainsworth, Omaha (SAC HQ), NE
- Egg Harbor, NJ
- Albuquerque (Kirtland AFB), NM
- Elmira, Hudson Falls, Remson, NY
- Beaufort, NC
- Devils Lake, Edinburg, Medora, ND
- Canton, OK
- Klamath Falls, Seneca, OR
- Harbor Creek, Gettysburg, Hawk Run, PA
- Little Compton, RI
- Kensington, SC
- Clark, SD
- Summerfield, TX
- Driver, VA
- Appleton, Spokane, Wenatchee, WA
- Mequon, WI

ground zero: The point on the surface of land or water vertically below or above the center of a planned (desired) or actual nuclear detonation. The term "surface zero" is used for a burst over or under water. (see also **actual ground zero, desired ground zero**)

group: 1. A combat organization consisting of two or more battalions or squadrons. **2.** In the Army, an organization comprising several field armies (Army group). **3.** In the Navy, an administrative unit of a naval type command (force). (see also **amphibious group, carrier group, cruiser-destroyer group, naval surface group, service group, special warfare group, submarine group, type command**)

Gryphon: 1. Program to provide survivable submarine communications for the National Command Authority and CINCs during and after a nuclear attack by modulation compression and coding of VLF signals. It contains many components, including **ELF, TACAMO, Verdin**, Integrated Submarine Communications System (ISCS), and **Clarinet Pilgrim**. **2.** Nickname for the Air Force **Ground-Launched Cruise Missile (GLCM)**.

Guarantee Reserve Fund (GRF): A multi-billion dollar fund established by Congress on 16 December 1980 to accommodate commercial and federal lending institutions unable to collect interest payments from indebted Third World countries that armed themselves in the 1970s through cheap loans taken out through the **security assistance program**. GRF was created to guarantee payments for delinquent or rescheduled **Foreign Mili-**

tary Sales **(FMS)** loans extended by the Federal Financing Bank (FFB) and commercial lending institutions. Prior to its establishment, funds for guarantee payments were maintained in segregated reserve within the FMS credit account. Since inception of the GRF, Congress has appropriated $109 million (FY 1985) and $532 million (FY 1988) into the fund. GRF is currently liable to the U.S. Treasury, the Federal Financing Bank, and private lenders for a total of $18 billion dollars. GRF disbursements are made to a lender when a guaranteed loan payment is missed by a borrowing nation. In this situation, the **Defense Security Assistance Agency (DSAA)**, as guarantor, makes payment to the FFB and, at the same time, attempts to collect the corresponding missed payment. GRF will benefit from refinancing of guaranteed loans under the **Foreign Military Sales Debt Reform/Restructuring** provisions to the extent that defaulted principal and interest due the GRF are included in the refinancing [Department of State, *Congressional Presentation of Security* Assistance Program FY 1990, p.37].

Guard and Reserve Forces: Program 5 of the 11 **major force programs** that represent all of the major missions of the services and that are the most basic structural elements of the **Five Year Defense Program**. It consists of national guard and reserve training units and individuals in support of strategic offensive, strategic defensive, general purpose, airlift, and support forces.

Guardrail: Army AN/USD-9 airborne ground-communications intelligence intercept system. Guardrail is used to intercept ground-based communications emitters, to calculate direction-finding data on them, and to transmit the data to a transportable ground station, which relays that information to combat forces. It utilizes **RC-12** aircraft and a mobile ground-mission processing facility. Beech Aircraft and ESL are the prime contractors.

guerrilla warfare: "Military and paramilitary operations conducted in enemy-held or hostile territory by irregular, predominantly indigenous forces" [*JCS Pub 1*, p. 164].

guided missile cruiser   (see **cruiser**)

guided missile destroyer (see **destroyer**)

guided missile frigate   (see **frigate**)

gun: Generally, a gun is a piece of ordnance consisting of a tube and firing projectiles. Specifically, a gun has a relatively long barrel (usually over 30 calibers) and a relatively high initial velocity and is capable of being fired at low angles of elevation.

gun-type weapon (gun assembly weapon): A **nuclear weapon** in which the assembly of two subcritical masses of highly enriched uranium (U-235) produces a supercritical mass, resulting in a nuclear explosion when the initiator is activated. The only remaining gun-type nuclear weapon in the U.S. stockpile at the end of 1989 is the W33 8-in (203 mm) artillery projectile. (see also **implosion-type weapon**)

H

H: Prefix designating **1.** Silo stored missile. **2.** Search and rescue aircraft (e.g., HC-130). **3.** Helicopter (rotary wing aircraft) (e.g., H-1).

HALO (see **High Altitude Large Optics**)

Hammer Ace: Air Force lightweight, secure, long-range air-transportable communications system for rapid response. Hammer Ace was designed at **Air Force Communications Command (AFCC)** to provide flexible communications from accident sites. Hammer Ace takes only two people to set up and is the size of a suitcase. It can operate for 72 hours on its own battery power and can work off of a car battery. Nineteen trained AFCC members and three Hammer Ace packages are kept on 24-hour alert and are ready to deploy within hours. It allows access to **AUTOSEVOCOM**. Hammer Ace conversations are transmitted from the site to the operations center at Scott AFB via satellite. The first Hammer Ace package was used in August 1982 at an airplane crash site in Cherokee National Forest.

Hammer Rick: Air Force program to provide lightweight man-transportable UHF **satellite communications** packages for crisis and contingency applications.

Hardened Intersite Communications System (HICS): The network of thousands of miles of electromagnetic pulse-hardened buried communications cables connecting the Strategic Air Command's underground ICBM silos. The system does not extend to SAC headquarters.

hard target: Any weapon site, command and control facility, production center, blast shelter, or other military target that has been hardened (fortified with layers of concrete, steel, earth, and other materials) for protection against the blast effects of nuclear attack. Hardness is measured by the power needed by a nuclear weapon, precision guided weapon, or directed energy weapon to destroy the target.

HARM (High Speed Anti-Radiation Missile) (AGM-88A): Air Force and Navy, supersonic, guided, conventionally armed, air-to-surface missile designed to suppress and destroy land and sea-based radars. Its guidance homes in on enemy radar emissions at a range of 50+ nm. In the

Air Force, it is carried by **F-4G** Wild Weasel aircraft, and is being integrated into the **F-16**, **EF-111 Raven**, **B-52**, and **F-15**. In the Navy **A-6E**, **A-7E**, **EA-6B**, and **F/A-18** aircraft can carry the missile. It replaces the first generation **Shrike** and ARM antiradiation missiles.

The missile became operational in the Air Force in 1984. By the end of 1988, 3,063 HARMs had been delivered to the Air Force, and it plans to acquire a total of 9,200 by the time production ends in 1994. In June 1988, Navy attack squadron 75 (VA-75) became the first fleet A-6 squadron to be armed with HARM missiles.

The prime contractor is Texas Instruments, Dallas, TX. The Navy's FY 1990 and FY 1991 budget request for 1,162 and 1,400 missiles each year is $302.5 million and $356.5 million, respectively, including RDT&E and military construction. The Air Force's FY 1990 and FY 1991 budget request for 326 and 200 missiles each year is $83.8 and $45.3 million, respectively.

Harpoon: Air Force and Navy all-weather, guided, medium-range, conventionally armed, anti-ship cruise missile launched from aircraft (AGM-84), ships (RGM-84) and submarines (UGM-84). The missile is turbojet powered and employs a low-level cruise trajectory. It has a range greater than 50 nm and an active-radar terminal guidance system. A 500 lb conventional warhead is employed. It was introduced into the fleet on ships and submarines in 1977 and on the **P-3 Orion** in 1979. It can also be carried by the A-6 and S-3Bs. Two squadrons

of Air Force B-52Gs have been converted to carry the Harpoon and are assigned secondary long-range anti-ship missions. The Navy is developing a new infrared Harpoon variant called **SLAM (Standoff Land Attack Missile)**.

The prime contractor is McDonnell Douglas of St. Louis, MO. The FY 1990 and FY 1991 budget request for 190 and 184 missiles each year is $222.9 and $233 million, respectively, including RDT&E.

Harrier   (see **AV-8**)

Have Glance: Infrared countermeasures system using low-powered lasers to confuse heat-seeking missiles. During its beginning stages, Have Glance will be used in strategic aircraft for air-to-air and air-to-ground applications. In the future, it will be incorporated into tactical aircraft. The Have Glance system would take effect once the silent attack warning system (SAWS) warns a pilot that he is under attack. Have Glance then points its laser at the target and tracks it, aims and fires the laser to deceive the heat-seeking function of the missile, and determines whether the missile has been effectively countered. In addition to SAWS technology, Have Glance also incorporates infrared (IR) technologies in developing the laser source.

Have Glance began development in the fall of 1988 and was first tested in a 22-in pod under the wings of an F-111 aircraft. Live wire testing is conducted at North Oscura Peak, White Sands Missile Range, NM. It will eventually work with the Integrated

Electronic Warfare System (INEWS). The **Air Force Systems Command's** Aeronautical Systems Division is in charge of the program.

Have Nap: An Air Force conventional, tactical missile program currently under development to provide long-range bombers with a conventional precision strike capability in support of worldwide theater commanders. Under the Have Nap program the Air Force has purchased Israeli-built Popeye medium-range TV-guided standoff missiles. The missiles are inertially guided, with terminal TV-homing guidance. If the decision is made to put Have Nap into production, the primary carrier of the missile will be the conventionally-dedicated **B-52G**. The value of the 16-month contract awarded in June 1988 to Rafael of Haifa, Israel for the missiles is $39 million. If the Have Nap goes into production Rafael will be teamed with Martin Marietta.

Have Quick: Air Force program to provide the tactical Air Forces with anti-jam voice communications. Airborne platforms are acquiring the Have Quick capability through a modification to the existing AN/ARC-164 radios. Selected ground locations are also installing the Have Quick-modified AN/ARC-164. Most of the ground Have Quick capability will be satisfied in the near term by 93 AN/GRC-171(V)4s, acquired for the **Tactical Air Control System**.

Hawk (MIM-23): Army and Marine Corps medium-range, guided surface-to-air missile designed to destroy high-speed aircraft flying from tree-top altitude to 22 mi. The whole Hawk **air defense** system consists of a high-power illuminator, continuous wave acquisition radar, the missile, and the launcher. The Hawk missile is guided by reflected radar energy and uses a proximity fuse to detonate its warhead. Developed by Raytheon, the Hawk was first deployed in July 1959. An improved Hawk entered the field in FY 1973. The Hawk's latest improvement (PIP III) will provide a low-altitude, simultaneous-engagement capability and enhanced electronic counter-countermeasures. It is scheduled to be fielded in FY 1989. The prime contractor is Raytheon Corp., West Andover, MA. The FY 1990 request for 358 missiles is $67.2 million including RDT&E.

Hawkeye   (see **E-2**)

Haystack: Long-range imaging radar owned by MIT's Lincoln Laboratory and located at Tyngsboro, MA. Haystack augments the Space Detection and Tracking System (see **Space Surveillance Network**) and provides radar images of near-Earth and deep-space satellites.

HC-130:   Air Force and Coast Guard, long-range, medium-sized, search and rescue version of the **C-130 Hercules**. It has an uprated engine and specialized search and rescue equipment for the recovery of aircrews and space hardware. The initial flight was made in 1964 and 43 were delivered. Crew complement is 10 to 12. An update program to improve navigation, night vision, and communications was announced in 1987 for

31 H-130Hs, 21 of which will also be equipped for inflight refueling. Seventeen HC-130Ps are similar but are adapted to refuel helicopters in flight. Four JHC-130H conversions were refitted with equipment for aerial recovery of space capsules. Another HC-130H was modified to a DC-130H standard with four pylons, each capable of carrying remotely piloted vehicles. Fifteen HC-130Ns with advanced direction-finding equipment were ordered in 1969; these aircraft can also refuel helicopters in flight. The HC-130 is the main aircraft of the Military Airlift Command's 23rd Air Force.

HE   (see **high explosive**)

headquarters (HQ):   Administrative and tactical element that exercises command, control, and administration of a combat or administrative unit or command. HQ size and compositions vary according to mission and combat organizations. The staff structure is normally fairly standard, based on the **general staff** model or the department model.

Headquarters, Department of the Army   (see **Department of the Army**)

Headquarters, Marine Corps   (see **Marine Corps**)

Health Services Command   (see **Army Health Services Command**)

heavy ballistic missile: An **ICBM** (intercontinental ballistic missile) which has a launchweight or throw-weight greater than that of the Soviet SS-19 ICBM. A heavy ballistic missile is one of two categories of ballistic missiles designated by the **SALT II** treaty for purposes of missile counting. (see also **light ballistic missile**)

heavy bomber: The term used for **SALT II** missile counting to describe those aircraft included in the aggregate limitations of the agreement. Heavy bombers consist of four categories of airplanes:

- "Current types," the U.S. **B-52 Stratofortress** and **B-1**, and the Tu-95 Bear and Myasishchev Bison for the Soviets;
- "Future types," including any bombers which can carry out the mission of a heavy bomber in a manner similar or superior to that of the bombers listed above (U.S. **B-2** and Soviet Blackjack);
- Types of bombers equipped for **cruise missiles** capable of a range in excess of 600 km;
- Types of bombers equipped for air-launched ballistic missiles (ASBMs).

(see also **bomber**)

HEDI   (see **High Endoatmospheric Defense Interceptor**)

height of burst (HOB):   "The vertical distance from the earth's surface or target to the point of burst" (*JCS Pub 1*, p. 170.) For nuclear weapons, the optimum height of burst for a particular target is the height at which it is estimated a weapon of a specific energy yield will produce a certain desired effect over the maximum possible area.

helicopter: An aircraft supported in flight by rotating airfoils instead of fixed wings. Helicopters are used for observation, rescue, transport, anti-submarine warfare, and antitank duties.

Hellfire: Army and Marine Corps, short-range, air-to-ground, guided, conventionally-armed anti-armor missile. It is a third generation anti-armor missile, the follow-on missile to the **TOW**. It is presently the main armament of the Army **AH-64 Apache** helicopter and Marine Corps attack helicopters. The missile is designed to accept a laser, imaging infrared, and a radar frequency/infrared seeker. Hellfire homes on a laser spot that can be projected from ground observers, other aircraft, and the launching aircraft itself. This enables the missile to be launched indirectly, in some cases without the firing aircraft seeing the target. The infrared seeker has a fire-and-forget capability, allowing the launching aircraft to leave the area after firing. The AH-64 Apache can carry up to 16 missiles. Hellfire is in full scale production and was fielded with the Apache in 1986. There is an improvement program underway to increase the missile's lethality against reactive armor and harden the seeker to countermeasures. Contractors are Rockwell International and Martin Marietta. In FY 1990 the Army requested $167.4 million for 3,102 missiles including RDT&E, and the Navy requested $51.5 million for 1,098 missiles for Marine Corps use.

HEMP (see **electromagnetic pulse**)

Hercules (see **C-130**)

HERT (Headquarters Emergency Relocation Team): Strategic Air Command mobile command center located at the Cornhusker Army Ammunition Plant, Grand Island, NE. (see also **Ground Mobile Command Center**)

Hexagon: **Byeman** code name for the former KH-9 class of photographic reconnaissance satellites. Nicknamed "Big Bird," it was initially developed as a backup to the Air Force's Manned Orbiting Laboratory (MOL). Nineteen Hexagon satellites were launched into north-south polar orbits between 15 June 1971 and 20 June 1984. It was a medium-altitude, film-return, area-surveillance satellite, capable of photographing large areas (e.g., entire base complexes, testing facilities, cities, etc.). Intelligence obtained by Hexagon and other imaging satellites is marked by the codeword **Ruff** [Jeffrey Richelson, *American Espionage and the Soviet Target*, 1987, pp. 229, 231]. (see also **keyhole**)

HH-3 (see **CH-3**)

HH-53 (see **CH-53**)

HH-60H Seahawk: Navy's helicopter combat support (HCS) aircraft, a derivative of the **SH-60F**. The helicopter has a crew of three and seating for up to 11 troops. The primary mission of the new HH-60H will be strike rescue, with secondary tasks involving special warfare missions. The HH-60Hs are the first new aircraft purchased for and operated exclusively by the Naval Air Reserve. The first HH-60H flight was conducted at Sikorsky Aircraft, Stratford, CT, on 17 August 1988. The first HH-60H squadron, Helicopter Combat Support Special Squadron (HCS) 5, was established on 1 October 1988 at NAS Point Mugu, CA. Its primary mission is combat search and rescue (strike rescue), with a secondary mission of special warfare support.

H-hour: **1.** The specific hour on **D-day** on which particular operations or hostilities commence or are to commence. **2.** Time zero, or time of detonation. (see also **military time**)

HI-CAMP (Highly Calibrated Airborne Measurements Program): Sensors aboard Lockheed U-2 reconnaissance aircraft to measure combinations of atmospheric, oceanic, and terrestrial backgrounds to build a data base of infrared (IR) signatures.

HICOM: Navy-operated command HF/SSB communications network for shore to ship and **TACAMO** to submarine communications. HICOM stations are located at Sigonella, Sicily, Italy; Nea Makri, Greece; Rota, Spain; Wahiawa, HI; Yokosuka, Japan; Guam; and San Miguel, Philippines.

high-altitude burst: A detonation of a nuclear weapon at an altitude over 100,000 ft. Above this level the distribution of the energy of the explosion between **blast** and thermal radiation changes appreciably with increasing altitudes due to changes in the fireball phenomena.

High Altitude Large Optics (HA-LO): DARPA project that tests imaging sensors in synchronous orbit for satellite capability to closely follow both aircraft and cruise missiles.

high earth orbit: An orbit around the Earth at an altitude greater than 3,000 nm (about 5600 km). Both geostationary and geosynchronous orbits are high earth orbits.

High Endoatmospheric Defense Interceptor (HEDI): Strategic Defense Initiative Organization and **U.S. Army Strategic Defense Command** ground-based, hypervelocity, high-acceleration, area-defense interceptor to engage ballistic missile reentry vehicles in the endoatmosphere. HEDI, under this description, must intercept short-range and depressed-trajectory SLBMs as well as ICBM reentry vehicles penetrating the midcourse defense layer. If used as a defense for short-range ballistic missiles, HEDI could be used as part of the antitactical ballistic missile defense in Europe. Mid-course sensors will provide target detection, tracking, and identification; determine the intercept point; select the trajectory; and issue the launch command to HEDI. The HEDI kill vehicle includes an optical window, an active cooling system for its infrared seeker, a propulsion system, a protective shroud, and a nonnuclear explosive warhead.

Three HEDI tests are planned at Launch Complex 37 at White Sands Missile Range, NM, with later interception tests planned for Kwajalein Atoll. The first of a series of experimental flights planned for 1989 as part of the Kinetic Kill Vehicle Integrated

Technology Experiment (KITE) program, has been delayed to early 1990. The series will test the integration of the kill vehicle into the interceptor, the removal of the segmented shroud and check of the cooling system, and the seeker and laser rangefinder to fuze the fragmenting warhead. McDonnell Douglas is the prime contractor and was awarded $330 million for RDT&E. FY 1989 funding was at $113 million. Major subcontractors are Hughes for the seeker and kill vehicle electronics and Aerojet Technical Systems for the controls and thrusters.

high explosive (HE): An explosive that, when used in its normal manner, detonates rather than deflagrates or burns: that is, the rate of advance of the reaction zone into the unreacted material exceeds the velocity of sound in the unreacted material.

high frequency (HF) (see **frequency**)

High Level Group (HLG): NATO group created in the 1970s to plan for the modernization of nuclear forces in Europe. The HLG recommended that NATO needed a land-based missile system with the capability to reach the Soviet Union. The recommendation resulted in the INF modernization decision of December 1979 to deploy **Pershing II** and **ground-launched cruise missiles** in Europe.

high risk area: **Civil defense** term referring to likely target areas such as strategic bases, major military installations, and metropolitan areas.

HILEX: NATO high-level **exercise**.

Holystone: Former code name for a Navy submarine-reconnaissance program established in 1959. It was previously called Bollard and Pinnacle, and is currently known as **Barnacle** [Jeffrey Richelson, *The U.S. Intelligence Community,* 2d Edition, pp. 190-191].

Homing   Overlay   Experiment (HOE): Army **ballistic missile defense** research project begun in 1978 to demonstrate the ability of optics to acquire targets in flight; to isolate reentry vehicles from accompanying chaff, penetration aids, and booster fragments; and to guide a missile to intercept with a goal of a miss distance small enough to permit destruction by other than a nuclear explosion. HOE consisted of four tests of ground-based, exoatmospheric nonnuclear kill vehicles made of large aluminum nets carrying metal weights equipped with sensors to detect long wave infrared emissions. The kill vehicle destroys its target by colliding into it at a speed high enough to disintegrate the target. The kill vehicle and a small infrared-guided homing device were carried atop a modified Minuteman ICBM in the experiments.

The first three tests, held in 1983, were all failures. During the fourth test flight on 10 June 1984, the HOE intercepted a dummy **Minuteman** warhead fired from Vandenburg AFB, CA, in the direction of Kwajalein Atoll. After this test, HOE became part of the **Exoatmospheric Reentry Vehicle Interception System (ERIS)**. In January 1984, the

Soviet Union protested that using the Minuteman to test HOE was in violation of the **ABM Treaty**. The U.S. response, published in an Arms Control and Disarmament Agency Bulletin, stated that "the test missile in question was observably different from Minuteman I, as were its performance characteristics. In any case, the Minuteman I is no longer deployed by the United States."

Hornet   (see **F/A-18**)

host nation support (HNS):   Civil or military assistance provided in peace or war to U.S. forces located on a host nation's territory. The basis of such assistance are commitments arising from bilateral and multilateral agreements concluded among the United States and host nations. The type and extent of assistance is agreed upon on the basis of the national laws and the actual support capabilities of the host nation. The form of reimbursement differs. Peacetime HNS is provided to U.S. forces by allies in such areas as skilled labor, transportation, construction services and materials, real property facilities, and pipelines. There are three primary U.S. programs to acquire wartime host nation support from NATO allies: the **collocated operating base (COB)** program, the **lines of communications (LOC)** program, and the Germany HNS program (similar to LOC arrangements, but a separate program recognizing the amount of HNS support required from West Germany).

hot box: The exercise term for a **defense emergency**.

Hot Line   (see **Direct Communications Link**)

howitzer: A cannon that combines certain characteristics of guns and mortars. The howitzer delivers projectiles with medium velocities, either by low or high trajectories. (see also **artillery**)

HQ: Abbreviation for **headquarters**.

human   intelligence   (HUMINT): Type of **intelligence** information collected from human sources, including military officers, agents, attachés, defectors, emigrés, and travelers.

Human Reliability Program (HRP): Air Force term applied to the **Personnel Reliability Program (PRP)**.

hunter-killer submarine   (see **attack submarine**)

Huron   (see **C-12 Huron**)

hydrophone: "In acoustic mines and underwater sound detecting equipment, the detecting element which converts the sound vibratory pressure into an electrical signal" [*NWP 3*]. (see also **anti-submarine warfare**, **Sound Surveillance System**)

Hydrus: EHF secure submarine-to-shore report-back satellite communications network using **Fleet Satellite Communications System**, **LES-8/9**, and **MILSTAR** in the future. A development program to enable ballistic missile submarine commanders to communicate with commanders on shore without revealing the submarine location or unduly constraining operations. Hydrus subprojects:

- Omen: ship-to-shore communications using satellite relay;
- Classic Mayflower: support to existing operational ship-to-shore communications systems;
- **Clarinet Merlin**: submarine emergency communications transmitter and automatic guard receiver terminal providing automatic shore notification of the loss of fleet ballistic missile submarines on patrol.

Hypersonic Glide Vehicle (HGV): Air Force/DARPA technology prototype research program to yield a long-range precision-strike vehicle capable of attacking high-value airborne and ground-based targets with nonnuclear warheads. Testing of flight vehicles is on **Minuteman I** rocket boosters. The HGV program includes **Loraine** radar and mid-course satellite navigation package and the Air Force high-speed submunition ejection experiment conducted for the **Air Defense Initiative**. HGV flies at speeds of Mach 20 to 25.

hypervelocity gun (see **electromagnetic gun**)

Hypervelocity Launcher (HVL): Kinetic energy electromagnetic accelerator used to propel projectiles at high velocities to destroy enemy ballistic missiles. The hypervelocity launcher has applicability to ground-based terminal defense and space-based boost and mid-course defense. Initial testing is being conducted on ground segments, with space-based testing planned for the early 1990s. The United States and Australia have cooperated in the development of a hypervelocity launcher. (see also **electromagnetic gun**, **kinetic energy weapon**)

I

I: Prefix designating aerial intercept vehicle.

IACS: Ship-to-submarine active sonar-initiated acoustic-signalling network.

Iberian Atlantic Command (IBER-LANT): Major subordinate command of NATO's **Allied Command Atlantic**, established September 1982. Its area extends from the **Allied Command Europe** boundary 500 miles to the west. It shares part of its area of responsibility with **Allied Naval Forces Southern Europe (NAV-SOUTH)**. It is commanded by a Portuguese officer.

Headquarters
Lisbon, Portugal

Principle Subordinate Command

• Island Command Madeira, Funchal, Madeira

ICBM (intercontinental ballistic missile): Land-based rocket-propelled **ballistic missile** capable of delivering a warhead to intercontinental range (5,500 km or more). An ICBM consists of a booster, one or more reentry vehicles, possibly penetration aids, and in the case

of a **MIRV**ed missile, a post-boost vehicle. Active U.S. ICBMs are **Minuteman** II, Minuteman III, and the **MX**. The **Small ICBM** (nicknamed Midgetman) is under development. Only land-based missiles are called ICBMs to differentiate them from **submarine-launched ballistic missiles**, which are not necessarily of intercontinental range.

Land-based ICBMs have redundant and intrusion-secure specialized communications that are considered the most survivable of all strategic forces. This includes hardened underground cables, HF and UHF radios, LF and VLF reception, and satellite links. The Air Force ICBM SHF Satellite Terminal will provide a Super High Frequency receive capability for SAC **launch control centers (LCCs)** and enhances the LCC ability to receive **emergency action message** information in nuclear-disrupted environments.

Iceland Defense Force (IDF): Sub-unified command of **U.S. Atlantic Command**. Under the terms of an agreement signed in 1951 by the United States and Iceland, the IDF is charged with the defense of Iceland on behalf of NATO. The agreement, renewed in 1974, provides that the United States retain the use of its military facilities in Iceland. U.S. operations centered around the Keflavik airport include naval and air facilities and components, radar centers and facilities, and Air Force fighter-interceptor and AWACS operating forces. In wartime, IDF air and naval forces are provided to the NATO Island Commander Iceland (see **Island Commanders**), which is subordinate to **Eastern Atlantic Command** (Allied Command Atlantic). It is commanded by Commander, Fleet Air Keflavik, who in wartime becomes the NATO Island Commander Iceland. IDF comprises approximately 3,000 U.S. service personnel.

Headquarters
Keflavik, Iceland
(APO New York 09571)

Service Component Commands

- Air Forces Iceland
- Naval Forces Iceland

Iceland Regional Operational Control Center (ICEROCC): Air defense command system capable of combining data from ground-based radars, **Airborne Warning and Control System** radars, and civil air-traffic radars. ICEROCC automatically computes intercepts and matches target data against existing flight plans. The system has 12 operator consoles, each with two cathode ray tubes for maintaining surveillance and directing intercepts. Hughes is the primary equipment contractor.

Identification, Friend or Foe (see **IFF**)

IFF (Identification, Friend or Foe): An electronic system of coded signals between aircraft and radar systems to provide positive friend identification and air traffic control capabilities. With the growing sophistication in the capabilities of radar-controlled missiles and aircraft, the chance of shooting down one's own aircraft has increased. The IFF system is designed to transmit and receive signals in a secure, jam resistant, and precise time mode. The next generation of IFF hardware is the Mark XV joint secure anti-jam system being developed by Bendix and Texas Instruments to replace Mark XII. Deployment of the Mark XV is planned for the **F-15, F-18**, EH-60 helicopter (see **EH-1**), I-**Hawk** missile, and Aegis and Spruance class destroyers.

IIR Maverick   (see **Maverick**)

imagery intelligence (IMINT): Type of **intelligence** information collected by optical or electronic means, including visual photography, infrared images, electro-optics, and radar images. Photographic and electro-optic imagery can only be produced in daylight and without heavy cloud cover. Radar images, obtained by bouncing radio waves off of an object to produce an image, are capable of being produced through cloud cover. Thermal infrared imagery may be produced in darkness. Means of collecting IMINT are by satellite and overhead reconnaissance systems. (see also **airborne reconnaissance, satellite reconnaissance, keyhole satellites, photographic intelligence**)

immediate: Precedence category assigned to a message to indicate the relative order and speed at which it is to be communicated. It is reserved for data relating to "situations that gravely affect the security of national/allied forces or populace." Immediate messages are marked "OO" and are to be handled within approximately 30 minutes. (see also **FLASH, Priority, Routine**)

implosion-type weapon (implosion weapon): A type of nuclear weapon in which a subcritical configuration of fissionable materials (called the "core") is compressed into a supercritical state by a surrounding high-explosive detonation. The implosion configuration can either be used by itself (and is subsequently called a **fission** weapon), or can be used as the first stage in a multi-stage thermonuclear weapon. (see also **gun-type weapon**)

Improved Emergency Message Automated Transmission System (IEMATS): A dedicated message processing and transmission system linking the **National Military Command Center**, the **Alternate National Military Command Center**, the command centers and alternate operations centers of the nuclear-capable unified and specified commands, and the operations centers of the service headquarters. It is the primary record means used by the JCS and the CINCs to prepare and transmit **emergency action messages (EAMs)**.

inactive aircraft inventory: Aircraft in storage, bailment, government furnished aircraft on loan or lease outside DOD, or otherwise not available to the military services.

Inactive National Guard: A category of **ready reserve** personnel who are temporarily unable to participate in training. Such members are unpaid and cannot receive retirement credits. They remain available for mobilization with their unit if so ordered. This category is only used by the **Army National Guard**. Its personnel strength is approximately 10,000.

indications & warning (I&W): 1. Forewarning of enemy actions or intentions, the imminence of hostilities, nuclear/nonnuclear attack on the United States or allied nations, hostile reactions to U.S. reconnaissance activities, terrorist attacks, and other similar events that would precede actual **tactical warning** of an attack. 2. Intelligence and command center activities intended to detect and report time-sensitive information that would provide indications and warning.

Indigo   (see **Lacrosse**)

individual mobilization augmentee (IMA): Army **manpower** term that refers to individuals counted in the **selected reserve** manning structure who fill active component billets upon mobilization. The program was adopted in October 1981 by transferring personnel of the Mobilization Designation (MOBDES) program from the **Individual Ready Reserve (IRR)** to the selected reserve. In peacetime, IMA program personnel are pre-assigned to active units, the

Selective Service System, or the Federal Emergency Management Agency to train for wartime duties. IMA billets are not included in the active component programmed manpower structure, but fill active Army wartime force structure requirements [DOD, *Manpower Requirements Report FY 1989,* March 1988, pp. III-44, B-2]. (see also **force structure**)

Individual Ready Reserve (IRR): A category of **ready reserve** personnel whose members are not assigned to the **Selected Reserve**. Many such personnel are former members of active duty forces completing their six-year military service obligation. They may participate in periodic training for retirement or promotion credit. They remain available for mobilization with their unit if so ordered. The total personnel strength of the IRR is approximately 450,000. The Army National Guard does not use this category, but refers to its inactive personnel as **Inactive National Guard**.

individuals: A **manpower** term that refers to personnel not filling spaces in the programmed manpower structure. Individuals include: "transients, trainees (includes reserve component training pipeline for the reserve component), patients, prisoners, holdees, cadets and students." The individual category is counted as a portion of the **end strength** figures [DOD, *Manpower Requirements Report FY 1989*, March 1988, p. B-2].

inertial guidance: A weapon guidance system designed to project a missile over a predetermined path, wherein the path of the missile is adjusted after launching by devices wholly within the missile and independent of outside information. The system measures and converts accelerations experienced to distance traveled in a certain direction [*JCS Pub 1,* p. 183].

Inertial Upper Stage   (see **IUS**)

INF (intermediate range nuclear forces): Category of nuclear weapons with a range less than 5,500 km.

infantry: **Branch** and combat arm of the Army, and the basic building block for five of the eight **maneuver battalions**, and five of six **divisions**. All infantry units have the same mission of closing with, destroying, or capturing the enemy. They have the capability to hold ground and conduct offensive and defensive operations in all types of terrain and weather, but their combat power is based upon the rifleman.

infantry battalion: Type of Army **maneuver battalion**, and the most common formation in Army combat forces. Infantry battalions are further classified into **light infantry, air assault, airborne, motorized**, and **mechanized** infantry battalions. There are two ways to classify infantry battalions: light (light infantry, air assault, airborne, and motorized) and heavy (which includes only mechanized battalions).

infantry division: A type of Army **division**, consisting of either **light infantry, air assault, airborne, mo-**

torized, or **mechanized** divisions. These divisions can conduct sustained close combat tasks including air assault, active defense, and riverine operations, either dismounted or mounted in armored personnel carriers or armored fighting vehicles. The infantry division is capable of operations in difficult weather and terrain and can operate as part of a joint airborne force.

Information Systems Command (see **Army Information Systems Command**)

information systems security: General term that encompasses the various security disciplines, including **communication security (COMSEC)**; compromising emanations (**TEMPEST**); computer security (COMPUSEC); **operations security (OPSEC)**; information security; personnel security; industrial security; resource protection; physical security; and some types of command, control, and communications systems security. (see also **security classification, National Security Agency/Central Security Service**)

Inform Net: Air Force HF radio communications system providing **U.S. Air Forces Europe (USAFE)** command and control functions. Inform Net also supports contingency operations, aircraft operations, and U.S. embassies. The Air Force Communications Command maintains and operates the Net under the operational control and management of USAFE headquarters. There are 13 active and 9 standby stations, capable of operations with 24 hours notice. Five of

the stations can also provide air-to-ground communications. Ground stations include Incirlik, Turkey; Torrejon, Spain; Aviano, Italy; Bitburg, Hahn, Zweibruecken, West Germany; and Alconbury and Bentwaters, UK. Air-to-ground stations include Rhein Main (network control station) and Ramstein (alternate network control station), West Germany; Mildenhall and Greenham Common, UK; and Athens, Greece. Standby stations include Spangdahlem and Sembach, West Germany; Zaragoza, Spain; Camp Amsterdam, Netherlands; Fairford, Schulthorp, Lakenheath, Upper Heyford, and Wethersfield, UK. The CINCEUR airborne command post can also act as the network control station [Maj. Louis J. Casamayou, USAF, *A Guide to U.S. Air Force Command Control Communications*, Air Command and Staff College, Air University, Maxwell AFB, AL, Report #83-0380, April 1983, released under the FOIA].

infrared (IR): Electromagnetic radiation lying in the wavelength interval from about 0.8 microns to an indefinite upper boundary, sometimes arbitrarily set at 1,000 microns (0.01 cm). At the lower limit of this interval, the infrared radiation spectrum is bounded by visible radiation, while on its upper limit it is bounded by microwave radiation of the type important in radar technology. An infrared sensor is a surveillance system used to detect weapons by sensing the thermal radiation emitted. In the case of ballistic missiles, for instance, thermal radiation is most easily detected during the boost phase of a missile trajectory or during the mid-course phase in space. IR sensors detect the temperature difference between a target and its ocean or land background. IR sensing cannot see through clouds or rain and must be done from a medium or low altitude.

Infrared detection research is a major part of **Strategic Defense Initiative** and **air defense** related surveillance programs. IR research began with **HI-CAMP**, using **U-2** surveillance aircraft to measure platforms and backgrounds to build a data base of IR signatures. Balloons and sounding rockets were also equipped with sensors to gather data on the IR signatures of ballistic and cruise missile targets. The **Teal Ruby** satellite was to have determined how well IR detection works from space. Satellite launch was set back by the destruction of the space shuttle Challenger on which it was to be launched. The satellite is now in storage but is slated for carriage on the shuttle in 1990.

INF Treaty: U.S.–Soviet arms control agreement signed in Washington by President Reagan and General Secretary Gorbachev on 8 December 1987. The treaty eliminated all ground-launched intermediate-range (1,000–5,500 km) and short-range (500–1,000 km) missiles and launchers and support equipment. The treaty entered into force on 1 June 1988. The Soviet Union is to destroy 1,846 missiles while the United States is to destroy 846 missiles. The INF negotiations were a series of talks that began after the Soviet Union deployed the first SS-20 missiles in late 1976 and after the 1979 NATO decision to deploy 572 intermediate-range **Pershing II** and **Ground-Launched Cruise Missiles (GLCMs)** in Europe.

When the negotiations began between the superpowers in November 1981, perspectives on the balance of intermediate-range nuclear weapons were vastly different. The United States claimed that the Soviet Union enjoyed a six-to-one missile-to-warhead advantage, while the Soviets maintained that "an appropriate balance" existed. The disagreement arose over which systems should be counted: U.S. exclusion and Soviet inclusion of British and French systems; U.S. inclusion and Soviet exclusion of SS-20s in the Asian region of the USSR; number of nuclear-capable aircraft to be included for each side — each side counted all such aircraft in the number for the other side but not in their own.

Initial U.S. negotiating goals formulated during the Carter Administration included reducing the level of Soviet SS-20s and deploying its own new systems. Initially, the Soviets hoped to block U.S. deployment of INFs in Europe and generally did not take up serious negotiations until the missiles were actually deployed. In 1981, the Reagan Administration proposed a "zero option" plan: the Soviet Union would scrap all of its SS-20, SS-4, and SS-5 missiles and the United States would cancel deployments in Europe. The Soviets, however, initially rejected this proposal, refusing to dismantle new SS-20s in return for the United States cancelling missiles that were only under development.

In July 1982, negotiators Paul Nitze and Yuli Kvitsinsky took their celebrated "walk in the woods," which would have foregone U.S. Pershing II deployments in Europe in exchange for a Soviet reduction in INFs, leaving a ceiling of Soviet and American missiles. Both governments, however, turned down this plan: the United States was too pro-Pershing II not to deploy it and the Soviet Union was too anti-INF deployments to sanction and give legitimacy to the long-range GLCM deployment.

Negotiations on strategic arms control were also deadlocked, creating more problems for the INF negotiations. The new U.S. missiles in Europe were capable of hitting Soviet territory while the Soviet SS-20s were not capable of striking the U.S. homeland. Some arms control advocates thus felt that it was therefore almost mandatory to set limits on the strategic forces first, look at the resulting balance, and then decide on INF limits.

The U.S. Congress, which had played a minimal role in the original 1979 NATO modernization decision to deploy the new missiles, funded the two weapons and supported deployment. Although public opinion in Europe ran strongly against the INF deployments, the missiles were deployed in November-December 1983. On 23 November 1983, the first Pershing II missiles arrived in West Germany for deployment; on the same day the Soviet delegation walked out of the INF negotiations in protest. On 1 January 1984, the first 16 GLCMs deployed in the UK become operational.

Negotiations to limit INF weapons did not begin again until 12 March 1985. At the Geneva summit meeting in November 1985, President Reagan and Secretary Gorbachev issued a joint statement committing both countries to early progress on nuclear and space arms control talks (strategic arms control), as well as pursuit of an interim INF agreement. In September 1986, the sixth round of INF talks begin in Geneva: The United States proposed that each side restrict its forces to 100 warheads in Europe and that the Soviet Union reduce to 100 warheads in Asia, with the United States storing 100 missiles and warheads in CONUS for potential deployment in "Asia" (e.g., Alaska).

On 11–12 October 1986, Reagan and Gorbachev met in Reykjavik, Iceland, and among other topics discussed, they agreed to the "zero option" for Europe with equal limits of 100 long-range INF warheads for each side. The Soviets dropped their demand that French and British nuclear forces be included in a U.S.-Soviet INF accord and agreed to include limits on short-range INF systems as well. On 12-15 April 1987, Secretary Shultz met with Gorbachev and Foreign Minister Shevardnadze in Moscow, and the Soviets proposed the total elimination of short-range INF missiles. Then, on 22 July 1987, Gorbachev proposed the "double zero-option" that would eliminate all short-range and long-range INF systems in Europe and all SS-20s in Asia, altering their previous position of maintaining 100 long-range INF warheads on each side outside of Europe. Completion of the treaty then proceeded smoothly, with only the verification provisions of the destruction of the missiles to be worked out.

The treaty's three types of verification procedures are the most detailed and stringent in arms control history. Verification includes on-site inspections, inspections by challenge, and national technical means (e.g., intelligence collection, primarily by signals intelligence and reconnaissance satellites). The provisions include

- A specified number of Americans to be stationed at the Votkinsk missile center for 13 years (Votkinsk man- ufactured the INF missiles);
- A comparable number of Soviet inspectors to be stationed at the U.S. missile plant in Magna, UT, for 13 years;
- On-site inspections to be conducted at INF facilities in the United States and the Soviet Union, and in allied countries in Eastern and Western Europe;
- Comprehensive data on missiles and launchers being eliminated to be exchanged;
- Actual destruction of prohibited missiles and launchers to occur within first three years of the treaty entering into force;
- During the first three years, 20 short-notice challenge inspections to be permitted for each side, at sites listed in the treaty;
- During the next five years, 15 short-notice challenge inspections to be permitted at listed sites;
- During subsequent five years, 10 short-notice inspections to be per- mitted at listed sites; and
- Soviet shorter-range missiles and launchers to be removed to elimina- tion facilities within 90 days of the treaty entering into force, with full destruction of these systems occur- ring within 18 months of the treaty entering into force.

initial operational capability (IOC): The date when the first combat unit is equipped and trained and logistic support is established to permit per- formance of combat missions in the field. An IOC date is also associ- ated with each new weapon system as a target date for delivery of com- bat equipment, repair parts, mainte- nance equipment, and publications, plus trained personnel. (see also **full operational capability**)

Inshore Underseas Warfare Group (IUWG): 1. "A specialized orga- nization of the [Navy's] operating forces established to fulfill the Navy's responsibility for inshore undersea warfare." [*NWP 3*] **2.** "A task orga- nization which provides surface and subsurface detection of enemy tar- gets in the seaward approaches to the amphibious objective area. It is ordi- narily composed of a mobile inshore surveillance unit and inshore warfare attack unit" [*NWP 3*]. IUWGs are naval **special operations** units and since 1980 have been part of the naval reserve. There are two groups: IUWG 1 at NAB Coronado, CA, and IUWG 2 at NAB Little Creek, VA. Each group comprises 16 **Mobile Inshore Underseas Warfare (MIUW)** units.

inshore undersea warfare (IUW): "Operations conducted with the inten- tion of denying the enemy effective use of his submarines, submarine- launched vehicles, surface craft, and swimmers in the inshore area." The inshore area is a "relatively shal- low water area in which the prox- imity and contour of the bottom and/or nearby coastline influences the actions and capabilities of the adversary. This area generally encom- passes water depths 0–500 fathoms but may include depths to 2,000 fathoms" [*NWP 3*].

inspection: By design and intent, an inspection is a graded evaluation of individual or unit performance or proficiency measured against established standards. Training is not a primary inspection objective; rather, inspections assess the effectiveness of prior training. Unit operational readiness inspection and annual aircraft inflight evaluations are perhaps the most typical examples of inspections. Inspections are fault or performance oriented; exercises are no-fault or training oriented [AF, *Air Force Participation in the Military Exercise Program*, AFR 55-37, 7 June 1985, p. 5, released under the FOIA].

Institute for Defense Analysis (IDA) (see **Federally-Funded Research** and **Development Centers**)

instrumentation: **1.** The installation and use of electronic, gyroscopic, and other instruments for the purpose of detecting, measuring, recording, telemetering, processing, or analyzing different values or quantities as encountered in the flight of an aircraft, a missile, or a spacecraft. Instrumentation applies to both airborne and ground-based equip- ; ment.   **2.** The assemblage of such instruments in an aerospace vehicle, each instrument designed and located so as to occupy minimum space, achieve minimum weight, yet function effectively.   **3.** A special field of engineering concerned with the design, composition, and arrangement of such instruments.

insurgency: "A struggle between a constituted government and organized insurgents frequently supported from without, but acting violently from within, against the political, social, economic, military, and civil vulnerabilities of the regime to bring about its internal destruction or overthrow. Such wars are distinguished from lesser insurgencies by the gravity of the threat to government and the insurgent object of eventual regional or national control" [*Army Dictionary*, p. 144].

Integrated Operational Nuclear Detection System (IONDS): Former name of the **Nuclear Detonation Detection System**.

intelligence: **1.** "The product resulting from the collection, processing, integration, analysis, evaluation and interpretation of available information concerning foreign countries or areas" [*JCS Pub 1*, p. 188].   **2.** Activities and organizations engaged in the production of such information. The three types of intelligence collection are

- **imagery intelligence (IMINT)**, which includes **photographic intelligence (PHOTINT)**;
- **signals intelligence (SIGINT)**, which includes **communications intelligence (COMINT), foreign instrumentation signals intelligence (FISINT), telemetry intelligence (TELINT), electronic intelligence (ELINT), radar intelligence (RADINT)**, and **laser intelligence (LASINT)**; and
- **human intelligence (HUMINT)**.

Intelligence and Communications: Program 3 of the 11 **major force programs** that represent all of the major missions of the services and are the most basic structural elements of the DOD **Five Year Defense Program**. Consists of intelligence, security, and communications program elements, including resources related primarily to centrally directed DOD support functions, such as mapping, charting, geodetic activities, weather service, oceanography, aerospace rescue and recovery, nuclear weapons operations, space boosters, satellite control, and aerial targets.

Intelligence and Security Command (INSCOM)   (see **Army Intelligence and Security Command**)

intelligence community: Collective term that refers to the various **intelligence** agencies of the Executive Branch: the office of the **Director of Central Intelligence (DCI)** and its Intelligence Community Staff, the **Central Intelligence Agency**, the **National Security Agency**, the **Defense Intelligence Agency**, the **National Reconnaisance Office**, the Department of State's Bureau of Intelligence and Research (INR), intelligence elements of the military services, and intelligence elements of the **Federal Bureau of Investigation**, Department of Treasury, Department of Energy, and Drug Enforcement Administration. Military- and defense-related intelligence agencies and offices are often referred to as the **defense intelligence community**.

Intelligence Oversight Board: A body formed by appointment of the President to provide him and the Attorney General with reports and advice on the legality and propriety of intelligence activities; membership and duties are expressed in Executive Order 12036.

Intelligence Priorities for Strategic Planning (IPSP):   One of six documents of the **Joint Strategic Planning System (JSPS)**, the IPSP is a midrange forecast covering years 1 to 10 in a 20-year cycle, and is published annually by 15 April. The IPSP provides military intelligence priorities and tasking for DOD intelligence collection, production, and support activities. It provides prioritized collection and production of military intelligence requirement categories to support developing, updating, and revising the **Joint Intelligence Estimate for Planning**.

Interagency Communications System (ICS):   The dedicated system for communications between the **FEMA Special Facility** and the **Alternate National Military Command Center**, and between civilian and military relocation sites in the federal arc.

intercept: 1. To detect and identify enemy aircraft beyond visual range by day methods or by all-weather and night methods.   **2.** To detect and identify distant electronic signals.

interceptor   (see **fighter interceptor**)

intercontinental ballistic missile(see **ICBM**)

interdepartmental group (see **National Security Council**)

Interdepartmental Group on Terrorism (IG/T): A committee of the **National Security Council (NSC)** as organized in the Reagan Administration charged with setting U.S. government **counter-terrorism** policy. The IG/T is chaired by the Director of the State Department Office for Counter-Terrorism. Permanent members include representatives from the Office of the Vice President; NSC staff; Department of Justice (which has interagency responsibility for domestic terrorism); the **Federal Bureau of Investigation**; the **Department of Defense**; the **Joint Chiefs of Staff**; the **Department of Energy**; the **Central Intelligence Agency**; and the **Federal Aviation Administration**. (see also **terrorism**)

interdiction: Mission of **air operations** associated with the destruction of roads, bridges, railroads, tunnels, supply facilities, and the like, to prevent the support of enemy front lines. Interdiction connotes operations to prevent or impede enemy use of an area or route.

interference: 1. See **MIJI**. **2.** A SALT II term that provides that neither party shall interfere with the other's use of **national technical means of verification (NTM)**. This means that neither side can destroy or attempt to negate the functioning of the NTM of the other side (e.g., blinding of photoreconnaissance satellites).

Interim Offensive Weapons Agreement (see **SALT I**)

Intermediate Nuclear Forces/Intermediate Range Nuclear Forces (see **INF**)

intermediate-range ballistic missile (IRBM): A land-based **ballistic missile** with a range 1,500 to 3,000 nm (2,750–5,500 km) less than that of an ICBM but greater than that of a short- or medium-range ballistic missile (10–1,000 km). Currently deployed IRBMs are the Soviet SS-20 and U.S. **Pershing II**, but these are being dismantled under the **INF Treaty**.

internal security: "The prevention of action against United States resources, industries, and institutions; and the protection of life and property in the event of **domestic emergency** by the employment of all measures, in peace and war, other than military defense" [*Army Dictionary*, p. 145].

International Military Education and Training (IMET): A type of grant-aid, low-cost **security assistance program** that brings foreign military personnel to the United States for training in military doctrine and technical skills and that provides the United States with access to civilian and military leadership of other countries. IMET program worldwide budget totals $54 million—the cheapest of the security assistance programs. El Salvador, Indonesia, Jordan, and the Philippines rank amongst the highest recipients of the IMET program. Military training is provided in specialties from professional military education through nation-building activities to basic technical skills. IMET supplements other countries' indigenous training capabilities. According to the Department of State's description of the program, "A significant number of IMET-trained military leaders are likely to hold future positions of prominence in their countries . . . over 1500 IMET-trained personnel hold [leadership] positions, including cabinet ministers, ambassadors, chiefs of military services and commandants of senior professional military schools." Since 1950, IMET has trained more than 500,000 foreign officers and enlisted personnel [*Department of State Congressional Presentation of Security Assistance Program FY 1990*, p. 18].

International Military Staff (IMS): The staff component of the **North Atlantic Treaty Organization (NATO)** military structure. It was established 10 February 1967 from the former Standing Group. It consists of six divisions, a Secretariat, and numerous agencies that report to the **Military Committee (MC)** through the IMS. The deputy chairman of the MC is specifically responsible for the coordination of nuclear-related affairs within the IMS. Divisions of the IMS include Intelligence, Plans and Policy, Operations, Management and Logistics, C3 Systems, and Armaments Standardization and Interoperability. Agencies reporting to the Military Committee through the IMS include

- Advisory Group for Aerospace Research and Development (AGARD);
- Allied Communications Security Agency (ACSA);

- Allied Data Systems Interoperability Agency (ADSIA);
- Allied Long Lines Agency (ALLA);
- Allied Naval Communications Agency (ANCA);
- Allied Radio Frequency Agency (ARFA);
- Allied Tactical Communications Agency (ATCA);
- Military Agency for Standardization (MAS);
- Military Command, Control and Information Systems Working Group (MCCISWG);
- Military Committee Meteorological Group (MCMG);
- Military Communications-Electronics Working Group (MCEWG);
- NATO Command and Information Systems and Automatic Data Processing Committee (NCCDAG);
- NATO Communications-Electronics Board (NCEB);
- NATO Defense College (NADEFCOL);
- NATO Electronic Warfare Advisory Committee (NEWAC); and
- Senior NATO Logisticians Conference (SNLC).

Its personnel strength is approximately 300 military personnel and 100 civilian employees (proportional representation of NATO countries).

International Staff (IS): A component of the **North Atlantic Treaty Organization's** civil structure. The IS provides support to the NATO **Secretary General**, Deputy Secretary General, the **North Atlantic Council** and the **Defense Planning Committee**. Staff divisions include Political Division, Division of Defense Planning and Policy, Division of Defense

Support, Division of Infrastructure, Logistics and Council Operations, and Division of Scientific Affairs.

interoperability: The ability of systems, units, or forces to effectively operate and exchange with each other. (see also **Rationalization, Standardization, and Interoperability**)

Inter-Service/Agency Automated Message Processing Exchange (I-S/A AMPE): An Office of the Secretary of Defense-directed effort to modernize record communications throughout switching centers, including a standardized base-level AMPE system replacement, an interface to the **Defense Data Network** for backbone trunking, and the capability to consolidate intelligence and common-user communications systems in a multilevel secure system certified to the highest level.

Intruder   (see **A-6**)

intrusion   (see **MIJI**)

intrusion detection: The process of **physical security**, normally referring to the system, consisting of a sensor or set of sensors capable of detecting one or more types of phenomena, signal media, annunciator(s), and energy source, for signaling the entry or attempted entry of a person or other target into a protected area, such as an ammunition storage point or individual bunker.

IOC   (see **initial operational capability**)

IONDS (Integrated Operational Nuclear Detection System) (see **Nuclear Detonation Detection System**)

Iowa class (BB-61): Battleship class modernized and reintroduced into the Navy during the Reagan Administration with major renovations in weapons, communications, electronic warfare, and habitability. The first modernized battleship, USS New Jersey (BB-62), was recommissioned 28 December 1982. The second, USS Iowa (BB-61), was recommissioned 28 April 1984. The third, USS Missouri (BB-63), was recommissioned 10 May 1986. The fourth, USS Wisconsin (BB-64) was recommissioned 22 October 1988. Battleships are the second largest ships in the U.S. fleet after aircraft carriers, displacing 58,000 tons. They are 887 ft long and have a beam of 108 ft. Eight boilers power four turbines and shafts, giving the ships a top speed of 35 kt. They retain their original armament of nine 16-in guns and 12 of their original 5 in/38 caliber guns. During modernization, eight four-celled armored box launchers for 32 **Tomahawk sea-launched cruise missiles**, four quad launchers for 16 **Harpoon** missiles and four Phalanx close-in-weapon systems were added. There are 123 officers and 1,699 enlisted personnel in the ship's complement.

IRBM   (see **intermediate-range ballistic missile**)

ISHTAR   (see **sensitive compartmented information**)

Island Commander: Regional organization of NATO's **Allied Command Atlantic** at the **major subordinate command (MSC)** level:

- Island Commander Azores: subordinate to Western Atlantic Command, headquartered at San Miguel, Azores.
- Island Commander Bermuda: subordinate to Western Atlantic Command, headquartered at Hamilton, Bermuda.
- Island Commander Faroes: subordinate to Eastern Atlantic Command, headquartered at Thorshavn, Faroes.
- Island Commander Greenland: subordinate to Western Atlantic Command, headquartered at Gronnedal, Greenland.
- Island Commander Iceland: subordinate to Eastern Atlantic Command, headquartered at Keflavik, Iceland.
- Island Commander Madeira: subordinate to Iberian Atlantic Command, headquartered at Funchal, Madeira.

Island Sun (see **Ground Mobile Command Center**)

issues: The name given to alternatives to program proposals contained in the annual **Program Objectives Memorandum (POM)**. Any **Defense Resources Board (DRB)** member or any commander-in-chief can review service POMs and propose candidate topics for development into issues for DRB consideration. In a typical year, over 200 candidates are submitted. From the candidates, a smaller number (about 80) worthy of DRB atten-

tion are selected for development. The Joint Chiefs of Staff and the Office of the Secretary of Defense develop issues (Issue Papers) and consolidate them into Issue Books. There are eight issue books, and an additional book, CINCs Issues (added in the FY 1987 process):

- Policy and Risk Assessment.
- Nuclear Forces.
- Conventional Forces.
- Modernization and Investment.
- Readiness and other Logistics.
- Manpower.
- Intelligence.
- Management Initiatives.
- CINCs Issues.

Issue papers contain analysis of military department POMs relative to the **Defense Guidance**, illuminate the significant issues, list the alternatives, evaluate the costs and effectiveness of the alternatives, and suggest program changes to the POMs. Following comment by the Joint Chiefs of Staff and the Services, they are submitted to the DRB.

IUS (Inertial Upper Stage): Boeing two-stage, solid rocket vehicle capable of putting 5,000 lb into geosynchronous orbit using the **space shuttle**, or 4,000 lb using a Titan rocket. There were numerous problems in development. IUS-1 was launched on 4 April 1983 aboard STS-6, but experienced a malfunction. IUS-2 was successfully launched on 30 October 1982 from a Titan rocket. (see also **expendable launch vehicle**)

Ivy Bells: Code name for a sophisticated reconnaissance system operated by the National Security Agency (NSA) and Navy intelligence between the mid-1970s and mid-1980s. Ivy Bells was "compromised" in 1981 by a former NSA employee, Ronald W. Pelton, who sold information regarding the program to the Soviet Union. "The project involved implanting a device to intercept the signals transmitted along a Soviet underwater cable in the Sea of Okhotsk between the Kamchatka Peninsula and the eastern Soviet coastline" [Jeffrey Richelson. *American Espionage and the Soviet Target*, 1987, p. 164]. The eavesdropping device was described as "a large tap pod that . . . had a wraparound attachment that 'tapped' into the cable electronically without direct physical contact with the individual wires in the cable. If the cable had to be raised by the Soviets for inspection or maintenance, there would be no physical evidence of a tap on it; the pod would easily break away from the cable and remain on the ocean floor, undetected. Tapes in the pod recorded messages and signals on various channels or communications links for four to six weeks, and the pod had been installed for only two recording sessions a year" [Bob Woodward. *Veil: The Secret Wars of the CIA 1981–1987*, p. 448]. Implantation and recovery of the device was done by Navy **SEALs** using either SEAL Delivery Vehicles or deep submergence vehicles released by submarines. The

intercepted communications included "information on the whereabouts (at given points in time) and activities of the Soviet submarines. Such information could be exploited by the United States not only to enhance her picture of the Soviet submarine fleet but also to fine tune the detection capability of the SOSUS arrays . . . employed to track Soviet submarines" [Woodward, p. 448]. Other intelligence probably included information on Soviet military movements, plans, weapon capabilities, and ballistic-missile tests.

Long before Ivy Bells became known to the Soviet Union or popularly to the American public, this type of cable-tapping technology was the subject of several mentions in public forums. In 1976, the Pike Committee reported that a "highly technical U.S. Navy submarine reconnaissance program, often operating within unfriendly water, has experienced at least 9 collisions with hostile vessels in the last ten years, over 110 possible detections, and at least three press exposures." Seymour Hersh in *The New York Times* reported the existence of submarine operations close to the Soviet Union that "were able to plug into Soviet land communication cables strewn across the ocean bottom and thus were able to intercept high-level military messages and other communications considered too important to be sent by radio or other less secure means."

J

J: Prefix designating **1. Joint Staff** offices and officers in the **general staff** model (e.g., J-1, J-2). **2.** Special test (temporary) aircraft or vehicle.

Jackpot: Nickname for the Joint Chiefs of Staff committed and controlled air deployable communications package containing long-range and satellite data-link systems [Air Force, *Disaster Preparedness: Planning and Operations*, AFR 355-1, 17 November 1986, p. 85, released under the FOIA].

JAG (see **Judge Advocate General**)

jamming: An **electronic warfare** technique to create deliberate radio or radar interference. It involves the intentional transmission of a signal (i.e. radio frequency energy) to drown out a signal transmitted by another radar or radio. "In the high frequency (HF) band, jamming is affected by propagation of both the desired signal and the jamming energy from source locations to the receiver location. HF propagation is affected by latitude, time of day, season, and solar activity, as well as distance. The jamming of ultra high frequency (UHF) satellite systems is affected principally by the power of the jammer, antenna gain, the ability to locate the satellite uplink frequency, and the jammer's location in the satellite footprint" [Joint Chiefs of Staff, *NMCS-DOD Emergency Communications Plan,* OPR OJCS/J6C, 1 April 1988, p. 2-10, released under the FOIA].

There are two general types of electronic jammers: expendable and repeater. An expendable jammer is "a transmitter designed for special use such as dropping behind enemy lines." A repeater jammer is "a receiver-transmitter device which, when triggered by enemy radar impulses, returns synchronized false signals to the enemy equipment. The returned impulses are spaced and timed to produce false echoes or bearing errors in the enemy equipment" [*NWP 3*].

There are several types of jamming that expendable and repeater jammers can accomplish

- Barrage: "Barrage jammers are wideband amplitude- or frequency-modulated transmitters that deny the use of frequencies over a wide portion of the electromagnetic spectrum. The jamming bandwidth is normally variable and, in some equipment, may be divided between two or more portions of the spectrum."

- Frequency-search-and-lock: "This type of jamming is characterized by a narrow-band jamming signal that can be tuned over a broad frequency band and locked on to a particular frequency. This is essentially spot jamming with the additional feature of automatic lock on."
- Spot: "Spot jammers are generally narrow-band, tunable transmitters which may be modulated in frequency or amplitude by random noise or by a periodic signal. They are visually employed on a one-jammer versus one-radar basis."
- Sweep: "Sweep jammers are generally narrow-band, automatically tunable transmitters that sweep through a frequency band at a specified rate. The frequency may be tuned either mechanically or electronically from a few sweeps per second to many thousand sweeps per second" [*NWP 3*].

(see also **Compass Call**, **EF-111 Raven**, **F-4G Wild Weasel**, **MIJI**, **Quick Fix**)

Jam Resistant Secure Communications (JRSC): Part of the architecture selected by the **Worldwide Military Command and Control System (WWMCCS)**, JRSC provides SHF jam-resistant secure voice and graphics communications through **Defense Satellite Communications System (DSCS) III** for strategic warning and critical command and control communications. JRSC is composed of **Defense Support Program (DSP)** mobile ground terminals placed at various sensor locations and command sites to provide warning and intel-

ligence data, to ensure command and control of the forces, and to communicate with subordinate commands. A total of 32 JRSC terminals are planned, as well as JRSC terminals in vans that will accompany mobile ground terminal trucks. Complementary to the **Ground-Wave Emergency Network (GWEN)**, JRSC is the only system fielded that is designed to withstand electromagnetic pulse full effects and at the same time be resistant to **jamming** and nuclear degradation of the transmission path. Satellite control is achieved through eight DSCS Operations Centers, two for each satellite area.

Japanese Security Treaty: On 8 September 1951, the Treaty of Peace with Japan was signed by representatives of 49 countries in San Francisco to conclude the Pacific phase of World War II and to begin the occupation of Japan. The treaty states that "Nothing in this provision shall . . . prevent the stationing or retention of foreign armed forces in Japanese territory under or in consequence of any bilateral or multilateral agreements which have been or may be made between one or more of the Allied Powers, on the one hand, and Japan on the other" (Article 6). In addition, the signatories recognized that "Japan as a sovereign nation possesses the inherent right of individual or collective self-defense . . . and that Japan may voluntarily enter into collective security arrangements" (Article 5).

On 19 January 1960, the United States and Japan signed the Treaty of Mutual Cooperation and Security Between the United States of America and Japan, which replaced the 1951 Treaty. The agreement is composed of the following main articles:

- Article I: Both parties will "refrain in their international relations from the threat or use of force against the territorial or political independence of any state."
- Article III: Both parties "will maintain and develop, subject to their constitutional provisions, their capacities to resist armed attack."
- Article V: "Each Party recognizes that an armed attack against either Party in the territories under the Administration of Japan would be dangerous to its own peace and safety and declares that it would act to meet the common danger in accordance with its constitutional provisions and processes."
- Article VI: "For the purpose of contributing to the security of Japan and the maintenance of international peace and security in the Far East, the United States of America is granted the use by its land, air and naval forces of facilities and areas in Japan."

JASON: An elite and somewhat secretive group of scientists composed mainly of physicists. Established in 1960, the 47-member group meets for a few weeks each summer in La Jolla, CA, largely sets its own agenda, and works by contract for the DOD, the intelligence agencies, and other government organizations that have need of its expertise. The name is either derived from their annual task force study meetings during *J*uly, *A*ugust, *S*eptember, *O*ctober, and *N*ovember

or possibly borrowed from the leader of the Argonauts.

JCS (see **Joint Chiefs of Staff**)

JCS-Coordinated Exercise: Joint and combined military exercises that require scheduling and coordination by the Joint Chiefs of Staff. (see also **exercise**)

JCS-Directed Exercise: Joint and combined military exercises that are specifically directed by the Joint Chiefs of Staff. (see also **exercise**)

Jezebel: Navy AN/SSQ-38 mobile airborne passive sonobuoy system that can detect low-frequency sounds originating from waterborne sources of energy used for localization of targets.

joint: Military planning, organization, or activity involving elements of more than one service of the same nation.

Joint Air Transportation Service (JATS): Air Force service that would "provide air transportation to and between" dispersed government relocation sites during a crisis or war to ensure **continuity of government**. This program provides emergency air transportation for key individuals from the entire executive branch during conditions that require operations from dispersed sites. The services are tasked to commit helicopters and fixed-wing aircraft to JATS. "Movement of Cabinet members shall take priority under JATS; then, requirements of utmost urgency and importance, mission-essential requirements, and other traffic" [DOD, *Continuity of Operations Policies and Planning*, DOD Dir 3020.26, 24 October 1985, p. 7-1]. Relocation may be a phased implementation of the **Joint Emergency Evacuation Plan (JEEP)** or a dispersal of key personnel before implementing JEEP.

Joint Chiefs of Staff (JCS): Corporate staff of senior military advisors to the President, the **National Security Council (NSC)** and the **Secretary of Defense (SecDef)**. The concept of a "unified high command" was first adopted by the U.S. armed forces in 1942. The Joint U.S. Chiefs of Staff operated with increasing influence throughout World War II. Following the war, the JCS was formally established by the **National Security Act of 1947**, as principal military advisors to the Secretary and the President. DOD Directive 5100.1 assigns the Joint Chiefs of Staff, supported by the Joint Staff, as the immediate military staff of the Secretary of Defense. This designation is not found in Title 10 U.S. Code, but is a clear statement that the Secretary of Defense will turn to the Joint Chiefs of Staff for staff support on military matters. Each amendment to the National Security Act of 1947 states that the Joint Staff is not to operate or be organized to be an overall General Staff; therefore, it has no authority over combatant forces.

Today, in accordance with amendments to the 1947 act and other laws, the JCS consists of the presiding **Chairman of the Joint Chiefs of Staff (CJCS)**; a Vice Chairman; the **Chief of Staff of the Army**; the **Chief of Staff of the Air Force**; the **Chief of Naval Operations**; and the Commandant of the **Marine Corps**. The Goldwater-Nichols **Department of Defense Reorganization Act of 1986** redesignated the CJCS, rather than the greater staff, as the principal military advisor to the President, the NSC, and the SecDef. The 1986 act also established the position of the Vice Chairman, chosen from a different service than the Chairman, who serves in a joint-capacity and during the Chairman's absence. The Chairman exercises exclusive direction over the **Organization of the Joint Chiefs of Staff**, which includes the JCS, the Joint Staff, and JCS agencies. The service chiefs are the highest ranking active members of their individual services, and as members of the JCS, serve in an advisory capacity and do not normally exercise operational control over their services or other armed forces. Any member of the JCS may submit advice or an opinion in disagreement with the CJCS to the NCA.

The formal process by which the JCS provides military advice to the President is through the **Joint Strategic Planning System (JSPS)**. JCS responsibilities in the strategic planning process are

- a. Preparing strategic plans and providing strategic direction for the armed forces.
- b. Providing adequate and timely joint intelligence for use within the DOD.
- c. Preparing for the SECDEF [Secretary of Defense], statements of military requirements based on national security policy and strategic war plans.

- d. Preparing the SECDEF military guidance for use in developing military aid programs.
- e. Preparing integrated plans for military mobilization.
- f. Preparing integrated logistic plans which may include assignments of logistics responsibilities to the armed forces and the Defense Logistics Agency.
- g. Reviewing major personnel, material, and logistics requirements of the armed forces in relation to strategic and logistics plans.
- h. Advising and assisting the SECDEF on research and engineering matters.
- i. Recommending to the SECDEF the establishment and force structure of unified and specified commands.

[Air Force, *War Planning: USAF Operation Planning Process*, AFR 28-3, 30 June 1986, p. 15, released under the FOIA]

The participation of the JCS in the **crisis action system** is described as the following: to "manage the planning process, provide options and recommendations to the NCA, and convey NCA decisions to the unified and specified commands. The Joint Chiefs of Staff also receive and analyze reports, task commanders to prepare estimates and COAs [courses of action], review those estimates and COAs, resolve conflicts and shortfalls or seek resolution from the NCA, and directly monitor the planning and execution process. The NCA have the final responsibility and authority in a crisis. They approve a course of action and direct the major actions to be taken, which might include the deployment or redeployment of forces. Authority to conduct military operations against a potential enemy . . . must be explicitly provided by the NCA before any such operations may take place" [JCS, *Joint Operation Planning System: Vol. IV (Crisis Action System)*, SM-502-85, 12 August 1985, pp. I-4 and 5, released under the FOIA].

JCS-originated instructions and reports include the **Joint Chiefs of Staff Memorandum (JCSM)**, Secretary's Memorandum (SM), **Memorandum, Joint Chiefs of Staff (MJCS)**, and **Memorandum of Policy (MOP)**.

Joint Chiefs of Staff Alerting Network (JCSAN): The primary joint nonsecure telephone network, installed in 1960. Operating over leased circuits, JCSAN links **unified and specified commands** and the Canadian Defence Headquarters with the **Joint Chiefs of Staff (JCS)**, the **National Military Command Center (NMCC)** and the **Alternate National Military Command Center (ANMCC)**. The Strategic Air Command (SAC) senior controller in the SAC underground command post has a direct line to the Emergency Actions section of the NMCC in Washington and then to the other major command headquarters via the JCSAN. JCSAN is the initial system for voice transmission of **emergency action messages** and **nuclear control orders (NCO)** by the JCS. JCSAN lines are configured for either two-way (crisis) or one-way (alert) patching, and they connect to the Washington Tactical Switchboard. Alert and launch orders from the Commander of SAC are passed via the voice telephone **Primary Alerting System (PAS)**. Separate routes connect HQ SAC with **launch control centers**, aircraft and subordinate command posts. Regional Operations Control Centers forward information on air-breathing threats directly to **NORAD** and pass information on a target that passes from one region to another to the adjacent ROCC. **AUTOVON** is the dedicated backup net [JCS, *Policy for the Joint Chiefs of Staff Alerting Network*, JCS MOP 163, released under the FOIA].

Joint Chiefs of Staff Memorandum (JCSM): A type of memorandum originated within the **Joint Chiefs of Staff (JCS)** to implement JCS decisions. A JCSM is addressed to agencies or individuals outside the JCS or the military services, for example, to the Office of the Secretary of Defense or a level comparable to that of the JCS. It is prepared for the signature of the Chairman or Vice Chairman of the JCS or the Director of the Joint Staff.

Joint Crisis Management Capability Level: U.S. European Command and **U.S. Pacific Command** air-transportable communications packages operable in either airborne or ground-based modes. They contain various standard radios and computer equipment to provide en-route and on-the-scene communications capability for crisis response teams.

Joint Deployment Agency (JDA): Former all-service deployment planning and execution agency, disestab-lished 1 October 1987 with the estab-lishment of the **U.S. Transportation Command**.

Joint Deployment System (JDS): The personnel, procedures, commu-nication systems, and data process-ing system to support time-sensitive (crisis) planning and execution, and to complement deliberate (peacetime) planning. JDS procedures bridge the gap between deliberate planning and time-sensitive planning described in the **Joint Operations Planning System (JOPS)**.

Joint Emergency Evacuation Plan (JEEP): Program to evacuate key military leaders in a crisis under **continuity of operations** plans. JEEP-1 cardholders are provided 24-hour helicopter transportation to emer-gency relocation sites and alternate headquarters. JEEP-2 cardholders are authorized helicopter transportation only during duty hours. JEEP is automatically implemented at declara-tion of **Defense Readiness Condition (DEFCON)** 3. The Army is tasked to airlift 22 JEEP-1 cardholders within three hours of execution of JEEP dur-ing duty or nonduty hours, and 132 people within four hours of imple-mentation of JEEP. The Air Force is tasked to airlift 24 JEEP-1 card-holders within three hours of exe-cution of JEEP during duty or non-duty hours, and 162 people within four hours of JEEP implementation. Overall, there are 46 JEEP-1 card-holders, and 248 JEEP-2 cardhold-ers (this includes 54 **Federal Emer-gency Management Administration (FEMA)** JEEP-2 cardholders).

Joint Intelligence Estimate for Planning (JIEP): One of six documents of the **Joint Strategic Planning System**, the JIEP is a midrange forecast covering years 1 to 10 in a 20-year cycle, published biennially (formerly annually) on 1 December. The JIEP is developed by the **Joint Staff**, the **Defense Intelligence Agency (DIA)**, and service intelligence offices. The JIEP is organized into seven parts—Global Appraisal, Regional Appraisals, USSR/Warsaw Pact, People's Republic of China, North Korea, Southeast Asia, and Cuba. The JIEP:

- Describes situations and developments throughout the world that could affect U.S. security interests;
- Provides global and regional appraisals and threat estimates, including estimates of the external and internal threat to countries of significance to the United States;
- Estimates Warsaw Pact and Asian military forces and potential threats in the Middle East-Persian Gulf region, Korea, and various Third World regions, including Soviet capabilities to project forces into these regions.

A JIEP supplement, a DIA publication, is not subject to approval by the Joint Chiefs of Staff, consists of significant changes in intelligence occurring between publications of the JIEP, and describes the military capabilities and vulnerabilities of armed forces or selected countries. The JIEP provides the principal intelligence basis for development of the **Joint Strategic Planning Document (JSPD)**, **Joint Program Assessment Memorandum (JPAM)**, **Joint Security Assessment Memorandum (JSAM)**, and the **Joint Strategic Capabilities Plan (JSCP)**.

Joint Interoperability Tactical Command and Control System (JINTACCS): System for the exchange of information between and among automated and manual tactical command and control facilities for the joint U.S. services through standard message formats and rules. JINTACCS was established to ensure compatibility, interoperability, and operational effectiveness of tactical command and control systems in support of ground and amphibious operations.

Joint Long Range Strategic Appraisal (JLRSA): Formerly one of seven documents of the **Joint Strategic Planning System (JSPS)**, a long-range intelligence forecast covering years 5 to 20 in a 20-year cycle, published every four years on 1 October, and reviewed biennially. It has been discontinued with the shift to two-year planning.

Joint Nuclear Accident Coordinating Center (JNACC): Joint agency of the **Defense Nuclear Agency (DNA)** and the **Department of Energy (DOE)**. JNACC coordinates the response to accidents involving nuclear weapons and radioactive materials. They maintain information regarding contacts for requesting the accident-response capabilities of the armed services, the DNA, and the DOE. [Air Force, *Disaster Preparedness: Planning and Operations*, AFR 355-1, 17 November 1986, p. 85, released under the FOIA]. The DOD element of JNACC was established at

DNA Field Command on 22 January 1982. The DOD element, however, was transferred to Headquarters DNA in Washington on 1 April 1987.

Joint Operations Planning and Execution System (JOPES): Joint Chiefs of Staff (JCS) system to succeed the **Joint Operations Planning System**, the **Joint Deployment-System**, and major portions of the **Joint Reporting Structure**. It will support planning and command and control of mobilization, deployment, employment, and sustainment activities using an improved information system. JOPES development efforts are intended to exploit fully the ongoing efforts to design and implement use of the **World-wide Military Command and Control System (WWMCCS) Information System (WIS)**. As a result of the **Department of Defense Reorganization Act of 1986**, the J-7—Operational Plans and Interoperability Directorate—was formed and is now the proponent for JOPES. The new **U.S. Transportation Command** will also act as the implementing agency for JCS-approved JOPES policy.

The JOPES-required operational capability, dated 5 July 1983, is the JCS-approved document that outlines a series of target objectives needed to resolve operational deficiencies in the current planning process. As described by the JOPES Required Operational Capability and the JOPES Concept of Operations approved in 1986, JOPES will be an integrated, conventional, command and control system designed primarily to satisfy the information needs of senior-level decisionmakers in conducting joint planning. The system will support the national, theater, and supporting organizational levels in both peacetime and wartime. A principal goal of JOPES is to develop one set of procedures for both deliberate and time-sensitive (crisis) planning, differentiated primarily by the length of the planning cycles; JOPES will work toward 45 days for deliberate planning and 2 to 3 days for crisis planning.

Joint Operations Planning System (JOPS): The **Joint Chiefs of Staff** system for the conduct of the joint planning process. JOPS established the system to be used in both deliberate and time-sensitive planning of joint operations. It is directed by Department Of Defense and does not include the Single Integrated Operational Plan. The JOPS planning cycle is initiated by the **Joint Strategic Capabilities Plan (JSCP)** and focuses on military planning. The JOPS is explained in four volumes:

- Volume I (**Deliberate Planning** Procedures): Provides guidance and procedures for the development, coordination, dissemination, review, and approval of joint operation plans during peacetime. In addition, it prescribes standard formats for operations plans.
- Volume II (Supplementary Planning Guidance): Provides directional, procedural, and planning guidance keyed to plan annexes.
- Volume III (Automated Data Processing Support): Establishes the **Worldwide Military Command and Control System (WWMCCS)**

standard computer-based system that supports the planning of joint operations.

- Volume IV (**Crisis Action System**): Provides guidance and procedures for the conduct of joint planning during emergency or time-sensitive situations.

The JOPS is normally based on an 18-month cycle. The cycle begins with publication of the JSCP and terminates at the end of the fiscal year to which the JSCP applies. Each unified and specified **operations plan (OPLAN)** is then revised to reflect changes in conditions or forces.

JOPS is an established, common, and orderly way of creating operations plans and operations orders. It is comprehensive and flexible enough to allow for the preparation of a concept of military operations and automated enough to handle enormous quantities of data. (see also **planning**)

Joint Program Assessment Memorandum (JPAM): One of six documents of the **Joint Strategic Planning System**, the JPAM covers the midrange period from years 2 to 10 in a 20-year cycle, is published annually following the **Program Objectives Memorandum (POM)**, and is based on the **Joint Strategic Planning Document**, the **Defense Guidance**, the **Five Year Defense Plan**, and service inputs. The JPAM provides the Secretary of Defense with a Joint Chiefs of Staff risk assessment of the service POM force recommendations—including JCS views on the allocation of resources—to use during the POM review. The JCS recom-

mends actions to improve overall joint defense capability within alternative POM funding levels directed by the Secretary of Defense. The JPAM is used by the Secretary in reviewing the POMs, in developing **issues**, and in drafting the **Program Decision Memorandums**.

Joint Publications Research Service: Central Intelligence Agency organization that monitors and translates publications in foreign languages for the purpose of providing intelligence information. The monitoring efforts are by subject area or by region, and technical or obscure publications are sought out to provide insight into foreign and domestic policies. The publications are often restricted-dissemination internal government or military publications that are obtained clandestinely. (see also **Foreign Broadcast Information Service**)

Joint Reporting Structure (JRS): Reports and reporting systems used throughout the military designed to furnish

- Military information to the **National Command Authorities (NCA)**;
- A central catalog of recurring reports to support command decisions on military operations and to minimize duplication;
- Standardization in reporting systems of the JCS, services, and DOD agencies; and
- Central management and standard rules for the application of message text formatting-to-reporting systems.

JRS has wide applications in command and control, operation and support planning, plan execution, and analysis. It portrays essential data on personnel, materiel, and equipment status; operational and logistic planning; and the overall military situation. It establishes

- Procedures for preparing reports;
- The framework for reporting systems for transferring data between participating commands and agencies; and
- The standards for automatic data processing.

Components of the JRS include: Standing Operating Procedures for Coordination of Atomic Operations (CAOSOP); **Unit Status and Identity** reports; **Operational Reports (OPREP)**; nuclear weapons reports; reconnaissance reports; **Joint Operations Planning System**; **situation reports**; and **logistics** reports. The JRS outlines five intelligence reports: **Defense Intelligence Notices**; **Special Defense Intelligence Notices**; **Spot Intelligence Reports**; the **Daily Intelligence Summary**; and the **DIA Periodic Intelligence Summary**.

Joint Security Assistance Memorandum (JSAM): One of six documents of the **Joint Strategic Planning System**, the JSAM covers the mid-range period from years 2 to 8 in a 20-year cycle and is published annually in September. It provides proposed funding levels and priorities for the **Security Assistance Program**, recommended manpower levels for security assistance organizations, and views of key arms-transfer matters.

Joint Special Operations Agency (JSOA): Former **Joint Chiefs of Staff** agency established in January 1984 as the interservice administrative command for **special operations**; responsible for the development and coordination of special operations and **counterterrorism** doctrine and plans. It was disestablished with the creation of the unified **U.S. Special Operations Command**.

Joint Special Operations Command (JSOC): Component of **U.S. Special Operations Command** established in 1981 to consolidate DOD's hostage rescue and **counterterrorism** forces and doctrine. Although DOD does not directly acknowledge its counterterror units, JSOC components are believed to include **Delta Force**, helicopter units known as the "Night Stalkers" of the Army's **Task Force 160**, and the Navy's **SEAL** Team Six. In addition, units of the 23d Air Force assist when designated. Combined personnel strengths are thought to be approximately 1,000.

Headquarters
Pope AFB, NC 28308

Joint Special Operations Support Element (JSOSE): Former **unconventional warfare** support element of the **U.S. Readiness Command**. It provided staff (command and control) augmentation to other unified command **Joint Unconventional Warfare Task Forces (JUWTF)** or **Special Operations Commands**, as well as to other joint task forces organized for a major conflict or special operations exercise. The responsibilities were transferred to the **U.S. Special Operations Command**.

joint staff: 1. Headquarters staff of a unified or specified command or subcommand, or of a joint task force, that includes members from the several services. Nominal joint staff organization of a command is

- Commander
- Deputy Commander
- Personal Staff (Aide, Political Adviser, Public Affairs, Legal Advisor, Inspector General)
- Chief of Staff and Deputy Chief of Staff
- Secretary, Joint Staff
- Special Staff (Comptroller, Engineer, Medical/Command Surgeon, Transportation)
- Joint Staff
- J-1, Personnel
- J-2, Intelligence
- J-3, Operations
- J-4, Logistics
- J-5, Plans and Policy
- J-6, Command, Control, and Communications Systems

2. The Joint Staff, a component of the Organization of the **Joint Chiefs of Staff (JCS)**, operating under the **Chairman of the Joint Chiefs of Staff**. The Goldwater-Nichols Act restricts the Joint Staff's size to 1,627 military and civilian personnel. The staff is composed of approximately even numbers of officers from the Army, Navy and Marine Corps, and Air Force. In practice, Marines make up about 20 percent of the number allocated to the Navy.

The Joint Staff is organized into the

- Office of the Chairman
- Office of the Director of the Joint Staff
- Secretary of the Joint Staff

- Manpower and Personnel Directorate (J-1)
- Operations Directorate (J-3)
- Logistics Directorate (J-4)
- Strategic Plans and Policy Directorate (J-5)
- Command, Control, and Communications Systems Directorate (J-6)
- Operational Plan and Interoperability Directorate (J-7)
- Force Structure, Resource, and Assessment Directorate (J-8)
- Directorate for Information and Resource Management
- Advisor for Mapping, Charting, and Geodesy Support
- Office of the Inspector General.

The Chairman, after consultation with other JCS members, selects the Director of the Joint Staff, to assist in managing the Joint Staff. The Director is authorized to review and approve issues when there is no dispute between the Services, when the issue does not warrant JCS attention, when the proposed action is in conformance with JCS policy, or when the issue has not been requested by a member of the JCS.

Joint Staff Communications Office: The message center at the **Alternate National Military Command Center** (Site R), operated by the Air Force.

Joint Strategic Capabilities Plan (JSCP): One of six documents of the **Joint Strategic Planning System (JSPS)**, the JSCP (pronounced "jay-scap") covers the two years following publication and is published biennially by April 1. It is the planning directive to the commanders-in-chief (CINCs) and the service chiefs for the accomplishment of military tasks based on projected military capabilities and conditions during the next two fiscal years (formerly single fiscal year). The JSCP is published in two volumes. Annexes to the JSCP provide planning guidance, indicate capabilities, and amplify Volume I taskings with the specified functional areas.

- Volume I (Concepts, Tasks, and Planning Guidance): contains national security objectives, derived military objectives, military strategic concepts, task assignments, and general planning guidance for each of the CINCs. It also provides planning guidance to the Services for the support of the unified and specified commands in the execution of assigned tasks.
- Volume II (Forces): identifies the major combat forces apportioned for planning in the development of operation plans. It also cites the Service planning documents, which specify for planning purposes the forces not specifically apportioned.
- Annex A (Intelligence)
- Annex B (Logistics)
- Annex C (Nuclear)
- Annex D (Psychological Operations)
- Annex E (Special Operations)
- Annex F (Chemical Warfare; Nuclear, Biological, and Chemical Defense; Riot Control Agents; and Herbicides)
- Annex G (Mapping, Charting, and Geodesy)
- Annex H (Counter Command, Control, and Communications; formerly the Nuclear Weapons Damage Considerations, Civil Defense, Recovery, and Reconstitution annex)
- Annex I (Command and Control Systems; formerly the Communications-Electronics annex)
- Annex J (Mobility)
- Annex K (Deception)
- Annex L (Civil Affairs)
- Annex M (Electronic Warfare)
- Annex N (Mobilization).

Joint Strategic Planning Document (JSPD): One of six documents of the **Joint Strategic Planning System (JSPS)**, the JSPD covers the mid-range period from years 2 to 10 in a 20-year cycle and is published biennially on 1 September (formerly annually). "The JSPD provides advice to the President, the NSC [National Security Council], and the Secretary of Defense on the military strategy and force structure required to attain the national security objectives of the United States. It provides a comprehensive military appraisal of the threat to U.S. interests and objectives worldwide, a statement of recommended military objectives derived from national objectives, and the recommended military strategy required to attain national objectives in the mid-range period. Planning forces required to execute the national military strategy are developed by the Joint Chiefs of Staff in consideration of national objectives, the threat, allied and friendly force levels, and recommended minimum-risk force levels provided by CINCs and the Chiefs of the Services." The JSPD Supporting Analysis is a document internal to the JCS that provides the principal support work for the JSPD. [JCS, *Joint Operations Planning System*, Volume I, p. I-5, released under the FOIA]. In the future the JSPD

Document	Years	Publication
Intelligence Priorities for Strategic Planning (IPSP)	1–10	Annually, 15 April
Joint Intelligence Estimate for Planning (JIEP)	1–10	Biennially, December
Joint Program Assessment Memorandum (JPAM)	2–10	Annually, following the POM
Joint Security Assistance Memorandum (JSAM)	2–8	Annually, September
Joint Strategic Capabilities Plan (JSCP)	2 years following publication	Biennially, 1 April
Joint Strategic Planning Document (JSPD)	2–10	Biennially, 1 September

Supporting Analysis will probably be replaced by three JSPD supporting documents—Planning Guidance, Military Net Assessment, and Planning Force.

A purpose of the JSPD is to serve as the foundation for the development of the **Defense Guidance**. It appraises current U.S. defense policy as stated in the last Defense Guidance and makes recommendations for change. It also establishes the Joint Chiefs of Staff position for Presidential and NSC actions and includes recommendations for risk reduction measures (i.e. which mission or program areas should receive emphasis if additional funds were available).

Joint Strategic Planning System (JSPS): The primary process used by the **Joint Chiefs of Staff** for formulating the nation's military strategy and resource needs. It translates national security policy into strategic guidance, direction, and objectives for force structure, resource programming, and operational planning. There are six JSPS documents listed

above, each of which has specific applications in planning within the intelligence community, in programming and budgeting at Military Department level, and in planning at the unified and specified command level.

The JSPD initiates the first phase of the **Planning, Programming, and Budgeting System (PPBS)**, which sets the pattern for the resource allocation process. The JSCP initiates and influences the nature of the **Joint Operations Planning System**. The shift from an annual to biennial planning process within DOD resulted in the discontinuation of the Joint Long Range Strategic Appraisal (JLRSA) document, which was incorporated into the JSPD.

At the beginning of a new administration and thereafter under the new system, the President sends to the Secretary of Defense his decision on the national purpose, policy, objectives, and strategy by means of a directive. With these are provisional budget levels for each of the five years of the programming period. The President directs a study of the national security situation and solicits options and recommendations in terms of military strategies, forces, and capabilities. Using the draft Policy Guidance, the Secretary of Defense, in turn, directs the Chairman of the Joint Chiefs to return a recommended strategy and range of options included in a military net assessment. It is planned that the JSPD and its supporting documents will serve as the JCS response to the Secretary. The Secretary holds a strategy and operations review after reviewing the JSPD. He then makes strategy recommendations to the President. With the Secretary's recommendations the President has an array of strategy and force options from which he makes a strategy and options decision. The President's decision is then incorporated into the Defense Guidance, which serves as the link between planning and programming.

Joint Strategic Target Planning Staff (JSTPS): The joint staff created in 1961 by Secretary of Defense Thomas Gates that develops the list of enemy targets and prepares target missions for various nuclear contingencies, namely, the **Single Integrated Operational Plan (SIOP).** As a joint staff, the JSTPS is composed of representatives of all the services. Its director, an Air Force general, is commander of the **Strategic Air Command (SAC)** and is designated the Director of Strategic Target Planning. The Deputy Director is a naval Vice Admiral. The JSTPS reports to **National Comand Authorities (NCA)** through the **Joint Chiefs of Staff.** Senio: officers rep-

resent their respective commanders from unified and specified commands and the supreme allied commands of NATO, and they participate in staff duties. A number of SAC personnel are assigned additional duty with the JSTPS. The JSTPS staff consists of the National Strategic Target List Directorate, which develops the target lists and contingencies, known as the National Strategic Target List; and the SIOP Directorate, which uses the List to employ all available strategic forces and weapons against the various targets. The SIOP Directorate also manages the SIOP Reconnaissance Plan (SRP), which integrates the reconnaissance plans of the unified and specified commands, and other DOD and government agencies.

Headquarters
Offutt AFB, NE 68113

Joint Surveillance System (JSS): Radar network operated by the Air Force and the **Federal Aviation Administration (FAA)**; activated in 1982 to replace the semiautomatic ground environment (SAGE) system of **NORAD**. The JSS controls access to U.S. sovereign airspace in peacetime. It will operate during crises as long as is possible, after which time the command and control of air defense forces will switch over to the **Airborne Warning and Control System**. JSS consists of 46 200-mi range radar sites around the perimeter of CONUS, 24 radar sites in the east and west of Canada, 14 radar sites in Alaska, and 2 radars in Hawaii. These radars have minimal military effectiveness against low-flying aircraft.

The information from these radars travels along telephone lines to **Regional Operational Control Centers (ROCCs)**: two in Canada (both at North Bay, Ontario); four in CONUS (Griffiss AFB, NY; March AFB, CA; Tyndall AFB, FL; and McChord AFB, WA); and one each in Hawaii and Alaska. The operation and costs of JSS are shared by the United States and Canada. Most of the CONUS sites are operated jointly with the FAA. Interceptors directed by JSS include Canadian CF-18s from Cold Lake, Alberta, and Bagotville, Quebec; Air Force F-15s and F-16s; and Air National Guard (ANG) F-4s and F-16s.

Joint Surveillance and Target Attack Radar System (JSTARS or Joint Stars): Joint Air Force and Army program for a common radar and attack control system to support the **airland battle** and **follow-on forces attack** doctrines. JSTARS is an airborne, wide-area, multimode radar system to detect, locate, disrupt and destroy second-echelon mobile forces by providing targeting information to tactical aircraft with standoff missiles or to artillery and missile units. Radar information detected from a range of over 100 km is transmitted directly to the ground stations through secure data links. The Air Force is responsible for the Prime Mission Equipment (PME) airborne portion of JSTARS (platform, radar, and data link) while the Army is responsible for the development of the ground station modules (GSMs). The JSTARS platform is the **E-8A** (formerly known as the C-18, a mil-

itarized Boeing 707) and includes an electronic scan, multimode radar, processing equipment, controller stations and command and control interfaces. The GSM data processing and evaluation centers link the JSTARS radars (through the data link) to the Army ground commanders and command, control and communications nodes at corps and division levels. The GSM processes data from both the JSTARS and **OV-1D Mohawk** radars. Enhancements to the GSMs will incorporate capabilities to process data from unmanned aerial vehicles and **North Atlantic Treaty Organization** airborne radars. Situation development information is transmitted through the All-Source Analysis System (ASAS) and targeting information is transmitted through the **Tactical Fire Directional Advanced Field Artillery Tactical Data System (TACFIRE/AFATDS)** to their users. The Block II GSMs will incorporate nuclear/blast hardening and NBC filtering.

The PME and GSM were in the full-scale engineering development phase as of September 1989, with a limited procurement order of 11 GSMs (one of which will go to the NATO Airborne Radar Demonstration System). A field test of a fully operational GSM and a full-scale development platform radar is planned for early 1992. The ground station contractor is Motorola, Tempe, AZ, and the simulator/trainer contractor is Honeywell, Minneapolis, MN. PME contractors are Grumman Aerospace, New York, NY, and Melbourne, FL; and Norden Systems Division of United Technologies, Norwalk, CT [*Army Weapon Systems*, 1989, p. 83].

Joint Tactical Fusion Program (JTFP): Joint Army and Air Force project to process, analyze, and disseminate intelligence and command, control, and communications information for battle management and execution. The primary project within JTFP is the **all source** analysis system/ enemy situation correlation element (ASAS/ENSCE). This is a transportable, semiautomatic tactical intel-system to give air and land battle managers a common and coherent perception of the battlefield. The intelligence will be gained through **signals intelligence (SIGINT), electronic intelligence (ELINT), human intelligence (HUMINT),** and **imagery intelligence (IMINT)**.

The Army is the lead service and is working on the ASAS portion, which will be the control system for the intelligence and electronic warfare area for command and control of the Army 21 warfighting doctrine. This doctrine emphasizes rapidly moving forces and the heavy use of electronic warfare and computer-controlled weapons. ASAS will support Army commanders at the brigade, division, corps, and above-corps levels.

The Air Force is managing the development of the ENSCE segment that will provide the intelligence necessary to support operations within Air Force tactical control centers. ENSCE is to correlate and aggregate sensor data, locate enemy forces, and develop ground battle situation displays. The U.S. European Command (USEUCOM) is the executive agent for the JTFP in Europe, and it has installed a Limited Operational Capability for Europe (LOCE) prototype in Stuttgart.

Program Management Office
McLean, VA 22102-5099

Joint Tactical Information Distribution System (JTIDS): High-capacity, reliable, jam-protected, secure digital-information distribution system to link ground and airborne command and control nodes, surveillance activities, intelligence centers, naval vessels, and combat and support aircraft. The JTIDS program began in September 1974 when the Air Force and Navy were directed to work on a joint system rather than separate communication and navigation aids. JTIDS operates in the L-band frequency range and its ability to frequency hop protects it from electronic countermeasures. The entire system operates on a single communications channel with all participants in continuous synchronization. Users beyond line-of-sight are connected by retransmission of JTIDS messages by other aircraft having the system. The small Class 2 terminal is being developed for Air Force, Army, and Navy tactical requirements.

Joint Task Force (JTF): An operational military force composed of assigned or attached elements of two or more of the services, formed for the purpose of carrying out a specific operation, mission, or a continuing task. It is established by the Secretary of Defense or the commander of unified or specified command, sub-unified command, or an existing JTF. Current JTFs include

- JTF 4: U.S. Atlantic Command task force established 8 February 1989 for the coordination and conduct of drug detection, monitoring, and interdiction operations along the east coast of the United States. It is commanded by a Coast Guard flag officer and when fully operational, will be staffed by 115 DOD and Coast Guard personnel and additional personnel from the Drug Enforcement Agency, the Customs Service, the Federal Bureau of Investigation, and the National Security Agency. It is headquartered at Key West, FL.

- JTF 5: U.S. Pacific Command task force established 8 February 1989 for the coordination and conduct of drug interdiction operations along the west coast of the United States. It will work in conjunction with JTF 4 on the east coast. It is commanded by a Coast Guard flag officer and is headquartered at Oakland, CA.

- JTF 110: U.S. Pacific Command task force to be activated in the case of **civil disturbances** in Guam, the Northern Marianas Islands, and Micronesia (with the exception of Kwajalein Atoll.)
[PACOM, *Command Relationships in the U.S. Pacific Command*, USCINCPACINST S3020.2J Ch-2, 5 July 1985, p. 6-2, released under the FOIA].

- JTF 119: U.S. Pacific Command task force located at Wheeler AFB, Oahu, and under the CINCPAC command center, probably responsible for the defense of Hawaii.

- JTF 120: A special command subordinate to the U.S. Atlantic Command, which assists in the planning and conduct of operations in areas specified by CINCLANT. Its commander is also commander of the U.S. Second Fleet.

- JTF 140: Task force of the U.S. Atlantic Command with unspecified duties.

- JTF 510: U.S. Pacific Command "primary action agency for operational matters relating to certain USPACOM contingency operations . . . out-of-theater contingency force." Commander is J30. Office of primary responsibility is Special Operations Division, J36 [CINCPAC, *Emergency Action Procedures (USCINCPAC—EAP), Volume V: Crisis Staffing*, 18 December 1985, p. 1-5, released under the FOIA].

- JTF Alaska: JCS-directed joint task force that would be responsible for the defense of Alaska, incorporated into the **Alaskan Command** on 7 July 1989.

- JTF Aleutians: JCS-directed, U.S. Pacific Command–controlled task force responsible for the defense of the Aleutians, incorporated into the **Alaskan Command** on 7 July 1989.

- JTF Middle East (JTFME): Task force established in August 1987 and responsible for all U.S. operations in the Persian Gulf and Northern Arabian Sea. The JTFME, which incorporated the Navy's **Middle East Force** in February 1988, is commanded by a single Rear Admiral and reports directly to the U.S. Central Command.

joint test assembly (JTA): An inert nuclear warhead or bomb employed in test projects. A JTA is installed with appropriate instrumentation (called the joint test subassembly) to simulate the operations of a nuclear warhead under conditions of launch without having the presence of nuclear materials.

Joint Vertical Lift Airlift (JVX) (see **CV-22**)

Jolly Green Giant   (see **CH-3**)

JSTARS (see **Joint Surveillance and Target Attack Radar System**)

Judge Advocate General (JAG):   1. Legal officer in the military services and the senior legal officer in the military department. The civilian legal advisor to the Secretary is called the General Counsel.   **2.** The Judge Advocate General's Corps, a **combat service support** branch of the Army.

Julie: Navy AN/SSQ-23A sonobuoy that releases charges that explode at predetermined depths to provide echo-ranging information.

Jumpseat: Byeman code name for a class of currently operable **signals intelligence (SIGINT)** satellites operating in tandem with the **Satellite Data System (SDS)**. Approximately four satellites have been launched since 10 March 1975 (one date being 6 August 1976). Jumpseat is in a highly elliptical orbit that brings the satellite within 240 mi of earth over the southern hemisphere and 24,000 mi above the earth over the Soviet Arctic. Intelligence obtained by Jumpseat and other SIGINT satellites is marked by the codeword **ZARF**.

Junior Reserve Officer Training Corps   (see **Reserve Officers Training Corps**)

K

K: Prefix designating tanker aircraft used for aerial refueling (e.g., KA-6, KC-135).

KA-3B Skywarrior: Naval Air Reserve aerial refueling aircraft based upon the A-3 attack aircraft fuselage. Aerial Refueling Squadron (VAK) 308 at NAS Alameda, CA, was disestablished on 30 September 1988. The last squadron of KA-3B aerial refueling aircraft, VAK-208, is scheduled to disestablish in 1989.

KA-6: Navy A-6 attack aircraft modified for carrier-based aerial refueling ("buddy" refueling). The KA-6 is capable of transferring more than 8,000 liters at a flight radius of 500 km. A typical carrier air wing has four KA-6 aircraft.

KATUSA (Korean Augmentation to the United States Army): The assignment of South Korean soldiers to selected American units to serve as fillers and to perform work details. (see also **host nation support**)

KC-10A Extender: Air Force strategic aerial-refueling tanker and transport aircraft assigned to the Strategic Air Command (SAC). The KC-10 is a derivative of the DC-10 widebody Series 30CF modified with air refueling to supplement the **KC-135** fleet. The KC-10 supports joint tactical and strategic air operations, and can deploy overseas. The first KC-10 flew in July 1980, and SAC took delivery of the first planes in March 1981. Some 60 aircraft are assigned to March AFB, CA; Barksdale AFB, LA; and Seymour Johnson AFB, NC. The Air Force Reserve provides associate crews. Douglas Aircraft Corp, a division of McDonnell Douglas, is the prime contractor. A multiyear contract for 44 aircraft was issued in 1982, and the FY 1987 buy of eight aircraft for $112.5 million completed the acquisition program. The KC-10A was called the Advanced Tanker Cargo Aircraft during development.

KC-130T: Navy and Marine Corps aerial-refueling transport aircraft updated for aerial refueling of fighter and attack aircraft and helicopters. The KC-130T is a version of the **C-130 Hercules** and is also capable of conventional or aerial delivery of personnel or cargo. The prime contractor is Lockheed-Georgia, Marietta, GA. The final two aircraft were purchased in FY 1989 at a total cost of $45 million, appropriated to National Guard and Reserve Equipment.

KC-135 Stratotanker: Air Force aerial-refueling aircraft assigned to the Strategic Air Command (SAC), and the primary aircraft providing **B-52** and **B-1** bombers intercontinental range with full weapons loads as part of the **Single Integrated Operational Plan (SIOP)**. The aircraft also provides general air refueling, along with the **KC-10**, to tactical Air Force, Marine Corps, and Navy units. Although based on the commercial Boeing 707 aircraft, the KC-135 is strengthened and redesigned to carry heavy loads. First flight of the KC-135A was in August 1956, and a total of 730 were built by 1966. Almost 600 remain in operational service in active SAC units of Air National Guard and Air Force Reserve units.

A KC-135R modernization program will provide new engines, nacelles, and pylons, as well as 34 total subsystem modifications designed to increase fuel off-load by as much as 200 percent. The modifications will enable the KC-135 to take off with maximum fuel loads, in shorter distances, and will nearly eliminate the adverse noise impact of the planes. First flight of a modified KC-135R was in August 1982, and the first plane was delivered to SAC in 1984. The operational fleet of some 395 aircraft will be modified through FY 1992. The French government is responsible for reengining 11 aircraft. KC-135As still assigned to the reserves are also being updated to KC-135E standard with new engines.

Prime contractors for the KC-135R are Boeing Military Aircraft, Wichita, KS, and General Electric, Evendale, OH. FY 1990 and 1991 budget requests for 44 modernizations were $387.3 million and $389.4 million, respectively.

K-day: The basic date for the introduction of a convoy system or any particular convoy lane. (see also **military time**)

Kennan: **Byeman** code name for the currently operating class of KH-11 photographic reconnaissance satellites contracted by the Air Force and used by the Central Intelligence Agency. KH-11s have been launched between December 1976 and 1987 and have nominal lifetimes of between two and three years. Until the **KH-12** series is developed, the KH-11 serves as the only U.S. digital-readout and imaging satellite. Its mission is the production of real-time images of Soviet civilian and military installations. Intelligence obtained by KH-11 and other imaging satellites is marked by the codeword **Ruff**. (see also **keyhole**)

Kernel: The first word of a two-word nickname (e.g., Kernel Potlatch) for **Third Fleet** amphibious exercises involving Marine Corps and Navy forces.

keyhole (KH): General code name for U.S. photographic reconnaissance satellites. The United States has employed imaging satellites for **intelligence** collection on the Soviet Union since the 1960s. The Air Force and the Central Intelligence Agency oper-

Past and Present Keyhole Satellites

Class	Code Name and number launched	Known Launch Dates
KH-1	SAMOS (Satellite and Missile Observation System)	11 Oct 1960–27 Nov 1963
KH-4	**Corona**/Discoverer	7 Mar 1962 26 Apr 1962 17 Jun 1962 18 Jul 1962 5 Aug 1962 11 Nov 1962
KH-5	Codename unknown (46 area surveillance)	28 Feb 1963–30 Mar 1967
KH-6	Codename unknown (38 close-look)	12 Jul 1963–4 Jun 1967
KH-7	Codename unknown (29 area surveillance)	9 Aug 1966–1972
KH-8	**Gambit** (30)	20 July 1966–15 Jun 1971
KH-9	**Hexagon** (19)	15 Jun 1971–20 Jun 1984
KH-10	(Manned Orbiting Laboratory (MOL))	cancelled
KH-11	**Kennan**	19 Dec 1976 4 Dec 1984 26 Oct 1987
KH-12	(4 planned high-resolution, digital)	
Lacrosse	(4 planned high-resolution, radar imaging)	3 Dec 1988

ated comparable photographic satellites systems until their consolidation during the Carter Administration. Their primary mission is intelligence collection, but they also possess capabilities for early warning, particularly **indications and warning**. KH satellites are placed in low earth orbit (400–500 km above the earth), and orbit the earth in 90-minute intervals. KH satellites vary in capabilities and specifications. All have nighttime capabilities, but they cannot operate in extreme darkness or cloud cover. Many of the classes are given a **Byeman** code name. Intelligence obtained by satellite photography is marked by the security code word **Ruff**. (see also **satellite reconnaissance**)

[Jeffrey Richelson, *American Espionage and the Soviet Target,* 1987, pp. 182, 192–5, 230, 232; William

E. Burrows, *Deep Black: Space Espionage and National Security,* 1986, pp. 191–2; John Pike, *The Case Against the Stealth Bomber*, Federation of American Scientists, 26 Sep 1988, pp. 87–89].

KH (see **keyhole**)

KH-12: Newest class of photographic reconnaissance (**keyhole**) satellites, more advanced than the KH-11 **Kennan** class. The first of the four planned satellites is scheduled to be launched in late 1989. All will follow a low earth orbit, with two placed at 57 degrees and two at 90–110 degree inclinations. They are high-resolution, digital transmission systems.

K-hour: The time at which fuzes are fired in a Navy demolition operation. (see also **military time**)

kill effects: Destructive effects upon detonation of a weapon. Kill effects are blast, penetration, perforation, fragmentation, cratering, earth shock, fire, nuclear and thermal radiation, and combinations of these in varying degrees.

kinetic energy weapon (KEW): Those weapons using nonexplosive projectiles moving at very high speeds to destroy a target on impact. A kinetic energy weapon is one that shoots unarmed projectiles at high velocity to destroy an object on impact, rather than through an explosion created by the projectile. The projectile may be launched from a rocket, conventional gun, or electromagnetic rail gun. (see also **electromagnetic gun**)

knuckle: "A wake turbulence having great persistence caused by a tight turn of a surface ship or submarine. Frequently misinterpreted as the target by the sonar operator" [*NWP 3*].

L

L: Prefix designating **1.** Silo-launched vehicle (e.g., LGM-118). **2.** Cold weather aircraft (e.g., LC-130).

L access (or clearance): Security **classification** category used by the Department of Energy (DOE), equivalent to DOD's **confidential** and **secret** categories. L security clearances may be granted by the DOE to its employees, consultants, assignees, contractors, or to other Federal employees. It may also be granted to craft or manual workers, management and service personnel, technicians, and the like on a limited basis. The clearance requires a personnel investigation (national agency check and/or records inquiry) by the Office of Personnel Management. It allows an individual to gain access on a **need-to-know** basis to confidential **restricted data**, secret and confidential **formerly restricted data**, and secret and confidential **national security information**. Excluded from access are **CRYPTO, Communications Security (COMSEC)**, or **intelligence** information. Access permits specify the type(s) of information an individual is eligible to receive [DOE, *Personnel Security Program*, DOE Order 5631.2, 13 November 1980, released under the FOIA]. (see also **Q access**)

Lacrosse: **Byeman** code name for the new **synthetic aperture radar (SAR)** photographic reconnaissance satellite previously called Indigo. The first of four planned satellites was launched on 3 December 1988. It follows a low earth orbit (700 km above the earth) with two planned for placement at 57 degrees and two at 90–110 degree inclinations. Its mission probably includes the monitoring of Soviet troop movements and mobile weapons. Lacrosse uses radar-imaging technology to produce the equivalent of photographs. Unlike other imaging satellite systems, it is capable of producing all-weather and nighttime photo reconnaissance. Intelligence obtained by Lacrosse and other imaging satellites is marked by the codeword **Ruff**. (see also **keyhole**)

LAMP (LODE Advanced Mirror Program): LAMP is a segment of the three-part **Strategic Defense Initiative (SDI)** directed energy research program, along with **Alpha** (a continuous wave HF chemical laser) and **LODE** (the large optics demonstration experiment). The LODE and LAMP experiments are designed to improve beam control and the quality of the mirrors that would be used in any laser system. The **Strategic Defense Initiative Organization (SDIO)** projects that LAMP may be able to achieve a reduction in density (kilograms/ square meter) over that of National Aeronautics Space Administration's space telescope, with segmented elements scalable to great sizes.

In 1987, the program produced a large primary mirror consisting of seven segments that can be moved to shape the beam to the required quality. The mirror will be modified and used on the **Zenith Star** space experiment. SDIO does not plan to test the mirror with the laser on the ground before the space test. However, plans call for the LODE and LAMP mirror segment to be integrated with Alpha in the early 1990s for ground-based testing against stationary ground targets (so as not to violate the **ABM Treaty**). The total cost of the program is approximately $40 million [General Accounting Office, *Strategic Defense Initiative Program: Zenith Star Space-Based Chemical Laser Experiment*, GAO/ NSIAD-89-118, April 1989, p. 15].

LAMPS (see **Light Airborne Multipurpose System**)

LAN (Local Area Network): Telecommunications system to allow a number of independent devices (host computers, workstations, terminals, and peripherals) to communicate with each other. LANs are generally restricted to relatively small geographic areas (rooms, buildings, or clusters of buildings) and utilize fairly high data rates. LAN is typically a subsystem of a larger information-processing system.

Lance: Model designation MGM-52C, Lance is an Army mobile, liquid-fuel, inertially guided, supersonic, spin-stabilized, short-range surface-to-surface dual-capable missile. When armed with the W70 nuclear warhead, Lance is used to provide timely, accurate nuclear and nonnuclear fire support in general support of the Corps at ranges beyond the capability of cannons and rockets.

The objective is to destroy, neutralize, disrupt, or delay enemy second echelon forces (thus decreasing the enemy's ability to reinforce and support the central battle) or to attack enemy missile-firing positions, airfields, transportation centers, and command and logistic installations. The Army has eight Lance battalions, six in Europe and two in the United States, plus an independent battery in South Korea (Battery B, 6th Bn, 33d FA at Camp Mercer). A tracked transport vehicle also serves as the Lance's launcher.

Lance development began in 1962. Missile production began in 1970 and the first battalion was deployed in 1972. It originally was deployed as a nuclear-only weapon. It has a range of 90 km with conventional munitions and 133 km with the lighter nuclear warhead. It is approximately 20 ft long, has a diameter of 22 in and weighs 2,400 lb. The missile is no longer in production, but the prime contractor was LTV Aerospace and Defense Co. of Dallas, TX. A successor missile, **Follow-On to Lance (FOTL)**, is under development to replace Lance in the mid to late 1990s.

Landing craft, air cushion (LCAC): Marine Corps transport air-cushion vehicle able to operate over both land and water. Amphibious ships (both currently deployed and future) can carry the LCAC in their well decks. It has a payload capability of 120,000 lb and speeds of up to 40 kt; it is 88 ft long and 47 ft wide. The range capability of the LCAC is 200 nm. The contractors are Bell Aerospace Textron, New Orleans, LA, and Avondale Gulfport Marine. FY 1990 and 1991 requests for 9 and 12 vessels per year were $223.2 million and $301.7 million, respectively. (see also **amphibious warfare landing craft**)

landing ship, dock (LSD): Navy conventionally powered **amphibious warfare ship** for carrying and launching amphibious warfare craft, vehicles, and Marines for amphibious assault operations.

landing ship, tank (LST): Navy conventionally powered **amphibious warfare ship** for carrying and landing amphibious vehicles, tanks, combat vehicles, and equipment for amphibious assault operations.

LANDSOUTH (see **Allied Land Forces, Southern Europe**)

LANDSOUTHEAST (see **Allied Land Forces, Southeastern Europe**)

LANTCOM (see **U.S. Atlantic Command**)

LANTIRN (Low Altitude Navigation and Targeting Infrared for Night System): Air Force air-to-ground fire-control system designed for night and adverse weather use on **F-15E Strike Eagle** and F-16C/D fighters. LANTIRN allows a single-seat fighter pilot to enter and leave target areas below enemy defenses at night and in conditions of limited visibility at low altitudes while targets are cited and weapons launched. LANTIRN also provides capability to find and attack tactical targets with the imaging infrared version of the **Maverick** missile, laser guided bombs, and conventional weapons. The prime contractor is Martin Marietta, Orlando, FL. FY 1990 and 1991 requests were $365.9 million and $277.9 million, respectively.

The first production navigation pod was delivered in March 1987; the first targeting pod was delivered in July 1988. The navigation pod consists of an infrared sensor in the upper section and terrain-following radar in the lower section. The targeting pod contains a laser designator, digital head-up **forward-looking infrared radar**, a missile boresight correlator for aligning the IIR Maverick missile, and processors and cooling units. Each pod can be operated and employed separately. The targeting pod portion has been approved for full-rate production, to reach 10 sets per month by the end of 1989. The system is scheduled to be operational in late 1989.

Laser (Light Amplification by Stimulated Emission of Radiation): A device producing a narrow beam of coherent radiation by a process called stimulated emission, which utilizes a natural molecular (and atomic) phenomenon whereby molecules absorb incident electromagnetic energy at specific frequencies, store this energy for short but usable periods, and then release the stored energy in the form of light at particular frequencies in an extremely narrow frequency band. A laser can be focused to provide force that has potential application for military weapons. It produces radiation of a given frequency and with all wavefronts in phase in very short optical waves. The beam does not widen out and diffuse like normal light radiation, so it is therefore directional and highly concentrated. Lasers would themselves thus destroy their targets by heating, melting, or vaporizing their surfaces. There are a number of different lasers in use

- Chemical laser: A laser in which chemical action is used to produce the pulses of coherent light.
- Continuous-wave laser: A laser in which the coherent light is generated continuously rather than at fixed time intervals.
- Excimer laser: A chemical laser that uses noble gases.
- Free-electron laser: A laser in which electrons are converted to coherent light. The electrons are supplied by an accelerator, and power for the laser by electrical energy.
- Repetitively pulsed laser: A laser that fires its beam in sequential short bursts, as opposed to a continuous beam or a single pulse.

laser designation: The use of a laser to illuminate a mid-course target with a low-power laser beam, thus allowing target engagement with laser-seeking munitions such as **Hellfire**, **Copperhead**, Marine Corps **Maverick** missiles, or Air Force laser guided bombs. Army designators are the **Fire Support Vehicle** (ground vehicular laser locator designator (G/VLLD)), **Aquila** remotely piloted vehicle, and the **OH-58D** helicopter. Laser homing weapons in production include the Hellfire missile and laser Maverick.

laser Hellfire   (see **Hellfire**)

laser intelligence (LASINT):   Type of **signals intelligence** information collected from laser beam emissions, such as the vibrations of sound waves. LASINT is a subcategory of electro-optical intelligence.

laser reconnaissance system: An active electro-optical night reconnaissance system that produces either photographic or TV-type images by detecting the reflected laser illumination. The small, intense laser beam rapidly sweeps the ground in contiguous scans as opposed to the conventional methods of illuminating targets using photoflash cartridges, flares, or condenser discharge strobe lights. The system also increases the coverage obtainable by other systems since it is not restricted by the amount of cartridges or flares that are carried or by the time required to recharge the strobe light condensers. (see also **electro-optics**)

LASINT   (see **laser intelligence**)

Latin American Nuclear Free Zone Treaty   (see **Treaty of Tlatelolco**)

launch control center (LCC) Underground manned **command post** used by the **Strategic Air Command** to launch **ICBMs** (intercontinental ballistic missiles). One hundred LCCs are currently active, each controlling ten ICBMs. LCCs can launch missiles only after receiving emergency action messages. Ground LCCs are supplemented with airborne launch centers. The ground LCCs are somewhat hardened against **electromagnetic pulse (EMP)** effects but are not expected to survive direct attack.

There are two types of countdowns to launch used by the LCCs: terminal and preterminal. A terminal countdown begins after two or more LCCs send the launch command to the missiles and may last from a second to more than an hour. A preterminal countdown means that only a single LCC issued the launch command, which activates a long-term launcher. A launch in a preterminal countdown could technically be stopped, but "cancelling an authorized launch of a missile in preterminal or terminal countdown is prohibited, even though orders directing immediate termination might have been received" [Bruce Blair, *Strategic Command and Control*, p. 232].

launch-on-warning (LOW): Retaliatory policy of launching strategic nuclear forces at the point of confirmation of an attack in preparation, or in progress, and before incoming warheads arrive. The missiles would be launched as soon as early warning of the attack is received. ("Launch under attack" connotes launching of the missiles as warheads are actually impacting in the United States.) A

decision to launch-on-warning would have to be taken in less than 30 minutes, and would follow first detection by the **Defense Support Program** early-warning satellites. The amount of time available to the National Command Authorities before the first missiles reached their targets would be only a matter of minutes. Despite the time limitations of detecting an attack, assessing its size and intentions, and choosing an option in the **Single Integrated Operational Plan** for a response, LOW has been a part of nuclear employment policy since the 1970s. U.S. official declaratory policy is to maintain the option to launch-on-warning.

launch-under-attack (LUA): A modification of **launch-on-warning,** with ICBMs (intercontinental ballistic missiles) launched only after an enemy attack has been confirmed, that is, when actual warheads have exploded. The Joint Chiefs of Staff define LUA as "execution by **National Command Authorities** of **Single Integrated Operational Plan** forces subsequent to tactical warning of strategic nuclear attack against the United States and prior to first impact" [*JCS Pub 1*, p. 208]. The President's Commission on Strategic Forces (the Scowcroft Commission) outlined a scenario in which Soviet ballistic missile submarine forces operating close to U.S. shores hit targets before ICBM forces arrived, and the United States would launch its ICBMs during that interval. The Commission stressed that this would not be a launch-on-warning or even a launch-under-attack, but rather a launch after attack [*Report of the President's Commission on Strategic Forces*, April 1983, p. 8].

launchweight: The weight of the fully loaded missile at the time of launch. It includes the aggregate weight of all booster stages, the post-boost vehicle (PBV), and the payload.

laydown: "A weapon employment concept that requires weapon survival upon ground impact following release from low-flying delivery aircraft and delayed fuzing and firing of the weapon in order to permit safe escape of the aircraft" [*DNA Dictionary*, p. 86].

LCAC Designation for **landing craft, air cushion**.

LCC: Designation for **amphibious command ship**.

LCM Designation for landing craft, mechanized.

LCPL Designation for landing craft, personnel, large.

LCU: Designation for landing craft, utility. (see also **amphibious warfare landing craft**)

LCVP Designation for landing craft, vehicle, personnel.

LEASAT (leased satellite): Navy-leased UHF **communications satellite** designed by Hughes (designated Syncom during development and prior to successful launch) as a follow-on and supplement to **FLTSATCOM**. The 2,900 lb satellite has 12 channels in the 200–400 MHz range and is launched by the space shuttle. LEASAT number 1 was launched by STS 41-D on 31 August 1984.

Lemonade: Secure worldwide communications system operated by the **National Security Agency**. The Lemonade system is a time division multiplex channel-packing system used for transmission of **signals intelligence** information.

Lemon Juice: Exercise term for **air defense warning** yellow.

LERTCON: Common acronym used for **alert condition**.

LES 8/9 (Lincoln Experimental Satellites 8 and 9): Experimental, two-way EHF secure **communications satellites** built by Lincoln Laboratories and used by the Air Force as part of the **Minimum Essential Emergency Communications Network (MEECN)**. LES 8 and LES 9 were launched on 4 March 1976, using a gyro that eliminated dependence on ground satellite control and employing EHF frequencies in space for the first time. The test satellites in near-synchronous orbit can communicate crosslink from satellite to satellite as well as with ground terminals. The LES satellites are designed for use by small mobile terminals, as well as by transportable or fixed ground terminals. They are a prototype to develop the **MILSTAR** system. Their power plants are designed to survive nuclear impacts by using radioisotope thermoelectric power rather than solar power. Each satellite has a ground visibility of 12,800 km in diameter, and when working together, they can cover more than three quarters of the earth's surface. Up- and down-link control communications are primarily in UHF.

LHA: Designation for **amphibious assault ship, aircraft carrier**.

LHD-1 Wasp class Amphibious Assault Ship A currently deployed Navy multipurpose amphibious assault ship. Its mission is to embark, deploy and land Marine elements in an assault on land by helicopters, landing craft, and amphibious armored vehicles. Wasp class ships displace 40,500 tons at full load and can accommodate almost 2,000 Marine troops, 42 helicopters (or a mix of 30 helicopters and six to eight **AV-8 Harrier** short take-off and landing jets), three **landing craft, air cushion**, and numerous cargo and assault vehicles. The lead ship in the class was launched in 1987 and commissioned in 1989. Three additional ships have been authorized by the Congress but a fifth ship, which had been scheduled for purchase in FY 1991 was deferred for budgetary reasons. The Navy ultimately wishes to have nine LHD ships. The prime contractor is Ingalls Shipbuilding, Pascagoula, MS. The FY 1989 procurement request for the fourth LHD was $757.9 million. FY 1990 and 1991 requests for outfitting and RDT&E were $10.7 and $60.9 million, respectively. (see also **amphibious warfare ship**)

L-hour: **1.** The specific hour on **C-day**, expressed in Greenwich Mean Time, that serves as a common reference time from which the movement of weapon systems, equipment, supplies, personnel, and transportation is measured during deployment operations. Preplanned deployment activities can be scheduled prior to or after L-hour. **2.** In the Navy, the time of touchdown of the first helicopter at the landing zone. **3.** Launch hour. (see also **military time**)

LHX (Light Armed Scout Helicopter): Joint two-crew, light helicopter under development by the Army. It is to be the Army's and Marine Corps' next-generation helicopter, which will replace aging unarmed **OH-6**, **OH-58** scout and **AH-1** attack helicopters. This aircraft in the Army's air cavalry and attack battalions will significantly expand the Army's capability to conduct day/night tactical operations in all types of terrain, adverse weather, and battle environments, with increased survivability. With its increased speed, air-to-air and air-to-ground capability and mission equipment, the LHX will enhance the combat operations of supported forces. The LHX was approved in June 1988 for entry into the demonstration/validation phase of development. It is scheduled for deployment in the mid-1990s. The helicopter will weigh 7,500 lb empty, have 170+ kt cruising speed, and have an endurance of 2.5 hours (.5 hours reserve). Its self-deployment ferry range will be 1,260 nm. FY 1990 and FY 1991 RDT&E budget requests are $292.4 million and $499.6 million, respectively.

life-cycle: The total of all the phases a **procurement** item passes through from the time it is initially developed until its consumption or disposal. Life-cycle cost is the total cost of an item or weapon system over its full life. It includes the cost of development, acquisition, ownership (operation, maintenance, support, etc.) and, where applicable, disposal.

Light Airborne Multipurpose System (LAMPS): Navy computer-integrated ship/helicopter system to increase the effectiveness of surface combatants. A remote helicopter platform—either **SH-2F Seasprite** or **SH-60 Seahawk** helicopters—deploy sonobuoys and torpedoes, process magnetic anomaly detector sensor information, and serve as elevated platforms for radar and electronic warfare support measures. LAMPS provides surface ships with greater anti-submarine warfare, anti-ship surveillance, and targeting capability. LAMPS Mk I ships carry the SH-2F and LAMPS Mk III ships carry the SH-60B.

light ballistic missile: One of two categories of **ICBMs** (intercontinental ballistic missiles) designated by the **SALT II** treaty for purposes of missile counting. The Soviet SS-19 ICBM is recognized as the heaviest of the existing light ICBMs. (see also **heavy ballistic missile**)

light infantry battalion: One of five types of **infantry** battalions, the light infantry battalion is an Army **maneuver battalion** with a total strength of 800 personnel, equipped to obtain the optimum degree of weight and strength to conduct sustained combat operations with some self-sufficiency, at the same time maintaining a degree of air transportability and mobility. Three rifle companies can be lifted entirely by utility helicopters, and heavy weapons, such as 107 mm mortars and **TOW**

antitank missiles, in the headquarters company can be quickly transported. A ground scout platoon, vehicular-mounted ground surveillance radar, and Redeye/**Stinger** air defense section are also assigned to the battalion.

light infantry division (LID): A type of Army infantry **division** that is smaller and more mobile than other division types, and consists of approximately 10,800 personnel. The LID is composed of nine **light infantry battalions**, three 105 mm towed howitzer artillery battalions, and one 155 mm towed howitzer artillery battalion. LIDs are capable of conducting sustained operations including those in difficult weather and terrain. They can operate as part of a joint force, and with less combat service support than other divisions. LID missions include **air assault** operations, active defense operations, and riverine or amphibious operations. The LID is limited however, in its ground vehicular mobility, organic airlift, and antitank protection capabilities.

In order to improve the Army's power-projection capability, two new light divisions were added to its inventory during the Reagan Administration (6th Infantry Div (Light), AK; and 10th Mountain Division (Light Infantry), Ft. Drum, NY). In addition, two existing divisions, the 7th Infantry at Ft. Ord, CA, and the 25th Infantry in Hawaii, are making transitions to the new design. The units are offensively oriented, training to attack by infiltration, air assault, ambush, and raid.

LIGHTSAT: The Advanced Space Technology (LIGHTSAT) Program is a research and development program to develop a system of lightweight communication, positioning, and targeting satellites that can be quickly launched in time of crisis or war. The LIGHTSAT concept administered by DARPA's Advanced Strategic Technology Office, began with another DARPA program—the global low-orbit message relay (GLOMR), which relayed signals from oceanographic sensors and identified their position.

DARPA plans to develop several different types of satellites under the LIGHTSAT concept, including **communications satellites**, position-locating satellites (which could fill in if **NAVSTAR** were destroyed), and sensor packages for weapons targeting. The LIGHTSAT program will not concentrate on surveillance and photographic reconnaissance capabilities. The Director of the DARPA Advanced Strategic Technology Office, which is administering the development of LIGHTSAT, envisions the program as a "warehouse truck loaded with a dozen satellites of different types accompanied by trucks with boosters in them. Then, when needed, the appropriate type of satellite could quickly be mated with a booster and launched" [James W. Rawles, "Lightsat: All Systems Are Go," *Defense Electronics*, May 1988, p. 68]. LIGHTSAT capabilities may also include the replenishment of military satellites destroyed by enemy **anti-satellite (ASAT)** weapons.

The LIGHTSAT launch system would be similar in size and mobility to that of the **Patriot** or **Pershing** missiles. The two most likely basing modes for a "pop-up system"

are the rail garrison (similar to or in conjunction with that planned for the **MX missile**) and mobile launchers installed on CONUS military reservations.

The rationale for a mobile LIGHTSAT system is that current U.S. launch facilities and satellites in orbit are susceptible to enemy attack and could be put out of commission during wartime, therefore necessitating the need for a survivable mobile system independent of large, fixed-position launch pads and mission control centers.

The first launch of an experimental LIGHTSAT is tentatively scheduled for the fall of 1989. The first payload to be placed into orbit from Vandenberg AFB, CA, will consist of two MACSATS (Multiple Access Communications Satellites) manufactured by Defense Systems, Inc., McLean, VA. Each MACSAT weighs 150 lb and will be placed into a circular polar orbit at an altitude of 400 nm and will be involved in test demonstrations during the following year. The MACSATs will have a global store-and-forward message relay capability at UHF frequencies and in orbit, will provide up to 15 passes daily with 14 minutes visibility each at the earth's poles and at minimum, 5 passes with an average visibility of 5–10 minutes each at the equator.

The LIGHTSAT program would eventually be relinquished by DARPA to either the Air Force or the Army.

limited access: Security control applied to the **operation plan (OPLAN)** information, restricting access to selected personnel and the

Worldwide Military Command and Control System terminals. (see also **close-hold access, normal access**)

limited area: A **restricted area** designated by a nuclear storage site or alert site commander that surrounds one or more **exclusion areas**. Within a limited area, guards and internal controls (depending on the nature of the activity) prevent access by unauthorized persons.

limited life component: Nuclear weapon component that is replaced periodically to maintain the design operational capability of a weapon. The term is usually used euphemistically to refer to tritium, which is used as a neutron generator or explosive yield booster in nuclear warheads.

limited nuclear options (LNOs): Preplanned options for selected nuclear attacks against discrete sets of military targets, as opposed to massive attacks. Secretary of Defense James Schlesinger is credited with introducing this concept into the **Single Integrated Operational Plan** in the 1970s, stressing that the selective use of U.S. forces requires "the indoctrination and the planning in anticipation of the difficulties involved. It is ill-advised to attempt to do that under the press of circumstances" [U.S. Congress, Senate Foreign Relations Committee, *U.S.-USSR Strategic Policies*, Hearing before Subcommittee on Arms Control, International Law, and Organization, 1974, p. 13].

LNOs were called for in **National Security Decision Memorandum 242 (NSDM-242)** issued by President Nixon and were also one of the four categories of attack outlined in the Carter Administration's Presidential Directive 59 **(PD-59)**. There were four target groups as determined by PD-59: nuclear forces, conventional military forces, military and political leadership, and economic and industrial targets. Attacks against these groups could be accomplished by

- Major attack options, such as all-out attack and the "no cities" attack against military, economic, and industrial resources;
- Selected attack options;
- Regional nuclear options; and
- Limited nuclear options.

The LNO would be accomplished with a small number of weapons, permitting selective attacks on fixed enemy military or industrial targets to achieve specific objectives.

Limited Test Ban Treaty (LTBT): Formally known as the Treaty Banning Nuclear Weapon Tests in the Atmosphere, in Outer Space and Under Water. The multilateral treaty was signed in Moscow by the United States, the United Kingdom, and the Soviet Union on 5 August 1963, ratified on 24 September 1963, and entered into force on 10 October 1963. Signed by over 100 nations (with the notable exceptions of France and China), the treaty prohibits nuclear explosions (both military and peaceful) underwater, in the atmosphere, and in outer space, that is, in an environment that would easily cause radioactive debris to be present outside the state conducting the explosion. This was the first significant step in nuclear arms control negotiations. The underground testing of nuclear weapons is permitted under the treaty. The treaty is of unlimited duration.

In 1955, the Soviet Union made the first proposal for a nuclear test ban as an initial step in a comprehensive disarmament plan. The United States linked these proposals to verification problems and other **comprehensive test ban** agreements under negotiation. In 1958, President Eisenhower modified the U.S. position and agreed to look at verification issues without linkage to other disarmament issues. Reports on verification were then released by an international conference, which stated that a control system utilizing 160–170 land-based and 10 shipborne posts with on-site inspections could monitor a nuclear test ban. In August 1958, the United States called for negotiations for a test ban based upon this report. At this time both the United States and the Soviet Union declared a moratorium on nuclear explosive testing. For four years, verification issues remained the stumbling block to an agreement. U.S. experts repudiated the conference report, and debate over the number of on-site inspections to be allowed deadlocked the talks, which adjourned in January 1962.

In March 1962, negotiations on the comprehensive ban resumed with the idea of manned control posts with automatic seismic recording stations (black boxes) taking hold. Still, the United States demanded six to seven more on-site inspections than the Soviet Union was willing to permit. By the spring of 1963, negotiations had shifted from a comprehensive to a limited test ban, most notably because of the Cuban missile crisis. In April 1963, Soviet Premier Khrushchev withdrew the Soviet on-site inspection offer. In June, President Kennedy,

at a speech at American University, announced that the United States had agreed to hold negotiations in Moscow on a comprehensive ban. In July 1963, Khrushchev called for an agreement banning nuclear tests in the atmosphere, outer space, and underwater, noting that on-site inspection would not be needed to verify tests in these environments. During this time, both countries had ceased to test nuclear weapons in the atmosphere.

The treaty was signed in Moscow on 5 August 1963, Kennedy stressed that the treaty required no cooperative verification mechanism because the United States already had the means to detect nuclear tests in these environments. The risks of violation were far outweighed, he argued, by the risks of unrestricted testing. Despite expressing some reservations (chances of Soviet violations and possible hampering of U.S. development of new nuclear weapons), the Senate ratified the treaty. Critics were mollified by Kennedy's promise to conduct an extensive underground testing program and to maintain the standby capability of atmospheric testing in case the Soviet Union violated the treaty [U.S. Congress, House Foreign Affairs Committee, in *Fundamentals of Nuclear Arms Control. Part 1— Nuclear Arms Control: A Brief Historical Survey*, 20 May 1985. pp. 9–11; ACDA, *Documents on Disarmament*, 1960, 1961, 1963]. In February 1985, President Reagan complained that Soviet underground test practices had produced radioactivity outside the Soviet Union. The complaint focused on the issue of debris versus fallout. The Soviet Union makes the same complaint about U.S. testing. (see also **arms control, Comprehensive Test Ban, Threshold Test Ban Treaty**)

limited war: "Armed conflict short of general war, exclusive of incidents, involving the overt engagement of military forces of two or more nations" [*JCS Pub 1*, p. 211]. Limited war connotes the use of U.S. military forces to protect "vital interests" even though no direct threat to national survival exists. (see also **general war**)

line officer   (see **officer**)

line of sight (LOS):   1. The straight line between two points; in the military the line between the target and the aiming reference. This line is in the plane of a great circle, but does not follow the curvature of the earth. **2.** The straight-line distance to the horizon or to an elevated point beyond the horizon from a given point.

Line of Sight-Forward-Heavy (LOS-F-H) missile system   (see **Forward Area Air Defense System**)

lines of communication (LOC): Land, sea, and air routes essential to the conduct of military operations, particularly the deployment of armed forces and associated logistic support. LOCs provide for the reception and onward movement of personnel, equipment, and other resources deployed forward to Europe, the Pacific, or the Middle East for wartime operations. Overseas unified commands conclude agreements with allied countries to obtain support for movement of war resources, including those already in the host countries. These include access

to hospitals, ports, airfields, transportation networks, civilian manpower resources, and prepositioned materiel. (see also **host nation support**)

LKA: Designation for **amphibious cargo ship**.

Local Area Network   (see **LAN**)

LODE (Large Optics Demonstration Experiment): A segment of the three-part **Strategic Defense Initiative (SDI)** experimental directed-energy program, along with **Alpha** (a continuous wave HF chemical laser), and **LAMP** (the LODE advanced mirror program). The LODE and LAMP experiments are designed to improve beam control and the quality of the mirrors that would be used in any laser weapon system. The LODE and LAMP mirror segment is to be integrated with Alpha in the early 1990s to be used for ground-based testing against stationary ground targets (so as not to violate the ABM Treaty) [*SDI Dictionary*, p. 9].

LODE Advanced Mirror Program (see **LAMP**)

logistics: The process of providing goods and services where and when they are needed, which in the military is the science of planning and carrying out the movement and maintenance of forces. Given new technology and more capable and sophisticated weapon systems, it is not a static process. Logistics includes a number of different functions:

• Supply: The procurement, distribution, maintenance while in storage, and salvage of supplies, including the determination of kind and quality of supplies.

- Maintenance: The sustaining of materiel in an operational status, restoring it to a serviceable condition, or updating/upgrading its utility through modification.
- Transportation: Services related to the movement of personnel and materials to meet the forces' needs.
- Services: That part of logistics that provides combat service support in the form of food, laundry, dry cleaning, clothing sales, fumigation and baths, property disposal, and graves registration. Its functional subdivisions are field, personnel, and medical services.
- Facilities: The part of logistics that pertains to real property management and consists of facility management, new construction, operation and maintenance.

The essential nature of adequate logistics is readily apparent in sustaining effective air combat. Air Force tactical fighter wings deployed outside the United States would not deploy the entire structure but rather just the flying squadrons and those maintenance and other functions appropriate to the nature and duration of the operation. Initial maintenance would be limited to "remove, repair, and replace" procedures, especially at limited standby bases. Within 30 days, a full intermediate-level maintenance capability, which includes the emergency manufacture of some unavailable parts, will be established. Other logistical support will be similarly phased in. Generally aircraft will not be deployed until they are required by the circumstances. In many cases wing aircraft will be deployed in separate squadron (or smaller detachment) packages, each with its own slice of initial maintenance support, to widely dispersed operating locations. Depending on host base facilities, combat support group personnel (e.g., security police, air traffic control) will also be deployed. The tactical airfield must have adequate runways, taxiways, parking, and all the other essential base support functions. Army Corps of Engineers may have to be called on to construct an expedient airfield in a forward combat area. Harvest Bare kits are available to allow Red Horse civil engineers to convert a base site (runways, taxiways, parking space, and water supply) into a combat-capable operating base. Prime Beef teams may be used to activate a standby base or to augment limited bases to support maintenance and logistics functions.

Logistic and administrative support includes those aspects of operations that deal with

- Research, development, test and evaluation;
- Acquisition, storage, movement, distribution, maintenance, evacuation, and disposition of materiel;
- Movement and evacuation of personnel;
- Medical services, including aeromedical evacuation;
- Communications services;
- Acquisition or construction, maintenance, operation, and disposition of facilities; and
- Other logistic and administrative services, comprising planning,

management, and execution of responsibilities.

Logistics Command: Navy type organization operating within the **Pacific Fleet**. The command is located at Pearl Harbor, HI.

logistic ships (A-):   Navy ships that provide services and support to combatant ships as well as general support to Navy missions. Such ships have an "A" as the first letter in their hull designation and include

- *Mobile Logistic-Type Ships*: Ships that have the capability to provide **underway replenishment** to fleet units and/or to provide direct material support to other deployed units operating far from home base.
- *Underway replenishment ships*: Multiproduct fast combat support ships (designated AOE) and replenishment oilers (AOR) that operate at sea as an integral part of a carrier battle group. Also, fleet oilers (AO), ammunition ships (AE), and stores ships (AFS), which operate in escorted, underway replenishment groups shuttling fuel, ammunition, and stores to and from advanced logistic bases or consolidation points at sea. (These shuttle ships are supplied in turn by merchant tanker and cargo ship deliveries from the United States. If an AOE or AOR is not available for a carrier battle group, AOs or AEs may be used to replace it.)
- *Material support ships*: Those destroyer tenders (AD), submarine tenders (AS), and repair ships (AR) that provide services and repairs to other ships and their weapons while in port.

- *Support Type Ships*: Ships designed to operate in the open ocean in a variety of sea states to provide general support to either combatant forces or shore-based establishments. This includes smaller auxiliaries that by the nature of their duties leave inshore waters. Fleet support ships include salvage ships (ARS), submarine rescue ships (ASR), fleet ocean tugs (ATF), and salvage and rescue ships (ATS). Other auxiliaries include miscellaneous (AG), deep submergence support ships (AGDS), miscellaneous command ships (AGF), missile range instrumentation ships (AG-M), oceanographic research ships (AGOS), surveying ships (AGS), auxiliary research submarines (AG-SS), hospital ships (AH), cargo ships (AK), vehicle cargo ships (AOG), gasoline tankers (AOG), transport oiler ships (AOT), transport ships (AP), cable repairing ships (ARC), small repair ships (ARL), aviation logistic support ships (AVB), guided missile test ships (AVM), and auxiliary aircraft-landing training ships (AVT).

Several classes of support and logistic ships can maintain or transport nuclear weapons. According to the U.S. Navy, "destroyer tenders have the capability for storage, assembly, and issue of ASROC to delivery ships." There are nine active destroyer tenders in the fleet. The three ships in the oldest class were commissioned from 1940–1944, and the six ships in the newest classes from 1967–1983. They range in size from 18,000–22,500 tons at full load. Destroyer tenders support the ASROC and Tomahawk capable cruisers, destroyers, and frigates, and also provide support for Terrier missiles and warheads.

Submarine tenders (ASs) have similar capabilities with respect to SUBROC, Tomahawk, Poseidon, and Trident missiles. There are 12 active submarine tenders divided among six classes. They were commissioned between 1941–1981 and range in size from 16,230–23,000 tons at full load. Typically, submarine tenders are docked in a port and service submarines moored alongside. Four submarine tenders support ballistic missile submarines and eight support attack submarines.

The ballistic missile submarine tenders have facilities for servicing submarine-launched ballistic missiles, reentry vehicles, and warheads. One is based at Holy Loch, Scotland, UK to support the forward-deployed Poseidon ballistic missile submarines. This tender is supplied by one Military Sealift Command cargo ship (TAK) converted to carry ballistic missiles and other submarine equipment (the need for this TAK will disappear in the late 1990s when the U.S. Navy achieves an all-Trident missile force based in the United States). The other ballistic missile submarine tenders are homeported in Charleston, SC, and King's Bay, GA.

The attack submarine tenders support SUBROC and Tomahawk missiles. Attack submarine tenders are home ported at New London, CT; Norfolk, VA; San Diego, CA; Charleston, SC; La Maddalena, Italy; and Guam.

According to the U.S. Navy, "ammunition ships and most fast combat-support ships are capable of transporting, storing, and providing underway replenishment for all Navy weapons except Polaris and Poseidon." Replenishment oilers also "have an emergency capability for transporting and providing underway replenishment for all Navy weapons except Polaris and Poseidon." Underway replenishment ships, in addition, "may be ordered to load Marine Corps" nuclear weapons "for transport to amphibious forces."

Underway transfer of nuclear weapons may occur either through connected replenishment (CONREP), where supply ships are joined to the ship to be supplied and cables and slings are used for transferring containers, or by vertical replenishment (VERTREP), depending on the availability of CH-46 or CH-53 helicopters. If the operational situation demands, small craft can also be used to transfer nuclear weapons, but this is the least desirable and the most hazardous method of transfer. Transfers of nuclear weapons are "generally made between support ships and combatants, but an exchange or consolidation could be ordered between ships of the same type," for example, from aircraft carrier to aircraft carrier using the underway replenishment ships as a conveyor. The U.S. Navy warns that "the transfer of nuclear weapons at sea presents one of the most hazardous of all shipboard operations. It contains all the dangers found in conventional ammunition transfer plus the grave consequences of accidental loss or contamination" [U.S. Navy, Office of the Secretary, *Classification of Naval Ships and Craft*, SECNAVINST 5030.1k, 4 February 1986, released under the FOIA; U.S. Navy, *Nuclear Warfare Operations (U) NWP 28 (Rev.D)*, November 1980, p. 4-8, released under the FOIA; U.S. Navy, *Loading and Underway Replenishment of Nuclear Weapons (U) NWP 14-1 (Rev. A)*, November 1979, p. 2-25; released under the FOIA].

Logistics Management Institute(see **Federally-Funded Research and Development Centers**)

Long Range Air ASW Capable Aircraft (LRAACA)   (see **P-7**)

Long-Term Defense Program (LTDP): 1978 **North Atlantic Treaty Organization (NATO)** program that set out medium-term spending force improvement goals in 10 areas: readiness; reinforcement capabilities; reserve mobilization; maritime posture; air defense; command, control and communications; electronic warfare; standardization and interoperability; logistics; and theater nuclear forces. The procedures were adopted in May 1980, and planning has a 15-year horizon. The first two planning guidelines issued dealt with air defense and **follow-on forces attack**. Current issues and goals include

- Improved Readiness: Increased national holdings of tanks, anti-armor weapons, missiles, armored helicopters, and air-to-surface weapons; purchase of protective equipment against chemical weapons; and pursuit of cooperative and coordinated development of next-generation anti-armor weapons and a common family of air-to-surface weapons.

- Reinforcement: Accelerate the movement of significant fighting units to forward areas; preposition the equipment for three heavy U.S. divisions (some allies will modify civil aircraft to carry equipment that cannot be prepositioned); and improve amphibious lift for British and Dutch marines.

- Reserve Mobilization: Bring national reserve forces up to NATO standards and improve readiness of certain reserve formations; a number of European countries will consider providing more reserve brigades.

- Maritime Posture: Improved command and control; improved air defense for naval units; better anti-missile defense for naval units; greater mine warfare capabilities.

- Air Defense: Improve ability to identify hostile aircraft and control NATO's own aircraft; improve fighter aircraft; and acquire improved surface-to-air weapons.

- Command, Control and Communications: Implementation of second phase of the **NATO Integrated Communications System**; cooperation and coordinated efforts in maritime communications, tactical trunk networks, single-channel radio access, NATO/national area interconnection, strategic automatic data processing, and war headquarters improvements.

- Electronic Warfare: Improved capability to counter Warsaw Pact electronic warfare; improved organization and procedures.

- Rationalization: New procedures for long-range armaments planning; improved formulation and utilization of standardization agreements;

continuation of work undertaken by the Conference of National Armaments Directors in the field of intellectual rights.

- Logistics: Policy and organizational improvements to harmonize and coordinate arrangements to improve logistics support; development of a logistics master-planning system; increased war reserve stocks; and improved flexibility in the use of ammunition stocks.

(see also **Conceptual Military Framework**)

look-down, shoot-down: Airborne radars that discriminate aerial targets from ground clutter below, combined with air-to-air weapons that can destroy those targets. The United States has four fighter planes with look-down capability: the **F-14**, **F-15**, **F-16**, and **F/A-18**. The **Airborne Warning and Control System (AWACS)** and the **E-2 Hawkeye** system also provide look-down surveillance capability.

Looking Glass: Nickname for the **airborne command post** operated by the **Strategic Air Command (SAC)**. Looking Glass is an **EC-135** aircraft containing a scaled-down version of the **SAC command post**, including a battle staff commanded at all times by a general officer able to take command of strategic forces. As part of the **Post Attack Command and Control System (PACCS)**, Looking Glass would take over the command and control of SAC missile and bomber forces if the SAC underground command post or terrestrial communications system were destroyed. It is able to launch the SAC aircraft force for survival and **Minuteman** missiles from its airborne launch control center (ALCC). By transmitting a coded UHF signal, Looking Glass could also order the launch of the **emergency rocket communications system (ERCS)**.

Looking Glass aircraft are always airborne and take off three times a day, one every eight hours, from the 2nd Airborne Command and Control Squadron (ACCS) at Offutt AFB, NE, and the 4th ACCS, Ellsworth AFB, SD. One aircraft remains airborne until the next achieves altitude and establishes communications with the SAC command post. The Looking Glass mission began at Offutt AFB in 1961. On 1 February 1989, Looking Glass celebrated its 28th year of continuous airborne operations, logging 267,180 flying hours without a major aircraft accident.

Loraine (DARPA Long-Range Intercepter Experiment): Candidate air-to-air and surface-to-air missile system for the **Air Defense Initiative**. Loraine is a nonnuclear, long-range, highly maneuverable anti-cruise missile. It is intended for continental and naval battle group air defense. Loraine will have a Swerve **phased-array** attack radar with a large search area whose speed will allow it to reach distant aircraft or cruise missiles in minutes. It is designed to complement long-range sensor systems such as the **OTH-B** radar.

LORAN (Long-Range electronic Navigation): A system of electronic navigation in which the time difference in the reception of pulse signals

382 low-altitude bombing system (LABS)

originated simultaneously at a master and slave station is used to locate a ship or aircraft. The LORAN network of navigation stations is operated by the **Coast Guard**.

low-altitude bombing system (LABS): A low-level aircraft-delivery technique for airburst or contact burst of parachute-retarded nuclear **gravity bombs**. The delivery method is a four-G pullup to an approximate 45 degree flight path with release of the nuclear bomb occurring 5–12 seconds later.

Low Altitude Navigation and Targeting Infrared for Night System (see **LANTIRN**)

low frequency (see **very low frequency**)

low intensity conflict (LIC): Level of hostilities constituting **limited war** but short of a conventional or **general war**. The U.S. military's developing doctrine for LIC necessitates that national political objectives are the determinants of military action but guards against the protracted commitment of U.S. forces in a combat role.

LIC tactics are analogous to those of "counter-**insurgency**," and counter-**guerilla warfare**. LIC missions include: peacekeeping operations, assistance to foreign law enforcement agencies, **foreign internal defense**, **anti-terrorism**, **counter-terrorism**, **strike operations**, and **unconventional** warfare. As of July 1985 the Commander, Army Combined Arms Center, acts as the Army's proponent for LIC doctrine.

LPD: Designation for amphibious transport dock ship. (see also **amphibious warfare ship**)

LPH: Designation for helicopter amphibious assault ship. (see also **amphibious warfare ship**)

LSD: Designation for **landing ship, dock**.

LSSC: Designation for light **SEAL** support craft.

LST: Designation for **landing ship, tank**.

LWT: Designation for amphibious warping tug.

M

M: Prefix designating **1.** Multimission aircraft (e.g, MC-130). **2.** Mobile missile launched from a ground vehicle or movable platform (e.g., MGM-52). **3.** Guided missile or drone. **4.** Maintenance vehicle for checking the launch vehicle. **5.** Meditate (see **sensitive compartmented information**).

M-1 Abrams: Army's primary main battle tank, featuring special armor and ballistic protection, compartmentalization of fuel and main gun ammunition, and automatic fire detection and suppression systems. The M-1 is a four-crew vehicle, mounts a 120 mm main gun and three secondary armament systems with day/night fire control and shoot-on-the-move capabilities. The 1500-horsepower turbine engine makes it capable of high speeds. It has improved fire control and shoot-on-the-move capabilities over the **M-60**, which it is replacing. Fielding of the M-1 began in 1981 and will continue into the early 1990s. Over 5,500 tanks are in the field as of the beginning of 1989. By the end of FY 1989, all armor units in Europe, and most active-component armor units in CONUS, will be equipped with the Abrams. The Abrams Block II (M-1A2) is slated to enter production in 1992 with enhanced survivability, improved target acquisition and fire control equipment, and improved reliability.

The Marine Corps also uses the M-1A1, which will eventually equip all active, reserve, and Maritime Preposition Support tank units. Improvements include the 120 mm cannon, nuclear, biological, and chemical (NBC) overpressure defense system, Commander's Independent Thermal Viewer, improved CO_2 laser rangefinder, improved armor protection, and various RAM-D improvements to the power train and suspension components.

Prime contractors are General Dynamics Land Systems Division, Sterling Heights, MI (the tank is manufactured at Lima, OH and Warren, MI); Cadillac Gage, Detroit, MI; GMC Detroit Diesel Allison, Indianapolis, IN; Hughes Aircraft, Culver City, CA; Textron Lycoming, Stratford, CT; Honeywell Inc., Hopkins, MN; Kollmorgen, Northampton, MA; Singer-Kearfoot, Little Falls, NJ; Garrett AiResearch, Torrance, CA; and Computing Devices of Canada, Nepean, Ontario. FY 1990 budget request for 448 vehicles is $1,440.6 million and for FY 1991 (261 vehicles) is $1,334.5 million. The FY 1990 Marine Corps request for 155 tanks is $526.6 million. The FY 1991 request for 255 tanks is $665.3 million.

M-2/M-3 Bradley Fighting Vehicle: Army full-tracked, lightly armored, Infantry Fighting Vehicle/Cavalry Fighting Vehicle (IFV/CFV). The IFV version provides cross-country mobility and mounted firepower in support of mounted and dismounted mechanized infantry operations. It has a crew of three: the commander, gunner, and driver. The CFV version is used by scout and armored cavalry units for screening, reconnaissance, and security missions. It has the same three-man crew as the IFV, plus two scouts.

Both the IFV and CFV versions have a two-person turret that mounts a stabilized 25 mm automatic cannon supported by **TOW** missiles and a coaxially mounted 7.62 machine gun. The M-2 and M-2A1 IFVs have in addition six 5.56 mm firing ports along the side and rear. The M-2A2 IFV has only two such ports in the rear. The M-2 has a road speed of 38 mph, a swim speed of 4.4 mph and a cruising range of 300 miles.

The first production model was delivered to the Army in May 1981. By 1989, 33 battalion-sized units, including Army National Guard battalions, fielded the Bradley. A major modification, fielded in 1987, incorporates the more lethal TOW 2 missile. The modified vehicles are designated M-2A1 and M-3A1. A decision to incorporate further survivability enhancements was approved in 1987. These modifications are being retrofitted into the M-2A1 and M-3A1 Bradleys currently fielded. Bradley's with more survivability enhancements are designated M-2A2 and M-3A3 vehicles.

Prime contractor is FMC Corporation, San Jose, CA. Other contractors are Ford Aerospace, Newport Beach, CA; General Electric, Pittsfield, MA; Honeywell, Minneapolis, MN; Cummins, Columbus, IN; RCA, Burlington, MA; Colt Industries, Hartford, CT; Chrysler Corp, Huntsville, AL; Hughes Aircraft Co., El Segundo, CA; and McDonnell Douglas, Mesa, AZ. The FY 1990 and FY 1991 budget requests for 600 vehicles in each year are $659.3 and $699 million, respectively, including RDT&E.

M-60 tank: Army and Marine Corps four-crew main battle tank being replaced by the **M-1 Abrams.** The tank has a road speed of 30 mph and a cruising range of 280 miles at 20 mph. It has a 105 mm rifled main gun and one 7.62 and one .50 caliber machine gun.

The original version has been in the field since 1961. Production of the latest version, the M-60A3TTS (for tank thermal sight) began in 1979 and ran through 1987 to fulfill foreign orders. The last new U.S. Army production model was delivered in 1983. Improvements made to the M-60A1 tank in the A3 upgrade program included gun stabilization, addition of a laser rangefinder, solid state computer and thermal shroud, and a tank thermal-imaging sight.

The Army has an inventory goal of some 7,300 M-60s. New-production

M-60A3 account for some 1,700 of this total, with the rest achieved by converting M-60A1 tanks to M-60A3 configurations. Conversions are done at the Anniston Army Depot, AL, and Mainz Army Depot, West Germany. (The M-60A2 version is no longer in service.) The last of the older M-60A1s was produced for the Marine Corps in May 1980.

M-101: Army and Marine Corps light 105 mm towed artillery gun used widely in the Korean and Vietnam Wars that has been largely replaced by the **M-102** in the active Army. It is airliftable by the **CH-47** helicopter. Its range is 11,500 meters with conventional rounds, or 14,500 meters with rocket-assisted projectiles. Each Marine division artillery regiment has 24 M-101A1s. The M-101A1 also equips one active duty Army artillery battalion in Alaska, and about 20 reserve component units. (see also **M-119**).

M-102: Army light 105 mm towed artillery gun being replaced by the **M-119**. It is airliftable by **CH-47** and **UH-60** helicopters and can be dropped by parachute. The M-102 has a range of 11,500 meters with conventional rounds, or 15,100 meters with rocket assist. There are three M-102 direct-support battalions in each **light infantry division,** the 101st Air Assault Division, and the 82nd Airborne Division.

M-109: Standard Army and Marine Corps 155 mm fully tracked amphibious self-propelled nuclear-capable artillery howitzer with a crew of six. The M-109A2/A3 is the stan-dard direct-support artillery weapon in armored and mechanized infantry units. It has secondary armament of a .50 caliber machine gun.

In service since 1963, the M-109 series has been converted with improvements to the M-109A1 and then to the M-109A3. The M-109A3 is a depot-modified M-109A1 with the same capabilities as the new-production M-109A2. The M-109 is air-portable in Air Force **C-5 Galaxy** transport aircraft. The Army Howitzer Improvement Program (HIP), begun in 1985, includes upgraded hydraulic and electrical systems, an automatic fire control system, and increased range. The HIP howitzers should begin entering field service in FY 1991. The prime contractor is BMY, a division of Harsco Corporation, York, PA. The guns fire the W48 **artillery fired atomic projectiles** and will fire the W82 when it is fielded in the early 1990s.

M-110: Army and Marine Corps 8-inch (203 mm) fully tracked self-propelled nuclear-capable artillery howitzer with a crew of five. Currently deployed in heavy division and Corps artillery units, and Marine Corps Force artillery, it is being slowly phased out of service in favor of the **Multiple Launch Rocket System (MLRS)** and improved 155 mm artillery. The gun provides general support to division combat units. Its maximum range is 22,900 meters or 30,000 meters with rocket assist. The guns fire the W33 and W79 **artillery fired atomic projectiles**.

M-113: Army basic-tracked armored personnel carrier, being replaced by the **M-2/M-3 Bradley Fighting Vehicle**. The M-113 has a crew of two and can carry 11 armed troops. Newer versions are equipped with **TOW** launchers. The M-113A3 is an improved version with engine and armor upgrades. The M-113 fleet will continue to be improved for service into the year 2000 and will operate in infantry and engineer squad roles and as mortar carriers, MEDE-VAC carriers, and maintenance support vehicles. Budgeted for FY 1988 at $65 million for 300 vehicles (appropriated to National Guard and Reserve Equipment). The prime contractors are FMC Corp., San Jose, CA; GMC Detroit Diesel Allison, of Detroit, MI, and Indianapolis, IN.

M-114: Army reserve and Marine Corps medium towed-artillery howitzer, provides direct or general support for Army reserve component infantry divisions and Marine divisions. It is airliftable by **CH-47** helicopters. The gun has a range of 14,600 meters. The newer M-114A2 is compatible with all projectiles used in the self-propelled **M-109** and can fire a rocket-assist projectile to 19,300 meters. Nine eight-gun M-114A1/A2 batteries in the Marine Corps are being replaced by **M-198**s.

M-119: Army 105 mm light artillery howitzer replacing the **M-101** and **M-102** guns, for issue to **light infantry divisions** starting in FY 1989. (As M-102s are replaced, they in turn are used to replace M-101s. Eventually, both gun models will be replaced by M-119s). The British-designed and -manufactured gun is airliftable by **UH-60** helicopters and can be

dropped by parachute. It has a range of 14,300 meters conventional round, or 19,500 meters with rocket assist. The weapon began production in the UK during 1987, and initial production in the United States began in 1988. The Army has a total requirement of 548 guns. The gun is produced at Watervliet Arsenal, NY, and Rock Island Arsenal, IL.

M-198: Army and Marine Corps lightweight, towed nuclear-capable 155 mm artillery howitzer. The M-198 will be employed as the primary direct-support weapon system in Army airborne and Marine divisions and will provide fire support in the Army **light infantry divisions**. It is replacing the **M-114,** providing increased range, improved reliability, and improved maintainability. It has a range of 30 km using rocket-assist ammunition. The M-198 is air-transportable by **CH-53E, C-130,** or larger fixed-wing aircraft. The gun was manufactured at Rock Island Arsenal, IL. The FY 1987 budget for the last 94 M-198s for the Marine Corps was $45.3 million.

MAC (see **Military Airlift Command**)

MACSAT (Multiple Access Communication Satellite) (see **LIGHTSAT**)

MAD (see **Mutual Assured Destruction**)

magazine: **1.** The holder for ammunition, particularly small arms ammunition. **2.** Compartment aboard a ship or at an onshore facility used for the storage of ammunition.

magnetic anomaly detection (MAD): "The detection of magnetic materials through the distortions they produce in the normal magnetic field of the earth. Although it has a relatively short range of initial detection, the equipment is useful in developing contacts originally made by other means of detection or intelligence" [*NWP 3*]. MAD is accomplished using a magnetic anomaly detector, an anti-submarine warfare device carried by low-flying maritime patrol aircraft designed to locate submarines. The aircraft carries a magnetometer, which is used to detect the disturbances of the Earth's normal magnetic field caused by submarines. It is used most prominently by the **P-3 Orion**.

Magnum: Byeman code name for a currently operating class of **signals intelligence (SIGINT)** satellites. It is the follow-on to the **Rhyolite/Aquacade** class, with increased power and potential "stealth" capabilities. Magnum is positioned in geosynchronous orbit and was first launched from the space shuttle Discovery on 25 January 1985. It has a single parabolic antenna and has a primary function of interception of military communications and telemetry signals (e.g., Soviet missile and nuclear tests and preparations). The satellite transmits its data to its ground control station at Pine Gap, Australia, or other ground stations. It is either stationed over the Soviet Union or Borneo. Intelligence obtained by Magnum and other SIGINT satellites is marked by the codeword **Zarf** [Jeffrey Richelson, *The U.S. Intelligence Community,* 2nd ed., pp. 173–74; and *American Espionage and the Soviet Target,* 1987, pp. 278, 280, 277, 244–46].

MAGTF (see **Marine Air-Ground Task Force**)

main operating base (MOB): 1. The primary airbase used by aircraft, strategic bombers, and ground-launched missiles. **2.** A base on which all essential buildings and facilities are erected. Total organizational and intermediate maintenance capability exists for assigned weapon systems. The intermediate maintenance capability may be expanded to support specific weapon systems deployed to the MOB [MAC, *Contingency Planning Policies and Procedures,* MACR 28-2, 29 December 1986, p. 103, released under the FOIA].

main stage: 1. In a single-stage rocket vehicle powered by one or more engines, the period when full thrust (at or above 90 percent) is attained. **2.** In a multistage rocket, the stage that develops the greatest amount of thrust, with or without boosters. **3.** A sustainer engine, considered as a stage after booster engines have fallen away.

maintenance: There are three categories of maintenance operations: user, intermediate, and depot. They are often referred to as organizational (1st echelon), organizational (2nd echelon), and intermediate (3rd echelon). User maintenance is preventive and minor maintenance performed at the unit, for example, by the unit motor pool. Intermediate maintenance can be of two types, direct support and general support. Direct support maintenance involves the repair and return of an item to the user. In the Army, this is mostly done at a **division support command** or a **corps support command (COSCOM)**. General support maintenance involves the repair and return of items to the theater supply systems. In the Army, this is done at a COSCOM or within a **communications zone**. Depot maintenance involves the rebuilding of equipment to support-service inventory objectives. This is done at the depots operated by the logistics commands. (see also **logistics**)

major attack options (MAO)   (see **limited nuclear options**)

major command: Major unit of organization (command) of a military department established, designated, and directly subordinate to its service headquarters. Army and Air Force component commands of **unified commands** and **specified commands** are also major commands. The two types of major naval commands are (1) **operating forces** (combat and combat support forces directed by the **Department of the Navy** and assigned to unified or specified commands); and (2) **shore establishments** (administrative and logistical support activities directed by the Navy). (see also Air Force **separate operating agencies,** Air Force **direct reporting units,** Army **field operating agencies**)

Air Force Major Commands

- **Air Force Communications Command (AFCC)**
- **Air Force Logistics Command (AFLC)**
- **Air Force Space Command (AF-SPACECOM)**
- **Air Force Systems Command (AFSC)**
- **Air Training Command (ATC)**
- **Alaskan Air Command (AAC)**
- **Electronic Security Command (ESC)**
- **Military Airlift Command (MAC)**
- **Pacific Air Forces (PACAF)**
- **Strategic Air Command (SAC)**
- **Tactical Air Command (TAC)**
- **U.S. Air Forces Europe (USAFE)**
- **Air University (AU)**

Army Major Commands

- **Army Corps of Engineers (USACE)**
- **Army Criminal Investigation Command (CIDC)**
- **Army Health Services Command (HSC)**
- **Army Information Systems Command (ISC)**
- **Army Intelligence and Security Command (INSCOM)**
- **Army Materiel Command (AMC)**
- **Eighth U.S. Army (EUSA)**
- **First Special Operations Command (1st SOCOM)**
- **Forces Command (FORSCOM)**
- **Military District of Washington (MDW)**
- **Military Traffic Management Command (MTMC)**
- **Training and Doctrine Command (TRADOC)**
- **U.S. Army Europe (USAREUR)**

- U.S. Army Forces, Atlantic Command (USARLANT)
- U.S. Army Forces, Central Command (USARCENT)
- U.S. Army Pacific (USARPAC)
- U.S. Army South (USARSO)
- U.S. Army Space Command (USASPACECOM)
- U.S. Army Strategic Defense Command (USASDC)

Major Marine Corps Commands

- Fleet Marine Force, Atlantic (FMFLANT)
- Fleet Marine Force, Pacific (FMFPAC)
- Marine Corps Air-Ground Combat Center (MCAGCC)
- Marine Corps Combat Development Command (MCCDC)
- Marine Corps Research, Development and Acquisition Command (MCRDAC)

Major Naval Organizations

Operating Forces

- Atlantic Fleet (LANTFLT)
- Military Sealift Command (MSC)
- Mine Warfare Command
- Naval Reserve Force
- Naval Special Warfare Command
- Operational Test and Evaluation Force (OPTEVFOR)
- Pacific Fleet (PACFLT)
- U.S. Naval Forces Central Command (NAVCENT)
- U.S. Naval Forces Europe (NAVEUR)
- U.S. Naval Forces Southern Command (NAVSO)

Shore Establishment

- Chief of Naval Education and Training (CNET) Command
- Naval Air Systems Command (NAVAIR)
- Naval Data Automation Command
- Naval District of Washington
- Naval Facilities Engineering Command (NAVFAC)
- Naval Intelligence Command (NIC)
- Naval Investigative Service Command (NISC)
- Naval Legal Service Command
- Naval Medical Command
- Naval Military Personnel Command
- Naval Oceanography Command (NAVOCEANCOM)
- Naval Sea Systems Command (NAVSEA)
- Naval Security Group Command (NSGC)
- Naval Space Command (NAVSPACECOM)
- Naval Supply Systems Command (NAVSUP)
- Naval Telecommunications Command (NAVTEL)
- Space and Naval Warfare Systems Command

Major Coast Guard Commands

- Atlantic Area
- Coast Guard Headquarters
- Pacific Area

major component (MC): An assembly of components, piece parts, hardware, material, and the like designed to perform a specific operational function for which a developing agency specifies the design and performance requirements and delineates manufacturing processes. The MC is normally designated with a four-digit number (e.g., MC-1561). Examples of MCs include **aircraft monitor and control (AMAC)** systems, **limited life components**, and **permissive action links**.

major disaster: Any hurricane, tornado, storm, flood, highwater, wind-driven water, tidal wave, earthquake, volcanic eruption, landslide, mudslide, snowstorm, drought, fire, explosion, or other catastrophe in any part of the United States, which in the determination of the President, causes damage of sufficient severity and magnitude to warrant major disaster assistance under 42 U.S.C. 5121.

- a. The terms as used herein do not include emergencies resulting from
(1) An enemy attack;
(2) Accident involving vehicles, aircrafts, missiles, spacecrafts, or weapons of the military services, or any department or agency of the federal government.
(3) Accidents involving hazardous materials which are the property of or in the custody of any contractor to any department or agency of the federal government.
(4) **Civil disturbances**.
(5) Work stoppages.
(6) An outbreak of an epidemic disease or pestilence.
- b. Additionally, these terms are not applicable to the following emergencies, unless the President or the **Federal Emergency Management Agency** determine otherwise:
(1) Oil and industrial chemical spills.

(2) Disorders.
(3) **Explosive ordnance disposal** incidents.
[Air Force, Disaster Preparedness: Planning and Operations, AFR 355-1, 17 November 1986, p. 86, released under the FOIA]. (see also **civil emergency**)

Major Force Program: The structure of data in the DOD **Five Year Defense Program (FYDP)** used for internal program review. There are eleven major force programs—six combat force and five support:

1. **Strategic Forces.**
2. **General Purpose Forces.**
3. **Intelligence and Communications.**
4. **Airlift and Sealift Forces.**
5. **Guard and Reserve Components.**
6. **Research and Development.**
7. **Central Supply and Maintenance.**
8. **Training, Medical, and other Personnel Activities.**
9. **Administration and Associated Activities.**
10. **Support of other Nations.**
11. **Special Operations Forces.**

Each MFP consists of a number of **program elements (PEs)**.

major installation: An installation at which fulltime flying or missile operations are conducted by a permanently assigned squadron, its equivalent, or higher active or reserve Air Force units. A major installation is also one at which flying or missile operations are not conducted but which does have assigned to it a wing headquarters, its equivalent, or a higher-level Air Force organization. (see also **Air Force base, Air Base**)

major NATO command (MNC): One of three major military commands of the **North Atlantic Treaty Organization** alliance. All MNCs are established, designated, and directly subordinate to a regional allied command under a **Supreme Allied Commander** or NATO Commander-in-Chief. In turn, each MNC is composed of several **major subordinate commands (MSCs)**. The MNCs report to the NATO **Military Committee** and to the **North Atlantic Council/Defense Planning Committee**.

Major NATO commands

- **Allied Command, Atlantic (ACLANT)**
- Allied Command, Europe (ACE)
- Allied Command Channel (ACCHAN)

major subordinate command (MSC): A military organization (command) of the **North Atlantic Treaty Organization** subordinate to a **major NATO command (MNC)**. Each is operationally responsible to its MNC for an allocated geographical area or function.

Major subordinate commands

- **ACE Mobile Force**
- **Allied Forces Northern Europe**
- **Allied Forces Central Europe**
- **Allied Forces Southern Europe**
- **Allied Maritime Air Force Channel Command**
- **Benelux Channel Command**
- **Eastern Atlantic Command**
- **Iberian Atlantic Command**

- **NATO AWAC Force Command**
- **Nore Channel Command**
- **Plymouth Channel Command**
- **Striking Fleet Atlantic Command**
- **Standing Naval Force Atlantic**
- **Standing Naval Force Channel**
- **Submarines Allied Command Atlantic**
- **United Kingdom Air Command Region**
- **United States European Command**
- **Western Atlantic Command**

major system acquisition: An **acquisition** of a weapon system or other military system where research, development, test, and evaluation costs exceed $250 million (FY 1987$) or production costs exceed $1.5 billion (FY 1987$).

maneuverable reentry vehicle (MaRV): A **reentry vehicle** with terminal guidance and capable of performing flight maneuvers during the reentry phase. The only U.S.-deployed MaRV is on the **Pershing II** missile.

maneuver battalion: A type of Army combat **battalion** that includes infantry, light infantry, air assault, airborne, motorized, mechanized, tank (armor), armored cavalry, and attack helicopter battalions.

maneuver brigade: An Army unit subordinate to the **division** that is either a ground maneuver brigade or a **combat aviation brigade**. The ground maneuver brigade is a tactical headquarters capable of controlling from two to five maneuver battalions for extended operations. The composition remains relatively fixed in peacetime, but can be tailored in wartime for specific missions. The combat aviation brigade, a new type of unit, incorporates the aviation assets of the division formerly assigned to the division base.

manpower: Military and civilian personnel in active or reserve status. The DOD manpower program is developed based on the forces required to carry out approved plans and strategies. The programmed manpower structure is "the aggregation of **billets** describing the full manning requirement for all units and organizations in the programmed force structure" not including **individuals** or **individual mobilization augmentees**. The term "programmed manning" is synonymous with

- Army: force structure allowance;
- Navy: distributable billets;
- Air force: structure authorization, funded peacetime authorizations, and;
- Marine Corps: authorized strength report.

[DOD, *Manpower Requirements Report FY 1989*, March 1988, pp. B-3, II-1]. (see also **active component**, **reserves**, **Total Force**, **force structure**)

Marine aircraft group (MAG): Air combat unit of the **Marine Corps**, smaller than a **Marine aircraft wing**. It usually operates as the aviation element of a **Marine expeditionary brigade**. Established as units of a task organization, type MAGs vary in size and composition depending on their assigned mission. There are five types of MAGs: Marine Wing Support Group; Marine Air Control Group; Marine Aircraft Group, Fighter Attack; Marine Aircraft Group, Helicopter; and Marine Training Group.

Marine aircraft wing (MAW): The basic air combat organization of the **Marine Corps**, generally comparable to a numbered air force. A MAW operates as a component of a **Marine expeditionary force**, providing aviation support to a **Marine division** and other combat support forces. MAWs serve as organic elements of the **fleet marine forces (FMFs)** (Atlantic and Pacific). They are organization units, and vary in size and composition depending on their assigned mission. They are not functionally organized according to types of aircraft but include a variety of fighter, attack, reconnaissance, transport, and helicopter aircraft, as well as light anti-aircraft missile units. A typical MAW consists of a wing headquarters group, eight various **Marine aircraft groups**, a tactical electronic warfare squadron, a tactical reconnaissance squadron, and an aerial refueling transport squadron.

The basic aviation unit within a wing is a **squadron**. Two or more tactical squadrons plus a headquarters and maintenance squadron and an airbase squadron are normally included in a Marine aircraft group. Two or more groups make a wing. Depending on the type of aircraft assigned, a squadron will have from 12–24 aircraft. FMF aviation units, whose aircraft permit carrier operations, are trained to serve aboard aircraft carriers.

A MAW operates a variety of aircraft—approximately 250 tactical fixed-wing aircraft and 190 helicopters—and is composed of 14,000 Marine and Navy personnel. The Marine Corps has four organized MAWs:

- 1st MAW (FMFPAC), Okinawa, Japan
- 2d MAW (FMFLANT), MCAS Cherry Point, NC 28533
- 3d MAW (FMFPAC), MCAS El Toro, CA 92709
- 4th MAW (Reserve), New Orleans, LA 70142.

Marine Air-Ground Task Force (MAGTF): Integrated combat organization of the **Marine Corps**, which serves as an element of a **fleet marine force** for specific amphibious assault missions. The three types of MAGTFs, varying in size, are: **Marine expeditionary forces (MEFs), Marine expeditionary brigades (MEBs)**, and **Marine expeditionary units (MEUs)**. Each MAGTF typically consists of a Command Element (CE), a Ground Combat Element (GCE), an Aviation Combat Element (ACE), and a Combat Service Support Element (CSSE). Other temporary organizations may also be added to perform specific functions, such as landing support, engineering, reconnaissance, artillery, and electronic warfare. As a task organization, MAGTF composition varies according to assigned mission.

Marine amphibious brigade (MAB): Former name of **Marine expeditionary brigade**.

Marine amphibious force (MAF): Former name of **Marine expeditionary force**.

Marine amphibious unit (MAU): Former name of **Marine expeditionary unit**.

Marine Barracks: 1. A Marine Corps guard unit that protects a naval base and, specifically, nuclear weapons, nuclear materials or nuclear power reactors. **2.** The ceremonial and special security unit assigned to Washington, DC, and located at the Marine Barracks, 8th and I Streets, SE.

Marine Corps (U.S. Marine Corps): A separate military service functioning within the **Department of the Navy**, established 10 November 1775 by the Continental Congress, and designated a separate service within the Navy Department on 11 July 1798. The statutory basis for its functions and compositions is found at 10 U.S. Code §5041 and within 10 U.S. Code Subtitle C. The primary role of the Marine Corps is to support and maintain the operational **fleet marine forces (FMFs)** (Atlantic and Pacific) with naval, air, ground and support forces. Additionally, it provides security aboard aircraft carriers and battleships, at selected naval shore activities, and at U.S. embassies and diplomatic missions. Its basic combat organization is the **Marine expeditionary force (MEF)**, comprising divisions, wings, and service support groups.

The highest ranking Marine Corps officer is the **Commandant of the Marine Corps**, who is also a member of the **Joint Chiefs of Staff (JCS)**. As the Commandant's role is administrative, he does not exercise operational control of combat forces, except when assigned by the Secretary of Defense or the JCS to to so. Operational control of the Marine Corps is exercised through the FMFs by the Atlantic and Pacific commanders-in-chief or other unified commanders. Headquarters, Marine Corps, is a component of the Department of the Navy (Secretariat). Marine Corps personnel are assigned to Navy staffs, including those within the offices of the **Secretary of the Navy** and the **Chief of Naval Operations**. The Marine Deputy Chief of Staff/Naval Aviation is also the Assistant Deputy Chief of Naval Operations (Air Warfare). Combat forces include four Marine divisions and four Marine aircraft wings. The total Marine force strength is about 197,000 active-duty military personnel and 89,000 **Marine Corps Reserve** personnel.

Headquarters, USMC

- Commandant of the Marine Corps
- Deputy Chief of Staff (Manpower)
- Deputy Chief of Staff (Installation and Logistics)
- Deputy Chief of Staff (Plans, Policy, and Operations)
- Deputy Chief of Staff (Aviation)
- Deputy Chief of Staff (Reserve Affairs)
- Assistant Chief of Staff (Requisition and Programs)
- Assistant Chief of Staff (Training)
- Assistant Chief of Staff (to be determined)

Commandants of the Marine Corps

Gen Lemuel C. Shepard
    1 Jan 1952–31 Dec 1955
Gen Randolph McC. Pate
    1 Jan 1956–31 Dec 1959
Gen David M. Shoup
    1 Jan 1960–31 Dec 1963

Gen Wallace M. Greene, Jr.
    1 Jan 1964–31 Dec 1967
Gen Leonard F. Chapman, Jr.
    1 Jan 1968–31 Dec 1971
Gen Robert E. Cushman, Jr.
    1 Jan 1972–30 Jun 1975
Gen Louis H. Wilson
    1 Jul 1975–1 Jul 1979
Gen Robert H. Barrow
    1 Jul 1979–30 Jun 1983
Gen Paul X. Kelley
    1 Jul 1983–1 Jul 1987
Gen Alfred M. Gray, Jr.
    1 Jul 1987–present

Marine Corps Air Facility (MCAF)/ Marine Corps Air Station(MCAS): Operating, testing, overhaul, and personnel facility for Marine aviation units.

Marine Corps Air-Ground Combat Center: Major command of the U.S. Marine Corps with its headquarters at Twentynine Palms, CA.

Marine Corps Combat Development Command (MCCDC): Major command of the U.S. **Marine Corps** established from the **Marine Corps Development and Education Command (MCDEC)** in 1987. Its missions are to develop Marine Corps concepts, plans, and doctrine; to identify and assess changes in doctrine, training, MAGTF force structure, and materiel; to serve as proponent for warfare mission areas; to develop and implement policy and programs for the training and education of all regular and Reserve Marines, units, and schools; to develop (in coordination with other services, unified and specified commands, and allied commands) joint doctrine, tactics, and warfighting techniques; and to provide for Marine corps wargaming.

Headquarters
Quantico, VA 22134

Centers

- MAGTF Warfighting Center
- Training and Education Center
- Intelligence Center
- Wargaming and Assessment Center
- Information Technology Center

Marine Corps Research Development and Acquisition Command (MCRDAC): Major command of the U.S. **Marine Corps,** established November 1987 from the former Development Center of the Marine Corps Development and Education Command (MCDEC). It is responsible for acquisition of tactical equipment to meet requirements of the Marine Corps. It consists of two deputies (Support and Programs); 14 program managers; and a variety of offices.

Headquarters
Quantico, VA 22134

Marine Corps Reserve: The federal reserve component of the **Marine Corps**. It consists of a division/wing team with combat, combat support, and combat service support forces. The reserves consist of one marine division, one marine wing, and one service support group. All Marine Corps reserve units report to the **Commandant of the Marine Corps**. The Marine Corps Reserve receives about two percent of the total reserve appropriations. It constitutes about 15 percent of the Marine Corps personnel strength. The total personnel strength

of the component is about 96,000 for FY 1987, including 42,000 in the **Selected Reserve**, 44,000 in the **Individual Ready Reserves**, 1,400 in the **Standby Reserve**, and 8,000 in the **Retired Reserve**.

Marine Detachment afloat: A **Marine Corps** detachment assigned for duty on board an armed vessel of the Navy as a distinct and integral part of the complement of the ship to provide a unit organized and trained for operations ashore, either as part of a landing force from vessels of the fleet or as an independent force for limited operations; to provide gun crews as required; and to provide internal security for the ship, particularly for the ship's nuclear weapons.

Marine division: The basic ground combat organization of the **Marine Corps**. A division operates as a component of a **Marine expeditionary force (MEF)** to conduct amphibious assault operations or operations ashore under condition of limited or general war. Marine divisions serve as organic elements of the **fleet marine forces** (Atlantic and Pacific). A typical division of approximately 16,000 Marines consists of a headquarters battalion, three **Marine infantry regiments** (each consisting of three infantry battalions), an artillery regiment, one tank battalion, one reconnaissance battalion, one combat engineer battalion, and one assault amphibian battalion. It is employed—in conjunction with a **Marine aircraft wing**, a **force service support group**, and other combat support forces—as an integral part of a MEF. There are currently four Marine divisions:

- 1st Marine Division (FMFPAC), Camp Pendleton, CA 92055
- 2d Marine Division (FMFLANT), Camp Lejeune, NC 28542
- 3d Marine Division (FMFPAC), Okinawa, Japan
- 4th Marine Division (Reserve), New Orleans, LA 70142

Marine division/wing team: A **Marine Corps** air-ground unit consisting of one **Marine division** and one **Marine aircraft wing**.

Marine expeditionary brigade (M-EB):   Middle-sized **Marine air-ground task force (MAGTF)** consisting of approximately 16,000 Marine and Navy personnel. It is composed of a **regimental landing team**, a **Marine aircraft group**, and a Brigade Service Support Group. A MEB may deploy to **marine prepositioning force** ships. It is commanded by a Brigadier General.

MEB Notional Task Organization

- Ground Combat Equipment: 17 tanks, 47 amphibious assault vehicles, 36 light armored vehicles, 24 155 mm towed howitzers, and 6 155 mm self-propelled howitzers.
- Aircraft: 40 AV-8B or 19 A-4M, 24 F/A-18 or F-4, 10 A-6, 4 EA-6, 4 RF-4, KC-130, 5 OA-4M, 5 OV-10, 8 CH-53E, 20 CH-53D, 48 CH-46, 12 UH-1, and 12 AH-1.

There are five organized Marine Expeditionary Brigades in the Marine Corps:

- 1st MEB (FMFPAC), Camp H.M. Smith, HI 96602

- 4th MEB (FMFLANT), Camp Lejeune, NC 28542
- 5th MEB (FMFPAC), Camp Pendleton, CA 92055
- 6th MEB (FMFLANT), Camp Lejeune, NC 28542
- 7th MEB (FMFPAC), Twentynine Palms, CA 92278

Marine expeditionary force (MEF): Largest **Marine air-ground task force (MAGTF)**, consisting of approximately 52,000 Marine and Navy personnel and 50 ships. It is composed of a **Marine division**, a **Marine aircraft wing**, and a **force service support group**, and supporting units. MEFs are established to "command, control, direct, plan, and coordinate air-ground operations of assigned forces." It is commanded by a Lieutenant General.

MEF Notional Task Organization

- Major Ground Combat Equipment: 70 tanks, 208 amphibious assault vehicles, 147 light armored vehicles, 90 towed 155 mm howitzers, and 12 8-inch self-propelled howitzers.
- Aircraft: 100 AV-8B or 38 A-4M, 48 F/A-18 or F-4, 20 A-6, 8 EA-6, 8 RF-4, 9 TA-4/OA-4, 12 KC-130, 12 OV-10, 16 CH-53E, 32 CH-53D, 60 CH-46, 24 UH-1, and 24 AH-1.

The Marine Corps currently has three active MAFs:

- *I Marine Expeditionary Force (I MEF):*   A subordinate command of the **Fleet Marine Force Pacific (FMFPAC)**, and a **major command** of the U.S. Marine Corps. Its mission is to plan contingencies and amphibious and air-ground exercises in the eastern Pacific. In wartime, when directed, its commanding general assumes operational control of forces assigned by FMFPAC and reports for operational control to the **Third Fleet** or other unified, subunified, or joint task force commands. Administrative command of I MEF always rests with FMFPAC. Its major fighting units are air/ground teams consisting of tanks, medium and heavy artillery, engineer elements, and service units. Its forces are drawn from the 1st Marine division, 3d Marine aircraft wing, the 1st Force Service Support Group (Camp Pendleton, CA), the 5th and 7th Marine Expeditionary Brigades, and the Marine Corps (Helicopter) Air Station (Tustin, CA). It also operates Marine air-ground task force Training facilities at Twenty-nine Palms, CA.

Headquarters
Camp Pendleton, CA 92055

- *II Marine Expeditionary Force (II MEF):* A subordinate command of the **Fleet Marine Force Atlantic (FMFLANT)**, and a **major command** of the U.S. Marine Corps. Its mission is to plan contingencies and amphibious and air-ground exercises in support of the **Second Fleet**, **Sixth Fleet**, or other unified, subunified, or joint task force commands. In wartime, when directed, it assumes operational control of forces assigned by FMFLANT. Administrative control of II MEF always rests with FMFLANT. Its forces are drawn from the 2d Marine Division, the 2d Marine Aircraft Wing, 2d Force Service Support Group (Camp Lejeune, NC), and the 4th and 6th Marine Expeditionary Brigades.

Headquarters
Camp Lejeune, NC 28542

- *III Marine Expeditionary Force (III MEF):* A subordinate command of the **Fleet Marine Force Pacific (FMFPAC)**, and a **major command** of the U.S. Marine Corps. Its mission is to plan contingencies and amphibious and air-ground exercises in the western Pacific. In wartime, when directed, its commanding general assumes operational control of forces assigned by FMFPAC, and reports for operational control to the **Seventh Fleet** or other unified, subunified, or joint task force commands. Administrative command of III MEF always rests with FMFPAC. Its major fighting units are seaborne Marine air-ground task forces, usually consisting of a reinforced Marine battalion, aviation elements, and readily deployed reinforcement units. Its landing forces are drawn from the 3d Marine division, the 1st Marine air wing, and the 3d Force Service Support Group (MCAS Iwakuni, Japan). Its crisis reinforcement force is the 1st Marine Expeditionary Brigade, consisting of the 3d Marine Regiment, an aircraft group of 20 squadrons, support artillery, combat service units and Marine Aircraft Group 24.

Headquarters
Camp Butler, Okinawa, Japan

Marine expeditionary unit (MEU): Smallest **Marine air-ground task force (MAGTF)**, approximately the size of a battalion, composed of 2,000 Marine and Navy personnel. MEUs are forward-deployed and consist of a

Battalion Landing Team, a composite aviation squadron (with two or more types of helicopters and support units, as well as in some cases, vertical/short take-off and landing aircraft), and a MEU Service Support Group. It is commanded by a Colonel.

Marine expeditionary unit (Special Operations Capable) (MEU(SOC)): A **Marine expeditionary unit** organized for maritime **special operations** and **unconventional warfare** tasks. Eight battalions are assigned to the MEU(SOC) rotation base to form MEU(SOC)s in peacetime. The 26th MEU became the first SOC unit in December 1985 and is deployed with the Sixth Fleet in the Mediterranean. The 22d and 24th are the second and third units to receive SOC training.

Marine infantry regiment: Basic tactical element of a **Marine division**. It is normally combined with aviation and combat service support units to form the basis of a specially-tasked **Marine air-ground task force**. The Marine infantry regiment is composed of a headquarters company and three infantry battalions. The battalions are the basic tactical units with which the regiment accomplishes its mission. Each battalion consists of a headquarters and service company, three rifle companies, and a weapon company. The primary mission of the infantry regiment is to locate, close with, and destroy the enemy by fire and maneuver or to repel an assault by fire and close combat. The regiment is the major element of close combat power of the Marine division and, with its

three organic battalions, is a permanent organization with a staff capable of integrating the efforts of organic, attached, and supporting units.

Marine regiment: The major close-combat element of a **Marine division**. Types of regiments include the **Marine infantry regiment**, and the Marine artillery regiment, which is typically composed of a headquarters battery, three direct support battalions, and one or two support battalions.

MARISAT (maritime satellite): Three commercial **communications satellites** whose UHF portions were leased in 1976 by the Navy from the Communications Satellite Corporation (COMSAT) under the program name Gapfiller. MARISAT transmits messages from shore to the Navy fleet, and by the end of the 1970s about 99 percent of the fleet was able to pick up the MARISAT broadcasts. The Navy then gave permission to the unified and specified command aircraft to access MARISAT but since the satellites were positioned for maximum coverage of ocean areas, only the **National Emergency Airborne Command Post (NEACP)** and CINCLANT's **airborne command post (Scope Light)** could receive communications via MARISAT. The operational **Fleet Satellite Command** system was the follow-on to MARISAT. The first MARISAT launch took place on 19 February 1976.

Maritime Defense Zones (MARDEZ or MDZ): U.S. Atlantic and Pacific coastal areas designated for peace and wartime defense against hostile activities and forces. The MDZ concept was established in March 1984 by a memorandum of understanding between the Secretaries of Navy and Transportation (for the Coast Guard). The MDZ program is planned, exercised, and operated (when directed) by the **Coast Guard**, although its Atlantic and Pacific commands are components of the Atlantic and Pacific Fleets. Two MDZ contingency commands (Atlantic and Pacific) were established to provide defense of coasts, harbors, and nearby sea lines of communication. Activities include **port security**; mine countermeasures (see **mine warfare**); **inshore undersea warfare**; limited **anti-submarine warfare**; harbor clearance; **intelligence**, **reconnaissance**, and surveillance; **anti-terrorism** and countersabotage; **interdiction**; and shipping control. The Commander of the Pacific Area Coast Guard acts as Commander, U.S. Maritime Defense Zone Pacific (CTF 16). The commander of the Atlantic Area Coast Guard acts as Commander, U.S. Maritime Defense Zone Atlantic (CTF 89).

maritime prepositioning force (M-PF): Equipment and supplies prepositioned at overseas locations in special ships and available for rapid movement to nearby ports or available for offloading at the homeport. Under the MPF concept, approximately 16,500 Marines would be airlifted from their home bases directly to the area where they would "marry up with" maritime prepositioning ships. There are three MPF squadrons administratively assigned to the

Military Sealift Command, each consisting of four to five specially configured, Navy-commanded, civilian-crewed merchant vessels with combat equipment and supplies for a combined arms Marine brigade. The brigade's tactical aircraft, except for those aboard MPF ships, flight-ferry to nearby airfields. The timetable calls for the brigade to be combat-capable and ready to move on designated objectives within five days—less in some cases—after the MPF squadron arrives in the expeditionary area. There are sufficient supplies for the brigade to fight for up to 30 days without resupply. A total of 13 maritime prepositioning ships—5 Maersk class, 3 Waterman class, and 5 Braintree class—are divided among the three squadrons. They displace from 44,000 to 52,000 tons and have speeds from 16 to 20 knots. The ships are capable of offloading at piers or from offshore with special equipment with which they have been fitted. However, the ships themselves have no amphibious capability.

The first squadron, completed and loaded in 1984, operates in eastern and northern Atlantic waters. The second, which was completed and loaded in 1985, replaced five prepositioned ships homeported in Diego Garcia. The third, completed and loaded in 1986, is homeported in Guam/Tinian and operates in the Western Pacific.

Maritime Strategy: Navy strategy codified in 1982 representing a consensus of professional naval judgement on how best to implement the maritime aspects of U.S. national security as stated in **NSDD 32**, "**U.S.**

National Security Strategy." The Maritime Strategy is a warfighting **doctrine** and assumes that the U.S. Navy is superior and that it should "attack and destroy, rather than stay on the defense" [United States Naval Institute Professional Seminar Series, *The Maritime Strategy*, Naval Air Station Jacksonville, FL, 29 May 1986, p. 6].

The are six underlying concepts of the Maritime Strategy: war will be conventional; it will be a global conflict; it will be a "conditional" (limited) war; war will be protracted; there will be allied involvement; and war will end with only one superpower. The Maritime Strategy seeks to provide the President with a nonnuclear naval option for putting at risk Soviet nuclear forces. A central premise of the strategy is to deny the Soviets an option to fight in a single theater, and it designates the Pacific equal in importance to other theaters.

The Maritime Strategy originated in the late 1970s. Admiral Thomas B. Hayward, Chief of Naval Operations, began arguing that the Navy should be used offensively against the Soviet Union. At the same time the U.S. Navy began hedging about its superiority over the Soviet Navy. In 1981 testimony before Congress, Admiral Hayward, for instance, refused to claim any margin of superiority for the U.S. Navy: "it would be misleading to continue speaking of a 'narrow margin' when, in fact, we have entered a period in which any reasonable estimate of the balance falls within the range of uncertainty. In other words, the situation today is so murky one cannot, with confidence, state that the U.S. possesses a margin

of superiority" [U.S. Congress, *House Appropriations Committee, FY 1982 DOD Appropriation, Part 1*, p. 540].

There are three phases of the Maritime Strategy:

- *Phase I, "Transition to War" or "Deterrence or transition to war"*: This phase would be triggered "by recognition that a specific international situation has the potential to grow to a global superpower confrontation" [Adm James D. Watkins, "The Maritime Strategy," *Proceedings*, January 1986 (Special Supplement), p. 9]. With speed and decisiveness being essential, naval forces would move to maximize warning time of attack, would decrease their tactical vulnerability and avoid maldeployments, and Naval and Marine forces would position forward. Attack submarines and carrier battlegroups would move forward toward the Soviet Union, and a battleship surface action group would be moved into the South China Sea. According to Admiral James D. Watkins, former Chief of Naval Operations, "as the battlegroups move forward, we will wage an aggressive campaign against all Soviet submarines, including ballistic missile submarines" [Watkins, p. 11]. Strategic sealift to overseas theaters would begin during phase I and the reserves would be activated and control of the Coast Guard would be transferred to the Navy.
- *Phase II, "Seizing the initiative"*: During this phase, sea control would be established in key maritime areas as far forward and as rapidly as possible. **Anti-**

submarine, anti-air, anti-surface, mine warfare, command and control countermeasures, strike operations, amphibious operations, and **special operations** would be conducted. One objective would be to seize key terrain and "fight our way toward Soviet home waters" in the Norwegian Sea, eastern Mediterranean, and Pacific approaches to the Soviet Union [Watkins, p. 11]. One of the objectives of phase II is to divert Soviet attention from central Europe. It "is possible that, faced with our determination, the Soviets can be induced to accept war termination while still in this phase" [Watkins, p. 11].

- *Phase III, "Carrying the Fight to the Enemy":* During the final phase, strike operations and amphibious warfare would be accelerated, including direct attacks on the Soviet homeland in order to threaten the bases and support structure of the Soviet navy, and threaten Soviet strategic reserve forces. According to Admiral Watkins, carrying the fight to the enemy means "winning the battle and bringing the war to termination on terms favorable to the United States" [U.S. Congress, *House Armed Services Committee, The 600-Ship Navy and the Maritime Strategy*, Hearings, June 24, September 5, 6, and 10, 1985, p. 32]. "Anti-submarine warfare forces would continue to destroy Soviet submarines, including ballistic missile submarines, thus reducing the attractiveness of nuclear escalation by changing the nuclear balance in our favor" [Watkins, p. 13].

Since the Maritime Strategy was publicly unveiled in 1986, it has received much attention, and some aspects of it, including plans to attack ballistic missile submarines and make strikes against the Soviet homeland, have been criticized for being too provocative or having unclear war termination objectives. Modifications to the strategy since 1986 have included more emphasis on forward submarine operations and less on aircraft carriers.

martial law: "The exercise of partial or complete military control over domestic territory in time of emergency because of public necessity. In the U.S., it is usually authorized by the President, but may be imposed by a military commander in the interests of public safety" [*Army Dictionary*, p. 163].

"Conditions may arise necessitating the imposition of martial law over specific areas. An essential objective of martial law is to create conditions wherein civil government can be rapidly reconstituted. The justification for martial law is public necessity. Such necessity gives rise to the imposition justification, and limited duration of martial law. The extent of the military force used and the legal propriety of the measures taken, consequently, will depend upon the actual threat to order and public safety that exists at the time. In most instances, the decision to impose martial law is made by the President. Normally, the President announces the decision by a proclamation usually containing instructions concerning the exercise of martial law and any limitations thereon. However, the decision to impose martial law may be made by the local commander if circumstances demand immediate action and time and if available communications facilities do not permit obtaining prior approval from higher authority. . . . In every case, control will be returned to civil authorities upon receipt of notification from a recognized civilian authority, at an authorized level, that civil authorities, are prepared to exercise control" [JCS, *Basic Planning Directive for Land Defense of the Continental United States and Military Support of Civil Defense*, 15 February 1983, pp. 20–21, released under the FOIA]. (see also **civil emergency**, **Continuity of Government**)

MaRV   (see **maneuverable reentry vehicle**)

MASER (Microwave Amplification by Stimulated Emission of Radiation):   Beams of very short **electromagnetic radiation** waves that can be focused to provide energy that has potential applications for military weapons.

MASINT   (see **measurement and signature intelligence**)

massive retaliation: U.S. nuclear strategy dating from the early 1950s for countering aggression of any type, particularly in Europe, with a nuclear response to any armed provocation deemed serious enough to warrant military action. The massive retaliation policy was proclaimed by Secretary of State John Foster Dulles, and it led to the creation of the "tripwire" strategy. Prior to the adoption

of **flexible response** by **NATO** in 1967, the basic strategy in Europe was one of massive retaliation. For strategic nuclear forces, massive retaliation existed as the main option for retaliation against any nuclear attack on the United States. With creation of the **Single Integrated Operational Plan (SIOP)**, a number of additional, more limited, options were added to U.S. nuclear strategy. Massive retaliation was replaced by flexible response at the strategic level as well. The most destructive option in current SIOPs is often referred to as the massive retaliation option. (see also **NSDM 242, "Planning Nuclear Weapons Employment for Deterrence"**)

material breach: As defined by the Vienna Convention, a material breach is "the violation of a provision essential to the accomplishment of the object or purpose of the treaty. A material breach of a bilateral treaty by one of the parties entitles the other to invoke the breach as a ground for terminating or suspending its operation in whole or in part." A treaty party has the right to invoke a material breach as grounds for terminating a treaty, but this does not automatically nullify the treaty. Legal steps would have to be taken to relieve all signatories of treaty obligations.

Maverick (AGM-65):   An Air Force, Marine Corps, and Navy supersonic, conventionally armed air-to-ground missile. It has a range of 12 nm and can be fired from **A-4M**, **A-6**, **A-7**, **AV-8B**, **F-4E**, **F-4G**, **F-16**, and **F/A-18** aircraft. There are several versions of the Maverick including television (TV) guided, imaging-infrared

(IIR) guided, and laser-guided types. The basic Air Force AGM-65A Maverick has TV guidance. Production of the missile was initiated in 1971. The Air Force AGM-65B has scene magnification and better optics. The AGM-65C has laser guidance. The Air Force AGM-65D has a launch-and-leave IIR radar seeker optimized against armored fighting vehicles and fortified structures. The AGM-65E is a Marine Corps version of AGM-65F warhead and fuzing but with laser seeker optimized for close air support. The Navy AGM-65F has a IIR seeker and is optimized for attacking ships, with a larger warhead and delayed fuzing. The AGM-65G uses the IIR seeker with an alternate 298 lb blast fragmentation warhead for use against hardened targets and increased targeting capability. Software has been added to provide the option of targeting ships and large land targets as well as armor. The first successful launch took place in November 1987.

Prime contractors are Hughes Aircraft Corp., Tucson, AZ, and Raytheon Corp., Lowell, MA. The Navy's FY 1990 and FY 1991 budget request for 560 and 2,135 copies of both IIR and laser Mavericks is $67.8 and $193.3 million, respectively. The Air Force's FY 1990 and FY 1991 budget request for 2,270 and 2,020 of IIR Mavericks is $193.1 and $179.2 million, respectively.

MC-130 Combat Talon: Air Force medium size, turboprop, **special operations** and tactical transport aircraft. The aircraft has a cruise speed of 290 kt and can operate at an altitude of 35,000 ft. The range is 4,200 nm with a payload of 30,000 lb. The MC-130 is a specially modified **C-130 Hercules** and is used to infiltrate, resupply, and extract troops from hostile territory. Special features include electronic countermeasure subsystems, inflight refueling, and capability to refuel helicopters. The combat Talon is also capable of conducting **Special Operations Low Level (SOLL)** missions. Fourteen C-130Es have been modified to MC-130E Combat Talon I, and are used in low-level deep-penetration missions. The MC-130E is being supplemented by the improved, all-weather, MC-130H Combat Talon II, equipped with terrain-following radar, precision navigation, inflight refueling, and self-protection. First flight was in December 1987, with initial operations planned in early FY 1990. Combat Talon is assigned to the 1st Special Operations Squadron (SOS) at Clark AB, the Philippines; 7th SOS at Ramstein AB, West Germany; and 8th SOS at Eglin AFB, FL. FY 1990 and 1991 budget requests are $298.3 million in 1990 for the two final aircraft, and $59.3 million in FY 1991 for support and initial spares. IBM and Lockheed-Georgia are the prime contractors.

MCM: Designation for mine countermeasures ship. (see also **mine warfare ships**, **mine-sweeper**)

McMahon Act (see **Atomic Energy Act**)

M-day: The day on which mobilization commences or is to commence. (see also **military time**)

meaconing: System of receiving enemy beacon signals and rebroadcasting them on the same frequency to confuse enemy navigation. (see also **MIJI (Meaconing, Interference, Jamming and Intrusion)**)

measurement and signature intelligence (MASINT): Type of **electronics intelligence** information collected from technical sensors for the purpose of identifying any distinctive features associated with the source, emitter, or sender and to facilitate subsequent identification and/or measurement of the same. MASINT is obtained by analyses of metric, angle, spatial, wavelength, time dependence, modulation, plasma, and hydromagnetic data.

mechanized infantry battalion: One of eight types of **maneuver battalions** in the Army, and the heaviest of the **infantry** battalions. The mechanized infantry battalion has a total strength of about 880 personnel, being the largest and most versatile of the infantry battalions. All personnel are mounted in armored personnel carriers or infantry fighting vehicles. As mounted infantry, this battalion is compatible with the tank battalion for rapid ground movement for use in deep penetration, exploitation, and pursuit roles. When occasions arise where tasks unique to foot infantry must be carried out, the rifle companies may be dismounted to fight on foot or to conduct air assault operations. Much of the battalion's mobility is lost when rifle companies are dismounted. Self-propelled 81 mm mortars are organic to the rifle company. Self-propelled 107 mm mortars and TOW antitank missiles

are organic to the headquarters company to furnish close fire support. Because of the tracked vehicles, additional radios, and heavier weapons, the combat service support elements of the battalion are larger than those of other infantry battalions.

mechanized infantry division: Type of Army **division** consisting of approximately 17,100 personnel and including at least five tank and five mechanized infantry battalions. The mechanized infantry division can conduct sustained combat operations; accomplish rapid movement, deep penetration, and pursuit; operate as a mobile counterattack force; disperse over great distances and concentrate rapidly from widely separated areas; conduct limited air assault operations; and conduct covering-force operations. Its limitations are limited air assault capability; restricted vehicular mobility in dense forests, in untrafficable, steep, or rugged terrain; requirement for large quantities of fuel, supplies, logistical support, and ammunition; and the requirement for rail or highway movements of tracked vehicles in long administrative moves.

Medium Atomic Demolition Munition (MADM): A low-yield, team portable, **atomic demolition munition** used by Army and Marine Corps engineers. The device can be detonated either by remote control or a timer device. The last MADM, with its W45 warhead, was retired in 1985.

medium launch vehicle (see **naval nuclear propulsion**)

medium-range ballistic missile: A **ballistic missile** with a range capability from about 600 to 1,500 nm.

medium-range bomber: A bomber designed for a tactical operating radius of under 1,000 nm at design gross weight and design bomb load.

MEECN   (see **Minimum Essential Emergency Communications Network**)

meltdown: The overheating of a reactor core as a result of the failure of reactor cooling systems, leading to melting of the fuel and the structures that hold it in place.

Memorandum, Joint Chiefs of Staff (MJCS):   A type of memorandum originated by the **Joint Chiefs of Staff (JCS)** and used to implement JCS decisions. It is signed on behalf of the **Chairman of the Joint Chiefs of Staff** by either the Director of the **Joint Staff** or the head of the JCS directorate.

Memorandum of Policy (MOP):   A statement of policy approved by the **Joint Chiefs of Staff (JCS)** and issued as guidance for the services, unified and specified commands, and the **Joint Staff**. MOPs are published and circulated as consecutively numbered memorandums. They are also referred to as Policy Memorandums (PMs).

Merchant Marine: All nonmilitary vessels of the nation, publicly and privately owned, together with crews, that engage in domestic and/or inter-national trade and commerce. In wartime, the U.S. Merchant Marine would provide more than 75 percent of the national sealift capability.

message: The main form of rapid communications within the military. A message may be transmitted electronically, or may be sent via courier, depending on requirements for security and speed of delivery. **Precedence** categories indicate the relative order in which a message is processed in the telecommunications system and the speed with which it must be handled during internal headquarters and staff processing.

meteor burst communications: **Burst communications** systems designed to use intermittent meteor trails as the medium to transmit data. Those meteors with useful trails for propagating radio waves for beyond line of sight (BLOS) communications are near a milligram in size. The meteors collide with the Earth's atmosphere traveling at thousands of mph and the friction causes the meteors to heat up and vaporize. The vaporized atoms escape from the meteor's surface and collide with those of the atmosphere, ionizing them and leaving trails of free electrons. The trails range from 10–20 miles in length and have an altitude of between 50 and 75 miles. The trails dissipate rapidly, usually only lasting one-half of a second. The surface of the trails are then used to reflect radio waves back to the Earth's surface. To provide communications between two points, the radio wave must be reflected off the trail at an angle that would bounce the signal back down to a receiver station.

The largest meteor-burst communications system is the Department of Agriculture's SNOTEL system built by the Meteor Communications Corp., Kent, WA. It has two stations, one in Boise, ID, and one in Ogden, UT, and approximately 560 unmanned, remote stations throughout the western United States. The stations are assigned to one of eight polling groups based 15 miles away from any other remote in the same polling group. Operational since 1978, the stations compile reports on snow pack, precipitation, and temperature for water resource planning.

The Alaskan Meteor Burst Communications System (AMBCS) is composed of nodes in the Alaskan wilderness that collect aeronautical and environmental data as well as provide message communications service to remote manned camps. The Alaskan Air Command, National Weather Service, Bureau of Land Management, Soil Conservation Service, U.S. Geological Survey, and the Army Corps of Engineers all use the long-range radar sites. The radars collect and store information ready for transmission. Antennas monitor the sky for meteor trails, and when a trail is detected, the stored data is transmitted twice. Computer systems at the collection station assemble and collate the data.

By 1990, the Defense Communications Agency and the Air Force have planned to complete an emergency meteor burst communications network to span the United States. The network, under construction by the Air Force Rome Air Development Center, Rome, NY, will be used by all government agencies in the event of a nuclear war or other communications-disrupting national emergency. The network is expected to be inherently survivable in the sense that the recovery of communications disrupted by the electromagnetic pulse of a nuclear explosion is much faster for meteor burst transmissions than for conventional radio transmissions.

MH-47E: An Army four-crew, twin-rotor, medium-lift **special operations** helicopter currently under development. Its missions include rapid deployment, strategic strikes, and other operational missions supported by the **Special Forces**. The MH-47E is a modified version of the medium-lift **CH-47D Chinook** helicopter. It will have a low-level, night, adverse weather, extended-range precision navigation capability through unfamiliar mountainous terrain and an extended-range fuel system including an aerial refueling capability. The helicopter has an upgraded engine, global communications equipment, an integrated cockpit that will dramatically reduce pilot workload, and improved terrain-following/terrain-avoidance radar and **forward-looking infrared (FLIR)** sensors. The MH-47E has a mission weight of 54,000 lb, a cruise speed of 138 knots, an unrefueled endurance of 9.8 hours, and a maximum unrefueled range of 1,260 nm. It is armed with two 50-caliber machine guns and can carry up to 42 troops.

MH-47E production was scheduled to begin in FY 1989, with the first unit to be equipped in FY 1991. Fifty-one MH-47E helicopters are to be converted from CH-47s. The contractors are Boeing Helicopter Co., Philadelphia, PA; Sikorsky Aircraft Division, Stratford, CT; and IBM Federal Services Division, Owego, NY.

MH-53E Super Stallion II: Navy, three-engine airborne mine-sweeping helicopter based on the **CH-53E** heavy-lift helicopter. MH-53Es have significantly enhanced mine-sweeping capability over the presently deployed **RH-53D**. The first two were delivered in 1986. The contractors are Sikorsky Aircraft Division, Stratford, CT (airframe) and General Electric Company, West Lynn, MA (engine). The FY 1989 and FY 1990 budget request for 17 CH/MH-53E aircraft is $317.5 million, including RDT&E. (see also **minesweeper, mine warfare**).

MH-53H/J Pave Low: Air Force **special operations** helicopter based on the **CH-53E** heavy-lift helicopter. These long-range air-refuelable helicopters have an installed **forward-looking infrared (FLIR)** system, new navigation system, and a computer-projected map display. The Pave Low III enhanced MH-53J upgrade includes terrain-following and terrain-avoidance systems, greater armor, and advanced **electronics countermeasures**. Nine of the aircraft are flown at Hurlburt Field, FL; all will be upgraded to the J version by 1990.

MH-60G Pave Hawk Helicopter: Air Force combat search-and-rescue and **special operations** helicopter based on an upgraded **UH-60A Black Hawk**. All Air Force H-60s are being upgraded to the MH-60G Pave Hawk standard. Future UH-60As will be upgraded to MH-60G configuration. The helicopter allows day and night missions, including operations in marginal weather conditions, although it is not capable of operating in adverse weather. Cost in FY 1989 for six aircraft was $56.5 million.

MH-60K: An Army four-crew, single rotor, **special operations** helicopter currently under development. Its missions include rapid deployment, strategic strikes, and other operational missions supported by **Special Forces**. The MH-60K is a modified version of the **UH-60A Black Hawk** helicopter. The MH-60K is smaller than the MH-47E, but like the MH-47E, it will have low-level, night, adverse weather, and extended-range precision navigation capabilities through unfamiliar mountainous terrain. It will also have an extended-range fuel system including aerial refueling capability, upgraded engines, global communications equipment, an integrated cockpit that will dramatically reduce pilot workload, and improved terrain-following/terrain-avoidance radar and **forward looking infrared (FLIR)** sensor capabilities. The MH-60K has a mission weight of 24,500 lb, a cruise speed of 122 knots, and unrefueled endurance of 7.6 hours, and a maximum unrefueled range of 755 nm. It is armed with two 50-caliber machine guns and can carry up to 12 troops.

The first unit with MH-60Ks will be equipped in FY 1992. Twenty-three MH-60K helicopters are to be converted from UH-60s. The contractors are Boeing Helicopter Co., Philadelphia, PA; Sikorsky Aircraft Division, Stratford, CT; and IBM Federal Services Division, Owego, NY.

Microwave/Millimeter Wave Monolithic Integrated Circuit (MIMIC): DOD and tri-service program to develop cost-effective integrated circuits, complementary to the **Very High Speed Integrated Circuit (VHSIC)** program. While the VHSIC program is to develop new chip technologies, the MIMIC program was established to find ways to keep the costs of integrated circuits at an affordable level. Specifically, MIMIC is to develop pilot production lines, to create computer-aided design (CAD) and computer-aided manufacturing (CAM) techniques, to encourage the building of chip foundries, and to devise new testing and packaging processes. MIMIC chips, made from monolithic slabs of gallium arsenide, are to be used initially in the **Joint Tactical Information Distribution System (JTIDS)** and the Identification, Friend or Foe (**IFF**) system. MIMIC does, however, have a limited commercial use, while VHSIC chips can be readily used outside of military applications.

Phase 1 of the MIMIC program, from January 1987 to January 1988, funded 11 concept definition studies. Phase 1 contract winners were announced in 1988, and began three-year demonstration projects. Phase 2 (set to begin in 1992) goals include demonstrations of MIMIC chips in naval/military hardware and software systems.

MIDAS   (see **Corona**)

mid-course correction: 1. Adjustment of a ballistic or cruise missile flight path during flight. **2.** In the **Strategic Defense Initiative (SDI),** the mid-course phase indicates the point in a missile's flight where the missile has released its warheads and decoys and is no longer a single object but a mass of reentry vehicles, decoys, and debris falling freely along preset trajectories in space. The reentry vehicles travel on a ballistic course toward their targets during the mid-course, a phase that can last up to 20 minutes.

Middle East Force (MIDEAST-FOR): Operating Commander **Task Force** 109 of the **Sixth Fleet** and the principle force assigned to the **Naval Forces Central Command**. It operates in the Red Sea, Persian Gulf, and northwest Indian Ocean area. Its Surface Action Group, a five-ship forward-deployed force in the Persian Gulf, is composed of the USS Lasalle (AGF-3) command ship and four rotational destroyers or frigates. Currently, the MIDEASTFOR is assigned to the temporary **Joint Task Force Middle East**. The consolidated command reports directly to CINC-NCCENTCOM. MIDEASTFOR headquarters personnel strength is 110.

Administrative Headquarters

Bahrain
(APO New York 09501-6008)

Homeport
Norfolk, VA 23511

Midgetman   (see **Small ICBM**)

Mid-Infrared Advanced Chemical Laser   (see **MIRACL**)

MIJI (Meaconing, Interference, Jamming and Intrusion): Electronic warfare program to protect U.S. frequency bands against intrusion. The MIJI program keeps track of and analyzes MIJI events to determine the status of foreign electronic warfare capabilities and the trend of hostile activities. The Air Force Electronic Warfare Center (AFEWC) is responsible for investigating all MIJI reports submitted by the individual operators who have experienced MIJI. The other services provide trained personnel to AFEWC to accomplish this mission. The four components of MIJI are

- *Meaconing:* The transmission or retransmission of actual or simulated navigation signals to confuse navigation;
- *Intrusion:* The intentional insertion of electromagnetic energy into transmission paths to deceive operators or cause infusion;
- *Jamming:* The deliberate radiation, reradiation, or reflection of electromagnetic energy to impair the use of electronic devices, equipment, or systems; and
- *Interference:* The radiation, emission, or indication of electromagnetic energy, unintentionally causing degradation, disruption, or complete obstruction of the designed function of the electronic equipment affected. Meaconing, intrusion or jamming events caused by friendly countries or other U.S. components are reported as interference rather than as deliberate actions by unfriendly forces.

[AFR 55-3, AR 105-3, OPNAVINST 3430.18B, MCO 3430.3A, *Reporting Meaconing, Intrusion, Jamming, and Interference of Electromagnetic Systems*, 13 August 1980, released under the FOIA]

Military Affiliated Radio System (MARS): An amateur/volunteer global radio network operated by the Army, Navy, and Air Force that provides emergency military communications as an adjunct to normal channels of communications. MARS also serves as an HF backup to defense communications. The MARS program was conceived in 1948 as a way to stimulate interest in military communications by amateur radio operators and to train people who could be called on in an emergency.

There are two categories of MARS stations: (1) base or unit stations on a military installation operated by military personnel during duty hours and utilizing military equipment, and (2) affiliates in the Individual Member program—licensed radio amateurs who volunteer their services to MARS. Using their own equipment, these operators provide service on voice, continuous-wave and radioteletype circuits during the hours when base stations are not in service.

Military amateur radio operations were first organized in 1925 under the Army Amateur Radio System. Members were trained in Army radio procedures and practices and by the beginning of World War II, there were about 8,000 operators. In December 1941, the Federal Communications Commission (FCC) terminated all amateur radio operations in the United States. In 1948, the Army and the new Air Force jointly formed the Military Amateur Radio

System. In 1950, membership was expanded to include radio amateurs outside of military personnel and reservists.

In 1952, the MARS mission was expanded to encompass the transmission of American Red Cross messages. MARS would also handle Air Force message traffic when established systems were not operational and would assist in civil defense emergency communications. The word "amateur" in the title of the program was changed to "affiliate." In 1959, MARS was deemed a backup to Air Force communications circuits and responsive to domestic emergency plans of numbered air forces in CONUS.

The **Air Force Communications Command** manages the over 300 MARS stations and over 3,000 volunteer affiliates. There are ten MARS regions: six in CONUS; one in Alaska; one in Central America; one in the Pacific; and one in Europe. There are four 24-hour stations that are responsible for the ten regions: Scott AFB, IL; Andrews AFB, MD; Travis AFB, CA; and Rhein Main AB, West Germany. Although most often used to transmit birthday messages home, MARS has also served in the following instances:

- On 14 February 1979, the U.S. embassy in Tehran was attacked and normal communications were cut off. The **National Military Command Center** in the Pentagon requested the MARS station at Andrews AFB, MD, to make contact with any Iranian radio station it could reach. In less than one and a half hours, MARS had made

contact with an Iranian amateur radio station that served (for the next two and a half hours) as the link between U.S. officials and Iran. The next day, the Andrews MARS station made contact with a station in Tehran, which served as a communications channel for over a week.

- During the Vietnam war, commercial telephone facilities were limited and MARS radio stations were airlifted into troop areas to send messages home, especially during the holiday times. Message relay stations in Alaska were assisted by volunteers and passed thousands of messages per month.

- The first news to reach the Department of State of the 1985 earthquake in Mexico City was transmitted from the Robins AFB, GA MARS station.

Military Airlift Command (MAC): A **major command** of the Air Force and a component command of **U.S. Transportation Command**. MAC predecessor agencies include the Air Corps Ferrying Command (ACFC), Air Transport Command (ATC), and Military Air Transport Service (MATS) (redesignated 1 June 1948). MAC was a specified command from 1 February 1977 until the establishment of the unified U.S. Transportation Command.

MAC provides peacetime and wartime airlift and air logistics support as directed by the JCS and USAF. On 1 March 1983, MAC also assumed responsibility for Air Force special operations and consolidated its 23rd Air Force with the Aerospace Rescue and Recovery Service. Additional missions include providing airlift support to the President and government VIPs. It contracts with 30 commercial air carriers for their airlift support. MAC operates over 1,000 aircraft, 14 bases in CONUS, 2 bases overseas, and 340 locations throughout the world. It employs approximately 94,000 active-duty personnel. When fully mobilized, MAC would gain 22,000 Air National Guard and 46,000 Air Force Reserve personnel.

Headquarters Scott AFB, IL 62225

Subordinate Units

• 21st AF (airlift), McGuire AFB, NJ 08641
• 22d AF (airlift), Travis, AFB, CA 94535
• 23d AF (combat rescue, special operations, aeromedical airlift), Scott AFB, IL 62225
• 89th Military Airlift Wing (presidential, VIP airlift), Andrews AFB, MD 20331
• Air Weather Service, Scott AFB, IL 62225
• Aerospace Audiovisual Service, Norton AFB, CA 92409

[MAC Directorate of Public Affairs letter to IPS, 30 Aug 1988]

Military Airlift Command (MAC) Command, Control, and Communication (C3) network: The MAC Command Center, located at Scott AFB, IL, is the highest level in the worldwide command and control system to support airlift forces. The next level down is the MAC Air Force Operations Center (AFOC), which provides direction, mission routing authority, and monitoring of all MAC missions and aircraft within its geographical area of responsibility. MAC AFOCs are located at 21st AF, McGuire AFB, NJ, and 22d AF, Travis AFB, CA. The AFOC at McGuire is also the MAC Command Center Alternate (MACALT). There are also theater Airlift Control Centers (ALCCs) at two Airlift Divisions: the 322d at Ramstein AB, West Germany, and 834th at Hickam AFB, HI. These ALCCS provide operational control over theater-assigned airlift forces and may assume AFOC duties for assigned airlift forces operating in their area. MAC command posts supplement both ALCCs and AFOCs by providing centralized command and control for airlift support activities and aircraft and crews on MAC missions at their stations.

The MAC mobile segment consists of deployable ALCCs, Airlift Control Elements (ALCEs) and **Combat Control Teams** (CCTs). ALCCs function either as a part of the Tactical Air Control System or alone in support of the Commander of Airlift Forces in a particular theater area. Once deployed, they function as a theater ALCC. ALCEs are tailored to support airlift missions in locations without adequate C3 facilities. CCTs are extensions of ALCCs, which are deployed into forward areas to establish and operate landing, drop, and extraction zones, as well as to provide long-range communication, weather, and navigational aid support [Maj Louis J. Casamayou, *A Guide to U.S. Air Force Command Control Communications,* Air Command and Staff College Student Report, 83-0380, released under the FOIA].

MAC Commanders/CINCMACS

BG Robert Olds	(ACFC)	29 May 1941	31 Mar 1942
LTG Harold L. George	(ACFC)	1 Apr 1942	19 Jun 1942
	(ATC)	20 Jun 1942	19 Sep 1946
MG Robert M. Webster	(ATC)	20 Sep 1946	30 Jun 1947
MG Robert W. Harper	ATC)	1 Jul 1947	31 May 1948
LTG Laurence S. Kuter	(MATS)	1 Jun 1948	14 Nov 1951
LTG Joseph Smith	(MATS)	15 Nov 1951	30 Jun 1958
LTG William H. Tunner	(MATS)	1 Jul 1958	31 May 1960
Gen Joe W. Kelly	(MATS)	1 Jun 1960	18 Jul 1964
Gen Howell M. Estes, Jr.	(MATS)	19 Jul 1964	31 Dec 1965
	(MAC Commander)	1 Jan 1966	31 Jul 1969
Gen Jack J. Catton	(MAC Commander)	1 Aug 1969	11 Sep 1972
LTG George B. Simler	(MAC Commander) killed en route to assume command		
LTG Jay T. Robbins	(MAC Commander)	12 Sep 1972	25 Sep 1972
Gen Paul K. Carlton	(MAC Commander)	26 Sep 1972	1 Feb 1977
	(CINCMAC)	2 Feb 1977	31 Mar 1977
Gen William G. Moore, Jr.	(CINCMAC)	1 Apr 1977	30 Jun 1979
Gen Robert E. Huyser	(CINCMAC)	1 Jul 1979	25 Jun 1981
Gen James R. Allen	(CINCMAC)	26 Jun 1981	29 Jun 1983
Gen Thomas M. Ryan, Jr.	(CINCMAC)	30 Jun 1983	20 Sep 1985
Gen Duane H. Cassidy	(CINCMAC)	21 Sep 1985	

Military Assistance Advisory Group (MAAG): Military mission to oversee implementation of the **foreign military sales** and **security assistance programs** in its assigned area. MAAG delegations, located in some 50 foreign countries, conduct background work on pending sales negotiations prior to review by the Office of the Assistant Secretary of Defense (International Security Affairs).

Military Assistance Program (MAP): A type of **security assistance program** that assists U.S. allies in government-to-government purchases of defense articles and services. The Department of Defense describes MAP as a program that permits recipient countries to arm themselves without devoting scarce resources to defense. "The principal channel used for exporting arms is the MAP program, augmented during the Vietnam War by the Military Assistance Service-Funded program (MASF). These grant programs peaked in FY 1973 (the final year of the Nixon Administration's 'Vietnamization' effort) at $4.7 billion, then dropped precipitously" [Michael Klare, *American Arms Supermarket,* Austin, TX: University of Texas Press, 1984, p. 14].

Since FY 1982, MAP funds have been merged with recipient countries' funds and/or with Foreign Military Sales (FMS) financing credits in the FMS Trust Fund. By 1988, the major recipients of MAP funds were base rights countries and countries in Central America and East Asia, such as Honduras and Pakistan. In the FY 1990 request to Congress, the State Department requested that all FMSF be in the form of direct grants, thereby effectively removing MAP as a category of security assistance other than in the category of Peacekeeping Operations (PKO). Under the new proposal, selected recipients will be able to apply part of or all of their FMS financing to commercial purchases, previously prohibited under MAP, which was designed exclusively for purchasing material from the U.S. government. Under the new arrangement, the U.S. government subsidizes the defense industry by paying directly for countries' commercial defense purchases.

military capability: The ability to achieve a specified wartime objective (e.g., winning a battle or destroying a target). The four supporting components of military capability are

- **Force structure:** numbers, size, and composition of the units that constitute defense forces—divisions, ships, airwings.
- Modernization: technical sophistication of forces, units, weapon systems, and equipment.
- **Readiness:** ability of forces, units, weapon systems, or equipment to deliver the output for which they were designed (includes the ability to deploy and employ without unacceptable delays).
- **Sustainability:** the "staying power" of forces, units, weapon systems, and equipment, often measured in numbers of days.

Reporting on military capability is accomplished through two reports—the **Commander's Situation Report (SITREP)** and the combat-readiness status portion of the **Unit Status and Readiness Report (UNITREP)**.

Military Committee (MC): The highest-level military organization of the **NATO** alliance. It was established by the **North Atlantic Treaty** and conducted its first meeting 6 October 1949 in Washington, DC. The roles of the MC are to make recommendations regarding military matters to the **North Atlantic Council** and the **Defense Planning Committee** and to provide military guidance to NATO allied commanders. The MC is composed of the chiefs of staff of member countries taking part in NATO's integrated defense system.

This excludes France, which does not formally participate in NATO military planning and sends no representative, and Iceland, which has no military forces but sends a civilian representative. Spain participates on a limited basis even though its forces are not formally integrated into the military planning. France and Greece, though withdrawn from NATO's Integrated Defense System, are represented in the MC by nonvoting liaison missions.

The national chiefs of staff (e.g., the U.S. Chairman of the Joint Chiefs of Staff) normally meet three times a year. At other times, MC activities are handled by permanent military representatives of the chiefs of staff. The **major NATO commands** all report to the MC. The presidency of the MC rotates annually in alphabetical order of countries. The chairman is elected by the committee with a term of two to three years and represents the MC on the North Atlantic Council. The deputy chairman is specifically responsible for the coordination of nuclear-related and arms control affairs within the **International Military Staff**.

Military Communications Electronics Board (MCEB): Joint body under the **Defense Communications Agency** that establishes and coordinates joint communications and electronics operating methods and procedures in support of the unified and specified commands. It operates under the direction of the Secretary of Defense and the Joint Chiefs of Staff. Under the supervision of the MCEB, combined methods and procedures are published in the following publications:

• Allied Communications Publications (ACPs): produced in conjunction with allied nations, and are approved for U.S. use by the Chairman of the JCS. ACPs are reviewed biennially.
• Joint Army-Navy-Air Force Publications (JANAPs): used when no ACP covers a specific topic; to expedite information to U.S. forces; or to meet specific requirements of U.S. operations.
• U.S. Supplements to ACPs.

[JCS, *Unified Action Armed Forces (UNAAF),* JCS Pub 2, December 1986, p. 3-86].

military deception: "Actions executed to mislead opposition decision-makers, causing them to derive and accept desired appreciations of military capabilities, intentions, operations, or other activities that evoke actions that contribute to the originator's objectives" [JCS, *Joint Operations Planning System, Vol. II,* p. C-77, released under the FOIA]. (see also **cover and deception**)

Military Department (see **Department**)

Military District of Washington (M-DW): Army **major command,** established 5 May 1942, with administrative jurisdiction over units assigned to the Washington, DC area, including those in Maryland and Virginia at Ft. Myers, Ft. McNair, Cameron Station, Suitland Annex, and Davison U.S. Army Airfield. MDW also supervises Arlington National Cemetery and the U.S. Army Service Center for the Armed Forces, servicing Pentagon office logistics and personnel. Its logistical functions include personnel support for 34,000 military and civilian employees in the MDW region, building maintenance, and administration of commissaries. Additional MDW missions include the emergency security, rescue, and evacuation of the President and White House staff; defense of the U.S. Capitol and the federal government; **civil disturbance assistance;** and ceremonial functions such as receptions for foreign heads of state, state and special funerals; and participation in the Presidential Inaugural Parade. Its ceremonial units include the 3rd U.S. Infantry (Old Guard), and the U.S. Army Band (Pershing's Own). (see also **Air Force District of Washington, Naval District of Washington**)

Headquarters
Ft. McNair, Washington, DC
20319

military exercise   (see **exercise**)

Military Intelligence: Combat Support branch of the Army.

Military Net Assessment: Future Joint Chiefs of Staff report that is likely, with the **Planning Guidance** and the **Planning Force** document, to replace the **Joint Strategic Planning Document** Supporting Analysis in the future.

military occupational specialty (M-OS): Numerical system used by the Marine Corps and the Army to identify job skills of an individual. (see also **Navy enlisted classification code (NEC),** Appendix F)

Military Police Corps: Combat service support and **combat support** branch of the Army.

Military Sealift Command (MSC): Navy **operating force** and service component command of **U.S. Transportation Command**. Its primary mission is to provide strategic mobility in support of wartime and peacetime national security objec-

tives through the Strategic Sealift Force, the Naval Fleet Auxiliary Force (NFAF), and the Special Mission Support Force. The NFAF is composed of oilers, stores ships, and ocean surveillance ships. The Special Mission Support Force is composed of scientific and technical support ships.

MSC forces are drawn from U.S. government-owned ships, and ships chartered from the U.S. **Merchant Marine**. MSC is organized by area: MSC Europe, MSC Mediterranean, MSC Atlantic, MSC Pacific, and MSC Far East. These area commands also respond to duties assigned by their respective fleets. MSC consists of approximately 129 ships, including 74 government-owned and bareboat chartered ships; a commercial fleet of 55 ships; 80 Ready Reserve Force ships. Its commander reports directly to the Chief of Naval Operations. MSC personnel strength is approximately 7,000 active duty military and civilian personnel, plus over 2,200 contract merchant mariners in peace time. When fully mobilized, MSC would gain 2,300 personnel from the reserve forces.

Headquarters
Washington Naval Yard,
Washington, DC 20003

military service: A branch of the U.S. armed forces established by Congress and operated and administered by a military department: the **Department of the Air Force, Department of the Army, Department of the Navy,** and the U. S. **Marine Corps**. A service may also be operated by an executive department, as is the case with the U.S. **Coast Guard**.

Military Support of Civil Defense (MSCD): "Those military activities and measures taken by DOD components to assist the civilian population during time of military conflict. MSCD is designed to minimize the effects upon the civilian population caused by an enemy attack upon the United States, and/or United States territories and possessions; deal with the immediate emergency conditions that would be created by any such attack; and effect emergency repairs to or the emergency restoration of vital utilities and facilities destroyed or damaged by any such attack. MSCD will complement and not substitute for civil participation in civil defense operations. Military plans and plans developed by civil authority will recognize that civil resources must be the first used to support civil requirements and that military resources must be used only when available and with resource capability to supplement the civil resources. . . . Military support will be provided within the capabilities of the commanders and will not supersede essential combat, combat support, or self-survival operations" [JCS, *Basic Planning Directive for Land Defense of the Continental United States and Military Support of Civil Defense*, 15 February 1983, released under the FOIA].

In addition, the JCS manual on MSCD states that: "in event of nuclear, biological, chemical (NBC), or conventional weapon attack on the United States . . . military operations have first priority. Other missions that have precedence over MSCD missions include continuity of Federal Government operations" [JCS, *Military Support of Civil Defense System Description*, 1 December 1983, p. I-4, released under the FOIA].
(see also **civil defense, continuity of government**)

military time: 1. Time expressed in **zulu time** with the required number and alphabetic letters as indicated:

Day	(01–31)	2 digits
Hour	(00–23)	2 digits
Minute	(00–59)	2 digits
Zulu	(Z)	1 letter
Month	(Jan–Dec)	3 letters
Year	(Last 2 digits of year)	

Example: 312359Z Mar 84 (31 Mar 1984, 2359 hours zulu).   **2.** The day or hour that designates the timing of a military operation or activity and is used for planning purposes.

Days

- *C-day*: **1.** The unnamed day for planning on which movement from origin in a deployment operation in support of a crisis commences or is to commence. The deployment may be movement of troops, cargo, or weapon systems, or a combination of these elements utilizing any or all types of transport. All movement required for C-day preparatory actions or prepositioning of deployment support are expressed relative to this day as negative days (e.g., N-5). For execution the actual day is established under the authority and direction of the Secretary of Defense [JCS, *Joint Operation Planning System, Volume I: Deliberate Planning Procedures*, p. xxii, released under the FOIA]. **2.** The day on which USCENTCOM deployment/

redeployment commences or is scheduled to commence. This applies to movement of USCENT-COM deploying elements from onload air bases, surface ports or embarkation, and tactical unit departure bases. The movement of select deployment-support elements to prepositioned locations may precede C-day. USCENTCOM operations plans (OPLANS) designate C-day [HQ, USCENTCOM, *Emergency Action Procedures, Volume I: System Description*, 20 February 1986, p. 4-2, released under FOIA].

• *D-day*: **1.** The unnamed day on which a particular operation, such as a land assault, air strike, naval bombardment, parachute assault, or amphibious assault, commences or is to commence. It may be the commencement of hostilities or the date an employment phase is implemented. The senior headquarters directing the operation will specify the D-day. (C-, D-, M-days end at 2400Z and are assumed to be 24 hours long for planning) [USCENTCOM, *Emergency Action Procedures, Volume I: System Description*, 20 February 1986, p. 4-3, released under FOIA]. **2.** The unnamed day on which a nuclear test takes place. $D+7$ means seven days after D-day.

• *E-day*: The day on which an exercise commences [*JCS Pub 1*, p. 112].

• *G-day*: The day on which the decision to deploy a specific force or forces is directed by competent authority.

• *K-day*: The basic date for the introduction of a convoy system or any particular convoy lane.

• *M-day*: The day on which mobilization commences or is to commence.

• *N-day (Negative Day)*: An unnamed day prior to C-day in which a unit is notified for deployment or redeployment [JCS, *Joint Operation Planning System, Volume I: Deliberate Planning Procedures*, p. xxii].

Hours

• *A-hour (Alert hour)*: **1.** The time designated by the Joint Chiefs of Staff at which generation of nonalert forces will commence. **2.** The hour nuclear forces begin force generation.

• *E-hour*: **Single Integrated Operational Plan** (**SIOP**) execution hour.

• *F-hour*: The effective time of announcement by the Secretary of Defense to the military department of a decision to mobilize reserve units.

• *H-hour*: **1.** The specific hour on D-day on which particular operations or hostilities commence or are to commence. **2.** Time zero, or time of detonation.

• *K-hour*: The time at which fuzes are fired in a Navy demolition operation.

• *L-hour*: **1.** The specific hour on C-day at which a deployment operation commences or is to commence. **2.** In the Navy, the time of touchdown of the first helicopter at the landing zone. **3.** Launch hour.

• *P-hour*: Navy; **1.** In daylight operations, the predetermined time of rendezvous of underwater demolition craft and the swimmers they retrieve. **2.** In night operations, the time at which all swimmers possible must have been retrieved by their parent boat.

- *R-hour*: Navy; **1.** In daylight operations, the time at which underwater demolition craft, with swimmer personnel aboard, cross the fire support line in the approach to the beach to discharge the swimmers. **2.** In night operations, the time at which the underwater demolition crafts are launched from the parent surface ship.
- *X-hour*: Navy; **1.** In daylight SEAL operations, the time at which all swimmers possible must have been retrieved and the underwater demolition craft must be seaward of the fire support line en route to their parent surface ship. **2.** In night operations, the time at which all rubber boats have been retrieved by their parent underwater demolition craft.
- *Z-hour*: In the Navy, the time at which all underwater demolition craft have been retrieved by their parent ship.

Times

- *Slew time*: The time needed for a weapon to re-aim at a new target after having just fired at a previous one.
- *Zone time*: The time kept in sea areas in a 15 degree zone of longitude, the central meridian of each zone being 15 degrees or a multiple of 15 degrees removed from the Greenwich Meridian. The times of successive zones differ by one hour.

Military Traffic Management Command (MTMC): Army **major command** established as the Military Traffic Management and Terminal Service on 15 February 1965 and renamed MTMC on 31 July 1974. It is also the Army component command of **U.S. Transportation Command** (USTRANSCOM) and a joint executive agent for a number of transportation duties. It manages DOD passenger and freight land transportation, military port usage, and container transport in both peace and wartime. It provides transportation planning to the JCS through USTRANSCOM and its deployment directorate, as well as to the other military services in cooperation with the **Military Airlift Command** and **Military Sealift Command,** unified and specified commands, and the commercial transportation industry. MTMC administers national defense programs for use of civil highways, ports, rail-roads, inland waterways, pipelines, and airways in CONUS. Annually MTMC manages approximately 17 million short tons of freight traffic, transports 5 million passengers within CONUS, and transships 14 million measurement tons of cargo through ports worldwide. It is jointly commanded and staffed by the services with an Army Major General serving as its Commander, an Air Force Brigadier General as Vice Commander, and a civilian as its Executive Director for Operations and Plans. Its personnel strength is approximately 4,000 military and civilian personnel in peacetime, plus over 4,400 Army reservists.

Headquarters
Falls Church, VA 22041

Subordinate Commands and Offices

- Eastern Area, Bayonne, NJ 07002
- Western Area, Oakland Army Base, CA 94626

- Transportation Terminal Command, Europe, Rotterdam, The Netherlands
- Transportation Engineering Agency, Newport News, VA 23604

Millstone Hill: Mechanical tracking radar in Lexington, MA, owned and operated by Lincoln Laboratories, Massachusetts Institute of Technology. It provides space object identification data on deep space satellites, typically those with periods greater than 220 minutes. (see also **Spacetrack, ALCOR**)

MILSTAR (Military Strategic, Tactical and Relay): Joint service EHF **satellite communications** system under development to provide worldwide jam-resistant two-way connectivity to strategic and tactical forces before, during, and after a nuclear attack. MILSTAR was the first satellite communications system designed from the outset to have the endurance characteristics needed to support the management of strategic nuclear forces in a protracted war. MILSTAR connects Army brigades in the field; Navy surface ships and submarines; Air Force strategic aircraft, **airborne command posts,** and ICBM **launch control centers;** and mobile Marine Corps forces. The National Command Authorities can conduct critical conferencing through MILSTAR, connecting through airborne command posts or ground **mobile command centers**.

The EHF communications payload will provide 45 GHz for the uplink and 20 GHz for the downlink. It offers limited service in the SHF and UHF spectrum (225 to 400 MHz).

MILSTAR will replace **AFSATCOM** as part of the **Minimum Essential Emergency Communications Network (MEECN)**. MILSTAR will use frequency-hopping on the uplink to confuse enemy jamming. Phased-array antennas on the satellite will also protect against jamming. As the first operational military communications satellite employing direct satellite-to-satellite link for global coverage, there is no need to relay signals via intermediate ground terminals. (This crosslink technology was first demonstrated in the **LES-8/9** satellites.) The mobile MILSTAR control terminal is called the Network Communication Control Station.

Expected to be deployed in the early 1990s, MILSTAR will consist of seven active satellites in circular orbits: four geostationary and one spare (covering the Pacific, Atlantic, and Indian Oceans and North and South America) and three geosynchronous (covering Europe, Africa, Western Asia, and the polar regions). The satellites will be launched by Titan-IV/Centaur booster rockets.

Various types of MILSTAR terminals will be produced for the Air Force and the Navy for use in aircraft, ships, submarines, and ground facilities. The Air Force requires three different types of MILSTAR terminals

1. Airborne/ground command posts and terminals required for secure voice and data communications
   - **National Emergency Airborne Command Post**
   - **EC-135** airborne command post

- **National Military Command Center**
2. Attack warning and attack assessment sensor facilities to transmit data and secure voice communications
- **PAVE PAWS**
- **BMEWS** (Ballistic Missile Early Warning System)
- **RC-135s**
3. Airborne/ground-based force elements to provide teletype and higher-speed data service but no voice communications
- B-1B bomber
- B-2 bomber
- B-52 bomber
- **launch control centers** (LCCS) for MX and Minuteman missiles

Navy terminals, designated the AN/USC-38, include a shore-based facility, a shipboard terminal, and a terminal for mounting on a submarine periscope. The ship terminal has been tested aboard the USS David R. Ray; the submarine terminal, aboard the USS Blueback. The Navy **TACAMO** E-6A aircraft will use the same airborne terminals developed for the Air Force. A mini-MILSTAR transponder has been on the Navy **Fleet Satellite Command** satellite number 7 since late 1986 to test MILSTAR operations.

The entire MILSTAR program involves approximately $22 billion. Lockheed Missile and Space Company, Sunnyvale, CA, was granted a five-year $1.05 billion cost-plus-incentive fee contract to build one satellite and buy long lead items for a second one. TRW Electronic Systems Group has subcontracts for EHF com-

munications payload; Hughes subcontracted to TRW for the SHF downlink program. Raytheon, Rockwell, and Textron/Bell have teamed to produce the MILSTAR terminals for the Air Force and Navy. The small mobile Army terminals, designated AN/TSC-124, are provided by Magnavox.

The program has received criticism from Congress for cost overruns and management problems. On 1 July 1989, the House Armed Services Committee froze spending of $103 million slated for MILSTAR until the DOD produces a procurement plan for the program. The Senate Armed Services Committee requested a new launch schedule and an assessment of MILSTAR's availability in its 19 July budget report. And on 28 July, the House Appropriations defense subcommittee voted to terminate the MILSTAR program.

mine countermeasures ship (see **mine warfare ship**)

minesweeper: 1. A device used to detect land mines so they can be neutralized and/or removed.   **2.** A ship that carries devices for the detection, neutralization, and/or destruction of naval mines. (see also **mine warfare ship**)

mine warfare: 1. In land warfare, an explosive charge or other substance (e.g., chemical and biological agent) used to kill personnel or to damage or destroy equipment. It may be detonated by the action of its victim, by the passage of time, or by controlled means.   **2.** In naval warfare, an explosive device laid in the water with the intention of damaging or sinking ships or of deterring shipping from entering an area. "The term does not include devices attached to the bottoms of ships or to harbor installations by personnel operating underwater, nor does it include devices that explode on expiration of a predetermined time after laying" [*JCS Pub 1,* p. 233]. Also, controlled mines are no longer a part of active Navy stocks.

Modern influence mines do not require physical contact with the target to fire. They are activated by the presence of the target as sensed by magnetic, acoustic, or pressure devices. A mine field is an area of ground or sea containing mines laid with or without a pattern. Mines are considered to be both weapons for attacking and destroying personnel and material and obstacles used to limit or channel the movement of opposing forces. Land mines are usually for anti-personnel or antitank purposes. Sea mines are for destroying ships and submarines.

Mines are described as being offensive or defensive weapons. When used offensively they are placed in the enemy's territory, waterways, harbors, anchorages, and channels or may be planted in territory or sea lanes removed from the enemy's home territory to attack his military and commercial transportation and shipping. When used defensively, mines may be placed near friendly positions (perimeter defense) or in friendly ports, harbors, channels, anchorages, and the like, and in open water to protect against enemy offensive attacks in these areas. The actual threat of mines is often of equal importance with the destruction of enemy forces, since the presence or threat of mines requires countermeasures to sweep or neutralize them and causes delays or diversions in shipping or transportation schedules.

Mines can be hand-placed, scattered from mine-laying vehicles, dispersed from artillery shells, dropped from aircraft, and launched from ships or submarines. Aircraft- and submarine-laid mines are normally employed in offensive operations. Surface ship-launched mines are no longer in the U.S. stockpile of active service mines. Naval mines can be moored or allowed to drift. There are also a variety of practice and inert mines used for training purposes.

A typical land mine is composed of a fuze that ignites the detonator, which in turn ignites the booster that then sets off the main charge, all of which is contained with a body or casing.

Types of land mines include

- Anti-personnel (AP) mines: Includes the bouncing fragmentation mine, the "Bouncing Betty," which when activated by pressure or a trip wire pops out of the ground to a height of about six feet and explodes; and the directional fragmentation mine, the "Claymore," which when activated by electrical, nonelectrical, command, or tripwire means, projects steel fragments horizontally forward in a 60-degree horizontal arc.
- Antitank: Generally take a greater pressure to activate than anti-personnel mines (300–500 lb rather than 8–20 lb) and use high explosive blasts or steel plates propelled

by high explosives to disable or destroy a vehicle.

A typical sea mine is composed of the firing mechanism with accessories, the explosive filler, the case, and the anchor (if one is used). Methods of actuating sea mines include

- Acoustic: "A naval influence mine designed to be actuated by the acoustic emissions from a target ship."
- Contact: "A naval influence mine designed to be actuated by contact with the target ship."
- Pressure: "A naval influence mine designed to be actuated by the pressure wave of a target ship."
- Magnetic: "A naval influence mine designed to be actuated by the magnetic signature from a target ship." [*NWP 3*]

Some mines contain combinations of all three of these influence devices. This combination makes mine countermeasures more difficult and also reduces spurious firings.

Sea mines can also be classified as to their deployment location

- Drifting: "A mine with positive or neutral buoyancy, free to move under the influence of wind, tide, or current. International law requires a drifting mine to become harmless within 1 hour after it is free to drift." U.S. forces do not use drifting mines.
- Moored: "A mine having a buoyant case maintained at a predetermined depth by means of a cable attached to an anchor."
- Bottom: "A nonbuoyant mine designated for planting on the sea

bottom (Formerly called a 'ground mine')."
[*NWP 3*].

Types of sea mines include

- Mk25: An aircraft-deployed bottom mine, using magnetic induction and equal to a 2,000 lb bomb. It is being phased out of the inventory as it is a World War II era mine.
- Mk52: An aircraft-deployed bottom mine, designed primarily to attack submarines and equal to a 1,000 lb bomb.
- Mk53: An aircraft-deployed moored mine equal to a 500 lb bomb; its purpose when planted with other mines in a field is to destroy an enemy's minesweeping gear.
- Mk55: An aircraft-deployed bottom mine identical to the Mk52, except it is a nominal 2,000 lb rather than a 1,000 lb bomb sized mine.
- Mk56: An aircraft-deployed moored mine equal to a 2,000 lb bomb and designed specifically for effectiveness against high-speed, deep-operating submarines.
- Mk57: A submarine-deployed 2,000 lb class moored mine with a magnetic firing mechanism. It is nearly identical to the air-deployed Mk56 mine.

There is also a class of mines called "destructors" (DSTs). A modification kit installed on Navy general-purpose 500 lb Mk82 or 1,000 lb Mk83 bombs or Air Force 750 lb Mk117 bombs converts these, respectively, to DST Mk36 or DST Mk40 or DST Mk117D destructor magnetically actuated mines. DSTs became the first mines to be useful as both land mines and sea mines. When buried in the ground after impact, they would be set off by motor vehicles or personnel-carrying metal objects, and the like. When dropped in rivers or coastal waters they would be set off by freighters, coastal craft, small craft, or any metal-carrying or metal craft. (see also **Captor**)

Mine Warfare Command: Navy **operating force** that coordinates with the fleet commanders and other navy forces on all **mine warfare**, readiness, tactics, and doctrine above the level of the individual mine-capable surface ship, squadron, and submarine. It also provides technical advice to the Atlantic Fleet, Pacific Fleet, and U.S. Navy Europe. It exercises operational control over mobile mine assembly groups, mine warfare inspection groups, Mine Warfare Group 1 (Seattle, WA), and fleet mine divisions.

Headquarters
Charleston, SC 29408-5500

mine warfare group: A **task organization** of ships and helicopters that conducts offensive and defensive mine operations in support of the amphibious task force.

mine warfare ship (M-): Navy conventionally armed ship designed for clearing the bottom of the sea and water volume of mines. There are ocean minesweepers (MSOs) as well as coastal minesweepers (MHCs), which perform coastal mine clearance operations of up to five days duration without replenishment, with

the objective of allowing the breakout of U.S. combatants and resupply ships from mined continental U.S. military and commercial ports. Mine countermeasures ships (MCMs) are wooden hulled and will be used to clear mines from the ocean bottom and surrounding water. The craft-of-opportunity-program (COOP) makes use of converted fishing boats and former Naval Academy training boats for harbor mineclearing.

Newly constructed Avenger (MCM-1) class ships displace 1,350 tons at full load, are 224 ft long, have a beam of 39 ft, a speed of 14 kt, are armed with two .50 caliber machine guns and have a crew of 74. MHC-51 class ships under construction will displace 785 tons at full load, are 188 ft long, have a beam of 36 ft, and a crew of 45.

For many years the Navy paid little attention to its mine counter-measures program. The last ocean-going minesweeper was included in the 1954 shipbuilding program and was commissioned in 1958. But in the early 1980s the Navy embarked on a program to replace the aging minesweeper fleet with new MCM ships. In December 1982 the keel was laid for the first of the planned 14 Avenger (MCM-1) class ships. But construction problems delayed the delivery of the first ship until mid-1987. Eleven of the fourteen ships were funded as of FY 1989.

Seventeen minesweeper hunters (MSHs) also were in the Navy plans, and the contract for the first of these was awarded in FY 1984 to Textron Marine Systems. Shock test problems with the glass-reinforced plastic hull led to the cancelling of the program, and to a decision to adopt a design perfected by Intermarine SPA, an Italian shipyard. A design contract for a coastal minehunter (MHC-51) class was awarded to Intermarine in August 1986, and the construction contract for the lead ship of a 17-ship class was awarded to Intermarine USA in May 1987. Construction commenced at Intermarine's Savannah, GA, shipyard in May 1988, with the first ship to be completed in 1991. Until these new ships enter the fleet in sizable numbers, the Navy will continue to rely on the 3 active MSOs in the fleet and the 18 assigned to the Naval Reserve.

The prime contractors for the MCM-1 class are Peterson Boatbuilders Inc., and Marinette Shipyard, Sturgeon Bay, WI. The FY 1990 budget request for the last three MCMs is $358.3 million. The FY 1990 and FY 1991 budget request for three MHCs each year is $235.4 and $227.7 million, respectively, including RDT&E.

miniature homing vehicle (MHV): Air Force air-launched, direct-ascent, **anti-satellite** kinetic energy interceptor weapon to disable enemy satellites. The MHV would directly collide with its target at a high rate of speed and destroy it through kinetic energy. The MHV, one ft in diameter and one ft long, is designed to be carried into space by an 18 ft missile launched by a two-staged rocket from an **F-15**. Two tests of the MHV against points in space were held in 1984. The first test was successful, but DOD has not stated whether the second one was, although press reports suggest that it was not.

miniature receive terminal (MRT): Air Force communications program to provide a small receiver for **B-1B, B-52,** and **FB-111** Strategic Air Command (SAC) bomber aircraft to allow them to receive **emergency action messages (EAMs)** over VLF/LF frequencies. The MRT will also provide the high-survivability LF communications from CINCSAC and the National Command Authorities (NCA) to SAC bomber forces for passing EAMs. Low-frequency MRTs will be on bombers, allowing **EC-135s** to transmit EAMs to the MRTs, thereby providing a new communications link for bombers that will be unaffected by atmospheric disturbances.

Minimum Essential Emergency Communications Network (MEECN): The network of land-based, satellite, and airborne communications systems expected to survive a nuclear attack and remain operable for the command of strategic nuclear forces. Established as a special JCS-controlled network in 1970, MEECN "consists of communications systems specifically designed to operate during a nuclear attack and to provide a communications capability for the dissemination of nuclear execution and termination orders during various phases of conflict [transmitting **emergency action messages**] . . . [and to] exercise deliberate and precise control of strategic nuclear options for the SIOP [**Single Integrated Operational Plan**] execution and termination" [U.S. Congress, House Armed Service Committee, *FY 1983, DOD Authorizations, Part 3,* p. 141].

MEECN is composed of the following:

• **Airborne command posts** and radio relays, including the **National Emergency Airborne Command Post** (NEACP), the **Post-Attack Command and Control System,** the Worldwide Airborne Command Post Fleet, and **TACAMO**;
• **Emergency Rocket Communications System (ERCS)**;
• **Survivable Low Frequency Communications System (SLFCS)**;
• Air Force Satellite Communications System (**AFSATCOM**);
• **Ground Wave Emergency Network (GWEN)**;
• **LES-8/9, GAPFILLER,** and **Fleet Satellite Command** satellites; and
• **MILSTAR.**

minimum risk force: The force, developed in the **Joint Strategic Program Document** that achieves national objectives with virtual certainty of success. It is not constrained by fiscal, manpower, logistic, mobility, or other limitations. (see also **Planning Force**)

Minuteman missile: Model designation LGM-30. An Air Force, long-range, nuclear-armed, three-stage, solid-propellant, guided ICBM, launched from underground silos and assigned to the Strategic Air Command. The Minuteman I was introduced in 1962 and is no longer deployed, having been replaced by the Minuteman II and Minuteman III.

The Minuteman II (LGM-30F) carries one W56/Mk-11C **reentry vehicle** with a yield of 1.2 megatons. It

has a range of over 6,000 miles and an accuracy (CEP) of 0.2–0.34 nm. Minuteman II became operational in 1966, and there are currently 450 deployed. The missiles are organized into three wings of 150 missiles each. Wing I is located with the 341st Strategic Missile Wing (SMW) at Malmstrom AFB, MT. Wing II is with the 44th SMW at Ellsworth AFB, SD. Wing IV is with the 351st SMW at Whiteman AFB, MO. The Minuteman II was the first U.S. ICBM to carry **penetration aids**. Its guidance set is being improved to increase accuracy, and it provides remote retargeting and expanded execution plan capability.

Minuteman IIIs (LGM-30G) carry two or three W62/Mk-12 warheads with 170 kt yield or the more accurate and powerful W78 Mk-12A warheads with 335–350 kt yields. They have a range of over 7,000 miles and an accuracy (CEP) of some 600 ft for the Mk-12A and 900–1,000 ft for the Mk-12. Minuteman III became operational in June 1970 and there are currently 500 deployed. They are organized into four wings, one with 50 missiles and three with 150. Wing I with 50 missiles is located with the 341st SMW at Malmstrom AFB, MT. Wing III is with the 91st SMW at Minot AFB, ND. Wing V is with the 90th SMW at F. E. Warren AFB, WY. Wing VI is with the 312th SMW at Grand Forks AFB, ND. The Minuteman III was the first missile to make use of **MIRVs (multiple independently targetable reentry vehicles)**. Fifty Minuteman III missiles at F. E. Warren AFB, WY were withdrawn and replaced by **MX missiles**.

Motors and guidance systems in both missiles are being replaced and/or improved, and restorations and additions to the launch facilities are also occurring to maintain the viability of the force well beyond the year 2000. Boeing Aerospace, Seattle, WA, was the prime contractor.

Minuteman Radio Communication Services: A Washington, DC, mobile VHF radio-telephone network used to support the command and control requirements of the **National Military Command System**. Subscribers are key selected general or flag officers, or equivalent civilian officials, whose functions contribute directly to the decision-making process of the Office of the Secretary of Defense, of the decision-making process relating to the planning, deployment, and/or direction of the armed forces [Air Force, *Washington Tactical Switchboard and Minuteman Radio Communication Services*, HOI 100-7, 20 July 1981, released under the FOIA].

MIRACL (Mid-Infrared Advanced Chemical Laser): High-energy ground-based laser research-and-development project located at White Sands, NM. MIRACL is a technology-development and risk-reduction program that supports several ground- and space-based laser research programs, such as tactical testing against low-flying target drones for the Navy, and lethality, tracking, and atmospheric propagation experiments for the Strategic Defense Initiative's **ballistic missile defense** studies. In the future, the MIRACL system may be used to counter Soviet surveillance satellites that threaten U.S. and allied-forces, particularly naval forces. And by 1990, along with the Satellite Beam Director, MIRACL could be upgraded to provide an interim, very limited, and very near-term **anti-satellite** capability.

MIRV (Multiple Independently Targeted Reentry Vehicle): Two or more warheads carried by a single **ballistic missile** booster, each of which can be directed to a separate target. The dispensing and targeting mechanism, the post-boost vehicle (PBV or "bus"), maneuvers to achieve successive desired positions and velocities to dispense each **reentry vehicle (RV)** on a trajectory to attack the desired target. Alternately, the RVs might themselves maneuver toward their targets after they reenter the atmosphere. MIRVed missiles in the U.S. arsenal are: **Minuteman** III, **Poseidon**, and **Trident** I. MIRVed missiles under development include the **MX** and the Trident II.

missile: An unmanned weapon that is propelled to its target by some kind of an engine. **Cruise missiles** are powered by jet engines and resemble unmanned aircraft. **Ballistic missiles** are propelled into the upper atmosphere by chemical rockets. After the rocket burns out, the missile returns to earth due to gravitational pull. Ballistic missiles are categorized by range:

- 600–1,500 miles: **Medium-range ballistic missile**.
- 1,500–4,000 miles: **Intermediate-range ballistic missile**.
- 4,000 or more miles: **ICBM** (Intercontinental ballistic missile).

mission: A function or task assigned to a specific armed force or unit.

MITRE Corporation (see **Federally Funded-Research and Development Centers**)

MK-15 CIWS (see **Phalanx**)

MK-46 Torpedo: Navy conventional lightweight **torpedo** for delivery by surface vessel torpedo tubes, **ASROC** missiles, and fixed- and rotary-wing aircraft. The torpedo was first deployed in 1967, and production ended in FY 1987. The torpedo is the backbone of the Navy's inventory. Neartip is the updated version of MK-46 and features improved acoustics and countermeasures resistance. The prime contractor is Honeywell, Minneapolis, MN. FY 1987 cost for the final 500 torpedoes was $85.7 million. The MK-46 is being replaced by the MK-50.

MK-48 Torpedo: Submarine-launched, conventional, wire-guided acoustic-homing, anti-submarine and anti-surface **torpedo**. First deployed in 1972, the torpedo is no longer in production. An ADCAP (additional capability) program will modify current torpedoes to go faster, deeper, and farther than the MK-48. Contractors were Hughes Aircraft, Fullerton, CA, and Westinghouse Electric, Cleveland, OH. FY 1990 and FY 1991 budget requests for 320 ADCAPs each year are $554.9 million and $473.6 million, respectively.

MK-50 Barracuda Torpedo: Navy submarine-, ship-, or aircraft-launched **torpedo** under development with capabilities to counter deeper-diving, faster, and quieter submarines of the future. The MK-50 is the follow-on to the MK-46 and was called the Advanced Lightweight Torpedo (ALWT) in early development. The MK-50 will provide the payload for the **Sea Lance** anti-submarine warfare (ASW) weapon. The prime contractor is Honeywell Inc., Minneapolis, MN. Westinghouse Electric Corp, Cleveland, OH, has been selected as the second source. It will be deployed in the early 1990s. FY 1990 budget request for purchase of 200 MK-50s is $336.1 million.

MOB (see **main operating base**)

MOBEX (Mobilization Exercise): An Army **exercise** to test the service's ability to mobilize reserve forces and to reinforce deployed forces.

mobile command center (see **Ground Mobile Command Center**)

mobile ground station (MGS): Mobile ground terminal for command and control and information readout from communications and surveillance satellites. The mobile ground stations operated by the Air Force Space Command for the **Defense Support Program** early-warning satellites are called mobile ground terminals (MGTs).

Mobile Inshore Underwater Warfare (MIUW) units: Special operations units of the **Naval Reserve** that are mobile, self-contained, and quickly deployable. MIUWs conduct surface and subsurface surveillance of inshore areas: ports, harbors, straits, and advance bases. Their secondary mission is to provide command and control in surveillance areas, including control of mine warfare helicopters, surface craft, and ship movements. "The smallest mobile tactical IUW unit capable of systematic observation and interpretation of contacts in an assigned inshore area for the purpose of identifying, localizing, and attacking hostile forces" [*NWP 3*]. Seven west coast MIUWs are subordinate to **Inshore Underseas Warfare Group (IUWG)** 1. Nine MIUWs operate on the east coast under IUWG 2.

Mobile Subscriber Equipment (MSE): Army program to provide mobile, secure, automatic tactical communications in active and reserve corps and divisions. MSE includes radio, telephone, and data services for command and control. Prime contractor is General Telephone and Electronics (GTE). The FY 1990 budget request is $984.7 million.

mobilization: The act of preparing for war or other emergencies by assembling and organizing raw materials, focusing industrial efforts on national security objectives, marshalling and readying Reserve and National Guard units and individuals for active military service, and/or readying new military organizations filled with personnel inducted from civilian life. There are four levels of mobilization:

- Partial: Expansion of the active Armed Forces (short of full mobilization) resulting from actions by Congress or the President to mobilize Reserve component units and/or individual reservists to meet all

or part of the requirements of a particular contingency or operational war plans or to meet requirements incident to hostilities.

- Full: Expansion of the active armed forces resulting from action by Congress and the President to mobilize all reserve component units in the existing approved force structure, all individual reservists, and the material resources needed for their support. Neither full nor partial mobilization represents more than activating additional military forces.

- Total: Expansion of the active armed forces by the organization and/or generation of additional units or personnel beyond the existing approved active and reserve structures to respond to the requirement generated by the contingency, including mobilization of all national resources needed to create and sustain such forces.

- General: Mobilization of military forces of a nation, either to engage in hostilities already begun or in preparation for an all-out war.

mod: Modifications made to a major assembly of a weapon system.

modernization: 1. A major component of **military capability**. 2. "The process of modifying a weapon system such that its characteristics or components are altered in order to improve the performance capabilities for that weapon system. **SALT II** provides that, subject to provisions to the contrary, modernization and replacement of strategic offensive arms may be carried out" [ACDA, *SALT II: Glossary of Terms,* 1979].

modern large ballistic missile (ML-BM): An **ICBM**, deployed since 1964, capable of being launched from a launcher and having a volume significantly greater than the largest light ICBM operational in 1972 (the Soviet SS-11). The term was coined in an agreed understanding of the Interim Agreement of the **SALT I** accords. The United States has no MLBMs. The Soviet Union has produced two types of MLBMs: the SS-9 (no longer deployed) and the SS-18.

MOLINK: The secure teletype system between the U.S. and Soviet governments; operated from the **National Military Command Center** by a Presidential translator team and used only when approved by the President. An identical facility is operated at the **Alternate National Military Command Center**. MOLINK is part of the **Direct Communications Link** [JCS, *Crisis Staffing Procedures of the Joint Chiefs of Staff*, SM-481-83, 12 July 1983, p. 4-44, released under FOIA].

monitored retrievable storage (MRS): A Department of Energy program to develop a temporary disposal site for high-level **nuclear waste**. As envisioned by the Nuclear Waste Policy Act of 1982, the MRS site would be near Oak Ridge, TN. It would serve as a center for waste packaging and consolidation and for preparation of spent nuclear fuel for transit to a permanent western repository. However, in the Omnibus Reconciliation Act of 1987 (PL 100-203), Congress required that the search for an MRS site be reconducted and it required a commission report by November 1987.

Montebello Decision: A NATO **Nuclear Planning Group** agreement concluded in Montebello, Canada, in October 1983. The decision agreed to unilaterally withdraw 1,400 U.S. nuclear warheads from Europe. The United States also agreed to withdraw one additional warhead for every **Ground-Launched Cruise Missile** and **Pershing II** warhead deployed. The NATO countries pledged to modernize their short-range nuclear forces as a compensation for the lower number of warheads by introducing new nuclear artillery projectiles, by developing the **Follow-on to Lance** missile, and by developing the new **Tactical Air-to-Surface Missile (TASM)** for delivery from aircraft.

Moon Agreement: Formally known as the Agreement Governing the Activities of States on the Moon and Other Celestial Bodies. The agreement was opened for signature on 18 December 1979 and entered into force on 11 July 1984. As of 31 July 1988, it had seven signatories. The agreement complements the **Outer Space Treaty** in that it bans the use of the moon and planets for military purposes. The use of force on the moon, the planting of any weapons, including nuclear weapons, on or in orbit around it, or any kind of militarization of it or other celestial bodies, is prohibited.

Moray: Control-marking and security-clearance level for the least sensitive type of **special intelligence** at the confidential level. (see also **Spoke, Umbra**)

MOS (see **military occupational specialty**)

MOTIF (Maui Optical Tracking and Identification Facility): Air Force operated visible-light and long-wave infrared sensors for collecting data on both near-Earth and deep-space satellites. MOTIF is located at Maui, HI, at 10,000 ft atop Mount Haleakala. It searches deep space for objects not cataloged by NORAD when it is not being used to obtain positional or signature information on known satellites. MOTIF is an element of the **Space Surveillance Network** ("Spacetrack").

motorized infantry battalion: One of eight types of **maneuver battalions** in the Army, and the newest type. The battalion grew out of the "High Technology Test Bed" created at Ft. Lewis, WA, by former Chief of Staff of the Army General Edward Meyer. The intent was to allow a division commander the flexibility of developing equipment, tactics, and doctrine unhampered by regulations. The results include experimentation with motorcycles, "fast attack vehicles" (dune buggies), remotely piloted vehicles, and the like. The battalion retains the basic **infantry** mission but differs in its equipment and mode of transport. It is basically a wheeled vehicle unit.

motorized infantry division: A type of Army **division** that conducts combat operations against light infantry, tank, and motorized units. The motorized division has capabilities against light infantry and tanks and motorized forces in close terrain

to destroy, defend, and delay; and against tanks and motorized infantry in open terrain to conduct standoff attack, to defend, and to delay. Its limitations are organic airlift capability and protection against armor. The division is designed to fill the gap between heavy (armored and mechanized) and light (airborne and light infantry) divisions. Its division base consists of three ground maneuver brigades comprising nine **maneuver battalions** (five combined arm battalions (heavy), two combined arm battalions (light), and two light attack battalions). Additionally, the division consists of an air attack cavalry brigade; three artillery battalions; and engineer, air defense, intelligence, and signal battalions. The 9th Infantry Division (Motorized), Ft. Lewis, WA, is the only division of this type.

mountain division (see **light infantry division**)

MOVREPS (movement report system): "A system established to collect and make available to certain commands vital information on the status, location, and movement of flag commands, commissioned fleet units, and ships under operational control of the Navy" [*JCS Pub 1*, p. 241].

MPS (maritime prepositioning ships) (see **maritime prepositioning force**)

MRBM (see **medium-range ballistic missile**)

MRV (see **multiple reentry vehicle**)

MSB: Designation for minesweeping boat. (see also **mine warfare ship, minesweeper**)

MSH: Designation for **minesweeper** hunter. (see also **mine warfare ship**)

MSO: Designation for ocean going minesweeper. (see also **mine warfare ship**)

MSSC: Designation for medium **SEAL** support craft.

Mt. Weather (see **FEMA Special Facility**)

Multiple Access Communications Satellite (MACSAT) (see **LIGHT-SAT**)

Multiple-Launch Rocket System (MLRS): Army all-weather, short-range, conventionally armed, free-flight, indirect, area-fire, solid-fuel, artillery rocket system being fielded to fill a void in conventional fire support at the division and corps levels. The MLRS includes a tracked, three-crew, self-propelled launcher/loader with two disposable launch-pod containers holding six 13-ft rockets in each pod. The primary missions of MLRS are fire suppression and suppression of enemy air defenses. MLRS supplements cannon artillery fire by delivering large volumes of firepower in a short time against critical, time-sensitive targets. This high-rate-of-fire weapon can fire its load of 12 rockets in less than a minute, covering an area the size of six football fields with approximately 7,700 grenade-like submunitions effective against both person-

nel and lightly armored targets. The basic warhead carries improved conventional submunitions (ICM), and the missiles can be armed with a scatterable mine warhead developed in West Germany. Growth potential exists to add a terminally guided warhead (TGW) to defeat armor, a **sense-and-destroy armor (SADARM)** warhead to improve counter-battery fires, and a binary chemical warhead (see **binary chemical munitions**). The MLRS launcher vehicle will likely be the launcher for the nuclear **Follow-on to Lance** missile if it is developed. Additionally, the Army plans to adapt the **Tacit Rainbow** cruise missile so that it can be fired from the MLRS launcher. TGW development is a multinational effort that includes the United States, the United Kingdom, France, and West Germany to enter full scale development in FY 1990.

Development of MLRS began in 1977. The original system was modified to accommodate a NATO requirement for a scatterable mine warhead in 1978. The first unit achieved operational status in 1983. Starting in FY 1989, the MLRS will be coproduced by the United States, the United Kingdom, West Germany, France, and Italy.

The prime contractor for the rocket is Vought Corp., Dallas, TX, and for the tracked launcher-loader, FMC, San Jose, CA. The FY 1990 and FY 1991 budget request for 24,000 rockets each year is $336.2 and $326.2 million, respectively.

Multiple reentry vehicle (MRV): A **ballistic missile** reentry vehicle in which the missile does not have the capability to independently target the reentry vehicles—as distinct from a missile equipped with **MIRVs** (Multiple Independent Reentry Vehicles). The United States does not currently have any missiles with MRVs deployed.

munitions: General term applying to all types of nuclear and non-nuclear weapons, to general-purpose force missiles, and to chemical/biological agents designed for use by combat elements, including those elements training to be capable of inflicting or aiding in inflicting damage to or for the neutralization of enemy personnel, equipment, or facilities. It includes bombs, rockets, missile warheads, small arms and cartridges, bulk explosives, smoke agents, incendiaries, and nonexplosive practice and training devices.

Mutual and Balanced Force Reduction Talks (MBFR): Talks conducted until 1989 on arms control; begun in 1973 between the United States, Britain, Canada, West Germany, Belgium, the Netherlands, Luxembourg, East Germany, Poland, Czechoslovakia, and the Soviet Union. A stumbling block in the talks was the alleged lack of conventional parity between Soviet and U.S. forces. The United States argued that the Soviet Union had a numerical advantage and therefore should have deeper cuts, while the Soviets maintained that there was parity between the two and that cuts should be symmetrical. The last series of MBFR talks was held in February 1989. The 15-year talks did result in some agreements and a model for conventional arms control in subsequent fora:

- NATO and the Warsaw Pact are each allowed manpower totals of 900,000 in the central area;
- Reductions to manpower forces will occur in phases, with the U.S. and Soviet troops reduced in the first phase;
- Information on these reductions and on large-scale military movements will be exchanged before and after the fact;
- On-site inspection, permanent observation posts, satellites, and a consultative committee were established for verification.

No agreement has been reached on the following points:

- The number of phases of force reductions: the Warsaw Pact wanted two phases while NATO wanted four;
- Restriction proposed by the Warsaw Pact that no one state may provide over 50 percent of the 900,000 manpower total (aimed at West Germany's military);
- The reported number of soldiers currently kept by the Soviet Union is not accepted by NATO;
- Number and type of inspections: NATO wanted 18 on-site inspections while the Warsaw Pact wanted inspection only by challenge;
- Banning maneuvers of over 50,000 troops; and
- Excluding the Rapid Deployment Force from the total number of forces.

Mutual Assured Destruction (MAD): The doctrine of reciprocal **deterrence** that rests on the ability of two opponents to inflict unacceptable damage on each other after surviving a nuclear first strike. The phrase "assured destruction" was coined by Secretary of Defense Robert McNamara in 1964.

MX missile (LGM-118A): Nicknamed the Peacekeeper. An Air Force long-range, MIRVed, nuclear-armed, four-stage, solid-propellant, guided, intercontinental ballistic missile launched from underground silos and assigned to the Strategic Air Command. It has a greater range and accuracy and more warheads than **Minuteman** missiles.

MX missiles carry 10 W87/Mk21 warheads with a yield of 300 kt each. They have range of 7,000+ miles with an accuracy CEP of less than 400 ft, allowing them to attack all hardened targets. Deployment of 50 MX missiles in existing Minuteman III silos as part of the 90th Strategic Missile Wing at F. E. Warren AFB, WY, began in June 1986. The first MX was operational in December 1986; full operational capability with 50 missiles occurred in December 1988.

Plans are under consideration to base existing and additional MX missiles on railroad cars. MXs in this "rail garrison basing mode" will be placed on railroad cars during peacetime at military installations around the country. During times of national emergency the MX missiles could be randomly dispersed in the civil rail system. The FY 1990 and FY 1991 budget request for 12 missiles each year is $2,360.4 and $3,141 million, respectively, including RDT&E and military construction.

Mystic Star: Code name for the high frequency communications system used aboard **Air Force One** and other VIP aircraft operated by the 89th Military Air Wing, Andrews AFB, MD. The original Mystic Star system became operational in 1967. Updates of the system began in 1985. Whereas the original system had only 100 phone lines and 5 data circuits available for its special air missions, the improved Mystic Star Presidential Radio System will possess 5,000 phone lines and 72 data links. The new Mystic Star will also improve communications security aboard VIP aircraft as a result of improvements in its cryptographic equipment. The Mystic Star system assists the **National Military Command System (NMCS)** and utilizes **Scope Control** equipment. It is augmented by **Global Command and Control System** stations. Ground entry stations are located at:

- Andrews AFB, MD 20331 (network control station)
- McClellan AFB, CA 95652
- Scott AFB, IL 62225
- Hickam AFB, HI 96853
- Yokota AB, Japan (APO San Francisco 96328)
- Clark AB, Philippines (APO San Francisco 96274)

The improved system will possess 18 satellite terminals for the maintenance of worldwide communications. UHF-equipped satellite stations are located at:

- Brandywine, MD
- Wahiawa, HI
- San Vito, Italy

[Air Force, *Standard Procedures for Operation of USAF Global Command Control System Stations*, AFCC R100-20, 1 May 1984, released under the FOIA]. (see also **Nationwide**)

N

N: Prefix designating **1.** Probe vehicle. **2.** Special test aircraft or vehicle (permanent).

NABS (NATO Airbase SatCom Terminal System): Air Force program to develop a transportable satellite ground system and control segment to provide survivable, jam resistant communications for U.S. forces deployed in support of NATO.

NADGE (NATO Air Defense Ground Environment): Air defense radar network with continuous north-south coverage through Norway, Denmark, West Germany, the Netherlands, Belgium, France, Italy, Greece, and Turkey. France participates only in reporting and control, and UK-based radars interface indirectly with NADGE. The original system consisted of 84 sites, 37 of which contained processing systems with digital computers for real-time processing, analysis, and distribution of target information from its own sensors and from data links to other stations.

Information on targets acquired by NADGE is sent by data link to the Command Reporting Center. The information appears as a target reflection on a display console; a video processor simultaneously determines whether the reflection is caused by jamming, video clutter, or a genuine target. A correlator then determines target tracking for genuine targets. **Identification, Friend or Foe (IFF),** voice identification, and computer comparison are used to identify the target. A NATO commander will then direct forces to intercept the target or command surface-to-air missiles. Salty Net provides the data interconnection between NADGE and the Air Force **Tactical Air Control System** tactical air warfare capability.

The NADGE radars are of different types, having been incorporated at different times. Fourteen of the original NADGE radars are Marconi Radar System S269 long-range height finders. As of 1977, the new S669 has been installed in Italy to expand the NADGE southern flank coverage. The UK air defense network is using the Plessey/ITT-Gilfillan AR-320 three-dimensional advanced radar. In 1983, the United Kingdom ordered six AR-329 radars, three of which were NATO-funded. The Hughes air defense radars are three-dimensional, multirole systems to detect, classify, and report target information. They have a range of 250 nm and are capable of detecting objects up to 100,000 ft in altitude.

The NADGE update to integrate NATO **Airborne Warning and Control System** (**AWACS**) information is called the Airborne Early Warning/Ground Environment Integration Segment (AEGIS). Real-time radar information from the 18 NATO AWACS aircraft will be relayed to more than 40 ground stations in Europe, spanning from Turkey to Norway. AEGIS will use the **Joint Tactical Information Distribution System** to provide voice and digital communications between AWACS and ground stations. NADGE will also be augmented by the German Air Defense ground environment (GEAD-GE), which adds southern Germany to the European system, and by the Coastal Radar Integration System (CRIS), which adds data links from Danish coastal radars. Initiated by Denmark in 1984, CRIS gathers data from coastal radars surveying the western Baltic. In the mid-1980s, a new NATO radar station was installed on the Algarve coast of Portugal and three new air-defense radars were delivered to Norway, along with 18 low-level altitude surveillance radars and a control system.

NADS (North Atlantic Defense System): Air Force program to install a new set of automated radars and communications systems in Iceland, including both interim installations and new systems.

National Aeronautics and Space Administration (NASA): Independent civilian space agency operating under the Executive branch. It was created by President Eisenhower on 2 April 1958 as the National Aeronautics and Space Agency from the National Advisory Council of Aeronautics (1915–1958). It was established by law on 29 July 1958 as NASA. At that time, many military space programs were transferred to NASA from the Advanced Research Projects Agency (now DARPA). The NASA-DOD relationship has become closer with development of the **space shuttle**, which is managed by NASA. Other examples of DOD-NASA cooperation in space: early NASA astronauts were formerly service pilots, and current astronauts are almost always active officers; NASA has launched a number of military satellites; and the DOD lobbies extensively to increase NASA's budget. [see also **National Aerospace Plane (NASP)**]

Headquarters
Washington, DC 20546

National Aerospace Plane (NASP): Model designation X-30A. Joint DOD and NASA research program to develop a hypersonic aerospace vehicle to deliver payloads into orbit. The Air Force has been assigned overall responsibility for the program, with participation from DARPA, the Navy, and the Strategic Defense Initiative Organization. Envisioned as an air-breathing, hydrogen-fueled, single-stage-to-orbit horizontal takeoff and landing vehicle, the NASP is seen as a flexibly-based military aircraft, low-cost space launch platform, and economical civil hypersonic transport. The technology development phase began in April 1986. General Electric, Pratt & Whitney, Boeing, Lockheed, General Dynamics, McDonnell Douglas, and Rockwell International all have contracts. Selection of contractors for X-30 fabrication is expected in 1991 with a first flight planned for the mid-1990s. The FY 1990 budget request for RDT&E is $299.7 million, and for FY 1991, $3,889.5 million.

National Agency Check (NAC): A cursory review of an individual's background, usually restricted to search of Federal Bureau of Investigation and police files for derogatory material. Successful completion of an NAC is sufficient to receive a **secret** clearance. (see also **security classification**)

National Capitol Region: The area that includes the District of Columbia; Arlington, Fairfax, Loudon, and Prince William counties and Alexandria, Fairfax, and Falls Church cities in Virginia; and Montgomery and Prince George's counties in Maryland. (see also **Military District of Washington, Air Force District of Washington, Naval District of Washington**)

national censorship: Censorship of communications to, from, and within the borders of the United States, including telecommunications censorship, postal and travelers censorship, and **public media censorship**. (see also **censorship**)

national command: An organization established by and functioning under the authority of a specific nation. A national command may be placed under a NATO commander.

National Command Authorities (NCA): 1. "The National Command Authorities consist only of the President and the Secretary of Defense or their duly deputized alternates or successors. The **chain of command** runs from the President to the Secretary of Defense and through the Joint Chiefs of Staff to the commanders of unified and specified commands. The channel of communications for execution of the [**Single Integrated Operational Plan**] **SIOP** and other time-sensitive operations shall be *from the President* through the Chairman, Joint Chiefs of Staff, representing the Joint Chiefs of Staff, to the executing commanders" [JCS, *Emergency Action Procedures, Vol. I*, 1 April 1984, pp. 1-16–17, released under the FOIA, emphasis added]. **2.** "The NCA consists only of the President and the Secretary of Defense or their duly deputized alternates or successors. The chain of command runs from the President to the Secretary of Defense and through the Joint Chiefs of Staff to the commanders of Unified and Specified Commands. The channel of communication for execution of the Single Integrated Operational Plan (SIOP) and other time-sensitive operations shall be *from the NCA* through the Chairman of the Joint Chiefs of Staff, representing the Joint Chiefs of Staff, to the executing commanders" [*World-Wide Military Command and Control System*, DOD Directive 5100.30, 2 December 1971, with change 1, pp. 1–2, emphasis added].

After the assassination attempt against President Reagan in 1981, a memo was sent from DOD General Counsel William H. Taft IV to Richard Hauser, Deputy Counsel to the President, on 31 March 1981, about the NCA, stating

> The term National Command Authority (NCA) refers to those persons with the authority to command or direct the activities of the Armed Forces of the United States. The NCA consists only of the President and the Secretary of Defense or their duly deputized alternates or successors. The chain of command runs from the President, who at all times is the Commander-in-Chief of the Armed Forces under the Constitution, directly to the Secretary of Defense who, subject to the direction of the President, has authority over the Department of Defense and its component Armed Services.
>
> In case of the death or inability of the President to discharge the powers and duties of his office, the order of succession to the Presidency is as prescribed in the 20th and 25th Amendments to the Constitution and the implementing legislation codified at 3 U.S.C., Section 19. Whoever may succeed to the Presidency pursuant to these provisions of law and the Constitution becomes the Commander-in-Chief and simultaneously a part of the National Command Authority. At all times during March 30, 1981, Secretary of Defense Weinberger exercised authority over the activities of the Department of Defense and its component Armed Services subject to the direction of President Reagan. . . .

Some confusion over the NCA and the chain of **operational command** was clarified in the **Department of Defense Reorganization Act of 1986**. As a result of the act, NSDD-281, "United States Nuclear Weapons Command and Control," 21 August 1987, was signed, creating new procedures for the control of nuclear weapons and establishing the **Nuclear Command and Control System**.

The NCA dates from a National Security Council document, "United States Policy on Atomic Weapons," 10 September 1948, which states that "the decision as to the employment of atomic weapons in the event of war is to be made by the Chief Executive [the President] when he considers such decision to be required" [J. L. Gaddis and T. Etzold, *Containment: Documents on American Policy and Strategy, 1945–1950*, New York: Columbia University Press, 1978]. (see also **National Military Command System**)

National Communications System (NCS): Established on 21 August 1963, the NCS provides "a centrally planned, programmed and operational federal government telecommunications system that would be responsive to the federal government's needs under all conditions ranging from normal situations to national emergencies and international crises including nuclear attack" [NCS, *Organization and Functions*, September 1982, p. 1; White House, Memorandum to the Heads of Executive Departments and Agencies, *Subject: Establishment of the NCS*, 21 August 1963].

The NCS consists of the **Defense Communications System (DCS)** and selected telecommunications assets from the **Department of State**, the **Federal Aviation Administration**, the **National Aeronautics and Space Administration**, the General Services

Administration, the Department of the Interior, the Federal Communications Commission, the Department of Commerce, the U.S. Information Agency, and the **Department of Energy**. The NCS plans, allocates, restores, reallocates, and reconstitutes these systems, each operated and funded by its respective agency, for and during national emergencies. The Secretary of Defense, as the Executive Agent and director of the Defense Communications Agency (DCA), serves as the NCS manager.

In 1979, President Carter's directive PD-53 on national security telecommunications policies increased the role of the NCS. Capital improvements in parts of the NCS, or augmentations to support **continuity of government**, have included a **Federal Emergency Management Agency** network of high-frequency, long-range radio stations (e.g., the Northeast Regional Communication System) and **meteor burst communications**.

national defense area (NDA): The temporary establishment within the United States of "federal areas" for the protection or security of DOD resources. Normally, NDAs are established for emergency situations such as accidents. NDAs may be established, discontinued, or their boundaries changed as necessary to provide protection for or security of DOD resources. Commanders of major commands or installations have the authority to establish NDAs. [Air Force, *Disaster Preparedness: Planning and Operations,* AFR 355-1, 17 November 1986, p. 86, released under the FOIA]. "The land owner's consent and cooperation will be obtained whenever possible; however, military necessity will dictate the final decision regarding location, shape, and size of the NDA" [DNA, *Nuclear Weapon Accident Response Procedures (NARP) Manual*, January 1984, p. 157, released under the FOIA]. (see also **national security area**)

National Defense University (NDU): Joint service school, established 16 January 1976, from the recommendations of the DOD Committee on Excellence in Education. The NDU operates under the direction of the Joint Chiefs of Staff and is composed of three senior-level educational institutions:

- National War College, Ft. McNair, Washington, DC, 20319;
- Industrial College of the Armed Forces, Ft. McNair, Washington, DC, 20319; and
- Armed Forces Staff College, Norfolk, VA, 23511.

National Emergencies Act: Congressional act signed into law on 14 September 1976 (PL 94-412, 50 U.S. C. §§ 1601–1651). It outlines specific requirements regarding the exercise of Presidential powers in **national emergencies**.

- *Sec. 1601*: Terminated "all powers and authorities" that existed as a result of declared emergencies, effective 14 September 1978.
- *Sec. 1621*: Regarding acts of Congress authorizing the exercise of any special or extraordinary power during the period of a national emergency, the President is authorized to declare such national emergency.

Congress is to be notified immediately of such a declaration as it is to be printed in the *Federal Register*.

- *Sec. 1622*: Termination of emergencies; Congress, by concurrent resolution, may terminate any national emergency declared by the President. The President, by proclamation, may also terminate such an emergency. Congress will conduct a review of the emergency within six months of its declaration and every six months thereafter for its possible termination.
- *Sec. 1631*: The legal basis for powers and authorities exercised in a declared national emergency must be stated in advance of the actions, either in the declaration or in one or more executive orders transmitted to Congress and published in the *Federal Register*.
- *Sec. 1641*: Files and indexes of orders pertaining to national emergencies and war must be kept by the President and executive agencies; all orders, rules, and regulations of the President shall be transmitted to the Congress; expenditure reports must be submitted to the Congress.

[DOD, *Compendium of Emergency Authorities*, April 1981, released under the FOIA].

national emergency: A state of emergency declared either by the Congress or the President by which a partial, full, or total **mobilization** of the armed forces may be called for [*JCS Pub 1*, p. 243]. (see also **civil emergency**)

National Emergency Airborne Command Post (NEACP): One of five **airborne command posts** that back up land-based command centers and that could assume the command and control of strategic forces in the pre-, trans-, and post-attack phases of nuclear war. NEACP (pronounced "kneecap") is one of three **National Military Command Centers (NM-CCs)**, with the main NMCC located in the Pentagon and the **Alternate National Military Command Center** located at Raven Rock, PA. When the **National Command Authorities** are on board, NEACP operates as the primary control center and JCS and Secretary of Defense battle-station, providing a war-fighting capability not provided by **Air Force One**. Unlike Air Force One, NEACP also has the ability to transmit **emergency action messages** and is a component of the **Minimum Essential Emergency Communications Network**. Once airborne, NEACP can stay aloft for up to 72 hours.

NEACP consists of four Boeing **E-4B** aircraft converted from Boeing 747 commercial planes. The E-4Bs are divided into six functional areas: command work area, conference room, briefing room, battlestaff work area, communications control center, and a rest area. The communications control center contains data and voice areas with access to the **Worldwide Military Command and Control System**, including **AUTODIN, AFSAT-COM, Nuclear Detonation Detection System** consoles and LF/VLF control leads. The LF/VLF system includes a five-mile-long trailing-wire antenna that is unreeled through the rear fuselage floor to transmit a message. Through it, NEACP can link with **TACAMO** and **EC-135** airborne command post aircraft used by SAC's **Post Attack Command and Control System**. Transmissions received through the **Defense Satellite Communications System** give the President the capability to communicate from his airborne command post via SHF **satellite communications** channels worldwide. The communication systems also include HF, MF, VHF, and UHF band two-way radio channels. Modifications include adding **Ground-Wave Emergency Network** and **MILSTAR** receive capabilities.

The aircraft are assigned to the 1st Airborne Command and Control Squadron at Offutt AFB, NE, with a forward detachment at Grissom AFB, IN. The alert force aboard the aircraft consists of a JCS joint service operations team, a SAC flight crew, a maintenance crew, security forces, and a communications team from the **Air Force Communications Command**. The E-4B is also known as the Advanced Airborne Command Post (AABNCP) or the "Doomsday plane." The JCS codename for NEACP is Night Watch.

National Foreign Intelligence Board (NFIB): A body formed to provide the **Director of Central Intelligence** with advice concerning production, review, and coordination of foreign intelligence. It is composed of representatives of the **intelligence community.** (see also **satellite reconnaissance**, **National Intelligence Estimate**)

National Foreign Intelligence Program (NFIP): A portion of the government budget consisting of the programs of the Central Intelligence Agency, the Consolidated Cryptologic Program, the General Defense Intelligence Program, and other national **intelligence** and **counterintelligence** activities.

National Guard (NG): The armed militia of the 50 U.S. states, Puerto Rico, the District of Colombia, and the Virgin Islands. NG missions include disaster and emergency assistance, **civil disturbance** control, and drug eradication and interdiction. Operational control of the NG is exercised by State Adjutant Generals reporting to the Governor. Each state's Guard serves a dual function as a component of the federal reserves, as part of the **Army National Guard** and **Air National Guard**. In case of federal mobilization, the state functions of the National Guard may be assumed by **State Defense Forces**.

National Guard Bureau (NGB): A joint Bureau of the Departments of the Army and Air Force created in 1908 as the Division of Militia Affairs and redesignated the NGB in 1933. It is responsible for the federal functions and missions of the **Air National Guard** and the **Army National Guard**. The Chief, NGB, is appointed by the President and reports to the Secretaries of the Army and Air Force.

Headquarters
Pentagon
Washington, DC 20310-2500

National Intelligence Estimate (NIE): A thorough national-level intelligence assessment of a specific situation, written for the purpose of providing a prediction of future courses. A NIE is structured to illuminate differences of view within the **intelligence community.** NIEs are issued by the **Director of Central Intelligence** with the advice of the **National Foreign Intelligence Board**. They are prepared by teams working for National Intelligence Officers (NIOs) who are located at the Central Intelligence Agency. (see also **Special National Intelligence Estimate**)

National Military Command Center (NMCC):   One of the four **National Command Authority (NCA)** command centers. Established in October 1962 when the Joint War Room was designated as an NMCC resource, this Pentagon facility serves as the day-to-day center of command for the highest level of military authority within the Joint Chiefs of Staff. Prior to 1962, the JCS shared the Air Force command post facilities in the basement of the Pentagon.

The NMCC is the primary military command center supporting the NCA in the operational direction of the U.S. Armed Forces. To accomplish its mission, the NMCC is staffed by a highly qualified OT [operations team] on a 24-hour-a-day basis to monitor the worldwide situation, report significant activities, and take necessary actions as directed by the NCA, Joint Chiefs of Staff and Joint Staff. The NMCC is supervised by a DDO, a general/flag officer, who represents the Director of Operations, Joint Staff. During the development of a crisis situation, the NMCC becomes the focal point for crisis-related matters and assumes certain responsibilities in addition to normal daily activities [JCS, *Crisis Staffing Procedures of the Joint Chiefs of Staff*, SM-481-83, 12 July 1983, pp. 1-2–1-3, released under the FOIA].

The NMCC has direct communications links with the White House Situation Room, the State Department, and NATO military forces worldwide. It contains the Washington terminal of the **Direct Communications Link (DCL)** (the "hotline") with the Soviet Union and is adjacent to the **National Military Intelligence Center**. The NMCC is also the national-level element of the **Worldwide Military Command and Control System (WWMCCS)**. In wartime, the JCS would likely disperse to airborne command posts or the **Alternate National Military Command Center** located at Raven Rock, PA.

National Military Command System (NMCS):   Created in May 1963, NMCS consists of the national-level command centers and the communications that link them to intelligence systems and other subordinate command centers. It is the priority component of the **Worldwide Military Command and Control System (WWMCCS)**, designed to support the **National Command Authorities (NCA)** and the JCS in the direction of military forces under all conditions of peace and war, including providing the NCA with the capability to command strategic forces during national crises. DOD Directive 5100.30 states that "since survival of the command and control capability of NMCS is fundamental to **continuity of operations,** a composite command structure with survivable communications is required.

This includes the **National Military Command Center**, the **Alternate National Military Command Center** [which can take full control of operations], the **National Emergency Airborne Command Post** and such other command centers as may be designated by the Secretary of Defense" (such as a mobile command center at Island Sun). NMCS also includes the communications systems linking the command centers to the headquarters of the **combatant commanders**, Service headquarters, and other agencies and commands supported via WWMCCS. [DOD, *Worldwide Military Command and Control System*, 2 December 1971, released under the FOIA].

The four national command centers are emergency operating locations supporting the NCA. **PAVE PAWS** SLBM radars and **Defense Support Program** early-warning satellites send simultaneous data directly to all four centers. Alternative ground and mobile command centers and airborne command posts also send information to the NCA centers:

- **National Military Command Center (NMCC)**;
- **Alternate National Military Command Center (ANMCC)**;
- **NORAD Cheyenne Mountain Complex (NCMC)**; and
- **SAC Command Post**.

National Military Establishment (NME): Predecessor agency of the **Department of Defense** created by the **National Security Act of 1947**.

National Photographic Interpretation Center (NPIC): Facility operated by the Central Intelligence Agency and charged with imagery analysis of satellite reconnaissance. (see also **keyhole**)

Headquarters
Washington Navy Yard,
Washington, DC 20003

National Reconnaissance Office (NRO): National-level **intelligence** organization with management responsibility for U.S. **satellite reconnaissance** programs, including the routine operation of satellites and satellite systems security. The NRO was established 25 August 1960 in response to the failures of the first missile and satellite programs (including the 1960 shootdown of an Air Force/CIA U-2 over the Soviet Union). Its predecessor organization was the Directorate of Advanced Technology within the office of the Air Force Chief of Staff. The first satellite system to be handled by the office was the Air Force's SAMOS program. The existence of the office is not acknowledged by the DOD, but it is believed to operate under the "cover" of the Under Secretary of the Air Force and the Office of Space Systems. Its existence was mistakenly revealed in a Congressional report in 1973, but it is still considered a **black program**. It consists of the Special Projects Office (Air Force), a CIA component headed by the Deputy Director for Science and Technology, and a naval component within the Space and Sensor Systems Program Directorate of the Naval Space and Warfare Command. It reports to the National Reconnaissance Executive Committee. Its Director is usually the Under Secretary of the Air Force.

Its Deputy Director is an Air Force civilian official. The NRO staff director is usually an Air Force Brigadier General. The NRO's annual budget is believed to be in the $3–4 billion range. [Jeffrey Richelson, *U.S. Intelligence Community*, 2d ed., pp. 26-9]. (see also **Corona, keyhole**)

Headquarters
Pentagon, Washington, DC 20301

national security: "A collective term encompassing both national defense and foreign relations of the United States. Specifically, the condition provided by: a. a military or defense advantage over any foreign nation or group of nations, or b. a favorable foreign relations position, or c. a defense posture capable of successfully resisting hostile or destructive action from within or without, overt or covert" [*JCS Pub 1*, p. 244].

National Security Action Memorandum (NSAM): Presidential directives issued by Presidents Kennedy and Johnson. Kennedy NSAMs include establishing greater police assistance programs in less developed countries and authorizing logistical support to the Congo for contingency purposes. While President Kennedy issued 273 NSAMs, President Johnson issued only about 99. Many of Johnson's NSAMs dealt with operations in the Vietnam war. (see also **National Security Decision Directive, National Security Decision Memoranda, National Security Directive**)

National Security Act of 1947: Congressional act signed into law on 26 July 1947 (5 U.S.C. §§ 101, 102, 5312(3), 5313(16–18), 5315(7–

9, 14–16); 10 USC §§ 101(5,7), 131–33, 141, 143, 171, 718, 743, 3011, 3012, 3062, 5012, 5013, 8011–13; 50 USC §§ 401–5, 409–11). It created the National Military Establishment (NME) composed of the **Department of the Army**, the **Department of the Navy**, an independent **Department of the Air Force** (all separately administered executive departments); a **Secretary of Defense**, the **Joint Chiefs of Staff** (with a **Joint Staff** of 100 officers); the **Central Intelligence Agency** (50 USC § 403); and the **National Security Council**. The stated intent of this establishment was "To promote the national security . . . and for the coordination of the activities of the National Military Establishment with other departments and agencies of the Government concerned with the national security." It was amended by the **National Security Act of 1949**.

National Security Act of 1949: Congressional amendment to the **National Security Act of 1947**, signed into law 10 August 1949 (various sections of 5 U.S.C., 10 U.S.C., and 50 U.S.C.). It was intended to mandate more forcefully the cooperation, unity, and flexibility of the separate military departments. To that end, the National Military Establishment was redesignated the **Department of Defense**; the executive military departments were redesignated as subordinate military departments; and an **Office of the Secretary of Defense** was mandated. The act also included the Vice President as a member of the **National Security Council**, increased the powers of the Secretary of Defense, established the position of the **Chairman of the Joint Chiefs of Staff**, increased the personnel strength of the **Joint Staff** from 100 to 210 officers, and created the offices of Comptroller and Deputy Comptroller in the service departments.

National Security Advisor: The Assistant to the President for National Security Affairs, responsible for the daily operations of the **National Security Council**.

Assistants to the President for National Security Affairs

Robert Cutler	1953–1955
Dillon Anderson	1955–1956
William A. Jackson (acting)	1956
Robert Cutler	1957–1958
Gordon Gray	1958–1961
McGeorge Bundy	1961–1966
Walt W. Rostow	1966–1969
Henry A. Kissinger	1969–1975
Brent Scowcroft	1975–1977
Zbigniew Brzezinski	1977–1981
Richard V. Allen	1981–1982
William P. Clark	1982–1983
Robert C. McFarlane	1983–1985
John M. Poindexter	1985–1986
Frank C. Carlucci	1986–1987
Colin L. Powell	1987–1989
Brent Scowcroft	1989–present

National Security Agency/Central Security Service (NSA/CSS): One of 13 agencies of the **Department of Defense**, established 5 December 1952 from the Armed Forces Security Agency. The statutory basis for its composition, mission, and functions are the National Security Agency Act of 1959 (50 U.S.C. § 402 note). Its primary missions, as outlined in National Security Council Intelligence Directive 6 (17 January 1972), are national level **signals intelligence (SIGINT)** and **communications security (COMSEC)**. The Director, NSA (DIRNSA), also develops and approves all U.S. government **cryptographic** systems and techniques and acts as liaison with foreign governments and international intelligence organizations. The Central Security Service (CSS) was established in 1971 as a separate service functioning under the command of NSA. CSS is responsible for the supervision of all **Service Cryptological Authorities (SCAs)** (the **Army Intelligence and Security Command**, the Air Force **Electronics Security Command**, and the **Naval Security Group Command**).

In its SIGINT role, NSA has **operational control** over the worldwide network of electronic listening posts and the land-based, ship-based, and airborne collection systems. Its functions include

- Coordination of telecommunications requirements in support of the U.S. SIGINT system with the Defense Communications Agency, the JCS, the military services, and the commanders of the unified and specified commands;
- Validation of circuit requirements for the **Critical Intelligence Communications System (CRITICOMM)**, including appropriate Defense Special Security Communications System (DSSCS) access lines to **AUTODIN** switching centers;
- Development and promulgation of the DSSCS operating instructions; and
- Assignment of routing indicators

for the integrated activities of the AUTODIN/DSSCS.

[JCS, *Joint Operation Planning System, Volume II (Supplementary Planning Guidance)*, SM-142-85, 22 March 1985, p. K-6, released under the FOIA].

SIGINT operations are conducted by the Office of Signals Intelligence Operations. Its activities are geographically divided into four areas: Group A (Soviet Union and Eastern Europe), Group B (China, Korea, Vietnam, and communist Asia), Group G (all other nations), and Group W (space SIGINT). Subordinate to Group W is the **Defense Special Missile and Astronautics Center (DEFSMAC)** (which receives intelligence regarding) Soviet, Chinese, and other foreign space and missile launches and transmits such knowledge to monitoring systems including **COBRA BALL** aircraft) and the National Telemetry Processing Center (NTPC), which processes electronic signals intelligence obtained from Soviet, Chinese, and foreign missile test flights. The SIGINT office also operates the National SIGINT Operations Center (NSOC), which directs SIGINT activities in crisis situations and serves as an **indication & warning** center.

In its COMSEC role, the NSA authorizes and manages the communications procedures and codes used by government agencies including the Departments of Defense and State, the Defense Intelligence Agency, and the Federal Bureau of Investigation, as well as those used by the President in crisis situations. It also manages the security for codes for strate-gic weapons systems such as the MX and Minuteman. Additionally, NSA's COMSEC role was expanded in September 1984 to include the management of **information security (INFOSEC)** for all national automated information systems, including the computer and data banks of some 1,000 federal offices, departments, and agencies. COMSEC and computer security functions are managed through the Office of Information Security. Guidance is provided by the Systems Security Steering Group, a senior-level policy group consisting of the Secretaries of State, Transportation, and Defense, the Attorney General, the Directors of the Office of Management and Budget, the Central Intelligence Agency, and the Assistant to the President for National Security Affairs (the National Security Advisor). Subordinate to the steering group is the operational interagency National Telecommunications and Information Systems Security Committee (NTISSC)—which consists of a telecommunications subcommittee and an automated information systems security subcommittee—and the National Computer Security Center, which focuses on industry computer security.

Supervision of the NSA/CSS staff is provided by the office of the Assistant Secretary of Defense (Command, Control, Communications, and Intelligence). NSA/CSS personnel strength is believed to be approximately 20,000–24,000. Its total budget is thought to be in the $3 billion range.

Headquarters
Ft. Meade, MD 20755

Directors of the National Security Agency/Central Security Service

LTG Ralph J. Canine, USA	Jul 1951	Nov 1956
Lt GEN John A. Samford, USAF	Nov 1956	Nov 1960
VADM Laurence H. Frost, USN	Nov 1960	Jun 1962
Lt GEN Gordon A. Blake, USAF	Jul 1962	May 1965
LTG Marshall S. Carter, USA	Jun 1965	Jul 1969
VADM Noel Gayler, USN	Aug 1969	Aug 1972
Lt GEN Samuel C. Phillips, USAF	Aug 1972	Jul 1973
Lt GEN Lew Allen, Jr., USAF	Aug 1973	Jul 1977
VADM Bobby R. Inman, USN	Jul 1977	Mar 1981
Lt GEN Lincoln D. Faurer, USAF	Apr 1981	Apr 1985
LTG William E. Odom, USA	May 1985	Jul 1988
VADM William O. Studeman, USN	Aug 1988	present

NSA Offices

- Director's Staff (D Group)
- Inspector General (I Group)
- General Counsel (U Group)
- Legislative Affairs (J Group)
- Office of Programs and Resources (N Group)
- Office of Plans and Policy (Q Group)
- Office of Signals Intelligence Operations (P Group)
- Office of Research and Engineering (R Group)
- Office of Information Security (S Group)
- Office of Telecommunications and Computer Services (T Group)
- Office of Installations and Logistics (L Group)
- Office of Administration (M Group)

national security area (NSA): "An area established on non-Federal lands located within the United States, its possessions, or Territories, for the purpose of safeguarding classified and/or restricted data information, or protecting DOE [Department of Energy] equipment and/or material. Establishment of an NSA temporarily places such non-Federal lands under the effective control of the DOE and results only from an emergency event. The senior DOE representative having custody of the material at the scene will define the boundary, mark it with a physical barrier, and post warning signs. The landowner's consent and cooperation will be obtained whenever possible; however, operational necessity will dictate the final decision regarding location, shape, and size" [DNA, *Nuclear Weapon Accident Response Procedures (NARP) Manual,* January 1984, p. 157, released under the FOIA]. (see also **national defense area**)

National Security Council (NSC): An advisory body within the Executive office of the President, created by the **National Security Act of 1947**, 26 July 1947. Its mission, as stated in 50 U.S.C. § 402, is to provide advice to the President "with respect to the integration of domestic, foreign, and military policies relating to the national security so as to enable the military services and the other departments and agencies of the Government to cooperate more effectively in matters involving the national security." Its statutory functions are

1. To assess and appraise the objective, commitments, and risks of the United States in relation to our actual and potential military power, in the interest of national security, for the purpose of making recommendations to the President on connection therewith.
2. To consider policies on matters of common interest to the departments and agencies of the Government concerned with the national security, and to make recommendations to the President in connection therewith.

The four statutory members of the NSC are the President, Vice President, the Secretary of State, and the **Secretary of Defense**. Statutory advisors to the NSC are the **Chairman of the Joint Chiefs of Staff**, and the **Director of Central Intelligence**. Daily operation of the NSC is the responsibility of the Assistant to the President for National Security Affairs (the **National Security Advisor**), who also attends NSC meetings. Others who attend, as invited by the President, have included the Directors of the U.S. Arms Control and Disarmament Agency and the U.S. Information Agency.

The organization of the NSC has undergone many changes since its conception. Recently, under the Reagan Administration, its structure consisted of Senior Interdepartmental Groups (SIGs) and Interdepartmental Groups (IGs), created to support the NSC. Six SIGs were created: Defense Policy (SIG-DP), Foreign Policy (SIG-FP), Emergency Planning (SIG-EP), Intelligence (SIG-I), International Economic Policy (SIG-IEP), and Senior Arms Control Policy Group (SACPG). Each SIG included representatives from the Departments of Defense and State, the CIA, and the NSC staff, plus invited individuals who have expertise on specific matters under consideration. IGs were established under SIGs to consider issues in greater detail and to prepare papers for SIG review. In addition, on 12 January 1982, the Special Situation Group (SSG) was established under Vice President Bush to be specifically in charge of crisis management. The SSG was assisted by the Crisis Pre-Planning Group (CPPG), a working-level body monitoring crises throughout the world. Toward the end of the Administration, changes in organization (influenced by the Tower Commission) included the addition of an office of NSC Legal Adviser and the activation of the Policy Review Group—the senior sub-Cabinet forum for interagency coordination of policy.

Today, as established by the Bush Administration in National Security Directive (NSD)-1, the council comprises three NSC Sub-Groups:

- NSC Principals Committee (NSC/PC): The senior interagency forum responsible for the review, coordination, and monitoring of national security policy. It is chaired by the President's advisor, and members are the Secretaries of Defense and State, Director of Central Intelligence, Chairman of the JCS, Chief of Staff to the President, and other participants as invited.

- NSC Deputies Committees (NSC/DC): The senior sub-Cabinet interagency forum for consideration of policy issues affecting national security. "It shall review and monitor the work of the NSC interagency process . . . and make recommendations concerning the development and implementation of national security policy." The deputy NSA assistant to the President chairs the NSC/DC. Members are the Under Secretary of Defense (Policy), the Under Secretary of State (Political Affairs), the Deputy Director of Central Intelligence, the Vice Chairman of the JCS, and other participants as invited. A representative of the Attorney General is included in meetings regarding covert actions.
- NSC Coordinating Committees (NSC/PCC): Regional or functional committees acting as "the principal interagency forum for the development and implementation of national security policy" for their area. Regional NSC/PCCs, chaired by the Secretary of State, are Europe, Soviet Union, Latin America, East Asia, Africa, and Near East/South Asia. Functional committees are: defense (chaired by the Secretary of Defense), international economics (chaired by the Secretary of the Treasury), intelligence (chaired by the Director of Central Intelligence), and arms control (chaired by the Assistant to the President for National Security Affairs). Members are representatives at the Assistant Secretary level. The interagency NSC/PCCs may receive tasking from the NSC/DC.

Presidential national security decision documents (named differently by each administration) have included: **Presidential Directives**/National Security Council (PD/NSC) (Carter Administration), **National Security Decision Memorandums (NSDMs)** (Nixon and Ford Administrations), **National Security Decision Directives (NSDDs)** (Reagan Administration), **National Security Action Memorandums (NSAMs)** (Kennedy and Johnson Administrations), and **Executive Orders (EOs)** (various administrations). The presidential directives of the Bush Administration are called **National Security Directives (NSDs)**. The NSC staff, which supports the NSC assistant, is headed by a civilian executive secretary, and comprises approximately 60 personnel.

Headquarters
Washington, DC 20506

National Security Decision Directive (NSDD): Presidential national security directive of the Reagan Administration. The NSDD replaced the term **Presidential Directive** used during the Carter Administration. National Security Council initiatives were put forth as National Security Study Directives to present policy options for consideration. Once approved by the President, specific directives are implemented through the National Security Council (NSC) to other government operations, most commonly the Departments of Defense, State, and Treasury, and the CIA and the Arms Control and Disarmament Agency. NSDDs vary in length from 1 to 15 pages and cover no specific time period unless so stated. President Reagan issued about 300 NSDDs, most of which were in the form of policy papers or summaries rather than memoranda.

National Security Decision Directives

NSDD-1   National Security Council Directives. 25 February 1981. Revised 17 December 1981.

NSDD-2   National Security Council Structure. 12 January 1981.

NSDD-3   Crisis Management—Special Situation Group. 1981.

NSDD-4   Creation of Contras to interdict supplies. 9 March 1981.

NSDD-5   Conventional Arms Transfer Policy. 8 July 1981.

NSDD-6   United States Non-Proliferation and Peaceful Nuclear Cooperation Policy. 16 July 1981. Funding in support of NSDD-6 (Confidential). July 1983.

NSDD-8   Space Transportation System Policy. 1 October 1981.

NSDD-11 subject unknown (Secret). Date unknown.

NSDD-12 Strategic Forces Modernization Program. 1 October 1981.

NSDD-13 Nuclear Weapons Employment Policy. October 1981. Funding for NSDD-13 (Top Secret). December 1981.

NSDD-14 Scientific Communication and National Security. 23 December 1981.

NSDD-16 Economic and Security Decisions for Libya. 15 December 1981.

NSDD-17 Deterring Cuban Models/Covert Action in Nicaragua. 23 November 1981.

NSDD-18 subject unknown (Secret). January 1982.

NSDD-19 Protection of Classified National Security Council and Intelligence Information. 12 January 1982.

NSDD-20 subject unknown (Secret). January/February 1982.

NSDD-22 Designation of Intelligence Officials Authorized to Request FBI Collection of Foreign Intelligence. 29 January 1982.

NSDD-23 Civil Defense. 3 February 1982.

NSDD-24 subject unknown (Secret). February 1982.

NSDD-25 Preparations for the Economic and NATO Summits, [of] June 1982. 12 February 1982.

NSDD-26 U.S. Civil Defense Policy. 16 March 1982. This is almost the same as NSDD-23 but is the unclassified version. NSDD-47 states that NSDD-26 is Secret and dated 26 February 1982.

NSDD-27 subject unknown (Secret). March 1982.

NSDD-28 subject unknown (Secret). March/April 1982.

NSDD-29 Nuclear Weapons Stockpile Memorandum FY 1983–87. 17 March 1982.

NSDD-74 subject unknown (Secret). January 1983.

NSDD-75 Strategy Regarding Soviet Union/Covert Operation. 19 January 1983.

NSDD-76 subject unknown (Secret). January 1983.

NSDD-77 Management of Public Diplomacy Relative to National Security. 14 January 1983.

NSDD-79 subject unknown (Secret). February 1983.

NSDD-80 Shuttle Orbiter Production Capability. 3 February 1983.

NSDD-81 DOE's Role in Nuclear Test Monitoring and Verification. February 1983.

NSDD-83 subject unknown (Confidential). March 1983.

NSDD-84 Safeguarding National Security Information. 11 March 1983.

NSDD-85 Eliminating the Threat from Ballistic Missiles. 25 March 1983.

NSDD-86 subject unknown (Secret). March 1983.

NSDD-87 subject unknown (Top Secret). April 1983.

NSDD-88 subject unknown (Confidential). April 1983.

NSDD-89 Export Administration Act. 5 April 1983.

NSDD-90 United States Arctic Policy. 14 April 1983.

NSDD-91 ICBM Guidance/Penaids. April 1983.

NSDD-92 subject unknown (Secret). April 1983.

NSDD-93 Refugee Policy and Processing Refugees from Indochina. 13 May 1983.

NSDD-94 Commercialization of Expendable Launch Vehicles. 16 May 1983.

NSDD-95 subject unknown (Secret). May 1983.

NSDD-97 National Security Telecommunications Policy. 3 August 1983.

NSDD-99 Lebanon (Top Secret). July 1983.

NSDD-100 Enhanced U.S. Military Activity and Assistance for the Central American Region. 28 July 1983.

NSDD-102 U.S. Response to Soviet Destruction of KAL Airliner. 5 September 1983.

NSDD-103 subject unknown (Secret). September 1983.

NSDD-104 subject unknown (Top Secret). September 1983.

NSDD-105 subject unknown (Top Secret). October 1983.

NSDD-107 subject unknown (Secret). October 1983.

NSDD-109 subject unknown (Top Secret). October 1983.

NSDD-110 U.S. Troops to Grenada. 23 October 1983.

NSDD-111 Middle East Policy. 29 October 1983.

NSDD-112 subject unknown (Top Secret). November 1983.

NSDD-113 Radio Telephone COMSEC Government Limousines. November 1983, possibly March 1984?

NSDD-114 subject unknown (Top Secret). November 1983.

NSDD-115 subject unknown (Secret). November 1983.

NSDD-116 SDI, Congressional and Allied Consultation. 2 December 1983.

NSDD-117 subject unknown (Top Secret). December 1983.

NSDD-118 subject unknown (Confidential). December 1983.

NSDD-119 Strategic Defense Initiative. 6 January 1984.

NSDD-120 subject unknown (Secret). January 1984.

NSDD-121 subject unknown (Secret). January 1984.

NSDD-122 subject unknown (Secret). January 1984.

NSDD-123 Nuclear Weapons Stockpile Memorandum FY 1984–89. 16 February 1984.

NSDD-124 U.S. Objectives in Central America and Mexico. February/March 1984.

NSDD-125 subject unknown (Secret). March 1984.

NSDD-126 subject unknown (Secret). February 1984.

NSDD-127 Strategic Policy. February 1984.

NSDD-129 subject unknown (Top Secret). March 1984.

NSDD-130 International Communications Policy. 9 March 1984.

NSDD-131 subject unknown (Secret). March 1984.

NSDD-132 subject unknown (Unclassified). March 1984.

NSDD-133 subject unknown (Secret). March 1984.

NSDD-134 subject unknown (Secret). April 1984.

NSDD-135 subject unknown (Top Secret). April 1984.

NSDD-136 subject unknown (Secret). April 1984.

NSDD-137 subject unknown (Secret). April 1984.

NSDD-138 Counterterrorism. 3 April 1984.

NSDD-140 subject unknown (Secret). April 1984.

NSDD-? Improving U.S. posture to respond to developments in the Iran/Iraq War. May 1984.

NSDD-? U.S. policy to keep Strait of Hormuz open. June 1984.

NSDD-142 subject unknown (Confidential). July 1984.

NSDD-143 U.S. Third World Hunger Relief: Emergency Assistance. 9 July 1984.

NSDD-144 National Space Strategy/ Shuttle. 15 August 1984.

NSDD-145 National Policy on Telecommunications and Automated Information Systems Security. 17 September 1984.

NSDD-147 subject unknown (Secret). October 1984.

NSDD-150 subject unknown (Secret). December 1984.

NSDD-151 subject unknown (Secret). December 1984.

NSDD-? Terrorism. Date unknown.

NSDD-? Training Lebanese Units v. Terrorists. November 1984.

NSDD-155 subject unknown (Secret). January 1985.

NSDD-156 U.S. Third World Food Aid: A Food For Progress Program. 3 January 1985.

NSDD-157 Rules for covert actions. 14 January 1985.

NSDD-158 subject unknown (Secret). January 1985.

NSDD-159 Covert Action Policy Approval and Coordination Procedures. 18 January 1985.

NSDD-160 subject unknown (Secret). January 1985.

NSDD-161 subject unknown (Special Access). February 1985.

NSDD-162 subject unknown (Secret). February 1985.

NSDD-163 subject unknown (Secret). February 1985.

NSDD-? Nuclear Weapons Stockpile Memorandum FY 1985–90. February 1985.

NSDD-164 National Security Launch Strategy. 25 February 1985.

NSDD-? Arms Control Geneva Talks. March 1985.

NSDD-166 U.S. Support to Afghan Rebels. April 1985.

NSDD-167 Food For Progress Program Implementation. 29 April 1985.

NSDD-168 U.S. Policy Towards North Africa. 30 April 1985.

NSDD-169 Nuclear weapons (Secret restricteddata).May1985.

NSDD-? Draft NSDD by Oliver North on selling arms to Iran. Rejected. June 1985.

NSDD-170 Nuclear weapons (Top Secret restricted data). May 1985.

NSDD-171 Nuclear weapons (Secret restricted data). June 1985.

NSDD-172 Strategic Defense Initiative Fact Sheet. 1 June 1985.

NSDD-173 Soviet Violations of Arms Control and Other Treaties. 10 June 1985.

NSDD-174 Nuclear weapons (Secret restricted data). 12 June 1985.

NSDD-175 Establishment of a Blue Ribbon Commission on Defense Management. 17 June 1985.

NSDD-177 Southern Africa. August 1985.

NSDD-178 Strategic Policy Creating the Air Defense Initiative. July 1985.

NSDD-179 Vice President's Task Force on Combating Terrorism. 20 July 1985.

NSDD-180 Nuclear weapons (Secret restricted data). July 1985.

NSDD-181 Space Shuttle Pricing Policy. 1 August 1985.

NSDD-185 subject unknown (Unclassified). September 1985.

NSDD-186 subject unknown (Unclassified). September 1985.

NSDD-187 subject unknown (Unclassified). September 1985.

NSDD-188 Government Coordination for National Security Emergency Planning. 20 September 85.

NSDD-189 National Policy on the Transfer of Scientific, Technical and Engineering Information. 21 September 1985.

NSDD-191 Nuclear Weapons Deployment Authorizations. October 1985.

NSDD-192 SDI/Narrow Interpreta-

tion of ABM Treaty. 12
October 1985.
NSDD-193 Nuclear weapons (Secret
restricted data). October
1985.
NSDD-194 Nuclear weapons (Secret
restricted data). October
1985.
NSDD-196 Counterintelligence/Coun-
termeasure Implementa-
tion Task Force. 1 Nov-
ember 1985.
NSDD-197 Reporting Hostile Contacts and Security Aware-
ness. 1 November 1985.
NSDD-201 National Security Emergency Preparedness Tele-
communications Funding.
17 December 1985.
NSDD-202 Arms Control and Test
Ban Violations. Decem-
ber 1985.
NSDD-203 Nuclear weapons (Secret restricted data). December 1985.
NSDD-204 Nuclear weapons (Secret restricted data). December 1985.
NSDD-205 subject unknown (Un-
classified). January 1986.
NSDD-206 subject unknown (Secret).
January 1986.
NSDD-207 Protection of Spouse of
Foreign Heads of State.
20 January 1986.
NSDD-208 subject unknown (Secret).
February 1986.
NSDD-209 subject unknown (Con-
fidential). February
1986.
NSDD-211 subject unknown (Secret).
March 1986.
NSDD-212 subject unknown (Secret).
February 1986.

NSDD-213 subject unknown (Secret).
February 1986.
NSDD-215 subject unknown (Secret).
February 1986.
NSDD-216 Counterintelligence. 10
March 1986.
NSDD-? Nuclear Weapons Stock-
pile Memorandum FY
1986–91. 4 March 1986.
NSDD-219 Blue Ribbon Commission
on Defense Management.
1 April 1986.
NSDD-220 Narcotics and National
Security Fact Sheet. 8
April 1986.
NSDD-221 subject unknown (Secret).
April 1986.
NSDD-222 SALT Treaty. Date
unknown.
NSDD-223 subject unknown (Confi-
dential). May 1986.
NSDD-? Central America. 16 May
1986.
NSDD-225 subject unknown (Un-
classified). May 1986.
NSDD-226 subject unknown (Con-
fidential). May 1986.
NSDD-227 subject unknown (Secret).
May 1986.
NSDD-228 subject unknown (Un-
classified). May 1986.
NSDD-229 subject unknown (Secret).
June 1986.
NSDD-? Libya Covert Action. 16
August 1986.
NSDD-? Cuban Immigration. Aug-
ust 1986.
NSDD-252 subject unknown (Secret).
April 1987.
NSDD-254 United States Space
Launch Strategy. 27 De-
cember 1986.
NSDD-255 subject unknown (Top
Secret). January 1987.

NSDD-256 subject unknown (Secret). January 1987.

NSDD-257 subject unknown (Secret). February 1987.

NSDD-259 U.S. Civil Defense Policy. 4 February 1987.

NSDD-260 subject unknown (Secret). February 1987.

NSDD-261 Resolving Conflict between the ABM Treaty and SDI. February 1987.

NSDD-263 subject unknown (Secret). February 1987.

NSDD-264 subject unknown (Secret). March 1987.

NSDD-265 subject unknown (Confidential). March 1987.

NSDD-266 Implementation of the Recommendations of the President's Special Review Board. 31 March 1987.

NSDD-267 subject unknown (Secret). April 1987.

NSDD-268 subject unknown (Secret). April 1987.

NSDD-269 subject unknown (Top Secret). April 1987.

NSDD-270 subject unknown (Secret). May 1987.

NSDD-271 subject unknown (Secret). May 1987.

NSDD-272 subject unknown (Secret). May 1987.

NSDD-273 subject unknown (Secret). May 1987.

NSDD-274 subject unknown (Secret). May 1987.

NSDD-276 National Security Council Interagency Process. 9 June 1987.

NSDD-278 subject unknown (Secret). June 1987.

NSDD-280 National Airlift Policy. 24 June 1987.

NSDD-281 subject unknown (Top Secret). September 1987.

NSDD-282 subject unknown (Confidential). October 1987.

NSDD-283 subject unknown (Secret). October 1987.

NSDD-284 subject unknown (Confidential). October 1987.

NSDD-285 subject unknown (Secret). October 1987.

NSDD-286 Review of "Special Activities." August or October 1987.

NSDD-287 subject unknown (Confidential). November 1987.

NSDD-288 subject unknown (Secret). November 1987.

NSDD-289 subject unknown (Secret). November 1987.

NSDD-291 subject unknown (Secret). December 1987.

NSDD-292 subject unknown (Confidential). December 1987.

NSDD-? National Space Policy. 5 January 1988.

NSDD-298 National Operations Security Program. 22 January 1988.

[Lawrence J. Korb, "National Security Organization and Process in the Carter Administration," in *Defense Policy and the Presidency: Carter's First Years*, Sam C. Sarkesian, ed., Boulder, CO: Westview Special Studies in National Security and Defense, 1983; National Archives; People for the American Way, *Government Secrecy: Decisions Without Democracy*, Washington, DC: 1988; Paul E. Taibl, *Graduated Mobilization Response: A Key Element of National Deterrent Strategy*, MCDC Monograph, Mobilization Concepts Development Center,

Institute for National Strategic Studies, NDU: Ft. McNair, Washington, DC, April 1988; JCS Register of Papers, released under the FOIA].

National Security Decision Memorandum (NSDM): Presidential national security directive of the Nixon and Ford Administrations. NSDMs were often preceded by in-depth studies, National Security Study Memoranda, which were looked at by the **National Security Council** before producing a policy decision. At least 318 NSDMs resulted from these Memoranda. (see also **National Security Decision Directive**, **National Security Action Memoranda**, and **National Security Directive**)

*National
Security Decision Memorandums*

NSDM 3   The Direction, Coordination, and Supervision of Interdepartmental Activities Overseas.
NSDM 15   East-West Trade.
NSDM 21   Peru.
NSDM 33   Preliminary Strategic Arms Limitation Talks.
NSDM 35   United States Policy on Chemical Warfare Program and Bacteriological/Biological Research Program.
NSDM 40   Responsibility for the Conduct, Supervision, and Coordination of Covert Action Operations.
NSDM 44   United States Policy on Toxins.
NSDM 49   Preparation of Detailed SALT Options.
NSDM 51   SALT Talks.
NSDM 64   Panama Canal.

NSDM 69   Strategic Arms Limitation Talks.
NSDM 71   United States Antarctic Policy and Program.
NSDM 89   Cambodia Strategy.
NSDM 98   Coordination of Foreign Affairs Research Sponsored by the Federal Government.
NSDM 112 Country Programming.
NSDM 115 Panama Canal Treaty Negotiations.
NSDM 119 Disclosure of Classified United States Military Information to Foreign Governments and International Organizations.
NSDM 131 Panama Canal Negotiations.
NSDM 136 Policy on Cases of Expropriation.
NSDM 139 Fishing Negotiations with Chile, Ecuador, and Peru.
NSDM 143 United States International Exchange Programs.
NSDM 144 United States Arctic Policy and Arctic Policy Group.
NSDM 151 Next Steps with Respect to U.S.-Soviet Trading Relationships.
NSDM 187 Launch Assistance for Space Satellite Projects.
NSDM 189 GE-SNECMA Jet Engine Joint Venture.
NSDM 194 Fisheries Negotiations with Ecuador.
NSDM 202 Arctic Program Review and Recommendations.
NSDM 215 U.S.-Soviet Bilateral Issues.
NSDM-242 Planning Nuclear Weapons Employment for Deterrence.
NSDM 244 International Energy Review Group.

NSDM 302 Panama Canal Treaty Negotiations.
NSDM 305 Termination of U.S. Restrictions on Third Countries Trading with Cuba.
NSDM 318 U.S. Policy for Antarctica.

National Security Directive (NSD): Bush Administration term for **presidential directives** relating to national security affairs. NSD-1 was issued in April 1989 to organize the **National Security Council (NSC)** system for the Bush Administration to assist the President with his national security responsibilities. NSD-1 takes precedence over National Security Decision Directives (NSDDs) 266 and 276 and all other presidential guidance on the organization of the NSC. NSD-1 includes the following:

- The NSC shall be the principal forum for consideration of national security policy issues requiring presidential determination.
- The functions of the NSC shall be as set forth in the **National Security Act of 1947**, as amended, and by NSD-1.
- The NSC shall advise and assist the President in integrating all aspects of national security policy as it affects the United States — domestic, foreign, military, intelligence, and economic.
- Along with its subordinate bodies, the NSC will be the President's principal means for coordinating Executive departments and agencies in the development and implementation of national security policy.
- In addition to its statutory members and statutory advisors, the Chief of

Staff to the President and the Assistant to the President for National Security Affairs (the National Security Advisor) shall attend NSC meetings.
- The Secretary of the Treasury normally will attend NSC meetings except that, on occasions when the subject matter so dictates, he will be asked not to attend.
- The Attorney General will be invited to attend meetings pertaining to his jurisdiction, including covert actions.
- Heads of other Executive departments and agencies, the special statutory advisors to the NSC, and other senior officials will be invited to attend meetings of the NSC where appropriate in light of the issues to be discussed.
- The Assistant to the President for National Security Affairs shall be responsible, at the President's direction and in consultation with the Secretaries of State and Defense, for determining the agenda and ensuring that the necessary papers are prepared.
- Established within the NSC are three interagency subgroups.

national security information: General term referring to information that "requires protection in the interest of national defense or foreign relations of the United States and classified in accordance with an Executive order." National security information does not fall within the categories of **Restricted Data** or **Formerly Restricted Data**. [DOE, *Personnel Security Program*, DOE Order 5631.2, 13 November 1980, released under the FOIA]. (see also **security classification**)

National Security Telecommunications Advisory Committee (NST-AC): President's Committee established by E.O. 12382, 13 September 1982, to provide industry support to national telecommunications and to the **National Communications System**. The NSTAC consists of Chief Executive Officers from 30 of the major communications companies in the United States and it reports to the President and the Secretary of Defense.

national technical means of verification (NTM): Methods of monitoring compliance with treaty provisions, including satellites, aircraft-based systems, and sea- and ground-based data collection systems and signals intelligence systems. Use of NTMs to verify arms control treaties and an implicit agreement not to interfere with the collection of information by NTMs were agreed upon during the **SALT I** negotiations. The **SALT II** agreement provides that the sides undertake neither to interfere with the NTM of the other party nor to use **deliberate concealment** measures that impede verfication by NTM of compliance with the provisions of the agreement.

National Test Bed (NTB): Program within the Strategic Defense Initiative (SDI) to compare, evaluate, and test architectures for a layered strategic defense and its battle management. NTB is a number of geographically separated experiment facilities electronically linked to simulate a layered ballistic missile defense system. At the center is the National Test Facility, which serves as the central control

and coordinating point for the NTB as well as the major simulation point for SDI programs. The NTB is managed by a Joint Program Office reporting to the Air Force Systems Command's Electronic Systems Division and the Strategic Defense Initiative Organization.

Nationwide: White House Communications Agency–operated Presidential UHF/FM radio voice communications network incorporating 41 CONUS stations. (see also **Mystic Star**)

NATO (see **North Atlantic Treaty Organization**)

NATO Airbase SatCom Terminal System (see **NABS**)

NATO Airborne Early Warning Force (NAEWF): Major subordinate command of NATO's **Allied Command Europe**. Activated in 1980, it controls NATO's **Airborne Warning and Control System** aircraft flown by a 12-nation multilateral force. Forward bases are located in Konya, Turkey; Oerland, Norway; Preveza, Greece; and Trapani, Italy.

Headquarters
Geilenkirchen, West Germany

NATO Air Defense Ground Environment (see **NADGE**)

NATO Alert System: Set of instructions prescribed in advance by NATO's **North Atlantic Council** and **Defense Planning Committee** that trigger military responses. It is activated in times of rising tension and is similar to DOD's **Defense Readiness**

Conditions. The three components of the system are

- State of military vigilance: Used in periods of tension and for low-scale preparatory military actions by individual nations.
- Formal alert system: Simple alert, reinforced alert (both of which call for actions on the part of individual nations to prepare for and transfer forces to NATO control) and general alert (the final stage in preparations for combat).
- Countersurprise system: Consists of two warning conditions and requires immediate military action. State Orange indicates that an enemy attack is imminent (within a matter of hours), and State Scarlet indicates that an enemy attack is imminent (within an hour).

Under extreme emergency conditions, a **major NATO commander** has the authority to declare alert measures without Defense Planning Committee approval [LANTCOM, *Atlantic Command Alert System*, CIN-CLANTINST S3301.3B, 13 January 1982, released under the FOIA].

NATO Guidelines Area: A **Mutual Balanced Force Reduction (MBFR)** term often used, inaccurately, as a definition of NATO's **Allied Forces Central Europe**. It is the area including Belgium, the Netherlands, West Germany, East Germany, Czechoslovakia, and Poland.

NATO Integrated Communications System (NICS) (NATO III): NATO communications system that provides rapid and secure communications among NATO members via a network of ground and shipborne stations operated by the individual NATO countries. NATO III consists of four geosynchronous satellites positioned at an approximate altitude of 19,300 nm above the Atlantic Ocean. The ground segment consists of over 20 fixed and mobile terminals. NICS has a three-channel transponder that operates in the 7–8 GHz range. Signals for all three channels are received by a wide-beam receiver antenna and then amplified, shifted in frequency, further amplified, and transmitted back to earth through the appropriate transmit antenna (narrow-beam, wide-beam, or common receive). An X-band beacon is used for ground station acquisition, tracking, and identification of individual satellites. Command and control for the satellite is provided by an onboard S-band receiver.

For 17 years, NICS acquisition and development was handled by the International Satellite Communications System Program Office. Responsibility was then transferred

Satellite	Launch Date	Booster	Function
IIIA	22 Apr 1976	Delta 2914	Died December 1982
IIIB	28 Jan 1977	Delta 2914	Operational
IIIC	18 Nov 1978	Delta 2914	Backup
IIID	14 Nov 1984	Delta 3914	Operational
IIIE	1986		

to the Program Office for the **Defense Satellite Communications System (DSCS).** Operational responsibility rests with the NICS Central Operating Agency. Air Force Satellite Control Facility provides the telemetry, tracking, and command. . The satellites were launched from Cape Canaveral, FL, by NASA Delta space boosters under management of the Air Force System Command's Space Division. Ford Aerospace and Communications Corp., Palo Alto, CA, is the prime contractor. NATO III is funded entirely by NATO.

NATO Maintenance and Supply Organization (NAMSO): NATO organization that provides logistics coordination support and supplies for common systems used by the alliance. It is operated by the NATO Maintenance and Supply Agency with depots at Taranto, Italy; Paris, France; and Ft. Bliss, TX, which together house 100,000 line items. Its main workshop is at Capallan, Luxembourg. (see also **supply categories**)

NATO Operations Plan (NOP): The set of NATO **plans** based upon strategy and guidance promulgated by the **Military Committee** and prepared by the **major NATO commands**. The two basic types of NATO plans are General Defense Plans (GDPs) and Contingency Operation Plans (COPs). Both type plans have associated support plans (SUPs).

naval air facility (NAF): Naval base established to meet a specific requirement of naval aviation, typically providing small degrees of maintenance support to operating aircraft.

A NAF may or may not be dependent upon a parent administrative activity and does not necessarily possess an aircraft runway. A NAF is smaller than and not as well developed as a **naval air station**. It comprises approximately 200 personnel.

naval air force: Naval **type command** with broad administrative responsibility for fleet aviation. It establishes policy regarding the organization, maintenance, and employment of fleet aviation; advises fleet commanders on air operations; and develops operational doctrine for certain types of aircraft. Naval Air Forces are assigned to the Atlantic and Pacific Fleets. Each is composed of subordinate **carrier groups**, and task-oriented and regionally oriented **carrier air wings** and units. Air Forces maintain liaison with the Department of the Navy's Deputy Chief of Naval Operations (Air). Fleet aviation does not include Marine Corps aviation.

*Naval Air Force Atlantic
(NAVAIRLANT),*
NAS Norfolk, VA 23511-5188

- Fighter/Medium Attack/AEW Wings, NAS Oceana, VA 23460
- Fleet Air Caribbean
- Fleet Air Mediterranean
- Helicopter Wings, NAS Jacksonville, FL 32212
- Patrol Wings, NAS Brunswick, ME 04011
- Strike Fighter Wings, NAS Cecil Field, FL 32215
- Tactical Support Wing 1, NAS Norfolk, VA 23511

*Naval Air Force Pacific
(NAVAIRPAC),*
NAS North Island, CA 92135-5100

- Anti-Submarine Warfare Wing, NAS North Island, CA 92135
- Fighter/AEW Wing, NAS Miramar, CA 92145
- Fleet Air Western Pacific, NAS Atsugi, Japan
- Light Attack Wing, NAS Lemoore, CA 93230
- Medium Attack/Tactical AEW Wing, NAS Whidbey Island, WA 98277
- Patrol Wings, NAS Moffett Field, CA 94035

naval air station (NAS): Naval base providing operating, testing, overhaul training, maintenance, and personnel support facilities in support of naval aviation missions. A NAS is comprised of at least one runway and approximately 3,000–4,000 personnel. There are between 25 and 30 NASs in the Navy establishment. (see also **naval air facility**)

Naval Air Systems Command (NAVAIR): Navy **shore establishment** and one of five navy systems commands reporting directly to the Chief of Naval Operations. It was redesignated from the Bureau of Naval Weapons in 1966. It conducts research, development, test and evaluation, procurement, and logistics support of Navy and Marine Corps aircraft systems, including air-launched weapon systems, avionics, air-launched underwater sound systems, airborne pyrotechnics, airborne mine countermeasure equipment, droned and towed target systems, remotely piloted vehicles, and aircraft/missile range and evaluation instrumentation. NAVAIR includes eight Naval Air Rework Facilities and seven Naval Plant Representative Offices.

Headquarters
Washington, DC 20361-0900

Operations

- Naval Weapons Engineering Support Activity, Washington, DC
- Naval Avionics Center, Indianapolis, IN
- Pacific Missile Test Center, Pt. Mugu, CA
- Naval Air Test Center, Patuxent River, MD
- Naval Air Engineering Center, Lakehurst, NJ
- Naval Air Propulsion Center, Trenton, NJ
- Naval Weapons Evaluation Facility, Albuquerque, NM
- Naval Aviation Logistics Center, Patuxent River, MD
- Naval Air Technical Services Facility, Philadelphia, PA
- Naval Aviation Engineering Service Unit, Philadelphia, PA
- Naval Environmental Prediction Research Facility, Monterey, CA.

[Naval Air Systems Command, *Headquarters Organization Manual,* NAVAIRINST 5400.1A, 17 May 1977 Ch 7; *NWP 2*].

naval base: A shore command providing administrative and logistic support to the **operating forces** and integrating all naval shore activities in the assigned area. (see also **naval air facility, naval air station**)

naval beach group: Naval command within an amphibious force, comprising a beachmaster unit, an amphibious construction battalion, and a boat unit.

naval communications area master station (NAVCAMS): Naval communications station designated to direct and control naval communications broadcasts, ship/shore, air/ground, and other tactical circuitry and assets within the naval communications area. (see also **Naval Telecommunications Command**)

naval communications station (NAVCOMMSTA): "An activity which operates and maintains those facilities, systems, equipment, and devices necessary to provide requisite fleet support and fixed communication services for a specific area" [*NWP3*]. (see also **Naval Telecommunications Command**, **naval communications unit**)

naval communications unit (NAVCOMMU): An activity that is smaller in personnel, resources, and facilities than a **naval communications station** and that is assigned a more limited or specialized functional mission. (see also **Naval Telecommunications Command**)

Naval Construction Force (NCF): The deployable naval construction units together with their command and support units. The force includes active and reserve units; naval construction battalions (Atlantic and Pacific Fleets); naval construction brigades (NCBs); naval construction regiments (NCRs); naval mobile construction battalions (NMCBs); naval construction force support units (NCFSUs); naval construction battalion maintenance units (CBMUs); underwater construction teams

(UCTs); amphibious construction battalions (PHIBCBs); and naval construction battalion units (CBUs).

Naval Control of Shipping: Control and coordination of the routing and movement of merchant convoys and independently sailed merchant ships subject to the directives of the operational control authority.

Naval Data Automation Command: Navy **shore establishment** reporting to the Chief of Naval Operations, which administers and coordinates the Navy Information Systems Program. It provides guidance and planning for naval information systems, career development and training, systems development, and acquisition. The command operates through a network of Regional Data Automation Centers and Facilities at naval bases.

Headquarters
Washington, DC 20374

naval district: A geographic area assigned to one naval commander reporting directly to the Secretary of the Navy and the Chief of Naval Operations. A district commander is responsible for naval defense and security and coordination of naval activities in his or her specific area.

Naval District of Washington: Navy **shore establishment** responsible for the coordination of naval activities in the Washington, DC, area and the administration of military and civilian personnel and facilities in the national capital region. (see also **Air**

Force District of Washington, Military District of Washington)

Headquarters
Washington Navy Yard,
Washington, DC 20003

Naval Electronic Systems Command (NAVELEX): Former Navy shore establishment, redesignated **Space and Naval Warfare Systems Command** on 1 May 1985.

naval establishment: Unofficial term for the entire Navy organization, consisting of the **Department of the Navy**, its **operating forces**, and the **shore establishment**. (see also **major command**)

Naval Facilities Engineering Command (NAVFAC): Navy **shore establishment** and one of five naval systems commands reporting directly to the Chief of Naval Operations. Established as the Bureau of Yards and Docks in August 1842, and redesignated as NAVFAC on 1 May 1966. It plans, designs, procures, constructs, and inspects all naval shore facilities, including family housing. It also conducts ocean engineering and support of naval construction forces and assists in the management, repair, and upkeep of shore and ocean facilities. It is composed of three Construction Battalion Centers and nine Public Works Centers.

Headquarters
Alexandria, VA 22332

Operations
- Naval Energy and Environmental Support Activity
- Naval Civil Engineering Laboratory
- Naval Support Facility

- Naval Support Unit State Department

Field Divisions
- Northern Division, Philadelphia, PA
- Chesapeake Division, Washington, DC
- Atlantic Division, Norfolk, VA
- Southern Division, Charleston, SC
- Western Division, San Bruno, CA
- Pacific Division, Honolulu, HI

Naval Forces Caribbean/Fleet Air Caribbean (see **U.S. Naval Forces Caribbean/Fleet Air Caribbean**)

Naval Forces Central Command (NAVCENT) (see **U.S. Naval Forces Central Command**)

Naval Forces Iceland (NAVICE) (see **U.S. Naval Forces Iceland**)

Naval Forces Southern Command (NAVSO) (see **U.S. Naval Forces Southern Command**)

Naval Intelligence Command (NIC): Navy **shore establishment** reporting to the Chief of Naval Operations through the Director of Naval Intelligence. NIC directs and manages naval **intelligence** activities, including collection, processing, analysis, and dissemination of intelligence information in support of fleet commanders and higher authorities, with the exception of signals intelligence, which is under the **Naval Security Group Command**.

Headquarters
Washington, DC 20389–5000
(Suitland, MD)

Component Commands

- Naval Intelligence Support Center (NISC): processes, analyzes, produces and disseminates scientific and technical intelligence on foreign naval systems.
- Naval Intelligence Processing Systems Support Activity (NIPSSA): plans, sponsors, develops, and manages automated intelligence, information processing, and communications systems.
- Navy Operational Intelligence Center (NOIC): produces finished operational intelligence, including ocean surveillance information, and analyses of Soviet strategy and tactics.
- Task Force 168/Naval Intelligence Operations Group: collects intelligence in support of fleets through its forward area support teams (FASTs); manages naval **human intelligence (HUMINT)** collection activities.

Naval Investigative Service Command (NISC): Navy **shore establishment** reporting directly to the Chief of Naval Operations. Originally established as the Naval Investigative Service; elevated to a command on 8 August 1985 and redesignated NISC from the Naval Investigative Service. It conducts law enforcement and security functions, criminal investigations, **counterintelligence**, and **counterterrorism** activities in support of the Navy and Marine Corps. It operates 10 regional offices, more than 150 Naval Investigative Service Resident Agencies (NISRAs), and regional fraud units. NISC special agents are also placed fulltime aboard major fleet combatant vessels. NISC is a member of DOD's Defense Counterintel-

ligence Board, established December 1979, and is the Navy's liaison to federal law enforcement and counterintelligence agencies.

Headquarters
Suitland, MD 20746

Naval Legal Service Command: Navy **shore establishment** headquartered in Alexandria, VA.

Naval Material Command (NAVMAT): Former Navy shore establishment, disestablished 9 May 1985. Its functions were fully assumed by the five naval systems commands:

- **Naval Air Systems Command**
- **Naval Facilities Engineering Command**
- **Naval Sea Systems Command**
- **Naval Supply Systems Command**
- **Space and Naval Warfare Systems Command** (formerly Naval Electronics Systems Command)

Naval Medical Command: Navy **shore establishment** headquartered in Washington, DC.

Naval Military Personnel Command: Navy **shore establishment** headquartered in Washington, DC.

naval nuclear propulsion: The Navy's nuclear propulsion program was conceived in the late 1940s. Its first prototype and operational **nuclear reactors** for submarines were constructed in the early 1950s. The first nuclear-powered ship, the submarine USS Nautilus (SSN-571), was commissioned in 1954. The first nuclear-powered surface ship, the USS Long Beach (exDLGN/CGN-9), was commissioned in 1961.

Originally both pressurized water and liquid metal (sodium) reactor designs were pursued. However, the first operational liquid metal cooled reactor (S2G) aboard the USS Seawolf (SSN-575) proved to be unsatisfactory and the design was abandoned in favor of pressurized water reactors (the Seawolf received its new reactor, S2W, in the late 1950s).

Since the 1950s, 198 nuclear reactors have been built to power approximately 160 nuclear-powered submarines and 15 nuclear-powered surface ships. Several land prototypes have also been constructed. Each nuclear-powered submarine has one reactor. One twin-reactor submarine, the USS Triton (SSN-586) was built in the late 1950s, but the submarine has since been decommissioned. All nuclear-powered aircraft carriers are powered by two reactors each, except the USS Enterprise (CVN-65), the first nuclear-powered aircraft carrier that is powered by eight. All the nuclear-powered cruisers are powered by two nuclear reactors. A new reactor is under development for the Seawolf (SSN-21) class attack submarines.

Some 30 nuclear-powered submarines have been decommissioned as of 1989. Eight have had their reactor vessels removed and shipped for storage at the Hanford Nuclear Reservation, WA.

Reactors currently operating on U.S. ships and submarines are

- A2W Large Ship Reactor: Eight reactors installed in the single-ship Enterprise (CVN-65) class aircraft carrier. Pressurized water reactors built by Westinghouse, together the eight deliver some 280,000 shp. A

two-reactor A1W prototype nuclear reactor plant was constructed at Arco, ID.
- A4W Large Ship Reactor: Two reactors installed in each Nimitz (CVN-68) class aircraft carriers. Pressurized water reactors built by Westinghouse, two provide some 280,000 shp.
- C1W Cruiser Reactor: Two reactors installed on the single-ship Long Beach (CGN-9) class cruiser. Pressurized water reactors built by Westinghouse, together they deliver some 80,000 shp.
- D2G Destroyer Reactor: Two reactors installed in Virginia (CGN-38), California (CGN-36), Truxtun (CGN-35), and Bainbridge (CGN-25) class cruisers. Pressurized water reactors built by General Electric, two can provide 60,000 shp.
- NR1 Submersible Reactor: A single reactor installed on the NR1 deep sea research submersible. It is a pressurized water reactor built by Westinghouse.
- S5G Natural Circulation Reactor: One installed on the single-ship Narwhal (SSN-671) class attack submarine. A pressurized water, natural circulation reactor built by General Electric, it can provide up to approximately 17,000 shp. A land-based prototype was built at Arco, ID. The natural circulation reactor uses natural convection rather than pumps for heat transfer/coolant transfer at slow speeds, reducing self-generated machinery noises. This concept was used in the subsequent Los Angeles and Ohio class submarines.
- S6G Natural Circulation Reactor: One each installed on Los Angeles

(SSN-688) class attack submarines. A pressurized water, natural circulation reactor built by General Electric, it can provide up to approximately 30,000 shp.

- S8G Natural Circulation Reactor: One each installed in Ohio (SSBN-726) class ballistic missile submarines. A pressurized water, natural circulation reactor built by General Electric, it was originally planned to provide up to 60,000 shp, but now reportedly has a horsepower just greater than 30,000 shp. An S7G land-based prototype reactor plant for the Ohio was built at West Milton, NY.
- S5W Submarine High Speed Reactor: One each installed in Lafayette (SSBN-616), James Madison (SSBN-627), and Benjamin Franklin (SSBN-640) class ballistic missile submarines, and in Sturgeon (SSN-637), Permit (SSN-594), Ethan Allen (SSN-608), and Skipjack (SSN-585) class attack submarines. A pressurized water reactor built by Westinghouse, it can provide approximately 15,000 shp.
- S5Wa Submarine High Speed Reactor: One installed on the USS Glenard P. Lipscomb (SSN-685). A pressurized water reactor built by Westinghouse, it can provide approximately 15,000 shp.

Naval Oceanography Command (NAVOCEANCOM): Navy **shore establishment** reporting to the Chief of Naval Operations. Established 1 October 1978 by consolidating the Oceanographic Office and the Naval Weather Service Command, NAVOCEANCOM provides oceanographic information and environmental/prediction services to Navy air, surface, and subsurface forces and the **Defense Mapping Agency**, and it manages the Naval Oceanographic Program as well as all naval oceanographic activities, including meteorology, mapping, charting, hydrography, and geodesy. Its environmental surveys are conducted from 12 data-collecting ships operated by the Military Sealift Command, 3 specially equipped aircraft (Oceanographic Development Squadron 8), and 70 shore activities.

Headquarters
Bay St. Louis, MS 39529

Operations

- Naval Oceanographic Office, Bay St. Louis, MS 39529
- Fleet Numerical Oceanography Center, Monterey, CA
- Naval Oceanography Centers:
  - Western: Pearl Harbor, HI
  - Eastern: Norfolk, VA 23511
  - Polar: Suitland, MD
- Naval Oceanography Command Facility, Bay St. Louis, MS 39529

Naval On Call Force Mediterranean (NAVOCFORMED): NATO's sole operating naval force in the Mediterranean Sea, first activated in April 1970. Unlike NATO's other two standing naval forces, the **Standing Naval Force Atlantic** and the **Standing Naval Force Channel**, NAVOCFORMED is not a permanent force but is activated twice a year for one month at a time. It consists of destroyers and frigate-type ships. It has never been called to active duty in the region for a real-world crisis but has participated in joint exercises.

Naval Reserve: The federal reserve component and an **operating force** of the Navy. It comprises the Fleet, Organized Volunteer, and Merchant Marine Reserves. It consists of the Naval Surface Reserve Force comprising 16 Naval Reserve Readiness Command Regions, the Naval Reserve Construction Force, and the Naval Support Activity; the Naval Air Reserve Force comprising six reserve air wings, six naval air stations, two naval air facilities, seven Naval Air Reserve sites, and one anti-submarine warfare training center; and the Naval Reserve Intelligence Program. Its shore activities include the Personnel Support Activity, the Financial Information Processing Center, and the Consolidated Civilian Personnel Office. All activities and units report to the Chief of Naval Operations through the Commander, Naval Reserve Forces, who also serves as the Director, Naval Reserve. The reserves contribute approximately 20 percent of the Navy's total personnel strength, 16 percent of its frigates, 35 percent of its maritime air patrol squadrons, and 65 percent of its mobile construction battalions. The naval reserve receives approximately 15 percent of the total reserve appropriations.

Headquarters
New Orleans, LA 70146–5000

Naval Sea Systems Command (NAVSEA): Navy **shore establishment** and one of five naval systems commands reporting directly to the Chief of Naval Operations. It conducts research, development, testing and evaluation, acquisition, logistics support, and maintenance of ships, craft, and shipboard weapons systems for the Navy and Marine Corps. NAVSEA also coordinates shipbuilding, conversion, and repair for the Navy and DOD. The command includes two Naval Ordnance Stations and five Naval Weapons Stations responsible for the storage and handling of ammunition, including nuclear weapons. The industrial base includes 4 Naval Plant Representative Offices, 2 Naval Sea Support Centers, 8 Naval Shipyards, and 16 Supervisors of Shipbuilding, Conversion, and Repair at civil shipyards.

Headquarters
Washington, DC 20362

Subcommands

- Naval Explosive Ordnance Disposal Technology Center, Indian Head, MD 20640
- Naval Undersea Warfare Engineering Station, Keyport, WA 98345
- Naval Mine Warfare Engineering Activity
- Naval Ship Weapons Systems Engineering Station, Pt. Hueneme, CA 93043
- Trident Command and Control Systems Maintenance Activity, Newport, RI 02841
- Naval Ship Engineering Station, Philadelphia, PA 19112
- Naval Weapons Support Center, Crane, IN 47522
- Navy Experimental Diving Unit, Panama City, FL 32407
- Naval Sea Combat Systems Engineering Station, Norfolk, VA 23511

Naval Security and Investigative Command (NSIC) (see **Naval Investigative Command**)

Naval Security Group Command (NSGC): Navy **shore establishment** reporting to the Chief of Naval Operations and the naval component (Service Cryptological Authority) of the Central Security Service of the **National Security Agency**. NSGC was formerly the Communications Security Section of the Office of Naval Communications. NSGC missions are naval **communications security** monitoring and naval cryptologic and **signals intelligence** through Naval Security Group Activities and detachments. It provides personnel support to **Classic Wizard**, **Classic Outboard** and Classic **Bullseye** ocean surveillance systems. It is directed by the Deputy Director of Naval Intelligence.

Headquarters
Washington, DC 20390

naval shipyard: An industrial activity charged with building, repairs, alterations, overhauling, docking, converting, and outfitting of ships, together with the necessary replenishment. There are eight naval shipyards assigned to the **Naval Sea Systems Command**.

Naval Space Command (NAVSPACECOM): Navy **shore establishment** reporting to the Chief of Naval Operations. A service component command of **U.S. Space Command (USSPACECOM)** and established 1 October 1983, NAVSPACECOM operates and maintains naval space systems and resources in support of naval forces worldwide, as well as to USSPACECOM. Current satellite programs managed by NAVSPACECOM are the **Fleet Satellite Communications System (FLTSATCOM)**, a leased satellite system (**LEASAT**), and the Navy Navigation Satellite System (**TRANSIT**). Satellite systems in development are **NAVSTAR**, Navy **Remote Ocean Sensing System (NROSS)**, and **MILSTAR**. It also serves as the fleet support portion of the **Tactical Exploitation of National Capabilities (TENCAP)** program.

Headquarters
Dahlgren, VA 22448-5170

Field Operations

- **Navy Astronautics Group**, Pt. Mugu, CA 93042
- Fleet Surveillance Support Command, Chesapeake, VA 27322: operates and maintains Navy's Relocatable **Over-the-Horizon Radar** (ROTHR) system, a high-frequency radar under development to provide oceanic surface and air surveillance information in support of fleet units.
- Naval Space Surveillance Center, Dahlgren, VA 22448: operates the **Naval Space Surveillance System (NAVSPASUR)**. (see also **satellite communications**, **satellite reconnaissance**)

Naval Space Surveillance System (NAVSPASUR): System of the **Naval Space Command** that maintains surveillance 6,000 nm into space and 3,000 miles across the southern United States from Georgia to California in support of fleet units, **NORAD**, and **U.S. Space Command (USSPACECOM)**. The system has been functioning since 1959 and consists of three powerful transmitter stations and six receivers. Transmitters are located at Gila River, AZ; Lake Kickapoo, TX; and Jordan Lake, AL. Receivers are at San Diego, CA; Elephant Butte, NM; Silver Lake, MI; Red River, AR; and Ft. Stewart and Hawkinsville, GA. NAVSPASUR serves as USSPACE-COM's Alternate Space Surveillance Center. The system is a dedicated component of the **Space Surveillance Network**.

naval special warfare (NSW): "That set of naval operations generally accepted as being unconventional in nature and, in many cases, covert or clandestine in character, including the use of specially trained forces assigned to support and contribute to coastal and riverine interdiction and to conduct special action operations, **unconventional warfare**, **psychological operations**, beach and coastal reconnaissance, **cover and deception**, certain intelligence collection operations, and other clandestine/covert operations that may be required" [*NWP* 3]. (see also **special operations**)

Naval Special Warfare Command: A service component command of **U.S. Special Operations Command**. Its mission is to develop **naval special warfare** and **special operations** doctrine in support of the Maritime Strategy and to train naval special operations units in support of the Navy, U.S. Special Operations Command, and other unified and specified commands as designated. Its subordinate units include two **naval special warfare groups** and specialized special

operations groups and units assigned to the fleets.

Headquarters
NAB Coronado, CA 92155

naval special warfare group (NSWG): The fundamental organizational unit of naval **special operations** subordinate to the **Naval Special Warfare Command**. "An amphibious force asset specializing in the conduct of **naval special warfare**. The group is composed of a staff, **SEAL** teams, and beach jumper units" [*NWP* 3]. NSWGs consist of forward-deployed naval special warfare units (NSWUs) of Navy SEAL Teams and elements, Inshore Underseas Warfare Groups and detachments, and **Mobile Inshore Underseas Warfare** units. All underwater demolition teams (UDTs) were redesignated as SEAL and swimmer delivery vehicle (SDV) teams on 1 May 1983. NSWGs of the Naval Surface Force are NSWG 1, assigned to PACFLT and headquartered at Coronado, CA, and NSWG 2, assigned to LANTFLT at Little Creek, VA. Their three active NSWUs are forward-based at Subic Bay and Roosevelt Roads, PR, and Machrihanish, Scotland. NSWG subordinate units include 11 active and reserve SEAL teams, 5 reserve detachments, 2 Special Delivery Vehicles teams (SD-VT), 4 special boat squadrons (SBR), and one light attack helicopter (HAL) squadron supporting LANTFLT. Total personnel strength of naval units is over 5,000.

Naval Submarine Force: Naval **type command** with broad operational and administrative responsibility for submarine activities. Naval Submarine Forces are assigned to the Atlantic and Pacific Fleets. As the only type command with continuing operational duties, Submarine Force Atlantic reports directly to the Commander, **Second Fleet**, and Submarine Force Pacific reports directly to the commander of the **Third Fleet** or **Seventh Fleet**, as appropriate. Its subordinate organization is the **submarine group**.

Naval Submarine Force Atlantic
Norfolk, VA 23511

Naval Submarine Force Pacific
Pearl Harbor, HI 96860-6550

Naval Supply Systems Command (NAVSUP): Navy **shore establishment** and one of five naval systems commands reporting to the Chief of Naval Operations. Established 1 May 1966, NAVSUP serves as the logistics and supply center for the Navy. Its functions include the development and management of materiel transportation systems, nuclear weapons material supplies, contracting programs, inventory and information systems, financial management systems, logistics technology programs, publications and printing programs, food service programs, fuel management systems, and naval security assistance programs. It operates 25 major field activities. In a typical year, it stocks over $20 billion worth of equipment and supplies and acquires $10 billion worth of materials and services. Operations include eight Naval Supply Centers, three Inventory Control Activities, four Navy Regional Contracting Centers, the Navy Publications and Forms Center (Philadelphia, PA), the Fleet Material Support Office (Mechanicsburg, PA), and the Navy Resale and Services Support Office (Staten Island, NY). Personnel strength is approximately 50,000 (95 percent civilian). If it were a private corporation, NAVSUP would rank in the top 25 of the Fortune 500.

Headquarters
Washington, DC 20376

Naval Surface Force: Naval **type command** with broad administrative responsibility for all warships except aircraft carriers, submarines, and submarine support ships. It develops surface warfare, logistics, and operating doctrine; operates various shore activities; and trains, maintains, and assigns forces to operating commands as directed. Subordinate organizations are

- **Naval surface groups**
- **Cruiser-destroyer groups**
- **Amphibious groups**
- **Naval special forces groups**
- **Service groups**

Naval Surface Force Atlantic
Norfolk, VA 23511-6292

Naval Surface Force Pacific
NAB Coronado, CA 92155-5035

naval surface group (NAVSURF-GRU): A permanent **Navy Surface Force** organization—both administrative and operational—comprising battleships, cruisers, destroyers, and attendant repair ships. It provides intermediate-level maintenance to combatant units; coordinates depot level maintenance; coordinates team and unit training in anti-submarine, anti-surface, and anti-air operations, and strike warfare; and provides combat ships to numbered fleet and task force commanders when directed. It generally supports a regional area. NAVSURFGRUs are

- Naval Surface Group 4, Newport, RI 02841
- Naval Surface Group Mediterranean, APO New York 09521
- Naval Surface Group Mid-Pacific, Pearl Harbor, HI 96860
- Naval Surface Group Western Pacific, Subic Bay, Phillipines (APO San Francisco 96601-6011)

naval tactical data system (NTDS): "A shipboard system using high-speed digital computers, special symbolic displays, and digital data links, whereby tactical data is gathered, processed, and exchanged instantaneously between units, providing commanders of forces and units with a comprehensive display of the tactical situation within the force sensor capability." [*NWP 3*] Terms commonly used when referring to the NTDS:

- *Condition IV operational program*: "Those NTDS computer programs designed to provide maximum capability for operation in readiness Condition IV (peacetime cruising), using one computer only. Emphasis is on detection, tracking, surface maneuvering, communications, and aircraft vectoring functions required for peacetime cruising."
- *Data display equipment*: "Those NTDS consoles normally manned and used to display symbology,

radar video, and alphanumeric information. These consoles are referred to as data input consoles (DIC), data utilization consoles (DUC), and data readout consoles (DRO)."
- *Data readout (DRO)*: "A matrix of display cells used to provide alphanumeric information pertinent to a target or operator request."
- *Full capability program (FOC)*: "Those NTDS computer programs which are designed to provide a maximum operational capability for readiness Condition I and which require the full capability of the NTDS."
- *Input functions*: "Those programmed functions primarily concerned with entering, updating, and amplifying information on air, surface, and subsurface targets."
- *Keyset (KS)*: "A device used to manually enter operational data and instructions in the computer."
- *Local track*: "A track for which all primary data being entered into that ship's display complex is coming from the ship's own sensors."
- *Mode III*: "The situation aboard an NTDS unit in which the NTDS displays are not available because of the loss of power or critical equipment failure. The result is loss of that ship's own sensors."
- *Reduced operational capability program (ROC)*: "Those NTDS computer programs designed to provide the maximum operational capability for readiness Condition I, using the full capability of the NTDS hardware system less one computer. ROC programs provide the highest degree of automated capability in situations where a computer is

not available because of casualty or other reason. ROC programs are basically FOC programs modified by deletion of less essential functional areas and reduction in programmed system capacity."

- *Remote track*: "A target for which all primary data are received via digital communication links from other NTDS ships."
- *System tracks*: "Tracks which are candidates for transmission over digital data links."
- *Training program*: "Basically, a fully operational capability computer program modified to provide simulated target video and means for problem control. This program is designed for use when live targets are not available or when the complexity of the problem is to be controlled."
- *User functions (also utilization functions)*: "Those programmed functions which are used to provide recommendations for solution of tactical problems."

[*NWP 3*]

Naval Telecommunications Command (NAVTEL): Navy **shore establishment** reporting to the Chief of Naval Operations, established 1 June 1973. Its missions are the operation and management of the Naval Telecommunications System (NTS); development of planning, programming, and implementation of telecommunications systems, equipment, facilities, and personnel; as well as serving as the Operations and Maintenance Manager of systems assigned from the **Defense Communications System**. Four Naval Com-

munication Area Master Stations—EASTPAC, Honolulu, HI; WESTPAC, Guam; Atlantic, Norfolk, VA; and Mediterranean, Naples, Italy—command 13 Naval Communications Stations and four Naval Communications Units. NAVTEL's personnel strength is approximately 8,000 military and 3,000 civilians, including 800 foreign civilians.

Headquarters
Washington, DC 20390

NAVSTAR/GPS (Navigation Satellite Tracking and Ranging/Global Positioning System): A space-based radio navigation system operated jointly by the Army, Navy, and Air Force to provide U.S. and allied military forces with concise, continuous, all-weather, common-grid, three-dimensional, world-positioning and navigation, and time reference information on land, sea, and in the air. When the system is fully operational, NAVSTAR/GPS satellites will give receivers position data accurate to a 50-ft diameter circle anywhere on the globe and in some cases will be accurate to within 10 ft. This information can be used for accurate target location, route planning, and weapon delivery by aircraft, artillery, ships, tanks, and other weapon delivery systems. The satellites will also provide time data based on their internal atomic clocks, which are accurate to within one second every 300,000 years.

NAVSTAR/GPS equipment includes satellites; ground control stations to monitor the satellites, including a master control station at the **Consolidated Space Operations Center**

(**CSOC**); three upload stations and five worldwide monitor stations; and receiving equipment, including radio receivers, for military users to provide a common navigation system. In addition to the coded military signal, there is a less accurate clear acquisition signal for civilian users.

The NAVSTAR/GPS program is to develop one-, two-, and five-channel radio receivers to be integrated into over 200 different types of aircraft, land vehicles, surface ships, and submarines. These user sets will have antenna, receiver, signal-processor, flexible modular-interface and control/display units. The user set will automatically select the four satellites most favorably located in relationship to the receiver, lock onto their signals, and compute the user's position, velocity, and time. The Army is responsible for the testing and use of the one- and two-channel receivers. NAVSTAR/GPS has progressed along the following time line:

- Milestone I: Concept validation, 1973
- Milestone II: Full-scale development, 1979
- Milestone IIIA: Limited-rate initial production, June 1986
- Milestone IIIB: Full-rate production decision, scheduled for FY 1990

The full NAVSTAR/GPS constellation is to include 21 satellites, with three on-orbit spares, by the end of FY 1992. The satellites will orbit the earth in six different planes at an altitude averaging 11,000 miles. The Air Force plans to launch a new satellite every 60 days and to phase out the test satellites. The NAVSTAR/GPS master control station at Falcon AFS, CO, will monitor and control the satellites while five monitor stations, interconnected via wideband satellite communications, will track the satellites. Information from these stations will be processed at the master control station and uplinked to satellites via the upload antenna. Original plans were to have the satellites launched on the space shuttle, but in January 1987, the Air Force contracted with McDonnell Douglas for the Delta II to be the dedicated NAVSTAR/GPS booster.

By 14 Febuary 1989, seven test satellites (Block I) had been placed into orbit. On 21 October 1989, the fourth second-generation NAVSTAR/GPS satellite was launched by an Air Force Delta II rocket booster. A fifth Block II satellite is planned to be launched by the end of 1989, bringing the total number of NAVSTAR/GPS satellites in orbit to 12.

The United States and Soviet Union have agreed to develop joint operational performance standards for their NAVSTAR/GPS and Glonass satellite-based navigation systems. The compatibility will allow the civil aviation sector to use data from both satellite networks for highly accurate, reliable navigation.

The NAVSTAR/GPS system will provide basic two-dimensional coverage worldwide within two years, with full three-dimensional coverage worldwide to be accomplished by 1992 or 1993 depending on the launch rate. As of March 1989, DARPA is seeking the development of a miniaturized GPS navigation and guidance package. The package will include a GPS receiver, an inertial measurement unit, and control processors.

The package is being developed to provide a small, low-cost, mass-producible guidance system for platforms including strike weapons, high-performance aircraft, and unmanned vehicles. The Naval Ocean Systems Center is DARPA's agent for the project.

The DOD executive agency for the NAVSTAR/GPS system is the Air Force Systems Command's Space Division, Los Angeles AFB, CA.

The prime contractors are Rockwell, Seal Beach, CA; and General Dynamics, San Diego, CA. The FY 1986 estimated cost of the entire program was placed at $6.538 billion. Funding for FY 1990 and FY 1991 is $103.6 million and $231.5 million, respectively. The Air Force has ordered 28 Block 2 satellites from Rockwell and competition is on to purchase another 20 Block 2R satellites. The contract was scheduled to be awarded in the summer of 1989. The additional satellites will be used to replenish the constellation, with first launch planned for FY 1995.

The Air Force has put McDonnell Douglas on an incentive program: the company receives a bonus of $3 million for each successful launch and a $1 million bonus each year if all contractual obligations are met. With just one failure, however, the company forfeits all bonus payments; two failures would forfeit all incentives and half of the profits; three failures would forfeit all incentives and profits.

Navy Astronautics Group (NAV-ASTROGRU): Commissioned in 1962 to control and operate the ground tracking and control stations,

subsystems, and spacecraft of the **TRANSIT** Navy Navigation Satellite System (NNSS), NAVASTROGRU became operational in 1968. The NNSS satellites provide navigation, land survey, geodesic research, and precision time information to commercial, private, and U.S. military ships, aircraft, and spacecraft. The NNSS space segment consists of five operational navigation satellites, as well as two modified TRANSIT satellites: one used in the Range Safety program at Pacific Missile Test Center, Point Mugu, CA, and the other for an Air Force Space Test Program experiment. The ground system consists of four tracking and injection centers located in Maine, Minnesota, California, and Hawaii; a Communications Center, Operations Center, and Computer Center at HQ, Point Mugu, CA; and a Satellite Prelaunch-Checkout Facility at Vandenberg AFB, CA. In October 1983 the **Naval Space Command** consolidated the Navy space activities of NAVASTROGRU, **Naval Space Surveillance System,** and **Fleet Satellite Communications System (FLTSATCOM)** elements within the Naval Telecommunications Command into one operating command under the Chief of Naval Operations.

Headquarters
Point Mugu, CA 93042

Navy Department (see **Department of the Navy**)

Navy enlisted classification (NEC) code: System for identifying special skills and knowledge for enlisted personnel. Every sailor has at least two of the four-digit NEC codes: a primary and a secondary. Details are contained in the Manual of Navy Enlisted Classification.

NCMC (see **NORAD Cheyenne Mountain Complex**)

N-day (Negative day): An unnamed day prior to C-day in which a unit is notified for deployment or redeployment. (see also **military time**)

NDEW (Nuclear Directed-Energy Weapon): A directed-energy weapon with a specially designated nuclear explosive as its source of energy. It would most likely be an x-ray laser, a gamma-ray laser or an electromagnetic pulse weapon.

near real time: The delay in the time between the occurrence of an event and the receipt of related data at another location [*JCS Pub 1*, p. 248]. (see also **real time**)

need-to-know: "A determination made by a possessor of classified information that a prospective recipient, in the interest of national security, has a requirement for access to, or knowledge, or possession of the classified information in order to accomplish lawful and authorized Government purposes" [DOD, *Information Security Program Regulation*, DOD Dir 5200.1-R, 28 April 1987, p. 20]. (see also **security classification**)

net assessment: A dispassionate comparison of capabilities possessed by two competing countries or alliances to ascertain which is best able to achieve its objectives, despite opposition by the other. Studies may be comprehensive, or survey special subjects, such as technology and naval power. (see also **Military Net Assessment**)

Network Communication Control Station: The mobile control terminal of the **MILSTAR** system.

neutral particle beam (NPB) accelerator: Experimental technology used in the **Strategic Defense Initiative** effort as a potential follow-on phase of a strategic defense system. The NPB technology would be used to discriminate between enemy reentry vehicles and decoys and could be used to kill missile boosters and warheads. The first successful test of the NPB accelerator in space, conducted 13 July 1989, will provide further information about the strategic applicability of the beam technology in a space environment.

new type of ICBM: "The US and the Soviet Union have agreed, for the period of **SALT II**, to limit each side to only one new type of **ICBM**. Specific technical criteria have been established to distinguish between new types of ICBMs and existing types of ICBMs. These criteria include such physical parameters as missile length, maximum diameter, throwweight, launch-weight, and fuel type" [ACDA, *SALT II: Glossary of Terms*, 1979]

NFZ (see **nuclear free zone**)

nickname: "A combination of two separate unclassified words which is assigned an unclassified meaning and is employed only for unclassified administrative, morale, or public information purposes" [*JCS Pub 1*, p. 249]. (see also **code word**)

NICS (see **NATO Integrated Communication System**)

Nifty Nugget 78: Large scale JCS-sponsored and -conducted **command post exercise** conducted in October 1978 to test worldwide mobilization procedures and capabilities. It was the first joint exercise following the Army's **MOBEX** 76 to practice and assess procedures and preparedness for protracted conventional war. Nifty Nugget was the most ambitious effort to measure military mobilization preparedness since World War II. It was held simultaneously with **REX** 78, a civil exercise sponsored by the Federal Preparedness Agency. The results were disastrous and precipitated a major review of **mobilization** capabilities. Several of the problems noted could be traced to divided responsibility for deployment planning and to the lack of a single, authoritative list of deployment. The result was the creation of the Joint Deployment Agency in 1979, as well as a new series of biennial mobilization exercises (the next was Proud Spirit).

Night Blue/Night Watch: Joint Chiefs of Staff codename for the **National Emergency Airborne Command Post (NEACP)** and other **airborne command posts**.

Nimitz class (CVN-68): Navy nuclear-powered **aircraft carrier** class, capable of supporting a **car-**

rier air wing of about 95 planes. Nimitz-class carriers have two reactors and nuclear fuel for 15 years of normal operations, the equivalent of more than 11 million barrels of fuel oil. They are the largest and most capable of the Navy's aircraft carriers. The Nimitz class includes six carriers: USS Nimitz (CVN-68), USS Dwight D. Eisenhower (CVN-69), USS Carl Vinson (CVN-70), and the USS Theodore Roosevelt (CVN-71), the USS Abraham Lincoln (CVN-72) have been delivered; and USS George Washington (CVN-73) were authorized in the FY 1983 Defense budget. On 13 February 1988, the Abraham Lincoln was launched. On 19 December 1988, the name John C. Stennis was approved by the Secretary of the Navy for use on CVN-74. The Theodore Roosevelt (CVN-71) departed Norfolk, VA, on 30 December 1988 for its first operational deployment to the Mediterranean. The Roosevelt had completed an earlier two-month deployment to the North Atlantic and Norwegian Sea where it participated in a number of exercises.

Nine Lives: Joint Chiefs of Staff/ **Federal Emergency Management Agency** limited-participation, joint civil/military procedural **command post exercise (CPX)** dealing with **Presidential succession** and **continuity of government**. (see also **Treetop**)

NOCONTRACT: Control marking on national security-related information used to indicate that the release of information to contractors or consultants (regardless of security clearances) is prohibited. (see also **security classification**)

node: A point in a communications network at which several branches come together.

no fire area (NFA): A certain area within a military theater that is declared an NFA because of operational, political, cultural, and/or religious reasons. **Unconventional warfare** components "will identify NFA around established guerilla operating areas/refugee centers and pre-planned Direct Action (DA) targets" [CENTCOM, *Operations SOP*, p. B-4–B-1, released under the FOIA].

NOFORN: Control marking on national security-related information standing for "Special Handling Required–Not Releasable to Foreign Nationals." It is used to control the release of intelligence information and nuclear weapons information to foreign governments when:

> (1) the possible compromise of the status of relations with collaborating foreign governments or officials [and] (2) jeopardizing the continuing viability of vital technical collection programs.

[DCID (Director Central Intelligence Directive] 1/7, "Control of Dissemination of Intelligence Information," quoted in Jeffrey Richelson, *The U.S. Intelligence Community*, 2d ed., p. 431]. (see also **security classification**)

non-circumvention: "**SALT II** provides that each Party undertakes not to circumvent the provisions of this Treaty, through any other state or states, or in any other manner. This provision simply makes explicit the inherent obligation any state assumes when party to an international agreement not to circumvent the provisions of that agreement. This provision will not affect existing patterns of collaboration and cooperation with our allies, including cooperation in modernization of allied forces" [ACDA, *SALT II: Glossary of Terms*, 1979].

noncombatant evacuation: **1.** JCS: "DOD-sponsored personnel, Department of State personnel, other U.S. Government-sponsored personnel, and U.S. citizens and designated aliens who must be moved from a threatened geographic area or theater of operations" [JCS, *Joint Operations Planning System, Volume I*, p. xviii, released under the FOIA]. **2.** Air Force: "All dependents of U.S. armed forces personnel, employees of any U.S. government agency, and their dependents; U.S. citizen residents; tourists who are U.S. citizens; and certain designated aliens" [USAF, *U.S. Noncombatant Evacuation Operations*, HQ Operating Instruction 55-11, 7 May 1980, released under the FOIA].

The Department of State, assisted by overseas military commands, prepares evacuation plans. "Planning for, and evacuation of, U.S. noncombatant and certain non-U.S. persons abroad [will be] in accordance with the provisions of . . . 'State-Defense Policies and Procedures for the Protection and Evacuation of US Citizens and Certain Designated Aliens Abroad in Time of Emergency' " [JCS, *Unified Command Plan*, 28 October 1983, released under the FOIA]. At any given time, nearly two million American citizens who are not members of the U.S. armed forces reside abroad. In addition, a substantial number are traveling overseas for business or vacation.

non-commissioned officer (NCO): An enlisted person appointed in the grade E-4 or higher, excluding specialists, normally to fill positions wherein the qualities of leadership are required. (see also **officer**)

Non–Line of Sight (NLOS) missile (see **Fiber Optic-Guided Missile**)

Non-Proliferation Act: Congressional legislation signed into law on 10 March 1978. The act mandates the licensing and regulating of nuclear exports to negate the chance that U.S. nuclear exports would be used militarily by other states.

Non-Proliferation Treaty (NPT): Formally known as the Treaty on the Non-Proliferation of Nuclear Weapons, the NPT opened for signature on 1 July 1968 in London, Moscow, and Washington, to nuclear and nonnuclear states. It was ratified by the United States on 24 November 1968 and entered into force on 5 March 1970. According to Secretary of State Dean Rusk, the treaty's objective was "to make nuclear war less likely by preventing the spread of nuclear weapons to additional countries" [U.S. Congress, Senate Foreign Relations Committee, *Non-Proliferation Treaty, Hearings*, July 10-12, 17, 1968, p. 28]. The treaty defines the obligations of both nuclear and nonnuclear weapon states regarding the prevention of the further spread of nuclear weapons. Nonnuclear weapon states are prohibited from acquiring nuclear weapons, and nuclear weapon states (United States, Soviet Union, France, China, and United Kingdom) are prohibited from transferring nuclear explosives to nonnuclear weapon states. With the notable exceptions of France, China and India, over 140 nations have signed the treaty.

In 1946, the United States put forward the Baruch plan, which would have given the United Nations all control over nuclear weapons. In the period 1957–1961, several plans limiting the transfer of nuclear weapons to nonnuclear states were put forward by several European nations and the United States. In August 1965, the United States submitted a proposal to the United Nations for a multilateral nuclear force (MLF), whereby West Germany would get access to nuclear weapons (and tie the NATO countries even closer together). The Soviet Union did not accept this, and for a variety of other political reasons, the multilateral force plan was dropped.

In May 1966, the U.S. Congress approved the Pastore Resolution (S.R. 179, 89th Congress, 2nd sess.), which favored completion of a nonproliferation agreement. The United States and Soviet Union submitted identical draft treaties to the United Nations in August 1967. The treaties called for the superpowers to pursue nuclear disarmament and to share nuclear research technology. However, the nonnuclear states were worried that their promises not to obtain nuclear technologies would put them at a political and military disadvantage. To alleviate these fears, the United States, the United Kingdom, and the Soviet Union passed a March 1968 Security Council resolution stating that any nuclear aggression or threat of aggression would be immediately addressed by the U.N. Security Council. This satisfied the nonnuclear states, and on 1 July 1968 the NPT was opened for signature at the United Nations.

The NPT was submitted to the U.S. Congress almost immediately, and despite the Soviet invasion of Czechoslovakia during Treaty hearings, the Senate reported in favor of the NPT. However, ratification was held over until after the 1968 presidential election and it was not until March 1969 that the NPT was ratified under the Nixon Administration.

Key NPT provisions:

• Verification will be maintained by inspections of peaceful nuclear operations by the International Atomic Energy Agency (IAEA). In December 1980, the United States and the IAEA negotiated an agreement that allowed the United States to determine which of its nuclear facilities would be subject to IAEA inspection. On 21 February 1985, the Soviet Union signed a similar agreement with the IAEA.
• All states retain the right to "develop research, production and use of nuclear energy for peaceful purposes" (Article IV).

• "Potential benefits from any peaceful applications of nuclear explosions will be made available to non-nuclear-weapon states" (Article V).
• All parties are to pursue both an end to the arms race and disarmament (nonnuclear nations do not believe that the nuclear nations are living up to this responsibility).
• Amendments to the treaty must be approved by a majority of the signatories; the treaty is open for signature to all states.
• Withdrawal from the treaty is permitted if a party decides that "extraordinary events have jeopardized the supreme interests of its country." Written notification must be made three months in advance and must state the precipitating extraordinary events (Article X).
• Twenty-five years after the NPT entered into force (March 1995), a review conference of the signatories will decide whether or not to extend the treaty. Review conferences have been held in May 1975, August 1980, and June 1985. As of 1989, France and China still had not signed the treaty.

[CRS, *Fundamentals of Nuclear Arms Control, Part I—Nuclear Arms Control: A Brief Historical Survey*, report prepared for the House Committee on Foreign Affairs, 20 May 1985].

non-strategic nuclear forces: "Those general purpose forces assigned to United Commanders which are capable of delivering tactical nuclear weapons in a spectrum of conflict ranging from localized engagements to general nuclear war" [CINCPAC, *CINC-*

PAC Standing Operating Procedures (SOP) for Nuclear Operations, 18 April 1983, released under the FOIA].

NOPLAN (No Plan available or prepared):   A JCS term for "a contingency for which no **operation plan** has been published."

NORAD (North American Aerospace Defense Command):   U.S.-Canadian **combined command** established in 1957 to provide surveillance and control of North American airspace and warning, assessment, and defense against aerospace attack. The countries signed the formal agreement on 12 May 1958 and declared that the "problem of air defense of our two countries could best be met by delegating to an integrated headquarters, the task of exercising operational control over combat units of the national forces made available for the air defense of both countries" [1958 NORAD Agreement]. The original NORAD agreement was for a period of ten years. Subsequent extensions have renewed the agreement, and in 1981 its name was changed from the North American Air Defense Command to the North American Aerospace Defense Command to reflect its "aerospace surveillance and missile warning related responsibilities" [1981 NORAD Agreement].

In its ballistic missile warning role, NORAD transmits data on a continual basis to the National Command Authority (NCA) command centers and the Canadian Defense headquarters in Ottawa over the circuits that would be used in the event of an actual attack. In its space-related role, NORAD tracks, catalogues, and makes predictions on space objects. It established the **Space Defense Operations Center (SPADOC)** to serve as the focal point for national space defense operations. Its space mission includes space surveillance, a role NORAD has performed for over 20 years. Data on every piece of orbiting hardware detected by a sensor is transmitted to SPADOC computers in the NORAD command post. The observation is compared with predicted locations of catalogued satellites. SPADOC then makes follow-on reports of the object, determines whether it is a new object or already catalogued, and follows satellites when they reenter the earth's atmosphere to alert the missile warning community that it is not an incoming warhead. This function satisfies the 1967 U.N. **Outer Space Treaty**, which calls for all signatories to be responsible for any damage incurred by one of its returning satellites.

CINCNORAD also serves as Commander of **U.S. Space Command** and **Air Force Space Command**. CINCNORAD reports to the U.S. President through the JCS and the Secretary of Defense and to the Canadian Prime Minister through the Canadian Chief of Defence Staff and Minister of National Defence. **Tactical Air Command's** 1st Air Force is responsible for management of resources for continental air defense, including fighter interceptors, radar sites, and control centers; **Alaskan Air Command** operates air defense units in Alaska. Other interceptors are provided by the Air National Guard, Navy, and Marine Corps.

Headquarters
Peterson AFB, CO 80914

NORAD Regions

- Alaskan NORAD Region, Elmendorf AFB, AK 99506
- 23rd NORAD Region, Tyndall AFB, FL 32403
- 24th NORAD Region, Griffiss AFB, NY 13441
- 25th NORAD Region, McChord AFB, WA 98438
- 26th NORAD Region, March AFB, CA 92518
- Canadian NORAD Region, CFB North Bay, Ontario, Canada

Operations Centers

- Missile Warning Center
- **NORAD Combat Operations Center (COC)**
- **Space Defense Operations Center (SPADOC)**
- Space Surveillance Center
- **Air Defense Operations Center (ADOC)**

NORAD Cheyenne Mountain Complex (NCMC): Hollowed-out mountain near Colorado Springs and Pikes Peak, CO, that contains the **NORAD Combat Operations Center (COC)** in 15 steel buildings. NORAD's worldwide air, missile, and space attack warning systems terminate at NCMC, and first alert warnings would be sent from here. Preliminary planning for NCMC began in 1956 when defense officials defined the need for a survivable underground air defense combat operations center. The first dynamite blasting began in 1961, and in 1966, NORAD discontinued operation of its above-ground command post in Colorado Springs and moved to the mountain complex. The NCMC is self-sufficient, with an operating force of over 1,700 people. The complex could be sealed off from the outside world except for communications and remain self-sufficient for over a month in the event of war.

NORAD computer systems are the Command Center Processing and Display System (CCPDS) and the Missile Warning and Space Surveillance System. They receive, process, and store data on air defenses, early warning, satellites, and enemy submarines. The CCPDS, operational since September 1979, consolidates information on missile warnings and space surveillance into a single computer system.

In addition to the COC, the NCMC houses the Missile Warning Center; the **Space Defense Operations Center**; the Space Surveillance Center; the **Air Defense Operations Center**, which maintains status of air defense forces and high interest air traffic; the FEMA National Warning Center for **civil defense**; a weather support unit; and communications and intelligence centers. The NORAD Alternate Command Post (ALCOP) is located at Malmstrom AFB, MT.

NORAD Combat Operations Center (COC): Command center housed within the **NORAD Cheyenne Mountain Complex** that receives information from early-warning sensors for both ballistic and air-breathing attack. The COC receives information from satellites and radar on space and missile launches. This information is automatically translated into symbols on maps of the world for assessment of whether the launch is a threat to North America. In case of an attack, NORAD would send warning and assessment information to the National Command Authorities (NCA) and SAC on the following types of launch:

- Type I Launch: a domestic or cooperative launch that could become a reportable event.
- Type II Launch: a domestic or cooperative launch, other than a Type I, whose detection by NORAD sensors is expected.
- Type III Launch: a domestic or cooperative launch, other than a Type I, whose detection by NORAD sensors is not expected, but possible.
- Type IV Launch: a domestic or cooperative launch, other than a Type I, whose detection by NORAD sensors is not expected.

Nore Sub Area: Major subordinate command of NATO's **Allied Command Channel** headquartered at Pitreavie, U.K.

normal access: Security control placed on **operation plan (OPLAN)** information allowing access by most **Joint Deployment System** personnel. (see also **close-hold, limited access**)

North American Aerospace Defense Command (see **NORAD**)

North Atlantic Assembly: An unofficial interparliamentary organiza-

tion of the **North Atlantic Treaty Organization (NATO)**. It was founded in 1955 and has 172 members with each country's representation determined by its population. Its purpose is to encourage governments to take NATO needs into account when drawing up national legislation. The Assembly consists of five committees that meet twice a year: economic, cultural and information, military, political, and scientific and technical.

North Atlantic Council (NAC): The supreme decisionmaking body of the **North Atlantic Treaty Organization (NATO)**, established by Article 9 of the **North Atlantic Treaty**. It is composed of heads of state from all 16 member countries. Together with the **Defense Planning Committee**, the NAC implements the treaty in all areas of foreign, political, and security affairs. Decisions by the body are reached by consensus and are then binding. The Council itself meets only twice a year, but its functions are carried out throughout the year by permanent representatives, subsidiary committees, and the **International Staff**. The chairman of the Council is the NATO **Secretary General**.

North Atlantic Defense System (see **NADS**)

North Atlantic Treaty: The basis for the **North Atlantic Treaty Organization (NATO)**. The western alliance agreement was signed in Brussels on 4 April 1949, and it entered into force on 24 August 1949. The original 12 signatories were Britain,

France, Belgium, Canada, the Netherlands, Luxembourg, the United States of America, Denmark, Norway, Iceland, Italy, and Portugal. Greece and Turkey both signed the treaty in 1952; West Germany signed in 1955; and Spain in 1982. France withdrew from the military organization of NATO in 1966.

The treaty provides for mutual support in the event of an attack on personnel or territory north of the Tropic of Cancer of any of the participating nations. Article V states, ". . . an attack against one or more of them in Europe or North America shall be considered an attack against them all . . . ." The goals of its members as outlined in the treaty are to preserve peace and international security, to further stability and well-being in the North Atlantic region, to eliminate possible interalliance conflicts regarding international economic policies, and to encourage economic collaboration.

North Atlantic Treaty Organization (NATO): The civil and military alliance formed in 1949 to implement the **North Atlantic Treaty**. It now consists of 16 member nations. NATO's civil structure comprises the **North Atlantic Council (NAC)**, the supreme decisionmaking body concerning foreign, political, and security affairs; the **Defense Planning Committee (DPC)**, which deals only with defense matters; and the **International Staff**. Both the NAC and the DPC are chaired by NATO's **Secretary General**. NATO's military structure consists of the **Military Committee (MC)**, made up of member nations' chiefs of staff (e.g., the U.S.

Chairman of the Joint Chiefs of Staff), who make recommendations regarding military matters to the Council and the DPC, and the **International Military Staff (IMS)**, formerly the Standing Group, which consists of six divisions and numerous agencies.

The strategic area covered by NATO is divided among three **major NATO commands (MNCs)** and numerous subordinate and principal subordinate NATO commands. Each major command is headed by a **Supreme Allied Commander** responsible for the operation of forces under his command and the development of defense plans for his area. Commanders receive military policy guidance, direction, and information from the Military Committee and may communicate directly with defense ministers and heads of state of member nations. Some combat forces are assigned to or earmarked for NATO commands, and others are under the operational control of a NATO command. But generally, the forces of member countries remain under national command and control.

Within the U.S. system, either the Secretary of Defense or the President makes decisions regarding final U.S. positions. If the matter is primarily a military one, the U.S. position is made known to the U.S. representative on the Military Committee. In certain cases, U.S. authorities may request a matter to be brought before the NAC/DPC.

Headquarters
Brussels, Belgium
(APO New York 09667)

Major NATO Commands
- **Allied Command Atlantic**
- **Allied Command Channel**
- **Allied Command Europe**

Northern Army Group (NORTH-AG): Principle subordinate command of NATO's **Allied Forces Central Europe**. It is responsible for land defense of northern West Germany up to the Elbe River. It is commanded by a British general (Commander of the British Army of the Rhine) and includes army corps from Belgium, the Netherlands, West Germany, and the United Kingdom with a combined peacetime strength of 240,000 and reinforcements from the United States (III Corps). In peacetime, each force remains under its national command.

Headquarters
Moenchen-Gladbach, West Germany

North Warning System (NWS): Air defense early-warning radar system operated by NORAD to replace the 31 **DEW Line** (sometimes called "SEEK FROST") radars stretching from Alaska to Labrador, Canada. The NWS will complement long-range, all-altitude coverage of **over the horizon**-backscatter (OTH-B) radar surveillance by providing tactical early warning of bomber or cruise missile attacks on North America. Scheduled for completion in 1992, the full NWS system will consist of 54 radar stations: 15 long-range AN/FPS-117 air defense radars and 39 short-range unattended gap filler radars. In November 1987 the first five radars became operational in the western Arctic and have been used to detect Soviet long-range bombers over the Beaufort Sea. The NWS radars are augmented by SEEK IGLOO radars, four OTH-B radars, and **Joint Surveillance System (JSS)** radars in CONUS. The NORAD Cheyenne Mountain Complex will be upgraded by 1991 with $1 billion in improvements for data processing to provide better characterization of a Soviet air or ballistic missile attack against U.S. satellites. The NWS is tied into regional operati ROCCS at Elmendorf AFB, AK, and North Bay, Canada, via satellite communications. The United States is funding 60 percent of the project, and the Canadians are funding the remaining 40 percent. Funding for procurement of the radars in FY 1990 is $207.1 million and in FY 1991 is $10.1 million.

NOSS (Naval Ocean Surveillance Satellite) (see **White Cloud**)

NOTAL: Not to (nor needed by) all, a term used in messages to refer to previous communications and references.

notice to airmen (NOTAM): Information issued periodically concerning any facility or aid relating to air navigation, or concerning modification of safety conditions necessitating changes in flight plans, affecting civil safety, or creating a potential hazard.

notice to mariners: Information giving latest changes to navigational charts and other aid, including modification of safety conditions necessitating changes in ship traffic patterns or affecting civilian boating in any way. Notices are published by the **Defense Mapping Agency's** Hydrographical Topographic Center and are prepared jointly with the National Ocean Service and the U.S. **Coast Guard**. They are used to report gunnery exercises, fleet maneuvers, missile tests, and the like.

NSA (see **National Security Agency/Central Security Service**)

NSC (see **National Security Council**)

NSDD (see **National Security Decision Directive**)

NSDD-13, "Nuclear Weapons Employment Policy": Reagan Administration **National Security Decision Directive** that sets U.S. policy on the deployment, employment, and acquisition of nuclear forces. NSDD-13 replaces **PD-59** of the Carter Administration. According to then Secretary of Defense Casper Weinberger, U.S. nuclear policy (as stated by NSDD-13) is as follows

The current nuclear policy guidance generally reaffirms the fundamental principles of previous U.S. nuclear deterrence policy. There are, however, some differences between the current nuclear guidance and the previous administration's guidance. The current guidance:

- Clarifies and emphasizes the direct link between nuclear weapon deterrence strategy and acquisition policy; i.e., our objectives and national security requirements if we fail to deter in a conflict will directly determine our systems acquisition and weapons requirements in peacetime.
- Deterrence strategy should determine basic nuclear weapons requirements, force acquisitions and force structure.
- Deterrence strategy should evolve in parallel with improvements in force capabilities.

- Places greater emphasis on the importance and need for diversity in nuclear weapon systems and basing modes.
- Diversity in force structure strengthens flexibility, survivability and endurance which, in turn, strengthens deterrence.
- Diversity complicates Soviet defense and attack planning.
- Hedges against unforeseen degradation in the effectiveness or survivability of our force elements and the possibility of Soviet technological breakthroughs.
- Recognizes better than previous guidance the importance of command, control and communications for the U.S. deterrence forces and their significant contribution to stable deterrence.

In addition, the current guidance was prepared as a part of a broader policy review which includes significant strengthening of our conventional deterrent. [U.S. Congress, Senate Foreign Relations Committee, *U.S. Strategic Doctrine, Hearings*, 14 December 1982, p. 100].

NSDD-32, "U.S. National Security Strategy": The basic national security strategy statement of the Reagan Administration, signed by President Reagan on 20 May 1982. The strategy of the **National Security Decision Directive** designated the Soviets as the main military threat, rather than the more common but less significant adversaries in the Third World. The strategy stated that a war with the Soviet Union is likely to be global and that military planning should envision sequential, rather than simultaneous, operations in different theaters. To counter the threat, the strategy placed increasing importance on conventional forces, including allied contributions, and directed the forward basing of U.S. forces in peacetime. The heavy reliance upon military forces deployed overseas—forces capable of responding to a spectrum of contingencies in overseas areas of primary national interest—also focused more attention on the maritime links to those forces. The emphasis on prolonged conventional conflict and on denying the Soviets the ability to choose the geographic limits of a conflict also served as the basis for the **Maritime Strategy**, the Navy strategy to support campaigns in ground theaters of operations both directly and indirectly.

NSDM-242, "Planning Nuclear Weapons Employment for Deterrence": Nixon/Ford **National Security Decision Memorandum** issued on 17 January 1974 that was later replaced by **PD-59** in the Carter Administration and **NSDD-13** in the Reagan Administration. The complete text is as follows

The fundamental mission of U.S. nuclear forces is to deter nuclear war, and plans for the employment of U.S. nuclear forces should support this mission. Our deterrence objectives are:

1. To deter nuclear attacks against the United States, its forces, and its bases overseas.
2. In conjunction with other U.S. and allied forces, to deter attacks—conventional and nuclear—by nuclear powers against U.S. allies and those other nations whose security is deemed important to U.S. interests.
3. To inhibit coercion of the United States by nuclear powers and, in

conjunction with other U.S. and allied forces, help inhibit coercion of U.S. allies by such powers.

The United States will rely primarily on U.S. and allied conventional forces to deter conventional aggression by both nuclear and non-nuclear powers. Nevertheless, this does not preclude U.S. use of nuclear weapons in response to conventional aggression.

Planning Limited
Nuclear Employment Options

Should conflict occur, the most critical employment objective is to seek early war termination, on terms acceptable to the United States and its allies, at the lowest level of conflict feasible. This objective requires planning a wide range of limited nuclear employment options which could be used in conjunction with supporting political and military measures (including conventional forces) to control escalation.

Plans should be developed for limited employment options which enable the United States to conduct selected nuclear operations, in concert with conventional forces, which protect vital U.S. interests and limit enemy capabilities to continue aggression. In addition, these options should enable the United States to communicate to the enemy a determination to resist aggression, coupled with a desire to exercise restraint.

Thus, options should be developed in which the level, scope, and duration of violence is limited in a manner which can be clearly and credibly communicated to the enemy. The options should (a) hold some vital enemy targets hostage to subsequent destruction by survivable nuclear forces, and (b) permit control over the timing and pace of attack execution, in order to provide the enemy opportunities to reconsider his actions.

Planning for General War

In the event that escalation cannot be controlled, the objective for employment of nuclear forces is to obtain the best possible outcome for the United States and its allies. To achieve this objective, employment plans should be developed which provide to the degree practicable with available forces for the following:

1. Maintenance of survivable strategic forces in reserve for protection and coercion during and after major nuclear conflict.
2. Destruction of the political, economic, and military resources critical to the enemy's postwar power, influence, and ability to recover at an early time as a major power.
3. Limitation of damage to those political, economic, and military resources critical to the continued power and influence of the United States and its allies.

Further Guidance and Presidential Review of Employment Plans

The Secretary of Defense shall issue guidance consistent with this NSDM to serve as the basis for the revision of operational plans for the employment of nuclear forces by the Joint Chiefs of Staff. An information copy of this guidance should be provided to the President and Secretary of State.

Within three months, the Secretary of Defense shall present for Presidential review an initial set of limited employment options. At quarterly intervals thereafter, the Secretary of Defense shall present for Presidential review a summary of available options and an analysis of any additional recommended options. Each presentation should include illustrative scenarios for each limited employment option.

Within six months the Secretary of Defense shall submit to the President an analysis of the political, economic, and selected military targets considered critical to potential enemy's post war power, influence, and recovery as a major power. Appropriate aspects of this analysis should be coordinated with the Secretary of State and the Director of Central Intelligence.

In addition, the Secretary of Defense shall submit to the President an evaluation of the effectiveness, limitations and risks of the resultant operational plans. Interim results of this evaluation should be reported approximately every six months at significant points in the process of revision.

Command, Control and Crisis Management

To insure that nuclear forces are responsive to the national command authorities, employment planning for command, control, communications and surveillance must support decision-making and force execution, taking into account U.S. nuclear employment objectives and options, the survivability of the forces themselves, and the consequences of direct attack on the command control systems. At a minimum, this planning should provide for:

1. Essential support to decision-making and execution of retaliatory strikes in the event of large attacks on the United States.
2. Adequate support for decision-making and flexible use of nuclear forces in attempts to control escalation in local conflict. Employment planning for this function may assume that the national level command, control, and communications systems and associated sensors supporting the National Command Authorities are not subject to direct attack.

With regard to crisis management procedures:

1. The Secretary of State, Secretary of Defense, and the Director of Central Intelligence shall refine their crisis management procedures to provide timely political-military assessments and recommendations to the National Command Authority to support potential nuclear employment decisions. The revised procedures should be submitted to the President for review by 31 March 1974.
2. The Secretary of Defense shall in addition submit to the President by March 31, 1974, detailed recommendations on the desirability, composition, operations, facilities, and physical location of a senior level staff to provide prompt military advice to the National Command Authority on the possible use of nuclear forces in a crisis.
3. The Assistant to the President for National Security Affairs, in consultation with the Secretaries of State and Defense and the Director of Central Intelligence, shall conduct a continuing evaluation of the national level crisis management procedures. Within six months, the Defense Program Review Committee shall prepare an initial report on the adequacy of present interagency organizational arrangements for Presidential review. Future annual reports shall contain evaluations of appropriate tests and exercises of these procedures.

Additional Actions

The Secretary of State shall prepare an analysis of any necessary actions related to informing the NATO Alliance and other states, including the Soviet Union and the PRC, of changes in U.S. nuclear policy. The analysis should include a discussion of the extent to which we need to inform other states and the key considerations in making decisions on these issues. This study should identify for each alliance and, as applicable, on a nation-by-nation basis, those aspects whose disclosures should be avoided. In support of this effort the Director of Central Intelligence should prepare a special assessment of likely Soviet and PRC reactions to the new policies, and how these might be influenced by US statements and actions.

The Secretary of Defense should prepare an analysis, from the point of view of military preparedness, of the desirability of any changes in current arrangements for allied participation in NATO nuclear planning.

The results of these additional actions should be submitted for review by the Verification Panel by 31 March 1974.

NUCFLASH: Flagword used on an **OPREP-3 PINNACLE** message to describe an event or incident where creating a risk of outbreak of nuclear war exists. NUCFLASH is used to provide the National Command Authorities with immediate notification of accidental or unauthorized launchings of nuclear weapons that could create risk of outbreak of war with the Soviet Union:

- Any accidental, unauthorized, or other unexplained nuclear detonation or possible nuclear detonation.
- The accidental or unauthorized launch of a nuclear-armed or nuclear-capable missile in the direction of or having the capability to reach the USSR, other Warsaw Pact countries, or the People's Republic of China.

• Unauthorized flight of, or deviation from an approved flight plan by, a nuclear-armed or nuclear capable aircraft with the capability to penetrate the airspace of the USSR, other Warsaw Pact countries, or the People's Republic of China.

• The detection of unidentified objects by a missile-warning system or interference (experienced by such a system or related communications) that appear to be threatening and could create a risk of nuclear war.

(see also **nuclear weapons accident**, **nuclear weapons incident**)

Nuclear and Space Talks (NST): U.S.-Soviet negotiations begun in Geneva on 12 March 1985 to discuss defense and space weapon systems, INF, and strategic nuclear weapons arms control. U.S. Ambassador Max Kampelman was placed in charge of all three subnegotiations, as well as serving as the negotiator for the space and defense talks covering **Strategic Defense Initiative** and anti-satellite weapons; Yuliy Vorontsov headed the Soviet delegation. Congressional observers attend the talks occasionally and are briefed by the U.S. delegation, but do not attend any of the actual negotiating sessions. The anti-satellite negotiations and **START** negotiations continue even with successful conclusion of the **INF Treaty**.

nuclear-capable unit: "A unit or activity assigned responsibilities for assembling, maintaining, transporting, or storing war reserve nuclear weapons, their associated components and ancillary equipment" [DNA, *Department of Defense Nuclear Weapons Technical Inspection System*, TP 25-1, p. 3, released under the FOIA]. Many units within the military possess a theoretical capability to stow, handle, or fire nuclear weapons; however, only a unit with an assigned nuclear mission is considered nuclear-capable. (see also **nuclear-certified unit**)

nuclear-certified unit: "A **nuclear-capable unit** which has been certified" [DNA, *Department of Defense Nuclear Weapons Technical Inspection System*, TP 25-1, p. 3, released under the FOIA]. (see also **nuclear weapons technical inspection**)

nuclear command and control: "The exercise of authority and direction by the President, as Commander in Chief, through established command lines, over nuclear weapon operations of military forces; as Chief Executive over all Government activities that support those operations; and as Head of State over required multinational actions that support those operations" [DOD, *United States Nuclear Command and Control System Support Staff*, DOD Dir 3150.6, 3 February 1988, p. 1]. (see also **Nuclear Command and Control System**)

Nuclear Command and Control System (NCCS): The system established by the DOD on 21 August 1987 by **National Security Decision Directive** (NSDD)-281 for the conduct of **nuclear command and control**. The NCCS is defined as

The designated combination of flexible and enduring elements including facilities, equipment, communications, procedures, personnel, and the structure in which these elements are integrated, all of which are essential for planning, directing, and controlling nuclear weapon operations of military forces and the activities that support those operations. The NCCS supports the exercise of authority and direction by the President as Commander in Chief, through established command lines, over nuclear weapon operations of military forces; as Chief Executive over all Government activities that support those operations; and as Head of State over required multinational actions that support those operations [DOD, *United States Nuclear Command and Control System Support Staff*, DOD Dir 3150.6, 3 February 1988, p. 1].

The Nuclear Command and Control System Support Staff was created in 1988 under the Secretary of Defense, who also serves as the Executive Agent for the NCCS.

nuclear control orders (NCO): "An EAM [**emergency action message**] which authorizes or directs the transfer, employment, termination of employment, destruction, or disabling of nuclear weapons" [USCINCLANT *Emergency Action Procedures*, 17 July 1985, Ch 10, pp. 2–7, released under the FOIA]. Within execution of the **Single Integrated Operational Plan**, NCOs direct the selective release of nuclear weapons. The two types of NCOs are

• Nuclear execution messages: 12 options
• Nuclear termination messages: 6 options

[JCS, *Emergency Action Procedures, Nuclear Control Orders*, 20 March 1985, released under the FOIA]. (see also **nuclear weapons release**)

Nuclear Defense Affairs Committee (NDAC): A NATO committee established in 1967 to make policy proposals on matters regarding NATO's nuclear inventory. Membership on the NDAC is open to any interested NATO country, thus including nonnuclear states in nuclear planning. (see also **Nuclear Planning Group**)

Nuclear Detonation Detection System (NDDS): Previously known as the Integrated Operational Nuclear Detection System (IONDS), NDDS replaces the aging Vela satellites as a new generation of sensors to monitor nuclear explosions. The NDDS satellite sensors are one segment of the **Atomic Energy Detection System**, which also includes sea-bottom detectors, aircraft, submarines, and ground stations. NDDS sensors are carried on **NAVSTAR/GPS** satellites with 40 small, mobile read-out terminals for retargeting and assessment. NDDS will be able not only to detect detonations but to determine the type of warhead, size, and location (within 100 meters) anywhere in the world. The system will be used in command centers, including airborne command posts, to assess U.S. nuclear strikes worldwide, the targeting of follow-on nuclear strikes, and the reconstitution of military forces and communications facilities during and after a nuclear war. [*Nuclear Battlefields*, p. 20].

nuclear device: Fission and **fusion** materials, along with the arming, fuzing, firing, and chemical explosive elements that are not yet part of an operational weapon but are used for experimental purposes such as nuclear testing.

nuclear directed-energy weapon (NDEW): A **directed-energy weapon (DEW)** concept within the **Strategic Defense Initiative** pursued by the Department of Energy for using nuclear explosions to drive DEW technologies. A portion of the energy released in a nuclear explosion would be converted into a concentrated and directed form over long ranges onto ballistic missiles and warheads. Some concepts, such as the **X-ray laser**, would be ground-based pop-up interceptors to intercept missiles in the trajectory stage.

nuclear dud: "A nuclear weapon that when launched at or emplaced on a target, fails to provide any explosion of that part of the weapon designed to produce the nuclear yield" [*JCS Pub 1*, p. 254].

nuclear emergency search team (NEST): A Department of Energy (DOE) organization established in January 1975 under the management of the DOE Nevada Operations Office to enhance the department's ability to search for and identify lost or stolen nuclear weapons and **special nuclear materials**, and to respond to nuclear bomb threats or radiation dispersal threats. It involves sophisticated radiation detection systems developed and operated by scientific personnel from Lawrence Livermore and Los Alamos National Laboratories, and EG&G Inc., the civilian contractor. Depending on the situa-

tion, NEST resources would be made available to DOD or other federal agencies. NEST teams in the United States are located at the Nevada Test Site, NV; and Andrews AFB, MD. An overseas NEST is maintained at Ramstein AB, West Germany.

nuclear free zone (NFZ): Site that has been declared off limits to the design, testing, production, and deployment of nuclear weapons. The size of NFZs can vary from an individual home to entire regions, such as those established by the **Treaty of Tlatelolco** and the **Treaty of Raratonga**. The specifics for each NFZ are determined on a case-by-case basis.

Nuclear Non-Proliferation Treaty (see **Non-Proliferation Treaty**)

Nuclear Planning Group (NPG): North Atlantic Treaty Organization (NATO) organization established in 1967 to provide multilateral political input into tactical nuclear planning. It reviews NATO's nuclear program and receives reports from NATO military authorities and NPG working groups on nuclear matters. Only seven NATO nations sit on the NPG at any one time (Iceland and Luxembourg do not but can attend as observers); smaller countries rotate membership. In theory, the **Nuclear Defense Affairs Committee** supervises the NPG, but in practice the NPG directly influences nuclear policy by reporting back to NATO as a whole. The NPG meets twice a year at Ministerial level, and more often at Permanent Representative level. Past NPG meetings have resulted in the decision to modernize **intermediate range nuclear forces**, the **Montebello Agreement**, and subsequent offerings of INF arms control.

nuclear power   (see **nuclear reactor**, **naval nuclear propulsion**)

nuclear reactor: An apparatus in which nuclear **fission** may be initiated, maintained, and controlled. The usual components of a nuclear reactor are

- Fissionable material (fuel), such as uranium or plutonium
- Moderating material (unless it is a fast reactor)
- Usually, a reflector to conserve escaping neutrons
- Provision for heat removal
- Measuring and controlling elements

Types of Nuclear Reactors

- Boiling water reactor (BWR): a type of commerical light-water reactor produced by General Electric, in which water passing through the reactor core is converted directly to steam, which drives a turbine to generate electricity.
- Clinch River Breeder Reactor (CR-BR): a proposed prototype nuclear reactor near Oak Ridge, TN, that Congress canceled in 1983. Breeder reactors are intended to produce more fissionable nuclear fuel than they use.
- Light water reactor (LWR): the most common type of commercial nuclear reactor. Because it uses regular water to cool the reactor core and moderate the nuclear reaction, it can be fueled only with enriched uranium. Canadian "Candu" heavy water reactors can operate on natural uranium.
- Pressurized water reactor (PWR): the most common type of U.S. light water reactor. Cooling water that goes through the reactor core is kept in a pressurized loop and not allowed to boil. The heat from the pressurized loop is then transferred to a second loop of water, which is turned to steam to drive an electric generator.

The term *reactor* is used interchangeably with the term *pile*, from the earliest reactors, which were piles of graphite blocks and uranium slugs. (see also **naval nuclear propulsion**)

nuclear reactor accident: Codename "Faded Giant," a reactor accident is defined as: "an uncontrolled reactor critically resulting in damage to the reactor core, or an event, such as a loss of coolant, that results in a significant release of fission products from the reactor core." The Defense Nuclear Agency further defines a nuclear reactor accident as a

loss of control of radioactive material which presents or could present a hazard to life, health, or property or which may result in any member of the general population exceeding exposure limits for ionizing radiation; any unexpected event involving radioactive materials or radiation exposure which prudence dictates to be of such consequence to warrant the informational interest of appropriate government officials through the NMCC [**National Military Command Center**], including events having domestic or international implications and those that would be of significant interest to the public.

Criteria for determining whether an accident within this general description has occurred include

a) Fatality or lost workday injury to an individual as a direct result of the accident. Also included is the loss of any reactor fuel;
b) Damage to property in excess of $100,000;
c) Release of radioactive material exceeding 5,000 times the limits specified for material listed in appendix B, table II, Title 10, CFR Part 20, when averaged over a period of 24 hours;
d) Exposure of the whole body of any individual to 25 **rems** or more of radiation; exposure of the skin of the whole body to 150 rems or more of radiation; or exposure of the feet, ankles, hands, or forearms to 375 rems or more of radiation;
e) A loss of one workweek or more of operation of the facilities.

[DNA, *Notification Procedures for Accidents and Significant Incidents Involving Nuclear Weapons, Reactors and Radioactive Materials*, DNA Instruction 7730.2D, 22 February 1978, released under the FOIA; Army, *Safety: Accident Reporting and Records*, AR 385-40, 1 September 1980; DOD, Assistant to the Secretary of Defense (Public Affairs), *Nuclear Accident and Incident Public Affairs Guidance*, DOD Directive 5230.16, 7 February 1983; DOD, Assistant to the Secretary of Defense (Atomic Energy), *Notification Procedures for Accidents and Significant Incidents Involving Nuclear Weapons, Reactors, and Radioactive Materials*, DOD Instruction 7730.12, 1 August 1976; Chief of Naval Operations (OP-981N), *Nuclear Reactor and Radiological Accidents: Procedures and Reporting Requirements*

for, OPNAVINST 3040.5B, 3 April 1981; all released under the FOIA]. (see also **nuclear reactor incident**)

nuclear reactor incident: Significant nuclear reactor incidents are defined as unexpected events resulting from any of the following:

a) Exceeding a safety limit as defined in the technical specifications;
b) Exposure of personnel to any radiation in excess of allowable limits;
c) Release of radioactive material in excess of 500 times the limit for materials listed in appendix B, table II, Title 10, CFR Part 20, when averaged over a period of 24 hours;
d) A loss of one day or more of the operation of the facilities;
e) Damage to property in excess of $10,000;
f) Unusual interest in the public or news media.

[Army, *Safety: Accident Reporting and Records*, AR 385-40, 1 September 1980, released under the FOIA]. (see also **nuclear reactor accident**)

nuclear reserve force: A part of strategic nuclear forces that is expected to survive a protracted nuclear war and be available and under control for use in bargaining or subsequent strikes. The nuclear reserve force includes a set of **ICBMs, bombers, submarines,** and **Tomahawk sea-launched cruise missiles** that would not be employed in initial nuclear strikes. It is also called a strategic reserve force. (see also **Single Integrated Operational Plan**)

nuclear risk reduction center   (see **Agreement on the Establishment of Nuclear Risk Reduction Centers**)

nuclear surety: Personnel, material, and procedures that provide for the security, safety, and reliability of nuclear weapons and that lend assurance that no **nuclear weapon(s) accident**, **nuclear weapon(s) incident**, unauthorized detonation or degradation will occur.

nuclear test: Test to provide information on the design and improvement of nuclear weapons and/or to study the effects of nuclear explosions. Both the Departments of Energy and Defense conduct nuclear tests. The three main types of DOE tests are

- One-point safety test: verifies that detonating a high nuclear explosive by initiation at any one point has a probability of not more than one in one million of producing a nuclear yield in excess of four pounds TNT equivalent;
- Proof test: determines the yield of nuclear weapons already in the stockpile or possible additions to it;
- Weapon development test: a physics experiment designed to test new theories and/or techniques of a new device or design.

The two main types of DOD tests are

- Nuclear weapon effects test (NWET): determines effects of nuclear detonations on the environment (atmosphere, materials, equipment, structures, and personnel) and the effects of the environment on nuclear detonations;
- Operational test: checks the functions of a military system in the system's operating nuclear environ-

ment to develop confidence in the system and to develop tactics and doctrine associated with the system.

Nuclear Warfare Status Group (NWSG): "The NWSG serves as the **Joint Staff** element responsible for matters pertaining to monitoring and executing SIOP (**Single Integrated Operational Plan**) nuclear options and determining the residual nuclear capability of the United States and the residual enemy threat." The NWSG is located at the Nuclear Warfare Status Branch, Strategic Operations Division, J-3, Joint Chiefs of Staff (JCS). As the primary staff group on the conduct of nuclear warfare, the NWSG "provides sufficient information to assist the JCS and the NCA [National Command Authority], as necessary, in formulating decisions involving SIOP execution and termination" [JCS, *Crisis Staffing Procedures of the Joint Chiefs of Staff*, SM-481-83, 12 July 1983, pp. 3-35, 3-36, released under the FOIA].

nuclear warhead: An item normally consisting of the explosive system, the nuclear system, and the electrical circuitry. It may be implosion type, gun assembly, or thermonuclear type.

nuclear waste: The biproduct of **nuclear reactor** operations and the production of nuclear weapons. Nuclear waste is categorized as either high-level or low-level waste. High-level nuclear waste consists of spent nuclear fuel rods, irradiated reactor elements, and other radioactive waste that can remain dangerous for more than 10,000 years. Most high-level waste currently is stored in pools of water at nuclear reactor sites, awaiting permament disposal in underground repositories being developed by DOE. Low-level nuclear waste consists of radioactive waste from nuclear reactors, industrial processes, and medical facilities that generally decays to safe radiation levels within a few decades. Low-level waste is divided into classes A, B, and C, with class A being the least dangerous and class C remaining dangerous for hundreds of years. The Nuclear Regulatory Commission allows low-level nuclear waste to be buried in shallow trenches.

A typical U.S. nuclear reactor produces about 30 tons of highly radioactive waste each year. Nuclear power plants have been operating since the early 1950s and have generated more than 10,000 metric tons of spent nuclear fuel. It is estimated that approximately 40,000 metric tons of nuclear waste will have accumulated by the year 2000 and approximately 10,000 metric tons of high-level waste from the production of nuclear weapons will have piled up by the year 2020.

The Nuclear Waste Policy Act of 1982 (PL 97-425) called for the Department of Energy to open a permanent deep repository by 1998 for high-level waste, and to recommend a second site that would begin receiving waste about five years later. The act also created the **nuclear waste fund** to cover the multibillion dollar cost of developing and operating the repositories. On 28 May 1985, the Reagan Administration announced that the search for a second site would be postponed, due to lower-than-anticipated waste volumes. On 28 May 1986, President Reagan named three sites—the Hanford reservation in Washington, Yucca Mountain in Nevada, and Deaf Smith County in Texas—as the candidates for the first permanent repository of nuclear waste. Congress agreed in 1987 to cancel the second repository search and restrict further characterization work for the first repository to Yucca Mountain. The new law allows compensation for the state of Nevada and authorizes a **monitored retrievable storage** facility for storing and packaging spent nuclear fuel before its trip to the permanent respository.

nuclear waste fund: A special Department of Treasury fund that pays for the Department of Energy's high-level **nuclear waste** disposal program. The fund is financed primarily by a per-kilowatt-hour fee on nuclear utilities and the DOE's nuclear weapons program.

nuclear weapon: "A complete assembly (i.e., implosion type, gun type, or thermonuclear type), in its intended ultimate configuration which, upon completion of the prescribed arming, fusing and firing sequence, is capable of producing the intended nuclear reaction and release of energy" [*JCS Pub 1*, Ch 2, 1 December 1984, p. B-23]. A nuclear weapon is a device yielding a reaction by **fission, fusion,** or a combination of both that results in an explosion. The A-bomb (atomic) and H-bomb (hydrogen) are both nuclear weapons; however, it has become common to refer to weapons created by fission as A-bombs and those created by a thermonuclear (fusion) reaction of hydrogen isotopes as H-bombs. Specific types of nuclear weapons are as follows

- Atomic bomb: fission weapon.
- Boosted fission weapon: neutrons produced in thermonuclear reactions enhance the fission process.
- **Clean weapon**: the amount of residual radioactivity is reduced.
- Controlled effects nuclear weapons varies in intensity for specific effects other than normal blast effect.
- Convertible weapon: insertable nuclear component (INC) with both nuclear and conventional capabilities.
- **Dirty weapon**: fission weapon that distributes larger than normal amounts of radioactivity when exploded.
- Dummy weapon: inert weapon with the same configuration and ballistic characteristics as the one it represents.
- **Enhanced radiation weapon**: produces more neutrons, gamma, or x-rays than a normal weapon of the same yield (the so-called "neutron bomb").
- Finished weapon: certified by DOE as ready for the stockpile.
- Fission weapon: nuclear weapon utilizing only fission energy.
- Free-fall weapon: no device, such as a parachute, to stop its fall rate after its release in the air.
- Hydrogen bomb: same as a thermonuclear weapon.
- **Insertable nuclear component (INC)**: weapon from which all the nuclear materials can be removed for storage away from the weapon.

- Laydown weapon: detonation at a finite time after the weapon lands on water or land.
- Maneuver weapon: taken from storage to use in training operations.
- Minimum residual radioactivity weapon: reduces after-detonation fallout, rainout, and burst-site radio activity.
- Operational suitability test weapon (OST unit): produced by DOE and transferred to DOD for evaluation of delivery and targeting systems. It is common for OST units to utilize dummies or mockup weapons rather than active material counterparts.
- Retarded-fall weapon: a parachute is activated after the weapon is dropped from the air to allow the delivery aircraft time to escape radioactive weapon debris.
- Salted weapon: at the time of explosion, certain elements or isotopes capture neutrons and produce radioactive products over the usual amount.
- Service-produced weapon: nuclear weapon minus nuclear components and warhead; produced by a DOD agency and maintained by DOD.
- Suppressed radiation weapon: type of clean weapon that reduces the amount of radiation emitted during explosion and/or reduces the activation of any surrounding material.
- Thermonuclear weapon: fission generates very high temperatures to bring about fusion of light nuclei, causing the release of great amounts of energy. These are clean weapons, unlike fission weapons, because they do not result in contaminating fission products except for the fissionable material needed to detonate them.

• Training weapon: contains no HE components; produced for instruction and training.

nuclear weapon(s) accident: Codename Broken Arrow:

An unexpected event involving nuclear weapons or radiological nuclear weapon components that results in any of the following:

a) Accidental or unauthorized launching, firing, or use by U.S. forces or U.S. supported allied forces, of a nuclear-capable weapon system that could create the risk of an outbreak of war;

b) Nuclear detonation;

c) Nonnuclear detonation or burning of a nuclear weapon or radiological nuclear weapon component;

d) Radioactive contamination;

e) Seizure, theft, loss or destruction of a nuclear weapon or radiological nuclear weapon component, including jettisoning;

f) Public hazard, actual or implied.

The Air Force codifies a Broken Arrow as:

a) The destruction of a nuclear weapon from any cause in which there is a nuclear contribution to the yield, or;

b) The loss of destruction of war reserve nuclear bombs, components or warheads, or other systems employing nuclear energy, in which a nuclear reaction did not contribute to the energy released;

c) An occurrence from any cause leading to radioactive contamination of sufficient magnitude to adversely affect the community.

[DNA, *Notification Procedures for Accidents and Significant Incidents Involving Nuclear Weapons, Reactors and Radioactive Materials*, DNA Instruction 7730.2D, 22 February 1978, released under the FOIA; Army, *Safety: Accident Reporting and Records*, AR 385-40, 1 September 1980; DOD, Assistant Secretary of Defense (Public Affairs), *Nuclear Accident and Incident Public Affairs Guidance*, DOD Directive 5230.16, 7 February 1983; DOD, Assistant to the Secretary of Defense (Atomic Energy), *Notification Procedures for Accidents and Significant Incidents Involving Nuclear Weapons, Reactors, and Radioactive Materials*, DOD Instruction 7730.12, 1 August 1976; Navy, Chief of Naval Operations (OP411-F3) and Commandant of the Marine Corps (POG), *Minimum Criteria and Standards for Navy and Marine Corps Nuclear Weapons Accident and Incident Response*, OPNAVINST 3440.15 CH-1, 13 June 1983; Chief of Naval Operations (OP-981N), *Nuclear Reactor and Radiological Accidents: Procedures and Reporting Requirements for*, OPNAVINST 3040.5B, 3 April 1981; all released under the FOIA. *JCS Pub 1*, 1 April 1984, p. 256]. (see also **nuclear weapon(s) incident**)

nuclear weapon accident/significant incident assistance:

That assistance provided after an accident or significant incident involving nuclear weapons or radiological nuclear weapons components to:

a. Evaluate the radiological hazard.

b. Accomplish emergency rescue and first aid.

c. Minimize safety hazards to the public.

d. Minimize exposure of personnel to radiation and/or radioactive material.

e. Establish security, as necessary, to protect classified government material.

f. Minimize the spread of radioactive contamination.

g. Minimize damaging effects on property.

h. Disseminate technical information and medical advice to appropriate authorities.

i. Inform the public (as appropriate) to minimize public alarm and to promote orderly accomplishment of emergency functions.

j. Support recovery operations of damaged weapons or weapon components.

k. Support the removal of radiological hazards.

[DNA, *Nuclear Weapon Accident Response Procedures (NARP) Manual*, January 1984, p. 158, released under the FOIA].

Nuclear Weapon(s) Deployment Authorizations: Annual guidance provided by the Joint Chiefs of Staff on the deployment of nuclear weapons worldwide, including in foreign countries. The authorizations include the number of allied weapons authorized to fire U.S. nuclear warheads and the contingency weapons that would be moved overseas under operations plans.

nuclear weapon(s) incident: 1. Codename Bent Spear, a nuclear incident is one that involves a nuclear weapon/warhead or nuclear component that does not fall into the category of a **nuclear weapons accident** but:

a. Results in damage to a nuclear weapon or component requiring a major rework, complete replacement, or examina-

tion/recertification by the Department of Energy.

b. Requires immediate action in the interest of safety or nuclear weapons security.

c. May result in adverse public reaction (national or international) or premature release of classified information.

d. Could lead to a nuclear weapons accident and warrants the informational interest or action by the recipients of Bent Spear messages.

e. Army: the striking of a nuclear weapon by lighting or when a commander suspects that lighting has degraded the safety or reliability of a nuclear weapon system and/or when it is known or suspected that the nuclear weapon has been partially or fully armed.

The Air Force classifies a Bent Spear as the following:

a. Any damage to war reserve nuclear bombs or warheads from any cause that does not meet classification of accident as defined in AFR 136-9.

b. Loss or destruction of full-scale nuclear training items from any cause.

c. Damage to full-scale nuclear training bombs or warheads requiring any repair or replacement of components.

d. Loss or destruction of scaled training items when employed with nuclear weapon suspension and release systems.

e. Inadvertent release of full-scale or scaled training items.

f. Inadvertent release of any item using the nuclear weapon suspension and release systems (e.g., fuel tanks, pylons, bomb dispenser, etc.).

g. Damage to or failure of handling and test equipment during any part of the stockpile-to-target sequence of a war reserve weapon or a training item.

h. Individual error or unauthorized act committed in handling, assembly, testing, loading, transporting, and, during training operations, using war reserve nuclear bombs, warheads, or training items.

i. Individual error or unauthorized act that is in violation of nuclear safety procedures or rules and that would degrade the safety of the nuclear weapon system.

2. Codename Dull Sword

Any unexpected event involving a nuclear weapon/component (including war reserve, test, and training weapons or BDU) or associate test and handling equipment which does not fall under the category of a broken arrow or bent spear but meets one of the following criteria:

a. The possibility of detonation or radioactive contamination is increased;
b. Errors are committed in the assembly, testing, loading or transporting of equipment which could lead to a substantially reduced yield, increased dud probability, or to unintentional operation of all or part of a weapons arming and/or firing sequence;
c. The malfunctioning of equipment and material which could lead to a substantially reduced yield, increased dud probability, or to unintentional operation of all or part of a weapons arming and/or firing sequence;
d. Any natural phenomena over which man has no control which results in damage to a weapon or component;
e. Any unfavorable environment or condition, however produced, which subjects a nuclear weapon to vibration, shock, stress, extreme temperatures, or other environments sufficient to cause questioning of the reliability or safety of the weapon. This includes exposure or suspected exposure of the weapon or major components to electrical or electromagnetic energy which could energize or damage weapons components.

The Army classifies a Dull Sword as the following:

a. Damage to the warhead section or warhead that Army organizations are authorized to repair, or malfunctions of associated equipment that could result in damage to the warhead section or warhead. (Associated equipment includes test handling, launch, control, arming, and monitoring systems.)
b. Damage, loss, or destruction of a nuclear-type training weapon. Of particular concern are instances where the same technical procedures and equipment prescribed for use with nuclear weapons were being used when the trainer was damaged or the equipment failed.
c. Unauthorized acts which degrade the safety of a nuclear weapon, unless they are reportable as accidents or significant incidents.
d. The failure to unlock or lock, or other inoperable condition of a permissive action link (PAL) device when it is installed in or attached to a nuclear weapon.
e. A nuclear-capable missile system accident in flight which does not meet the definition of a NUCFLASH or while being transported or stored, even though no nuclear warhead or warhead joint flight test assembly is attached at the time. Missile system accidents will be reported and contain the flagword Dull Sword, in addition to the missile accident flagword.
f. Any other condition which is reportable in the judgement of the commander or custodian of a nuclear weapon.

[Army, *Safety: Accident Reporting and Records*, AR 385-40, 1 September 1980; DOD, Assistant Secretary of Defense (Public Affairs), *Nuclear Accident and Incident Public Affairs Guidance*, DOD Directive 5230.16, 7 February 1983; DOD, Assistant to the Secretary of Defense (Atomic Energy), *Notification Proce-*

dures for Accidents and Significant Incidents Involving Nuclear Weapons, Reactors, and Radioactive Materials, DOD Instruction 7730.12, 1 August 1976; Chief of Naval Operations (OP-981N), *Nuclear Reactor and Radiological Accidents: Procedures and Reporting Requirements for*, OPNAVINST 3040.5B, 3 April 1981; Navy, Chief of Naval Operations (OP411-F3) and Commandant of the Marine Corps (POG), *Minimum Criteria and Standards for Navy and Marine Corps Nuclear Weapons Accident and Incident Response*, OPNAVINST 3440.15 CH-1, 13 June 1983; DNA, *Notification Procedures for Accidents and Significant Incidents Involving Nuclear Weapons, Reactors and Radioactive Materials*, DNA Instruction 7730.2D, 22 February 1978; all released under the FOIA].

nuclear weapon(s) release: Elaborate **National Command Authority (NCA)** instructions permitting the release of nuclear weapons. The JCS has identified certain **nuclear control orders (NCOs)** to the forces that would have to be verified using sealed authentification procedures and then retransmitted to the subordinate units. As coding and decoding take place at each stage, the process can be stopped if verification requirements are not met and are therefore invalid. Once nuclear weapons are used, there is no freedom of choice by commanders to use nuclear weapons again. Once the decision to use nuclear weapons has been made, procedures for coordinating and reporting on nuclear operations (Coordination of Atomic Operations Standing Operating Procedures

(CAOSOP)) are under JCS authority. The CAOSOP consists of at least 12 reports required for reporting on the course of nuclear war.

The procedures by which nuclear release would take place are as follows

1. An **emergency action message (EAM)** from the NCA is sent by the JCS to unified and specified commands or joint task forces that control nuclear weapons. EAMs to submarines go via **TACAMO** (VLF) links and other links from Atlantic and Pacific Fleets.
2. Two persons copy and decode the EAM if it is an NCO. NCOs received by submarines are checked with the onboard fire control computer to select the prestored target assignment package containing flight data for each missile and its warheads from a specific launch area. Four crewpeople will have to act in unison to validate launch orders and execute the attack.
3. The "Red Safe" is opened in ICBM **launch control centers (LCCs)** or individual bombers and the Sealed Authenticators and keying ensembles are removed.
4. The NCO is authenticated, matching with duplicates kept in the Red Safe.
5. The Emergency War Order (EWO) procedures check-list is started in LCCs to prepare proper timing of launch of missiles.
6. Access is established to missile-arming and -firing circuits directly, or through the **Airborne Launch Control System**

(**ALCS**) if LCCs are inoperable. For land-based missiles, each LCC of each squadron (five per 50 Minuteman missiles) is connected to and can fire all 50 missiles. If contact between the LCCs and the missiles is broken, they can be launched by ALCS, whose crew members can transmit the secure launch codes to the missiles against preprogrammed targets.

7. Options are implemented and selected for missiles—the option dialed on two-digit selector, corresponding with NCA-approved options as stated in the NCO. The ALCS has two preparatory commands to implement launch option: preparatory launch command alpha—allowing the crew to select any of 100 preplanned targets and timing modes—and preparatory launch command bravo, which allows the crew to select any targets in the missiles' memories and provide timing and targeting for individual missiles.

8. "Launch Enable" is established, allowing missiles to accept a "Launch Execute" order at the proper time as specified in the NCO; or "Auto" is established, which combines the enable and launch votes in a single action for immediate launch.

9. The time delay is determined for missiles.

10. At this point, a "Launch Inhibit" command is possible, interrupting the next step to execute launch command by second missile LCC. If a second LCC puts in a launch inhibit signal, a sec-

ond launch vote from a third LCC can override.

11. "Launch Execute" by turning keys providing two launch votes for an enabled missile. "Execute" in a bomber or submarine requires similar cooperative efforts among the crew to launch weapons.

12. If ALCS, toggle switch third vote by pilot of **EC-135 airborne command posts** or by battle staff coordinator of **E-4B National Emergency Airborne Command Post (NEACP)**.

Nuclear Weapons Personnel Reliability Program (see **Personnel Reliability Program**)

nuclear weapon(s) technical inspection (NWTI): "A Service or DNA inspection of a **nuclear-capable unit** conducted to examine nuclear weapons technical assembly, maintenance, storage functions, logistic movement, handling, and safety and security directly associated with these functions." All nuclear-capable units must receive an NWTI, certifying that they can execute their assigned nuclear missions. The NWTI is encompassed within the following inspections:

• Defense Nuclear Surety Inspection (DNSI) conducted by DNA;
• Nuclear Surety Inspection (NSI) conducted by the Army;
• Navy Technical Proficiency Inspection (NTPI) and Nuclear Weapons Acceptance Inspection (NWAI) conducted by the Navy;
• Nuclear Surety Inspection (NSI) and Initial Nuclear Surety Inspection conducted by the Air Force.

According to the Department of Defense, nuclear-capable units must be certified at least once every 18 months in order to retain their certification [DNA, *Department of Defense Nuclear Weapons Technical Inspection System*, TP 25-1, p. 2, released under the FOIA].

nuclear weapon war risk accident: Flagword **NUCFLASH**. As defined by the Army, an event that results in either of the following:

1. An accidental, unauthorized, or unexplained nuclear detonation.
2. An accidental or unauthorized launch of a nuclear-armed or -capable missile in the direction of and/or having the capability to reach the Soviet Union or other Warsaw Pact countries.

[Army, *Safety: Accident Reporting and Records*, AR 385-40, 1 September 1980, released under the FOIA].

nuclear yield: "The energy released in the detonation of a nuclear weapon, measured in terms of kilotons or megatons of trinitrotoluene explosive (TNT) required to produce the same energy release" [*JCS Pub 1*, pp. 256–7]. Yields are categorized by DOD as

- Very low: less than one kiloton
- Low: one to ten kilotons
- Medium: 11 kilotons to 50 kilotons
- High: 51 kilotons to 500 kilotons
- Very high: over 500 kilotons

The total energy yield is manifested as nuclear radiation, thermal radiation, and blast and shock energy.

numbered air force: Central organization of aircraft, air combat and combat support units, and personnel operationally assigned to an operating Air Force **major command**— e.g., 1st **Air Force** (Tactical Air Command). The U.S. Air Force has 14 active air forces and three in the Air Force Reserve.

numbered fleet: Central organization of naval ships, aircraft, and personnel operationally assigned and subordinate to an area fleet (Atlantic or Pacific Fleet). A commander of a numbered fleet exercises operational control over assigned Commander **task forces**. The numbered fleets of the U.S. Navy are the **Second Fleet** in the western Atlantic, the **Third Fleet** in the eastern and northeastern Pacific, the **Fifth Fleet** (inactive) in the Indian Ocean, the **Sixth Fleet** in the Mediterranean Sea, and the **Seventh Fleet** in the western and northwestern Pacific. (see also **operational chain of command, fleet, operating forces**)

O

O: Prefix designating an observation aircraft (e.g., OH-58).

OA-10: Air Force single-seat, twin-engine, turboprop, forward air control (FAC) aircraft. It is modified from the **A-10 Thunderbolt** aircraft. In addition to its FAC capability, the OA-10 is designed for combat escort, search and rescue, and visual reconnaissance missions. Like the A-10s, OA-10s are equipped with a 30 mm gun and up to 16,000 lb of ordnance. In October 1987, 24 operational and 2 backup OA-10s were assigned to the 23rd Tactical Air Support Squadron for FAC operations. The OA-10 will replace the OA-37 Dragonfly based at Davis-Mothan AFB, AZ.

observable difference (OD): Externally observable design feature used to distinguish between current types of **heavy bombers** that are capable of performing a particular **SALT**-limited function and those types that are not. A difference may not be functionally related but must be a design feature that is externally observable.

occupation: "The specialty skill requirement of a **billet**, and the skill qualifications of personnel" (DOD, *Manpower Requirements Report FY 1989*, March 1988, p. B-2). Occupation codes used by the services are as follows

- Army: SSI (officer); military occupational specialty (enlisted)
- Navy: NOBC (officer); Rating/NEC (enlisted)
- Air Force: Air Force Specialty Code (officer and enlisted)
- Marine Corps: military occupational specialty (officer and enlisted).

(see also **Appendix F**)

oceanographic research ship (T-AGOR): Specially configured ships of the **Military Sealift Command** that perform research in support of naval oceanography. A new AGOR class is under construction that will be able to operate worldwide in all seasons and will be suitable for use by Navy laboratories, contractors, and academic institutions. These ships will meet changing oceanographic requirements for general, year-round, worldwide ocean research that includes launching, towing, and recovering a variety of large and heavy equipment and sensors involved in acoustic and nonacoustic research. Mizar (T-AGOR 13) participated in the search for the sunken submarine Thresher (SSN-593) in 1964 and the Scorpion (SSN-589) in 1968, as well as helping to locate a Soviet Golf-class submarine that sank near Hawaii and the U.S. hydrogen bomb lost at sea off Palomares, Spain, in 1966. FY 1990 funding for three ships is $278.1 million.

Ocean Safari: A biennial series of NATO maritime exercises held to exercise the alliance's ability to protect sea **lines of communications** carrying supplies and military reinforcements from North America to Europe in wartime. The exercises are conducted between the east coast of the United States and Canada to the Norwegian Sea and Norwegian coastal waters. The **Supreme Allied Commander Atlantic** sponsors the exercise. Eleven NATO nations participated in the 1980s: the United States, Belgium, Canada, Denmark, France, Iceland, West Germany, the Netherlands, Norway, Portugal, and the United Kingdom. In Ocean Safari 85, 157 ships participated, involving some 80,000 NATO personnel. Ocean Safari 87 (31 August–18 September 1987) included the participation of some 150 ships and 250 aircraft from 11 NATO countries, including the USS Forrestal (CV-59) aircraft carrier battle group.

Ocean Surveillance Information System (OSIS):   A Navy network of personnel, facilities, computers, communications, and procedures designed to receive, process, correlate, and disseminate evaluated ocean surveillance information to naval forces. OSIS is a confederation of different collection systems that provides near real-time, all-source **indications & warning**; threat assessment; positional and movement information; and over-the-horizon targeting support to national, theater, and fleet users. The OSIS central elements, created in 1977–1978, consist of two primary subsystems: Sea Watch and the OSIS Baseline Subsystem (OBS). Sea Watch supports the Naval Ocean Surveillance Information Center (NOSIC) located in Suitland, MD. Its prime responsibility is providing ocean surveillance information to the National Command Authorities, the Chief of Naval Operations, and other high-level users in Washington. The OBS supports the Atlantic and Pacific fleets and the numbered fleet commanders and fleet subordinates. (see also **anti-submarine warfare, Bullseye, Classic Wizard, Sound Surveillance System**)

Ocean Venture: Field-training exercise **(FTX)** directed by the JCS and sponsored by the **U.S. Atlantic Command**. This biennial, live-fire exercise is conducted in the Caribbean, Gulf of Mexico, and Puerto Rico areas. Ocean Venture exercises command and control of forces, rapid deployment and employment, and integration of military reserve units into the active force. Operations normally include **carrier battle group** maneuvers, infantry operations, strategic and tactical air activity, air and sealift support, **special operations**, amphibious landings, **port security**, and harbor defense. Ocean Venture 88, held 1–22 April 1988, included more than 40,000 military personnel, including Dutch Royal Marines.

Office of Munitions Control (O-MC): Part of the Department of State's Bureau of Politico-Military Affairs that administers the U.S. government's program to control commercial exports of defense articles and services, including related technical data. The OMC is responsible for granting export licenses to private defense firms who sell weapons through the commercial sales program of the **security assistance program**. The OMC serves as a regulatory agency that either approves or disapproves of license applications in accordance with the provisions of the **Arms Export Control Act**.

office of primary responsibility (O-PR): Any headquarters, agency, or activity having primary functional interest in and responsibility for a specific action, project, plan, program, or problem.

Office of the Secretary of Defense (OSD) (see **Secretary of Defense**)

officer: General term for a military person holding a commission or warrant in one of the armed services. Categories and functional types of officers include:

- *Commissioned officer:* An officer holding a grade and office under a commission issued by the President. In the Army, those officers in a grade of second lieutenant or higher are commissioned.
- *Warrant officer:* An officer holding a warrant issued by the Secretary of

his or her service used to fill specialized technical positions above the enlisted level. A warrant officer ranks below second lieutenant or ensign but above cadet.
- *Non-commissioned officer:* An enlisted soldier in a pay grade of E-4 or higher, excluding specialist, usually used to fill leadership positions.

Commissioned and warrant officers are often referred to in a number of different ways:

- *Action officer:* A staff officer with responsibility for a specific project or action.
- *Flag officer:* A General Officer authorized to fly a personal flag.
- *General officer:* An officer, either a General or Admiral.
- *Line officer:* ("officer of the line"). An officer belonging to a combat branch of the service.
- *Staff officer:* An officer belonging to an administrative staff.

(see also **commander/commanding officer**, **Appendix F**)

officer in tactical command: The senior naval officer present and eligible to assume command, or the officer given tactical command functions by a superior [*JCS Pub 1*, p. 260].

OH-58 Kiowa: Army single-engine, single four-bladed, light observation and scout helicopter assigned to the division attack helicopter battalion, to artillery units, and to cavalry units. The helicopter provides adjustment of conventional artillery, as well as spotting and **laser designa-**

tion for **Hellfire** and other precision-guided munitions. The OH-58 provides day/night real-time reconnaissance and target acquisition support to antitank, air cavalry, and field artillery units. The OH-58A is modified with television, a thermal imaging system (TIS), and a laser rangefinder and designator incorporated into a Mast-Mounted Sight (MMS) above the rotor. An aerial fire support officer usually operates the laser rangefinder-designator (LRFD). The *A* version is being upgraded to *mod D* under the Army Helicopter Improvement Program (AHIP). *Mod D* is fitted with an IR-suppressed exhaust. A highly accurate navigation system permits precise target location information that can be handed off to other aircraft or artillery elements via the airborne target handover system. **Stinger** missiles have also been placed in OH-58D types beginning in FY 1989. The first OH-58Ds joined the 2d Armored Division Artillery in March 1987, and 115 aircraft were fielded through December 1988. Current fielding plans call for each of 10 active divisions to receive six OH-58Ds. Separate artillery brigades in support of the XVIII Airborne Corps, VII Corps, and V Corps will also receive OH-58D helicopters. The prime contractor is Bell Helicopters, Fort Worth, TX, and the engines are produced by Detroit Diesel Allison, Indianapolis, IN. Costs for FY 1990 and 1991 for purchase of 36 helicopters per year are $299.1 million and $327.9 million, respectively.

oiler (AO): Designation for **fleet oiler**.

older heavy ballistic missile launcher: A **ballistic missile** launcher capable of launching ICBMs deployed before 1964 that has a volume significantly greater than the largest light ICBM operational in 1972. The term was coined in an agreed understanding of the Interim Agreement of the **SALT I** accords. Examples of older heavy ballistic missile launchers are the U.S. Titan II (no longer deployed), the Soviet SS-7 launcher, and the SS-8 launchers.

Omega: Subsurface and surface V-LF worldwide radio navigation system managed by the **Coast Guard** that uses phase differences for positioning. Omega, and **LORAN-C** navigation transmitters, are subject to errors as large as two miles, making them 100 times less accurate than NAV-STAR satellites. Omega stations are located in La Moure, ND, Haiku, Japan, and the Soviet Union (three stations: Novosibirsk, Siberian military district; Komsomolsk-na-Amure, Far East military district; and Krasnodar, North Caucasus military district).

Omen   (see **Hydrus**)

On-Site Inspection Agency (OSIA): One of 13 agencies of the **Department of Defense**, established following the ratification of the Intermediate-range Nuclear Forces **(INF) Treaty** between the United States and Soviet Union. It is responsible for monitoring Soviet compliance with the treaty through inventory and "challenge" on-site inspections of missile sites, vehicles, and support facilities and for the destruction of

U.S. medium-range missiles in accordance with the treaty. There are 110 Soviet sites and 25 U.S. sites (12 of which are in Europe) subject to inspection. OSIA is composed of two inspection/escort teams of up to 200 people each. The "red" team, operating in the Soviet Union (including a team of permanent inspectors at the Votkinsk missile production plant), inspects Soviet military facilities and elimination sites. The "blue" team, operating in the United States and Europe, escorts Soviet verification teams on their inspection tours of U.S. facilities and conducts **counterintelligence** activities. Teams include specialists in Soviet affairs and language, missile technology, and technical support. Votkinsk inspectors are rotated every six to nine weeks for "medical and psychological reasons." The on-site verification process will span 13 years. OSIA is headed by an Army Brigadier General, and it reports to the office of the Under Secretary of Defense (Acquisition). Its executive committee is chaired by the Under Secretary and includes the Chairman of the Joint Chiefs of Staff, the Assistant Secretary of Defense (International Security Policy), and deputy directors of the Department of State and the Arms Control and Disarmament Agency. It does not include members of the U.S. intelligence community or National Security Council. Its total personnel strength is approximately 600, and its FY 1988 budget is approximately $200 million [DOD, Under Secretary of Defense (Acquisition), *Organization and Functions Guidebook*, December 1988, p. 72.; Department of State. "U.S. Teams Ensure INF

Treaty Implementation, *Update From State*, January–February 1989, p. 3].

Headquarters
Dulles International Airport,
Chantilly, VA 20041-0498

on station: 1. A code phrase used in air intercept operations meaning, "I have reached my assigned station." **2.** Airborne aircraft in position to attack targets or perform a support or interdiction mission (*JCS Pub 1*, p. 462).

OO: Marking for **immediate** messages.

OP: The short title for an office or individual within the Office of the Chief of Naval Operations; when so used it is always followed by a number or number and letter designation (e.g., OP 50, OP 09D).

operating forces: The operating forces of the Navy are the **numbered fleets**, seagoing forces, **fleet Marine forces (FMFs)** and other assigned Marine Corps forces, **Military Sealift Command**, and such **shore activities** of the Navy and other forces as may be assigned to the operating forces of the Navy by the President or the Secretary of the Navy. The CNO is responsible to the Secretary of the Navy for the command, use, and administration of the operating forces of the Navy. When forces are assigned to unified or specified commands, this responsibility is discharged in a manner consistent with the full **operational command** vested in the combatant commands. The operating forces of the Marine Corps are the fleet Marine forces, the Marine complements aboard Navy ships, the security forces, and Marine combat forces not otherwise assigned. (see also **major command**)

operating location (OL):   1. A unit of the Air Force below the level of **detachment** or smaller than a detachment and lacking any logistic support. **2.** An Air Force member's permanent duty station.

operating strength: An Army **manpower** term referring to the portion of the **end strength** figure assigned to units in the programmed structure. The term is synonymous with

• Navy: distributable strength
• Air Force: assigned strength
• Marine Corps: chargeable strength
• Selected Reserve: trained strength in units.

[DOD, *Manpower Requirements Report FY 1989*, March 1988, p. B-2]

operational chain of command: Command hierarchy established for a particular operation or a series of continuing operations. The **Department of Defense Reorganization Act of 1986** clarified the unified chain of command that runs from the President to the Secretary of Defense to the commanders of the **combatant commands** (i.e., the unified commands and specified commands).

The Navy's typical operational chain of command is illustrated below. Note that the fleet commanders-in-chief fall in the administrative chain of command, as do group, ship squadron, and air wing commanders. Commander Submarine Forces Atlantic and

Pacific are exceptions in that they are the only type commanders that exercise operational control of their forces.

President
:
Secretary of Defense
:
Chairman of the Joint Chiefs of Staff
:
unified or specified command
:
naval component commander
(i.e. CINCLANTFLT or CINCPACFLT)
:   :   :
ASW com-   :   submarine
mander ashore : commander ashore
:
Operational Fleet Commander
:
Task Force Commander
:
Task Group Commander
:
Task Unit Commander
:
Task Element Commander
:
Commanding Officer of ship

(see also **operational control, administrative chain of command**, and **task organization**)

operational command (OPCOM):

OPCOM is the authority to perform those functions of command involving the composition of subordinate forces, assignment of tasks, designation of objectives, and authoritative direction necessary to accomplish the mission. OPCOM includes directive authority for logistics and training. OPCOM should be exercised through the commanders of assigned normal organizational units or through the commanders of subordinate forces established by the commander exercising OPCOM. OPCOM provides full authority to organize forces as the operational commander deems necessary to accomplish assigned missions, and to retain or delegate operational control or **tactical control** as necessary. OPCOM does not, of itself, include such matters as administration, discipline, internal organization, and unit training. OPCOM is exercised solely by the commanders of unified and specified commands [JCS, *Unified Action Armed Forces*].

OPCOM is a concept that is not shared with other echelons of command. **Combatant commanders** exercise OPCOM through service **component** commanders, functional component commanders, subordinate unified commanders, commanders of single-Service forces, and commanders of joint task forces. Within DOD, operational command is often used synonymously with **operational control**, although they mean different things. OPCOM is associated with the authority of the commanders of unified and specified commands, and generally cannot be delegated. (see also **administrative command, commander/commanding officer, commander-in-chief**)

operational control (OPCON): A level of authority used in the execution of joint military operations. OPCON is authority delegated to echelons below the **combatant commander**. Normally, this is authority exercised through the commander of established subordinate commands and the service **component** commanders. Limitations on OPCON as well as additional authority not normally

included in OPCON are specified by a delegating commander. OPCON is

the authority delegated to a commander to perform those functions of command over subordinate forces involving the composition of subordinate forces, the assignment of tasks, the delegation of objectives, and the authoritative direction necessary to accomplish the mission. OPCON includes directive authority for joint training. OPCON should be exercised through the commanders of assigned normal organizational units or through the commanders of subordinate forces established by the commander exercising OPCON. OPCON normally provides full authority to organize forces as the operational commander deems necessary to accomplish assigned missions, and to retain or delegate OPCON or **tactical control** as necessary. OPCON may be limited by function, time, or location. It does not, of itself, include such matters as administration, discipline, internal organization, and unit training [JCS, *Unified Action Armed Forces*].

"Command" and "control" are used in slightly different contexts in the combined arena. Operational control is not synonymous with **operational command**. OPCON is only associated with the authority of a major commander or that delegated to a lower echelon by the commander of a unified or specified command. (see also **administrative command, commander/commanding officer**)

operational readiness inspection (ORI): An Air Force or Navy inspection to assess the **readiness** of combat units. Units receive combat ratings (**C-ratings**) based on the level and condition of unit resources and training through the **Status of Resources and Training System (SORTS)** (formerly the Unit Status and Identity Report).

Operational Report (OPREP): D-OD "reporting system used to advise the Joint Chiefs of Staff, Services, and U.S. Government agencies of an event or incident that may attract national interest; current operations and recommended **operations plans** describing the deployment or employment of military units; and the results of activities associated with military operations. The system is designed to satisfy all echelons of command with a single reporting system." An OPREP is usually a narrative report and is transmitted via **AUTODIN** or the **Worldwide Military Command and Control System (WWMCCS) Intercomputer Network**. Of the five levels of reports, only OPREP-3 is "implemented worldwide continually." An OPREP is transmitted by any level of command directly to the **National Military Command Center (NMCC)**. OPREPs 1, 2, 4, and 5 are transmitted by service commanders or by the commanders of unified or specified commands. When activities do not justify the use of the OPREP system, plans and data are usually relayed via a **situation report (SITREP)**. There are five OPREP categories:

1. *OPREP-1 (Operation(s) Planning Report)*: The OPREP-1 is used to describe planned operations for current situations during a succeeding time period, normally 24 hours
2. *OPREP-2 (Operation(s) Start Re-*

port): The OPREP-2 is used to advise that an operation has started; used in conjunction with OPREP-1 or alone.
3. *OPREP-3 (Event/Incident Report)*: The OPREP-3 is used by any unit for timely notification of appropriate commanders of any incident that has occurred or is in progress. The report will be submitted to provide "as it happens" information on

- Incidents that have either seriously changed or may seriously change current operations;
- Events that have indications of national-level interest involving military operations, natural disasters, and/or civil disorders; and
- Other events as directed.

An OPREP-3 is normally the first indication to senior authority that an incident has occurred that will or may generate high-level interest. It is an initial telephone or radio report, followed by a teletype report for record and confirmation purposes. The goal is to report within 5 minutes, with written confirmation within 20 minutes. OPREP-3 PINNACLE is used to provide the National Command Authorities (NCA) (through the NMCC) with information on any significant event or incident where national interest is indicated.
4. *OPREP-4 (Operation(s) Stop/Result Report)*: The OPREP-4 is used to advise of the completion of an operation or a phase of an operation.
5. *OPREP-5 (Operation(s) Summary Report)*: The OPREP-5 is designed to provide daily summary statistics

pertaining to deployment of joint force operations for the JCS.

The most common OPREP report used on a day-to-day basis is the OPREP-3, which is used to notify **component commands, services, sub-**unified commands, and **major commands** of activity, and which is directed to the national level. An OPREP-3 that denotes that an event or incident is of possible national-level interest uses the flagword PINNACLE. It is sent directly from the originator to the NMCC. An OPREP-3 PINNACLE is one of two formal reports (the other is a **CRITIC**) that could initiate actions under the JCS **Crisis Action System**. There are a number of other flag-words used in OPREP-3 messages, each with specific purposes:

- OPREP-3 BEELINE: Serious incident report of interest to the Air Force only.
- OPREP-3 BENT SPEAR: Incidents involving nuclear weapons that are of significant interest but are not categorized as PINNACLE NUCFLASH or PINNACLE BROKEN ARROW and that are originated at the lowest level of command. A service headquarters can further transmit an OPREP-3 PINNACLE BENT SPEAR.
- OPREP-3 FADED GIANT: Nuclear reactor and/or radiological accidents originated at the lowest level of command. A service headquarters can further transmit an OPREP-3 PINNACLE FADED GIANT.
- OPREP-3 Navy Blue: Serious incident report of interest to the Navy or Marine Corps only.

- OPREP-3 PINNACLE BROKEN ARROW: An unexpected event involving nuclear weapons or nuclear components where a risk of outbreak of nuclear war does not exist but where nuclear detonation, nonnuclear detonation, radioactive contamination, or public hazard could exist.
- OPREP-3 PINNACLE COMMAND ASSESSMENT: A Commander-in-Chief's assessment of a local event or crisis, stating what forces are readily available, the timeframe for their earliest commitment, the major constraints to their employment, and what action, if any, the commander is taking or proposing within the current rules of engagement.
- OPREP-3 PINNACLE EMERGENCY DESTRUCTION/DISABLEMENT: Used to report operations involving the emergency destruction or disablement of nuclear weapons.
- OPREP-3 PINNACLE EMERGENCY EVACUATION: Used to report operations involving the emergency evacuation of nuclear weapons.
- OPREP-3 PINNACLE FRONT BURNER: Report that involves any harassment or attack of U.S. forces.
- OPREP-3 PINNACLE LERTCON: A Commander-in-Chief's alert used to immediately notify the NMCC of unified or specified command actions relative to the **alert condition** of forces. There are five LERTCON messages, one, a Declaration, that may be satisfied by an **emergency action message**, and four that respond to higher authority relat-

ing to the status of forces placed on alert: Attainment, Deviation, Exception, and Progress.

- OPREP-3 PINNACLE **NUCFLASH**: Report where creating a risk of outbreak of nuclear war exists.
- OPREP-3 WHITE PINNACLE: Exercise report of the OPREP-3 system.

operational storage site (OSS): CONUS nuclear weapons storage site designated to provide for storage and maintenance of allocated undeployed nuclear weapons and/or JCS-allocated weapons. (see also **nuclear stockpile**)

operational support: 1. Those pieces of equipment, skills, techniques, and forces that come into play during operations but that are not normally identified as components of the operational combat system. (see also **support**) **2.** That portion of the overall research and development program devoted to the development of individual items of equipment, skills, or techniques that support combat tasks but that are not normally identifiable as components of a specific weapon, support, or command and control system. Operational support presupposes a decision to produce for the inventory.

Operational Test and Evaluation Agency: Army Staff **field operating agency** headquartered at Falls Church, VA.

Operational Test and Evaluation Force (OPTEVFOR): Navy **operating force** reporting to the Chief of Naval Operations; it conducts tests and evaluations of specific na-

val weapons systems, ships, aircraft, equipment, tactics, and procedures. It also assists other agencies with evaluations and tests when directed. It operates the OPTEVFOR, Pacific; Test and Evaluation Force Detachment, Sunnyvale, CA; and is assigned three test and evaluation squadrons.

Headquarters
Norfolk, VA 23511-6388

operations and maintenance (O&M): Day-to-day operations and maintenance costs including fuels, travel and transportation, civilian pay, contract services for maintenance of equipment and facilities, supplies, modification kit installation, and repair parts for weapon systems and equipment. O&M is normally allocated to three classes of combat and support forces:

- Program 1: **Strategic Forces**
- Program 2: **General Purpose Forces**
- Program 3: **Intelligence and Communications.**

operations center: Any of a type of military **command centers**, alternate command centers, **command posts** (mobile and fixed), alternate command posts (**ALCOPs**), emergency actions elements, combat alert/operations centers, **airborne command posts**, and similar facilities of the Navy afloat.

Operations Deputies (OPSDEPS): A body of senior **flag officers** within the Joint Chiefs of Staff (JCS) that resolve operational matters not requiring JCS corporate-body attention. Each service Chief appoints an operations deputy who works with the

Director of the **Joint Staff** to form a subsidiary body known as the Operations Deputies of the Joint Chiefs of Staff. The OPSDEPS are generally the three-star chiefs of operations for the services. The body is chaired by the Director of the Joint Staff and considers issues of lesser importance on behalf of the JCS or screens major issues before consideration by the JCS. A similar body known as the Deputy Operations Deputies (DEPOPSDEPS) serves the same functions but deals primarily with plans. DEPOPSDEPS is chaired by the Vice Director of the Joint Staff.

operations order (OPORD): 1. A directive issued by a commander to subordinate commanders for the purpose of effecting the coordinated execution of an operation (*JCS Pub 1*, p. 264). **2.** An order prepared by the supported commander to implement the National Command Authorities' decision for the execution of an operation. **3.** A directive (issued by unified and specified commands, **Joint Task Force** commanders, or other high-level operational commanders, usually in response to a JCS **alert order**) that sets forth details regarding activities necessary to implement the commander's decisions and accomplish the mission of the command. An OPORD can be a printed hard copy or a message transmitted via **AUTODIN**. (see also **operations plan**)

operations plan (OPLAN): "Any plan, except for the SIOP [**Single Integrated Operational Plan**], for the conduct of military operations in a hostile environment prepared by the commander of a unified or specified command in response to a requirement established by the Joint Chiefs of Staff. Operations plans are prepared in either complete or concept format" [JCS, *Joint Operations Planning System, Volume I*, p. xix, released under the FOIA].

- *Operation Plan in Complete Format (OPLAN)*: An operation plan for the conduct of joint operations that can be used as a basis for development of an **operations order**. "OPLANs are normally prepared only for those situations that would be sufficiently critical to national security to require detailed prior planning. Such situations would normally tax the total resources made available for planning" [JCS, *Joint Operations Planning System, Volume I*, p. II-1, released under the FOIA]. OPLANs resulting from **Joint Strategic Capabilities Plan (JSCP)** tasking and other JCS directives are submitted to the JCS for review and approval.

- *Operation Plan in Concept Format (CONPLAN)*: An operations plan in an abbreviated format that would require considerable expansion or alteration to convert it into an OPLAN or operations order. "CONPLANs are normally prepared when the contingency is not sufficiently critical to national security to require detailed prior planning, the probability of occurrence in the JSCP timeframe is low, or planning flexibility is desired to prepare additional concepts of operations for a wider range of contingencies" [JCS, *Joint Operations Planning System, Volume I*, p. II-1, released under the FOIA]. CONPLANs resulting from JSCP tasking and other JCS directives are submitted to the JCS for review and approval.

operations security (OPSEC): Measures designed to protect information concerning plans and operations (past, present, and future) against unauthorized disclosure.

OPREP (see **Operational Report**)

oral communications: "Crisis that could require U.S. military operations may develop with little or no warning and may require accelerated decisions by the National Command Authority (NCA), the Joint Chiefs of Staff (JCS), and the CINCs [Commanders-in-Chief]. As a result the CAS [**Crisis Action System**] planning process may use rapid oral communications with all concerned. Information and direction provided by oral means should be confirmed by record communications as soon as possible" [JCS, *Joint Operations Planning System, Vol. IV*, p. I-7, released under the FOIA].

oralloy: Nickname for uranium enriched to 93.5 percent in the uranium-235 isotope, a primary **fission** material for nuclear weapons.

ORCON: Control marking on national security-related information standing for "Originator Controlled." Used by the Central Intelligence Agency to indicate that dissemination and extraction of information from a document is under the strict control of the office that originated the material. (see also **security classification**)

order: A communication by a commander to a subordinate commander or unit carrying instructions for a task. An order may be written, oral, or automated. It is used synonymously with "**command**"; however, an order "implies discretion as to the details of execution" [*JCS Pub 1*, p. 266]. (see also **general order**)

order of battle: "The identification, strength, command structure, and disposition of the personnel, units, and equipment of any military force" [*JCS Pub 1*, p. 266].

ordnance: **1.** Collective term for guns, missiles, torpedoes, bombs and related equipment. **2.** The Ordnance Corps, a **combat service support** branch of the Army.

organic: An essential part of a military organization. Organic units, for example, are those listed in the **table of organization** for the Army, Air Force, and Marines, as well as those assigned to the administrative organizations of the Navy.

Organization of the Joint Chiefs of Staff (OJCS): An element of the Department of Defense that provides overall administrative, analytical, and command and control functions in support of the **Chairman of the Joint Chiefs of Staff (CJCS)**. The OJCS consists of

- The **Joint Chiefs of Staff (JCS)**
- The **Joint Staff**
- The agencies of the JSC.

The Joint Staff operates under the exclusive direction of the CJCS, and provides assistance with planning and reporting duties regarding the unified strategic direction of combatant forces, the operation of the **combatant commands**, and the integration of land, naval, and air forces. It also provides support as directed to the Vice Chairman, as well as other JCS members. It is directed by the CJCS and managed by the Director of the Joint Staff.

JCS agencies include organizations reporting to the CJCS and those reporting through the CJCS to the SecDef. JCS agencies reporting *to* the CJCS include the Joint Staff; the **Joint Special Operations Agency**; the **National Defense University**; the Joint Materiel Priorities and Allocations Board; the Joint Transportation Board; and military representatives to NATO, the United Nations, the Inter-American Defense Board, the Mexican-U.S. Defense Commission; the Permanent Joint Board on Defense Canada-U.S., and the Canada-U.S. Military Cooperation Committee. Organizations reporting *through* the CJCS to the National Command Authorities are the **unified and specified commands**, the **Joint Strategic Target Planning Staff**, the Military Communications-Electronic Board, the **Joint Special Operations Command**, and the designated combat support agencies of the Department of Defense (i.e., the **Defense Intelligence Agency**, the **Defense Logistics Agency**, the **Defense Mapping Agency**, the **Defense Communications Agency**, and the **Defense Nuclear Agency**).

The OJCS consists of approximately 1,600 personnel of which 900 are officers. Staff positions are made up of an equal number of officers from the three main services, with Marines occupying 20 percent of the personnel spaces allotted to the Navy. By law, the Joint Staff consists of not more than 400 officers. J-2 was disestablished in 1963 and its functions were assumed by the Director of the Defense Intelligence Agency. The CJCS and Vice Chairman are appointed by the President for a maximum of three two-year terms. Term limitations may be waived in wartime.

The Joint Staff—Organization

- Office of the Chairman of the Joint Chiefs of Staff
- Office of the Director of the Joint Staff
- Secretary of the Joint Staff
- J-1, Manpower and Personnel Directorate
- J-3, Operations Directorate
- J-4, Logistics Directorate
- J-5, Strategic Plans and Policy Directorate
- J-6, Command, Control and Communications Systems Directorate
- J-7, Operational Plans and Interoperability Directorate
- J-8, Force Structure, Resource, and Assessment Directorate
- Directorate for Information and Resource Management (DIRM)
- Adviser for Mapping, Charting, and Geodesy Support
- Office of the Inspector General
- Directorate for JCS Support (JS), Defense Intelligence Agency

organize: "To arrange or group the components and or functions of a unit or establishment. Such actions establish the levels of supervision, internal relationships and responsibilities" [*Air Force Glossary*, AFM 11-1, 2 January 1976, p. 28].

ORI (see **operational readiness inspection**)

Orion (see **P-3 Orion**)

OSD (Office of the Secretary of Defense) (see **Secretary of Defense**)

OTD (Other Than D): Documents for contingencies (other than a **Federal Emergency Plan D** situation) that justify applications of emergency measures on a national scale. The OTD plan, managed by the **Federal Emergency Management Agency**, was first approved in November 1972. It includes national crises not involving attacks upon the United States. (see also **contingency plan**)

OTH/OTH-B radar (see **over-the-horizon radar**)

Outer Space Treaty: Formally known as the Treaty on Principles Governing the Activities of States in the Exploration and Use of Outer Space, including the Moon and Other Celestial Bodies. Negotiated at the United Nations in 1967 and signed by the United States, Soviet Union, and United Kingdom on 27 January 1967, the treaty was ratified by the United States on 24 May 1967 and entered into force on 10 October 1967. As of 31 July 1988, 88 countries had signed the treaty.

The treaty limits the use of celestial bodies to peaceful purposes and prohibits the orbiting of nuclear weapons and the stationing of any weapons of mass destruction on any celestial body or in space. Military activities and weapon testing on celestial bodies are also banned by the treaty. Although intended to ban the militarization of outer space, the treaty is broadly interpreted by the United States and the Soviet Union to exclude **anti-satellite** testing and **Strategic Defense Initiative** components. The treaty does not cover the use of satellites for military communication and intelligence missions. The treaty does provide that:

- Peaceful exploration and use of outer space, including celestial bodies, is for the use of all countries, regardless of economic or scientific development.
- Claims of national sovereignty may not be made upon celestial bodies.
- Treaty parties will "undertake not to place in orbit around earth any objects carrying nuclear weapons or any other kinds of weapons of mass destruction, install such weapons on celestial bodies, or station such weapons in outer space in any other manner"; all celestial bodies, including the moon, are to be used for peaceful purposes: "the establishment of military bases, installations and fortifications, the testing of any type of weapons and the conduct of military maneuvers on celestial bodies shall be forbidden" (Article IV).
- The use of military personnel for scientific purposes is not forbidden.
- Astronauts are considered "envoys of mankind" and are to be given assistance by all states in emergency situations.

- Any country launching an object into outer space is fully responsible for any effects that object may cause to another state.
- International cooperation in the exploration and use of outer space is to be promoted; that is, launches and the nature, conduct, locations, and results of missions are to be made public.
- Any state may accede to the treaty; amendments may be proposed; withdrawal may be made one year after entry by written notification to the United States, Soviet Union, and the United Kingdom.

"It is worthy of note that during the negotiations the United States did not insist on formal verification provisions. This was indicative of growing U.S. confidence during the 1960s in the capabilities of its intelligence-gathering, space tracking systems to detect launchings, and devices in orbit" [ACDA, *Arms Control and Disarmament Agreements: Texts and Histories*, 1982 ed. p. 49].

In December 1979, the U.N. opened for signature the Agreement on Celestial Bodies, which established further guidelines for scientific use of the moon. As of December 1988, the United States (like most nations) had not signed the agreement.

outlays: Gross payments less reimbursements, refunds, and loan repayments received and credited to the appropriation or fund account. Consists of expenditures and net lendings. The terms "outlay" and "expenditures" are virtually synonymous since the only difference is a relatively insignificant amount of net lending. Out

lays are the actual expenditure of money from the U.S. Treasury, which generally lags behind the obligation. Congress approves sufficient budget authority to complete a program even though completion and final payment may be several years away.

OV-1D Mohawk: Army, two-crew, twin-engine turboprop, medium-range surveillance aircraft deployed in military intelligence battalions. The OV-1D is equipped with airborne side-looking radar (AN/APS-94F) and a photographic (KA-60/76) camera capable of monitoring enemy movements in daylight, darkness, and inclement weather. The primary sensor is the AN/UPD-7 airborne radar surveillance system. When used in conjunction with a data link, the radar information is transmitted to a ground-based receiving system that has the capability to convert the received signals back to film for near real-time viewing analysis. The AN/UPD-7 system is capable of interfacing with the ground station modules (GSMs) of the **Joint Surveillance and Target Attack Radar System**. The Block improved OV-1D program will increase the structural life of the airframe, upgrade the on-board avionics, and incorporate a controls-and-display system in the cockpit. Also, the engines and the radar surveillance system will be upgraded. The aircraft has a cruise speed of 210 kt with an endurance of 4 hours. The maximum range is 820 nm. The OV-1D is deployed in military intelligence battalions (Aerial Exploitation): three OCONUS, two in the Forces Command, and two in the Army National Guard. The contractors are Grumman Aerospace,

Stuart, FL; Motorola Inc., Tempe, AZ; and Lycoming, Stratford, CT.

OV-10 Bronco: Air Force and Marine Corps, two-crew, two-engine turboprop, short-range, light-attack aircraft used for forward air control, aerial reconnaissance, and limited quick-response ground support pending the arrival of tactical fighters. The Bronco was first flown in 1967 as a **counterinsurgency** aircraft; a total of 157 were delivered to the Air Force before production ceased in April 1969. It is deployed with the Tactical Air Command, the Alaskan Air Command, and the Pacific Air Forces. The Marines operate three squadrons of 18 aircraft—9 OV-10As and 9 OV-10Bs (night observation system platforms, operating night surveillance sensors, laser target designators, and radar homing and warning systems). The OV-10 replaced the **OV-1 Mohawk**, which is still used as a surveillance aircraft in the Army. The aircraft can be used for short takeoff and landings on aircraft carriers without the use of catapults. By removing the second seat, the OV-10 can carry 3,200 lb of cargo, five paratroopers, or two litter patients and an attendant. The plane has an unloaded top speed at sea level of 281 mph. It has a 228 nm range (fully loaded and no loiter) in its attack role and a 1,430 nm ferry range. It is armed with four 7.62 mm machineguns and can carry bombs, rocket pods, missiles, and fuel tanks on four wing and one fuselage stations. The contractor was Rockwell International.

overhaul: The period during which a ship undergoes scheduled and/or unscheduled maintenance and repair. These periods vary in length, intensity, and effect on the ship's ability to be deployed quickly. Overhaul periods frequently include extra crew training as well as work on the ship. The variety of overhauls include

- Regular overhaul (ROH) phase: "The ROH phase follows an operational phase, and consists of a regular overhaul period and a refresher training period" [*NWP 3*].
- Regular overhaul (ROH) period: "In the ROH period, the ship is in a shipyard, naval or civilian, undergoing depot level maintenance" [*NWP 3*]. ROHs are regular and extensive, and generally occur during planned periods. ROHs tend to be the only form of repair officially referred to as overhauls. Most other shorter and more contingent repair periods are known as "availabilities," which is defined as the "period of time assigned a ship by a competent authority for the uninterrupted accomplishment of work which requires services of a repair activity ashore or afloat" [*NWP 3*].

There are three different levels of availability:

- Restricted availability: "An availability for the accomplishment of specific items of work by a repair activity, with the ship present, during which period the ship is rendered incapable of fully performing its assigned mission and task due to the nature of the repair work. The work may be accomplished with the ship not present at a repair activity, all or part of the period, when the determination is made by the authority granting the availability" [*NWP3*].

- Technical availability: "An availability for the accomplishment of specific items of work by a repair activity, with the ship not present, during which period the ship's ability of fully performing its assigned mission and tasks is not affected by the nature of the repair work. The work may be accomplished with the ship present at a repair activity, all or part of the period, when this determination is made by the authority granting the availability" [*NWP3*].
- Post-shakedown availability (PSA): shakedown cruises take place after a ship is commissioned or after a major overhaul to ensure that all ship systems are working properly. PSAs are conducted after shakedown cruises to make repairs and correct deficiencies uncovered in the course of the shakedown cruise.

(see also **Service Life Extension Program**)

overseas military program management: A program that places military and civilian personnel overseas to ensure in-country planning and management of U.S. **security assistance programs**. Individuals who are part of this program in a given country constitute the security assistance organization and serve under the direction and supervision of the Chief of the United States Diplomatic Mission. They provide a direct liaison among the mission, the Department of Defense, and the host country defense establishment in relation to security assistance matters.

Of the 80 countries participating in the U.S. security assistance programs nearly 60 have separate organizations dedicated solely to the security assistance mission—for example, the Joint U.S. Military Mission for Aid to Turkey (JUSMAAT) or the Office of Defense Representative, Pakistan (ODRP). In 16 other countries, security assistance programs are administered by the **defense attaché** office with additional personnel assigned for security assistance functions. In countries that have a lesser U.S. security assistance program, embassy personnel manage the program [Department of State, *Congressional Presentation of Security Assistance Program FY 1990*, pp. 50–51].

over-the-horizon (OTH) radar: **Radar** whose signals hug the earth's surface to distances well beyond line of sight, bounce off the ionosphere, and return to earth several times in saw-toothed waves, activating a receiver, either on the far side of the globe (forward scatter) or near the transmitter (backscatter). The effective detection range is about 1,800 mi. The over-the-horizon backscatter (OTH-B) radar is the primary method for Air Force and Navy long-range **early-warning** and attack assessment of bomber aircraft and air- and sea-launched cruise missiles. These radars bounce their radio signals off the ionosphere and scan airspace at all altitudes from 500–1,800 nm. The return signals, indicating airframes, bounce back to a receiver, providing over three hours of warning of subsonic objects, and one-and-one-half hours warning for supersonic objects.

The Air Force AN/FPS-118 radar system is a long-range, wide-area surveillance of aircraft and cruise missile threats approaching North America. An eastern-looking OTH-B radar system is in Maine, with the transmitter near Moscow, ME, with the receiving antennas (one mile long) near Columbia Falls, and with the operations center at Bangor ANGB. The radar is able to track targets at all altitudes up to the ionosphere at ranges between 500–2,000 mi. The east coast OTH-B began limited operations in FY 1988 and in March 1989 tested successfully the ability to simultaneously detect and track targets along the east coast of the United States. The western-looking system will have its transmitter at Buffalo Flat near Christmas Valley, OR, the receiver at Rimrock Lake near Alturas, CA, a support site at Klamath Falls, OR, and the operations center at Mountain Home AFB, ID. A third south-looking OTH-B system is planned for the Midwest, and a fourth radar is planned for Alaska, with the transmitter at Gulkana and the receiver at Tok.

The Navy AN/TPS-71(XN1) relocatable over-the-horizon-radar (ROTHR) is a land-based ionospheric backscatter radar system to detect, track, and estimate the composition of groups of ships and aircraft in a fixed annular sector with ranges of 1,800 nm in a 60 degree arc. The ROTHR program began in FY 1983 in support of maritime air defense of the Navy's carrier battle groups and selected sea lanes. According to the Navy, it will be capable of providing early warning to U.S. ships of possible enemy action, particularly air and cruise missile attack. The first site is located at Amchitka Island in the Aleutians and will probably become operational in late 1989. It is expected that the facility will be manned year round by 225 military and civilian personnel. The second facility is planned for Guam and Tinian islands. The Navy is reportedly planning nine such radars, and Japan is working on a north-facing over-the-horizon-radar to be a part of the network as well.

The program is estimated to eventually cost $1 billion and involve 2,000 personnel worldwide. Total funding for FY 1990 and FY 1991 was $237.8 million and $276.4 million, respectively.

P

P: Prefix designating **1.** Soft-pad launching environment. **2.** Patrol aircraft (e.g., P-3).

P-3 Orion: Navy long-range, shore-based, 10-crew, four-engine turboprop, day-and-night, all-weather, nuclear-capable, **anti-submarine warfare** and maritime **patrol** aircraft developed from the commercial Lockheed "Electra" aircraft design. The Orion replaced the P-2 Neptune and will itself be partially replaced by the **P-7**. Three versions are currently deployed, and there are a number of non–anti-submarine warfare configurations, such as the electronic warfare EP-3. Most active squadrons are equipped with P-3Cs, while most reserve squadrons fly P-3A/Bs. The first P-3 became operational in 1961. The P-3C became operational in 1969. The P-3C has a series of improvements (updates). Update III entered fleet service in May 1984 and some 21 planes had been updated by the end of FY 1988. Update IV is under development and will be produced by Boeing into 80 P-3Cs and 125 P-7s. The retrofit program will begin in FY 1991 with first delivery in FY 1993. Orions can spend 10–14 hours flying 1,300–1,500 nm on patrol. Orions use **sono-** buoys, **radar**, **forward-looking infrared radar**, and **magnetic anomaly detectors** to detect, classify, and locate submarines. Armament includes the B57 nuclear depth bomb, conventional lightweight **Mk-46 torpedoes**, **Harpoon**, or mines in combination in a weapons bay and wing points. Standard load is four torpedoes and four conventional depth bombs.

A force of over 350 P-3s is organized into 37 squadrons—24 active, 13 reserve—with nine planes to each squadron. P-3s are permanently stationed at NAS Moffett Field, CA; NAS Barbers Point, HI; NAS Brunswick, ME; NAS Jacksonville, FL; and numerous temporary deployment sites worldwide.

Contractors are Lockheed Aircraft, Burbank, CA (prime/airframe), and Detroit Diesel, Allison Division, Indianapolis, IN (engines). FY 1988 was the last year money was appropriated for procuring P-3Cs (six planes for the reserves). The recurring flyaway cost of the P-3C is $34.7 million. (see also **patrol wing**)

P-7: Navy land-based, four-engine, subsonic, long-range, nuclear-capable **anti-submarine warfare patrol** plane to be the replacement for the **P-3A/B**

Orion. Called the Long Range Air Anti-submarine Capability Aircraft (LRAACA) prior to its designation as the P-7, the plane will have greater range, better survivability and maintainability, increased payload, and state-of-the-art acoustic and nonacoustic sensor processing equipment.

On 14 October 1988, the Navy selected Lockheed Aeronautical Systems Company, Burbank, CA, to develop the P-7. The engine contractor is General Electric, Lynn, MA. Boeing is developing the P-3C Update IV system, which will be installed in the P-7. First delivery is expected in 1994.

FY 1989, 1990, and 1991 RDT&E costs are $65.8, $205.1, and $231.6 million, respectively. First procurement funds are scheduled in FY 1991 at $19.9 million.

PACBAR (Pacific Barrier Radar): AN/GPS-10 radar for detection and tracking of satellites to be used as part of **anti-satellite** surveillance programs. Radars are located at San Miguel, Philippines, and at Saipan in Micronesia.

PACCS(see Post-Attack Commandand Control System)

Pacific Air Forces (PACAF): Air Force **major command** and air component command of the **U.S. Pacific Command (USPACOM)**. Redesignated from the Far East Air Forces, 1 January 1957. It plans and conducts offensive and defensive air operations in the Pacific and Asian theaters, including tactical reconnaissance and air defense. It operates approximately 330 aircraft at 10 major locations and employs approximately 39,000 military and civilian personnel.

Headquarters
Hickam AFB, HI 96853

Subordinate Commands

- 5th Air Force (north Asia region), Yokota AB, Japan (APO San Francisco 96328)
- 7th Air Force, Osan AB, South Korea (APO San Francisco 96570)
- 13th Air Force (Southeast Asia), Clark AB, Philippines (APO San Francisco 96274)
- 15th Air Base Wing, Hickam AFB, HI 96853

Pacific Air Forces (PACAF) Command and Control System: Network of command centers and communication links from the Commander of PACAF to the numbered air forces, air divisions, wings and other units, and between units. Its main CD centers are located at PACAF headquarters and the numbered air forces. The command centers have both voice and record communications capabilities, including the CINC-PACAF Voice Alerting Network (CVAN), **AUTOVON**, and a direct circuit to **Commando Escort**. Aircraft units also have UHF transceivers, HF/FM radio, and tactical secure voice equipment. Record communications centers are equipped with **AUTODIN**. The Yokota AB and Clark AB command and control systems are joint U.S./allied systems [Maj Louis J. Casamayou, *A Guide to U.S. Air Force Command Con-*

trol Communications, Air Command and Staff College Student Report, 83-0380, released under the FOIA].

Pacific Command (PACOM) (see **U.S. Pacific Command**)

Pacific Fleet (PACFLT): Navy **operating force** and service component command of the **U.S. Pacific Command**. Its mission area includes the entire Pacific and Indian Oceans, or approximately 94 million square miles of ocean. The Commander-in-Chief, Pacific Fleet (CINCPACFLT) falls in both the administrative and operational chains of command. In his administrative role, CINCPACFLT readies and provides naval forces for the **Third Fleet**, the **Seventh Fleet**, and other commands as directed. In his operational role, CINCPACFLT exercises command of the **Fifth Fleet** *task forces* (CTFS), when activated, and directs operations of the Commanders of the Third and Seventh Fleets. He also exercises **operational control** of assigned commander task forces, when activated. The Pacific Fleet consists of approximately 220 ships, 2,600 Navy and Marine aircraft, 55 shore activities, and 238,000 personnel.

Headquarters
Pearl Harbor, HI 96860

Subordinate Operating Forces

• Third Fleet
• Fifth Fleet (when activated)
• Seventh Fleet

Type Commands

• **Naval Submarine Force** (CTF 14), Pearl Harbor, HI 96860

• **Naval Surface Force** (CTF 15), NAB Coronado, CA 92155
• **Naval Air Force** (CTF 17), NAS North Island, CA 92135
• **Fleet Marine Force Pacific** (CTF 19)

Special Commands

• Temporary Operations Force (CTF 10)
• Training Command (CTF 11)
• **Naval Logistics Command** (CTF 13), Pearl Harbor, HI 96860

(see also **Atlantic Fleet**)

package: In nuclear operations, a grouping of nuclear weapons by specific yields planned for employment in a specified area during a short time period, as specified in **nuclear control orders**.

packet switching: A communications system, pioneered by DARPA, wherein a message is broken into small units called packets, each containing up to about 250 characters and a destination address. Each packet is then routed along one of several alternative paths from its initial node to its destination node. The packet incurs a delay of only a fraction of a second at each node, causing a total delay time across the network averaging 1/10 of a second. Packet switching nodes can typically operate without an attendant and are small, reliable, and inexpensive; they can therefore be installed at multiple nodes to provide alternate routing capabilities for networks and greater efficiency in overloaded circuits, as well as increased survivability for an entire network.

PAL   (see **permissive action link**)

Panama Canal Zone Treaties: In 1978, the U.S. Senate ratified two treaties dealing with the United States and the Panama Canal, and on 1 October 1979 these two treaties entered into force. The first, the Panama Canal Treaty, governs the U.S. operation and defense of the Canal through 31 December 1999, after which both Panama and the United States are responsible for its defense. The second, the Treaty Concerning the Permanent Neutrality and Operation of the Panama Canal, affirms the canal's neutrality. The United States is charged with defending the Canal against threats to ships passaging through the Canal, and U.S. warships are accorded the right to transit the Canal without restrictions. Upon the signing of these treaties, the U.S.-administered Panama Canal Zone ceased to exist. However, the United States is still permitted to use facilities in the area necessary to maintain and defend the Canal. **U.S. Southern Command** units still operate from bases in Panama and would be used to defend the Canal.

The Panama Canal Act of 1979 was passed by Congress to implement the treaties. The act:

- Specified the basis for fixing tolls;
- Provided for U.S. participation in binational bodies set up by the treaties, such as the Joint Commission on the Environment;
- Set up an employment system; and
- Directed the President to report back to Congress on an annual basis on the status of the treaties.

The act also established the Panama Canal Commission to manage and operate the Canal until the year 2000, as dictated in the Panama Canal Treaty. The Commission is supervised by a board of directors composed of five Americans and four Panamanians.

PARCS   (see **Perimeter Acquisition Radar Attack Characterization System**)

Partial Test Ban Treaty (PTBT): Formally known as the Treaty Banning Nuclear Weapon Tests in the Atmosphere, in Outer Space and Under Water. The treaty was signed in Moscow on 5 August 1963 by the United States, the United Kingdom, and the Soviet Union, and was entered into force on 10 October 1963. The treaty bans all nuclear explosions (both military and peaceful) in the atmosphere, in space, and underwater. Underground testing is not covered by the treaty; however, the treaty explicitly states that these provisions are made "without prejudice to the conclusion of a treaty resulting in the permanent banning of all nuclear test explosions, including all such explosions underground." Since 1963, the United States, the Soviet Union, and the United Kingdom have conducted their nuclear tests underground. China, although not a signatory, also conducts its nuclear tests underground, while France continues to test in the atmosphere. Terms of the PTBT are

- Any party may propose amendments, which then must be passed by a majority of signatories;

- The treaty is open to all states for signature; ratification by signatory states is required;
- The treaty is of unlimited duration; and
- If "extraordinary events, related to the subject matter of this Treaty, have jeopardized the supreme interests" of the nation, then that nation retains the right to withdraw from the treaty.

(see also **Comprehensive Test Ban**, **Threshold Test Ban Treaty**)

particle beam weapon (PBW): A stream of atoms or subatomic particles that accelerate to nearly the speed of light and then destroy the target from the inside. Unlike **laser** beams (which use light energy), particle beams produce electrons or protons and accelerate their motion to almost the speed of light. When the beam hits a target, the atoms of the target are pulled apart. This produces a shattering shock wave that smashes through the target. Military applications for particle beams would be as **electronic countermeasures** (a particle beam can destroy semi-conductors in guidance systems or erase programming in computer memories) or as the inducement of premature **fission** in nuclear warheads. Some advantages of particle beams over laser beams are that particle beams do not need to be held on target for as long a time and they are not vulnerable to countermeasures that protect ICBMs (e.g., smoke, reflectors, spinning). Development of particle beam weapons is years behind that of laser beams for several reasons: the energy needed to produce subatomic particles is in excess of ten billion volts; the particles leaving the accelerator are all negatively charged and repel each other, thus spreading out the beam; and the earth's magnetic field bends the beam. Theoretically, some of these problems can be overcome with a beam neutralizer. A proton beam, however, is not problem free: as it penetrates the earth's atmosphere it strips electrons from the air. These then combine with the beam's protons to form hydrogen atoms that combine with atmospheric oxygen to form water (i.e., a giant water pistol). (see also **Strategic Defense Initiative**, **Space-Based Neutral Particle Beam**)

pathfinder: 1.   Name for an aircraft crew that leads a formation to the drop zone, release point, or target.   **2.**   An air team dropped or landed at an objective to establish and operate navigational aids for oncoming aircraft and/or to determine the best approach and withdrawal lanes, landing zones, and sites for aircraft and helicopters.   **3.**   A radar device used for navigating or homing to an objective when visual sighting is limited.

Patriot: Model designation MIM-104. Army surface-to-air, all-weather, high-and medium-altitude, conventionally-armed **air defense** missile replacing the **Nike Hercules** and **Hawk** missiles. The entire Patriot system consists of a radar set, an engagement control station, a power plant, and up to eight remotely located launchers. Each launcher contains four ready-to-fire missiles sealed in canisters that serve the dual purpose of shipping containers and launch tubes. Guidance is track via missile (TVM). The system uses a single phased-array radar coupled with a rapid and responsive fire control computer. The system can engage multiple targets simultaneously. Patriot is integrated with other forward-area air defense weapons and the Air Force for overall defense of the theater of operations. The system is highly automated and the missile is designed to minimize maintenance. It has a faster reaction time, higher firepower, and greater ability to operate in an electronic countermeasures environment than the missiles it is replacing. The system combines high-speed digital processing with various software routines to control the battlespace effectively.

The missile was first deployed to Europe in 1985, and West Germany, the Netherlands, and Italy are currently participating in allied acquisition programs. Nine battalions are operational in 1989 with one additional battalion scheduled to join the force in 1991. A Patriot air defense artillery battalion at the Field Army level includes six fire units. The first NATO unit was delivered in 1986. Japan has been licensed for the production of 26 fire units. Prime contractors are Raytheon, West Andover, MA, and Martin Marietta, Orlando, FL. FY 1990 and 1991 requests for the purchase of 815 and 817 missiles per year are $1,025.8 and $889.5 million, respectively.

patrol combatant (P-): Smaller patrol craft whose mission may extend beyond coastal duties and whose characteristics include adequate endurance and sea keeping to provide a capability for operations exceeding 48 hours on the high seas without support. The Navy operates six conventionally armed Pegasus (PHM-1) class hydrofoil patrol boats and a number of smaller inshore and **naval special warfare** patrol craft. The six patrol hydrofoil boats are homeported at Key West, FL. They displace 265 tons at full load and can achieve a top speed of 50 kt when foil-borne. They are armed with one 76 mm/.62 caliber gun and two quad **Harpoon** anti-ship missile canisters. The other Navy patrol boats are smaller (some 40 tons at full load), conventionally powered types armed with 40 mm or 20 mm cannon or .50 caliber machine guns. Some were specifically designed to operate in the Panama Canal Zone area.

patrol wing (PATWING): Navy **P-3 Orion** aircraft unit with subordinate patrol squadrons. Approximately six squadrons are in each patrol wing. The Atlantic and Pacific Fleets also have patrol wings that serve as the administrative headquarters for subordinate wings: Patrol Wings Atlantic (COMPATWINGSLANT) and Patrol Wings Pacific (COMPATWINGSPAC). COMPATWINGSLANT also operates the Atlantic training and readiness squadron (VP-30) at NAS Jacksonville, FL, and the oceanographic squadron (VXN-8), which operates out of NAS Patuxent River, MD. COMPATWINGSPAC also controls the Pacific training and readiness squadron (VP-31).

Patrol Wings, Atlantic,
NAS Brunswick, ME

- Patrol Wing 5, NAS Brunswick, ME 04011
- Patrol Wing 11, NAS Jacksonville, FL 32212

Patrol Wings, Pacific,
NAS Moffett, CA 94035

- Patrol Wing 1, Kamiseya, Japan
- Patrol Wing 2, NAS Barbers Point, HI 96860
- Patrol Wing 10, NAS Moffett, CA 94035

PAVE PAWS: Model designation 474N. Air Force network of four AN/FPS-155 dual-faced, long-range, **early-warning**, **phased-array radars**. PAVE PAWS would be the first ground-based radars to detect SLBMs launched towards the east and west coasts of the United States from close-in ocean areas. The radars have a range of 3,000 nm, can count incoming warheads, and can predict missile impact points. The network is a part of the major sensor system to confirm early-warning detection from the **Defense Support Program** satellites and to provide attack assessment. The four radar sites are at Beale AFB, CA; Otis ANGB, MA; Robins AFB, GA; and near Goodfellow AFB, TX. Each PAVE PAWS high-speed digital data circuit is routed two ways from the site to NORAD and Strategic Air Command (SAC) command centers and the **National Military Command Center**. The PAVE PAWS radars also have a secondary peacetime mission of tracking objects in space. The name of the radars is sometimes incorrectly called an acronym for both words. PAVE is a general Air Force code word and has no meaning. PAWS stands for "phased array warning system."

payload: **1.** The weapons, bombs, missiles, reentry vehicles and penetration aids or cargo capacity carried by a delivery vehicle.   **2.** Satellite or research vehicle of a space probe or research missile.

PB: Designation for patrol boat. (see also **patrol combatant**)

PBR: Designation for river patrol craft. (see also **patrol combatant**)

PCF: Designation for fast patrol craft. (see also **patrol combatant**)

PD   (see **Presidential Directive**)

PD-59, "Nuclear Weapon's Employment Policy":   President Carter's 25 June 1980 document stating national guidance to the military on targeting objectives and articulating U.S. strategic nuclear strategy, also known as flexible response, or counterforce/ "countervailing" strategy. PD-59 replaced **National Security Decision Memorandum (NSDM)-242**, adopted by the Nixon Administration. PD 59 opened the way for the Reagan Administration strategy of protracted nuclear war in **National Security Decision Directive (NSDD)-13**. PD-59 arose from an initial 18-month study sponsored by the White House to identify the targets that could paralyze, disrupt, and dismember the Soviet government by annihilating the ruling group within the Soviet state. (see also **Presidential Directive**)

PDM   (see **Program Decision Memorandum**)

Peaceful Nuclear Explosion Treaty (PNET): Formally known as the Treaty between the United States and the Soviet Union on Underground Nuclear Explosions for Peaceful Purposes. It was signed by the United States on 28 May 1976. Under the direction of President Carter, who was looking for a **Comprehensive Test Ban Treaty**, the PNET was never ratified by the U.S. Senate. However, both the United States and the Soviet Union have agreed to abide by the treaty's provisions. The treaty limits the yield of individual peaceful underground nuclear explosions used for civilian development purposes to 150 kt, and the yield of group explosions to 1,500 kt. A protocol provides for on-site observation and measurement of yields for group explosions whose aggregate yields are greater than 150 kt. The treaty is tied to the **Threshold Test Ban Treaty (TTBT)**, in that neither party could withdraw from the PNET while the TTBT was still in effect.

Peacekeeper: Official name for the MX missile.

Peacekeeping Operations (PKO): A **security assistance program** authorized by the **Foreign Assistance Act of 1961**, as amended, to grant assistance to friendly countries and international organizations for peacekeeping operations that further U.S. national security interests. The Congress authorizes

funding for United Nations Force in Cyprus (UNFICYP) and for Multinational Force and Observers (MFO) as a direct result of the 1979 Egypt-Israel Peace Treaty.

pedestal-mounted Stinger (PMS) (see **Forward Area Air Defense System**)

penetration aids (PENAIDS):   Devices and/or techniques used in offensive weapon systems, such as ballistic missiles and bombers, to increase the probability of penetrating enemy defenses. They are frequently designed to simulate or to mask an aircraft or ballistic missile warhead in order to mislead enemy radar and/or divert defensive anti-aircraft fire. Reentry vehicle (RV) penetration aids include decoys, chaff, and electronic jammers. Air-to-surface missiles and air-to-air missiles are also referred to as active penetration aids.

Penguin: Navy conventional anti-ship missile launched by LAMPS Mark III and allied helicopters. The Penguin is 120 inches long and 11 inches in diameter, and it has a range of 19 miles. It has been in full-scale engineering development and is undergoing aircraft integration testing. FY 1989 procurement funds for the Penguin were requested but denied by Congress for budgetary reasons. The missile is Norwegian designed and under the overall responsibility of the Royal Norwegian Navy Material Command.

Perimeter   Acquisition   Radar Attack   Characterization   System (PARCS):   Air   Force   AN/FPQ-16

early-warning, phased-array radar located at Cavalier AFS, Concrete, ND. PARCS was originally designed as the target-tracking radar for the **Sentinel** and **Safeguard ABM** systems, but when the Safeguard program was canceled, PARCS was transferred from Army to Air Force responsibility and made a part of the early-warning system. PARCS is now used mostly for warning of ICBMs launched over the North Pole toward the United States, and particularly for attack characterization. Its coverage area includes 80 percent of CONUS. PARCS provides more detail on the size and objectives of a missile attack than the Ballistic Missile Early Warning System **(BMEWS)**(PARCS can track 450 golf ball-sized objects at 1,800 miles) and has the ability to track and count individual reentry vehicles after they are deployed. It was designed to track ballistic missiles in their terminal phase beginning at a maximum range of about 1,000 miles, which has been extended to 2,500 nm, and to predict probable impact points. It would transmit to NORAD approximately 17–23 minutes following a ballistic missile launch.

permissive action link (PAL): "A system included in or attached to a nuclear weapon or nuclear weapons system to preclude arming or launching until the insertion of a prescribed discrete code or combination. It may include equipment and cabling external to the weapon or weapon system to activate components with the weapon or weapon system" [Air Force, *Communications Security for Nuclear Command and Control Communications,* AFR 205-28, 10 August 1973, released under the FOIA].

Pershing II: Army solid-fuel, mobile, guided, nuclear-armed, surface-to-surface ballistic missile; part of the U.S. long-range/intermediate-range nuclear forces (LRINF) eliminated under the **INF Treaty**. The missile is armed with one .3–80 kt range W85 nuclear warhead. The missile is carried by a wheeled truck that also serves as its launcher (transporter-erector-launcher). The missile is described by the Army as a modular, evolutionary improvement over the Pershing 1a ballistic missile deployed in Europe 1964–1983, which it replaced. The Pershing II provides a ten-fold accuracy improvement over the Pershing 1a and provides more than twice the range (1,800 km). The accuracy improvement si achieved by a technique called Radar Area Correlation. As a Pershing II reentry vehicle descends in the target area, it compares a live radar reflection from the target area with reference scenes stored prior to launch. It then makes course adjustments based on the comparison, producing almost pinpoint accuracy. This is thus the first deployed **maneuvering reentry vehicle (MaRV)**. The major military use of the missile was to provide a survivable, quick-reaction nuclear force that could strike targets deep in eastern Europe or in the western Soviet Union.

Under development in the 1970s; in 1979 NATO made its "dual-track" modernization decision, which provided for the deployment of the Pershing II and **Ground-Launched Cruise Missiles (GLCMs)** in Europe, while simultaneously pursuing arms control negotiations for their limitation. Engineering development started in 1979 after the NATO decision. The missile achieved its initial operational capability in December 1983 when it was first deployed in Mutlangen, West Germany. Full operational capability was achieved in December 1985 when deployment of 108 launchers in West Germany was completed. The final missile was produced in late 1987.

The missile is to be eliminated under the INF Treaty, and all missiles will be withdrawn from deployed status by 1992. The prime contractor was Martin Marietta, Orlando, FL. Other contractors were Loral Corporation, Akron, OH; Singer Co., Kearfott Division, Little Falls, NJ; Bendix Corp., Teterboro, NJ; and Hercules, Inc., Salt Lake City, UT.

personnel: "Individuals required in either a military or civilian capacity to accomplish the assigned mission" [*JCS Pub 1,* p. 276]. (see also **manpower**)

Personnel Reliability Program (PRP): A DOD program "implemented for all personnel who control, handle, have access to, or control access to nuclear weapon systems. The program covers selection, screening, and continuous evaluation of the personnel assigned to various nuclear duties. The program seeks to insure that personnel coming under its purview are mentally and emotionally stable and reliable" [DNA, *Nuclear Weapon Accident Response Procedures (NARP)*

Manual, January 1984, p. 159, released under the FOIA]. PRP applies individual reliability, safety, and accountability standards to personnel with access to nuclear weapons, nuclear weapon systems, nuclear components, or code systems used in releasing nuclear weapons, such as sealed authenticators. According to the DOD PRP directive, "the national security and welfare require . . . that only those personnel who have demonstrated unswerving loyalty, integrity, trustworthiness, and discretion of the highest order shall be employed in nuclear weapon PRP positions." PRP applies to all personnel filling critical or controlled positions, units, services, combatant commands, the offices of the Secretary of Defense, the JCS, and defense agencies responsible for operations associated with nuclear weapons. It is designed as a peacetime program; however, "while adherence to PRP procedures during wartime may be impractical, particularly in a combat theater, the philosophy of the PRP remains in effect."

Qualifying standards of reliability are

- Physical competence, mental alertness, and technical proficiency commensurate with job or duty requirements.
- Evidence of dependability in accepting responsibilities and effectively performing in an approved manner; flexibility in adjusting to changes in working environment.
- Evidence of good social adjustment and emotional stability and ability to exercise sound judgment in meeting adverse or emergency situations.

- Positive attitude toward nuclear weapon duty, including the purpose of the PRP.

Disqualifying standards are

- Alcohol abuse.
- Drug abuse. It is not intended that isolated or experimental use of cannabis derivatives, such as marijuana or hashish, be automatically disqualifying. The Certifying Official must judge whether such experimental or isolated use has adversely affected the individual's reliability.
- Negligence or delinquency in performance of duty.
- Conviction(s) by a military or civil court of serious offense(s), or a pattern of behavior or actions that is reasonably indicative of a contemptuous attitude toward the law or other duly constituted authority.
- Any significant physical or mental condition substantiated by competent medical authority, or characteristic or aberrant behavior considered by the Certifying Official as prejudicial to reliable performance of the duties of a particular critical or controlled position.
- Poor attitude or lack of motivation.

PRP procedures include initial screening of an individual (based on security investigation and security clearance, medical evaluation, review of personnel files, personal interview, and proficiency qualification), certification, continuing evaluation, decertification, review of permanent decertification, and subsequent screening [DOD, *Nuclear Weapon Personnel Reliability Program*, DOD Dir 5210.42, 6 December 1985, released under the FOIA].

PG: Designation for patrol ship. (see also **patrol combatant**)

Phalanx: Model designation MK-15 Close-In Weapon system (CIWS). Navy light-weight, ship-mounted, fast-reaction, rapid-fire 20 mm gun **air defense** and anti-missile system. It is an automatic, autonomous gun used as a last ditch defense against cruise missiles and other anti-ship missiles. It combines on a single mount a fire control radar and a six-barrel Gatling gun firing depleted uranium bullets. Phalanx uses an electronic spotting system to direct projectile line of fire against closing targets. It can fire 3,000 rounds per minute. The Navy will install 676 systems aboard 44 classes of ships. Prime contractors are General Dynamics Corp., Pomona, CA, and General Electric Corp., Pittsfield, MA. The FY 1990 and 1991 budget requests for 20 and 19 units per year are $65.1 and $74.3 million, respectively.

Phantom (see **F-4 Phantom/Phantom II**)

phased-array radar: A **radar** that scans the field of view electronically rather than through moving an antenna dish across the target area. It is composed of small stationary radar elements linked to give a three dimensional view. The beam is electronically steerable and can switch rapidly from one target to another. The radar can scan large expanses of space in fractions of a second. (see also

AEGIS, Burke class guided missile destroyer, Perimeter Acquisition Radar Attack Characterization System, PAVE PAWS)

PHM: Designation for patrol ship, hydrofoil; specifically the Pegasus class. (see also **patrol combatant**)

Phoenix missile: Model designation AIM-54A/C. Navy supersonic, all-weather, long-range, conventionally armed, **air-to-air missile** with semi-active mid-course and active terminal guidance, providing long-range standoff capability for **F-14 Tomcat** air superiority fighters. The Phoenix entered the fleet with the F-14A aircraft and its AN/AWG-9 weapons-control system in 1974. The AN/AWG-9 is capable of long-range tracking of multiple air targets and can launch up to six missiles against six targets simultaneously. The Phoenix/F-14 combination was developed to respond to Soviet Naval Aviation's long-range aircraft ability to launch anti-ship cruise missiles to attack U.S. **carrier battle groups**. The missile has a range in excess of 104 nm and a speed in excess of 3,040 mph. It uses a proximity fuse with a 135 lb warhead. The AIM-54A was provided to the Iranian Air Force prior to the overthrow of the Shah of Iran in 1979. The AIM-54A is no longer in production. The AIM-54C version entered production in FY 1980, has improved **electronic counter-countermeasures** features (relative to earlier models), and costs approximately $1.3 million each. The prime contractor is Hughes Aircraft Company, Tucson, AZ. Raytheon Corp., Low-ell, MA, is a second production source. Quality control problems have surrounded Hughes' production of the missile and have led Congress to limit the missile's production rate. The Navy requested $382.3 million for 420 missiles in FY 1990.

phonetic alphabet: Standard words representing each letter of the alphabet, used by military personnel to identify letters in a message transmitted by radio or telephone:

Alfa	Juliet	Sierra
Bravo	Kilo	Tango
Charlie	Lima	Uniform
Delta	Mike	Victor
Echo	November	Whiskey
Foxtrot	Oscar	X-ray
Golf	Papa	Yankee
Hotel	Quebec	Zulu
India	Romeo	

[*JCS Pub 1*, p. 277]

photographic intelligence (PHOTINT): Type of **imagery intelligence** produced by the interpretation of photographic images. PHOTINT is obtained from visible light using either film-based, conventional camera equipment or television-type electro-optical equipment, which converts a picture (analog) image into a digital image for electronic transmission, reconstruction, and enhancement. The **National Photographic Interpretation Center** is the primary PHOTINT analysis organization, handling material from both satellites and strategic reconnaissance aircraft. (see also **keyhole** satellites)

P-hour: **1.** In daylight Navy operations, the predetermined time of rendezvous of underwater demolition craft and the swimmers they retrieve. **2.** In night Navy operations, the time at which all swimmers possible must have been retrieved by their parent boat [*NWP 3.*] (see also **military time**)

physical security: Procedures and measures intended to "a. Safeguard personnel, property and operations. b. Prevent unauthorized access to equipment, facilities, materiel, and information. c. Protect personnel, property, and operations against espionage, damage, and theft."

> Physical security will provide the means to counter threat entities during peacetime, mobilization and wartime. These include—
> 1. Hostile intelligence services.
> 2. Paramilitary forces.
> 3. Terrorists or saboteurs.
> 4. Criminal elements.
> 5. Protest groups.
> 6. Disaffected persons.

[Departments of the Army, Air Force, Navy, and the DLA, *Physical Security*, AR 190-16, AFR 207.4, OPNAVINST 5530.15, MCO 5500.13, 15 March 1984]. (see also **counterintelligence, counterterrorism**)

picket: Armed boat that performs sentry, security, and patrol duty, usually at night.

pig: Nickname for the container used to ship or store radioactive materials. A pig is usually made of lead, and its thick walls provide protection from human exposure to radiation.

ping   (see **sonar**)

Pinnacle: 1. Former code name for the Navy's HOLYSTONE submarine reconnaissance system, now called **Barnacle**.   **2.** An **Operational Report** (**OPREP**)-3 message designator (flagword) that denotes that an event or incident is of possible national-level interest; includes Broken Arrow, Emergency Destruction, Emergency Evacuation, Front Burner, LERTCON, and NUCFLASH.

Pioneer: Navy short-range **remotely piloted vehicle** (**RPV**) under development to provide day or night real-time reconnaissance, battlefield surveillance, target acquisition, artillery/gun support, and battle damage assessment. The Pioneer system was originally designed to operate from a fixed base using a runway or pneumatic launcher for takeoff and a runway for landing. An added capability to operate from selected ships (e.g., battleships) was developed.

   In July 1985, the Secretary of the Navy directed the procurement of an unmanned aerial vehicle (UAV) as soon as possible, using proven RPV technology in order to provide a minimum operational capability. This procurement was intended to correct shortfalls in tactical reconnaissance capabilities experienced during Grenada, Lebanon, and Libya operations. In April 1986, the Secretary of the Navy initiated a program to accelerate the use of RPVs by Navy and Marine Corps units. The Pioneer system was first installed aboard the battleship USS Iowa (BB-61) in August 1986. Operational assessment and tactical employment with Navy and Marine Corps units continue.

pipeline: That part of the logistics cycle that includes all program weapons, aircraft, or weapon systems in support of the operating segment of the inventory. The logistic pipeline includes systems in, en route to, and awaiting, either standard or special rework; and those systems awaiting or in transit to operating forces from standard or special rework. The category does not include new systems in process of first delivery or in storage.

pit: The components of a nuclear warhead located within the inner boundary of the explosive assembly but not including safing materials.

planning   (see **plans**)

Planning Force: 1. The level of forces considered necessary to execute the national strategy with a reasonable assurance of success. Fully structured, manned, and supported with active and reserve forces, it considers the possibility of simultaneous world conflicts and allied and friendly capabilities. It is based on the **minimum risk force** and Service-recommended planning forces levels, resource availability, industrial capacity, and technological capability. The Planning Force is specified in the **Joint Strategic Planning Document** Supporting Analysis. **2.** Future JCS report that is likely, with the **Military Net Assessment** and the **Planning Guidance** document, to replace the **Joint Strategic Planning Document** Supporting Analysis in the future.

Planning Guidance: Future JCS report that is likely, with the **Military Net Assessment** and the **Planning Force** document, to replace the **Joint Strategic Planning Document** Supporting Analysis in the future.

planning order: Order issued by the Chairman of the Joint Chiefs of Staff to initiate execution planning. It follows a Commander's estimate and precedes an **alert order**. The issuance of a planning order does not require approval by the National Command Authority (NCA). A planning order may be substituted for a warning order when the Joint Chiefs of Staff have selected a course of action and require execution planning before submission to the NCA for approval. "If the crisis warrants change in the alert status of units or prepositioning of units (if this has not been done in a warning order), the planning order can contain a deployment preparation/deployment order. The planning order is normally approved by the Chairman, Joint Chiefs of Staff. However, if the order directs a change in alert status or a deployment of forces, Secretary of Defense approval is required" [JCS, *Joint Operations Planning System Vol. IV*, released under the FOIA].

Planning, Programming, and Budgeting System (PPBS): The comprehensive decisionmaking process used by the DOD for managing the allocation of resources. PPBS translates force requirements developed in the **Joint Strategic Planning Document (JSPD)** into budgetary requirements that result in the **Five Year**

Defense Program (FYDP) and the DOD portion of the President's budget presented to Congress. The PPBS cycle involves simultaneous and overlapping activities within the Office of the Secretary of Defense, the JCS, and the Services. The overall responsibility for managing the system has been assigned to the **Defense Resources Board (DRB)**, chaired by the Deputy Secretary of Defense. The JCS provide inputs to the PPBS through the **Joint Strategic Planning System**.

The PPBS, which follows a biennial cycle, is made up of the following actions:

- The JCS, based upon service input, develop strategy and force-planning guidance recommendations in the Joint Strategic Planning Document.
- The Secretary of Defense provides guidance for planning and programming to departments and agencies in the Defense Guidance.
- Each military department and agency develops a **Program Objective Memorandum (POM)** that provides its recommendation for the allocation of its resources.
- Based upon the **Defense Guidance (DG)** and the JSPD and using the POMs and the **Joint Program Assessment Memorandum (JPAM)**, the JCS and OSD develop **issues** for consolidation into Issue Papers (consolidated into Issue Books). Issue Papers contain analysis of military department POMs relative to the DG, illuminate the significant issues, list the alternatives, evaluate the costs and effectiveness of the alternatives, and suggest program changes to the POMs. Following comment by the

Joint Chiefs of Staff and the Services, they are submitted to the DRB.
- The DRB recommends specific changes that are codified by the Secretary of Defense in **Program Decision Memorandums (PDMs)**.
- PDM-directed changes to the POMs are taken by the military departments and translated into the budget estimate submission.
- After review by the OSD and Office of Management and Budget (OMB), military department budget submissions are approved by the Secretary of Defense. Program Budget Decisions issued by OSD are used to resolve most differences between the service budget estimate submission (BES) and OSD/OMB pricing. Remaining issues are resolved by the DRB or the Secretary of Defense. The result is the President's budget.

During the 1984 program review, several unified and specified commanders-in-chief (CINCs) expressed concern regarding their limited participation in POM development. As a result, the Deputy Secretary of Defense solicited their views for enhancing the CINCs' role in the PPBS, with emphasis on POM development and program review. In November 1983, the Deputy Secretary directed that three actions be taken to enhance the role of the CINCs in program development. First, the CINCs were directed to submit a list of their higher priority needs to the Secretary of Defense. This list is referred to as an Integrated Priority List (IPL). Second, the services were directed to report in the POMs the extent of funding support for each IPL requirement. Third, the CINCs were permitted to take direct exception to the service POMs by submitting their own Issue Papers in the process.

The DOD was directed to establish a biennial PPBS system on 1 April 1986 (National Security Decision Directive-219) as a result of recommendations of the President's Blue Ribbon Commission on Defense Management (Packard Commission). Under the new system, no POM or FYDP update will be conducted during the odd year, while the even year will continue the major review.

plans: Any plan for the conduct of military operations prepared in response to a requirement established by national authority, the Joint Chiefs of Staff, or a military department. Plans can either be the result of the **deliberate planning** process or the **time-sensitive planning** process. The five basic categories of plans are

1. The **Single Integrated Operational Plan (SIOP)**.
2. **Operations plan (OPLAN)**: plans other than the SIOP prepared for the conduct of military operations in a hostile environment. These plans are based upon national guidance and are approved by the JCS.
3. Plans other than operations plan: plans for the conduct of military operations in a peacetime or nonhostile environment. This includes disaster relief (see **domestic emergency**), **noncombatant evacuation**, protection of U.S. citizens, nuclear weapon recovery and evacuation, and **continuity of operations**.

These plans generally do not need JCS approval.
4. **Special plans**: **unconventional warfare**, deception, focal point, and other compartmented plans.
5. Bilateral military plans and military plans of international treaty organizations (e.g., NATO operations plans) or combined commands. NATO, for instance, has three types of war plans:

- General Defense Plans (GDP)
- Contingency Operation Plans
- Support Plans (SUPS)

The planning process is one in which the scenarios for warfare, the tasks before military forces, the threat posed by enemy forces, and the objectives of military operations are put into a coherent and systematized format to guide military forces. Planning for the DOD takes place in the planning phase of the **Planning, Programming, and Budgeting System (PPBS)**. The **Joint Strategic Planning System (JSPS)** reports form the basis for the preparation of operations plans under the **Joint Operations Planning System** or the preparation for crises under the **Crisis Action System**.

In the **Joint Strategic Capabilities Plan (JSCP)**, the JCS tasks the unified and specified commanders, and other combatant commanders, to develop operations plan. The extent of planning is not limited by JSCP taskings. Each commander-in-chief (CINC) also has broad responsibilities assigned in the **Unified Command Plan** and the Unified Action Armed Forces directive and may prepare whatever plans he deems necessary to discharge those responsibilities. The plans are kept up-to-date and relevant as forces, scenarios, resources, and strategies change. Planning is also done in combined commands.

There are four interrelated systems in existence that affect the development of plans:

- The national-level National Security Council System, which generates Presidential Directives;
- The JSPS, which generates the JSCP and other documents;
- The PPBS, which generates the **Defense Guidance**, budget documents, and the budget;
- The Joint Operation Planning System, which specifies procedures and guidance for the development of plans and the conduct of the military in a crisis.

Each Service Chief, under the respective departmental Secretary, is responsible for the efficiency of his service and its planning and preparedness for military operations. Each has designed a Service-unique planning system to complement the joint planning system. On the basis of strategic guidance provided in JSPS documents and program and budget guidance, the Chiefs develop a series of documents that support the PPBS, and provide direction and guidance for subordinate major commanders in the Service chain of command. Service documents that describe the Service-unique planning systems are

- Army Mobilization and Operations Planning System;
- Naval Operational Planning (NWP 11);
- USAF Operational Planning Process (AFR 28-3); and

- Command and Staff Action (FMFM 3-1).

Principal Service-planning documents that have specific application in the development of operations plan and that support the JSCP are

- Army Strategic Capabilities Plan (ASCP);
- Naval Capabilities Plan and Mobilization Plan (NSMP);
- USAF War and Mobilization Plan (WMP);
- Marine Corps Capabilities Plan (MCCP-FY); and
- Marine Corps Mobilization Management Plan.

platoon (plt): The smallest standard fighting formation commanded by a commissioned officer in the Army and Marine Corps, and the basic tactical element of a **company**. Platoons vary in size depending on type (e.g., a tank platoon consists of approximately 20 personnel and five tanks; a mechanized infantry platoon consists of approximately three squads of 11 personnel each, each mounted in an armored personnel carrier). Platoons are commanded by lieutenants.

PLRS (see **Army Data Distribution System**)

Plymouth Channel Command: Major subordinate command of NATO's **Allied Command Channel**.

Headquarters
Plymouth, UK

point defense: Defense of critical military assets perceived to be vulnerable to attack, such as a missile silo, air base, command post, or individual ship.

POLAD   (see **Political Advisor**)

Pole Vault 76:   JCS worldwide **command post exercise (CPX)** held 1–12 March 1976. Pole Vault 76 was conducted in a post–nuclear-attack environment, and was a follow-on to exercise **Prime Rate 75**. The exercise was designed to "portray a simulated post-strategic nuclear attack environment at home and abroad with massive destruction and casualties, degraded communications and information systems, civil disorder, and widespread uncertainty concerning the worldwide politico-military situation" [JCS, *Exercise Pole Vault 76 Final Report*, 11 August 1976, released under the FOIA]. Canada participated in the exercise as a member of NORAD. The exercise was held concurrent with the civil exercise REX 76 (see **REX Bravo**).

Policy Guidance for Contingency Planning (PGCP): Annual planning document submitted by the Secretary of Defense to provide guidance for the preparation of **operations plan** and for initiation of the **Joint Strategic Planning System**. The PGCP was first issued in August 1980 as a result of the **Nifty Nugget 78** and **Proud** Spirit exercises, which identified a number of planning weaknesses relating to mobilization. The PGCP focuses on near-term guidance for military planning (with the exception of nuclear contingency planning, which is provided in the Policy Guidance for the Employment of

Nuclear Weapons (NUWEP)). "The primary purpose of the PGCP is to ensure that military contingency planning reflects existing capabilities, is based on valid assumptions, and addresses contingencies considered vital by the National Command Authority (NCA)." The PGCP is updated annually. [DOD, *Policy Guidance for Contingency Planning,* January 1980, released under the FOIA].

Policy Memorandums   (see **Memorandums of Policy**)

Political Advisor (POLAD): A Department of State foreign service officer who serves as the point of contact between the commander of a military organization and the Department of State on matters pertaining to political-military affairs. POLADs are assigned to the staffs of unified or specified commands, NATO commands, or other special commands, where political-military advice is required on a regular basis. In addition to providing information and advice on political affairs, the POLAD is responsible for command issues, such as basing rights, overflight clearances, landing rights, Status of Forces agreements, emergency evacuation operations, contingency plans for spacecraft/astronaut recovery, and fleet visit clearances.

Poll Station 81: JCS **command post exercise (CPX)** held in the Pentagon, 9–21 March 1981, and a follow-on to **Power Play 79**. The exercise tested procedures in the **Joint Deployment System**, alert system, **Crisis Action System**, command center operations, chemical and nuclear release, civil-military interface (including **noncombatant evacuation** and **host nation support**), and **Worldwide Military Command and Control System** operations. Poll Station 81 was held simultaneously with the NATO exercise **WINTEX/CIMEX** 81.

Polo Hat: JCS-sponsored, regularly held **National Military Command System** procedural and timing **command post exercise (CPX)** of the **Worldwide Military Command and Control System**. The exercise ensures that "the system is maintained in a high state of readiness and to identify deficiencies and improvements involving procedures, manpower, and equipment" [JCS, *Polo Hat Exercise Plan for CY 86*, 21 February 1986, released under the FOIA]. Participants include National Military Command System elements, CINC command centers, **airborne command posts**, **launch control centers**, bombers/tankers, ballistic missile submarines, and designated ground and mobile units. **Emergency Action Message (EAM)** dissemination, conferencing (emergency conference call procedures and connectivity), warning, and force management are exercised. There are usually three or four Polo Hat exercises held per year. Polo Hat exercises are held in conjunction with, or are supplemented by, Strategic Connectivity Performance Tests, which focus on EAM dissemination, connectivity of forces, and certain elements of force management [SAC, *SAC Exercise Program,* SACR 55-38, Vol. I, p. 2-2, released under the FOIA].

POMCUS (pre-positioned materiel configured to unit sets): Pre-positioned military equipment in Europe for rapid deployment of reinforcements from the United States. Sufficient materiel exists to deploy by airlift the personnel of about four divisions to Europe in ten days. (see also **REFORGER**)

Pony Express: Code name for special aerial reconnaissance and sampling operations conducted for the Joint Chiefs of Staff to support collection of intelligence about Soviet missile testing. The planes monitor flight testing over the Pacific Ocean. Support is provided by specially equipped **WC-130**, **WC-135**, and **HC-130** aircraft of the Military Airlift Command, and by Navy **P-3 Orion** aircraft, ships, and submarines.

popcorn: Dust particles caused by thermal radiation hitting a surface.

port security program: "Within the United States and its possessions, this is the administration and operation of a **Coast Guard** organization provided primarily for the protection of ships and all waterfront facilities within a harbor from damage caused by fire, sabotage, accidents, and negligence. The port security organization of any port is under the command of a Coast Guard officer specifically designated as 'Port Security Officer (geographical location).' The jurisdiction of a Coast Guard port security officer in wartime extends from within the harbor out to the submarine and/or torpedo nets or (when such nets are not provided) out to the line mutually agreed upon by harbor defense forces and port security forces in each port area" [*NWP 3*].

Poseidon: Model designation UGM-73A. Navy submarine-launched, solid-fuel, two-stage, inertially guided, nuclear-armed, MIRVed, **ballistic missile**. The missile can carry 6–14 W68 40 kt warheads, although 10 is the average number of warheads currently loaded on missiles. It has a range of some 2,500 nm with an accuracy (CEP) of .25 nm. It is 34 ft long and weighs some 65,000 lb. Its targets are primarily soft targets such as military airfields, large bases, command and communications installations, and cities.

The missile was developed as a replacement for the Polaris SLBM and became operational on 31 March 1971 aboard the USS James Madison (SSBN-627). Between 1969–1977, 31 ballistic missile submarines were converted from Polaris to Poseidon. The missile is currently deployed on just over a dozen ballistic missile submarines of the Lafayette (SSBN-616) class and James Madison (SSBN-627) class. Twelve of these have been further converted to carry **Trident I C4** missiles. As of 1989, six submarines with Poseidon missiles have been retired; several more are in the process of being decommissioned as the submarines reach the end of their operating life. Lockheed Missiles and Space Co., Sunnyvale, CA, was the prime contractor. From 1969–1974, 619 operational missiles were procured at a cost of some $3,487 million.

position   (see **billet**)

positive   control: A   system   of authentication codes and communications procedures used in strategic forces to ensure survival of ground alert aircraft under attack, while preserving orders to proceed to targets. The SAC Commander-in-Chief has the authority to order bombers and tankers airborne if warning of an attack is received from NORAD. After reaching a certain prearranged orbit point on their routes (the "positive control" turnaround point), well outside enemy territory, the bombers will be returned to their bases unless they receive positive authenticated voice instructions from the National Command Authorities to proceed to their targets. Positive control procedures are tested repeatedly in **Global Shield** and other exercises. The act of launching alert aircraft is often referred to as positive control launch (PCL).

Positive Leap 80:   JCS **command post exercise (CPX)** held in the Spring of 1980. It tested both the newly formed **Joint Deployment Agency (JDA)** and the **Rapid Deployment Joint Task Force**. Exercise play included command center procedures, the **Joint Deployment System**, civil/military interface, and **Worldwide Military Command and Control System** support.

Posse Comitatus Act: Congressional act signed into law on 18 June 1878 (18 U.S.C. §1385) that governs the use of the military in civilian law enforcement activities. It outlaws the use of the Army and Air Force as a "posse comitatus," that is, as a police force or law enforcement force able to be summoned by civil authorities.

Although not specifically mentioned in the act, the Navy has complied with the intent of the act by its own regulations. The act was amended for the first time in 1981 by 10 U.S.C., Chapter 18, "Military Cooperation with Civilian Law Enforcement Officials," primarily to allow the use of the military in illegal drug interdiction activities. However, the act is not issue-specific. The amendment allows the use of military resources for non-military purposes in certain circumstances, including

- Use of military equipment and facilities by civilian law enforcement;
- Assignment of military personnel to train, operate, maintain, or assist in the use of equipment;
- Transfer of information collected during the normal course of military operations to civilian law enforcement officials;
- Assignment of personnel to assist civilian law enforcement OCONUS in "emergency" circumstances.

Assistance provided to civil authorities is made on a reimbursable basis and is not to interfere with or adversely affect military "preparedness." The statute still restricts the military from "direct participation . . . in an interdiction of a vessel or aircraft, a search and seizure, [or] arrest" unless otherwise allowed by law. Further amendment of the law was made on 27 October 1986 (10 U.S.C. §379) by mandating the assignment of Coast Guard personnel on board naval ships during operations for drug law enforcement purposes. As civilian employees of the Department of Transportation, Coast Guard personnel are granted arrest, search, and seizure powers.

post-attack: The period of war beginning when the "last" nuclear detonation has been identified, by either negotiation, surrender, or exhaustion of assets. Post-attack is characterized by national recovery, reconstitution, and force regeneration. However, it assumes the international situation has reverted to surveillance and warning of any new attack conditions or resumption of hostilities. Thus, the primary post-attack function is similar to that of **pre-attack**, but is accomplished in a very different environment. According to the Air Force, post-attack is "the indefinite period from the end of the enemy attack until another attack or the end of hostilities" [Air Force, *Disaster Preparedness: Planning and Operations,* AFR 355-1, 17 November 1986, p. 87, released under the FOIA]. (see also **trans-attack**)

Post-Attack Command and Control System (PACCS): SAC-operated **airborne command post (ABNCP)** system providing the National Command Authorities and the JCS a survivable command and control capability for the direction of strategic nuclear forces during wartime. PACCS would also serve as an alternate SAC airborne command and control facility to manage forces during the trans- and post-attack periods and to ensure the survivability of the SAC bomber and tanker force. It provides the means to order the launch of **Minuteman** and **MX** (Peacekeeper) missiles and to transmit attack orders to bombers. PACCS is a part of the **Minimum Essential Emergency Communications Network** and is managed by the Air Force Logistics Command. Upgrades to the system in the 1990s include the ability to interface with the **Ground-Wave Emergency Network (GWEN)**, **MILSTAR**, and the **Nuclear Detonation Detection System (NDDS)**. The various components of the PACCS include

- **SAC airborne command post (ABNCP)**: **EC-135** aircraft continuously airborne over central CONUS with a SAC General Officer and battle staff on board. The aircraft, nicknamed **Looking Glass**, are stationed at Offutt AFB, NE. Operational since 1961, the ABNCP is tied into the **National Military Command Center (NMCC)** and the **SAC Command Post** and alternate command post by a UHF radio link. Other radio links (each EC-135 has four links) connect the ABNCP to other PACCS aircraft. The ABNCP can also transmit and receive HF, VLF, LF, and UHF over the **AFSATCOM** system. VLF communications can be established with the **National Emergency Airborne Command Post (NEACP)**, **TACAMO**, and SAC strategic bombers. While the **E-4B** NEACP aircraft have the mission of directing the full range of U.S. strategic forces, the PACCS EC-135 aircraft are tasked with the narrower mission of commanding and controlling only SAC's nuclear assets.

- Auxiliary Command Posts (AUX-CPs): The East Auxiliary Command Post is located at Offutt AFB, NE; the West Auxiliary Command Post is located at Ellsworth AFB, SD. The AUXCPs are on ground alert and would launch upon direction

to link with the ABNCP through the UHF air-to-air link. The AUXCPs support the ABNCP and act as nodes in the airborne radio link between the Airborne Launch Control Center aircraft in the West and the NEACP in the East. Two aircraft on ground alert at two other bases act as relay platforms in this link.

- Radio relay aircraft: Radio Relays 1 and 2 are stationed at Grissom AFB, IN.
- Airborne Launch Control Center (ALCC) aircraft: ALCCs 1, 2, and 3 are based at Ellsworth AFB, SD. The ALCC for the Minuteman force offers only one-way communications between the aircraft and the missiles. The ALCC for the MX is being designed for two-way communications between the airborne command post and the missile system, which will permit the battlestaff on the aircraft to receive missile status reports before issuing launch orders.

Power Play 79: JCS-sponsored and -conducted worldwide **command post exercise (CPX)** that included testing of the relocation to the **Alternate National Military Command Center**, alert systems, **Joint Deployment System**, **rules of engagement**, war powers, **Crisis Action System**, **Worldwide Military Command and Control System**, and chemical and nuclear weapon release. Power Play 79 was a follow-on to Prime Target 77, and was held in conjunction with NATO **WINTEX/CIMEX** 79. Power Play 79 was followed by **Poll Station 81**.

Power Sweep 87: JCS-sponsored and -conducted worldwide **command**

post exercise (CPX) to test crisis management procedures, mobilization capabilities, and deployment of forces for conventional war in a multitheater environment. The exercises included extensive civil agency participation. Exercise activity included relocation to the **Alternate National Military Command Center (ANMCC)**, alert systems, **rules of engagement**, war powers, **Crisis Action System**, and chemical and nuclear release. It was held 27 October–7 November 1986.

PP: Marking on **priority** messages.

PPBS (see **Planning, Programming, and Budgeting System**)

Prairie Schooner: Code word for submarine surveillance operations conducted by the Navy. The program includes optical system technology, acoustic processing applications, photographic developments, direction finding and displays, digital recording applications, and laser signal detection capabilities. The types of intelligence collection equipment used fall into four categories: acoustic, electromagnetic, electro-optical, and recording and reporting. The work is sponsored by the Naval Ocean Systems Center [U.S. Congress, *Senate Appropriations Committee, FY 1978* DOD, Part 4, p. 750]. (see also **acoustical intelligence**, **electronics intelligence**, **electro-optics**)

pre-attack: The first phase of general war that is used for planning purposes. "The period from the present until the first enemy weapon impacts." It exists until the first surveillance report of a missile launch is put on the data circuits [Air Force, *Disaster Preparedness: Planning and Operations*, AFR 355-1, 17 November 1986, p. 87, released under the FOIA]. (see also **post-attack**, **trans-attack**)

precedence: **1.** In communications, categories that indicate the relative order in which a message is processed in the telecommunications system and the speed with which it must be handled during internal headquarters processing. There are four precedence categories:

Precedence	Code	Time Objective
FLASH	ZZ	As fast as possible (less than 10 minutes)
Immediate	OO	30 minutes
Priority	PP	3 hours
Routine	RR	6 hours

2. In **reconnaissance**, "A letter designation, assigned by a unit requesting several reconnaissance missions, to indicate the relative order of importance, within an established priority, of the mission requested" [*JCS Pub 1*, p. 283].

Precision Location Strike System (PLSS):   Air Force all-weather standoff location/strike system that will detect and collect targeting information on enemy emitters to direct attack aircraft and weapons against enemy targets. The PLSS will be carried on the **TR-1** tactical reconnaissance aircraft. It uses distance-measuring equipment to locate and classify enemy radar emitters and provide near real-time target locations to tactical air units for attacks against enemy **air defense** systems. Lockheed Missiles and Space Co. is the prime contractor for the prototype system.

preinitiation: The process by which a nuclear weapon is exposed to a sufficient number of neutrons during assembly of the fissionable material, such that there is an appreciable probability that a premature sustained nuclear reaction will be produced that will cause the warhead to detonate prematurely with a significantly reduced yield.

pre-positioned materiel configured to unit sets (see **POMCUS**)

pre-positioned war reserve requirement (PWRR): Amount and type of materiel determined by the Secretary of Defense to be "reserved and positioned at or near the point of planned use or issue to the user before hostilities to reduce reaction time and to ensure timely support of a specific force or project until replenishment can be effected" [*JCS Pub 1*, p. 284]. Pre-positioned war reserve stock (PWRS) is that materiel designated to fulfill the PWRR. (see also **Maritime Prepositioning Force**, **POMCUS**)

prescribed nuclear load: A specified quantity of nuclear weapons to be carried by a delivery unit, particularly in the Army. The establishment and replenishment of this load after the use of nuclear weapons is dependent on the tactical situation, the logistics support, and the continuing capability of the unit to transport and use the load.

Present Arms 86: JCS-sponsored and -conducted worldwide **command post exercise (CPX)** that evaluated policies, plans, and procedures during sequential periods of worldwide crisis, nuclear attack, strategic communications connectivity, and **postattack** reconstitution. The exercise included participation by the **Federal Emergency Management Agency** and state-level **civil defense** offices.

Presidential Directive (PD): 1. System for announcing and circulating, within the Executive Branch, decisions on domestic, foreign, and military policies. The directives establish policy, direct the implementation of policy, and/or authorize the commitment of government resources. The directives are signed or authorized by the President and issued by the **National Security Council** (NSC). Most of the PDs issued from 1947 to 1960 have been declassified; however, most of the directives issued since 1961 remain classified. Since 1961, at least 1,000 directives have been issued but only 247 have been publicly released. The NSC is not required to notify Congress when a PD is issued even though the directives involve foreign and military policy. Proposed House legislation (H.R. 5092), put forth in the Spring of 1989, would establish the Presidential Directives and Records Accountability Act. The bill would require presidential directives to be registered in the *Federal Register* and to be disclosed to the Speaker of the House of Representatives and the President Pro Tempore of the Senate.

In 1947, the NSC began producing policy papers. Papers recommending policies were presented to President

Truman for his approval and signature. When Eisenhower took office, there were already over 100 NSC policy papers in existence, and by the end of his administration, 320 policy papers and NSC Actions (numbered records of NSC decisions) had been approved. The Kennedy and Johnson Administrations named their presidential directives **National Se-** **curity Action Memoranda**; Nixon and Ford later changed the name to **National Security Decision Memoranda** in their Administrations. President Carter was the only one to retain the term Presidential Directive for the NSC decisions made during his term. The Reagan Administration used the name **National Security Decision Directives**; the Bush NSC

Carter Administration Presidential Directives

PD/NSC-1	Establishment of Presidential Review and Directive Series/NSC. 20 January 1977.
PD/NSC-2	The National Security Council System. 20 January 1977.
PD/NSC-3	Disposition of National Security Decision Memoranda. 11 February 1977.
PD/NSC-4	The Law of the Sea Policy Review. 8 March 1977.
PD/NSC-5	Southern Africa. 9 March 1977.
PD/NSC-6	Cuba. 15 March 1977.
PD/NSC-7	Resulted from PRM-2, SALT.
PD/NSC-8	Nuclear Non-Proliferation. 24 March 1977.
PD/NSC-9	Army Special Operations Field Office in Berlin. 30 March 1977.
PD/NSC-10	Instructions for the Tenth Session of the Standing Consultative Commission. 20 April 1977.
—	Presidential Decision on Proliferation. 22 April 1977.
—	Presidential Determination on Arms Transfers. 16 April 1977.
—	Foreign Intelligence Electronic Surveillance Legislation. 25 April 1977.
PD/NSC-11	Micronesian Status Negotiations. 5 May 1977.
PD/NSC-12	U.S. Policy in Korea. 5 May 1977.
—	Sale of Hawk Missiles to the Republic of China. 21 May 1977.
—	AWACS for Iran. 19 May 1977.
PD/NSC-13	Conventional Arms Transfer Policy. 13 May 1977.
PD/NSC-14	Disposition of National Security Action Memoranda and National Security Decision Memoranda. 10 June 1977.
PD/NSC-15	Chemical Warfare. 16 June 1977.
PD/NSC-16	Law of the Sea. 16 June 1977.
—	Presidential Determination #77-77: Eligibility of Egypt for the Purchase of Defense Articles and Defense Services Under the Arms Export Control Act as Amended. 2 August 1977.

PD/NSC-17   Reorganization of the Intelligence Community.
4 August 1977.

PD/NSC-18   U.S. National Strategy and Military Posture. 24 August 1977.

PD/NSC-19   Intelligence Structure and Mission (Electronic
Surveillance Abroad and Physical Searches for
Foreign Intelligence Purposes). 25 August 1977.

PD/NSC-20   SALT. 9 September 1977.

PD/NSC-21   Policy Toward Eastern Europe. 6 October 1977.

PD/NSC-22   ABM Treaty Review. 11 October 1977.

—   Strategic and Critical Materials Stockpile.
6 October 1977.

—   FY-78 Underground Nuclear Test Program (CRESSET).
20 October 1977.

PD/NSC-23   Standing Consultative Commission. 18 November 1977.

PD/NSC-24   Telecommunications Protection Policy.
22 November 1977.

PD/NSC-25   Scientific or Technological Experiments with
Possible Large Scale Adverse Environmental Effects
and Launch of Nuclear Systems into Space.
22 December 1977.

PD/NSC-26   Nuclear Weapons Stockpile Memorandum FY 1979–81.
11 January 1978.

PD/NSC-27   Procedures for Dealing with Non-Military
Incidents. 30 January 1978.

PD/NSC-28   U.S. Policy on Chemical Warfare Program and
Bacteriological/Biological Research Program.
3 February 1978.

PD/NSC-29   Nuclear Weapons Deployment Authorization
FY 1978–79. 7 February 1978.

PD/NSC-30   Human Rights.

PD/NSC-34   Micronesian Status Negotiations.

PD/NSC-37   National Space Policy. 11 May 1978.

PD/NSC-41   Civil Defense and Government Continuity. 1979.

PD/NSC-42   Civil and Further National Space Policy.

PD/NSC-44   Nuclear Weapons Stockpile Memorandum FY 1980–82.
5 January 1979.

PD/NSC-50   Arms Control.

PD/NSC-53   National Security Telecommunications Policy. 1979.

PD/NSC-54   Civil Operational Remote Sensing. 16 November 1979.

PD/NSC-55   subject unknown (Top Secret). date unknown.

PD/NSC-57   U.S. Mobilization Planning.

PD/NSC-58   Continuity of Government. June 1980.

PD/NSC-59   Nuclear Weapons Employment Policy.

PD/NSC-3   Nuclear Weapons Stockpile Memorandum FY 1981–83.
24 October 1980.

PD/NSC-62   subject unknown (Secret). date unknown.

PD/NSC-63   subject unknown (Secret). date unknown.

is using the name **National Security Directive** [GAO, *National Security: The Use of Presidential Directives to Make and Implement U.S. Policy,* GAO/NSIAD-89-31, December 1988.] **2.** Presidential directive issued by the Carter Administration.

Presidential succession: Current succession to the Presidency is stated in the Presidential Succession Act of 1947, which requires, after the Vice President, that two popularly elected officials serve in the line of succession to become the President. The successors, in sequence, are

1. Vice President.
2. Speaker of the House.
3. President Pro Tempore of the Senate.
4. Secretary of State.
5. Secretary of the Treasury.
6. Secretary of Defense.
7. Attorney General.
8. Secretary of the Interior.
9. Secretary of Agriculture.
10. Secretary of Commerce.
11. Secretary of Labor.
12. Secretary of Health and Human Services.
13. Secretary of Housing and Urban Development.
14. Secretary of Transportation.
15. Secretary of Education.
16. Secretary of Veterans Affairs.

(see also **continuity of government, Treetop**)

pressure vessel: A strong-walled container housing the core of most types of **nuclear reactors**; it usually also contains a moderator, the reflector, the thermal shield, and the control rods.

Price-Anderson Act: The common name for Section 170 of the **Atomic Energy Act** of 1954, which establishes a liability limit for nuclear accidents to protect nuclear power operators from overwhelming liability claims, and to provide a mechanism for limited compensation for victims of nuclear accidents. Under the Price-Anderson Act, which was revised and extended for 15 years in August 1988, all licensed nuclear power plants must contribute up to $63 million per reactor, in installments of up to $10 million a year, to pay for public damages caused by a nuclear reactor accident. In addition, the act requires the Department of Energy to provide protection for its nuclear contractors operating weapons-related facilities from accident liabilities and to provide public compensation of up to $7 billion.

primary aircraft authorization: The number and types of aircraft authorized to a unit for its ongoing missions. The unit receives personnel, support equipment, and flying-hours funds based upon this authorization [*JCS Pub 1,* p. 286].

Primary Alerting System (PAS): Air Force voice communications network for one-way communications from SAC headquarters to units around the world, including all 152 underground missile **launch control centers (LCCs)** and 35 unit **command posts**. It is popularly known as the "red phone." The PAS prime function is to transmit coded messages giving notice of an actual or practice **alert order** or launch order.

It is a telephone hookup consisting of a leased, dedicated landline. CONUS units have two dedicated PAS lines: one to headquarters SAC called "Frontdoor" and one to its numbered Air Force command post called "Backdoor." SAC can also contact the command posts through the Backdoor. When SAC transmits an alert message, it goes over both circuits to the unit command posts. Message reception is acknowledged by pushing a button at the receiving location, which extinguishes the lamp on the SAC underground command post consoles. Bomber and tanker crews are patched via radio to the unit command post. SAC airborne command posts (**Looking Glass**) have full access through UHF ground entry points. HQ SAC can patch the **Joint Chiefs of Staff Alerting Network (JCSAN)** into PAS for direct transmission of JCS orders to the units. These orders are then patched to UHF transmitters by the units for broadcast to aircraft. (see also **SAC Command Post**)

Prime BEEF (Base Engineer Emergency Forces): Air Force worldwide base civil engineer forces organized to provide trained military civil engineer elements used in direct **combat support** or emergency recovery from natural disasters. Six incremental teams are organized to respond to worldwide contingencies on a 28-hour notice. The teams are postured from the peacetime base civil engineering real property maintenance forces. Prime BEEF teams deploy with personal weapons, tools, and mobility equipment [Air Force, *Disaster Pre-*

paredness: Planning and Operations, AFR 355-1, 17 November 1986, p. 87, released under the FOIA].

prime contract: As used by DOD, any contract entered into directly by a military department or procurement activity of DOD. A prime contractor is the main corporation engaged to develop and/or manufacture a weapon system. A second source prime contractor can also be selected to increase competition and quality assurance of manufacture. Other prime contractors selected by the government will cooperate with the overall prime contractor, who acts as the integrator of different components into the whole. Vendors engaged by the prime contractor to provide components but not contracted directly by the government are called subcontractors.

Prime Rate 75: JCS-sponsored and -conducted **command post exercise (CPX)** that practiced procedures during a simulated period of deteriorating worldwide politico-military relations resulting in a strategic nuclear exchange. The exercise was followed by **Pole Vault 76**.

Prime Ribs: Air Force deployable base services emergency force consisting of engineers and other logistics experts. (see also **Prime BEEF**)

principle subordinate command (PSC): A **North Atlantic Treaty Organization** command subordinate to a **major subordinate command** and responsible for a specific region of operations.

priority: Precedence category assigned to a message to indicate the relative order and speed at which it is to be communicated. Usually reserved for messages containing essential information regarding an operation in progress or requiring expeditious action by the recipient. Priority messages are marked "PP" and are to be handled within approximately three hours. (see also **FLASH**, **Immediate**, **Routine**)

Privacy Act of 1974: Congressional act signed into law 31 December 1974 (5 U.S.C. §552a). As popularly used, the act allows U.S. citizens and legal aliens in permanent U.S. residence to gain access to personal information about themselves held by government agencies of the Executive Branch of the federal government. The act only covers records about individuals that are maintained in a "system of records," and does not apply to records held by state and local governments or private organizations. It also outlines procedures for those seeking amendment of any incorrect or incomplete information in their files and provides certain protections against the misuse of personal records. An appeal procedure for denied records is available to the requester by many agencies, although it is not required by law. Court appeals may also be sought. All records maintained by the Central Intelligence Agency are exempt from the act, as are certain records maintained by an agency whose principal function relates to criminal law enforcement. In addition, there are seven specific exemptions to the Privacy Act that can be applied to certain records to withhold their release:

- (k)(1): Applies to information and material properly classified pursuant to an Executive Order in the interest of national defense or foreign policy;
- (k)(2): Certain investigatory material, compiled for law enforcement purposes, other than material covered by the general law enforcement exemption;
- (k)(3): Records maintained in connection with providing protective services to the President of the United States or other individuals pursuant to section 3056 of Title 18;
- (k)(4): Records required by statute to be maintained and used solely as statistical records;
- (k)(5): Applies to investigatory material compiled solely for the purpose of determining suitability, eligibility, or qualifications for federal civilian employment, or access to classified information, release of which would disclose a confidential source;
- (k)(6): Testing or examination material used to determine individual qualifications for appointment or promotion in federal government service, the release of which would compromise the testing or examination process; and
- (k)(7): Evaluation material used to determine potential for promotion in the armed services, if such information would reveal the identity of a confidential information source.

Prize Gauntlet 80: JCS-sponsored and -conducted **command post exer-**

cise (CPX) that tested command center operations, civil-military interface, and the operations of the **Worldwide Military Command and Control System**.

procurement: 1. Aircraft procurement: aircraft weapon systems, modifications, direct ground support equipment, aircraft industrial facilities, spares, war consumables, and technical data. **2.** Missile procurement: missile weapon systems, operational space systems, modifications, spares, component improvements, missile industrial facilities, site activation, and technical data. **3.** Other procurement: direct and indirect ground weapon support materiel (munitions and associated equipment; vehicular equipment; electronic and telecommunications equipment, including cryptologic equipment; other base maintenance and support equipment), base-procured local purchase equipment, industrial preparedness measures, equipment modifications, and spare and repair parts. Includes installation and emplacement of equipment, testing of production items, and technical data and handbooks procured with end-item equipment.

production (aircraft): New aircraft accepted from the contractor by a Service. Production aircraft include aircraft that were procured for operational and training purposes (i.e., all aircraft except those procured solely for experimental purposes). In this sense, aircraft are either "experimental" or "production."

production phase: The period from production approval until the last system is delivered and accepted. The objective is to efficiently produce and deliver effective and supportable systems to the operating units. It includes the production and deployment of all principal and support equipment.

program acquisition cost: Total recurring and nonrecurring procurement expenditures required to produce and deploy a weapon system with associated initial spares plus total research, development, test and evaluation, and military construction. It is composed of procurement cost plus research, development, test and evaluation, and military construction. Additional costs, such as production base support, first destination transportation, and modifications, are not included.

Program Budget Decision (PBD): Decision issued by the Office of the Secretary of Defense (OSD) to resolve any differences between Service budget estimate submissions and OSD or Office of Management and Budget pricing. If issues cannot be resolved by a PBD, they are resolved by the **Defense Resources Board** or the Secretary of Defense.

program change decision (PCD): Decision documenting the Secretary of Defense's changes in the **Five Year Defense Program**. (see also **program change request**)

program change request (PCR): A request by a Service or DOD agency to change the **Five Year Defense Program** other than at the time for **Program Objective Memorandums**,

Budget Estimates Submission, or President's Budget. (see also **program change decision**)

Program Decision Memorandum (PDM): 1. Secretary of Defense memorandum to the Services indicating the results of the OSD review of the **Program Objective Memorandum(POM)** and Joint Forces Memoranda. It comes at the end of the **Issue Paper** cycle. **2.** A final decision promulgated by the **Defense Resources Board** in the programming portion of the DOD review of the Service Program Objective Memorandums. The PDM directs adjustments to the POMs, in essence approving the POMs as modified by these decisions, and forms the basis for the Services to compile their Budget Estimate Submissions. A separate PDM is issued for each Service.

program element (PE): The basic building block of the **Five Year Defense Program (FYDP)**, representing a mission of the DOD and its associated units and resources. Each DOD program element is assigned a five digit standardized PE number. DOD PEs are used and can be deciphered by determining PE status, Service, and general mission. The first digit of a typical PE number (e.g., 64568N) determines the DOD **major force program** area:

1. **Strategic Forces**.
2. **General Purpose Forces**.
3. **Intelligence and Communications**.
4. **Airlift and Sealift Forces**.
5. **Guard and Reserve Forces**.
6. **Research and Development**.

7. **Supply and Maintenance**.
8. **Personnel Activities**.
9. **Administration**.
10. **Support of other nations**.
11. **Special Operations Forces**.

The second digit determines **research and development (R&D)** category:

1. Research.
2. Exploratory Development.
3. Advanced Development.
4. Engineering Development.
5. Management and Support.

The third digit denotes budget activity:

1. Military sciences.
2. Aircraft and related equipment.
3. Missiles and related equipment.
4. Military Astronautics and related equipment.
5. Ships, Small Craft, and related equipment.
6. Ordnance, Combat Vehicles and related equipment.
7. Other equipment.
8. Program management and support.

The fourth and fifth digits are the serial number of the project. The letter suffix denotes the DOD component.

PEs describe all forces, manpower, equipment, facilities, activities, and support required to accomplish the mission with associated costs for a five-year period. Program element costs, by appropriation, are provided. There are over 1,600 PEs in DOD. For each PE, there is normally a Service or agency program element monitor.

Program Management Directive (PMD): Official Air Force management directive used to provide direction to the implementing commands and to satisfy documentation requirements. It will be used during the entire **acquisition cycle** to state requirements and request studies as well as to initiate, approve, change, transition, modify or terminate programs.

programmed force structure   (see **force structure**)

programmed manning   (see **manpower**)

programmed manpower structure (see **manpower**)

Program Objective(s) Memorandum (POM): The document used by the Services to transmit their programmatic requirements to DOD, which is done each May, and to update the **Five Year Defense Program (FYDP)**. Each military department and defense agency prepares a biennial POM, which contains a detailed presentation of the forces and manpower needed to attain the objectives of the **Defense Guidance (DG)** for the next five years and includes rationale in support of the planned changes from the previously approved FYDP baseline. The POM is based upon inputs from the CINCs, the major commands, and the Service staffs. It ranks and recommends programs for implementation within the fiscal ceiling for each of the five years in the DG. The POMs are reviewed by the CINCs, the Joint Staff, the Office of the Secretary of Defense staff, and the Office of Management and Budget. Alternatives and disagreements are developed into **Issue**

Papers, which are reviewed by the **Defense Resources Board**. Secretary of Defense decisions on the alternatives are provided in a **Program Decision Memorandum (PDM)**. The POM, as modified by the PDM, serves as a baseline for the start of the budgeting process.

prohibition: Restriction relating to the release of nuclear weapons, derived from guidance provided in Annex C, Nuclear Weapons, of the **Joint Strategic Capabilities Plan**.

propaganda: "Any form of communication in support of national objectives designed to influence the opinions, emotions, attitudes, or behavior of any group in order to benefit the sponsor, either directly or indirectly" [*JCS Pub 1,* p. 291].

PROPIN: Control marking on national security-related information standing for "Caution—Proprietary Information Involved." Used to indicate that protection of information obtained from U.S. private businesses is necessary to protect the proprietary and competitive interests of the company source. (see also **security classification**)

protected   distribution   system (PDS): Component of a **secure** communications system used to augment encrypted communications. PDS has physical and electromagnetic safeguards to minimize the risks associated with communications cables carrying classified clear-text information through unrestricted areas. Cables installed in unrestricted areas must be under sufficient control (**physical**

security and/or surveillance) to preclude covert tapping. PDS includes all equipment and cabling needed for the clear-text transmission of classified information and may be used in either fixed or tactical environments. (see also **communications security**)

Proud: Biennial JCS-sponsored and -conducted worldwide mobilization and deployment **command post exercises (CPXs)**. Senior DOD and Cabinet-level officials often participate in the exercises. They generally focus on plans, policies, and procedures utilized during **mobilization**; the **Joint Deployment System**; command center operations; civil-military interface; and operations of the **Worldwide Military Command and Control System** in a multiple theater environment:

• Proud Spirit 80: Exercise held 6–26 November 1980, similar in scenario to **Nifty Nugget 78**, and a follow-on to that exercise and **Positive Leap 80**. The exercise was held simultaneously with **REX-80 Bravo**.
• Proud Saber 83: Exercise concentrated on crisis management and coordination, particularly testing of the OSD crisis management system.
• Proud Scout 88: Exercise held 12–20 November 1987, all State-area commands (STARCs) participated for the first time. Concurrent with Proud Scout 88, the Army conducted the first "no-notice" exercise of the President's statutory authority under 10 U.S.C. §673(b) to call up to 200,000 members of the Selected Reserve to active duty.
• Proud Eagle 89: Details unknown.

Prowler   (see **EA-6B Prowler**)

psychological operations (PSYOPS): The use of **propaganda** against enemy forces and civilians (psychological warfare) in both peace and wartime; and the "political, military, economic, and ideological actions planned and conducted to create in neutral or friendly foreign groups the emotions, attitudes, or behavior to support the achievement of national objectives" [*JCS Pub 1*, p. 292]. PSYOPS are used in **special operations** as well as in conventional military operations. In Vietnam, PSYOPS were controlled by the Joint U.S. Public Affairs Office (JUSPAO), supervised by the U.S. Information Agency and the PSYOP directorate of the Military Assistance Command, Vietnam (MACV). Programs included the "third party inducement program," which offered dispensations to persons who successfully persuaded their relatives to cease fighting U.S. forces and allies; the "voluntary informant program," which offered money to persons in exchange for enemy weapons or information; "operation family tree," which "presented leaflets and tapes which contrasted our enemy casualty figures with enemy dead as reported by the enemy" to cause confusion and distrust [Army, IMA SC 811D, *Introduction to Psychological Operations*, September 1974, pp. 1-7–9].

In recent operations, PSYOPS have been employed in Grenada, the Libya bombings, and Central American operations. Four Army PSYOP groups—one in the active component (4th PSYOP Group, Ft. Bragg, NC)

and three in the Army Reserve—
are located within **Special Forces**
("Green Berets") and are subordinate to the Army's **First Special
Operations Command**. The active
unit comprises approximately 970
personnel. The reserve groups are stationed in 19 U.S. states.

public media censorship: "The voluntary withholding from publication
by the domestic mass media industries of military and other information which should not be released
in the interest of the safety and
defense of the United States and its
allies" [Army, *Armed Forces Censorship,* FM 30-28, January 1964].

purple: Former Joint Chiefs of Staff
slang for a written proposal of
changes to a **buff**.

Q

Q: Prefix designating a drone.

Q access (or clearance): Security **classification** category used by the Department of Energy, equivalent to DOD's **top secret** category. Q security clearances may be granted by DOE to its employees, consultants, assignees, contractors, or to other federal employees. The clearance requires a full field investigation by the Federal Bureau of Investigation, Office of Personnel Management, or other government investigator agency. It allows an individual to gain access on a **"need to know"** basis to top secret, secret, and confidential **restricted data**, **formerly restricted data**, national security information, or category I or II **special nuclear material**. Access permits specify the type(s) of information an individual is eligible to receive [DOE, *Personnel Security Program*, DOE Order 5631.2, 13 November 1980, released under the FOIA]. (see also **L access**)

Quadripartite Agreement: Four-power agreement between the United States, the Soviet Union, the United Kingdom, and France that determined the status of Berlin. Since 1945, Berlin had been under the divided control of the victorious allies of World War II.

In September 1971, the four powers agreed that this situation would not change. The Western powers agreed that:

- West Berlin was not a part of West Germany; and
- They would discourage the Federal Republic of Germany from holding sessions of the Bundestag and Bundesrat and from conducting federal elections in West Berlin.

The Soviet Union agreed that:

- The Bonn government could perform certain consular, nonpolitical services for West Berliners; and
- The transportation of persons and goods between West Germany and West Berlin would be unimpeded.

The agreement marked a change from the Soviet position that West Berlin was a part of East Germany and therefore subject to control by the East German government.

quarantine: **1.** As applied during the Cuban Missile Crisis of 1962, "a collective, peaceful process involving limited coercive measures interdicting the unreasonable movement of certain types of offensive military weapons and associated material by one state into the territory of another." The

United States imposed a quarantine on military shipments to Cuba and not a **blockade** because Vice President Johnson had earlier described a blockade as "an act of war." **2.** A period during which a vessel is detained in isolation until free of contagious disease. When both definitions are combined, the meaning becomes an act, short of war, designed to exclude specific items from movement into or from a state.

Quartermaster Corps: Combat service support branch of the Army.

Queen Match: Experimental rocket program at Shemya Island in the Aleutians to develop **infrared (IR)** sensors for mid-course and terminal phase interceptors. Test vehicles will be rocket launched to observe Soviet ballistic missile tests for information on how to better design U.S. missile defenses, as well as to test sensor prototypes against realistic targets.

Queen Match, previously known as Designating Optical Tracker (DOT), uses a sensor similar to that of the **Homing Overlay Experiment (HOE)**. DOT had already been tested at the Kwajalein Missile Range. The specially configured Optical Aircraft Measurement Program (OAMP) C-135 aircraft, a research predecessor to the **Airborne Optical Adjunct**, is also located at Shemya AFB under the **Cobra Eye** program. Tests of DOT and OAMP are planned up to the early 1990s.

Quick Fix I/II: Army tactical **electronic warfare jamming** system mounted in **EH-1H/X** and **EH-60A** helicopters. Each aircraft has the ability to intercept and jam radio transmissions, and the EH-1X and EH-60 (Quick Fix II) versions can also locate communications transmitters. Three Quick Fix aircraft will be organic to each division, separate brigade, or armored cavalry regiment. Interim Quick Fix systems are currently fielded and have ended production. The EH-60A Quick Fix II will replace the interim systems—Quick Fix IB (EH-1H) and II (EH-1X). The Quick Fix II system mounted in the EH-60A will provide HF/VHF jamming and VHF transmitter-location capability. The first unit was equipped with Quick Fix II in May 1988. Contractors are Electromagnetic Systems Laboratories, Inc., Sunnyvale, CA; Sikorsky Aircraft, Stratford, CT; and TRACOR, Inc., Austin, TX. The Army plans to purchase 66 Quick Fix II aircraft. The procurement request in FY 1987 was $129.6 million. (see also **UH-60 Black Hawk**)

Quick Look: Army two-person, automatic, airborne, noncommunications-emitter location and identification system to conduct **electronics intelligence (ELINT)** collection. Quick Look electronic equipment is mounted on the RV-1D Mohawk. The RV-1D fleet is planned to be replaced by the EC-12 Guardrail common sensor. The first RV-1D set will be retired in FY 1991, with full retirement by FY 1995. The remainder of the equipment is on surface vehicles. Quick Look is operational with the Army's military intelligence (Aerial Exploitation) battalions and can operate both day and night in all weather conditions. The RV-1D has a cruise speed of 210 kt and a mission endurance of four hours. Its maximum range is 820 nm. It does not carry armament. Prime contractors are Grumman Aerospace, Stuart, FL, and UTL Corporation, Dallas, TX.

quick reaction alert (QRA): Common name for nonstrategic nuclear weapons that are kept in constant readiness for prompt use, normally ready to be fired within 15 minutes. QRA applies exclusively to Air Force and Army nuclear weapons in Europe. Those weapons on QRA status are long range and are generally targeted for pre-planned strikes, rather than for use against invading military forces. During peacetime, weapons normally on QRA include **Ground Launched Cruise Missiles, Pershing II** missiles, and **F-111**, **F-16**, and **Tornado** aircraft. During generated alerts, short-range nuclear weapons such as **Lance** missiles, Navy **Tomahawk sea-launched cruise missiles**, and carrier-based aircraft (**A-6, A-7**, and **F/A 18**) can also be added to the QRA force. Quick reaction alert is officially referred to as "combat alert status" to downplay the readiness to use nuclear weapons.

R

R: Prefix designating **1.** Reconnaissance aircraft (e.g., RC-135). **2.** Rocket.   **3.** Vehicle launched from a surface vessel, such as a ship or barge.

radar (Radio Detection and Ranging): Equipment to determine the distance and usually the direction of objects by transmission and return of **electromagnetic** energy. Waves are generated that then reflect off the target and back to the radar sensors. Reflected waves (returns or echoes) give information on distance to target and velocity of target.

radar cross-section: The image produced by **radar** signals reflected off a given target surface. Because the size of the image is a function not only of the target's size, but of structural shape and the refractory characteristics of its materials, radar cross-section is an important design characteristic for air and space vehicles.

radar intelligence (RADINT): A type of **signals intelligence** information obtained by nonimaging **radar**. RADINT is produced by the emission of electronic signals (radio waves) that are then reflected back to the source. RADINT includes information on missile flight paths, speed, trajectory, angles of flight, and maneuverability.

radiation absorbed dose (rad): The traditional unit for measuring energy that is deposited by radiation in any material (i.e., the absorbed dose). The unit was recommended and adopted by the International Commission on Radiological Units at the Seventh International Congress of Radiology, held in Copenhagen, Denmark, in July 1953. The effect of one rad of highly penetrating gamma radiation equals one **rem**. The unit is being replaced by the "gray." There are a number of different classifications for rad exposure by military personnel, particularly on the battlefield:

- *Latent lethality dose: 600 rads.* Persons receiving such a dose will become functionally impaired within two hours of exposure. Personnel may respond to medical treatment if available and survive this dose; however, the majority of the exposed personnel will remain functionally impaired until death (in several weeks).

- *Immediate transient incapacitation dose: 3,000 rads.* Persons receiving this dose will become incapacitated within five minutes of exposure and will remain incapacitated for 30–45 minutes. Persons will partially recover from the dose but will remain functionally impaired until death (in 4–6 days).

- *Immediate permanent incapacitation dose: 8,000 rads.* Persons receiving such a dose will become incapacitated within five minutes of exposure and will remain incapacitated until death (in 1–2 days).

radiation intelligence (RINT): Type of **intelligence** information derived from the unintentional emission of radioactive sources or through nuclear detonations. RINT is collected by air-, ground-, sea-, and space-based systems, most as part of the **Atomic Energy Detection System**. Ground-based methods of RINT collection include seismic monitoring, cryogenic distillation, and **electromagnetic pulse (EMP)** sensing. Air-based systems include air filtering and aerial sampling. Ocean-based collection is by hydroacoustic detection (Digital "O") systems. RINT is a secondary mission of the **Defense Support Program** and **NAVSTAR** satellites, which have **Nuclear Detonation Detection System (NDDS)** sensors aboard.

RADINT   (see **radar intelligence**)

radio frequency   (see **frequency**)

radius of action   (see **range**)

ramjet: A jet propulsion engine containing neither compression nor turbine. It depends on the air compression accomplished by the forward motion of the engine for its operation.

RAND Corporation (Research and Development)   (see **Federally Funded Research and Development Centers**)

R&D   (see **research and development**)

range: **1.** The distance between any point and a target.   **2.** The limit of an operation, such as the range of an aircraft. The maximum distance a vehicle may travel with its normal payload without returning for refueling is also referred to as its "radius of action."

Rangers: Nickname for the Army's 75th Infantry Regiment, which specializes in long-range **reconnaissance** and **special operations**. It was formally established in 1984, but the unit traces its history back to Major Robert Rogers' "Rangers"—nine companies of American colonists who employed guerrilla-type tactics during the French and Indian wars. Ranger missions include strikes, tactical reconnaissance, long-range patrol, and special light infantry missions. Ranger operations take two forms: quick response and deliberate offensive operations. Deliberate operations rely on planning, detailed reconnaissance, deceptive countermeasures, and secrecy. Both types of missions require that the unit be extracted from behind enemy lines before the enemy can react in strength.

The 75th Regiment is subordinate to the **First Special Operations Command**. It comprises three Ranger battalions, each composed of 575 total personnel; 45 officer and 530 enlisted.

The battalions alternately serve as the Ranger Ready Force, available for rapid deployment. Total personnel strength is approximately 1,800 personnel.

Headquarters
Ft. Benning, GA 31905

Battalions

- 1st Ranger Bn, Hunter Army Airfield, GA 31409
- 2d Ranger Bn, Ft. Lewis, WA 98433
- 3d Ranger Bn, Ft. Benning, GA 31905

rank: The relative position of an **officer** or enlisted person within a particular grade. (see also Appendix E)

Rapid Deployment Joint Task Force (RDFJTF): Joint task force established by the Carter Administration to prepare for military contingencies in the Persian Gulf region. It was transitioned to the unified **U.S. Central Command** in 1984. The U.S. Central Command is still popularly called the Rapid Deployment Force.

Rapid Engineer Deployment, Heavy Operational Repair Squadrons, Engineering (RED HORSE): Air Force squadrons established to provide a highly mobile, self-sufficient, rapidly deployable civil engineering capability required in potential theaters of operation.

Rapier (Rapid Emergency Reconstitution Team): NORAD/U.S. Space Command ground mobile command center for **post-attack, early-warning**, and attack assessment reception and evaluation. Rapier would consist of a staff of 60–100 people who, at a heightened level of alert or upon the direction of the Commander of **Air Force Space Command (AFSPACE COM)**, would disperse to preselected sites in the central United States and reconstitute NORAD and AFSPACE-COM headquarters. These new headquarters will be able to operate for at least 30 days. Rapier vans are located in Colorado Springs, CO, in peacetime.

rate: Navy personnel occupation identity designation by pay grade. Within a **rating**, a rate reflects levels of aptitude, training, experience, knowledge, skills, and responsibilities. There are six rates: master chief, senior chief, chief petty officer, and first, second, and third class petty officers. These correspond respectively to pay grades E-9, E-8, E-7, E-6, E-5 and E-4. Personnel in pay grades E-1 through E-3 do not possess rates because their occupations are too broad in context and too limited in technical content and responsibility. (see also Appendix F)

rating: System used by the Department of the Navy to designate the occupation of a petty officer requiring related aptitudes, knowledge, training, and skill. Boatswain's Mate (BM), Gunner's Mate (GM), and Aviation Electronics Technician (AT) are examples of ratings. A rating is subdivided into six **rates** [Navy, *Navy Military Personnel Statistics,* NAVPERS 15658, 31 December 1987, p. III, released under the FOIA]. (see also Appendix F)

rationalization: Actions that improve NATO's capabilities through more efficient or effective use of defense resources, including consolidation, revised national priorities, standardization, specialization, mutual support, better interoperability, and greater allied cooperation. (see also **rationalization, standardization, and interoperability**)

rationalization, standardization, and interoperability (RSI): Term that refers to cooperative efforts among NATO allies to standardize weapon systems and equipment procured for and used by their forces. The objectives of RSI are to increase military capability of NATO forces, to improve political cohesion among the allies, and to benefit industrial cooperation. The Department of Defense (DOD) RSI directive states that

". . .it is the policy of the United States that equipment procured for U.S. forces employed in Europe under the terms of the North Atlantic Treaty Organization should be standardized or at least interoperable with equipment of other members of NATO. Accordingly, the Department of Defense shall initiate and carry out methods of cooperation with its Allies in defense equipment acquisition. . . . The Department of Defense will also seek greater compatibility of doctrine and tactics to provide a better basis for arriving at common NATO requirements. The goal is to achieve standardization of entire systems, where feasible, and to gain the maximum degree of interoperability throughout Alliance military forces" [DOD, *Standardization and Interoperability of Weapons Systems and Equipment within the North Atlantic Treaty*

Organization, DOD Directive 2010.6, 5 March 1980, pp. 1–2].

RSI priorities of DOD are established annually in the Consolidated Guidance. Further, the JCS has established and the NATO **Military Committee** has endorsed five top priority areas for interoperability and standardization:

1. Command, control, and information systems;
2. Cross-servicing of aircraft;
3. Ammunition;
4. Compatible battlefield surveillance/target designation/acquistion systems; and
5. Components and spare parts.

To further RSI objectives, many existing allied-produced weapons have been selected for use by the armed forces of individual nations, and others are developed by individual nations for use by other NATO members. Some systems have been codeveloped or coproduced by member nations. Examples of U.S. systems developed for procurement and use by NATO allies are the **forward-looking infrared (FLIR)** sensor, the **Harpoon** anti-surface ship missile, **Airborne Warning and Control System (AWACS)** aircraft, and the **NAV STAR/GPS.** Examples of systems codeveloped or coproduced by the U.S. and allies include the **Multiple-launch Rocket System (MLRS),** and the **AV-8 Harrier** V/STOL aircraft [DOD, *Standardization of Equipment within NATO,* 31 January 1984]. (see also **interoperability, rationalization, standardization**)

Raven (see **EF-111A Raven**)

Raven Rock: Nickname for the **Alternate National Military Command Center** located at Raven Rock, PA.

RC-12: Army twin turbo-prop platform for the Improved **Guardrail** V combined airborne and ground **communications intelligence (COMINT)** system capable of intercepting and locating communications emitters. The Guardrail system consists of mission-configured RC-12Ds and a mobile ground mission processing facility. Two Improved Guardrail V systems were deployed in 1985. The Guardrail V system currently being replaced is flown in the RU-21H. A RC-12K Guardrail Common Sensor System is under development and will enter the inventory in 1991. Improved Guardrail V sensors will then be upgraded. The prime contractor for the aircraft is Beech Aircraft, Wichita, KS. Avionics are produced by ESL, Inc., of Sunnyvale, CA. UTL Corporation, Dallas, TX, and IBM, Owego, NY, are other contractors. FY 1990 and FY 1991 budget requests for 5 and 10 RC-12D aircraft in each year are $71.3 million and $121.1 million, respectively.

RC-135: Air Force versatile airborne reconnaissance platform operated by the Strategic Air Command for the collection of **signals intelligence**. The RC-135 versions of the C-135 Stratolifter are equipped with specialized equipment to fulfill a wide variety of signals intelligence roles. There are 18 RC-135s in the inventory, varying in mission and capabilities. The first aircraft, model RC-135B, was deployed in December 1965. Fourteen of the planes—modified RC-135V and RC-135M aircraft—operate under the code name **Rivet Joint** and are general signals intelligence platforms. Rivet Joint missions are called "Burning Wind." An average of 70 flights are conducted per month in western Europe and the Far East, and 12 flights per month are conducted around Central America. Two RC-135S models operate under **Cobra Ball** and monitor Soviet missile testing. The remaining two are RC-135U models, nicknamed **Combat Sent**. The aircraft have a cruising speed of 460 mph at an operational altitude of 34,990 ft, and an operating radius of 5,500 km. RC-135 planes operate from bases at Eielson AFB and Shemya AFB, AK; Offutt AFB, NE; Howard AB, Panama; RAF Mildenhall, UK; Hellenikon AB, Greece; and Kadena AB, Japan.

RDT&E (research, development, test, and evaluation) (see **research and development**)

reactor (see **nuclear reactor**)

reactor vessel: A container surrounding either the core or the entire structure of a **nuclear reactor**.

readiness: An indicator of precombat status that affects the ability of a force to achieve a wartime objective. Further, unit readiness is a subset of force readiness that involves unit integration and coordination through command, control, and communication to form a cohesive, effective force. Unit readiness is further broken down into two major categories: personnel and materiel readiness. Personnel readiness consists of the personnel available and their training. Materiel readiness consists of equipment and supplies on hand and equipment condition.

For years, DOD, Congress, and others have been concerned over the inadequacies of readiness reporting systems in terms of their design, their accuracy in reporting military status/capability, and their use in determining appropriations levels. One problem with readiness reporting has been the absence of a standard definition of readiness. For example, a 1980 House readiness panel report concluded that "readiness" was an imprecise term and that DOD did not have a definition of readiness applicable to broad congressional concerns. This conclusion was borne out by a March 1980 study sponsored by the Air Force that cited 44 different readiness definitions and readiness-related terms used within DOD. This issue was at least partially addressed in mid-1982 when DOD approved a definition of **military capability** with readiness being one of four major components used to judge or evaluate DOD's ability to undertake military actions successfully.

DOD does not have a single quantitative measurement of readiness. The Army Unit Status Report (USR) evaluates four elements of a combat unit: personnel, equipment on hand, equipment readiness, and training. Each element is rated on a standard criterion that compares what the unit actually has on hand to that which is needed to perform its wartime mission.

Each area is assigned a readiness status (a **C-rating**) as follows

- C-1: Combat ready, no deficiencies.
- C-2: Combat ready, minor deficiencies.
- C-3: Combat ready, major deficiencies.
- C-4: Not combat ready.
- C-5: Not combat ready, undergoing reorganization or major equipment conversion or in cadre status.

(see also **readiness conditions**)

Readiness Command (REDCOM): Predecessor to the U.S. Strike Command, and a former unified command; disestablished in 1988 with the creation of the **U.S. Special Operations Command**, which took over the headquarters complex and basic staff at MacDill AFB, FL. The functions of REDCOM were transferred to the specified **Forces Command** of the Army.

readiness conditions: A designation of the state of military and civil defense forces in peacetime and their readiness to respond to orders to implement crisis or wartime plans. Readiness conditions are not the same as the actual readiness deployment state of a unit during military operations. There are three types of readiness conditions:

- **Defense Readiness Conditions (DEFCONS);**
- **Civil Readiness Conditions; and**
- **Civil Defense Readiness Conditions.**

"During **REX-82 Bravo**, and in previous **mobilization** exercises, confusion arose concerning the relationship of the readiness terms used to describe military forces and those that apply to the civil government. In fact, there is no intended relationship between the three Civil Readiness Conditions and the five DEFCONs. The former refer to increased preparedness stages to ensure continuity of essential government operations. The latter increase military responsiveness. . . . Neither is related to the four categories of actions that the Federal Government recommends to State and local governments to increase civil defense readiness" [FEMA, *REX-82 Bravo Evaluation Report,* 25 February 1983, pp. 3–12, released under the FOIA].

Ready Reserve: Category of reserve personnel consisting of members of the **Selected Reserve**, the **Individual Ready Reserve**, and the **Inactive National Guard**.

real time: The absence of delay, except for the time required for the transmission by electromagnetic energy, between the occurrence of an event or the transmission of data and the knowledge of the event or reception of the data at some other location. (see also **near real time**)

rear area protection: Actions taken to counter the enemy threat to units, and to reduce damage to activities and installations in the **corps** rear area. The mission is normally assigned to the **corps support command**. Rear area security includes all actions to prevent or neutralize the effect of enemy nuclear, chemical, and biological weapons; airborne forces; guerilla

infiltrators; and saboteurs. Area damage control includes all measures taken to avoid, control, or repair damage from any type of disaster or enemy action.

Rebound Echo: Code name for dispersal bases used by the **National Emergency Airborne Command Post** and other airborne command posts during emergencies or attacks upon primary bases at Offutt AFB, NE, and Grissom AFB, IN [JCS, *Strategic Connectivity Study*, March 1979, p. D-109, released under the FOIA].

reconnaissance (RECON or RECCE): An operation undertaken to obtain **intelligence** information by visual observation or other detection methods. RECON normally refers to airborne intelligence collection, particularly by photographic means. (see also **satellite reconnaissance**)

reconnaissance squadron: Army **cavalry** squadron assigned to a **light infantry division**, but with only one ground troop rather than two, although its mission remains the same.

RED/BLACK Concept: The separation of electrical and electronic circuits, components, equipment, and systems that handle classified plain language information in electric form (RED) from those that handle encrypted or unclassified information (BLACK). RED and BLACK terminology is used to clarify specific criteria relating to and differentiating between such circuit components, equipment, and systems and the areas in which they are contained [*DIC Glossary*].

Redeye (see **Stinger**)

Red Flag: Recurring **Tactical Air Command** live-fire intense-training **exercise** designed to provide realistic multithreat opportunities to aircrews. Red Flag establishes an environment that reflects all the threats a pilot and crew might encounter in a real combat situation. It has grown from 522 training sorties flown in one month in 1975 to a culmination of more than 217,000 missions as of 1987. The five-week exercise is held at Nellis AFB, NV. While Air Force personnel are the main Red Flag participants, joint exercises are conducted with the other services and with allied units. [SAC, *SAC Exercise Program*, SACR 55-38, Vol. I, p. 2-2, released under the FOIA].

redout: "The blinding, or dazzling, of infrared detectors because of nuclear explosions in the upper atmosphere. High levels of infrared radiation could cause a kind of radar blackout of terminal-phase airborne optical sensors. The use of airborne optical sensors is viewed by scientists as an important supplement to the use of ground-based radars; therefore, overcoming redout is a major problem" [*SDI Dictionary*, p. 116].

red phone: Nickname for the **Primary Alerting System (PAS)**.

red rocket: A type of **emergency action message (EAM)** used to transmit urgent instructions simultaneously from the National Command Author-

ities to several commands and echelons of command. The red rocket message is part of the **emergency action procedures** of the JCS and the unified and specified commands. The message requires voice receipt acknowledgement to the **National Military Command Center**. A white rocket message is the exercise version of a red rocket message [CENTCOM, *Emergency Action Procedures, Vol. 1*, p. 13-1, released under the FOIA].

reentry body (RB): A Navy term for **reentry vehicle**.

reentry vehicle (RV): The portion of a space vehicle designed to reenter the earth's atmosphere in the terminal portion of its trajectory. A "reentry body," as designated by the Air Force and Navy, connotes that part of a ballistic missile or any other vehicle that reenters the earth's atmosphere after flight. When used by the Navy, it implies that the body contains a warhead and its components with the mission to ultimately detonate on a predetermined target. A "reentry system," as used by the Air Force and Navy, identifies the portion of a ballistic missile designed to place one or more reentry vehicles or bodies on terminal trajectories so as to arrive at selected targets. **Penetration aids**, spacers, deployment modules, and control-and-sensing devices are included in the reentry system. "Nuclear reentry vehicle" is a term used by the Air Force to identify a component of a system designed to reenter the earth's atmosphere. It may include a nuclear warhead and fuzing, arming, and triggering devices, as well as devices for programming, correlating, sequencing, deployment, survival, target sensing, safing, and vehicle-booster separation [DNA, *Technical Manual—Glossary of Nuclear Weapons Materiel and Related Terms*, TP4-1, 15 November 1975, released under the FOIA].

refire time: For a **ballistic missile**, the time required after the initial firing to launch a second missile from the same pad or launcher.

reflector: A layer of material immediately surrounding a **nuclear reactor** core that scatters back, or deflects, into the core many neutrons that would otherwise escape. The returned neutrons cause more **fission** and improve the neutron economy of the reactor. Common reflector materials are graphite, beryllium, and natural uranium.

REFORGER (Return of force to Germany):   The name given the deployment of U.S. Army forces to Europe to participate in maneuvers with European-based U.S. and allied forces. The two primary purposes of REFORGER are to fulfill the understandings of the 1967 Trilateral Talks and to practice war plans for the reinforcement of Europe.

In 1967, the United States entered into a Trilateral Agreement with the United Kingdom and West Germany to return up to 35,000 U.S. soldiers and airmen to U.S. bases for their stations in Europe. The agreement stipulated that returning U.S. forces would be held in a high state of readiness to ensure their capability to return rapidly to Europe in an emergency. The NATO **Defense Planning Committee** concurred in the agreement. The United States also agreed that, to demonstrate its resolve and ability to meet its commitments under the **North Atlantic Treaty**, the withdrawn forces would return annually to Germany for exercises (named REFORGER for Army forces and **Crested Cap** for Air Force units). The addition of major U.S. combat units (i.e., Army brigades and tactical air squadrons) to Europe during 1975 and 1976 brought U.S. combat forces to their pre-1967 agreement level and provoked the House Appropriations Committee to argue that the 1967 agreement, as a reason for conducting annual REFORGER exercises in their present scale and scope, were obviated.

REFORGER exercises provide opportunities for practicing the plans and procedures that have been developed for the reinforcement of U.S. forces in West Germany during an emergency. Units earmarked for European deployment prepare for deployment in the United States, deploy to Europe, move to their prepositioned equipment, withdraw equipment, withdraw and upload supplies, move to an assembly area, and organize for combat within a relatively short period. In 1978, the Secretary of Defense provided guidance stipulating that major reinforcement units, deploying to prepositioned material configured to unit sets (**POMCUS**), be operationally ready for combat and be released to NATO shortly after mobilization.

Regency Net: Army-operated HF voice and data communications system in Europe and South Korea for nuclear weapons command and control to replace the **Cemetery Net**. Regency Net command consoles and computers are nuclear hardened. They control and store messages, assign priority of dissemination, and then relay data to appropriate users. The Army awarded Magnavox an initial $82.6 million contract in 1984 to upgrade emergency HF communications under the Regency Net program.

regiment (regt):   Army and Marine Corps administrative and tactical unit, subordinate to a **division** and made up of **battalions**. A regiment is larger than a battalion and smaller than a division or brigade. In the Army, a regiment is organized as a self-contained unit and is capable of independent operations over a wide area and of light-armor, reconnaissance, and security operations. An armored cavalry regiment usually consists of a headquarters and headquarters troop, three armored cavalry squadrons, and one air cavalry troop. It is usually assigned to a **corps** and commanded by a colonel. In the Marine Corps, a regiment is organized similarly to a **brigade** in the Army. (see also **U.S. Army Regimental System**)

Regimental System (see **U.S. Army Regimental System**)

Regional Operational Control Center (ROCC):   NORAD-controlled **air defense** command center operated jointly with the **Federal Aviation Administration**. ROCCs process data from **Joint Surveillance System (JSS)** radars monitoring North American airspace to detect intruders and control interceptor aircraft

as required. ROCCs are continuously informed of the current status of the air defense resources available in the area. In the event of air attack, a ROCC will perform the primary command and control functions for intercepting aircraft for as long as it survives, after which its functions would be taken over by an **E-3A Sentry AWACS** aircraft. There are eight ROCCs: four in CONUS (McChord, March, Griffiss, and Tyndall AFBs), two in Canada (both at North Bay, Ontario; one a back-up for the other), one in Alaska (Elmendorf AFB), and one in Hawaii (Wheeler AFB).

release: "Authorization for the employment of nuclear weapons. Release is granted by the President, through the Joint Chiefs of Staff, to the commander of a unified or specified command or other commanders" [JCS, *Emergency Action Procedures, Vol. I*, 1 April 1984, p. 1–21, released under the FOIA]. (see also **emergency action procedures**)

relocatable over-the-horizon radar (ROTHR) (see **over-the-horizon radar**)

rem (roentgen equivalent man): The traditional unit for measuring the biological effect of a dose of radiation (i.e., the dose equivalent). The damage from one **rad** of gamma radiation equals one rem. The average annual natural radiation exposure is between 100 and 200 millirems (thousandths of a rem). Standards imposed by international bodies and the Environmental Protection Agency (EPA) set exposure limits at 500 millirems per year for the public from a nuclear facility, and 5 rems per year for nuclear workers. The measurement rem is being replaced by the "sievert."

remotely piloted vehicle (RPV): "An unmanned air vehicle capable of being controlled by a person from a distant location through a communications link. It is normally designed to be recoverable" [*JCS Pub 1*, p. 309]. An RPV is "an unmanned/mission-oriented airborne weapon system capable of preprogrammed or commanded flight from a land-based or shipboard ground station. RPVs can be used to perform a variety of independent missions, such as **reconnaissance**, communications relay, **electronic warfare**, target designation, and **strike**, as well as to complement existing/future manned aircraft systems" [*NWP 3*]. (see also **Aquila, drone, unmanned aerial vehicle, Unmanned Air Reconnaissance Vehicle**)

render safe procedures: The application of **explosive ordnance disposal (EOD)** methods and tools to provide for the interruption of functions or separation of essential components of explosive ordnance items to preclude a detonation or munition function.

repair ship (AR): Navy material support ship capable of providing full repair and logistics support, at anchor or moored to a pier, in a peacetime or wartime environment. ARs can simultaneously repair a large number of ship systems and subsystems and can be forward deployed in wartime. The Navy operates four repair ships of the Vulcan (AR-5) class, two in the active fleet and two in the reserves. The ships displace approximately 16,270 tons full load, are 529 ft long, have a beam of 73 ft, a top speed of 19.2 kt, and a complement of 1,000 personnel. They were built by New York Shipbuilding and Los Angeles Shipbuilding and Drydock between 1934 and 1940.

Republic of Korea/U.S. Combined Forces Command (CFC) (see **Combined Forces Command**)

request message: Message of the JCS **emergency action procedures** used by commanders of unified and specified commands to **release** chemical or nuclear weapons. "A commander's request or warning must contain sufficient information to insure complete understanding of the situation at the highest level of government" [JCS, *Emergency Action Procedures, Vol. I*, 15 March 1983, p. 7-1, released under the FOIA].

Required operational capability (ROC): A formal, serially-numbered document used to identify an operational need and to request a new or improved capability for the operating forces that cannot be satisfied by existing equipment, or to propose a significant reduction in the cost of current operations. The capability sought is described in terms of the operational objective, operational environment, support and maintenance concepts, and concepts of operation.

research and development (R&D): Program 6 of the 11 **major force programs** that represent all of the major missions of the services and are the most basic structural elements of the **Five Year Defense Program**. RED consists of all research and development programs and activities that have not yet been approved for operational use. The research and development program is divided into five "categories," the second digit designating the category:

- *6.1 Research:* All scientific study and experimentation directed toward increasing knowledge and understanding in those fields of the physical, engineering, environmental, biological-medical, and behavioral-social sciences directly related to explicitly stated long-term national security needs.
- *6.2 Exploratory Development:* All efforts directed toward the solution of specific military problems, short of major development projects.
- *6.3 Advanced Development:* All projects that have moved into the development of hardware for experimental or operational test. It is characterized by line item projects, and program control is exercised on a project basis. 6.3A is Technology Demonstration. 6.3B is Engineering Prototype.
- *6.4 Engineering Development:* Development programs being engineered for service use but not yet approved for procurement or operation.
- *6.5 Management and Support:* Includes research and development effort directed toward support of installations or operations required for general research and development use. Included are test ranges,

military construction not included elsewhere, and operation and maintenance of test aircraft.

Research & Development activities are also divided into "budget activities" identified by the third digit of a major force program 6 **program element**:

- 6X1XX: Technology Base.
- 6X2XX: Advanced Technology Development.
- 6X3XX: Strategic Programs.
- 6X4XX: Tactical Programs.
- 6X5XX: Intelligence and Communications.
- 6X6XX: Defense-wide Mission Support.

research, development, test, and evaluation (RDT&E)   (see **research and development**)

Reserve Officers Training Corps (ROTC): Officer recruiting and training program of the Army, Navy, and Air Force, established by the National Defense Act of 1916. The Senior ROTC programs are designed to recruit, educate, and commission officer candidates through civilian educational institutions. Junior ROTC provides citizenship training and science programs at the secondary education level.

Reserves: Component of the **Total Force** consisting of service members not on active duty but subject to call up to active federal duty. The role of the reserve forces was significantly altered by the adoption of the Total Force concept by the Department of Defense in 1973. Under the program, which ended the draft and instituted the All Volunteer Force, reserve components are slated as the primary and initial military personnel to augment active forces in national military emergencies. According to the Reserve Forces Policy Board of the Office of the Secretary of Defense, the policy intends that reserve forces are to be "equal partners, on and off the battlefield, and must be as ready as their active counterparts." U.S. Reserve components include the **Air Force Reserve; Air National Guard; Army Reserve; Army National Guard; Naval Reserve; Marine Corps Reserve;** and the **Coast Guard Reserve**. The three categories of reserve personnel are

- **Ready Reserve**: Consisting of the **Selected Reserve**, the **Individual Ready Reserve**, and the **Inactive National Guard;**
- **Standby Reserve**; and
- **Retired Reserve**.

In addition to the Reserve Forces Policy Board, the Assistant Secretary of Defense (Reserve Affairs) is responsible for the overall supervision of reserve components. Each service (except the Coast Guard) has an Assistant Secretary for Manpower and Reserve Affairs and a Chief or Director of its reserve component. The President may call up any unit or category of the reserves upon declaration of war or a state of national emergency for a period of up to 24 consecutive months. As many as 1,000,000 reservists may serve on active duty at any given time under the law. Total appropriations for reserve components in a typical year are

approximately $20 billion (FY 1988), or 6.8 percent of the total. The personnel strength of the Selected Reserve, the largest category of reserve personnel, increased during the fiscal years 1980–1987 by 32 percent, while active duty personnel strength increased only 7 percent (approximately). The total strength of all the U.S. reserve components for FY 1987 was just over 2,000,000.

response force: A force of 15 or more security force personnel, in addition to those on established guard posts, capable of responding to attempted penetrations of security or unauthorized access to nuclear weapons. A response force must be able to react to a nuclear security emergency in less than five minutes.

restricted area: Any area to which entry is subject to special restrictions or controls for reasons of security or safeguarding of property or materiel, exclusive of those designated areas over which aircraft flights are restricted. (see also **exclusion area, limited area**)

restricted data (RD):   Type of classified information designated by the DOD and the Department of Energy that applies to weapons data concerning the design and manufacture of nuclear weapons and the production of special nuclear materials. Differs from classified material in that RD specifically refers to nuclear weapons information as defined in the **Atomic Energy Act**, but does not include information declassified or removed from the restricted data category under Section 142 of the Act. (see also **formerly restricted data**)

Retired Reserve: A category of reserve personnel, in addition to the **Ready Reserve** and the **Standby Reserve**, whose members have retired status after completing the required years of military service or due to a physical disability. Such members are available for mobilization only upon a declaration of war or national emergency. Total personnel strength of the Retired Reserve is about 380,000 (see also **Reserves**).

retrograde: The movement of personnel and/or cargo from the area of operations back to their points of origin.

REX-Alpha: Biennial Federal Emergency Management Agency-sponsored national/regional joint civil/military nuclear attack exercise designed to provide for the participation of senior government officials in the coordination of civil and military operations to maintain **continuity of government**, in military support of **civil defense**, in economic recovery, and in resource management.

- REX-82 Alpha was played in coordination and simultaneously with the DOD exercise **Ivy League** 82.
- REX-84 Alpha (5–13 April 1984) was played in coordination and simultaneously with the JCS/DOD exercise Night Train 84.
- REX-86 Alpha was played in coordination and simultaneously with the JCS/DOD exercise **Present Arms 86**.

- REX-88 Alpha was played in coordination and simultaneously with an unknown JCS exercise.

REX-Bravo: Biennial Federal Emergency Management Agency (FEMA)–sponsored national/regional joint civil-**mobilization** and civil-**readiness command post exercise (CPX)** designed to provide civil agencies an opportunity to identify and address resource problems involved in sustaining an expanding military mobilization process during a protracted conventional war. REX-Bravo are large-scale command post exercises dealing with national mobilization that began in 1976, when the Army conducted MOBEX-76.

- REX-76 was held by the Federal Preparedness Agency concurrently with **Pole Vault 76**. The exercise focused on "testing the civil and military policies, plans, systems, and procedures to be used in an early post attack period and for projecting the redirection, recovery, and reconstitution goals of the Nation" [JCS, *Exercise Staff Participation and Administrative Support Requirements for Exercise POLE VAULT 76*, 13 January 1976].
- REX-78 (10–30 October 1978) was held by the Federal Preparedness Agency in coordination and simultaneously with JCS exercise **Nifty Nugget 78**.
- REX-80 Bravo (6–18 November 1980) was held concurrently with and parallel to JCS exercise **Proud Spirit 80**. FEMA, DOD, and 19 federal departments and agencies

participated. "The exercise demonstrated the low priority that had been accorded mobilization planning in preceding years. Plans, where they could be found, were out of date, and planning had been given little priority within the civil agencies. FEMA, created from a number of disparate Federal organizations, was unable to provide effective direction or cohesion. FEMA lacked the prestige and the authority to serve as the focal point for civil agency mobilization planning" [FEMA, *REX 82 Bravo Evaluation Report*, 25 February 1983, p. 1–2, released under the FOIA.]

- REX-82 Bravo (25 October–5 November 1982) was held by FEMA simultaneously with Proud Saber 83. "It was more ambitious, lasted longer, involved more participants, and in general presented a more demanding test of the Federal Government's ability to support a full mobilization than any previous exercise" [FEMA, *ibid.*, p. 1–1].

RF-4 (see **F-4 Phantom/Phantom II**)

RH-53D Sea Stallion: Navy single main rotor head, all-weather, airborne, mine countermeasures helicopter. The specially modified helicopters, based on the **CH-53** airframe, are capable of land- and ship-based operations. The RH-53 is capable of mine sweeping, spotting, and neutralization, as well as surface towing. The helicopter was used extensively in mine countermeasures operations in the Persian Gulf in 1987–1988. The Navy operates two active and one reserve airborne mine countermeasures squadrons.

R-hour: 1. In daylight Navy operations, the time at which underwater demolition craft, with swimmer personnel aboard, cross the fire support line in the approach to the beach to discharge the swimmers. **2.** In nighttime Navy operations, the time at which the underwater demolition crafts are launched from the parent surface ship. [*NWP 3*]. (see also **military time**)

Rhyolite: Initial code name for a retired class of **signals intelligence (SIGINT)** satellites, renamed **Aquacade**. Five Rhyolite spacecraft were launched into geosynchronous orbit between 19 June 1970 and 7 April 1978. The primary targets were **communications intelligence** and **radar intelligence**, as well as **telemetry intelligence** from missile testing. Its successor system is **Magnum**. The system was controlled from the Pine Gap, Australia, facility. Intelligence obtained by Rhyolite and other SIGINT satellites is marked by the codeword **Zarf**.

RICHTER (see **sensitive compartmented information**)

RINT (see **radiation intelligence**)

Rio Treaty: Formally known as the Inter-American Treaty of Reciprocal Assistance. The Rio Treaty was signed in Rio de Janeiro on 2 September 1947 by the United States and 21 Latin American countries. It entered into force on 3 December 1948. The treaty establishes a collective security agreement among the signatories if a member nation is attacked by a nonsignatory. However, the treaty does not stipulate the amount or type of aid allies are obliged to give. The Organization of American States (OAS) supplements this treaty by offering provisions for the settling of internal disputes. Cuba was expelled from treaty membership in 1962, and Nicaragua and Ecuador remain outside the treaty.

riverine force: "The forces organized or assembled in order to conduct riverine operations and composed of naval, air, and ground forces operating from riverine bases or land bases" [*NWP 3*].

Rivet Joint   (see **RC-135**)

rocket: "A self-propelled vehicle whose trajectory or course, while in flight, cannot be controlled" [*JCS Pub 1,* p. 316].

rocket assisted projectile (RAP): An artillery projectile that has been modified with a post-launch boost to achieve greater range.

roentgen   equivalent   man   (see **rem**)

Rolling Airframe Missile (RAM): Navy high-firepower, low-cost, lightweight, self-defense system to engage anti-ship missiles. RAM is a joint development with West Germany. The missile uses the infrared seeker of the **Stinger** missile and the rocket motor, fuze, and warhead from the **Sidewinder**. It can be fired from

Sea Sparrow launchers and from a 21-cell dedicated launcher. The missile is scheduled to become operational in 1990. Limited production was approved in April 1987. Major contractors are General Dynamics of Ponoma, CA, and RAMSYS of West Germany. FY 1990 and 1991 budget requests for 580 and 540 missiles per year are $96.5 and $90.7 million per year, respectively.

ROTHR (relocatable over-the-horizon radar)   (see **over-the-horizon radar**)

Round House: Exercise term to describe the **Defense Readiness Condition (DEFCON) 3**.

round out: Army Reserve and **Army National Guard** units that bring understructured active Army units (divisions and separate brigades) up to a standard configuration by affiliation and augmentation. Reserve maneuver battalions and brigades are designated round out units. For FY 1989, six reserve brigades and eight maneuver battalions will round out active units. Nine of 18 active divisions, including 2 light divisions, will have round out units [DOD, *Manpower Requirements Report FY 1989*, March 1988, p. III-9].

routine: Precedence category assigned to a message to indicate the relative order and speed at which it is to be communicated. Used for communication of all types of messages, routine messages are marked "RR" and are to be handled within approximately six hours. (see also **FLASH, Immediate, Priority**)

RPV   (see **remotely piloted vehicle**)

RR: Marking on **routine** messages.

Ruff: Control marking and security clearance applied to **talent-keyhole** information relating to the products of imaging satellites. (see also **security classification**)

rules of engagement (ROE):   "Directives issued by competent military authority that delineate the circumstances and limitations under which United States forces will initiate and/or continue combat engagement with other forces encountered" [*JCS Pub 1*, p. 317]. ROEs are usually issued by the Joint Chiefs of Staff (JCS) or the unified and specified commands. Peacetime ROEs are directives issued by military authorities that delineate the circumstances and limitations under which military forces will operate short of wartime or U.S.-initiated hostilities. They are essentially defensive in nature. Commanders of unified and specified commands publish, consistent with JCS guidance, peacetime ROEs for their respective forces and forward copies to the JCS. The compilation of peacetime, ROEs are available in the national command centers. In some cases, higher authority may provide ad hoc guidance that modifies ROEs when informed of a confrontation involving U.S. forces. Guidance to escalate a conflict or confrontation may require implementation of **operation plans**. The implementation of such plans, unless otherwise directed, invokes the ROE cited in those plans and discontinues applicability of peacetime ROE.

RV   (see **reentry vehicle**)

S

S: Prefix designating anti-submarine aircraft (e.g., S-2, S-3).

S-3 Viking: Navy, four-person, all-weather, high-endurance, carrier-based, twin-engine, nuclear-capable **anti-submarine warfare** and maritime patrol aircraft. The S-3 replaced the S-2 Tracker starting in the mid-1970s. The S-3 Viking uses **sono buoys**, **electronic warfare support measures**, **forward-looking infrared radar (FLIR)**, and a **magnetic anomaly detector (MAD)** to detect, locate, and classify submerged submarines. It is armed with B57 nuclear depth bombs, Mk-46 lightweight torpedos, **Harpoon** anti-ship missiles, conventional bombs, or mines in combination in a weapons bay and on wing points. The Viking has a patrol endurance of nine hours. It generally patrols several hundred miles from an aircraft carrier, providing an outer screen against submarines (the **SH-3** and **SH-60F** provide the inner screen). The plane is no longer in production (the last of 187 was delivered in 1978), but a Weapons System Improvement Program (WSIP) will convert 148 S-3As to S-3Bs at a rate of two per month. The S-3B will have an increased radar detection range, advanced acoustic processing, and upgraded electronic warfare support measures. By the end of 1988, 20 S-3As had been upgraded. An additional 16 S-3As are being converted to ES-3A signals intelligence aircraft to replace the **EA-3B**. One S-3 squadron of 10 aircraft is assigned to each **carrier air wing**, except the Midway and Coral Sea wings. Home bases for Atlantic and Pacific Fleet squadrons are NAS Cecil Field, FL; and NAS North Island, CA. Contractors are Lockheed California Co., Burbank, CA (prime/airframe); and General Electric, West Lynn, MA (engines). (see also **SH-2F, P-3**)

sabotage: "An act or acts with intent to injure, interfere with, or obstruct the national defense of a country by willfully injuring or destroying, or attempting to destroy, any national defense or war material, premises or utilities, to include human and natural resources" [*JCS Pub 1*, p. 319].

SAC   (see **Strategic Air Command**)

SAC airborne command post   (see **Looking Glass, SAC Command Post**)

SAC Automated Command and Control System (SACCS): Model designation 465L. Two-way, dedicated, high-speed, secure data processing and teletype communications network that links the **Strategic Air Command (SAC)** headquarters with subordinate command posts. It is one of the three main data processing systems used in the command and control of nuclear weapons and is the SAC counterpart of the **WWMCCS Information System (WIS)** used for the storage and retrieval of operational, weather, force movement, strength, readiness, and planning data. In times of war, SACCS would process strike reports and give the battle staff immediate and continuous updates on the status of the **Single Integrated Operational Plan**. Access to SACCS is through the 200 field unit terminals of the **SAC Digital Information Network (SACDIN)**. Information is available in printed form, on monitors, or on screen projections. There are six screens in the **SAC Command Post**, each 16 ft by 16 ft.

SAC Command Post (SAC CP): A specially designed, reinforced underground concrete structure with the capacity to become self-contained for an extended period of time. The headquarters building at Offutt AFB, NE, has seven floors: three aboveground, one basement, and three underground. The underground floors are limited access areas and contain more than three acres of floor space. Housed there are the SAC command center, the communications center, the **SAC Automated Command and Control System** ADP center, the **SAC Digital Information Network (SACDIN)**, a portion of the **Joint Strategic Target Planning Staff,** and intelligence, logistics, and operations activities of SAC headquarters. In wartime, the three underground floors would be sealed off.

"The fixed alternate command centers of SAC are the CONUS NAF [numbered Air Force] operational headquarters. The NAF Commanders are designated alternates to CINCSAC. When the SAC Command Post is incapacitated, command of SAC devolves to the Airborne Emergency Action Officer (AEAO) in the ABNCP [**airborne command post**], and then to the alternate command centers" [JCS, *Strategic Connectivity Study,* March 1979, p. D-79, released under the FOIA]. The two alternate ground command posts for the SAC CP are at 8th Air Force, Barksdale AFB, LA, and 15th Air Force, March AFB, CA. The SAC airborne command post, **Looking Glass,** is constantly airborne on its **EC-135** platform.

Communication systems used to link SAC command posts and tactical units are:

- **Primary Alerting System (PAS);**
- **Giant Talk;**
- **Green Pine;**
- **Emergency Rocket Communications System (ERCS);**
- **Survivable Low Frequency Communications System (SLFCS)**
- **SAC Digital Information Network (SACDIN);**
- **SAC Automated Command and Control System (SACCS); and**
- **Air Force Satellite Communications System (AFSATCOM).**

SAC Digital Information Network (SACDIN): Two-way, dedicated, secure data command and control communications system connecting the **Strategic Air Command (SAC)** headquarters and subordinate forces, and ensuring **positive control** over SAC missile launch sites and aircraft wings. SACDIN has terminals at every ICBM **launch control center** and wing **command post**. It is not its own communications network but uses existing transmission media such as **AUTODIN**, the Defense Data Network (DDN), **AFSATCOM**, the **Survivable Low-Frequency Communications System (SLFCS)**, and the **Post-Attack Command and Control System (PACCS)** to relay its information. **Emergency action messages** and **nuclear control orders** would be transmitted through SACDIN. SACDIN is the communications portion of the **SAC Automated Command and Control System (SACCS)**.

SACEUR (see **Supreme Allied Commander Europe**)

SACLANT (see **Supreme Allied Commander Atlantic**)

SAC Telephone Network (STN): Dedicated, non-secure telephone network providing two-way command and control voice communications. It connects **Strategic Air Command (SAC)** locations, key Air Force personnel and the **Federal Aviation Administration**, to pass along aircraft movement information. STN also connects SAC headquarters to the major subordinate commands. It

serves as a back-up to the **Primary Alerting System (PAS)**.

SADARM (see **sense-and-destroy armor**)

Safeguard: Army **ballistic missile defense** system designed to protect land-based ICBMs against attack, or to protect the entire United States against an accidental missile launch or small-scale attack. Formerly called the Sentinel, the **ABM** system was developed in the 1960s to protect population centers. Under President Nixon, Sentinel was renamed Safeguard and given the more limited task of protecting missile sites. Safeguard was deployed in 1974 at Grand Forks, ND, but was deactivated a year later because of ineffectiveness and high costs. The principal subsystems were the Sprint (short-range) and Spartan (long-range) missiles, the Missile Site Radar, the Perimeter Acquisition Radar, and the Safeguard data processing system. (see also **Perimeter Acquisition Radar Attack Characterization System**)

Safe Haven: **1.** Code name for the program in which the Department of Defense supports Department of Energy shipments of nuclear materials, nuclear weapons components, and nuclear warheads by providing temporary storage of DOE shipments or, in the event of natural disasters, **civil disturbances**, or other emergencies, such as accidents, by providing secure facilities for the transportation units on military bases. **2.** "An area of safety, within or outside the CONUS, to which noncombatants are evacuated for temporary residence until they return to the location they were evacuated from or moved onward to a designated location. (The State Department designates primary safe havens. The service secretaries may designate additional safe havens)" [Air Force, *U.S. Noncombatant Evacuation Operations*, HQ Operating Instruction 55-11, 7 May 1980, released under the FOIA]. (see also **noncombatant evacuation**)

Safe Wind: The nickname signifying an ordered condition of emergency security operations in an emergency and applicable to all Air Force commands and units possessing priority resources.

safing: The prevention of a nuclear yield in the event of accidental detonation of the high-explosives of high-explosive assembly weapons or ignition of the propellant of a gun assembly weapon.

SAGE (see **Semi-Automated Ground Environment**)

SALT (Strategic Arms Limitation Talks):   A series of arms control talks between the United States and the Soviet Union from 1969–1979 dealing with strategic weapons. The SALT process achieved:

- **Agreement on Measures to Reduce the Risk of Outbreak of Nuclear War** (1971)
- Hot Line Improvement Agreement (1971), an improvement to the **Direct Communications Link**;
- **ABM Treaty** (1972);
- Interim Agreement on the Limita-

tion of Strategic Offensive Nuclear Weapons (1972) (**SALT I**);
- Agreement to make removal of the danger of nuclear war a "prime objective" of both countries (1973);
- **Threshold Test Ban Treaty** (1974);
- **Vladivostok Aide-Memoire** (1974);
- Peaceful Nuclear Explosions Treaty (1976); and
- **SALT II** Treaty (1979).

The talks were replaced by the Strategic Arms Reduction Talks (**START**) in the Reagan and Bush Administrations, and the ongoing **nuclear and space talks**. (see also **SALT I, SALT II**)

SALT I (Strategic Arms Limitation Talks I):   Formally known as the "Interim Agreement between the United States of America and Union of the Soviet Socialist Republics on Certain Measures with Respect to the Limitation of Strategic Offensive Arms and the **ABM Treaty**." SALT I is a series of arms control talks that opened in Helsinki, Finland, in November 1969 between the United States and the Soviet Union. The talks lasted for over two years and included seven negotiating sessions. The first year of the talks brought little progress, as the Soviet Union insisted that, within any agreement limiting offensive forces, it be compensated for U.S. forward-based systems (FBSs) in Europe and Asia. The United States argued that FBSs were theater weapons, outside of the scope of SALT, and offset by Soviet intermediate- and medium-range missiles.

   In May 1971, a Nixon–Kosygin joint statement reaffirmed the desire to limit anti-ballistic missile systems and future offensive missile deployments. In April 1972, it was agreed that each side would limit itself to two ABM deployments. (In 1974, this was reduced to one system each.) It was also agreed to include Intercontinental Ballistic Missile (**ICBM**) and Submarine-launched Ballistic Missile (**SLBM**) limits in an interim agreement. The Soviet Union was lagging behind the United States in SLBM development and was hesitant to commit itself to limits until it was assured that it could expand its force in exchange for dismantling old ICBMs and SLBMs. Acceptable figures on SLBM launchers and ballistic missile submarines were finally reached, and, on 26 May 1972, President Nixon and General Secretary Brezhnev signed the ABM Treaty and the Interim Offensive Agreement.

The Interim Offensive Agreement was presented to Congress as an executive agreement rather than as a treaty. The Soviet numerical advantages in ICBM and SLBM launchers were the main points of contention. The Senate approved the agreement on 20 September 1972, with an amendment by Senator Henry Jackson (D–WA) that "urges and requests the President to seek a future treaty that . . . would not limit the United States to levels of intercontinental strategic forces inferior to the limits provided for the Soviet Union" [H. J. Res. 1227, S. J. Res. 241. Public Law 92-448, 30 September 1972, known as the "Jackson Amendment"]. The Interim Offensive Agreement entered into force on 3 October 1972. The Agreement expired on 3 Octo-

ber 1977, but both parties agreed to refrain from breaking the provisions nonetheless. The **Vladivostok Accord** in 1974 revised the limits on launchers set by the SALT I agreement.

The agreement:

- Established numerical limits on land-based ICBM launchers (United States: 1,054; Soviet Union: 1,618) and SLBM launchers (United States: 710 on 44 submarines; Soviet Union: 950 launchers on 62 submarines);
- Fixed land-based ICBM launcher construction halted after 1 July 1972;
- Limited the number of SLBM launchers to the number operational in May 1972;
- Allowed for modernization and replacement of older missiles and launchers on a one-for-one basis; and
- Allowed for verification by **national technical means**, with a mutual pledge not to use deliberate concealment measures that impede verification.

There have been a number of U.S. accusations of Soviet violations of SALT I agreements, including the exceeding of its SLBM launcher limit of 740 during 1976–77. Soviet accusations of U.S. violations included complaints on the use of shelters over **Minuteman** launchers during maintenance, an impediment to verification by national technical means.

SALT II (Strategic Arms Limitation Talks II): Formally known as the "Treaty between the United States of America and the Union of the

Soviet Socialist Republics on the Limitation of Strategic Offensive Arms." The SALT II process began in 1972 and was completed in 1979. The SALT II agreement was signed on 18 June 1979 but was never ratified by the United States. Nonetheless, both countries agreed to abide by SALT II provisions. This was the case until May 1986, when the Reagan Administration announced it no longer felt constrained by the SALT II Treaty limits.

The treaty provided the following numerical limits:

- A ceiling of 2,400 each on intercontinental ballistic missile (**ICBM**) and submarine-launched ballistic missile (**SLBM**) launchers and on **heavy bombers** (to be reduced to 2,250 by the end of 1981 after ratification);
- A limit of 1,320 launchers on **MIRV**ed ICBMs, SLBMs, and heavy bombers armed with long-range air-launched **cruise missiles**;
- A sublimit of 1,200 on launchers for MIRVed ICBMs and SLBMs; and
- A sublimit of 820 on launchers for MIRVed ICBMs.

The treaty banned

- Construction of additional fixed ICBM launchers and increases in the number of fixed **heavy ballistic missile** launchers;
- Heavy mobile ICBM launchers, launchers of heavy SLBMs, and **air-to-surface** ballistic missiles;
- Flight testing or deployment of new types of ICBMs, with the exception of one new type of light ICBM for each side;

- Increases in the numbers of warheads on existing types of ICBMs;
- Conversion of light ICBM launchers to launchers of heavy ICBMs;
- Rapid-reload ICBM systems; and
- Certain new types of strategic offensive systems that were technologically feasible but which had not yet been deployed (including long-range ballistic missiles on surface ships, and ballistic and cruise missile launchers on the sea-bed).

The treaty also established the following numerical limits on nuclear warheads:

- 10 warheads on each new type of ICBM allowed;
- 14 warheads on SLBMs;
- 28 (average) long-range cruise missiles per heavy bomber; and
- 20 long-range cruise missiles per existing heavy bomber.

The treaty also established ceilings on the launcher weights and throwweights of ballistic missiles, mandated advance notification of certain ICBM test launches, and established an agreed data base for systems included in the various SALT-limited categories. In a separate letter not actually part of the treaty, General Secretary Brezhnev agreed that the Soviet Union would not deploy the SS-16 mobile missile, would not give the Backfire bomber intercontinental capabilities, and would not produce more than 30 Backfires per year. The United States agreed in a protocol not to deploy SLCMs or **Ground-Launched Cruise Missiles** (**GLCMs**) of greater than 600-km ranges before 31 December 1981.

The treaty text included provisions to enhance verification (verification of MIRV limits was to be carried out according to a treaty provision that stated that all missiles tested as MIRVs would be counted as MIRVed missiles), a ban on circumvention, and a provision outlining the duties of the Standing Consultative Committee, which hears proposals for amendments or modifications and resolves verification disputes. Either party was entitled to withdraw from the treaty with six months advance notice. The treaty officially expired at the end of 1985.

During the negotiations, a number of contested issues were dealt with. In keeping with the "Jackson Amendment" to **SALT I**, the United States wanted to remove the numerical advantage given to the Soviet Union in ballistic missile launchers, as well as reach equal levels in the aggregate payload/throwweight of each side's missiles and bombers. The Soviets accepted equal limits on ballistic missiles and bombers but not on missile throwweight.

The United States was looking for lower numbers than was the Soviet Union. A Ford Administration proposal in December 1974 suggested a ceiling of 2,400 on ICBMs, SLBMs, and bombers. President Carter reduced the ceiling proposal to 1,800–2,000 in March 1977 (his "Deep Cuts" proposal). The final compromise was to accept the 2,400 ceiling but require a reduction to 2,250 by 31 December 1981. This reduction, however, was never implemented, since the treaty never entered into force.

The United States wanted to minimize the use of MIRVing whereas the Soviets, with their larger missiles, wanted to maximize. The Soviets were eager, however, to limit the deployment of cruise missiles, where the United States had the lead. Compromise was reached by counting cruise missile-carrying aircraft and launchers for MIRVed missiles in the 1,320 limit.

Despite concerns about Soviet heavy missiles, SALT permitted the Soviets to maintain 308 SS-18 ICBMs in return for dropping their complaints against U.S. forward-based systems (FBSs) raised under SALT I. Some Congressional members saw this as contradicting the Jackson Amendment. In March 1977, the Soviets rejected a proposal banning the testing or deployment of new ICBMs or SLBMs. The Soviets then presented a proposal banning flight tests of new ICBMs and SLBMs, except for one new missile of each type.

Throughout the SALT II talks, the Executive Branch was mindful of Congressional opinion, issued several progress reports on the negotiations, and invited Congressional observers to take part. The growing disillusionment with détente and U.S.–Soviet relations, fear of Soviet military strength, and foreign policy failures such as the U.S. hostages in Iran all served to complicate Congressional approval for the treaty. Allegations in August 1979 that a Soviet combat brigade was in Cuba became linked to the treaty and, although later dismissed, delayed ratification for several months. After the Soviet invasion of Afghanistan, it was evident that Congressional opposition to the treaty was substantial. It became apparent that the treaty would not be ratified before Carter left office, and it was withdrawn. The United States publicly stated that it would not undercut the treaty, and President Reagan, despite his stated dissatisfaction with aspects of the treaty, followed its provisions until May 1986.

U.S. accusations of Soviet violations of the SALT II treaty have included:

- Deliberate concealment activities impeding verification (e.g., encoding missile test data and encrypting telemetry on new ballistic missiles);
- Deployment of the banned SS-16 mobile ICBM at the Plesetsk test range;
- Falsifying the SALT II data base identifying specific systems and their numbers; and
- Testing the SS-X-25 missile, claimed by the United States to be a second new missile and so banned by the treaty because the Soviet Union already had identified the SS-X-24 as its one new missile. (The Soviets claim it fits within the volume and throwweight restrictions of SALT to be a modification of an existing SS-13 missile.)

Soviet accusations of U.S. violations have been less significant and are tied to ratification and future systems. The Soviet Union has complained that the United States failed to seek a permanent solution with respect to SLCMs and GLCMs; that deployment of **Pershing IIs** and GLCMs circumvents the treaty through the use of other states and international commitments that contradict the treaty; and that the development of both the **MX** and **Small ICBM** missile violate the pro-

vision of one new ICBM allowed to each side [ACA, *Background Paper on Compliance Issues Contained in Reagan Administration Report*, 27 February 1984; ACA, *Arms Control Today*, Vol. 14, No. 3, March/April 1984; U.S. Congress, House Foreign Relations Committee, *Fundamentals of Nuclear Arms Control: Part I— Nuclear Arms Control: A Brief Historical Survey*, 20 May 1985].

salted weapon: A nuclear weapon that has, in addition to its normal components, certain elements or isotopes that capture neutrons at the time of the explosion and produce radioactive products over and above the usual radioactive weapon debris.

SAM (see **surface-to-air missile**)

SAMOS (see **Corona**)

Sanguine: Former Navy program intended to be a survivable ELF submarine communications system. Sanguine was canceled in the late 1970s when it was clear that it would not survive a direct attack. It was followed by the **Seafarer** system. The proposed Sanguine system consisted of an underground grid in CONUS composed of transmitters and antennas in concrete capsules. Its ELF transmittal radio signals were thought to be safe from enemy jamming and the effects of nuclear explosions in the atmosphere.

satellite communications (SATCOM): Voice and data communications using satellites for either point-to-point or bulk transmission. More than 75 percent of all general-purpose military communications are carried by satellites. Current DOD SATCOM systems can be divided into five categories:

1. Global, wide-band, high-data rate, dedicated SHF communications provided by satellites in the **Defense Satellite Communications System (DSCS)**;
2. Global, voice-and-data, dedicated UHF communications provided by **Fleet Satellite Communications System (FLTSATCOM), MARISAT (Gapfiller)**, and the **Satellite Data System** satellites;
3. Global, specialized UHF communications systems for the nuclear-capable forces provided by **AFSATCOM**;
4. Global, voice-and-data EHF communications to be provided by dedicated **MILSTAR** satellites and currently operating as additional circuits on FLTSATCOM and the experimental **LES 8-9** satellites; and
5. Leased UHF and SHF communications services from commercial carriers, including Intelsat.

The military satellite communications system is responsible for operating the DSCS, FLTSATCOM, and AFSATCOM. Air Force Space Division of **Air Force Systems Command** develops and acquires the space segments of these systems and the telemetry, tracking, and command elements. Operators of the systems include **Air Force Communications Command** and **Naval Telecommunications Command**. The Army's satellite communications program consists of the ground portion of the DSCS and the ground mobile force (GMF) satellite communications

program. The GMF program provides single-channel, multi-channel, and special-purpose tactical satellite ground terminals and control systems for long-range, jam-resistant communications. The Army is procuring the single-channel AN/PSC-3 and AN/VSC-7 UHF terminals for Ranger and Special Forces units. Full-scale development of the highly mobile Single Channel Objective Tactical Terminal (SCOTT) for the MILSTAR satellite communications system is underway.

NATO SATCOM, the military satellite communications system of the alliance, was established in 1965. It is in its third stage of development and consists of 22 ground terminals (21 fixed and 1 mobile) and 2 active satellites. NATO SATCOM III, an all-digital system, provides the majority of telephone and telegraph transmissions for the **NATO Integrated Communications System**. The next phase of the system, NATO SATCOM IV, will consist of two new satellites, the first of which is planned to be launched in 1990. As of 1988, NATO SATCOM had cost approximately $1 billion.

Satellite Data System (SDS): Air Force UHF, two-way, secure, transpolar **communication satellites** in critically inclined elliptical orbits. SDS provides communications coverage of the polar regions and, for the command and control of nuclear forces, complements **Fleet Satellite Communications System (FLTSATCOM)** satellites over the equator. Together, FLTSATCOM and SDS comprise the coverage needed by onboard **AFSATCOM** transponders for command and control of strategic forces. SDS also supports the Air

Force Satellite Control Facility communications network by linking the tracking station at Thule, Greenland, with CONUS ground stations further south. In addition, SDS is linked to the Satellite Tracking Center (STC) at Sunnyvale, CA, for the command and control of U.S. reconnaissance and intelligence satellites.

The SDS program began in the early 1970s with initial funding of $18 million. The primary contractor was Hughes Aircraft, El Segundo, CA. The first SDS satellite was launched by a Titan IIIB/Agena D rocket and became operational during FY 1978. In the early 1980s, it was decided to switch from Titan boosters to deployment by the space shuttle. (see also **Jumpseat**)

satellite early-warning system (see **Defense Support Program**)

satellite reconnaissance: The collection and transmission of electronic **signals intelligence (SIGINT)** and **photographic intelligence (PHOTINT)** from space. The United States currently employs six types of satellite reconnaissance systems:

- **KH-12** photographic imaging satellites;
- **Ferret** electronics intelligence (ELINT) satellites;
- **White Cloud** and follow-on ocean surveillance satellites;
- **Magnum** SIGINT satellites;
- **Chalet/Vortex** SIGINT satellites; and
- **Jumpseat** polar SIGINT satellites.

Management of satellite imaging operations is conducted by the **National Foreign Intelligence Board** and committees (in the areas of satellite collection and implementation) and by the National Reconnaissance Executive Committee (NREC), created in 1965. NREC reports directly to the Secretary of Defense and is chaired by the Director of Central Intelligence. Classes of reconnaissance satellites are given a **Byeman** code name. Intelligence obtained by satellite photography is marked by the code word **Ruff**; that obtained by SIGINT satellites is marked **Zarf**.

Operational support to satellite systems is provided by a worldwide network of ground control stations centered at the headquarters of the Air Force Satellite Tracking Center (STC) at Vandenberg AFB, CA. STC stations are located at New Boston, NH; Kaena Pt., HI; Thule AB, Greenland; Mahe, the Seychelles; Andersen AFB, Guam; and RAF Oakhanger, UK. CIA- and NSA-operated satellite down-links to receive intelligence information are located at Alice Springs (Pine Gap), Australia; Bad Aibling, West Germany; and Menwith Hill, UK. (see also **keyhole** satellites)

SIGINT Satellites

Code Name	Known Launch Dates
Rhyolite/Aquacade	19 Jun 1970
	6 Mar 1973
	23 May 1977
	11 Dec 1977
	7 Apr 1978
Jumpseat	10 Mar 1975
	6 Aug 1976
Chalet	10 June 1978
Vortex	1 Oct 1979
	31 Oct 1981
	22 Dec 1984
Magnum	24 Jan 1985

satellite tracking   (see **Space Surveillance Network**)

SATKA   (see **Surveillance, Acquisition, Tracking, and Kill Assessment**)

Scope Light: Code name for the **EC-135** airborne command post of the **U.S. Atlantic Command**. It is part of the **Worldwide Airborne Command Post (WWABNCP)** system.

Scope Signal: Air Force worldwide, ground-to-air and contingency weather broadcast and HF/SSB communications system. Scope Signal is upgrading and replacing the **Giant Talk** system. Scope Signal includes command and control missions such as **Mystic Star** and the **Global Command and Control Stations** of the Military Airlift Command. It is connected to the **Post-Attack Command and Control System (PACCS)** and provides **emergency action message** transmission to airborne forces. The new system of radios and antennas will allow a reduction of manpower and an upgrade in capabilities over Giant Talk. **Commando Escort** upgrades in the Pacific HF network are also under the Scope Signal program. The objective of the Contingency Weather Broadcast System is to support Army- and Air Force-deployed forces with secure environmental data during contingencies, exercises, and natural disasters. The Scope Signal program is divided geographically into phases for completion of conversion:

- Phase II: Pacific. Stations at Hickam AFB, HI; Yokota AB, Japan; Clark AB, Philippines; Kadena AB, Okinawa, Japan; Andersen AFB, Guam; and Kunsan AB, South Korea.
- Phase IV: Europe. Stations at Croughton, UK; Incirlik, Turkey; Lajes, Azores, Portugal; Mt. Edheri, Greece; and Southwest Asia.
- Phase V: Western Hemisphere. Stations at Elmendorf AFB, AK; McClellan AFB, CA; Puerto Rico; Andrews AFB, MD; Loring AFB, ME; Patrick AFB, FL; Thule AB, Greenland; Ascension Island; Offutt AFB, NE; and Keesler AFB, MS.

Scout: DOD and NASA **expendable launch vehicle** capable of putting maximum 377 lb payloads into 310-mile polar orbits. Scout rockets have been used to launch a number of DOD communications and navigation satellites, as well as commercial payloads. The current Scout has an improved fourth stage. It can send a 100 lb payload more than 16,000 miles into space. (see also **Atlas II, Delta II, Titan 34D/II/IV**)

scram: In a **nuclear reactor**, the rapid shutdown (to prevent or minimize a dangerous condition) initiated when some operational parameter reaches a level determined by operational or safety regulations. A scram is usually initiated by rapid insertion of the safety rod.

SDI   (see **Strategic Defense Initiative**)

SDV: Designation for swimmer-delivery vehicle.

Sea-Bed Treaty: Formally known as the "Treaty on the Prohibition of the Emplacement of Nuclear Weapons and Other Weapons of Mass Destruction on the Sea-Bed and the Ocean Floor and in the Subsoil Thereof." The Sea-Bed Treaty opened for signature in Moscow, London, and Washington on 11 February 1971. It was ratified by the United States on 26 April 1972 and entered into force on 18 May 1972. Since then, over 80 nations have signed the treaty, with the significant abstentions of France and India. The treaty bans the placement of nuclear or other weapons of mass destruction and facilities for such weapons on the sea-bed or ocean floor beyond the 12-mile limit from the coast line. Treaty provisions are:

- Nuclear or other mass destruction weapons will not be deployed, tested, or stored on the ocean floor 19 km (12 miles) beyond a nation's coastline. However, within this 12 miles, the placing of nuclear weapons is permitted. Nuclear weapons are also permitted to be carried in international waters aboard ships and submarines. These are the only likely scenarios for putting nuclear weapons on the sea floor;
- Verification by observation and, if doubts exist, by inspection is permitted;
- Violations are to be reported to the Security Council of the United Nations;
- Existing international rights on territorial seas, contiguous zones, and continental shelves are not to be prejudiced;
- Negotiations toward disarmament are to continue;

- The treaty is open to signature and amendment by all states;
- Review conferences will be held to consider technological advances and treaty conformance. One was held in 1977 and another in 1983; and
- Withdrawal in the face of "extraordinary events" is permitted with written notification to all parties and the United Nations Security Council three months in advance.

The treaty originated as part of a larger effort to govern the use of ocean floors that lay beyond national jurisdictions. In 1967, a special Sea-Bed Committee of the U.N. General Assembly and the 18-nation Committee on Disarmament met in Geneva. In March 1968, the Soviet Union put forth a draft treaty that would ban all military uses of the sea-bed beyond the 12-mile zone. This was turned down by the United States, in part because of the loosely defined "military uses" and in part to protect its **Sound Surveillance System (SOSUS)** submarine detection systems. In May 1969, the United States offered its own draft treaty, which prohibited only nuclear weapons or other weapons of mass destruction beyond the 3-mile territorial limit. After compromise, a final draft treaty was presented to the General Assembly [U.S. Congress, Senate Foreign Relations Committee, *Seabed Arms Control Treaty*, Executive Report 92-18, 10 February 1972].

SeaBee: Nickname for a naval construction battalion unit or specialist.

Sea Cobra   (see **AH-1 Sea Cobra**)

sea control: The employment of naval forces, supplemented by land and aerospace forces as appropriate, to destroy enemy naval forces, suppress enemy ocean-going commerce, protect shipping, and establish local superiority in areas of naval operations. (see also **Maritime Strategy**)

Seafarer: Navy **ELF** radio submarine communications system canceled in the 1970s. Seafarer involved vast antenna grids and followed the hardened, underground **Sanguine** system, which was canceled in the mid-1970s. The more modest Seafarer system also fell prey to environmental and technical opposition (the large area of antenna grids to be deployed throughout CONUS made the program particularly unpopular). In 1981, the Reagan Administration ordered the creation of a new, more scaled down ELF system to communicate with U.S. submarines.

Sea Knight (see **CH-46 Sea Knight**)

SEAL (Sea, Air, and Land): Primary operating unit of **naval special warfare groups**. SEAL teams were first commissioned in 1962 alongside underwater demolition teams (UDTs) and were redesignated as separate SEAL teams in 1983. They specialize in **special operations** and **unconventional warfare** operations, including pre-combat reconnaissance of beaches, coasts, and waterways; harbor defense; interdiction of enemy shipping; underwater demolition; and sabotage of enemy plans and resources. SEALs also train foreign navies in **counterinsurgency** and interdiction tactics. They have the capability to use **Special Atomic Demolition Munitions**.

There are six active SEAL teams as of 1989. There are two active SEAL Delivery Vehicle Teams. Each SEAL team has an authorized personnel strength of 175. There are five Naval Reserve SEAL detachments, which support and augment active teams. SEAL Team 6, Dam Neck, VA, designated for **counterterrorism** operations, is subordinate to the **Joint Special Operations Command (JSOC)**.

Sea Lance: Navy long-range, **anti-submarine warfare** standoff weapon (ASWSOW) under development to replace the nuclear-armed **SUBROC** missile on attack submarines and the **Vertical Launch ASROC (VLA)** on surface ships. The Sea Lance will launch the **Mk-50** advanced lightweight torpedo under development. In 1990, the Navy will decide whether to equip Sea Lance with a nuclear depth charge as well. The prime contractor is Boeing Aerospace Company, Seattle, WA. FY 1990 and 1991 budget requests for development of the Sea Lance are $129.6 and $186.2 million, respectively.

sea-launched cruise missile (SLCM) (see **cruise missile, Harpoon, Tomahawk**)

sealed pit weapon: A hollow sealed nuclear warhead, in which no portion of the pit is accessible.

sea lines of communication (SLOC): Sea routes essential to the conduct of military operations, particularly the deployment of armed forces and associated logistic support. Because U.S. forces are forward-deployed overseas, an important objective of U.S. military strategy, according to the Navy, is to keep open the Atlantic and Caribbean SLOCs (or other regional SLOCs) so that a war in Europe (or other regions) could be supplied by sea. (see also **lines of communication**, **Maritime Strategy**)

Sea Nymph: Model designation AN/WLQ-4. Navy **electronic warfare support measures** surveillance system installed on Sturgeon class attack submarines. The equipment enables the tracking of enemy submarines through the "acquisition, identification, recording, analysis and exploitation of electromagnetic signals." It replaces the AN/WLR-6 Waterboy system. It operates in support of **Barnacle** missions [Jeffrey Richelson, *The U.S. Intelligence Community,* 2d ed., p. 192].

Sea Stallion   (see **CH-53 Sea Stallion**)

Sea Wolf (SSN-21) class submarine: Navy new-design, high-speed, nuclear-powered attack submarine class under development to be a follow-on to and replacement for the Los Angeles class and earlier classes of attack submarines. The single-screw submarine will displace 9,150 tons and be 353 ft long. The submarine will be armed with Mk-48 **torpedoes**, **Sea Lances**, **Harpoons**, **Tomahawks**, **mines**, and other submarine weapons. It will be capable of long-endurance submerged patrols. The contract will be competitively selected between Newport News Shipbuilding and Electric Boat

Company. The first funding for development was in the FY 1985 budget. FY 1989 was supposed to be the initial funding for construction, but problems with the development of the combat system delayed the initial ship request. The FY 1990 budget request for development and advanced procurement was $1,061.7 million. The FY 1991 request for the first two submarines was $3,343.9 million.

Second Allied Tactical Air Force (TWOATAF): NATO air organization assigned to **Allied Air Forces, Central Europe (AAFCE)**. It is responsible for air defense over Belgium, the Netherlands, the northern part of West Germany, and parts of the North Sea, and for close air support of the **Northern Army Group**. It is commanded by a British Air-Marshal (also the commander of Royal Air Forces Germany). Its forces are provided by the Netherlands, Belgium, the United Kingdom, West Germany, and the United States.

Headquarters
Moenchen-Gladbach, West Germany

Second Fleet (2d FLT): One of the four **numbered fleets** in the Navy, and the primary operating force assigned to the **Atlantic Fleet (LANTFLT)**. It was established in 1945 as the Eighth Fleet and renamed in January 1947. Its mission areas comprise the north and south Atlantic and the Caribbean Sea. It functions as the NATO strike force and has historically operated as a training fleet and an anti-submarine warfare force. Its Commander "plans for and, when directed, conducts battle force operation in the Atlantic Command in support of designated unified or allied commanders; directs movements and exercises operational control of assigned units to carry out scheduled ocean transits and other special operations, as directed by CINCLANT-FLT, in order to maximize fleet operational readiness to respond to contingencies in the Atlantic Command area of operations; plans fleet intertype training exercises; and participates in joint and combined exercises as directed" [*NWP 2*, Rev. D, Chapter 18]. Commander, Second Fleet exercises operational control over assigned (commander) **task forces (CTFs)**. Ships rotate at regular intervals to the **Sixth Fleet** in the Mediterranean Sea. The Second Fleet is composed of approximately 305 active ships, 2,100 active aircraft, and 220,000 personnel.

Fleet Headquarters
Norfolk, VA 23511

Fleet Flagship
USS Mount Whitney (LCC 20)

Operating Task Forces

- CTF 20 Battle Force
- CTF 21 Battle Force Readiness and Training
- CTF 22 Amphibious Force
- CTF 23 Landing Force
- CTF 24 Anti-Submarine Warfare and Surveillance Task Force
- CTF 25 Mobile Logistic Support Force
- CTF 26 Patrol Air Force (VP)
- CTF 27 Battle Force Tactical Development
- CTF 28 Special Mission [Caribbean] Contingency Force
- CTF 29 Ready Alert Force

second strike: "The first counterblow of a war. Generally associated with nuclear operations." Second strike capability is "the ability to survive a **first strike** with sufficient resources to deliver an effective counterblow" [*JCS Pub 1*, p. 326]. Second strike excludes preemptive actions before the onset of war.

secret (S): Security classification category applied to national security-related information "that requires a substantial degree of protection and the unauthorized disclosure of which could reasonably be expected to cause serious damage to the national security. Examples of 'serious damage' include disruption of foreign relations significantly affecting the national security; significant impairment of a program or policy directly related to the national security; revelation of significant military plans or intelligence operations; and compromise of significant scientific or technological developments relating to national security" [*JCS Pub 1*, p. 328]. Of the three major classification levels, secret is a higher category than **confidential (C)** but is lower than **top secret (TS)**.

The transmission of secret information is controlled in accordance with **communications security (COMSEC)** guidelines. Transmission is generally done through the **Protected Distribution System (PDS)** (formerly named "approved circuits"), which includes "all equipment and cabling used for the clear text transmission of classified information." However, "during hostilities, Confidential and Secret information may be electrically transmitted in-the-clear by unsecured means (such as telephone, teletypewriter, and radio) as an emergency measure." Prior to the transmission of secret information, a PDS must be evaluated, approved, and authorized at the Service staff and major command levels. In a tactical environment, the authority to approve circuits for transmission of secret information lies with the battalion commander and higher echelons.

Authorized access to secret information is granted to an individual by a government agency based upon a **National Agency Check** to try to determine that the recipient is not a criminal or spy. In FY 1986, secret clearances were held by approximately 1,933,000 DOD and industry personnel [GAO, *DOD Clearance Reduction and Related Issues*, GAO/NSIAD-87-170BR, September 1987, p. 12; Department of the Army, *Communications Security*, AR 530-2, 1 September 1982, pp. 10–11, released under the FOIA].

Secretary General: Ultimate administrative head of the **North Atlantic Treaty Organization**. The Secretary General serves as the chairman of both the **North Atlantic Council** and the **Defense Planning Committee**, and is head of the **International Staff**. Support is provided by the International Staff and the Office of the Secretary General, which includes the Office of the Legal Adviser, Executive Secretariat, Office of Security, Office of Management and of Administration and Personnel, and the Office of the Financial Controller.

NATO Secretary Generals

Lord Ismay, UK	1952–1957
Paul-Henri Spaak, Belgium	1957–1961
Dirk W. Stikker, The Netherlands	1961–1964
Manlio Brosio, Italy	1964–1971
Joseph M.A.H. Luns, The Netherlands	1971–1984
Lord Peter Carrington, UK	1984–1988
Manfred Woerner, West Germany	1988–present

Secretary of Defense (SecDef):   Civilian executive director of the **Department of Defense** and statutory member of the **National Security Council**. The Secretary originally only held general authority over the department, a power shared by the Service secretaries. The **National Security Act of 1949**, which redesignated the National Military Establishment as the DOD, established the Secretary of Defense as the sole authority, subordinated the military departments within the **Office of the Secretary of Defense**, and assigned budgetary authority to the Secretary. Today, the Secretary "is the principal defense policy advisor to the President and is responsible for the formulation of general defense policy and policy related to all matters of direct and primary concern to the DOD, and for the execution of approved policy. Under the direction of the President and subject to the provisions of the **National Security Act of 1947**, as amended, the Secretary exercises direction, authority, and control over the Department

Secretaries of Defense

James V. Forrestal	17 Sep 1947	27 Mar 1949
Louis A. Johnson	28 Mar 1949	19 Sep 1950
George C. Marshall	21 Sep 1950	12 Sep 1951
Robert A. Lovett	17 Sep 1951	20 Jan 1953
Charles E. Wilson	28 Jan 1953	8 Oct 1957
Neil H. McElroy	9 Oct 1957	1 Dec 1959
Thomas S. Gates, Jr.	2 Dec 1959	20 Jan 1961
Robert S. McNamara	21 Jan 1961	29 Feb 1968
Clark M. Clifford	1 Mar 1968	20 Jan 1969
Melvin R. Laird	22 Jan 1969	29 Jan 1973
Eliot L. Richardson	30 Jan 1973	24 May 1973
James R. Schlesinger	2 Jul 1973	19 Nov 1975
Donald H. Rumsfeld	20 Nov 1975	20 Jan 1977
Harold Brown	21 Jan 1977	20 Jan 1981
Caspar W. Weinberger	21 Jan 1981	23 Nov 1987
Frank C. Carlucci	24 Nov 1987	21 Jan 1989
Richard B. Cheney	21 Mar 1989	present

of Defense." The **Department of Defense Reorganization Act of 1986** formalizes the responsibilities of the Secretary of Defense to issue guidance on the Services' programs and budgets and clarifies the Secretary's position in the operational chain of command. Regarding NATO affairs, the Secretary has certain final decision-making power on U.S. positions. The Secretary is appointed by and reports to the President (as chief executive and Commander-in-Chief of the armed forces) and is confirmed by the Senate. The DOD agencies, the Chairman of the Joint Chiefs of Staff, the DOD staff, military departments, and DOD field activities all report directly to the Secretary.

Office of the Secretary of Defense

- Secretary of Defense
- Deputy Secretary of Defense
- Under Secretary of Defense (Acquisition)
- Under Secretary of Defense (Policy)
- Assistant Secretary of Defense (Comptroller)
- Assistant Secretary of Defense (Health Affairs)
- Assistant Secretary of Defense (Force Management and Personnel)
- Assistant Secretary of Defense (Legislative Affairs)
- Assistant Secretary of Defense (Public Affairs)
- Assistant Secretary of Defense (Reserve Affairs)
- Assistant Secretary of Defense (Program Analysis and Evaluation)
- Assistant Secretary of Defense (Special Operations and Low-Intensity Conflict)
- Director, Operational Test and Evaluation
- Director, Administration and Management
- Inspector General
- General Counsel
- Defense Advisor, U.S. Mission to NATO
- Assistant to the Secretary of Defense (Intelligence Oversight)

Secretaries of the Air Force

W. Stuart Symington	18 Sep 1947	24 Apr 1950
Thomas K. Finletter	24 Apr 1950	20 Jan 1953
Harold E. Talbott	4 Feb 1953	13 Aug 1955
Donald A. Quarles	15 Aug 1955	30 Apr 1957
James H. Douglas, Jr.	1 May 1957	10 Dec 1959
Dudley C. Sharp	11 Dec 1959	20 Jan 1961
Eugene M. Zuckert	23 Jan 1961	30 Sep 1965
Harold Brown	1 Oct 1965	14 Feb 1969
Robert C. Seamans, Jr.	15 Feb 1969	14 May 1973
John L. McLucas (Acting)	15 May 1973	18 Jul 1973
John L. McLucas	19 Jul 1973	23 Nov 1975
James W. Plummer (Acting)	24 Nov 1975	1 Jan 1976
Thomas C. Reed	2 Jan 1976	5 Apr 1977
John C. Stetson	6 Apr 1977	18 May 1979
Hans M. Mark (Acting)	18 May 1979	26 Jul 1979
Hans M. Mark	26 Jul 1979	9 Feb 1981
Verne Orr	9 Feb 1981	30 Nov 1985
Russell A. Rourke	6 Dec 1985	7 Apr 1986
Edward C. Aldridge, Jr.	8 Apr 1986	16 Dec 1988
Donald B. Rice	30 May 1989	present

Secretary of the Air Force (SAF): Civilian executive director of the **Department of the Air Force**. The SAF is "responsible for and has the authority necessary to conduct all affairs of the Department of the Air Force to include supervision of space programs" [DOD, OSD Directorate for Organizational and Management Planning, *Organization and Functions Guidebook*, June 1987]. The Secretary is responsible for the training, administration, logistical support and maintenance, welfare, preparedness, and overall effectiveness of the Air Force. This authority also extends to interactions with Congress, other government organizations and persons, and non-governmental organizations and persons. The SAF is appointed by the President, approved by the Senate, and reports to the President through the Secretary of Defense. He exercises authority through civilian assistants and the **Chief of Staff of the Air Force**.

*Office of the
Secretary of the Air Force*

- Secretary of the Air Force
- Under Secretary of the Air Force
- Assistant Secretary (Acquisition)
- Assistant Secretary (Readiness and Support)
- Assistant Secretary (Manpower, Reserve Affairs, and Installations)
- Comptroller of the Air Force
- Inspector General
- Auditor General
- Director of Legislative Liaison
- Public Affairs
- Administrative Assistant

Secretaries of the Army

Kenneth C. Royall	9 Nov 1945	27 Apr 1949
Gordon Gray	20 Jun 1949	11 Apr 1950
Frank Pace, Jr.	12 Apr 1950	20 Jan 1953
Robert T. Stevens	4 Feb 1953	20 Jul 1955
Wilber M. Brucker	21 Jul 1955	20 Jan 1961
Elvis J. Stahr, Jr.	24 Jan 1961	30 Jun 1962
Cyrus R. Vance	5 Jul 1962	27 Jan 1964
Stephen Ailes	28 Jan 1964	1 Jul 1965
Stanley R. Resor	7 Jul 1965	30 Jun 1971
Robert F. Froehkle	1 Jul 1971	14 May 1973
Howard H. Callaway	15 May 1973	3 Jul 1975
Martin R. Hoffmann	5 Aug 1975	13 Feb 1977
Clifford L. Alexander, Jr.	14 Feb 1977	20 Jan 1981
John O. Marsh, Jr.	30 Jan 1981	14 Aug 1989
Michael P. W. Stone	14 Aug 1989	present

Secretary of the Army (SA): The civilian executive of the **Department of the Army**, reporting to the President through the Secretary of Defense. The SA is appointed by the President and is approved by Congress. The Secretary is responsible for the training, administration, logistical support and maintenance, welfare, preparedness, and overall effectiveness of the Army. The SA directs and supervises the activities of the Army but does not exercise operational control of forces. He exercises his authority through civilian assistants and through the **Chief of Staff of the Army**.

Office of the Secretary of the Army

- Secretary of the Army
- Under Secretary of the Army
- Deputy Under Secretary of the Army
- Administrative Assistant
- General Counsel
- Assistant Secretary of the Army (Civil Works)
- Assistant Secretary of the Army (Manpower and Reserve Affairs)
- Assistant Secretary of the Army (Acquisition)
- Assistant Secretary of the Army (Installations and Logistics)
- Assistant Secretary of the Army (Financial Management)
- Director of Information Systems
- Chief of Public Affairs
- Chief of Legislative Liaison
- Inspector General
- Auditor General

Secretary of the Navy (SecNav): The civilian executive of the **Department of the Navy**, reporting to the President through the Secretary of Defense. The SecNav is "responsible for the policies and control of the Department of the Navy, including its organization, administration, operation, and efficiency" [*NWP 2*, Rev., Chapter 5]. The Secretary is responsible for the training, administration, logistical support and maintenance, welfare, preparedness, and overall effectiveness of the Navy. This authority also extends to interactions with Congress, other government organiza-

Secretaries of the Navy

John L. Sullivan	18 Sep 1947	24 May 1949
Francis P. Matthews	25 May 1949	30 Jul 1951
Dan A. Kimball	31 Jul 1951	20 Jan 1953
Robert B. Anderson	4 Feb 1953	2 May 1954
Charles S. Thomas	3 May 1954	31 Mar 1957
Thomas S. Gates, Jr.	1 Apr 1957	2 Dec 1959
William B. Franke	8 Jun 1959	20 Jan 1961
John B. Connally	25 Jan 1961	20 Dec 1961
Fred H. Korth	4 Jan 1962	1 Nov 1963
Paul H. Nitze	29 Nov 1963	1 Jul 1967
Paul R. Ignatius	1 Sep 1967	24 Jan 1969
John H. Chafee	31 Jan 1969	4 May 1972
John W. Warner	4 May 1972	8 Apr 1974
J. William Middendorf II	10 Jun 1974	20 Jan 1977
W. Graham Claytor, Jr.	14 Feb 1977	26 Jul 1979
Edward Hidalgo	27 Jul 1979	20 Jan 1981
John F. Lehman	5 Feb 1981	10 Apr 1987
James Webb	10 Apr 1987	22 Feb 1988
William L. Ball III	23 Mar 1988	15 May 1989
H. Lawrence Garrett III	15 May 1989	present

tions and persons, and non-governmental organizations and persons. The SecNav exercises authority through civilian assistants and the **Chief of Naval Operations**.

Office of the Secretary of the Navy

- Secretary of the Navy
- Under Secretary of the Navy
- Public Affairs
- Judge Advocate General
- Legislative Affairs
- Auditor General
- General Counsel
- Inspector General
- Research, Engineering, and Systems Acquisition
- Shipbuilding and Logistics Acquisition
- Manpower and Reserve Affairs
- Financial Management, Comptroller, Information Management

secure: An electronic data or voice communications transmission system that uses various techniques to prevent the information content of friendly signals from being exploited by hostile elements. Secure visual communications involves the transmission of an encrypted digital signal consisting of animated visual and audio information. The transmission distance may vary from a few hundred feet to thousands of miles. (see also **communications security**)

Secure Voice System (SVS):   National Security Agency program to develop a new generation of secure voice telephone units to replace the **AUTOSEVOCOM (Automatic Secure Voice Communications System)**. The Secure Voice Improvement Program will provide new Secure

Telephone Units (STUs), and the Secure Conferencing Project (SCP) will provide worldwide secure voice and graphics conferencing capability.

Security Assistance Program: The multi-billion dollar U.S. government program, evolving from the Marshall Plan, whereby Congress authorizes the provision of defense equipment, services, and military training to foreign countries by grant, credit, or cash sales. Security assistance programs are broken down into four principal forms of aid:

- **Foreign Military Sales (FMS);**
- **Military Assistance Program (MAP);**
- **International Military Education and Training (IMET);** and
- **Economic Support Fund (ESF).**

Security assistance programs are currently directed primarily at Third World and developing countries: Latin America and the Caribbean, the Horn of Africa, southeast Asia, the Pacific, the Middle East, and Mediterranean countries where the United States maintains military bases. In the FY 1990 budget request, Israel, Egypt, Jordan, Pakistan, and El Salvador were the five highest ranking recipients of security assistance aid. Security assistance programs permit the United States to engage in and support governments as well as non-governmental military forces without the direct involvement of U.S. military forces. The Department of Defense's FY 1990 report to Congress stated that "Military assistance enhances our allies' ability to deter and combat aggression without the direct involvement of U.S. forces. . . . Security assistance provides the principal policy instrument for assisting nations engaged in **low intensity conflict.**"

Loans to purchase weapons and defense-related material have increased the foreign debts of many of the countries that participate in the security assistance program. Congress has approved a series of three programs to re-finance loans, particularly for the high-ranking recipients of FMS and MAP: **Foreign Military Sales Financing (FMSF), Foreign Military Sales Debt Reform/Restructuring**, and the **Guarantee Reserve Fund (GSF)**.

The security assistance program is organized in each recipient country by the Overseas Military Program Management Team. The Secretary of State is responsible for the day-to-day general supervision of security assistance programs, including commercial sales, through the Bureau of Politico-Military Affairs. The Office of Security Assistance and Sales (SAS) administers FMS and MAP. When a foreign government wishes to purchase a particular item, it makes the request either through the U.S. ambassador or through the local **Military Assistance Advisory Group** chief. SAS then reviews the request, assigns it to the relevant category (FMS, commercial sales, weapons vs. services, cash vs. credit sales, etc.), and dispatches it to the appropriate regional government departments in DOD and the State Department for further review. The Secretary of Defense has the administrative responsibilities through the

Defense Security Assistance Agency (DSAA). The DOD agency responsible for the overall administration of security assistance programs, in conjunction with the military services, the JCS, and the Office of the Assistant Secretary of Defense (International Security Affairs) (OASD/ISA). The Agency for International Development (AID) administers and disburses the Economic Support Fund (ESF). Congress votes on security assistance programs each year, as codified in the **Foreign Assistance Act of 1961** and the **Arms Export Control Act of 1976 (AECA).**

security classification: The process by which access to and distribution of national security-related information is controlled by official U.S. government agencies. A document or device is determined to be of a specific classification category (level) according to the type of information it contains (i.e., its subject matter and national security value or sensitivity).

Categories of classified information employed by the Departments of Defense and Energy, NATO, and the intelligence community include

- **Top Secret, Secret,** and **Confidential;**
- **"Q"** and **"L";** and
- **Atomal** and **Cosmic.**

Types of classified information and material include

- **critical nuclear weapon design information;**
- **extremely sensitive information;**
- **restricted data** and **formerly restricted data;**
- **Sigma;**

- **sensitive compartmented information;**
- **sensitive nuclear material production information;** and
- **special nuclear material (and information),** as well as any eligible national security information.

Control markings are code words attached to classified materials that place specific restrictions on the dissemination of and access to information. Control markings include

- Not Releasable to Foreign Nationals (**NOFORN**);
- Originator-Controlled (**ORCON**);
- Not Releasable to Government Contractors (**NOCONTRACT**);
- Proprietary Information Involved (**PROPIN**); and
- Warning Notice—Intelligence Sources and Methods (**WNINTEL**).

National security information is currently classified under E.O. 12356, "National Security Information," and implemented by Directive No. 1 of the Information Security Oversight Office (ISOO) of the General Services Administration. The E.O. includes definitions of national security information; types of classifiable information; limits on classification; procedures for declassifying and downgrading and for safeguarding national security information; and descriptions of **special access** programs. The authority for original classification of information at the Top Secret, Secret, and Confidential level lies with the Secretary of Defense, the secretaries of the military departments, and other officials to whom the authority is further delegated in writing.

Security Clearances Held by DOD and Industry Personnel

	FY 1984	FY 1985	FY 1986	FY 1987	FY 1988
Top Secret	597,000	493,000	356,000	441,000	473,000
Secret	3,188,000	2,526,000	1,933,000	2,008,000	2,180,000
Confidential	324,000	408,000	427,000	415,000	375,000
TOTAL	4,100,000	3,426,000	2,715,000	2,863,000	3,028,000

Information classified under E.O. 12356 may be declassified or downgraded "as soon as national security considerations permit," in accordance with guidelines prepared by the appropriate agency. "Decisions concerning declassification shall be based on the loss of sensitivity of the information with the passage of time or on the occurrence of an event that permits declassification." Declassification authority rests with the Director of ISOO or the original or exclusive classification authority. Security classification restrictions are not applied to certain official records and materials. However, the disclosure of unclassified (U) information is considered by the DOD to be potentially "subject to control for other reasons" (see **for official use only** and **unclassified controlled nuclear information**).

Access to classified information and materials is controlled by personnel security regulations. All persons handling classified information or materials are specifically investigated for competency, "certified," and granted security "clearance(s)" to do so. Access is then further determined on a **need to know** basis. The different types of personnel security investigations used to determine access to levels of classified information are

- National Agency Check (NAC): "Consists of record searches of selected agencies for information bearing on the loyalty, trustworthiness and suitability of individuals under investigation." A NAC may include records at the Defense Central Index of Investigations, the FBI, Office of Personnel Management, Immigration and Naturalization Service, and the Department of State. A NAC is required for granting of a Secret level clearance.
- National Agency Check and Inquiries (NACI): A NAC plus written inquiries covering the past five years of an individual's background.
- Background Investigation (BI): A NACI plus a credit check and personal interviews with selected sources. It covers up to the past seven, but not less than five years of an individual's background. A BI is required for granting of a Top Secret level clearance.
- Special Background Investigation (SBI): A BI which covers the past 15 years of an individual's background or to the individual's 18th birthday, whichever is shorter. An SBI is required for granting a Special Intelligence/Codeword clearance.
- Periodic Reinvestigation (PR): An investigation to update a BI or SBI,

*Total Classification Actions, FY 1981–87 ***

FY	Total	Number and Percent Change
1981	17,374,102	
1982	17,504,611	+ 130,509 (0.8%)
1983	18,005,151	+ 500,540 (3%)
1984	19,607,736	+ 1,602,585 (9%)
1985	22,322,895	+ 2,715,159 (14%)
1986	15,120,298	− 4,350,650 (29%)
1987	10,769,648	+ 1,086,250 (10%)

* FY 1981–1984 and FY 1985–1987 data were computed using different sampling techniques.

required every five years. It requires at least an updated Personal Information Questionnaire and review of personnel and security files. It may include a NAC, subject interview, record search, credit search, and the resolution of issues raised since the last background investigation.

[*Glossary of Terms and Acronyms,* Attachment VI to statement of Bill W. Thurman, Deputy Director, GAO/NSIAD before Senate Subcommittee on Investigations, 16 April 1985, S. Hrg 99-166, pp. 56–58]
Oversight of security classification programs is conducted by the Information Security Oversight Office; Defense Investigative Service; the DOD and department Inspectors General; the Government Accounting Office; and the House and Senate Committees on Intelligence and Government Operations [DOD, *Information Security Program Regulation,* DOD 5200.1-R, 28 April 1987; *JCS Pub 1,* p. 383; GAO, *DOD Clearance Reduction and Related Issues,* GAO/NSIAD-87-170BR, September 1987, p. 12; U.S. Information Security Oversight Office, *Annual Report* from Frederick M. Kaiser, "The Amount of Classified

Information: Causes, Consequences, and Correctives of a Growing Concern," *Government Information Quarterly,* 1989]

SEEK FROST: Nickname for the **DEW (Distant Early Warning) Line**. (see also **North Warning System**)

SEEK IGLOO: Air Force program to replace 13 long-range **air defense** radars along the coasts and in the interior of Alaska at remote sites with AN/FPS-117 minimally attended long-range radars. The radars are connected to the Alaskan **NORAD** Region for airspace control, as well as to the radars of the **North Warning System** in Canada and Greenland.

SEEK SKYHOOK: Air Force set of two "aerostat" **air defense** radars that hang in tethered balloons off Cudjoe Key, FL; and Cape Canaveral, FL. The radars, tethered at 12,000 ft, provide surveillance of low-flying aircraft. SEEK SKYHOOK is part of the **Joint Surveillance System**.

Selected Reserve: A category of Ready Reserve personnel whose members are assigned to reserve or active units. The Selected Reserve includes all members of the **Air National Guard** and nearly all members of the **Army National Guard**. Many selected reservist members are serving out the terms of their initial training, which require them to complete at least 48 periods of inactive duty training (usually one weekend drill per month) and one active duty training stint of at least 14 days. The President may mobilize as many as 50,000 Selected Reservists into active federal service for up to 90 days without any declaration of war or national emergency. The Selected Reserve is the largest of all reserve personnel categories. Its total personnel strength is 1,200,000. (see also **Individual Ready Reserve**)

self-propelled artillery (see **M-109, M-110**)

Semi-Automated Ground Environment (SAGE): Obsolete Air Force-operated peacetime-and-wartime surveillance and control system, the forerunner to the **Regional Operational Control Centers** of NORAD. SAGE was a network of air defense command centers built in the late 1950s to correlate information from radars about enemy aircraft and to direct interceptor aircraft against them. For over 25 years, SAGE provided command and contrul for the NORAD air defense mission.

Senior Crown/Senior Year: Code words to designate **SR-71** or **U-2** aerial reconnaissance operations and information.

Senior Interdepartmental Group (see **National Security Council**)

senior officer present afloat (SOPA): The senior naval **line officer** present in an area and in command of any unit at sea. SOPA is responsible for the overall administration of naval units operating in the prescribed area [*JCS Pub 1*, p. 329].

sense-and-destroy armor (SADARM): Army research program to develop a fire-and-forget artillery submunitions that could be delivered by the **Multiple Launch Rocket System (MLRS)** and by 155 mm artillery howitzers. After launch, the SADARM submunitions disperse over the target area and search for appropriate targets using a dual-mode (combination millimeter-wave and infrared) sensing mechanism. As targets are detected, the SADARM submunitions orient, stabilize, and descend by parachute over the target area. The SADARM then fires an explosive-projected penetrator, which travels at an extremely high velocity to penetrate the top of an armored target vehicle. Two submunitions are carried in the 155 mm projectile, six in the MLRS rocket.

SADARM was approved in March 1988 for full-scale development and is scheduled for fielding in FY 1993. Honeywell, Minneapolis, MN; and Aerojet, Aczusa, CA, are the contractors.

sensitive compartmented information (SCI): Security classification category applied to "information and material that requires (sic) special controls for restricted handling within compartmented intelligence systems and for which compartmentation is established" [DOD, *Infor-*

mation Security Program Regulation, DOD 5200.1 R, 28 April 1987, p. 21]. SCI is considered more sensitive than traditional categories of national security information; as such, its level of protection is more strict than Top Secret. Systems that produce SCI include imaging and signals intelligence **reconnaissance satellites**; strategic aerial reconnaissance aircraft (e.g., **SR-71**, **U-2**, and **RC-135**); submarine and ship covert-reconnaissance programs such as **Barnacle**; and ground stations for foreign signals intercept. SCI also includes information about the characteristics of satellites and surveillance systems themselves. SCI is subject to great physical security measures, and access to such information is granted on a **need to know** basis and requires a special security clearance. The personnel security standards for SCI clearances are more rigorous than those for Top Secret information. Within the SCI category are four basic types of security information (and clearances):

- **Special Intelligence (SI)**: Clearance for basic **signals intelligence** information;
- **Talent Keyhole (TK)**: Clearance for satellite and air surveillance intelligence;
- Combined **SI-TK** clearance; and
- **Byeman (B)**: Clearance for signals intelligence satellites and imaging satellites.

SCI materials may also be marked by a code word referring to a sensitive information source. Some of these markings are or have been

- DIKTER: Information obtained from Norway;

- DRUID: Information obtained by a third party intercept;
- ISHTAR: Information obtained from Japan;
- RICHTER: Information obtained from West Germany;
- SETEE: Information obtained from South Korea; and
- SYNAMO: Information obtained from Denmark.

Other SCI systems used by intelligence agencies include VER, used by the National Security Agency, standing for "Very Restricted Knowledge" and probably regarding satellite imagery and intercepts; and SNCP, standing for "Special Navy Control Program" and regarding covert submarine intelligence collection. The U.S. Navy further labels its programs with a single-letter designation, such as "M,'" an abbreviation for "MEDITATE" and meaning **Ivy Bells**-type operations [DOE, *Personnel Security Program*, DOE Order 5631.2, 13 November 1980; Jeffrey Richelson, *The U.S. Intelligence Community*, 2d ed., pp. 415, 417–418].

sensitive nuclear material production information: A type of classified information designated by the DOD and the Department of Energy. It includes

"a. Secret production rate or stockpile quantity information relating to plutonium, tritium, enriched lithium 6, uranium 235 and 233.
b. Classified gaseous diffusion technology.
c. Classified gas centrifuge technology."

[DOE, *Control of Classified Documents and Information*, DOE Order

5635.1, Change 1, 14 April 1981, released under the FOIA] (see also **special nuclear material**)

sensor: An electronic instrument to detect **electromagnetic radiation** from objects at either near or great distances. Sensors acquire information for tracking, aiming, discrimination, attack, and kill assessment. There are two broad groups of sensors, active and passive. Active sensors generate stimuli to produce a detectable response (e.g., radar). Active sensors illuminate the target to produce return secondary radiation, which is detected in order to track and/or identify the target. Passive sensors depend on an object's radiated energy for detection and detect naturally occurring emissions from a target for tracking and identifying purposes.

Sentinel: Anti-ballistic missile program proposed in 1967 to protect the United States from the "Chinese nuclear threat," accidental nuclear launches, and nuclear terrorism. Sentinel interceptors were to be placed around the nation's largest cities for protection from ballistic missile attacks. Popular opposition forced the proposal to be withdrawn, and the **Safeguard** system, with a different deployment scheme and a more limited mission of protecting military facilities, replaced it.

Sentry   (see **E-3 Sentry AWACS**)

separate brigade: Army unit with a similar mission to a **division**, but where the threat or geographical area requires less than a division force. A separate brigade is capable of sustaining itself in battle; however, it obviously has less staying power, less firepower, and less capability than a division. A separate brigade is larger than a divisional **maneuver brigade**, but it rarely has more combat power, as each is made up of the same number of combat maneuver battalions. The primary difference between the two brigades is that, in separate brigades, maneuver units, combat support, and combat service support units are organic. In a divisional brigade, support units are attached to the brigade or support the brigade as part of the division support command or divisional artillery. Separate brigades operate in task forces or are attached to the corps on an as-needed basis. The types of separate brigades include infantry, light infantry, armor, mechanized, and air cavalry combat. Organized Army separate brigades include

- Berlin Bde, Berlin, West Germany
- 29th Infantry Bde, Honolulu, HI
- 30th Infantry Bde (Mech), Clinton, NC
- 30th Armored Bde, Jackson, TN
- 31st Armored Bde, Northport, AL
- 32nd Infantry Bde (Mech), Milwaukee, WI
- 33rd Infantry Bde, Chicago, IL
- 39th Infantry Bde, Little Rock, AR
- 41st Infantry Bde, Portland, OR
- 45th Infantry Bde, Edmond, OK
- 53rd Infantry Bde, Tampa, FL
- 73rd Infantry Bde, Columbus, OH
- 81st Infantry Bde (Mech), Seattle, WA
- 92nd Infantry Bde, San Juan, PR
- 157th Infantry Bde (Mech), Horsham, PA
- 177th Armored Bde, Ft. Irwin, CA 92311

- 187th Infantry Bde, Ft. Devens, MA 01433
- 193rd Infantry Bde, Ft. Clayton, Panama
- 194th Armored Bde, Ft. Knox, KY 40121
- 197th Infantry Bde (Mech), Ft. Benning, GA 31905
- 205th Infantry Bde (Light), Ft. Snelling, MN 55111
- 218th Infantry Bde (Mech), Newberry, SC

separate operating agency (SOA): Air Force organizational entity smaller than a **major command**. Separate operating agencies usually perform specialized services and operate from one location. They report directly to the Air Staff and the Office of the **Chief of Staff of the Air Force**.

Air Force
Separate Operating Agencies

- **Air Force Accounting and Finance Center (AFAFC)**
- **Air Force Audit Agency (AFAA)**
- **Air Force Commissary Service (AFCOMS)**
- **Air Force Engineering and Services Center (AFESC)**
- **Air Force Inspection and Safety Center (AFISC)**
- **Air Force Intelligence Service (AFIS)**
- **Air Force Legal Services Center (AFLSC)**
- **Air Force Management Engineering Agency (AFMEA)**
- **Air Force Military Personnel Center (AFMPC)**
- **Air Force Office of Medical Support (AFOMS)**
- **Air Force Office of Security Police (AFOSP)**
- **Air Force Office of Special Investigations (AFOSI)**
- **Air Force Operational Test and Evaluation Center (AFOTEC)**
- **Air Force Reserve (AFRES)**
- **Air Force Service Information and News Center (AFSINC)**
- Air Reserve Personnel Center (ARPC)

(see also **major command**, **direct reporting units**. For the equivalent Army unit of organization, see also **field operating agency**)

service: 1. A military service; an arm of the U.S. armed forces: the **Department of the Air Force**, **Department of the Army**, or **Department of the Navy**. **2.** A **branch** of the Army that performs logistics or administrative functions in support of combat arms operations (e.g., Army Corps of Engineers). (see also **combat support**, **combat service support**)

Service Cryptological Authority (SCA): A military department's intelligence agency with cryptological missions: the **Army Intelligence and Security Command**; Air Force **Electronics Security Command**; and **Naval Security Group Command**. Supervision of the SCAs is exercised by the Central Security Service, a component of the **National Security Agency/Central Security Service (NSA/CSS)**. The Director of the NSA is dual-hatted as director of the CSS. (see also **cryptology**)

service group (SERVGRU): Permanent **Naval Surface Force** administrative organization that provides logistic support, including fuel; petroleum, oils, and lubricants (POL) products; ammunition and weapons components; repair parts and other provisions; salvage operations; and towing services for naval combatant forces. A service group provides mobile logistic support force ships and tugs to numbered fleet commanders when directed. Subordinate units are service squadrons. Assigned ships include Destroyer Tenders (AD), Repair Ships (AR), Ammunition Ships (AE), Fast Combat Support Ships (AOE), and other ocean going support ships. One service group is assigned to each fleet:

- Service Group 1: Oakland, CA 94625 (Pacific Fleet)
- Service Group 2: Norfolk, VA 23511 (Atlantic Fleet)

Service Life Extension Program (SLEP): Navy ship refurbishment program designed to upgrade the capabilities of an **aircraft carrier** and add 15 years to its normal service life (20–30 years). Each carrier's SLEP takes 2–3 years to complete and is more extensive than the **overhauls** undergone in the course of its normal operations. The USS Independence (CV-62) was the last carrier to complete SLEP. The USS Kitty Hawk (CV-63) is currently in SLEP and the USS Constellation (CV-64) is the next carrier scheduled to enter the program.

services: Services can be divided into three functional sub-areas: field services, personnel services, and medical services. Field services include graves registration, clothing exchange and bath, laundry and textile and clothing renovation, bakery, airdrop, and salvage. (see also **logistics**)

service storage facility (SSF): A service-operated and -controlled nuclear weapons storage facility that does not have the capability for maintenance and modifications of weapons and components. (see also **nuclear stockpile**)

servicing: A logistical function performed by one military organization (usually a service) in support of another. The three types of servicing are

- Cross-servicing: Where one service provides support to another for which reimbursement is required (e.g., aircraft servicing of a Navy aircraft at an Air Force base);
- Common servicing: Where a function performed by one service to another does not require reimbursement (usually when a particular service has responsibility for providing all items of a certain type to the various services); and
- Joint servicing: Where a function is performed by a jointly staffed and financed activity in support of two or more military services (e.g., medical, transportation, and graves registration).

(see also **logistics**)

SETAF (see **Southern European Task Force**)

SETEE (see **sensitive compartmented information**)

Seventh Fleet (7th FLT): One of four **numbered fleets** of the Navy, and one of two operating fleets assigned to the Navy's **Pacific Fleet** (the other is the **Third Fleet**). Its mission area is the Western Pacific and Indian Oceans, or approximately 52 million square miles. Its Commander "exercises operational control over assigned ships, aircraft, and submarines; plans and conducts fleet training (including combined, joint, and inter-type) exercises; and conducts operations to ensure control of the sea in order to defend the United States against attack through the Western Pacific and Indian Oceans, to maintain the security of the [**U.S.**] **Pacific Command**, and to support the operations of adjacent Allied and national commanders" [*NWP* 2, Rev. C, Chapter 19]. Commander, Seventh Fleet exercises operational control over assigned commander **task forces** (CTFs). Most of the ships rotate from homeports in Hawaii or the west coast of the United States, although some are homeported in Japan. The day-to-day fleet is composed of approximately 70–80 ships, including 2–3 aircraft carriers, 3–4 cruisers, 18–20 destroyers/frigates, 7 attack submarines, 1 marine expeditionary unit, 440 aircraft, and 60,000 personnel.

Fleet Headquarters
Yokosuka, Japan
(APO SF 96601-6003)

Fleet Flagship
USS Blue Ridge (LCC-19)

Operating Task Forces

- CTF 70 Commander Battle Force
- CTF 71 Commander Command and Coordination Force
- CTF 72 Commander Patrol and Reconnaissance Force
- CTF 73 Commander Logistic Support Force
- CTF 74 Commander Submarine Force
- CTF 75 Commander Surface Combatant Force
- CTF 76 Commander Amphibious Force
- CTF 77 Commander Carrier Strike Force
- CTF 79 Commander Landing Force

SH-2F Seasprite LAMPS (Light Airborne Multi-Purpose System) Mk I: Navy, two-seat, twin-turbine, surface ship-based helicopter, designed to augment the **anti-submarine warfare (ASW)** capability of surface combatants. Its missions are to detect, localize, classify, and attack submarines initially detected by another source, usually surface ship sonar. The SH-2 is projected to remain the primary ASW system for over 80 surface ships through the year 2010. Secondary missions include anti-ship surveillance and targeting, search and rescue, medical evacuation, and communications relay. The helicopter is equipped with a search radar, **electronic warfare support measures**, **magnetic anomaly detectors**, an acoustic data link, and passive and active **sonobuoys**. Armament includes two **Mk-46** light torpedoes. The SH-2 is deployed on frigates and a single class of cruisers. The frigates generally cannot accommodate the larger **SH-60 LAMPS Mk III** deployed on destroyers and cruisers. When not embarked, helicopters are stationed at NAS Norfolk, VA; Mayport, FL; NAS Cubi Point, Philippines; NAS North Island, CA; and NAS Barbers Point, HI. The first SH-

2 flew in 1959. Since then, many versions have been produced for the Navy. In 1988, there were approximately 125 SH-2Fs in the inventory. No further procurement is anticipated. Recurring flyaway cost is $8.6 million each in FY 1987. The prime contractor is Kaman Aerospace Corporation, Bloomfield, CT.

SH-3D/H Sea King: Navy twin engine, four-person, all-weather, carrier-based, nuclear-capable, **anti-submarine warfare (ASW)** helicopter. The helicopter is the current Navy inner-zone (50 mi around ships) ASW system for the protection of aircraft carriers. It is equipped with a variable-depth active dipping **sonar**, active and passive **sonobuoys**, a data link, a **magnetic anomaly detector**, electronic countermeasures systems and **chaff**, and a tactical navigation system. Its primary missions are to detect, classify, track, and destroy enemy submarines. Secondary missions include logistic support and search and rescue. The helicopter exists in two variants, the SH-3D and the SH-3H, both upgraded from earlier models. All of the SH-3Ds are being converted to SH-3Hs. The SH-3 is to be eventually replaced by the **SH-60F**, which began deployment in 1987. Under FY 1990 plans, all SH-3s will be replaced by 1999. Armaments include one B57 nuclear depth bomb or two **Mk-46** light torpedoes. When not embarked, helicopters are based at NAS North Island, CA; and NAS Jacksonville, FL. There were about 200 helicopters in the Navy inventory in 1989. The first SH-3 became operational in 1961; the SH-3D became operational in 1966. The prime contractor is Sikorsky Aircraft Division of United Technologies Corporation.

SH-60B Seahawk LAMPS (Light Airborne Multi Purpose System) Mk III: Navy three-person, twin-engine, surface ship-based **anti-submarine warfare (ASW)** helicopter. It is a modified version of the Army's **UH-60 Blackhawk**. LAMPS Mk III is a computer-integrated ship/helicopter system that increases the ASW effectiveness of surface ships. The air vehicle is the SH-60B helicopter, which provides a remote platform for the deployment of active and passive **sonobuoys**, weapons, and systems for the processing of acoustic and **magnetic anomaly detection** sensor information, as well as an elevated platform for radar surveillance and **electronic warfare support measures** collection. The SH-60B passes sonobuoy information through an advanced data link to the LAMPS Mk III ship for processing, but it also possesses full processing capability for over-the-horizon surveillance. Its primary mission is ASW. Secondary missions include anti-ship surveillance and targeting, search and rescue, medical evacuation, and vertical replenishment. The range is 50 nm with three hours on station. Armament includes two **Mk-46** light torpedoes and the **Penguin** anti-ship missile. The SH-60B was first deployed on four frigates in 1985. It is scheduled for deployment on newer Oliver Hazard Perry class frigates; Spruance, Burke, and Kidd class destroyers; and Ticonderoga class cruisers that do not carry the **SH-2F**. The original Navy plan was to purchase 204 aircraft, but the program has been so successful that some ships will be modified to carry two helicopters, and the number of helicopters to be procured is being increased. The recurring fly-away cost is $12.2 million each in FY 1987. Contractors include International Business Machines, Owego, NY (prime system contractor); Sikorsky Aircraft Corporation, Stratford, CT (helicopter); and General Electric Company, Lynn, MA (engine). FY 1990 and FY 1991 requests for the purchase of six helicopters each year, together with support, are $199.5 million and $180.2 million, respectively.

SH-60F Seahawk: Navy four-person, carrier-based **anti-submarine warfare** helicopter modified from the **SH-60B**. The SH-60F will replace the **SH-3D/H Sea King** helicopter as the Navy's inner-zone (50 mi around ships) protection for aircraft carriers. It is equipped with an improved tethered variable-depth active-dipping sonar, and active and passive **sonobuoys**. Armament includes either the B57 nuclear depth bomb or two **Mk-46** light torpedoes. The first production model was delivered in late 1986. When not embarked, SH-60Fs are deployed at NAS North Island, CA; and NAS Jacksonville, FL. The Navy plans to buy 175 Seahawks, although budget constraints may cancel the program before that number is reached. Sikorsky Aircraft Division, United Technologies Corporation, Stratford, CT, is the prime contractor, and General Electric Company, Lynn, MA, is the engine contractor. FY 1990 and FY 1991 requests to purchase 18 helicopters each year, together with support,

are $313.7 million and $271.6 million, respectively.

shakedown: Period of adjustment, clean-up, and training for a ship after **commissioning** or a major **overhaul**. Following commissioning, a ship also makes a shakedown cruise.

SHAPE   (see **Supreme Headquarters Allied Powers Europe**)

Sherpa   (see **C-23 Sherpa**)

shore establishment: The collection of all activities of Navy organizations not included in the **operating forces** or in the Department of the Navy headquarters. Shore activities exist solely for the support of the operating forces. Class I shore activities are in the chain of command of either the CNO or the Commandant of the Marine Corps and receive primary support from that official. Class II activities are in the same chain of command but receive primary support from an organizational element not under the command of either. Class III activities are in the chain of command or under the supervision of an official other than the CNO or CMC. (see also **major command**)

Short-Range Attack Missile   (see **SRAM/SRAM II**)

short-range ballistic missile (SRBM): A **ballistic missile** with a range of up to 600 nm. The only actively deployed U.S. SRBM is the **Lance** missile.

show of force: The purposeful exhibition of armed might before an enemy or potential enemy, usually in a **crisis** situation, to reinforce demands. A show of force is normally considered an extension of the presence of U.S. forces that stops short of bringing opposing forces together in combat. It has been referred to as "gunboat diplomacy," "muscle flexing," or "saber rattling." A show of force may be intended as a deterrent to prevent the further escalation of hostilities.

SI   (see **special intelligence**)

Sidearm: Model designation AGM-122A. Navy and Marine Corps, short-range, air-to-ground anti-radiation missile that can be carried by most attack aircraft and helicopters. The missile is a modification of the **Sidewinder** air-to-air missile. FY 1988 cost for the purchase of the final 276 missiles was $25.9 million.

side-looking airborne radar (SLAR): An airborne radar that views at right angles to the axis of the vehicle, which produces a presentation of terrain or targets.

Sidewinder: Model designation AIM-9. Air Force and Navy short-range, air-to-air infrared homing missile carried by fighter and attack aircraft. It is designed for combat in visual encounters. Prime contractors are Raytheon, Lowell, MA; and Ford Aerospace and Communications, Newport Beach, CA. The final year of Air Force procurement was FY 1989, when the Air Force was appropriated $37.1 million for 760 missiles.

sievert   (see **rem**)

SIGINT   (see **signals intelligence**)

Sigma: Department of Energy categories of classified nuclear weapons information (i.e., **restricted data** and/or **formerly restricted data**) used to further identify information regarding the "design, manufacture, or utilization of atomic weapons, or utilization of atomic weapons or nuclear explosive devices." Sigma 1 and Sigma 2 generally relate to **Critical Nuclear Weapon Design Information (CNWDI)**. The Sigma categories of data are

- *Sigma 1*: "Theory of operation (hydrodynamic and nuclear) or complete design of thermonuclear weapons or their unique components."
- *Sigma 2*: "Theory of operation or complete design of fission weapons or their unique components. This includes the high explosive system with its detonators and firing unit, pit system, and nuclear initiation system as they pertain to weapon design and theory."
- *Sigma 3*: "Manufacturing and utilization information not comprehensively revealing the theory of operation or design of the physics package. Complete design and operation of nonnuclear components but only information as prescribed below for nuclear components. Utilization information necessary to support the stockpile to target sequence. Information includes
(a) General external weapon configuration, including size, weight, and shape.
(b) Environmental behavior, fuzing, ballistics, yields, and effects.
(c) Nuclear components or subas-

semblies which do not reveal theory of operation or significant design features.

(d) Production and manufacturing techniques relating to nuclear components or subassemblies.

(e) Anticipated and actual strike operations."

- *Sigma 4*: "Information inherent in preshot and postshot activities necessary in the testing of atomic weapons or devices. Specifically *excluded* are the theory of operation and the design of such items. Information includes

(a) Logistics, administration, other agency participation.

(b) Special construction and equipment.

(c) Effects, safety.

(d) Purpose of test, general nature of nuclear explosive tested including expected or actual yields and conclusions derived from tests not to include design features."

- *Sigma 5*: "Production rate and/or stockpile quantities of nuclear weapons and their components."

- *Sigma 9*: "General studies not directly related to the design or performance of specific weapons or weapon systems, e.g., reliability studies, fuzing studies, damage studies, aerodynamic studies, etc."

- *Sigma 10*: "Chemistry, metallurgy, and processing of materials peculiar to the field of atomic weapons or nuclear explosive devices."

- *Sigma 11*: "Information concerning inertial confinement fusion which reveals or is indicative of weapon data."

[DOE, *Control of Weapon Data*, DOE Order 5610.2, 1 August 1980, released under the FOIA]

Signal Corps: Army **combat support** branch and **combat service support** arm that provides command, control, communications, and audiovisual support to combat forces. Signal Corps units install, operate, and maintain communications–electronic and audiovisual equipment and participate in combat operations when required.

signals intelligence (SIGINT): General term for a type of **intelligence** information collected by the interception of electronic signals. SIGINT includes

- **Communications intelligence (COMINT)**;
- **Foreign instrumentation signals intelligence (FISINT)**;
- **Telemetry intelligence (TELINT)**;
- **Electronic intelligence (ELINT)**;
- **Radar intelligence (RADINT)**;
- **Laser intelligence (LASINT)**; and
- Non-imaging infrared.

SIGINT is collected by satellites; by reconnaissance aircraft; and by land stations, ships, and submarines. Information sought by such systems includes diplomatic, scientific, economic, and military intelligence from foreign governments, outposts, and individuals. The Secretary of Defense is the government's executive agent for SIGINT activities, and the **National Security Agency/Central Security Service (NSA/CSS)** acts as the operational program manager. SIGINT requirements and priorities are established by the SIGINT Committee of the **National Foreign Intelligence Board**. Intelligence offices within the military departments conduct SIGINT operations in coordination with the NSA, and in accordance with intelligence requirements, goals, and priorities established by the Director of Central Intelligence.

Basic SIGINT doctrine and regulations are contained in U.S. Signals Intelligence Directives (USSIDs), particularly USSID 3, "SIGINT Support to Military Commanders," 1 July 1974; USSID 18, "Limitations and Procedures in Signals Intelligence Operations of the USSS [United States SIGINT System]," 26 May 1976; and USSID 40, "ELINT Operating Policy," 24 October 1975.

There are a number of prominent SIGINT collection systems, each of which has specific attributes, including frequency coverage, mobility, and sensitivity. These collection systems include SIGINT satellites and **Guardrail**, **Quick Fix**, **Quick Look**, **RC-135**, **SR-71**, **TR-1**, and **U-2** aircraft. Systems whose primary missions are not SIGINT but that collect signals for use in direct support of combat forces are called **electronic warfare support measures**. (see also **satellite reconnaissance**)

signals security (SIGSEC): Generic term that includes electronic security (ELSEC) and **communications security (COMSEC)** and encompasses measures to deny or counter the hostile exploitation of electronic emissions. In combat situations, SIGSEC has an active role in the shore and afloat environments relative to **electronic warfare**, **electronic countermeasures (ECM)**, and **electronic counter-countermeasures (ECCM)**. SIGSEC is also a major ingredient in **command, control, and communications countermeasures (C3CM)**. SIGSEC data bases and surveys can contribute to deception planning, as transmission security can be used to convey deceptive information. SIGSEC encompasses

- Cryptosecurity: The provision of technically sound cryptosystems and their proper uses.
- Transmission security: All measures designed to protect transmissions from interception and exploitation by means other than cryptanalysis.
- Emissions security: All measures taken to deny unauthorized persons information of value that might be derived from the interception and analysis of compromising emanations from crypto-equipment and telecommunications systems.
- Physical security: All physical measures necessary to safeguard classified equipment, materiel, and documents from access thereto or observation thereof by unauthorized persons.

Silk Purse: Code name for the **EC-135** airborne command post of the **U.S. European Command**, including ground support vans and fixed ground entry points providing access to the **Defense Communications System (DCS)**.

silo: A hardened, underground facility for a fixed-site missile, designed to provide pre-launch protection and to serve as a launching platform. Silos have facilities either to lift the missile into a launch position or to launch the missile directly from the shelter. Normally applied to ballistic missiles, a silo can also house an anti-ballistic missile. U.S. silo-based missiles are **Minuteman** II, Minuteman III, and **MX**.

single-channel ground and airborne radio system (SINCGARS): Army small, easily maintained, frequency-hopping VHF-FM (30–87.975 MHz) short-range (8–35 km) radio, replacing the existing standard radios such as the AN/PRC-25/77 backpack, AN/VRC-12 vehicular, and AN/ARC-54/114/131/186 airborne radios. The radio can be configured to specified net architectures by attaching one or more of nine modules, and it provides **electronic counter-counter-measures**. It is the primary means of command and control for infantry, armor, airborne, and artillery units. The first radios fielded did not contain integrated **communications security (COMSEC)** but used external Vinson devices. The first SINCGARS ground radios were delivered in January 1988. First-source contracts for 44,100 ground radios are expected in 1990 and 1991. Of this quantity, 27,625 will have integrated COMSEC (ICOM). Second-source ICOM SINCGARS radios were contracted in July 1988, with options for FYs 1990 and 1991. Full competition among first- and second-source contractors and other bidders will begin in FY 1992. The first radios were delivered to the 2nd Infantry Division in South Korea. Major unit deliveries will begin in January 1990. Up to $5 billion could be spent on as many as 400,000 units in the Army procurement program. ITT Aerospace/Optical Division, Fort Wayne, IN, developed the radio and is the first-source prime contractor for ground and airborne radios. General Dynamics Electronics Systems, San Diego, CA, is the second-source prime contractor for ground radios.

SINCGARS began as an Army program for jam-resistant voice communication in the UHF-FM band. The Air Force is acquiring the Army-developed ground SINCGARS and is developing a SINCGARS-compatible radio to replace its airborne AN/ARC-186 radio in selected platforms. The FY 1990–1991 procurement award will be split between ITT and General Dynamics. The FY 1990 request is for $330.4 million, and the FY 1991 request is for $315.9 million.

Single Integrated Operational Plan (SIOP): The central strategic nuclear war **operations plan** of the United States, first drawn up in 1960 under President Eisenhower. It includes all of the nuclear forces of the Strategic Air Command, and all Navy ballistic missile submarines. Numerous options concerning size of attack and target base are created. Also, individual force elements (e.g., warheads on missiles, bombers with bombs, or cruise missiles) are assigned targets (and routing, in the case of bombers), and their timing and non-interference is structured. Support forces, such as aerial refueling aircraft, are also directed. Options range from a show of force to attacks in the trans- and post-nuclear periods. Attacks are categorized as either major attack options (MAOs), selected attack options (SAOs), limited nuclear options (LNOs), or regional nuclear options (RNOs). Targets are divided into four principal classes: counterforce, other military targets, leadership, and economic.

The SIOP is coordinated with the nuclear war plans of the unified commands, and the **NATO [Nuclear] Operations Plan (NOP)**. SIOP applies only to preplanned strikes, although new developments in future SIOPs will also create options for "adaptively planned" strikes. A portion of the strategic forces are withheld from even the most major strikes as the Nuclear Reserve Force.

The SIOP is prepared by the **Joint Strategic Target Planning Staff (JSTPS)** at Offutt AFB, NE. The CINCSAC is also dual-hatted as the Director of Strategic Target Planning, reporting to the JCS. The Deputy head of the JSTPS is a Navy Admiral. The SIOP as of late 1989 is SIOP-6F, adopted in January 1989. It is the sixth revision of SIOP-6, first adopted on 1 October 1983. Revisions are made to the SIOP every six months to accommodate changes in the target base, force capabilities, and national guidance. Each revision is designated with a letter (e.g., SIOP-6A, SIOP-6B).

The first SIOP went into effect 1 July 1961. The next SIOP (SIOP-63) went into effect on 1 August 1963. SIOP-4 went into effect in the mid-1960s. SIOP-5 took effect on 1 January 1976. SIOP-5 introduced more selective, relatively small options in addition to the large-scale options. SIOP-6 highlights attacks on the Soviet command structure (the military, party, and internal security apparatus), Soviet power projection forces, and the Soviet industrial and "economic recovery base." It extends the possible timespan of a nuclear war to 60 days and calls for command, control, and communications support

of nuclear weapons that are at least as robust and survivable as the weapons themselves. With each new SIOP, the number of targets and weapons grows, to where, in 1989, the SIOP plans for the use of about 13,000 warheads.

National guidance from the President is provided in the form of a Presidential Directive dealing with "Nuclear Weapons Employment Policy" (e.g., **Presidential Directive 59**, **National Security Decision Memorandum 242**, and **National Security Decision Directive 13**). The Office of the Secretary of Defense provides guidance for nuclear contingency planning in the "Policy Guidance for the Employment of Nuclear Weapons (NUWEP)". Preparation of the SIOP is further based on guidance provided by the Joint Chiefs of Staff in Annex C, Nuclear Weapons, to the **Joint Strategic Capabilities Plan** [JCS, *Joint Operations Planning System*, Vol. I., p. II-2, released under the FOIA]. The JSTPS develops a list of enemy targets and prepares the National Strategic Target List (Annex C of the SIOP), develops the SIOP, and maintains the SIOP Reconnaissance Plan (SRP) and the Reconstituted Nuclear Strike Plan (RNSP) for protracted warfare. (see also **SIOP ESI**)

single-sideband   (see **SSB**)

SIOP ESI: Code word marking classified national security information ("extremely sensitive information") dealing with the **Single Integrated Operational Plan (SIOP)**. The JCS considers that the "compromise" of SIOP ESI "would seriously degrade the effective execution of the SIOP," and thus security for the information is very strict. SIOP ESI messages and material are controlled as Top Secret JCS documents and are tracked by a receipt system. Information is transmitted only by approved message systems or courier. Electrically transmitted messages are marked "SPECAT." Two couriers are usually required for the hand delivery of SIOP ESI materials. Other special security measures are taken for briefings and debriefings, training, reproduction, destruction, and declassification regarding SIOP ESI material. Access is granted on a **need-to-know** basis. To possess an ESI security clearance, personnel must be U.S. citizens with final Top Secret clearance and must undergo a special background investigation (SBI), a more extensive investigation than a national agency check or background investigation. There are eight access categories of SIOP ESI information (01–08) designed to give access to specific types of information only to those with responsibilities in those areas. The categories themselves do not necessarily reflect certain levels of sensitivity, but the JCS states that "scrupulous discrimination must be used when granting access to Category 01, 02, or 04" [JCS, *Safeguarding the Single Integrated Operational Plan*, SM-36-76, 15 January 1976, released under the FOIA]. (see also **security classification**)

Site R: The nickname of the underground bunker near Fort Ritchie, MD, housing the **Alternate National Military Command Center (ANMCC)** and the **Alternate Joint Communications Center (AJCC)**. The "R" prob-

ably stands for "Raven Rock," the mountain in which the bunker is located.

SI-TK: One of the four major types of **sensitive compartmented information**, a combination of **special intelligence (SI)** and **talent-keyhole (TK)** categories. SI-TK is used to mark the products of **electronic intelligence, communications intelligence**, and other **signals intelligence** collection systems (but not including information regarding the systems themselves). Joint SI-TK security clearances are granted more commonly than separate SI and TK clearances. (see also **security classification**)

situation monitoring: "The continuous review and analysis of events transpiring worldwide, using all available agencies and resources, to detect situations that could affect U.S. policy or interests. Also situation monitoring requires a communications network capable of providing access to worldwide information sources" [JCS, *Joint Operations Planning System*, Vol. IV, p. II-4, released under FOIA].

situation report (SITREP): 1. A special report, generally of an informal nature, required to keep higher authorities advised of the tactical situation. SITREPs are prescribed under certain circumstances, but they may also be required at any time. Most combat commanders are required to submit a SITREP to higher authority at regular specified intervals. **2.** The Commander's Situation Report of the **combatant commanders**, used to keep the JCS, CINCs, Services, and agencies of the government advised of

• Critical national and international situations;
• Existing political, military, and operational situations and plans;
• The readiness of combatant commanders to meet the requirements of JCS-approved plans;
• The progress of ongoing large-scale military exercises; and
• Any significant intelligence event.

The daily SITREP of the combatant commanders is submitted effective 2400Z to ensure its receipt in Washington, DC, no later than 0400Z the following day. The contents of the 30 September and 31 March semiannual SITREPs and SITREP updates are specified by the JCS.

Sixth Allied Tactical Air Force (SIXATAF): NATO air organization assigned to **Allied Air Forces Southern Europe**, established 14 October 1953. It is responsible for the air defense of Turkey. When operational, its forces are provided by Turkey.

Headquarters
Izmir, Turkey
(APO New York 09224)

Subordinate Air Forces

• 1st Tactical Air Force, Eskisehir, Turkey
• 2d Tactical Air Force, Diyarbakir, Turkey

Sixth Fleet (6th FLT): One of the four **numbered fleets** in the U.S. Navy, and the primary operating force assigned to the **U.S. Naval Forces,** **Europe**. It was originally established as the Naval Forces Mediterranean, redesignated the Sixth Task Fleet in 1948, and established as the Sixth Fleet in 1950. Its mission area is the Mediterranean Sea and Black Sea. Its Commander "plans for and conducts offensive and/or defensive naval combat operations, when directed by CINCNAVEUR or other competent authority, in order to establish and maintain control of the waters of, and air space over, the Mediterranean Sea, approaches thereto, adjacent inland areas, and the Black Sea; plans for and conducts contingency operations, including evacuation of U.S. citizens and/or protection of U.S. interests, when directed by higher authority; provides a U.S. Navy presence in the Mediterranean area in support of U.S. Navy overseas diplomacy objectives and U.S. foreign policy; and carries out training operations in order to maintain fleet readiness to carry out the above wartime, contingency, and peacetime responsibilities" [*NWP 2*, Rev. C, pp. 17-1–17-8]. Commander, Sixth Fleet exercises operational control over assigned commander **task forces** (CTFs). When under NATO command, COMSIXTHFLT becomes Commander, Naval Striking and Support Forces, Southern Europe of the **Allied Forces Southern Europe**. The Sixth Fleet participated in evacuations from Beirut, Lebanon, in June 1982; supported the U.S. Marine contingent of the multinational peacekeeping force in Lebanon in 1982; assisted in minesweeping operations in the Suez Canal in 1984; and conducted the counterterrorist intercept of the Achille Lauro in October 1985. It has been the primary combat organization involved in the 1986 and earlier attacks upon Libya. Most ships rotate from the **Second Fleet** area in the Atlantic, and virtually all of the ships of the Sixth Fleet are homeported on the east coast of the United States. Some support ships are homeported in Italy. The day-to-day fleet is composed of approximately 30 ships, 6 submarines, 100 aircraft, and 20,000 personnel.

Fleet Headquarters
Gaeta, Italy
(APO New York 09501-6002)

Fleet Flagship
USS Belknap (CG 26)

Operating Task Forces

- CTF 60 Commander Battle Force
- CTF 61 Commander Amphibious Force
- CTF 62 Commander Landing Force
- CTF 63 Commander Service Force
- CTF 64 Commander Fleet Ballistic Missile Submarine Force
- CTF 66 Commander Area Antisubmarine Force
- CTF 67 Commander Maritime Surveillance Reconnaissance Force
- CTF 68 Commander Special Operations Force
- CTF 69 Commander Attack Submarine Force
- Commander Fleet Air Mediterranean (COMFAIRMED)
- CTF 109 Commander **Middle East Force**

Skyhawk   (see **A-4 Skyhawk**)

Skywarrior   (see **EA-3 Skywarrior**)

sky wave: High-frequency (HF) radio wave that leaves the transmitting antenna and travels upward from the Earth's surface until it is bent back toward the Earth by the ionosphere. The ionosphere, about 100–400 km above the Earth's surface, contains free ions and electrons, which reflect radio signals of some frequencies back to Earth, sometimes to locations thousands of miles from the transmitting station. The highest frequency that is reflected for vertical incidence on the ionosphere is called the "critical frequency." For any given path and time, there is an upper frequency limit for long-distance HF transmission via the ionosphere. Above this frequency—the maximum usable frequency (MUF)—the wave will not be reflected. The MUF varies with the time of day, season of the year, and sunspot activity. During the summer months, the MUF varies over a restricted band of frequencies, and the HF spectrum is usually usable throughout day and night with higher frequencies of 10–28 MHz. During the winter months, these higher frequencies are not usable past sunset, and signal quality at the lower spectrum (2–10 MHz) improves. Since HF communications are prone to long-term fading due to absorption and short-term fading due to interference, using frequencies near the MUF reduces fading and multi-path disturbances. (see also **ground wave**, **skip zone**)

SLAM (Standoff Land Attack Missile):   Navy derivative of the infrared-seeking **Harpoon** missile, designed for deployment from carrier-based aircraft. It allows an aircraft to attack land targets and ships in port or at sea from an extended range, in excess of 60 nm. The Navy's first SLAM came off the production line at McDonnell Douglas's facility in St. Charles, MO, on 3 November 1988. The missile will enter the fleet in 1989.

slant: Obsolete JCS term indicating a divergent view submitted by a Service in the form of a Memorandum for the Joint Chiefs of Staff. It is currently called a Chief of Naval Operations Memorandum (CNOM).

SLBM (submarine-launched ballistic missile): A **ballistic missile** carried in and launched from a submarine, which affords mobility and concealment. (see also **fleet ballistic missile submarine**, **Poseidon**, **Trident I**, **Trident II**)

SLBM Boost-Phase Engagement Project: Strategic Defense Initiative kinetic-energy sea- or air-based system for intercepting SLBMs during their boost phases. Since SLBMs have potentially short flight times, space-based interceptors would not always be useful. However, mobile sea- or air-based platforms could move close to submarine patrol areas and intercept SLBMs near the atmosphere.

SLCM (sea-launched cruise missile) (see **cruise missile**, **Tomahawk**)

SLEP (see **Service Life Extension Program**)

slew time: The time needed for a weapon to aim at a new target after having just fired at a different one. (see also **military time**)

SLFCS (see **Survivable Low-Frequency Communications System**)

SM-1 (see **Standard missile**)

SM-2 (see **Standard missile**)

Small ICBM ("Midgetman"): Air Force mobile, three-stage, single-warhead, solid-propellent missile under development. The missile will weigh no more than 30,000 lb, have a range of approximately 6,000 nm, and be cold-launched. The missile will have a liquid post-boost deployment system for its warhead. The leading contender for the basing mode is a hard mobile transport on pre-existing government reservations. The Small ICBM entered full-scale development in FY 1987, but the amended FY 1988–1989 DOD budget proposal in February 1988 terminated the program. Instead, $250 million was requested to keep the missile alive and allow the Bush Administration to revive the program and move forward with development. The last defense report of the Reagan Administration stated that "in light of the current fiscal environment . . . this administration has concluded that we cannot afford both [the SICBM and the rail-based **MX**] and that the Peacekeeper [MX] is the more cost effective choice. . . . Because we have not proposed SICBM funding in the FY 1990–1991 budget, a decision to continue the SICBM program would require budget adjustments for FY 1990–91" [DOD, *Annual Report to Congress*, FY 1990, p. 187]. Congress decided in deliberations for the FY 1990–1991 defense budget to fund continued development of the Small ICBM.

SNCP (Special Navy Control Program (see **sensitive compartmented information**)

Snow Man: Exercise term for **Air Defense Warning** White.

Solid Shield: JCS-directed, U.S. Atlantic Command-sponsored annual **exercise** conducted in the Atlantic Ocean, Caribbean Sea, Gulf of Mexico, and Puerto Rico. Started in 1963, Solid Shield is the largest exercise held by the Atlantic Command, involving more than 50,000 U.S. military personnel in a typical year.

sonar (sound navigation and ranging): Equipment for the detection and location of underwater objects. Surface ships and submarines have snar systems, normally mounted in the bow or towed behind the ship. Helicopters also carry sonars, either a dipping sonar tethered to the helicopter or an expendable **sonobuoy**. A variable-depth sonar (VDS), a "sonar whose transducer is towed beneath its parent ship with the object of improving sonar detection ranges by permitting the sonar to operate beneath a layer," is fitted on most ASW surface vessels [*NWP 3*].

There are two major types of sonar and sonar detection:

• Active: "Information concerning a distant underwater object is obtained by reflecting a sound signal from the object into receiving and processing equipment" [*NWP 3*]. The equipment includes a trans-

ducer to provide the beam, transmitting antenna, and a receiver-transducer-amplifier to process the returning beam. This is also known as "echo-ranging" or "pinging." An active sonar can also direct voice communications by transmitting the voice as modulated ultrasonic energy. For navigation and target detection, active sonar can provide a realistic picture, as the scanning beam is rotated and the reflected beams show objects as "echo blips," similar to those from radar. The range of the object is figured by timing the rate of return of the reflected beam to the transmittal point. To control weapons, acoustic-homing torpedoes are guided by a locked-on sonar device, a programmer that converts target position data into directional instructions, and a servo-mechanism that activates the torpedo control surfaces. These torpedoes are launched from ordinary deck tubes and aircraft, although they are also used as the terminal stages for the **ASROC**.

• Passive: "Information from a distant underwater object is obtained by receiving and processing the sound generated by the object itself" [*NWP 3*].

There are also various types of sonar ranges:

• Best-depth range (BDR): "The estimated range at which the return from a submarine operating at its best depth to avoid detection will be identified 50 percent of the time."

• Periscope-depth range (PDR): "The estimated range at which return from a submarine at periscope depth will be identified 50 percent of the time."

- Predicted sonar range (PSR): "The range estimated by consideration of factors which influence the propagation of sound, such that the target returns will be identified by an average unalerted sonar operator 50 percent of the time."
- Surface sonar range: "The estimated range at which a surface target will be identified 50 percent of the time."
- Tactical sonar range (TSR): "The TSR is based on PSRs; however, it may also make allowances for operator alertness, level of unit efficiency, and so forth" [*NWP 3*].

Sonar detection also makes use of, or can be complicated by, the refraction of sound energy in water. One of the more common phenomena is the convergence zone. The convergence zone is that distance at which sound energy reaches the surface after it is directed downward from a source and is refracted upwards to the surface. This distance varies from about 7.5 miles in Arctic regions to about 40 miles in equatorial regions. The sound is successively reflected and refracted so that it appears at the surface in a ring-like pattern at intervals out to several hundred miles.

sonobuoy: A **sonar** device used in active-hunting **anti-submarine warfare (ASW)** operations. Most types of sonobuoys consist of a hydrophone and/or sound transducers that detect submarine noises and transmit detection information by radio to the plane or helicopter that launched and controls the sonobuoy. Standard sonobuoy types include

- AN/SSQ-36: Bathythermograph sonobuoy that provides a vertical water temperature profile from the surface to a depth of 1,000 ft. Data are relayed to ASW aircraft to aid crew in the selection of optimum hydrophone depths and tactics to be utilized.
- AN/SSQ-41 (LOFAR): Passive sonobuoy used in search, localization, and tracking.
- AN/SSQ-47: Active echo-ranging sonobuoy with a self-contained sonar that provides non-directional target information to the ASW aircraft during the localization and attack of submerged submarines.
- AN/SSQ-50 (CASS): Command-activated, non-directional sonobuoy that operates only on command from the attack aircraft. It has several selectable sonar signals to optimize performance under differing water conditions. It provides range information during the localization and attack of submerged submarines.
- AN/SSQ-53 (DIFAR): Passive directional sonobuoy used during the target-localization phase of air ASW missions. It is dropped after initial contact has been made by the AN/SSQ-41. It is able to obtain a line of bearing to noise emitters as well as monitor selected sectors around the sonobuoy.
- AN/SSQ-57: Passive acoustic- and sound pressure-level data sonobuoy used to measure ambient noise. It is a specially calibrated passive buoy similar to the AN/SSQ-41 and is used primarily for intelligence gathering and special exercises.
- AN/SSQ-62 (DICASS): Active directional sonobuoy that provides

target-bearing information to fix the submarine.

- AN/SSQ-77 (VLAD): Passive directional sonobuoy utilizing a line array of omni-directional hydrophones and a DIFAR element.
- AN/SSQ-86: One-way acoustic communicator sonobuoy that provides a link between ASW aircraft and submerged submarines.

Sonobuoys are frequently deployed in a sonobuoy barrier, which is "a pattern of sonobuoys or one or more lines of sonobuoys so designed and planted that a submarine attempting to pass, enter, or leave an area should be detected. A barrier pattern is usually identified as to position or purpose, such as containing barrier, flank barrier, intercepting barrier" [*NWP 3*]. (see also **Jezebel**, **Julie**, **P-3**, **S-3**, **SH-3**, **SH-60**, **SH-2F**)

SOOS (Stacked Oscars on Scout): Navy navigation satellites launched by Scout boosters in August 1985 and September 1987. General Electric was the prime contractor. (see also **TRANSIT**)

SOP (standard operating procedures): "A set of instructions covering those features of operations which lend themselves to a definite or standardized procedure without loss of effectiveness. The procedure is applicable unless ordered otherwise" [*JCS Pub 1*, Ch. 2, December 1984, p. B-31].

sortie: 1. A sudden attack made from a defensive position, often called a "sally." **2.** One operational flight by one aircraft. **3.** To depart from a port or station for operations or maneuvers. (see also **mission**)

Sound Surveillance System (SOSUS): Network of passive hydrophone arrays operated by the Navy for the collection of **acoustic intelligence** as part of the **Ocean Surveillance Information System (OSIS)**. SOSUS functions as an **anti-submarine warfare** asset by locating submarines with its mounted or moored passive hydrophones placed at choke points and likely submarine-operating areas off U.S. and allied shores. The arrays are composed of clusters of hydrophones in oil storage-sized tanks, connected to ground processing stations. The hydrophones, each of which is tuned to a different frequency, listen for the sound signatures of submarines.

The first SOSUS array, code-named Caesar, was laid on the continental shelf of the Atlantic and Gulf coasts and reached completion in 1954. Colossus, the next array, was laid along the Pacific continental shelf. Other arrays in the system reportedly include Barrier, which screens the approaches to the Murmansk and Kola Peninsula base complex in the Soviet Union; Bronco, placed off of the Kamchatka peninsula in the Soviet Union; arrays laid between Norway and Bear Island; an array that covers the Scotland, Iceland, and Greenland gaps; and an array off the Atlantic coast of Spain to monitor entrance and exit from the Mediterranean Sea. In the Mediterranean Sea, a separate SOSUS system monitors the channel between Italy and Corsica. Other systems have been laid in the Indian Ocean near the U.S. base at Diego Garcia and in the Pacific to monitor Hawaiian waters.

The newest SOSUS arrays are linked with fiber optic cables to minimize the interception of data. SOSUS data are initially sent to Naval Facilities (NAVFACs) and Naval Regional Processing Centers (NRPCs). Naval Facilities are located at Argentia, Newfoundland, Canada; Bermuda; Brawdy, Wales, UK; Keflavik, Iceland; Adak, AK; Coos Head, Charleston, OR; Ferndale, CA; Guam; Pacific Beach, WA; and Whidbey Island, WA. The processed data are transmitted to Naval Ocean Processing Facilities at Dam Neck, VA, and Ford Island, HI, via the **Fleet Satellite Communication System (FLTSATCOM)**. The data are then fused with other sources of ocean surveillance information to provide the Atlantic and Pacific Fleets with a picture of worldwide submarine movements.

source material: As listed in the **Atomic Energy Act of 1954**, one of the two categories of substances used to produce nuclear weapons or nuclear materials: uranium, thorium, or other material determined to be source material, or ores containing these materials. Concentrations are regulated by the Department of Energy. (see also **special nuclear material**)

source term: The amount of radioactive material (primarily cesium and iodine) that reaches the environment following a **nuclear reactor** accident.

Southern Command (SOUTHCOM) (see **U.S. Southern Command**)

Southern European Task Force (SETAF): Army headquarters subordinate to **U.S. Army Europe (USAREUR)** and whose area of operation includes Italy, Greece, and Turkey. The 1,000 person 1st Bn, 509th Airborne Battalion Combat Team, stationed at Vicenza, Italy, since 1973, is the only combat unit assigned to SETAF, and it is committed as the U.S. representative of the **ACE Mobile Force (AMF)**. SETAF also supervises nuclear weapons custodial detachments in Italy, Greece, and Turkey.

Headquarters
Vicenza, Italy
(APO New York 09221)

Southern Region Amendment (SRA): A **security assistance** term used interchangeably with Section 516 of the **Foreign Assistance Act of 1961**, specifically with reference to excess defense articles (EDAs). As originally enacted, SRA authorized the President to provide, on a no-cost basis, excess or programmed-to-be-excess U.S. defense equipment to security assistance countries in NATO's southern region that were integrated into NATO's military structure. Congress amended the authority of SRA to extend eligibility to Israel and Egypt while restricting the definition of available equipment. A provision was also added to require that any SRA assistance provided to Greece and Turkey be provided in the same ratio as their military assistance funding (7:10). SRA items are not the same as EDA items—EDA items are publicly reported whereas SRA items are not. Congress receives notification of items transferred under SRA in a classified report under the provisions of Section 516.

SP-100:   Code name for the Space Nuclear Power Development Program. After a ten-year hiatus in the development of U.S. nuclear reactors for space, DOE, NASA, and the Strategic Defense Initiative Organization are producing the 100–300 kilowatt SP-100 nuclear reactor. Its most likely purpose is to support directed-energy weapons in the **Strategic Defense Initiative** second stage. Other possible uses for space nuclear power include powering the **Space Surveillance and Tracking System (SSTS)** or orbital space mirrors, radars, hypervelocity guns, and lasers. Launch of the SP-100 nuclear power plant was originally planned for the mid-1990s but has been delayed. Due to funding shortfalls, the ground demonstration of the reactor, originally scheduled for 1991, is now planned for 1994 and the demonstration of a complete system has been terminated. General Electric is the prime contractor.

Space and Naval Warfare Systems Command: Navy shore establishment, redesignated from Naval Electronics Systems Command (NAVELEX) on 9 May 1985. It conducts research, development, test and evaluation, procurement, and logistics support of Navy shore-based, airborne, and shipboard electronics, including naval space; command, control, communications, and intelligence; electronic warfare; navigation; surveillance; air traffic control; and cryptography. The command is composed of four Naval Electronic Systems Engineering Centers, a Naval Electronic Systems Security Engineering Center, and the Navy Space Systems Activity.

Headquarters
Washington, DC 20363

Space-Based Chemical Laser Research (SBCLR):   DARPA program of directed-energy laser experiments to be used as a part of the **Strategic Defense Initiative**. The project consists of the **Talon Gold** pointing and tracking component, the Large Optics Demonstration Experiment (**LODE**) mirror system, and the **Alpha** hydrogen-fluoride chemical infrared laser. The Talon Gold telescope would be attached to a space-based laser and used to aim the laser at its target. The system will probably not be ready for on-orbit demonstration until the mid- to late-1990s.

Space-Based Imaging Radar and Imaging Laser: **Strategic Defense Initiative (SDI)** air- and space-based sensor development program to distinguish decoys from warheads. Prior to their incorporation into the SDI program, the imaging radar and laser were under development for missions other than missile defense. Full-scale demonstration in space of either system could be achieved by the early 1990s.

Space-Based Interceptor (SBI or Sabir):   Strategic Defense Initiative

(**SDI**) kinetic-energy missile interceptor that would launch multiple small, guided missiles without explosive warheads from a space-based platform to destroy ballistic missiles during their boost and post-boost phases. SBI might also be able to destroy individual reentry vehicles. One SDI architecture would require 250–300 SBI platforms. The Advanced Launch System (ALS) was planned to be used to launch SBI into orbit, but, with delays in its production, the Strategic Defense Initiative Organization (SDIO) is attempting to get approval to build a new launch vehicle specifically for SBI and the Exoatmospheric Reentry Vehicle Interceptor Subsystem (**ERIS**).

A series of laboratory flight tests, named ONTARGET (On-board Navigation, Transition, and Real-time Guidance Experimental Test) were conducted in September 1989 on the detection and tracking capabilities of the SBI, elements of the first phase of the SDI. The prime contractor for the test series was Martin Marietta's Electronics and Missiles Group.

The program is managed for the SDIO by the Air Force Space Systems Division. As of October 1988, the projected cost for SBI was $17.7 billion.

Space-Based Kinetic Kill Vehicle: Advanced kinetic-energy rocket interceptor component of the **Strategic Defense Initiative** for boost and post-boost interception of ballistic missiles and reentry vehicles. A large number of satellites would be deployed in low Earth orbits, with each satellite carrying interceptor rockets similar to the miniature homing vehicle

anti-satellite system formerly under development. Testing of this type of system is planned for the mid-1990s. (see also **kinetic-energy weapon**)

Space-Based Laser (see **Space-Based Chemical Laser Research**)

Space-Based Neutral Particle Beam: Directed-energy weapon component of the **Strategic Defense Initiative**. Funding problems within the Strategic Defense Initiative Organization have cut back the research on using **neutral particle beams** to distinguish missile warheads from decoys. Most of the effort is going to basic ground-based neutral particle beam development. There are two Air Force experimental programs:

- Beam Experiment Aboard a Rocket (BEAR): Uses an Aires rocket to launch a low-energy neutral particle beam generator into a ballistic trajectory up to an altitude of about 125 miles for brief tests in space; and
- Integrated Space Experiment (ISE): Launch of a moderate-power neutral particle beam accelerator on a satellite with two smaller spacecraft, one of which would serve as a target while the other would measure the effects of beam radiation on the target.

space boosters (see **Delta**, **Scout**, **Titan 34D/II/IV**)

Space Defense Operations Center (SPADOC): Air Force center located in the **NORAD Cheyenne Mountain Complex**. The SPADOC, established in October 1979 by NORAD, is the center for information on the space situation. SPADOC monitors space activity by tracking, identifying, and reevaluating all objects in space continually. A worldwide network of sensors, called the **Space Surveillance Network (SSN)**, is used to obtain tracking information on satellites. Ford Aerospace is the prime contractor for a SPADOC upgrade to support satellite and space surveillance processing capabilities.

Space Detection And Tracking System (SPADATS): Former network of space surveillance sensors for detecting and tracking space vehicles from the Earth and reporting their orbital characteristics to a central control facility. SPADATS has been incorporated into the **Space Surveillance Network (SSN)**.

Space Nuclear Power Development Program (see **SP-100**)

space shuttle: The Space Transportation System (STS) operated by the National Aeronautics and Space Administration (NASA). The shuttle is a reusable heavy-lift launch vehicle that can bring objects either into low Earth orbits or to approximately 250 miles above the Earth's surface, where the payload's thrusters take the object into geosynchronous orbit or launch it towards its ultimate destination. For its first 24 flights, the shuttle was basically a payload delivery system for taking satellites into orbit. Although it will continue to deliver free-flying payloads, most of the commercial payloads will be transferred to **expendable launch vehicles**.

After the Challenger accident of January 1986, the space shuttle pro-gram was put on hold while the solid rocket booster was redesigned and ground-tested and the main engines were modified. The space shuttle Discovery was launched into orbit at 11:37 A.M. on 29 September 1988 from Cape Canaveral, FL. This marked the end of a 32-month lapse in U.S. space flights. At launch, the shuttle weighed approximately 2,048,350 kg (including external tank, engine, fuel, cargo, and the shuttle itself). The primary payload was the **Tracking and Data Relay Satellite (TDRS)**, which was deployed six hours, six minutes into the flight. The shuttle performed 11 scientific experiments and touched down at Edwards AFB, CA, on 3 October 1988. The space shuttle Atlantic completed a successful liftoff at 9:31 A.M. on 2 December 1988 from Cape Canaveral, FL. Four days later, after deploying its payload, the shuttle landed at Edwards AFB, CA.

A new orbiter is planned for 1991. For 1994, NASA plans to replace the booster rocket used for the shuttle with the Advanced Solid Rocket Motor. Also to be added is the Extended Duration Orbiter, which will extend the astronauts' stay in space from 8 to 16 days.

DOD direct expenses in support of space shuttle operations include procurement of upper-stage vehicles that place operational satellites into orbit, and procurement of ground support equipment for launch of DOD payloads from the space shuttle. The FY 1990 and FY 1991 requests for DOD support are $110.8 million and $85.6 million, respectively.

Space Surveillance and Tracking System (SSTS): Strategic Defense Initiative sensor program using cryo-

Space Shuttle Flights

1. Columbia	12 April 1981	Flight instrumentation
2. Columbia	12 November 1981	OSTA-1, first RMS, flight instrumentation
3. Columbia	22 March 1982	OSS-1, flight instrumentation
4. Columbia	27 June 1982	DOD, flight instrumentation
5. Columbia	11 November 1982	SBS-C, Telesat E
6. Challenger	4 April 1983	TDRS A
7. Challenger	18 June 1983	SPAS-01, OSTA-2, Telesat F, Palapa B-1
8. Challenger	30 August 1983	PDRS/PFTA, OIM, INSAT 1-B
9. Columbia	28 November 1983	Spacelab 1
10. Challenger	3 February 1984	SPAS-01A, Palapa B-2, Westar 6
11. Challenger	6 April 1984	LDEF, SMM Repair
12. Discovery	30 August 1984	OAST-1, SBS-D, Telastar 3-C, Syncom IV-1
13. Challenger	5 October 1984	OSTA-3, ERBS, LFC/ORS
14. Discovery	8 November 1984	HS-376 RETV(2), Telesat H, Syncom IV-1
15. Discovery	24 January 1985	DOD
16. Discovery	12 April 1985	Telesat I, Syncom IV-3
17. Challenger	29 April 1985	Spacelab 3
18. Discovery	17 June 1985	Spartan, Morelos A, Arabsat 1-B, Telestar 3-D
19. Challenger	29 July 1985	Spacelab 2
20. Discovery	27 August 1985	Aussat 1, ASC-1, Syncom IV-4
21. Atlantis	3 October 1985	DOD
22. Challenger	30 October 1985	Spacelab D-1
23. Atlantis	26 November 1985	EASE/ACCESS, Morelos B, Satcom KU-2, Aussat 2
24. Columbia	12 January 1986	MSL-2, Satcom KU-1, Gas Bridge
25. Challenger	28 January 1986	TDRS B
26. Discovery	29 September 1988	TDRS 3
27. Atlantis	2 December 1988	DOD

genically-cooled infrared sensors to detect and track warheads and decoys in the post-boost, midcourse, and terminal phases of flight. SSTS will use a fleet of at least four spacecraft with infrared- and visible-wavelength sensors to monitor Soviet satellites. The object of SSTS is to define in precise terms what Soviet satellites do and what their capabilities are, as well as to provide early warning of an attack on U.S. space systems. Target tracking and identification information would be relayed for use by midcourse interceptors. SSTS was originally under development as part of the **Satellite Surveillance Network (SSN)** ground-based satellite tracking network.

Space Surveillance Network (SSN): Network of radars and tracking sensors for tracking objects in orbits around the Earth, cataloging these objects, and predicting their locations in future orbits. The SSN was formerly the Space Detection and Tracking System (SPADATS) and is commonly called Spacetrack. Space Object Identification (SOI), a part of **U.S. Space Command**'s surveillance mission, conducts about 30,000 observations each day of over 5,000 objects in space, of which 73 percent are "space junk." The information collected is transmitted to and analyzed by the **Space Defense Operations Center (SPADOC)**.

The SSN is composed of three sensor categories: dedicated, collateral, and contributing:

- Dedicated sensors: Sensors operationally controlled by U.S. Space Command and used solely for satellite tracking. These include

  - **Baker-Nunn** cameras at St. Margarets, New Brunswick, Canada; and San Vito, Italy.
  - The **Ground-based Electro-optical Deep Space Surveillance System (GEODSS)**.
  - The Maui Optical Tracking and Identification Facility (**MOTIF**), Maui, HI.
  - The **Naval Space Surveillance System (NAVSPASUR)**.
  - **Pacific Barrier Radars (PACBAR)**.

- Collateral: Radars operationally controlled by U.S. Space Command with a primary mission other than space surveillance, often ballistic missile warning. These include

  - **PAVE PAWS radars** (AN/FPS-115).

  - The Ballistic Missile Early-Warning System (**BMEWS**).
  - **Cobra Dane** (AN/FPQ-16).
  - Radar facility at Pirinclik, near Diyarbakir, Turkey.
  - **Perimeter Acquisition Radar Attack Characterization System.**

- Contributing: Radar sites not under the control of NORAD or U.S. Space Command but under contract or agreement to support space surveillance when requested. These include tracking radars associated with the Eastern Test Range (e.g., Ascension Island, Antigua) and the Western Test Range (e.g., Kaena Point, HI, and Kwajalein), and private and research sensors:

  - Haystack, Tyngsboro, MA; and Millstone Hill, Lexington, MA. MIT Lincoln Lab sensors provide accurate deep-space metric data.
  - DARPA Maui Station (AMOS), Maui, HI.

Spacetrack: Common name for the **Space Surveillance Network**.

Space Transportation System (STS) (see **space shuttle**)

SPADATS (see **Space Surveillance Network**)

SPADOC (see **Space Defense Operations Center**)

Sparrow: 1. Model designation AIM-7F/M. Navy and Air Force air-to-air, all-weather, semi-active, radar-guided intercept missile, designed to give fighter aircraft air superiority. It is a primary weapon for use on **F-4**, **F-14**, **F/A-18**, and **F-15** series aircraft. The missile has undergone several design changes since its initial introduction in the Navy in the 1950s. The AIM-7F version was delivered in 1976; the AIM-7M began procurement in FY 1980 and was delivered for use in 1983. The AIM-7F replaced the AIM-7E/E2 version and had increased performance, reliability, range, lethality, and countermeasures protection. The AIM-7M version incorporated active fuze and seeker improvements to enhance performance in the **electronic countermeasures** environment, and it has greater look-down/shoot-down capabilities than the AIM-7F. The range of the AIM-7F/M is 30 nm. Its warhead is either high-explosive continuous rod (AIM-7F/H) or blast fragmentation (AIM-7M). The Air Force finished procurement of the Sparrow in FY 1989 with 174 missiles for $25 million. The Navy completed procurement of the Sparrow in FY 1989 with 450 missiles for $52.3 million. The Sparrow will be replaced by **AMRAAM**. **2.** Model designation RIM-7H/M, known as the NATO Seasparrow. Navy surface-to-air missile, the nearly identical surface ship-launched version of the AIM-7M, with folding wings and clipped tail fins, used for point defense against aircraft, anti-ship missiles, and air-launched weapons. It is used in the NATO Seasparrow launcher. Seasparrow is deployed on U.S. surface ships that do not have Tartar/**Terrier**/**Standard** missile capability. These include Spruance class destroyers and a variety of amphibious and support ships and aircraft carriers. The missile range is 10 nm. Prime contractors

are Raytheon Corporation, Lowell, MA; General Dynamics, Camden, AK, and Pomona, CA (missile and control sections); and Hercules (rocket motor).

special access program (SAP): "Any program imposing **need-to-know** or access controls beyond those normally required for access to Confidential, Secret, or Top Secret information. Such a program includes, but is not limited to, special clearance, adjudication, or investigative requirements; special designation of officials authorized to determine need-to-know; or special lists of persons determined to have a need-to-know" [DOD, *Information Security Program Regulation*, DOD 5200.1-R, 28 April 1987, p. 21]. The existence of some special access programs is publicly stated by DOD; others remain classified in their entirety. Current special access programs include general stealth technology such as the **B-2** and **Advanced Cruise Missile** programs, and the Navy's **A-12 Advanced Tactical Aircraft**. Programs are also referred to as "carve-out contracts," as most involve defense industry contracts and are made exempt from the normal periodic inspection programs conducted by the Defense Industry Security Program. The selection of a program as requiring special access is supposed to be determined primarily on the basis of security considerations and not according to program type (such as "stealth") or to avoid Congressional or public oversight. The authority to create such programs is outlined in E.O. 12356, "National Security Information." It is exercised by the Secretary of Defense through the Deputy Under Secretary of Defense (Policy) or the secretaries of the military departments. Oversight is conducted by the Defense Investigative Service, the DOD and department Inspectors General, the Government Accounting Office, and the Senate and House Committees on Intelligence.

The number of special access programs is unknown; however, the Government Accounting Office estimated the number of contracts in 1983 to be "several thousand" [GAO, *Information Security: Need for DOD Inspections of Special Access Contracts*, GAO/NSIAD-86-191, August 1986, p. 5]. Also, according to the 1985 Commission to Review DOD Security Policies and Practices (Stilwell Commission), "such programs have proliferated in DOD in recent years" out of a concern for security [DOD, *Keeping the Nation's Secrets: A Report to the Secretary of Defense by the Commission to Review DOD Security Policies and Practices*, (Stilwell Commission), 19 November 1985, p. 58]. (see also **security classification**, **black program**)

special activities: **1.** A control mechanism for categories of compartmented information that deal with "activities of an international, joint, liaison, diplomatic, political, research, or other special purpose nature" [*Army Dictionary*]. **2. Satellite reconnaissance activities**. The acronym SAO (Special Activities Office) is often used to refer to the compartmented information itself that deals with satellite reconnaissance.

special airlift missions: Air Force airlift mission, conducted mostly by the 89th Military Airlift Wing (MAW), Andrews AFB, MD, but also by other units, involved in transport of the President, key officials of the government, or foreign dignitaries, or of passengers and cargo that the Chief of Staff of the Air Force specifies. The 89th MAW conducts approximately 1,000 airlift missions per year.

special ammunition (see **special weapons**)

Special Atomic Demolition Munition (SADM): A very low-yield, man-portable **atomic demolition munition** that is detonated by a time device. The SADM is used solely by **special operations** forces for detonations behind enemy lines. It is employed by the Army **Special Forces** and by Navy **SEALS**.

special category (SPECAT): "Projects or subjects requiring security protection or handling not guaranteed by the normal **security classification** and requiring that the message be handled and viewed only by specially cleared or authorized personnel" [*Army Dictionary*].

Special Defense Acquisition Fund (SDAF): Part of the **security assistance program** created in FY 1982 by the Reagan Administration and authorized by the Arms Export Control Act to "stockpile arms in anticipation of future **foreign military sales (FMS)** requests . . . . The stockpile is financed by monies received from previous FMS sales, and consists of basic combat gear . . . commonly used by Third World forces" [Department of State, *Congressional Presentation of Security Assistance Program FY 1990*, pp. 33–35]. The Department of Defense proposes to Congress a list of stockpiled defense material to be made available under "the Fund": communications security equipment, tactical vehicle and personnel radios, military vehicles, infantry/cavalry fighting vehicles, towed howitzers, machine guns and mortars, infantry equipment, ordnance and support items, ammunition and ordnance of all types, antitank missiles, rockets and projectiles, air-to-air missiles and ordnance, air-to-surface missiles and munitions, surface-to-air missiles and gun systems, anti-shipping and anti-radiation missiles, multiple-launch rocket systems (MLRS) and rockets, tactical radars, counterbattery radars, utility helicopters and ASW platforms, and aircraft long lead-support. The Department of Defense is responsible for the management of SDAF, and the **Defense Security Assistance Agency (DSAA)** is the executive agency responsible for its day-to-day operation.

SDAF has helped the **National Security Agency (NSA)** implement more orderly planning and management and stabilize procurements to foster interoperability of U.S. secure communications with Australia and New Zealand. Also, it has expedited replenishing the Air Force for security assistance-related withdrawals of **communications security** assets later needed for U.S. communications systems. Congress sets dollar limits each year on stockpile reserves. SDAF's investment of $50 million

in a Supply Support Procurement program with the **Defense Logistics Agency (DLA)** is helping DOD to respond more efficiently to **low-intensity conflict (LIC)** pressures without drawing directly upon U.S. forces. Procurements and sales from the Fund also help force modernization planning and accelerate deliveries to NATO's Southern Flank and sales to Australia and Japan. By keeping equipment on hand that those countries will later purchase with FMS loans, the DSAA can fill material requests rapidly without having to use stockpiles meant for use directly by U.S. forces.

Special Defense Intelligence Notice (SDIN): Defense Intelligence Agency intelligence report to the JCS, the unified and specified commands, the Services, and selected government agencies that gives intelligence about events that could have immediate and significant effects on current planning and operations. (see also **Defense Intelligence Notice**)

special facility   (see **FEMA Special Facility**)

Special Forces: Army **special operations** personnel and organization, popularly referred to as the **Green Berets**. Their special operations missions include foreign military and paramilitary training; **foreign internal defense**; **direct action**; special reconnaissance; and **counterterrorism**. Special Forces are a component of the Army's **First Special Operations Command**. The major unit of organization is the **special forces group (SFG)**. (see also **PSYOPS**, **Civil Affairs**, **Task Force 160**)

special forces group (SFG): 1.
Basic unit of Army **Special Forces**
organization, composed of Green Berets. SFGs are subordinate to the **First
Special Operations Command**. An
SFG is typically composed of three
battalions, signals units, combat support units, and service units. There are
eight SFGs—four in the active component and four in the reserves—all
with regional missions and areas of
concentration, and specially trained
linguists and area officers. An additional SFG to specialize on sub-
Saharan Africa is planned for activation in the 1990s.

Army Special Forces Groups

• 1st SFG, Ft. Lewis, WA 98373:
  East Asia and the Pacific.
• 3d SFG (planned): sub-Saharan
  Africa.
• 5th SFG, Ft. Campbell, KY 42223:
  Southwest Asia and northeast
  Africa.
• 7th SFG, Ft. Bragg, NC 23824:
  Latin America.
• 10th SFG, Ft. Devens, MA 01433:
  Europe and the Mediterranean
  region.
• 11th SFG (USAR), Ft. Meade, MD
  22427
• 12th SFG (USAR), Arlington
  Heights, IL
• 19th SFG (UTARNG), Salt Lake
  City, UT 84065
• 20th SFG (ALARNG), Birming-
  ham, AL 35217

The 1st Bn, 1st SFG is forward-
deployed at Torii Station, Okinawa,
Japan. The 3rd Bn, 7th SFG is forward-deployed at Ft. Davis, Panama.

The 1st Bn, 10th SFG is forward-
deployed at Bad Toelz, West Germany. **2.** Naval special operations unit
(see **naval special forces group**).

special intelligence (SI): One of
the four major types of **sensitive
compartmented information** used to
mark intelligence produced by **signals intelligence (SIGINT)** systems.
Access to SI requires a special security clearance. The three levels of SI
are **UMBRA**, the most sensitive SI
type (Top Secret level); **SPOKE** (Secret level); and **MORAY**, the least
sensitive SI type (Confidential level).
SI material is normally limited to
ground-based and aircraft collection
systems. (see also **SI-TK**)

**Special National Intelligence Esti-
mate (SNIE):   National intelligence
estimate (NIE)** relevant to specific policy problems that need to be addressed in the immediate future.

special nuclear material (SNM): As
listed in the **Atomic Energy Act of
1954**, SNM falls into one of the
two categories of substances used to
produce nuclear weapons: plutonium, uranium enriched in isotopes 233
or 235 (U-233 or U-235), or other
nuclear material, or any material arti-
ficially enriched, but not including
source material (uranium, thorium,
or other material). SNM is also called
active material. Two categories are
used for purposes of storage, shipment, and security of SNM:

Category I

• **1.** "Uranium 235 (contained in Uranium enriched to 20 percent or more

in the isotope U-235) alone, or in combination with Plutonium and Uranium 233 when (multiplying the Plutonium and Uranium 233 content by 2.5), the total is 5,000 grams or more."

- **2.** "Plutonium and Uranium 233 when the Plutonium and Uranium 233 content is 2,000 grams or more."
- **3.** "SNM in lesser quantities but which is located in the same area or shipment with other SNM with which it could be selectively combined to produce the equivalent quantities in" the above.

Category II

- **1.** "Uranium 235 (contained in Uranium enriched to 20 percent or more in the isotope U-235) alone, or in combination with Plutonium and Uranium 233 when (multiplying the Plutonium and/or Uranium 233 content by 2.5) the total is 1,000 to 4,999 grams."
- **2.** "[Plutonium] and Uranium 233 when the Plutonium and Uranium 233 content is 400 grams to 1,999 grams."
- **3.** "SNM in lesser quantities but which is located in the same area or shipment with other SNM with which it could be selectively combined to produce the equivalent quantities in subparagraphs (1) or (2) of this category" [DOE, *Personnel Security Program*, DOE Order DOE 5631.2, 13 November 1980, released under the FOIA].

(see also **sensitive nuclear material production information**, **unclassified controlled nuclear information**)

special operations: "Operations conducted by specially trained, equipped, and organized DOD forces against strategic or tactical targets in pursuit of national military, political, economic, or psychological objectives. These operations may be conducted during periods of peace or hostilities. They may support conventional operations, or they may be prosecuted independently when the use of conventional forces is either inappropriate or infeasible" [*JCS Pub 1*, p. 339].

The peacetime missions assigned are

- Assisting foreign governments or elements of the U.S. government, such as the Central Intelligence Agency, or unified and specified commands in the conduct of their missions;
- Training, advising, and supporting foreign military and paramilitary forces;
- Acquiring specific information in support of strategic collection plans;
- Conducting humanitarian operations;
- **Counter-terrorism**;
- Safeguarding U.S. citizens and property abroad;
- Conducting detainee rescue and evacuation operations;
- Recovering sensitive items;
- Conducting show-of-force operations;
- Supporting **foreign internal defense** operations; and
- Providing clandestine support of other operations.

In wartime, the special forces (SF) conduct strategic, operational, and tactical missions. Strategic missions include the employment of SF at the highest level of command having direct responsibility for the mission (unified command). These strategic missions include

- Foreign internal defense;
- **Unconventional warfare**;
- Strategic reconnaissance;
- **Strike** operations;
- Special light infantry;
- Strategic **psychological operations**;
- **Civil Affairs** support of general-purpose forces;
- Civil Administration;
- Rescue and evacuation; and
- Collective security.

Operational support missions are integrated into the execution of strategic missions. Operational support missions are the same as strategic missions, except that tactical reconnaissance is conducted rather than strategic reconnaissance, and civil administration, rescue and evacuation, and collective security are not conducted. Tactical operations are conducted at the corps level and below. They are not normally conducted by Special Forces or Ranger units, but they do include PSYOP and civil affairs elements.

Special Operations Command (SOC): Subunified command, subordinate to a unified command for the conduct of **special operations** in its theater.

Special Operations Commands

- SOC, Atlantic (SOCLANT), Ft. Bragg, NC 28307
- SOC, Central (SOCCENT), MacDill AFB, FL 33608
- SOC, Europe (SOCEUR), Stuttgart, West Germany
- SOC, Pacific (SOCPAC), Camp H. M. Smith, HI 96861

(see also **U.S. Special Operations Command**)

special operations forces (SOF):   1. Program 11 of the 11 **major force programs** that represent all of the major missions of the Services and are the most basic structural elements of the **Five-Year Defense Program (FYDP)**. It consists of resources identified with SOF forces, including acquisition and operating and support costs. Also included are resources for Air Force Reserve and Air National Guard SOF units. **2.** Elite military units whose primary mission is the conduct of **special operations** and unconventional warfare. All CONUS-based SOF are operationally commanded by the unified **U.S. Special Operations Command**, including **Naval Special Warfare Groups**. **Joint Unconventional Warfare Task Forces** or **Special Operations Commands** exist within each unified command or joint task force to coordinate special operations in the theater. **Counter-terrorism** units are organized in each service and are controlled by the **Joint Special Operations Command**. U.S. Special Operations Forces include:

Unified Command

- **U.S. Special Operations Command (USSOC)**

Subunified Commands

- **Special Operations Command**, Atlantic

- Special Operations Command, Europe
- Special Operations Command, Pacific
- Special Operations Command, Central

Joint Commands

- **Joint Special Operations Command (JSOC)**

Army

- **First Special Operations Command**
- **Special Forces**
- **Delta Force** (Special Operations Detachment, Delta)
- **Rangers**
- **Task Force 160 (TF160)**
- **Psychological Operations (PSYOPS)** units
- **Civil Affairs (CA)** units

Air Force

- 1st **Special Operations Wing**
- 39th Special Operations Wing

Navy

- **Naval Special Warfare Command**
- **Naval Special Warfare Groups**

Marine Corps

- **Marine Amphibious Units (Special Operations Capable) (MAU (SOCs))**

Special Operations Low-Level (SOLL): Category of **special operations** capability composed of Air Force aircrews trained to perform low-level drops of personnel and equipment under hostile conditions. About 130 aircrews are designated as SOLL I-capable. Aircrews also qualified in night-vision goggle use during low-level flights and airland operations are designated SOLL II-capable. Primary Air Force SOLL aircraft are **MC-130 Combat Talons**.

special operations squadron (SOS) (see **special operations wing**)

special operations wing (SOW): Air Force combat wing configured for the conduct of **special operations**. There are two SOWs, subordinate to the 23d Air Force of the Military Airlift Command: the 1st SOW, Hurlburt Field, FL; and the 39th SOW, Eglin AFB, FL. The wings are composed of CONUS-based special operations squadrons; overseas squadrons forward-deployed at Clark AB, Philippines, and Rhein-Main AB, West Germany; special operations groups; Detachment 1 at Howard AFB, Panama; special operations **combat control teams**; and **special operations low-level (SOLL)** aircraft augmentation wings. Dedicated Air Force SOF aircraft include the **MC-130E Combat Talon**, **AC-130H Spectre** gunships, the **MH-60 Pave Hawk**, and **HH/MH-53 Pave Low** helicopters.

special plans: High-priority sensitive or classified programs having to do with activities that may include deception, perception management and public diplomacy, **psychological operations**, **unconventional warfare**, **foreign internal defense**, **special activities**, **counter-terrorism**, military civic action, nation building, **special operations**, and crisis response management. Special plans branches or offices have existed within the JCS Special Operations Division, the Principal Deputy Assistant Secretary of Defense (International Security Affairs), the Defense Intelligence Agency, the Army's Special Operations Office, and the Air Force Directorate of Plans, as well as with some unified, specified, and service combat commands. A Defense Special Plans Office (DSPO) was established by a DOD Directive, 21 April 1982, but it was subsequently disestablished lacking specific authorization from Congress. Some Air Force special plans projects in the Pacific have code words, such as Heavy Sword, Sage Scarab, Heavy Stone, Proper Lady, Heavy Key, and Heavy Door.

special weapon(s): "A term sometimes used to indicate weapons grouped for special procedures, for security, or other reasons. Specific terminology, e.g., nuclear weapons, guided missiles, is preferable" [*JCS Pub 1*, pp. 339–40]. Special weapons include "**a.** Nuclear and nonnuclear warhead sections, atomic demolition munitions, nuclear projectiles, and associated spotting rounds, propelling charges, and repair parts. **b.** Missile bodies (less missiles combining high density, low maintenance and conventional ammunition features), related components of missile bodies (less repair parts), and missile propellants. A complete round is included within the meaning of the term special ammunition . . . **c.** Lethal and incapacitating chemical agents/ammunition" [*Army Dictionary*].

specified command: Operational **combatant command** composed of forces from a single Service, with a continuing and functional mission.

The establishment of specified commands was first authorized by the **National Security Act of 1947**. A command is established by the President and receives orders from the **National Command Authorities (NCA)** through the **Joint Chiefs of Staff**. Operational command is exercised by a single specified commander (the **commander-in-chief (CINC)**) through the commanders of subordinate components. The chain of command specifies that communications between the NCA and the combatant commanders may pass through the **Chairman of the Joint Chiefs of Staff (CJCS)**. The CJCS also acts as the spokesman for CINCs of specified commands on matters including programming and budgets and provides general oversight of the commands regarding their function and mission requirements. The general responsibilities of the CINCs are outlined in the **Unified Command Plan (UCP)**.

There are currently two specified commands: **Forces Command (FORSCOM)** in the Army and **Strategic Air Command (SAC)** in the Air Force. The **Military Airlift Command (MAC)** is now incorporated into the **U.S. Transportation Command** and is no longer a specified command. As mandated by the **Department of Defense Reorganization Act of 1986**, all forces under the jurisdiction of the military departments are assigned to the unified and specified commands, with the exception of those performing specific service missions (e.g., training, administration, supply, maintenance). The individual military departments maintain responsibility for the administrative and logistical support of assigned units and components.

spent fuel: Nuclear fuel that can no longer sustain a chain reaction. The fuel is highly radioactive and contains some recoverable nuclear materials, including uranium and plutonium. Spent fuel is considered high-level **nuclear waste** and is currently stored in pools of water adjacent to nuclear power plants.

SPOKE: Control marking and security clearance level for the moderately sensitive type of **special intelligence**, at the Secret level. (see also **MORAY**, **UMBRA**, **security classification**)

spot intelligence report: "Provides essential **intelligence** covering events or conditions that may have an immediate and significant effect on current planning and operations" [*NWP 3*].

squad: The smallest unit of Army or Marine Corps organization, of which **platoons** are composed. Squads vary in size depending on type (infantry, artillery, engineer, etc.) and are led by a noncommissioned officer called a "squad leader."

squadron: **1.** Basic administrative aviation unit of the Army, Navy, Marine Corps, and Air Force. A squadron is subordinate to a **group** or **wing** in the Navy, Marine Corps, and Air Force. **2.** In the Army, an armored or air **cavalry** unit, equivalent in size to a **battalion**. Army cavalry squadrons are subordinate to regiments or brigades. **3.** In the Navy, two or more divisions of ships or flights of aircraft. Aircraft are normally of the same type. Navy ship squadrons

are normally assigned to groups. Aircraft squadrons are assigned to groups or wings. (see also **type command**)

SR-71 Blackbird: Air Force-operated, multisensor, strategic aerial reconnaissance aircraft. The SR-71 is the fastest flying production aircraft built and it has conducted overflight reconnaissance missions since 1966. SR-71s were assigned to the 9th Strategic Reconnaissance Wing of Strategic Air Command at Beale AFB, CA, until 1989 when they were temporarily retired. The program received an additional $200 million in FY 1990 for restructuring, including transfer of the SR-71 mission to the Air National Guard.

SRAM (Short-Range Attack Missile):   Model designation AGM-69. Air Force nuclear-armed, air-to-surface, supersonic strategic missile carried by **B-52**, **FB-111**, and **B-1B** bombers. The missile, with an effective range of about 60 miles, is used to destroy enemy air defenses to increase the bomber's chances of successfully penetrating to its target. SRAM was initially deployed in 1972, and 1,500 were produced. About 1,100 were left in the Air Force inventory as of 1989. The missile is to be replaced by the **SRAM II** in the early 1990s.

SRAM II (Short-Range Attack Missile II):   Model designation AGM-131. Air Force nuclear-armed, air-to-surface, supersonic strategic missile under development to replace the **SRAM**. The missile will arm **B-1B** and **B-2** bombers and will have offensive missions against mobile targets as well as the defense suppression missions currently available with the SRAM. Higher missile velocity, greater accuracy, and greater range will be provided. Boeing Aerospace won the contract for the Full-Scale Development in December 1986. The SRAM II will be capable of penetrating advanced defensive threats from stand-off range to strike hardened/defended and mobile targets. It will have a range of 250 km.

Planned procurement is for 1,633 missiles. Boeing Aerospace Corporation is the prime contractor. Previous funding profiles and development paces were to have procured the first missile in FY 1990, with a scheduled operational date of April 1993. The FY 1990 budget request was only $227.8 million, and the first year of procurement slipped to FY 1991. The request for the purchase of 25 missiles in FY 1991 is $296 million. The missile is now likely to be operational in 1994. A tactical version of the SRAM II, designated SRAM-T (Short-Range Attack Missile—Tactical) is the main candidate to become the Air Force's nuclear-armed **tactical air-to-surface missile (TASM)** for deployment in Europe.

SS/SSN: Designation for a diesel-powered/nuclear-powered attack submarine. (see also **attack submarine, Los Angeles, naval nuclear propulsion, Sea Wolf (SSN-21) class submarine**)

SSB (single-sideband): High-frequency communications operating mode that performs the same function as AM (amplitude modulation) but with greater efficiency. The SSB transmitter transmits only an upper sideband (USB) or lower sideband (LSB) with very little carrier. All of the transmitted signal is therefore used, with clearer intelligence. An SSB transmitter, consuming no more power than an AM transmitter, provides about eight times the communications capability and so conserves the radio spectrum. SSB also provides longer range.

SSBN: Designation for a nuclear-powered ballistic missile submarine. (see also **fleet ballistic missile submarine, naval nuclear propulsion, Poseidon, Trident**)

SSM (surface-to-surface missile): A surface-launched missile designed to operate against a target on the surface.

SSN-21 (see **Sea Wolf (SSN-21) class submarine**)

staff officer: An officer belonging to an administrative staff. (see also **officer**)

STANAVFORCHAN (see **Standing Naval Force Channel**)

STANAVFORLANT (see **Standing Naval Force Atlantic**)

Standard ARM: Model designation AGM-78. Air Force passive homing air-to-surface anti-radiation missile originally designed as a follow-on to the Shrike.

standardization: Processes by which allied forces achieve the closest practicable cooperation and the most efficient use of research, development, and production resources, by agreeing to adopt on the broadest possible bases common, compatible, interchangeable, and/or interoperable criteria and procedures, supplies, components, weapons, equipment, organization, and doctrine. (see also **rationalization, standardization, and interoperability (RSI)**)

Standard missile (SM): Model designation RIM-66/RIM-67. A family of Navy supersonic, medium- and extended-range surface-to-air and surface-to-surface missiles. Standards provide all-weather anti-aircraft and surface-to-surface armament for cruisers, destroyers, and guided missile frigates. It has replaced the Tartar and **Terrier** surface-to-air missiles and is equipping about 100 ships. The missile has four configurations (sequential upgrades are called "blocks"):

• Standard-1 (SM-1) Medium-Range (MR);
• Standard-1 (SM-1) Extended-Range (ER);
• Standard-2 (SM-2) Medium-Range (MR); and
• Standard-2 (SM-2) Extended-Range (ER).

In recent years, the SM-1 (MR) Block VI, SM-2 (MR) Block II, and SM-2 (ER) Block II have been procured. The Navy has identified a need to increase SM-2 inventories for new cruiser deliveries. Greater low-altitude fuze enhancements will be incorporated into the SM-2 missile after FY 1988 to improve its effectiveness against sea-skimming anti-

ship missiles. These will be designated SM-2 Block III missiles.

SM-1 MR (RIM-66B) is a medium-range (15–20 nm) missile using passive or semi-active homing. It is propelled by an integral dual-thrust rocket motor. SM-1 MR is installed on frigates, destroyers, and cruisers equipped with Tartar and AEGIS combat systems. SM-1 ER (RIM-67B) is an extended-range surface launch missile using passive/semi-active homing or midcourse command guidance. It is propelled by a detachable rocket booster and integral sustainer rocket motor. SM-1 ER is installed on cruisers and destroyers equipped with Terrier combat systems.

SM-2 MR (RIM-66C) is a medium-range (up to 90 nm) missile incorporating midcourse guidance, allowing the missile to be launched on cueing from search radar information only. The missile is redirected in midflight and then again during the terminal homing phase. It also has electronic counter-countermeasures (ECCM) improvements that provide immunity to a broad scope of electronic jamming. SM-2 MR is installed on Tartar New Threat Upgrade (NTU) and AEGIS-equipped destroyers and cruisers. The SM-2 (MR) Block II/III missile is the primary air defense weapon for Ticonderoga class (CG-47) cruisers. Arleigh Burke class (DDG-51) destroyers and the 10 ships in the California, Virginia, and Kidd classes will receive SM-2 MR capability with the Tartar NTU conversion. In the future, Oliver Hazard Perry class (FFG-7) guided missile frigates will also be upgraded with SM-2 MR and NTU. The SM-2 (ER) Block II/III missile, with a range of approximately 65 nm, will be the primary air defense weapon for Leahy, Belknap, Bainbridge, Truxton, and Long Beach class Terrier guided missile cruisers planned to receive the NTU conversion when Terrier missiles are removed. In combination with the AEGIS and NTU systems, the SM-2 provides the ability to conduct simultaneous multiple engagements against high- and low-profile missiles and aircraft. An AEGIS Extended Range version of SM-2 Block IV may be deployed on future Ticonderoga and Burke class ships.

Plans were to equip the SM-2s with a W81 low-kiloton enhanced radiation nuclear warhead and designate it the SM-2(N). These plans, however, were canceled in 1986. SM-2 missile contractors are General Dynamics of Pomona, CA, and Raytheon of Lowell, MA. The budget request for FY 1990 procurement of 590 missiles was $485.1 million. The FY 1991 request for 900 missiles is $646 million.

standard operating procedure   (see **SOP**)

standby base: An austere base, designated for wartime use, having adequate airfield facilities to accept deployed aircraft. Standby bases will be maintained in a caretaker status until augmented, at which time they will be capable of receiving and employing assigned aircraft. To initiate and sustain operations, all supporting personnel, supplies, and equipment must be provided. Fuel and munitions may be pre-positioned in a state of readiness for use by the deploying forces.

Standby Reserve: A category of reserve personnel, in addition to the **Ready Reserve** and the **Retired Reserve**, whose members are temporarily unavailable for immediate mobilization. Such members are not paid and do not participate in training, although they have the option of training for retirement credit. Members in active status are completing their statutory military terms of service, being retained in an active status, requesting assignment to the active status list from the Ready Reserve, or temporarily unassigned due to temporary physical disability, hardship, or other reason. Those in inactive status are not required by law or regulation to remain in active status but retain their reserve affiliation for possible future activation. Mobilization of the Standby Reserve may begin upon the Congressional declaration of a national emergency. Total personnel strength of the Standby Reserve is about 38,000. The Army and Air National Guards do not use this category. (see also **Army Reserve**, **Air Force Reserve**)

stand-down: The   period   during which forces cease routine activities and concentrate on maintenance, supply, personnel actions, and other steps to improve performance in preparation for maximum operational efforts and active military operations. A standdown period usually follows intense training periods, overseas deployments, or field exercises.

Standing Consultative Commission (SCC): U.S.–Soviet group established by the **SALT I** Treaty to deal with compliance and verification issues and obligations. In June 1979, the SCC also assumed these duties for the **SALT II** Treaty. The SCC is composed of equal numbers of American and Soviet representatives who meet twice a year in month-long sessions to discuss amendments to the treaties and verification disputes. (see also **ABM Treaty**)

Standing Naval Force Atlantic (STANAVFORLANT): One of two permanent international maritime forces, and a **major subordinate command** of NATO's **Allied Command Atlantic (ACLANT)**. STANAVFORLANT is the only force assigned to ACLANT in peacetime and normally consists of four destroyer-type ships.

Headquarters
Afloat (FPO New York 09501)

Standing Naval Force Channel (STANAVFORCHAN): One of two permanent international maritime forces, and a **major subordinate command** of NATO's **Allied Command Channel (ACCHAN)**, established in 1973. It is the only force assigned to ACCHAN in peacetime and consists of mine countermeasures ships provided from Belgium, West Germany, the Netherlands, and the United Kingdom. It is commanded by the Allied Commander-in-Chief Channel (CINCHAN), a British Admiral.

Headquarters
Afloat (APO New York 09083)

Starlifter (see **C-141 Starlifter**)

START (Strategic Arms Reduction Talks): Current set of U.S.–Soviet negotiations to achieve strategic arms control. Previous arms control negotiations, such as **SALT I** and **SALT II**, had concentrated on limiting the number of launchers rather than the number of warheads, and on achieving greater "stability" regardless of reductions in nuclear force size. With the increase in MIRVed missiles, however, the Reagan Administration moved to reduce the actual number of nuclear weapons, especially those on **ICBMs**, while at the same time embarking on its Strategic Modernization Program unveiled in October 1981. In May 1982, the official U.S. START position was unveiled in a speech by President Reagan, who called for equal numbers of ballistic missile warheads, at two thirds the current level with no more than half of the warheads on ICBMs, with a second phase to address equal ceilings on other forces, including equal amounts of missile throwweight. In June 1982, the START negotiations opened.

The U.S. delegation tabled a proposal of a ceiling of 5,000 ballistic missile warheads with no more than 2,500 of these on ICBMs and a maximum of 850 ballistic missiles. This would have meant a severe cut in Soviet land-based forces and a less drastic cut in U.S. forces. The Soviets countered this proposal with one offering an 1,800-launcher ceiling with no sublimits on types of launchers and warheads. This resembled the Carter SALT II "deep cuts" proposal put forth in March 1977, which was rejected at that time by the Soviet delegation.

In December 1983, the United States deployed **Ground-Launched Cruise Missiles** and **Pershing II** missiles in Europe, and the Soviet Union walked out of the START negotiations in protest. The original proposals were at a stalemate, although some compromises had been proffered. The United States offered to raise the ceiling of 850 missiles to 1,250; to consider additional bomber limits; and to have a "build-down" to reach limits. The Soviet Union offered subceilings on MIRVed ballistic missiles and ICBMs.

In 1984, the United States tried to resume the talks, using START as a precondition for anti-satellite negotiations, but the Soviet Union declined. In 7 January 1985, Secretary of State George Shultz and Soviet Foreign Minister Andrei Gromyko met in Geneva to discuss the status of U.S.–Soviet arms control. Agreement was reached on a three-part "umbrella" approach to arms control covering strategic defensive, strategic offensive, and intermediate offensive systems (the **Nuclear and Space Talks**). The Soviet Union considered this to be an arms control package, whereas the U.S. negotiators operated under the assumption that progress could be made in one area regardless of the status of the other two. In November 1985, President Reagan and General Secretary Gorbachev met for the first time in Geneva. They agreed in principle to seek 50 percent reductions in strategic offensive forces and to meet again in Washington in 1986 and in Moscow in 1987.

In October 1986, Reagan and Gorbachev met in Reykjavik, Iceland, for their second summit. Tentative agreement was reached on a plan to reduce all strategic nuclear forces by 50 percent within the first five years of a ten-year accord, and a framework was devised for reducing INF missiles to 100 warheads per side, not deployed in Europe. The issue of nuclear testing was also discussed, but the United States was not willing to accept a comprehensive test ban as the basis for any testing negotiations. No final agreement was reached at Reykjavik because of differences over SDI and the interpretations of the ABM Treaty.

On 8 May 1987, the United States presented a draft treaty at the START talks in Geneva. This draft reflected most of the areas of agreement settled on at Reykjavik. The Soviet Union presented a draft treaty on 31 July 1987. These treaties serve as the elements for the joint draft treaty presently being negotiated. At the Washington summit meeting in December 1987, in addition to signing the INF Treaty, Reagan and Gorbachev agreed to work toward the completion of a START agreement at the earliest possible date. The basic provisions called for a ceiling of no more than 1,600 strategic offensive delivery systems, 6,000 warheads, and 1,540 warheads on a maximum of 154 heavy missiles. It was later decided to put a sublimit of 4,900 on the total number of ballistic missile warheads. Also, a method for counting warheads on existing ballistic missiles was agreed to, and guidelines for effective verification were set down. As of 1989, differences remained in the areas of mobile ICBMS, long-range sea-launched cruise missiles

(SLCMs), counting rules for air-launched cruise missiles, and certain aspects of verification.

On 29 May 1988, Reagan and Gorbachev met in Moscow for their fourth summit. They exchanged the instruments of ratification used for the **INF Treaty**, and Secretary of State George Shultz and Soviet Foreign Minister Eduard Shevardnadze signed two minor agreements establishing the Joint Verification Experiment (for measuring the yields of nuclear tests at each other's test sites) and the requirement that both parties give 24-hour notice of ICBM and SLBM test launches. Gorbachev asked the United States to sign an agreed statement of "peaceful coexistence," but the United States declined on the ground that the text was "ambiguous [and] freighted with the baggage of the past." In December 1988, Gorbachev addressed the United Nations and met with Reagan and President-elect George Bush in New York. In his U.N. speech, Gorbachev proposed unilateral Soviet cuts in conventional weapons and manpower and stated that START, a chemical weapons ban, and the Conventional Stability Talks were the leading issues of the U.S.–Soviet arms control agenda.

In June 1989, the START talks reopened in Geneva under the Bush Administration and centered on several main unresolved issues. The first was the problem of how to count air-launched cruise missiles (ALCMs). In Reykjavik, the U.S. and Soviet delegations took the position that ICBM, SLBM, and ALCM warheads would be counted one-for-one. Now, however, the United States wanted to count ALCMs by the "notional counting rule," meaning they would assign a value in relation to how many warheads a loaded bomber could theoretically carry. In addition, despite calls for more stringent verification practices, the United States refused to allow Soviet on-site inspections of bomber loadings.

The second question dealt with SLCMs. In Reykjavik, Reagan and Gorbachev agreed that SLCMs would be controlled separately from the central treaty limits of 6,000 warheads. The Soviet Union originally proposed an SLCM limit of 400 nuclear and 600 conventional warheads. The U.S. position, however, was that both sides should exchange "non binding declarations" of force size and deployments and keep one another informed of SLCM developments, but that no cuts should be made in SLCM levels. Again, the United States position was that it would not permit Soviet on-site inspections of SLCM loadings on ships that are not themselves counted in the treaty.

On mobile missiles, the Soviet position was to permit mobile missiles on land but with numerical limits of approximately 1,600 reentry vehicles in mobile modes. The U.S. delegation took the position that mobile missiles should be banned, although DOD is planning to build at least one, if not two, mobile missiles itself, and the Bush Administration will likely remove the U.S. proposal for a mobile missile ban. Verification of mobile missiles is centered on road-mobile systems, with not much attention to rail-mobile models. And the question of deploying any type of SDI system while at the same time reducing offensive forces is still a matter of debate between the two countries. The Bush Administration has also linked the START negotiations with cuts in conventional forces, a link some critics say decreases the chance for agreements on both conventional and strategic forces.

The current reduction numbers agreed upon by the U.S. and Soviet delegations are for no more than 6,000 warheads on 1,600 ICBMs, SLBMs, and heavy bombers, with sublimits of 4,900 on the aggregate number of ICBM and SLBM warheads and 1,540 on heavy missile warheads (applicable to Soviet SS-18s and follow-ons). The agreed-upon reduction period is seven years [CRS, *Fundamentals of Nuclear Arms Control. Part I—Nuclear Arms Control. A Brief Historical Survey*, Report for the House Committee on Foreign Affairs, Subcommittee on Arms Control, International Security and Science, 20 May 1985; ACA, *Brief History of U.S.–Soviet Summit Conferences: 1955–1988*, December 1988; Michele Flournoy, "START Cutting Soviet Strategic Forces," *Arms Control Today*, June 1989; ACA Press Briefing, "Resumption of U.S.–Soviet START Negotiations in Geneva," 19 June 1989].

State Defense Force (SDF): A temporary state militia that serves as a state military reserve force and becomes active upon the federalization of the state **National Guard**. SDFs, originally called "Home Guards" and sometimes called "Militias," functioned sporadically in World Wars I and II and during the Korean War. Today, 22 states maintain State Defense Forces in addition to their National Guard formations.

Status of Resources and Training System (SORTS): The primary **Worldwide Military Command and Control System** (**WWMCCS**) data source of force availability, which describes by **C-rating** each registered unit in terms of personnel, equipment and supplies on hand, equipment condition, and training. The category level compares current status against the required resources and training. This automated file supports operation planning and command and control functions. DOD Directive S-5100.44, "Master Plan for the National Military Command System," directs that the **National Military Command Center** and the **Alternate National Military Command Center (ANMCC)** have access to all information required for normal operations and for an analysis of any crisis situation. SORTS reports the registration of each unit, the unique unit status and identity information, basic identity data elements of units and changes to support, and the status of a selected registered organization of foreign nations committed to combined operations. Organization and unit identity and status information is accumulated, refined, updated, and filed for rapid recall. SORTS submissions are made via **AUTODIN**, with **WWMCCS Intercomputer Network (WIN)** used as a backup.

SORTS was formerly the Unit Status and Identity Report (UNITREP), which is being incorporated into the new formats. The UNITREP is one of numerous reporting systems constituting the **Joint Reporting Struc-**

ture, which is designed to provide the National Command Authority (NCA) with information on logistics, communications, nuclear operations, and other functions during both peacetime and wartime conditions. All military services are required to report basic unit status and identity information through the UNITREP system. It maintains an inventory of military units, tracks their locations, and reports the activities they are involved in. Specific information elements include

- Home and present locations;
- Operational and administrative chains-of-command;
- Current activity, such as deploying to station or training;
- Level and type codes;
- Parent organization;
- Nuclear and conventional equipment;
- Equipment crew status; and
- The status of JCS-controlled- and transportable communications equipment.

UNITREP also reports on the **readiness** of combat, combat support, and service-selected combat service support units (both active and reserve). These units report in terms of combat readiness ratings (C-ratings), which measure a unit's ability to perform wartime tasks by assessing the peacetime availability and status of resources possessed or controlled by the unit or its parent unit in four resource areas. These are

- Equipment and supplies on hand;
- Equipment condition;
- Personnel; and
- Training.

Generally, units report UNITREP data to a major command, which in turn relays the data to the ANMCC for the JCS. UNITREP data are reported as changes occur and reach the JCS within 24 hours of the change. The UNITREP data base is maintained by the JCS, and from it over 50 reports are periodically generated and used by various elements of DOD. The data base is used for general unit status monitoring and management purposes, such as highlighting resource shortages that affect unit readiness. UNITREP was adopted in April 1980 and replaced the Force Status and Identity Report (FORSTAT) reporting system, which had been established in 1968. UNITREP information is the basic source of data to compile the SORTS.

stealth: A technology designed to reduce the vulnerability of aircraft and cruise missiles to detection by enemy forces by reducing the **radar cross-section**. Stealth technologies include shapes, materials, and chemical coverings that reduce visibility to radar, infrared, or optical sensors. The "Stealth" bomber, formally known as the **B-2**, is the main stealth program, although an **F-117A** tactical stealth fighter and the stealth **Advanced Cruise Missile** also use stealth technologies. The Air Force is developing a new tactical fighter, the **Advanced Tactical Fighter**, and the Navy is developing the **A-12 Advanced Tactical Aircraft**; both of these incorporate stealth characteristics. Stealth programs and technologies are categorized and controlled as **special access programs**.

stick: 1. A succession of missiles fired or released separately at predetermined intervals from a single aircraft. 2. The number of parachutists who jump from one aperture or door of an aircraft during one run over a dropping zone.

Stinger: Air Force, Army, Marine Corps, and Navy man-portable, shoulder-fired, infrared-guided, disposable surface-to-air missile replacing the Redeye missile. The missile comes in a disposable launch tube with a reusable grip stock and an Identification, Friend or Foe (IFF) unit. It is used for air defense against jet, prop-driven, and helicopter aircraft. The missile is 1.52 meters in length and has a range of 5 km. It can attack much faster targets than Redeye can. Prime contractors are General Dynamics Valley Systems Division, Ontario, CA; and Raytheon Corporation, Lowell, MA. A follow-on seeker (Stinger–POST) improvement program gives Stinger greater capability in certain infrared countermeasures environments. The Stinger-Reprogrammable microprocessor (RMP) further enhances performance in infrared countermeasures environments and provides the capability to make future changes to the missile through a replaceable software module. The basic Stinger was operationally deployed with U.S. forces in West Germany in 1981. Basic Stinger production is completed. Stinger–POST entered production in FY 1983, and first deliveries were made in September 1986. Production was completed in August 1987. Stinger-RMP initial production and deliveries occurred in FY 1989.

The Navy activated its first Stinger missile detachment in 1987. Its final buy was made in FY 1988. Stinger missiles were deployed aboard Sixth Fleet ships in the Mediterranean in 1983 in response to the possibility of terrorist attacks upon U.S. ships. The Marine Corps uses Stingers for forward-area units, troops on the move, and rear installations. The final year of Marine Corps procurement was FY 1989, when 3,115 Stingers were purchased for $141.1 million.

The Pedestal-Mounted Stinger (PMS) is an Army program of incorporating eight ready-fire Stinger missiles, integrated with sensors, on a High-Mobility Multipurpose Wheeled Vehicle (HMMWV). PMS has a two-person crew and can fire on the move. This will provide low-altitude air defense in divisions, armored cavalry regiments, and corps-level air defense brigades. The prime contractor is Boeing Corporation, Huntsville, AL.

stockpile: 1. A stored and maintained supply of ordnance, fuel, or other war materiel, usually available for generated combat operations or for use by deployed forces. Stockpiled supplies are used to allow the sustainment of combat operations for certain periods of time, before external supplies have to be brought in.   2. Nuclear weapons and components whose custody has been transferred from the Department of Energy (DOE) to DOD with the following exceptions: weapons and components transferred from DOD to DOE, retired weapons, and weapons dropped from accountability due to use or loss.

Commanders-in-Chief, Strategic Air Command

GEN George C. Kenney, USAF	21 Mar 1946	18 Oct 1948
GEN Curtis E. LeMay, USAF	19 Oct 1948	30 Jun 1957
GEN Thomas S. Power, USAF	1 Jul 1957	30 Nov 1964
GEN John D. Ryan, USAF	1 Dec 1964	21 Jan 1967
GEN Joseph J. Nazzaro, USAF	1 Feb 1967	28 Jul 1968
GEN Bruce K. Holloway, USAF	29 Jul 1968	30 Apr 1972
GEN John C. Meyer, USAF	1 May 1972	31 Jul 1974
GEN Russell E. Dougherty, USAF	1 Aug 1974	31 Jul 1977
GEN Richard H. Ellis, USAF	1 Aug 1977	31 Jul 1981
GEN Bennie L. Davis, USAF	1 Aug 1981	31 Jul 1985
GEN Larry D. Welch, USAF	1 Aug 1985	30 Jun 1986
GEN John T. Chain, Jr., USAF	1 Jul 1986	present

stockpile-to-target sequence (STS): The process involved in removing a nuclear weapon from storage and assembling, testing, transporting, and delivering it to the target. For each nuclear weapon, the logistical and employment concepts and physical environments important to its delivery are included in a stockpile-to-target report, which is then used to guide the weapon's handling. The STS is constantly reviewed to evaluate flaws in handling, operations, and security.

strategic: 1. The nation's offensive and defensive military potential, including its geographic location and its economic, political, and military strength. **2.** Weapons or forces capable of directly affecting another nation's strategic position and warfighting capacity. **3.** Weapons capable of delivering a nuclear warhead at ranges in excess of 5,500 km.

Strategic Air Command (SAC): Air Force **major command** and JCS **specified command**, established as the Continental Air Forces on 15 December 1944 and redesignated as SAC on 21 March 1946. It is the Air Forces' long-range strike force and is composed of strategic bombers, strategic reconnaissance aircraft, aerial tankers, and **ICBMs**. It also operates the **National Emergency Airborne Command Post** fleet and the SAC airborne command post fleet in the **Post-Attack Command and Control System**. SAC flies over 2,000 aircraft, including over 400 bombers, and maintains over 1,000 ICBMs. Up to 30 percent of its bomber and tanker force and nearly all of its ICBMs are on constant alert. SAC operates at 24 bases in CONUS and one overseas base, with units located at 55 additional bases of other commands worldwide. Its personnel strength is approximately 115,000 civilian and military personnel.

Headquarters
Offutt AFB, NE 68113

Subordinate Commands

- 8th Air Force, Barksdale AFB, LA 71110
- 15th Air Force, March AFB, CA 92518
- 544th Strategic Intelligence Wing, Offutt AFB, NE 68113

strategic airlift: **1.** The continuous or sustained movement of units, personnel, and materiel in support of all DOD agencies between area commands, between CONUS and overseas areas, or within an area of command when directed. This mission, the responsibility of the **Military Airlift Command**, is performed by C–5 and C-141 aircraft. **2.** Long-range transport that allows the projection of forces quickly to any point on the globe. Strategic airlift resources possess the capability to airland or airdrop troops, supplies, and equipment over long distances for the augmentation of tactical forces when required.

Strategic Arms Limitation Talks (SALT) (see **SALT I, SALT II, ABM Treaty**)

Strategic Arms Reduction Talks (see **START**)

strategic attack: "An attack by means of aerospace forces directed at selected vital targets of an enemy nation so as to destroy its war-making capacity or will to fight" [*Air Force Glossary*, AFM 11-1, Vol. 1, 2 January 1976].

strategic defense: Strategies and forces designed primarily to protect the nation from **general war**, including defense against ballistic missiles, bombers, and cruise missiles. This defense depends on weapons that can shoot down other weapons.

Strategic Defense Command (see **U.S. Army Strategic Defense Command**)

Strategic Defense Initiative (SDI): Program formally created by President Reagan in his "Star Wars" speech of 23 March 1983 in which he proposed "a comprehensive and intensive effort to define a long-term research and development program to begin to achieve our ultimate goal of eliminating the threat posed by strategic nuclear missiles." In January 1984, the **Strategic Defense Initiative Organization (SDIO)** was established under DOD to undertake "a comprehensive program to develop the key technologies associated with concepts for defense against ballistic missiles." In June of the same year, the **Homing Overlay Experiment (HOE)** successfully intercepted and destroyed a mock ballistic missile warhead in its midcourse phase of flight; this laid the foundation for the **ERIS (Exoatmospheric Reentry Vehicle Interceptor Subsystem)**. On 18 March 1985, Secretary of Defense Caspar Weinberger invited 18 allied governments to participate in the SDI program. In September 1985, two SDI experiments were conducted: a ground-based directed-energy experiment in which the Mid-Infrared Advanced Chemical Laser (**MIRACL**) successfully destroyed a Titan booster at White Sands Missile Range, NM; and one in which a laser beam, adjusted for atmospheric distortion, was propagated from the ground into space at the Maui Optical Site, HI.

In October 1985, President Reagan decided to define the **ABM Treaty** in its broadest sense, and, in November, the U.S. delegation at the Nuclear and Space Talks offered an "open laboratory" arrangement with the Soviet Union on strategic defense research.

From April–June 1986, a series of kinetic-energy tests of guidance technologies for warhead interception were run with the **Flexible Lightweight Agile Guided Experiments (FLAGE)**. In July 1986, following a particle beam experiment that irradiated an anti-satellite miniature homing vehicle with a proton beam, President Reagan proposed that both the United States and the Soviet Union agree not to deploy advanced strategic weapons through 1991, at which time plans for sharing strategic defenses and eliminating ballistic missiles would be negotiated.

U.S. testing of SDI components continued, and, in September 1986, the Delta 180 rocket launched the first laser radar ever flown in space, collecting data for characterizing rocket plumes during their boost phases. The next month, at the Reykjavik summit, President Reagan and General Secretary Gorbachev came close to achieving dramatic reductions of offensive ballistic missiles, but Soviet objections to SDI precluded a final agreement. Over a year later, on 30 November 1987, the Soviet Union admitted to conducting research similar to SDI. Gorbachev stated in an interview with NBC-TV that "practically, the Soviet Union is doing all that the United States is doing, and I guess we are engaged in research, basic research, which relates to those aspects which are covered by SDI in the United States." At the summit meeting in Washington in December 1987, Reagan and Gorbachev agreed to instruct their Geneva delegations to observe the ABM Treaty as before while researching, developing, and testing SDI systems. In February 1988, the Delta 181

rocket was launched from Cape Canaveral, FL, with SDI sensors and 14 test objects. The objects were deployed into space, and active and passive sensors were used to characterize the objects in a variety of space environments. On 14 March 1988, at a conference assessing the first five years of SDI, President Reagan stated that the United States "will continue to research SDI, to develop and test it. And, as it becomes ready, we will deploy it." The next week, on 23 March, the groundbreaking for the construction of the SDI National Test Facility was held. The facility serves as the coordinating point for various electronically linked facilities, including the **National Test Bed**.

The SDI research program is divided into five key technology areas: directed-energy weapons; kinetic-energy weapons; surveillance, acquisition, tracking, and kill assessment systems; surveillance and analysis/-battle management; and survivability, lethality, and key technologies (space logistics and power). SDI research is aimed at a 1990s decision deploying ground- and space-based weapons, but program goals are being altered by the Bush Administration. Sensors, kinetic-energy weapons, and battle management systems will receive emphases. More exotic weapons, such as neutral particle beams, are not expected to emerge as weapons deployment candidates until the late 1990s or beyond. During FY 1987, the Defense Acquisition Board recommended that certain SDI technologies enter the demonstration and validation phase of the defense acquisition process. The purpose of this phase is to evaluate, through analysis, experimentation, and simulation, the feasibility of critical elements of a potential SDI system.

In October 1988, the SDI Phase I space-based system deployment costs were estimated at $70 billion. There is some discussion, however, of replacing Phase I space-based deployment with a concept called **Brilliant Pebbles**, a program deploying free-flying singlets of interceptors rather than clustered groups. Brilliant Pebbles does not include the midcourse sensors a multi-layered full-Phase I deployment would have.

SDI programs and components include **Surveillance, Acquisition, Tracking, and Kill Assessment (SATKA); Battle Management/-Command, Control, and Communications**; and **Survivability, Lethality, and Key Technologies (SLKT)**.

SDI **sensors** under development include

- **Boost Surveillance and Tracking System (BSTS);**
- **Space Surveillance and Tracking System (SSTS);**
- **Ground-Based Surveillance and Tracking System (GSTS);**
- **Airborne Optical Adjunct (AOA);**
- **Terminal Imaging Radar (TIR);**
- **Space-Based Imaging Radar and Imaging Laser**; and
- **Ground-Based Radar (GBR).**

Directed-energy weapons under development include

- **Space-Based Laser;**
- **Ground-Based Laser;**
- **Space-Based Neutral Particle Beam;**
- **Nuclear-Directed Energy Weapon (NDEW);**

- **Talon Gold;**
- **Delphi**; and
- **Alpha/LODE/LAMP.**

Kinetic-energy weapons under development include

- **Space-Based Interceptor;**
- **Hypervelocity Launcher;**
- **SLBM Boost-Phase Engagement;**
- **Space-Based Kinetic Kill Vehicle;**
- **Homing Overlay Experiment (HOE);**
- **ERIS** (Exoatmospheric Reentry Vehicle Interception System);
- **High Endoatmospheric Defense Interceptor (HEDI):**
- **Flexible Lightweight Agile Guided Experiment (FLAGE)**; and
- **Extended-Range Interceptor (ER-INT).**

In FY 1989, $3,793.4 million was appropriated for SDI. The FY 1990 request was for $4.6 billion, and the FY 1991 request was for $5.4 billion.

Strategic Defense Initiative Organization (SDIO):   One of 13 agencies of the **Department of Defense**, established 23 July 1984. Its mission is the management of DOD, non-DOD, and private research on advanced technologies, namely anti-ballistic missile systems in support of the **Strategic Defense Initiative** program. Its organizations and functions document states, "the goal of the SDIO is to eliminate the threat posed by nuclear ballistic missiles and to increase the contribution of defensive systems to the U.S. and Allied security." The three program areas of the SDIO are basic and applied research; feasibility experiments; and demonstration of new technologies. In addition to its nine program offices, SDIO consists of a Chief Scientist, who serves as liaison to the scientific and technical community, and an Assistant for Countermeasures, who oversees a "Red Team" of senior-level representatives from DOD, the Services, DOD agencies, and the intelligence community; these personnel continually evaluate U.S. technical and tactical countermeasures to Soviet ballistic missile offenses.

SDIO reports directly to the Secretary of Defense. Guidance and oversight of the SDI program is provided by an Executive Committee. Committee members include Deputy Secretary of Defense (chair); Chairman of the Joint Chiefs of Staff; the Under Secretaries of Defense; Assistant Secretary of Defense (Comptroller); Chair, Nuclear Weapons Council; Director, Defense Advanced Research Projects Agency; and Director, Defense Nuclear Agency.

Headquarters
Pentagon, Washington, DC 20301

Offices

- Kinetic Energy
- Survivability, Lethality, and Key Technologies
- Resource Management
- Directed Energy
- Systems
- External Affairs
- Sensors
- Innovative Science and Technologies
- Support Services

[DOD, OSD, *Management of the Strategic Defense Initiative*, 24 April 1984; *Functions of the Strategic Defense Initiative Organization*, n.d.].

strategic forces: Program 1 of the 11 **major force programs**, which represent all of the major missions of the Services and are the most basic structural elements of the **Five-Year Defense Program**. It consists of strategic offensive forces and strategic defensive forces, including operational management headquarters, logistics, and associated support organizations.

strategic offense: Strategy and forces designed primarily to destroy the enemy's war-making capacity by degrading it to the point that the opposition collapses.

strategic reserve: 1. A reinforcement combat force not committed in advance to a specific NATO **major subordinate command**. It may be deployed to any area for a mission designated by the major NATO commander [*JCS Pub 1*, Ch. 2, p. B-31]. **2.** Common designation for nuclear weapons systems assigned to the **nuclear reserve force**.

strategic warning: Intelligence information or intelligence regarding the threat of the initiation of hostilities against the United States or hostilities in which U.S. forces may become involved. Strategic warning may be received at any time prior to the initiation of hostilities. (see also **indication & warning**, **tactical warning**, **early warning**)

Stratofortress   (see **B-52**)

Streaker: Model designation MGM-107A/B/D. Air Force and Army recoverable, variable-speed, standard, subscale target drone. The B version was ordered in quantity in April 1983, and deliveries were made between August 1984 and May 1985. The D version has a more powerful engine and is used to test and evaluate air-to-air missiles. Streakers are assigned to Tyndall AFB, FL, and Wallace AS, Philippines, for use in training.

Streamliner: National Security Agency-controlled secure communications system for the transmission of **signals intelligence (SIGINT)** material.

strike mission: 1. In NATO and the Navy, nuclear weapons missions, particularly those involving dual-capable aircraft. **2.** In **special operations**: interdiction, raids, and personnel recovery operations. These are specific acts conducted in an overt, covert, clandestine, or low-visibility mode in hostile or denied areas.

Striking and Support Force Southern Europe (STRIKFORSOUTH): A **principle subordinate command** of NATO's **Allied Forces Southern Europe**. It is responsible for naval operations in southern Europe, including the Mediterranean Sea; from the Straits of Gibraltar to the coast of Syria, including the Adriatic, Ionian, and Agean Seas; plus the Sea of Marmara and the Black Sea outside Soviet waters. It is commanded by an American admiral (commander of the U.S. **Sixth Fleet**). When operational, STRIKFORSOUTH consists of the U.S. Sixth Fleet and eight **task forces** of about 40 ships and 200 aircraft.

Headquarters
Naples, Italy
(FPO New York 09524)

Fleet Flagship
USS Puget Sound

Task Forces

- TF 60 Carrier Strike Force (TF 502 when NATO-assigned)
- TF 61 Amphibious Task Force, shipping (TF 503 when NATO-assigned)
- TF 62 Main element (TF 504 when NATO-assigned)
- TF 63 Logistics Support Force (TF 505 when NATO-assigned)
- TF 69 (SUBMED when NATO-assigned)
- Commander Maritime Air Forces, Mediterranean (COMFAIRMED)
- **Naval On-Call Forces, Mediterranean (NAVOCFORMED)**

Striking Fleet Atlantic Command: A **major subordinate command** of NATO's **Allied Command Atlantic**. Its **principle subordinate command** is the Carrier Striking Force, which consists of Carrier Striking Groups 1 and 2 of the Atlantic Fleet.

Headquarters
Afloat (FPO New York 09501)

submarine: A warship designed for under-the-surface operations. **Attack submarines** (designated SS/SSN) have the primary mission of locating and destroying enemy ships, including other submarines. Current U.S.

nuclear-powered attack submarine classes include the Permit, Skipjack, Narwhal, Lipscomb, Ethan Allen, Sturgeon, Skate, and Los Angeles classes. Diesel-powered submarines include the Darter and Barbel classes. The Sea Wolf class is under development. **Ballistic missile submarines** (designated SSBN) have the mission of attacking land targets. Current U.S. ballistic missile submarine classes include Ohio, Benjamin Franklin, Lafayette, and James-Madison. Ballistic missile submarines fire either **Poseidon** or **Trident** missiles. The USS Nautilus, commissioned in 1954, was the first U.S. nuclear-powered submarine (see **naval nuclear propulsion**).

submarine group (SUBGRU): A permanent **Naval Submarine Force** organization that exercises administrative and operational command of assigned submarine units; monitors shipboard training, personnel, supply, and material readiness; conducts training; conducts inspections of assigned units (including nuclear weapons inspections); and coordinates weapons movement and handling. Subordinate units are submarine squadrons. Ships assigned include submarines and submarine support ships. Navy submarine groups are:

- Submarine Development Group 1, San Diego, CA 92106
- Submarine Group 2, Groton, CT 06349-5100
- Submarine Group 5, San Diego, CA 92106
- Submarine Group 6, Charleston, SC 29408
- Submarine Group 7, Yokosuka, Japan (APO Seattle 98762-0061)
- Submarine Group 8, La Maddalena, Sardinia, Italy (APO New York 09521)
- Submarine Group 9, Bremerton, WA 98315-5100

submarine-launched ballistic missile (SLBM): A **ballistic missile** carried in and launched from a submarine. U.S. SLBMs include **Poseidon** C3, **Trident I** C4, and **Trident II** D5.

Submarines Allied Command Atlantic: A **major subordinate command** of NATO's **Allied Command Atlantic**. Together with the Western and Eastern Atlantic area commands, it coordinates and plans the activities of the submarine forces in those areas.

Headquarters
Norfolk, VA 23511

Submarine Satellite Information Exchange System (SSIXS): A subsystem of the **Fleet Satellite Communications System (FLTSATCOM)** that is used for non-urgent shore-to-submarine broadcasting. FLTSATCOM in the SSIXS mode uses a teletype and cannot connect a submarine with another submarine or a surface vessel.

subordinate area command: NATO command operating under the **Commander-in-Chief Allied Forces Channel (CINCHAN)** within a designated geographical area. (see also **Allied Forces Channel**)

subpackage: A grouping of division and lower-echelon nuclear weapons to be used on the battlefield. Sub-packages are employment schemes for a portion of a corps **package**.

SUBROC (submarine rocket): Model designation UUM-44A. Navy submarine-launched, 20–30 nm range, inertially guided, rocket-powered nuclear **depth bomb**. The SUBROC can be fired from a submerged torpedo tube: it breaks the surface of the water, travels through the air, and reenters the water to attack an enemy submarine. It carries a 1–5 kt W55 nuclear warhead. The SUBROC was originally deployed in 1965 and armed attack submarines of the Permit, Sturgeon, Narwhal, Lipscomb, and Los Angeles classes. It began retirement in 1989 and will finish in 1990. The **Sea Lance** anti-submarine stand-off weapon may replace the SUBROC in the nuclear role, but, as of 1989, only a conventionally armed version was under development.

subunified command: An operational command subordinate to a **unified command**, composed of components of two or more Services and having a broad continuing mission, either regionally or functionally based. A command is established by the President through the Secretary of Defense or by a unified commander, with authorization by the Joint Chiefs of Staff. A sub-unified commander exercises operational command over assigned forces and functions within a specified area of responsibility. Its service components, however, communicate directly with the service components of the unified command on service matters, unless otherwise directed.

Subunified Commands

- Alaskan Command
- Iceland Defense Force (LANTCOM)
- Special Operations Command Atlantic (LANTCOM)
- Special Operations Command Central (CENTCOM)
- Special Operations Command Europe (EUCOM)
- Special Operations Command Pacific (PACOM)
- U.S. Forces Azores (LANTCOM)
- U.S. Forces Japan (PACOM)
- U.S. Forces Korea (PACOM)

subversion: "Action designed to undermine the military, economic, psychological, morale, or political strength of a regime" [Air Force, *USAF SOF Master Plan*, 1985, released under the FOIA].

sufficiency: Applied to strategic nuclear forces, a term introduced by President Nixon in 1969 to denote a posture in which the United States possesses a nuclear capability to (1) maintain an adequate second-strike capability in the face of a massive Soviet first strike; (2) provide no incentive for the Soviet Union to strike the United States first in a crisis; and (3) prevent the Soviet Union from gaining the ability to cause considerably greater urban/industrial destruction than the United States could inflict on the Soviet Union in a nuclear war.

supply categories: DOD– and NATO–designated classes covering the range of military items used for the equipment, maintenance, and operation of military forces.

DOD Supply Category Class Codes

- I: Subsistence (food and rations), including health and welfare items;
- II: General support items (clothing, organizational tool sets and tool kits, tentage, administrative and housekeeping supplies, and individual equipment);
- III: POL (petroleum, oils, and lubricants);
- IV: Construction materials, fortification/barrier materials;
- V: Ammunition and explosives (all types, including chemical, biological, nuclear, etc.);
- VI: Personal demand items (nonmilitary sales items sold in exchange facilities);
- VII: Major end items (e.g., launchers, missiles, tanks, trucks, vehicles);
- VIII: Medical materiel, including medical repair parts;
- IX: Repair parts and components, including kits and assemblies; and
- X: Materiel to support military assistance and civic action programs (e.g., agricultural and economic development items).

[Air Force, *War Planning: USAF Operation Planning Process*, AFR 28-3, 30 June 1986, pp. 432–433, released under the FOIA]

NATO Supply Category Class Codes

- I: Rations;
- II: Clothing, spare parts, tools, weapons;
- III: Fuels, lubricants;
- IV: Barrier material, construction material; and
- V: Ammunition.

support: The assistance, protection, or supplies provided to combat organizations, or the assisting unit itself (e.g., reserve force). Supporting forces are combat forces stationed in, or to be deployed to, an operations area in fulfillment of an operations order. Operational command is not transferred to the supported commander.

support of other nations: Program 10 of the 11 **major force programs**, which represent all of the major missions of the Services and are the most basic structural elements of the **Five-Year Defense Program (FYDP)**. It consists of resources in support of international activities, including service support to the **Military Assistance Program (MAP)**, **Foreign Military Sales (FMS)**, and **North Atlantic Treaty Organization (NATO)**.

Supreme Allied Commander (SAC): Highest-level military commander of a **major NATO command**.

Supreme Allied Commander Atlantic (SACLANT): Commander of NATO's **Allied Command Atlantic**. SACLANT is also the Commander-in-Chief of **U.S. Atlantic Command** and is equal in rank to the **Supreme Allied Commander Europe (SACEUR)** and **Allied Commander-in-Chief Channel (CINCHAN)**. SACLANT is always a U.S. Admiral. The U.S. Liaison Officer to SACLANT is located in the Pentagon.

Supreme
Allied Commanders Atlantic

ADM Lynde D. McCormick	Jan 1952
ADM Jerault Wright	Apr 1954

ADM Robert L. Dennison	Dec 1959
ADM H. P. Smith	Apr 1964
ADM Thomas H. Moorer	May 1965
ADM Ephraim P. Holmes	Jun 1967
ADM Charles K. Duncan	Oct 1970
ADM Ralph W. Cousins	Oct 1972
ADM Isaac C. Kidd	May 1975
ADM Harry D. Train	Oct 1978
ADM Wesley L. McDonald	Nov 1982
ADM Lee Baggett, Jr.	Nov 1985
ADM Frank B. Kelso II	Nov 1988

Supreme Allied Commander Europe (SACEUR): Commander of NATO's **Allied Command Europe**. The SACEUR is also the Commander-in-Chief of **U.S. European Command** and is equal in rank to the **Supreme Allied Commander Atlantic (ACLANT)** and **Allied Commander-in-Chief Channel (CINCHAN)**. SACEUR is always a U.S. General. (see also **Supreme Headquarters Allied Powers Europe**)

Supreme
Allied Commanders Europe

GEN Dwight D. Eisenhower	Dec 1950
GEN Mathew B. Ridgway	May 1952
GEN Alfred B. Gruenther	Jul 1953
GEN Lauris Norstad	Nov 1956
GEN Lyman L. Lemnitzer	Jan 1963
GEN Andrew J. Goodpaster	Jul 1969
GEN Alexander M. Haig, Jr.	Dec 1974
GEN Bernard W. Rogers	Jun 1979
GEN John R. Galvin	Jun 1987

Supreme Headquarters Allied Powers Europe (SHAPE): The administrative headquarters of NATO's **Allied Command Europe**. Fourteen NATO-member countries have National Military Representatives at SHAPE who serve as liaisons with their chiefs of staff. France has a military liaison mission at SHAPE. The U.S. Liaison Officer to SHAPE is located in the Pentagon.

Location
Casteau Mons, Belgium
(APO New York 09055)

(see also **Supreme Allied Commander Europe**)

surface action group (SAG): Navy battlegroup that does not contain an aircraft carrier. A SAG normally consists of two guided-missile cruisers, seven destroyers, and one nuclear-powered attack submarine. A battleship battlegroup, with a battleship at the center, is also considered a surface action group.

surface-to-air missile (SAM): Surface-launched air defense missile designed to intercept and destroy enemy aircraft. Current U.S. surface-to-air missiles include **Chaparral**, **Hawk**, **Patriot**, **Standard**, **Stinger**, and **Terrier**.

surface-to-surface missile (see **SSM**)

SURTASS (Surface-Towed Array Sensor): Navy passive hydrophone array 8,575 ft in length towed from a **TAGOS Ocean Surveillance Ship** at speeds of three knots and at depths typically from 500–1,500 ft, depending on the ocean environment. A satellite relay is used to transmit acoustic data to a shore facility for processing and display. SURTASS extends sound surveillance coverage to areas not routinely monitored by the **Sound Surveillance System (SOSUS)** and supplements SOSUS in other areas. The Navy says SURTASS is necessary because of the vulnerability of the fixed SOSUS arrays and because of the quietness of new generations of Soviet submarines. Under development since the early 1970s, it was first operationally deployed in FY 1984.

Surveillance, Acquisition, Tracking, and Kill Assessment (SAT-KA): Strategic Defense Initiative program providing the research to identify and validate sensors for surveillance, acquisition, tracking, and kill assessment of enemy ballistic missiles from launch to detonation. The SATKA program is divided into three parts:

- *Technology base development*: Programs including infrared (IR) sensors, laser radars, microwave radars, interactive discrimination, signal processing, and the **Terminal Imaging Radar (TIR)**.
- *Data collection and measurement*: Facilities, measurement equipment, and test targets for the collection and interpretation of signature data on ballistic missiles, reentry vehicles (RVs), and space backgrounds.
- *Technology integration experiments*: Basic sensor development programs including boost-phase sensors, midcourse surveillance and discrimination sensors, and terminal-phase surveillance. Boost-phase sensors detect rocket plumes, provide attack alerts, and give tracking data to boost-phase interceptors. Included is the **Boost Surveillance and Tracking System (BSTS)**. Midcourse surveillance and discrimination sensors track post-boost vehicles, RVs, decoys, chaff, and other debris, discriminate between warheads and decoys, provide target position data, and assist with

kill assessment. Included is the **Space Surveillance and Tracking System (SSTS)** program. Terminal-phase surveillance acquires, tracks, and collects data on objects reentering the atmosphere for discrimination databases; predicts intercept points; and helps with kill assessment. Included is the **Airborne Optical Adjunct (AOA)**.

[SDIO, *Report to the Congress on the Strategic Defense Initiative*, April 1987]

survivability: "The ability to continue to exist and function satisfactorily after, or in spite of, nuclear conflict, conventional conflict, hostile countermeasures, sabotage, or natural disaster. This includes the additional qualities of deception, denial, dispersion, hardness, mobility, diversity, and redundancy. It may also include the ability to continue to function through alternate existing means or through regeneration of a system to perform the required function" [JCS, SM-101-81].

Survivability, Lethality, and Key Technologies (SLKT) Program: A set of Strategic Defense Initiative Organization–sponsored research projects into technologies necessary for the deployment of the **Strategic Defense Initiative**, specifically:

- *Survivability Project*: Developing the technology base for the survival of defense forces in hostile environments;
- *Lethality and Target-Hardening Project*: Reducing uncertainties in predicting Soviet vulnerability to SDI;

- *Space Power and Power-Conditioning Project*: Coordinating and stimulating the development of power systems;
- *Space Transportation and Support Project*: Developing space transportation systems; and
- *Materials and Structures Project*: Identifying, formulating, and managing research and development programs and needed equipment.

Survivable Low-Frequency Communications System (SLFCS): Air Force very-low-frequency/low-frequency (VLF/LF) anti-jam strategic command and control communications system. SLFCS provides a general SAC command channel and reserve communications system for long-range bomber and aircraft communications and "provide[s] essential command control communications in support of SAC EWO [emergency war order] operations before, during, and after a nuclear attack" [Strategic Communications Division (AFC-C), *1st Aerospace Communications Group*, SCD Regulation 23-2, 31 July 1981, p. 4, released under the FOIA]. In 1968, SAC deployed two SLFCS radio transmitters on the ground, at Hawes, CA, and Silver Creek, NE, and equipped over 200 receive-only sites at launch control centers, bomber wing command posts, submarines, and Green Pine UHF radio facilities. The SLFCS antennas were buried in the ground at launch centers, since LF waves are able to penetrate the earth. SAC airborne command posts and the **National Emergency Airborne Command Post** were also equipped with SLFCS transceivers

using two-mile-long trailing wires. The airborne terminals are, for the most part, immune to direct immediate attack but are prone to technical problems, whereas the ground transmitting stations and the Green Pine sites are more reliable but are more vulnerable. SLFCS links to the Navy's **Verdin** and **TACAMO** systems as a part of the **Minimum Essential Emergency Communications Network (MEECN)**.

sustainability: A major component of **military capability**; a measure of "staying power" concerned with supporting sustained battle, logistics pipelines, war reserves, shortages, and industrial capacity.

SWATH (Small Waterplace Area Twin Hull) (see TAGOS (SURTASS) Ocean Surveillance Ship)

SWCL: Designation for special warfare craft, light.

SWCM: Designation for special warfare craft, medium.

swimmer-delivery vehicle (SDV): "A power-driven device used to propel swimmers through the water either surfaced or submerged. The device is used in conjunction with scuba for submerged operations" [*NWP 3*]. Navy **SEAL** delivery vehicle teams operate SDVs.

SYNAMO (see sensitive compartmented information)

synchronous orbit: 1. An orbit in which a satellite makes a limited number of equatorial crossing points, which are then repeated in synchronism with some defined reference, usually the Earth or the sun. **2.** In common usage, the equatorial, circular, 24-hour orbit in which a satellite appears to hover over a specific point of the Earth. (see also **geosynchronous orbit**)

Syncom   (see **LEASAT**)

synthetic aperture radar (SAR): **Radar** that picks up signal echoes given off at different points of a satellite's orbit, an airplane's flight path, or a ship's travels. In theory, the highest resolution achievable by SAR is equivalent to that of a single, large antenna as wide as the distance between the most widely spaced points along the orbit that are used for transmitting positions. In practice, however, resolution will be limited by the radar receiver's signal-processing capability or by the limited coherence of the radio signal emitted by the radar transmitter.

System Report Verification: An assessment by command center personnel of the validity of an **early-warning** report pertaining to a space, missile, or explosive event. The SRV is based on site systems reports, intelligence data, and other judgements of the operators. "The sensor site personnel conduct the site investigation and report the site System Report to USSPACE-COM [**U.S. Space Command**] as soon as possible but no later than 1 minute after the event is reported or system reporting has been requested by USSPACECOM." The assessment

is either false, under investigation, or valid:

- False: "Investigation is complete; and in the judgement of the operations personnel, the event was caused by hardware or software malfunction, personnel error, or environmental conditions."
- Under investigation: "Preliminary investigation reveals the event may not have been an actual missile launch, reentering object, or nuclear detonation. Investigation is continuing."
- Valid: "Investigation is complete and in the judgement of operations personnel, the event is an actual missile launch, reentering object, or nuclear detonation."

[JCS, *EAP–Emergency Conferences for Tactical Warning and Attack Assessment,* 1 December 1986, p. II-B-2, released under the FOIA]

Systems Generated Electromagnetic Pulse (SGEMP): The fields and currents generated by the interaction of weapons–produced radiation (principally x-rays and gamma rays) with a weapon system or portion of a weapon system. Internal EMP (IEMP), referring to the electromagnetic fields interior to systems and containers and generated by gamma rays or high-energy x-rays, is included in SGEMP. **TREE (transient radiation effects on electronics)** are excluded from SGEMP. "SGEMP is most important for electronic components in satellites and ballistic systems above the deposition region that would be exposed directly to the nuclear radiations from a high-altitude burst. The system–generated EMP can also be significant for surface and moderate–altitude bursts if the system is within the deposition region but if not subject to damage by other weapons effects. This could possibly occur for surface systems exposed to a burst of relatively low yield or for airborne (aircraft) systems and burst of higher yield" [DNA, *Capabilities of Nuclear Weapons* DNA EM-1. Part 1, Chapter 7, "Electromagnetic Pulse (EMP) Phenomena," 1 July 1972, released under the FOIA]. (see also **electromagnetic pulse**)

T

T: Prefix designating **1.** Trainer aircraft (e.g., T-45). **2.** Ships belonging to the Navy's Military Sealift Command (e.g., TAGOS).

T-2 Buckeye: Navy twin-engine, two-seat, basic jet trainer; to be replaced by the **T-45 Goshawk**.

T-28 Trojan: Navy high-performance, two-seat, single-engine, propeller aircraft used for basic pilot training, including carrier landing training.

T-37 Tweet: Air Force standard, two-seat jet trainer used in the primary phase of undergraduate pilot training. Originally introduced in the 1950s, the T-37B version replaced all earlier A versions by the end of the 1950s. Some 600 remain in the **Air Training Command** inventory as of 1989. Following cancellation of the T-46, a service life extension program was undertaken for the T-37 fleet. Prime contractor is Cessna Aircraft Company.

T-38 Talon: Air Force lightweight, twin-jet, two-seat advanced trainer used in the basic phase of undergraduate pilot training. Originally introduced in 1959, some 800 aircraft remain in the **Air Training Command** and **Strategic Air Command** inventories. Northrop Corporation is the prime contractor.

T-41 Mescalero: Air Force light, piston-engine aircraft used in flight screening for pilot candidates and for cadet flight training at the Air Force Academy. First introduced in 1964, some 100 remain in the Air Force inventory. Cessna Aircraft Company is the prime contractor.

T-43: Air Force navigation trainer derived from the Boeing 737, and introduced in 1973. Fourteen are assigned to the **Air Training Command** and **Air National Guard**.

T-44: Navy twin-engine, commercial FAA-certified trainer aircraft. It is used for multi-engine pilot training for land based **P-3 Orion** maritime patrol and transport aircraft. Beech Aircraft, Wichita, KS, is the prime contractor. The FY 1990 budget request for five aircraft is $12.3 million.

T-45 Goshawk: Navy primary two-seat, carrier-capable jet trainer under development, scheduled to become the Navy's primary aircraft for training naval aviators. The aircraft is a derivative of the British Aerospace Hawk trainer. The T-45A made its maiden flight at Douglas Aircraft Company, Long Beach, CA, on 16 April 1988. The plane is to be operational in 1991, when the T-45 will begin replacing current Navy intermediate- and advanced-phase training aircraft. The Navy plans to purchase over 300 aircraft. FY 1990 budget request for 24 aircraft was $484.6 million, and FY 1991 request for 48 aircraft is $658.3 million.

table of distribution and allowance (TDA): Standard table used in the Army and Marine Corps prescribing the organizational structure, personnel, and equipment requirements of a military unit for the performance of a specific mission for which there is no appropriate **table of organization and equipment (TOE)**.

table of organization and equipment (TOE): Standard table used in the Army and Marine Corps that prescribes the organizational structure, personnel, and equipment requirements for a military unit. A modified TOE (MTOE) is a version of the TOE based upon a specific unit's assigned mission or geographical environment and are the authorizing documents for the allocation and requisition of personnel and equipment.

TACAMO (Take Charge and Move Out): Navy unarmed VLF/LF radio relay aircraft serving as a one-way communications relay system linking the National Command Authorities to the submarine force. TACAMO is a part of the **Minimum Essential Emergency Communications Network (MEECN).** TACAMO's mission is to survive a nuclear attack long enough to relay an **emergency action message (EAM)** to the nuclear forces. This presupposes that the ground-based VLF stations that carry messages to the submarines would not survive an attack.

There are two squadrons of TACAMO aircraft: the Atlantic squadron (Fleet Air Reconnaissance Squadron Four (VQ-4)), based at NAS Patuxent River, MD and the Pacific squadron (Fleet Air Reconnaissance Squadron Three (VQ-3)), formerly stationed in Guam and now at NAS Barbers Point, HI. A normal TACAMO mission lasts about 11 hours. A TACAMO plane is airborne at all times in the Atlantic area. During operations, TACAMO aircraft transit to and are deployed from a number of U.S. and overseas air bases.

TACAMO aircraft receive messages over a wide variety of communication links (including LF/VLF, HF/UHF/SHF, and satellite systems such as Air Force Satellite Communications System **(AFSATCOM)** and **Fleet Satellite Communications System (FLTSATCOM)**. The high-power VLF transmitter then retransmits the messages to the submarines in their operating area. Downlink messages are routed to Verdin transmit terminals for encryption and anti-jam coding. The planes trail antennas five miles long that hang below the aircraft in a spiral after the plane goes into a very tight turn. For a submarine to receive a message, it must trail an antenna at or very close to the ocean surface, since VLF/LF signals can penetrate only a few feet into the water. TACAMO have limited receiving and transmitting radii since they must stay within EAM receiving range.

Since 1964, the two squadrons of **EC-130** modified Hercules aircraft have provided the TACAMO mission. The EC-130G/Q aircraft are now being replaced with **E-6A Hermes** TACAMO aircraft, which are faster and have a larger radius of operations, enabling TACAMO to remain within the EAM receiving area while having its signal reach a wider group of submarines.

TACFIRE (see **Tactical Fire Direction**)

Tacit Rainbow: Model designation AGM-136A. Joint Navy/Air Force passive anti-radiation, air-to-surface, jet-powered, loitering drone under development to augment the **HARM** missile. The missile is intended to arm both Air Force **B-52G** bombers and Navy **A-6E** attack aircraft. The drone carries a 40 lb high-explosive fragmentation warhead. The missile will be able to fly ahead of a main air strike force to a range of about 50 miles and autonomously seek out and attack and disable air defense radar warning and tracking systems. A Tacit Rainbow test at China Lake in March 1989 required the use of unplanned manual guidance to reach the target area because the mid-course guidance did not work as a result of computerized navigation data being erased before the flight. The first free flight launch of a Tacit Rainbow missile from an A-6E Intruder occurred on 12 April 1989. Beginning in FY 1990, the Navy will no longer fund Tacit Rainbow, but the Air Force will continue development. Full-scale development

is scheduled for completion in FY 1991. Prime contractor is Northrop Ventura, Perry, GA.

tactical: Relating to battlefield operations rather than **theater** or **strategic** operations. Tactical weapons are designed for direct combat with enemy forces—unlike theater or strategic weapons, which are designed for over-the-horizon use to reach the rear areas of the battlefield, or the opponent's homeland. Tactical nuclear weapons, often called "battlefield" nuclear weapons or "nonstrategic" nuclear weapons, are short-range weapons intended solely for battlefield combat use.

Tactical Air Command (TAC): Air Force **major command** and service component command of **U.S. Atlantic Command**. It was established on 21 March 1946 and redesignated from the Continental Air Command on 1 December 1950. TAC is the Air Force's tactical strike force comprising tactical fighter, fighter bomber, and tactical reconnaissance aircraft. Its operations include air interdiction, air support, bombing, tactical reconnaissance, electronic combat, tactical air control, and strategic air defense. When activated as Air Forces Atlantic (USAFLANT), its responsibilities include operations in the North Atlantic and Caribbean in support of the unified command. In addition, TAC's tactical subordinate numbered **Air Forces** (the 9th Air Force and 12th Air Force) serve as components of other unified commands (**U.S. Central Command** and **U.S. Southern Command**, respectively). When activated as Air Forces Central Command (US-

CENTAF) in support of U.S. Central Command, the 9th Air Force provides units for joint operations in Southwest Asia. In its role as the Air Forces Southern Command (US-SOUTHAF), the 12th Air Force provides air defense, tactical air support, and command and control for U.S. Southern Command operations in Latin America. The TAC Commander serves as CINC, USAFLANT and CINC, USCENTAF. Commander, 9th Air Force serves as the air component commander for USCENTAF. Commander, 12th Air Force serves as the air component commander for USSOUTHAF.

The TAC Command and Control System is led by the TAC Command Post at Langley AFB, VA. It supports the TAC Commander as COMTAC, CINCAFRED and CINCAFLANT by providing data support systems, facilities, communications, and administration for the Contingency Support Staff. It also provides immediate responses to **emergency action messages (EAMs)** and changes in readiness posture. The 9th Air Force, Shaw AFB, SC, and 12th Air Force, Bergstrom AFB, TX, have alternate command posts. Most communications from the TAC Command and Control System are accomplished via **AUTOVON, AUTODIN**, and direct lines. The 1st Tactical Fighter Wing's 6th Airborne Command and Control Squadron at Langley AFB, VA, is responsible for operating the **EC-135 airborne command posts** supporting the unified Atlantic Command. Other airborne command and control elements include the EC-130E Airborne Battle Command and

Control Center (ABCCC), **E-3 Sentry AWACS** aircraft, and the EC-135K Tactical Deployment Control Aircraft (TDCA). All of these aircraft are operated by squadrons based at the 552d Airborne Warning and Control Wing, Tinker AFB, OK.

Air Defense, TAC (ADTAC), provides daily management for the ground-based radars, control centers, and interceptor units providing air defense for the United States and Canada. In times of national emergency, these functions would be transferred to **NORAD**. The 1st Air Force provides air defense interceptor forces. ADTAC operates in coordination with NORAD on a day to day basis by organizing, training, equipping, maintaining, and providing air defense forces. NORAD has operational control over these ADTAC-provided forces. The ADTAC Operational Readiness Center, collocated with the 48th Fighter Interceptor Squadron at Langley AFB, VA, monitors the readiness of the ADTAC forces and is the ADTAC command and control element.

TAC operates at over 100 locations worldwide, and its combined peacetime and mobilized combat strength includes over 4,000 aircraft. Its active personnel strength is approximately 119,000 military and civilian personnel, with an additional 70,000 Air National Guard and Air Force Reserve personnel assigned to TAC units when mobilized. (see also **tactical air force**)

Headquarters
Langley AFB, VA 23665

Subordinate Commands

- 1st Air Force, Langley AFB, VA 23665
- 9th Air Force, Shaw AFB, SC 29152
- 12th Air Force, Bergstrom AFB, TX 78743
- 28th Air Division, Tinker AFB, OK 73145
- Southern Air Division (SOUTH-COM), Howard AFB, Panama
- Tactical Air Warfare Center, Eglin AFB, FL 32542
- Tactical Fighter Weapons Center, Nellis AFB, NV 89191

tactical air control: **1.** "The organization and equipment necessary to plan, direct, and control tactical air operations and to coordinate air operations with other Services" [*JCS Pub 1*, p. 360]. **2.** In the Navy, the direction of aircraft in close support of amphibious troops, exercised from aboard ship or from the beach. Naval personnel are organized into tactical air control squadrons (TACRONs) and tactical air control groups (TACGRUs). (see also **Tactical Air Control System**)

Tactical Air Control System (TACS): Main Air Force command and control system providing an Air Force component commander of joint operations with the organization and equipment necessary to operate tactical air forces in support of ground operations. First deployed in the late 1960s and early 1970s, TACS is a flexible structure of mobile command and control elements, including the **Tactical Air Control Center (TACC)**,

the operations center of the tactical air commander. TACC provides flexible capability for centralized control of assigned or attached air resources; decentralized execution of operations; rapid coordination; and close integration of operations, mobility, alternate facilities, and dispersion. TACS can integrate all air operations, including air defense and centralized airspace control over the combat zone. TACS elements are employed through Tactical Air Control Wings and Tactical Control Groups in CONUS and overseas. The basic operating element of the TACS is the Tactical Air Control Party (TACP) consisting of officers, technicians, and other support personnel; airborne and ground vehicles; and communications equipment needed to obtain, coordinate, and control tactical air support for ground forces. Parties are collocated at corps, division, brigade, and battalion levels.

Ground-based surveillance and control elements of the TACS include

- Tactical Air Control Center (TACC): Controls and coordinates missions assigned by the Air Control Center (ACC). TACC plans airspace control procedures and coordinates airspace management and use. The Combat Operations Division and the Enemy Situation Correlation Element are physically integrated within TACC.
- Control and Reporting Center (CRC): Directly subordinate to TACC, the CRC is the senior radar element of TACS to direct regional and sector air defense operations, to provide aircraft guidance for offensive and defensive missions, to

relay mission changes to airborne aircraft, and to coordinate mission control with other TACS agencies.

- Control and Reporting Post (C-RP): Subordinate to the CRC, the CRP provides radar surveillance and control within an assigned area, but does not assign aircraft.
- Forward Air Control Post (FA-CP): Subordinate to the CRC, the FACP is a small, mobile radar element that is deployed at the front lines. With limited surveillance and control capabilities, two or more FACPs operate subordinate to a CRP.
- Message Processing Center (MPC): The MPC assures data linkage between TACS, airborne **E-3 Sentry AWACS**, and other command and control systems. The Center may also be used for defensive counterair operations, management of data conflicts, and preparation and dissemination of tactical data.
- Air Support Radar Team (AS-RT): Provides tracking and aircraft guidance in forward areas with ground-directed bomb delivery in areas where aircrew visibility is poor. ASRT also provides control of special airlift operations.

While E-3 sentry AWACS and EC-130 Airborne Battlefield Command and Control Center (ABCCC) aircraft belong to the 552nd Airborne Warning and Control Wing of TAC, they are assigned to the Air Component Commander for specific operations in the theater.

Air support coordination and control elements in direct support of ground forces include

- **Air Support Operations Center (ASOC):** Located within the Army Corps Tactical Operations Center, the Center plans, coordinates, and directs tactical air operations in support of ground forces.
- Corps G-3 Fire Support Element: Located within the fire support center of the Corps command post, it coordinates close air support.

tactical air force: Active and reserve tactical fighter, reconnaissance, and command and control unit that is primarily oriented toward tactical air operations—those that produce direct effects on the field of battle. Tactical air forces are deployed worldwide, principally in the CONUS-based **Tactical Air Command (TAC)** and the **Air National Guard** and reserve units that are attached to it, and three major air commands in the theaters: **U.S. Air Forces Europe, Pacific Air Forces**, and **Alaskan Air Command**.

tactical airlift: Airlift providing the immediate and responsive air movement and delivery of combat troops and supplies directly into objective areas through air-landing, airdrop, Low Altitude Parachute Extraction (LAPES) or other delivery techniques. Tactical airlift also provides air logistic support of all theater forces, including those engaged in combat operations, to meet specific theater objectives and requirements. Resupply and rapid battlefield mobility are given with the theater of operations. The **C-130** is the primary tactical airlifter.

The basic tactical airlift unit is the tactical airlift wing (TAW). All TAWs are assigned to the **Military Airlift Command (MAC)** or to the **Air National Guard** and **Air Force Reserve** for assignment to MAC. Current TAWs include

- 94th TAW*, Dobbins AFB, GA 30069
- 118th TAW#, Nashville, TN 37217
- 123d TAW#, Louisville, KY 40213
- 133rd TAW#, St. Paul, MN
- 136th TAW#, Dallas, TX 75211
- 137th TAW#, Oklahoma City, OK
- 146th TAW#, Channel Island, CA
- 302nd TAW*, Peterson AFB, CO 80914
- 314th TAW, Little Rock AFB, AR 72099
- 317th TAW, Pope AFB, NC 28308
- 374th TAW, Clark AB, Philippines (APO SF 96274)
- 403d TAW*, Keesler AFB, MS 39534
- 435th TAW, Rhein-Main AB, West Germany (APO NY 09097)
- 440th TAW*, Gen. Billy Mitchell Field, WI 53207
- 463rd TAW, Dyess AFB, TX 79607

*Air Force Reserve.
#Air National Guard.

tactical air-to-surface missile (TA-SM): Air Force medium-range, nuclear-armed, **air-to-surface missile** under development for deployment to Europe. It is designed to meet NATO targeting requirements predating the **INF Treaty**, as agreed as part of a package of modernization projects at Montebello, Canada, in October 1983. Two new nuclear weapons,

the TASM and the **Follow-on to Lance (FOTL)** were approved for development. The TASM requirement was stated as a missile with a range of 400 km. As a standoff nuclear missile, the TASM will extend the effective range of NATO **F-15E Strike Eagle, F-16**, and **Tornado** dual-capable aircraft. A modified **SRAM II** air-to-ground missile (designated SRAM-Tactical or SRAM-T) was proposed in the FY 1990 budget to meet the TASM requirement. In the FY 1990/1991 budget, the Air Force requested $173.1 million for research and development. The "imperative" deployment date identified by the **Supreme Allied Commander Europe** is 1995. (see also **Montebello Decision**)

tactical control: "The detailed and usually local direction and control of movements or maneuvers necessary to accomplish missions or tasks assigned" [JCS, *United Action Armed Forces (UNAAF)*]. (see also **operational command, operational control**)

Tactical Exploitation of National Capabilities (TENCAP): Joint program to improve the combat effectiveness of the military services through more effective use of national **satellite reconnaissance** systems at the tactical level. With TENCAP, tactical intelligence bypasses analysts at the national level and goes directly to headquarters and forces in the field. TENCAP will use the **KH-12** photographic reconnaissance satellite and the **MILSTAR** communications satellite to relay real-time imagery directly to Army, Navy, and Air Force field commands. Field commanders will also be able to task reconnaissance satellites for imagery they require and receive it directly upon production.

tactical fighter wing (TFW): Air Force basic tactical combat unit. Normally, wings are organized into three tactical fighter squadrons of 24 aircraft each (plus a few spares). As of 1989, there are 45 TFWs, 14 assigned to **Tactical Air Command (TAC)**, 1 in the **Alaskan Air Command (AAC)**, 5 assigned to **Pacific Air Forces (PAC-AF)**, 9 assigned to **U.S. Air Forces Europe (USAFE)**, and 16 in the **Air National Guard (ANG)** and **Air Force Reserve (AF-RES)** earmarked for other commands. An additional 22 tactical fighter groups of two squadrons are assigned to the Air National Guard.

Tactical Fighter Wings

- 1st TFW (TAC), Langley AFB, VA 23665
- 3rd TFW (PACAF), Clark AB, Philippines (APO San Francisco 96274)
- 4th TFW (TAC), Seymour Johnson AFB, NC 27531
- 8th TFW (PACAF), Kunsan AB, South Korea (APO San Francisco 96264)
- 10th TFW (USAFE), RAF Alconbury, UK (APO New York 09238)
- 18th TFW (PACAF), Kadena AB, Okinawa, Japan (APO San Francisco 96239)
- 20th TFW (USAFE), RAF Upper Heyford, UK (APO New York 09194)
- 21st TFW (AAC), Elmendorf AFB, AK 99506
- 23rd TFW (TAC), England AFB, LA 71311
- 27th TFW (TAC), Cannon AFB, NM 88103
- 31st TFW (TAC), Homestead AFB, FL 33039
- 33rd TFW (TAC), Eglin AFB, FL 32542
- 36th TFW (USAFE), Bitburg AB, West Germany (APO New York 09132)
- 37th TFW (TAC), George AFB, CA 92394
- 48th TFW (USAFE), RAF Lakenheath, UK (APO New York 09150)
- 49th TFW (TAC), Holloman AFB, NM 88330
- 50th TFW (USAFE), Hahn AB, West Germany (APO New York 09122)
- 51st TFW (PACAF), Osan AB, South Korea (APO San Francisco 96570)
- 52nd TFW (USAFE), Spangdahlem AB, West Germany (APO New York 09126)
- 81st TFW (USAFE), RAF Bentwaters/Woodbridge, UK (APO New York 09755)
- 86th TFW (USAFE), Ramstein AB, West Germany (APO New York 09094)
- 108th TFW (TAC),† McGuire AFB, NJ 08641
- 113th TFW (TAC),† Andrews AFB, MD 20331
- 116th TFW (TAC),† Dobbins AFB, GA 30069
- 121st TFW (TAC),† Rickenbacker ANGB, OH 43217
- 122nd TFW (TAC),† Fort Wayne, IN 46809
- 127th TFW (TAC),† Selfridge ANGB, MI 48045

- 128th TFW (TAC),† Truax Field, WI 53704
- 132nd TFW (TAC),† Des Moines, IA 50321
- 131st TFW (TAC),† St. Louis, MO 63145
- 140th TFW (TAC),† Buckley ANGB, CO 80011
- 174th TFW (TAC),† Syracuse, NY 13211-7099
- 301st TFW (TAC),* Carswell AFB, TX 76127
- 343rd TFW (AAC), Eielson AFB, AK 99702
- 347th TFW (TAC), Moody AFB, GA 31699
- 354th TFW (TAC), Myrtle Beach AFB, SC 29579
- 363rd TFW (TAC), Shaw AFB, SC 29152
- 366th TFW (TAC), Mountain Home AFB, ID 83648
- 388th TFW (TAC), Hill AFB, UT 84056
- 401st TFW (USAFE), Torrejon AB, Spain (APO New York 09283)
- 419th TFW (TAC),* Hill AFB, UT 84056
- 432nd TFW (PACAF), Misawa AB, Japan (APO San Francisco 96519)
- 442nd TFW (TAC),* Richards-Gebaur AFB, MO 64030
- 474th TFW (TAC), Nellis AFB, NV 89191
- 482nd TFW (TAC),* Homestead AFB, FL 33039
- 917th TFW (TAC),* Barksdale AFB, LA 71110

*Air Force Reserve
†Air National Guard

Tactical Fire Direction (TACFIRE): Army integrated, computer-based command and control system that automates field artillery with computers linked to artillery headquarters at corps, division, and battalion levels. TACFIRE correlates targets by location and type and stores this information for retrieval. The computers can also plan and schedule fires—matching firing units against targets, determining the best allocation of weapons, considering the requirement for unimpeded air corridors for air operations, ensuring that firing rounds do not hit friendly forces, and allocating targets appropriate for the stocks of ammunition on hand. TACFIRE entered full-scale production in 1978 and completed final fielding in 1987. It will be replaced by the **Advanced Field Artillery Tactical Data System (AFATDS)**.

tactical warning/attack assessment (TW/AA): Notification that enemy offensive operations are in progress (particularly strategic attack operations), information which may be received at any time from the moment the attack is launched until its effect is felt. Tactical warning differs from **strategic warning** in that it is the actual alert of an attack. Attack assessment provides instantaneous data on the size, characteristics, and postulated effects of an attack. The DOD program to provide TW/AA of strategic missile and bomber attacks on the United States is called the Integrated Tactical Warning and Assessment System (ITW&AS). The program was formerly called the Attack Warning/Attack Assessment System (AW/AA) and was expanded from the Ballistic Missile Tactical Warning/Attack

Assessment System to include space-based and air-breathing threats to the United States, as well as the integration of intelligence information providing supplemental **early warning**. The ITW&S system provides an aid to National Command Authorities (NCA) survivability, NCA decision-making, and force application in the execution of the **Single Integrated Operational Plan**.

TAGOS (SURTASS) Ocean Surveillance Ship: Navy conventionally powered ocean surveillance ships operated as units of the Military Sealift Command. TAGOS supports the towed arrays and data processing/transmitting equipment of the **SUR-TASS** system. Its mission is to extend sound surveillance coverage to areas not routinely monitored by the **Sound Surveillance System (SOSUS)** and to supplement SOSUS in areas it already covers. The monohull ships (Stalwart class) displace 2,285 tons at full load, are 224 ft long, have a beam of 43 ft, a speed of 11 kt, and a crew of 25. The first two ships became operational in FY 1984. Congress authorized 22 ships, although the Navy is seeking 27 TAGOS ships overall, 11 of which had been delivered by FY 1989. The first 18 ships were monohulled. Due to poor seakeeping in sea states in the higher latitudes, the 19th and subsequent ships will have a Small Waterplace Area Twin Hull (SWATH) configuration. They will be 224 ft long and 94 ft wide, have a twin screw, and be capable of speeds of 9 kt. Tacoma Boatbuilding Co. and Halter Marine built the first 18 boats; McDermott Marine, Inc., LA, is building the SWATH ships.

Three SWATH ships were appropriated in FY 1989 at a cost of $167 million. An additional SWATH ship is requested in the FY 1990 budget for $169.1 million.

tail hook: The hook lowered from the aft part of a carrier aircraft that engages the arresting gear of an airplane upon landing. In slang, a "tailhooker" is a naval aviator qualified in carrier operations.

Take Charge and Move Out (see **TACAMO**)

talent keyhole (TK): One of the four major types of **sensitive compartmented information** used to mark intelligence produced by certain overhead intelligence collection systems such as satellites and surveillance aircraft (e.g., U-2 and SR-71). Access to TK information requires a special security clearance. The three TK clearances are

- **RUFF:** deals with the products of imaging (**Keyhole**) satellites;
- **ZARF:** probably deals with satellite-obtained **signals intelligence**; and
- **CHESS:** relates to **U-2** or **SR-71** photography.

(see also **SI-TK**, **security classification**)

Talon Gold: Pointing and tracking telescope used as part of the **Space-Based Chemical Laser Research**, a component of the **Directed-Energy Weapon (DEW)** program of the **Strategic Defense Initiative**. The Talon Gold telescope would be attached to the Space-Based Laser and used to aim the laser at its target.

Initially, experiments with Talon Gold called for two tests aboard the space shuttle in mid-1987 and mid-1988. These tests were delayed until 1988–89 to include a second telescope with additional surveillance and targeting capabilities. Congressional budget cuts then dictated that a newer and more capable Talon Gold system be developed, probably under a new program name, with the first space test to occur in the early 1990s. (see also **Alpha, LODE**)

tamper: A heavy, dense material surrounding the fissionable material in an atomic weapon, for the purpose of (1) holding the supercritical assembly together longer by its inertia, and (2) reflecting neutrons, thus increasing the fission rate of the active material. U-238 is a commonly used tamper in U.S. nuclear warheads.

tank landing ship (LST): A naval ship that transports and lands amphibious vehicles, tanks, combat vehicles, and equipment in an amphibious assault [*JCS Pub 1*, p. 364]. (see also **amphibious warfare ship**)

target: "A geographical area, complex, or installation planned for capture or destruction by military forces" [*JCS Pub 1*, p. 364].

target acquisition: "The detection, identification, and location of a target in sufficient detail to permit the effective employment of weapons" [*JCS Pub 1*, p. 364]. (see also **target analysis**)

target analysis: "An examination of potential targets to determine the mil-

itary importance, priority of attack, and weapons required to obtain a desired level of damage or casualties" [*JCS Pub 1*, p. 364]. (see also **target acquisition**)

target data inventory (TDI): "A basic **target** program which provides standardized target data in support of the requirements of the Joint Chiefs of Staff, military departments, and unified and specified commands for target planning coordination and weapons application" [*JCS Pub 1*, p. 364]. The TDI is compiled by the **Defense Intelligence Agency (DIA)** and contains the identification, location, relative importance, and physical vulnerability of installations and complexes that have been evaluated as possessing current or potential target significance. The TDI is further refined in the National Target Base (NTB) compiled by the **Joint Strategic Target Planning Staff**, from which targets for the **Single Integrated Operational Plan** are drawn. DIA produces the Accepted Change List to the TDI monthly.

target recognition attack multi sensor (TRAM): Navy bombing system on **A-6 Intruder** attack aircraft that utilizes a **forward-looking infrared (FLIR)** sensor, a combination laser designator and ranger, and a forward air-controller laser energy receiver. The TRAM is integral to the A-6E and improves its effectiveness by providing the crew with a TV-like picture of potential targets at night, by improving bombing accuracy by using the FLIR for precision aimpoint selection and laser ranging, and by improving bombing accuracy when using laser-guided bombs. The TRAM also allows bomb damage assessment through the use of video tape to record the attack.

task element (TE):   The lowest echelon of naval operational organization below the **task unit**. (see also **task organization**)

task fleet: Naval operational organization organized in such a way to meet specific operational requirements levied by higher authority. (see also **task organization**)

task force (TF):   The highest echelon of naval operational organization above the **task group**. A TF is formed for the purpose of carrying out a specific operation, a mission, or a continuing task (e.g., carrier strike force or combat support force). It may be temporary, activated only in times of war; or semi-permanent, existing also in peacetime. It is under the operational control of a single commander and is operationally subordinate to an operational **numbered fleet** commander. TFs are commonly called Commander Task Forces and are designated as CTFs. (see also **task organization**, **joint task force**)

Task Force 160 (TF 160):   Army **special operations** aviation unit, a composite organization of the 160th Aviation battalion of the 101st Air Assault Division, Ft. Campbell, KY. Established in 1981, it specializes in personnel transportation, air support of **counterterrorism** operations, and air assault. The TF is subordinate to the **Army's First Special Operations**

Command, except for its specialized counterterrorism helicopter elements (called the "Night Stalkers"), which are believed to be subordinate to the **Joint Special Operations Command**.

Headquarters
Ft. Campbell, KY 42223

task group: The second echelon of naval operational organization; below the **task force** and above the **task unit**. (see also **task organization**)

task organization: Operational command structure of the U.S. Navy. Command of ships is normally exercised by a **fleet** commander through the formation of task organizations composed of task forces, task groups, task units, and task elements.

Sample Task Organization

Commander Atlantic Fleet
|
Commander Second Fleet
|
Commander Task Force 20
(Battle Force Second Fleet)
|
Task Group 20.2
(Carrier Battle Group 2)

Task Unit 20.2.1 (Aircraft Carrier)		Task Unit 20.2.3 (Surface Attack Unit)

Task Unit 20.2.2
(Destroyer Screen)
|
Task Element 20.2.2.1
(ASW Search Unit)

task unit: The third echelon of naval operational organization; below the **task group** and above the **task element**. (see also **task organization**)

TDY: Temporary duty or temporary additional duty.

Teal Ruby: DARPA-sponsored and managed by the Air Force Space Command, Teal Ruby is an experimental **early warning** space sensor to detect aircraft and cruise missiles from space, to demonstrate supporting technology, and to collect multispectral infrared background data in support of follow-on infrared surveillance systems (including tactical surveillance of theater battlefields). The Teal Ruby program was initiated in 1974 with a high-resolution sensor using large, light-weight optics and a multispectral mosaic focal plane. Teal Ruby includes (1) a servo system that allows the sensor to stare at earth backgrounds, and (2) onboard signal processors capable of detecting and tracking moving targets. Teal Ruby will have a 350–450 nm orbit at a minimum 72 degrees inclination. It is expected to contain over 100,000 infrared detectors and will be deployed by the space shuttle. Rockwell is the prime contractor. (see also **High Altitude Large Optics**)

Team Spirit: JCS-directed and sponsored by the U.S. Pacific Command, Team Spirit is an annual field training exercise **(FTX)** and deployment exercise for U.S. forces stationed in South Korea and for forces from the Republic of Korea (ROK). It has been termed the "largest Free World combined training exercise" by the Joint Chiefs of Staff [JCS, *FY 1989*, p. 74]. The purpose of Team Spirit is "to improve defense readiness of ROK and U.S. Forces through participation in combined/joint operations, to include receiving, staging, employing and redeploying out of country forces. Particular emphasis [is] given to improvement of ROK/U.S. Force interoperability and teamwork. ROK/U.S. combined participation [demonstrates] their mutual determination to preserve the freedom of the Republic of Korea." Other Pacific Command and CONUS forces, including **Capstone** aligned active and reserve forces from the United States and the Pacific, take part in the exercise as well. The 14th annual Team Spirit field training exercise was held on 14–23 March 1989. The first Team Spirit exercise was held in June 1976 [DOD News Release No. 93 89, *Team Spirit '89*, 3 March 1989].

technical control systems program (TCSP): Air Force program to upgrade, extend, and build new worldwide technical control facilities to support the **Defense Communication System (DCS)**. Included in this program are

- Automated Audio Remote Test System (AARTS);
- Base Central Test Facilities (BCTF): program to provide automated testing capability and systems for on-base voice and data transmission circuits and systems;
- Defense Communications System Orderwire program;
- Digital Patch and Access System (DPAS): program to provide auto-

mated switching and access to DCS circuits at the di-group level;

- Data Transmission Network (DTN): program to incorporate a digital transmission of low speed data into the DCS. Composed of the LSTDM (Low Speed Division Multiplex) and the DCS Timing and Synchronization Program;
- Transmission Monitoring and Control System (TRAMCON): program to monitor and control transmission equipment for the Digital European Backbone (DEB) program and related DCS transmission systems;
- Technical Control Improvement Program (TCIP): program to procure and install more modern and logistically supportable signalling, console, patching, supervisory interface, and conditioning equipment at technical control facilities worldwide;
- Manual Technical Control Improvement Program (MTCIP): program to procure and install more logistically supportable equipment at technical control facilities worldwide.

technical proficiency inspection: "An inspection of a nuclear weapons storage support or delivery organization to determine its capability to meet operational commitments in nuclear weapons as directed in its current mission, while adhering to standard procedures in storage, maintenance, safety testing, handling, and assembly" [*Army Dictionary*].

telemetry: Measurement and transmission of data from a space vehicle to detached receiving stations where the data can be displayed, interpreted, or recorded. Two types of data are collected and relayed: payload data, concerning the complete mission, and state-of-health data, relating to the operational status of the object.

telemetry intelligence (TELINT): Type of **foreign instrumentation signals intelligence** information derived from intercepting, processing, and analyzing foreign telemetry. TELINT intercepts the signal a missile, missile stage, or warhead sends back to earth about its performance during a test flight. TELINT can provide information about the missile payload, throwweight, accuracy, and number and size of warheads on a missile.

TEMPEST: Short name referring to technical investigations and studies of compromising emanations. Computer and automated data processing equipment are protected using TEMPEST requirements to ensure that the systems do not emanate signals that would inadvertently provide intelligence information for hostile interception. TEMPEST is used synonymously for the term "compromising emanations." The program is supervised by the **National Security Agency**. (see also **communications security**)

TENCAP (see **tactical exploitation of national capabilities**)

TERCOM (see **terrain contour matching**)

terminal guidance: In-flight corrections to the trajectory of a ballistic or cruise missile (or an air-to-air or air-to-surface rocket or missile) during its final approach to the target for the purpose of improving accuracy. Corrections can occur as a result of the guidance seeking a target with a sensor, such as a radar or acoustic detector or an infrared or millimeter wave detector.

Terminal Imaging Radar (TIR): Ground-based terminal defense radar system under development to defend cities and military targets. As part of the **Strategic Defense Initiative** sensor program, TIR would probably be deployed in a mobile mode for survivability; however, unless it is deployed as a fixed, ground-based system, it would violate Article V(1) of the **ABM Treaty** banning the development, testing, or deployment of mobile, ground-based ABM components.

terminal phase: The stage of a **ballistic missile** trajectory in which the warhead reenters the atmosphere, usually at the altitude of about 100 km. The phase lasts for only 30 to 100 seconds.

termination: ". . . [T]he process of perceiving a willingness on the part of the enemy to negotiate termination of hostilities, projecting the results of current U.S. and enemy activity, and assessing enemy intent and residual capability. The process includes developing plans for recovery and redeployment to deter renewed conflict and monitoring the achievement of the directed recovery posture to insure that the conflict terminates under conditions favorable to the United States" [JCS, *Policy and Procedures for Management of Joint Command and Control Systems*, 11 January 1982, p. 6].

terrain contour matching (TERCOM): The guidance employed in U.S. long-range cruise missiles, which correlates preprogrammed contour map data with the terrain being overflown in order to take periodic fixes and adjust the flight path accordingly. TERCOM improves the accuracy of the missile beyond the capability of inertial guidance alone. It is employed on the **Advanced Cruise Missile, Air-launched Cruise Missile, Ground-launched Cruise Missile**, and the **Tomahawk sea-launched cruise missile**.

Terrier: Model designation RIM-2F. Navy tactical, short-range, nuclear-armed **surface-to-air missile** (with limited surface-to-surface capability). Several versions were fielded since its original introduction in 1956, but the only remaining Terrier missiles in the inventory are nuclear-armed with a range of about 25 miles. Once the target has been detected and tracked, the missile is readied and loaded by automatic magazines, and the launcher is aimed at the target. Terrier is a beam-riding missile with semiactive terminal radar homing and proximity fuzing. It uses a 1 kiloton W45 nuclear warhead. Some 280 Terrier nuclear missiles were deployed on Mk-10 twin-rail launchers as of mid-1989 and have been carried aboard 31 cruisers and destroyers and three aircraft carriers. The missile will be retired by 1991 and will be replaced by the **Standard 2**. Prime contractors are General Dynamics, Pomona, CA (guidance); Allegheny Ballistic Laboratory (motors); and Atlantic Research (booster).

terrorism: "The unlawful use or threatened use of force or violence against individuals or property to coerce or intimidate governments or societies, often to achieve political, religious or ideological objectives" [Approved definition for future volume of *JCS Pub 1* in *Joint LIC Final Report*, Vol. 1, 1 August 1986]. (see also **antiterrorism, counterterrorism, terrorist threat condition**)

terrorist threat condition (THREATCON): An alert level used to create a standard level of terrorist threat to U.S. military facilities or personnel. There are three different levels:

- THREATCON WHITE: Nonspecific threat in a general geographic area (may be based on information that terrorists in the area have general plans for attack against a military facility).
- THREATCON YELLOW: Specific threat within a particular geographical area (may be based on information that terrorists are preparing for an attack in a particular area).
- THREATCON RED: Imminent threat against a specific military facility or personnel (may be based on information regarding plans and preparations for attack against a specific target).

test and training launcher: For the purposes of **SALT II**, these are launchers of **ICBM**s or **SLBM**s used only for test and training purposes. New test and training launchers may be constructed only at test ranges. Test and training launchers may be replicas or partial launchers without an actual launch capability, or they may be launchers used to launch missiles for test and training purposes.

Theater Army: Army component of a unified command operating in an established theater of operations. It is at the combat echelon above corps, and is established by the President through the Secretary of Defense, with advice from the Chairman of the Joint Chiefs of Staff. It conducts both operational and support missions, prepares long-range strategic and operational plans, and develops land campaign plans in support of the unified command. Forces are assigned on the basis of mission. The Theater Army commander is under the operational command of the theater (unified) commander but reports to the Department of the Army on uniservice administrative and training matters.

Theater Army area command (TAACOM): Army area support organization in the theater responsible for the **communications zone (COMMZ)**. The TAACOM is composed of area support groups that vary in number depending on the size of the COMMZ. Types of functions provided by the area support groups include

- Direct support (less medical, COMSEC, and map supply) and support to units located in the COMMZ;
- Direct support to units passing through the COMMZ;
- General support, as directed by the Theater Army commander, to units in the combat area;
- Rear-area protection in the COMMZ;
- Area emergency warning to the COMMZ;
- Nuclear, biological, and chemical services and support;
- Combat military police support;
- Procurement;

- Explosive ordnance disposal; and
- Automatic data processing services.

theater nuclear force (TNF): Nuclear weapons with a longer range and larger yield than **tactical** nuclear weapons, and used in theater operations. Many strategic nuclear weapons are usable in theater operations, but not all theater nuclear weapons are designed for strategic use. In the Reagan Administration, the term "theater nuclear forces" was replaced by intermediate-range nuclear forces (**INF**) to remove the stigma of nuclear weapons intended for use outside of the United States, particularly on allied soil. Theater nuclear forces are also referred to as nonstrategic nuclear forces.

theater/theater of operations: A geographical area outside of the United States for which a **unified command** has been assigned military responsibility. The term "theater of operations" is used synonymously with the term "area of operations." It denotes an area of conflict used for military operations according to an assigned mission and is established by the President, through the Secretary of Defense, with advice from the Chairman of the Joint Chiefs of Staff.

The Tank: Slang for the room in the Pentagon (Room 2E924) where the Joint Chiefs of Staff and the operations deputies of the services meet. It is also called the "gold room."

Third Fleet (3d FLT): One of the four operating fleets of the U.S. Navy, and one of two **numbered fleets** assigned to the **Pacific Fleet**.

It was established 15 March 1943 under the command of ADM William F. "Bull" Halsey, was designated a reserve fleet 17 October 1945, and was returned to active status 1 February 1973, assuming the duties of the former 1st Fleet and the Anti-Submarine Warfare Force, U.S. Pacific Fleet. Its mission area is the eastern and middle Pacific Ocean areas, ranging from the west coast of North America to a line approximately halfway between Midway Island and Japan from pole to pole (approximately 50 million square miles). Its Commander "exercises operational control over assigned ships, aircraft, and submarines; commands assigned shore activities; plans, conducts, and evaluates fleet training (including combined, joint, and intertype) and tactical development exercises; and conducts operations to ensure control of the sea, in order to defend the United States against attack through the eastern Pacific Ocean and the Bering Sea, to maintain the security of the **U.S. Pacific Command**, and to support the operations of adjacent Allied and national commanders." Commander, Third Fleet, exercises operational control over assigned commander **task forces** (CTF). The fleet comprises approximately 115 surface combatant ships and submarines, including four aircraft carriers, five helicopter carriers, 15 cruisers, 25 destroyers, 30 frigates, and 30 attack submarines [*NWP* 2, Rev. 2, Chapter 19].

Fleet Headquarters
Ford Island,
Pearl Harbor, HI 96860

Fleet Flagship
USS Coronado (AFG 11)

Operating Task Forces

- CTF 30 (Commander Battle Force 3d FLT)
- CTF 31 (Commander Combat Support Force 3d FLT)
- CTF 32 (Commander Patrol and Reconnaissance Force 3d FLT)
- CTF 33 (Commander Logistic Support Force 3d FLT)
- CTF 34 (Commander Submarine Force 3d FLT)
- CTF 35 (Commander Surface Combatant Force 3d FLT)
- CTF 36 (Commander Amphibious Force 3d FLT)
- CTF 37 (Commander Carrier Strike Force 3d FLT)
- CTF 39 (Commander Landing Force 3d FLT, when activated)

third generation: New class of mission-specific nuclear weapons following atomic **fission** bombs (first generation) and thermonuclear bombs (second generation). Enhanced radiation ("neutron bombs") are considered third-generation weapons, as are the weapons under development to provide other special effects in support of **Strategic Defense Initiative** missions, such as nuclear-driven x-ray lasers and nuclear-driven hypervelocity pellets.

THREATCON   (see **Terrorist Threat Condition**)

threshold: Limit imposed by the Secretary of Defense on program changes, the basis for which is the DOD **Five Year Defense Program (FYDP)**. It is expressed in terms of dollars and physical resources.

Threshold Test Ban Treaty (TTBT): Formally known as the Treaty between the United States and the Soviet Union on the Limitation of Underground Nuclear Weapon Tests. The TTBT was signed by the United States on 3 July 1974 but has never been ratified by the U.S. Senate. The Ford Administration delayed hearings on the treaty until after the 1976 presidential elections, and it was not until the summer of 1977 that hearings were finally held with support from the Carter Administration. However, the treaty never progressed further than this stage, partly because the Carter Administration appeared to be having some success with the Soviets on negotiating a comprehensive test ban. Some Congressional members felt that passing the TTBT would undermine the opportunity to obtain a total test ban, and while some thought that the treaty restrictions on the development of new weapons were too strict, others thought them too loose. The usual quagmire of verification and measurement technologies (particularly the adequacy of seismic monitoring) also stonewalled ratification. However, despite U.S. nonratification, both the United States and the Soviet Union agreed to abide by the 150 kt limit on underground tests—but with no formal provisions for specific verification.

The TTBT is a follow-on to the **Partial Test Ban Treaty** of 1963 to limit the number of tests to a minimum and their yield to 150 kt. The treaty does not cover nuclear explosions for peaceful purposes. A protocol provides for the exchange of geological and geophysical data on the tests and test sites to supplement seismic verification. Duration of the treaty was for five years with automatic five-year extensions unless either country terminated the agreement. On 19 July 1982, the United States decided to renegotiate the treaty to improve verification measures. In January 1984 both countries accused the other of numerous violations of the treaty.

throwweight: The useful weight of a ballistic missile that is placed on a trajectory toward the target by the boost or main propulsion stages. The **SALT II** Treaty defines the throwweight of an ICBM, SLBM, or ASBM as "the sum of the weight of: a) its reentry vehicle or reentry vehicles; b) any self-contained dispensing mechanisms or other appropriate devices for targeting one reentry vehicle, or for releasing or for dispensing and targeting two or more reentry vehicles; and c) its penetration aids, including devices for their release" [Article II(7), Second Agreed Statement; Article IV(7), Second Agreed Statement]. "Other appropriate devices" is further defined to exclude devices that would impart added velocity to reentry vehicles in excess of 1,000 meters per second. Since 1981, reducing the amount of Soviet missile throwweight has been a negotiating position of the U.S. government in the **START** negotiations.

Thunderbolt II (see **A-10 Thunderbolt II**)

time (see **military time**)

time sensitive planning: Planning under the **Crisis Action System** for the development of response actions during time-constrained operations. "To facilitate OPSEC [**operations security**], crisis planning can be, and often is, conducted in a close-hold mode, with extremely limited access to the deployment data" [JCS, *Joint Operations Planning System, Vol. IV,* p. I-3, released under the FOIA].

Titan: Air Force **expendable launch vehicle** used to launch satellites, Titan is based upon retired Air Force Titan ICBMs. The types of Titan launchers currently in use are the Titan II and the Titan IV, and until recently, the Titan 34D. Titan II rockets were refurbished Titan II ICBMs that were retired between 1982 and 1987. The ICBMs were converted into launch vehicles with the ability to put 4,200 lb payloads into low-earth polar orbits. The first launch of a refurbished Titan II took place in September 1988 and the second on 5 September 1989. As of early 1989, 14 of the 56 available Titan II missiles were scheduled for conversion to launch vehicles. These replaced the Atlas E. Titan IIs will launch the **Defense Meteorological Satellite Program (DMSP)** satellites and Navy ocean surveillance satellites.

The Titan 34D was based on the Titan II ICBM and replaced the Titan III-C and III-D configurations. It included two solid strap-on boosters and was able to accommodate either the Boeing inertial upper stage (IUS) developed for the space shuttle, or Transtage, an upper stage capable of functioning both in the boost phase of flight and as a restartable space propulsion vehicle. The Titan 34D was capable of placing a 4,000 lb payload into geosynchronous orbit or a 27,000 lb payload into low-earth polar orbit. Sixteen Titan 34Ds were ordered by the Air Force, and the first was launched from Cape Canaveral, FL, on 30 October 1982 — the first launch of the IUS System Satellites and two Defense Satellite Communications System Satellites. However, the Air Force launch program was seriously interrupted by two failures of Titan 34Ds in August 1985 and April 1986. Air Force Systems Command Space Division's reassessment of the Titan 34D was completed in the summer of 1987, and the rocket was launched successfully in October 1987 and November 1987. The last Titan 34D was launched on 4 September 1989. It is replaced by the Titan IV.

The Titan IV was selected in February 1985 to augment the space shuttle and to allow greater flexibility in launching military satellites. The Titan IV has stretched first and second stages and two solid rocket boosters. It can accommodate the Centaur G prime upper stage, enabling it to launch the Department's heavier space payloads (a 10,200 lb payload into geosynchronous orbit, 31,100 lb into low earth polar orbit, or 39,100 lb into low equatorial orbit). Titan IV can also carry the IUS, which can place 5,300 lb into geosynchronous orbit. The Air Force originally contracted for 23 Titan IVs, and the first was launched from Cape Canaveral on 14 June 1989. Launches from Vandenberg AFB, CA, are scheduled to begin in 1990. The Air Force now plans to buy an additional 18 Titan IV vehicles, with options for six more, to support launches through 1995. The FY 1990 budget request includes three

Titan IVs at a cost of $759.4 million, and the FY 1991 budget request includes two Titan IVs at a cost of $556.8 million. The prime contractor for the Titan IV is Martin Marrieta, Denver Aerospace, Denver, CO.

Tomahawk sea-launched cruise missile (SLCM): Model designation BGM-109. Navy subsonic (about 760 mph), dual-capable, long-range, submarine- and surface ship–launched **cruise missile**. Tomahawk has three basic versions: the conventionally armed anti-ship missile (TASM) with a range of 250 + nm, the conventionally armed land-attack missile (TLAM/C) with a range of 450 + nm, and the nuclear-armed land-attack missile (TLAM/N) with a range of 1350 nm (1500 miles). The TASM guidance system has passive and active radar search; TLAM missiles have inertial guidance, with **terrain contour matching (TERCOM)** guidance. All versions are propelled by solid boosters for launch and small turbofan engines for cruise flight. The TLAM/-N is armed with the W80-0 5–150 kt nuclear warhead; the TLAM/C carries a 1,000 lb high-explosive warhead or sub-munitions dispenser with combined-effects bomblets (designated TLAM-D); and the TASM has a high-explosive warhead. All three have an accuracy/CEP of about 30 meters.

Tomahawk missiles are 18 ft, 3 inches long, and 20 ft, 6 inches long with booster. The missile diameter is 20.4 inches. The missile weighs 2,650 lb, or 3,200 lb with booster. Tomahawk's small radar cross section, its ability to fly at low altitude, and its low heat emission make it difficult to detect in flight.

Tomahawk nuclear targets are primarily naval related: ports, air bases, and surface ship concentrations. The Tomahawks are launched from submarine 21-in torpedo tubes (called Torpedo Tube Launched (TTL) Tomahawk), armored box launchers on surface ships, or **vertical launching systems**. Current plans call for Tomahawks to be deployed on at least 192 surface ships and submarines: four Iowa (BB-61) class battleships; one Long Beach (CGN-9) class nuclear-powered cruiser; four Virginia (CGN-38) class nuclear-powered cruisers; 22 Ticonderoga (CG-47) class cruisers (CG-52 and later); 31 Spruance (DD-963) class destroyers; 29 Arleigh Burke (DDG-51) class destroyers; and 62 Los Angeles (SSN-688) and 39 Sturgeon (SSN-637) class nuclear-powered attack submarines.

As of January 1989, 950 Tomahawks had been delivered to the Navy, including 295 of the nuclear versions. During 1988, nine surface ships were converted to fire Tomahawks, for a total of 27 (three battleships, five nuclear-powered cruisers, seven cruisers, and 12 destroyers). Six submarines were made Tomahawk-capable, for a total of 37 (29 Los Angeles class and eight Sturgeon class).

The Tomahawk production order calls for a total of 3,994 missiles, of which 758 will be the TLAM/N version. Prime contractors are General Dynamics-Convair, San Diego, CA, and McDonnell-Douglas, St. Louis, MO. The FY 1990 and FY 1991 budget request for 400 missiles each year is $631.0 and $716.0 million, respectively, including RDT&E and military construction. The FY 1980 fly-away cost per missile was $3.167 million without nuclear warhead. (see also **Air-launched Cruise Missile**, **Ground-launched Cruise Missile**, **Harpoon**)

Tomcat   (see **F-14**)

tonnage: The unit of measurement to describe a naval ship, expressed in short tons (2000 lb); long tons (2240 lb); or metric tons (2205 lb) to describe weight; or measurement tons (40 cubic ft); or register tons (100 cubic ft) to describe volume. There are four categories of ship tonnage:

• Deadweight cargo: difference between displacement loaded and displacement light.
• Displacement: weight of a ship in long tons either with cargo, fuel, water, and the like (loaded) or without (light).
• Gross register: entire cubic capacity of a ship expressed in register tons.
• Net register: cubic capacity, less certain non-cargo spaces, expressed in register tons.

tooth-to-tail ratio: Army term used to describe the proportion of combat forces to administrative and logistic support force.

top secret (TS):   Security classification category applied to national security-related information "that requires the highest degree of protection and the unauthorized disclosure of which could reasonably be expected to cause exceptionally grave damage to the national security. Examples of 'exceptionally grave damage' include armed hostilities against the United States or its allies; disruption of foreign relations vitally affecting the national security; the compromise of vital national defense plans or complex cryptologic and communications intelligence systems; the revelation of sensitive intelligence operations; and the disclosure of scientific or technological developments vital to national security" [*JCS Pub* 1, p. 327]. Of the three major classification levels, top secret is a higher category than both **secret (S)** or **confidential (C)**. Authorized access to TS information is granted to an individual by a government agency based upon a background investigation. In FY 1986, TS clearances were held by approximately 356,000 DOD and industry personnel [GAO, *DOD Clearance Reduction and Related Issues,* GAO/NSIAD 87 170BR, September 1987, p. 12].

According to **communications security (COMSEC)** guidelines, "information classified TOP SECRET may not be electrically transmitted in-the-clear over unsecured means at any time." Secure communication of TS information is done through **protected distribution system (PDS)** safeguards (formerly named approved circuits), which include "all equipment and cabling used for the clear text transmission of classified information." Prior to the transmission of TS information, a PDS must be evaluated, approved, and authorized at the service staff and major command level [Department of the Army, *Communications Security*, AR 530-2, 1 September 1982, p. 10].

Tornado: A fighter developed by a British, Italian, and West German consortium, the Tornado replaces the F-104 in the Italian and West German air forces. Tornado's used by the Italian and German Air Forces are certified by the United States to deliver U.S. nuclear bombs stored in these two countries.

torpedo: Self-propelled underwater explosive weapon that is aimed at or seeks a target and detonates by contact, sound, or magnetic force. There are several general types of torpedoes characterized by their guidance and type of run:

- *Pattern-running:* "An aimed torpedo that carries out a present course/depth/spiral search pattern."
- *Straight-running:* "An aimed torpedo for use against surface craft. It is fitted with special tracing gear which permits setting up a predetermined course for a straight run to a chosen point at constant depth."
- *Target-seeking (acoustic homing):* "A torpedo guided to its target by the interception of signals emanating from or reflected by the target. It may be an active, passive, or combination active-passive homing torpedo."
- *Wire-guided:* "A torpedo capable of receiving guidance commands over a connecting wire from the firing ship after the torpedo has left the tube" [*NWP 3*].

Specific models are identified by mark and modification numbers. Three models are currently deployed in the U.S. Navy: the **Mk-37, Mk-46**, and **Mk-48**. A few older Mk-37 torpedoes are maintained for diesel-powered submarines of the Darter (SS-576) class. The Mk-46 is a lightweight torpedo launched from aircraft, ships, **ASROC** missiles, or **Captor** mines. A near-term torpedo improvement program (NEARTIP) is underway to upgrade the Mk-46. The heavyweight Mk-48 is a submarine-launched, long-range torpedo. A Mk-48 ADCAP (advanced capability) torpedo is being procured to upgrade the Mk-48's capability against new Soviet submarines. The torpedoes are primarily for anti-submarine use, though the Mk-48 and Mk-37 can be used against surface targets. In addition, a **Mk-50** advanced lightweight torpedo (ALWT) is being developed as a replacement for the MK-46 and to arm the **Sea Lance** ASW standoff weapon.

torpedo countermeasures: "The material and tactical measures that are adopted by ships for protection against submarine torpedoes." For example:

- **Fanfare:** "An electronic noisemaker; an acoustic torpedo decoy."
- **Noisemaker: 1.** "A towed decoy device (such as fanfare) which generates underwater sounds to mislead acoustic homing torpedoes and paralyze their steering mechanisms." **2.** "A type of submarine evasion device (masking beacon) used to confuse sonar operators by obscuring the submarine's self-noise or by blanking echo ranging signals." [*NWP 3*]

torpedo danger zone: "An area which the submarine must enter in order to be within maximum effective torpedo range" [*NWP 3*].

torpedo swim-out: "A torpedo which is designed to egress from the torpedo tube under its own power" [*NWP 3*].

total active aircraft authorization: The total number of primary and backup aircraft authorized to an Air Force unit.

total active aircraft inventory (TAAI): The sum of the primary and backup aircraft assigned to meet the **total active aircraft authorization.**

Total Force: The force structure of the U.S. Armed Forces, officially named the DOD Total Force Policy, "which recognizes that all elements of the structure contribute to success. Those elements include the **Active [component]** and **Reserve Components**, civilian workforce, and retired military, host nation support, and DOD contractors." The concept was adopted by the Department of Defense in 1973. Under the program, which ended the draft and instituted the All Volunteer Force, reserve components are slated as the primary and initial military personnel to augment active forces in national military emergencies and are to be considered "equal partners, on and off the battlefield" with the active components [DOD, *Manpower Requirements Report FY 1989*, March 1988].

The Total Force (FY 1989)

Component	Personnel (millions)
Active	2.1
Selected Reserve	1.2
Other Reserve	.8
Civilian	1.1
Mobilizable Retirees	.8
Total	6.0

total obligational authority (TOA):
A DOD term synonymous with **budget authority (BA)**, a Congressional term. TOA is the authority to enter into obligations for immediate or future payments (outlays) of government funds. Obligations may be incurred from one to five years depending on the type of appropriation. TOA is set in the **Defense Guidance** and reflects Presidential/Office of Management and Budget decisions concerning the amount of real growth and the inflation rates to be used when developing DOD programs.

total overall aircraft inventory: The total inventory of active and inactive aircraft in the Air Force.

TOW   (tube-launched   optically tracked wire-guided antitank missile   system): Model   designation BGM-71. Army and Marine Corps, heavy, antitank, wire-guided missile consisting of a missile, launcher system, missile guidance set, and ground support equipment. The TOW primary mission is to destroy tanks and other armored vehicles, but it can also be used against bunkers and has a limited self-defense capability against helicopters. It is crew portable or can be mounted on M-2/M-3 **Bradley Fighting Vehicles**, trucks, armored personnel carriers, jeeps,   and   **AH-1S Cobra** attack helicopters. With a range of 3,750 meters, TOW receives automatic corrections in flight through two thin wires that unwind from the missile and link it to the launcher. A sensor in the launcher tracks a beacon in the tail of the missile. The gunner needs to keep his crosshairs on the target; a computer in the launcher corrects

any deviation of the missile from the crosshair aim and sends corrections to the missile via the wires.

The TOW program consists of four different missiles: the basic TOW; improved TOW (ITOW); TOW 2; and TOW 2A. The basic TOW has been fielded with the Army since 1970 and has been adopted by the Marine Corps and 39 foreign countries. A two-phased TOW improvement program began in 1979. Phase 1 was designed to meet current and near-term threats, and produced ITOW, which was fielded in March 1981. The ITOW improved five-inch warhead is fitted with a probe. Phase 2, to meet future armor threats, produced TOW 2, which included a six-inch warhead with probe and improvements to the missile guidance system enabling the gunner to track through smoke, fog, and other battlefield obscurants. The first-production TOW 2 units were delivered to the Army in May 1983. TOW 2s were delivered to combat units in Europe in October 1983. The latest improvement, TOW 2A, was delivered to the Army in Europe beginning in September 1987. It was developed to counter Soviet reactive armor. A TOW 2B warhead development effort is underway for FY 1990 production.

Prime contractors are Hughes Aircraft Company, Tucson, AZ, for the missiles and Emerson Electric, St. Louis, MO, for the launchers. A second source was scheduled to be chosen during FY 1989. The FY 1990 Army budget request for 9,455 TOW 2 missiles is $138 million. The FY 1990 Marine Corps budget request for 839 TOW 2 missiles is $10 million. TOW is to be replaced by the **Advanced**

Antitank Weapon System—Heavy in the early 1990s.

towed array: Passive **hydrophones** formed into linear arrays that are fitted onto surface warships and submarines. First developed in the 1960s, the arrays are streamlined to permit towing at high speeds. Towed arrays can be longer in length than the towing ship and are physically remote from ship machinery and propeller noises. The towed lines are also more easily replaced than hull-mounted systems. Each hydrophone is omnidirectional, and each beam is formed by computer control. Limitations of the towed arrays are that they are not effective in shallow water and even less effective under ice and that they impose limitations on the speed and maneuverability of the towing ship.

Surface ship towed arrays

- AN/SQR-15: Garcia class frigates, early Spruance-class destroyers;
- AN/SQR-17A: Knox class frigates;
- AN/SQR-18A(V)1: Knox class ships with VDS;
- AN/SQR-18A(V)2: Knox class without VDS, Oliver Hazard Perry class frigates in the naval reserve;
- AN/SQR-19: Ticonderoga class destroyers beginning with the Antietam (CG-54), Arleigh Burke class destroyers, later Spruance class destroyers, Oliver Hazard Perry class active force ships.

Submarine towed arrays

- AN/BQQ-5: Los Angeles class, Sturgeon class, Permit class, Glenard P. Lipscomb class, Narwhal class;

- AN/BQR-15: Lafayette class;
- AN/BQQ-6/9: Ohio class.

SURTASS (surface towed arrays) are designed for very long range detection of submarines in regions where the **Sound Surveillance System (SOSUS)** is not deployed or has been destroyed. There are 28 **TAGOS (SURTASS) Ocean Surveillance Ships** in the program, both of the Stalwart class and the new SWATH design. The converted Ethan Allen (SSN-608) class special operations and transport submarines also launch the AN/UQQ-2 towed array.

TR-1A: Air Force, single-seat, single-engine, subsonic, high-altitude, long-range, unarmed, tactical **reconnaissance** aircraft assigned to the **Strategic Air Command**. It is a derivative of the **U-2R** strategic reconnaissance aircraft designed for high-altitude standoff surveillance missions in Europe. Each TR-1 is equipped with sensors to provide continuously available, all weather surveillance of the battle area, or potential battle area, day or night in direct support of U.S. and allied ground and air forces during peacetime, crises, or wartime. The TR-1s are equipped with a high-resolution Advanced Synthetic Aperture Radar System (ASARS-2) in a side-looking airborne radar (SLAR) form and with modern electronic countermeasures. This provides high-quality imagery at long standoff ranges in strip mapping and spotlight modes. Real-time images are processed on the ground at the TRS Ground Station. The TR-1 maximum cruising speed at an altitude of over 70,000 ft is more than

430 mph, and the range is more than 3,000 miles.

Initial funding for the TR-1A was provided in the FY 1979 budget. A total of 29 aircraft have been ordered, including 2 two-seat TR-1B trainers and one ER-2 for NASA. The first TR-1A flew on 1 August 1981, and pilot training at Beale AFB, CA, began later that year. The first active squadron of TR-1s was the 95th tactical reconnaissance squadron at RAF Alconbury, UK, where aircraft arrived in February 1983. Lockheed Corporation is the prime contractor.

Tracking and Data Relay Satellite (TDRS) System: NASA communications relay satellite serving as an orbiting ground station for communications between space-borne satellites and earth via a dedicated facility at White Sands, NM. Geosynchronous satellites are more often within range of TDRS satellites than within range of normal ground stations; therefore, the TDRS satellites can increase communications coverage from about 15 percent to 50 percent within a given satellite's orbit, with increases of even higher percentages with more than one TDRS in use. TDRSs operates in S-band, C-band, and Ku-band and can transmit 300 million bits of information per second.

TDRS-1 became operational in April 1983, while TDRS-2 was destroyed on the space shuttle Challenger in January 1986. TDRS-3 is the second in a three-satellite constellation and was deployed from the Discovery space shuttle on 29 September 1988.

TDRS-4 was launched on 13 March 1989 replacing TDRS-1, which became an in-orbit spare. The active satellites are located at 41 degrees west longitude over the Atlantic Ocean off the coast of Brazil, and at 171 degrees west longitude over the Pacific Ocean southwest of the Hawaiian Islands. The spare is located between the two active satellites.

When the TDRS system became fully operational in late 1989, NASA closed most if its ground stations in Bermuda and Merritt Island, FL. Three Deep Space Network Stations at Goldstone, CA; Canberra, Australia; and Madrid, Spain, will also provide emergency back-up communications. The satellites are built by TRW for Contel, which leases them to NASA [GAO, *Space Operations: NASA's Communications Support for Earth Orbiting Spacecraft*, GAO/IMTEC 89-41, April 1989].

traffic analysis: The cryptologic discipline that develops information from communications about the composition and operation of communications structures and the organizations they serve. The process involves the study of traffic and related materials, and the reconstruction of communications plans, to produce **signals intelligence**.

Training and Doctrine Command (TRADOC): Army **major command** established in 1973, TRADOC is responsible for the development of Army combat doctrine and training of individual personnel. It also serves as the Army's point of contact for joint and allied doctrinal matters. It operates in coordination with other service and DOD agencies on operational matters, including the development of joint weapons and equipment. TRADOC operates 6 Integrating Centers; the U.S. Army Command and General Staff College; 20 mission-oriented **branch** centers, specialist centers, and schools; 8 basic training centers; and 11 test, experimentation, and analysis activities. In addition, TRADOC manages DOD's public affairs school and the Defense Language Institute, and supervises the Army **Reserve Officer Training Corps** program at four ROTC Centers.

Headquarters
Ft. Monroe, VA 23651

training, medical, and other personnel activities: Program 8 of the 11 **major force programs** that represent all of the major missions of the services and that are the most basic structural elements of the **Five Year Defense Program (FYDP)**. It consists of resources related to training and education, accessions, personnel services, health care, permanent change-of-station travel, transients, family housing, and other support activities associated with personnel. It excludes training specifically related to and identified with another major program. It also excludes housing, subsistence, health care, recreation, and similar costs and resources in a program element, such as base operations, of another major program.

TRAM   (see   **target   recognition attack multi-sensor**)

trans-attack: 1.   "In nuclear warfare, the period from the initiation of the attack to its termination. The period from the impact of the first weapon until the attack ceases" [Air Force, *Disaster Preparedness: Planning and Operations,* AFR 355-1, 17 November 1986, p. 87, released under the FOIA]. **2.** As applied to the **Single Integrated Operational Plan (SIOP)**, "the period which extends from execution (or enemy attack, whichever is sooner) to termination of the Single Integrated Operational Plan" [*JCS Pub 1*, p. 377.] **3.** The middle phase of **general war** used for planning purposes.
(see also **pre-attack**, **post-attack**)

TRANSIT: The first Navy navigation satellite providing all-weather, passive-user navigation capabilities to worldwide military and civilian users. The satellites use a radio-doppler navigation method in which an object's position is calculated from the observed change in the received frequency of the satellite's radio transmissions as the satellite passes across the sky. Initially intended to be a navigation tool solely for Polaris submarines, TRANSIT benefits were quickly transferred to other military users. The complete TRANSIT system consists of three subsystems:

- A constellation of five radiating satellites in circular polar orbit at an altitude of 1,075 km;
- Ground tracking and control stations in Maine, Minnesota, and Hawaii operated by the **Navy Astronautics Group** (a part of Naval Space Command) to monitor and update satellite data—and a control center at Point Mugu, CA;
- 4,000 military and 30,000 commercial users. The U.S. Coast Guard

requires ships in U.S. waters to use either **LORAN-C** or TRANSIT for position determination.

Four solar-cell panels power the satellites' internal batteries. Signals are sent to earth by an antenna kept pointing toward the earth by a gravity-gradient stabilization boom. The accuracy of a fix determined by the satellites is usually within 100 meters, but the time lag between usable satellite passes (generally about 90 minutes) is a shortcoming of the system.

In continuous operation since January 1964, TRANSIT was made available for civilian use in July 1967. Since 1964, 22 TRANSIT satellites were successfully launched by either **Scout** or Thor-AbleStar boosters. The name TRANSIT was discarded in 1964 in favor of Navy Navigation Satellite (NNS), NavSat, and Oscar. Newer satellites are called Nova. As of 1989, there were four Oscar satellites and one Nova satellite performing TRANSIT functions. **NAVSTAR/GPS** will replace TRANSIT once it becomes fully operational. RCA is the prime contractor; the Johns Hopkins Applied Physics Laboratory is the design and development agent.

Transportation Command (see **U.S. Transportation Command**)

transportation operating agencies (TOAs): 1. Major commands including the **Military Airlift Command**, **Military Sealift Command**, and **Military Traffic Management Command**. TOAs coordinate preliminary deployment estimates with **U.S. Transportation Command** for each course of

action (COA). "When the NCA [National Command Authorities] select a military COA, the TOAs develop movement schedules and, upon execution, provide deploying military forces common-user lift, land transportation, and port and terminal services, as required" [JCS, *Joint Operation Planning System, Vol. IV,* August 1985, p. I-6]. **2.** Civil transportation agencies with national emergency responsibilities. Also referred to as Federal Modal Agencies or Federal Transport Agencies [*JCS Pub 1*, p. 378].

transport ship (AP): Navy support ship operated by the **Military Sealift Command** for transport of troops. Only a few of these World War II era ships are in service.

Treaty Banning Nuclear Weapon Tests in the Atmosphere, in Outer Space and Under Water (see **Limited Test Ban Treaty**)

Treaty of Rarotonga: Also known as the South Pacific Nuclear Free Zone Treaty. Signed on 6 August 1985 by Australia, Cook Islands, Fiji, Kiribati, New Zealand, Niue, Tuvalu, and Western Samoa. Papua New Guinea, Nauru, and the Solomon Islands later signed the treaty. It entered into force on 11 December 1986 and was then deposited with the United Nations. The treaty originated from proposals and initiatives of the early 1960s from the Australian and New Zealand Labour parties for a southern hemisphere **nuclear free zone (NFZ)** adjacent to the Latin American zone.

The treaty is the fifth regional nuclear free zone treaty, preceded by the **Treaty of Tlatelolco** (Latin American NFZ treaty, the only other one to cover a populated area), the Antarctic, Outerspace, and Seabed treaties. The territory covered by the Treaty of Rarotonga extends to areas covered by the Antarctic Treaty to the south and by the Latin American Treaty to the east. The treaty also restates the pledge made by nonnuclear nations in the **Nonproliferation Treaty** not to acquire or possess nuclear weapons.

Three protocols were added to the treaty for signature by the five nuclear weapons states:

- **Protocol I:** Prohibits the stationing, manufacturing, and testing of any nuclear explosive device within treaty boundaries. (Open for signature by the United States, France, and the United Kingdom; refers to the U.S. territory of American Samoa, French Polynesia, and Britain's colony of Pitcairn Island.)
- **Protocol II:** Requires the five nuclear states to promise not to use or threaten to use any nuclear weapon against any South Pacific country that is a signatory to the treaty.
- **Protocol III:** Requires the five nuclear weapon states not to test any nuclear device anywhere in the zone.

The United States refused to sign any of the above protocols. One of the U.S. concerns is maintaining good relations with France, whose underground nuclear testing program in the Pacific would be prohibited by the treaty. The Soviet Union signed Protocols II and III with the added condition that they would continue to target U.S. facilities and ships in the treaty zone that are involved in nuclear activities. France and the United Kingdom have not signed any of the protocols; China signed all three in February 1987.

Treaty of Tlatelolco: Formally known as the Treaty for the Prohibition of Nuclear Weapons in Latin America. The Treaty of Tlatelolco created a **nuclear free zone (NFZ)** in over 7.5 million square miles of Latin America. Named after the suburb of Mexico City in which it was negotiated, this multilateral treaty opened for signature on 14 February 1967 and entered into force on 22 April 1968. Signature of the treaty remains open indefinitely to all republics of Latin America and to all sovereign states south of latitude 35 degrees north in the western hemisphere. As of December 1988, the treaty had been signed by all of the Latin American states except for Cuba and Guyana, although Argentina had not yet ratified it and Brazil had not brought itself into accordance. The main provisions of the treaty include

- Testing, use, manufacture, production, acquisition, receipt, storage, installation, deployment, and possession of nuclear weapons for nonpeaceful means is prohibited;
- Nuclear materials and facilities located within the territory are to be used only for peaceful purposes: "Nothing in the provisions of this Treaty shall prejudice the rights of the Contracting Parties, in conformity with this Treaty, to use nuclear energy for peaceful purposes, in particular for their economic development and social progress" (Article 17);

- Explosions for peaceful purposes, either singly or in collaboration, are permitted, provided the Agency for the Prohibition of Nuclear Weapons in Latin America (OPANAL) (headquartered in Mexico City) and the International Atomic Energy Agency (IAEA) are notified;
- OPANAL is responsible for monitoring treaty compliance and periodic review;
- Each treaty signatory will negotiate an agreement with the IAEA on its nuclear activities and will file semiannual reports with the IAEA on nuclear activities;
- Special inspections may be called by the Agency or the IAEA when deemed necessary; and
- In the event of nonconformance with the treaty, the General Conference of the Agency will report to the United Nations Security Council and General Assembly and to the Council of the Organization of American States.

Protocol I to the treaty states that France, the Netherlands, the United Kingdom, and the United States will extend the treaty to apply to their territories located within its physical boundaries. For the United States, which signed Protocol I on 26 May 1977 and ratified it in November 1981, this refers to the Panama Canal Zone, Guantanamo Bay Naval Base, PR, and the U.S. Virgin Islands. Protocol II, signed by the United States on 1 April 1968 and ratified on 12 May 1971, states that the five nuclear nations, all of whom signed and ratified the protocol, agree to respect the denuclearized zone and will not use or threaten to use nuclear weapons against Latin American signatories. This protocol entered into force on 11 June 1971.

Treaty on Principles Governing the Activities of States in the Exploration and Use of Outer Space, Including the Moon and Other Celestial Bodies (see **Outer Space Treaty**)

Treaty on the Non Proliferation of Nuclear Weapons (see **Non-Proliferation Treaty**)

TREE (transient radiation effects on electronics): ". . . Those effects occurring in electronics as a result of the transient radiation from a nuclear weapon explosion or as a result of an environment designed to simulate that radiation." "Transient" refers to the radiation, not to the effects: The effects may be transient, semipermanent, or permanent. The electronics that are affected include electronic component parts; electronic component parts assembled into a circuit; circuits assembled into a system; and electromagnetic components connected to the electronics, such as gyros and inertial equipment. Specifically excluded are hydraulic cylinders and systems and fuel lines and systems.

The weapon-burst radiations that TREE deals with are neutrons, gamma rays, x-rays, and electrons. Even though the radiation lasts for only a short time, the effects can be permanent on the electronics [DNA, *Capabilities of Nuclear Weapons*, DNA EM-1, 1 July

Examples of system responses to TREE:

Temporary Effects in Systems	Typical Consequence
Change in logic state in missile borne guidance computer.	Program jump or disturbance of key data causing mission failure.
Spurious (ill timed) fluxing signal.	Warhead dudding or premature detonation.
Excess currents in transistors and capacitors in servo control loop.	Excessive steering maneuvers causing structural instability.
Excess currents in memory write circuits.	Writing erroneous data in memory, usually causing mission failure.
Microcircuit latchup following ionization pulse.	Functional disabling of microcircuit until power is cycled off and on.

Permanent Effects in Systems	Typical Consequence
Neutron induced loss of gain in lower frequency transistors.	Loss of power supply regulation; decreased servo loop gain.
Delamination of semiconductor wire bonds due to thermomechanical shock.	Functional failure of the affected device, usually leading to mission failure.
Neutron induced loss of gain in higher frequency transistor structures.	Decreased fan out capability in computer logic.
Metallization burnout due to excess ionization induced currents.	Functional failure of affected device, usually causing mission failure.

1972. Chapter 6, "Transient Radiation Effects on Electronics (TREE) Phenomena," released under the FOIA].

Treetop: Plan for controlled **presidential succession** under the **continuity of government** program, managed jointly by the **Federal Emergency Management Agency (FEMA)** and the Joint Chiefs of Staff. The plan is called the "Presidential Successor Emergency Support Plan." On 29 January 1982, FEMA issued a 120-page top-secret document titled, *Standing Operating Procedures for Treetop Teams.* The current plan is called "TREETOP II." It outlines guidance and procedures for the establishment of numerous teams consisting of civilian and military advisors to presidential successors and for the maintenance of emergency kits that include war plans, regulations and instructions, fact sheets, and so forth, so that the successors would be able to make decisions. The **National Security Agency** is involved in the preparation of unique authenticators for successors and in the system of codewords and tools used to confirm proper succession.

The 16 Presidential successors are tracked on a day-to-day basis using the "Automated Central Locator System" operated by the **White House Communications Agency**. The locator keeps travel itineraries and feeds constant information to "observer stations" within FEMA, the Pentagon, the **Alternate National Military Command Center (ANMCC)**, and the White House. Treetop is practiced through command post exercise **Nine Lives**, a joint FEMA/JCS mock test. More than one exercise is conducted every year. Nine Lives 1 was conducted 6–8 May 1980. There are also a number of other Presidential-related exercises: Flash Burn, Jackpot, Log Tree, Logex, Log Horn, Pine Ridge, Sage Brush, Ski Jump, Snow Fall, Snow Storm, Southern Pine, Surf Board, Swarmer, and Timber Line.

Triad: Nickname for the strategic offensive force structure that consists of three arms: **ICBMs**, **submarine launched ballistic missiles (SLBMs)**, and **bombers**. The capabilities and characteristics of each system complement the others' for survivability, prompt response, penetration, and reliability. Disproportionate reliance on any one system is avoided, so that the ends of **deterrence** and stability are served and the risks of technological surprise are reduced. Reverence for the Triad also ensures a rationale for a mix of Air Force and Navy systems and a mix of missiles and bombers in the Forces.

Trident I C4: Navy three-stage, solid-propellant, **submarine-launched ballistic missile (SLBM)** with greater range (4,000 nm) than the Polaris A3 and Poseidon C3 missiles it replaced. The longer range of this missile compared to earlier SLBMs means that submarines equipped with Trident I do not have to be based overseas and can patrol a larger portion of the oceans

and still be in range of targets in the Soviet Union. The missile has little hard-target capability, and its accuracy in terms of circular error probable is 750–1,500 ft. The Trident I C4 can carry eight W76/Mk-4 nuclear warheads/reentry vehicles of 100 kt explosive power each. Missile throwweight is 2,900 lb. The missile is guided by a stellar-aided **inertial guidance** digital computer.

Trident I is deployed on the first eight Ohio class SSBNs and on 12 converted Poseidon SSBNs. The first Poseidon SSBN backfitted with Trident I C4 became operational on 20 October 1979, and the last was converted in FY 1983. Each backfit of 16 Trident I C4 missiles into a Poseidon submarine cost about $200 million, not counting the costs of the warheads. The Ohio class submarines were equipped with Trident I missiles as they became operational in the Pacific. They will be backfitted with the **Trident II D5** missile starting in 1992 as Ohio class submarines undergo regular overhauls. The Poseidon submarines armed with Trident I missiles will be retired starting in 1993, or sooner under a **START** agreement. The flyaway cost of each Trident I C4 missile in FY 1980 was $6.934 million, and a total procurement program of 740 missiles was appropriated. The prime missile and RV contractor is Lockheed Missiles and Space Co., Sunnyvale, CA. A consortium of General Electric, Raytheon, and MIT has contracted for the guidance system, and Hercules (Wilmington, DE) and Thiokol have contracted for propulsion.

Trident II D5: Navy three-stage, **submarine-launched ballistic missile (SLBM)** to "deter nuclear war by means of assured destruction in response to a major attack on the United States; to enhance nuclear stability by providing no incentive for enemy first strike" [DOD, *Program Acquisition Costs, FY 1990*]. The Trident II is planned for initial deployment on the ninth Ohio class submarine, the USS Tennessee (SSBN 734), in March 1990 and will replace the **Trident I C4** missile by the mid-1990s. The Trident II D5 has improved accuracy over the Trident I (400–600 ft versus 750–1,500 ft). Its range is virtually the same as Trident I (4000 nm), but can be increased to 6000 nm with reduced RVs. The Trident II D5 can carry up to 14 nuclear warheads, but will not be armed with more than eight warheads under the **START** agreement. The missile can be armed with either the W76/Mk4 nuclear warhead/reentry vehicle of 100 kt each or the W88/Mk5 nuclear warhead/reentry vehicle of 475 kt each. The throwweight of the missile is estimated to be 5,075 lb. It can be targeted at all hardened targets and has an instant retargeting capability as well as a stellar-aided **inertial guidance** system and **NAVSTAR/GPS** reception.

Trident II D5 will be deployed on Ohio class SSBNs starting with the ninth submarine and will be backfitted onto the first eight submarines during their regular overhauls in the 1990s. The Navy plans to have a 21-submarine Trident force by the end of the century. The DOD program cost for 21 Ohio class submarines and their Trident II missile is estimated at $70.3 billion. Backfit of the Trident II missile into the first eight Ohio class submarines will cost $3.6 billion. The 899 Trident II missiles planned for procurement, plus their nuclear warheads, is estimated to cost $40 billion. The prime contractor is Lockheed Missiles and Space Co, Sunnyvale, CA. As of FY 1989, 153 Trident II missiles had been procured at a cost of $5.9 billion, excluding research and development and production costs. The FY 1990 budget request for 63 Trident II D5s, including RDT&E and military construction, is $2,045 million. The FY 1991 request for 52 missiles is $1,714.2 million.

Trident Ohio class ballistic missile submarine: Newest and largest of the nuclear-powered **ballistic missile submarines**, fitted with 24 tubes for either **Trident I C4** or **Trident II D5** submarine-launched ballistic missiles (SLBMs). Its mission is to "provide an undersea strategic missile system in order to ensure that the United States continues to maintain a credible, survivable strategic deterrent independent of foreseeable threats" [DOD, *Program Acquisition Costs*, FY 1990]. Originally labeled ULMS (Undersea Long-range Missile System) during preliminary development in the 1960s, it was renamed Trident in 1972. The first submarine was authorized in FY 1974 and commissioned the USS Ohio (SSBN-726) in November 1981. The submarine is designed for a nine-year operating cycle between overhaul and refueling, plus an operating life in excess of 20 years. Twenty-one submarines are to be built by 1998 at an average cost of more than $2 billion dollars each. Nine submarines are homeported at Bangor, WA. Kings Bay, GA, will be the homeport on the Atlantic Coast for the remaining submarines. The first eight submarines were deployed with the Trident I C4 missile; the ninth and subsequent submarines will have the Trident II D5 missile, which will be backfitted on the first eight submarines during planned overhauls in the 1990s. The prime contractor is Electric Boat Division, General Dynamics, Groton, CT. The FY 1989 budgeted cost for one submarine was $1,257.6 million. The FY 1990 request for one submarine is $1,276.8 million. (see also **naval nuclear propulsion**)

TRI-TAC: Joint service program to provide mobile, high-speed voice-and-data switched digital telephone, facsimile, and message transmission services. TRI-TAC message switches, troposcatter radios, message centers, and user instruments replace antiquated equipment of the 407L analog system. It provides **Tactical Air Control System (TACS)** operations and support personnel with survivable battlefield and bare base communications capability.

TRI-TAC equipment includes

- AN/TAC-1: mobile digital fiber optic interface unit;
- AN/TRC-170 V2/3: mobile digital tropospheric scatter radio, with up to 150-mile ranges;
- AN/TTC-39: mobile 600 line digital circuit switch, which provides

secure and non-secure voice-and-data switching capability;
- AN/TYC-39: mobile 50 line digital message switch, with interoperability to **AUTODIN**;
- AN/TSQ-146: mobile digital group multiplex (DGM) assemblage for concentration/breakout of TRI-TAC circuits;
- Digital Non-Secure Voice Terminal (DNVT): 16/32 kbps digital non-secure telephone instrument for use with TRI-TAC family of circuit switches;
- AN/UXC-7 Lightweight Digital Facsimile (LDF): NATO interoperable, 75 baud to 32 kbps operation, black-and-white medium resolution graphic transmission;
- Modular Tactical Communications Center (MTCC): mobile telecommunications center with ten-line remote terminal message-switching capability for direct service to on-base customers;
- SB-3865: mobile 30-line digital automatic switchboard. secure and non-secure voice-and-data switching capability;
- Secure Digital Net Radio Interface Unit (SDNRIU): semiautomatic interface device to convert ANDVT, Parkhill, and Vinson encrypted radio transmissions to 16/32 kbps TRI-TAC protocol encrypted signals for connection into the TRI-TAC switched network;
- AN/UGC-137 Single Subscriber Terminal (SST): mobile AUTODIN model I and TRI-TAC mode IV message terminal with automatic message preparation/format/address capability;

- TCM-608B Tropo/Satellite Support Radio (TSSR): short-range digital wideband radio;
- Digital Subscriber Voice Terminal (DSVT) (TSEC/KY-68): 16/32 kbps digital secure-voice telephone for use with TRI-TAC family of circuit switches.

troop/troops: **1.** Troop: Army armored or air cavalry unit, equivalent in size to a **company**. **2.** Troops: A collective term referring to military personnel (e.g., airborne troops, combat support troops).

TUSLOG (Turkish-U.S. Logistics Group): Administrative headquarters for U.S. forces in Turkey that serves as the liaison with the Turkish government. Operated by the Air Force, TUSLOG provides base and logistics support, and common services. TUSLOG is subordinate to the 16th Air Force of **U.S. Air Forces Europe**. It supervises the 39th Tactical Group at Incirlik; the 7217th Air Base Group, Ankara AS; and the 7241st Air Base Group, Izmir AS.

Headquarters
Ankara AS, Turkey

TW/AA (see **tactical warning/attack assessment**)

two-man rule: The procedure designed to prohibit access by one individual to nuclear weapons and release codes by requiring the presence at all times of at least two authorized persons capable of detecting unauthorized procedures in certain **restricted areas**, such as **exclusion areas** where weapons are stored or areas containing **nuclear control orders** in command centers. Also referred to as the "two-man concept" or "two-man policy" [DNA, *Nuclear Weapon Accident Response Procedures (NARP) Manual*, January 1984, p. 161, released under the FOIA].

type command: The highest echelon in the Navy's administrative command structure for forces afloat. The organization is based on groupings of a specific "type" of ship or function. Type command organization is a permanent administrative organization of the Atlantic and Pacific Fleets. Type commanders are responsible for the administration, upkeep, maintenance, and training of their assigned forces. Each command is commanded by a Vice Admiral. The Navy type commands and their major subordinate units are

- **Naval Air Force**

    Carrier Groups
    Carrier Air Wings

- **Naval Submarine Force**

    Submarine Groups

- **Naval Surface Force**

    Amphibious Groups
    Cruiser Destroyer Groups
    Naval Special Warfare Groups
    Naval Surface Groups
    Service Groups

- **Fleet Marine Force**

    Force Service Support Groups
    Marine Division
    Marine Aircraft Wing

(see also **Mine Warfare Command, Logistics Command, Fleet Training Command**)

U

U: Prefix designating **1.** Underwater attack vehicle. **2.** Utility aircraft for battlefield support, localized transport, and special light missions (e.g., U-21).

U-2: Air Force all-weather, day-or-night, single-crew, single-engine, subsonic (430 mph), unarmed, high-altitude, photo-reconnaissance and air-sampling aircraft assigned to the **Strategic Air Command**. The long, wide, straight wings of the U-2 give it glider-like characteristics and increase its load capacity to accommodate cameras and data collection instruments. The plane can operate above 70,000 ft and linger in an area for hours. It has a range of more than 3,000 nm. U-2s can carry a variety of high-resolution cameras or the Advanced Synthetic Aperture Radar System (ASARS), as well as an all-weather, day-or-night, digital imaging system.

Since 1957, specially equipped U-2s have conducted flights to sample radioactive debris in the stratosphere. They have also flown missions in support of the U.S. Department of Agriculture land management and crop estimate programs (to make photographs for the Army Corps of Engineers for flood control studies) and for state governments (to determine damage from floods, hurricanes, and tornadoes). Other U-2 projects include obtaining data for the geothermal energy program and participating in search missions for missing boats and aircraft.

The U-2 made its first flight in August 1955. Fifty-five are believed to have been built in various forms, and some eight remain in service. The U-2R with increased span and length is now the primary version. Two U-2Rs equipped with "superpods" are due for delivery in 1989. The U-2s are assigned to the 9th Strategic Reconnaissance Wing at Beale AFB, CA. Lockheed Aircraft Corp., Burbank, CA, is the prime contractor. (see also **TR-1A**)

UCMJ (see **Uniform Code of Military Justice**)

UH-1 Huey/Iroquois: Air Force, Army, and Marine Corps multipurpose utility helicopter. The Air Force twin-engine UH-1H Iroquois is the replacement for the HH-1H Iroquois, a single-engine, two-seat military version of the Bell Model 205. The UH-1H has a maximum speed of 130 kt and a maximum 260 nm range without fuel reserves.

The UH-1N Huey is an Air Force and Marine Corps twin-engine, two-seat version of earlier models. It can carry up to 16 people, including the pilot or weight equivalent. The aircraft is unarmed but can carry two General Electric 7.62 mm miniguns or two 40 mm grenade launchers and two seven-tube 2.75 inch rocket launchers.

All services use the UH-1 for administrative duties. In the Air Force, the UH-1N is used mostly for missile site support duties, providing rapid movement of security forces and supplies to ICBM sites in the United States. The Army uses the UH-1 in its special operations forces and in air assault, air cavalry, and aeromedical evacuation. In the Marine Corps, the UH-1 is used for ship-to-shore movement in amphibious assault and subsequent support operations, and for aeromedical evacuation.

The original Hueys entered service in 1959 with the Army. HH-1H Iroquois military versions of the Bell Model 205 entered service with the Air Force in 1970. The last delivery to the Army was in December 1976. The Hueys entered the Marine Corps in March 1964. Some 3,700 UH-1Hs Hueys are in U.S. service. They are being replaced by the **UH-60 Black Hawk** in the Army. Bell Helicopter Textron, Inc., is the prime contractor.

UH-60 Black Hawk: Army, three-crew, twin-engine, subsonic, troop-carrying/utility helicopter replacing the **UH-1 Huey**. The Black Hawk can carry more than twice the UH-1 payload and is the Army's first helicopter capable of transporting an entire 11-person, fully equipped squad. Alternate seating arrangements can accommodate 14 troops and a crew of three. It can reposition a 105 mm howitzer, its crew of six, and up to 30 rounds of ammunition in a single lift. Its critical components and systems are armored or redundant to enable it to withstand multiple small-arm hits, and its airframe is designed to deform progressively on impact to protect crew and passengers in a crash. It is also designed to be easier to maintain. The Black Hawk has a cruise speed of 145 kt, a maximum range of 330 nm, and endurance of 2.3 hours. The crew consists of two pilots and a crew chief. The helicopter can be armed with two 7.62 mm machine guns. **Hellfire** air-to-surface missiles are also scheduled to be added to UH-60s in 1990, and **Stinger** air-to-air missiles will be added in 1991.

The UH-60 is replacing the UH-1 Huey in air assault, air cavalry, and aeromedical evacuation missions as follows:

- Fifteen UH-60As for 23 UH-1s in combat support aviation companies;
- Seven UH-60As for eight UH-1s in air cavalry units; and
- One UH-60A for one UH-1 in aeromedical evacuation and **Special Forces** units.

The UH-60A entered service in 1978. The 1,000th Black Hawk was delivered to the Army in October 1988. The original planned buy of 1,107 aircraft has been increased to 2,253. Aircraft beyond the 1,107th will be improved UH-60s by a multistage improvement program (MSIP) to restore the original performance characteristics of the aircraft, which have been eroded by increasing aircraft weight from improvements added since 1978.

There will be new rotor composites, upgraded engines, greater fuel capacity, Stinger missile capability, increased external lift capability, and structural modifications to allow for heavier mission weights. The prime contractor is Sikorsky Aircraft, Stratford, CT. The FY 1990 and FY 1991 budget requests for 72 aircraft each year is $439 and $480.6 million, respectively, including RDT&E.

UMBRA: Control-marking and security-clearance level for the most sensitive type of **special intelligence** at the top secret level. (see also **MORAY**, **SPOKE**, **security classification**)

unclassified (see **security classification**)

unclassified controlled nuclear information (UCNI): Controlled but not classified information pertaining to the design or security of nuclear facilities and material (e.g., safeguards information regarding security of **special nuclear materials**). The authority to prohibit the unauthorized disclosure of UCNI was given to the Nuclear Regulatory Commission (NRC) by the **Atomic Energy Act**, Section 147 (amended 1980). Section 148, added in December 1981, also gives the Department of Energy (DOE) the authority to prohibit the disclosure of such "sensitive" information "in the interest of protecting both the health and safety of the public and the common defense and security of the Nation." The restriction of information under Section 148 must be based on the determination that its release could have a significant adverse effect on public health and safety or on the "common defense and security by significantly increasing the likelihood of illegal production of nuclear weapons, or theft, diversion, or sabotage of nuclear materials, equipment, or facilities." The legislative exceptions to the withholding of UCNI include: UCNI already in the public domain, nongovernmental or non-atomic energy defense program information, information already restricted under Section 147, "basic scientific information," employee and public safety information, and data regarding the transport of low-level radioactive waste. DOE does not consider UCNI to be subject to release under the **Freedom of Information Act**. The maximum civil penalty for unauthorized disclosure of UCNI is $100,000. (see also **security classification**)

unconventional warfare (UW): "A broad spectrum of military and paramilitary operations conducted in enemy-held, enemy-controlled or politically sensitive territory. UW includes, but is not limited to, the interrelated fields of guerrilla warfare, evasion and escape, subversion, sabotage, and other operations of a low visibility, covert, or clandestine nature. These interrelated aspects of unconventional warfare may be prosecuted singly or collectively by predominantly indigenous personnel, usually supported and directed in varying degrees by (an) external source(s) during all conditions of war or peace" [*JCS Pub 1*,

p. 383]. As a mission of the special forces, UW operations include

- Peacetime and wartime operations "to exploit military, political, economic, or psychological vulnerabilities of an enemy";
- Providing "support and advice to indigenous resistance forces";
- "Exploiting the existing potential of a resistance movement";
- Concentrating on "guerrilla warfare, evasion and escape, subversion, sabotage and the gathering of intelligence (strategic)"; and
- "Military and paramilitary operations conducted in hostile territory by indigenous forces."

[Armed Forces Staff College. *U.S. Army Organization and Capabilities*, Vol. I, p. 10–5] (see also **Special Forces**, **special operations**)

underwater construction team (UCT): "A unit of the **naval construction force** that provides underwater engineering, construction, and repair capability" [*NWP 3*].

underwater demolition team (UDT): Navy **special operations** team of specially trained "frogmen" who conduct underwater reconnaissance, demolition work, and mine clearing along the beaches just prior to an amphibious assault.

underway replenishment (UNREP): All forms of replenishing ships while underway by transfer-at-sea operations. The primary mission is to keep a naval task force supplied until such time as operations permit return of the task force to a supply point for complete replenishment. During

transits and other cruising operations, the surface force will normally require fuel every three to five days. During high-speed operations, refueling will normally be accomplished every two to five days. Ammunition is rarely required more frequently than fuel. Perishable foods are required about once a month.

Aircraft carrier replenishment is accomplished by fixed-wing aircraft, employed in **carrier onboard delivery (COD)**. Critical items of material and personnel are commonly transferred to the carrier while it is operating at sea. The carrier also receives supplies for further distribution to other ships. Vertical replenishment (VERTREP) is a form of underway replenishment of ships employing helicopters for transport of cargo. VERTREP has the advantage of being able to make deliveries to most types of ships with little or no interference in the operations of the ships. The standard tensioned replenishment alongside method (STREAM) of transfer is used "in the movement of missile components from storage on the delivery ship through the intership transfer and the strikedown operation on the combatant ship. Proper use of missile/cargo STREAM will ensure delivery of 'go' missiles; will reduce time alongside, deck handling, and hazard to crew; and will increase heavy weather replenishment" [NWP 3].

The Navy underway replenishment group (URG) is the organization of the naval Combat Logistics Force (CLF) that accomplishes resupply of combat forces at sea. CLF (formerly known as the Mobile Logistics Support Force) ships include: fast combat support ships (AOE), fleet replenishment oilers (AOR), oilers (AO and TAO), ammunition ships (AE and TAE), and stores ships (AFS and TAFS). A typical URG would be made up of oilers, a provision ship, an ammunition ship, and a stores ships.

Unified Action Armed Forces (UNAAF): Joint Chief of Staff publication containing the principles, doctrines, and functions governing the unified activities of two or more services. Formerly designated JCS Pub 2, the UNAAF has been redesignated JCS Pub 0–2.

unified command: "[A] command with a broad continuing mission, under a single commander and composed of significant assigned components of two or more services . . . . The primary purpose of a unified command or **specified command** is to provide the optimum effectiveness of US military forces in combat operations for the projection of US military power, as required, to support and advance national policies" [JCS, *Unified Command Plan*, SM-729-83, 28 October 1983, and SM-314-84, 17 May 1984, p. 1, released under the FOIA]. Unified commands are operational **combatant commands**, either regionally or functionally-based. The establishment of unified commands was first authorized by the **National Security Act of 1947**. A command is established by the President and receives orders from the **National Command Authorities (NCA)** through the **Joint Chiefs of Staff**. **Operational command** is exercised by a single unified commander (**commander-in-chief (CINC)**)

through the commanders of subordinate commands and components. The unified chain of command specifies that communications between the NCA and the combatant commanders pass through the **Chairman of the Joint Chiefs of Staff (CJCS)**. The CJCS also acts as the spokesman for unified commanders on matters including programming and budgets and provides general oversight of the commands regarding their function and mission requirements. The general responsibilities of the CINCs are outlined in the **Unified Command Plan (UCP)**.

The current unified command organization consists of eight unified commands (five with geographic area responsibilities and three with functional responsibilities), subordinate unified commands, **component commands** provided by the Services, and special commands (**joint task forces** and functional component commands). As mandated by the **Department of Defense Reorganization Act of 1986**, all forces under the jurisdiction of the military departments are assigned to the unified and specified commands with the exception of those performing specific service missions (e.g., administration, training, supply, and maintenance). "In the event of a major emergency that necessitates the use of all available forces, commanders of unified and specified commands are hereby granted the additional authority to assume temporary operational command of all forces in their general areas of responsibility. Not included arc thosc forces scheduled for or engaged in executing missions, under plans approved by the Joint Chiefs of

Staff, that would be interfered with by such use. The determination of the existence of such a major emergency is the responsibility of the commander of the unified or specified command and may not be delegated" [*Unified Command Plan*, pp. 5–6]. The individual military departments maintain responsibility for the administrative and logistical support of assigned units and components.

The commander of a unified or specified command shall

a. Maintain the security of the command and protect the United States, its possessions, and bases against attack or hostile incursion.
b. Carry out assigned missions, tasks, and responsibilities.
c. Assign tasks to, and direct coordination among, the command's subordinate commands to insure unity of effort in the accomplishment of the commander's assigned missions.
d. Communicate directly with

   (1) The Chiefs of the Military Services on uni-Service matters as the commander deems appropriate.
   (2) The Joint Chiefs of Staff on other matters, including the preparation of strategic and logistic plans, strategic and operational direction of the command's assigned forces, conduct of combat operations, and other necessary functions of command required to accomplish the missions.
   (3) The Secretary of Defense, in accordance with applicable directives.

e. Carry out planning and implementing responsibilities for the evacuation of US noncombatants and certain non-US persons aboard in accordance with the provisions of the current "State-Defense Policies and Procedures for the Protection and Evacuation of US Citizens and Certain Designated Aliens in Time of Emergency."
f. [Deleted for security reasons by the JCS.]
g. Provide for US military representation, within the commander's general geographic area of responsibility, where required, to all supranational, international, and US national agencies and furnish US military representation, advice, and assistance to Chiefs of US Diplomatic Missions for negotiation of rights, authorizations, security assistance responsibilities, and facility arrangements, except as otherwise directed by the Joint Chiefs of Staff." [*Unified Command Plan*, pp. 6–8].

Unified Commands

U.S. Atlantic Command (USLANTCOM)

Component Commands

- Atlantic Fleet (LANTFLT)
- U.S. Army Forces Atlantic Command (USARLANT)
- U.S. Air Forces Atlantic (USAFLANT)

Subordinate Unified Commands

- Iceland Defense Forces (IDF)
- U.S. Forces Azores
- Special Operations Command Atlantic (SOCLANT)

U.S. Central Command (USCENTCOM)

Component Commands

- U.S. Army Central Command (USARCENT)
- U.S. Naval Forces Central Command (USNAVCENT)
- U.S. Air Forces Central Command (USCENTAF)

Subordinate Unified Command

- Special Operations Command Central (SOCCENT)

U.S. European Command (USEUCOM)

Component Commands

- U.S. Army Europe (USAREUR)
- U.S. Naval Forces Europe (USNAVEUR)
- U.S. Air Forces in Europe (USAFE)

Subordinate Unified Command

- Special Operations Command Europe (SOCEUR)

U.S. Pacific Command (USPACOM)

Component Commands

- U.S. Army Pacific (USARPAC)
- Pacific Fleet (PACFLT)
- U.S. Pacific Air Forces (USPACAF)

Subordinate Unified Commands

- Alaskan Command
- U.S. Forces Japan (USFJ)
- U.S. Forces Korea (USFK)
- Special Operations Command Pacific (SOCPAC)

U.S. Southern Command (USSOUTHCOM)

Component Commands

- U.S. Army South (USARSO)
- U.S. Naval Forces Southern Command (USNAVSO)
- U.S. Air Forces Southern Command (USAFSO)

U.S. Space Command (USSPACECOM)

Component Commands

- U.S. Army Space Command (USASPACECOM)
- Naval Space Command (NAVSPACECOM)
- Air Force Space Command (AFSPACECOM)

U.S. Special Operations Command (USSOCOM)

Component Commands

- First Special Operations Command (1st SOCOM)
- Air Force Component Command (see special operations wings)
- Naval Special Warfare Command (NAVSPECWARCOM)

U.S. Transportation Command (USTRANSCOM)

Component Commands

- Military Traffic Management Command (MTMC)
- Military Sealift Command (MSC)
- Military Airlift Command (MAC)

Unified Command Plan (UCP): Joint Chiefs of Staff directive that "sets force basic guidance for commanders of unified and specified commands and promulgates their general geographic areas of responsibility and functions" [JCS, *Unified Command Plan*, SM-729-83, 28 October 1983, and SM-314-84, 17 May 1984, p. 1, released under the FOIA]. Such guidance includes the identification of areas of responsibility, assignment of tasks, definition of command authority, establishment of command relationships, and guidance on the exercise of **operational command**. The UCP requires presidential approval and is published by the Chairman of the JCS. It is reviewed biennially. (see also **unified command**, **specified command**)

Uniform Code of Military Justice (UCMJ):   Code of laws enacted by Congress (10 U.S.C. §§801-940) which govern the conduct of all persons in the Armed Forces or subject to military law.

unit: **1.** A military organization structured according to an authority such as a table of organization and equipment.   **2.** In the Navy, a unit subordinate to a task group in a **task force**.

UNITAS: Annual series of naval **exercises** conducted between the U.S. and South American military forces. Begun in 1960, the exercises are conducted through internavy cooperation without any formal agreements between governments. Some Army, Air Force, Marine Corps, and Coast Guard elements may participate. Generally, a U.S. naval task group of some half-dozen ships and several aircraft begins the exercise in the Caribbean Sea with some Latin

American participation and proceeds through the Panama Canal, continuing counter-clockwise around South America. Bilateral and multilateral training exercises are conducted with South American navies along the way. The exercises usually commence in the summer and take place over a period of four to five months. The operation is generally under the command of Commander, South Atlantic Force, Atlantic Fleet, headquartered at Roosevelt Roads, PR.

United Kingdom Air Command Region (UKAIR):   NATO **major subordinate command** of **Allied Command Europe (ACE)**, established in 1975. It is the only single-nation major subordinate command of NATO. It is responsible for air defense of the United Kingdom, is commanded by a British commander, and consists of forces provided by the Royal Air Force (approximately 500 combat aircraft). It has no primary subordinate commands, but has three subordinate RAF formations.

Headquarters
High Wycombe, UK
(APO New York 09241)

Subordinate RAF Formations

• No. 1 Group (Strike/Attack)
• No. 11 Group (Air Defense)
• No. 38 Group (Support and Air Transport)

United Nations Command (UNC):   International combat command established 7 July 1950 for the defense of the Republic of Korea. Today, it operates to carry out the terms and conditions of the 27 July 1953

Armistice agreement. It remains the only international command of its kind. Its participants include Australia, Canada, France, New Zealand, the Republic of the Philippines, Thailand, Colombia, the United Kingdom, and the United States. However, only the United States maintains troops under the UNC. CINCUNC, a four-star U.S. Army General, also serves as Commander of **U.S. Forces Korea (USFK)**, Commander of the ROK/US **Combined Forces Command**, and Commanding General of the **Eighth U.S. Army**.

Headquarters
Seoul, South Korea
(APO San Francisco 96301)

unit equipment (aerospace vehicles): The number of operating active aerospace vehicles authorized to a unit for performance of its operational mission. The unit equipment authorization forms the basis for the allocation of operating resources to include manpower, support equipment, and flying hour funds.

unit identification code (UIC): A six-character, alphanumeric code that uniquely identifies each Active, Reserve, and National Guard unit of the Armed Forces.

Unit Manning System (UMS): Army **manpower** system for active components "based on the precepts of stabilization and unit replacements, operating within the framework of the regimental system" [DOD, *Manpower Requirements Report FY 1989*, March 1988, p. III-28]. The Army implemented the UMS to improve com-

bat effectiveness by reducing personnel turbulence and fostering unit cohesion, esprit de corps, and loyalty in Army units. Components of UMS are the **Cohesion Operational Readiness and Training (COHORT)** unit replacement program and the **U.S. Army Regimental System (USARS)**.

UNITREP (Unit Status and Identity Report): Principle report providing essential information regarding the operational status of units and organizations, now part of the **Status of Resources and Training System (SORTS)**.

unmanned aerial vehicle (UAV): Pilotless aircraft that resemble small aircraft or helicopters and that are remotely controlled or preprogrammed to be controlled by on-board equipment. Also called a **remotely piloted vehicle (RPV)**, but UAV is a more contemporary term. Missions for UAVs include reconnaissance and surveillance, identification and location of targets, relay of communications, and jamming. In the future, UAVs may also be employed in bombing operations when air-, sea-, and ground-based manned systems require additional capabilities to operate within acceptable attrition rates. Usually, UAV systems include the air vehicle, launch and recovery systems, and a ground station for controlling UAV flights and processing collected information.

Typically, the DOD does not consider air vehicles that attack radars or other targets UAVs, although such weapons may share some of the same technology and characteristics. Although target drones technically fit the definition for UAVs or RPVs, they are not generally referred to as such.

In the 1980s the military services sponsored numerous RPV development programs that have resulted in the Navy's **Pioneer** and Amber UAVs, the Army's **Aquila** and Corps Operations UAVs, and the Air Force's **Tacit Rainbow**. In addition, the DOD is developing payloads under separate programs. In the early 1990s, the DOD plans to spend $6 billion on these and other UAV programs.

Due to Congressional concern over redundant programs, the FY 1988 Defense Appropriations Act consolidated UAV and RPV funding within the Office of the Secretary of Defense (OSD) to promote commonality and required a master plan to be submitted to Congress. The Services entered into negotiations to merge the programs, and on 25 February 1988 an agreement in principle among the Air Force, Army, and Navy on acquisition was forwarded to OSD for consideration. OSD submitted its master plan to Congress on 27 June 1988. The master plan grouped ongoing and planned UAV programs into four range categories: close, short, medium-range, and endurance. It generally continued previous Service programs, but it did not reconcile Service UAV requirements or eliminate duplications in the near term. It put off attempts to achieve full commonality until FY 1990.

The OSD UAV joint program provides management supervision of Department of Defense UAVs to ensure cost-effective approaches for fielding a needed capability for conventional forces. The principal objective in the near term is procurement of a short-range UAV system to meet all Service needs. These UAVs will provide capabilities complementary to manned systems in the areas of electronic warfare; intelligence collection; reconnaissance; and command, control, and communications. The FY 1989 budget request for UAVs was $90.0 million, including RDT&E and spares. Continued RDT&E budget requests for FY 1990 and FY 1991 were $152.5 and $152.1 million, respectively.

The Army developed the short-range Aquila to provide reconnaissance, surveillance, and artillery target identification. A production contract for Aquila was cancelled in FY 1987 due to budget considerations, but the DOD UAV master plan allows for continuation of the program. The Army also plans to initiate another short-range UAV (Corps Operations UAV) to provide reconnaissance and surveillance.

The Navy is acquiring the short-range Pioneer system to perform reconnaissance, surveillance, and target identification for naval gunfire support and Marine Corps artillery.

unmanned air reconnaissance vehicle (UARV):   Joint unmanned, subsonic, reconnaissance **remotely piloted vehicle** under development. UARV is part of the Advanced Tactical Air Reconnaissance System (**ATARS**) series of upgrades to improve tactical reconnaissance capabilities, for which the Air Force is the lead service. UARV will carry ATARS sensors, which consist of electro-optical sensor suites (sensors, recorders, a video management system, and data-link sets), fly at subsonic speed, and incorporate signature-reduction features to enhance survivability. Both the Air Force and Navy plan to procure this system. The Air Force will deploy UARV in existing **RF-4C** squadrons, recovering vehicles after each flight. The Navy will put air-launched and expendable UARVs aboard aircraft carriers and also plans to procure target drone versions. The Marine Corps will air-launch the mid-range UARV from **F/A-18D Hornet** fighter aircraft.

U.S. Air Forces Atlantic Command (USAFLANT): Air Force component command of the unified **U.S. Atlantic Command**. The AFLANT organization is collocated with **Tactical Air Command**. USAFLANT is commanded by a four-star Air Force General.

Headquarters
Langley AFB, VA 23665

U.S. Air Forces Central Command (USCENTAF): Air Force component command of **U.S. Central Command**. Its mission is to plan for the employment of air forces assigned to the command. It comprises the 9th Air Force, seven subordinate tactical fighter wings, electronic combat squadrons, tactical reconnaissance squadrons, and tactical air command and control squadrons—all drawn from the **Tactical Air Command**—and tactical airlift squadrons from the **Military Airlift Command**. Reserve forces make up about 65 percent of the **C-130** airlift force, over 50 percent of the tactical reconnaissance squadrons, and nearly 60 percent of communications support. USCENTAF also has operational command of **E-3 Sentry AWACS** aircraft flying along the Persian Gulf approaches to Saudi Arabia in support of the Saudi government. USCENTAF is commanded by an Air Force Lieutenant General.

Headquarters
Shaw AFB, SC 29152

U.S. Air Forces in Europe (USAFE): Air Force **major command** and service component command of **U.S. European Command (USEUCOM)**, redesignated from United States Strategic Air Forces in Europe on 7 August 1945. Its mission is to support NATO in the European theater and to support U.S. military plans in portions of Africa, including close air support, air defense, reconnaissance, strategic and tactical airlift, and maritime support. CINCUSAFE also serves as the commander of NATO's **Allied Air Forces Central Europe (AAFCE)**, and in wartime the two forces are combined and commanded by CINCAAFCE. Further, the commander of USAFE's 16th Air Force in Spain serves as the Commander of **Allied Air Forces Southern Europe**; and the Commander, 17th Air Force, in West Germany serves as Commander, Sector Operations Center III of NATO. USAFE operates 21 major bases in countries between the United Kingdom and Turkey and flies over 650 tactical fighter aircraft. Its personnel strength is over 72,000. It is commanded by a four-star General.

The USAFE major command center is a fixed underground bunker near Ramstein AB at Kindsbach, West Germany, (the USAFE Command Center), which connects with subordinate unit command posts at USAFE tactical wings and groups. The USAFE Command Center supports CINCUSAFE by disseminating information to and collecting data from the unit command posts. The unit command posts have direct voice circuits to the USAFE Command Center, as well as UHF/HF transceivers for ground/air communications, **Primary Alerting System** voice circuits, **AUTODIN** and **AUTOVON** circuits, and HF/SSB **Inform Net** station access lines. The mobile portion of the USAFE C3 system is the USAFE **Tactical Air Control System (TACS)**. Provided by the 601st Tactical Control Wing at Sembach AB, West Germany, TACS is a modular command and control system supporting tactical air support of ground forces. USAFE also operates the CINCEUR **airborne command post** (Silk Purse) with crews from the 10th Airborne Command and Control Squadron, RAF Mildenhall, UK.

Headquarters
Ramstein AB, West Germany
(APO New York 09012)

Subordinate Units

- 3d Air Force, RAF Mildenhall, UK, (APO New York 09127)
- 16th Air Force, Torrejon AB, Spain (APO New York 09283)
- 17th Air Force, Sembach AB, West Germany (APO New York 09130)

U.S. Air Forces Korea: Air Force subordinate component command of **U.S. Forces Korea**, providing logistical and administrative support for all air units assigned in South Korea.

U.S. Air Forces Southern Command (USAFSO):   Air Force component command of **U.S. Southern Command**, responsible for the air defense of the Panama Canal; providing air support of U.S. forces in Central and South America; providing assistance, advice, and training to Latin American air forces through the Inter-American Air Forces Academy; and conducting search and rescue operations. It reports directly to the 12th Air Force of the **Tactical Air Command**. The 830th Air Division (formerly Southern Air Division) represents the U.S. Southern Air Force in Panama. Personnel strength of USAFSO in Panama is approximately 2,300. It is commanded by a Lieutenant General.

Headquarters
Bergstrom AFB, TX 78743

U.S. Army Europe (USAREUR)/7th Army: Army **major command** and component command of **U.S. European Command**. Its wartime mission is to provide logistical and administrative support to U.S. Army units in Europe and to support U.S. military forces operating in portions of Africa. USAREUR's area of responsibility includes 77 countries in Europe, Africa, and parts of the Middle East. Most tactical and CONUS-based Army units are committed to NATO under the operational command of CINC-EUCOM and Supreme Allied Commander Europe and are administratively supported by USAREUR. Major forces include the V Corps and VII Corps, U.S. Command Berlin, U.S. Army **Southern European Task Force**, 32d Army Air Defense Command, 56th Field Artillery Command, 4th Transportation Command, and four general support commands. The USAREUR commander is also the commander of NATO's **Central Army Group (CENTAG)**. USAREUR units are scattered over 40 communities and 800 occupied installations, with a personnel strength of approximately 200,000. It is commanded by a four-star Army General.

Headquarters
Heidelberg, West Germany
(APO New York 09403)

U.S. Army Forces, Atlantic Command (USARLANT): Army **major command** and service component command of **U.S. Atlantic Command**, assigned to the Army **Forces Command (FORSCOM)**. It consists of up to three combat ready divisions assigned to FORSCOM. It is commanded by a four-star Army General.

Headquarters
Ft. McPherson, GA 30050

U.S. Army Forces, Central Command (USARCENT): Army **major command** and component command of **U.S. Central Command**. USARCENT's (and the 3d U.S. Army's) mission is to plan for the operational employment of Army combat, combat support, and combat service-support units assigned to it in wartime. It is composed of one corps headquarters, one airborne division, one air assault division, one mechanized infantry division, one light infantry division, one mechanized brigade, and one cavalry brigade (air combat). It is commanded by a Lieutenant General.

Headquarters
Ft. McPherson, GA 30050

U.S. Army Japan (USARJ)/IX Corps: Army **major command** and subordinate component command of **U.S. Forces Japan**. It is also the U.S. component of the U.S. Army-Japan Ground Self Defense Force (JGSDF). Formerly a separate Army command, USARJ/IX Corps was made subordinate to **U.S. Army Western Command (WESTCOM)** (27 March 1987) and will be transferred to U.S. Army Pacific with WESTCOM's disestablishment in 1990. USARJ missions are to conduct contingency planning for the defense of Japan, to provide logistical support of WESTCOM, and, in wartime, to command all Army units assigned in Japan. There are no combat units permanently assigned to USARJ, but it maintains a headquarters and approximately 20 logistical and storage facilities. Its headquarters (merged with headquarters IX Corps since 15 May 1972), conducts three major annual command post exercises in cooperation with the JGSDF: **Yama Sakura**, Orient Shield, and North Wind.

Headquarters
Camp Zama, Japan
(APO San Francisco 96503)

U.S. Army Nuclear and Chemical Agency (USANCA): Army **field operating agency** that provides advice and assistance to Army organizations and other government agencies on nuclear and chemical warfare matters. It also participates in chemical and nuclear R&D programs and weapons effects studies and testing. USANCA is responsible for Army nuclear and chemical weapons systems safety and surety, participates in survivability programs and evaluation, supports the Army Staff in determining nuclear weapons stockpile requirements, participates in the Army's on-call nuclear and chemical accident command post, and augments the Nuclear Accident and Incident Response and Assistance Center and the Army Nuclear Accident Investigation Board. Its director is also director of the Army's Nuclear and Chemical Office on the Army Staff. USANCA reports to the Office of the Deputy Chief of Staff for Operations and Plans [Army, *United States Army Nuclear and Chemical Agency*, AR 10-16, 15 March 1984, released under the FOIA].

Headquarters
Springfield, VA 22150

U.S. Army Pacific (USARPAC): Future Army **major command** and component of **U.S. Pacific Command** to be redesignated from **U.S. Army Western Command (WEST-COM)** pending Congressional approval in 1990. USARPAC will gain command of **U.S. Army Japan** and other units subordinate to WEST-COM, including the Alaskan 6th Light Infantry Division, transferred from the operational command of Forces Command. The WESTCOM commander will become the USARPAC commander.

U.S. Army Regimental System (USARS): A subsystem of the **Unit Manning System** designed to enhance combat effectiveness of Army units. Under the system, a **regiment** is organized as "a single unit or a group of like-type units designed with a unique regimental color and formed for the purpose of providing an affiliated soldier with an opportunity for long term identification, the potential for recurring assignments, and the basis to perpetuate historical customs and traditions." A total of 197 regiments have been or are slated for reorganization under the USARS system. Under the system, 13 "whole branch" regiments have also been reorganized, while aviation was established as a separate combat arms branch with 29 new regimental designations of its own. Approximately one quarter of the units are assigned to the **Training and Doctrine Command** [*Army Posture Statement*, FY 1988, p. 15]. (see also **Cohesion Operational Readiness Training,** **branch**)

U.S. Army South (USARSO): Component command of **U.S. Southern Command**. It was deactivated in 1974, then reactivated in FY 1985 and designated an Army **major command** on 4 December 1986. Its missions are to provide ground defense of the Panama Canal and to support other regional missions, including support of deployments to 12 Latin American countries for training, engineering, medical, and intelligence operations. It maintains control of all Army combat and support units assigned to USSOUTHCOM. Its major combat element is the 193d Infantry Brigade (Canal Zone), which comprises the 3d Battalion of the 7th Special Forces Group and the Jungle

Operations Training Center. USARSO personnel strength is about 7,000. It is commanded by a Major General.

Headquarters
Ft. Clayton, Panama
(APO Miami 34009)

U.S. Army Space Command (USA-SPACECOM): Army **major command** and component command of **U.S. Space Command**. It was established 7 April 1988 from the U.S. Army Space Agency. Since the Fall of 1987, it has exercised operational control of the ground control elements of the **Defense Satellite Communications System (DSCS)**. Elements transferred to USASPACE-COM include the former U.S. Air Force DSCS Operations Center at Onizuka AFB, CA; all DSCS ground control facilities transferred from the Army Information Systems Command; and a planned Navy DSCS Operations Center. The Command will also take over the Regional Space Support Center from the DSCS. Technical control of DSCS remains with the **Defense Communications Agency**, and satellite command functions remain with the **Air Force Space Command**. In addition, the Command performs some SpaceTrack radar functions (see Space Surveillance Network); provides operational crews for the **NAVSTAR/GPS**; coordinates the operation of the Army Kwajalein Atoll space surveillance radars in the south Pacific; and forms "the operational nucleus of any Army portion of a layered ballistic missile defense system, should the decision be made to proceed with deployment." The Command also

acts as the lead service in the development of a national kinetic energy anti-satellite weapon and is responsible for the command and control planning for the **ERIS (Exoatmospheric Reentry Vehicle Intercept System)** and the **Ground-based Surveillance and Tracking System (GS-TS)**. Its personnel strength is 100 personnel, expected to grow to approximately 450 by the mid-1990s. It is commanded by a Brigadier General.

Headquarters
Peterson AFB, CO 80914

U.S. Army Strategic Defense Command (USASDC): Army staff **field operating agency** and component of DOD's **Strategic Defense Initiative Office (SDIO)**. It was preceded by components of the Army Ballistic Missile Defense Agency, established in 1957. The Command was established on 1 July 1985 from the Ballistic Missile Defense Office. USASDC exercises executive authority for the Army portion of the **Strategic Defense Initiative**, and conducts a coordinated research program toward the development of ballistic missile defense technologies. The focus of the research is in support of the Strategic Defense System (SDS). Army components of Phase I of the SDS are **ERIS (Exoatmospheric Reentry Vehicle Interceptor System)**; the Ground-based Surveillance and Tracking System (GSTS); the Battle Management, Command, Control and Communications (BM/C3) support systems; and the **Ground-Based Radar (GBR)**. Other Army-operated programs include **Cobra**

Judy; the Optical Aircraft Measurement Program (OAMP); the **Airborne Optical Adjunct (AOA)**; **Terminal Imaging Radar (TIR)**; **Flexible Lightweight Agile Guided Experiment (FLAGE)**; SENTRY; and **High Endoatmospheric Defense Interceptor (HEDI)**. USASDC represents approximately one third of the SDIO budget or $1.3 billion (FY 1989).

Headquarters
Arlington, VA 22215-0280

Directorates

- Survivability, Lethality and Key Technologies
- Advanced Technology
- Kinetic Energy Weapons
- Sensors
- Systems Analysis/Battle Management

U.S. Army Western Command (WESTCOM): Army **major command** and component command of **U.S. Pacific Command (PACOM)** to be redesignated as U.S. Army Pacific pending Congressional approval in 1990. On 1 January 1975, U.S. Army Pacific was disestablished and redesignated the U.S. Army CINCPAC Support Group (USACSG). On 23 March 1979, USACSG and U.S. Army Support Command Hawaii (USASCH), a subordinate element of Forces Command, merged to form the U.S. Army Western Command (WESTCOM).

WESTCOM's mission is the support of Army units assigned to PACOM, less responsibilities for South Korea. It consists of the 25th Light Infantry Division (LID) in Hawaii; Support Command Hawaii;

45th Support Group; Army Readiness Group; IX Corps (augmentation) in Hawaii; the Army Chemical Activity at Johnston Atoll; and the 6th Light Infantry Division in Alaska (as of 1 October 1989). The Command also exercises operational control of the 1st Battalion, 1st Special Forces Group, and, as of 27 March 1987, exercises operational control of **U.S. Army Japan**, formerly a separate Army command. For uniservice matters, WESTCOM administrates the **Eighth U.S. Army** in South Korea, although this command falls under the operational command of **U.S. Forces Korea**. Through the International Activities Program (IAP), established in 1978, WESTCOM maintains security assistance and civic action contact with approximately 33 foreign armies in the Asian-Pacific area, conducting joint seminars and information exchanges. It is commanded by a Lieutenant General.

Headquarters
Ft. Shafter, Oahu, HI 96858

U.S. Atlantic Command (USLANTCOM): Unified command established 1 December 1947 with operational command of all U.S. forces in the Atlantic from the North to South Poles, including the Norwegian, Greenland, and Barents Seas; the Caribbean Sea and the waters surrounding Africa to the Cape of Good Hope; and the Pacific Ocean west of Central America. "The Commander in Chief, US Atlantic Command (USCINCLANT), with present headquarters at Norfolk, VA, is the commander of a unified command comprising all forces assigned for the accomplishment of his missions. USCINCLANT's general geographic area of responsibility for the conduct of normal operations, less security assistance responsibilities for Iceland and Cape Verde, is the Atlantic Ocean west of 17 degrees E. longitude; the Caribbean Sea; the Pacific Ocean east of 92 degrees W. longitude; the Arctic Ocean east of 95 degrees W. longitude and west of 100 degrees E. longitude; Greenland; and other islands (less the UK and Ireland) in all assigned water areas" [JCS, *Unified Command Plan*, SM-729-83, 28 October 1983, and SM-314-84, 17 May 1984, p. 11, released under the FOIA].

Primarily a maritime command, USLANTCOM consists of over 300 active and reserve ships from the Atlantic Fleet as well as Army and Air Force forces. In wartime, such forces would be provided to NATO's **Allied Command Atlantic**. CINCLANT-COM, a four-star Navy Admiral, also serves as the **Supreme Allied Commander Atlantic (SACLANT)**. USLANTCOM conducts the annual joint exercises **Ocean Venture** (in even years) and **Solid Shield** (in odd years) and regularly participates in NATO exercises Northern Wedding and **Ocean Safari**.

Headquarters
Norfolk, VA 23511

Component Commands

- **Atlantic Fleet (LANTFLT)**
- **U.S. Air Forces Atlantic (USAFLANT)**
- **U.S. Army Forces Atlantic (USARLANT)**

Subunified Commands

- **Iceland Defense Force (IDF)**
- **Special Operations Command**, Atlantic (SOCLANT)
- **U.S. Forces Azores**

Special Commands

- **Joint Task Force 4**
- Joint Task Force 120
- Joint Task Force 140

Commanders-in-Chief Atlantic

ADM Lynde D. McCormick	Dec 1947
ADM Jerault Wright	Apr 1954
ADM Robert L Dennison	Dec 1959
ADM H.P. Smith	Apr 1964
ADM Thomas H. Moorer	May 1965
ADM Ephraim P. Holmes	Jun 1967
ADM Charles K. Duncan	Oct 1970
ADM Ralph W. Cousins	Oct 1972
ADM Isaac C. Kidd	May 1975
ADM Harry D. Train	Oct 1978
ADM Wesley L. McDonald	Nov 1982
ADM Lee Baggett, Jr.	Nov 1985
ADM Frank B. Kelso II	Nov 1988

U.S. Atlantic Fleet (see **Atlantic Fleet**)

U.S. Central Command (USCENTCOM): Unified command redesignated from the Rapid Deployed Joint Task Force (RDJTF) on 1 January 1983. USCENTCOM exercises operational command of all U.S. forces in Southwest Asia, the Middle East, and East Africa, encompassing 19 countries and 3,100 miles east to west and 3,400 miles north to south. "The Commander in Chief, US Central Command (USCINCCENT), with present headquarters at MacDill Air Force Base, Tampa, Florida, is the commander of a unified command comprising all forces assigned for the accomplishment of his missions. USCINCCENT's general geographic area of responsibility for the conduct of normal operations includes Egypt, Sudan, Djibouti, Ethiopia, Kenya, Somalia, Jordan, Saudi Arabia, Kuwait, Oman, Qatar, United Arab Emirates, Yemen Arab Republic, People's Democratic Republic of Yemen, Bahrain, Iran, Iraq, Afghanistan, and Pakistan, plus the Persian Gulf and Red Sea" [JCS, *Unified Command Plan*, SM-729-83, 28 October 1983, and SM-314-84, 17 May 1984, pp. 12–13, released under the FOIA].

The mission of USCENTCOM is the defense of U.S. interests in its region, including protection of its strategic oil reserves, import and export shipping, international waterways such as the Suez Canal and Bab el Mandeb accesses, and the Straits of Hormuz. **Maritime Prepositioning Force** ships with heavy military equipment and stores have been prepositioned in ports including Mombasa (Kenya) and Diego Garcia in the Indian Ocean. Other base facilities have been prepared for U.S. use in Kenya, Somalia, and Oman. USCENTCOM forces may also be assigned to NATO in wartime. USCENTCOM manages the **Security Assistance Program** for 13 countries in the region, totalling approximately $1.5 billion for FY 1989. Its major field training exercise, conducted in odd-numbered years, is Bright Star. Its major CONUS exercises, conducted in even-numbered years, are the command post exercise Gallant Knight

and the field training exercise Gallant Eagle. USCENTCOM is often still popularly called the Rapid Deployment Force. Its CINC is a four-star Marine Corps General. (see also **Middle East Force**, **Joint Task Force Middle East**)

Headquarters
MacDill AFB, FL 33608

Component Commands

- **U.S. Air Forces Central Command (USCENTAF)**
- **U.S. Army Central Command (USARCENT)**
- **U.S. Marine Forces Central Command (USMARCENT)**
- **U.S. Naval Forces Central Command (USNAVCENT)**

Subunified Command

- **Special Operations Command, Central (SOCCENT)**

Special Command

- **Joint Task Force Middle East (JTFME)**

Commanders-in-Chief USCENTCOM

GEN Robert C. Kingston, USA
1 July 1983 — 22 Nov 1985
GEN George B. Crist, USMC
22 Nov 1985 — 1 Nov 1988
GEN H. Norman Schwarzkopf, USA
1 Nov 1988 — present

USCINCSPACE Assessment: An evaluation by the Commander-in-Chief of the **U.S. Space Command** of the likelihood that an attack is in progress or has occurred against a space system. The assessments are as follows

- "No": In the judgment of USCINC-SPACE, an attack against a space system has not occurred nor is one in progress.
- "Concern": In the judgment of USCINCSPACE, events are occurring that have raised his level of concern. Further assessment is necessary in order to determine the nature of the activity involved. Pending completion of the ongoing assessment, precautionary measures to enhance responsiveness or survivability are suggested.
- "Medium": In the judgment of USCINCSPACE, an attack against a space system may have occurred or may be in progress; USCINC-SPACE is still assessing the situation.
- "High": In the judgment of USCINCSPACE, a verified attack against a space system has occurred. This means that all source data confirms that the hostile event has occurred or is occurring.

[JCS, *Emergency Action Procedures—Emergency Conferences for Tactical Warning and Attack Assessment*, 1 December 1986, p. II-B-2, released under the FOIA]

USCINCPAC Voice Alert Network (CVAN): Primary **U.S. Pacific Command (PACOM)** non-secure voice alerting system connecting the Commander-in-Chief, PACOM and the alternate command post **(AL-COP)**, to all other PACOM command posts and critical communication centers.

U.S. European Command (USEU-COM): Unified command and a **major subordinate command** of NATO's **Allied Command Europe (ACE)**. It was established 1 August 1952 with operational command of all U.S. forces in the European theater—from the north cape of Norway, through the Mediterranean and parts of the Middle East, to the tip of southern Africa—encompassing 13 million square miles, 77 countries, and 119 diplomatic posts. "The US Commander in Chief, Europe (USCINCEUR), with present headquarters at Patch Barracks, Stuttgart, FRG, is the commander of a unified command comprising all forces assigned for the accomplishment of his missions. USCINCEUR's general area of responsibility for the conduct of normal operations is: Europe including eastern European countries (German Democratic Republic, Poland, Czechoslovakia, Hungary, Bulgaria, Romania, Yugoslavia, Albania), the UK, and Ireland; the Mediterranean Sea and the islands therein; the Mediterranean littoral (excluding Egypt); and the continent of Africa (less Egypt, Sudan, Kenya, Ethiopia, Somalia, and Djibouti). In addition, USCINCEUR is responsible for planning for and the administration of the military aspects of security assistance for Iceland and Cape Verde" [JCS, *Unified Command Plan*, SM-729-83, 28 October 1983, and SM-314-84, 17 May 1984, p. 13, released under the FOIA].

EUCOM's primary mission is to support NATO in conventional and nuclear operations. In support of U.S. objectives, its missions are to con-

Commanders-in-Chief USEUCOM

GEN Mathew B. Ridgway, USA	1 Aug 1952
GEN Alfred M. Gruenther, USA	11 Aug 1953
GEN Lauris Norstad, USAF	20 Nov 1956
GEN Lyman L. Lemnitzer, USA	1 Nov 1962
GEN Andrew J. Goodpaster, USA	5 May 1969
GEN Alexander M. Haig, USA	1 Nov 1974
GEN Bernard W. Rogers, USA	27 Jun 1979
GEN John R. Galvin, USA	25 Jun 1987

duct crisis management and contingency operations, such as humanitarian relief to allies and evacuation of U.S. noncombatants residing in the region; to coordinate military intelligence activities; and to manage security assistance programs. Combat and combat support units are transferred to NATO during wartime, while administrative control of forces is retained by EUCOM. EUCOM also retains both responsibility for the custody of nuclear weapons and operational control of theater airlift through **U.S. Air Forces in Europe (USAFE)**—as well as operational control of tactical fighter and reconnaissance forces, in some cases. CINCEUCOM, a four-star Army General, also serves as NATO's **Supreme Allied Commander Europe (SACEUR)**. Major EUCOM exercises include **Autumn Forge**, conducted with the cooperation of Allied Command Europe, and its annual U.S. reinforcement exercise, **REFORGER** (Return of Forces to Germany). Joint personnel strength is 317,000, with a headquarters staff of 625.

Headquarters
Patch Barracks, Stuttgart-Vaihingen, West Germany
(APO New York 09128)

Component Commands

- **U.S. Air Force in Europe (USAFE)**
- **U.S. Army Europe (USAREUR)**
- **U.S. Naval Forces Europe (USNAVEUR)**

Subunified Command

- **Special Operations Command**, Europe (SOCEUR)

U.S. Forces Azores: Subunified command of **U.S. Atlantic Command (USLANTCOM)**. Its maritime patrol mission includes surveillance and anti-submarine warfare. It also serves as a refueling base in support of U.S. air and sea reinforcements to NATO and **U.S. Central Command**. Its personnel strength is approximately 1,400. It is commanded by an Air Force Brigadier General.

Headquarters
Lajes Field, Terceira, Azores
(APO New York 09406)

U.S. Forces Caribbean: Former subunified command of **U.S. Atlantic Command (USLANTCOM)**, disestablished on 30 June 1989. Its facilities and assets were transferred to **Joint Task Force (JTF)** 4, a multi-service drug interdiction force.

U.S. Forces Command   (see **Forces Command**)

U.S. Forces Japan (USFJ): Sub-unified command of **U.S. Pacific Command**, responsible for the "maintenance of peace and security in the Far East" under the U.S.–Japanese Treaty of Mutual Cooperation and Security, signed in 1952 and revised January 1960. USFJ operates over 100 air, naval, and communications bases and facilities in Japan. Many of the bases and activities are jointly operated with the Japanese Self Defense Forces (SDF), and Japan maintains major logistics depots for U.S. forces. U.S. forces have priority use of the railway system, radio frequencies, and the like. Japan expends approximately $600 million annually in support of U.S. forces. The commander of USFJ is also the commander of the 5th Air Force. USFJ conducts combined training exercises with the SDF, including the biennial RIMPAC (rim of the Pacific) exercise, and a variety of ground and air exercises. Total personnel strength is approximately 47,000. It is commanded by a three-star Air Force Lieutenant General.

Headquarters
Yokota AB, Tokyo, Japan
(APO SF 96328)

Component commands

- **5th Air Force (PACAF)**
- **U.S. Army, Japan (USARJ)**
- **U.S. Naval Forces Japan**

U.S. Forces Korea (USFK): Sub-unified command of **U.S. Pacific Command** and U.S. component of the ROK/U.S. **Combined Forces Command (CFC)**, with operational control of U.S. forces operating in South Korea under the provisions of the bilateral U.S.-Republic of Korea mutual defense treaty. Total personnel strength is about 44,000. It is commanded by a four-star Army General.

Headquarters
Yongsan, S. Korea (APO SF 96301)

Component commands

- **Eighth U.S. Army**
- **U.S. Air Forces Korea**
- **U.S. Marine Forces Korea**
- **U.S. Naval Forces Korea**

U.S. Marine Forces Central Command (USMARCENT): Component command of **U.S. Central Command**, when designated. It is a Marine Corps planning force consisting of the 1st Marine Expeditionary Force and the 7th Marine Expeditionary Brigade. For combat operations, these units deploy by sea and air to join their prepositioned equipment or deploy with available task forces.

Headquarters
Camp Pendleton, CA 92055

U.S. Naval Forces Caribbean/Fleet Air Caribbean: Navy command of the Atlantic Fleet, formerly assigned to the disestablished **U.S. Forces Caribbean** (LANTFLT). Its drug interdiction mission and assets were assumed by the **Joint Task Force (JTF)** 4. Naval facilities at Guantánamo Bay, Cuba; Roosevelt Roads, P.R.; and Antigua remain assigned to the Atlantic Fleet.

U.S. Naval Forces Central Command (USNAVCENT): Navy operating force and component command of **U.S. Central Command**, with overall command and operational control of naval forces assigned to the area (except those under the operational control of the Commander Joint Task Force Middle East). Its principle operating force is the **Middle East Force (MIDEASTFOR)**, which conducts peacetime and wartime operations in the Red Sea, Persian Gulf and northwest Indian Ocean area. An additional planning force is composed of three aircraft carrier battle groups of over 50 surface and subsurface ships; two amphibious ready groups; five maritime patrol squadrons; 13 ocean going minesweepers; and one mine countermeasures helicopter squadron. It is commanded by a Navy Rear Admiral.

Headquarters
Pearl Harbor, HI 96860

U.S. Naval Forces Europe (USNAVEUR): Navy component command of **U.S. European Command** responsible for the operation and management of all naval forces in Europe from the eastern shores of Greenland through the North Atlantic and Mediterranean Sea. **USNAVEUR** would also provide U.S. forces and logistical support to NATO in wartime. The Deputy CINCUSNAVEUR also serves as the Commander of (U.S.) Atlantic Fleet's

Eastern Atlantic Command. It is commanded by a four-star Navy Admiral.

Headquarters
London, UK
(APO New York 09510)

Subordinate Commands

• Fleet Air Mediterranean
• **Sixth Fleet**
• U.S. Naval Activities, UK

U.S. Naval Forces Iceland (NAVICE): Highest-level naval command in Iceland and, in wartime, the U.S. Navy component command of the **Iceland Defense Force**. Its primary facility is the U.S. Naval Station, Keflavik. Its tenant facilities provide operational logistic and administrative support to deployed units and tenants. NAVICE includes the U.S. Naval Communication Station, Iceland, which provides support of U.S. and NATO commands and the American Embassy in Reykjavik. It has one receiver site at Rockville, and a transmitter site at Grindavik. It also includes the Naval Weather Service Environmental Detachment, Keflavik, which supports all U.S. and NATO forces in the area, as well as civilian and non–NATO consumers; a U.S. Naval Security Group Activity; a **P-3** squadron on rotation from NAS Brunswick, ME; and the Fleet Air Keflavik Operations Control Center. NAVICE is commanded by Commander, Fleet Air Keflavik, which is responsible to Naval Air Force Atlantic. In wartime, the commander becomes NATO's Island Commander Iceland.

Headquarters
NS Keflavik, Iceland
(APO New York 09571)

U.S. Naval Forces Japan: Navy component command of **U.S. Forces Japan**, providing logistical and administrative support to the naval support forces assigned to the region.

Headquarters
Yokosuka, Japan
(APO San Francisco 98762-0051)

U.S. Naval Forces Korea: Navy component command of **U.S. Forces Korea**, providing logistical and administrative support to the naval support forces assigned to South Korea and Korean military missions. The headquarters personnel strength is about 400.

Headquarters
Yongsan, South Korea
(APO San Francisco 96301-0023)

U.S. Naval Forces Marianas: Navy command responsible for administrative command of naval activities in Micronesia, Guam, and the Marshall Islands.

Headquarters
Guam
(APO San Francisco 96630-0051)

U.S. Naval Forces Philippines: Navy command responsible for administrative command of naval activities in the Philippines and for operation of the naval complex at Subic Bay.

Headquarters
Subic Bay, Philippines
(APO San Francisco 96651-0051)

U.S. Naval Forces Southern Command (USNAVSO): Navy **operating force** and component command of **U.S. Southern Command**. It maintains a special boat unit and provides fleet support to the unified command. It also manages the operation of the U.S. Naval Small Craft Instruction and Technical School in Panama. Its personnel strength is about 400.

Headquarters
Ft. Amador, Panama
(APO Miami 34059)

U.S. Naval Ship (USNS): "A public vessel of the United States in the custody of the Navy" [*NWP 3*]. A USNS is either operated by the **Military Sealift Command (MSC)** and consists of a civil service crew, or it is operated by a commercial company under contract to the MSC and staffed by a **Merchant Marine** crew.

U.S. Pacific Command (USPACOM): Unified command established on 1 January 1947, with operational command of all U.S. forces in the Pacific area—from the west coast of the Americas to the east coast of Africa, and from the Arctic to the Antarctic—an area of more than 100 million square miles. "The Commander in Chief US Pacific Command (USCINCPAC), with present headquarters at Camp H. M. Smith, Oahu, Hawaii, is the commander of a unified command comprising all forces assigned for the accomplishment of his missions. USCINCPAC's general area of responsibility for the conduct of normal operations is the Pacific Ocean west of 92 degrees W. longitude, the Bering Sea,

Commanders-in-Chief Pacific

FADM Chester W. Nimitz	3 Apr 1942	24 Nov 1945
ADM Raymond A. Spruance	24 Nov 1945	1 Feb 1946
ADM John H. Towers	1 Feb 1946	28 Feb 1947
ADM Louis E. Denfeld	28 Feb 1946	3 Dec 1947
ADM Dewitt C. Ramsey	12 Jan 1948	30 Apr 1949
ADM Arthur W. Radford	30 Apr 1949	10 Jul 1953
ADM Felix B. Stump	10 Jul 1953	31 Jul 1958
ADM Harry D. Felt	31 Jul 1958	30 Jun 1964
ADM U.S. Grant Sharp	30 Jun 1964	31 Jul 1968
ADM John S. McCain, Jr.	31 Jul 1968	1 Sep 1972
ADM Noel A.M. Gayler	1 Sep 1972	30 Aug 1976
ADM Maurice F. Weisner	30 Aug 1976	31 Oct 1979
ADM Robert L.J. Long	31 Oct 1979	1 Jul 1983
ADM William J. Crowe, Jr.	1 Jul 1983	18 Sep 1985
ADM Ronald J. Hayes	18 Sep 1985	30 Sep 1988
ADM Huntington Hardisty	30 Sep 1988	present

the Arctic Ocean west of 95 degrees W. longitude and east of 100 degree E. longitude, the Indian Ocean east of 17 degrees E. longitude (including the Gulf of Oman and the Gulf of Aden), Japan, the ROK, the Democratic People's Republic of Korea, the People's Republic of China, the countries of Southeast Asia and the southern Asian landmass to the western border of India, and Madagascar and the other islands in all assigned water areas. In addition, USCINPAC's general geographic area of responsibility for the conduct of normal operations other than air defense is the Aleutian Island (excluding the Alexander Archipelago, Kodiak, Nunivak, and Little Diomede Islands)" [JCS, *Unified Command Plan*, SM-729-83, 28 October 1983, and SM-314-84, 17 May 1984, pp. 13–14, released under the FOIA].

PACOM implements security agreements with Japan, the Republic of Korea, Thailand, the Republic of the Philippines, and Australia, and bilateral relationships with members of the Association of Southeast Asian Nations (ASEAN). USPACOM also manages all security assistance programs in the theater. USPACOM conducts approximately 86 annual bilateral and multilateral exercises. The CINCPAC alternate command post **(ALCOP)** is located at Hickam AFB, HI. Its personnel strength is approximately 380,000. The commander is a four-star Navy Admiral.

Headquarters
Camp H. M. Smith,
Oahu, HI 96861

Component Commands

- **Fleet Marine Force, Pacific**
- **Pacific Fleet (PACFLT)**
- **U.S. Army Western Command (WESTCOM)**
- **U.S. Pacific Air Forces (USPACAF)**

Subunified Commands

- **Alaskan Command**
- **Special Operations Command**, Pacific (SOCPAC)
- **U.S. Forces Japan (USFJ)**
- **U.S. Forces Korea (USFK)**

Special Commands

- **Joint Task Force** 5
- Joint Task Force 110
- Joint Task Force 119
- Joint Task Force 510

U.S. Pacific Fleet (PACFLT) (see **Pacific Fleet**)

U.S. Southern Command (US-SOUTHCOM): Unified command established 6 June 1963 from the U.S. Caribbean Command. It exercises operational command of all U.S. land forces in South America, Central America (except Mexico), and the Panama Canal. "The Commander in Chief, US Southern Command (USCINCSO), with present headquarters at Quarry Heights, Panama, is the commander of a unified command comprising all forces assigned for the accomplishment of his missions. USCINCSO's general geographic area of responsibility for the conduct of normal operations other than air defense and the protection of sea communications is Central and South America (excluding Mexico) . . . . For the purpose of security assistance activities and coordination of security assistance organization only, the geographic area of responsibility of USCINCSO includes all of Central America, South America, and Mexico. USCINCSO's pri-

mary responsibility is for the defense of the Panama Canal and Panama Canal area, and such other contingency planning responsibilities as directed by the Joint Chiefs of Staff" [JCS, *Unified Command Plan*, SM-729-83, 28 October 1983, and SM-314-84, 17 May 1984, pp. 14–15, released under the FOIA].

USSOUTHCOM's missions include defense of the southern approaches to the United States, support for combined inter-American training exercises, search and rescue missions, disaster relief, and evacuation missions. Specific USSOUTHCOM missions: to provide support for counterinsurgency operations in El Salvador; to assist Latin American militaries in combating insurgency, terrorism, and narcotics trafficking; and to "reverse Soviet, Cuban and Nicaraguan influence and their attempts to destabilize democratic processes in Latin America." USSOUTHCOM's forward-deployed force consists of an Army combat brigade, an Army Special Forces battalion, a Navy small boat unit, an Air Force tactical air support squadron, and support elements. There are 16 military groups (MIL-GROUPS) stationed in central and south American countries to coordinate training and security assistance. Additionally, there are approximately 1,200 military personnel stationed in Honduras. Combined personnel strength of USSOUTHCOM is approximately 10,000. The command headquarters is being relocated to CONUS as part of a phased military withdrawal from Panama. The Panama Canal Treaty will expire on 31 December 1999.

Commanders-in-Chief U.S. Southern Command

GEN Andrew P. O'Meara	Jun 1963	Feb 1965
GEN Robert W. Porter, Jr.	Feb 1965	Feb 1969
GEN George R. Mather	Feb 1969	Sep 1971
GEN George V. Underwood, Jr.	Sep 1971	Jan 1973
GEN William B. Rosson	Jan 1973	Jul 1975
LTG Dennis P. McAuliffe	Jul 1975	Oct 1979
LTG Wallace H. Nutting	Oct 1979	May 1983
GEN Paul F. Gorman	May 1983	Mar 1985
GEN John R. Galvin	Mar 1985	Jun 1987
GEN Frederick F. Woerner, Jr.	Jun 1987	Oct 1989
GEN Maxwell R. Thurman	Oct 1989	present

CINCUSSOUTHCOM is a four-star Army General.

Headquarters
Howard AFB, Panama
(APO Miami 34001)

Component Commands

- **U.S. Air Forces Southern Command (USAFSO)**
- **U.S. Army South (USARSO)**
- **U.S. Naval Forces Southern Command (USNAVSO)**

U.S. Space Command (USSPACE-COM): Unified command activated 23 September 1985, with operational command of all Service space, air, and ballistic missile defense operations. Its missions include integrated tactical warning and assessment of aerospace attacks on CONUS; operation of satellites; "space control" through surveillance of enemy spacecraft and threats; protection of U.S. space assets; and providing warning and assessment support to **NORAD**, a combined U.S.-Canadian command for the strategic aerospace defense of North America. Its command center operates in coordination with several other centers in the **NORAD Cheyenne Mountain Complex**, and was opened on 14 August 1987. CINCUSSPACECOM, a four-star Air Force General, also serves as CINCNORAD and Commander, **Air Force Space Command**. Although the resources and operational responsibilities of NORAD and USSPACE-COM overlap, USSPACECOM provides a specific chain of command for U.S. space activities and unilateral actions. USSPACECOM exercises operational command of the **Defense Satellite Communications System**, the **Fleet Satellite Communications System**, and **LES** (Lincoln Experimental Satellites) 8 and 9. Staff personnel strength is 600, split about 50 percent Air Force, 30 percent Navy/Marine Corps, and 20 percent Army. Command strength is programmed to reach 10,000.

Headquarters
Peterson AFB, CO 80914-5001

Component Commands

- **Air Force Space Command (AF-SPACECOM)**

- **Naval Space Command (NAV-SPACECOM)**
- **U.S. Army Space Command (USASPACECOM)**

Operational Centers

- Air Force Space Operations Support Center
- Naval Space Operations Support Center, Dahlgren VA
- Space Defense Operations Center, Cheyenne Mountain, CO
- Unified Space Operations Center, Peterson AFB, CO

Commanders-in-Chief
U.S. Space Command

GEN Robert T. Herres   23 Sep 1985
GEN John L. Piotrowski   Feb 1987

U.S. Special Operations Command (USSOCOM): Unified command established 16 April 1987 with operational command of all CONUS-based **special operations forces (SOF)** and activities, including **naval special warfare groups**. Its missions include providing SOF for rapid reinforcement of other unified commands; development and implementation of special operations strategy, doctrine, and tactics; special operations training; planning, programming, and budgeting; and management of special operations intelligence support. USSOCOM organization includes a special operations plans division, programs division, and a counterterrorism/antiterrorism division. USSOCOM headquarters personnel strength is 250. CINCUSSOCOM is a four-star Army General.

Headquarters
MacDill AFB, FL 33608

Component Commands

- Air Force Component Command (see **special operations wings**)
- **First Special Operations Command (1st SOCOM)**
- **Naval Special Warfare Command (NAVSPECWARCOM)**

Joint Command

- **Joint Special Operations Command**

Subunified Commands

- **Special Operations Command, Atlantic (SOCLANT)**
- Special Operations Command, Central (SOCCENT)
- Special Operations Command, Europe (SOCEUR)
- Special Operations Command, Pacific (SOPAC)

Commanders-in-Chief
Special Operations Command

GEN James J. Lindsay   16 Apr 1987

U.S. Transportation Command (USTRANSCOM): Unified command activated 1 October 1987 from a recommendation by the Blue Ribbon Commission on Defense Management (the Packard Commission). USTRANSCOM was made fully operational 1 October 1988. It is responsible for all the Services' wartime transportation systems and needs, and the support of other unified and specified commands through management of the Service's air, land, and sea transportation needs and activities. As such, the command consolidates the peacetime and wartime efforts of DOD's **transportation operating agencies** (Air Force's **Mil-**

itary **Airlift Command**, the Navy's **Military Sealift Command** and the Army's **Military Traffic Management Command**). During peacetime, each Service remains in command of its respective transportation component. Its Deployment Directorate (formerly the Joint Deployment Agency) operates the Joint Deployment System, an automated data-processing system for multiservice mobilization/transportation information. It is developing the **Joint Operation Planning and Execution System (JOPES)** in order to integrate crisis action and deliberate planning. Its combined peacetime personnel strength is over 107,000, with an additional 70,000 National Guard and reserve personnel when fully mobilized. Its headquarters personnel strength is approximately 550. CINCUSTRANSCOM is a four-star Air Force General who also serves as the commander of the Military Airlift Command. (see also **Civil Reserve Air Fleet, Merchant Marine, Maritime Prepositioning Force**)

Headquarters
Scott AFB, IL 62225

Component Commands

- **Military Airlift Command (MAC)**
- **Military Sealift Command (MSC)**
- **Military Traffic Management Command (MTMC)**

Commanders-in-Chief
U.S. Transportation Command

GEN Duane H. Cassidy	1 Oct 1987–
	1 Oct 1989
GEN Hansford T. Johnson	1 Oct 1989–
	present

UV-18B Twin Otter: Air Force version of the DHC-6 Twin Otter short take-off and landing utility transport. The twin-turboprop helicopter can accommodate a crew of two and up to 20 passengers. It weighs 12,500 lb and has a maximum cruising speed of 210 mph, a service ceiling of 26,700 ft, and a range of 806 miles with a 2,500 lb payload. Two UV-18Bs were procured in FY 1977 for parachute jump training at the Air Force Academy. The prime contractor is de Havilland Aircraft of Canada Ltd. The engine contractor is Pratt and Whitney of Canada.

V

V: Prefix designating **1.** Marine Corps or naval aviation unit designation (e.g., VA: attack squadron; VMA: Marine Corps attack squadron; VP: patrol squadron). **2.** Staff aircraft, modified mission (e.g., VC-25A). **3.** Vertical take-off and landing/short take-off and landing (VTOL/STOL) aircraft (e.g., V-22).

V-22 Osprey: Joint tiltrotor, multimission, **vertical/short take-off and landing (V/STOL)** aircraft under development. The Navy is the lead Service in development. The V-22 will be able to fly 2,000 nm without refueling; its tiltrotor design will allow it to combine V/STOL helicopter characteristics with the high-speed, high-altitude flight characteristics of a fixed wing aircraft. Once airborne, the engine nacelles mounted on each wing tip rotate forward 90 degrees for horizontal flight, converting the V-22 to a fuel-efficient turboprop airplane. The aircraft will be capable of carrying 24 combat equipped troops or 10,000 lb of cargo. The aircraft will fold for compact stowage aboard ship.

The V-22 was called the Joint Service Advanced Vertical Lift Aircraft during development (and designated JVX). It is based on Bell's XV-15 experimental aircraft. Bell and Boeing were awarded a seven-year $1,714 million, firm fixed price, full-scale engineering development contract in May 1986. It made its debut during rollout ceremonies at Bell Helicopter's Flight Research Center in Arlington, TX, on 23 May 1988. The first flight was made on 19 March 1989. Under the FY 1990 budget's five-year plan, production deliveries to the Marine Corps are scheduled for 1992.

A number of different missions are identified for the basic V-22 airframe:

- CV-22: Air Force transport for delivery of Army **Special Forces** over long ranges and for combat search and rescue to replace **HH-53** helicopters and supplement **C-130** transports;
- HV-22: Navy combat search and rescue aircraft; special operations aircraft for infiltration and exfiltration of special warfare teams; and logistics transport for ship-to-shore operations, replacing **HH-3** helicopters;
- MV-22: Marine Corps airborne assault transport for troops, equipment, and supplies, operating from amphibious ships or bases ashore, replacing **CH-46 Sea Knight** and **CH-53A/D** helicopters; and

- SV-22: Navy carrier-based anti-submarine warfare aircraft to replace the **SH-3** helicopters and **S-3 Viking** fixed wing aircraft.

Some 650 Ospreys are planned for the Services. The Army had planned to use the MV-22 for aeromedical evacuation, special forces infiltration and exfiltration, and long-range logistics support, but withdrew from the program in 1988. Prime contractors are Bell Helicopter Textron, Fort Worth, TX; and Boeing Vertol, Philadelphia, PA. Other contractors are Allison Gas Turbine Division, General Motors, Indianapolis, IN (engine); Grumman (tail unit); and General Electric (flight controls). The FY 1989 RDT&E costs were $636.8 million. The FY 1990 RDT&E budget request was $1,639.8 million.

Valiant: First word of a two word nickname (e.g., Valiant Usher) for Seventh Fleet amphibious exercises involving Marine Corps and naval forces. Third Fleet amphibious exercises use the initial nickname "Kernel."

VC-25A: Designation for the Presidential transportation aircraft that will replace the **Air Force One** C-137C transports starting in late 1989. The VC-25 is a modified Boeing 747-200B airframe with state of the art communications equipment and a special interior. The VC-25A will have a crew of 23 and will be able to carry about 70 passengers.

Vela: The first nuclear detonation detection system, used as a **national technical means of verification** for the **Limited Test Ban Treaty** (1963) and the **Threshold Test Ban Treaty** (1974). The Vela program emerged from two special panel meetings in Washington and the Conference of Experts in Geneva during 1959. Vela was to serve as a surveillance program for both arms control and military intelligence purposes. Expanding mission requirements led to the development of the satellite Integrated Operational Nuclear Detection System (IONDS), now called the **Nuclear Detonation Detection System (NDS)**. The Vela program was divided into three components to monitor nuclear explosions:

- Vela Hotel: The use of satellites working in pairs to detect nuclear explosions on the surface of the earth or in space;
- Vela Uniform: The use of seismic and other detection equipment to pick up vibrations of underground and underwater explosions; and
- Vela Sierra: The use of earth-bound measurement instruments to spot atmospheric and space-related detonations.

Responsibility for developing the Vela program went to DARPA, with the Air Force serving as the main military adviser and eventually becoming the Vela operator. The Sierra and Uniform segments were handled by the **Air Force Technical Applications Center (AFTAC)** at Patrick AFB, FL, while Hotel was handled by the Air Force Space Division of the Air Force Systems Command. The first seismic sensor in the Vela Uniform program became operational in October 1960 at the Wichita Mountain Seismological Observatory near Lawton, OK. The station had an array of ten short period vertical seismometers spaced at intervals of about 3,000 ft, along with 21 seismographs.

The Vela Hotel satellites were placed in circular 60,000-mile orbits. A total of 12 satellites were launched: the first pair was launched 16 October 1963, and the last pair went up on 8 April 1970. The system was retired on 27 September 1984, when the last satellite ceased operation. (see also **Atomic Energy Detection System**)

VER (very restricted knowledge) (see **sensitive compartmented information**)

Verdin: Navy VLF/LF multichannel shore-to-submarine broadcast system. Fixed VLF stations are at Annapolis, MD; Cutler, ME; North West Cape, Australia; Jim Creek, WA; Lualualei, HI; and Yosami, Japan. The stations in Maine and Australia provide VLF signals to virtually all ocean areas. During peacetime, the other stations provide backup to these two main stations. The largest and most powerful site at Cutler, ME, uses a 75-mile antenna to broadcast messages to ranges up to 5,000 miles. A submarine is able to receive these signals to a depth of about 150 ft via a small, fixed loop antenna attached to the hull or the telescopic mast, or by unreeling a 2,000-ft-long trailing wire antenna or an antenna buoy. The stations are equipped with 67-word-per-minute, multichannel, encrypted transmitters that transmit messages to patrolling submarines. The Verdin system was developed to correct deficiencies in VLF and LF radio transmission and reception capabilities. Verdin uses the same cryptographic keystream block as the Air Force 616A **Survivable Low Frequency Communications System (SLFCS)**. The enhanced Verdin program will extend operational capability with the Air Force, with some aircraft receiving airborne VLF/LF processors. Downlink messages from the **TACAMO** radio relay aircraft are routed to Verdin transmit terminals for encryption and anti-jam modulation and coding before retransmission to patrolling submarines.

The shore-based VLF system, because of its slow words-per-minute transmission rate, is primarily a "bell ringer" system, although it is also capable of delivering **emergency action messages (EAMs)**. Standard messages are repeated three times over a period of several hours to confirm to the patrolling submarines that the United States and Soviet Union are at peace. Nonreceipt of these messages signals the submarine to deploy alternative reception antennae and await information from other communications systems. Atmospheric conditions sometimes force this to occur.

Vertical Launched ASROC (VLA): Ship-launched **anti-submarine warfare** weapon that can be fitted with a Mk-46 acoustic-homing conventional torpedo. VLA provides a short-term, 12-mile-range, all weather, quick-reaction, anti-submarine capability for ships receiving the vertical launching system, including the Spruance class (DD-963), Burke class (DDG-51), and Ticonderoga class (from CG-52 on). For these ships, the VLA is to be replaced by **Sea Lance** when it is deployed in the mid 1990s. The program was almost cancelled in FY 1989, but the Navy was directed by Congress to produce 300 weapons to fill a shortfall pending deployment of the Sea Lance. Plans to provide the VLA with a nuclear depth bomb payload were cancelled in 1987. Major contractors are Loral Systems Group, Akron, OH; and Martin Marietta, Orlando, FL. FY 1989 costs were $134.3 million for 300 weapons.

Vertical Launching System (Mk-41 VLS): An armored magazine of either 29 or 61 missiles, each stowed vertically below the deck of a ship within a sealed canister in an individual cell. The canister serves as both launch tube and shipping container. The magazine consists of either three or seven identical eight-cell modules and one module containing five cells and a servicing ("breakdown") crane. The hatches atop the cells lie almost flush with the deck and the cells extend vertically below deck. All missiles are available for firing, with the launcher capable of rapid fire launches against air, surface, and underwater targets. The VLS is deployed on three ship classes: 22 newly produced Ticonderoga class (CG-47) cruisers (hull CG-52 and later ships), 29 newly produced Burke class (DDG-51) destroyers, and backfitted on 24 Spruance class (DD-963) destroyers. The first VLS-equipped ship, the USS Bunker Hill (CG-52), was commissioned in September 1986. The USS Spruance (DD-963) started her backfit in June 1986. The Burke class destroyers are still to

be built. The cruisers will have two 61-cell launchers. The Burke class will have a 61-cell launcher aft and a 29-cell launcher forward. The Spruance class have one 61-cell launcher. Spruance class ships will carry **Tomahawk sea-launched cruise missiles** and **Vertical Launched ASROC (VLA)**. Ticonderoga and Burke class ships will carry Tomahawk, **Standard Missile** 2 (SM-2 Blk-II) surface-to-air missiles, and VLA. Los Angeles class (SSN-688) attack submarines will also have a vertical launch capability. Hulls SSN-719 and later will have a Mk-45 capsule launch system (CLS) with 12 tubes exterior to the pressure hull in the forward part of the submarine for launching Tomahawk sea-launched cruise missiles.

vertical onboard delivery (VOD): The delivery of passengers and/or light freight on board a ship at sea by helicopter. (see also **underway replenishment**)

vertical/short take-off and landing (V/STOL): Aircraft capable of taking off from the ground with little or no runway distance required. These can be used on improvised runways (such as highways) or from smaller ships. V/STOL aircraft currently deployed or under development include the Marine Corps **AV-8 Harrier** fighter and the joint Service **V-22 Osprey** tiltrotor aircraft.

very low frequency (VLF)/low frequency (LF) communications: 1. Principal means for shore-to-submarine communications utilizing a redundant system of VLF and LF transmitting sites supported by an interconnecting landline and microwave communications network under the **Verdin** program. **2.** The Air Force **Survivable Low Frequency Communications System** located at Silver Creek, NE; and Hawes, CA, used for ground to air communications, and emergency worldwide general communications. **3.** Navy **TACAMO** (Take Charge and Move Out) radio relay aircraft. The TACAMO aircraft trail a wire antenna five miles in length; the aircraft goes into a very sharp turn, and the antenna hangs down below the aircraft in a spiral to transmit and receive signals. Aircraft operated by the Air Force **airborne command post** can also send VLF/LF signals.

VH-60: Modified VIP version of the UH-60A Blackhawk helicopter, operated by the Marine Corps and intended to replace the VH-1N, a modified version of the **UH-1 Huey**. New VH-60s will be assigned to the Executive Flight Detachment of Marine Helicopter Squadron One (HMX-1) at Anacostia Naval Station, Washington, DC, and will be used to provide transportation for the President and other government officials. Airframes by Sikorsky Aircraft and engines by General Electric.

VHSIC (Very High Speed Integrated Circuits): DOD program initiated in 1981 to develop and demonstrate two new generations of advanced data- and signal-processing (integrated circuit) technologies for smaller and cheaper—yet more powerful—computers. VHSICs will be used in combat and noncombat systems, specifically cruise missiles,

military satellites, fire-and-forget missiles, radar, command and control, wideband data communications, undersea search, electronic warfare, and signals intelligence equipment. Systems expected to use VHSIC circuits include the Navy **Mk-50 Barracuda** torpedo, **MILSTAR** satellites, the **EA-6B Prowler** electronic warfare aircraft, and the **F-14** and **F/A-18** fighter aircraft. The VHSIC development program began in the late 1970s when DOD found that commercial manufacturers were not producing the kinds of integrated circuit chips that were needed in military systems.

The most advanced VHSIC devices will demonstrate applications that should yield a 50- to 100-fold increase in signal-processing capability over early-generation VHSIC devices. Microwave and millimeter wave transmissions are capable of higher frequencies and shorter wavelengths. A parallel program is the **Microwave/Millimeter Wave Monolithic Integrated Circuit (MIMIC)**, which is oriented toward providing improvements in sensor electronics. This effort will focus on monolithic, gallium arsenide, integrated circuit technology and will emphasize analog functions for microwave and millimeter wave military applications. The MIMIC program calls for rapid technology insertion into existing and future military systems. MIMIC will provide advanced capabilities in analog circuitry for applications in aircraft, missiles, surveillance, and other military systems.

The VHSIC program is divided into two phases. Phase 1, which began in March 1981, concentrated on chip fabrication using circuitry of 1.25 microns in diameter. Six prime contractors participated in this phase: TRW, Honeywell, Hughes Aircraft, IBM, Texas Instruments, and Westinghouse. By February 1983, the TRW/Motorola team had produced the first fully functional VHSIC chip, but at a low yield and high price. In 1984, the VHSIC office established a Yield Enhancement Program to correct the yield and economic problems. In December 1985, the Air Force conducted the first successful test of a VHSIC within a military system (an electronic warfare countermeasures pod). This pod was then flight tested in July 1986 in an Air Force A-10 close air support fighter. In August 1986, the Navy successfully demonstrated VHSIC technology with the VHSIC Signal Conditioner (VSC), a subsystem of the AN/UYS 1 computer used on ASW aircraft. The VSC prefiltered data received from sonobuoys in the water and converted the data from an analog mode (continuous electronic waves) to a digital mode (discontinuous on/off pulses needed for military computers). In December 1986, the Army tested VHSIC components used in the Enhanced Position Location Reporting System (EPLRS), used to locate both friendly and enemy forces by detecting electronic signals.

Phase 2 began in October 1984 to develop .5 micron integrated circuits that will operate four times faster than the Phase 1 chips. Contracts were awarded to IBM, TRW, and Honeywell, requiring the three contract winners to develop a common set of specifications that would ensure interoperability. The chips to be produced in Phase 2 are invisible to the naked eye and must be made with the use of electron beam lithography—a computer-guided machine engraves circuit paths by projecting an electron beam onto silicon chip wafers. Interoperability between the 100 MHz .5 micron technology chips manufactured by the three contractors was reached in June 1988.

Most of the Phase 1 VHSIC 1.25 micron integrated circuits are functional with thousands of sample chips available for weapon system insertion. A number of smaller chips at the leading edge of technology are also operational. The VHSIC program is managed by the OSD. As of 1989 total research and development cost of the VHSIC program was projected at $781 million [DOD, *VHSIC Program Security Classification Guide*, DOD Directive 5210.75, 27 November 1985, released under the FOIA].

Vice Chairman of the Joint Chiefs of Staff (see **Joint Chiefs of Staff, Chairman of the Joint Chiefs of Staff**)

Viking (see **S-3 Viking**)

Vladivostok Aide-Memoire or "Vladivostok Accords": In November 1974, President Ford and General Secretary Brezhnev met in Vladivostok in the Soviet Union and signed an Aide-Memoire establishing the basic framework for **SALT II** negotiations and agreement. Since 1972, arms control discussions between the two superpowers had concentrated on the weapons systems to be included, bans on new systems, qualitative and quantitative limits, and forward-based systems in Europe and the Pacific. These discussions raised many concerns and questions on arms control but few points of agreement. At the Vladivostok meeting, the United States and Soviet Union were able to reach consensus on a number of significant issues. The Aide-Memoire set forth the following:

- 2,400 equal aggregate limits on strategic nuclear delivery vehicles (ICBMs, SLBMs, and heavy bombers) for both sides;
- 1,320 equal aggregate limits on MIRVed systems;
- A ban on construction of new land-based ICBM launchers;
- Limits on deployment of new types of strategic offensive arms; and
- Elements of the Interim Agreement (**SALT I**) would be incorporated into the new agreement (SALT II).

The Aide-Memoire set new numerical limits (as opposed to those established by SALT I) on the number of weapons the United States and the Soviet Union could deploy. Unlike the SALT I limitations, the new limits were numerically equal: no compensation was allowed for technological superiority. And for the first time, limits were imposed on nuclear weapons with more than one warhead. Also, the Soviet Union was allowed to continue deploying heavy missiles without interference, while the United States was permitted to maintain nuclear weapons overseas (e.g., forward based systems).

VLF (see **very low frequency (VLF)/low frequency (LF) communications**)

Volcano: Army rapid mine-dispensing system, capable of launches from helicopters or ground vehicles. Volcano (also called the Multiple Delivery Mine System) incorporates Gator antitank and anti-personnel mines in dispenser racks. A single **UH-60 Black Hawk** helicopter with Volcano will be capable of delivering 960 mines. Volcano has been in procurement since FY 1987 and is being fielded in motorized and light infantry divisions. Honeywell, Hopkins, MN, and Day & Zimmerman, Texarkana, TX, are the prime contractors. (see also **mine warfare**)

Vortex: **Byeman** code name for a class of geosynchronous **signals intelligence (SIGINT)** satellites, formerly called Chalet. Chalet was redesignated following the disclosure of its name in the *New York Times*. The first Chalet was launched on 10 June 1978; Vortex satellites were launched on 1 October 1979, 31 October 1981, and (probably) 22 December 1984. The original mission was **communications intelligence (COMINT)** collection only, but the system was modified to conduct **telemetry intelligence (TELINT)** as well. Intelligence information obtained by Chalet/Vortex and other SIGINT satellites is marked by the codeword **Zarf** [Jeffrey Richelson, *The U.S. Intelligence Community*, 2d ed., p. 174; and *American Espionage and the Soviet Target*, 1987, pp. 233, 245, 277, 278, 280]. (see also **security classification**)

VP: Navy shore based **anti-submarine warfare** patrol aircraft squadron, currently flying the **P-3 Orion**.

V/STOL (see **vertical/short takeoff and landing**)

W

W: Prefix designating weather mission aircraft (e.g., WC-135).

War and Mobilization Plan (WMP): The Air Force plan in support of the **Joint Strategic Capabilities Plan (JSCP)** and DOD mobilization planning directives. The WMP comes in five volumes:

- *WMP-1, Basic Plan:* Provides Air Staff and major command planners with a single source of current policies and guidance concerning mobilization planning and the conduct and support of all conditions of warfare.
- *WMP-2, Plans Listing and Summary:* Contains a listing of Air Force and unified and specified command planning documents that reflect Air Force tasking.
- *WMP-3, Combat and Support Forces:* Reflects wartime availability data for combat and support forces.
- *WMP-4, Wartime Aircraft Activity:* Reflects the planned force.
- *WMP-5, Basic Planning Factors and Data:* Reflects sortie and flying-hour data used in planning war and mobilization requirements.

[Air Force, *The Air Force Budget Process*, 1 October 1987]

warhead: "That part of a missile, projectile, torpedo, rocket, or other munition which contains either the nuclear or thermonuclear system, high-explosive system, chemical or biological agents or inert materials intended to inflict damage" [*JCS Pub 1*, p. 393]. The warhead and carrier together are referred to as the weapon or weaponized warhead. A warhead section (WHS) is "a completely assembled warhead including appropriate skin sections and related components" [DNA, *Nuclear Weapon Accident Response Procedures (NARP) Manual*, January 1984, p. 161, released under the FOIA].

warning message: Message of the Joint Chiefs of Staff **emergency action procedures (EAPs)** used by commanders of unified and specified commands to request release of nuclear or chemical weapons. "A commander's request or warning must contain sufficient information to insure complete understanding of the situation at the high level of government" [JCS, *Emergency Action Procedures*, Volume I, 15 March 1983, p. 7-1, released under the FOIA].

warning order: An order that initiates development of course(s) of action (Phase III of the Joint Chiefs of Staff (JCS) **Crisis Action System**) and requests that a Commander's Estimate be submitted. After the decision is made that a crisis situation warranting military preparation or action exists, the JCS normally publish a warning order. If the crisis warrants change in the alert status of units, then the warning order can contain a deployment preparation/deployment order. "The warning order is normally approved by the Chairman, Joint Chiefs of Staff. However, if the order contains deployment of forces, Secretary of Defense approval is required" [JCS, *Joint Operations Planning System*, Volume IV, p. B-1, released under the FOIA].

War Powers Resolution: Congressional act passed on 7 November 1973 (PL 93-148—50-U.S.C. 1541-1548). The Resolution, passed overriding President Nixon's veto, outlines the executive-legislative relationships with regard to the deployment and use of U.S. military forces in war situations and places specific limitations on the war powers of the executive branch.

Key provisions of the resolution include

- *Sec. 2c*: "The constitutional powers of the President as Commander-in-Chief to introduce United States Armed Forces into hostilities, or into situations where imminent involvement in hostilities is clearly indicated by the circumstances, are exercised only pursuant to (1) a dec-laration of war, (2) specific statutory authorization, or (3) a national emergency created by attack upon the United States, its territories or possessions, or its armed forces."
- *Sec. 3*: "The President in every possible instance shall consult with Congress before introducing United States Armed Forces into hostilities."
- *Sec. 4*: "In the absence of a declaration of war," Presidential notification of Congress prior to the intended actions is required whenever forces are introduced (1) "into hostilities or into situations where imminent involvement in hostilities is clearly indicated by the circumstances," or (2) in numbers that escalate U.S. involvement in a situation, or (3) "into the territory, airspace, or waters of a foreign nation, while equipped for combat." The President is to report to Congress the status of the entered conflict at least once every six months.
- *Sec. 5*: "Within sixty calendar days after a report was submitted pursuant to section 4(a)(1) . . . the President shall terminate any use of United States Armed Forces with respect to which such report was submitted (or required to be submitted), unless the Congress (1) has declared war or has enacted a specific authorization for such use of United States Armed Forces, (2) has extended by law such sixty-day period, or (3) is physically unable to meet as a result of an armed attack upon the United States. Such sixty-day period shall be extended for not more than an additional thirty

days if the President determines and certifies to the Congress in writing that unavoidable military necessity respecting the safety of United States Armed Forces requires the continued use of such armed forces."

- *Sec. 8*: Authority to engage the Armed Forces in any hostilities "shall not by inferred" from any law or treaty that does not specifically authorize the use of forces in a specific instance. "Introduction" of U.S. Armed Forces, as defined, includes "the assignment of members of such armed forces to command, coordinate, participate in the movement of, or accompany the regular or irregular military forces of any foreign country or government when such military forces are engaged, or there exists an imminent threat that such forces will become engaged, in hostilities."

warrant officer: A category of **officer** senior to all noncommissioned officers but lower in rank than commissioned officers. The warrant officer is normally a specialized technician (e.g., pilot, intelligence analyst, nuclear weapons technician) who does not command troops or units, but performs a specific technical task. A warrant officer's authority is derived from a warrant issued by the Secretary of Defense. The highest-ranking warrant officer is commissioned under the authority of the President.

war reserve materiel (WRM): Quantities of military materiel required, in addition to peacetime assets, to ensure immediate availability of resources to support the initial phase of war plans in the event of an emergency. WRM includes station sets, housekeeping sets, munitions, tanks, adapters, pylons, spares and repair parts, vehicle reserve sets, chemical equipment, aviation and ground fuel, and rations. (see also **pre-positioned war reserve requirement**)

WASHFAX (Washington Area Secure High Speed Facsimile System): The secure-document transmission terminal that links the **National Military Command Center (NMCC)**, the **Alternate National Military Command Center (ANMCC)**, the White House, the Department of State, the Central Intelligence Agency, the National Security Agency/Central Security Service, the Defense Intelligence Agency, the Department of the Treasury, and the National Photographic Interpretation Center. It was formerly called the LDX system, for "long-distance xerography" [JCS, *Crisis Staffing Procedures of the Joint Chiefs of Staff*, SM-481-83, 12 July 1983, p. 4-42, released under the FOIA].

Washington Tactical Switchboard: The specialized, direct, and timely telephone service supporting the command and control requirements of the **National Military Command Center (NMCC)**, the Air Force Operations Center, DOD, JCS, and other government agencies. Telephone and mobile radio-telephone (Minuteman) services are provided to the offices and residences of DOD or government personnel supporting the **National Military Command System** who must be available for consultation in an emergency [AF, *Washington Tactical Switchboard and Minuteman Radio Communication Services*," HOI 100-7, 20 July 1981, released under the FOIA]. (see also **Minuteman Radio Communications Service**)

watchlist: For censorship purposes, a list composed of civilians or groups believed to pose a threat to a military-controlled command or area [Department of the Army, *Civil Censorship*, FM 45-20, December 1965]. (see also **civil censorship**)

WC-130:   Air Force specially modified version of the **C-130 Hercules** transport aircraft. WC-130s are used for weather reconnaissance duties including hurricane forecasting, following, and penetration of the eye of the hurricane. WC-130s are assigned to the **Military Airlift Command**.

WC-135:   Air Force specially modified version of the **KC-135 Stratotanker** aerial refueling aircraft. WC-135s are used for weather reconnaissance and atmospheric sampling and are assigned to the **Military Airlift Command**.

weaponeering: The process of calculating the probability of damage given target vulnerability, weapon systems, munitions, and damage criteria. The number of the weapons required to attain the desired damage will determine the sorties required for each target. The focus is on economy of forces—the best target, weapon system, and munition combination. Targeting personnel and combat planners determine jointly whether avail-able aircraft can attack the tar-get or if deception and electronic countermeasures are more appropriate. Other considerations include rules of engagement, timing, availability of support forces, target resilience and recuperability, and proximity to friendly forces.

weapon system accuracy trials (WSAT):   Navy test conducted on a three-dimensional underwater range by **anti-submarine warfare** surface ships and submarines to demonstrate the capability of an installed anti-submarine warfare weapon system to successfully discover, attack, and destroy its assigned target in its normal operating environment.

Western Atlantic Command (WEST-LANT):   A major subordinate command of NATO's **Allied Command Atlantic**.

Headquarters
Norfolk, VA 23511-5102

Principle Subordinate Commands

- Canadian Atlantic Sub-Area, Halifax, Canada B3K 2XO
- Island Commander Azores, San Miguel, Azores
- Island Commander Bermuda, Hamilton, Bermuda
- Island Commander Greenland, Gronnedal, Greenland
- Ocean Sub-Area, Norfolk, VA 23511-5101
- Submarine Forces, Western Atlantic Area: Norfolk, VA 23511

Western Command (WESTCOM) (see **U.S. Army Western Command**)

Wheelhouse: UHF air-to-ground strategic communications system, used as part of the **National Military Command System** [JCS, *Strategic Connectivity Study*, March 1979, p. D-23, released under the FOIA].

White Cloud: Navy code name for the space-based ocean surveillance component of **Classic Wizard**, a ground-based ocean surveillance system. Nine White Cloud satellites were launched between 1976 and 1988. Each launch placed one mother ship and three subsatellites in a near-circular 63 degree orbit 700 miles above the earth. Quartets were launched on 30 April 1976, 8 December 1977, 3 March 1980, 9 February 1983, 9 June 1983, 6 February 1984, 9 February 1986, 15 May 1987, and 5 September 1988. The system is equipped with passive infrared scanners, millimeter wave radiometers, and radio-frequency antennas that collect radio communications and radar emissions [Jeffrey Richelson, *The U.S. Intelligence Community*, 2d ed., pp. 200–201].

White Dot: Code name for NATO **emergency action messages (EAMs)** originated by the **Supreme Allied Commander Europe (SACEUR)**. White Dot Echo messages are nuclear execution orders; White Dot Romeo messages are nuclear release orders. White Dot messages are numbered with updates.

White House Communications Agency (WHCA): Component of the **Defense Communications Agency** that provides telecommunication and other related audiovisual support to the President and White House staff, the first family, the Vice-President and family, the Secret Service, and others as directed. WHCA was established in 1962 to operate the Console Control Section, also known as the White House Signal Switchboard (or "White House signals"). Its preceding organization was the Signal Detachment of the Army, established in 1942 at the White House. Originally, the Detachment placed mobile communication stations aboard President Roosevelt's car and in 31 White House automobiles and outfitted Presidential aircraft and ships during travel. Today, in addition to the telephone system WHCA consists of two radio nets: the Washington Area System (WAS) ("Crown" Control), and the **Nationwide** System.

Divisions

- Office of the Adjutant: Staff advisor and action office in personnel, security, finance, personnel management, administrative services, and accounting functional areas;
- Automated Services Division: Provides general purpose computer support for the National Security Council (NSC) and the President's office and provides automated teleprocessing communications support for the President, his staff, and the NSC;
- Operations Division: Receives, coordinates, and develops procedures for all operational requirements for which WHCA is responsible; that is, coordinates trips and communications; and
- Plans Division: Responsible for planning, programming, and budgeting.

Subordinate Units

- Defense Communications Administrative Unit (DCAU): Provides and maintains logistical, transportation, electronics maintenance, communications security, graphics, and photographic laboratory support for the WHCA;
- Defense Communications Operations Unit (DCOU): Provides communications support (secure and nonsecure voice and record), audiovisual support, and emergency power facilities for the President, Vice-President, and their families and staff within the White House complex and outside the complex as necessary; and
- Defense Communications Support Unit (DCSU): Provides communications support to the President and designated members of the White House staff at fixed facilities during travel and in contingency operations. Provides personnel and equipment to respond to any presidential emergency movement. Provides interface between the Office of the President and the **National Military Command System** and other government offices during emergencies. Detachments are at Andrews AFB, MD; Camp David, MD; and Ft. Ritchie, MD.

[DCA, *DCA Organization and Functions Manual*, DCA Circular 640-45-21, April 1984, released under the FOIA]

white rocket: An "unclassified **exercise** flag-word designated for use with messages containing simulated time-critical information from the NCA [National Command Authority] to operating units" [REDCOM, *Emergency Action Procedures*, p. 9-1, released under the FOIA]. It is a practice **red rocket** message used as part of the Joint Chiefs of Staff **emergency action procedures**.

wing: 1. In general, a flank unit or a part of a military force to the right or left of the main body. **2.** In the Marine Corps, a balanced Marine Corps task organization of aircraft groups and squadrons called a **Marine aircraft wing**, complemented by command, air control, administrative, and maintenance units. Usually provides support to a Marine division as part of a Fleet Marine Force or Marine Expeditionary Force. **3.** In the Navy, the basic organizational and administrative unit of a fleet for naval, land, and tender-based aviation. The **carrier air wing** is subordinate to the naval air force. **4.** In the Air Force, the basic operational and administrative aviation unit designed for immediate and sustained combat operations. It typically consists of a wing commander (acting as the tactical commander), a vice-commander, special staff, a deputy commander for operations, a deputy commander for maintenance, a deputy commander for resource management, assigned squadrons, and a combat support group and Air Force hospital or clinic when necessary. Its mission is to provide command supervision over primary mission units and assigned support units. The **tactical fighter wing (TFW)** is the lowest echelon of organization that contains all the combat, combat support, and combat service support necessary for sustained combat operations.

The wing is usually organized in three fighter squadrons of 24 aircraft each (plus a few spares). The wing commander shares functional responsibilities with three deputies. The deputy commander for operations directs the day-to-day activities of the flying squadrons as well as the combat-oriented staff functions: intelligence, operational planning, tactics, command and control, and training. Maintenance functions are centrally managed under a second deputy commander. About 75 percent of the maintenance crews are assigned to the flight line and are directly involved in sortie production. Most of the other logistical concerns are under the third deputy commander for resources management. (see also **tactical air forces, tactical airlift, type command**)

WINTEX/CIMEX (Winter Exercise/Civil Military Exercise): Biannual NATO crisis management **command post exercise (CPX)** held in odd years to test the NATO alert system, political consultation for the release of nuclear weapons, activation of NATO civil wartime agencies, host nation support, civil emergency planning—including military use of civil resources such as rail, sea, and air transportation—noncombatant evacuation, and refugee control. WINTEX/CIMEX 79 was held simultaneously with **Power Play 79**; WINTEX/CIMEX 81 was held simultaneously with **Poll Station 81**; WINTEX/CIMEX 85 was held simultaneously with Ivy League 85.

withhold (nuclear): The limiting of authority to employ nuclear weapons

by denying their use within specified geographical areas or certain countries. Restrictions relating to the release of nuclear weapons are derived from Annex C of the **Joint Strategic Capabilities Plan**, which is the JCS guidance for preparation of the **Single Integrated Operational Plan (SIOP)** and other nuclear war plans [*JCS Pub 1*, p. 397].

WNINTEL (Warning Notice—Intelligence Sources and Methods Involved): A warning notice placed on classified documents containing certain sensitive foreign intelligence information. It is used to protect sources and methods of collection. (see also **security classification**)

Worldwide Airborne Command Post System (WWABNCP): System comprising the **airborne command posts** of the five nuclear capable unified and specified commands. WWABNCP is designed to "provide a survivable command and control facility for the SIOP [**Single Integrated Operational Plan**] CINCs that will support the National Command Authority during all phases of a **general war**" [Air Force, *Supporting Data for FY 1984 Budget Estimates Submitted to Congress, Descriptive Summaries, RDTE, FY 1984*. 31 January 1983, p. 320]. WWABNCP aircraft (**EC-135s**) are supplied with the communications equipment, codes, and plans needed to take command of military forces and nuclear weapons in an emergency. The aircraft are electromagnetic pulse–hardened and are equipped with high-power extended transmission range communications systems, including VLF/LF antennae, and satellite equipment. The command posts are assigned as follows

- U.S. Atlantic Command: Four aircraft. Codename: **Scope Light**;
- U.S. Central Command: Four aircraft. Codename: unknown;
- U.S. European Command: Four aircraft. Codename: **Silk Purse**;
- U.S. Pacific Command: Four aircraft. Codename: Blue Eagle; and
- Strategic Air Command: 27 aircraft. Codename: **Looking Glass**, and portions of the **Post-Attack Command and Control System**;
- Joint Chiefs of Staff: **National Emergency Airborne Command Post (NEACP)**. Codename: **Night Watch**.
- CINCSAC. Codename Cover All (also referred to as WWMCCS Airborne Resources (WABNRES).

Worldwide Military Command and Control System (WWMCCS): Established in October 1962, the WWMCCS (pronounced "Wimex") is composed of the facilities, equipment, communications, procedures, and personnel that provide the means for operational direction and technical and administrative support for the command and control of U.S. military forces. The WWMCCS comprises some 35 computer systems at 26 locations, which provide "current situation monitoring, formulating responses to warning, selecting options, employing forces, assessing damage, reconstituting forces, and conducting activities necessary to terminate a fight" [*DOD Statement before the U.S. Congress*, House Armed Services Committee, 24 March 1983, p. 6].

The primary mission of WWMCCS is to support the National Command Authorities. The **National Military Command System (NMCS)** is the main component of the WWMCCS that provides the President and Secretary of Defense with warnings and intelligence on which to base decisions, apply the resources of the military departments, and assign military missions and direction to the unified and specified commands. The NMCS also provides support of the JCS.

The secondary mission of WWMCCS is to support the command and control systems of the unified and specified commands and WWMCCS-related management information systems of other DOD components.

WWMCCS is composed of

National-level Subsystems

- National Military Command System (NMCS) (the priority system);
- Command and control (C2) systems of the Service headquarters; and
- C2 systems of other DOD agencies and offices (e.g., DNA, DIA, and DCA).

Theater-level Subsystems

- C2 systems of the unified and specified commands;
- C2 systems of established and assigned joint task forces; and
- C2 systems of the component commands.

The WWMCCS, through its automatic data-processing systems, provides the capability for data acquisition, storage, processing, and display to support decisionmakers in carrying out the following tasks:

- Monitoring the current situation, including the status of U.S. and non-U.S. forces;
- Formulating responses to warning and threat assessment;
- Selecting options, deploying/employing forces, and implementing operation plans;
- Performing attack, strike and damage assessments, and residual capability assessments;
- Reconstituting and redirecting forces; and
- Terminating hostilities and active operations.

The WWMCCS automatic data-processing system includes four major functional applications:

- *Resource and Unit Monitoring:* Supports readiness assessment, situation assessment, and operations. Can provide current information such as the status and location of forces, aircraft, airfields, ammunition, civil engineering, communications, electronic warfare/reconnaissance, facilities, medical, missiles, nuclear weapons, personnel, fuel, seaports, ships, supply, transportation, units, war reserve materials, and weapon systems.
- *Conventional Planning and Execution:* Supports joint planning, mobilization, and deployment—including plan development, course of action development, execution planning, execution, movement monitoring, sustainment, and redeployment from origin to designation.
- *Tactical Warning and Attack Assessment, Space Defense:* Supports warning, damage assessment, and space defense planning, execution,

termination, and reconstitution.
- *Nuclear Planning and Execution:* Supports Strategic Single Integrated Operational Plan (SIOP) and tactical (non-SIOP operations) planning, execution, termination, and reconstitution. This subsystem is available to the NMCC, Alternate Military Command Center, Strategic Air Command, U.S. European Command, U.S. Pacific Command, U.S. Atlantic Command, U.S. Central Command, and Defense Intelligence Agency.

A post-attack WWMCCS development program, including a prototype ground mobile capability, was started in 1980 to supplement airborne command and control systems after the first days of a nuclear war. (see also **WWMCSS Information System [WIS], WWMCSS Intercomputer Network [WIN]**)

Worldwide Secure Voice Conferencing System (WWSVCS): Automatic Secure Voice Communications Network (**AUTOSEVOCOM**) emergency network connecting the JCS, **National Military Command Center (NMCC)**, and NORAD with command centers worldwide. The USPACOM command center is connected through a "receive only" terminal and is referred to as the "Snatcher."

WWMCCS Information System (WIS): The automatic data-processing (ADP) program of the **Worldwide Military Command and Control System (WWMCCS)**. WIS is an arrangement of personnel, equipment (including ADP equipment and software), communications, facilities, and procedures employed in planning, directing, coordinating, and controlling the operational activities of U.S. military forces. The system is in the process of replacing elements of the WWMCCS ADP system, including the **Joint Reporting Structure**, the operational reporting procedures, formats, and executive aids.

WIS includes the existing command and control systems of the unified and specified commands, the command and control and related management information systems used by the headquarters of the military departments, the command and control systems of the headquarters of the Service component commands, and the command and control support systems of DOD agencies. WIS is intended to provide the National Command Authorities with a capability to

- Receive early warning and intelligence information;
- Apply the resources of the military departments;
- Assign military missions; and
- Provide direction to the unified and specified commands while supporting the JCS in carrying out their responsibilities.

WIS provides the means for coordination and liaison with activities outside DOD, including the White House Situation Room, the State Department Operations Center, the Central Intelligence Agency Indications Office, the U.S. Intelligence Board National Indications Center, the United Nations Military Mission, the Federal Emergency Management Agency, U.S. Coast Guard Operations Center, the Federal Aviation Administration Executive Communications Control Center, and NATO. Information is exchanged directly or indirectly between and among these differing activities via the **National Military Command System (NMCS)**.

In the early 1960s, WIS capabilities consisted of a loosely knit federation of 1,158 different computer systems using 30 different general purpose software systems at 81 separate locations. The systems were found not responsive to national-level requirements, were not fully integrated, were in some cases incompatible, and were expensive to acquire and maintain. In 1966, the present-day WIS was established to resolve some of these problems. Beginning in 1970, various study groups began to criticize WIS, including the General Accounting Office and Congress. False nuclear alerts at NORAD in 1980 and ADP support problems during a number of crises in 1978–1980 highlighted weaknesses in the system. On 7 February 1980, the DOD submitted its initial improvement plan, titled "Planning for the Modernization of the WWMCCS Information System (WIS)," and followed it up in January 1981 with a detailed modernization plan, called "Modernization of the WWMCCS Information System (WIS)." The modernization plan called for the improvement of the capability of WIS to provide timely, accurate, and complete information to commanders, particularly during times of crisis.

The WIS network is unique because of the dispersion of netted sites, the massive amount of time-sensitive data that is transmitted between sites, and the security requirements of transmitting secure information. All traffic passing through the network is encrypted. (see also **Strategic Air Command, NORAD Command Center Processing and Display System**)

WWMCCS Intercomputer Network (WIN): The dominant command and control interconnection network supporting the **Worldwide Military Command and Control System (WWMCCS)**. WIN provides users with teleconferencing and electronic mail capabilities. It has the ability to access the resources of any other computer in the network, to read and update files, to retrieve information from remote systems, to transfer entire data bases between computers, and to share workloads. With the advent of distributed/shared processing capabilities, WIN has become an important component of the **WWMCCS Information System (WIS)**.

In September 1971, the JCS issued a report (JCSM-593-71) stating the need to develop the Prototype WWMCCS Intercomputer Network (PWIN) to provide faster and more accurate information to support crisis management actions and continuity of operations for the national command authorities. Specific requirements called for on-line or remote responses in a timely manner from computer terminals and multilevel computer security features. The interconnecting of WWMCCS automatic data processing began in 1975 when three geographically dispersed computer systems were connected in PWIN. In 1976, PWIN was expanded to six sites. From 1973 to 1976, the Defense Communications Agency and program contractors debated on whether PWIN would be declared an operational system. Major reliability problems were noted, as well as difficulty in achieving multilevel computer security (as of March 1976, the PWIN system crashed every 35 minutes). However, on 18 July 1977, the JCS approved and validated an operational requirement for WIN despite the problems with the system, and the system was declared operational. WIN was expanded to serve 19 key commands by early 1980, and was further expanded to include the entire WWMCCS net in the 1980s.

X

X: Prefix designating experimental and research aircraft, rockets, guided missiles, and vehicles (e.g., XV-15).

X-29: NASA lightweight, single-seat, forward-swept wing demonstrator aircraft undergoing flight testing at the Dryden Flight Research Center at Edwards AFB, CA. The Air Force provides flight test support. The first supersonic flight occurred in December 1985. On 8 June 1988, the X-29 made its 200th flight, a record for a single X-series aircraft. The prime contractor is Grumman Aerospace Corporation, which built two demonstrators.

X-30 (see **National Aerospace Plane**)

X-hour: 1. In the Navy, in daylight **SEAL** operations, the time at which all swimmers must have been retrieved, and the underwater demolition craft must be seaward of the fire support line en route to their parent surface ship. **2.** In night SEAL operations, the time at which all rubber boats have been retrieved by their parent underwater demolition craft [*NWP 3*]. (see also **military time**)

XO: Common designation for an **executive officer**, the second in command on a naval vessel or the second person in charge of a staff office. The deputy commander or deputy director of an organization may also be called an XO.

X-ray laser: Theoretical single shot **laser** weapon that generates x-rays (electromagnetic radiation with wavelengths less than 10 nanometers) as the primary kill mechanism. The X-ray laser would receive its power from a nuclear explosion. This use of x-rays from a nuclear explosive source would make up the **third generation** of nuclear weapons (following atomic fission and hydrogen fusion weapons). The X-ray laser would use the same amount of energy as atomic or hydrogen weapons but would direct that energy more into the booster rather than scattering it. The design of the weapon is as follows: thin layers of phasing material are powered by pulsed radiation; the heat of the nuclear explosion would raise electrons of the lasant atoms to upper energy levels; lasing occurs as the electrons fall back to lower energy levels. The beam would be focused by special optical elements (conventional lenses and mirrors do not work with x-rays). Targets would be damaged from impulse kill. Studies on the X-ray laser are attempting to come up with different wavelengths, since changes in wavelength cause changes in penetrating capability.

Although President Reagan stated that the Strategic Defense Initiative program should only use nonnuclear weapons, DOD and DOE research on the X-ray laser continues.

Y

Y: Prefix designating a prototype model suitable for evaluation of design, performance, and production potential (e.g., YAV-8).

Yama Sakura: Bilateral U.S.–Japanese Self Defense Force training exercise held in Japan to practice ground reinforcements of Japan and the ground defense of Japanese territory. Yama Sakura exercises have include the deployment of elements of the 25th Light Infantry Division in Hawaii to Japan.

Yankee/Zulu: VHF presidential radio voice network connected to the **National Emergency Airborne Command Post** and operated by the **White House Communications Agency**.

yard and service craft: Any self-propelled or non–self-propelled noncombatant naval craft intended primarily for harbor or base support duties. The "N" suffix in this category indicates that the craft is non–self-propelled [DIA, *Glossary of Naval Ship Types*, DDB-1200-47-81, June 1981].

YAG   Miscellaneous service craft: Service craft whose function is not covered by other definitions, or is so general as to preclude precise definitions.

YAGE   Experimental service craft: A service craft employed in weapons, communications, hydrodynamics, propulsion, navigation, or sensor related RDT&E.

YC   Open barge: Non–self-propelled open barge of any size.

YCF   Car barge: Non–self-propelled barge of any size intended for transporting vehicles or railroad cars. Must have roll on/roll off capability. (see also YFB in this list)

YD   Floating crane: Floating crane of any capacity, either self-propelled or non–self-propelled.

YDG   Deperming/degaussing craft: Craft used either for support of a degaussing range or for deperming.

YDT   Diving tender: Self-propelled craft equipped primarily to provide support for divers.

YE   Ammunition lighter: Self-propelled craft configured for local transport of munitions.

YF   Covered lighter: Self-propelled craft configured for local transport of dry bulk cargo.

YFB   Ferry: Self-propelled craft configured for local transport of personnel and/or vehicles along fixed routes between prepared berths.

YFDB   Large floating drydock: Any floating drydock with a lift capacity of 20,000 metric tons or greater. (Equates to USN AFDB.)

YFDL   Small floating drydock: Any floating drydock with a lift capacity below 5,000 metric tons. (Equates to USN AFDL.)

YFDM   Medium floating drydock: Any floating, open-ended drydock with a lift capacity between 5,000 and 20,000 metric tons. (Equates to USN AFDM.)

YFL   Launch: Self-propelled craft intended to transport personnel within sheltered waters. (see also YFB)

YFNB   Large covered barge: Non–self-propelled cargo craft for transport of dry bulk cargo, capable of being employed on the open ocean and equipped with cargo transfer gear.

YFND   Drydock companion barge: Non–self-propelled craft equipped to provide machinery and hull repair facilities in direct support of a floating drydock.

YFP   Floating power barge: Non–self-propelled craft equipped to provide electrical power and/or steam to other ships and craft or to shore facilities.

YFR   Refrigerated lighter: Self-propelled refrigerator cargo craft intended for local transport of provisions.

YFU   Harbor utility transport: Self-propelled general-purpose craft for local and coastal transport of general cargo, vehicles, and personnel. It must be capable of beaching. The designation is generally applied to former or converted utility landing craft (LCU).

YG   Garbage lighter: Self-propelled craft intended for transporting garbage to a disposal area or for the processing and disposal of human waste.

YGS   Survey craft: Hydrographic survey craft intended for operation in sheltered waters, harbors, or rivers.

YGT   Target service craft: Self-propelled craft intended to act as a live target, an "aim-to-miss" target, a high-speed target tow craft, or a controller craft for remote-controlled targets, either surface or airborne.

YH   Ambulance craft: Self-propelled craft intended to provide small scale emergency medical facilities, floating clinic, or casualty evacuation capability.

YM   Dredge: Self-propelled craft employed as a dredge for the deepening of channels, harbor entrances, and/or inland waterways, and for the improvement of berths.

YNG   Gate craft: Service craft, normally non–self-propelled, intended to service and/or control harbor defense nets.

YO   Fuel lighter: Self-propelled craft intended for local transport of ship, vehicle, or aircraft fuel and for in-port replenishment of other naval units. May be capable of limited coastal operations.

YOSR   Nuclear waste disposal barge: Non–self-propelled craft intended to transport and dispose of radioactive waste products.

YPL   Barracks barge: Non–self-propelled craft employed primarily as an accommodations facility. (Equates to USN APL and YRBM.)

YPT   Torpedo retriever: Self-propelled craft intended to recover exercise torpedoes. May also be able to perform post firing maintenance and readout on torpedoes; may also be used to recover other floating expended ordnance.

YR   Floating workshop barge: Non–self-propelled craft equipped to serve in any naval ship-related repair or maintenance capacity; intended to be capable of performing its duties independent of other service craft or auxiliaries.

YRC   Cable tender: Self-propelled craft intended for laying, retrieval, and/or repair of underwater cables within harbors or sheltered waters.

YRD   Auxiliary repair dock: Float-

ing drydock with a ship-configured bow to enable higher-speed ocean towing and a stern gate to permit ships and craft to enter. Also any floating dock intended to permit transport of deep-draft ships or submarines on limited depth inland waterways (i.e., "transporter dock"). (Equates to USN ARD.)

YRG   Tank cleaning craft: Service craft (self-propelled or non–self-propelled) intended to steam-clean ships' fuel and cargo tanks and bilges and to transport and/or process the accumulated waste.

YRRN   Radiological repair barge: Service craft (normally non–self-propelled) intended to repair and/or service radioactive equipment—generally limited to propulsion system.

YRS   Salvage craft: Craft intended to support salvage operations through the provision of heavy-lift capabilities, pumps, salvage pontoon stowage, and/or specialized salvage diver support.

YSR   Sludge removal craft: Service craft intended to support dredging operations by transporting sludge. Generally equipped with hopper bottoms to permit sludge dumping.

YSS   Service submersible: A manned military submersible supported by either surface ships or submarines, used primarily for research, rescue, or special operations. Normally will not have indigenous weapons capability.

YTB   Large harbor tug: Tug intended for harbor and coastal service and equipped with a propulsion plant of over 1,200 horsepower.

YTL   Small harbor tug: Tug intended primarily for harbor service and equipped with a propulsion plant of less than 300 horsepower.

YTM   Medium harbor tug: Tug intended primarily for harbor service, but capable of limited coast operations and equipped with a propulsion plant of between 300 and 1,200 horsepower.

YTR   Fireboat: Self-propelled craft equipped primarily for firefighting duties. May also be employable as a tug.

YTS   Sail training craft: Craft primarily configured for sail propulsion and intended to provide basic navigational, maneuvering, and/or seamanship training in sheltered waters.

YXT   Training craft: Engine propelled craft intended to provide basic navigational, maneuvering, and/or seamanship training in sheltered waters. (Equates to USN YP.)

YVS   Seaplane service craft: Self-propelled craft especially configured to support seaplanes by means of towing, fueling, fairway marker laying, and so on.

YW   Water lighter: Self-propelled craft intended for local transport of water and for inport replenishment of other naval units. May be capable of limited coastal operations.

(see also **ammunition ship, oceanographic research ship**)

yeoman: Navy petty officer who performs clerical and secretarial duties.

YF-22A/YF-23A (see **Advanced Tactical Fighter**)

Z

Z: Prefix designating **1.** A lighter-than-air vehicle such as a blimp or balloon. **2.** A planning aircraft or vehicle.

Zarf: Control marking and security clearance applied to **talent-keyhole** information relating to satellite obtained **signals intelligence (SIGINT)**. (see also **security classification**)

Z-hour: In the Navy, the time at which all underwater demolition craft have been retrieved by their parent ship. (see also **military time**)

zone time: The time kept in sea areas in a 15 degree zone of longitude, the central meridian of each zone being 15 degrees or a multiple of 15 degrees removed from the Greenwich Meridian. The times of successive zones differ by one hour. (see also **military time**)

Zulu time: Universal Coordinated Time (Greenwich Mean Time). "The mean solar time of the meridian of Greenwich, England, used as the prime basis of standard time throughout the world. Zulu time is used in all **emergency action messages** [and all other military messages]" [USCENT-COM, *Emergency Action Procedures, Volume I: System Description*, 20 February 1986, p. 4–8, released under the FOIA].

APPENDIXES

APPENDIX A
Aircraft Designations

All DOD aerospace vehicles, including aircraft, are assigned a mission-designation-series (MDS). A prescribed arrangement of letters and numbers constitutes an MDS. An aircraft MDS designation identifies the status, mission, type, and design series of the aircraft. Positions one through four and six are letters; position five is a number. A sample MDS is given below with a complete list of the various letter designations and their meanings.

1. Status Prefix This symbol is used only when necessary, to indicate that an aircraft's test, modification, or experimental or prototype design does not make it standard. The symbol appears to the immediate left of the modified mission or basic mission symbol.

Description

G Permanently grounded Aircraft permanently grounded or used for ground training.

J Special test (temporary) Aircraft in special test program by authorized organization, on bailment contract with a special test configuration, or with installed property temporarily recovered to accommodate a test.

N Special test (permanent) Aircraft in special test program by authorized activities or on bailment contract and whose configuration is so drastically changed that returning to original operational configuration is beyond practical or economical limits.

X Experimental Aircraft in developmental or experimental stage. The basic design number of this vehicle has been designated but the vehicle has not been established as a standard vehicle.

Y Prototype A model suitable for evaluation of design, performance, and production potential.

Z Planning Aircraft in the planning or predevelopmental stage.

Letter and Number Designations
(EH-60B Quick Fix)

	1	2	3	4 -	5	6
	Y		E	H-	60	B

Status prefix (*prototype*) ⎦
Modified mission (*none*)
Basic mission (*electronics*)
Type (*helicopter*)
Design number (*60th helicopter design*)
Design series (*2nd version of this design*)

2. Modified Mission This symbol is used to identify modifications to the basic mission of an aircraft. It appears to the immediate left of the basic mission symbol. Only one modified mission symbol should be used in any one MDS.

Description

A   Attack   Aircraft modified to search out, attack, and destroy enemy land or sea targets using conventional or special weapons. This symbol also describes aircraft used for interdiction and close–air support missions.

C   Transport   Aircraft modified to carry personnel and cargo. May be classified according to range: Short-range: does not exceed 1,200 nm at normal cruising conditions, Medium-range: between 1,200 and 3,500 nm at normal cruising conditions, Long-range: exceeds 3,500 nm at normal cruising conditions.

D   Director   Aircraft modified for controlling drone aircraft or missiles.

E   Special electronic installation   Aircraft modified with electronic devices for one or more of the following missions: electronic counter-measures; airborne early-warning radar; airborne command and control, including communications relay; or tactical data communications link for all non-autonomous modes of flight.

F   Fighter   Aircraft modified to intercept other aircraft or missiles.

H   Search and rescue   Aircraft modified for search and rescue missions.

K   Tanker   Aircraft modified to refuel other aircraft in flight.

L   Cold Weather   Aircraft modified for operation in Arctic and Antarctic regions. Includes skis, special insulation, and other equipment for extreme cold-weather operations.

M   Multimission   Aircraft modified to perform several different missions.

O   Observation   Aircraft modified to observe (through visual or other means) and report tactical information concerning composition and disposition of enemy forces in a combat area.

P   Patrol   Long-range, all-weather, multi-engine aircraft that operate from land or water bases modified for independent anti-submarine warfare, maritime reconnaissance, and mining.

Q   Drone   A land, sea, or air vehicle modified to be remotely or automatically controlled.

R   Reconnaissance   Aircraft modified for photographic or electronic reconnaissance missions.

S   Anti-submarine   Aircraft modified to search, identify, attack, and destroy enemy submarines.

T   Trainer   Aircraft modified for training purposes.

U   Utility   Aircraft modified to perform multiple missions such as battlefield support, localized transport, and special light missions.

V   Staff   Aircraft modified to provide accommodations such as chairs, tables, lounges, and berths for transporting staff personnel.

W Weather Aircraft modified and equipped for meteorological missions.

3. Basic Mission This symbol identifies an aircraft's primary function and capability. It appears to the immediate left of the vehicle type symbol or design number.

Description

A Attack Aircraft designed to search out, attack, and destroy enemy land or sea targets using conventional or special weapons. This symbol also describes aircraft used for interdiction and close–air support missions.

B Bomber Aircraft designed for bombing enemy targets.

C Transport Aircraft designed to carry personnel and cargo. May be classified according to range: Short-range: does not exceed 1,200 nm at normal cruising conditions. Medium-range: between 1,200 and 3,500 nm at normal cruising conditions. Long-range: exceeds 3,500 nm at normal cruising conditions.

E Special electronic installation Aircraft designed with electronic devices for one or more of the following missions: electronic countermeasures; airborne early-warning radar; airborne command and control, including communications relay; or tactical data communications link for all non-autonomous modes of flight.

F Fighter Aircraft designed to intercept other aircraft or missiles. Includes multipurpose aircraft also designed for ground support missions such as interdiction and close air support.

O Observation Aircraft designed to observe (through visual or other means) and report tactical information concerning composition and disposition of enemy forces in a combat area.

P Patrol Long-range, all-weather, multi-engine aircraft that operate from land or water bases designed for independent anti-submarine warfare, maritime reconnaissance, and mining.

R Reconnaissance Aircraft designed for photographic or electronic reconnaissance missions.

S Anti-submarine Aircraft designed to search out, identify, attack, and destroy enemy submarines.

T Trainer Aircraft designed for training purposes.

U Utility Aircraft designed to perform multiple missions such as battlefield support, localized transport, and special light missions. Included are aircraft designed for small payloads.

X Research Aircraft designed for testing highly experimental configurations. These aircraft are not generally intended for use as operational aircraft.

4. Vehicle Type This symbol is required only for rotary wing, vertical takeoff and landing, short takeoff and landing, and glider aircraft. It must be accompanied by a basic mission or modified mission symbol and appears to the immediate left of the design number.

Description

G Glider Engineless, fixed-wing aircraft flown by using air currents to keep it aloft.

H   Helicopter   Rotary-wing aircraft (deriving its lift from a rotating lifting surface).

V   VTOL and STOL   Aircraft designed to take-off and land vertically or in a very short distance.

Z   Lighter-than-air-vehicle   Nonrigid or semi-rigid aircraft carried aloft by hot gases or lighter-than-air gases (includes blimps and balloons).

5. Design Number   This number identifies major design changes within the same mission category. Design numbers run consecutively; "1" is used to begin each category. A dash is used to separate the design number from the symbol to its immediate left.

6. Series   This symbol identifies the first production model of a particular design and any subsequent models representing modifications that significantly alter the relationship of the aircraft to its nonexpendable system components or change its logistic support. Consecutive series symbols begin with "A" and are placed to the immediate right of the design number. To avoid confusion, the letters "I" and "O" are not used for this symbol.

Block Numbers   This number identifies a production group of identically configured aircraft within a particular design series. The numbers are assigned in multiples of five (05, 10, etc.). Intermediate block numbers are reserved for field modifications that the military departments apply. Block numbers are not considered part of the MDS.

Sources: USAF, *Designing and Naming Defense Equipment: Military Aerospace Vehicles*, AF Regulation 82-1, 17 July 1984; Department of the Army, AR 70-50; Department of the Navy, NAVMATINST 8800.4D.

APPENDIX B
Missile Designations

All DOD aerospace vehicles, including rockets and missiles, are assigned a mission-designation-series (MDS). A prescribed arrangement of letters and numbers constitutes an MDS. A rocket or missile MDS designation identifies the status, launch environment, mission, type, and design series of the vehicle. Positions one through four and six are letters; position five is a number. A sample MDS is given below for the Ground-Launched Cruise Missile (GLCM) with a complete list of the various letter designations and their meanings.

1. Status Prefix This symbol is used only when necessary, to indicate that a rocket's or missile's test, modification, or experimental or prototype design does not make it standard. The symbol appears to the immediate left of the launch environment symbol or mission symbol.

Description

C Captive Vehicle designed to be carried on a launch platform but incapable of being fired.

D Dummy Nonflyable vehicle used for training.

J Special test (temporary) Vehicle in special test program by authorized organization, on bailment contract with a special test configuration, or with installed property temporarily removed to accommodate tests.

M Maintenance Vehicle designed for conducting maintenance checks of the launch vehicle.

N Special test (permanent) Vehicle in special test program by authorized activities or on bailment contract and whose configuration is so drastically changed that returning it to its original operational configur-

Letter and Number Designations

(Example: Ground-Launched Cruise Missile (GLCM)-Designation BGM-109G)

	1	2	3	4 -	5	6
		B	G	M -	109	G
Status prefix(*none*) ⌐						
Launch environment (*multiple*)						
Mission (*surface attack*)						
Vehicle type (*guided missile*)						
Design number (*109th missile design*)						
Series (*7th version of this design*)						

ation is beyond practical economical limits.

X   Experimental   Vehicle in developmental or experimental stage. The basic mission symbol and design number of this vehicle have been designated but the vehicle has not been established as a standard vehicle.

Y   Prototype   A model suitable for evaluation of design, performance, and production potential.

Z   Planning   Vehicle is in the planning or predevelopment stage.

2. Launch Environment   This symbol identifies the launch environment or platform parameter and appears to the immediate left of the mission symbol. Only one of these symbols should be used in any one MDS.

Description

A   Air   Vehicle air-launched.

B   Multiple   Vehicle capable of being launched from more than one environment.

C   Coffin   Vehicle stored horizontally or at a less-than-45-degree angle in a protective enclosure (regardless of structural strength) and launched from ground level.

F   Individual   Vehicle hand-carried and launched by combat personnel.

G   Runway   Vehicle launched from a runway.

H   Silo-stored   Vehicle vertically stored but not launched below ground level.

L   Silo-launched   Vehicle vertically stored and launched from below ground level.

M   Mobile   Vehicle launched from a ground vehicle or movable platform.

P   Soft Pad   Vehicle partially protected or unprotected in storage and launched from ground level.

R   Ship   Vehicle launched from a surface vessel (ship or barge).

U   Underwater attack   Vehicle launched from a submarine or other underwater device.

3. Mission   This symbol identifies the basic function and capability of the rocket or missile and appears to the immediate left of the rocket or missile type symbol.

Description

D   Decoy   Vehicle designed or modified to confuse, deceive, or divert enemy defenses by simulating an attack vehicle.

E   Special electronic installation   Vehicle designed or modified with electronic equipment for communications, countermeasures, electronic radiation sounding, or other electronic recording or relay mission.

G   Surface attack   Vehicle designed to destroy enemy land or sea targets.

I   Aerial intercept   Vehicle designed to intercept aerial targets in defensive or offensive roles.

Q   Drone   Land, sea, or air vehicle remotely or automatically controlled.

T   Training   Vehicle designed or permanently modified for training purposes.

U Underwater attack Vehicle designed primarily to detonate underwater and destroy submarines or other underwater targets.

W Weather Vehicle designed to observe, record, or relay meteorological data.

4. Vehicle Type This symbol identifies an unmanned vehicle. It appears with a dash to the immediate left of the design number.

Description

M Guided missile or drone Unmanned vehicle that flies in and above the atmosphere and whose trajectory or flight path can be controlled by an external or internal guidance system.

N Probe Nonorbital, instrumented vehicle used to penetrate the aerospace environment and transmit information back to earth stations.

R Rocket Vehicle propelled by an engine that derives its thrust from the ejection of hot gases generated by liquid or solid propellants carried in the vehicle. It does not require an intake of air (i.e., it carries its own oxidizer) or water.

5. Design Number This number identifies major design changes within the same mission category. Design numbers run consecutively: "1" is used to begin each category. A dash is used to separate the design number from the symbol to its immediate left.

6. Series This symbol identifies the first production model of a particular design and any subsequent models representing modifications that significantly alter the relationship of the rocket or missile to its nonexpendable system components or change its logistic support. Consecutive series symbols begin with "A" and are placed to the immediate right of the design number. To avoid confusion, the letters "I" and "O" are not used for this symbol.

Configuration or Component Number This number is used only to denote configuration changes that affect performance or tactics, or integral components of a weapons system that require the same operations or logistics reporting as the rocket or missile. This number appears separated by a dash on the immediate right of the series symbol. Each military department determines its own method for assigning configuration numbers, and they are not considered part of the MDS.

Sources: Departments of the Air Force, the Army, and the Navy, *Designating and Naming Defense Equipment: Military Aerospace Vehicles,* AFR 82-1, AR 70-50, NAVMATINST 8800.4D., Washington, DC, 17 July 1984.

APPENDIX C
Ship Designations

A. Warship Classifications

Aircraft Carrier Type

CV	Multipurpose Aircraft Carrier
CVA	Attack Aircraft Carrier
CVN	Multipurpose Nuclear-Powered Aircraft Carrier
CVS	Anti-Submarine Warfare Aircraft Carrier

Surface Combatant Type

BB	Battleship
CA	Gun Cruiser
CG	Guided-Missile Cruiser
CGN	Nuclear-Powered Guided-Missile Cruiser
DD	Destroyer
DDG	Guided-Missile Destroyer
FF	Frigate
FFG	Guided-Missile Frigate

Submarine Type

SS	Attack Submarine
SSN	Nuclear-Powered Attack Submarine
SSBN	Nuclear-Powered Ballistic Missile Submarine

B. Other Combatant Classifications

Patrol Combatant Type

PG	Patrol Combatant
PHM	Hydrofoil Guided-Missile Patrol Combatant

Amphibious Warfare Type

LCC	Amphibious Command Ship
LHA	General-Purpose Amphibious Assault Ship
LHD	Multipurpose Amphibious Assault Ship
LKA	Amphibious Cargo Ship
LPA	Amphibious Transport
LPH	Helicopter Amphibious Assault Ship
LSD	Dock Landing Ship
LST	Tank Landing Ship

Mine Warfare Ships

MCM	Mine Countermeasures Ship
MSH	Minesweeper Hunter
MSO	Ocean Minesweeper

C. Auxiliary Ship Classifications

Mobile Logistic Type Ships—Underway Replenishment

AE	Ammunition Ship
AF	Stores Ship
AFS	Combat Stores Ship
AO	Oiler
AOE	Fast Combat Support Ship
AOR	Replenishment Oiler

Mobile Logistic Type Ships—Material Support

AD	Destroyer Tender
AR	Repair Ship
AS	Submarine Tender

Support Type Ships—Fleet Support

ARS	Salvage Ship
ASR	Submarine Rescue Ship
ATF	Fleet Ocean Tug
ATS	Salvage and Rescue Ship

Support Type Ships—Other Auxiliaries

AG	Miscellaneous
AGDS	Deep-Submergence Support Ship
AGF	Miscellaneous Command Ship

AGM	Missile Range Instrumentation Ship
AGOR	Oceanographic Research Ship
AGOS	Ocean Surveillance Ship
AGS	Surveying Ship
AGSS	Auxiliary Research Submarine
AH	Hospital Ship
AK	Cargo Ship
AKR	Vehicle Cargo Ship
AOG	Gasoline Tanker
AOT	Transport Oiler
AP	Transport
ARC	Cable Repairing Ship
ARL	Small Repair Ship
AVB	Aviation Logistic Support Ship
AVM	Guided Missile Ship
AVT	Auxiliary Aircraft Landing Training Ship

D. Combatant Craft Classifications

Coastal Patrol Combatants
| PB | Patrol Boat |
| PCF | Fast Patrol Craft |

River/Roadstead Craft
| ATC | Mini-Armored Troop Carrier |
| PBR | River Patrol Craft |

Amphibious Warfare Type— Landing Craft
LCAC	Landing Craft, Air Cushion
LCM	Landing Craft, Mechanized
LCPL	Landing Craft, Personnel, Large
LCU	Landing Craft, Utility
LCVP	Landing Craft, Vehicle, Personnel
LWT	Amphibious Warping Tug
SLWT	Side Loading Warping Tug

Amphibious Warfare Type— Special Warfare Craft
LSSC	Light SEAL Support Craft
MSSC	Medium SEAL Support Craft
SDV	Swimmer–Delivery Vehicle
SWCL	Special Warfare Craft, Light
SWCM	Special Warfare Craft, Medium

Mine Warfare Type Craft
| MSB | Minesweeping Boat |

E. Support Craft Classifications

Dry Docks (non–self-propelled)
AFDB	Large Auxiliary Floating Dry Dock
AFDL	Small Auxiliary Floating Dry Dock
AFDM	Medium Auxiliary Floating Dry Dock
ARD	Auxiliary Repair Dry Dock
ARDM	Medium Auxiliary Repair Dry Dock
YFD	Yard Floating Dry Dock

Tugs (self-propelled)
YTB	Large Harbor Tug
YTL	Small Harbor Tug
YTM	Medium Harbor Tug

Tankers (self-propelled)
YO	Fuel Oil Barge
YOG	Gasoline Barge
YW	Water Barge

Lighters and Barges (self-propelled)
| YF | Covered Lighter |
| YFU | Harbor Utility Craft |

Lighters and Barges (non–self-propelled)
YC	Open Lighter
YCF	Car Float
YCV	Aircraft Transportation Lighter
YFN	Covered Lighter
YFNB	Larger Covered Lighter
YFNX	Special Purposes Lighter
YFRN	Refrigerated Covered Lighter
YFRT	Range Tender
YGN	Garbage Lighter
YON	Gasoline Barge
YOS	Oil Storage Barge
YSR	Sludge Removal Barge
YWN	Water Barge

Other Craft (self-propelled)
| DSRV | Deep Submergence Rescue Vehicle |
| DSV | Deep Submergence Vehicle |

NR	Submersible Research Vehicle	YRB	Repair and Berthing Barge
YAG	Miscellaneous Auxiliary Service Craft	YRBM	Repair, Berthing, and Messing Barge
YFB	Ferry Boat or Launch	YRDH	Floating Dry Dock Workshop (hull)
YM	Dredge		
YP	Patrol Craft, Training	YRDM	Floating Dry Dock Workshop (machine)
YTT	Torpedo Trials Craft		
		YRR	Radiological Repair Barge

Other Craft (non–self-propelled)

YRST   Salvage Craft Tender

APL	Barracks Craft
YD	Floating Crane
YDT	Diving Tender
YFND	Dry Dock Companion Craft
YFP	Floating Power Barge
YLC	Salvage Lift Craft
YMN	Dredge
YNG	Gate Craft
YPD	Floating Pile Driver
YR	Floating Workshop

Unclassified Miscellaneous Units

IX   Unclassified Miscellaneous Unit

Source: U.S. Navy, Office of the Secretary of the Navy, *Classification of Naval Ships and Craft*, SECNAV Instruction 5030.1K, 4 February 1986.

APPENDIX D
Electronic Nomenclature Designations

All DOD electronic systems, including radars, radios, and computers, are assigned a unique designation based on the Joint Electronics Type Designation System (JETDS). A JETDS designation is a prescribed arrangement of five or six letters and numbers identifying the platform, type of equipment, purpose, model number, and modifications. It also gives miscellaneous identification. The "AN" that precedes a designation indicates that the designation is in fact a joint service system (i.e., an Army/Navy) designation, although not all systems may be in use by more than one service. Frequently, the AN is omitted when a system is referred to by its designation. A sample designation is given below with a complete listing of the various letter designations and their meanings.

1. Platform Prefix Symbols

A Airborne (installed and operated in aircraft)
B Underwater mobile, submarine
C Air transportable (an inactive designation)
D Pilotless carrier
G Ground, mobile (includes two or more ground-type designations)
K Amphibious
M Ground, mobile (installed as operating unit in a vehicle that has no function other than transporting the equipment)
P Pack or portable (animal or human)
S Water surface craft
T Ground transportable
U General utility (multiplatform, i.e., installed on two or more general installation classes, airborne, shipboard, and ground)

Letter and Number Designations
(Example: APS-59)

	1	2	3-	4	5	6
	A	*P*	*S-*	*59*		

Platform (*airborne*)
Type of equipment (*radar*)
Purpose (*detecting and/or range bearing, search*)
Model number (*59th model*)
Modification letter (*none*)
Miscellaneous identification (*none*)

V Ground, vehicular (installed in vehicle designed for functions other than carrying electronic equipment)
W Water surface and underwater

2. Type of Equipment Symbols

A Invisible light, heat radiation
B Pigeon
C Carrier
D Radiac
E Nupac
G Telegraph or teletype
I Interphone and public address
J Electromechanical or inertial wire-covered
K Telemetering
L Countermeasures
M Meteorological
N Sound in air
P Radar
Q Sonar and underwater sound
R Radio
S Special types, magnetic, etc., or combinations of types
T Telephone (wire)
V Visual and visible light
W Armament (peculiar to armament, not otherwise covered)
X Facsimile or television
Y Data processing

3. Purpose Symbols

A Auxiliary assemblies (incomplete operating sets used with or part of two or more sets or series)
B Bombing
C Communications (receiving and transmitting)
D Direction finder, reconnaissance, and/or surveillance
E Ejection and/or release
G Fire-control or searchlight, directing

H Recording and/or reproducing (graphic, meteorologic, and sound)
K Computing
L Searchlight-control (inactivated; "G" used instead)
M Maintenance and test assemblies (including tools)
N Navigational aids (including altimeters, beacons, compasses, racons, depth sounding, approach, and landing)
P Reproducing (no longer used)
Q Special, or a combination of purposes
R Receiving, passive detecting
S Detecting and/or range and bearing, search
T Transmitting
W Automatic flight, remote control, or weapons control
X Identification and recognition
Y Multifunction

Examples

AN/APS-50 Airborne search radar
AN/GRC-20 Ground radio transmitter/receiver
AN/PRC-77 Portable radio transmitter/receiver
AN/URD-4 General-purpose radio direction finder
AN/VRC-46 Ground radio transmitter/receiver
AN/WLR-1 Surface/underwater passive countermeasures receiver

Sources: U.S. Army Command and General Staff College, *Navy and Marine Corps CGSC Student Text 100-1.* 30 June 1987; Departments of the Army, the Navy, and the Air Force, *Joint Electronics Type Designation System*, AR 105-19, AFR 82-

2, NAVMATINST 10550.14, MCO 10550.8, Washington, DC, February 1974; Department of the Air Force, *Designating Aeronautical and Support Equipment*, AFR 82-4, Washington, DC, January 1980; Department of the Air Force, *Designating and Redesignating Air Force Electronics Equipment*, AFR 82-7, Washington, DC, 30 August 1983.

APPENDIX E
Military Rank

Commissioned Officers

Army General of the Army (GA)
Navy Fleet Admiral (FADM)
Air Force General of the Air Force (Gen AF)

O-10 (four-star)

Army General (GEN)
Marine Corps General (GEN)
Navy Admiral (ADM)
Air Force General (GEN)
Coast Guard Admiral (ADM)

O-9 (three-star)

Army Lieutenant General (LTG)
Marine Corps Lieutenant General (LtGen)
Navy Vice Admiral (VADM)
Air Force Lieutenant General (Lt Gen)
Coast Guard Vice Admiral (VADM)

O-8 (two-star)

Army Major General (MG)
Marine Corps Major General (Maj-Gen)
Navy Rear Admiral (upper half) (RADM)
Air Force Major General (Maj Gen)
Coast Guard Rear Admiral (RADM)

O-7 (one-star)

Army Brigadier General (BG)
Marine Corps Brigadier General (BGen)

Navy Rear Admiral (lower half) (RADM); Commodore (COMO)
Air Force Brigadier General (Brig Gen)
Coast Guard Commodore (COMO)

O-6

Army Colonel (COL)
Marine Corps Colonel (Col)
Navy Captain (CAPT)
Air Force Colonel (Col)
Coast Guard Captain (CAPT)

O-5

Army Lieutenant Colonel (LTC)
Marine Corps Lieutenant Colonel (LtCol)
Navy Commander (CDR)
Air Force Lieutenant Colonel (Lt Col)
Coast Guard Commander (CDR)

O-4

Army Major (MAJ)
Marine Corps Major (Maj)
Navy Lieutenant Commander (LCDR)
Air Force Major (Maj)
Coast Guard Lieutenant Commander (LCDR)

O-3

Army Captain (CPT)
Marine Corps Captain (Capt)
Navy Lieutenant (LT)
Air Force Captain (Capt)
Coast Guard Lieutenant (LT)

O-2

Army   First Lieutenant (1LT)
Marine Corps   First Lieutenant (1stLt)
Navy   Lieutenant Junior Grade (LTJG)
Air Force   First Lieutenant (1Lt)
Coast Guard   Lieutenant Junior Grade (LTJG)

O-1

Army   Second Lieutenant (2LT)
Marine Corps   Second Lieutenant (2ndLt)
Navy   Ensign (ENS)
Air Force   Second Lieutenant (2Lt)
Coast Guard   Ensign (ENS)

Warrant Officers

W-4

Army   Chief Warrant Officer (CW4)
Marine Corps   Chief Warrant Officer (CWO4)
Navy   Chief Warrant Officer (CWO-4)
Air Force   Chief Warrant Officer (CWO-4)
Coast Guard   Chief Warrant Officer (CWO-4)

W-3

Army   Chief Warrant Officer (CW3)
Marine Corps   Chief Warrant Officer (CWO3)
Navy   Chief Warrant Officer (CWO-3)
Air Force   Chief Warrant Officer (CWO-3)
Coast Guard   Chief Warrant Officer (CWO-3)

W-2

Army   Chief Warrant Officer (CW2)
Marine Corps   Chief Warrant Officer (CWO2)
Navy   Chief Warrant Officer (CWO-2)

Air Force   Chief Warrant Officer (CWO-2)
Coast Guard   Chief Warrant Officer (CWO-2)

W-1

Army   Warrant Officer (WO1)
Marine Corps   Warrant Officer (WO)
Navy   Warrant Officer (WO-1)
Air Force   Warrant Officer (WO)
Coast Guard   Warrant Officer (WO-1)

Enlisted Personnel

E-10

Army   Sergeant Major of the Army (SMA)
Marine Corps   Sergeant Major of the Marine Corps (SgtMajMC)
Navy   Master Chief Petty Officer of the Navy (MCPON)
Air Force   Chief Master Sergeant of the Air Force (CMSAF)
Coast Guard   Master Chief Petty Officer of the Coast Guard (MCPOCG)

E-9

Army   Command Sergeant Major (CSM); Sergeant Major (SGM)
Marine Corps   Sergeant Major (Sgt-Mjr); Master Gunnery Sergeant (MGySgt)
Navy   Fleet/Command Master Chief Petty Officer; Master Chief Petty Officer (MCPO)
Air Force   Chief Master Sergeant (CMSgt); First Sergeant
Coast Guard   Master Chief Petty Officer (MCPO)

E-8

Army   First Sergeant (1SG); Master Sergeant (MSG)

Marine Corps   First Sergeant (1st Sgt); Master Sergeant (MSgt)
Navy   Senior Chief Petty Officer (SCPO)
Air Force   Senior Master Sergeant (SMSgt); First Sergeant
Coast Guard   Senior Chief Petty Officer (SCPO)

E-7

Army   Platoon Sergeant (PSG); Sergeant First Class (SFC)
Marine Corps   Gunnery Sergeant (GySgt)
Navy   Chief Petty Officer (CPO)
Air Force   Master Sergeant (MSgt); First Sergeant
Coast Guard   Chief Petty Officer (CPO)

E-6

Army   Staff Sergeant (SSG); Specialist 6 (SP6)
Marine Corps   Staff Sergeant (SSgt)
Navy   Petty Officer First-Class (PO1)
Air Force   Technical Sergeant (TSgt)
Coast Guard   Petty Officer First Class (PO1)

E-5

Army   Sergeant (SGT); Specialist 5 (SP5)
Marine Corps   Sergeant (Sgt)
Navy   Petty Officer Second Class (PO2)
Air Force   Staff Sergeant (SSgt)

Coast Guard   Petty Officer Second Class (PO2)

E-4

Army   Corporal (CPL); Specialist 4 (SP4)
Marine Corps   Corporal (Cpl)
Navy   Petty Officer Third Class (PO3)
Air Force   Sergeant (Sgt); Senior Airman (SrA)
Coast Guard   Petty Officer Third Class (PO3)

E-3

Army   Private First Class (PFC)
Marine Corps   Lance Corporal (LCpl)
Navy   Seaman (Seaman)
Air Force   Airman First Class (A1C)
Coast Guard   Seaman (Seaman)

E-2

Army   Private (PV2)
Marine Corps   Private First Class (PFC)
Navy   Seaman Apprentice (SA)
Air Force   Airman (Amn)
Coast Guard   Seaman Apprentice (SA)

E-1

Army   Private (PV1)
Marine Corps   Private (Pvt)
Navy   Seaman Recruit (SR)
Air Force   Airman Basic (AB)
Coast Guard   Seaman Recruit (SR)

APPENDIX F
Military Occupational
Specialties and Ratings

The occupational specialties, ratings, and codes listed in this appendix are used by the military to classify personnel with respect to their occupations. The appendix is separated by Service (Air Force, Army, Navy, and Marine Corps) and by officer, warrant officer, and enlisted personnel categories.

The Air Force uses *Specialty Codes* in its personnel structure. Officers are assigned to a broad career area and then to a particular utilization field within that area. An officer's job is further channeled with the assignment of an *Air Force Specialty Code (AFSC)* number and title. Enlisted AF personnel are assigned specific AFSC numbers and titles within broader career fields. Personnel numbers are provided for 31 December 1987 and are presented for each utilization field (officers) and career field (enlisted).

The Army uses the term *Military Occupational Specialties (MOS)* and assigns officers to specific branches. Warrant Officers are assigned MOS numbers and titles, which are broken down into subcategories within the particular MOS. Enlisted personnel are assigned MOS numbers and titles within a broad CMF. The corresponding pay grade is given for each enlisted MOS. Personnel statistics are

provided for 9 November 1988 (officers) and 7 November 1988 (warrant officers and enlisted).

The Marine Corps also uses the term *Military Occupational Specialties (MOS)* in categorizing its personnel. Both officers and enlisted corpsmen are assigned specific MOS numbers and titles within general fields. Personnel statistics are provided for 1 January 1988 and are presented for individual MOS numbers and titles.

The Navy uses *Officer Billet Designator Codes* and *Enlisted Rating Structures*. Billet and officer designator codes are grouped into several categories of line and staff officers. Each officer is assigned a billet code, which may correspond to an officer code (all billets do not have corresponding officer codes). Enlisted personnel are assigned rates with codes and titles. Pay grades are given for each rate. More detailed information is provided in the Navy section of this appendix. Personnel statistics are provided for 31 December 1987 and are given for officer codes, general warrant officer categories, and enlisted rates.

It should be noted that the personnel numbers provided in this appendix are accurate only for the date listed. Changes to the statistics occur continually, as people move in and out and up and down the MOS ladder. However, these numbers are useful in that they give an indication of the trends and tendencies of assigning personnel to specific tasks.

A list of abbreviations used in this appendix appears on page 839.

1. Air Force Specialty Codes (AFSCs)

Officers

Career Area (Code)	Utilization Field	AFSC	Title	Number as of 12/31/87
International Political-Military Affairs (02)	Int Pol-Mil Aff			294
		0216	Int Pol-Mil Aff	
Disaster Preparedness (05)	Dis Prep			166
		0516	Dis Prep Staff	
		0524	Dis Prep	
Operations (10–22)	Pilot			6,145
		1025	Hel	
		D	T/UH-1F/P	
		E	CH-3	
		F	CH-53	
		G	UH-1N	
		H	HH-1H	
		J	HH-3	
		K	HH-53	
		L	HH-60	
		M	UH-60	
		N	MH-53	
		Z	Other	
		1035	S&R	
		B	HC-130	
		Z	Other	
		1045	Trans	
		F	C-131	
		H	C-135, C-137	
		K	C-140, C-20	
		L	C-141	
		M	C-9	
		N	C-5	
		P	C-12	
		Q	T-39, C-21	
		R	T-43, SAM	
		Z	Other	
		1055	TAC Alft	
		B	C-130	
		C	C-23 (EDSA)	
		D	JC-130	
		Z	Other	
		1065	Tanker	
		C	KC-135	
		D	KC-10	
		Z	Other	
	Pilot			5,099
		1115	Fighter	

Career Area (Code)	Utilization Field	AFSC	Title	Number as of 12/31/87
Operations	Pilot			
		B	F-15	
		C	F-106	
		F	F-4	
		G	F-111	
		H	F-5	
		J	F-4	
		K	A-7	
		M	F-15	
		N	A-10	
		P	AT-38	
		Q	F-16	
		R	RF-4	
		V	EF-111	
		Z	Other	
		1145	Forward Air Ctrl	
		E	OV-10	
		F	O-2A	
		G	OA-10	
		H	OA-37	
		Z	Other	
		1165	Mission Spt	
		A	T-33	
		B	T-37	
		C	T-38	
		D	MPQM, QF-100, QF-102	
		Z	Other	
	Pilot			1,185
		1235	Strat Bomber	
		C	B-52	
		E	FB-111	
		N	B-1	
		Z	Other	
	Pilot			3,177
		1315	Spl Ops	
		A	AC-130	
		B	MC-130	
		Z	Other	
		1325	EW, Abn C2, Spl Recon	
		G	RC-135	
		Q	WC-130	
		S	EC-135	
		T	E-3	
		U	E-4	
		V	WC-135	
		W	EC-130	
		Z	NC-135, NKC-135	
		1335	Strat Recon	
		A	TR-1/U-2	
		B	SR-71	

Career Area (Code)	Utilization Field	AFSC	Title	Number as of 12/31/87
Operations				
		Z	Other	
		1355	Flt Tng Inst	
		B	T-37	
		C	T-38	
		D	T-47	
		E	TTB	
	Pilot	Z	Other, T-41	5,147
		1406	Air Ops Staff Dir	
		A	Strat Recon	
		B	Tac Recon	
		C	Trans/Alft	
		D	Strat Bomber/Tanker	
		E	Tac Air Ctrl	
		F	Fighter	
		G	Spl Ops	
		H	EW, Abn C2, Spl Recon	
		J	Hel	
		K	S&R	
		Y	Gen	
		1415	Air Ops/Strat Recon	
		A	TR-1/U-2	
		B	SR-71	
		D	Strat Recon-Gen	
		Y	Gen	
		1425	Air Ops/Trans	
		A	C-5	
		C	C-9	
		G	C-130	
		H	C-141	
		J	Strat Alft, Gen	
		K	Tac Alft, Gen	
		L	Spec Air Msn	
		M	C-23	
		Y	Gen	
		1435	Air Ops/Strat Bomber	
		A	B-52	
		B	FB-111	
		C	KC-135	
		E	KC-10	
		N	B-1	
		V	Bomber, Gen	
		W	Tanker, Gen	
		Y	Gen	
		1445	Air Ops/Tac Air Ctrl	
		F	FAC	
		J	ALO Jt Duty	
		K	ALO Jt Duty	
		L	ALO Jt Duty	
		Y	Gen	

Career Area (Code)	Utilization Field	AFSC	Title	Number as of 12/31/87
Operations	Pilot			
		1455	Air Ops/Fighter	
		A	F-15	
		B	F-4	
		C	RF-4	
		E	F-4	
		G	F-5	
		H	A-7	
		J	A-10	
		K	F-15	
		M	F-106	
		N	F-16	
		T	F-111	
		U	EF-111	
		V	Air Ground, Gen	
		W	AT-38	
		Y	Gen	
		Z	Air-Air, Gen	
		1465	Air Ops/Spl Ops	
		A	AC-130	
		B	MC-130	
		Y	Gen	
		1475	Air Ops/EW/C2	
		K	WC-130	
		M	EC-135	
		N	RC-135	
		P	WC-135	
		T	E-3	
		U	E-4	
		V	EC-130	
		Y	Gen	
		1485	Air Ops/Hel	
		B	HH-1H	
		C	UH-1H, UH-1N, T/UH-1F	
		E	CH-3,CH-53	
		F	HH-3, HH/MH-53, HH/UH-60	
		N	HC-130	
		P	Hel S&R	
		R	Spl Ops	
		S	Tac Air Ctrl Sys	
		Y	Gen	
		1495	Air Ops/Other	
		A	Physiological Spt	
		D	Undergrad Pilot Tng	
		Y	Gen	
	Nav			5,559
		1505	Wpn Sys/Strat Recon	
		A	SR-71	
		Z	Other	

Career *Area (Code)*	Utilization *Field*	AFSC	*Title*	Number as *of 12/31/87*
Operations	Nav			
		1525	Strat Bombardier	
		A	B-52 Nav	
		C	B-52 RN	
		E	FB-111	
		N	B-1	
		Z	Other	
		1535	Tanker	
		G	KC-135	
		Z	Other	
		1545	Alft/Trans	
		A	C-5	
		G	C-130	
		H	C-130	
		J	C-135, C-137	
		L	C-141	
		Z	Other	
		1555	Wpn Sys/Fighter	
		B	F-15	
		C	F-4	
		E	F-111	
		R	RF-4	
		Z	Other	
		1565	EW, Abn C2, Spl Recon	
		J	WC-130	
		K	EC-135	
		L	RC-135	
		M	WC-130	
		S	HC-130	
		T	E-3	
		U	E-4	
		W	EC-130	
		Z	Other	
		1575	EW	
		A	F-4	
		C	B-52	
		G	EC-130	
		H	MC-130	
		J	AC-130	
		L	RC-135	
		N	B-1	
		Q	EF-111	
		Z	Other	
		1585	Spl Ops	
		C	MC-130	
		D	AC-130 (Nav)	
		F	AC-130 (FCO)	
		Z	Other	
		1595	Flt Tng Inst	
		A	SUNT	

Career Area (Code)	Utilization Field	AFSC	Title	Number as of 12/31/87
Operations	Nav			
		B	TTB	
		C	EWOT	
		D	FAR	
		Z	Other	
	ATC			409
		1616	ATC Staff Off	
		1634	ATC Ops Off	
		A	Ops/Eval Off	
		B	Ops Off	
		1645	Cbt Ctrl Off	
	Air Wpn Dir			2,239
		1716	Air C2 Staff Off	
		1745	Air Wpn Dir	
		A	Manual Sys	
		F	407L	
		G	AWACS	
		H	JSS/GEADGE/222	
		K	OTH-B Sys	
		Z	Other	
		1796	Battle Mgt Dir	
	Missile Ops			2,983
		1816	Missile Ops Staff	
		1825	Missile Launch	
		C	BGM-109	
		F	LGM-25, Titan II	
		G	WS-133A, WS-133A/M MMII	
		H	WS-118A, Peacekeeper	
		K	WS-133A/M, MMIII	
		L	WS-133B, MMIII	
		M	WS-133A/M, MMII	
		Z	Other	
		1835	Missile Ops Off	
		1896	Missile Ops Dir	
	Ops Mgmt			960
		1916	Ops Mgmt Staff Off	
		1925	Ops Mgmt Off	
		1996	Ops Mgmt Dir	
	Space Ops			1,580
		2016	Space Ops Staff	
		2025	Space Ops Anal	
		2035	Space Ops Off	
		A	Surv & Comm Sys	
		B	Space Sys Ctrl	
		C	Space & Missile Warning C2	
		D	Space Wpn Sys	
		2045	Manned SpaceFlt Ops Off	
		2055	Sat Ops Off	
		2066	Astronaut	
		A	Pilot	
		B	Msn Spec	

Career Area (Code)	Utilization Field	AFSC	Title	Number as of 12/31/87
Operations	Space Ops			
		2096	Space Ops Dir	
	Navigator			3,212
		2206	Air Ops Staff Dir	
		A	Strat Recon	
		B	Tac Recon	
		C	Trans/Alft	
		D	Strat Bomber/Tanker	
		E	Tac Air Ctrl	
		F	Fighter	
		G	Spl Ops	
		H	EW, Abn C2, Spl Recon	
		Y	Gen	
		2215	Air Ops/Strat Recon	
		A	SR-71	
		D	Strat Recon, Gen	
		Y	Gen	
		2225	Air Ops/Bomber/Tanker	
		C	B-52 RN	
		E	FB-111	
		F	B-52 EWO	
		N	B-1 Off Sys Off	
		P	B-1 Def Sys Off	
		R	Bomber, Gen	
		S	Tanker, Gen	
		Y	Gen	
		2245	Air Ops/Trans/Alft	
		A	C-5	
		G	C-130	
		H	C-130 (AWADS)	
		J	C-135, C-137	
		L	C-141	
		M	ALO Jt Duty	
		N	Strat Alft, Gen	
		P	Tac Alft, Gen	
		Y	Gen	
		2255	Air Ops/Fighter	
		B	F-15	
		C	F-4	
		E	F-111	
		G	ALO Jt Duty	
		J	F-4	
		K	EF-111	
		L	ALO Jt Duty	
		R	RF-4	
		V	WSO, Gen	
		W	ESO, Gen	
		Y	Gen	
		2265	Air Ops/EW/Abn C2	
		J	WC-130	
		K	EC-135	

Career Area (Code)	Utilization Field	AFSC	Title	Number as of 12/31/87
Operations	Space Ops			
		L	RC-135 RN	
		M	WC-135	
		N	RC-135 EWO	
		S	HC-130	
		T	E-3	
		U	E-4	
		V	EC-130 Nav	
		W	EC-130 EWO	
		Y	Gen	
		2285	Air Ops/Spl Ops	
		C	MC-130 Nav	
		D	AC-130 Nav	
		E	MC-130 EWO	
		F	AC-130 EWO	
		G	EWO, Gen	
		H	Nav, Gen	
		Y	Gen	
		2295	Air Ops/Other	
		A	Physiological Spt	
		D	Undergrad Nav Tng	
		V	Nav, Gen	
		W	EWO, Gen	
		Y	Gen	
Visual Information (23)	Vis Info			104
		2316	Vis Info Staff	
		2324	Vis Info	
Weather (25)	Weather			1,396
		2516	Weather Staff	
		2524	Weather Off	
		2534	Aerial Recon Weather Off	
		2546	Adv Weather Off	
Scientific & Development Engineering (26–28)	Sci			1,641
		2616	Sci Mgr	
		2625	Comp Res Sci	
		2635	Physicist	
		2645	Chem Res	
		2665	Nuclear Res	
		2675	Behavioral Sci	
		A	Human Factors Eng	
		2685	Sci Anal	
	Acq			2,540
		2716	Acq Mgt	
		2724	Acq Proj Off	
		2736	Comp Sys Acq Mgr	
	Dev Eng			5,911
		2816	Staff Dev Eng Mgr	
		2825	Elec Eng	
		2835	Mech Eng	

Career Area (Code)	Utilization Field	AFSC	Title	Number as of 12/31/87
Scientific & Development Engineering	Dev Eng	2845	Astronautical Eng	
		2855	Aeronautical Eng	
		2865	Exp Test Pilot	
		A	Alft/Tanker/Strat Bomber	
		B	Fighter/Recon	
		E	Hel/VSTOL	
		Z	Other	
		2875	Exp Test Nav	
		A	Alft/Tanker/Strat Bomber	
		B	Fighter/Recon	
		Z	Other	
		2885	Comp Sys Eng	
		2895	Project Eng	
Logistics (31–40)	Missile Maint			448
		3116	Missile Maint Staff	
		3124	Missile Maint	
		C	BGM-109	
		F	LGM-25	
		G	WS-133A/M, WS-133B	
		Z	Other	
		3196	Missile Maint Dir	
	Acft Maint & Munitions			3,928
		4016	Maint Staff	
		4024	Acft Maint	
		4054	Munitions	
		A	Munitions	
		B	EOD	
		4096	Aero Maint Dir	
Communications— Computer Systems	Comm–CompSys			6,900
		4916	Staff Off	
		4925	Programming & Anal Off	
		4935	Sys Eng	
		4945	Sys Off	
		A	Ops	
		B	Maint	
		C	Plans & Prog	
		4996	Sys Dir	
Civil Engineering (55)	Civ Eng			2,213
		5516	Civ Eng Staff	
		5525	Civ Eng Off	
		A	Architect	
		C	Civ Eng	
		D	Industrial Eng	
		E	Elec Eng	
		F	Mech Eng	
		G	Gen Eng	
		5596	Civ Eng Dir	

Career Area (Code)	Utilization Field	AFSC	Title	Number as of 12/31/87
Cartography & Geodesy (57)	Cartography/ Geodesy			95
		5716	Staff Off	
		5734	Cartography/Geodesy Off	
Logistics (60–66)	Trans			998
		6016	Trans Staff Off	
		6054	Trans Off	
	Svc			440
		6216	Svc Staff Off	
		6224	Svc Ops Off	
		6234	Svc Sales Off	
		6244	Food Svc Off	
	Supply Mgmt			1,257
		6416	Staff Off	
		6424	Supply Ops Off	
	Acq Cont			1,653
		6516	Acq Cont/Manu Staff Off	
		6524	Prod/Manu Off	
		6534	Acq Cont Off	
		6544	Manu Eng Off	
		6596	Acq Cont/Manu Dir	
	Log Plans & Prog			1,100
		6616	Staff Off	
		6624	Off	
Comptroller (67)	Fin			1,555
		6716	Staff Off	
		6724	Off	
		6736	Budget Off	
		6746	Cost Anal Off	
		6756	Comptroller Staff Off	
		6784	Auditor	
		6796	Auditor, Staff	
Personnel Resource Management (70–75)	Admin			2,333
		7016	Exec Spt Staff Off	
		7024	Exec Spt Off	
		7034	Admin Mgmt Off	
		7046	Admin Mgmt Off, Staff	
	Pers			1,786
		7316	Pers Prog Staff Off	
		7324	Pers Prog Off	
		7364	Social Actions Off	
		A	Equal Opportunity/Human Relations	
		B	Drug/Alcohol Abuse Ctrl	

Career Area (Code)	Utilization Field	AFSC	Title	Number as of 12/31/87
Personnel Resource Management	Pers	7376	Social Actions Off, Staff	
	Man Mgmt			576
		7416	Man Mgmt Staff Off	
		7424	Man Mgmt Off	
	Educ & Tng			600
		7516	Educ & Tng Staff Off	
		7524	Educ & Tng Off	
Public Affairs (79)	Pub Aff			565
		7916	Pub Aff Staff Off	
		7924	Pub Aff Off	
Intelligence (80)	Intel			3,427

		8016	Intel Plans, Prog,
			    Resources, & Sys
			    Staff Off	

		8025	Human Resources Intel Off	
		8035	Signals Intel Off	
		8045	Imagery Intel Off	
		8075	Intel Applications Off	
		8085	Target Intel Off	
		8096	Intel Dir	
Security Police (81)	Sec Pol			1,143
		8116	Sec Pol Staff Off	
		8124	Sec Pol Off	
Special Investigations (82)	Spl Inv			575
		8216	Spl Inv Staff Off	
		8224	Spl Inv Off	
Band (87)	Band			34
		8716	Band Staff Off	
		8724	Band Off	
Legal (88)	Legal			1,337
		8816	Judge Advocate, Staff	
		8824	Judge Advocate	
Chaplain (89)	Chaplain			821
		8916	Staff Chaplain	
		8924	Chaplain	
Medicine (90–99)	Health Svc			1,272
		9016	Health Svc Admin, Staff	
		9025	Health Svc Admin	
	Biomed Sci			1,100
		9116	Biomed Eng Staff	
		9125	Bioenv Enr	
		A	Gen	
		B	Industrial Hygiene	

Career Area (Code)	Utilization Field	AFSC	Title	Number as of 12/31/87
Medicine	Biomed Sci	C	Med Const	
		D	Env	
		E	Architecture	
		F	Biomed Eng	
		H	Bioenv/Health Phys	
		9136	Med Entomologist	
		9146	Staff Biomed Sci	
		9156	Biomed Lab Off	
		A	Biomed Lab Sci	
		B	Microbiology	
		C	Clinical Chem	
		E	Env & Industrial Hygiene Chem	
		G	Blood Bank	
		H	Other	
		9166	Aero Physiologist	
		9176	Health Phys	
		A	Med	
		9186	Clin Psychologist	
		B	Clin Neuro–Psychologist	
		9196	Clin Social Worker	
	92			1,255
		9216	Dietician	
		9226	Occupational Therapist	
		9236	Physical Therapist	
		9246	Pharmacist	
		9256	Optometrist	
		9266	Biomed Spl	
		B	Audiologist	
		C	Speech	
		D	Other	
		9276	Podiatrist	
		9286	Phys Asst	
		A	Orthopedics	
		B	Otalaryngology	
		C	Gen Surgery	
		9296	Env Health Off	
	Physician			2,337
		9316	Staff Clinician	
		9326	Gen Practice Phys	
		9346	Family Phys	
		9356	Aero Med Phys	
		A	Aero Med Spec	
		B	Preventive Med	
		C	Occupational Med	
		D	Family Practice Spec	
		9366	Pediatrician	
		B	Adolescent Med	
		C	Cardiology	

Career Area (Code)	Utilization Field	AFSC	Title	Number as of 12/31/87
Medicine	Physician			
		D	Dev Pediatrics	
		E	Endocrinology	
		F	Neonatology	
		G	Gastroenterology	
		H	Hematology	
		J	Neurology	
		L	Infectious Diseases	
		M	Med Genetics	
		N	Nephrology	
		9376	Physical Med Physician	
		9386	Internist	
		B	Oncology	
		C	Cardiology	
		E	Endocrinology	
		G	Gastroenterology	
		H	Hematology	
		J	Rheumatology	
		K	Pulmonary Diseases	
		L	Infectious Diseases	
		N	Nephrology	
		R	Nuclear Med	
		9396	Emergency Service Phys	
		A	Emergency Med Spec	
	94			930
		9416	Surgeon	
		A	Thoracic Surgery	
		B	Colon & Rectal Surgery	
		C	Cardiac Surgery	
		D	Pediatric Surgery	
		E	Peripheral Vascular Surgery	
		F	Neurological Surgery	
		G	Plastic Surgery	
		9426	Urologist	
		9436	Ophthalmologist	
		9446	Otorhinolaryngologist	
		9486	Orthopedic Surgeon	
		A	Hand Surgery	
		B	Pediatrics	
		C	Biomed	
		D	Sports Med	
		E	Spine Surgery	
		F	Oncology	
		G	Replacement Arthroplasty	
		9496	OB/GYN	
		A	Endocrinology	
		B	Oncology	
		C	Pathology	
		D	Maternal-Fetal Med	

Career Area (Code)	Utilization Field	AFSC	Title	Number as of 12/31/87
Medicine	95			619
		9526	Pathologist	
		E	Neuropathology	
		9536	Diagnostic Radiologist	
		B	Neuroradiology	
		C	Nuclear Med	
		E	Spl Procedures	
		9556	Dermatologist	
		A	Dermatologic Surgery	
		B	Dermatopathology	
		9566	Anesthesiologist	
		9576	Neurologist	
		9586	Psychiatrist	
		A	Child Psychiatry	
		9596	Radiotherapist	
	96			28
		9636	Allergist	
		9656	Critical Care Med	
		A	Pediatrics	
	Nurse			5,228
		9716	Nursing Admin	
		9726	Mental Health Nurse	
		A	Mental Health Spec	
		9736	Operating Room Nurse	
		9746	Nurse Anesthetist	
		9756	Clin Nurse	
		A	OB/GYN Nurse Practitioner	
		B	Pediatric Nurse	
		C	Primary Care Nurse	
		D	Staff Dev Off	
		9766	Flight Nurse	
		9776	Nurse-Midwife	
		9786	Env Health Nurse	
	Dental			1,570
		9816	Dental Staff Off	
		9826	Dental Off	
		A	Comprehensive	
		B	Adv Clinical	
		C	Gen Clinical	
		9836	Oral Surgeon	
		9846	Periodontist	
		9856	Prosthodontist	
		9866	Orthodontist	
		9876	Oral Pathologist	
		9886	Endodontist	
		9896	Pedodontist	

Career Area (Code)	Utilization Field	AFSC	Title	Number as of 12/31/87
Medicine	Biomed Sciences			17
		9936	Veterinary Sci	
		B	Toxicology/Pharma-cology	
		C	Radiology/Biophysics	
		D	Psychology	
		E	Physiology/Biochem	
		H	Microbiology	
		9946	Veterinary Clinician	
		A	Surgery	
		B	Internal Med	
		C	Radiology	
		D	Pathology	
		G	Laboratory Animal	

Source: AFVA 36-1. 30 April 1988. Washington, DC: GPO. Numbers obtained through the FOIA.

Enlisted Personnel

Airman Classification: The Airman Classifications are divided into the following skill levels and corresponding job titles and AFSC designations:

Level		Job Title	AFSC
1.	Input or Unskilled	Helper	XXX1X
2.	Semiskilled	Apprentice	XXX3X
3.	Skilled	Specialist/Operator	XXX5X
4.	Advanced	Technician	XXX7X
5.	Superintendent	Superintendent	XXX9X
6.	Chief Enlisted Manager	Manager	XXX00

The following describes the six separate skill levels for AFSC 111X0, Defensive Aerial Operations. The main job title remains the same throughout the skill levels, with the AFSC numbers following the sequence outlined above.

11110	Defensive Aerial Gunner Helper
11130	Apprentice Defensive Aerial Gunner
11150	Defensive Aerial Gunner
11170	Defensive Aerial Gunner Technician
11190	Defensive Aerial Gunner Support
11100	Defensive Aerial Gunner Manager

The AFSCs used in the following section for Air Force Enlisted Personnel contain an "X" where the skill level numbers should be inserted (1,3,5,7,9,00). Where anomalies in the numbering system exist, an * appears next to the AFSC number in the table. The note "no 3,4" means that no skill levels 3 or 4 exist for that AFSC; other notes should be interpreted similarly.

Career Field (Number)	AFSC	Title (exceptions to skill levels)	Number as of 12/31/87
First Sergeant (10)			1,734
	100X0	First Sgt	
Aircrew Ops (11)			9,225
	111X0	Def Aerial Gunner	
	112X0	In–Flt Refueling Oper	
	113X0	Flt Eng	
	B	Hel	
	C	Performance Qualified	
	114X0	Acft Loadmaster	
	115X0	Pararescue/Recovery	
	116X0	Abn Command Sys	
	117X0	Abn Warning C2 Sys	
	118X0	Abn Comp Sys	
	*11899	Abn C2 Msn Elec Sys Spt	
	*11800	Abn C2 Msn Elec Sys Mgr	
	118X1	Abn C2 Comm Eqmt (no 5,6)	
	118X2	Abn Radar Sys (no 5,6)	
Aircrew Protection (12)			3,103
	121X0	Survival Tng	
	122X0	Aircrew Life Spt	
Intelligence (20)			13,069
	201X0	Intel Ops	
	*20199	Intel Ops & Targeting	
	*20600	Intel Ops & Exploitation	
	201X1	Target Intel (no 5,6)	
	202X0	Radio Comm Anal	
	205X0	Elec Intel Ops	
	206X0	Imagery Interpreter	
	207X1	Morse Sys (no 5,6)	
	*20799	Comm Collection/Sys Spt	
	*20200	Radio Comm Anal Mgr	
	207X2	Printer Sys (no 5,6)	
	208X1	Germanic Cryptolinguist (no 3,5,6)	
	A	German	
	B	Dutch	
	C	Flemish	
	D	Swedish	
	208X2	Romance Cryptolinguist (no 3,5,6)	
	A	Spanish (Latin America)	
	B	Portuguese (Latin America)	
	C	French	
	D	Italian	
	E	Romanian	
	208X3	Slavic Cryptolinguist (no 3,5,6)	
	A	Russian	
	B	Polish	
	C	Czech	
	D	Serbo–Croatian	
	E	Russian (White)	

Career Field (Number)	AFSC	Title (exceptions to skill levels)	Number as of 12/31/87
Intelligence			
	F	Hungarian	
	G	Lithuanian	
	H	Slovenian	
	J	Bulgarian	
	208X4	Far East Cryptolinguist (no 3,5,6)	
	A	Chinese (Mandarin)	
	B	Vietnamese	
	C	Thai	
	D	Cambodian	
	E	Lao	
	F	Japanese	
	G	Korean	
	H	Chinese (Cantonese)	
	J	Tagalog	
	208X5	Mid East Cryptolinguist (no 3,5,6)	
	A	Arabic	
	B	Arabic (Syrian)	
	C	Hebrew	
	D	Persian	
	E	Turkish	
	F	Greek	
	G	Indonesian	
	H	Hindi–Urdu	
	209X0	Def C3CM	
Geodetic (22)			120
	222X0	Geodetic	
Visual Information (23)			3,081
	231X0	Vis Info Media	
	231X1	Graphics (no 5,6)	
	231X2	Still Photographic (no 5,6)	
	231X3	Prod–Documentation (no 5,6)	
	233X0	Imagery Prod (no 6)	
Safety (24)			1,436
	241X0	Safety	
	242X0	Dis Prep	
Weather (25)			3,219
	251X0	Weather	
	A	Forecaster (no 1,4,5,6)	
C2 System Operations (27)			16,893
	271X1	Airfield Mgmt	
	*27100	Air Ops Mgr	
	271X2	Ops Resources (no 6)	
	272X0	ATC	
	273X0	Cbt Ctrl	
	274X0	C2	
	275X0	Tac Air C2	
	276X0	AC & W	
	A	Manual Sys (no 3,4,5,6)	
	B	416L SAGE (no 3,4,5,6)	
	277X0	Space Sys Ops	

Career Field (Number)	AFSC	Title (exceptions to skill levels)	Number as of 12/31/87
Communications– Electronic Systems(30)			25,454
	302X0	Weather Eqmt	
	*30100	Comm–Elec Sys Man	
	303X1	ATC Radar (no 6)	
	A	GPN-20/FPN-62 (no 3,4,5,6)	
	B	GPN-20/GPN-22 (no 3,4,5,6)	
	C	GPN-12/FPN-62 (no 3,4,5,6)	
	D	GPN-12/GPN-22 (no 3,4,5,6)	
	E	MPN-14/GPN-20/GPN-22 (no 3,4,5,6)	
	303X2	AC&W Radar (no 5,6)	
	303X3	Auto-Tracking Radar (no 5,6)	
	*30399	Ground Radar Spt	
	304X0	Wideband Comm Eqmt (no 5,6)	
	*30499	Ground Radio Comm Spt	
	304X1	Nav Aids (no 5,6)	
	304X4	Ground Radio Comm (no 5,6)	
	304X5	Television Eqmt (no 5,6)	
	304X6	Space Comm Sys Eqmt (no 5,6)	
	A	DSCS (no 3,4)	
	B	AFSATCOM (no 3,4)	
	C	GMF (no 3,4)	
	305X4	Elec Comp & Switching Sys (no 6)	
	E	Gen Comp Sys (no 3,4,5)	
	F	465L/EDTCC/SACCS (no 3,4,5)	
	G	465L/RCC-EDLCC/SACCS (no 3,4,5)	
	H	465L/Display Eqmt/SACCS (no 3,4,5)	
	K	HM-4118/407L (no 3,4,5)	
	L	SACDIN (no 3,4,5)	
	M	AN/FYQ-93 (no 3,4,5)	
	P	490L OS AUTOVON (no 3,4,5)	
	Q	AN/TTC-30 Elec Switching Sys (no 3,4,5)	
	R	427M Comp Maint (no 3,4,5)	
	T	Abn Comp Maint (no 3,4,5)	
	306X0	Elec Comm & Crypto Eqmt (no 6)	
	306X3	Telecom Sys Maint (no 5,6)	
	309X0	Space Sys Eqmt Maint (no 6)	
Instrumentation (31)			638
	316X3	Instrumentation	
Precision Measurement (32)			NA
	324X0	Precision Measurement Eqmt Lab	
Training Devices (34)			1,092
	341X2	Def Sys Tng	
	*34199	Tng Devices Supt	
	*34100	Tng Devices Mgr	

Career Field (Number)	AFSC	Title (exceptions to skill levels)	Number as of 12/31/87
Training Devices	341X4	Flt Simulator (no 5,6)	
	341X6	Nav/Tac Tng Devices (no 5,6)	
	341X7	Missile Tng (no 5,6)	
Wire Communications Systems Maintenance (36)			4,377
	361X0	Ant/Cable Sys Proj/Maint	
	*36200	Tel/Cable & Ant Maint	
	361X1	Cable Splicing Proj/Maint (no 5,6)	
	362X1	Tel Switching (no 5,6)	
	*36299	Tel & Missile Ctrl Comm Sys Supt	
	362X3	Missile Ctrl Comm Sys (no 5,6)	
	362X4	Tel & Data Circuitry Eqmt (no 5,6)	
Maintenance Management (39)			3,296
	391X0	Maint Data Sys Anal	
	392X0	Maint Scheduling	
Intricate Equipment Maintainence (40)			313
	404X0	Vis Info Eqmt Maint	
	*40490	Photographic Sys Maint Supt	
	*40400	Photographic Sys Maint Mgr	
Missile Systems Maintenance (41)			5,551
	411X0	Missile Sys Maint	
	A	WS-133AM/WS-133AM/ CDB/WS-133B/ CDB/LGM-118A (no 5,6)	
	B	AGM-69A/AGM-69B (no 5,6)	
	C	BGM-109 GLCM (no 5,6)	
	411X1	Missile Maint (no 5,6)	
	A	WS-133A/M/WS-133B/ LGM-118A	
	411X2	Missile Facilities (no 5,6)	
	A	WS-133B/WS-133A/M/ LGM-118A	
Aircraft Systems Maintenance (42)			45,989
	423X0	Acft Elec Sys	
	*42399	Acft Accessory Sys Supt	
	*43200	Acft Maint Mgr	
	423X1	Acft Env Sys (no 5,6)	
	427X0	Machinist	
	*42799	Fabrication Supt	
	*42700	Fabrication Mgr	
	427X1	Corrosion Ctrl (no 5,6)	
	427X4	Metals Processing (no 5,6)	
	427X5	Airframe Rpr (no 5,6)	

Career Field (Number)	AFSC	Title (exceptions to skill levels)	Number as of 12/31/87
Manned Aerospace Maintenance (45)			11,344
	451X4	F-15 Avionics Test Stn	
	A	Auto Test Stn (no 4,5,6)	
	B	Manned & EW Test Stn (no 4,5,6)	
	*45199	Avionics Test Stn Supt	
	*45100	Avionics Sys Mgr	
	451X5	F-16/A-10 Test Stn (no 5,6)	
	451X6	F/FB-111 Test Stn (no 5,6)	
	A	Auto Eqmt (no 4)	
	B	Manned & EW Eqmt (no 4)	
	451X7	B-1B Test Stn (no 5,6)	
	452X1	F-15 Avionics Sys (no 5,6)	
	A	Attack Ctrl Sys (no 4)	
	B	Instrumentation & Flt Ctrl Sys (no 4)	
	C	Comm Nav & Penetration Aids (no 4)	
	*45299	Tac Airlift Supt	
	*45200	Acft Mgr	
	452X2	F-16 Avionics Sys (no 5,6)	
	A	Attack Ctrl Sys (no 4)	
	B	Instrumentation & Flt Ctrl Sys (no 4)	
	C	Comm Nav & Penetration Aids (no 4)	
	452X3	F/FB-111 Avionics Sys (no 5,6)	
	A	Attack Ctrl Sys (no 4)	
	B	Instrumentation & Flt Ctrl Sys (no 4)	
	C	Comm Nav & Penetration Aids (no 4)	
	452X4	Tac Acft Maint (no 5,6)	
	A	F-15	
	B	F-16	
	C	F/FB-111	
	D	F-4 (no 3,4)	
	E	A-10 (no 3,4)	
	F	A-7 (no 3,4)	
	G	F-5 (no 3,4)	
	H	OV-10 (no 3,4)	
	J	T-38 (no 3,4)	
	K	T-37,OA-37 (no 3,4)	
	L	T-33 (no 3,4)	
	M	Gen (no 1,2)	
	Z	All Other (no 3,4)	
	454X0	Aero Propulsion	
	A	Jet Engines (no 5,6)	
	B	Turboprop & Turboshaft (no 5,6)	
	454X1	Aero Ground Eqmt (no 6)	
	454X2	Aircrew Egress Sys (no 5,6)	
	*45499	Sys Supt	

Career Field (Number)	AFSC	Title (exceptions to skill levels)	Number as of 12/31/87
Manned Aerospace			
Maintenance	454X3	Acft Fuel Sys (no 5,6)	
	454X4	Acft H/P Sys (no 5,6)	
	A	MAC/SAC Aero Repair	
	455X0	Photographic & Sensors Maint (no 5,6)	
	A	Tac/Recon Elec Sensors	
	B	Recon/Electro-optical Sensors	
	*45599	Conv Avionics Supt	
	*45100	Avionics Sys Mgr	
	455X1	Avionics Guidance & Ctrl Sys (no 5,6)	
	A	MAC	
	B	SAC	
	C	TAF	
	455X2	Comm and Nav Sys (no 5,6)	
	A	MAC	
	B	SAC	
	C	TAF	
	455X3	Wpn Ctrl Sys (no 5,6)	
	A	F-4E/G/AC-130/F-5E	
	B	A-7D/K	
	C	F-4D	
	455X4	Abn Warning & Ctrl Radar (no 5,6)	
	455X5	Avionics Spt Eqmt (no 5,6)	
	A	F/RF-4 Peculiar Spt Eqmt	
	B	A-7/C-5 Avionics Spt Eqmt	
	455X6	Abn Command Post Comm Eqmt (no 5,6)	
	456X0	Bomb–Nav Sys (no 5,6)	
	*45699	Off/Def Avionics Supt	
	456X1	EW Sys (no 5,6)	
	A	Strat (no 3,4)	
	B	Tac (no 3,4)	
	456X2	Def FC Sys (no 5,6)	
	A	AN/ASG-15	
	B	AN/ASG-21/AN/ASG-33	
	457X0	Strat Acft Maint	
	A	B-1 (no 4,5,6)	
	B	B-52 (no 4,5,6)	
	C	C-18/C-135/E-3/E-4/VC-25/ VC-137 (no 4,5,6)	
	D	KC-10 (no 4,5,6)	
	E	SR-71/TR-1/U-2 (no 4,5,6)	
	457X1	Hel Maint (no 5,6)	
	457X2	Alft Acft Maint (no 5,6)	
	A	C-23/C-130 (no 4)	
	B	C-5 (no 3,4)	

Career Field (Number)	AFSC	Title (exceptions to skill levels)	Number as of 12/31/87
Manned Aerospace Maintenance	C	C-9/C-20/C-22/C-140/ C-141/T-39/T-43 (no 3,4)	
	D	C-5/C-9/C-20/C-22/C-140/- C-141/T-39/T-43 (no 1,2,4)	
	457X3	B-1B Avionics Sys (no 5,6)	
	A	Off Avionics Sys (no 4)	
	B	Instrumentation & Flt Ctrl Comp (no 4)	
	C	Comm Nav & Def Avionic Sys (no 4)	
	*45793	Adv Avionic Sys Supt	
	458X1	Nondestructive Insp (no 5,6)	
	*45899	Acft Fabrication Spt	
	458X3	Fabrication & Parachute (no 5,6)	
Munitions & Weapons (46)			26,103
	461X0	Munitions Sys	
	462X0	Acft Armament Sys	
	C	A-10 (no 3,4,5,6)	
	D	F-4 (no 3,4,5,6)	
	E	F-15 (no 3,4,5,6)	
	F	F-16 (no 3,4,5,6)	
	H	F-111 (no 3,4,5,6)	
	J	FB-111 (no 3,4,5,6)	
	K	B-52G/H (no 3,4,5,6)	
	L	B-1B (no 3,4,5,6)	
	Z	All Other	
	463X0	Nuclear Wpns	
	464X0	EOD	
	465X0	Munitions Ops	
Vehicle Maintenance (47)			5,961
	472X0	Spl Purpose Veh & Eqmt	
	*47299	Veh Maint Supt	
	*47200	Veh Maint Mgr	
	472X1	Spl Veh Maint (no 4,5,6)	
	A	Firetrucks	
	B	Refueling Veh	
	472X2	Gen-Purpose Veh Maint (no 5,6)	
	472X3	Veh Body Mech (no 4,5,6)	
	472X4	Veh Maint Con & Anal (no 5,6)	
Communications/ Computer Systems (49)			20,346
	491X1	Comm–Comp Sys	
	491X2	Comm–Comp Sys Prog (no 5,6)	
	492X1	Comm Sys Radio (no 6)	
	492X2	Comm Sys Electromagnetic Spectrum (no 3)	
	493X0	Comm–Comp Sys Ctrl	
	496X0	Comm–Comp Sys Prog Mgt	

Career Field (Number)	AFSC	Title (exceptions to skill levels)	Number as of 12/31/87
Mechanical/Electrical (54)			10,404
	542X0	Elec	
	542X1	Elec Power Line (no 5,6)	
	542X2	Elec Power Prod (no 5,6)	
	*54999	Mech Spt	
	*54500	Mech Mgr	
	545X0	Refrigeration & Air Conditioning (no 5,6)	
	545X1	Liquid Fuel Sys Maint (no 5,6)	
	545X2	Heating Sys (no 5,6)	
	545X3	Comm–Elec Ctrl Sys (no 3,5,6)	
Structural/Pavements (55)			12,311
	551X0	Pavements Maint	
	551X1	Construction Eqmt (no 5,6)	
	552X0	Structural	
	552X2	Metal Fabricating (no 5,6)	
	552X5	Plumbing (no 5,6)	
	553X0	Eng Asst	
	555X0	Prod Ctrl	
Sanitation (56)			1,722
	566X0	Pest Mgmt (no 5,6)	
	*56699	Sanitation Spt	
	*56600	Sanitation Mgr	
	566X1	Env Spt (no 5,6)	
Fire Protection (57)			6,457
	571X0	Fire Protection	
Marine (59)			57
	591X0	Seaman (no 4,5,6)	
	*59170	Boatmaster	
	*59199	Marine Spt	
	*59100	Marine Mgr	
	591X1	Marine Eng (no 5,6)	
Transportation (60)			14,427
	602X0	Passenger (no 4,5,6)	
	*60273	Traffic Mgmt Spvr	
	*60299	Traffic Mgmt Spt	
	*60200	Traffic Mgr	
	602X1	Freight & Packaging (no 4,5,6)	
	603X0	Veh Oper/Dispatcher (no 4,5,6)	
	*60370	Veh Ops Sprv	
	*60390	Veh Ops Supt	
	*60300	Veh Ops Mgr	
	605X0	Air Passenger (no 4,5,6)	
	*60572	Air Trans Supr	
	*60599	Air Trans Supt	

Career Field (Number)	AFSC	Title (exceptions to skill levels)	Number as of 12/31/87
Transportation			
	*60500	Air Trans Mgr	
	605X1	Air Cargo (no 4,5,6)	
Commissary Services (61)			3,072
	612X0	Meatcutting (no 4,5,6)	
	*61272	Subsistence Ops Tech	
	*61299	Subsistence Ops Spt	
	*61200	Subsistence Mgr	
	612X1	Subsistence Ops (no 3,4,5)	
Services (62)			4,592
	623X0	Svc	
Fuels (63)			6,886
	631X0	Fuel	
Supply (64)			25,458
	645X0	Inventory Mgmt (no 5,6)	
	*64599	Supply Mgmt Spt	
	*64500	Supply Mgr	
	645X1	Materiel Storage & Distribution (no 5,6)	
	645X2	Supply Sys Anal (no 5,6)	
Contracting (65)			1,752
	651X0	Cont	
Logistics (66)			1,158
	661X0	Log Plans	
Finance (67)			6,397
	672X1	Fin Mgmt	
	672X2	Fin Svc (no 4,5,6)	
	673X0	Auditing (no 3)	
	674X0	Cost Anal	
Administrative (70)			24,793
	702X0	Admin	
	703X0	Reprographic	
Personnel (73)			14,772
	732X0	Pers	
	732X1	Personal Aff (no 5,6)	
	732X4	Career Advisory (no 3,5,6)	
	733X1	Man Mgmt (no 3)	
	734X0	Social Actions (no 3)	
	A	Equal-Opportunity/Human Relations (no 5,6)	
	B	Drug/Alcohol Abuse Ctrl (no 5,6)	
Morale, Welfare, & Recreation (74)			1,853
	741X1	Fitness & Recreation	
	742X0	Open Mess Mgmt	
Education & Training (75)			3,913
	751X0	Educ	

Career Field (Number)	AFSC	Title (exceptions to skill levels)	Number as of 12/31/87
Education & Training			
	751X1	Tng Sys (no 3,5,6)	
	753X0	Cbt Arms Tng & Maint	
	753X1	Gunsmith (no 3,5,6)	
Public Affairs (79)			1,321
	791X0	Pub Aff	
	791X1	Radio & TV Broadcasting (no 5,6)	
	792X2	Historian	
Security Police (81)			40,345
	811X0	Sec	
	811X2	Law Enforcement (no 5,6)	
	A	Mil Working Dog Qualified	
Special Investigation (82)			926
	821X0	Spec Invest (no 3)	
Band (87)			1,120
	871X0	Band (no 5, 6 for all)	
	A	Clarinet	
	B	Saxophone	
	C	Bassoon	
	D	Oboe	
	E	Flute or Piccolo	
	F	French Horn	
	G	Cornet or Trumpet	
	H	Baritone or Euphonium	
	J	Trombone	
	K	Tuba	
	L	Percussion	
	M	Piano	
	N	Guitar	
	P	Music Arranger	
	R	Vocalist	
	S	Electric Bass/String Bass	
	T	Mil Band Supt	
	V	Audio & Lighting	
	Z	ANG Band	
	872X0	Instrumentalist (no 3,5,6)	
Paralegal (88)			NA
	881X0	Paralegal	
Chapel Management (89)			NA
	893X0	Chapel Mgmt	
Medical (90)			19,139
	901X0	Aeromed	
	902X0	Med Svc	
	A	Allergy/Immunology (no 5,6)	
	B	Neurology (no 5,6)	
	902X2	Surgical Svc (no 5,6)	
	B	Urology	
	C	Orthopedics	
	D	Otorhinolaryngology	
	903X0	Radiologic	

Career Field (Number)	AFSC	Title (exceptions to skill levels)	Number as of 12/31/87
Medical			
	903X1	Nuclear Med (no 3,5,6)	
	904X0	Cardiopulmonary Lab	
	905X0	Pharmacy	
	906X0	Med Admin	
	907X0	Bioenv Eng	
	908X0	Env Med	
91			3,942
	911X0	Aero Physiology	
	912X5	Optometry	
	A	Ophthalmology (no 5,6)	
	913X0	Physical Therapy (no 5,6)	
	*91399	Biomed Therapy Supt	
	*91300	Biomed Therapy Mgr	
	913X1	Occupational Therapy (no 5,6)	
	914X0	Mental Health Clinic/Svc	
	914X1	Mental Health Unit (no 5,6)	
	915X0	Med Materiel	
	918X0	Biomed Eqmt Maint	
	919X0	Orthotic	
92			2,695
	924X0	Med Lab	
	924X1	Histopathology (no 5,6)	
	925X0	CytoTechology (no 5,6)	
	926X0	Diet Therapy	
Dental (98)			3,677
	981X0	Dental Asst/Tech	
	982X0	Dental Lab	
Reporting/Special (99)			13,173
	99XXX	NA	

Source: AFVA 39-1, Airman Classification Structure Chart. 31 October 1988. Number of personnel in each AFSC obtained through the FOIA.

2. Army Military Occupational Specialties (MOSs)

Officers

Branch	Title	Number as of 11/09/88
11	Infantry	10,696
12	Armor	5,741
13	Field Artillery	8,565
14	Air Defense Artillery	3,597
15	Aviation	6,933
18	Special Operations	1,106
21	Corps of Engineers	4,777
25	Signal Corps	5,337
31	Military Police Corps	2,276
35	Military Intelligence	5,235
38	Civil Affairs	RC
41	Personnel Management	6
42	Adjutant General Corps	3,054
44	Financial Corps	890
45	Comptroller	30
46	Public Affairs	21
47	Permanent Faculty	71
48	Foreign Area	4
49	Operations Research/System Analysis	78
50	Force Development	1
51	Research & Development	43
52	Nuclear Weapons	30
53	System Automation	119
54	Operations, Plans, Training	1
55	Legal Corps	1,758
56	Chaplain Corps	1,547
60–62	Medical Corps	5,242
63	Dental Corps	1,629
64	Veterinary Corps	452
65	Army Medical Specialist Corps	471
66	Army Nurse Corps	4,492
67–68	Medical Service Corps	5,059
74	Chemical Corps	1,738
88	Transportation Corps	2,278
91	Ordnance Corps	3,865
92	Quartermaster Corps	3,622
97	Contracting & Ind Management	107
99	Combat Developments (converted to branch code 51)	NA

Warrant Officers

MOS	Title	Number as of 11/07/88	
13	Field Artillery		241
130A	Pershing Tech	92	
130B	Lance Tech	17	
131A	Radar Tech	96	
131B	RPV Tech	5	
132A	Meterology Tech	31	
14	Air Defense Artillery		410
140A	C2 Tech	22	
140B	Chaparral–Vulcan Tech	143	
140C	Custodial Sys Tech	1	
140D	Hawk Tech	140	
140E	Patriot Tech	104	
15	Aviation		6,468
150A	ATC	35	
151A	Avn Maint	291	
152B	OH-58A/C Scout Pilot	546	
152C	OH-6 Scout Pilot	43	
152D	OH-58D Scout Pilot	141	
152F	AH-64 Pilot	578	
152G	AH-1 Pilot	1,022	
153A	Rotary Wing Aviator	1	
153B	UH-1 Pilot	1,469	
153C	OH-58A/C Observer Pilot	101	
153D	UH-60 Pilot	1,291	
154A	CH-54 Pilot	0	
154B	CH-47A/B/C Pilot	75	
154C	CH-47D Pilot	401	
155A	Fixed Wing Aviator	0	
155D	U-21 Pilot	87	
155E	C-12 Pilot	294	
156A	OV-1/RV-1 Pilot	93	
18	Special Operations		188
21	Corps of Engineers		403
210A	Utilities Ops & Maint	56	
213A	Eng Eqmt Rpr	285	
215A	Photomapping Tech	14	
215B	Survey Tech	11	
215C	Reproduction Tech	9	
215D	Terrain Analysis Tech	28	
25	Signal Corps		924
250A	Telecom Tech	384	
251A	Data Processing Tech	148	
252A	TMDE Maint Spt	38	
256A	Comm-Elec Rpr	300	
257A	Data Processing Rpr	54	
31	Military Police		628
35	Military Intelligence		994
350B	Order of Battle Tech	116	
350D	Imagery Intel Tech	75	

MOS		Title	Number as of 11/07/88	
	350L	Attache Tech	54	
	351B	Counterintel Tech	243	
	351C	Area Intel Tech	10	
	351E	Interrogation Tech	100	
	352C	Traffic Anal Tech	162	
	352D	Emitter/Identification Tech	18	
	352G	Voice Intercept Tech	55	
	352H	Morse Intercept Tech	25	
	352J	Emanations Anal Tech	51	
	352K	Non-Morse Intercept Tech	16	
	353A	IEW Tech	69	
42		Adjutant General's Corps		499
	420A	Mil Pers Tech	430	
	420C	Bandmaster	56	
	420D	Club Mgr	13	
55		Judge Advocate General's Corps		69
60		Medical Corps		539
64		Veterinary Corps		60
67		Medical Service Corps		85
88		Transportation Corps		152
	880A	Marine Deck Off	69	
	881A	Marine Eng Off	83	
91		Ordnance		1,144
	910A	Ammo Tech	115	
	911A	Nuclear Wpns Tech	177	
	912A	Land Cbt Missile Tech	73	
	913A	Armament Rpr	116	
	914A	Allied Trades Tech	77	
	915B	Light Track Sys Tech	47	
	915C	FA Tech	58	
	915D	Armor/Cavalry Tech	96	
	915E	Spt/Staff Tech	385	
92		Quartermaster Corps		1,228
	920A	Property Book Tech	629	
	920B	Rpr Parts Tech	387	
	921A	Airdrop Eqmt Tech	43	
	922A	Food Svc Tech	169	

Enlisted Personnel

CMF	MOS	Grade	Title	Number as of 11/07/88	
	00D	3-9	Spec Duty Asst[a]	NA	
	00U	6-9	Enlisted Off NCO	39	
	00Z	9-9	CSM	1,286	
09			For reporting purposes only		856
	09D		College Trainee	3	
	09S		Commissioned Off Candidate	71	
	09W		Warrant Off Candidate	782	

CMF	MOS	Grade	Title	Number as of 11/07/88
11			Infantry	79,554
	11B	3-8	Infantryman	50,110
	11C	3-8	Indirect Fire	9,355
	11H	3-8	Heavy Anti-armor Wpn	8,327
	11M	3-8	Fighting Veh	9,212
	11X		Accession Code[b]	2,264
	11Z	9-9	Infantry Sr Sgt	286
12			Combat Engineer	17,370
	12B	3-7	Cbt Eng	13,502
	12C	3-7	Bridge Crewmember	2,281
	12E	3-7[c]	ADM Spec	3
	12F	3-7	Eng Tracked Veh	1,120
	12Z	8-9	Cbt Eng Sr Sgt	464
13			Field Artillery	47,498
	13B	3-7	Cannon Crewmember	26,042
	13C	3-7	Tacfire Ops	1,176
	13E	3-7	Cannon Fire Direction	2,711
	13F	3-7	Fire Spt	6,557
	13M	3-7	MLRS	2,208
	13N	3-7	Lance	2,119
	13P	3-7	MLRS/Lance/Fire Direction	445
	13R	3-7	Firefinder Radar	838
	13T	3-7	RPV	47
	13Z	8-9	FA Sr Sgt	1,063
	15E	3-7	Pershing	1,944
	17B	3-7	FA Radar	RC
	21G	3-7	Pershing Elec	413
	82C	3-7	FA Surveyor	1,845
	93F	3-7	FA Meteorology	460
16			Air Defense Artillery	14,262
	16D	3-7	Cannon Crewmember	1,289
	16E	3-6	Hawk FC	659
	16F	3-7	Light Air Def	RC
	16G	3-7	Roland	RC
	16H	3-7	ADA & Intel	1,332
	16J	3-6	Def Acq Radar	482
	16P	3-7	Chaparral	1,863
	16R	3-7	Vulcan	2,576
	16S	3-7	MANPADS	4,436
	16T	3-7	Patriot	1,210
	16Z	8-9	ADA Sr Sgt	415
18			Special Operations	3,498
	18B	6-7	Wpns Sgt	705
	18C	6-7	Eng Sgt	606
	18D	6-7	Med Sgt	533
	18E	6-7	Comm Sgt	792
	18F	6-7	Intel Sgt	177
	18Z	8-9	Sr Sgt	685
19			Armor	29,937
	19D	3-7	Cavalry Scout	9,222
	19E	3-7	M48 M60 Crewman	6,153
	19K	3-7	M1 Crewman	13,641

CMF	MOS	Grade	Title	Number as of 11/07/88
	19Z	8-9	Sr Sgt	921
23			Air Defense Systems Maintenance	3,266
	24C	3-6	Hawk Firing Section Mech	513
	24E	3-6	Hawk FC Mech	38
	24G	3-6	Hawk Info Coord Central Mech	381
	24M	3-7	Vulcan Mech	509
	24N	3-7	Chaparral Mech	282
	24R	7-8	Hawk Master Mech	207
	24S	3-7	Roland Mech	RC
	24T	3-8	Patriot Ops Mech	999
	24U	3-7	Nike-Hercules Custodial Mech	122
	25L	3-7	AN/TSQ-73 ADA C2 Ops/Rpr	187
	26H	3-6	Radar Rpr	28
25			Audio–Visual	1,601
	25Z	8-9	AV Chief	15
	26T	3-6	Radio/TV Spec	297
	41E	3-5	AV Eqmt Rpr	5
	81E	3-6	Illustrator	428
	84B	3-7	Still Photographer Spec	461
	84C	3-5	Motion Picture Spec	22
	84F	3-6	Audio/TV Spec	319
	84T	7-7	TV/Radio Broadcast Ops Chief	54
27			Land Combat/Air Defense System Intermediate Maint	4,473
	21L	3-8	Pershing Elec Rpr	299
	24H	3-7	Hawk FC Rpr	167
	24K	3-7	Hawk Continuous Wave Radar Rpr	209
	24V	7-9[c]	Hawk Maint Chief	149
	27B	3-7	LCSS Test Spec	396
	27C	3-7	Roland Rpr	RC
	27D	3-6	Roland Field Rpr	RC
	27E	3-6	TOW/Dragon Rpr	1,267
	27F	3-6	Vulcan Rpr	418
	27G	3-7	Chaparral/Redeye Rpr	347
	27H	3-7	Hawk Fire Section Rpr	184
	27J	3-7	Hawk Pulse Acq Radar Rpr	136
	27K	3-7	Hawk FC/Cont Wave Radar Rpr	new
	27L	3-6	Lance Sys Rpr	78
	27M	3-6	MLRS Rpr	313
	27N	3-6	Forward Area Alert Radar Rpr	242
	27V	8-9	Hawk Maint Chief	new
	27Z	8-9	Maint Chief	74
	46N	3-7	Pershing Elec-Mech Rpr	194
28			Aviation Communications Electronic Systems Maintenance	2,542
	35K	3-5	Avionics Mech	851
	35L	3-5	Avionics Comm Eqmt Rpr	515
	35M	3-5	Avionics Nav/Flight Ctrl Rpr	303
	35P	6-9	Avionics Eqmt Maint Spvr	469
	35R	3-5	Avionics Spec Eqmt Rpr	404
29			Signal Maintenance	13,329
	29E	3-6	Radio Rpr	1,816

CMF	MOS	Grade	Title	Number as of 11/07/88
	29F	3-6	Fixed Comm Sec Eqmt Rpr	1,025
	29G	3-6	Digital Comm Eqmt Rpr	137
	29H	3-6	Auto Digital Message Switch Rpr	65
	29J	3-6	Teletypewriter Rpr	1,221
	29M	3-6	Tac Sat/Microwave Rpr	620
	29N	3-6	Tel Central Rpr	1,112
	29P	7-7	Comm Sec Rpr	164
	29S	3-6	Field Comm Sec Eqmt Rpr	1,133
	29T	7-7	Sat/Microwave Comm Chief	219
	29U	7-7	Digital Eqmt Maint Chief	60
	29V	3-6	Strat Microwave Sys Rpr	955
	29W	7-7	Comm Maint Spt Chief	678
	29X	8-8	Comm Eqmt Maint Chief	244
	29Y	3-6	Sat Comm Sys Rpr	1,014
	29Z	9-9	Elec Maint Chief	59
	35H	3-8	Calibration Spec	980
	39B	3-6	Automatic Test Eqmt Ops/Maint	284
	39C	3-6	Target Acq/Survey Radar Rpr	235
	39D	3-6	Auto Svc Spt Rpr	529
	39E	3-6	Spec Elec Devices Rpr	344
	39K	3-6	IBM Data Proc Rpr	29
	39L	3-6	FA Digital Sys Rpr	62
	39T	3-6	Tac Comp Rpr	109
	39V	7-7	Comp Sys Maint Group	50
	39W	7-7	Radar/Spec Elec Devices Maint Chief	36
	39X	8-8	Elec Eqmt Maint Group	39
	39Y	3-6	FA Tac Fire Direction Rpr	170
31			Signal Operations	48,306
	31C	3-6	Single Channel Radio Oper	10,520
	31D	3-6	Mob Subscriber/Trans Oper	153
	31F	3-6	Mob Subscriber Switching Sys Oper	90
	31G	6-7	Tac Comm Chief	2,409
	31K	3-5	Cbt Signaler	8,412
	31L	3-6	Wire Sys Installer	4,295
	31M	3-6	Multichannel Comm Sys Oper	8,442
	31N	3-6	Comm Sys/Circuit Controller	2,442
	31Q	3-6	Tac Sat/Microwave Sys Oper	1,905
	31V	3-5	Unit Level Comm Maint	4,467
	31W	7-9	Mob Subscriber Eqmt Comm Chief	33
	31Y	7-7	Comm Sys Spvr	1,492
	31Z	8-9	Comm Ops Chief	120
	36L	3-6	Switching Sys Ops/Maint	545
	36M	3-6	Switching Sys Oper	1,763
	72E	3-7	Tac Telecom Center Oper	4,615
	72G	3-7	Auto Data Telecom Center Oper	3,307
33			EW/Intercept Systems Maintenance	2,020
	33M	5-7	Anal & C2 Subsys Rpr	210
	33P	3-6	Receiving Subsys Rpr	341
	33Q	3-6	Processing/Storage Subsys Rpr	375
	33R	3-7	Avn Sys Rpr	334

CMF	MOS	Grade	Title	Number as of 11/07/88
	33T	3-7	Tac Sys Rpr	607
	33V	3-6	Aerial Sensor Rpr	113
	33Z	8-9	Sys Maint Spvr	40
46			Public Affairs	948
	46Q	3-7	Journalist	572
	46R	3-7	Broadcast Journalist	301
	46Z	8-9	Pub Aff Chief	77
51			General Engineering	12,120
	00B	3-7	Diver	104
	51B	3-5	Carpentry/Masonry Spec	2,609
	51G	3-5	Materials Quality Spec	63
	51H	6-7	Const Eng Spvr	938
	51K	3-5	Plumber	505
	51M	3-7	Firefighter	251
	51R	3-5	Interior Electrician	615
	51T	6-7	Tech Eng Spvr	77
	51Z	8-9	Spvr	266
	52E	5-7	Prime Power Prod Spec	244
	52G	3-7	Transmission/Distribution	61
	62E	3-5	Heavy Const Eqmt Oper	2,630
	62F	3-5	Crane Oper	898
	62G	3-6	Quarrying Spec	85
	62H	3-6	Concrete/Asphalt Eqmt Oper	222
	62J	3-5	Gen Const Eqmt Oper	1,469
	62N	6-7	Const Eqmt Spvr	609
	81B	3-5	Tech Drafting Spec	279
	82B	3-5	Const Surveyor	195
54			Chemical	9,449
	54B	3-9	Chem Ops Spec	9,449
55			Ammunition	6,152
	55B	3-7	Ammo Spec	3,547
	55D	3-9	EOD	848
	55G	3-7	Nuclear Wpns Spec	831
	55R	3-6	Stock Ctrl/Acct	535
	55X	6-7	Insp	220
	55Z	8-9	Spvr	171
63			Mechanical Maintenance	70,960
	41C	3-6	FC Instrument	356
	41J	3-7[c]	Office Machine Rpr	23
	44B	3-5	Metal Worker	1,416
	44E	3-7	Machinist	827
	45B	3-5	Small Arms Rpr	635
	45D	3-5	Self-Propelled FA Turret Mech	358
	45E	3-5	M-1 Abrams Turret Mech	790
	45G	3-6	FC Sys Rpr	253
	45K	3-6	Tank Turret Rpr	1,446
	45L	3-5	Artillery Rpr	492
	45N	3-5	M60A1/A3 Tank Turret Mech	363
	45T	3-5	Bradley Turret Mech	588
	45Z	7-7	Armament/FC Spvr	292
	52C	3-6	Utilities Eqmt Rpr	2,194

CMF	MOS	Grade	Title	Number as of 11/07/88
	52D	3-6	Power Generation Eqmt Mech	8,233
	52F	3-6	Turbine Engine Driven Gen Rpr	193
	52X	7-7	Spl Purpose Eqmt Rpr	415
	62B	3-7	Const Eqmt Rpr	4,059
	63B	3-8	Light Wheeled Veh Mech	18,914
	63D	3-8	Self-Prop FA Sys Mech	2,009
	63E	3-8	M1 Abrams Mech	2,830
	63G	3-5	Fuel & Elec Sys Rpr	961
	63H	3-7	Track Veh Rpr	5,387
	63J	3-5	Quartermaster & Chem Eqmt Rpr	1,902
	63N	3-8	M60A1/A3 Tank Mech	1,156
	63S	3-5	Heavy-wheel Veh Mech	3,301
	63T	3-8	Bradley Mech	4,930
	63W	3-5	Wheel Veh Rpr	4,581
	63Y	3-5	Track Veh Mech	1,465
	63Z	8-9	Mech Maint Spvr	598
67			Aircraft Maintenance	20,668
	66G	5-6	Utility Airplane Tech Insp	8
	66H	5-6	Obs Airplane Tech Insp	34
	66J	6-6	Armament Tech Insp	148
	66N	5-6	Utility Hel Tech Insp	315
	66R	5-6	AH-64 Tech Insp	104
	66S	5-6	Scout Hel Tech Insp	39
	66T	5-6	Tac Trans Hel Tech Insp	250
	66U	5-6	Medium Hel Tech Insp	177
	66V	5-6	Obs/Scout Hel Tech Insp	191
	66X	5-6	Heavy Lift Hel Tech Insp	RC
	66Y	5-6	AH-1 Tech Insp	185
	67G	3-7	Utility Airplane Rpr	33
	67H	3-7	Obs Plane Rpr	237
	67N	3-6	Utility Hel Rpr	2,557
	67R	3-7	AH-64 Rpr	856
	67S	3-6	Scout Hel Rpr	184
	67T	3-7	Tac Trans Hel Rpr	2,688
	67U	3-7	Medium Hel Rpr	2,009
	67V	3-6	Obs/Scout Hel Rpr	2,369
	67X	3-6	Heavy Lift Hel Rpr	RC
	67Y	3-7	AH-1 Rpr	2,035
	67Z	8-9	Sr Sgt	541
	68B	3-6	Acft Powerplant Rpr	843
	68D	3-6	Acft Powertrain Rpr	696
	68F	3-6	Acft Electrician	665
	68G	3-6	Acft Structural Rpr	969
	68H	3-6	Acft Pneudralics Rpr	220
	68J	3-7	Acft Armament/Missile Sys Rpr	2,025
	68K	7-7	Components Rpr Spvr	290
71			Administration	47,065
	00J	5-9	Club/Community Activities Mgr	257
	71C	4-6	Exec Admin Spec	470
	71D	3-9	Legal Spec	1,949
	71E	5-7	Court Reporter	105

CMF	MOS	Grade	Title	Number as of 11/07/88
	71L	3-9	Admin Spec	18,954
	71M	3-9	Chaplain Asst	1,681
	73C	3-7	Fin Spec	3,942
	73D	3-7	Acct Spec	539
	73Z	8-9	Fin Sr Sgt	194
	75B	3-6	Pers Admin Spec	6,795
	75C	3-6	Pers Mgmt Spec	3,013
	75D	3-6	Pers Records Spec	3,392
	75E	3-6	Pers Actions Spec	1,694
	75F	3-6	Pers Info Sys Mgmt	1,042
	75Z	7-9	Pers Sgt	3,034
74			Automatic Data Processing	3,931
	74D	3-7	Comp/Machine Oper	1,861
	74F	3-7	Programmer/Anal	1,887
	74Z	8-9	Data Processing NCO	183
76			Supply and Service	46,850
	43E	3-8	Parachute Rigger	2,049
	43M	3-7	Fabric Rpr Spec	281
	57E	3-8	Laundry & Bath Spec	491
	57F	3-8	Graves Registration	375
	76C	3-5	Eqmt Records & Parts Spec	8,264
	76P	3-7	Material Ctrl & Acct	6,151
	76V	3-7	Material Storage & Handling	7,239
	76X	3-7	Subsistence Supply Spec	1,259
	76Y	3-7	Unit Supply Spec	19,472
	76Z	8-9	Sr Supply/Svc Spec	1,254
77			Petroleum and Water	10,945
	77F	3-9	Petroleum Supply Spec	9,893
	77L	3-7	Petroleum Lab Spec	200
	77W	3-7	Water Treatment Spec	852
79			Recruitment and Reenlistment	4,362
	00E	5-9	Recruiter	1
	00R	5-9	Recruiter/Retention NCO	4,359
	79D	6-9	Reenlistment NCO	2
81			Topographic Engineer	1,257
	41B	3-5	Topographic Instrument Rpr	35
	81C	3-7	Cartographer	170
	81Q	3-7	Terrain Anal	340
	81Z	8-9	Topographic Eng Spvr	31
	82D	3-7	Topographic Surveyor	130
	83E	3-6	Photo and Layout Spec	152
	83F	3-7	Printing and Bindery Spec	399
88			Transportation	22,705
	88H	3-7	Cargo Spec	1,460
	88K	3-7	Watercraft Oper	720
	88L	3-7	Watercraft Eng	517
	88M	3-7	Motor Trans Oper	17,513
	88N	3-7	Traffic Mgmt Coordinator	2,164
	88P	3-7	Locomotive Rpr	RC
	88Q	3-7	Railway Car Rpr	RC
	88R	3-5	Airbrake Rpr	RC

CMF	MOS	Grade	Title	Number as of 11/07/88
	88S	3-6	Locomotive Electrician	RC
	88T	3-7	Railway Section Rpr	RC
	88U	3-7	Locomotive Oper	RC
	88V	3-7	Train Crewmember	RC
	88W	3-7	Railway Movement Coordinator	RC
	88X	8-9	Railway Sr Sgt	RC
	88Y	8-9	Marine Sr Sgt	16
	88Z	8-9	Trans Sr Sgt	315
91			Medical	48,062
	01H	4-6	Bio Sci Asst	297
	35G	3-5	Biomed Eqmt Spec, Basic	366
	35U	5-9	Biomed Eqmt Spec, Adv	417
	42C	4-7	Orthotic Spec	95
	42D	3-7	Dental Lab Spec	435
	42E	3-9	Optical Lab Spec	183
	71G	3-8	Patient Admin Spec	1,684
	76J	3-9	Med Supply Spec	1,934
	91A	3-5	Med Spec	17,232
	91B	5-9	Med NCO	5,509
	91C	5-9	Practical Nurse	4,569
	91D	3-8	Operating Room Spec	1,805
	91E	3-9	Dental Spec	2,232
	91F	3-7	Psychiatric Spec	374
	91G	3-7	Behavioral Sci Spec	800
	91H	3-7	Orthopedic Spec	329
	91J	3-7	Physical Therapy Spec	278
	91L	3-7	Occupational Therapy Spec	136
	91N	3-7	Cardiac Spec	203
	91P	3-8	X-Ray Spec	1,392
	91Q	3-8	Pharmacy Spec	1,043
	91R	3-9	Veterinary Food Insp	1,260
	91S	3-9	Preventive Med Spec	770
	91T	3-7	Animal Care Spec	535
	91U	3-7	Ear, Nose, & Throat Spec	209
	91V	4-7	Respiratory Spec	349
	91W	4-7	Nuclear Med Spec	66
	91X	5-7	Health Physics Spec	58
	91Y	3-7	Eye Spec	385
	92B	3-9	Med Lab Spec	2,362
	92E	5-7	Cytology Spec	41
	94F	3-9	Hospital Food Svc Spec	731
93			Aviation Operation	4,457
	93B	3-6	Aero Observer	294
	93C	3-9	ATC Oper	1,776
	93D	3-9	ATC Sys, Subsys, & Eqmt Rpr	368
	93P	3-9	Flt Ops Coordinator	2,019
94			Food Service	18,363
	94B	3-9	Food Svc Spec	18,363
95			Military Police	26,443
	95B	3-9	MP	24,338

CMF	MOS	Grade	Title	Number as of 11/07/88
	95C	5-9	Corrections NCO	1,551
	95D	5-9	Spl Agent	554
96			Military Intelligence	8,820
	96B	3-8	Intel Anal	3,181
	96D	3-8	Imagery Anal	892
	96F	3-8	Psychological Ops Spec	316
	96H	3-7	Aerial Intel Spec	169
	96R	3-8	Ground Surveillance Sys Op	1,212
	96Z	9-9	Intel Sr Sgt	32
	97B	3-8	Counterintel Agent	1,520
	97E	4-8	Interrogator	1,014
	97G	3-8	Counter SIGINT Spec	478
	97Z	9-9	Counterintel/Human Intel Sr Sgt	6
97			Bands	2,844
	02B	4-7	Cornet or Trumpet Player	395
	02C	4-7	Baritone or Euphonium	116
	02D	4-7	French Horn	157
	02E	4-7	Trombone	241
	02F	4-7	Tuba	172
	02G	4-7	Flute or Piccolo	120
	02H	4-7	Oboe	47
	02J	4-7	Clarinet	254
	02K	4-7	Bassoon	59
	02L	4-7	Saxophone	243
	02M	4-7	Percussion	194
	02N	4-7	Piano	72
	02S	5-9	Spl Bands Member	563
	02T	4-7	Guitar	69
	02U	4-7	Electric Bass	62
	02Z	8-9	Bands Sr Sgt	80
98			Electronic Warfare/Cryptologic Operations	12,596
	05D	3-6	Emitter Identifier/Locator	437
	05H	3-7	Morse Interceptor	1,634
	05K	3-7	Non-Morse Interceptor	1,279
	98C	3-7	Anal	2,871
	98G	4-8	Voice Interceptor	4,876
	98J	3-7	Noncomm Interceptor	1,173
	98Z	8-9	Chief	326

[a] This serves as a duty MOS only and is not counted into the total personnel count.

[b] This code is applied to those personnel pending assignment to CMF 11 MOS (Infantry) upon completion of training.

[c] MOS codes 12E, 24V, and 41J are in the process of being phased out or revised. The personnel in these codes will be reclassified. 24V will be converted to either 24H, 24K, 27H, 27J, or 27V.

3. Marine Corps Military Occupational Specialties (MOSs)

Officers

Field	MOS	Title	Number as of 01/01/88
00		no title	16
01		Personnel & Administration	
	0101	Basic Pers & Admin Off	6
	0107	Civ Aff Off	NA
	0160	Postal Off	8
	0170	Pers Off	189
	0180	Adjutant	334
02		Intelligence	
	0201	Basic Intel Off	52
	0202	Intel Off	259
	0205	Tac Intel Off	60
	0210	Counterintel Off	53
03		Infantry	
	0301	Basic Infantry Off	159
	0302	Infantry Off	2,628
04		Logistics	
	0401	Basic Log Off	54
	0402	Log Off	621
	0430	Embarkation Off	66
08		Field Artillery	
	0801	Basic FA Off	124
	0802	FA Off	1,138
11		Utilities	
	1120	Utilities Off	1
13		Engineering, Construction, & Equipment	
	1301	Basic Eng, Const, Eqmt Off	50
	1302	Eng Off	438
	1310	Eng Eqmt Off	59
14		Drafting, Surveying, & Mapping	
15		Printing & Reproduction	
18		Tank & Assault Amphibian	
	1801	Basic Tank/Amph & Veh Off	37
	1802	Tank Off	293
	1803	Assault Amphibian Veh Off	178
21		Ordnance	
	2102	Ordnance Off	10
	2110	Ordnance Veh Maint	40
	2120	Wpn Rpr Off	23
23		Ammunition & Explosive Ordnance Disposal	
	2305	EOD Off	23
	2340	Ammo Off	35
25		Operational Communications	
	2501	Basic Operational Comm Off	72
	2502	Comm Off	625
26		Signals Intelligence/ Ground Electronic Warfare	

Field	MOS	Title	Number as of 01/01/88
	2601	Basic SIGINT Ground EW Off	22
	2602	SIGINT/EW Off	195
28		Data/Communications Maintenance	
	2802	Elec Maint Off	80
30		Supply Admin & Operations	
	3001	Basic Supply Admin & Ops Off	106
	3002	Ground Supply Off	688
	3010	Ground Supply Ops Off	44
	3050	Warehousing Off	17
	3060	Avn Supply Off	219
	3070	Avn Supply Ops Off	42
31		Traffic Management	
	3102	Traffic Mgmt Off	15
33		Food Service	
	3302	Food Svc Off	30
34		Auditing, Finance, & Accounting	
	3401	Basic Auditing, Fin, & Acct Off	37
	3402	Disbursing Off	29
	3404	Fin Mgmt Off	275
	3406	Fin Acct Off	18
	3410	Auditing Off	19
35		Motor Transportation	
	3501	Basic Motor Trans Off	36
	3502	Motor Trans Off	348
	3510	Motor Trans Maint Off	57
40		Data Systems	
	4001	Basic Data Sys Off	12
	4002	Data Sys Off	241
	4006	Data Sys Ops Off	13
	4010	Data Sys Software Off	21
41		Marine Corps Exchange	
	4130	Exchange Off	18
43		Public Affairs	
	4301	Basic Pub Aff Off	5
	4302	Pub Aff Off	71
44		Legal Services	
	4401	Stu Judge Advocate	63
	4402	Judge Advocate	442
	4420	Legal Svc Off	1
	4430	Legal Admin Off	13
46		Training & Audiovisual Support	
	4602	Spt Off	17
55		Band	
	5502	Band Off	11
	5505	Drum & Bugle Corps Off	1
57		Nuclear, Biological, & Chemical	
58		Military Police & Corrections	
	5801	Basic MP & Corrections Off	19
	5803	MP Off	115
	5804	Corrections Off	16

Field	MOS	Title	Number as of 01/01/88
59		Electronics Maintenance	
	5902	Elec Maint Off—Avn	59
60		Aircraft Maintenance	
	6001	Basic Acft Maint Off	14
	6002	Acft Maint Off	202
	6004	Eng Off	75
63		Avionics	
	6302	Avionics Off	62
65		Aviation Ordnance	
	6502	Avn Ordnance Off	54
68		Weather Service	
	6802	Weather Svc Off	13
70		Airfield Services	
72		Air Control/Air Support/Anti-air Warfare	
	7201	Basic Air Ctrl/Anti-air Off	67
	7204	Surface-to-Air Wpns Off	172
	7208	Air Spt Ctrl Off	154
	7210	Air Def Ctrl Off	191
73		Air Traffic Control & Enlisted Flight Crews	
	7301	Basic ATC Off	9
	7320	ATC Off	106
75		Pilots/Naval Flight Officer	
	7500	Pilot VMA	10
	7501	A-4 Qualified	214
	7507	FRS Basic AV-8B Pilot	22
	7508	AV-8A/C Qualified	27
	7509	AV-8B Qualified	171
	7510	FRS Basic A-6E Pilot	12
	7511	A-6 Qualified	190
	7521	FRS Basic F/A-18 Pilot	37
	7522	F-4S Qualified	223
	7523	F/A-18 Qualified	242
	7540	FRS Basic RF-4B Pilot	6
	7541	FRS Basic EA-6A/B Pilot	4
	7542	EA-6A Qualified	2
	7543	EA-6B Qualified	38
	7545	RF-4B Qualified	42
	7550	Maritime Adv (NATC)	29
	7556	KC-130 Copilot	79
	7557	KC-130 Acft Commander	131
	7558	FRS Basic CH-53A/D Pilot	22
	7560	FRS Basic CH-53E Pilot	17
	7561	FRS Basic CH-46 Pilot	50
	7562	CH-46 Qualified	868
	7563	UH-1N Qualified	324
	7564	CH-53 A/D Qualified	440
	7565	AH-1 Qualified	361
	7566	CH-53E Qualified	196
	7567	FRS Basic UH-1N Pilot	29

Field	MOS	Title	Number as of 01/01/88
	7568	FRS Basic AH-1 Pilot	19
	7575	FRS Basic OV-10 Pilot	11
	7576	Pilot VMO	103
	7578	NFO Stu	52
	7579	FRS Basic RF-4B Airborne Recon	3
	7580	Tac Nav Flt Stu	13
	7581	FRS Basic A-6E Bombadier/Nav	19
	7582	FRS Basic EA-6A/B EW Off	5
	7583	Qualified A-6E Bombadier/Nav	176
	7584	Qualified EA-6A EW Off	2
	7585	Qualified RF-4B Airborne Recon	63
	7587	F-4S Radar Intercept Off	205
	7588	Qualified EA-6B EW Off	124
	7597	Basic Rotary Wing Pilot	141
	7598	Basic Fixed Wing Pilot	179
	7599	Flt Stu	663
96		Special Education Program	
	9602	Educ Off	1
99		Identifying & Reporting MOSs	
	9901	Basic Off	279
	9903	Gen Off	65
	9904	Colonel, Logistician	78
	9906	Colonel, Ground	355
	9907	Colonel, Aviator/Flt Off	195
	9908	Colonel, Supply	1
	9914	Colonel, Judge Advocate	22

Enlisted Personnel

Field	MOS	Title	Number as of 01/01/88
01		Personnel & Administration	
	0100	Basic Admin Marine	623
	0121	Pers Clerk	1,555
	0131	Unit Diary Clerk	1,597
	0151	Admin Clerk	4,737
	0161	Postal Clerk	474
	0193	Pers/Admin Chief	2,119
02		Intelligence	
	0200	Basic Intel Marine	72
	0211	Counterintel Spec	151
	0231	Intel Spec	630
	0241	Imagery Interpretation Spec	126
	0251	Interrogation/Translation	136
	0291	Intel Chief	35
03		Infantry	
	0300	Basic Infantryman	3,360
	0311	Rifleman	17,033

Field	MOS	Title	Number as of 01/01/88
	0313	Crewman	611
	0331	Machinegunner	3,131
	0341	Mortarman	3,230
	0351	Assaultman	2,926
	0352	Antitank Assault Guided Missile	1,351
	0369	Infantry Unit Leader	2,856
04		Logistics	
	0400	Basic Log	240
	0411	Maint Mgmt Spec	893
	0431	Log/Embarkation Spec	960
	0451	Air Delivery Spec	201
	0481	Landing Spt Spec	975
	0491	Cbt Spt Chief	353
08		Field Artillery	
	0800	Basic FA Man	357
	0811	FA Cannoneer	3,445
	0842	FA Radar Oper	106
	0844	FA FC Man	1,032
	0847	Artillery Meteorological Man	74
	0848	FA Ops Man	239
	0861	Fire Spt Man	484
11		Utilities	
	1100	Basic Utilities Marine	253
	1141	Electrician	853
	1142	Electrical Eqmt Rpr	677
	1161	Refrigeration Mech	481
	1169	Utilities Chief	244
	1171	Hygiene Eqmt Oper	956
	1181	Fabric Rpr Spec	143
13		Engineering, Construction, & Equipment	
	1300	Basic Eng, Const, & Eqmt	791
	1316	Metal Worker	312
	1341	Eng Eqmt Mech	1,283
	1345	Eng Eqmt Ops	1,467
	1349	Eng Eqmt Chief	197
	1371	Cbt Eng	2,937
	1391	Bulk Fuel Spec	1,926
14		Drafting, Surveying, & Mapping	
	1400	Basic Drafting, Surveying, & Mapping	32
	1411	Const Drafter	94
	1431	Map Compiler	119
	1441	Const Surveyor	55
	1442	Geodetic Surveyor	53
	1453	Mapping Chief	7
15		Printing & Reproduction	
	1500	Basic Printing & Reproduction	17

Field	MOS	Title	Number as of 01/01/88
	1521	Offset Press Oper	122
	1532	Process Camera Oper	24
	1541	Reproduction Chief	57
	1542	Reproduction Eqmt Rpr	1
18		Tank & Assault Amphibian	
	1800	Basic Tank & Assault Amphibian	205
	1811	Tank Crewman	1,269
	1833	Assault Amphibian Crewman	1,809
21		Ordnance	
	2100	Basic Ordnance Marine	326
	2111	Small Arms Rpr/Tech	1,196
	2131	Towed Artillery Rpr/Tech	289
	2141	Assault Amphibian Veh Rpr	633
	2143	Self-propelled Artillery Rpr	199
	2145	Cbt Tank Rpr/Tech	517
	2147	Light Armored Veh Rpr	268
	2149	Ordnance Veh Maint Chief	66
	2161	Machinist	180
	2171	Optical Instrument Rpr	312
	2181	Ground Ordnance Wpns Chief	52
	2182	Ordnance Elec Eqmt Chief	1
23		Ammunition & Explosive Ordnance Disposal	
	2300	Basic Ammo & EOD	158
	2311	Ammo Tech	1,172
	2336	EOD Tech	164
25		Operational Communications	
	2500	Basic Operational Comm	956
	2512	Field Wireman	2,012
	2513	Const Wireman	149
	2519	Wire Chief	204
	2531	Field Radio Ops	6,082
	2532	Microwave Eqmt Ops	130
	2534	High-Frequency Comm Central Ops	124
	2535	FLTSATCOM Terminal Ops	11
	2536	Ground Mobile Forces SATCOM Ops	38
	2537	Radio Chief	493
	2538	FLTSATCOM Radio Chief	3
	2539	Ground Mobile Forces Radio Chief	6
	2542	Comm Center Ops	1,547
	2549	Comm Center Chief	366
	2591	Operational Comm Chief	437
26		Signals Intelligence/ Ground Electronic Warfare	
	2600	Basic SIGINT/Ground EW	267
	2621	Manual Morse Intercept Ops	318
	2629	SIGINT Anal	207
	2631	Non-Morse/ELINT Intercept Oper	171
	2651	Spl Intel Comm	347
	2671	Cryptologic Linguist, Persian	83

Field	MOS	Title	Number as of 01/01/88
	2673	Cryptologic Linguist, East Asian	55
	2674	Cryptologic Linguist, Spanish	122
	2675	Cryptologic Linguist, Russian	74
	2691	SIGINT/EW Chief	57
28		Data/Communications Maintenance	
	2800	Basic Data/Comm Maint Marine	930
	2811	Tel Tech	370
	2813	Cable Sys Tech	93
	2818	Teletype Tech	240
	2819	KG-13 Teletype Tech	33
	2822	Elec Switching Eqmt Maint	102
	2823	Tech Controller	47
	2825	Fixed Ciphony Tech	23
	2827	Mobile Data Terminal Tech	37
	2828	KW-26 Terminal Tech	34
	2829	Mobile Comm Central Tech	44
	2831	Microwave Eqmt Tech	85
	2833	FLTSATCOM Terminal Tech	21
	2834	Ground Mobile Forces SATCOM Tech	9
	2841	Ground Radio Rpr	1,244
	2861	Radio Tech	526
	2871	Test Measurement/Diagnostic Eqmt	78
	2874	Metrology Tech	83
	2881	Comm Sec Eqmt	150
	2882	KG-30 COMSEC Tech	21
	2884	Ground Radar Rpr	48
	2885	Artillery Elec Sys Rpr	19
	2887	Counter Mortar Radar Rpr	26
	2889	Ground Radar Tech	55
	2891	Data/Comm Maint Chief	40
30		Supply Administration & Operations	
	3000	Basic Supply Admin & Ops	551
	3043	Supply Admin & Ops Clerk	4,589
	3044	Purchasing & Cont Spec	93
	3051	Warehouse Clerk	3,784
	3052	Packaging Spec	269
	3061	Subsistence Supply Clerk	399
	3072	Avn Supply Clerk	2,132
	3073	Comp Ops	114
31		Traffic Management	
	3100	Basic Traffic Mgmt Marine	45
	3112	Traffic Mgmt Spec	735
33		Food Service	
	3300	Basic Food Svc Marine	455
	3311	Baker	632
	3372	Cook Spec	11
	3381	Food Svc Spec	3,434
34		Auditing, Finance, & Accounting	
	3400	Basic Auditing, Fin, & Acct	110
	3421	Personal Fin Records Clerk	704

Field	MOS	Title	Number as of 01/01/88
	3431	Travel Clerk	140
	3432	Disburser/Disbursing Chief	345
	3441	NAFI Audit Tech	59
	3451	Acct Tech	407
35		Motor Transportation	
	3500	Basic Motor Trans Marine	1,035
	3513	Body Rpr Mech	76
	3521	Organizational Automotive Mech	3,409
	3522	Intermediate Automotive Mech	727
	3523	Veh Recovery Mech	211
	3524	Fuel & Elec Sys Mech	103
	3529	Motor Trans Maint Chief	650
	3531	Motor Veh Ops	6,819
	3533	Tractor-Trailer Ops	754
	3534	Semitrailer Refueler Ops	260
	3537	Motor Trans Ops Chief	651
40		Data Systems	
	4000	Basic Data Sys Marine	123
	4034	Comp Ops	737
	4041	Teleprocessing Spec	15
	4063	Programmer, COBOL	501
	4069	Sys Programmer	70
	4071	Database Mgmt Sys Spec	36
41		Marine Corps Exchange	
	4100	Basic MC Exchange Marine	35
	4131	Exchange Marine	139
	4132	Club Mgr/Treasurer	173
43		Public Affairs	
	4300	Basic Pub Aff Marine	27
	4313	Broadcast Journalist	75
	4321	Print Journalist	291
	4391	Pub Aff Chief	21
44		Legal Services	
	4400	Basic Legal Svc Marine	51
	4421	Legal Svc Spec	594
	4425	Notereader/Transcriber	55
	4429	Reporter	41
46		Training & Audiovisual Support	
	4600	Basic Tng & AV Spt	44
	4611	Graphics Spec	113
	4621	Tng Eqmt & Library Spec	108
	4641	Cbt Still Photographer	124
	4642	Cbt Photographic Tech	123
	4653	Cbt AV Eqmt Tech	79
	4671	Cbt Photographer/Motion Media	90
	4691	Tng & AV Spt Chief	33
55		Band	
	5500	Basic Musician	108
	5519	Enlisted Band Member	7
	5521	Band Drum Major	9

Field	MOS	Title	Number as of 01/01/88
	5523	Instrument Rpr Spec	7
	5526	Oboe/English Horn	3
	5528	Bassoon	4
	5534	Clarinet	33
	5536	Flute and Piccolo	28
	5537	Saxophone	70
	5541	Cornet/Trumpet	114
	5543	Baritone Horn/Euphonium	27
	5544	French Horn	26
	5546	Trombone	74
	5547	Tuba and String/Electric Bass	48
	5563	Percussion	58
	5565	Piano/Accordian/Guitar	7
	5571	Drum & Bugle Corps Drum Major	5
	5574	Bugler, Soprana or Mellophane	66
	5577	Bugler, Bass Baritone	42
	5593	Drummer, Drum & Bugle Corps	53
57		Nuclear, Biological, & Chemical	
	5700	Basic Nuclear, Bio, & Chem	31
	5711	Def Spec	628
58		Military Police & Corrections	
	5800	Basic MP & Corrections Marine	240
	5811	MP	3,049
	5812	MP Dog Handler	126
	5813	Accident Investigator	107
	5821	Criminal Investigator	160
	5831	Correctional Spec	823
59		Electronics Maintenance	
	5900	Basic Elec Maint Marine	407
	5921	IHAWK FC Rpr	91
	5922	IHAWK Info Coordination Central	75
	5923	IHAWK Firing Section Rpr	99
	5924	IHAWK Pulse Radar Tech	25
	5925	IHAWK Continuous-Wave Radar Tech	45
	5926	IHAWK Fire Distribution/Engagement	4
	5927	IHAWK FC Tech	49
	5928	IHAWK Missile Sys Maint	67
	5929	IHAWK Mech Sys Rpr	55
	5937	Avn Radio Rpr	154
	5938	Avn Meterological Eqmt	57
	5939	Avn Radio Tech	81
	5942	Avn Radar Rpr	41
	5943	Avn FC Rpr	36
	5944	Avn Radar Rpr	53
	5945	Avn Radar Rpr	42
	5947	Avn FC Tech	42
	5948	Avn Radar Tech	67
	5952	ATC Nav Aids	136
	5953	ATC Radar Tech	158
	5954	ATC Comm Tech	172

Field	MOS	Title	Number as of 01/01/88
	5959	ATC Ctrl Sys Maint Chief	36
	5962	Tac Air Cmd Central Rpr	49
	5963	Tac Air Ops Central Rpr	90
	5964	Tac Data Comm Central Rpr	75
	5974	Tac Central Tech	27
	5977	Tac GP Comp Tech	114
	5978	Tac Data Comm Central Tech	42
	5979	Tac Air Ops Central	72
	5982	Digital Data Sys Tech	38
	5993	Elec Maint Chief	5
	5994	Tac Data Sys Maint Chief	9
60/61		Aircraft Maintenance	
	6000	Basic Acft Maint Marine	815
	6011	Acft Mech, Trainees	199
	6012	Mech, A-4/TA-4/OA-4	327
	6013	Mech, A-6/EA-6	288
	6014	Mech, F-4/RF-4	292
	6015	Mech, AV-8/TAV-8	340
	6016	Mech, KC-130	187
	6017	Mech, F/A-18	374
	6018	Mech, OV-10	121
	6019	Maint Chief	70
	6022	Acft Power Plants Mech, J-52	215
	6023	Power Plants Mech, T-76	61
	6024	Power Plants Mech, J-79	142
	6025	Power Plants Mech, Pegasus	92
	6026	Power Plants Mech, T-56	138
	6027	Power Plants Mech, F-104	81
	6031	Flt Eng, KC-130, Trainee	17
	6032	Flt Eng, KC-130	83
	6035	Power Plants Test Cell Ops	65
	6044	Non-Destructive Inspection Tech	132
	6046	Maint Admin Clerk	794
	6047	Maint Data Anal Tech	255
	6051	H/P Mech, Trainee	174
	6052	H/P Mech, A-4/TA-4/OA-4	157
	6053	H/P Mech, A-6/EA-6	166
	6054	H/P Mech, F-4/RF-4	227
	6055	H/P Mech, AV-8/TAV-8	125
	6056	H/P Mech, KC-130	108
	6057	H/P Mech, F/A-18	165
	6058	H/P Mech, OV-10	44
	6060	Flt Eqmt Marine	615
	6071	Ground Spt Eqmt Mech, Trainee	208
	6072	Ground Spt Eqmt Mech	590
	6075	Cryogenics Eqmt Ops	139
	6076	Ground Spt Eqmt H/P Structural Mech	291
	6077	Ground Spt Eqmt Elec	361
	6078	Ground Spt Eqmt Refrigeration Mech	191

Field	MOS	Title	Number as of 01/01/88
	6081	Safety Eqmt Mech, Trainee	38
	6082	Safety Eqmt Mech, A-4/TA-4/OA-4	81
	6083	Safety Eqmt Mech, A-6/EA-6	111
	6084	Safety Eqmt Mech, F-4/RF-4	106
	6085	Safety Eqmt Mech, AV-8/TAV-8	99
	6086	Safety Eqmt Mech, KC-130	51
	6087	Safety Eqmt Mech, F/A-18	101
	6088	Safety Eqmt Mech, OV-10	50
	6091	Structures Mech, Trainee	155
	6092	Structures Mech, A-4/TA-4/OA-4	137
	6093	Structures Mech, A-6/EA-6	107
	6094	Structures Mech, F-4/RF-4	198
	6095	Structures Mech, AV-8/TAV-8	139
	6096	Structures Mech, KC-130	108
	6097	Structures Mech, F/A-18	184
	6098	Structures Mech, OV-10	38
	6111	Hel Mech, Trainee	244
	6112	Hel Mech, CH-46	708
	6113	Hel Mech, CH-53	483
	6114	Hel Mech, U/AH-1	675
	6115	Hel Mech, CH-53E	355
	6119	Hel Maint Chief	29
	6122	Hel Power Plants Mech, T-58	237
	6123	Hel Power Plants Mech, T-64	310
	6125	Hel Power Plants Mech, T-400	193
	6132	Hel Dynamic Components Mech	211
	6135	AC Power Plants Test Cell Oper	34
	6142	Hel Structures Mech, CH-46	249
	6143	Hel Structures Mech, CH-53	244
	6144	Hel Structures Mech, U/AH-1	207
	6152	H/P Mech, CH-46	196
	6153	H/P Mech, CH-53	152
	6154	H/P Mech, U/AH-1	169
	6155	H/P Mech, CH-53E	153
63/64		Avionics	
	6300	Basic Avionics Marine	609
	6311	Comm/Nav Sys Tech, OMA/IMA	184
	6312	Comm/Nav Sys, A-4/TA-4/OA-4	115
	6313	Comm/Nav Sys, A-6/TC-4C/EA-6A	143
	6314	Comm/Nav Sys, RF-4/F-4	111
	6315	Comm/Nav Sys, AV-8	127
	6316	Comm/Nav Sys, KC-130/OV-10	133
	6317	Comm/Nav Sys, F/A-18	119
	6322	Comm/Nav Sys, CH-46	184
	6323	Comm/Nav Sys, CH-53	161
	6324	Comm/Nav Sys, U/AH-1	156
	6331	Elec Sys Tech, Trainee	182
	6332	Elec Sys Tech, A-4/TA-4/OA-4	145
	6333	Elec Sys Tech, A-6/EA-6/TC-4C	234
	6334	Elec Sys Tech, RF-4/F-4	238

Field	MOS	Title	Number as of 01/01/88
	6335	Elec Sys Tech, AV-8	99
	6336	Elec Sys Tech, KC-130/OV-10	128
	6337	Elec Sys Tech, F/A-18	202
	6342	Elec Sys Tech, CH-46	295
	6343	Elec Sys Tech, CH-53	137
	6344	Elec Sys Tech, U/AH-1	163
	6345	Elec Sys Tech, CH-53E	141
	6351	Adv Avionics Tech, Trainee	46
	6352	Wpn Sys Spec, A-4/TA-4/OA-4	37
	6353	Wpn Sys Spec, A-6/TC-4C	121
	6354	Wpn Sys Spec, F-4J/S	132
	6355	Wpn Sys Spec, AV-8	126
	6357	Wpn Sys Spec, F/A-18	155
	6363	Radar Recon Sys Tech, RF-4	42
	6364	Wpn Sys Spec, A-6/OV-10/F/A-18	59
	6365	Comm/Nav/Radar Sys Tech EA-6B	53
	6367	Integrated Wpn Sys, F/A-18	89
	6372	Aerial Camera Sys Tech	41
	6374	Imagery Interpretation Eqmt Rpr	9
	6386	ECM Sys, EA-6B	91
	6391	Avionics Maint Chief	203
	6411	Comm/Nav Sys Tech, Trainee	100
	6412	Comm Sys Tech	341
	6413	Nav Sys, IFF/RADAR/TACAN	610
	6414	Adv Acft Comm/Nav Sys	177
	6423	Elec Micro-Mini/Instrument Rpr	70
	6431	Elec Sys Tech, Trainee	41
	6432	Elec/Instrument/Flt Ctrl	293
	6434	Adv Acft Elec/Instrument/Flt Cntl	135
	6462	Avionics Test Set Tech	24
	6463	Radar Test Sys Tech	24
	6464	Inertial Nav Sys Tech	54
	6465	Hybrid Test Set Tech	35
	6466	FLIR Tech	47
	6467	RADCOM/CAT IIID Tech	154
	6468	Elec Eqmt Test Set Tech	44
	6469	Adv Automatic Test Eqmt Tech	133
	6474	Wpn Sys Tech, AWG-10	50
	6475	Radar/IR Recon Sys Tech	23
	6476	Aerial Camera/ADAS Sys Tech	44
	6478	Adv Acft Wpn Sys Tech	43
	6482	ECM Sys, Fixed Wing	141
	6483	ECM Sys, Hel	94
	6484	ECM Sys, EA-6	70
	6485	Adv Acft ECM Sys Tech	49
	6492	PME Calibration Tech	325
65		Aviation Ordnance	
	6500	Basic Avn Ordnance Marine	200
	6511	Trainee	120
	6521	Munitions Tech	582

Field	MOS	Title	Number as of 01/01/88
	6531	Tech, A-6E/EA-6	1,009
	6541	Eqmt Rpr Tech	552
	6591	Avn Ordnance Chief	95
68		Weather Service	
	6800	Basic Weather Svc Marine	34
	6821	Weather Observer	132
	6842	Weather Forecaster	114
70		Airfield Services	
	7000	Basic Airfield Svc Marine	174
	7011	Acft Recovery Spec	302
	7041	Avn Ops Spec	859
	7051	Firefighting & Rescue Spec	1,073
72		Air Control/Air Support/Air Warfare	
	7200	Basic Air Ctrl/Air Spt/Anti-air	153
	7212	Low–Altitude Air Def Gunner	530
	7222	HAWK Missile Sys Ops	506
	7234	Air C2 Elec Ops	184
	7236	Tac Air Def Ctrl	86
	7242	Air Spt Oper	210
73		Air Traffic Control & Enlisted Flight Crews	
	7300	Basic ATC/Enlisted Flt Crew	135
	7311	ATC Trainee	89
	7312	ATC Tower	209
	7322	ATC Radar	327
	7371	Aerial Nav Trainee	4
	7372	First Nav	38
	7381	Airborne Radio Ops Trainee	5
	7382	Airborne Radio Ops	98
8000–9599		"B" MOS	
9800–9999		Identifying & Reporting MOSs	
	9811	Member U.S. Marine Band	141
	9900	Basic Marine, Gen Svc	2,988
	9956	Ground Safety Spec	1
	9971	Basic Marine w/Enlistment	4,949
	9991	Sgt Major	1
	9999	Sgt Major/First Sgt	1,335

Sources: U.S. Marine Corps, *Military Occupational Specialties Manual (MOS Manual).* MCO P1200.7. (Washington, DC: U.S. Marine Corps, n.d.), released through the FOIA. MOS Count for Enlisted and Officer personnel as of 1 January 1988 obtained through the FOIA.

4. Navy Officer Billet Designator Codes and Enlisted Rating Structure

Officer Billet Designator Codes

The officer billet designator codes are four-digit numbers used to group officers by categories for personnel accounting and administrative purposes and to identify the status of officers. These codes identify, from the first three digits, the categories in which officers are appointed and/or designated and, from the fourth digit, the status of the officers within the various categories.

Line officers are those eligible for command at sea. Restricted line officers are designated for engineering duty, aeronautical engineering duty, special duty, and limited duty. Limited-duty officers are qualified for command at sea when it is determined that they are qualified and authorized. Staff Corps officers are those in the medical, dental, medical service, judge advocate general, nurse, supply, chaplain, and civil engineer corps.

Fourth Digit Officer Billet Designator Codes

0	Officer of the Regular Navy whose permanent grade is Ensign or above.
1	Officer of the Regular Navy whose permanent status is Warrant Officer.
2	Temporary officer of the Regular Navy whose permanent status is Enlisted.
3	Officer of the Regular Navy who is on the retired list.
4	Restricted Line or Staff Corps officer of the Regular Navy who is Material Professional (MP)–designated.
5	Officer of the Naval Reserve.
6	Restricted Line or Staff Corps Officer of the Naval Reserve who is MP–designated.
7	Officer of the Naval Reserve on active duty in the TAR Program (Training and Administration of Reserves).
8	Officer of the Naval Reserve who was appointed in the Naval Reserve Integration Program from Enlisted status or whose permanent status is Warrant Officer or Enlisted.
9	Officer of the Naval Reserve who is on the retired list.

Billet Code	Description	Code	Description	Number as of 12/31/87
Unrestricted Line Officers				
1000	Appropriate skill & experience			NA
1050	Warfare Specialist			NA
NA	NA			
		110X	Gen, not warfare qualified	3,166
1110	Surface Warfare			
		111X	Surf Warfare	8,684
1120	Submarine Warfare			
		112X	Sub Warfare	3,153

Billet Code	Description	Code	Description	Number as of 12/31/87
1130	Underwater Demolition Team/ SEAL			
		113X	Spl Warfare	327
1140	Special Operations			
		114X	Spl Ops/EOD	372

In Training

1160	Surface Warfare			
		116X	Surface Warfare	4,531
1170	Anti-Submarine Warfare			
		117X	ASW	1,913
1180	Student, Special Warfare			
		118X	Spl Warfare	67
1190	Special Operations			
		119X	Spl Ops	98

Materiel Professional

NA	NA			
		120X	Gen, not warfare qualified	6
1210	Surface Warfare			
		121X	Surf Warfare	85
1220	Submarine Warfare			
		122X	Sub Warfare	45
1230	Aviation Warfare			
		123X	Pilot	138
1231	Aviation Warfare			
1232	Aviation Warfare			
1240	Naval Flight Officer			
1241	Naval Flight Officer			
1242	Naval Flight Officer			
		124X	NFO	35
1250	Pilot/Naval Flight Officer			
1251	Pilot/Naval Flight Officer			
1252	Pilot/Naval Flight Officer			
		125X	Rating as Pilot/NFO terminated	
1260	Spec Warfare Underwater Demolition Team/SEAL			
		126X	Spl Warfare	3
1270	Special Operations			
		127X	Spl Ops	NA
1280	(Appropriate Officer)			
1290	Warfare Specialist			
1300	Air Warfare/Pilot/Naval Flight Officer			

Billet Code	Description	Code	Description	Number as of 12/31/87
1301	Air Warfare/Pilot/Naval Flight Officer			
1302	Air Warfare/Pilot/Naval Flight Officer			
		130X	Air Warfare	279
1310	Aviation Warfare/Pilot			
1311	Aviation Warfare/Pilot			
1312	Aviation Warfare/Pilot			
		131X	Pilot	10,354
1320	Aviation Warfare/Naval Flight Officer			
1321	Aviation Warfare/Naval Flight Officer			
1322	Aviation Warfare/Naval Flight Officer			
		132X	NFO	5,866
1372	Student, Naval Flight Officer			
		137X	Tng, NFO	902
1392	Student, Pilot			
		139X	Tng, Pilot	2,106

Restricted Line

Billet Code	Description	Code	Description	Number as of 12/31/87
		14XX	Eng Duty	1,346
		141X	Eng Duty	
1440	Engineer Duty			
		144X	Ship Eng Spec	
1444	Engineer Duty			
1460	Engineer Duty			
		146X	Eng Duty Off in program leading to Designation 144X	
1500	Aeronautical Engineer			
1504	Aeronautical Engineer			
		15XX	AED	1,061
		150X	AED Flag Off or Captain	
1510	Aeronautical Engineer			
1511	Aeronautical Engineer Duty Pilot/Naval Flight Officer			
1512	Aeronautical Engineer Duty Pilot/Naval Flight Officer			
1514	Aeronautical Engineer Duty Officer			
		151X	AED Off	
1520	Aeronautical Engineer Duty Aeronautical Maintenance			

Billet Code	Description	Code	Description	Number as of 12/31/87
1524	Aeronautical Engineer Duty Aeronautical Maintenance			
		152X	Avn Maint	
1531	Aeronautical Engineer Duty Pilot/Naval Flight Officer			
1532	Aeronautical Engineer Duty Pilot/Naval Flight Officer			
1540	Aviation Duty/Pilot			
1541	Aviation Duty/Pilot			
1542	Aviation Duty/Pilot			
		154X	Avn Duty Off	119
		16XX	Spl Duty	2,209
1610	Special Duty/Cryptology			
		161X	Spl Duty/Cryptology	
		162X	Spl Duty/Merchant Marine	
1630	Special Duty/Intelligence			
		163X	Spl Duty/Intel	
		164X	Spl Duty/Photography	
1650	Special Duty/Public Affairs			
		165X	Spl Duty/Pub Aff	
		166X	Spl Duty/Merchant Marine	
		167X	Spl Duty/Merchant Marine	
		168X	Spl Duty/Gen Admin	
		169X	Spl Duty/Merchant Marine	
		18XX	Spl Duty Geophysic	451
1800	Special Duty/Oceanography			
		180X	Spl Duty/Oceanography	
1802	Special Duty/Pilot/Naval Flight Officer			

Unrestricted Line—Prospective Staff Corps

Billet Code	Description	Code	Description	Number as of 12/31/87
		19XX	Under Instruction for Staff	205
1910	Senior Medical Student Program			
		191X	Sr Med Std	
1920	Student Dental Corps			
		192X	Dental Corps Off	
1930	Medical/Optometry			
		193X	Med/Optometry	
		194X	Chaplain Corps	
		195X	Judge Advocate Gen Corps	
1960	Medical/Osteopathic			
		196X	Med/Osteopathic	
		197X	Med/Osteopathic	
		198X	Dental	
		199X	Med Svc Corps	

Billet Code	Description	Code	Description	Number as of 12/31/87

Staff Corps

2000	Medical Administration			
2100	Medical			
		210X	Med Corps Off	3,846
2102	Flight Surgeon			
2200	Dental			
		220X	Dental Corps	1,709
2300	Medical Service			
		230X	Med Svc Corps	2,425
2302	Aviation Physiologist/Experimental Psychologist			
2500	Law Specialist			
		250X	Judge Advocate Gen Corps	967
2900	Nursing			
		290X	Nurse Corps	3,095
3100	Supply			
		310X	Supply Corps	4,224
3104	Supply Specialist			
4100	Chaplain			
		410X	Chaplain Corps	1,160
5100	Civil Engineer			
		510X	Civ Eng Corps	1,610
5104	Civil Engineer			

Limited-Duty Officer—Line (Surface)

		6XXX	Limited-Duty (Surface)	3,163
6110	Deck Specialist			
		611X	Deck	
6120	Operations Specialist			
		612X	Ops	
6130	Engineering/Repair			
		613X	Eng/Rpr	
6160	Ordnance			
		616X	Ordnance	
6180	Electronics			
		618X	Elec	
6190	Communications			
		619X	Comm	

Limited-Duty Officer—Line (Submarine)

6210	Deck Specialist			
		621X	Deck	
6230	Engineering/Repair			
		623X	Eng/Rpr	

Billet Code	Description	Code	Description	Number as of 12/31/87
6260	Ordnance			
		626X	Ordnance	
6280	Electronics			
		628X	Elec	
6290	Communications			
		629X	Comm	

Limited-Duty Officer—Line (Aviation)

		Code	Description	
		6XXX	Limited-Duty (Avn)	1,064
6300	Aviation Warfare/Pilot			
		630X	Naval Aviator	
6301	Aviation Warfare/Pilot			
6302	Aviation Warfare/Pilot			
6310	Aviation Deck			
		631X	Avn Deck	
6320	Aviation Operations			
		632X	Avn Ops	
6321	Anti-Submarine Warfare			
6330	Aviation Maintenance			
		633X	Avn Maint	
6360	Aviation Ordnance			
		636X	Avn Ordnance	
6380	Avionics			
		638X	Avionics	
6390	Air Traffic Control			
		639X	ATC	

Limited-Duty Officer—Line (General)

6400	Nuclear Power			
		640X	Nuclear Power	
6410	Administration			
		641X	Admin	
6420	Data Processing			
		642X	Data Processing	
6430	Bandmaster			
		643X	Bandmaster	
6440	Cryptology			
		644X	Cryptology	
6450	Intelligence			
		645X	Intel	
6460	Meteorology/Oceanography			
		646X	Meter/Oceanography	
6470	Photography			
		647X	Photography	
6480	Explosive Ordnance			
		648X	Explosive Ordnance	

Billet Code	Description	Code	Description	Number as of 12/31/87
6490	Security			
		649X	Security	

Limited-Duty Officer—Staff Corps

		65XX	Sup–Mess Mgnt/Civil Eng	307
6510	Supply			
		651X	Supply	
6530	Civil Engineering			
		653X	Civ Eng Corps	
6550	Paralegal			
		655X	Judge Advocate Gen Corps	

Warrant Officers

Billet Code	Billet Description	Off Code	Off Description	Number as of 12/31/87
Chief Warrant W-4				1,017
Chief Warrant W-3				836
Chief Warrant W-2				1,057

Chief Warrant Officer—Line (Surface)

7110	Boatswain			
		711X	Boatswain	
7120	Operation Technician Specialist			
		712X	Ops Tech	
7130	Engineering			
		713X	Eng Tech	
7140	Repair Technician			
		714X	Rpr Tech	
7150	Special Warfare Technician			
		715X	Spl Warfare Tech	
7160	Ordnance Technician			
		716X	Ordnance Tech	
7180	Electronics Technician			
		718X	Elec Tech	
7190	Communications Specialist			
		719X	Comm Tech	

Billet Code	Billet Description	Off Code	Off Description	Number as of 12/31/87
Chief Warrant Officer—Line (Submarine)				
7210	Boatswain Specialist			
		721X	Boatswain	
7230	Engineer Specialist			
		723X	Eng Tech	
7240	Repair Technician			
		724X	Rpr Tech	
7260	Ordnance Technician			
		726X	Ordnance Tech	
7280	Electronics Technician			
		728X	Elec Tech	
7290	Communications Specialist			
		729X	Comm Tech	
Chief Warrant Officer—Line (Aviation)				
7310	Aviation Boatswain			
		731X	Avn Boatswain	
7320	Aviation Operations Technician			
		732X	Avn Ops Tech	
7321	Anti-Submarine Warfare Technician			
7340	Aviation Maintenance			
		734X	Avn Maint Tech	
7360	Aviation Ordnance			
		736X	Avn Ordnance Tech	
7380	Aviation Electronics Technician			
		738X	Avn Elec Tech	
		739X	ATC Tech	
Chief Warrant Officer—Line (General)				
7400	Nuclear Power Technician			
		740X	Nuclear Power Tech	
7410	Ship's Clerk			
		741X	Ship's Clerk	
7420	Data Processing Technician			
		742X	Data Processing Tech	
7430	Bandmaster			
		743X	Bandmaster	
7440	Cryptologic Technician			
		744X	Cryptologic Tech	
7450	Intelligence Technician			
		745X	Intel Tech	

Billet Code	Billet Description	Off Code	Off Description	Number as of 12/31/87
7460	Aerographer			
		746X	Aerographer	
7470	Photographer			
		747X	Photographer	
7480	Explosive Ordnance Disposal			
		748X	EOD	
7490	Security Technician			
		749X	Sec Tech	

Chief Warrant Officer—Staff Corps

7510	Supply Corps			
		751X	Supply Corps	
7520	Food Service			
		752X	Food Svc	
7530	Civil Engineer			
		753X	Civ Eng	
7540	Physician's Assistant			
		754X	Phys Asst	

Enlisted Personnel

Rate: Rate identifies personnel occupationally by pay grade.   Within a rating, a rate reflects levels of aptitude, training, experience, knowledge, skills, and responsibilities.   Thus, the rating of Boatswain's Mate is reducible to the following rates:

Master Chief Boatswain's Mate (BMCM)

Senior Chief Boatswain's Mate (BMCS)

Chief Boatswain's Mate (BMC)

Boatswain's Mate First-Class (BM1)

Boatswain's Mate Second-Class (BM2)

Boatswain's Mate Third-Class (BM3)

Pay grades E-3, E-2, and E-1 are also rates.

Rating: An occupation for a petty officer that requires related aptitudes, knowledge, training, and skill. Ratings are divided into six rates, which correspond to pay grades. Personnel in pay grades E-3, E-2, and E-1 do not have ratings, since their occupations are too broad in content and too limited in technical content and responsibility. The service rating is used when applicable to provide specialization in training and utilization of personnel in complex work areas.

Rate				*Pay Grade*
Master Chief				E-9
Senior Chief				E-8
Chief Petty Officer				E-7
First, Second, and Third Class Petty Officers				E-6, E-5, E-4

Rate	*Rate Code*	*Grade*	*Description*	*Number as of 12/31/87*
AA	7800	2	Airman Apprentice	6,270
AB	6700	8-9	Avn Boatswain's Mate	174
ABE	6704	1-7	Launch/Recovery Eqmt	2,797
ABF	6705	1-7	Fuels	1,848
ABH	6706	1-7	Acft Handling	3,114
AC	6600	1-9	ATC	2,971
AD	6200	1-8	Avn Machinist's Mate	12,777
AE	6800	1-8	Avn Elec Mate	9,128
AF	6080	9	Acft Maint Tech	334
AG	7100	1-9	Aerographer's Mate	1,539
AK	7300	1-9	Avn Storekeeper	5,641
AM	6900	8	Avn Structural Mech	393
AME	6903	1-7	Safety Eqmt	2,796
AMH	6902	1-7	Hydraulics	5,275
AMS	6901	1-7	Structures	9,119
AN	7800	3	Airman	9,743
AO	6500	1-9	Avn Ordnanceman	7,665
AQ	6520	1-8	Avn FC Tech	3,070
AR	7800	1	Airman Recruit	7,654
AS	7500	6-9	Avn Spt Eqmt Tech	720
ASE	7501	1-5	Elec	832
ASH	7502	1-5	Hydraulics/Structures	NA
ASM	7503	1-5	Mech	1,278
AT	6300	1-8	Avn Elec Tech	12,157
AV	6180	9	Avionics Tech	362
AW	6400	1-9	Avn ASW Ops	3,766
AX	6310	1-8	Avn ASW Tech	2,179
AZ	7400	1-9	Avn Maint Admin	4,355
BM	0100	1-9	Boatswain's Mate	12,160
BT	4000	1-9	Boiler Tech	10,543
BU	5600	1-8	Builder	2,874
CA	6000	2	Const Apprentice	84
CE	5300	1-8	Const Elec	1,549
CM	5500	1-8	Const Mech	1,686
CN	6000	3	Const Man	58
CR	6000	1	Const Recruit	386
CT			Comm Tech	
CTA	1622	1-9	Cryptologic Tech (Admin)	1,260

Rate	Rate Code	Grade	Description	Number as of 12/31/87
CTI	1666	1-9	Cryptologic Tech (Interpret)	1,341
CTM	1633	2-9	Cryptologic Tech (Maint)	2,253
CTO	1644	1-9	Cryptologic Tech (Comm)	2,005
CTR	1655	1-9	Cryptologic Tech (Collection)	2,168
CTT	1611	1-9	Cryptologic Tech (Tech)	2,321
CU	5080	9	Constructionman	43
DA	8300	2	Dental Apprentice	172
DC	4500	1-9	Damage Controlman	1,071
DK	2100	1-9	Disbursing Clerk	3,053
DM	3200	3-9	Draftsman Illustrator	330
DN	8300	3	Dentalman	1,318
DP	1900	1-9	Data Processing Tech	3,720
DR	8300	1	Dental Recruit	59
DS	1010	1-9	Data Sys Tech	2,624
DT	8300	4-9	Dental Tech	2,150
EA	5100	1-9	Eng Aide	391
EM	4100	1-9	Elec Mate	14,645
EN	3800	1-9	Engineman	9,799
EO	5410	1-8	Eqmt Ops	2,034
EQ	5380	9	Eqmt Man	30
ET	1000	1-9	Elec Tech	20,796
EW	0350	1-9	Elec Warfare Tech	3,112
FA	5000	2	Fireman Apprentice	5,440
FC	0700	1-9	FC Man	9,127
FN	5000	3	Fireman	9,666
FR	5000	1	Fireman Recruit	6,668
FT	0800	8-9	FC Tech	252
FTB	0803	3-7	Ballistic Missile	884
FTG	0801	1-7	Gun	1,384
GM	0600	7-9	Gunner's Mate	1,105
GMG	0604	1-6	Gun	4,267
GMM	0601	1-6	Missiles	2,403
GS	4400	8-9	Gas Turbine Sys Tech	110
GSE	4401	2-7	Elec	1,186
GSM	4402	1-7	Mech	1,779
HA	8000	2	Hospital Apprentice	1,565
HM	8000	4-9	Hospital Corpsman	17,764
HN	8000	3	Hospitalman	6,711
HR	8000	1	Hospital Recruit	465
HT	4300	1-9	Hull Maint Tech	12,541
IC	4200	1-8	Interior Comm Elec	6,271
IM	1100	1-8	Instrumentman	724
IS	2300	1-9	Intel Spec	1,655
JO	2600	1-9	Journalist	947
LI	3100	2-9	Lithographer	458
LN	1750	5-9	Legalman	549

Rate	Rate Code	Grade	Description	Number as of 12/31/87
MA	0150	5-9	Master at Arms	1,714
ML	4700	1-9	Molder	282
MM	3700	1-9	Machinist's Mate	29,864
MN	0900	1-9	Mineman	634
MR	3900	1-9	Machinery Rpr	3,095
MS	2200	1-9	Mess Mgmt Spec	17,055
MT	0810	1-7	Missile Tech	2,013
MU	3300	1-9	Musician	767
NC	1400	5-9	Navy Counselor	1,530
OM	1200	1-8	Opticalman	417
OS	0300	1-9	Ops Spec	12,062
OT	0450	9	Ocean Sys Tech	16
OTA	0451	1-8	Anal	1,545
OTM	0452	3-8	Maint	387
PC	2700	1-9	Postal Clerk	1,236
PH	7600	1-9	Photographer's Mate	1,673
PI	1080	9	Precision Instrumentman	6
PM	4600	1-7	Patternmaker	190
PN	1800	1-9	Pers Man	7,656
PR	7000	1-9	Survival Aircrew Eqmt	2,577
QM	0200	1-9	Quartermaster	5,418
RM	1500	1-9	Radioman	18,129
RP	2500	1-9	Religious Prog Spec	1,054
SA	3600	2	Seaman Apprentice	14,575
SH	2490	1-9	Ship's Serviceman	5,158
SK	2000	1-9	Storekeeper	10,063
SM	0250	1-9	Signalman	3,644
SN	3600	3	Seaman	18,783
SR	3600	1	Seaman Recruit	16,523
ST	0400	9	Sonar Tech	84
STG	0401	1-8	Surface	6,418
STS	0404	1-8	Sub	3,475
SW	5700	1-8	Steelworker	990
TD	7200	4-9	Tradesman	66
TM	0500	1-9	Torpedoman's Mate	4,090
UC	5280	9	Utilities Constructionman	22
UT	5800	1-8	Utilitiesman	1,352
WT	0610	1-9	Wpns Tech	1,151
YN	1700	1-9	Yeoman	13,301

Source: NWP 3 (Rev. D) for rating definitions; Department of the Navy, *Navy Military Personnel Statistics, First Quarter FY 1988,* NAVPERS 15658, 31 December 1987, released through the FOIA. Active Duty Enlisted Data Elements Catalog, Part 25 Item Code Tables, Table 5 Rate Abbreviation, released through the FOIA.

Abbreviations

Abn	Airborne	Comm	Communications
AC&W	Aeronautic Control and Warning	Comp	Computer
		COMSEC	Communications Security
Acct	Accounting		
Acft	Aircraft	Const	Construction
Acq	Acquisition	Cont	Contracting
ADA	Air Defense Artillery	Conv	Conventional
ADM	Atomic Demolition Munition	CSM	Command Sergeant Major
		Ctrl	Control/Controller
Admin	Administration	Def	Defense/Defensive
Adv	Advanced	Dev	Development
AED	Aeronautical Engineer Duty	Dir	Director
		Dis	Disaster
Aero	Aerospace	ECM	Electronic Countermeasures
Aff	Affairs		
Alft	Airlift	Ed	Education
Ammo	Ammunition	Elec	Electronic/Electrical
Anal	Analyst	Eng	Engineering/Engineer
Ant	Antenna	Env	Environmental
Asst	Assistant	EOD	Explosives Ordnance Disposal
ASW	Anti-Submarine Warfare		
ATC	Air Traffic Control	Eqmt	Equipment
Auto	Automatic	ESO	Electronic System Officer
AV	Audio-Visual		
Avn	Aviation	Eval	Evaluation
Biomed	Biomedical	EW	Electronic Warfare
C2	Command and Control	EWO	Electronic Warfare Officer
C3CM	Command, Control, and Communications Countermeasures		
		Exec	Executive
		Exp	Experimental
Cbt	Combat	FA	Field Artillery
Chem	Chemical/Chemistry	FC	Fire Control
CID	Criminal Investigative Division	Fin	Financial
		FLIR	Forward-Looking Infrared
Civ	Civil	Flt	Flight
Clin	Clinical	FLTSATCOM	Fleet Satellite Communications
Cmd	Command		

FRS	Fleet Replacement Squadron	Pub	Public
Gen	General	RC	Reserve Component
Hel	Helicopter	Recon	Reconnaissance
H/P	Hydraulic/Pneumatic	Res	Research
IHAWK	Improved HAWK	Rpr	Repair
Info	Information	RPV	Remotely Piloted Vehicle
Insp	Inspector	Sat	Satellite
Inst	Instructor	SATCOM	Satelite Communications
Int	International		
Intel	Intelligence	Sci	Scientist/Scientific
Inv	Investigation	Sec	Security
Jt	Joint	Sgt	Sergeant
Log	Logistics	SIGINT	Signals Intelligence
Maint	Maintenance	Spec	Specialist
Man	Manpower	Spl	Special
Manu	Manufacturing	Spt	Support
Mech	Mechanic	Spvr	Supervisor
Med	Medical	Sr	Senior
Mgmt	Management	S&R	Search and Rescue
Mgr	Manager	Stn	Station
Mil	Military	Strat	Strategic
Mob	Mobile	Stu	Student
MP	Military Police	Sub	Submarine
Msn	Mission	Supt	Superintendent
Nav	Navigation	Surf	Surface
NCO	Non-Commissioned Officer	Svc	Service
		Sys	Systems
NFO	Naval Flight Officer	Tac	Tactical
Obs	Observer/Observation	Tech	Technician
Off	Officer/Offensive	Tel	Telephone
Oper	Operator	Telecom	Telecommunications
Ops	Operations	Tng	Training
Org	Organizational	Trans	Transport/Transportation
Pers	Personnel	UDT	Underwater Demolition Team
Phys	Physician		
Pol	Political/Police	Veh	Vehicle
Prep	Preparedness	Vis	Visual
Prod	Production	Wpn	Weapon
Prog	Program	WSO	Weapons System Office

BIBLIOGRAPHY

Anderson, Frank W., Jr. *Orders of Magnitude: A History of NACA and NASA, 1915–1980.* The NASA History Series, NASA SP-4403. Washington, DC: Scientific and Technical Information Branch, NASA, 1981.

Arkin, William, M., and Richard Fieldhouse. *Nuclear Battlefields: Global Links in the Arms Race.* Cambridge, MA: Ballinger Books, 1985.

_____. "Nuclear Weapon Command, Control and Communications." In *World Armaments and Disarmament. SIPRI Yearbook 1984.* London: Taylor & Francis, 1984.

Arms Control Association. "A Glossary of Arms Control Terms." Reprinted from *Negotiating Security*, edited by William H. Kincade and Jeffrey D. Porro. Washington, DC: Carnegie Endowment for International Peace, 1979.

Blacker, Coit D., and Gloria Duffy. *International Arms Control: Issues and Agreements.* 2nd ed. Stanford Arms Control Group. Stanford, CA: Stanford Univ. Press, 1984.

Blair, Bruce G. *Strategic Command and Control: Redefining the Nuclear Threat.* Washington, DC: Brookings, 1985.

Brittin, Burdick H. *International Law for Seagoing Officers.* 5th ed. Annapolis, MD: Naval Institute Press, 1986.

Burrows, William E. *Deep Black: Space Espionage and National Security.* New York: Random House, 1986.

"Canada–U.S. Defence Cooperation and the 1986 Renewal of the NORAD Agreement." 4th Report of the Standing Committee on External Affairs and National Defence, Canada. February 1986.

Cannon, Don L., and Gerald Luecke. *Understanding Communications Systems.* Understanding Series. Dallas, TX: Texas Instruments, 1980.

Casamayou, Major Louis J. "A Guide to U.S. Air Force Command Control Communications," Report No. 83-0380. Master's thesis, Air Command and Staff College. Air University, Maxwell AFB, AL, 1983.

Cochran, Thomas B., William M. Arkin, and Milton M. Hoenig. *U.S. Nuclear Forces and Capabilities.* Natural Resources Defense Council, Nuclear Weapons Databook Series, Vol. I. Cambridge, MA: Ballinger, 1984.

Cochran, Thomas B., *et al. U.S. Nuclear Warhead Facility Profiles.* Natural Resources Defense Council, Nuclear Weapons Databook Series, Vol. III. Cambridge, MA: Ballinger, 1987.

——————. *U.S. Nuclear Warhead Production.* Natural Resources Defense Council, Nuclear Weapons Databook Series, Vol. II. Cambridge, MA: Ballinger, 1987.

Collins, John M. *U.S. and Soviet Special Operations.* A Study by the Congressional Research Service, Library of Congress, prepared at the request of the Special Operations Panel of the Readiness Subcommittee of the Committee on Armed Services, House of Representatives. 100th Congress, 1st Sess. Committee Print No. 6. Washington, DC: Government Printing Office, 28 April 1987.

——————. *U.S.–Soviet Military Balance: Concepts and Capabilities 1960–1980.* New York: McGraw-Hill, 1980.

——————, and Bernard C. Victory. Congressional Research Service Report 88-425-S. *U.S.–Soviet Military Balance: Statistical Trends, 1980–1987.* Washington, DC: Government Printing Office, April 1988.

Defence Update 1988–89. Presented to the House of Commons Standing Committee on National Defence. Ottawa, Ontario: National Defence Headquarters, Director General Information, March 1988.

Defense Electronics. *Command, Control, Communications, Intelligence Handbook.* 1st ed. Palo Alto, CA: EW Communications, 1986.

"Department of Defense Material Organizations," *National Defense*, October 1988, pp. 57–88.

Flynn, Capt. John P., and Ted E. Senator. "DARPA Naval Battle Management Applications," *Signal*, January 1986.

Foley, Theresa. "U.S. Developing Survivable Warning/Antimissile Satellites." *Aviation Week & Space Technology*, 23 January 1989, pp. 34–37.

"Gallery of USAF Weapons." *Air Force Magazine.* Arlington, VA: Air Force Association. Annual publication.

General Dynamics. *The World's Missile Systems.* 7th ed. Pomona, CA: General Dynamics, April 1982.

Goldich, Robert L. *Department of Defense Organization: Current Legislative Issues.* Congressional Research Service Report IB86036. Washington, DC: Library of Congress, January 1987.

Gregory, Nathaniel. *The Role of Congress in the Department of Defense Reorganization Act of 1958.* Congressional Research Service Report 75-161F. Washington, DC: Library of Congress.

"Guide to Major Air Force Installations." *Air Force Magazine*, May 1988.

"Guide to Military Installations in the U.S." Rev. 1988–89 ed. Supplement to *Army Times, Navy Times, Air Force Times.* Springfield, VA: Times Journal Co., April 1988.

Gunston, Bill. *The Illustrated Encyclopedia of the World's Rockets and Missiles*. New York: Crescent Books, 1979.

Hayward, Daniel. *The Air Defense Initiative*. Issue Brief No. 9. Canadian Centre for Arms Control and Disarmament. Ontario, Canada, October 1986.

Hersh, Seymour M. *"The Target is Destroyed": What Really Happened to Flight 007 and What America Knew About It*. New York: Random House, 1986.

Jane's All the World's Aircraft. 1987–88 ed. Edited by John W. R. Taylor. London: Jane's Publishing Co., 1987.

Jane's Fighting Ships. 1988–89 ed. Edited by Captain Richard Sharpe. London: Jane's Publishing Co., 1988.

Jane's Weapons Systems. 1987–88 ed. Edited by Bernard Blake. London: Jane's Publishing Co., 1987.

Jungerman, John A. *The Strategic Defense Initiative: A Primer and Critique*. San Diego, CA: University of California, San Diego, Institute on Global Conflict and Cooperation, 1988.

Keiser, Gordon W. *The U.S. Marine Corps and Defense Unification 1944–74*. Washington, DC: National Defense University Press, 1982.

Klare, Michael. *American Arms Supermarket*. Austin, TX: University of Texas Press, 1984.

Lewis, Kevin, and Mark Lorell. "Confidence-Building Measures and Crisis Resolution: Historical Perspectives." *Orbis*. XXVIII, No. 2, Summer 1984.

Luttwak, Edward. *A Dictionary of Modern War*. London: Penguin Press, 1971.

Missiles of the World. 1980 ed. Edited by Michael J. H. Taylor. New York: Charles Scribner's Sons, 1980.

National Guard Almanac. Edited by Lt. Col. Sol Gordon and Col. Al Ungerleider. Washington, DC: Uniformed Services Almanac, 1987.

NATO and the Warsaw Pact: Force Comparisons. 1984 ed. Brussels: NATO Information Service, 1984.

"Naval Review Issue." *Proceedings*. Annapolis, MD: U.S. Naval Institute, annual publication.

Noel, Captain John V., Jr., U.S. Navy (Ret), and Captain Edward L. Beach, U.S. Navy (Ret). *Naval Terms Dictionary*. 4th ed. Annapolis, MD: Naval Institute Press, 1978.

North American Aerospace Defense Command. *Code Words, Nicknames, and Exercise Terms*. Vol. 1. N/A Reg. 11-12. Peterson AFB, CO: HQ North American Aerospace Defense Command, March 1985.

——————— , Aerospace Defense Command, and Aerospace Defense Center. *Organization and Mission—Headquarters NORAD/ADCOM/ADC Organization and Functions*. N/A/A Pamphlet 20-4. Peterson AFB, CO: HQ North American Aerospace Defense Command, 15 June 1982.

——————— , Aerospace Defense Command and Space Command. *Commonly Used Terms in NORAD, ADCOM, and Space Command*.

N/A/S Pamphlet 11-3. Peterson AFB, CO: HQ North American Aerospace Defense Command, August 1985.

North Atlantic Treaty Organization. *The North Atlantic Treaty Organization: Facts and Figures.* Brussels: Nato Information Service, 1984.

Pocket Military Dictionary: A–Z of the World's Military Technology. Edited by Ernest Kay, Cornwall, England: K-Books Limited.

Polmar, Norman. *The Ships and Aircraft of the U.S. Fleet.* 14th ed. Annapolis, MD: Naval Institute Press, 1987.

Pringle, Peter, and William M. Arkin. *S.I.O.P.: The Secret U.S. Plan for Nuclear War.* New York: W. W. Norton, 1983.

Ravenstein, Charles A. *The Organization and Lineage of the United States Air Force.* Washington, DC: Office of Air Force History, USAF Warrior Studies, 1986.

Reserve Forces Almanac. Edited by Lt. Col. Sol Gordon. Washington, DC: Uniformed Services Almanac, 1987.

Richelson, Jeffrey. *American Espionage and the Soviet Target.* New York: William Morrow, 1987.

——————. *The U.S. Intelligence Community.* 2nd ed. Cambridge, MA: Ballinger, 1989.

——————. *The U.S. Intelligence Community.* 1st ed. Cambridge, MA: Ballinger, 1985.

Seminar on Command, Control, Communications and Intelligence. Incidental Paper, Program on Information Resources Policy. Cambridge, MA: Center for Information Policy Research, Harvard University, various years.

Semler, Eric, James Benjamin, and Adam Gross. *The Language of Nuclear War: An Intelligent Citizen's Dictionary.* New York: Harper and Row, 1987.

Sheehan, Michael, and James Wyllie. *The Economist Pocket Guide to Defence.* Oxford, England: Basil Blackwell and The Economist, 1986.

Sivard, Ruth Leger. *World Military and Social Expenditures.* Washington, DC: World Priorities, annual publication.

Stephenson, Michael, and John Weal. *Nuclear Dictionary.* Essex, England: Longman, 1985.

Stevens, Paul Schott. "The National Security Council: Past and Prologue." *Strategic Review*, Winter 1989, pp. 55–62.

Systems Research and Applications Corporation. *Compendium of Emergency Authorities.* Prepared for Office of the Under Secretary of Defense for Policy. Arlington, VA: April 1981. Mimeographed, released under the FOIA.

"The Almanac of Seapower." *Sea Power.* Arlington, VA: Navy League, annual publication.

"The Green Book." *Army.* Arlington, VA: Association of the U.S. Army, annual publication.

The Military Balance. London: International Institute for Strategic Studies, annual publication.

"The Unified and Specified Commands." *Defense 87.* Washington, DC: Government Printing Office, November–December 1987.

Thorpe, George C. *Pure Logistics: The Science of War and Preparation.* Washington, DC: National Defense University Press, 1986.

Uniformed Services Almanac. Edited by Lee E. Sharff and Lt. Col. Sol Gordon. Washington, DC: Uniformed Services Almanac, 1987.

"USAF Almanac." *Air Force Magazine.* Arlington, VA: Air Force Association, annual publication.

"USAF Will Develop Major Radar Upgrade for Its E-3 AWACS Fleet." *Aviation Week & Space Technology*, 23 January 1989, p. 45.

U.S. Arms Control and Disarmament Agency. *Arms Control Impact Statement.* U.S. Congress, for the use of the Senate Foreign Relations Committee and House Foreign Affairs Committee. Prepared by the Arms Control and Disarmament Agency, Joint Committee Print. Washington, DC: Government Printing Office, annual publication.

—————. Bureau of Nuclear and Weapons Control. Defense Program and Analysis Division. *World Military Expenditures and Arms Transfers.* Edited by Daniel Gallik. Washington, DC: Government Printing Office, annual publication.

—————. Office of Public Affairs. *Strategic Defense Initiative: A Chronology: 1983–1988.* Issues Brief. Washington, DC: 1988.

U.S. Atlantic Command. *Altantic Command Alert System; promulgation of.* CINCLANT Instruction S3301.3B. Norfolk, VA: CINCLANT, 13 January 1982, Released under the FOIA.

—————. *Commander in Chief, Atlantic, Commander in Chief, U.S. Atlantic Fleet, Commander in Chief, Western Atlantic Area, and Commander, Ocean Sub-Area Staff Organization and Regulations Manual.* CINCLANT/CINCLANT FLT/CINCWEST-LANT/COM-OCEANLANT Staff Instruction 5200.1N. Norfolk, VA: CINCLANT, 29 July 1981, released under the FOIA.

—————. *USCINCLANT Staff Responsibilities for Operation Plans and Time-Phased Force and Deployment Data (TPFDD) File Preparation.* USCINCLANT Staff Instruction 3020.5C. Norfolk, VA: CINCLANT, 8 August 1985, released under the FOIA.

U.S. Central Command. *Emergency Action Procedures, Volume I, System Description.* MacDill AFB, FL: HQ USCENTCOM, 20 February 1986, released under the FOIA.

—————. *Emergency Action Procedures, Volume II, Alert System.* MacDill AFB, FL: HQ USCENTCOM, 20 February 1986, released under the FOIA.

—————. *Emergency Action Procedures, Volume III, SAS/COMSEC.* MacDill AFB, FL: HQ USCENTCOM, 20 February 1986, released under the FOIA.

—————. *Master Briefing Index.* MacDill AFB, FL: HQ USCENTCOM, 1 October 1985, released under the FOIA.

_____. *Military Operations — Crisis Action Team Standing Operating Procedures.* USCENTCOM Reg. No. 525-15. MacDill AFB, FL: HQ USCENTCOM, 1 February 1984, Released under the FOIA.

_____. *Operations Standing Operating Procedures.* Central Command Reg. 525-1. MacDill AFB, FL: USCENTCOM, 30 March 1984, released under the FOIA.

_____. "Statement of Major General Christian Patte, U.S. Army, Director of Logistics and Security assistance before the Readiness, Sustainability and Support Subcommittee of the Senate Armed Services Committee on the Status of the United States Central Command." 23 March 1988.

_____. *U.S. Central Command Organization and Functions.* USCENTCOM Reg. No 10-2. MacDill AFB, FL: HQ USCENTCOM, 1 February 1985, released under the FOIA.

U.S. Central Intelligence Agency. CIA History Staff. *Directors and Deputy Directors of Central Intelligence: Dates and Data: 1946–1983.* Washington, DC: November 1983.

U.S. Coast Guard. *Coast Guard at War,* by Dr. Robert L. Scheina, Coast Guard Historian. Commandant's Bulletin 4087.

_____. *U.S. Coast Guard: Overview 1988.*

U.S. Congress. House. Department of Defense Subcommittee of the Committee of Appropriations. *Department of Defense Appropriations.* Washington, DC: Government Printing Office, various fiscal years.

_____. House. Energy and Water Development Subcommittee of the Committee of Appropriations. *Energy and Water Development Appropriations.* Washington, DC: Government Printing Office, various fiscal years.

_____. House. Committee on Armed Services. *Defense Department Authorization and Oversight.* Washington, DC: Government Printing Office, various fiscal years.

_____. House. Committee on Armed Services. *Department of Energy National Security Programs Authorization Act.* Washington, DC: Government Printing Office, various fiscal years.

_____. Office of Technology Assessment. *Anti-Satellite Weapons, Countermeasures, and Arms Control.* OTA-ISC-281. Washington, DC: Government Printing Office, September 1985.

_____. Senate. Department of Defense Subcommittee of the Committee of Appropriations. *Department of Defense Appropriations.* Washington, DC: Government Printing Office, various fiscal years.

_____. Senate. Energy and Water Development Subcommittee of the Committee of Appropriations. *Energy and Water Development Appropriations.* Washington, DC: Government Printing Office, various fiscal years.

_____. Senate. Committee on Armed Services. *Department of Defense Authorization for*

Appropriations. Washington, DC: Government Printing Office, various fiscal years.

_____. Senate. Committee on Armed Services. *Defense Organization: The Need for Change.* Washington, DC: Government Printing Office, 16 October 1985.

_____. Senate. Committee on Armed Services. *Department of Energy National Security Programs Authorization Act.* Washington, DC: Government Printing Office, various fiscal years.

U.S. Congressional Budget Office. *Strategic Command, Control and Communications: Alternative Approaches for Modernization.* Washington, DC: Government Printing Office, October 1981.

_____. *Reforming the Military Health Care System.* Washington, DC: Government Printing Office, January 1988.

U.S. Congressional Research Service. "Fundamentals of Nuclear Arms Control. Part I: Nuclear Arms Control: A Brief Historical Survey." Committee Print 99th Congress, 1st sess. Report prepared for the Subcommittee on Arms Control, International Security, and Science of the Committee on Foreign Affairs, U.S. House of Representatives. Washington, DC: Government Printing Office, 20 May 1985.

U.S. Defense Communications Agency. *Overseas AUTOVON Network Control Procedures.* DCA Circular 310-V70-44. Washington, DC: August 1972, released under the FOIA.

U.S. Defense Intelligence Agency. *Defense Intelligence Organization, Operations, and Management.* Manual No. 56-3. Washington, DC: HQ DIA, 8 July 1979, released under the FOIA.

_____. Soviet/Warsaw Pact Division, Directorate for Research. *Glossary of Naval Ship Types.* DDB-1200-47-81. Washington, DC: June 1981, released under the FOIA.

U.S. Defense Intelligence College. *Glossary of Intelligence Terms.* Washington, DC: n. d.

U.S. Defense Nuclear Agency. *Capabilities of Nuclear Weapons.* DNA EM-1, Part 1. Washington, DC: HQ DNA, 1 July 1972, released under the FOIA.

_____. *Glossary of Terms: Nuclear Weapon Phenomena and Effects,* by Kenneth E. Gould. DASIAC-SR-208. Washington, DC: February 1985, released under the FOIA.

_____. *Nuclear Accident Response Capability Listing.* DNA 5100.1L. Prepared by the Joint Nuclear Accident Coordinating Center (JNACC). Washington, DC: April 1988, released under the FOIA.

_____. *Nuclear Weapon Accident Response Procedures (NARP) Manual.* Washington, DC: January 1984, released under the FOIA.

_____. Interservice Nuclear Weapons School. *Glossary of Terms.* Kirtland AFB, NM: October 1975.

U.S. Defense Security Assistance Agency. *Fiscal Year Series.* Washington, DC: Data Management Division, Comptroller, DSAA.

U.S. Department of Defense. *A Report to Congress on the Anti-Ballistic Missile Treaty.* Washington, DC: 21 September 1987.

_____. *Defense Almanac.* Washington, DC: Government Printing Office, annual publication.

_____. *Electrical Power Modernization Program for Critical Command, Control, and Communications Facilities.* DOD Instruction 4630.7. Washington, DC: December 1984, released under the FOIA.

_____. *FY 1988 Annual Report of the Director, Operational Test & Evaluation.* Unclassified version. Washington, DC: 19 January 1989.

_____. *List of Military Installations (Including FY 1987 Authorized Full-Time Assigned Personnel).* Washington, DC: 1988.

_____. *Management of War Reserves.* DOD Instruction 4140.2. Washington, DC: 4 December 1974.

_____. *Organization and Functions.* Washington, DC: n.d.

_____. *Policies and Procedures for the DOD Master Urgency List (MUL).* DOD Dir. 4410.3. Washington, DC: April 1978, released under the FOIA.

_____. *Program Acquisition Costs by Weapon Systems: Department of Defense Budget.* Washington, DC: annual publication.

_____. *Program for Research, Development and Acquisition.* Washington, DC: Government Printing Office, annual publication.

_____. *Security: Information Security Program Regulation.* DOD Dir. 5200.1-R. AFR 20501. Washington, DC: HQ, USAF, 28 April 1987.

_____. *Standardization and Interoperability of Weapons Systems and Equipment within the North Atlantic Treaty Organization.* DOD Dir. 2010.6, 5 March 1980, released under the FOIA.

_____. *Telephone Directory.* Washington, DC: Government Printing Office, annual publication.

_____. Directorate for Defense Information. Office of the Assistant Secretary of Defense (Public Affairs). *Fact Book.* Washington, DC: September 1985.

_____. Directorate for Organizational and Management Planning. *Organization and Functions Guidebook.* Washington, DC: Government Printing Office, June 1987.

_____. Office of the Assistant Secretary of Defense for Public Affairs. *Freedom of Information Act Program CY 1987: Summary of the Report to Congress.* Washington, DC: 1988.

_____. Office of the Secretary. *Annual Report to the Congress by the Secretary of Defense.* Washington, DC: Government Printing Office, annual publication.

_____. Office of the Secretary. *Manpower Requirements Report.* Washington, DC: Government Printing Office, annual publication.

_____. Office of the Secretary. *Manpower Requirements Report—Unit Annex.* Washington,

DC: Government Printing Office, annual publication.

_____. Office of the Secretary. *Report to the Secretary of Defense of the Defense Agency Review.* Washington, DC: March 1979.

_____. Office of the Secretary. *Standardization of Equipment within NATO: A Report to the United States Congress.* Washington, DC: January 1984.

_____. Office of the Secretary. Historical Office. *The Department of Defense: Documents on Establishment and Organization 1944–1978.* Edited by Alice C. Cole, Alfred Goldberg, Samuel A. Tucker, and Rudolph A. Winnacker. Washington, DC: Government Printing Office, 1978.

_____. Office of the Under Secretary of Defense (Acquisition). *Organization and Functions Guidebook.* Washington, DC: December 1988.

_____. Office of the Under Secretary of Defense (Acquisition). *Report of the Defense Science Board Task Force Subgroup on Strategic Air Defense.* SDI Milestone Panel. Washington, DC: May 1988.

U.S. Department of Defense Reorganization Study Project. *Departmental headquarters Study: A Report to the Secretary of Defense.* 1 June 1978.

U.S. Department of Energy. *Control of Classified Documents and Information.* Washington, DC: 14 April 1981.

_____. *Control of Weapon Data.* DOE Dir. 5610.2. Wash-

ington, DC: 1 August 1980, released under the FOIA.

_____. *Personnel Security Program.* DOE Order 5631.2. Washington, DC: 13 November 1980, released under the FOIA.

_____. *Tenth Anniversary: United States Department of Energy.* October 1987.

U.S. Department of Justice. Office of the Attorney General. *Annual Report of the Organized Crime Drug Enforcement Task Force Program.* Washington, DC: March 1985.

U.S. Department of State. *Congressional Presentation for Security Assistance Programs.* Annual publication.

U.S. Department of the Air Force. *Administrative Practices: Communications–Electronics Terminology.* AFM 11-1. Vol. III. Washington, DC: HQ USAF, November 1973.

_____. *Air Force Address Directory.* AFR 10-4. Washington, DC: HQ USAF, 31 December 1985.

_____. *Air National Guard Operation and Maintenance.* Presentation to the House Armed Services Committee by Brigadier General Philip G. Killey, Director, Air National Guard. 9 March 1989.

_____. *Appropriation Symbols and Budget Codes.* AFR 172-1. Vol. IV. Washington, DC: HQ, USAF, 1 October 1986. Change 1, June 1987.

_____. *FY 1989 Air Force Acquisition Statement.* Presented to the 100th Congress by Assistant Secretary (Acquisition) John J. Welch, Jr., and Principal Deputy

Assistant Secretary (Acquisition) Lt. Gen. George L. Monahan, Jr. Washington, DC: HQ USAF, 29 February 1988.

——————. *High-Frequency Single-Sideband (HF/SSB) Radio Facility Consolidation/Regionalization Scope Signal II, IV and V and HF Contingency Weather Broadcast System*. PMD No. 3087 (2)/33112/35117. Washington, DC: HQ USAF, September 1984, released under the FOIA.

——————. *Military Aerospace Vehicles*. AFR 82-1/AR 70-50/NAVMATINST 8800.4D. Washington, DC: July 1984.

——————. *Nicknames and Exercise Terms*. AF Pamphlet 11-6. Washington, DC: HQ USAF, 30 June 1982.

——————. *Organization and Functions Chartbook*. HP 21-1. Washington, DC: HQ USAF, March 1986.

——————. *Program Management Directive for Worldwide Airborne Command Post System Program*. PMD No. 1018(2). Washington, DC: HQ USAF, released under the FOIA.

——————. *Questions and Answers About Your United States Air Force*. AFP 190-1. Washington, DC: HQ USAF, February 1977.

——————. *Safety Design and Evaluation Criteria for Nuclear Weapon Systems*. AFR 122-10. Washington, DC: HQ USAF, 5 January 1982, released under the FOIA.

——————. *USAF Command Organization Chart Book*. AFP 23-21. Washington, DC: HQ USAF, 10 April 1987.

——————. *USAF Command Posts*. AFR 55-23. Washington, DC: HQ USAF, 2 July 1982.

——————. *USAF FY88: Report to the 100th Congress of the United States of America*. Washington, DC: HQ USAF.

——————. *U.S. Air Force Glossary of Standardized Terms*. Vol. 1. AF Manual 11-1. Washington, DC: HQ USAF, 2 January 1976.

——————. Air Command and Staff College. *ACSC Readings and Seminars. Vol. 10: Strategic Planning and Operations*. Maxwell AFB, AL: Air University, January 1982.

——————. Air Command and Staff College. *Big Stick War Exercise: A Strategic Nuclear War Simulation*. Maxwell AFB, AL: Air University, April 1983.

——————. Air Force Communications Command, DCS Comptroller. *Information Handbook*. July 1987.

——————. Air Force Intelligence Service. Target Intelligence Division. *An Introduction to Air Force Targeting*. AFP 200-17. Washington, DC: October 1978.

——————. Air Force Issues Team. Office of the Vice Chief of Staff. *Air Force Issues Book*. Washington, DC: HQ USAF, 1986.

——————. Air Force Systems Command. Office of History, HQ Space Division. *Space and Missile Systems Organization: A Chronology, 1954–1979*. n. d.

——————. Air Force Systems Command. Office of Public

Affairs. *Alphabet Soup*. Fact sheet. Andrews AFB, MD: Air Force Systems Command, September 1982.

_____. Air Training Command. *NATO Orientation: Flying Training, Euro-NATO Joint Jet Pilot Training*. ATC Study Guide P-V4A-N-NO-SG. Randolph AFB, TX: HQ, Air Training Command, October 1981.

_____. Air University. *United States Air Force. Commands and Agencies: Basic Information*. 1986–87 ed. AU-23. Maxwell AFB: Air University Press, September 1986.

_____. Alaskan NORAD Region; HQ, Alaskan ADCOM Region; and HQ, Alaskan Air Command. *AAC/ANR/AFFOR Exercises*. AND/AADR/AAC Regulation 50-1. Elmendorf AFB, AK: 3 November 1982.

_____. Assistant Chief of Staff, Intelligence. *Trends in U.S. and Soviet Military Forces*. Washington, DC: HQ USAF, June 1976, released under the FOIA.

_____. Assistant Chief of Staff, Intelligence. *Summary Review of Selected U.S. and Soviet Military Forces*. Washington, DC: HQ USAF, 15 April 1975, released under the FOIA.

_____. Directorate of Cost, DCS Comptroller. *Air Force Com- munications Command Information Handbook*. HQ AFCC: July 1987.

_____. Directorate of Programs and Evaluation. *A Primer: The Planning, Programming and Budgeting System (PPBS)*. Interim ed. Washington, DC: January 1987.

_____. Economics and Field Support Division. Directorate of Cost, Comptroller of the Air Force. *United States Air Force Summary*. Washington, DC: 7 March 1986.

_____. Military Airlift Command. *Contingency Planning Policies and Procedures*. MAC Reg. No. 28-2. Scott AFB, IL: HQ Military Airlift Command, 23 November 1984, released under the FOIA.

_____. Military Airlift Command. *Emergency Action Procedures of the Military Airlift Command (EAP MAC)*. MAC Reg. No. 5-3. Scott AFB, IL: HQ Military Airlift Command, 3 May 1982, released under the FOIA.

_____. Military Airlift Command. *HQ MAC Crisis Action Team Guidance*. MAC Reg. No. 55-28. Scott AFB, IL: HQ Military Airlift Command, 16 October 1985, released under the FOIA.

_____. Office of the Comptroller. *The Air Force Budget*. Washington, DC; HQ, USAF, annual publication.

_____. Office of the Comptroller. *The Air Force Budget Process*. AFP 172-4. Washington, DC: 1 October 1987.

_____. Military Airlift Command. *HQ MAC Crisis Action Team Guidance*. MAC Reg. No. 55-28. Scott AFB, IL: HQ Military Airlift Command, 16 October 1985, released under the FOIA.

_____. Office of the Comptroller. *The Air Force*

Budget. Washington, DC: HQ, USAF, annual publication.

————————. Office of the Comptroller. *The Air Force Budget Process*. AFP 172-4. Washington, DC: 1 October 1987.

————————. Office of the Secretary (Public Affairs). *Air Force Base Guide*. Fact Sheet 82-47. Washington, DC: HQ USAF, 1982.

————————. Office of the Secretary. *Transition Issue Papers*. Washington, DC: January 1981.

————————. Pacific Air Forces. *313AD Operational Reporting System*. 313AD Reg. No. 55-1. APO San Francisco: HQ 313th Air Division (PACAF), 29 October 1982, released under the FOIA.

————————. Strategic Air Command. *Processing the JCS Commander's Situation Report (SITREP)*. SAC Reg. No. 11-38. Offutt AFB, NE: Department of the Air Force, 10 September 1980, released under the FOIA.

————————. Strategic Air Command. 376th Strategic Wing. *Pyramid Alert System*. 376 SW Reg. No. 55-3. APO San Francisco: HQ 376th Strategic Wing (SAC), 25 February 1983, released under the FOIA.

————————. Strategic Air Command. *Strategic Air Command Regulation, Operations, SAC Exercise Program*. SACR 55-38. Vol. 1. Offutt AFB, NE: Strategic Air Command, 17 November 1984, released under the FOIA.

U.S. Department of the Army. *Artillery Handbook*. ST 7-163. Fort Benning, GA: U.S. Army Infantry School, 1973.

————————. *Authorized Abbreviations and Brevity Codes*. AR 310-50. Washington, DC: HQ, Department of the Army, January 1971. Change 5, 28 November 1973.

————————. *Communications Security*. AR 530-2. Washington, DC: HQ, Department of the Army, 1 September 1982.

————————. *Department of the Army Manual*. Washington DC: October 1985.

————————. *Dictionary of United States Army Terms*. AR 310-25. Washington, DC: HQ, Department of the Army, 15 October 1983.

————————. *EW—A Weapons Qualification Course*. TC 100-32-1. Washington, DC: HQ, U.S. Army, September, 1977.

————————. *Fire Support in Combined Arms Operations*. FM 6-20. Washington, DC: HQ, Department of the Army, 30 September 1977.

————————. *Nuclear Special Ammunition Direct and General Support Unit Operations*. FM 9-84. Washington, DC: HQ, Department of the Army, 30 July 1981.

————————. *Nuclear Weapons Fundamentals*. 9th ed. Army Correspondence Course—Subcourse IS0216. Fort Rucker, AL: n. d.

————————. *Office Management: Office Symbols*. AR 340-9. Washington, DC: HQ, Department of the Army, February 1978.

————————. *Organization and Functions*. AR 10-5. Washington, DC: HQ, Department of the Army, 1 November 1978.

_____. *Organization of the United States Army*. ODCSOPS. October 1980.

_____. *Planning, Programming, Budgeting, and Execution System*. DA Pamphlet 5-9. Washington, DC: HQ, Department of the Army, August 1986.

_____. *The United States Army Posture Statement*. Washington, DC: annual publication.

_____. *United States Army Weapon Systems*. Washington, DC: annual publication.

_____. Army Armament, Munitions, and Chemical Command. *Emergency Employment of Army and Other Resources—Notification Procedure for Emergency Action Messages*. AMCCOM Reg. No. 500-4. Rock Island, IL: Department of the Army, 26 November 1984, released under the FOIA.

_____. Army Aviation Center. *Capabilities of Army Aviation: Units and Aircraft*. Army Correspondence Course—Aviation Sub Course AV0709. Fort Rucker, AL: U.S. Army Aviation Center, March 1985.

_____. Army Command and General Staff College. *Electronic Warfare*. RB 32-20. Fort Leavenworth, KS: July 1975.

_____. Army Command and General Staff College. *Navy and Marine Corps*. RB 110-2. Fort Leavenworth, KS: 1 July 1978.

_____. Army Command and General Staff College. *Navy and Marine Corps*. Student Text 100-1. Fort Leavenworth, KS: 30 June 1987.

_____. Army Command and General Staff College. *Unified Direction of the Armed Forces*. RB 101-32. Fort Leavenworth, KS: July 1982.

_____. Army Command and General Staff College. *U.S. Air Force Basic Data*. Student Text 100-2. Ft. Leavenworth, KS: May 1987.

_____. Army Command and General Staff College. *U.S. Air Force Basic Data*. RB 110-1. Ft. Leavenworth, KS: May 1987.

_____. Army Communications Command. *Communications-Electronics—Handling of Red Rocket/White Rocket Messages*. USACC Reg. No. 105-10. Ft. Huachuca, AZ: Department of the Army, 19 September 1977, released under the FOIA.

_____. Army Communications Command. *Organization and Functions: Mission, Organization, and Functions of the U.S. Army Communications Command*. CCR 10-1. Fort Huachuca, AZ: HQ, USACC, August 1981.

_____. Army Signal Center and School. *Signal Communications for All Arms and Services*. SIG 045-4. Fort Monmouth, NJ: Army Signal Center and School, n. d.

_____. Army Strategic Defense Command. Historical Office. *The U.S. Army Strategic Defense Command: Its History and Role in the Strategic Defense Initiative,* by Ruth Currie-McDaniel. Washington, DC: January 1987.

_____. Army War College. Department of Military Strategy,

Planning, and Operations. *Forces/ Capabilities Handbook. Vol. 1: Organizations.* Carlisle Barracks, PA: AY 1987.

————. Army War College. Department of Military Strategy, Planning, and Operations. *Forces/Capabilities Handbook. Vol. II: Weapon Systems.* Carlisle Barracks, PA: August 1986.

————. Army War College. Department of Military Strategy, Planning, and Operations. *NATO Armed Forces.* Carlisle Barracks, PA: February 1987.

————. Comptroller of the Army. *The Army Budget Fiscal Year 1988–89.* Washington, DC: February 1987.

————. Legislative Liaison. *Fact Book for the 97th Congress.* Washington, DC: January 1981. Change 1, May 1981.

————. Office of the Assistant Secretary. *Equipping the United States Army.* Statement to the Congress. FY 1989 Army RDT&E and Procurement Appropriations. Washington, DC: February 1988.

————. Office of the Chief of Staff. *Army Staff Relationships with the Federal Emergency Management Agency (FEMA).* Chief of Staff Regulation 500-1. Washington, DC: 11 February 1985.

————. Office of the Chief of Staff. *Planning, Programming, and Budgeting System (PPBS) Handbook.* Washington, DC: annual publication.

————. Office of the Chief of Staff. *Planning, Programming, and Budgeting System (PPBS) Handbook. Annex B. Program Formulation, Review and Approval.* Washington, DC: annual publication.

————. Office of the Chief of Staff. *Planning, Programming, and Budgeting System (PPBS) Handbook. Annex C. Budget Formulation, Justification, and Execution.* Washington, DC: annual publication.

————. Office of the Deputy Chief of Staff for Operations and Plans. *Department of the Army Emergency Action Procedures. Annex M to Vol. IV: Army Crisis Action System.* Washington, DC: 12 February 1982, released under the FOIA.

————. Department of the Air Force, Department of the Navy, and Defense Logistics Agency. *Military Police: Physical Security.* Army R190-16, AFR 207-4, OPNAVINST 5530.15, MCO 5500.13, DLAR 5710.4. Washington, DC: 15 March 1984.

U.S. Department of the Navy. *A Report to the Congress on the Navy's Total Force.* Washington, DC: HQ, USN, February 1985.

————. *U.S. Naval Ship Battle Forces.* 31 May 1989, released under the FOIA.

————. *U.S. Navy Guide Book for Joint Actions (Navy Green Book).* OPNAVINST 5216.10H. Washington, DC: November 1988, released under the FOIA.

————. Assistant Secretary, Research, Engineering, and Systems. *RDT&E Management Guide.* NAVSO P-2457 (Rev. 12-79). Washington, DC: Government Printing Office, December 1979.

_____. CINCPACFLT Public Affairs Office. *Ships and Aircraft of the U.S. Pacific Fleet*. FPO San Francisco: CINC U.S. Pacific Fleet.

_____. Naval Education and Training Command. *U.S. Fleet Operations: A Primer for Cryptologic Direct Support Personnel*. NAVEDTRA 10095-A. February 1978, released under the FOIA.

_____. Naval Forces, Japan. *Special Incident Reporting (OPREP-3)*. COMNAVFORJAPAN Instruction 3100.2D. FPO Seattle: Department of the Navy, 2 September 1982, released under the FOIA.

_____. Office of Information. *Navy Fact File*. 8th ed. Washington, DC: October 1987.

_____. Office of Information. *Navy Fact File*. 7th ed. Washington, DC: October 1984.

_____. Office of Information. *Ships, Aircraft and Weapons of the United States Navy*. Washington, DC: August 1984.

_____. Office of Information. *Ships, Aircraft and Weapons of the United States Navy*. Washington, DC: 2 January 1980.

_____. Office of the CNO. *Allowances and Location of Naval Aircraft*. OPNAV Notice C3110. Washington, DC: 31 March 1986, released under the FOIA.

_____. Office of the CNO. *Characteristics and Capabilities of U.S. Navy Aircraft*. NWP 11-3, Rev. B. Washington, DC: HQ, USN, March 1985, released under the FOIA.

_____. Office of the CNO. *Naval Reserve, Navy Command Center 106, Support of the Navy Command Center*. OPNAV Instruction 5400.34B. Washington, DC: 5 November 1983.

_____. Office of the CNO. *Naval Terminology*. NWP 3, Rev. D. Washington, DC: February 1985.

_____. Office of the CNO. *Organization of the U.S. Navy*. NWP 2, Rev. C. Washington, DC: March 1985.

_____. Office of the CNO. *Standard Navy Distribution List, Part 1*. 123 ed. OPNAV PO9B2-107 (87). Washington, DC: HQ, USN, November 1987.

_____. Office of the CNO. *Standard Navy Distribution List, Part 2 and Catalog of Naval Shore Activities*. 72 ed. OPNAV PO9B2-105(87). Washington, DC: HQ, USN, September 1987.

_____. Office of the Secretary. *Civil Disturbances*. SECNAVINST 5400.12A. 12 March 1975.

_____. Office of the Secretary. *Classification of Naval Ships and Craft*. SECNAVINST 5030.1K/OP-902K. Washington, DC: February 1986.

_____. Office of the Secretary. *Transition Issue Papers*. Washington, DC: 1981.

U.S. European Command. *Annex F to Appendix I to USJTF HQ SOP—References*. ED 55-11, App. I, Annex F. Stuttgart-Vaihingen, W. Germany: HQ, USEUCOM, n. d., released under the FOIA.

_____. *Operations—Command Center Operations*. ED 55-15. Stuttgart-Vaihingen, W. Germany:

HQ, USEUCOM, 13 March 1981, released under the FOIA.

_____. *Organization—HQ USEUCOM Modern Aids to Planning Program (MAPP) Terms of Reference*. Staff Memorandum No. 20-3. Stuttgart-Vaihingen, W. Germany: HQ, USEUCOM, 29 November 1985, released under the FOIA.

_____. *Plans and Policy— JCS Joint Operations Planning System (JOPS), Vol. I (SM-362-84), 28 June 1984 Supplement*. USEUCOM Supplement 1 to JCS JOPS. Stuttgart-Vaihingen, W. Germany: HQ USEUCOM, 28 June 1985, released under the FOIA.

_____. *Plans and Police— The USEUCOM Theater Modern Aids to Planning Program (Theater MAPP)*. ED 56-3. Stuttgart-Vaihingen, W. Germany: HQ, USEUCOM, 9 December 1986, released under the FOIA.

U.S. General Accounting Office. Comptroller General of the United States. *Marine Amphibious Forces: A Look at Their Readiness, Role and Mission*. Unclassified report to Congress No. LCD-78-417A. Washington, DC: General Accounting Office, February 1979.

_____. *Air Defense Initiative: Program Cost and Schedule Not Yet Determined*. GAO/NSIAD-89-2FS. Washington, DC: October 1988.

_____. *An Unclassified Version of a Classified Report Entitled "The Navy's Strategic Communications Systems—Need for Management Attention and Decisionmaking"*. PSAD-79-48A. Washington, DC: Office of the Comptroller General, 2 May 1979.

_____. *DOD Clearance Reduction and Related Issues*. GAO/NSIAD-87-170BR. Washington, DC: September 1987.

_____. *Force Structure: Army Needs to Further Test the Light Infantry Division*. GAO/NSIAD-88-115. Washington, DC: April 1988.

_____. *National Security: The Use of Presidential Directives to Make and Implement U.S. Policy*. GAO/NSIAD-89-31. Report to the Chairperson, Committee on Government Operations, House of Representatives. Washington, DC: December 1988.

_____. *Quality Assurance: Concerns About Four Navy Missile systems*. GAO/NSIA-88-104. Washington, DC: March 1988.

_____. *Reserve Components: Opportunities to Improve National Guard and Reserve Policies and Programs*. GAO/NSIAD-89-27. Washington, DC: November 1988.

U.S. General Services Administration. Information Security Oversight Office. *Annual Report to the President FY 1988*. Washington, DC.

U.S. Joint Chiefs of Staff. *Alert System of the Joint Chiefs of Staff, Part I—Concepts*. Washington, DC: 29 January 1981, released under the FOIA.

_____. *Crisis Staffing Procedures of the Joint Chiefs of Staff*. SM-481-83. Washington, DC: 12 July 1983, released under the FOIA.

_____. *Crisis Staffing Procedures of the Joint Chiefs of Staff*.

SM-205-80. Washington, DC: 27 March 1980, released under the FOIA.

_____. *Dictionary of Military and Associated Terms*. JCS Publication 1. Washington, DC: Government Printing Office, April 1984. Change 1, July 1984. Change 2, December 1984.

_____. *Emergency Action Procedures of the Joint Chiefs of Staff, Vol. I, General*. J3M-485-84. Washington, DC: 1 April 1984, released under the FOIA.

_____. *Emergency Action Procedures of the Joint Chiefs of Staff, Vol. I, General*. J3M-538-83. Washington, DC: 15 March 1983, released under the FOIA.

_____. *Emergency Action Procedures of the Joint Chiefs of Staff, Vol. I, General*. SM-272-81. Washington, DC: April 1981, released under the FOIA.

_____. *Emergency Action Procedures of the Joint Chiefs of Staff, Vol. I, General*. SM-204-80. Washington, DC: 24 March 1980, released under the FOIA.

_____. *Emergency Action Procedures of the Joint Chiefs of Staff, Vol. I, General*. SM-244-79. Washington, DC: 17 April 1979, released under the FOIA.

_____. *Emergency Action Procedures of the Joint Chiefs of Staff—Authentication (EAP–JCS Vol. III)*. J3M 644-86. Washington, DC: 15 July 1986, released under the FOIA.

_____. *Emergency Action Procedures of the Joint Chiefs of Staff—Nuclear Control Orders (EAP–JCS Vol. V)*. J3M 398-85. Washington, DC: 20 March 1985, released under the FOIA.

_____. *Emergency Action Procedures of the Joint Chiefs of Staff—Emergency Conferences for Tactical Warning and Attack Assessment (EAP–JCS Vol. VI)*. Washington, DC: 1 December 1986, released under the FOIA.

_____. *Joint Operation Planning System, Vol. I (Deliberate Planning Procedures)*. SM-362-84. Washington, DC: 28 June 1984, released under the FOIA.

_____. *Joint Operation Planning System, Vol. II (Supplementary Planning Guidance)*. SM-142-85. Washington, DC: March 1985, released under the FOIA.

_____. *Joint Operation Planning System, Vol. III (ADP Support)*. SM-524-85. Washington, DC: 7 August 1985, released under the FOIA.

_____. *Joint Operation Planning System, Vol. IV (Crisis Action System)*. SM-502-85. Washington, DC: August 1985, released under the FOIA.

_____. *Organization and Functions of the Joint Chiefs of Staff*. JCS Publication 4. Washington, DC: 1 July 1983.

_____. *Policy and Procedures for Management of Joint Command and Control Systems*. SM-7-82. Washington, DC: 11 January 1982, released under the FOIA.

_____. *Unified Action Armed Forces (UNAAF)*. JCS Publication 2. Washington, DC: December 1986.

_____. *United States Military Posture*. Prepared by the Joint

Staff. Washington, DC: annual publication.

_____. *WWMCCS Objectives and Management Plan*. Vols. I, II, III, IV. JCS Publication 19. Washington, DC: April 1977–October 1982, released under the FOIA.

_____. Armed Forces Staff College. *Armed Forces Staff College Joint Planning Document*. Publication 6. Norfolk, VA: National Defense University, September 1985.

_____. Armed Forces Staff College. *Joint Planning Problem. Vol. II: Situation and Intelligence Data*. Norfolk, VA: National Defense University, November 1985.

_____. Armed Forces Staff College. *Joint Staff Officer's Guide 1986*. AFSC Publication 1. Washington, DC: Government Printing Office, July 1986.

_____. Armed Forces Staff College. *Joint Staff Officer's Guide 1988*. AFSC Publication 1. Washington, DC: Government Printing Office, July 1988.

_____. Armed Forces Staff College. *Organization and Command Relationships. Vol. II: Organization and Command Relationships*. Norfolk, VA: National Defense University, September 1985.

_____. Armed Forces Staff College. *U.S. Air Force Organization and Capabilities. Vol. I: Student Guidance*. Course 8S30. Norfolk, VA: National Defense University, August 1987.

_____. Armed Forces Staff College. *U.S. Air Force Organization and Capabilities. Vol. II: Faculty Guidance/Student Scripts*. Course 8S30. Norfolk, VA: National Defense University, January 1986.

_____. Armed Forces Staff College. *U.S. Army Organization and Capabilities. Vol. I*. Norfolk, VA: National Defense University, January 1986.

_____. Armed Forces Staff College. *U.S. Army Organization and Capabilities. Vol. II*. Norfolk, VA: National Defense University, January 1986.

_____. Armed Forces Staff College. *U.S. Navy/Marine Corps/Coast Guard Organization and Capabilities. Vol. I: Student Guidance*. Course 8S20. Norfolk, VA: National Defense University, August 1987.

_____. Armed Forces Staff College. *U.S. Navy/Marine Corps Organizations and Operations. Vol. I: Group Discussion Study Guides*. 220/230SP. Norfolk, VA: National Defense University, January 1979.

_____. Armed Forces Staff College. Department of Command, Control, and Communications. *Acronyms, Abbreviations and Terms*. Norfolk, VA: National Defense University, August 1981.

_____. Historical Division, Joint Secretariat. *Role and Functions of the Joint Chiefs of Staff: A Chronology*. JCS Special Historical Study. Washington, DC: January 1987.

_____. Military Communications–Electronics Board. *Joint*

Department of Defense Plain Language Address Directory (JDOD PLAD). Washington, DC: 9 August 1982.

——————. Studies, Analysis, and Gaming Agency. *Catalog of Wargaming and Military Simulation Models*, by LTC Anthony F. Quattromani, USA. 9th ed. SAGAM 120-82. Washington, DC: May 1982.

——————. Joint Staff. Operations Directorate. *Crisis Staffing Procedures*. J-3 Instruction 3180.11B. Washington, DC: 29 September 1983.

U.S. Marine Corps. *Basic Principles, Fundamentals, and Concepts: Administration*. HB 1-3. Arlington, VA: Marine Corps Institute, March 1987.

——————. *Basic Principles, Fundamentals, and Concepts: Command and Staff Action*. HB 1-1. Arlington, VA: Marine Corps Institute, March 1987.

——————. *Basic Principles, Fundamentals, and Concepts: Communications*. HB 1-6. Arlington, VA: Marine Corps Institute, 1987.

——————. *Basic Principles, Fundamentals, and Concepts: Intelligence*. HB 1-2. Arlington, VA: Marine Corps Institute, March 1987.

——————. *Basic Principles, Fundamentals, and Concepts: Materiel Management*. HB 1-5. Arlington, VA: Marine Corps Institute, March 1987.

——————. *Basic Principles, Fundamentals, and Concepts: Support Arms*. HB 1-7. Arlington,

VA: Marine Corps Institute, March 1987.

——————. *Commandant of the Marine corps Posture Statement*. Washington, DC: HQ, USMC, annual publication.

——————. *List of Marine Corps Activities (LMCA)*. NAVMC 2766. Washington, DC: HQ, USMC, March 1984.

——————. *Marine Air–Ground Task Force Doctrine*. FMFM 0-1. Washington, DC: HQ, USMC, June 1983.

——————. *Weapons and Equipment*. Washington, DC: HQ, USMC, December 1983.

——————. *USMC Weapons and Equipment*. PAM:JCF: mat 5720. Washington, DC: 22 December 1983.

——————. Development and Education Command. *Close Air Support (CAS) Handbook*. OH 5-4. Quantico, VA: November 1979.

——————. Development and Education Command. *Cold Weather Operations Handbook*. OH 8-5. Quantico, VA: 28 December 1979.

——————. Development and Education Command. *Comparison of Power Projections Options*. IP 0-4. Quantico, VA: June 1984.

——————. Development and Education Command. *Fleet Marine Force Aviation*. IP 5-7. Quantico, VA: September 1984.

——————. Development and Education Command. *Magis Intelligence Analysis Center: Characteristics, Deployment, and Operation*. DB 4-80. Quantico, VA: September 1980.

_____. Development and Education Command. *Maritime Pre-positioned Deployment*. OH 4-11. Quantico, VA: June 1984.

_____. Development and Education Command. *Mechanized Combined Arms Task Forces (MCATF)*. OH 9-3, Rev. A. Quantico, VA: March 1980.

_____. Development and Education Command. *Missions, Functions and Organizations Manual*. MCDECO P5400.4E. Quantico, VA: May 1986.

_____. Development and Education Command. *Modular Universal Laser Equipment (MULE) and Its Employment*. DB 2-80. Quantico, VA: June 1980.

_____. Development and Education Command. *Radio Operator's Handbook*. OH-10-3. Quantico, VA: September 1980.

_____. Development and Education Command. *Search*. Quantico, VA: January 1985.

_____. Development and Education Command. *Ship-to-Shore Control Agencies*. IP 3-5. Quantico, VA: August 1983.

_____. Fleet Marine Force, Atlantic. *Fleet Marine Force, Atlantic and II Marine Amphibious Force*. FMFLANT 6-0200. Norfolk, VA: n. d.

U.S. National Security Council. *Organizational History of the National Security Council during the Kennedy and Johnson Administrations*, by Bromley K. Smith. Washington, DC: September 1988.

_____. Subcommittee on National Policy Machinery. *Organizational History of the National Security Council during the Truman and Eisenhower Administrations*, by James S. Lay and Robert H. Johnson. Washington, DC: August 1960.

U.S. Pacific Command. *Base/Installation Security during Increased Alert Conditions (LERT CONs) and other Emergency Situations*. CINCPAC Instruction 5510.12C. Camp H. M. Smith, HI: CINCPAC, 10 August 1981, released under the FOIA.

_____. *Commander in Chief, U.S. Pacific Command Emergency Action Procedures, Volume V, Crisis Staffing*. Camp H. M. Smith, HI: CINCPAC, 18 December 1985, released under the FOIA.

_____. *Command Relationships in the U.S. Pacific Command Change Transmittal 2—Enclosures 3 and 6*. CINCPAC Instruction S3020.2J. Camp H. M. Smith, HI: CINCPAC, 21 June 1984, released under the FOIA.

_____. *Event/Incident Report (Short Title: OPREP-3)*. CINCPAC Instruction 3480.6F. Camp H. M. Smith, HI: CINCPAC, 14 April 1982, released under the FOIA.

_____. *Headquarters of the Commander in Chief, U.S. Pacific Command Organizations and Functions Manual FY 84*. CINCPAC Instruction 5400.6K. Camp H. M. Smith, HI: CINCPAC, 5 December 1983, released under the FOIA.

_____. *Pacific Command Nuclear Biological Chemical Warning and Reporting System (Short Title: PACOM NBCWRS)*. CINCPAC Instruction 3401.3J. Camp H.

M. Smith, HI: CINCPAC, 6 February 1981, released under the FOIA.

_____. *Support of U.S. Pacific Command (USPACOM) Single Integrated Operational Plan SSBNs by Fleet Air Reconnaissance Squadron Three (VQ-3).* CINCPAC Instruction S3120.28B. Camp H. M. Smith, HI: CINCPAC, 8 February 1984, released under the FOIA.

_____. *The U.S. Pacific Command.* Camp H. M. Smith, HI: CINCPAC, Public Affairs Office.

_____. *USCINCPAC Fleet Ballistic Missile (FBM) Submarine Policy.* CINCPAC Instruction S3350.1A. Camp H. M. Smith, HI: CINCPAC, 24 October 1985, released under the FOIA.

_____. *U.S. Pacific Command (USPACOM) Special Operations Folder Program.* CINCPAC Instruction 3020.10. Camp H. M. Smith, HI: CINCPAC, 6 May 1985, released under the FOIA.

_____. U.S. Pacific Fleet. Commander, U.S. Naval Forces Marianas/Commander, U.S. Naval Base Guam. *Nuclear Biological Chemical Warning and Reporting System (NBCWRS).* COMNAVMARIANAS/COMNAVBASE GUAM Instruction 3401.3. FPO San Francisco: CINCPACFLT, 22 March 1982, released under the FOIA.

_____. *USPACOM Crisis Command and Control Procedures.* USCINCPAC Instruction C3100.1F. Camp H. M. Smith, HI: CINCPAC, 16 May 1985, released under the FOIA.

U.S. Readiness Command. *Crisis Action Procedures.* USREDCOM Manual 525-6, Ch. 2. MacDill AFB, FL: USREDCOM, 25 August 1982, released under the FOIA.

_____. *Crisis Action Procedures Manual.* USREDCOM Manual 525-6, with Ch. 1, MacDill AFB, FL: USREDCOM, 15 April 1980, released under the FOIA.

_____. *Index of USCINCRED Plans.* USREDCOM Dir. No. 310-2. MacDill AFB, FL: USREDCOM, 27 February 1986, released under the FOIA.

_____. *Readiness Emergency Action Procedures (REAP).* USREDCOM Manual No. 525-2. MacDill AFB, FL: USREDCOM, 30 March 1984, released under the FOIA.

_____. *USREDCOM Reporting Structure (REDCOMREP), Vol. I.* USREDCOM Manual 525-1. MacDill AFB, FL: HQ, USREDCOM, 22 November 1982, released under the FOIA.

_____. *USREDCOM Reporting Structure (REDCOMREP), Vol. II.* USREDCOM M525-1. MacDill AFB, FL: HQ, USREDCOM, July 1984, released under the FOIA.

U.S. Southern Command. *Headquarters USSOUTHCOM Organization and Functions Manual.* SC Reg. No. 10-1. Quarry Heights, Panama: USCINCSO, 1 October 1984, released under the FOIA.

_____. *Organization and Functions—USSOUTHCOM Joint Operations Center and Alternate Command Post Operation.* SC Reg. No. 10-3. Quarry Heights, Panama: USCINCSO, 17 October 1983, released under the FOIA.

_____. *USSOUTHCOM Emergency Action Procedures, Vol. I, General.* Quarry Heights, Panama: USCINCSO, 1 October 1983, released under the FOIA.

_____. *USSOUTHCOM Emergency Action Procedures, Vol. II, The Alert System.* Quarry Heights, Panama: USCINCSO, 12 November 1982, released under the FOIA.

U.S. Strategic Defense Initiative Organization. *Report to the Congress on the Strategic Defense Initiative.* Washington, DC: April 1987.

Waldman, Harry. *The Dictionary of SDI.* Wilmington, DE: SR Books, 1988.

Walsh, Edward J. "Foundaries of Progress." *Sea Power,* May 1988, pp. 39–43.

Woodward, Bob. *Veil: The Secret Wars of the CIA 1981–1987.* New York: Simon & Schuster, 1987.

"World Defence Almanac." *Military Technology.* McLean, VA: Monch Media, annual publication.

"World's Air Forces." *Flight International.* Annual publication.

Zarin, Michael N. *Intermediate-Range Nuclear Forces Treaty: Chronology, Major Provisions, and Glossary of Key Terms.* Congressional Research Service Report for Congress 88-44 F. Washington, DC: Library of Congress, January 1988.

About the Authors

William M. Arkin is Director of the Nuclear Information Unit at Greenpeace USA. He was formerly the Director of the National Security Program and a Fellow at the Institute for Policy Studies, Washington, DC, from 1981 to 1989. He is a former intelligence analyst for the U.S. Army, serving in West Berlin (1974–1978), and was an analyst at the Center for Defense Information.

Mr. Arkin writes frequently on military affairs and is a columnist and member of the Editorial Board for *The Bulletin of Atomic Scientists*. His articles have appeared in the *Washington Post, New York Times, Los Angeles Times,* and *International Herald Tribune*, as well as numerous other newspapers and magazines in the United States and overseas. He is a consultant to a number of organizations and news establishments.

Mr. Arkin has authored numerous books and monographs, including *Research Guide to Current Military and Strategic Affairs* (1981); *S.I.O.P.: The Secret U.S. Plan for Nuclear War* (with Peter Pringle) (1983); *Nuclear Battlefields: Global Links in the Arms Race* (with Richard W. Fieldhouse) (1985); *The Nuclear Arms Race at Sea* (1987); *Nuclear Warships and Naval Nuclear Weapons: A Complete Inventory* (with Joshua Handler) (1988); and *Naval Accidents: 1945–1988* (with Joshua Handler) (1989). His books have been published in Japan, Spain, and West Germany. With Thomas B. Cochran and Robert S. Norris, he is coeditor of the *Nuclear Weapons Databook* series, an encyclopedia of nuclear weapons, and coauthor of *Volume I: U.S. Forces and Capabilities* (with Cochran and Milton M. Hoenig) (1984); *Volume II: U.S. Nuclear Warhead Production* (with Cochran, Hoenig, and Norris) (1987); *Volume III: U.S. Nuclear Production Facilities* (with Cochran, Hoenig and Norris)(1987); and *Volume IV: Soviet Nuclear Weapons* (with Cochran, Norris, and Jeffrey I. Sands) (1989).

Joshua M. Handler is the Research Coordinator for the Greenpeace International Nuclear Free Seas Campaign. Prior to this he was a Research Assistant with the Arms Race and Nuclear Weapons Research Project at the Institute for Policy Studies, where he specialized in naval strategy and weaponry. He received his B.A. in 1982 from the University of Illinois and his M.A. in International Relations from the University of Chicago in 1988. He has coauthored several articles and publications, including *Nuclear Warships and Naval Nuclear Weapons: A Complete Inventory* (1988), and *Naval Accidents: 1945–1988* (1989).

Julia A. Morrissey was a Research Assistant with the Arms Race and Nuclear Weapons Research Project at the Institute for Policy Studies from 1985 to January 1990. She received a B.A. in Political Sociology from Harpur College, State University of New York at Binghamton in 1983, and is currently pursuing a Master's degree.

Jacquelyn M. Walsh is a Research Associate with the Nuclear Information Unit at Greenpeace USA. She was formerly the Assistant to the Director of the National Security Program at the Institute for Policy Studies. She received a B.A. from the College of William and Mary in 1984 and an M.A. in World Politics from the Catholic University of America in 1990.